THE WILEY BLACKWELL COMPANION TO MEDICAL SOCIOLOGY

WILEY BLACKWELL COMPANIONS TO SOCIOLOGY

The *Wiley Blackwell Companions to Sociology* provide introductions to emerging topics and theoretical orientations in sociology as well as presenting the scope and quality of the discipline as it is currently configured. Essays in the Companions tackle broad themes or central puzzles within the field and are authored by key scholars who have spent considerable time in research and reflection on the questions and controversies that have activated interest in their area. This authoritative series will interest those studying sociology at advanced undergraduate or graduate level as well as scholars in the social sciences and informed readers in applied disciplines.

The Wiley Blackwell Companion to Medical Sociology
Edited by William C. Cockerham

The Wiley Blackwell Companion to Sociology, Second Edition
Edited by George Ritzer, and Wendy Wiedenhoft Murphy

The Wiley Blackwell Companion to Social Movements, Second Edition
Edited by David A. Snow, Sarah A. Soule, Hanspeter Kriesi, and Holly J. McCammon

The Wiley Blackwell Companion to the Sociology of Families
Edited by Judith Treas, Jacqueline Scott, and Martin Richards

The New Blackwell Companion to the Sociology of Religion
Edited by Bryan S. Turner

The New Blackwell Companion to Social Theory
Edited by Bryan S. Turner

The Wiley-Blackwell Companion to Political Sociology
Edited by Edwin Amenta, Kate Nash, and Alan Scott

The Blackwell Companion to the Sociology of Culture
Edited by Mark Jacobs and Nancy Hanrahan

The Wiley-Blackwell Companion to Major Social Theorists
Edited by George Ritzer & Jeffrey Stepnisky

The Blackwell Companion to Major Contemporary Social Theorists
Edited by George Ritzer

The Blackwell Companion to Criminology
Edited by Colin Sumner

The Blackwell Companion to Social Inequalities
Edited by Mary Romero and Eric Margolis

The Blackwell Companion to Law and Society
Edited by Austin Sarat

The Blackwell Companion to Major Classical Social Theorists
Edited by George Ritzer

Also available:

The Blackwell Companion to Globalization
Edited by George Ritzer

The New Blackwell Companion to the City
Edited by Gary Bridge and Sophie Watson

THE WILEY BLACKWELL COMPANION TO

Medical Sociology

EDITED BY

WILLIAM C. COCKERHAM

WILEY Blackwell

This edition first published 2021

Registered Offices
John Wiley & Sons, Inc., 111 River Street, Hoboken, NJ 07030, USA
John Wiley & Sons Ltd, The Atrium, Southern Gate, Chichester, West Sussex, PO19 8SQ, UK

Editorial Office
9600 Garsington Road, Oxford, OX4 2DQ, UK
For details of our global editorial offices, customer services, and more information about Wiley products visit us at www.wiley.com.

Wiley also publishes its books in a variety of electronic formats and by print-on-demand. Some content that appears in standard print versions of this book may not be available in other formats.

Library of Congress Cataloging-in-Publication Data
Names: Cockerham, William C., editor.
Title: The Wiley Blackwell companion to medical sociology / edited by William C. Cockerham.
Description: Hoboken, NJ : John Wiley & Sons, [2021] | Series: Wiley Blackwell companions to sociology | Includes bibliographical references and index.
Identifiers: LCCN 2020043079 (print) | LCCN 2020043080 (ebook) | ISBN 9781119633754 (hardback) | ISBN 9781119637585 (paperback) | ISBN 9781119633785 (pdf) | ISBN 9781119633761 (epub) | ISBN 9781119633808 (ebook)
Subjects: LCSH: Social medicine.
Classification: LCC RA418 .W445 2021 (print) | LCC RA418 (ebook) | DDC 362.1—dc23
LC record available at https://lccn.loc.gov/2020043079
LC ebook record available at https://lccn.loc.gov/2020043080

Cover image: © studiocasper/Getty Images
Cover design: Wiley

Set in 10/12.5 Sabon LT Std by Integra Software Services Pvt. Ltd, Pondicherry, India

10 9 8 7 6 5 4 3 2 1

Contents

List of Contributors

Ronald J. Angel is Professor of Sociology at the University of Texas at Austin. He received his PhD in Sociology from the University of Wisconsin Madison in 1981. His research focuses on comparative welfare systems, retirement, and health care access and use among Hispanics and other minority populations. His work, which has been published in numerous books and journal articles, demonstrates the complex interaction of socioeconomic status, cultural and other social factors in determining individuals' and communities' opportunities for social advancement and exposure to health risks. Angel is currently working on a project focused on the role of the non-governmental sector in advocacy for and care delivery to older individuals in Mexico. The work appears in a book entitled *When Strangers Become Family: The Role of Civil Society in Addressing the Needs of Aging Populations* (Routledge 2020). This is part of a larger project on the role of civil society organizations in rapidly aging nations.

Jacqueline L. Angel is Professor of Public Affairs and Sociology and a Faculty Affiliate at the Population Research Center at The University of Texas at Austin. Her research examines health and retirement issues in the US, with a focus on older minorities, immigration processes, the impact of social policy on the Hispanic population and Mexican-American families. She is involved in several NIH/NIA projects, including a longitudinal study of older Mexican Americans (H-EPESE) since its inception in 1992 and for the past two decades a Conference Series on Aging in the Americas. Angel is author/coauthor/co-editor of numerous publications. This includes books such as *The Politics of a Majority-Minority Nation: Aging, Diversity and Immigration* (2019) and *Latinos in an Aging World* (2015). Major papers include "Institutional Context of Family Eldercare in Mexico and the United States" (2016) and "Medicaid Use among Older Low-Income Medicare Enrollees in California and Texas: A Tale of Two States" (2019).

Ellen Annandale is Professor of Sociology at the University of York, UK, where she was Head of Department between 2013 and 2017. She was Editor-in-Chief of the journal *Social Science & Medicine* between 2004 and 2012, a past Vice-President of the European Sociological Association (ESA) and is coordinator of ESA's Research Network 16 (Sociology of Health and Illness). She is Chair of the Trustees of the

Foundation for the Sociology of Health and Illness. Ellen has a long-standing interest in gender and health, particularly as it concerns feminist and gender theory, health inequalities, and the sociology of reproduction and childbirth. She is the author and editor of several books in this field, including *Women's Health and Social Change* (Routledge 2009) and, with Ellen Kuhlmann, *The Palgrave Handbook of Gender and Healthcare* (Palgrave 2012). She is currently working with colleagues on the research project Interactional Practices of Decision-making During Childbirth in Maternity Units funded by the UK's National Institute of Health Research.

Elyas Bakhtiari is Assistant Professor in the Department of Sociology at the College of William & Mary. His research examines how institutionalized social inequalities and boundary formation processes shape patterns of health outcomes and health disparities, particularly for racial and ethnic minorities and international migrants. His work relies on historical and cross-national comparison to understand the formation of health disparities, with current projects focusing on European migration to the US in the early twentieth century and Middle Eastern migrant health after September 11, 2001. His work has been published in the *Journal of Health and Social Behavior*, *Social Science & Medicine*, *American Behavioral Scientist*, *Socius*, and other outlets.

Ron Barrett is Associate Professor of Anthropology at Macalester College. His research focuses on the social determinants of infectious diseases and the anthropology of death and dying. His first book, *Aghor Medicine* (University of California Press), is an ethnography of religious healing and the stigma of leprosy in northern India. It was awarded the Wellcome Medal by the Royal Anthropological Institute. He also co-authored *An Unnatural History of Emerging Infections* (Oxford University Press) with George Armelagos, which explores the human determinants of disease in three transition periods occurring in the Neolithic, the Industrial Revolution, and today. Professor Barrett is also a former registered nurse with clinical experience in neuro-intensive care, brain injury rehabilitation, and hospice.

Shawn Bauldry is Associate Professor of Sociology at Purdue University. His interests in medical sociology include the interrelationship between education and health over the life course and across generations, the evolution of health lifestyles over the life course, and disparities in mental health and mental health care utilization. In addition, he works in the area of applied statistics with a focus on structural equation modeling and models for categorical data. His work has appeared in the *Journal of Health and Social Behavior*, *Social Science & Medicine*, *Sociological Methodology*, and *Sociological Methods & Research* among others.

Jaunathan Bilodeau is a postdoctoral researcher at the Department of Sociology at McGill University in Montreal, Canada. His work focuses on the relationship between work-family conflict and mental health, as well as the structural determinants of health inequalities such as gender and social policies. He recently published in *Stress & Health*, *Social Science & Medicine* and *Annals of Work Exposure and Health*.

Carol A. Boyer is former Associate Director of the Institute for Health, Health Care Policy and Aging Research and graduate faculty in the Department of Sociology at Rutgers University. She has devoted her career to health services research and policy and interdisciplinary studies informed by clinical experience in acute-care and emergency settings. With over 30 years' experience in mental health services research focusing on populations with severe mental illnesses and their medical co-morbidities, her studies addressed access, utilization, stigma, quality of life and the content and outcomes of treatment and services provided to individuals with a diagnosis of schizophrenia, psychosocial interventions and strategies to enhance adherence with antipsychotic medications and linking individuals successfully to home and community services. Her research informed developing and implementing training programs including both didactic and experiential learning components.

Hannah Bradby is Professor at the Sociology Department, Uppsala University, Sweden since 2013, having previously held a senior lectureship at the University of Warwick, UK. Her research interrogates the links between identity, structure and health with particular reference to racism, ethnicity and religion. She is Field Chief Editor for *Frontiers in Sociology* and blogs regularly at *Cost of Living*.

Cindy L. Cain is Assistant Professor of Sociology at the University of Alabama at Birmingham. Her interests in medical sociology include changes within the healthcare system, the experiences of healthcare workers, and care for vulnerable older adults. In addition, she specializes in qualitative and mixed methods approaches and is especially interested in how we can better integrate different methods. Her work has appeared in the *Journal of Health and Social Behavior*, *Sociology of Health & Illness*, *Journal of Contemporary Ethnography*, *The Gerontologist*, and other journals.

Yvonne Chen is a PhD student in the Department of Sociology at Vanderbilt University. Her major research interests center on race and ethnicity, mental health, social stratification, and social networks. Her work has appeared in *Sociology of Race and Ethnicity*.

Kirsten Ostergren Clark is a PhD candidate in medical sociology in the Department of Sociology at the University of Alabama at Birmingham. Her research interests are developmental disabilities, masculinity and fatherhood, and religion and health. She earned a Master of Social Work degree from the University of South Carolina and spent several years supervising group homes for individuals with developmental disabilities and working as a renal social worker in dialysis clinics. Her dissertation is a qualitative project involving fatherhood and developmental disabilities.

Adele E. Clarke is Professor Emerita of Sociology and History of Health Sciences at the University of California at San Francisco. Her books include *Disciplining Reproduction: Modernity, American Life Sciences, and "Problems of Sex"* (1998, Fleck Award, Society for Social Studies of Science; and Basker Award, Society for Medical Anthropology), *Situational Analysis: Grounded Theory after the Postmodern Turn* (2005, Cooley Award, Society for the Study of Symbolic Interaction), co-edited *The Right Tools for the Job in Twentieth Century Life Sciences* (1992), *Women's Health: Differences and Complexities* (1997), *Revisioning Women, Health, and Healing* (1999), *Biomedicalization: Technoscience, Health, and Illness in the US* (2010), *Situational Analysis in Practice* (2015), and co-authored *Situational Analysis: Grounded Theory After the Interpretive Turn* (2018). She received the Bernal Prize (Society for Social Studies of Science, 2012), the Reeder Award (Medical Sociology

Section, ASA, 2015), and sessions in her honor at American Anthropological Association (2012) and Pacific Sociological Association (2019) meetings.

William C. Cockerham is Distinguished Professor of Sociology and Chair Emeritus at the University of Alabama at Birmingham and Research Scholar of Sociology at the College of William & Mary. He is past president of the Research Committee on Health Sociology of the International Sociological Association and author or editor of several books and articles on medical sociology. Additionally, he is Deputy Editor of the *Journal of Health and Social Behavior* and previously served on the editorial boards of the *American Sociological Review*, *Society and Mental Health*, and other journals. He also has held editorial positions for several encyclopedias, including Editor-in-Chief of the *Wiley Blackwell Encyclopedia of Health, Illness, Behavior, and Society* (Wiley Blackwell 2014) and Associate Editor-in-Chief of the *International Encyclopedia of Public Health*, 2nd ed. (Academic Press 2017). His most recent books include *Social Causes of Health and Disease*, 3rd ed. (Polity 2021), *Sociological Theories of Health and Illness* (Routledge 2021), *Sociology of Mental Disorder*, 11th ed. (Routledge 2021), and *Medical Sociology*, 15th ed. (Routledge 2021).

Kaitlin Conway is a PhD student in Sociology at McGill University, Canada, under the supervision of Dr. Amélie Quesnel Vallée. Her research focuses on the life course health inequalities of marginalized populations in Canada and the US. Prior to beginning her PhD, Kaitlin worked in the non-profit sector in both research and program monitoring capacities, both with a focus on global health. She holds a Master of Science in Global Health from King's College London and an Honours Bachelor of Arts in International Development from McGill University.

Raymond De Vries is Associate Director of the Center for Bioethics and Social Sciences in Medicine, University of Michigan, visiting professor at the School for Public Health and Primary Care, University of Maastricht (Netherlands), and a fellow at the Hastings Center. He is a medical sociologist with broad experience in the study of the practice and profession of bioethics and the social and cultural influences on the organization of maternity care systems. He is the author of *A Pleasing Birth: Midwifery and Maternity Care in the Netherlands* (Temple University Press 2005), and co-editor of *Birth by Design: Pregnancy, Maternity Care and Midwifery in North America and Europe* (Routledge 2001), *The View from Here: Bioethics and the Social Sciences* (Blackwell 2007), *Qualitative Methods in Health Research* (Sage 2010), and co-edited special issues of *Medicine, Health Care, and Philosophy* (2008), *Social Science and Medicine* (2013), *Journal of Clinical Ethics* (2013), and the *AMA Journal of Ethics* (2019).

Christy L. Erving is Assistant Professor of sociology at Vanderbilt University. Using theories, concepts, and perspectives from several research areas, her program of research employs quantitative methods to clarify and explain social status distinctions in health. Her primary research areas explore: (1) how race, ethnicity, gender, and immigrant status intersect to produce health differentials, (2) the relationship between physical and mental health, (3) psychosocial determinants of Black women's health, and (4) the Black–White mental health paradox. In 2014–16, she was a post-doctoral fellow in the Robert Wood Johnson Foundation Health & Society

Scholars Program at University of Wisconsin, Madison. She completed a PhD and MA in Sociology at Indiana University-Bloomington, and received a BA in Sociology and Hispanic Studies from Rice University. Her research has been funded by the American Sociological Association, Ford Foundation, and Robert Wood Johnson Foundation.

Jonathan Gabe is Emeritus Professor of Sociology at Royal Holloway, University of London, UK. His research interests include pharmaceuticals, chronic illness, health professions, and health policy. He has edited or written 14 books (and 2 second editions) and published his research in journals such as *Health*, *Health, Risk & Society*, *Health Sociology Review*, *Social Science & Medicine*, *Sociological Review*, *Sociology*, *Sociology Compass*, and *Sociology of Health & Illness*. He is a past editor of the international journal *Sociology of Health & Illness* and a past chair of the European Sociological Association RN16, Sociology of Health and Illness. He is also a past President of the International Sociological Association RC15 Sociology of Health and a Fellow of the UK Academy of Social Sciences.

Frederic W. Hafferty is Professor of Medical Education, Associate Director of the Program for Professionalism & Values, and Associate Dean for Professionalism, College of Medicine at the Mayo Clinic in Rochester, Minnesota. He received his undergraduate degree in Social Relations from Harvard in 1969 and his PhD in Medical Sociology from Yale in 1976. He is past chair of the Medical Sociology Section of the American Sociological Association and currently sits on the American Board of Medical Specialties (ABMS) standing committee on Ethics and Professionalism, ABMS Professionalism Task Force, ABMS Stakeholder Council, and on the editorial board of *Academic Medicine*. He is the author of several books and a variety of academic papers that apply sociological frameworks to disability studies and issues of medical education, culture, and professionalism.

Terrence D. Hill is Associate Professor in the Department of Sociology at the University of Texas at San Antonio. His research examines social inequalities in health and human suffering. He is especially interested in the effects of religious involvement, neighborhood context, social relationships, and socioeconomic status. To date, he has published over 100 peer-reviewed journal articles and book chapters. His work appears in a range of journals, including the *Journal of Health and Social Behavior*, *Social Science & Medicine*, *The Journals of Gerontology*, *The Gerontologist*, *American Journal of Public Health*, *Labour Economics*, and *Social Work*. He has also published chapters in the *Handbook of Sociology of Aging*, *Annual Review of Gerontology and Geriatrics*, the *Handbook of the Sociology of Mental Health*, and the *Handbook on Religion and Society*. According to Google Scholar, his published work has been cited across a range of disciplines over 5,000 times.

Brian P. Hinote is Professor, Associate Vice Provost for Data Analytics & Student Success, and Chief Online Learning Officer at Middle Tennessee State University. In addition to clinical and research experience in areas as diverse as pediatrics, neurology, and cell biology, his interdisciplinary work appears in multiple books and peer-reviewed journals in social science, nursing, and medicine. His most recent work focuses on the various ways that social and behavioral science perspectives intersect and inform health care delivery and policy, clinical practice, and the work of various health professions. This line of inquiry culminates in his latest book project, *Social & Behavioral Science for Health Professionals* (Rowman & Littlefield 2020).

Ellen Idler is the Samuel Candler Dobbs Professor of Sociology, and Director of Emory's Religion and Public Health Collaborative, with additional Emory appointments at the Rollins School of Public Health, the Center for Ethics, the Graduate Division of Religion, and the Division of Geriatrics and Gerontology at the School of Medicine. Dr. Idler is a Fellow and past Chair of the Behavioral and Social Sciences Section of the Gerontological Society of America, and she served as Chair of the American Sociological Association's Section on Aging and the Life Course. She studies the influence of attitudes, beliefs, and social connections on health, including the effect of self-ratings of health on mortality and disability, and the impact of religious participation on health and the timing of death among the elderly. Her research papers have been cited over 20,000 times. She is an Academic Editor for *PLoS One* and serves on the editorial boards of the *Journal of Gerontology: Social Sciences*; *Innovation in Aging*; and *Palliative and Social Care*.

Melanie Jeske is a doctoral candidate in sociology at the University of California at San Francisco. Situated at the intersection of medical sociology and science and technology studies, her research explores the social, political and ethical dimensions of knowledge systems, emergent biotechnologies, and biomedical expertise. Her dissertation research explores the politics and values of translational medicine, and goals of commercialization in biomedical research. Melanie's research has been published in journals including *BioSocieties, Social Science & Medicine*, and *Engaging Science, Technology, and Society*.

Lei Jin is Associate Professor at the Department of Sociology and Jockey Club School of Public Health and Primary Care at the Chinese University of Hong Kong. She received her PhD at the University of Chicago and was a Robert Wood Johnson postdoctoral fellow in the Health Policy Program at Harvard University. Her research interests include social disparities in health and well-being, health lifestyle, healthcare policy and healthcare professions. Her work has appeared in prestigious international journals such as *Demography*, *Social Science Research*, *Social Science & Medicine*, and the *American Behavioral Scientist*. Professor Jin's current projects examine the following topics: (1) social disparities in health lifestyle in transitional China; (2) psychological well-being and power perception in different social and political contexts across the world; and (3) professionalization and professionalism among physicians in China's public hospitals.

Patrick M. Krueger is Associate Professor in Health & Behavioral Sciences at the University of Colorado Denver, and research faculty at the Population Program at the University of Colorado Boulder. His research focuses on race/ethnic and socioeconomic disparities in health, health behaviors, and mortality. His current hobby is reciting pi backward.

Laura Mamo (PhD Sociology) is Professor of Public Health at San Francisco State University. Her research focuses on the technoscientific, biomedical, and social and cultural dimensions of health inequalities largely in the US. She is the author of *Queering Reproduction: Achieving Pregnancy in the Age of Technoscience* (Duke University Press 2007); co-editor of *Biomedicalization: Technoscience, Health, and Illness in the US* (Duke University Press 2010); and co-author of *Living Green: Communities That Sustain* (New Society Press 2009). She is also a founding member of the Beyond Bullying Project, a multi-media and ethnographic project studying the circulation of sexuality at school. Her research has received funding from the National Science Foundation, the Ford Foundation, the Robert Wood Johnson Foundation, the Canadian Institutes of Health Research and the US National Institutes of Health.

Jane D. McLeod is Provost Professor and Chair of the Department of Sociology at Indiana University. Her research traverses social psychology, medical sociology, sociology of mental health, stratification, and the life course. She is currently working on projects concerned with the social psychology of inequality, the college experiences of youth on the autism spectrum, and mental health inequalities.

James Nazroo is Professor of Sociology at the University of Manchester, UK, where he is Deputy Director (formerly founding Director) of the Centre on Dynamics of Ethnicity. His research focuses on inequality, social justice and stratification in relation to ethnicity and aging. His research on ethnic inequalities has spanned more than twenty-five years and demonstrates how health and underlying socioeconomic inequalities are shaped by racism.

Hyeyoung Oh Nelson is Visiting Assistant Professor in the Department of Health and Behavioral Sciences at the University of Colorado-Denver. She is a medical sociologist and qualitative researcher. Her research interests include the medical profession, health care organizations, the doctor-patient relationship, racial health disparities, and maternal health. Her work has been published in the *Journal of Health and Social Behavior, Sociology of Health & Illness*, and *Qualitative Health Research*.

Sarah Nettleton is Professor of Sociology in the Department of Sociology, University of York, UK. Over three decades her research has focused on embodiment, experiences of illness, health promotion, recovery, sleep and more lately architecture in the context of health and social care. She is author of the textbook *Sociology of Health and Illness*, 4th edition (Polity 2020).

Alexandra "Xan" Nowakowski is Assistant Professor at Florida State University College of Medicine. They are a medical sociologist and program evaluator focused on health equity in aging with chronic disease. Currently they evaluate the Florida Asthma and REACH Geriatrics programs. They have published in numerous journals, including the *Sociology of Health & Illness*, *Symbolic Interaction*, and *Teaching Sociology* plus interdisciplinary sociomedical journals. They have served on editorial boards for *Inquiry*, *The Qualitative Report*, and *Sociological Spectrum*. Their books include the edited volume *Negotiating the Emotional Challenges of Deeply Personal Research in Health* (Routledge 2017) and the social fiction novel *Other People's Oysters* (Brill 2018). They also edit the Health and Aging in the Margins series (Rowman & Littlefield) and the Write Where It Hurts trauma informed scholarship project. Dr. Nowakowski is agender, which informs their intersectional scholarship on chronic illness, and uses they/them pronouns.

Kristina Orfali is Professor of Bioethics and a Fellow of the Institute for Social and Economic Research & Policy at Columbia University. She is a sociologist with broad cross-cultural experience in the study of the practice of bioethics and clinical ethics. She has published work on clinician and family decision making and on neonatal ethics; she is the co-editor of special issues of *Sociology of Health & Illness* (2007), *Social Science & Medicine* (2013) and of several books: *Who is my Genetic Parent? Assisted Reproduction and Donor Anonymity: A Cross-Cultural Perspective* (2012), *Families and End of Life Treatment. An International Perspective* (2013), *The Female Body: A Journey through Law, Culture and Medicine* (2014), *Reproductive Technology and Changing Perceptions of Parenthood around the World* (2014), *Protecting the Human Body: Legal and Bioethical Perspectives around the World* (2016), and *The Reality of Human Dignity in Bioethics and Law: Comparative Perspectives* (2018).

Bernice Pescosolido is Distinguished and Chancellor's Professor of Sociology at Indiana University, Founding Director of the Indiana Consortium for Mental Health Services Research (ICMHSR) and was Founding Co-Director of the Indiana University Network Science Institute (IUNI). Her research focuses on four areas – stigma, health care use, suicide, and social networks – primarily looking at mental illness and substance abuse and the role that social and organizational networks play in people's responses to problems. Trained as a medical sociologist at Yale University, her research has been published in sociology, anthropology, public health, and psychiatric journals and has been supported by the National Institute of Mental Health, the Fogarty International Center, the National Institute of Drug Abuse, the MacArthur Foundation, the Robert Wood Johnson Foundation, and the National Science Foundation, among others. She has served as the Vice President of the American Sociological Association, and has received several career, teaching, and mentoring awards in sociology and public health, including the NARSAD Distinguished Investigator Award and the Wilbur Lucius Cross Medal from Yale. In 2016, she was elected to the National Academy of Medicine.

Stella R. Quah is Adjunct Professor, Health Services and Systems Research, Duke-NUS Medical School, National University of Singapore. Prior to joining Duke-NUS in July 2009, she was Professor of Sociology at the National University of Singapore (NUS) where she was a faculty member from 1977 to 2009; and Research Sociologist at the Department of Social Medicine and Public Health from 1973 to 1975. In addition to her consultancy work, Stella Quah is also member of several Institutional Review Boards. Among her most recent publications on sociology of health and social epidemiology are the *International Encyclopedia of Public Health*, 2nd Ed., Editor-in-Chief (Elsevier 2017); and Section Editor of Epidemiology and Public Health, *Elsevier Reference Module in Biomedical Sciences* (since 2014). Her published research on family sociology includes the *Routledge Handbook of Families in Asia* (Routledge 2015); and *Families in Asia – Home and Kin* (Routledge 2009) among others. Her full list of publications by theme is available at https://www.stellarquah.website.

Amélie Quesnel-Vallée is the 2019–20 recipient of the Fulbright Canada Distinguished Chair in Quebec Studies, SUNY Plattsburgh. She is Professor at McGill University in Montreal where she holds the Canada Research Chair in Policies and Health

Inequalities and is jointly appointed across the faculties of Arts (Sociology) and Medicine (Epidemiology). She is the founding Director of the McGill Observatory on Health and Social Services Reforms. Her research examines the contribution of policies to social inequalities in health over the life course. It has appeared in journals such as *The Lancet*, the *International Journal of Epidemiology*, and *Social Science & Medicine* and was recognized through several international professional associations' awards, including from the American Sociological Association, the Population Association of America, and the American Public Health Association. Committed to furthering public understanding of science, she is frequently sought by the media such as National Public Radio, the *New York Times*, and *Business Week*.

Jarron M. Saint Onge is Associate Professor in Sociology at the University of Kansas and associate professor of Population Health at the University of Kansas Medical Center. His research focuses on social determinants of health disparities, with specific interests in health lifestyles and neighborhood contexts.

Lacee A. Satcher is a PhD Candidate in the Department of Sociology at Vanderbilt University. She received her BA in Psychology from Tougaloo College in 2013, MA in Sociology from Jackson State University in 2015, and MA in Sociology from Vanderbilt University in 2017. Her research interests include race, health, place and inequality, social psychology of health and inequality, health policy, environmental justice, and urban sociology. Her recent research focuses on the race-environment-health connection in the urban American South, specifically how various individual social identities/social locations structure our relations with and within space and place to shape health outcomes and health experiences.

Graham Scambler is Emeritus Professor of Sociology at University College London and Visiting Professor of Sociology at Surrey University, UK. He has published extensively in social theory and the sociology of health. Specific foci of his work have been the sociologies of stigma and health inequalities. Recent books include: *Sociology, Health and the Fractured Society: A Critical Realist Account* (Routledge 2018), which was awarded the Cheryl Frank Memorial Prize; *A Sociology of Shame and Blame: Insiders Versus Outsiders* (Palgrave 2020); and *Communal Forms: A Sociological Exploration of the Concept of Community* (with Aksel Tjora) (Routledge 2020). He is a Fellow of the Academy of Social Sciences, UK.

Teresa L. Scheid is Professor of Sociology at the University of North Carolina at Charlotte with joint appointments in Public Policy and Health Services Research. She is senior editor (with Eric Wright) of the *Handbook for the Study of Mental Health: Social Contexts, Theories, and Systems*, 3rd Ed. (Cambridge University Press 2017). She has published widely on the organization and delivery of mental health services and the work of mental health workers that resulted in her 2004 book *Tie a Knot and Hang On: Delivering Mental Health Care in a Turbulent Environment*. Her most recent books are *Comprehensive Care for HIV/AIDS: Community-Based Strategies* (Routledge 2015), *Reducing Race Differences in Direct-to-Consumer Pharmaceutical Advertising: The Case for Regulation* with Stephany De Scisciolo (Lexington 2018), and a forthcoming book with Megan S. Smith titled *Ties That Enable: Community Solidarity for Adults Living with Serious Mental Illness* to be published by Rutgers University Press.

Janet K. Shim is Professor of Sociology in the Department of Social and Behavioral Sciences at the University of California at San Francisco. Her current program of research focuses on two areas: the sociological analysis of health sciences, particularly how they understand social difference and health inequality, and the study of health-care interactions and how they produce unequal outcomes. Her work has been funded by the US National Institutes of Health and the National Science Foundation. She is a co-editor of *Biomedicalization: Technoscience, Health, and Illness in the US* (Duke University Press 2010) and the author of *Heart-Sick: The Politics of Risk, Inequality, and Heart Disease* (New York University Press 2014). Her articles have appeared in journals such as *American Sociological Review*, *Journal of Health and Social Behavior*, *Medical Anthropology Quarterly*, *Science, Technology & Human Values*, *Social Science & Medicine*, *Social Studies of Science*, and *Sociology of Health & Illness*.

Kim Shuey is Associate Professor of Sociology at the University of Western Ontario in Canada. Her research interests focus on life course sociology, and work and health. She has published in *Work and Occupations*, *Advances in Life Course Research*, and the *American Journal of Sociology*, among other venues.

Eeva Sointu is Senior Lecturer in Sociology at York St. John University, UK. She is the author of *Theorizing Complementary and Alternative Medicines: Wellbeing, Self, Class, Gender* (Palgrave Macmillan 2012). She studies configurations of power, legitimacy and meaning in the domains of health, well-being and medicine, and conceptualizes social identities and values as central to understanding medical work, health seeking, and the ways in which health practices are represented.

Lijun Song is Associate Professor in the Department of Sociology and the Center for Medicine, Health and Society at Vanderbilt University. Her major research interests include social networks and social capital, medical sociology and mental health, social psychology, social stratification, marriage and family, and comparative historical sociology. Her publications have appeared in journals such as *Social Forces*, *Journal of Health and Social Behavior*, *Society and Mental Health*, *Social Psychology Quarterly*, *Social Science & Medicine*, *Social Networks*, *Sociological Perspectives*, *American Behavioral Scientist*, *Chinese Sociological Review*, and *Research in the Sociology of Work*.

Mieke Beth Thomeer is Associate Professor of Sociology at the University of Alabama at Birmingham. Her research interests include aging, family, health, gender, and sexuality. In her research, she addresses questions about how family relationships influence and are influenced by physical and mental health, with particular attention to gender. She uses both qualitative and quantitative methods, with special emphasis on dyadic methods. Her research has been published in the *American Journal of Public Health*, *Journal of Marriage and Family*, *Journal of Gerontology*, *Social Science & Medicine*, *Journal of Health and Social Behavior*, and other journals. She currently serves as Deputy Editor for the *Journal of Marriage and Family*, on the editorial boards of several journals, and is Teaching Committee Chair for the American Sociological Association's Medical Sociology Section.

Jason Adam Wasserman is Associate Professor of Foundational Medical Studies at Oakland University William Beaumont School of Medicine, where he also holds an appointment in Pediatrics, is the course director for the Medical Humanities and Clinical Bioethics curriculum, serves as Faculty Advisor on Professionalism, and conduct ethics consultations for area hospitals. His first book, *At Home on the Street* (Lynne Rienner Publishers 2010) addressed the issue of homelessness, while his current scholarly work focuses on clinical bioethics as well as integrating social science into clinical medicine. The second edition of his book *Social and Behavioral Science for Health Professionals* (with Brian Hinote) was published in 2020 by Rowman and Littlefield. He has authored numerous articles in journals such as *Social Science & Medicine*, *American Journal of Bioethics*, *Hastings Center Report*, *Mayo Clinic Proceedings*, *JAMA-Pediatrics*, *Journal of Clinical Ethics*, *Journal of Preventive Medicine*, and *The New England Journal of Medicine*.

Andrea Willson is Associate Professor of Sociology at the University of Western Ontario in Canada. Her research focuses the investigation of health inequality over the life course and its transmission across generations. She is Principal Investigator (K. Shuey, co-investigator) of a grant from the Canadian Social Sciences and Humanities Research Council to investigate family context and the intergenerational persistence of health inequality. Her work has appeared in *Journal of Health and Social Behavior*, *International Sociology*, and the *American Journal of Sociology*.

Joseph D. Wolfe is Associate Professor of Sociology at University of Alabama at Birmingham. His interests include studying health disparities across periods of social change, multigenerational socioeconomic resources and longevity, and measurement of social hierarchies related to US health inequalities. His most recent research decomposes wealth into its multiple sources, such as housing and financial wealth, and then examines their relationships to mental and physical health among adults entering later midlife. His work has appeared in the *Journal of Health and Social Behavior*, *Social Forces*, *Research on Aging*, *Obesity*, and several other social science journals.

Chenyu Ye is a PhD candidate in the Department of Sociology at the Chinese University of Hong Kong. She completed her undergraduate studies at Sun Yat-sen University in Guangzhou, China. Her main research interests lie in the areas of medical sociology, sociology of professions, health policy, and family and marriage.

Preface

The Wiley Blackwell Companion to Medical Sociology is a follow-up to two earlier volumes of this book and the latest work currently in Wiley Blackwell's Companion series. The goal is to bring together leading scholars in medical sociology to provide discussion of the most important issues and review the current research in the field. This edition follows this practice by providing chapters on health-related topics of significant interest. The contributors are from Canada, China, Singapore, Sweden, the UK, and the US, who were carefully selected to write chapters on topics in which they were recognized experts.

As will be seen in several chapters, this book was organized and written during the 2019–20 COVID-19 global pandemic. Consequently, many of these chapters take the effects of COVID-19 into account. One chapter (Chapter 21) on newly emerging diseases by Ron Barrett (Macalester College), a recipient of the Wellcome Medal from the Royal Anthropological Institute in the UK, focuses directly on COVID-19 with an authoritative account of the pandemic. Part I of this volume begins with a chapter by Terrence Hill (Texas-San Antonio), myself, Jane McLeod (Indiana University), and Fred Hafferty (Mayo Clinic). It analyzes how medical sociology's former subfields of sociology *in* medicine and the sociology *of* medicine have changed as its subject matter has enlarged and expanded well beyond these two initial categories. Each of these co-authors addresses a particular area of contemporary research. Hill is one of the most prolific scholars in medical sociology, McLeod is Provost Professor and Chair of the Department of Sociology at Indiana University and recipient of both the James R. Greenley and Leonard I. Pearlin awards for distinguished contributions to the Sociology of Mental Health, and Hafferty is a past chair of the Medical Sociology Section of the American Sociological Association who is currently at the College of Medicine at Mayo Clinic in Rochester, Minnesota. He has spent his career as a sociologist working in medical institutions.

Next, I join Graham Scambler (University College London and Surrey University, UK) to provide an overview of sociological theory in medical sociology. Scambler is a Fellow of the Academy of Social Sciences, UK, and editor emeritus of the journal *Social Theory & Health*. Medical sociology's evolution from an applied and atheoretical field to a subdiscipline that not only draws from theory in sociology but contributes to it is noted. Current theories in the field are reviewed.

Chapter 3 focuses on research methods, which is a new yet important topic for this volume. This chapter is written by Joseph Wolfe (University of Alabama at Birmingham), Shawn Bauldry (Purdue University), and Cindy Cain (University of Alabama at Birmingham) – each of whom is an experienced and well-regarded methodologist. Next is Chapter 4 on the important relationship between culture and health in a global context. Stella Quah of the Duke-NUS Medical School in Singapore writes this chapter. She is past chair of the International Sociological Association (ISA) Research Council, past president of the ISA Research Committee on Health Sociology, and editor-in-chief of the 2nd edition of the *International Encyclopedia of Public Health*. Altogether, four past presidents of ISA's Research Committee on Health Sociology are authors of chapters in this volume (Cockerham, Gabe, Quah, and Quesnel-Vallée). The remaining introductory chapter is on bioethics by Kristina Orfali (Columbia University) and Raymond De Vries (University of Michigan). Orfali is a Fellow of the Institute for Social and Economic Research & Policy at Columbia and DeVries is Associate Director of the Center for Bioethics and Social Sciences in Medicine at Michigan,

The section (Part II) on theoretical approaches in medical sociology follows. Sarah Nettleton (University of York, UK) provides an update of research on the sociology of the body. Nettleton is a former senior editor of the journal *Social Science & Medicine*. Adele Clarke of the University of California Medical Center at San Francisco and her colleagues at U.C. San Francisco, Melanie Jeske, and Janet Shim, along with Laura Mamo at San Francisco State University reexamine biomedicalization theory in Chapter 7 on a return visit to the theory decades later. Clarke, the leading proponent of biomedicalization theory has received numerous prizes and awards from professional organizations, including the Medical Sociology Section of the American Sociological Association and the Societies for Medical Anthropology, the Study of Social Sciences, and the Study of Symbolic Interaction. Next (Chapter 8) is an update of health lifestyle theory by the editor with a focus on the significance of social structures in influencing the health-related behavior of individuals. This chapter is followed by a new chapter on life course theory by Andrea Willson and Kim Shuey of the University of Western Ontario in Canada. They have published substantial work in this area. Chapter 10 takes the next journey into theory with a chapter by Lijun Song and Yvonne Chin (Vanderbilt University) on social capital and health. Song is a former student of Nan Lin, a major figure in social capital theory who co-authored a chapter on social capital with her in earlier versions of this book.

Part III addresses health and social inequality, which is a focus of several studies in medical sociology. The section begins with a topic of major importance for medical sociologists, that of health and social class, by two experienced medical sociologists, Jarron Saint Onge (University of Kansas) and Patrick Krueger (University of Colorado-Denver). Next is Chapter 12 on health and gender by Ellen Annandale (University of York, UK). She is a former editor-in-chief of *Social Science & Medicine* and past vice-president of the European Sociological Association and the International Sociological Association's Research Committee on Health Sociology. Chapter 13 presents a European view of health, ethnicity, and race by two noted researchers in this area, Hannah Brady (Uppsala University, Sweden) and James Nazroo (University of Manchester, UK). A European perspective is often missing from similar accounts by American medical sociologists, and this chapter fills that void. Turning, however, to the US, Christy Erving and Lacee Satcher (Vanderbilt University) examine African American health, while senior scholars Ronald and Jaqueline Angel (University of Texas-Austin) look at Latinos and equity in access to health care. Both chapters are especially relevant topics today in the US. The concluding chapter in this section is on social policy and health inequality by Amélie Quesnel-Vallée, Jaunathan Bilodeau, and Kaitlin Conway of McGill University in Canada. Quesnel-Vallée holds the Canada Research Chair in Policies and Health Inequalities at McGill, is past president of International Sociological Association's Research Committee on Health Sociology, and has received awards from the American Sociological Association, the American Public Health Association, and the Population Health Association of America.

In Part IV, the emphasis is on health and various types of social relationships. Chapter 17 is on health and family, which is a new but highly significant topic for this volume. It is written by Mieke Thomeer and Kirsten Ostergren Clark of the University of Alabama at Birmingham. Thomeer is Deputy Editor of the *Journal of Marriage and Family*, on the editorial board of the *Journal of Health and Social Behavior*, and is Teaching Committee Chair for the American Sociological Association's Medical Sociology Section. Chapter 18 is an updated chapter on health and religion by the well-known scholar Ellen Idler (Emory University). She is the Samuel Candler Dobbs Professor of Sociology at Emory and Director of the Religion and Public Health Collaborative. She also is a Fellow and past chair of the Behavioral and Social Sciences Section of the Gerontological Society of America and the American Sociological Association's Section on Aging and the Life Course.

Next is a chapter (Chapter 19) on health and migration by a new scholar Elyas Bakhtiari (College of William & Mary) that investigates the increasingly important topic of the health of migrants by an expert on this topic. The section concludes with a chapter on another new subject for this volume, that of mental health, by Teresa Scheid (University of North Carolina-Charlotte). She is a well-known researcher in the sociology of mental health and a senior editor with Eric Wright of the third edition of the *Handbook for the Study of Mental Health: Social Contexts, Theories, and Systems.*

Part V contains two chapters on health and disease. One is by Barrett on emerging infectious diseases described earlier in this preface for its emphasis on COVID-19 and the other (Chapter 22) by Alexandra C. H. Nowakowski (Florida State University College of Medicine) is on chronic illness. As someone who has experienced a chronic illness over her life course, Nowakowski brings an insightful and personal view to this chapter.

The final section is Part VI on health care delivery. It begins with a chapter by rising scholars Jason Adam Wasserman (Oakland University Beaumont School of Medicine) and Brian Hinote (Middle Tennessee State University) on health professions and occupations. Hinote and Wasserman are co-authors of *Social and Behavioral Science for Health Professionals*. Another rising scholar is Hyeyoung Oh Nelson (University of Colorado-Denver), who analyzes the doctor-patient relationship in Chapter 24. Eeva Sointu (York St. John University, UK), who has extensively researched complementary and alternative forms of medicine, provides a chapter (Chapter 25) on that topic.

Part VI concludes with chapters on the health care systems of the US, the UK, and China – three important countries in health affairs. Chapter 26 is by Bernice Pescosolido (Indiana University) and Carol Boyer (Rutgers University), who contribute a chapter on the American health care delivery system. The chapter explores the current vortex of health care reforms, problems of access, and costs pertinent to the ongoing legal, legislative, and political disputes taking place in American society. Pescosolido is Distinguished and Chancellor's Professor of Sociology at Indiana University and Founding Director of the Indiana Consortium for Mental Health Services Research (ICMHSR). She has served as Vice President of the American Sociological Association, received several awards in sociology and public health, and elected to the National Academy of Medicine. Boyer has had a distinguished career at Rutgers where she is former Associate Director of the Institute for Health, Health Care Policy and Aging Research, and a well-known medical sociologist.

Chapter 27 on the British health care system by Jonathan Gabe (Royal Holloway, University of London, UK) is next, and he brings us up-to-date on that country's national health service and health issues. A noted scholar, he is a former editor of the journal *Sociology of Health & Illness*, past chair of the European Sociological Association's Research Network on the Sociology of Health and Illness, past president of the International Sociological Association's Research Committee on Health Sociology, and a Fellow of the Academy of Social Sciences in the UK. The book concludes with Chapter 28 on the Chinese health care delivery system by Lei Jin and Chenyu Ye of the Chinese University of Hong Kong. This chapter was written in difficult circumstances as Hong Kong was undergoing political protests at the time, and the Chinese University's campus was closed because of COVID-19. Nonetheless, they contribute an excellent chapter on China, including efforts to cope with the pandemic.

Finally, I would like to thank the efforts of several people at Wiley Blackwell in Oxford who had an important role in the development and publication of this book. These include Justin Vaughan, Charlie Hamlyn, Richard Samson, Merryl Le Roux, and Clelia Petracca. Katie McIntyre at Birmingham-Southern College worked on the index. The first volume of this book originated in a conversation with Justin in a bar in New York City one warm and pleasant afternoon during a long-ago American Sociological Association meeting. This version continues the venture. And thanks again to my wife, Cynthia, for her loving support.

William C. Cockerham
Williamsburg, Virginia

Part I

Introduction

1

Medical Sociology and Its Changing Subfields

Terrence D. Hill, William C. Cockerham, Jane D. McLeod, and Frederic W. Hafferty

The sociological study of health, illness, and healing systems in the US has expanded substantively and deepened theoretically over the past half century. While work in this area once fit under the single moniker of "Medical Sociology," we now use a range of alternative labels (e.g. Sociology of Medicine, Sociology of Health and Illness, Sociology of Health, Illness, and Healing, Sociology of Health, Health Sociology) and definitions to describe the field. Some definitions highlight topic areas:

> "Medical sociology is the study of health care as it is institutionalized in a society, and of health, or illness, and its relationship to social factors" (Ruderman 1981: 927).

> "The sociology of health and illness studies such issues as how social and cultural factors influence health and people's perceptions of health and healing, and how healing is done in different societies" (Freund et al. 2003: 2)

> "Medical sociology focuses on the social causes and consequences of health and illness" (Cockerham 2017: 4).

Others emphasize different aspects of the sociological perspective:

> "Medical Sociology is the subfield which applies the perspectives, conceptualizations, theories, and methodologies of sociology to phenomena having to do with human health and disease. As a specialization, medical sociology encompasses a body of knowledge which places health and disease in a social, cultural, and behavioral context" (Committee on Certification in Medical Sociology 1986).

The Wiley Blackwell Companion to Medical Sociology, First Edition. Edited by William C. Cockerham.

> "The most important tasks of medical sociology are to demonstrate and emphasize the important influence of cultural, social-structural, and institutional forces on health, healing, and illness..." (Weiss and Lonnquist 2016: 11).

> "An approach that emphasizes using the area of health, illness, and health care to answer research questions of interest to sociologists in general. This approach often requires researchers to raise questions that could challenge medical views of the world and power relationships within the health care world" (Weitz 2017: 346).

The many labels and definitions that have been offered suggest a lack of consensus on defining medical sociology's substantive scope and its most significant contributions to knowledge. Some suggest that it is "hard to find a comprehensible statement of what... medical sociology is" (Chaiklin 2011: 585). Others describe the field as a "loosely connected network of disparate subgroups" (Veenstra 2002: 748). This state of the field raises several fundamental questions. How can we characterize our field in a general and consistent manner? What are our contemporary disciplinary boundaries? What are our major subfields? In other words, who are we now, and what do we do?

In this chapter, we propose a disciplinary structure for medical sociology that attempts to answer these questions. By "disciplinary structure," we mean a representative model of our major subfields as defined by topic areas, theoretical orientations, and significant contributions to the study of health. All sciences invariably reflect on these important issues and, in doing so, define their scientific orientation and boundaries in relation to other sciences, including, for example, medical sociology (Bloom 1986; Gold 1977; Petersdorf and Feinstein 1980; Straus 1957), medical anthropology (Saillant and Genest 2007), health psychology (Baum et al. 2011), and health economics (Pauly et al. 2012). Explicit disciplinary structures are one way to set disciplinary boundaries, mark accomplishments, and direct future efforts toward a cumulative science. Substantive topics and concepts alone are too granular to signify a field's major organizing principles. As Zerubavel (1991) once pointed out, things become meaningful only when placed into categories, and the "islands of meaning" that are created in this process explain *what* matters to a particular social world (or in this case, medical sociology) and help to determine the *nature* of its social order (or field of knowledge). In short, it is through the process of classification that we establish our boundaries and identity and, by extension, distinguish ourselves from other fields within sociology and other disciplines concerned with health.

The identification of a disciplinary structure was once integral to the development of the field, as evidenced in Straus's (1957) classic distinction between the sociology *of* medicine and sociology *in* medicine. Six decades have passed since Straus offered his structure, and we believe it is time to consider a more contemporary scheme that acknowledges the expansion of our subject matter, the broadening of theoretical influences, and the resultant complexity. Our primary aim here is to stimulate a forward-looking conversation among medical sociologists by reviewing previous conceptualizations and proposing a new model to serve as a basis for discussion. Our model classifies medical sociology in terms of its major subfields as defined by substantive topics, theoretical orientations, and scientific contributions. We review the unique contributions of each subfield while recognizing an underlying unity driven by common training in sociological theory and methods. We end with several recommendations for a more refined and directed conceptualization of the field.

There are several reasons why we should be having these discussions. When we define our major subfields and contributions to the study of health, we (1) claim our independence from other health sciences (e.g. medicine), (2) maintain our status in the marketplace of health research (e.g. as health psychologists and public health researchers publish more and more on socioeconomic inequalities), and (3) develop as a cumulative science through a formal recognition of the expansion of our field's purview. Before Straus (1957), for example, some questioned whether sociology should be considered a "third branch to medicine" (Boulton 2017: 242). When we stop reflecting and leave our subfields undefined, we lose track of our major contributions across generations of medical sociologists and in the broader interdisciplinary field of health research, leaving scholars from other health sciences (e.g. public health) unable to identify them. We also create intellectual vacuums for less fruitful discussions. For example, when we stopped discussing subfields in the late 1980s, we began the great "moniker debate" over whether to continue using the term "medical sociology" or to rename ourselves something else to be more inclusive of work related more to health than medicine. Instead of taking up that debate, we intend to redirect the conversation to how best to represent our disciplinary structure. Ultimately, we believe that focusing more on our major subfields and contributions to sociology and the broader study of health will support more productive and substantive conversations about what medical sociology has to offer.

Previous Subfield Models

The establishment of subfields within medical sociology was a major advance in its early development. In the 1950s, Straus (1957) proposed a two-subfield structure that included the sociology *of* medicine and sociology *in* medicine. These subfields were important because they (1) organized studies depending on the extent to which they served the interests of sociology vs. medicine and (2) sought to highlight the unique contributions of sociology to the study of health, illness, and medical practice. In the 1980s, Petersdorf and Feinstein (1980) suggested a more elaborate six-subfield model that was still based on sociology's stance vis-à-vis professional medicine, including sociology *in* medicine, sociology *of* medicine, sociology *for* medicine, sociology *from* medicine, sociology *at* medicine, and sociology *around* medicine. Still others advocated for a sociology *with* medicine (Bury 1986; Horobin 1985; Levine 1987). Although elaborations on Straus' original model never really took hold (Cockerham 1983; Hollingshead 1973; Ruderman 1981; Straus 1999; Wardwell 1982), we argue that, after decades of scholarship, the two-subfield model no longer adequately represents our contemporary disciplinary structure or our contributions to the study of health. For example, many medical sociologists no longer define themselves primarily in relation to medicine (whether critical of, or allied with it), and areas of inquiry that have distinct sociological identities have become more prominent (e.g. social epidemiology). For these reasons, we take Straus' (1957) original concerns with disciplinary structure in a new direction by defining subfields that are distinguished by substantive topics, theoretical orientations, and contributions to the interdisciplinary study of health.

Handbooks and textbooks typically divide the field substantively. For example, the third edition of the *Handbook of Medical Sociology* (Freeman, Levine, and Reeder 1979) was organized into five parts: "Health and Illness," "Health Care Providers," "Individual and Organizational Behavior," "Health Policy Dimensions," and "Methods and Status in Medical Sociology." The most recent sixth edition of the *Handbook of Medical Sociology* (Bird et al. 2010) adopted a different set of three organizational categories: "Social Contexts and Health Disparities," "Health Trajectories and Experiences," and "Health-Care Organization, Delivery, and Impact." The *Handbook of Health, Illness, and Healing* (Pescosolido et al. 2011) offered yet another distinct seven-part scheme: "Rethinking Connecting Sociology's Role in Health, Illness, and Healing," "Connecting Communities," "Connecting to Medicine: The Profession and Its Organizations," "Connecting to the People: The Public as Patient and Powerful Force," "Connecting Personal & Cultural Systems," "Connecting to Dynamics: The Health and Illness Career," and "Connecting to the Individual and the Body."

When we turn to important textbooks, we find four major sections in Cockerham (2017) (Health and Illness, Seeking Health Care, Providing Health Care, and Health Care Delivery Systems) and four major sections in Weitz (2017) (Social Factors and Illness, The Meaning and Experience of Illness, Health Care Systems, Settings, and Technologies, and Health Care, Health Research, and Bioethics). In Weiss and Lonnquist (2016), we see a more complex structure with no major sections or organizational schemes. Although these formats are effective for textbook presentations of the literature, they are more a collection of topics than major subfields that might organize the field.

One of the challenges we face is defining our field's substantive scope and its most significant contributions to knowledge in a way that is contemporary, comprehensive, and efficient. Although Straus' (1957) original model was efficient, it no longer adequately represents the field. The organizational schemes of books are more contemporary, but their structures are inefficient in the sense that the categories are numerous and inconsistent across volumes. The compromise we propose is a modest elaboration on Straus (1957) that reflects contemporary developments in the field.

A New Four Subfield Model

Building on previous conceptualizations, Figure 1.1 identifies and describes four major subfields of medical sociology: (1) Social Epidemiology, (2) Social Psychology of Health and Illness, (3) Sociology *of* Medicine, and (4) Sociology *in* Medicine. These subfields are intended to represent the field according to substance, theory, and contributions to knowledge.

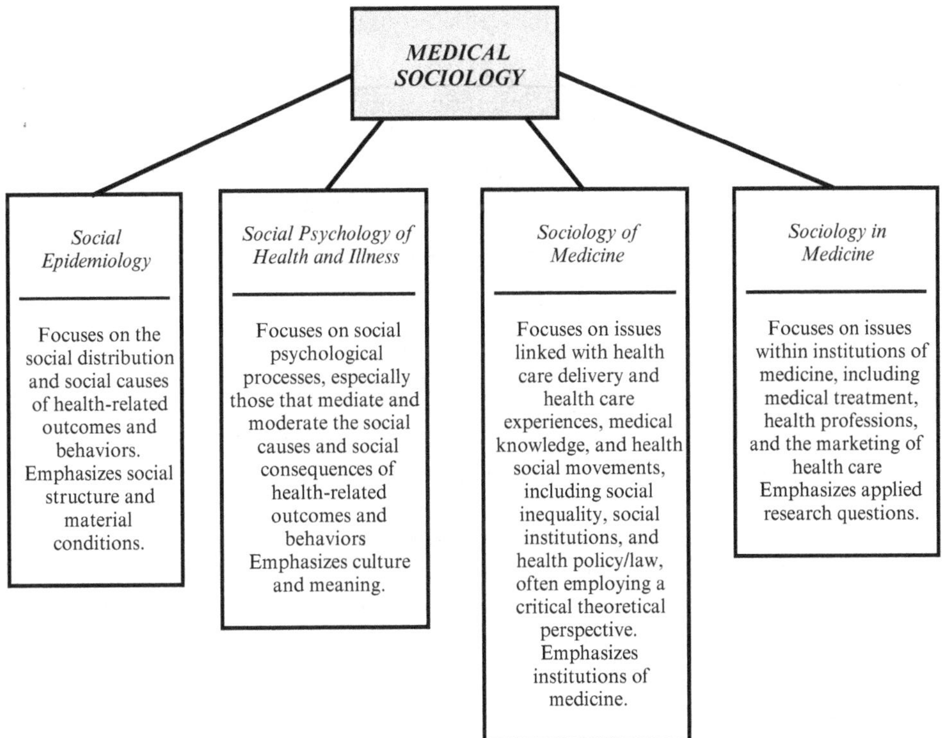

Figure 1.1 Major Subfields of Medical Sociology.

According to the ASA Committee on Certification in Medical Sociology (1986), our subject matter includes "*descriptions and explanations or theories relating to the distribution of diseases among various population groups; the behaviors or actions taken by individuals to maintain, enhance, or restore health or cope with illness, disease, or disability; people's attitudes, and beliefs about health, disease, disability and medical care providers and organizations; medical occupations or professions and the organization, financing, and delivery of medical care services; medicine as a social institution and its relationship to other social institutions; cultural values and societal responses with respect to health, illness, and disability; and the role of social factors in the etiology of disease, especially functional and emotion-related.*"

Our proposed subfields are intended to capture this broad range of topics, but not to be mutually exclusive or exhaustive. We fully acknowledge that some researchers may identify with more than one subfield. We believe that the diversity of research conducted in our field has and will continue to challenge the representativeness of our proposed disciplinary structure. With this in mind, our aim is not to find a perfect representation of the field or to dismiss other organizational schemes. Instead, our aim is to create a representative structure so that we can see the scope of our field more clearly. What does sociology contribute to the study of health and medicine? We argue that our subfield model answers this question in a clear way that better reflects where we are today.

Social Epidemiology

Social Epidemiology has been defined as "the branch of epidemiology concerned with the way that social structures, institutions, and relationships influence health" (Berkman et al. 2014:2). Research along these lines goes by many names, including Population Health, Social Determinants of Health, Health Disparities, Health Inequalities, Health Demography, and Biodemography. In our model, the subfield of Social Epidemiology focuses on the social distribution and social causes of health-related outcomes and behaviors. Health-related outcomes typically include indicators of mental health, physical health, and mortality risk. Health-related behaviors usually refer to risk factors such as exercise, smoking, alcohol consumption, illicit drug use, and broader health lifestyles. Relevant language from the Committee on Certification in Medical Sociology (1986) includes "descriptions and explanations or theories relating to the distribution of diseases among various population groups" and "the role of social factors in the etiology of disease."

Although the term "Social Epidemiology" is primarily associated with the field of public health, researchers across the health sciences examine the social distribution and social causes of health-related outcomes. Sociological social epidemiologists distinguish themselves by their emphasis on structural arrangements as determinants of health. Syme and Yen (2000:373) explain that while the social epidemiologist in public health "is fundamentally interested in learning about the nature of human disease by studying social characteristics," the social epidemiologist in sociology "seeks to learn about the social characteristics of human populations by studying the occurrence of disease." Social epidemiologists in public health believe that poor health is a problem to be solved or good health a goal to be achieved. Social epidemiologists in sociology believe that health is a consequence of social arrangements, especially those represented in social inequality, institutional ties, social relationships, and social roles (Mirowsky and Ross 2003). Social epidemiologists in public health primarily use analyses of health to direct health intervention programs and policy. Social epidemiologists in sociology primarily use analyses of health to shed light on the nature and function of social arrangements that cause or contribute to ill health.

Another important distinction is the use of theory. Although some health demography is descriptive rather than theoretical, most social epidemiology in sociology aims to document and explain health inequalities in the service of advancing sociological theory. Contemporary sociological social epidemiology is often informed by macro-structural theories of inequality, including, for example, fundamental cause theory (Link and Phelan 2000; Phelan and Link 2013), health lifestyle theory (Cockerham 2005; 2013), constrained choice theory (Bird and Rieker 2008), and life course theories (Ferraro and Shippee 2009; O'Rand 1996). What distinguishes these theories from those that dominate other subfields is their emphasis on broad structural and institutional factors that generate health inequalities.

While social epidemiology in sociology regularly engages in theoretical applications, social epidemiology in public health appears less enthusiastic about theory. In a recent review entitled "Social Epidemiology for the twenty-first Century," Kawachi and Subramanian (2018:240) concluded that social epidemiology "is no longer just for mavericks in fields such as sociology or economics where 'theoretical' research is often privileged over 'applied' research." This language is interesting to us since, in our judgment, the best analyses in sociological social epidemiology involve the use of theory. The conceptual framework provided by theory in social epidemiology in sociology is the medium through which reality is explained and understood. The use of sociological theory in empirical research is the key distinction between research conducted in sociology and public health. Social epidemiologists in public health are clearly able to distinguish their work from ours, but mainstream or generalist sociologists often view epidemiological research conducted in public health and sociology as typically "atheoretical," "applied," or simply "public health."

Social Epidemiology can also be distinguished from the other major subfields within medical sociology (discussed in greater detail below). While social epidemiologists describe the social distribution and social causes of health-related outcomes and behaviors, social psychologists of health and illness focus on social psychological processes, especially those that mediate and moderate the social causes and social consequences of health-related outcomes and behaviors. The Social Psychology of Health and Illness encompasses a range of theories that intersect with processes related to stratification and culture (Carr and Umberson 2013; George 2001; Kessler et al. 1995; McLeod et al. 2014; Schnittker and McLeod 2005; Simon 2000). Social Epidemiology and the Social Psychology of Health and Illness are nevertheless related through a natural scientific division of labor. Social epidemiologists identify social distributions and social causes. Social psychologists of health and illness analyze the social psychological processes that explain and modify the broader social distributions and social causes.

Social Epidemiology is more easily distinguished from the Sociology *of* Medicine and Sociology *in* Medicine. The Sociology *of* Medicine focuses on a range of theoretical issues related to institutions of medicine (Cockerham 2017). Sociology *in* Medicine focuses on applied issues within institutions of medicine, including medical treatment, health professions, and the marketing of health care (Cockerham 2017; McIntire 1894/1991; Weitz 2017). Social Epidemiology emphasizes the structures that drive health patterns within and across populations. The Sociology *of* Medicine and Sociology *in* Medicine focus on health patterns and practices within institutions of medicine and related social institutions. The Sociology *of* Medicine and Sociology *in* Medicine can also overlap with Social Epidemiology. Health and health-related behaviors are often tied to institutions of medicine. For example, gendered experiences within institutions of medicine (e.g. access to care) can contribute to broader gender disparities in population health.

Another way to see the contributions of Social Epidemiology is to review an excellent application of the subfield. Using data from the 1996–1997 Community Tracking Study and the pooled 1972–2000 General Social Survey, Schnittker (2004) examined "synergistic interactions between income and education" in the prediction of overall health status. The key question is whether the established association between income and health varies by level of education. The results of the study showed that "those with more education have better health for all levels of income, and fewer income-based disparities exist among the well educated than among the less" (Schnittker 2004: 286). We classify this study as Social Epidemiology because it focuses on the structural distribution of health and is primarily (not exclusively) descriptive in nature. In the end, this study contributes to the sociological study of health by specifying the educational or human capital conditions under which income is more or less relevant for overall health status. This study is distinguished from public health because it engages theories derived from medical sociology and health economics to support its examination of the synergistic interactions between income and education. This work also emphasizes social structure rather than health processes or health-related interventions.

Social Psychology of Health and Illness

The Social Psychology of Health and Illness is concerned with social psychological processes, especially those that explain or modify the structural causes of health and health-related behaviors or through which their social consequences are realized. It corresponds most closely to the following description from the Committee on Certification in Medical Sociology (1986): "the behaviors or actions taken by individuals to maintain, enhance, or restore health or cope with illness, disease, or disability; people's attitudes, and beliefs about health, disease, disability and medical care providers and organizations." For some researchers in the Social Psychology of Health and Illness, health is a lens into more general social psychological processes; for others, social psychology offers theories and concepts that illuminate health-related processes. Regardless of orientation, social psychologists of health and illness direct our attention to proximate health-related processes, especially those at the level of interpersonal interaction.

This subfield is as broad as sociological social psychology itself, encompassing interactionist analyses of self and identity in illness (Charmaz 1991), experimental studies of the health implications of small group processes (Taylor 2016), and multi-level analyses of the social determinants of health (House 2002). What distinguishes research in this subfield from descriptive Social Epidemiology is its emphasis on process (i.e. how outcomes are accomplished) and on subjective experience. Process and subjectivity are relevant to a range of topics, encompassing the onset and course of illness and disease, and individual and social responses, including help-seeking. The Social Psychology of Health and Illness can also be contrasted with health psychology (Taylor et al. 1997). Much like the distinction between sociological and psychological social psychology, the fundamental difference is defined by the primacy given to the analysis of social arrangements versus individual dispositions.

While research in the Social Psychology of Health and Illness draws inspiration from diverse theoretical traditions, among the most common orienting concepts are stress, identity, and stigma. The stress process framework and its constituent concepts (stressors, social support, and coping) provide explanations for health inequalities inasmuch as social groups differ in their exposure to stressors and their access to resources for managing stress (Aneshensel 1992; Pearlin 1989; Turner et al. 1995). Identity processes have been invoked to analyze variation in stress responses. For example, research shows that racial/ethnic identity can moderate or buffer the association between discrimination and health (Mossakowski 2003; Sellers et al. 2003). Identity processes have also been shown to have broader application in studies of how self and identity change in response to illness (Charmaz 1983). Stigma responses become incorporated into illness identities, shape the course of illness, and influence decisions about help-seeking (Pescosolido et al. 2008).

Because of its breadth, studies in this subfield defy easy categorization. Studies can address a broad range of topics. They can be quantitative or qualitative; based on surveys, interviews, or experiments. We offer two examples that illustrate the breadth, as well as the common elements, of research in the Social Psychology of Health and Illness.

Carr and colleagues (2017) used data from the Disability and Use of Time supplement from the Panel Study of Income Dynamics to evaluate the extent to which marital/partner strain and support moderate the association of disability with emotions among older adults, and whether those patterns differ by gender. They found that relationship support helps to protect women with severe impairment from feelings of frustration, sadness, worry, and negative mood, but the same support was associated with heightened distress for men, perhaps because men find support threatening to their sense of competence. The buffering effects for women suggest that emotional support may foster positive reinterpretations of disability and provide emotional resources to manage adjustments to roles and activities. This study exemplifies the Social Psychology of Health and Illness in that it uses social psychological concepts to shed light on health-related processes while also yielding insight into the social psychology of gender.

In a very different study, Kaiser (2008) analyzed in-depth interviews of women with breast cancer to explore how they interpret and use the survivor identity. She observed that, although some women embraced the identity, others rejected it. Women who rejected the identity cited fear of recurrence, not being sick enough to justify the label, and discomfort with the implied social identity as reasons for the rejection. Kaiser (2008) concluded that cultural images of cancer survivorship can be alienating and distressing to some women with cancer. By applying the concept of identity to the cancer illness experience, Kaiser (2008) highlights the centrality of the self to the experience of illness and to treatment responses.

Although different in their theoretical underpinnings and methodological approaches, these two studies are nevertheless related through their use of social psychological concepts to analyze the processes through which social conditions produce health and illness and the individual and social responses that follow. Both show how structural arrangements and cultural beliefs shape proximate life experiences and, finally, health.

Sociology of Medicine

The term "Sociology *of* Medicine," as previously noted, refers to half of Straus's (1957) original two-subfield model. The term is still appropriate for the broad subfield that takes medicine and its various activities pertaining to health and illness as an *object* of study. The Sociology *of* Medicine is characterized as research and analysis of the medical or health environment from a sociological perspective (Broom et al. 2013; Cockerham 2017; Straus 1957). The most relevant language from the Committee on Certification in Medical Sociology (1986) that pertains to the Sociology *of* Medicine today is that it covers "medical occupations or professions and the organization, financing, and delivery of medical care services; medicine as a social institution and its relationship to other social institutions; cultural values and societal responses with respect to health, illness, and disability."

Initially, the Sociology *of* Medicine encompassed the Social Psychology of Health and Illness and those facets of Social Epidemiology pertaining to the effects of social structures on health – essentially everything except sociological work that occurred within medical and health-related institutions (i.e. Sociology *in* Medicine). With the emergence of these other subfields as distinctive entities in medical sociology, the Sociology *of* Medicine is now primarily centered on issues linked with health care delivery and health care experiences, medical knowledge, and health social movements, including social inequality, social institutions, and health policy/law.

In its original conception, the Sociology *of* Medicine was centered in university sociology departments and characterized as "academic" rather than "applied" because of its grounding in sociological theory. This is the subfield where theory originated with Parsons' sick role and where theory has been closely identified in medical sociology. Although other subfields, particularly Social Epidemiology and the Social Psychology of Health and Illness, consistently test theories of health causation, Sociology *of* Medicine applies a broader range of sociological theories related to structure, culture, and social institutions. For example, social epidemiological research on structural health inequalities by race, class, and gender can spill over into the Sociology *of* Medicine when those disparities are linked to inequitable distributions of health insurance and health care within institutions of medicine (Lutfey and Freese 2005).

The Sociology *of* Medicine is perhaps best represented by the emergence of research on medicalization (Conrad 1992), pharmaceuticalization (Abraham 2010), biomedicalization (Clarke and Shim 2011), and health-related social movements (Brown et al. 2013). For example, Conrad's work on medicalization has uncovered the role of the medical profession in defining previously non-medical problems in medical terms, usually as an illness or disorder requiring a medical intervention. Conrad and others subsequently found that the forces driving medicalization have shifted to include biotechnology (Clarke and Shim 2011), patients and consumers (Barker 2002; Brown et al. 2001), and mass media advertising and the profit incentives in managed care systems (Conrad and Leiter 2004). Such critical perspectives on the roles of capitalism and social control in health care is one of the Sociology *of* Medicine's most important contribution to Medical Sociology.

Sociology in Medicine

Sociology *in* Medicine is the subfield of medical sociology primarily focused on applied research within institutions of medicine, with substantive focus on medical treatment, health professions, and the marketing of health care (Broom et al. 2013; Cockerham 2017; Straus 1957). The sociologist *in* medicine is one who collaborates directly with physicians and other health personnel in studying the social factors that are relevant to addressing problems in health care settings. The work of the sociologist *in* medicine is intended to be directly applicable to patient care or to solving issues related to public health. In these ways, Sociology *in* Medicine can be characterized as applied research and analysis that is more motivated by medical problems than sociological problems. Sociologists in medicine usually work in medical schools, nursing schools, public health schools, teaching hospitals, public health agencies, and other health organizations. They may also work for a government agency, such as the US Department of Health and Human Services or the Centers for Disease Control and Prevention, in the capacity of biostatisticians, researchers, health intervention planners, and administrators.

Straus's (1957) conception of Sociology *in* Medicine presented the emergent identity and hopes of a fledgling sociological sub-discipline. His survey of sociologists working on medical topics and in medical settings was one of several early publications (Anderson and Seacat 1957; Freeman and Reeder 1957; Mechanic 1966) that sought to claim a place and purpose for Sociology within Medicine's rapidly changing and culturally powerful institutional environment. The distinction between sociologists studying medicine from the outside (Sociology *of* Medicine) and sociologists located inside medical settings and engaged in collaborative work with medical insiders (Sociology *in* Medicine) remains relevant today. For Straus (1957:203), these two approaches tended to be "incompatible with each other." Correspondingly, Straus (1957) saw this tension as requiring those in the field to become "chameleons" in order to secure insider acceptance. Straus (1957: 203), argued that "there is a danger in this, for if the sociologist begins to talk like a physician, he [sic] may eventually come to act like a physician and even to think like a physician."

Straus' apprehensions were fundamentally about disciplinary identity and the dangers of over-identification with "the other" (i.e. physicians as an occupational group or medicine in general). More broadly, Straus and his contemporaries worried about the integrity of sociological objectivity along with the long-term independence of this new discipline. To read Straus and his peers (Bloom et al. 1960; Freeman et al. 1963) is to take a journey into the birth of a discipline at a time when neither acceptance nor a distinctive scholarly identity were foregone conclusions.

Now that medical sociology is a more established discipline, are Straus's concerns still relevant? How can we best understand the contributions of sociologists who work in medical settings? What can we say about the training model of sociologists who desire to work in medical settings to address problems of importance to Medicine using a sociological lens?

We believe that sociologists *in* medicine bring a unique perspective to the table (Constantinou 2015). In what might reflect a form of cultural bias, Medicine tends to define many of its educational and clinical challenges at the level of individuals rather than as reflections of organizational or structural challenges. Examples abound. "Problems" with learning outcomes, as reflected in student test scores on exams such as the National Board of Medical Examiners Licensing examinations, are "solved" by recruiting ever-higher scoring applicants. The recent upsurge of interest within Medicine regarding "burnout" (Dyrbye et al. 2017) has been followed by efforts to provide employees with tools to ameliorate its effects rather than to invest time and resources to address the structural conditions that might give rise to emotionally toxic work environments. Meanwhile, the possibility that organizational units, such as medical schools, might themselves suffer from burnout is not even on the radar. Even Medicine's recent attention to professionalism has remedially focused far more on teaching trainees and practitioners to be more professional, or to remediate "professionalism lapses" (a preferred term within medicine, but a sociologically evocative one) than on issues of contextual contributors, with concerns of "organizational professionalism" only recently gaining traction. Medicine still requires a sociological perspective to balance the prevailing lens of individualism.

Ospina and colleagues' (2019) recent study of physician-patient communication is an excellent example of Sociology *in* Medicine. Using secondary data collected from a random sample of 112 clinical encounters, this study found that clinicians elicit the patient's agenda in only 36% of encounters, with physicians interrupting the patient's story 11 seconds into their meeting. Key concepts in this article include "shared-decision making," "patient-centered care" and "patient-physician communication," all of which can be linked to broader sociological concerns with the structure and dynamics of dyadic communication exchanges. Furthermore, studies on physician-patient communication remain a staple in the social science literature (Cortez et al. 2019; Oh 2017; Ong et al. 1995, 2000; Stepanikova et al. 2012).

Key Contributions

In summary, medical sociology contributes to sociology and other health sciences by examining (1) the social causes of health-related outcomes and behaviors (Social Epidemiology), (2) the social psychological processes that mediate and moderate the social causes and social consequences of health (Social Psychology of Health and Illness), (3) issues linked with health care delivery and health care experiences, medical knowledge, and health social movements, including social inequality, social institutions, and health policy/law (Sociology *of* Medicine), and (4) problems within institutions of medicine, including medical treatment, health professions, and the marketing of health care (Sociology *in* Medicine). By distilling our major subfields and key contributions through an efficient and representative structure, we are able to see that medical sociology makes the broader study of sociology more meaningful by establishing explicit links between important sociological concepts (e.g. social structure, social institutions, and culture) and health, health care, and human suffering. Mirowsky and Ross (2003:3) note, for example, that few people would care about social inequality "if the poor, powerless, and despised were as happy and fulfilled as the wealthy, powerful, and admired." We are also able to discern the primacy of social arrangements and social processes in the study of health and medicine, which is medical sociology's unique contribution to the health sciences. Specifically, we describe patterns of health and health-related behaviors with greater attention to the complexities of social arrangements than one often sees in fields like public health. We offer unique and compelling analyses of the material and subjective conditions that explain the broader social distributions of health than fields like health psychology and health economics. We contribute more critical analyses of health care systems than medicine. Our discussion of major subfields also suggests a number of ways in which we might further develop as a field.

Recommendations

In this section, we offer several recommendations for a more refined and directed conceptualization of the field. Some of our suggestions stem from our core argument that the sociological study of health could use a more contemporary disciplinary structure that adequately represents the field. Others include more practical recommendations about graduate education. These recommendations are merely offered as possible directions for the field of medical sociology. Although these recommendations occurred to us, we realize they may be controversial to some. Our intent is to inspire even more discussions concerning the implications of our proposed model.

Recommendation #1. ***Explore explicit disciplinary structures.*** It is difficult to develop as a field when our disciplinary structure is little more than a collection of concepts and topics under several field identifiers (e.g. Medical Sociology, Sociology *of* Medicine, Sociology of Health and Illness, Sociology of Health, and Health Sociology). It is true that our field has developed in significant ways. We have accumulated an impressive body of research. We have multiple journals. We have the second largest section in the American Sociological Association. However, our field is underdeveloped in other ways that are also important. As indicated by the range of labels and definitions used to describe our field, we have little consistency in research identities across researchers and in the ways we define the purview of our field. Because medical sociology is often defined in terms of concepts and topics that are often non-unique to our field (e.g. health, illness, medicine, social factors), Sociology in general and other health sciences are often unclear about the nature of our work or our unique contributions to the study of health and medicine. Disciplinary structures that define Medical Sociology in terms of major subfields and key contributions is an important step toward a more efficient and contemporary representation of our unique contributions to the study of health.

Recommendation #2. ***Consider consistent research identities.*** It is difficult to develop as a field without consistent research identities. As medical sociologists, we should consider identifying with one or more of the four major subfields. The consistent use of shared labels will eventually help to crystalize our disciplinary structure and to better demonstrate our contributions. It is insufficient to simply identify the subfields that represent research conducted in medical sociology. Identifying with major subfields reinforces the structure of the field by consistently signifying the nature of our work. This recommendation in no way limits the ways in which researchers might identify themselves or their work. For example, in some circumstances, it may make sense to claim expertise in health care or medicalization. Our recommendation is that researchers also recognize where their interests fit into a broader disciplinary structure that distills our major subfields and key contributions to the sociological study of health and medicine.

Recommendation #3. ***Consider consistent graduate program identities.*** One potential strategy is for graduate programs to consider identifying as comprehensive or focused. Comprehensive graduate programs would represent the field as a whole. Focused graduate programs would represent one or more specific subfields. Precise program identities would contribute to more efficient graduate programs by dictating hiring decisions (who to hire), graduate recruitment strategies (who to recruit), and graduate curriculum (which courses and area examinations). For example, comprehensive programs could choose to require area examinations that cover the field whereas focused programs could require area examinations that correspond to selected subfields. Doing so would align examinations with faculty expertise, which is consistent with the American Sociological Association's *Code of Professional Ethics*.

Recommendation #4. ***Reconsider the role of Sociology in Medicine.*** Although we have excellent graduate programs in Social Epidemiology, Social Psychology of Health and Illness, and Sociology *of* Medicine, Sociology *in* Medicine is currently unrepresented in the graduate landscape. What role should Sociology *in* Medicine have in graduate education? Each year our graduates go on to work in medical schools, hospitals, government organizations, and health research firms. Non-academic job placements are likely to become even more common as the academic job market shrinks. We encourage conversations around the question of dedicating graduate courses or entire graduate programs to training graduate students to work in inter-disciplinary, inter-professional, and applied contexts. "Medical sociology's usefulness beyond its informative and educational function" has been called into question because our graduate programs are "still rather didactic and merely educational, not applied" (Constantinou 2015). Recent job ads for positions in institutions of medicine specify "a PhD in Psychology or Sociology with a specialty in Health Psychology or Medical Sociology." However, postings that encourage applications "from candidates in all disciplines… including the social and behavioral sciences…" are more and more common. Complicating this picture is a market that increasingly highlights skill sets rather than disciplinary background.

We also encourage conversations about how we can best support the long-term careers of sociologists placed in institutions of medicine. We may need to develop ways of embedding our graduates in ongoing training programs that are formed and nurtured not by medicine, but by sociology. When our graduates become disconnected from Sociology, the students we train so well may not remain sociologists for long. The Medical Sociology section of the American Sociological Association might consider devoting additional sessions and activities to applied medical sociology to maintain connections with sociologists in practice settings. Discussions along these lines could eventually facilitate the placement of even more graduate students in sparse hiring climates and increase our status across the health sciences. Success in these areas could lead to more resources being devoted to sociology programs in general.

Conclusion

In this paper, we argued that the sociological study of health in the US has failed to identify a contemporary disciplinary structure (an "island of meaning") that adequately represents the field. Instead of defining medical sociology conceptually, we defined its structure in terms of four major subfields: Social Epidemiology, Social Psychology of Health and Illness, Sociology *of* Medicine, and Sociology *in* Medicine. While recognizing an underlying unity driven by common training in sociological theory and research, we reviewed the unique contributions of each subfield. Specifically, medical sociology examines (1) the social causes of health-related outcomes and behaviors, (2) the social psychological processes that mediate and moderate the social causes and social consequences of health, (3) issues linked with health care delivery and health care experiences, medical knowledge, and health social movements, including social inequality, social institutions, and health policy/law, and (4) problems within institutions of medicine, including medical treatment, health professions, and the marketing of health care. We also recommended efforts toward a more refined and directed conceptualization of the field, including the establishment of a more explicit disciplinary structure that is supported by consistent research identities, relevant graduate program, and greater attention to Sociology *in* Medicine. Ultimately, we argued for a more efficient and representative organization of the field that more clearly demonstrates our contributions to the study of health. This is not the final statement on the organization of medical sociology. Our hope is to reintroduce these discussions as a matter of regular discourse. Much has changed since Straus (1957), and even more developments are on the horizon.

References

Abraham, John. 2010. "Pharmaceuticalization of Society in Context: Theoretical, Empirical and Health Dimensions." *Sociology* 44: 603–22.

Anderson, Odun and Milvoy Seacat. 1957. *The Behavioral Scientists and Research in the Health Field.* New York: Health Information Foundation, Research Series.

Aneshensel, Carol. 1992. "Social Stress: Theory and Research." *Annual Review of Sociology* 18: 15–38.

Barker, Kristin. 2002. "Self-Help Literature and the Making of an Illness Identity: The Case of Fibromyalgia Syndrome (FMS)." *Social Problems* 49: 279–300.

Baum, Andrew, Tracey Revenson, and Jerome Singer. 2011. *Handbook of Health Psychology.* New York: Taylor & Francis Group.

Berkman, Lisa, Ichiro Kawachi, and Maria Glymour. 2014. *Social Epidemiology*, 2nd *edition.* New York: Oxford University Press.

Bird, Chloe, Allen Fremont, and Stefan Timmermans. 2010. *Handbook of Medical Sociology*, 6th *edition.* Nashville, TN: Vanderbilt University Press.

Bird, Chloe and Patricia Rieker. 2008. *Gender and Health: The Effects of Constrained Choices and Social Policies.* New York: Cambridge University Press.

Bloom, Samuel. 1986. "Institutional Trends in Medical Sociology." *Journal of Health and Social Behavior* 27: 265–76.

Bloom, Samuel, Albert Wessen, Robert Straus, George Reader, and Jerome Myers. 1960. "The Sociologist as Medical Educator: A Discussion." *American Sociological Review* 25: 95–101.

Boulton, Richard. 2017. "Social Medicine and Sociology: The Productiveness of Antagonisms Arising from Maintaining Disciplinary Boundaries." *Social Theory & Health* 15: 241–60.

Broom, Dorothy, Cathy Banwell, and Don Gardner. 2013. "Antecedents of Culture-in-Health Research." Pp. 15–22 in *When Culture Impacts Health: Global Lessons for Effective Health Research*, edited by C. Banwell, S. Ulijaszek, and J. Dixon. London: Academic Press.

Brown, Phil, Stephen Zavestoski, Sabrina McCormick, Meadow Linder, Joshua Mandelbaum, and Theo Luebke. 2001. "A Gulf of Difference: Disputes over Gulf War-Related Illnesses." *Journal of Health and Social Behavior* 42: 235–57.

Brown, Phil, Stephen Zavestoski, Rachel Morello-Frosch, Sabrina McCormick, Brian Mayer, Rebecca Altman, et al. 2013. "Embodied Health Movements: Uncharted Territory in Social Movement Research." Pp. 600–15 in *The Sociology of Health & Illness: Critical Perspectives*, edited by P. Conrad. New York: Worth Publishers.

Bury, M. 1986. "Social Constructionism and the Development of Medical Sociology." *Sociology of Health & Illness* 8: 137–69.

Carr, Deborah, Jennifer Cornman, and Vicki Freedman. 2017. "Disability and Activity-Related Emotion in Later Life: Are Effects Buffered by Intimate Relationship Support and Strain?" *Journal of Health and Social Behavior* 58: 387–403.

Carr, Deborah and Debra Umberson. 2013. "The Social Psychology of Stress, Health, and Coping." Pp. 465–87 in *Handbook of Social Psychology*, edited by J. Delamater and A. Ward. New York: Springer.

Chaiklin, Harris. 2011. "The State of the Art in Medical Sociology." *Journal of Nervous and Mental Disease* 199: 585–91.

Charmaz, Kathy. 1983. "Loss of Self: A Fundamental Form of Suffering in the Chronically Ill." *Sociology of Health & Illness* 5: 168–95.

Charmaz, Kathy. 1991. *Good Days, Bad Days: The Self in Chronic Illness and Time*. New Brunswick, NJ: Rutgers University Press.

Clarke, Adele and Janet Shim. 2011. "Medicalization and Biomedicalization Revisited: Technoscience and Transformations of Health, Illness and American Medicine." Pp. 173–99 in *Handbook of the Sociology of Health, Illness, and Healing: A Blueprint for the 21st Century*, edited by B. Pescosolido, J. Martin, J. McLeod, and Anne Rogers. New York: Springer.

Cockerham, William. 1983. "The State of Medical Sociology in the United States, Great Britain, West Germany and Austria: Applied Vs Pure Theory." *Social Science & Medicine* 17: 1513–27.

Cockerham, William. 2005. "Health Lifestyle Theory and the Convergence of Agency and Structure." *Journal of Health and Social Behavior* 46: 51–67.

Cockerham, William. 2013. "Bourdieu and an Update of Health Lifestyle Theory." Pp. 127–54 in *Medical Sociology on the Move: New Directions in Theory*, edited by W. Cockerham. Dordrecht: Springer.

Cockerham, William. 2017. *Medical Sociology*, 14th *edition*. New York: Routledge.

Committee on Certification in Medical Sociology. 1986. Washington, D.C.: American Sociological Association.

Conrad, Peter. 1992. "Medicalization and Social Control." *Annual Review of Sociology* 18: 209–32.

Conrad, Peter and Valerie Leiter. 2004. "Medicalization, Markets and Consumers." *Journal of Health and Social Behavior* 45: 158–76.

Constantinou, Costas. 2015. "Individualized Medical Sociology: Placing Sociology in Medical Practice." *Journal of Applied Social Science* 9: 182–90.

Cortez, Dagoberto, Douglas Maynard, and Toby Campbell. 2019. "Creating Space to Discuss End-of-Life Issues in Cancer Care." *Patient Education and Counseling* 102: 216–22.

Dyrbye, Lotte, Tait Shanafelt, Christine Sinsky, Pamela Cipriano, Jay Bhatt, Alexander Ommaya, Colin West, and David Meyers. 2017. "Burnout among Health Care Professionals: A Call to Explore and Address this Underrecognized Threat to Safe, High-Quality Care." National Academy of Medicine July 5.

Ferraro, Kenneth and Tetyana Shippee. 2009. "Aging and Cumulative Inequality: How Does Inequality Get under the Skin?" *The Gerontologist* 49: 333–43.

Freeman, Howard, Sol Levine, and Leo Reeder. 1979. *Handbook of Medical Sociology*, 3rd *edition*. Englewood Cliffs, N.J.: Prentice-Hall.

Freeman, Howard and Leo Reeder. 1957. "Medical Sociology: A Review of the Literature." *American Sociological Review* 22: 73–81.

Freund, Peter, Meredith McGuire, and Linda Podhurst. 2003. *Health, Illness, and the Social Body: A Critical Sociology*. Upper Saddle River, NJ: Prentice Hall.

George, Linda. 2001. "The Social Psychology of Health." Pp. 217–37 in *Handbook of Aging and the Social Sciences*, edited by R. Binstock and L. George. Burlington, MA: Academic Press.

Gold, Margaret. 1977. "A Crisis of Identity: The Case of Medical Sociology." *Journal of Health and Social Behavior* 18: 160–8.

Hollingshead, August. 1973. "Medical Sociology: A Brief Review." *The Milbank Memorial Fund Quarterly* 51: 531–42.

Horobin, Gordon. 1985. "Medical Sociology in Britain: True Confessions of an Empiricist." *Sociology of Health & Illness* 7: 94–107.

House, James. 2002. "Understanding Social Factors and Inequalities in Health: 20th Century Progress and 21st Century Prospects." *Journal of Health and Social Behavior* 43: 125–42.

Kaiser, Karen. 2008. "The Meaning of the Survivor Identity for Women with Breast Cancer." *Social Science & Medicine* 67: 79–87.

Kawachi, Ichiro and S. Subramanian. 2018. "Social Epidemiology for the 21st Century." *Social Science & Medicine* 196: 240–5.

Kessler, Ronald, James House, Renne Anspach, and David Williams. 1995. "Social Psychology and Health." Pp. 548–70 in *Sociological Perspectives on Social Psychology*, edited by K. Cook, G. Fine, and J. House. Boston, MA: Allyn and Bacon.

Levine, Sol. 1987. "The Changing Terrains in Medical Sociology: Emergent Concern with Quality of Life." *Journal of Health and Social Behavior* 28: 1–6.

Link, Bruce and Jo Phelan. 2000. "Evaluating the Fundamental Cause Explanation for Social Disparities in Health." Pp. 33–46 in *Handbook of Medical Sociology*, edited by C. Bird, P. Conrad, and A. Fremont. Upper Saddle River, NJ: Prentice Hall.

Lutfey, Karen and Jeremy Freese. 2005. Toward Some Fundamentals of Fundamental Causality: Socioeconomic Status and Health in the Routine Clinic Visit for Diabetes. *American Journal of Sociology* 110: 1326–72.

McIntire, Charles. 1991. "The Importance of the Study of Medical Sociology." *Sociological Practice* 9: 30–7.

McLeod, Jane, Christy Erving, and Jennifer Caputo. 2014. "Health Inequalities." Pp. 715–42 in *Handbook of the Social Psychology of Inequality*, edited by J. McLeod, E. Lawler, and M. Schwalbe. New York: Springer.

Mechanic, David. 1966. "The Sociology of Medicine: Viewpoints and Perspectives." *Journal of Health and Human Behavior* 7: 237–48.

Mirowsky, John and Catherine Ross. 2003. *Social Causes of Psychological Distress*. Hawthorne, NY: Aldine de Gruyter/Transaction.

Mossakowski, Krysia. 2003. "Coping with Perceived Discrimination: Does Ethnic Identity Protect Mental Health?" *Journal of Health and Social Behavior* 44: 318–31.

O'Rand, Angela. 1996. "The Precious and the Precocious: Understanding Cumulative Disadvantage and Cumulative Advantage over the Life Course." *The Gerontologist* 36: 230–8.

Oh, Hyeyoung. 2017. "Resisting Throughput Pressures: Physicians' and Patients' Strategies to Manage Hospital Discharge." *Journal of Health and Social Behavior* 58: 116–30.

Ong, Lucille, Johanna De Haes, Alaysia Hoos, and Frits Lammes. 1995. "Doctor-Patient Communication: A Review of the Literature." *Social Science & Medicine* 40: 903–18.

Ong, Lucille, M. Frits Lammes Visser, and de Haes. Johanna 2000. "Doctor–Patient Communication and Cancer Patients' Quality of Life and Satisfaction." *Patient Education and Counseling* 41: 145–56.

Ospina, Naykky, Kari Phillips, Rene Rodriguez-Gutierrez, Ana Castaneda-Guarderas, Michael Gionfriddo, Megan Branda, and Victor Montori. 2019. "Eliciting the Patient's Agenda-Secondary Analysis of Recorded Clinical Encounters." *Journal of General Internal Medicine* 34: 36–40.

Pauly, Mark, Thomas McGuire, and Pedro Barros. 2012. *Handbook of Health Economics*. Waltham, MA: North Holland.

Pearlin, Leonard. 1989. "The Sociological Study of Stress." *Journal of Health and Social Behavior* 30: 241–56.

Pescosolido, Bernice, Jack Martin, Annie Lang, and Sigrun Olafsdottir. 2008. "Rethinking Theoretical Approaches to Stigma: A Framework Integrating Normative Influences on Stigma (FINIS)." *Social Science & Medicine* 67: 431–40.

Pescosolido, Bernice, Jack Martin, Jane McLeod, and Anne Rogers. 2011. *Handbook of the Sociology of Health, Illness, and Healing: A Blueprint for the 21st Century*. New York: Springer.

Petersdorf, Robert and Alvan Feinstein. 1980. "An Informal Appraisal of the Current Status of 'Medical Sociology'." Pp. 27–48 in *The Relevance of Social Science for Medicine*, edited by L. Eisenberg and A. Kleinman. Dordrecht: Springer.

Phelan, Jo and Bruce Link. 2013. "Fundamental Cause Theory." Pp. 105–26 in *Medical Sociology on the Move: New Directions in Theory*, edited by W. Cockerham. Dordrecht: Springer.

Ruderman, Florence. 1981. "What is Medical Sociology?" *Journal of the American Medical Association* 245: 927–9.

Saillant, Francine and Serge Genest. 2007. *Medical Anthropology: Regional Perspectives and Shared Concerns*. Malden, MA: Wiley-Blackwell.

Schnittker, Jason. 2004. "Education and the Changing Shape of the Income Gradient in Health." *Journal of Health and Social Behavior* 45: 286–305.

Schnittker, Jason and McLeod Jane. 2005. "The Social Psychology of Health Disparities." *Annual Review of Sociology* 31: 75–103.

Sellers, Robert, Cleopatra Caldwell, Karen Schmeelk-Cone, and Marc Zimmerman. 2003. "Racial Identity, Racial Discrimination, Perceived Stress, and Psychological Distress among African American Young Adults." *Journal of Health and Social Behavior* 44: 302–17.

Simon, Robin. 2000. "The Importance of Culture in Sociological Theory and Research on Stress and Mental Health: A Missing Link." Pp. 68–78 in *The Handbook of Medical Sociology*, edited by C. Bird, P. Conrad, and A. Freemont. Upper Saddle River, NJ: Prentice Hall.

Stepanikova, Irena, Qian Zhang, Darry Wieland, G. Eleazer, and Thomas Stewart. 2012. "Non-Verbal Communication between Primary Care Physicians and Older Patients: How Does Race Matter?" *Journal of General Internal Medicine* 27: 576–81.

Straus, Robert. 1957. "The Nature and Status of Medical Sociology." *American Sociological Review* 22: 200–4.

Straus, Robert. 1999. "Medical Sociology: A Personal Fifty Year Perspective." *Journal of Health and Social Behavior* 40: 103–10.

Syme, Leonard and Irene Yen. 2000. "Social Epidemiology and Medical Sociology: Different Approaches to the Same Problem." Pp. 365–76 in *Handbook of Medical Sociology*, edited by C. Bird, P. Conrad, and A. Fremont. Upper Saddle River, NJ: Prentice Hall.

Taylor, Catherine. 2016. "'Relational by Nature?' Men and Women Do Not Differ in Physiological Response to Social Stressors Faced by Token Women." *American Journal of Sociology* 122: 49–89.

Taylor, Shelley, Rena Repetti, and Teresa Seeman. 1997. "Health Psychology: What Is an Unhealthy Environment and How Does It Get under the Skin?" *Annual Review of Psychology* 48: 411–47.

Turner, R., Blair Wheaton, and Donald Lloyd. 1995. "The Epidemiology of Social Stress." *American Sociological Review* 60: 104–25.

Veenstra, Gerry. 2002. "Medical Sociology." Pp. 748–50 in *The Encyclopedia of Public Health*, edited by L. Breslow, L. Green, W. Keck, J. Last, and M. McGinnis. New York: Macmillan.

Wardwell, Walter. 1982. "The State of Medical Sociology – A Review Essay." *The Sociological Quarterly* 23: 563–73.

Weiss, Gregory and Lynne Lonnquist. 2016. *The Sociology of Health, Healing, and Illness*. Upper Saddle River, NJ: Pearson Prentice Hall.

Weitz, Rose. 2017. *The Sociology of Health, Illness, and Health Care: A Critical Approach*. Belmont, CA: Thomas Wadsworth.

Zerubavel, Eviatar. 1991. *The Fine Line: Making Distinctions in Everyday Life*. Chicago, IL: University of Chicago Press.

2

Medical Sociology and Sociological Theory

William C. Cockerham and Graham Scambler

The link between medical sociology and sociological theory is crucial to the subdiscipline. Theory binds medical sociology to the larger discipline of sociology more extensively than any other aspect of the sociological enterprise. Sociological theory is also what usually distinguishes research in medical sociology from socially oriented studies in allied fields, like public health, epidemiology, and health services research. Whereas seminal sociological contributions in quantitative and qualitative data collection and analysis, along with many fundamental concepts of social behavior, have been adopted by multidisciplinary approaches in several fields, sociological theory allows medical sociology to remain unique among the health-related social and behavioral sciences. This could be considered somewhat surprising because medical sociology has often been described in the past as atheoretical. It is true that much of the work in the field historically has been applied to practical problems rather than theoretical questions. That is, it was intended to help solve a clinical problem or policy issue, rather than develop theory or utilize it as a tool to enhance understanding.

Medical sociology was not established until after World War II when the American government provided extensive funding through the National Institutes of Health for joint sociological and medical research projects. The same situation prevailed in Western Europe, where, unlike in the US, few medical sociologists were affiliated with university sociology faculties and connections to the general discipline of sociology were especially weak (Claus 1982; Cockerham 1983). It was primarily through the stimulus of the availability of government funding that sociologists and health professionals embraced medical sociology as a new subdiscipline. Funding agencies were not interested in theoretical work, but sponsored research that had some practical utility in postwar society as Western governments had come to realize that social factors were important for health.

The Wiley Blackwell Companion to Medical Sociology, First Edition. Edited by William C. Cockerham.

By the end of the twentieth century, however, this situation had changed significantly. Most research in medical sociology remains oriented toward practical problem solving, but the use of sociological theory in this endeavor is now widespread. There has been a general evolution of work in medical sociology that combines both applied and theoretical perspectives, with the utilization of theory becoming increasingly common as a framework for explaining or predicting health-related social behavior. At the same time, medical sociology moved away from a state of dependence upon medicine for defining and guiding research agendas to a position of relative independence. Although the relationship between medical sociology and medicine has been important, it has not always been harmonious. Medical sociology tended to side with patients and call attention to instances of poor medical care, while some physicians have been contemptuous of medical sociologists in clinical settings. Yet medicine nurtured, funded, sponsored, and even named medical sociology early in its development and continues to do so today (Cockerham 2021). In fact, one could arguably state that medicine has supported medical sociology with funding, jobs, and research opportunities to a much greater extent than sociology. It can also be claimed that the increased use of theory in medical sociology represents more of an effort on the part of medical sociologists to establish and reinforce links to the parent discipline than vice versa. In many ways, medicine has been a better ally of medical sociology than sociology.

While medical sociology is moving closer to sociology, it has generally removed itself from a subordinate position to medicine. There are four reasons for this development. First, the shift from acute or infectious to chronic diseases as the primary causes of death in contemporary societies has made medical sociology increasingly important to medicine. This is because of the key roles of social behavior and living conditions in the prevention, onset, and course of chronic disorders. Previously, these social determinants were not considered prime causes of infectious diseases, but it appears this view is also changing as seen in social factors relevant to the origin and spread of the COVID-19 global pandemic (Abrams and Szefler 2020). Second, medical sociology has moved into a greater partnership with medicine as it has matured and fostered a significant body of research literature, much of it relevant to clinical medicine and health policy. Third, success in research has promoted the professional status of medical sociologists, in relation to both medicine and sociology. And fourth, medical sociology has generally set its own research agenda, which includes medical practice and health policy as an *object* of study. In doing so, medical sociologists have established themselves as objective professionals.

The movement of medical sociology toward greater connections with general sociology reflects the desire of a mature subdiscipline to expand its analytic capabilities and reinforce its potential. Changing social conditions associated with the transition in society from the postindustrial age to today's late modern period requires all of sociology to account for altered realities and formulate new concepts. This situation suggests that not only is medical sociology connecting with general sociology, but that sociology is moving toward a closer affiliation with it – given the considerations of health increasingly evident in the everyday social lives of people and medical sociology's capacity for explaining it. Under the current conditions of social change, medical sociologists are making greater use of sociological theory because theory promotes the explanatory power of their empirical findings. This development has led some to suggest that medical sociology may indeed prove to be the "leading edge" in some areas of the development of contemporary theory (Cockerham 2013a, 2021; Turner 1992). The extent to which this assertion will be fully realized is not yet certain, but it is clear that a considerable amount of theoretical work is taking place in medical sociology (Cockerham 2013a, 2013b, 2021a, 2021b; Collyer 2015; Conrad 2007, 2013; De Maio 2010; Link and Phelan 1995; Phelan and Link 2013; Scambler 2012, 2018). The remainder of this chapter will provide an overview of the field with respect to theory.

Talcott Parsons and Emile Durkheim

From 1946 to 1951, the new field of medical sociology was almost completely an applied area of research. Medical sociologists worked with psychiatrists and other physicians on government-funded projects to largely address medical problems; few were employed in university departments of sociology in the US and they were generally absent from sociology faculties in Europe and Asia. However, a pivotal event occurred in 1951 that oriented medical sociology toward theoretical concerns and initiated the establishment of its academic credentials. This was the publication of Talcott Parsons' long anticipated book, *The Social System*, which established the author at the time as the dominant figure in American sociology. Anything Parsons published attracted great attention because he was thought to be charting a course for all of sociology. This book, providing a structural-functionalist model of society, contained Parsons' concept of the sick role and was the first time a major sociological theorist included an analysis of the function of medicine in a general concept of society. Parsons (1951: 428–9) was interested in the differing roles of professionals in capitalist and socialist societies and decided to include physicians and their relationship to their clients in his analysis because this topic was an area of long-standing interest and one in which he felt he had familiarity.

Parsons had been strongly influenced by the ideas of the classic sociological theorists Emile Durkheim and Max Weber. He had completed his doctoral studies at Heidelberg University in Germany in the mid-1920s where he participated in the "Weber Circle" that continued to meet regularly to discuss sociology at the home of Max Weber's widow, Marianne Weber, following Weber's death in 1920. Parsons subsequently translated Weber's book on the *Protestant Ethic and the Spirit of Capitalism* (Weber [1904–5] 1958) into English, and reintroduced the theoretical work of both Weber and Emile Durkheim to European sociologists after the disruption of their work during World War II. In his concept of the sick role, Parsons incorporated Durkheim's ideas on moral authority and Weber's analysis of religion into his discussion of the normative requirement to visit physicians when sick and the dominant position of the physician in the doctor–patient role relationship.

Parsons' concept of the sick role is a clear and straightforward statement of four basic propositions outlining the normative pattern of physician utilization by the sick and their respective social roles. Parsons not only constructed the first theoretical concept directly applicable to medical sociology, but by utilizing the work of Durkheim and Weber, he did so within the parameters of classical sociological theory. His formulation was recognized as "a penetrating and apt analysis of sickness from a distinctly sociological point of view" (Freidson 1970a: 228), which indeed it was. Parsons' concept of the sick role remained a central theoretical proposition in medical sociology for decades, despite challenges. It still survives in a diminished status as an "ideal-type" explanation for physician–patient encounters in which the primary form of interaction is that of guidance on the part of the physician and cooperation by the patient in clinics or office settings.

Parsons also influenced the study of professions by using the medical profession as the model for professions based on expertise and a service orientation. Although extensive criticism was to subsequently lessen the acceptance of the Parsonian approach to theory, this outcome does not negate the significant influence Parsons initially had on promoting theory in medical sociology. Parsons, more so than any other sociologist of his time, made medical sociology academically viable by providing it with its inaugural theoretical orientation: structural-functionalism.

However, structural-functionalism, with its emphasis on value consensus, social order, stability, and functional processes at the macro-level of society, had a short-lived period as the leading theoretical paradigm in all of sociology, including medical sociology. It was under assault by critics in the 1960s and early 1970s and lost influence thereafter. Symbolic interactionists had objected to the relegation of individuals to passive roles in large social systems, while conflict theorists found structural-functionalism inadequate in explaining the process of social change and the social functions of conflict. The theory's emphasis on equilibrium and consensus also seemed to favor maintenance of the status quo and support for dominant elites. No one calls themselves a structural-functionalist today.

Durkheim ([1895] 1964), however, who was initially responsible for the theory in sociology, remains one of the greatest sociologists of time through his efforts to establish sociology as a science based on methodological procedures and empirical data. He emphasized the importance of macro-level social processes, structures, norms, and values external to individuals that integrated them into the larger society and shaped their behavior. People were depicted as constrained in exercising free will by the social order. Durkheim's ([1897] 1951) only work that had a direct application to medical sociology was his theory of suicide in which the act of taking one's life was determined by the individual's ties to his or her community or society. This is seen in his typology of three major types of suicide: (1) egoistic (social detachment), (2) anomic (state of normlessness), and (3) altruistic (a normative demand for suicide). A fourth type, fatalistic suicide, was never fully conceptualized. The merit of his approach is that it shows the capability of the larger society to create stressful situations where people are forced to respond to conditions not of their own choosing. Thus, Durkheim helps us not only to understand the social facets of suicide, but also to recognize that macro-level social events (like economic downturns) can affect health in a variety of ways through stress and that the effects of stress can be mitigated through social support.

Symbolic Interaction

The first major theoretical perspective to challenge Parsons and structural-functionalist theory in medical sociology was symbolic interaction, based largely on the work of George Herbert Mead (1934) and Herbert Blumer (1969). Symbolic interaction maintained that social reality is constructed on a micro-level by individuals interacting with one another on the basis of shared symbolic meanings. Human beings were seen to possess the capacity to think, define situations, and construct their behavior on the basis of their definitions and interpretations. "It is the position of symbolic interaction," states Blumer (1969: 55), "that the social action of the actor is *constructed* by him [or her]; it is not a mere release of activity brought about by the play of initiating factors on his [or her] organization." Social life was therefore produced by interacting agents choosing their own behavior and acting accordingly, not by large-scale social processes and structures channeling behavior down optionless pathways. Symbolic interaction had not only its particular (micro-level) orientation toward theory construction, but also its own qualitative research methodologies of participant observation focus groups, unobtrusive measures such as biographies and life histories, and situational analysis consisting of mapping the positions, situations, and social worlds of those being studied (Clarke et al. 2018; Denzin 2017; Denzin and Lincoln 2018). These methodologies focused on small group interaction in natural social settings. A related approach was ethnomethodology, which featured descriptions of taken-for-granted meanings in natural settings, rather than analysis.

The major figures in early medical sociology working in the symbolic interactionist tradition were Anselm Strauss and Erving Goffman. Strauss joined with Howard Becker and others in their now classic study of medical school socialization, *Boys in White* (Becker et al. 1961). Strauss made his own contributions to theory and methods in a number of areas, including seminal work on the social process of death and dying (Glaser and Strauss 1965, 1968); observation of the "negotiated order" of hospital routine featuring a minimum of "hard and fast" regulations and a maximum of "innovation and improvization" in patient care, especially in emergency treatment (Strauss et al. 1963); and formulation of grounded theory methodology featuring the development of hypotheses from data during analysis, rather than before (Glaser and Strauss 1967).

Goffman, who became a major theorist in sociology generally, began his research career in medical sociology by using participant observation to study the life of mental hospital patients. His classic work in this area, *Asylums* (1961), presented the concept of "total institutions" that emerged as an important sociological statement on the social situation of people confined by institutions. His observations also led to the development of his notions of impression management and the dramaturgical perspective in sociology that views "life as a theatre" and "people as actors on a stage," as well as his concept of stigma (Goffman 1959; 1967).

With the introduction of symbolic interactionist research into an area previously dominated by structural-functionalism, medical sociology became an arena of debate between two of sociology's major theoretical schools. By the mid-1960s, symbolic interaction came to dominate a significant portion of the literature in the field. One feature of this domination was the numerous studies conducted in reference to labeling theory, a variant of symbolic interaction, and the controversy it provoked. Labeling theory held that deviant behavior is not a quality of the act a person commits but rather is a consequence of the definition applied to that act by others (Becker 1973). That is, whether or not an act is considered deviant depends upon how other people react to it. Although labeling theory pertained to deviance generally, the primary center of argument was focused on the mental patient experience, with Thomas Scheff (1999) the principal proponent of the labeling approach. Labeling theory was also employed in studies of the medical profession as seen in Eliot Freidson's (1970b) alternative concept of the sick role.

By the 1980s, however, symbolic interaction entered a period of decline in medical sociology. Many of its adherents had been "rebels" intentionally subverting the dominant paradigm of structural-functionalism and giving voices to women and marginal social groups like mental patients, the physically handicapped, and the aged and their caretakers by entering their social world and observing it. Yet, as Norman Denzin (1991) points out, between 1981 and 1990, the canonical texts in the field had shifted from Mead to Blumer and Blumer himself was under attack on several methodological and substantive issues – but most importantly for not advancing the field to meet his own early criticisms; moreover, practitioners of the perspective were getting older ("the graying of interactionism"), the number of students espousing interactionism was decreasing, and the old enemy (structural-functionalism) had been largely vanquished. Elsewhere, in Britain, where interactionism had been the dominant theoretical perspective in medical sociology in the majority of published studies in the past (Annandale 2014), a related theoretical perspective – social constructionism – has now largely displaced it (Nettleton 2020; Seale 2008).

Unfortunately, symbolic interaction had taken on the image of a "fixed doctrine" and, except for Mead's (1934) concept of the "generalized other," was unable to satisfactorily link small group processes with social phenomena reflecting the behavioral influences of the larger social entities. It was particularly unable to account for interaction between institutions or societal – level processes that affect each other, not just individuals or groups. In addition, labeling theory, despite its merits in accounting for the powerful behavioral effects of "labels" placed on people, had not been able to explain the causes of deviance (other than the reaction of people to it), nor whether deviants themselves share common characteristics like poverty, stress, family, or class background.

But it would be a mistake to relegate symbolic interaction to history, as its methodologies remain the primary forms of qualitative research in medical sociology. Observed patterns of behavior and first-person accounts of social situations bring a sense of "real life" to studies that quantitative research is unable to capture. While symbolic interaction theory has not moved far beyond the original concepts of Mead and Blumer, it persists as an important theoretical approach to the study and explanation of social behavior among small groups of people interacting in ways that are relevant for health.

Conflict Theory

Conflict theory, with its roots in the work of Karl Marx and Max Weber, joined symbolic interaction in significantly reducing the influence of structural-functionalism, but did not achieve a dominant position in medical sociology. Conflict theory is based on the assumption that society is composed of various groups struggling for advantage, that inequality is a basic feature of social life, and conflict is the major cause of social change. Marx's perspective in conflict theory is seen in the rejection of the view expressed by structural-functionalism that society is held together by shared norms and values. Conflict theory claims that true consensus does not exist; rather, society's norms and values are those of the dominant elite and imposed by them on the less privileged to maintain their advantaged position. Weber adds, however, that social inequality is not based on just money, property, and relationships to the means of production, but also on status and political influence. Since all social systems contain such inequality, conflict inevitably results and conflict, in turn, is responsible for social change.

Whereas the Marxian-oriented features of conflict theory have emphasized systemic exploitation and class struggle, other theorists have moved toward emphasizing conflicts that occur between interest groups and the unequal distribution of political power (Dahrendorf 1959). According to Bryan Turner (1988), modern societies are best understood as having a conflict between the principles of democratic politics (emphasizing equality and universal rights) and the organization of their economic systems (involving the production, exchange, and consumption of goods and services, about which there is considerable inequality). Therefore, while people have political equality, they lack social equality. This unresolved contradiction is relatively permanent and a major source of conflict. Ideologies of fairness are constantly challenged by the realities of inequalities, and they influence governments to try to resolve the situation through politics and welfare benefits.

This situation represents one of conflict theory's most important assets for medical sociology; namely, the capacity to explain the politics associated with health reform. Conflict theory allows us to chart the maneuvers of various entities, like the medical profession, insurance companies, pharmaceutical companies, the business community, and the public, as they struggle to acquire, protect, or expand their interests against existing government regulations and programs and those under consideration. Other conflict approaches are connected more directly to classical Marxism by relying on class struggle to explain health policy outcomes and the disadvantages of the lower and working classes in capitalist medical systems where the emphasis is on profit (De Maio 2010; Muntaner et al. 2014; Scambler 2018). This view does not consider political struggles between interest groups as a sufficient strategy for understanding health inequalities and instead emphasizes class conflict and exploitation as the most complete explanation for the poor health of disadvantaged groups.

While versions of conflict theory emanating from the writings of Marx undoubtedly lost salience in the last quarter of the twentieth century, the global financial crisis of 2008–2009 and its aftermath have triggered a resurgence of interest. As material inequalities have increased in a politically uncertain and volatile world some medical sociologists have returned to mainstream Marxian analyses of capitalism's inherent contradictions to explain health inequalities (Scambler 2018). In this context Fredrich Engels too is often cited, not least because of his studies of Manchester in nineteenth-century England and the differential impact of rapid processes of industrialization on workers' health. For him, capitalist exploitation amounted to a murderous assault on the working classes. Unsurprisingly, explanations based on the theories of Marx and Engels emphasize the macro-sociology of social structure, sometimes at the expense of culture, interaction, and agency. As with most other theorists who have gained the attention of medical sociology, the contributions of conflict theorists throw light on limited aspects of health and healthcare. Their strength is a focus on the causal inputs of system and structure on institutions and individual behavior, their weakness a tendency to gloss over non-conflictual phenomena and the minutiae of everyday interactions through which individuals forge their projects and negotiate their way in the world.

Max Weber

None of the classical theorists – Comte, Spencer, Simmel, Marx, Durkheim, and Weber – concerned themselves with medical sociology. The canonized trio of Marx, Durkheim, and Weber did occasionally refer to health in their writings (Collyer 2010), but they did not establish medical sociology as a subdiscipline of sociology nor indicate they were even aware of it. Weber, nevertheless, had a major influence on the field. Among his most important contributions are his concepts of formal rationality and lifestyles. Weber ([1922] 1978) distinguished between two major types of rationality: formal and substantive. Formal rationality is the purposeful calculation of the most efficient means and procedures to realize goals, while substantive rationality is the realization of values and ideals based on tradition, custom, piety, or personal devotion. Weber described how, in Western society, formal rationality became dominant over its substantive counterpart as people sought to achieve specific ends by employing the most efficient means and, in the process, tended to disregard substantive rationality because it was often cumbersome, time-consuming, inefficient, and stifled progress. This form of rationality led to the rise of the West and the spread of capitalism. It is also linked to the development of scientific medicine and modern social structure through bureaucratic forms of authority and social organization that includes hospitals. The rational goal-oriented action that takes place in hospitals tends to be a flexible form of social order based on the requirements of patient care, rather than the rigid organization portrayed in Weber's concept of bureaucracy (Strauss et al. 1963). But his perspective on bureaucracy nevertheless captures the manner in which authority and control are exercised hierarchically and the importance of organizational goals in hospital work (Cockerham 2015).

Weber's notion of formal rationality has likewise been applied to the "deprofessionalization" of physicians. Deprofessionalization means a decline in power resulting in a decline in the degree to which a profession maintains its professional characteristics. Freidson's (1970a; 1970b) seminal work on the medical profession in the 1970s had depicted American medicine's professional dominance in its relations with patients and external organizations. Medicine was *the* model of professionalism, with physicians having absolute authority over their work and ranked at or near the top of society in status. However, George Ritzer and David Walczak (1988) noted the loss of absolute authority by physicians as their treatment decisions came under increasing scrutiny in the late twentieth century by patients, health care organizations, insurance companies, and government agencies.

Ritzer and Walczak found that government policies emphasizing greater control over health care costs and the rise of the profit motive in medicine identified a trend in medical practice away from substantive rationality (stressing ideals like serving the patient) to formal rationality (stressing rules, regulations, and efficiency). Government and insurance company oversight in reviewing and approving patient care decisions, and the rise of private health care business corporations, decreased the autonomy of medical doctors by increasingly hiring them as employees and monitoring their work. This, joined with greater consumerism on the part of patients, reduced the professional power and status of physicians. Thus, the "golden age" of medical power and prestige ended, as medicine's efforts to avoid regulation left open an unregulated medical market that invited corporate control and public demands for government control to contain costs.

Weber's work also provides the theoretical background for the study of health lifestyles. Weber ([1922] 1978) identified life conduct (*Lebensführung*) and life chances (*Lebenschancen*) as the two central components of lifestyles (*Lebensstil*). Life conduct refers to choice or self-direction in behavior. Weber was ambiguous about what he meant by life chances, but Ralf Dahrendorf (1979: 73) analyzed Weber's writings and found that the most comprehensive concept of life chances in his terminology is that of "class position" and that he associated the term with a person's probability of finding satisfaction for interests, wants, and needs. He did not consider life chances to be a matter of pure chance; rather, they are the chances that people have in life because of their social situation.

Weber's most important contribution to conceptualizing lifestyles is to identify the dialectical interplay between choices and chances as each works off the other to shape lifestyle outcomes (Abel and Cockerham 1993; Cockerham, Abel, and Lüschen 1993). That is, people choose their lifestyle and the activities that characterize it, but their choices are constrained by their social circumstances. Through his concept of *Verstehen* or interpretive understanding, Weber seems to favor the role of choice as a proxy for agency over chance as representative of structure in lifestyle selection, although both are important. Weber also made the observation that lifestyles are based not so much on what people produce, but what they consume. By connecting lifestyles to status, Weber suggests that the means of consumption not only *expresses* differences in social and cultural practices between groups, but *establishes* them as social boundaries (Bourdieu 1984).

Health lifestyles are collective patterns of health-related behavior based on choices from options available to people according to their life chances (Cockerham 2005, 2013b, 2021b; Cockerham et al. 1997). These life chances include class, age, gender, ethnicity, and other relevant structural variables that shape lifestyle choices. The choices typically involve decisions about smoking, alcohol use, diet, exercise, and the like. The behaviors resulting from the interplay of choices and chances can have either positive or negative consequences for health, but nevertheless form a pattern of health practices that constitute a lifestyle. Although positive health lifestyles are intended to produce good health, the ultimate aim of such lifestyles is to be healthy in order to use (consume) it for something, such as the capability to work, feel and look good, participate in sports and leisure activities, and enjoy life.

Health lifestyles originated in the upper middle class, yet have spread across class boundaries in varying degrees of quality (Cockerham, Kunz, and Lüschen 1988). While Weber did not consider the health aspects of lifestyles, his concepts allow us to view them as (1) associated with status groups and principally a collective, rather than individual, phenomenon; (2) patterns of consumption, not production; and (3) formed by the dialectical interplay between choices and chances. His conceptualization of lifestyles provides the foundation for current theorizing on health-related lifestyles (Cockerham 2005, 2013b, 2021a, 2021b).

Critical Theory and Jürgen Habermas

The term critical theory has a long history but in sociology has come to be associated with a group of philosophers and social theorists pre-eminent in a "culture critique" in Frankfurt in the interwar years and later, with the advent of Nazism, in California. Under the inspiration of Max Horkheimer and Theodor Adorno, and in the 1960s in the USA with Marcuse, the classical contributions of Marx and Weber were reworked and framed in response to fascism, Stalinism, and managerial capitalism (Outhwaite 1996). The name of Adorno, in particular, came to be linked with a profound and remorseless cultural pessimism: the logic of the twentieth century, even of modernity, was seen as one of ineluctable decline. The influential *Dialectic of Enlightenment*, written with Horkheimer during World War II and published in 1947, epitomizes this inexorable sense of decay. One of Adorno's assistants, Jürgen Habermas, did not share the gloom of his mentor and it is his contribution that came to dominate critical theory during the last decades of the twentieth century. Some medical sociologists turned to his work for theoretical inspiration. It was Habermas' concept of rationality that differentiated his theories from those of predecessors like Marx, Weber, Adorno, and Horkheimer. He rejected any suggestion that rationality be subsumed by Weber's *Zweckrationalität*, or instrumental rationality. In other words, rationality is more than that which governs the choice of means to given, usually material, ends. He developed the notion of what he came to call "communicative rationality," which refers to the activity of reflecting on our taken-for-granted assumptions about the world, bringing basic norms to the fore to be interrogated and negotiated. Not only does instrumental rationality bypass these norms, but it is on its own insufficient to capture the nature of either "cultural evolution" or even the economy and state, which are too complex to be seen merely as its product.

Basic to his early work is a distinction between work and interaction. Marx, Weber, and his Frankfurt predecessors had, he felt, fixated on the former and neglected the latter. In the case of Marxian theory, what Habermas understands as the reduction of interaction, or "communicative action," to work, instrumental or "strategic action," dramatically limited its scope both to account for modernity and to ground a project of human emancipation. The two-volume *Theory of Communicative Action*, published in Germany in 1981, took this analysis to a new level of subtlety and comprehensiveness (Habermas 1984; 1987). Locating his theories within the orbit of a "reconstructed" Enlightenment project, Habermas sought to bring together two long-standing, "rival" approaches to social theory. The first analyzes society as a meaningful whole for its participants (*Verstehen* theory); and the second analyzes society as a system that is stabilized behind the backs of the participants (system theory) (Sitton 1996). This goal gave rise to the celebrated distinction between the *lifeworld*, based on social integration, and the *system*, based on system integration.

The lifeworld is characterized by communicative action and has two aspects or sub-systems: the private sphere comprises the rapidly changing unit of the household, while the public sphere represents the domain of popular communication, discussion, and debate. The system operates through strategic action and it too has its sub-systems, the economy and the state. These four sub-systems are interdependent: each is specialized in terms of what it produces but is dependent on the others for what it does not produce. The private sphere of the lifeworld produces "commitment" and the public sphere "influence;" the economy produces "money" and the state "power." These products or "media" are traded between sub-systems. Thus the economy relies on the state to set up appropriate legal institutions such as private property and contract, on the public sphere of the lifeworld to influence consumption patterns, and on the private sphere to provide a committed labor force, and itself sends money into each other sub-system. Habermas argued that in the modern era, system and lifeworld have become "decoupled." Moreover, the system has come increasingly to dominate or "colonize" the lifeworld. Thus decision making across many areas owes more to money and power than to rational debate and consensus.

This notion of system penetration and colonization of the lifeworld has been taken up in medical sociology (Scambler 2001). It has been suggested that "expert systems" like medicine have become more answerable to system imperatives than to the lifeworlds of patients. Using Mishler's (1984) terms, the "voice of medicine" has grown in authority over the "voice of the lifeworld." Independently of the motivations and aspirations, and sometimes the reflexivity, of individual physicians, they have become less responsive to patient-defined needs, nothwithstanding ubiquitous rhetorics to the contrary. Habermas' framework of system and lifeworld, strategic and communicative action, continues to be used in the twenty-first century to analyze and explain macro-level changes to health care organization and delivery and micro-level changes to physician–patient interaction and communication.

Under the influence of Axel Honneth (Hazeldine 2017), contemporary critical theory has taken a different turn. Honneth has developed the concept of "recognition," seeking in doing so to acknowledge the false optimism of many critical theorists who anticipated progressive change and under-estimated the elasticity and durability of capitalism. Attention is switched in "recognition theory" away from distribution and towards identity. In this way feminist and post-colonialist movements are interpreted as rejecting "misrecognition" and in pursuit of active autonomy. For all that "identity politics" has proved controversial in both mainstream and medical sociology, with some regarding it as compromising critical theory's Marxian heritage, there is no doubt that notions of identity have gained significantly in salience in studies of health and health care (Scambler 2018).

Other Theories in the Twenty-First Century

The twentieth century ended with new social realities causing both sociology and medical sociology to adjust and consider new theoretical orientations, as well as adapt older ones to account for the changes. At the beginning of the twenty-first century, sociology's three once dominant theoretical perspectives – structural, functionalism, conflict theory, and symbolic interaction – were dead or on life support as "zombie theories" with a minimum of life (Ritzer and Yagatich 2012:105). The new theories and concepts in medical sociology that emerged in medical sociology suggest a shift away from a past focus on methodological individualism (in which the individual is the primary focus of analysis) toward a growing utilization of theories with a structural orientation as seen in (Cockerham 2013a, 2013b). Some built on the work of the classical theorists, such as health lifestyle theory and critical theory, while others take a different direction.

Michel Foucault

French theorist Michel Foucault, who focused on the relationship between knowledge and power, provided social histories of the manner in which knowledge produced expertise that was used by professions and institutions, including medicine, to shape social behavior. Knowledge and power were depicted as being so closely connected that an extension of one meant a simultaneous expansion of the other. In fact, Foucault often used the term "knowledge/power" to express this unity (Turner 1995). The knowledge/power link is not only repressive, but also productive and enabling, as it is a decisive basis upon which people are allocated to positions in society. A major contribution of Foucault to medical sociology is his analysis of the social functions of the medical profession, including the use of medical knowledge as a means of social control and regulation, as he studied madness, clinics, and sexuality. Foucault (1973) found two distinct trends emerging in the history of medical practice: "medicine of the species" (the classification, diagnosis, and treatment of disease) and "medicine of social spaces" (the prevention of disease). The former defined the human body as an object of study subject to medical intervention and control, while the latter made the public's health subject to medical and civil regulation. The surveillance of human sexuality by the state, church, and medicine subjected the most intimate bodily activities to institutional discourse and monitoring. Thus, bodies themselves came under the jurisdiction of experts on behalf of society.

Foucault's approach to the study of the body also influenced the development of a new specialty, the sociology of the body, with Bryan Turner's book *The Body and Society* (2008, originally published in 1984) the seminal work in this area. Theoretical developments concerning the sociological understanding of the control, use, and the phenomenological experience of the body, including emotions, have been most pronounced in Britain. One area of inquiry is directed toward understanding the dialectical relationship between the physical body and human subjectivity or the "lived" or phenomenological experience of both having and being in a body.

Foucault has his critics. Some suggest that Foucault's perspective on knowledge/power does not take limits on power into account, nor explain relations between macro-level power structures other than dwell on their mechanisms for reproduction; moreover, there is a disregard of agency in poststructural concepts. Giddens (1987: 98), for example, noted that Foucault's history tends to have no active subjects at all and concludes: "It is history with the agency removed." And he (Giddens 1987: 98) goes on to say that the "individuals who appear in Foucault's analyses seem impotent to determine their own destinies." Yet Foucault's knowledge/power equation, applied to the medical profession, remains a useful analysis of their role as "experts" in the social control of the body.

Social Constructionism

Social constructionism is based on the premise that social phenomena are not discovered but constructed through social interaction (Conrad and Barker 2010; Nowakowski and Sumerau 2019; Olafsdottir 2013; Turner 2004). That is, things are what they are defined as, even illness. In medical sociology, this perspective takes "the view that scientific knowledge and biological discourses about the body, health and illness are produced through subjective, historically determined human interests, and are subject to change and reinterpretation" (Gabe et al. 2004: 130). Illness is considered to be socially constructed in that the expression of symptoms is shaped by cultural and moral values, experienced through interaction with other people, and influenced by particular beliefs about what constitutes health and illness. The result is a transformation of physiological symptoms into a diagnosis which produces socially appropriate illness behavior and a modified social status, that of being sick. In medical sociology, one branch of the social constructionist approach is closely tied to Foucault and analyzes the body as a product of power and knowledge as previously discussed (Annandale 2014; Nettleton 2020). The other branch of social constructionism is based on the seminal work of Peter Berger and Thomas Luckmann in their book *The Social Construction of Reality* (1967), which is grounded in symbolic interaction and its emphasis on agency. This approach is also influenced by Eliot Freidson's (1970a, 1970b) analysis of medical professionalization. Freidson examined how the medical profession monopolized power and authority in health matters to advance its own interests. Given the significant differences between Berger and Luckmann in comparison to Foucault, it is obvious that social constructionism lacks a single, unified doctrine. According to Turner (2004: 43), "These different types of constructionism present very different accounts of human agency and thus have different implications for an understanding of the relationship between patients, doctors, and disease entities." The more social constructionist work is influenced by Berger and Luckmann, the more agency oriented it is; the closer to Foucault, the less agency has a role.

Medicalization/Biomedicalization

Medicalization is a major theoretical concept in medical sociology. According to Peter Conrad (2007; 2013), medicalization in its simplest form means "to make medical." It refers to the process by which previously nonmedical conditions become defined and treated as a medical problem, that is, as either a disease or disorder of some type. Conrad provides several examples of conditions which medicine assumed control over by defining them as a medical problem to be treated by medical means, even though in the past they were not necessarily considered as such. These include attention deficit hyperactivity disorder (ADHD), normal sadness, grief, shyness, premenstrual syndrome (PMS), sleep disorders, aging, obesity, infertility, learning disabilities, erectile dysfunction, surgical cosmetic enhancements, and baldness among others. The approach of the medicalization concept, however, is not to contest diagnoses but examine how a problem becomes defined as medical and the social consequences of doing so.

Conrad finds the sources or "drivers" of medicalization are now changing. Physicians are slowly being sidelined by new engines of medicalization making things medical, namely (1) biotechnology, especially the pharmaceutical industry and genetics, (2) consumers desiring treatments, and (3) managed care when health insurance companies make decisions about what is or is not included in their coverage. The changes connected to the increasing significance of biotechnology have led to the introduction of biomedicalization theory (Clarke et al. 2010). Biomedicalization consists of the rise of computer information and other new technologies to increase medical surveillance and treatment interventions by the use of genetics, bioengineering, chemoprevention, individualized designer drugs, multiple sources of information, patient data banks, digitized patient records, and other innovations. Also important in this process is the Internet making it easier to get medical information and merchandise, be exposed to advertising, and enhance the role of pharmaceutical companies in marketing their products.

Feminist Theory

Feminist theory in medical sociology has been linked in some instance to social constructionist accounts of the female body and its regulation by a male-dominated society. Social and cultural assumptions are held to influence our perceptions of the body, including the use of the male body as the former standard for medical training, the assignment of less socially desirable physical and emotional traits to women, and the ways in which women's illnesses are socially constructed (Annandale 2014). Other feminist theory is grounded in conflict theory or symbolic interaction, and deals with the sexist treatment of women patients by male doctors and the less than equal status of female physicians in professional settings and hierarchies (Riska and Wegar 1993; Hinze 2004). There is, however, no unified perspective among feminist theorists other than a "woman-centered" perspective that examines the various facets of women's health and seeks an end to sexist orientations in health and illness and society at large (Annandale 2014; Nettleton 2020).

Intersectionality theory, originating among American black feminist scholars has been one of the more promising feminist theoretical perspectives expanding into medical sociology (Collins 2015, 2019; Collins and Bilge 2016). It calls attention to the multiple forms of social inequality affecting black women and other disadvantaged individuals. In doing so, it expresses an activist orientation connected to community organizing, identity politics, coalition politics, and social justice. The approach focuses on examining forms of discrimination and inequality stemming from gender, race, ethnicity, class, age, nation, and sexual orientation, and makes the key point that such variables are not simply individual characteristics but operate simultaneously at multiple levels in people's lives. Thus, individual and group characteristics cannot be fully understood by prioritizing one variable (e.g. class) over another (e.g. gender) since all such variables combine to disadvantage some people in relation to others at the same time. People do not experience inequality only from the standpoint of one social characteristic but undergo all of them concurrently. Intersectionality theory therefore provides a perspective intended to investigate the interaction of numerous characteristics of a population, not only at the individual level but also at structural levels in order to capture the multiple factors that influence individual lives. Most of the research using intersectionality theory, however, has been qualitative because of the difficulty in measuring all variables simultaneously using quantitative methods.

Pierre Bourdieu

Once ranked as the leading intellectual in France, Bourdieu (1984) focused on how the routine practices of individuals are influenced by the external structure of their social world and how these practices, in turn, reproduce that structure. Through his key concept of habitus, Bourdieu connects social practices to culture, structure, and power (Swartz 1997). Bourdieu (1990) describes the habitus as a mental scheme or organized framework of perceptions (a structured structure operating as a structuring structure) that predisposes the individual to follow a particular line of behavior as opposed to others that might be chosen. These perceptions are developed, shaped, and maintained in memory and the habitus through socialization, experience, and the reality of class circumstances. While the behavior selected may be contrary to normative expectations and usual ways of acting, behavioral choices are typically compatible with the dispositions and norms of a particular group, class, or the larger society; therefore, people tend to act in predictable and habitual ways even though they have the capability to choose differently. Through selective perception, the habitus adjusts aspirations and expectations to "categories of the probable" that impose boundaries on the potential for action and its likely form.

Of all Bourdieu's works, the one most relevant for medical sociologists remains his book *Distinction* (1984), in which he systematically accounts for the patterns of cultural consumption and competition over definitions of taste of the French social classes. It includes an analysis of food habits and sports that describes how a class-oriented habitus shaped these particular aspects of health lifestyles. Cockerham (1999, 2000, 2007; Cockerham et al. 1997) follows Bourdieu's theoretical framework in his theory of health lifestyles and in identifying negative health lifestyles as the primary social determinant of ongoing downturn in life expectancy in Russia. The group most responsible for reduced longevity are middle-age, working-class males.

The living conditions of these men and their relatively low and powerless position in the social structure produced a habitus fostering unhealthy practices (heavy drinking and smoking, disregard for diet, and rejection of exercise) that resulted in a lifestyle promoting heart disease, accidents, and other health problems leading to a shortened life span. These behaviors were norms established through group interaction, shaped by the opportunities available to them, and internalized by the habitus. The structure of everyday life both limited and molded health-related choices to the extent that lifestyles led to premature deaths.

According to Williams (1995), the merit of Bourdieu's analysis for understanding the relationship between class and health lifestyles lies in his depiction of the relative durability of various forms of health-related behavior within particular social classes and the relatively seamless fashion in which he links agency and structure. "In particular," states Williams (1995: 601), "the manner in which his arguments are wedded to an analysis of the inter-relationship between class, capital, taste, and the body in the construction of lifestyles ... is both compelling and convincing." Although Bourdieu has been criticized for overemphasizing structure at the expense of agency and presenting an overly deterministic model of human behavior (Münch 1993), he nevertheless provides a framework for medical sociologists to conceptualize health lifestyles and for sociologists generally to address the agency–structure interface (Cockerham 2005).

Life Course Theory

Life course theory in medical sociology is intended to explain how social experiences and conditions of adversity and inequality in childhood and adolescence affect health later in life. The theory advances the proposition that people go through a sequence of age-based stages and social roles within particular families and social structures over the course of their lives. It maintains that socioeconomic disadvantages originating in childhood accumulate over the life course to disadvantage health in old age, while socioeconomic advantages over a person's lifetime likewise accumulate but do so to promote relatively good health when elderly. It considers both the early origins of chronic diseases whose symptoms are not obvious until later in life and the social processes and behaviors that promote susceptibility to these diseases until older ages or avoidance of such afflictions.

A subcategory of life course theory that is commonly utilized in medical sociology is the concept of cumulative advantage/disadvantage (Ferraro et al. 2016; Willson and Shuey 2019). It posits that the initial advantages or disadvantages that people have in life, including health, are typically associated with structural variables – especially SES, but others such as gender and race. The effects of these variables accumulate over time in either positive or negative ways to benefit or erode health. Another subcategory is cumulative inequality theory which likewise maintains that early disadvantage increases the later potential for risks to health, but it also acknowledges the potential use of resources at mid-life to mitigate or eliminate the effects of early life disadvantages before the onset of old age (Williams et al. 2019). Cumulative inequality theory begins with an initial position that negative life events and experiences place people at increased risk, positive experiences create opportunities for them, and both can alter life chances for individuals and groups for better or worse.

The Stress Process

Leonard Pearlin (1989) is known for the stress process model and his initial paper on this topic is the most cited paper in medical sociology. He states that stress involves a demanding situation whose experience of it is perceived as threatening or burdensome. In his view, stress originates in *situations*, yet what is also important is how people react to it in the *context* of their lives. This meant there is much more to stress research than simply looking at how people respond to certain stressors but also the social circumstances of stressed people. Pearlin maintained that the stress process consists of three components: (1) *stressors*, which he defines as any condition having the potential to arouse the adaptive capacity of the individual; (2) *moderators*, which consist of coping abilities, sense of mastery, and sources of social support; and (3) *outcomes*, the health effects of the distress experienced by the person. He identified two major types of social stressors: life events and chronic strain. The theory holds that not all people react to these stressors the same way because of differences in stress moderators which, in turn, influence different outcomes. The merit of Pearlin's stress process model is that it links the experience of stress directly to patterns of social stratification through its depiction of the origins of stress, its mediators, and outcomes.

Fundamental Cause Theory

The most popular theoretical concept in American medical sociology today is Bruce Link's and Jo Phelan's (1995; Phelan and Link 2013) theory of fundamental causes. The theory maintains that in order for a social variable to qualify as a fundamental cause of sickness and mortality, it must meet four basic criteria: First, it must influence multiple disease outcomes. Consequently, the association is not limited to affecting only one or a few diseases but many. Socioeconomic status qualifies, for example, because SES is related to virtually all major causes of death from disease. Second, it must impact the onset and outcomes of diseases through multiple risk factors, not just one or two. So there have to be more than a few ways it can cause people to become sick, such as stress, smoking, unhealthy diets, poor housing, obesity, drug and alcohol abuse, lack of exercise, and insufficient preventive health care. Third, it involves access to resources that can be used to avoid risks or minimize the consequences of a disease if a person does become ill. And fourth, the connection with health is reproduced over time. That is, the effects persist despite changes in risks, protective factors, and diseases which led Link and Phelan (1995: 87) to call them "fundamental" in the first place. In order to test the theory, empirical validation of these four core features are required.

SES meets all four of these criteria because a person's class position influences the risk and outcome of multiple diseases in multiple ways, higher SES persons have the resources to better avoid health problems or minimize them when they occur, and the association has endured indefinitely. The reason that SES is related to multiple disease outcomes through multiple pathways that change over time is that individuals and groups use their resources to avoid risks and adopt protective strategies. Consequently, the theory's basic principle is that a superior assortment of flexible resources permits higher SES persons to avoid disease and death in varying conditions. More recently, Phelan and Link (2015) have identified racism as another fundamental cause.

Critical Realism

Critical realism is a relatively new theoretical perspective that emerged in Britain and is based on the work of philosopher Roy Bhaskar (1994; 1998) and sociologist Margaret Archer (1995; 2000; 2003; Archer et al. 1998). Critical realist theory argues that social constructionism does not account for agency and provides an "oversocialized" view of individuals overemphasizing the effects of structure, while other theorists, like Bourdieu, opt for a "seamless" approach to agency and structure, but the operations of the two in reality are not synchronized. Consequently, critical realism treats agency and structure as fundamentally distinct but interdependent dimensions that need to be studied separately in order to understand their respective contributions to social practice. The "analytical decoupling of structure and agency" is necessary, states Williams (1999:809), "not in order to abandon their articulation, but, on the contrary, so as to examine their *mutual interplay across time*; something which can result both in *stable reproduction* or *change* through the *emergence* of new properties and powers."

Critical realism takes the position that social systems are open to process and change and that people as agents and actors have the critical capacity, reflexivity, and creativity to shape structure, yet, in turn, are shaped by structure. But the key factor for the critical realist is the capacity of the individual to transform structure and produce variable outcomes (Archer 1995). Structure, for its part, is relatively enduring, although it can be modified, and deep structures have generative mechanisms going beyond the observable that influence behavior. A goal of critical realism is to connect agency and structure in a way that the distinctive properties of both can be realistically accounted for without being reduced to a single entity. Among the studies in medical sociology employing critical realism to date are examinations of the body from the standpoint of chronic illness and disability, which focus on the interrelationship of biological and social factors in shaping outcomes (Williams 1999), an attempt to develop a sociology of health inequalities which goes beyond orthodox social epidemiological studies (Scambler 2002; 2018) and a study of psychiatric categories (Pilgrim 2014). That critical realism in relation to health is an ongoing project is evidenced by a new "practical handbook" published in the UK for researchers in that domain of study (Alderson 2020).

Conclusion

The notion that medical sociology is atheoretical is wrong. This chapter has provided a brief account of the history and variety of viewpoints in sociological theory that have been utilized within the field and provided influential statements on the relationship between society and health. Beginning with Parsons, medical sociology in reality has a rich theoretical tradition spanning almost 70 years and incorporating the work of both classical and contemporary theorists. Debates in general sociology, such as those involving the opposition of symbolic interactionists and conflict theorists to structural-functionalism and the agency versus structure dispute, became points of theoretical contention in medical sociology as well. During the latter part of the twentieth century, structural theories like structural-functionalism were largely abandoned in favor of agency oriented theories like symbolic interaction, labeling theory, and the agency side of social constructionism. However, improved statistical techniques to measure the effects of structure – such as hierarchical linear modeling – forecast a paradigm shift back to greater considerations of structure and structural approaches to theory. Although it is too early to determine the ultimate direction of theory in medical sociology this century with exact precision, these improved statistical procedures should provide a more comprehensive approach to research with theory guiding and adjusting to this capability. Already the theoretical basis for work in the field is extensive and its potential explanatory power is likely to increase. Medical sociology has become a theoretical subdiscipline.

References

Abel, Thomas and William C. Cockerham. 1993. "Lifestyle or *Lebensführung*? Critical Remarks on the Mistranslation of Weber's 'Class, Status, Party'." *Sociological Quarterly* 34(3): 551–6.

Abrams, Elissa M. and Stanley J. Szefler. 2020. "COVID-19 and the Impact of Social Determinants of Health." *Lancet* May 18. https://doi.org/10.1016/s2213-2600(20)30234-4.

Alderson, Priscilla. 2020. *Critical Realism for Health and Illness Research: A Practical Handbook*. Bristol: Policy Press.

Annandale, Ellen. 2014. *The Sociology of Health and Medicine: A Critical Introduction*, 2nd edition. Cambridge: Polity Press.

Archer, Margaret, Roy Bhaskar, Andrew Collier, Tony Lawson, and Alan Norrie. 1998. *Critical Realism: Essential Readings*. London: Routledge.

Archer, Margaret S. 1995. *Realist Social Theory: The Morphogenetic Approach*. Cambridge: Cambridge University Press.

Archer, Margaret S. 2000. *Being Human: The Problem of Agency*. Cambridge: Cambridge University Press.

Archer, Margaret S. 2003. *Structure, Agency, and the Internal Conversation*. Cambridge: Cambridge University Press.

Becker, Howard S. 1973. *Outsiders: Studies in the Sociology of Deviance*, 2nd edition. New York: Free Press.

Becker, Howard S., Blanche Greer, Everett Hughes, and Anselm Strauss. 1961. *Boys in White: Student Culture in Medical School*. Chicago, IL: University of Chicago Press.

Berger, Peter L. and Thomas Luckmann. 1967. *The Social Construction of Reality*. New York: Anchor.

Bhaskar, Roy. 1994. *Plato Etc.: The Problems of Philosophy and Their Resolution*. London: Verso.

Bhaskar, Roy. 1998. *The Possibility of Naturalism: A Philosophical Critique of the Contemporary Human Sciences*. London: Routledge.

Blumer, Herbert. 1969. *Symbolic Interactionism*. Englewood Cliffs, NJ: Prentice-Hall.

Bourdieu, Pierre. 1984. *Distinction: A Social Critique of the Judgement of Taste*. London: Routledge.

Bourdieu, Pierre. 1990. *The Logic of Practice*. Cambridge: Polity Press.

Clarke, Adele, Laura Mamo, Jennifer Ruth Fosket, Jennifer R. Fishman, and Janet K. Shim (eds.). 2010. *Biomedicalization: Technoscience, Health and Illness in the U.S.* Durham, NC: Duke University Press.

Clarke, Adele E., Carrie Friese, and Rachel Washburn. 2018. *Situational Analysis*, 2nd edition. Thousand Oaks, CA: Sage.

Claus, Elizabeth. 1982. *The Growth of a Sociological Discipline: On the Development of Medical Sociology in Europe*, Vol. I. Leuven, Belgium: Sociological Research Institute, Katholieke Universiteit Leuven.

Cockerham, William C. 1983. "The State of Medical Sociology in the United States, Great Britain, West Germany, and Austria." *Social Science & Medicine* 17: 1513–27.

Cockerham, William C. 1999. *Health and Social Change in Russia and Eastern Europe*. London: Routledge.

Cockerham, William C. 2000. "Health Lifestyles in Russia." *Social Science & Medicine* 51: 1313–24.

Cockerham, William C. 2005. "Health Lifestyle Theory and the Convergence of Agency and Structure." *Journal of Health and Social Behavior* 46(1): 51–67.

Cockerham, William C. 2007. "Health Lifestyles and the Absence of the Russian Middle Class." *Sociology of Health & Illness* 29(3): 457–73.

Cockerham, William C. 2013a. "Sociological Theory in Medical Sociology in the Early Twenty-first Century." *Social Theory & Health* 11(3): 241–55.

Cockerham, William C. (ed.). 2013b. *Medical Sociology on the Move: New Directions in Theory*. Dordrecht: Springer.

Cockerham, William C. 2015. "Max Weber: Formal Rationality and the Modern Hospital." Pp. 124–38 in *Palgrave Handbook of Social Theory on Health, Illness and Medicine*, edited by Fran Collyer. London: Palgrave.

Cockerham, William C. 2021a. *Social Causes of Health and Disease*, 3rd edition. Cambridge: Polity.

Cockerham, William C. 2021b. *Sociological Theories of Health and Illness*. New York: Routledge.

Cockerham, William C., Thomas Abel, and Lüschen. Günther. 1993. "Max Weber, Formal Rationality, and Health Lifestyles." *Sociological Quarterly* 34(3): 413–25.

Cockerham, William C., Gerhard Kunz, and Lüschen. Günther. 1988. "Social Stratification and Health Lifestyles in Two Systems of Health Care Delivery: A Comparison of the United States and West Germany." *Journal of Health and Social Behavior* 29(2): 113–26.

Cockerham, William C., Alfred Rütten, and Thomas Abel. 1997. "Conceptualizing Contemporary Health Lifestyles: Moving Beyond Weber." *Sociological Quarterly* 38(2): 321–42.

Collins, Patricia Hill. 2015. "Intersectionality's Definitional Dilemmas." *Annual Review of Sociology* 41: 1–20.

Collins, Patricia Hill. 2019. *Intersectionality as Critical Social Theory*. Durham, NC: Duke University Press.

Collins, Patricia Hill and Sirma Bilge. 2016. *Intersectionality*. Cambridge: Polity.

Collyer, Fran. 2010. "Origins and Canons: Medicine and the History of Sociology." *History of the Human Sciences* 23: 86–108.

Collyer, Fran (ed.). 2015. *The Palgrave Handbook of Social Theory in Health, Illness and Medicine*. Basingstoke: Palgrave Macmillan.

Conrad, Peter. 2007. *The Medicalization of Society*. Baltimore, MD: Johns Hopkins University Press.

Conrad, Peter. 2013. "Medicalization: Changing Contours, Characteristics, and Contexts." Pp. 195–214 in *Medical Sociology on the Move: New Directions in Theory, edited by William Cockerham*. Dordrecht: Springer.

Conrad, Peter and Kristin K. Barker. 2010. "The Social Construction of Illness: Key Insights and Policy Implications." *Journal of Health and Social Behavior* 51(extra issue): S67–S79.

Dahrendorf, Ralf. 1959. *Class and Conflict in Industrial Society*. Stanford, CA: Stanford University Press.

Dahrendorf, Ralf. 1979. *Life Chances*. Chicago: University of Chicago Press.

De Maio, Fernando. 2010. *Health and Social Theory*. Basingstoke: Palgrave Macmillan.

Denzin, Norman K. 1991. *Symbolic Interactionism and Cultural Studies*. Oxford: Blackwell.

Denzin, Norman K. 2017. *The Research Act*. New York: Routledge.

Denzin, Norman K. and Yvonna S. Lincoln (eds.). 2018. *The Sage Handbook of Qualitative Research*, 5th edition. Thousand Oaks, CA: Sage.

Durkheim, Emile. [1895] 1964. *The Rules of Sociological Method*. New York: Free Press.

Durkheim, Emile. [1897] 1951. *Suicide: A Study in Sociology*. Glencoe, IL: Free Press.

Ferraro, Kenneth F., Markus H. Schafer, and Lindsay R. Wilkinson. 2016. "Childhood Disadvantage and Health Problems in Middle and Later Life: Early Imprints on Physical Health?" *American Sociological Review* 81(1): 107–33.

Foucault, Michel. 1973. *The Birth of the Clinic*. London: Tavistock.

Freidson, Eliot. 1970a. *Profession of Medicine: A Study of the Sociology of Applied Knowledge*. New York: Dodd & Mead.

Freidson, Eliot. 1970b. *Professional Dominance*. Chicago, IL: Aldine.

Gabe, Jonathan, Mike Bury, and Mary Ann Elston (eds.). 2004. *Key Concepts in Medical Sociology*. London: Sage.

Giddens, Anthony. 1987. *Social Theory and Modern Sociology*. Stanford, CA: Stanford University Press.

Glaser, Barney G. and Anselm M. Strauss. 1965. *Awareness of Dying*. Chicago, IL: Aldine.

Glaser, Barney G. and Anselm M. Strauss. 1967. *The Discovery of Grounded Theory*. Chicago, IL: Aldine.

Glaser, Barney G. and Anselm M. Strauss. 1968. *Time for Dying*. Chicago, IL: Aldine.

Goffman, Erving. 1959. *The Presentation of Self in Everyday Life*. New York: Anchor.

Goffman, Erving. 1961. *Asylums*. New York: Anchor.

Goffman, Erving. 1967. *Stigma: Notes on the Management of Spoiled Identity*. Englewood Cliffs, NJ: Prentice-Hall.

Habermas, Jürgen. 1984. *The Theory of Communicative Action. Vol. 1: Reason and the Rationalization of Society*. London: Heinemann.

Habermas, Jürgen. 1987. *The Theory of Communicative Action. Vol. 2: Lifeworld and System: A Critique of Functionalist Reason*. Cambridge: Polity Press.

Hazeldine, Gary. 2017. "Pathologies of Recognition: Axel Honneth and the Renewed Possibility of a Critical Theory of Society." *Thought and Action* 40(1): 135–72.

Hinze, S. 2004. "'Am I Being Oversensitive?' Women' s Experience of Sexual Harassment During Medical Training." *Health* 8: 101 –27.

Link, Bruce G. and Jo C. Phelan. 1995. "Social Conditions as Fundamental Causes of Disease." *Journal of Health and Social Behavior* 36(extra issue): 80–94.

Mead, George H. 1934. *Mind, Self, and Society*. Chicago, IL: University of Chicago Press.

Mishler, Elliot. 1984. *The Discourse of Medicine: Dialectics of Medical Interviews*. Norwood, NJ: Ablex.

Münch, Richard. 1993. *Sociological Theory*. Chicago, IL: Nelson-Hall.

Muntaner, Carles, Ng Edwin, Haejoo Chung, and Seth J. Prins. 2014. "Two Decades of Neo-Marxist Class Analysis and Health Inequalities: A Critical Reconstruction." *Social Theory & Health* 13(3/4): 267–87.

Nettleton, Sarah. 2020. *The Sociology of Health and Illness*, 4th edition. Cambridge: Polity.

Nowakowski, Alexandra C.H. and J.E. Sumerau. 2019. "Reframing Health and Illness: A Collaborative Autoethnography on the Experience of Health and Illness Transformations in the Life Course." *Sociology of Health & Illness* 41(4): 723–39.

Olafsdottir, Sigrun. 2013. "Social Construction and Health." Pp. 41–59 in *Medical Sociology on the Move: New Directions in Theory*, edited by William Cockerham. Dordrecht: Springer

Outhwaite, William (ed.). 1996. *The Habermas Reader*. Cambridge: Polity Press.

Parsons, Talcott. 1951. *The Social System*. New York: Free Press.

Pearlin, Leonard I. 1989. "The Sociological Study of Stress." *Journal of Health and Social Behavior* 30(3): 241–56.

Phelan, Jo C. and Bruce G. Link. 2013. "Fundamental Cause Theory." Pp. 105–26 in *Medical Sociology on the Move: New Directions in Theory*, edited by William Cockerham. Dordrecht: Springer.

Phelan, Jo C. and Bruce G. Link. 2015. "Is Racism a Fundamental Cause of Inequalities in Health?" *Annual Review of Sociology* 41: 311–30.

Pilgrim, David. 2014. *Understanding Mental Health*. London: Routledge.

Riska, Elianne and Katarina Wegar (eds.). 1993. *Gender, Work, and Medicine*. London: Sage.

Ritzer, George and David Walczak. 1988. "Rationalization and the Deprofessionalization of Physicians." *Social Forces* 67(1): 1–22.

Ritzer, George and William Yagatich. 2012. "Contemporary Sociological Theory." Pp. 98–118 in *The Wiley-Blackwell Companion to Sociology*, edited by George Ritzer. Oxford: Wiley-Blackwell.

Scambler, Graham (ed.). 2001. *Habermas, Critical Theory and Health*. London: Routledge.

Scambler, Graham. 2002. *Health and Social Change: A Critical Theory*. Buckingham: Open University Press.

Scambler, Graham (ed.). 2012. *Contemporary Theorists for Medical Sociology*. London: Routledge.

Scambler, Graham. 2018. *Sociology, Health and the Fractured Society*. London: Routledge.

Scheff, Thomas J. 1999. *Being Mentally Ill*, 3rd edition. Hawthorne, NY: Aldine de Gruyter.

Seale, Clive. 2008. "Mapping the Field of Medical Sociology: A Comparative Analysis of Journals." *Sociology of Health & Illness* 5: 677 –95.

Sitton, John. 1996. *Recent Marxian Theory: Class Formation and Social Conflict in Contemporary Capitalism*. New York: State University of New York Press.

Strauss, Anselm, Leonard Schatzman, Danuta Ehrlich, Rue Bucher, and Melvin Sabshin. 1963. "The Hospital and its Negotiated Order." Pp. 147–69 in *The Hospital in Modern Society*, edited by Elliot Freidson. New York: Free Press.

Swartz, David. 1997. *Culture and Power: The Sociology of Pierre Bourdieu*. Chicago, IL: University of Chicago Press.

Turner, Bryan S. 1988. *Status*. Milton Keynes: Open University Press.

Turner, Bryan S. 1992. *Regulating Bodies*. London: Routledge.

Turner, Bryan S. 1995. *Medical Power and Social Knowledge*, 2nd edition. London: Sage.

Turner, Bryan S. 2004. *The New Medical Sociology: Social Forms of Health and Illness.* London: Norton.

Turner, Bryan S. 2008. *The Body and Society*, 3rd edition. London: Sage.

Weber, Max. [1904-5] 1958. *The Protestant Ethic and the Spirit of Capitalism*, translated by T. Parsons. New York: Scribner.

Weber, Max. [1922] 1978. *Economy and Society*, Vol. 2, translated by G. Roth and C. Wittich. Berkeley, CA: University of California Press.

Williams, Monica M., Blakelee R. Kemp, Kenneth F. Ferraro, and Sarah A. Mustillo. 2019. "Avoiding the Major Causes of Death: Does Childhood Misfortune Reduce the Likelihood of Being Disease Free in Later Life?" *Journals of Gerontology* 74B(1): 170–80.

Williams, Simon J. 1995. "Theorising Class, Health and Lifestyles: Can Bourdieu Help Us?" *Sociology of Health & Illness* 17(6): 577–604.

Williams, Simon J. 1999. "Is Anybody There? Critical Realism, Chronic Illness and the Disability Debate." *Sociology of Health & Illness* 21: 797–819.

Willson, Andrea E. and Kim M. Shuey. 2019. "A Longitudinal Analysis of the Intergenerational Transmission of Health Inequality." *The Journals of Gerontology* 74B(1): 181–91.

3

Research Methods in Medical Sociology

Joseph D. Wolfe, Shawn Bauldry, and Cindy L. Cain

Introduction

After accepting the task of writing a chapter on research methods in medical sociology, we were excited and then immediately overwhelmed at the breadth of the topic. Medical sociology is a diverse field in terms of methodological approaches. In the sections of this chapter that follow, we've tried our best to meaningfully condense this large literature into an introduction to key methodological issues and research in medical sociology (but many of the issues we review are relevant to all social science research). In an effort to speak to a broad audience within medical sociology, we rarely discuss more than the most basic technical details of specific methods. Instead, we highlight the underlying logic of research methods in medical sociology and the types of answers to research questions different methods can provide. To that end, before we outline the specific topics in this chapter, we need to mention a few basic requirements of sociological research.

The first requirement is a researchable question (Firebaugh 2008; Lieberson 1985). People often bring up broad existential questions to spark conversation – What's the true nature of humankind? Is world peace possible? These are examples of questions that we don't consider researchable, though they can inspire researchable questions. A researchable question in medical sociology is one that can be answered with empirical evidence collected and analyzed using acceptable research methods among contemporary medical sociologists. Researchable questions are also asked in such a way that their answer is capable of overturning one's assumptions about the social world. For example, is educational attainment associated with health in the US population? This is a question that is answerable with available data and research methods in medical sociology. Its answer also speaks to an underlying theory

The Wiley Blackwell Companion to Medical Sociology, First Edition. Edited by William C. Cockerham.

about education and health in the US, which brings us to our next requirement – a theoretical model.

The second requirement is a theoretical model informed by sociology. In very simple terms, theoretical models are abstract representations of social phenomena, and research methods are how sociologists investigate the empirical implications of theoretical models (Lieberson and Horwich 2008). Theory is thus critical to deciding which methodological approach, among many potentially appropriate approaches, is best suited for your research question. No single theoretical perspective dominates medical sociology, but a baseline – if often tacit – assumption is that the distribution of illness and disease in a population is determined by how exactly that population is socially organized. Continuing with our education-health example from above, we only arrived at our question because of an extensive body of research that finds an association between education and health. One explanation of the education-health association suggests that sweeping macroeconomic changes in the twentieth and twenty-first centuries transformed education into a social determinant of illness and disease in the US (Link and Phelan 1995; Masters et al. 2015; Phelan and Link 2015; Wolfe et al. 2018a; 2018b; Wolfe 2019). To extend this line of inquiry, we might elaborate on our initial question and ask whether the association between education and health changed for people who lived before and after the rapid expansion of higher education in the US. Although this is just a slight alteration to our original question, it has major implications for our research methods. Our point is that researchers should always strive to inform a broader theoretical model of health and society, and their choice of research methods should reflect and explicitly acknowledge that model.

The third requirement is reproducibility and transparency (Freese 2007; Long 2009). Reproducibility means that the investigators maintain all of the data and analysis files necessary to reproduce the results they publicly report, and transparency includes reporting pertinent information and decisions alongside the results. These are necessary for ensuring scientific accumulation and enhancing the credibility of findings. We should note that a study can be reproducible without being replicable. A study is replicable when multiple studies using different data (more on data coming up) come to the same overall conclusions. Reproducibility simply means that the researchers have preserved the instructions for recreating their study's results so that other researchers can extend or correct findings. Maintaining a study's reproducibility can be a time consuming and thankless job, but it's a necessary part of conducting good research and contributing to the scientific community.

Our examples thus far are quantitative, but these three requirements apply equally to qualitative work and even descriptive research exploring new areas without explicit guidance from sociological theory. Related, although we organize key topics in quantitative and qualitative research separately, we believe in a fluidity of research designs, taking a dynamic and flexible approach to our empirical investigating of the social world. Science is a cumulative effort, and different research methods shed light on sociological problems from different angles (Collins 1989; Gross 2009; Lieberson and Horwich 2008).

With our basic requirements out of the way, we can now provide a short outline of the sections to come. We begin our discussion by reviewing data and related issues such as the importance of conceptualization and choosing the appropriate level of analysis. We then discuss methods for analyzing data, beginning with quantitative issues like measurement and causality. Next we consider several qualitative methods, including special topics that offer interesting new avenues for research in medical sociology.

Data Reign

Assuming you have a health-related question inspired by sociological theory, how do you investigate it empirically? You need data. Without data – and good data at that – you'll never be able to empirically answer your questions. Unfortunately, data collection is one of the most challenging aspects of conducting original research in medical sociology. Researchers are often forced to make sacrifices as they move from the limitless world of ideas to the restrictive nature of rigorous, scientific observation. All research is pressed on either side by efficiency and bias. Normally these are statistical terms, but we think efficiency and bias are conceptually useful here, too. On the one hand, researchers must collect enough data to accurately answer their question but not so much that they waste precious resources, time and money, collecting extraneous information (we'll call this inefficiency). On the other hand, if researchers fail to collect enough information to sufficiently observe a sociological phenomenon, they will likely get incorrect (i.e. biased) answers to their questions. We review several of the challenges of collecting data and discuss why addressing them carefully is important for correctly answering research questions.

First and foremost, sociological phenomena are difficult to observe and even harder to measure consistently. This makes conceptualization a critical part of any sociological endeavor, and most researchers spend a large part of their time reviewing prior research in an effort to clearly define the unique pieces of their research questions. Human capital, for example, is a widely referenced concept in medical sociology, especially among scholars studying health behaviors (Mirowsky and Ross 1998). The basic idea is straightforward – human capital improves the constellation of behaviors that maintain health (e.g. avoiding sugar, staying physically active, etc.). Although years of schooling offers a sensible measure of human capital in the US, educational attainment is only an indirect measure of the wide array of cognitive and non-cognitive abilities (e.g. intelligence and self-discipline) that could potentially provide health-related advantages. By clearly conceptualizing these two distinct components of human capital, Herd (2010) found that cognitive human capital played a greater role than non-cognitive capital in mediating education and health among older adults in the Wisconsin Longitudinal Sample.

This brings us to the next challenge, choosing a level of analysis. Social action can be observed at micro, meso, and macro levels (Collins 1981; Fine 1991). Although some sociological theories lend themselves more clearly to specific levels of analysis, most of the major theoretical frameworks in medical sociology can be examined at multiple levels. For our investigation of education and health, should we collect rich descriptions of human experiences with health problems through a few dozen in-depth interviews from people with different educational backgrounds? Or, should we collect less detailed information from a sample of people who represent the entire US population? The answer usually depends on your research question. For example, the question "is the rate of college graduates in US cities associated with cardiovascular mortality rates?" would require a macro-level assessment of city demographics, whereas the question "how does physician-perceived human capital among patients affect patient-physician interactions in free health clinics?" would require micro-level data based on observations of social interactions. Both of these questions are inspired by sociological work on education and health, but each requires a much different approach to data collection. Studies of micro-level sociological phenomena often collect data on social interactions, attitudes, cognition, emotions, and decision-making (e.g. Spencer 2018). Studies of meso-level phenomena generally collect data on individuals, social groups, and social networks (e.g. Hallgren et al. 2020). Studies of macro-level phenomenon often consider country-level data on population trends, institutional and cultural change, laws, and health inequalities (e.g. Bakhtiari et al. 2018).

Data Collection

Research in medical sociology uses a variety of data collection techniques. What follows is a brief outline of the techniques contemporary medical sociologists use to obtain data. The most common tool for data collection is the questionnaire. Questionnaires are used in all types of research, ranging from in-person interviews to simple online surveys, and there's an entire science about developing them in ways that will improve the chances of actually getting respondents to answer questions (Couper 2017; Schaeffer and Presser 2003).

Non-experimental surveys that collect information with questionnaires are the most common source of data in sociology. Surveys like the General Social Survey (GSS, https://gss.norc.org) provide a wide array of information about the US population (currently around 330 million), including health information, by asking a carefully selected sample of only several thousand people. The GSS is also an example of secondary data, which are data collected by prior researchers. There are several prominent secondary data sources that appear frequently in medical sociology research, e.g. National Longitudinal Study of Adolescent to Adult Health (Add Health, https://www.cpc.unc.edu/projects/addhealth), National Longitudinal Surveys (NLS, https://www.bls.gov/nls), Behavioral Risk Factor Surveillance System (BRFSS, https://www.cdc.gov/brfss). These examples, like many other popular secondary datasets, are publicly available. Although researchers are unable to operationalize their theories exactly as they would please (increasing the potential for bias), secondary data removes the burden of data collection. Most social scientists don't have resources required to develop and implement national surveys. Publicly available data from larger surveys provides an essential resource for medical sociology.

Experimental and quasi-experimental methods of data collection are less common in sociology but still provide useful information for medical sociologists. Experimental methods have been used to good effect in, for instance, vignette studies in which researchers randomly manipulate characteristics of patients and study the conditions under which physicians treat them differently (Stepanikova 2012). Quasi-experimental methods exploit real-world interventions that "randomly" affect some groups of people more so than others. For instance, studies of the effect of education on health have exploited the uneven roll-out of changes in compulsory schooling laws and studies of the effect of trauma on mental health have exploited random variation in the communities exposed to a natural disaster, such as a tsunami (Courtin et al. 2019; Frankenberg et al. 2012).

Ethnography, participant/observation, and in-depth interviews are common techniques for creating the rich data necessary to understand social phenomena. Researchers who enter the field to collect qualitative data gain access to a more expansive social world than researchers who rely solely on questionnaires to gather information. Qualitative data collection allows for the observation of the serendipitous social action that so often goes unobserved in other data collection strategies and is especially good at integrating the context of social life. Qualitative researchers are themselves the data collection instruments, so these approaches require that researchers constantly reflect on how their own social positions affects what they observe (Fine and Hancock 2017).

"Found" data is another source of data that's having a growing influence on social science research. A creative researcher can develop unique datasets with information from administrative records, historical documents, social networks, and other publicly available data that is increasingly located online. For example, Cotti et al. (2015) merged the BRFSS with publicly available data on the Dow Jones Industrial Average, a stock index, and found that large drops in the stock market were associated with poorer mental health and higher levels of smoking, binge drinking, and fatal car accidents involving alcohol. Government websites in particular can have treasure troves of data for researchers willing to wade into the deep waters of internet data collection and organization. While offering an interesting new approach, inefficiency lurks. Data collection can go on ad infinitum if the researcher hasn't adequately conceptualized the key components of their research question.

Methods for Analyzing Data

Assuming a researcher has data in hand, they have a wide variety of research methods at their disposal to explore data in an effort to answer their research questions. In the sections that follow, we review the principal methods being used to understand data in ways that have helped advance medical sociology.

Quantitative Methods

If a researcher has numerical data, then they'll use quantitative methods for the analysis. A numerical array of data typically consists of columns representing study variables and rows containing observations of variables for each case/participant. For example, if we collected information about years of schooling from a sample of 100 adults, then each of the 100 rows would contain the education of a single participant. Variables are chosen through a process called operationalization (or simply measurement) in which researchers choose how to empirically represent concepts from their research questions. Because of the diversity of perspectives in medical sociology, most peer-reviewed journals require researchers to provide rigorous justifications for their measurement choices. This makes careful operationalization a critical feature of quantitative research in medical sociology (Aneshensel 2002; Link 2002; McAlpine et al. 2018).

Measurement

Operationalization involves two independent stages, identifying (or designing) a valid measure of a concept and then determining how exactly to incorporate that measure into a statistical model. The first stage involves a good deal of perseverance and creativity from researchers. Operationalizing complex sociological concepts generally requires a detailed review of prior studies in light of one's specific research question. The second stage is more circumscribed and can often depend on the availability of measures and the degree to which measurement models will help inform one's research question.

Researchers often take one of the following approaches to incorporating measures into statistical models: (1) single variable, (2) multiple variables, or (3) latent variable (Bollen et al. 2001). In some cases, the second step in operationalization is relatively straightforward. For example, if we are interested in estimating the extent to which age is related to alcohol use in a population, then we would look for data that includes respondents' age and some assessment of alcohol consumption. This would be a single variable approach because we only used one variable to represent each concept. We should note, however, that even in this simple example prior research offers multiple potential measures of age (e.g. in years, meaningful age ranges) and alcohol use (e.g. drinks on average, binge drinking, any drinking, etc.). In other cases, operationalization is less clear. Socioeconomic status (SES) is a recurring term in health disparities research, but despite its relative cohesiveness as a theoretical concept, researchers uses a wide variety of variables to operationalize SES. Generally, medical sociologists use a multiple variable approach to measuring SES by incorporating two or more variables related to educational, economic, and occupational attainments (Wolfe 2015). Although the single variable approach would be easier to interpret, the complexity of using multiple variables to represent SES is usually offset by the greater amount of information gained from results.

Working with latent variables requires an entirely different approach to measurement (Bollen 1989). For single and multi-variable operationalizations, researchers assume that sociological concepts can be directly observed. When we investigate variables such as years of age or schooling, we assume that people accurately know and report that information (with some random error being acceptable). Suppose, however, we're interested in the amount of depression in the general population. Do people always know if they're depressed? Does everyone have the same definition of depression? This is a trickier situation. Fortunately, the Center for Epidemiologic Studies Depression (CESD) scale, which originally included 20 items (Radloff 1977), is a well-established measure of depression. There are a number of statistical approaches to combining indicators of depression like the CES-D items into a single scale (e.g. Payton 2009; Perreira et al. 2005), but they all assume that we can create a latent variable for depression that avoids the measurement error we would encounter with a single question asking directly about depression.

Measurement concerns might seem pedantic at times but taking measurement issues seriously can generate important research. For example, Montez et al. (2012) evaluated models of US mortality with 13 different measures of education derived from Hummer and Lariscy (2011). The preferred functional form of education included a linear decline in mortality risk from 0 to 11 years, a notably larger reduction in mortality risk after high school completion, and a steep linear decline continuing after high school completion. Although their primary aims were methodological in nature, searching for the optimal form of education revealed an interesting theoretical insight – educational attainment benefits survival through both human capital accumulation and socially meaningful credentials (Collins 1979).

Research on health lifestyles offers another example of the importance of measurement (Cockerham 2005; Cockerham et al. 2020). Health lifestyles refer to meaningful combinations of health behaviors that people adopt. We can imagine a lifestyle involving regular exercise, a nutritious diet, and abstention from smoking and heavy drinking. Alternatively, we can also imagine a largely sedentary lifestyle with limited concerns about a nutritious diet. And one could continue with several other possible clusters of health behaviors that coalesce into recognizable health lifestyles. To investigate these potential lifestyles and their relationship to adult health, Cockerham et al. (2020) identified latent classes of different health lifestyles, and their results revealed a unique pattern of associations between health lifestyle and health status due to diagnosed conditions that affected lifestyles in middle adulthood.

Answering Descriptive Research Questions

Many questions of interest to medical sociologists are descriptive in nature. Their answers provide descriptions of circumstances without necessarily providing a sense of how they might be altered. For instance, we might be interested in knowing the extent to which immigrants exhibit better health than non-immigrants, trends in life expectancy among members of different communities over time, or differences in health care expenditures across countries. Answers to such questions not only provide valuable information for medical sociologists but are also critical for policymakers and other constituencies that rely on data to inform decision-making.

In some cases descriptive research questions can be addressed in a straightforward manner through calculating simple statistics such as means and proportions. In other cases, finding answers to descriptive research questions requires the use of a statistical model that takes into account multiple factors. For instance, in estimating trends in death rates due to cancer for different communities over time we might want to adjust for different age structures across the communities. A statistical model provides the means to make such an adjustment.

Various forms of regression models are the primary statistical models used in quantitative medical sociology research (Gelman and Hill 2007; Kalbfleisch and Prentice 2011; Long 1997). Regression models take the form of regressing an outcome or dependent variable on a set of predictors or independent variables, one of which is often considered the focal independent variable. The estimates from fitting a regression model provide a means for assessing the relationship between a focal independent variable and an outcome (e.g. years of schooling and self-rated health) while adjusting or controlling for one or more other independent variables. The outcome variable may be continuous (e.g. health care expenditures in constant dollars), categorical (e.g. an indicator for smoking in the past month), or even unobserved (e.g. the risk of dying in a given year). The independent variables may take any level of measurement.

Answering Causal Research Questions

Despite the value of answers to descriptive research questions, we often want to talk about the causes of the statistical associations we observe. In the physical sciences, causal research questions are addressed via experiments. As noted above, experiments are also used in medical sociology research, but more frequently we rely on observational data. Because observational data lack the statistical properties of experimental data, conclusions regarding causal processes are often tentative. However, over the past 20 to 30 years, methodologists have developed a framework for causal analysis with observational data referred to as the counterfactual framework (Morgan and Winship 2015; Pearl 2009).

The counterfactual framework has two components, the potential outcomes model and causal graphs. The potential outcomes model provides a precise statement of what we mean when we say that a focal independent variable has a causal effect on an outcome (Rubin 1974). In particular, we mean the difference in the outcome that would be observed if a given case experienced an alternative exposure of a focal independent variable than the exposure that was observed. Let us consider smoking during pregnancy as our focal independent variable and the child's birthweight as our outcome. Then the causal effect of smoking would be defined as the difference in a child's birthweight for a mother who smoked during pregnancy had she not smoked. It's impossible, however, to observe both of these states simultaneously (i.e. the birthweight of a child from a mother who smoked, and the birthweight of the same child had the same mother not smoked). Instead, we do the best we can to construct a comparison group to estimate what birthweight would have been observed had the mother not smoked.

The second component, causal graphs, provide a systematic approach to determining what strategies for causal analysis are available with a given set of data and which variables need to be included in the analysis (Pearl 2009). Causal graphs depict relevant variables for an analysis as nodes and causal relationships between the variables using directed edges from the predictor to the outcome. In addition, bidirected edges can be used to indicate that two variables share a common cause. The relationships indicated in a causal graph are non-parametric and include all possible interactions. Figure 3.1 illustrates an example of a causal graph of mortality. The graph indicates key confounders of the effect of education on mortality (X and U_1) as well as confounders of the effect of mediators on mortality (U_2). Confounders are variables that affect both the focal independent variable and the outcome. If confounders are not addressed, estimates of the causal effect of the focal independent variable on an outcome will be biased. In contrast, mediators are variables that are thought to transmit the effect of a focal independent variable to an outcome. A mediation analysis seeks to identify the mechanisms that underlie a causal process. In this causal graph, we see that some confounders are observed (e.g. education) while others are unobserved (e.g. noncognitive resources). The relationships depicted in this graph and the presence of observed and unobserved confounders have implications for strategies for estimating causal effects.

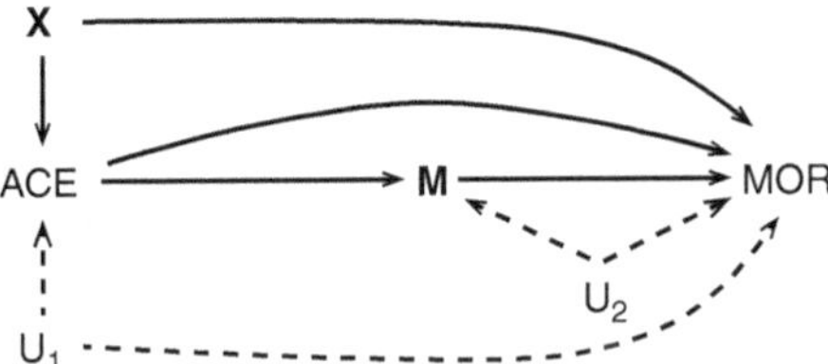

Figure 3.1 Causal graph of the relationships between adult children's education(ACE), a vector of mediators (M), and mortality(MOR). X represents a vector of pretreatment confounders (e.g., respondent education), and U1 and U2 represent potential unobserved pretreatment and posttreatment confounders, respectively.

Strategies for Estimating Causal Effects

In broad terms, there are three strategies for estimating causal effects that involve (1) conditioning on confounders, (2) identifying instrumental variables, or (3) specifying mechanisms. The first, and by far the most commonly used, involves conditioning on all confounders in a statistical model. For instance, it is likely that mother's education predicts both whether a mother smokes and the birthweight of her child. In this case, if we do not adjust for mother's education in our analysis of smoking and birthweight, then we would likely overestimate the causal effect of smoking on birthweight, as part of the effect is likely due to mother's education as a common cause of both. As noted above, a failure to incorporate all confounders in an analysis leads to biased estimates of causal effects. Well-articulated causal graphs allow researchers to identify the confounders that need to be included in an analysis. In practice, we never have measures of all possible confounders available, and therefore we need to rely on sensitivity analyses and/or more modest statements about our findings with respect to estimating causal effects.

The second strategy involves identifying an exogenous source of variation in the focal independent variable and often using statistical models based on instrumental variables. An exogenous source of variation refers to some feature of the world that induces a change in the focal independent variable for at least some cases but is otherwise unrelated to the outcome. Quasi-experiments fit into this category. Natural disasters can certainly cause changes in people's lives that may be otherwise unrelated to an outcome or policy-oriented changes can fulfill the same role. To give an example, some studies in medical sociology have leveraged changes in compulsory schooling laws to try to estimate the effect of education on health (Courtin et al. 2019). A source of exogenous variation can be treated as an instrumental variable, i.e. a variable that has an effect on the focal independent variable but not the outcome.

The third strategy, and least commonly used, involves (1) specifying all of the mechanisms that link a focal independent variable to an outcome, (2) estimating the effects of each mechanism, and then (3) adding up the effects to get a total causal effect. A mechanism refers to the process through which a variable has an effect on an outcome. If we return to the education and health example, there are a number of mechanisms thought to account for the positive relationship. To name a few, higher levels of education lead to better and higher paying jobs, which can be used to support health. Higher levels of education also come with greater knowledge of health promoting behaviors and how to navigate the health care system. In addition, higher levels of education tend to expose people to similarly more highly educated peers who might in turn reinforce health promoting behaviors. Each of these processes can be thought as one of the mechanisms linking education to health. As this example might suggest, however, such an approach is quite challenging. We rarely know all of the mechanisms linking a focal independent variable to an outcome, and even in cases where we might have a good grasp on all of the mechanisms, we often do not have measures for each.

With respect to causal research questions, the counterfactual framework provides a powerful approach to understanding the possibilities available for causal analysis with observational data and the assumptions needed to support a causal interpretation. The regression models described for descriptive outcomes are routinely used for causal analysis as well. The details of the research design (e.g. Are key confounders measured? Are there exogenous sources of variation?) dictate whether a causal interpretation is warranted.

Qualitative Methods

Although qualitative research strategies are diverse, qualitative scholarship is united by the use of non-numerical data. Qualitative data comes from observations of the world, interviews with people individually or in groups, examination of documents, or in-depth analysis of any other materials that help reveal the social world. Returning to our example of education and health, qualitative approaches can enrich our understanding of *why* education is associated with better health. Ethnographic studies may observe how patients with differing levels of education use their knowledge in interactions with health care professionals (Luftey and Freese 2005). Likewise, interviews with health care professionals could add to knowledge by revealing how doctors think about patients from differing educational levels (Thompson et al. 2015). Finally, someone interested in this question from a qualitative perspective may decide to look at training manuals for health care providers over several decades to understand the messages conveyed about patients with varying levels of education. In each of these, the focus is on linking the general finding about human capital and health to the larger social and medical context.

Ethnographic methods are primarily about observing and participating in the social world, which allows the researcher to bridge scholarly and folk understandings of the world. For example, classic medical sociologists observed health care organizations and medical training programs to understand how doctors are socialized to provide care in particular ways (Becker et al. 2002[1976]; Charmaz and Olesen 1997). There are many different approaches to ethnography that span from complete observer to complete participant. A complete observer of health care organizations may sit quietly in the back of a room, avoiding direct interaction with those in the setting. In contrast, a complete participant may be trained as a doctor or nurse and is actively involved in the interactions taking place. Most medical sociology ethnographies fall somewhere between these two and include deep levels of observation and some interactions. Ethnographic methods are especially useful for understanding the organizational context of healthcare, including how medical professionals work together and with patients (Cain 2019; Jenkins 2018). Ethnographers measure concepts through observing behaviors, the context surrounding the behaviors, and how actors talk about their behaviors.

Interviews are commonly used in medical sociology. Interviews range from unstructured, where the researcher may enter the conversation with a topic and a reason they selected a particular person, to structured, which includes a predetermined set of questions, probes to follow up, and the order in which the questions are asked. The level of structure to the conversation depends on many factors, including how much we already know about the phenomenon and how researchers want to speak to theory. Researchers using a "grounded theory" approach often use unstructured interviews, while those using other approaches may want more structure (Charmaz 2014; Strauss and Corbin 1997). Interviews with individuals are useful for gaining an in-depth understanding of their sense-making about the world (Barry et al. 2001). Interviews can also take place with a group of participants, sometimes called a focus group interview (Krueger 2014). Guiding the conversation when working with a group can be challenging and the researcher must keep in mind that small group dynamics (i.e. talking over one another, dominating the conversation, group think) can make analysis difficult. That said, group interviews can be an efficient way to learn about actors' perceptions and attitudes and are often used in qualitative studies of health and medicine. One advantage of group interviews is that participants engage with one another to agree, disagree, build on, contradict, or enrich others' perspectives. These group engagements are useful for understanding how people respond to changes in medical practices (Cain and McCleskey 2019). Interview researchers measure concepts through analyzing participants' verbal responses to questions, often grouping similar types of responses into codes, and then linking codes to one another through the development of themes.

Medical sociologists can also learn about the world through qualitatively analyzing content produced for another reason. Examples include newspaper articles about health, laws that govern health policies, billboards for public health campaigns, patient educational materials, television shows, or any other cultural product that one may use to understand the world. Content analysis is technique where the researcher establishes a selection process for finding relevant content and then develops codes and themes that represent the content (Hsieh and Shannon 2005). This often involves many hours of reading, re-reading, and re-coding the content to document its stable features and its variation across the sample. Content analysis can be especially helpful for studying cultural understandings of health and illness, such as documenting body size stigma in scientific and popular publications (Saguy and Almeling 2008). Historical methods are a form of content analysis which specializes in using a range of historical documents to provide a deeper understanding of how phenomena have changed or come to be. Researchers using content analysis measure concepts similarly to interviewers.

Special Topics in Qualitative Methods

Recent developments in qualitative methods have aimed to further enhance the theoretical contributions of qualitative research. While there have been many developments over time, here we focus on three that may be especially fruitful for medical sociology. First, recent analytical techniques have focused on abductive approaches (Timmermans and Tavory 2012). In contrast to deductive approaches that focus on testing hypotheses derived from existing literatures and inductive approaches that aim to generate knowledge "ground up" and often bracketing existing knowledge, abductive approaches balance existing and new knowledge. Abductive qualitative analyses use existing literature to set expectations about what the researcher will see or hear in their qualitative data, and then systematically identifies places where those expectations were not met. By focusing on "surprising" or contradictory findings, abductive analysis allows for greater refinement and development of theory. For example, in a study of interdisciplinary teamwork in end-of-life care, Cain (2019) used literature on team practices to set expectations about how health care professionals make decisions, but when these decision-making processes were not present, she used both interview and ethnographic data to document how policy changes made teamwork difficult to sustain. These findings come from iterating between expectations from the literature and findings that seem incompatible.

Relatedly, the extended case method also aims to improve the theoretical contributions of qualitative research (Burowoy 1998). In the extended case method, the researcher conceptualizes the data collection process as an "intervention" into the social world, which reveals processes of actors' lives. The researcher can then analyze observations for the structures that produce those processes, and then use data to reconstruct theories. In analyzing data for processes and structures, the extended case method is especially helpful for qualitative studies of the linkages across micro, meso, and macro levels of society. For example, Klawiter (2004) used multiple forms of qualitative data to document how social movements changed meaning systems around breast cancer, which then affected how individual people experience their illness. Importantly, the extended case method requires the researcher to be reflexive about how their social location affects what they see and hear.

Finally, one increasingly common site of development in qualitative research is a search for ways to blur the boundaries between qualitative and quantitative approaches. Some researchers do this by translating qualitative data from text into numerical data that can be analyzed statistically. Content analysis is especially amenable to this quantification process, but it can be used with any of the qualitative techniques discussed above. Analyses using fuzzy-set Qualitative Comparative Analysis requires the researcher to take complex qualitative data and classify cases by their degree of membership in a set of conceptual categories. The researcher then analyzes the combinations of concepts that produce a particular outcome. For example, one group of researchers defined different health care service contexts and patient characteristics as concepts and coded those concepts from interviews with vulnerable patients (Vickery et al. 2018). They then analyzed which service contexts and patient characteristics combined to produce the highest levels of improvement in quality of life. The focus on rich in-depth data and combinations of factors can be especially helpful for improving health policies or practices in the administration of care.

Conclusion

Like many other academic disciplines, consensus among medical sociologists is built from an accumulation of evidence from accepted research methods. On the one hand, the breadth of sociological methods available to study a topic is at times overwhelming. On the other hand, the triangulation of findings from multiple methods is a critical part of establishing consensus on sociological phenomenon as it relates to health and health systems. Throughout the chapters that follow in this volume, the integration of results from a variety of research methods will often offer answers to contemporary questions in medical sociology that no single study is able to provide. Thus, in our chapter of methods, we've tried to unpack some of the basic information about doing medical sociology research that can easily be skipped if one is too focused on pure statistical estimation.

We believe that doing good research is important beyond simply the improvement of science. Medical sociology has always had a more applied focus than other sub-disciplines of sociology, making it imperative that we use strong methodological approaches to answer a range of questions that also serve the public good. Some of these questions will take on the testing, refining, and creation of general social theory. Other questions will be more focused on using sociological insights to solve pressing problems in health and medicine. Both intentions are improved by attention to the issues we discuss here.

To end on a practical note, we'd like to take a moment to emphasize that a major component of both qualitative and quantitative analysis should be careful data management. The bulk of day-to-day work on research projects is keeping data organized and preparing it for analysis. Unfortunately, even the most cutting-edge methods can't overcome the errors created by incorrectly coded variables or misplaced field notes. This adds organizational pitfalls to the already difficult process of empirically testing a theoretical model. Although we won't advocate strongly for any specific one, we strongly suggest investing the time and energy to establish a good workflow of data analysis with your preferred method of analysis [e.g. see Long (2009) for an excellent approach integrated with Stata and Wickham and Grolemund (2017) for one using R].

References

Aneshensel, Carol S. 2002. "Answers and Questions in the Sociology of Mental Health." *Journal of Health and Social Behavior* 43(2): 236–46.

Bakhtiari, Elyas, Sigrun Olafsdottir, and Jason Beckfield. 2018. "Institutions, Incorporation, and Inequality: The Case of Minority Health Inequalities in Europe." *Journal of Health and Social Behavior* 59(2): 248–67.

Barry, Christine A, Fiona A Stevenson, Nicky Britten, Nick Barber, and Colin P Bradley. 2001. "Giving Voice to the Lifeworld. More Humane, More Effective Medical Care? A Qualitative Study of Doctor–Patient Communication in General Practice." *Social Science & Medicine* 53(4): 487–505.

Becker, Howard S., Blanche Geer, Everett C. Hughes, and Anselm L. Strauss. 2002[1976]. *Boys in White: Student Culture in Medical School.* Piscataway, NJ: Transaction Publishers.

Bollen, Kenneth A. 1989. *Structural Equations with Latent Variables.* New York: Wiley-Interscience.

Bollen, Kenneth A., Jennifer L. Glanville, and Guy Stecklov. 2001. "Socioeconomic Status and Class in Studies of Fertility and Health in Developing Countries." *Annual Review of Sociology* 27: 153–85.

Burowoy, Michael. 1998. "The Extended Case Method." *Sociological Theory* 16(1): 4–33.

Cain, Cindy L. 2019. "Agency and Change in Healthcare Organizations: Workers' Attempts to Navigate Multiple Logics in Hospice Care." *Journal of Health and Social Behavior* 60(1): 3–17.

Cain, Cindy L. and Sara McCleskey. 2019. "Expanded Definitions of the 'Good Death'? Race, Ethnicity and Medical Aid in Dying." *Sociology of Health & Illness* 41(6): 1175–91. 10.1111/1467-9566.12903.

Charmaz, Kathy. 2014. *Constructing Grounded Theory.* Thousand Oaks, CA: Sage Publishers.

Charmaz, Kathy and Virginia Olesen. 1997. "Ethnographic Research in Medical Sociology: Its Foci and Distinctive Contributions." *Sociological Methods & Research* 25(4): 452–94. doi: 10.1177/0049124197025004004.

Cockerham, W C. 2005. "Health Lifestyle Theory and the Convergence of Agency and Structure." *Journal of Health and Social Behavior* 46(1): 51–67. 10.1177/002214650504600105.

Cockerham, William C., Joseph D. Wolfe, and Shawn Bauldry. 2020. "Health Lifestyles in Late Middle Age." *Research on Aging* 42(1): 34–46. 10.1177/0164027519884760.

Collins, Randall. 1979. *The Credential Society: An Historical Sociology of Education and Stratification.* New York: Academic Press.

Collins, Randall. 1981. "On the Microfoundations of Macrosociology." *American Journal of Sociology* 86(5): 984–1014. 10.2307/2778745.

Collins, Randall. 1989. "Sociology: Proscience or Antiscience?" *American Sociological Review* 54(1): 124–39.

Cotti, Chad, Richard A. Dunn, and Nathan Tefft. 2015. "The Dow Is Killing Me: Risky Health Behaviors and the Stock Market." *Health Econ* 24(7): 803–21. 10.1002/hec.3062.

Couper, Mick P. 2017. "New Developments in Survey Data Collection." *Annual Review of Sociology* 34: 121–45. 10.1146/annurev-soc-.

Courtin, Emilie, Vahe Nafilyan, Mauricio Avendano, Pierre Meneton, Lisa F. Berkman, Marcel Goldberg, Marie Zins, and Jennifer B. Dowd. 2019. "Longer Schooling but Not Better Off? A Quasi-Experimental Study of the Effect of Compulsory Schooling on Biomarkers in France." *Social Science & Medicine* 220: 379–86. 10.1016/j.socscimed.2018.11.033.

Fine, Gary Alan. 1991. "On the Macrofoundations of Microsociology: Constraint and the Exterior Reality of Structure." *The Sociological Quarterly* 32(2): 161–77. 10.2307/4120955.

Fine, Gary Alan and Black Hawk Hancock. 2017. "The New Ethnographer at Work." *Qualitative Research* 17(2): 260–8.

Firebaugh, Glenn. 2008. *Seven Rules for Social Research.* Princeton, NJ: Princeton University Press.

Frankenberg, Elizabeth, Jenna Nobles, and Cecep Sumantri. 2012. "Community Destruction and Traumatic Stress in Post-Tsunami Indonesia." *Journal of Health and Social Behavior* 53(4): 498–514.

Freese, Jeremy. 2007. "Replication Standards for Quantitative Social Science Why Not Sociology?" *Sociological Methods & Research* 36(2): 153–72.

Gelman, Andrew and Jennifer Hill. 2007. *Data Analysis Using Regression and Multilevel hierarchical Models*, Vol. 1. New York: Cambridge University Press.

Gross, Neil. 2009. "A Pragmatist Theory of Social Mechanisms." *American Sociological Review* 74(3): 358–79.

Hallgren, Emily, Theresa A. Hastert, Leslie R. Carnahan, Jan M. Eberth, Scherezade K. Mama, Karriem S. Watson, and Yamilé Molina. 2020. "Cancer-Related Debt and Mental-Health-Related Quality of Life among Rural Cancer Survivors: Do Family/Friend Informal Caregiver Networks Moderate the Relationship?" *Journal of Health and Social Behavior* 61(1): 113–30.

Herd, Pamela. 2010. "Education and Health in Late-Life among High School Graduates: Cognitive Versus Psychological Aspects of Human Capital." *Journal of Health and Social Behavior* 51: 478–97.

Hsieh, Hsiu-Fang and Sarah E Shannon. 2005. "Three Approaches to Qualitative Content Analysis." *Qualitative Health Research* 15(9): 1277–88.

Hummer, Robert A. and Joseph T. Lariscy. 2011. "Educational Attainment and Adult Mortality." Pp. 241–61 in *International Handbook of Adult Mortality, International Handbooks of Population* 2, edited by R. G. Rogers and E. M. Crimmins. New York: Springer Science + Business Media.

Jenkins, Tania M. 2018. "Dual Autonomies, Divergent Approaches: How Stratification in Medical Education Shapes Approaches to Patient Care." *Journal of Health and Social Behavior* 59(2): 268–82.

Kalbfleisch, John D. and Ross L. Prentice. 2011. *The Statistical Analysis of Failure Time Data*. New York: Wiley.

Klawiter, Maren. 2004. "Breast Cancer in Two Regimes: The Impact of Social Movements on Illness Experience." *Sociology of Health & Illness* 26(6): 845–74. 10.1111/j.1467-9566.2004.421_1.x.

Krueger, Richard A. 2014. *Focus Groups: A Practical Guide for Applied Research*. Thousand Oaks, CA: Sage Publications.

Lieberson, Stanley. 1985. *Making It Count: The Improvement of Social Research and Theory*. Berkeley, CA: University of California Press.

Lieberson, Stanley and Joel Horwich. 2008. "Implication Analysis: A Pragmatic Proposal for Linking Theory and Data in the Social Sciences." *Sociological Methodology* 38(1): 1–50.

Link, Bruce G. 2002. "The Challenge of the Dependent Variable." *Journal of Health and Social Behavior* 43(2): 247–53.

Link, Bruce G. and Jo Phelan. 1995. "Social Conditions as Fundamental Causes of Disease." *Journal of Health and Social Behavior* 35(Extra Issue): 80–94.

Long, J Scott. 1997. *Regression Models for Categorical and Limited Dependent Variables*. London: Sage.

Long, J. Scott. 2009. *The Workflow of Data Analysis Using Stata*. College Station, TX: Stata Press.

Luftey, Karen and Jeremy Freese. 2005. "Toward Some Fundamentals of Fundamental Causality: Socioeconomic Status and Health in the Routine Clinic Visit for Diabetes." *American Journal of Sociology* 110(5): 1326–72. 10.1086/428914.

Masters, Ryan K., Bruce G. Link, and Jo C. Phelan. 2015. "Trends in Education Gradients of 'Preventable' Mortality: A Test of Fundamental Cause Theory." *Social Science & Medicine* 127: 19–28. 10.1016/j.socscimed.2014.10.023.

McAlpine, Donna D., Ellen McCreedy, and Sirry Alang. 2018. "The Meaning and Predictive Value of Self-Rated Mental Health among Persons with a Mental Health Problem." *Journal of Health and Social Behavior* 59(2): 200–14.

Mirowsky, John and Catherine E. Ross. 1998. "Education, Personal Control, Lifestyle and Health: A Human Capital Hypothesis." *Research on Aging* 20: 415–49.

Montez, Jennifer Karas, Robert A. Hummer, and Mark D. Hayward. 2012. "Educational Attainment and Adult Mortality in the United States: A Systematic Analysis of Functional Form." *Demography* 49: 315–36.

Morgan, Stephen L, and Christopher Winship. 2015. *Counterfactuals and Causal Inference: Methods and Principles for Social Research.* Cambridge: Cambridge University Press.

Payton, Andrew R. 2009. "Mental Health, Mental Illness, and Psychological Distress: Same Continuum or Distinct Phenomena?" *Journal of Health and Social Behavior* 50(2): 213–27. 10.1177/002214650905000207.

Pearl, Judea. 2009. *Causality.* Cambridge: Cambridge University Press.

Perreira, Krista M, Natalia Deeb-Sossa, Kathleen Mullan Harris, and Kenneth Bollen. 2005. "What Are We Measuring? An Evaluation of the Ces-D across Race/Ethnicity and Immigrant Generation." *Social Forces* 83(4): 1567–601.

Phelan, Jo C and Bruce G Link. 2015. "Is Racism a Fundamental Cause of Inequalities in Health?" *Annual Review of Sociology* 41(1): 311–30. 10.1146/annurev-soc-073014-112305.

Radloff, L S. 1977. "The Ces-D Scale: A Self-Report Depression Scale for Research in the General Population." *Applied Psychological Measurement* 1(3): 385–401.

Rubin, Donald B. 1974. "Estimating Causal Effects of Treatments in Randomized and Nonrandomized Studies." *Journal of Educational Psychology* 66(5): 688–701.

Saguy, Abigail C. and Rene Almeling. 2008. "Fat in the Fire? Science, the News Media, and the 'Obesity Epidemic'2." *Sociological Forum* 23(1): 53–83. 10.1111/j.1600-0838.2004.00399.x-i1.

Schaeffer, Nora Cate and Stanley Presser. 2003. "The Science of Asking Questions." *Annual Review of Sociology* 29: 65–88.

Spencer, Karen Lutfey. 2018. "Transforming Patient Compliance Research in an Era of Biomedicalization." *Journal of Health and Social Behavior* 59(2): 170–84.

Stepanikova, Irena. 2012. "Racial-Ethnic Biases, Time Pressure, and Medical Decisions." *Journal of Health and Social Behavior* 53(3): 329–43.

Strauss, Anselm and Juliet M Corbin. 1997. *Grounded Theory in Practice.* Thousand Oaks, CA: Sage.

Thompson, Mindi N., Rachel S Nitzarim, Odessa D Cole, Nickholas D Frost, Alyssa Ramirez Stege, and Pa Tou Vue. 2015. "Clinical Experiences with Clients Who Are Low-Income: Mental Health Practitioners' Perspectives." *Qualitative Health Research* 25(12): 1675–88. doi: 10.1177/1049732314566327.

Timmermans, Stefan and Iddo Tavory. 2012. "Theory Construction in Qualitative Research." *Sociological Theory* 30(3): 167–86. 10.1177/0735275112457914.

Vickery, K. D., N. D. Shippee, L. M. Guzman-Corrales, C. Cain, S. Turcotte Manser, T. Walton, J. Richards, and M. Linzer. 2018. "Changes in Quality of Life among Enrollees in Hennepin Health: A Medicaid Expansion Aco." *Med Care Res Rev* 2020 Feb;77(1):6073. 10.1177/1077558718769457. Epub 2018 May 11. PMID: 29749288.

Wickham, Hadley and Garrett Grolemund. 2017. *R for Data Science: Import, Tidy, Transform, Visualize, and Model Data.* O'Reilly Media, Inc.

Wolfe, Joseph D. 2015. "The Effects of Socioeconomic Status on Child and Adolescent Physical Health: An Organization and Systematic Comparison of Measures." *Social Indicators Research* 123(1): 39–58.

Wolfe, Joseph D. 2019. "Age, Cohort, and Social Change: Parental and Spousal Education and White Women's Health Limitations from 1967 to 2012." *Research on Aging* 41(2): 186–210. 10.1177/0164027518800486.

Wolfe, Joseph D., Shawn Bauldry, Melissa A. Hardy, and Eliza K. Pavalko 2018a. "Multigenerational Attainments, Racial Inequalities, and the Mortality of Silent Generation Women." *Journal of Health and Social Behavior* 59(3): 335–51.

Wolfe, Joseph D., Shawn Bauldry, Melissa A. Hardy, and Eliza K. Pavalko. 2018b. "Multigenerational Attainment and Mortality among Older Men: An Adjacent Generations Approach." *Demographic Research* 39: 719–52.

4

Health and Culture in the Global Context

STELLA QUAH

Is culture relevant to the study of health and illness? Yes. Culture is not just one of many factors associated with health but is the context within which health-related behavior unfolds. Over the past few decades the consensus among sociologists and anthropologists has been strengthened by increasing evidence-based research. Both disciplines produce the bulk of systematic research on health-related behavior by applying a wide range of conceptual perspectives and methodological approaches; and relevant psychology research contribute pertinent information. This analysis proposes and explains why the inclusion of the cultural context is central to our understanding of health, illness, and health-related behavior. The analysis unfolds in three steps: the definition of culture; the link between culture and health behavior; and the link between culture and healing systems.

DEFINING CULTURE

The meaning of the term "culture" varies widely across disciplines and conceptual perspectives. Let us begin with an historical glance at the efforts made in sociology and anthropology to define and understand "culture".

The Classics

One enduring contribution comes from Emile Durkheim, a pioneer of the discipline of sociology. In his *Rules of Sociological Method*, first published in 1895, Durkheim (1938) proposed guidelines for the study of social phenomena as *social facts*. He argued that social facts are "representations" of society in the mind of the individual.

The Wiley Blackwell Companion to Medical Sociology, First Edition. Edited by William C. Cockerham.

They are ways of thinking, feeling, and acting external to the person. Such "facts" include myths, popular legends, religious conceptions, moral beliefs, and social beliefs and practices in general. By treating social values, beliefs, and customs as social facts, Durkheim promoted the systematic study of culture. He introduced his concepts of social solidarity and, particularly, a collective consciousness, as reflective of culture and concurrently present within and external to the individual. Taylor and Ashworth (1987: 43) propose that these concepts are applicable to the study of medical sociology phenomena, such as attitudes toward death and the link between "changing forms of social solidarity and changing perceptions of health, disease, and medicine."

Another key pioneer in the study of culture was Max Weber. His research during the first two decades of the twentieth century brilliantly marked the initiation of the sociological analysis of culture. Among his voluminous work, two studies are particularly relevant: *The Protestant Ethic and the Spirit of Capitalism* (1904–5) and *Economy and Society* (first published in English in 1968). Weber highlighted the importance of culture as values and beliefs coexisting and shaping social action within the micro-cosmos of the individual actor as well as at the level of collectivities, institutions, and the larger society. Weber's conceptualizations of *ethnic group* and *traditional action* offer the most relevant insights to the study of culture.

Weber defined *ethnic* groups as human groups characterized by a "subjective belief in their common descent" given their real or perceived similarities in one or more characteristics (physical types or race, customs, language, religion), and in "perceptible differences in the conduct of everyday life" (Weber 1978: 389–390). The impact of these subjectively perceived similarities on social action is heightened by yet another essential feature of ethnicity: "the belief in a specific *honor* of their members, not shared by outsiders, that is, the sense of *ethnic honor*" Weber 1978: 391) explained:

> palpable differences in dialect and differences of religion in themselves do not exclude sentiments of common ethnicity... The conviction of the excellence of one's own customs and the inferiority of alien ones, a conviction which sustains the sense of ethnic honor, is actually quite analogous to the sense of honor of distinctive status groups.

Weber's concept of *traditional action* (one of four in his typology of social action) is also relevant to the link between culture and health. Weber defines *traditional* action as social action "determined by ingrained habituation." *Traditional* action, he wrote, "is very often a matter of almost automatic reaction to habitual stimuli that guide behavior in a course which has been repeatedly followed. The great bulk of all everyday action to which people have become habitually accustomed approaches this type" (Weber 1978: 4). The concepts of ethnicity and traditional action, as defined by Weber, elucidate the pervasiveness of customs, beliefs, and practices of different ethnic or cultural communities upon their health-related behavior. Weber's analyses have inspired subsequent research and contributed to the understanding of the pervasiveness of culturally inspired and culturally sustained health practices. Probably because of the profound influence and widespread incorporation of his conceptual insights into the body of general knowledge of sociology, these Weberian contributions are seldom cited directly in current medical sociology research. Two notable exceptions are the analysis of Weber's legacy in medical sociology (Gerhardt 1989) and his concept of lifestyles (Cockerham 2021a, 2021b).

This interest in culture continues among subsequent generations of social scientists. By 1951, Clyde Kluckhohn reported many different definitions of culture and many more have appeared since. Yet, in spite of the plurality of definitions, some common strands that make up the fundamental fabric of this important concept are found in the cumulative work of anthropologists and sociologists. Kluckhohn (1951: 86) defined "culture" in the widest sense, as a community's "design for living." He pointed out that despite the wide variety of definitions he and A. L. Kroeber (Kroeber and Kluckhohn 1952) found, an "approximate consensus" could be developed, in which:

> Culture consists in patterned ways of thinking, feeling, and reacting, acquired and transmitted mainly by symbols, constituting the distinctive achievements of human groups, including their embodiments in artifacts; ... traditional (i.e., historically derived and selected) ideas and especially their attached values. (Kluckhohn 1951: 86)

Kluckhohn proposed that this definition of culture be used as "a map" or "abstract representation" of the distinctive features of a community's way of life. This method is akin to the *ideal type*, the analytical tool introduced by Weber (1946) to identify general characteristics, patterns, and regularities in social behavior.

A direct connection between culture and health was articulated by Bronislaw Malinowski (1944: 37), who considered culture as a functional response to satisfy "the organic and basic needs of man and of the race." He defined culture as "the integral whole" encompassing "human ideas and crafts, beliefs and customs ... A vast apparatus, partly material, partly human and partly spiritual, by which man is able to cope with the concrete, specific problems that face him" (Malinowski 1944: 36). Malinowski saw those problems as human "needs" that prompted "cultural responses." These needs were metabolism, reproduction, bodily comforts, safety, movement, growth, and health. However, in his view, health is implied in all the other six human basic needs, in addition to the explicit need for "relief or removal of sickness or of pathological conditions" (1944: 93). The "cultural response" which addresses the problem of health is "hygiene", defined as all "sanitary arrangements" in a community, "native beliefs as to health and magical dangers," "rules about exposure, extreme fatigue, the avoidance of dangers or accidents," and the "never absent range of household remedies" (Malinowski 1944: 91, 108).

Another valuable contribution to the understanding of culture was provided by sociologist Talcott Parsons. Parsons was greatly influenced as a student by Durkheim and Weber. Among his colleagues, he acknowledged the influence of Kluckhohn concerning the problems of culture and its relation to society (Parsons 1970). He conceptualized social action as taking place within a three-dimensional context comprising personality, culture, and the social system. Parsons (1951: 327) defined culture as "ordered systems of symbols" that guide social action and are "internalized components of the personalities of individual actors and institutionalized patterns of social systems." For Parsons (1951: 11), the shared symbolic systems are fundamental for the functioning of the social system and they represent "a *cultural tradition*." Parsons (1951: 326–7) argued that a cultural tradition has three principal components or systems: value-orientations, beliefs, and expressive symbols.

His preoccupation with a balanced analysis of values and motives that would prevent us from falling into the extremes of "psychological" or "cultural" determinism, led him to invest considerable effort into the discussion of culture. Parsons (1951: 15) identified three main features:

> First, that culture is *transmitted*, it constitutes a heritage or a social tradition; secondly, that it is *learned*, it is not a manifestation, in particular content, of man's genetic constitution; and third, that it is *shared*. Culture, that is, is on the one hand the product of, on the other hand a determinant of, systems of human interaction.

Parsons' concepts of culture and cultural traditions and his identification of culture as transmitted, learned, and shared, together with the contributions from Durkheim, Weber, Kluckhohn, and Malinowski form the classical foundation for the study of culture. An additional heritage of the study of culture is the cross-fertilization of insights and research between sociology and anthropology. Most current studies on culture and on the link between culture and health have developed from this rich foundation.

By identifying the fundamental components of culture, the collective wisdom inherited from the classics permit us to consider culture and ethnicity as the same phenomenon. Although Margaret Mead (1956) and Benjamin Paul (1963) proposed that cultural differences cut across racial and religious lines, these two factors are very much part of the cultural landscape within which individuals and groups operate. This idea is captured by Stanley King (1962: 79), who proposed that what constitutes an ethnic group is the combination of "common backgrounds in language, customs, beliefs, habits and traditions, frequently in racial stock or country of origin" and, more importantly, "a consciousness of kind." Note that, from the perspective of individuals and collectivities, these ethnic similarities may be factual or perceived and may include a formal religion. The sharing of the same geographical settlement is not as important as it was once thought, mainly because large migrations (voluntary or not) of people from different ethnic groups have resulted in the formation of diaspora beyond their ancestral lands and the subsequent increase of multiethnic settlements. The process of assimilation (becoming a member of the host culture) is common when individuals settle in a new country.  Living in close proximity to each other leads individuals from different ethnic groups into another process, *pragmatic acculturation*, that is, the process of culture borrowing motivated by the desire to satisfy specific needs (Quah 1989a: 181). Assimilation and *pragmatic acculturation* have been found to influence health behavior significantly, as discussed later. But first, let us review some of the contemporary leading ideas on culture and health.

Main Contemporary Research Trends

The contributions of the classics are the foundation of our understanding of culture and of its impact on behavior. Research over the past six decades support their interpretation of culture. The corpus of contemporary sociological and anthropological research on culture is expanding rapidly and in different directions. "Neoclassical" approaches emerged from the work of Weber, Durkheim, and Marx but have taken a life of their own as seen, for example, in interpretations of religion, studies of social control, and feminist perspectives of the body and gender (Alexander 1990). Research is also advancing on multiple aspects of the impact of culture and ethnicity on health status (e.g. Fox et al. 2017; Gage-Bouchard 2017; Nelson and Wilson 2017; Versey et al. 2019); on utilization of healthcare services (e.g. Galbraith et al. 2016; Kikuzawa et al. 2019; Korous et al. 2017; Miller et al. 2019); and on the link of socioeconomic inequalities and health (e.g. Downing 2016; Lane et al. 2017), including the differential impact of the COVID-19 pandemic among ethnic minorities in the US (Borjas 2020), among other aspects.

Attention to the body as an important subject of social analysis was brought up by Michael Foucault's work on *The Order of Things* (1970), *The Birth of the Clinic* (1973), and *Discipline and Punish* (1977). He eschewed research in favor of formulating assumptions, but his effort at awakening alertness to the symbolic and perceived meaning of the body is, to me, his vital contribution. Research findings over the past two decades show that the symbolic meaning of the body in relation to health and illness, manipulation and completeness, varies across cultures. A dramatic illustration is the cultural interpretation of female genital mutilation/cutting (FGMC) by Western groups advocating the eradication of FGMC as opposed to the symbolic meaning of FGMC held by some African communities that are struggling to preserve it (e.g. Fox and Johnson-Agbakwu 2020; Greer 1999; Grose et al. 2020).

On the effort to elucidate how culture affects the individual's behavior, the work of Erving Goffman (1968a, 1968b) using the symbolic-interaction perspective is important. Goffman focuses on the person's subjective definition of the situation and the concept of stigma. He proposes a three-stage stigmatization process (1968b): the person's initial or "primary" deviation from a normative framework; the negative societal reaction; and the person's "secondary" reaction or response to the negative reaction that becomes the person's "master-status." Goffman's "normative framework" is socially constructed based on the community's predominant culture. Disability and disease, particularly mental illness (Goffman 1968a), are typically perceived as stigma and trigger the stigmatization process. Unfortunately, Goffman and many of his followers have neglected to apply his conceptual approach fully to their own studies: they overlook cross-cultural comparisons (e.g. Locker 1983; Scambler 1984; Strauss 1975).

The preceding discussion might suggest there is consensus on what culture is and how to study it. Jeffrey Alexander (1990: 25–6) suggests that while contemporary researchers agree on "the autonomy of culture from social structure," he finds "extraordinary disagreement over what is actually inside the cultural system itself." Is it symbols, or values, or feelings, or metaphysical ideas? He proposes that culture might embrace all these because culture cannot be understood "without reference to subjective meaning" and "without reference to social structural constraints." For the same reason he favors a multidisciplinary approach to the study of culture.

The multidisciplinary approach is indeed one of two main trends in contemporary research on the link between culture and health. Focusing on the understanding of culture and health behavior, the disciplines of sociology and anthropology have produced research findings confirming that culture or ethnicity influence health behavior and attitudes significantly. A second main trend in the literature is the wide variety of conceptual perspectives on the influence of culture, although no dominant theory has yet emerged to explain that influence systematically and comprehensibly.

Multiple angles of analysis are as important as multidisciplinary approaches. Renée Fox (Fox 1976, 1989; Parsons and Fox 1952a, 1952b) illustrated this decades ago. She demonstrated the advantages of close collaboration between sociology and anthropology in the study of health-related behavior, particularly on the aspect of culture. Fox has also contributed to the search for evidence on the impact of values and beliefs on health behavior at the micro-level through her analysis of individuals and at the macro-level by focusing on institutional aspects of medical care such as the medical school and the hospital.

A final note before moving on to culture and health: Researchers' attention to ethnicity is now common in international studies in medicine and medical sociology. However, despite the relevance of culture in understanding patterns of health and illness behavior, the research focus in the US is more on race. Cockerham (2021b) suggests that this is due to race being used as a standard variable in almost every study in order to measure racial health disparities. Nevertheless, efforts to assist clinicians and medical researchers to appreciate the complexity of culture continue (e.g. Fox et al. 2017; LaVeist 1994; Williams 1994). The social sciences and, in particular, sociology and anthropology remain the disciplines most dedicated to the study of culture or ethnicity per se and of its association with health and illness phenomena.

Culture and Health Behavior

The conceptual insights of the classic and contemporary sociologists and anthropologists on the significance of culture are confirmed by research on health behavior over the past five decades. A complete review of the vast body of sociological and anthropological literature dealing with the influence of culture upon the individual's health behavior is a formidable task beyond the scope of this chapter. Instead, I will highlight the nuances and significance of cultural variations in health behavior by discussing relevant findings within the framework of three types of health-related behavior, namely, *preventive health behavior, illness behavior*, *and sick-role behavior*. The two former concepts were proposed by Kasl and Cobb (1966). The concept of *sick-role* behavior was formulated by Talcott Parsons (1951: 436–8).

Preventive health behavior refers to the activity of a person who believes he or she is healthy for the purpose of preventing illness (Kasl and Cobb 1966: 246). Kasl and Cobb labeled this "health behavior" but the term *preventive* differentiates it clearly from the other two types of health-related behavior. Kasl and Cobb (1966: 246) defined *illness behavior* as the activity undertaken by a person who feels ill for the purpose of defining the illness and seeking a solution. In the sense intended for this discussion, *illness behavior* encompasses the time span between a person's first awareness of symptoms and his or her decision to seek expert assistance or "technically competent" help (to borrow Parsons' [1951: 437] term). *Illness behavior*, thus defined, includes activities such as initial self-medication or self-treatment and discussion of the problem with non-expert family members and others within one's primary or informal social network. *Sick-role behavior* is the activity undertaken by a person who considers himself or herself ill for the purpose of getting well (based on Parsons 1951: 436–8). *Sick-role behavior* is typically preceded by *illness behavior* and encompasses the sick person's formal response to symptoms, that is, the seeking of what he or she perceives as "technically competent" help. The sick person may seek technically competent or expert advice from whoever he or she perceives as or believes to be an expert including a traditional healer, modern medical practitioners, or a combination of these. *Sick-role behavior* also includes the relation between patient and healer, and the subsequent activity of the person as a patient.

Culture and Preventive Health Behavior

Preventive health behavior refers to the activity of a person who believes he or she is healthy for the purpose of preventing illness (Kasl and Cobb 1966: 246). In addition to the study of healthy individuals, relevant research on preventive health behavior also covers studies on substance addiction or abuse (drugs, alcohol, cigarettes), which seek to understand the path toward addiction and to identify the factors involved. The subjective evaluation of one's own health status may propel or retard preventive action against disease. Many studies on preventive health behavior report data on self-health evaluation but it is uncommon to report variations in the cultural meaning attached to health status. As health status is, in many respects, a value, cultural variations are common in people's evaluation of their own health status and the way in which they evaluate it.

An illustration of this phenomenon is the traditional Chinese notion of "ti-zhi" (Lew-Ting et al. 1998). "Ti-zhi" or "constitution" denotes "a long-term, pervasive characteristic that is central to their sense of self" and clearly different from the Western concept of health status. The latter is "a more temporal, fluctuating state" that varies with "the experience of illness" (Lew-Ting et al. 1998: 829). Their study illustrates the cultural similarity in the definition of constitution among people of the same ethnic group (Chinese elderly) living in two different parts of the world, Taipei and Los Angeles. In contrast, residing in the same geographical location does not secure a common meaning of health status. For example, significant cultural differences in self-evaluated health status were observed among three cultural groups living in close proximity of each other in south-central Florida (Albrecht et al. 1998).

Among the studies relevant to the prevention of substance abuse, is the work of Gureje et al. (1997). People in nine cities were interviewed on their values and perceptions concerning the meaning of drinking alcohol. The nine cities were Ankara (Turkey), Athens (Greece), Bangalore (India), Flagstaff (Arizona), Ibadan (Nigeria), Jebal (Romania), Mexico City, Santander (Spain), and Seoul (South Korea). These authors reported a "remarkable congruence" in the practitioners' criteria to diagnose alcoholism. But they found significant variations among people across the nine cities concerning "drinking norms, especially with regard to *wet* and *dry* cultures" (1997: 209). A *wet* culture, they stated, is that where alcohol drinking is permitted or encouraged by the social significance attached to the act of drinking and to the social context within which drinking takes place. In a *dry* culture, alcohol drinking is discouraged or prohibited altogether. Their study is part of the increasing body of research findings showing that the difficulties encountered in the prevention of alcoholism and other types of substance abuse are greater in some cultures than in others (e.g. Nelson and Wilson 2017).

The investigation into the relative influence of culture upon alcohol abuse was found by Guttman (1999) to be equivocal in situations where acculturation takes place. Guttman refers to the common definition of acculturation that is, "the process whereby one culture group adopts the beliefs and practices of another culture group over time" (1999: 175). His study of alcohol drinking among Mexican immigrants in the US highlighted several problems. He found it difficult to identify clearly the boundaries between cultures sharing the same geographical area. Some studies overcome this problem by following the symbolic-interaction postulate of the importance of subjective definition of self and of the situation and correspondingly accepting the subjects' self-identification as members of a given culture (e.g. Quah 1993). Some researchers assume that the length of time spent in the host country leads to acculturation and thus use other indicators, such as the proportion of the immigrant's life spent in the host country (i.e. Mandelblatt et al. 1999).

A second and more critical difficulty in the study of preventive and other types of health behavior involving alcoholism and other health disorders among immigrants and ethnic minorities is their concurrent exposure to multiple cultural influences. In this regard, Guttman's finding in the US is similar to findings in other countries. He observed that immigrants "are participants not only in the dissolution of older cultural practices and beliefs but are also constantly engaged in the creation, elaboration, and even intensification of new cultural identities" (Guttman 1999: 175). However, the presence of multiple cultural influences does not necessarily lead to the creation of new identities. Other outcomes are possible, such as one outcome I label *pragmatic acculturation*: the borrowing of cultural elements (concepts, ways of doing things, ways of organizing and planning) and adapting them to meet practical needs. Pragmatic acculturation is practiced in the search for ways to prevent illness, or trying different remedies to deal with symptoms (illness behavior), or seeking expert help from healers from other cultures (Quah 1985, 1989a, 2003, 2008). Individuals "borrow" healing options from cultures other than their own, but they may or may not incorporate those options or more aspects of the other cultures into their lives permanently. The borrowing and adapting is part of the ongoing process of dealing with health and illness. Solutions from other cultures tend to be adopted, or adapted to one's own culture, if and for as long as they "work" to the satisfaction of the user.

Yet another angle of analysis in the study of culture and health is the identification of cultural differences in health behavior among subgroups of a community or country assumed to be culturally homogeneous. Such is the case of differences commonly found between "rural" and "urban" ways of life and ways of thinking in the same country. Lyttleton's (1993) study of preventive health education on AIDS in Thailand illustrates well the urban–rural divide. The message of public preventive information campaigns designed in urban centers was not received as intended in rural villages. The concept of promiscuity that was at the center of the Thai AIDS prevention campaigns was associated by the villagers with the visiting of "commercial sex workers" only and not with the practice of "sleeping with several different village women" (1993: 143). The misperceptions of preventive public health campaigns occur between the rural, less educated, and dialect-speaking groups on the one hand, and the urban, educated civil servants and health professionals who design the campaigns, on the other hand. The misperception of the campaign message is not the only problem. An additional serious obstacle to reach the target rural population is the medium used to disseminate preventive health information. The Thai villagers perceived new technology including television broadcasts from Bangkok as "belonging to a different world – both physically and socioculturally" and, consequently, "increased exposure to these messages simply reinforces the [villagers'] perception that they are not locally pertinent" (Lyttleton 1993: 144). The search for, and testing, of effective approaches to "culturally tailored" health interventions continues (e.g. Galbraith et al. 2016; Kikuzawa et al. 2019; Miller et al. 2019).

Culture and Illness Behavior

As mentioned earlier, illness behavior refers to the activity undertaken by a person who feels ill for the purpose of defining the illness and seeking a solution (Kasl and Cobb 1966). What people do when they begin to feel unwell, the manner in which people react to symptoms, and the meaning they attach to symptoms vary across cultures.

Reviewing the work of Edward Suchman (1964, 1965) on illness behavior and ethnicity, Geertsen and his colleagues (1975) concluded that there was indeed an association between the two phenomena. They found that "Group closeness and exclusivity increases the likelihood" of a person responding to a health problem "in a way that is consistent with his subcultural background" (1975: 232). Further detailed data on the correlation between ethnicity and illness behavior was reported by, among others, Robertson and Heagarty (1975); Kosa and Zola (1975); and by Sanborn and Katz (1977) who found significant cultural variations in the perception of symptoms. In fact, the relative saturation of the literature regarding the ethnicity-illness behavior link was already manifested in Mechanic's observation in the late 1970s: "Cultures are so recognizably different that variations in illness behavior in different societies hardly need demonstration" (1978: 261).

Nevertheless, research on the association between culture and illness behavior continues (e.g. Nelson and Wilson 2017; Versey et al. 2019). One important theme is mental illness, given that symptoms are primarily manifested through alterations in what is culturally defined as "normal" or "acceptable" social interaction. A prominent contributor to the study of culture and mental illness is Horacio Fabrega (1991, 1993, 1995). Summarizing the crux of research in sociology and anthropology, Fabrega states that "empirical studies integral to and grounded in sound clinical and epidemiological research methods ... have succeeded in making clear how cultural conventions affect manifestations of disorders, aspects of diagnosis, and responses to treatment" (1995: 380).

The reactions of others, particularly family and significant others, play an important part in determining how the symptomatic person defines and handles symptoms and healthcare options (e.g. Perry et al. 2016). Such reaction varies across cultures. McKelvy et al. (1997) found that, in contrast to Americans, "the Vietnamese traditional culture has a much narrower definition of mental illness." They are more tolerant of behavioral disturbance triggered by distress, defining someone as mentally ill only if the person is "so disruptive" that he or she "threatens the social order or the safety of others". Even then, the family is the first source of care, which may include "physical restraint." The person is taken to the hospital only if the family is unable to control him or her (1997: 117).

From the perspective of psychiatry research, the cultural definition of symptoms tends to determine the disease outcome. Hahn and Kleinman (1983) proposed that beliefs in the etiology and prognosis of disease are as important to disease causation as microorganisms or chemical substances. In the case of the sudden nocturnal death syndrome or SUNDS among the Hmong refugees in the US, Adler (1994: 26) explains: "in the traditional Hmong worldview the functions of the mind and the body are not dichotomized and polarized." He identified a series of pathological circumstances leading to SUNDS. As refugees, the Hmong lost their traditional social support and were pressed to adapt to a different culture. Adler (1994: 52) found that "severe and ongoing stress related to cultural disruption and national resettlement" as well as "the intense feelings of powerlessness regarding existence in the US," and their "belief system in which evil spirits have the power to kill men who do not fulfill their religious obligations" together led "the solitary Hmong male" to die of SUNDS.

Illness behavior typically involves a "wait-and-see" attitude as the first reaction to symptoms, followed by self-medication; if the problem is judged to have worsened, then the person might be prepared to seek expert advice. In this process, cultural patterns of behavior may be superseded by formal education. In a comparative analysis of Chinese, Malays, and Indians, I found that education explains the practice of self-medication with modern over-the-counter medications better than culture. There was a significant difference among the three groups in the keeping of non-prescription and traditional medications at home. Yet, education served as an "equalizer" for self-medication with modern (i.e. Western) medicines. The more educated a person is, the more inclined he or she would be to practice self-medication with "modern" over-the-counter medicines before (or instead of) seeking expert advice, irrespective of his or her ethnic group (Quah 1985). A similar finding was reported in the treatment of malaria in the Philippines (Miguel et al. 1999).

Culture and Sick-Role Behavior

To recapitulate what was discussed in the first section, *sick-role behavior* is the activity undertaken by a person who considers himself or herself ill for the purpose of getting well (based on Parsons 1951: 436–8). Sick-role behavior encompasses the sick person's response to symptoms, in particular, the seeking of what he or she perceives as "technically competent" help (to borrow Parsons' term), as well as doctor–patient or healer–patient interaction. Lyle Saunders (1954) was among the first sociologists to observe that cultural differences in medical care manifested in the problems encountered when the physician and the patient were from different ethnic groups.

One of the earliest and most significant investigations on the actual influence of culture on sick-role behavior was Mark Zborowski's (1952, 1969) analysis of cultural differences in responses to pain. Investigating differences among war veterans warded in an American hospital, he observed that the Italian-American and Jewish-American patients differed significantly from the "old American" and Irish-American patients in their expression of pain and description of their symptoms. Zborowski proposed that cultural differences such as socialization, time-orientation, and the array of values outlining what is appropriate behavior in cultural communities explained the differences he observed among the four groups of patients. Similarly, Irving Zola (1966) analyzed how culture shapes the subjective perception of symptoms. His research confirmed Zborowski's findings on the presence of cultural differences in perception of, and reaction to, symptoms and pain. Zola (1973, 1983) continued his probe into the impact of cultural differences on the doctor–patient relationship, the perception of illness, and the importance given to health matters in different cultural communities. Twaddle (1978) conducted an exploratory replication of Zborowski's study, comparing 26 American married males who classified themselves as "Italian Catholics," "Protestants," and "Jewish." Twaddle found that Parsons' configuration of "sick role" varied among these groups. The relevance of cultural differences in responses to pain is well recognized and research on this important dimension continues. Some examples of findings on cultural differences are: Black Caribbean and White British cancer patients (Koffman et al. 2008); Saudi, Swedish and Italian patients with temporomandibular disorder (Al-Harthy et al. 2016); Japanese and British subjects' pain tolerance (Robertson et al. 2017); and chronic back pain among English-speaking Punjabi and white British people (Singh et al. 2018).

Similarly, studies continue to confirm the impact of culture on the doctor–patient relation and, correspondingly, on patient outcomes. Nitcher (1994) observed the use of the traditional term "mahina ang baga" (weak lungs) by doctors and lay persons in the Philippines. Nitcher found that doctors used the term when diagnosing tuberculosis in an effort to spare the patient the social stigma of the disease. However, "weak lungs" is a very ambiguous term in everyday discourse; thus, the unintended consequence was a negative patient outcome. Nitcher states "the sensitivity of clinicians to [the] social stigma [of tuberculosis] is laudatory." But he correctly points out that "the use of the term *weak lungs* has [serious] consequences" for public health because the diagnosis "*weak lungs* is not deemed as serious as TB" and thus people, especially the poor, do not comply with the prescribed treatment, which is a "six-month course of medication" (Nitcher 1994: 659).

A major direct implication of the concept of role is the symbolic, perceived or actual presence and agency of others. Sick-role behavior implies the presence of the healing expert (irrespective of what healing system is at work). A large body of research findings on the doctor–patient relationship has confirmed the relevance of culture. As expected, cultural similarities, such as physical appearance and language, among other characteristics, between doctor (or healer) and patient facilitate the relationship and increase the possibility of positive patient outcomes (Cockerham 2016:175–205; Kleinman 1980: 203–58). A note of caution, however: Similarities in culture do not secure success in the doctor–patient relationship. Many other aspects come into play, from ecological factors (e.g. Catalano 1989), to the differential understanding of metaphors (e.g. Glennon 1999), and structural features of the dyadic healer–patient relationship. Structural features – such as who is involved and how the interaction is conducted – vary across cultures. Haug and her colleagues (1995) found interesting differences in the manner in which the doctor-patient relationship develops in Japan and the US. Kleinman (1980: 250–310) shows how the direct involvement of the patient's family transforms that dyadic relationship in some communities. Furthermore, patients' subjective assessment of their interpersonal relationship with their healer may become as significant as "the technical quality" of the medical care they receive (Haddad et al. 1998).

Following the same premise on the significance of the presence of others, another important aspect of sick-role behavior is the availability of an informal social support network for the sick individual. The emotional, social, and instrumental support received from one's informal network of family and friends tends to guide the attitudes and actions of the ill person before, during, and after consulting experts. Just as cultural variations are observed among sick people searching for help from healing experts (whether traditional or modern), the seeking of emotional and social support and the presence and quality of informal social support from family and friends also vary across cultures. Some examples are: the comparative study of Asian-American and Anglo-American women's situations after breast cancer diagnosis (Kagawa-Singer et al. 1997); the systematic review of barriers to mammography screening (Miller et al. 2019); and the utilization of mental health services in Japan (Kikuzawa et al. 2019).

Culture and Healing Systems

The options available to people seeking health care vary greatly across countries and cultures. As Cockerham explains (2010: 208), even in a modern, developed country like the US, people may not look at modern medicine as the only or right option. In the discussion of culture and health, reference must be made to the wide range of healing options found in most societies today. For the sake of clarity, let us consider all healing options as falling into three general categories: the modern or *Western biomedicine* system; *traditional* medicine systems; and *popular* medicine. A medical system is understood as "a patterned, interrelated body of values and deliberate practices governed by a single paradigm of the meaning, identification, prevention and treatment of ... illness and/or disease" (Press 1980: 47). Traditional medical systems flourished well before Western biomedicine and their history goes back more than one millennium. Three ancient healing traditions are considered to be the most important: the Arabic, Hindu, and Chinese healing traditions (Leslie 1976: 15–7). However, there is a revival of interest in the two best-known traditional medicine systems: traditional Chinese medicine (Unschuld 1985) and Hindu or Ayurvedic medicine (Basham 1976). Popular medicine refers to "those beliefs and practices which, though compatible with the underlying paradigm of a medical system, are materially or behaviorally divergent from official medical practice" (Press 1980:48). Popular medicine is also labeled "complementary" and "alternative" medicine or therapies (Quah 2008; Sharma 1990).

In contrast to the modest attention given by researchers to power and dominance in the traditional healing system, the intense concern with the preponderance and power of Western biomedicine is evident in the work of Foucault (1973) and Goffman (1968a, 1968b), and has been documented and analyzed in detail by Freidson (1970), Starr (1982), and Conrad and Schneider (1992) among others. These authors refer to Western biomedicine as practiced in Western industrialized countries and beyond (Quah 1989b, 2003). Interestingly, in the second decade of the twenty-first century Western biomedicine continues its rapid scientific advance and leads in public health (Quah 2018), but, given increasing costs and the large migration waves of indigent communities across continents, Western biomedicine is less accessible to poor people compared to traditional and other healing systems (Benatar and Ashcroft 2017; Sanders et al. 2017).

Healing systems are constantly evolving and two features of their internal dynamics are relevant here: divergence and pragmatic acculturation. Divergence in a healing system is the emergence of subgroups within the system supporting different interpretations of the system's core values. The notion of "detached concern" in medical education is a good illustration of cultural divergence. In her comparative study of medical schools, Renée Fox (1976) investigated the assumed resilience of six value-orientations (in Parsons' sense) at the core of Western biomedicine: rationality, instrumental activism, universalism, individualism, and collectivism, all of which comprise the ethos of science and detached concern, a value she assigned specifically to Western biomedicine practitioners. Fox observed that these values of biomedicine are subject to reinterpretations across cultures. She found "considerable variability in the form and in the degree to which they [the six value-orientations] are institutionalized" (Fox 1976: 104–06) even within the same country as illustrated by the situation in four major medical schools in Belgium in the 1960s representing basic cultural rifts: "Flemish" versus "French," and "Catholic" versus "Free Thought" perspectives. Forty years later, in their systematic review of research on "detached concern," Underman and Hirsfield (2016) identified a divergent trend: the recognition of empathy as an important component of medical education and ethical medical practice.

A manifestation of pragmatic acculturation in a healing system is the inclination of its practitioners to borrow ideas or procedures from other systems to solve specific problems without necessarily accepting the core values or premises of the system or systems from which they do the borrowing (Quah 2003). To illustrate: some traditional Chinese physicians use the stethoscope to listen to the patient's breathing, or the sphygmomanometer to measure blood pressure, or the auto-clave to sterilize acupuncture needles, or a laser instrument instead of needles in acupuncture (Quah and Li 1989; Quah 1989a: 122–59). Norheim and Fonnebo (1998) illustrate the practice of pragmatic acculturation among young western biomedicine practitioners in Norway who learned and practiced acupuncture. Pragmatic acculturation has also facilitated the provision of western biomedical services to peoples from other cultures. Ledesma (1997) and Selzler (1996) studied the health values, health beliefs, and the health needs of Native Americans to improve the provision of relevant Western biomedical services to their communities. Adapting the type and mode of delivery of modern health care services to serve the needs of traditional peoples is receiving more serious attention from health care providers. Although pragmatic acculturation requires Western biomedicine practitioners to change or adapt their usual practices and assumptions, it is worthwhile if it attains the objective of making health care services more accessible to communities in need (e.g. Harmsen et al. 2008).

The presence and relative success of groups and institutions (for example, the medical profession, hospitals, and other health care organizations) involved in the provision of health care unfold in the context of culture. Arthur Kleinman (1980) highlights the relevance of the "social space" occupied by health systems. He identified significant differences among ethnic communities and the subsequent impact of cultural perceptions of mental illness upon the structure of mental health services. The influence of culture on the provision of mental health services is studied widely. Studying mental health in Vietnam, McKelvy and colleagues (1997: 117) found that "there is no profession specifically dedicated to hearing the woes of others. Talk therapy is quite alien to the Vietnamese". Similarly, the traditional Vietnamese perception of child behavior and their "narrow" definition of mental illness help to explain their skepticism on the need for child psychiatric clinics.

Adding to social science research on the link between culture and health is the systematic discussion of culture within the realm of bioethics, including the nuances of informed consent, its meaning and interpretation among different ethnic groups (Turner 2005). Similarly, governments and health authorities recognize the importance of culture in illness prevention and the provision of healthcare services. One interesting example is the US Surgeon General's Report on Mental Health (USDHHS 1999) and the supplement report on "Mental Health: Culture, Race and Ethnicity" (USDHHS 2001). The Supplement was intended as a collaborative document with social scientists and it became "a landmark in the dialogue – political and scientific – regarding health disparities in the United States" (Manson 2003: 395); and "more than a government document" as it discusses the significance of ethnicity in the planning and provision of preventive and curative mental health services (Lopez 2003: 420).

The Pervasiveness of Culture

In conclusion, culture has, does, and will continue to influence health-related behavior. There is a wealth of social science and, in particular, medical sociology research demonstrating the pervasiveness of cultural values and norms upon preventive health behavior, illness behavior, and sick-role behavior among individuals and groups as well as at the macro-level of healing systems.

The preceding discussion has highlighted three additional features of the study of culture in health and illness. The first of these features is the remarkable confluence of different and even opposite schools of thought in sociology concerning the need to analyze culture as an independent phenomenon, and the influence of culture upon agency and structure. The affective nature and subjectivity of one's perceived identity as member of an ethnic group and the permeability of cultural boundaries are ideas found implicitly or explicitly in Durkheim, Weber, Parsons, as well as in Goffman, Foucault, and Habermas, among others. The second feature is the divergence of healing systems. Healing systems are not always internally consistent; different interpretations of the core values or principles of the system may be held by subgroups within the system. The third feature is pragmatic acculturation, that is, the borrowing from other cultures of elements, ways of thinking and ways of doing things, with the objective of solving specific or practical problems. This borrowing is very prevalent in matters of health and illness and is found in all types of health-related behavior. Finally, a comprehensive review of the relevant literature is not possible in this chapter given the enormous body of medical sociology research on health and culture. Instead, illustrations and the list of references are offered for each main argument in this discussion in the hope that the reader be enticed to pursue his or her own journey into this engaging research topic.

References

Adler, Shelley R. 1994. "Ethnomedical Pathogenesis and Hmong Immigrants' Sudden Nocturnal Deaths." *Culture, Medicine and Psychiatry* 18: 23–59.

Albrecht, Stan L, Leslie L Clarke, and Michael K Miller. 1998. "Community, Family, and the Race/Ethnicity Differences in Health Status in Rural Areas." *Rural Sociology* 63: 235–252.

Alexander, Jeffrey C. 1990. "Analytic Debates: Understanding the Relative Autonomy of Culture." Pp. 1–27 in *Culture and Society. Contemporary Debates*, edited by J. C Alexander and Steven Seidman. Cambridge: Cambridge University Press.

Al-Harthy, Mohammad, R, Ohrbach, A Michelotti, and T List. 2016. "The Effect of Culture on Pain Sensitivity." *Journal of Oral Rehabilitation* 43: 81–88.

Basham, Arthur L. 1976. "The Practice of Medicine in Ancient and Medieval India." Pp. 18–43 in *Asian Medical Systems: A Comparative Study*, edited by Charles Leslie. Berkeley, CA: University of California Press.

Benatar, Solomon R, and Richard Ashcroft. 2017. "International Perspectives in Resource Allocation." Pp. 316–321 in *International Encyclopedia of Public Health*, edited by Stella R. Quah and William C Cockerham. 2nd ed. Vol. 4.

Borjas, George J. 2020. "Demographic Determinants of Testing Incidence and COVID-19 Infections in New York City Neighborhoods," *IZA Institute of Labor Economics*, Discussion Paper Series IZA DP No. 13115, http://ftp.iza.org/dp13115.pdf

Catalano, Ralph. 1989. "Ecological Factors in Illness and Disease." Pp. 87–101 in *Handbook of Medical Sociology*, edited by Howard E. Freeman and Sol Levine. 4th Ed. Englewood Cliffs, NJ: Prentice-Hall.

Cockerham, William C. 2010. *Medical Sociology*. 11th edition. Englewood Cliffs, NJ: Prentice-Hall.

Cockerham, William C. 2016. "Health Lifestyles: Bringing Structure Back." Pp. 159–183 in *The New Blackwell Companion to Medical Sociology*, edited by W C Cockerham. Oxford: Wiley Blackwell.

Cockerham, William C. 2021a. "Health Lifestyles: Bringing Structure Back." Pp. 151–170 in *The Wiley Blackwell Companion to Medical Sociology*, edited by W C Cockerham. Oxford: Wiley Blackwell.

Cockerham, William C. 2021b. *Sociological Theories of Health and Illness*. New York: Routledge.

Conrad, Peter and Joseph W Schneider. 1992. "Deviance and Medicalization. From Badness to Sickness." in *Expanded Edition*. Philadelphia, PA: Temple University Press.

Downing, Janelle. 2016. "The Health Effects of the Foreclosure Crisis and Unaffordable Housing: A Systematic Review and Explanation of Evidence." *Social Science & Medicine* 162: 88–96.

Durkheim, Emile. 1938. *The Rules of Sociological Method.* 8th Ed. New York: The Free Press.

Fabrega, Horacio. 1991. "Psychiatric Stigma in Non-Western Societies." *Contemporary Psychiatry* 326: 534–551.

Fabrega, Horacio. 1993. "A Cultural Analysis of Human Behavioral Breakdowns: An Approach to the Ontology and Epistemology of Psychiatric Phenomena." *Culture, Medicine and Psychiatry* 17: 99–132.

Fabrega, Horacio. 1995. "Cultural Challenges to the Psychiatric Enterprise." *Comprehensive Psychiatry* 36: 377–383.

Foucault, Michel. 1970. *The Order of Things: An Archaeology of the Human Sciences.* London: Tavistock.

Foucault, Michel. 1973. *The Birth of the Clinic: An Archeology of Medical Perception.* London: Tavistock.

Foucault, Michel. 1977. *Discipline and Punish: The Birth of the Prison.* London: Allen Lane.

Fox, Kathleen A., and Crista Johnson-Agbakwu. 2020. "Crime Victimization, Health, and Female Genital Mutilation or Cutting Among Somali Women and Adolescent Girls in the United States, 2017." *American Journal of Public Health* 110(1): 112–118.

Fox, Molly, Zaneta Thayer, and Pathik D Wadhwa. 2017. "Assessment of Acculturation in Minority Research." *Social Science & Medicine* 176: 123–132.

Fox, Renée C. 1976. "The Sociology of Modern Medical Research." Pp. 102–114." in *Asian Medical Systems: A Comparative Study*, edited by Charles Leslie. Berkeley, CA: University of California Press.

Fox, Renée C. 1989. *Medical Sociology. A Participant Observer's View.* New York: Prentice-Hall.

Freidson, Eliot. 1970. *Profession of Medicine: A Study of the Sociology of Applied Knowledge.* New York: Dodd Mead.

Gage-Bouchard, Elizabeth A. 2017. "Culture, Styles of Institutional Interactions, and Inequalities in Healthcare Experiences." *Journal of Health and Social Behavior* 58(2): 147–165.

Galbraith, Kayoll V, Julia Lechuga, Coretta M Jenerette, LTC Angelo D Moore, Mary H Palmer, and Jill B Hamilton. 2016. "Parental Acceptance and Uptake of the HPV Vaccine among African-Americans and Latinos in the United States: A Literature Review." *Social Science & Medicine* 159: 116–126.

Gerhardt, Uta. 1989. *Ideas about Illness: An Intellectual and Political History of Medical Sociology.* New York: New York University Press.

Glennon, Cheryl D. 1999. "Conceptual Metaphor in the Health Care Culture (Health Communicators)." *Unpublished Ph.D. Dissertation.* San Diego, CA: University of San Diego.

Goffman, Erving. 1968a. *Asylums: Essays on the Social Situation of Mental Patients and other Inmates.* Harmondsworth: Penguin.

Goffman, Erving. 1968b. *Stigma. Notes on the Management of Spoilt Identity.* Harmondsworth: Penguin.

Greer, Germaine. 1999. *The Whole Woman.* New York: Knopf.

Grose, Rose G, Julia S Chen, Katherine A Roof, Sharon Rachel, and Katheryn M Yount. 2020. "Sexual and Reproductive Health Outcomes of Violence Against Women and Girls in Lower-Income Countries: A Review of Reviews." *The Journal of Sex Research* January: 1–20.

Gureje, Oye, Venos Mavreas, J L Vazquez-Baquero, and Aleksandar Janca. 1997. "Problems Related to Alcohol Use: A Cross-Cultural Perspective." *Culture, Medicine and Psychiatry* 21: 199–211.

Guttman, Matthew C. 1999. "Ethnicity, Alcohol, and Assimilation." *Social Science & Medicine* 48: 173–184.

Haddad, Slim, Pierre Fournier, Nima Machouf, and Fissinet Yatara. 1998. "What Does Quality Mean to Lay People? Community Perceptions of Primary Health Care Services in Guinea." *Social Science & Medicine* 47: 381–394.

Hahn, Robert A, and Arthur Kleinman. 1983. "Belief as Pathogen, Belief as Medicine: 'Voodoo Death' and the 'Placebo Phenomenon' in Anthropological Perspective." *Medical Anthropology Quarterly* 14: 6–19.

Harmsen, J A M Hans, Roos M D Bernsen, Marc A Bruijnzeels, and Ludwien Meeuwesen. 2008. "Patients' Evaluation of Quality of Care in General Practice: What are the Cultural and Linguistic Barriers?" *Patient Education and Counseling* 72: 155–162.

Haug, Marie R, Hiro Akiyama, Georgeanna Tryban, Kyoichi Sonoda, and MMay Wykle. 1995. "Self-Care: Japan and the US Compared." Pp. 313–324 in *The Sociology of Medicine. International Library of Critical Writings in Sociology*, edited by William C. Cockerham. Aldershot: Elgar. Reprinted from *Social Science & Medicine* 1991, 33: 1011–22.

Kagawa-Singer, Marjorie, David K Wellisch, and Ramani Durvasula. 1997. "Impact of Breast Cancer on Asian American and Anglo American Women." *Culture, Medicine and Psychiatry* 21: 449–480.

Kasl, S V, and S Cobb. 1966. "Health Behavior, Illness Behavior, and Sick Role Behavior." *Archives of Environmental Health* 12: 246–255.

Kikuzawa, Saeko, B Pescosolido, M Kasahara-Kiritani, T Matoba, C Yamaki, and K Sugiyama. 2019. "Mental Health Care and the Cultural Toolboxes of the Present-day Japanese population: Examining Suggested Patterns of Care and their Correlates." *Social Science & Medicine* 228: 252–261.

King, Stanley H. 1962. *Perceptions of Illness and Medical Practice.* New York: Russell Sage Foundation.

Kleinman, Arthur. 1980. *Patients and Healers in the Context of Culture.* Berkeley, CA: University of California Press.

Kluckhohn, Clyde. 1951. "The Study of Culture." Pp. 86–101 in *The Policy Sciences. Recent Developments in Scope and Method*, edited by Daniel Lerner and Harold D. Lasswell. Stanford, CA: Stanford University Press.

Koffman, J., M. Morgan, P. Edmonds, P. Speck, and I.J. Higginson. 2008. "Cultural Meanings of Pain: A Qualitative Study of Black Caribbean and White British Patients with Advanced Cancer." *Palliative Medicine* 22: 350–359.

Korous, Kevin M., Jose M. Causadias, and Deborah N. Casper. 2017. "Racial Discrimination and Cortisol Output: A Meta-Analysis." *Social Science & Medicine* 193: 90–100.

Kosa, John, and Irving Kenneth Zola. 1975. *Poverty and Health. A Sociological Analysis.* Revised edition Ed. Cambridge, MA: Harvard University Press.

Kroeber, Alfred Louis, and Clyde Kluckhohn. 1952. "Culture: A Critical Review of Concepts and Definitions." *Papers of the Peabody Museum*, Vol. 41. Cambridge, MA: Harvard University.

Lane, Haylee, Mitchell Sarkies, Jennifer Martin, and Terry Haines. 2017. "Equity in Healthcare Resource Allocation Decision Making: A Systematic Review." *Social Science & Medicine* 175: 11–27.

LaVeist, T. A. 1994. "Beyond Dummy Variable and Sample Selection: What Health Services Researchers Ought to Know about Race as a Variable." *Health Services Research* 29: 1–16.

Ledesma, Rita V. 1997. "Cultural Influences upon Definitions of Health and Health Sustaining Practices for American Indian Children." *Unpublished Ph.D. Dissertation.* Los Angeles, CA: University of California.

Leslie, Charles (ed.). 1976. *Asian Medical Systems. A Comparative Study.* Berkeley, CA: University of California Press.

Lew-Ting, Chih-Yin, M., L. Hurwicz, and E. Berkanovic. 1998. "Personal Constitution and Health Status Among Chinese Elderly in Taipei and Los Angeles." *Social Science & Medicine* 47: 821–830.

Locker, David. 1983. *Disability and Disadvantage: The Consequences of Chronic Illness.* London: Tavistock.

Lopez, Steven R. 2003. "Reflections on the Surgeon's General Report on Mental Health, Culture, Race, and Ethnicity." *Culture, Medicine and Psychiatry* 27: 419–434.

Lyttleton, Chris. 1993. "Knowledge and Meaning: The AIDS Education Campaign in Rural Northeast Thailand." *Social Science & Medicine* 38: 135–146.

Malinowski, Bronislaw. 1944. *A Scientific Theory of Culture and Other Essays.* Chapel Hill, NC: University of North Carolina Press.

Mandelblatt, Jeanne S, K. Gold, A. S. O'Malley, K. Taylor, K. Cagney, J. S. Hopkins, and J. Kerner. 1999. "Breast and Cervix Cancer Screening Among Multiethnic Women: Role of Age, Health and Source of Care." *Preventive Medicine* 28: 418–425.

Manson, Spero M. 2003. "Extending the Boundaries, Bridging the Gaps: Crafting Mental Health: Culture, Race, and Ethnicity, a Supplement to the Surgeon General's Report on Mental Health." *Culture, Medicine and Psychiatry* 27: 395–408.

McKelvy, Robert S, David L Sang, and Cam Tu Hoang. 1997. "Is There a Role for Child Psychiatry in Vietnam?" *Australian and New Zealand Journal of Psychiatry* 31: 114–119.

Mead, Margaret. 1956. "Understanding Cultural Patterns." *Nursing Outlook* 4: 260–262.

Mechanic, David. 1978. *Medical Sociology.* 2nd Ed. New York: The Free Press.

Miguel, Cynthia A., V. L. Tallo, L. Manderson, and M. A. Lansong. 1999. "Local Knowledge and Treatment of Malaria in Agusan del Sur, The Philippines." *Social Science & Medicine* 48: 607–618.

Miller, Brittany C., Jennifer M. Bowers, Jackelyn B. Payne, and Anne Moyer. 2019. "Barriers to Mammography Screening Among Racial and Ethnic Minority Women." *Social Science & Medicine* 239: 112494.

Nelson, Sarah E., and K. Wilson. 2017. "The Mental Health of Indigenous Peoples in Canada: A critical Review of Research." *Social Science & Medicine* 176: 93–112.

Nitcher, Mark. 1994. "Illness Semantics and International Health: The Weak Lung/TB Complex in the Philippines." *Social Science & Medicine* 38: 649–663.

Norheim, Arne Johan, and Vinjar Fonnebo. 1998. "Doctors' Attitudes to Accupuncture – A Norwegian Study." *Social Science & Medicine* 47: 519–523.

Parsons, Talcott. 1951. *The Social System.* London: Routledge & Kegan Paul Ltd.

Parsons, Talcott, and Renée Fox. 1952a. "Introduction." *Journal of Social Issues* 8: 2–3.

Parsons, Talcott, and Renée Fox. 1952b. "Illness, Therapy, and the Modern Urban Family." *Journal of Social Issues* 8: 31–44.

Parsons, Talcott. 1970. *Social Structure and Personality.* New York: Free Press.

Paul, Benjamin. 1963. "Anthropological Perspectives on Medicine and Public Health." *Annals of the American Academy of Political and Social Science* 346: 34–43.

Perry, B.L., E. Pullen, and Bernice A. Pescosolido. 2016. "At the Intersection of Lay and Professional Social Networks: How Community Ties Shape Perceptions of Mental Health Treatment Providers." *Global Mental Health* 3: 1–17.

Press, Irwin. 1980. "Problems of Definition and Classification of Medical Systems." *Social Science & Medicine* 14B: 45–57.

Quah, Stella R. 1985. "Self-Medication in Singapore." *Singapore Medical Journal* 26:123–129.

Quah, Stella R. 1989a. "The Triumph of Practicality." Pp. 1–18 in *The Triumph of Practicality. Tradition and Modernity in Health Care Utilization in Selected Asian Countries*, edited by S R Quah. Singapore: Institute of Southeast Asian Studies.

Quah, Stella R. 1989b. "The Social Position and Internal Organization of the Medical Profession in the Third World: The case of Singapore." *Journal of Health and Social Behavior* 30(4): 450–466.

Quah, Stella R. 1993. "Ethnicity, Health Behavior, and Modernization: The Case of Singapore." Pp. 78–107 in *Health and Health Care in Developing Countries: Sociological Perspectives*, edited by Peter Conrad and Eugene B. Gallagher. Philadelphia, PA: Temple University Press.

Quah, Stella R. 2003. "Traditional Healing Systems and the Ethos of Science." *Social Science & Medicine* 57: 1997–2012.

Quah, Stella R. 2008. "In Pursuit of Health: Pragmatic Acculturation in Everyday Life." *Health Sociology Review* 17(4): 419–421.

Quah, Stella R. 2018. "Disability, Illness and Health Risks: Public Health and Epidemiology Approaches." *Elsevier Reference Module in Biomedical Sciences* 1–11. https://dx.doi.org/10.1016/B978-0-12-801238-3.66190-1.

Quah, Stella R, and Jing-Wei Li. 1989. "Marriage of Convenience: Traditional and Modern Medicine in the People's Republic of China." Pp. 19–42 in *The Triumph of Practicality. Tradition and Modernity in Health Care Utilization in Selected Asian Countries*, edited by Stella R. Quah. Singapore: Institute of Southeast Asian Studies.

Reed, Geertsen, Melville R. Klauber, Mark Rindflesh, Robert L. Kane, and Robert Gray. 1975. "A Re-Examination of Suchman's Views on Social Factors in Health Care Utilization." *Journal of Health and Social Behavior* 16: 226–237.

Robertson, Leon, and M. Heagarty. 1975. *Medical Sociology: A General Systems Approach.* New York: Nelson Hall.

Robertson, Olivia, S.J. Robinson, and R. Stephens. 2017. "Swearing as a Response to Pain: A Cross-cultural Comparison of British and Japanese Participants." *Scandinavian Journal of Pain* 17: 267–272.

Sanborn, K. O., and M. M. Katz. 1977. "Perception of Symptoms Behavior Across Ethnic Groups." Pp. 236–240 in *Basic Problems in Cross-Cultural Psychology*, edited by Y. H. Poortinga. Amsterdam: International Association for Cross-Cultural Psychology.

Sanders, D., N. Schaay, and S. Mohamed. 2017. "Primary Health Care." Pp. 5–14 in *International Encyclopedia of Public Health*, edited by Stella R. Quah and William C. Cockerham, 2nd Ed. Vol. 6.

Saunders, Lyle. 1954. *Cultural Differences and Medical Care.* New York: Russell Sage Foundation.

Scambler, Graham. 1984. "Perceiving and Coping with Stigmatizing Illness." Pp. 35–43 in *The Experience of Illness*, edited by Ray Fitzpatrick et al. London: Tavistock.

Selzler, Bonnie Kay. 1996. "The Health Experiences of Dakota Sioux and Their Perceptions of Culturally Congruent Nursing Care." *Unpublished Ph.D. Dissertation.* Denver, CO: University of Colorado Health Sciences Center.

Sharma, Ursula M. 1990. "Using Alternative Therapies: Marginal Medicine and Central Concerns." Pp. 127–139 in *New Directions in the Sociology of Health*, edited by Pamela Abbot and Geoff Payne. London: Falmer Press.

Shellae, Versey, H, Courtney C Cogburn, Clara L Wilkins, and Nakita Joseph. 2019. "Appropriated racial oppression: Implications for mental health in Whites and Blacks." *Social Science & Medicine* 230: 295–302.

Singh, Gurpreet, C., Newton, K. O'Sullivan, A. Soundy, and N.R. Heneghan. 2018. "Exploring the lived experience and chronic low back pain beliefs of English-speaking Punjabi and white British people: A qualitative study within the NHS." *BMJ Open* 8: 1–11.

Starr, Paul. 1982. *The Social Transformation of American Medicine.* New York: Basic Books.

Strauss, Anselm L. 1965. "Social Patterns of Illness and Medical Care." *Journal of Health and Human Behavior* 6: 2–16.

Strauss, Anselm L. 1975. *Chronic Illness and the Quality of Life.* St Louis, MI: Mosby.

Suchman, Edward. 1964. "Socio-Medical Variations Among Ethnic Groups." *American Journal of Sociology* 70:319–331.

Taylor, Steve, and Clive Ashworth. 1987. "Durkheim and Social Realism: An Approach to Health and Illness." Pp. 37–58 in *Sociological Theory & Medical Sociology*, edited by Graham Scambler. London: Tavistock.

Turner, Leigh. 2005. "From the Local to the Global: Bioethics and the Concept of Culture." *Journal of Medicine and Philosophy* 30: 305–320.

Twaddle, Andrew C. 1978. "Health Decisions and Sick Role Variations: An Exploration." Pp. 5–15 in *Dominant Issues in Medical Sociology*, edited by Howard D. Schwartz and Cary S. Kart. Reading, MA: Addison-Wesley.

US Department of Health and Human Services (USDHHS). 1999. *Mental Health: A Report of the Surgeon General.* Rockwille, MD: US Department of Health and Human Services.

US Department of Health and Human Services (USDHHS). 2001. *Mental Health: Culture, Race and Ethnicity. A Supplement to Mental Health: A Report of the Surgeon General.* Rockwille, MD: U.S. Department of Health and Human Services.

Underman, Kelly, and L.A. Hirsfield. 2016. "Detached Concern?: Emotional Socialization in Twenty-first Century Medical Education." *Social Science & Medicine* 160: 94–101.

Unschuld, Paul U. 1985. *Medicine in China. A History of Ideas.* Berkeley: University of California Press.

Weber, Max. 1905. *The Protestant Ethic and the Spirit of Capitalism.* Translated by Talcott Parsons. New York: Scribner.

Weber, Max. 1946 [1925]. *From Max Weber: Essays in Sociology.* Edited and translated by Hans H. Gerth and C. Wright Mills. New York: Oxford University Press.

Weber, Max. 1978 [1968]. *Economy and Society.* Berkeley: University of California Press.

Williams, D. 1994. "The Concept of Race in Health Services Research, 1966–1990." *Health Services Research* 29: 261–274.

Zborowski, Mark. 1952. "Cultural Components in Response to Pain." *Journal of Social Issues* 8: 16–30.

Zborowski, Mark. 1969. *People in Pain.* San Francisco, CA: Jossey-Bass.

Zola, Irving K. 1966. "Culture and Symptoms – An Analysis of Patients' Presentation of Complaints." *American Sociological Review* 31: 615–630.

Zola, Irving K. 1973. "Pathways to the Doctor – From Person to Patient." *Social Science and Medicine* 7: 677–687.

Zola, Irving K. 1983. *Socio-Medical Inquiries: Recollections, Reflections, and Reconsiderations.* Philadelphia, PA: Temple University Press.

5

Bioethics

A Study in Sociology

Kristina Orfali and Raymond de Vries

"In America the purely practical part of science is admirably understood, and careful attention is paid to the theoretical portion which is immediately requisite to application. In this respect, Americans always display a clear, free, original, and inventive spirit: but there is hardly anyone in the United States who devotes himself to the essentially theoretical and abstract portion of human knowledge."

Alexis de Tocqueville, Why the Americans are more addicted to Practical than to Theoretical Science p. 139 in *Democracy in America*, Vol. II, 1840

Introduction

Bioethics emerged in the 1960s as a movement concerned with the moral dimensions of life sciences and healthcare in the US from where it spread all over the world. There are multiple narratives around the birth of bioethics Jonsen (1998), attesting to the difficulties of defining a unified field or a clear object of classical sociological study (unlike, for example, education or religion). Despite its success, few can clearly define the field, often viewed as "in transition, if not confusion" (Faden 2004). Moreover, the sociology of bioethics is still an emerging field of study. That is somewhat surprising given the fact that sociology was defined by Durkheim as the "science of moral facts." While he did conceive sociology as the science of morality, medicine hardly caught his attention as a "moral fact" – it being a "technique" and an activity which, contrary to morality, "didn't regulate the ends."[1] Yet suicide caught his attention because, as Michel Foucault (1976) mentions, "[suicide] revealed at the

The Wiley Blackwell Companion to Medical Sociology, First Edition. Edited by William C. Cockerham.

borders and in the interstices of the power over life, the individual and private right to die ...."[2] In a way, this echoes the bioethical debates around the right to refuse therapy and around euthanasia, anticipating the prevailing "individualistic" principle of autonomy of contemporary bioethics.

Although bioethics was coming into its own in the late 1960s and early 1970s, sociological analysis of the field – as a distinct area of intellectual inquiry, as a social movement, as a service in clinical and research settings, and as a profession – did not begin until the mid-1980s. This tardiness, which we explore more fully below, is the result of several features of both sociology and bioethics, including sociological unease with matters ethical and bioethical displeasure with sociological descriptions of the field.

When medical sociology was starting to establish itself as a specific field, calling attention to the de-professionalization of medicine, emphasizing a lay perspective on medical knowledge, and fostering a more patient centered approach, it did not include study of the bioethics movement in such transformations. Yet both were advocating almost for the same changes. While today, medical sociology has moved closer to sociology, gaining its independence from medicine, this is not yet the case of the sociology of bioethics. Bioethics started as a challenge to medical authority but was co-opted by medicine (Keirns et al. 2009). We explore the social organization of bioethics as a new area of professional, interdisciplinary expertise, and consider the seeming reluctance of sociologists to address the place of bioethics in medicine.

The Birth of Bioethics in the US

The emergence of the bioethical enterprise

The principal characteristic of the socio-cultural movement that is American bioethics is the radical transformation of modes of accountability and oversight that took place in the context of medical care and research. These changes were driven, in part, by several infamous scandals, most notably the Tuskegee "experiment" and shifted the source of accountability from medical self/peer regulation to accountability to patients and lay people (Rothman 1991). Strikingly, this evolution was mostly an American phenomenon. While the ethical regulation of research (Belmont Report 1979) spread across the globe, bioethics outside of the US did not generate a drastic transformation within the care setting. In its early incarnation, American bioethics exposed the paternalistic context of healthcare, unveiling a world of secrets, taboos, power relationships, and benevolent lies, characteristics of medical practice examined earlier by medical sociologists.[3]

Several inter-related factors contributed to the emergence of the bioethics movement  in the US: the role of "moral entrepreneurs," the context of the anti-authoritarian movements in the 1960s, the impact of new medical technologies that created unprecedented ethical dilemmas in transplantation, end of life, and assisted reproduction, the transformation of medicine with the increasing erosion of trust, the lack of universal healthcare and the influence of the legal system. In addition, the changing character of illness, with the shift from acute to chronic illnesses, altered expectations within the healthcare system, creating a demand for more symmetrical partnerships between patients and physicians (Bury 1982; Charmaz 1991; Strauss and Glaser 1975; Strauss et al. 1985) and increasing the presence of a more powerful lay voice in medicine. Medical sociological literature emphasized patient experiences and narratives long before narrative ethics (Charon and Montello 2002) came into being. Bioethics translated this work into a call for the patient's ultimate authority through recognition of her absolute autonomy to make decisions regarding her health.

Scientific innovations and technological advances have made possible situations no one could foresee, leading to novel and often agonizing ethical dilemmas. Rothman (1991) argued that bioethics was established to find a way to live with new technology, and to find answers to questions that were unimaginable a few decades ago: When is someone "dead enough" to allow the harvesting of organs? What conditions justify creating a human clone? In 1973, Duff and Campbell's article on withdrawal of life support for severely compromised neonates and a plea for increased parental involvement drew considerable attention, revealing from within the clinic the ethical dilemmas of medical work and the secrecy surrounding them. Despite not supporting the complete shift to parental autonomy, the paper did, however, call for the courts' help to decide in case of disagreement "when death may be chosen, not (now) that generally death cannot be chosen" (p. 893). The question of who should draw the line of what is ethically acceptable became not only an issue between physicians – as it used to be – or even between doctors and parents, but a matter of *public* debate, a wider social issue.[4] Life and death decisions also became a flourishing field for sociologists who wished to study how ethical issues were managed within the medical setting.

The law has played an influential role in the shaping of bioethics and in the promotion of "a right to decide rather than in terms of the right thing to do" (Annas 1993; Annas and Miller 1994). The movement of law into American bioethics emphasized the shift from questions of substantive content of right and wrong to the search for practical answers to moral problems. In Evans' (2002) terms, this was a move from "thick" rationality (debates over ends) to "thin" or formal rationality, focusing more on who should decide and how decisions should be made. The 1976 *Quinlan* case, the 1990 *Cruzan* case, and the Patient Self Determination Act (1990) can be viewed as the legal milestones of bioethics, enacting the right to refuse life-sustaining treatments. These precedents created an arsenal of diverse means – from the durable power of attorney to living wills – to ensure that patient's autonomy as a decision maker could be respected even when the patient herself was no longer competent. The law – developed in the *Quinlan* case – turned to a "hospital ethics committee" to find a clear and convincing evidence "of what Karen Quinlan would have wanted had she been aware,"[5] gave bioethics the legitimation it lacked until then. The law validated bioethical expertise (Capron 1999) over medical expertise and triggered the extensive institutionalization of the field, as evidenced by the Joint Commission for Accreditation of Healthcare Organizations (JCAHO) linking hospital accreditation to the requirement of a process for resolving clinical ethics problems.

A jurisprudence of medical dying was taking place, giving bioethicists a greater role, not only in philosophical debates or in research ethics, but within the private world of the clinic. While life and death issues are not the sole topics of bioethics, they are the ones that are most relevant for lay people and the ones (as much as matters around birth or abortion) viewed as the most private issues. Yet these issues are the ones that are matters of public concern. In the US, the law played a role as an instrument of accountability in health care (Morreim 2001) that was unparalleled in other societies.

The institutionalization of Bioethics

When the Hastings Center was created in 1969, gathering scholars from different disciplines, including sociologist Renée Fox (Fox et al. 2008), it avoided any affiliation with academic institutions, thus providing an independent forum to discuss and disseminate analysis around bioethical issues such as death, genetic counseling, transplantation, and other topics. The Kennedy Institute, founded in 1971, fostered a more academic path to bioethics. Both organizations stimulated debates and were responsible for prompting federal activities in bioethics.

As mentioned by sociologist Charles Bosk (2007), there are today more than fifty medical schools which have established centers in bioethics in the US. Philosophy is often considered the core discipline of bioethics, although theology was first to appear on the scene (Evans 2014). The most spectacular growth of bioethics is certainly within the healthcare world. From IRB's to clinical ethics committees, bioethicists have found new employment opportunities. "Strangers at the bedside" (Rothman 1991) became advice givers to clinicians and "moral experts" before any specific qualification beyond theology, philosophy, or humanities was required. The role of an ethics consultant was seen as being the patient advocate, the guardian of her autonomy.

The Pragmatic Triumph of Autonomy

Autonomy emerged as the most powerful principle in American bioethics (Wolpe 1998), despite the insistence of Beauchamp and Childress (1979), the founders of principlism in bioethics, that equal moral weight should be given to the four core principles (autonomy, beneficence, non-maleficence, and justice). The efficiency of such formal principles, as reflected in Tocqueville's excerpt in the introduction, maybe more than his entrenched allusion to the American individualism, explains the success of the autonomy paradigm over all other principles in American Bioethics, making autonomy the *ideology* of bioethics. Wolpe (1998) gives an account of how autonomy became the central and most powerful principle in medical decision making, showing its practical value in decision-making, particularly in a society with no universal health coverage. Autonomy has its detractors. Some lament the overwhelming "mandatory" autonomy imposed upon vulnerable patients (Schneider 1998), while others denounce the triumph of autonomy over all other principles as an "ethnocentric phenomenon" (Fox et al. 2005). It also can be viewed as a way to resolve the apparently insurmountable contradiction between the reign of a universal reason and the resistance of particular cultures. Autonomy is, in a way, the "minimal" principle (Ogien 2018) that can hold together members of a multicultural and pluralistic society by promoting even minimally a stable, "rational" reference.

Bioethics as an American Product

Among the factors leading to the success of the bioethics movement, briefly reviewed above, many are not specific to the American context. After all, the anti- authoritarian movements of the 1960s and the debates around the ends of science were not unique to American culture. In fact, outside the US, matters of research ethics and clinical ethics remain mostly separate; the general landscape is often one of a State-regulated field of research ethics, coexisting with a still silent world of clinical ethics in which medical discretion prevails. The accountability of the researcher and the physician to the human research subject has not so easily expanded to the ordinary patient in other countries. From a sociological perspective, the articulation between research ethics and bedside ethics remains the specific attribute and contribution of the American bioethics movement. In many countries, despite recent legal changes to promote patients' rights, medical authority remains strong in the clinical context.

Among many of the factors that played a role in the coming of bioethics, the most salient to the American context is the importance of the law in formally promoting a lay voice in medical matters. Several authors (Annas 2004; Capron 1999) emphasize the crucial and "disproportionate influence" of American law in "shaping the content and methodology of the field." There is in American society an implicit reliance on courts, a commitment to "due process," and formal legal equality which translates "into an unwillingness to defer to expert authority" (Capron 1999: 296). California courts have been the most influential in shaping the doctrine of informed consent (*Cobbs v. Grant*, 502 P. 2d 1 (Cal 1972). Law played a crucial role in end of life issues, in the recognition of advance directives, and the right to refuse treatment. In Wolf's (2004) terms, law and medical ethics have been constructing as a "co-production" the field of American bioethics. Another feature of bioethics in the US is the public visibility given by the different cases that have shaped issues normally kept into the private world of doctor-patient relationship. Cases such as Florida's *Schiavo* case (2005) trigger media uproar and debates, that in turn sharpen thinking, helping define stakes, and allowing for mediation and a practical solution, vitalizing the public bioethical debate (Anspach 2010).

The autonomy paradigm is indeed an ethnocentric product; other cultural references may be more suitable to different healthcare systems, especially if these claim to be more oriented towards the "common good" than individual welfare. Not surprisingly, a stronger focus on vulnerability, dignity (Feuillet-Liger and Orfali 2018), and solidarity developed in the bioethics discourse outside the Anglo-Saxon world, particularly in cultures with socialized healthcare systems.

Sociology and Bioethics

Sociology has been conspicuously absent from the world of bioethics – although, bioethics developed at around the same time as medical sociology was taking root in the American landscape. Very much like medical sociology in the twentieth century (Cockerham 2001) bioethics was concerned with the same topics and was intended to help solve a clinical problem or a policy issue, often being funded by agencies less interested in theoretical work than practical utility. Their parallel development and their mutual unawareness of each other have been little explored. As much as medical sociology moved away from medicine, setting its own research agenda of "defining a medical practice and policy as an *object* of study" (Cockerham 2001: 4), the sociology of bioethics is slowly becoming a distinctive field of inquiry. In 2005, a Georgetown meeting focusing specifically on the intersection of sociology and bioethics (Fox and Swazey 2008) attracted 30 scholars from North America and England.[6] In 2006, the very first session entirely devoted to bioethics at the (ISA) International Sociological Association's World Congress took place in Durban.[7]

Yet, while the field of bioethics is about 50 years old, its emergence and growth have only recently become an object of study for social scientists (Bosk 2007; De Vries et al. 2007). The body of work in the recent sociology of bioethics can be classified into three main strands. The first line of work is a recurrent critique of the bioethical project and is strongly embedded in a contentious relationship which nevertheless has forced bioethics to define more clearly the task of bioethics (Callahan 1999). The second body of work develops in linkage to more classical approaches and topics in medical sociology around ethical dilemmas, information control, medical decision-making, and patient autonomy. The third approach focuses on both the bioethical work in specific new areas generated by the bioethics movement, such as ethics consultation or research ethics, IRB reviews, and on the professionalization of bioethics.

The Social Science Critique of bioethics: an uneasy relationship, an uncertain object of study

An uneasy relationship

The relationship between sociology and bioethics has been an uneasy one (Turner 2009). Although sociology had (and has) much to offer to the work of bioethics in the way of theoretical insights and well-tested strategies for data collection, bioethics remained a lonely outpost for a few sociologists until the twenty-first century. Why this lack of interest in bioethics on the part of sociology? For a number of reasons, sociologists have been reluctant to mix themselves up in bioethics. From its beginning, bioethics was seen as a task for philosophers, physicians, and lawyers, not for sociologists. Sociologists and bioethicists have, after all, different approaches to the study of medicine: sociologists attempt to study the medical world as it is while bioethicists write about medicine as it ought to be. Sociology tends to be a descriptive discipline that eschews explicit moral judgments. Conversely, bioethics is a prescriptive discipline, and its basic work is moral evaluation. Bioethics takes social science into the uncertain area of "values" (Sheehan and Michael 2013), a place that social scientists are taught to avoid. Speaking of his graduate school years, Bosk (2008, 228) notes: "In graduate school nothing so much attracted my teachers' attention, ire, and red pen as any sentence containing the grammatical structure *ought*, *should*, or, *must* plus a verb form. I learned first to give up this grammatical structure, then, like some subject trapped in some elaborately bizarre socio-psycho-linguistic experiment, I stopped thinking in these terms altogether. It was as if I had developed an allergy to normative arguments." Although sociological work is, of course, rife with values, sociologists have generally steered clear of *studying* values.

Second, bioethicists are not easy to study. Sociologists find it easier to "study down" rather than to "study up." Sociologists are quick to study prostitutes, drug users, and "street corner men," and less likely to study CEOs. Although some high status members of society are flattered by the attention of researchers, bioethicists are counted among those who do not necessarily enjoy the sociological spotlight. Bioethicists welcome the methods of sociology when those methods are used to study already bioethically defined "problems," but they are less eager to have those methods turned to the analysis of bioethics itself. For example, bioethicists were not pleased when a sociologist pointed out that they are training far too many students: using data collected by the American Society for Bioethics and the Humanities (ASBH), Bosk concluded that in ten years' time, "close to 2500 bioethicists[8] will be chasing 600 jobs." Thinking sociologically about this fact, Bosk (2002: 21–23) notes, "a buyer's market does not encourage fledgling bioethicists to take positions that go against the grain, to do work that ruffles feathers, or to take positions that challenge the conventional wisdom." Bioethicists, who view themselves as advocates for patients and research subjects facing the power of medicine and the medical-industrial complex, are made uneasy by this type of sociological analysis. Although we sociologists find this kind of analysis both interesting and useful – after all, effective bioethics must understand how the health system can deflect its goals – critical commentary has not eased the entree of sociologists into the worlds of bioethics.

The sociology of bioethics has thus been mostly a critique of bioethics. Several authors, among them Evans (2002), emphasize how government agencies recruited bioethicists to "translate" the thick reasoning into a formally rational discourse, transforming the "watchdogs," protecting the public against the scientific elite, into "lapdogs" of the research establishment regarding, for example, human genetic engineering. Others (Stevens 2000) contend that the bioethics movement fostered the illusion of lay ethical oversight but, in fact, served the needs of physicians and biomedical researchers in an area of newly emerging biomedical technologies. Many sociological narratives of the bioethics movement tend to denounce a hidden agenda, a manipulation, a flawed conceptual framework, a blindness to issues of social justice and resource allocation, a cultural myopia. Fox and Swazey (2005, 2008) show the weakness of the bioethical enterprise – a moral enterprise – that, despite its incredible growth, went awry, unable to live up to its initial expectations.

Bioethics as an undefined object of sociological study

As Daniel Callahan (1999), the co-founder of the Hastings Center, expresses it, bioethics, despite its strong institutionalization, has a "lingering uncertainty about its purpose and value." Like other inter-disciplines, bioethics continues to struggle with the well-known institutional impediments to interdisciplinarity – including problems related to funding, tenure, and promotion – and with the challenge of bringing together different disciplinary "languages," cultures, and methods of research.

But détente among the disciplines of bioethics also is hampered by *peculiar* features of the field, including the identity problem of bioethics, an unusual share of discipline-centrism, the "quandary of critical distance", and varied "moralities of method." While some of these peculiarities stand in the way of progress in bioethics, others are important sources of bioethical insight. If all players in bioethics "got along", the generative tensions of the field would be lost.

The identity problem – "Are you fish or fowl?" – exists for all interdisciplinarians, but it is especially acute in bioethics. Unlike other interdisciplines, several scholars in bioethics actively disavow the identity of bioethicist. While some descriptive social scientists proudly call themselves bioethicists; there are many prescriptive bioethicists who eschew the moniker, describing themselves as "philosophers (or theologians, or lawyers) who study bioethical issues." This identity problem presents a structural challenge to bioethics: if bioethicists cannot agree on who is, and is not, a member of the discipline, it will be nigh unto impossible to secure a distinct place for themselves. An unusual share of discipline centered thinking contributes to this problem of identity. Scholars tend to be reductionist, to see the world through the lenses of the disciplines to which they have devoted their lives. This tendency is aggravated in bioethics where members of different disciplines vie for the last word on what is *morally* right and wrong.

Another tension among the disciplines of bioethics is found in their varied "moralities of method." One of the strengths of interdisciplines is their ability to bring many methods of inquiry to bear on a research question, for example, on life and death decisions (Botti et al. 2010). Scholars in science and technology studies use historical research methods, surveys, qualitative methods (including focus groups, in-depth interviews, and ethnographies), and philosophical reflection to explore the emergence, adoption, and consequences of new biotechnologies. Bioethicists also rely on multiple methods, but the nature of their work demands reflection on the moralities embedded in these different methods. We do not refer here to whether the research is done ethically (i.e. no cheating, no harm to subjects), but rather to the moral standpoint assumed by the method. What is the moral vision that drives the sociological imagination? How is that similar to, and different from, the moral vision of the philosophical imagination?

Another hindrance to the peaceful co-existence of the disciplines of bioethics is the quandary of critical distance. Bioethics was born as a critique of harmful research and clinical practices: when bioethicists reflect on their history, they see themselves as speaking truth to (medical) power and advocates of vulnerable patients and research subjects. What happens when the critics are welcomed into the system they criticize? Yes, being admitted to the institutions of medicine and medical research allows one to work for change from the inside out, but it also weakens the critical distance that generated the original wisdom of bioethics. Bioethics gains both power and insight to the extent that there is a conversation between those who work in the system and those who remain outside. Bosk and Frader (1998), in their paper on clinical ethics committees, speculated about sociology's unexpected lack of interest in studying the social construction of ethical authority. According to these authors (Bosk and Frader 1998: 113) it might be that ethicists' role is "nothing more than an attempt to preserve professional power by internalizing a critique and thereby disarming it."

A growing, original, but still limited work

While the sociology of bioethics is a recent endeavor, the sociological study of ethical problems in medicine has a long history. Many sociologists have focused on the moral issues of medicine (Bosk 1979; Fox 1959; Fox and Swazey 1974; Gray 1975) well before the emergence of a specific field called bioethics.

The sociology of bioethics can be viewed as a subfield within medical sociology, one that has been ignored by bioethicists preoccupied by the very same topic, namely the often-powerless patient, or more generally, the promotion of a lay voice in medicine. Just as sociologists were seen as "imperialist rivals" to medical professionals (Strong 1979), they have become rivals to bioethicists as the field of bioethics itself grew more and more medicalized (Keirns et al. 2009).

In the 1990s a sociological perspective on *bioethics* began to develop more clearly with empirical studies of ways in which right and wrong were interpreted and justified and emerged out of the complex social situations of patients, families, and teams in the clinical setting (Clark et al. 1991; Muller 1991). Zussman (1997) examined how medical decision-making in intensive care units was negotiated, while Guillemin and Holmstrom (1986), Anspach (1993), Heimer and Staffen (1998), Orfali and Gordon (2004), Orfali (2004; 2017) looked at similar issues in neonatal intensive care units. From studies of life and death decisions, to descriptions of genetic counselors doing mop up work (Bosk 1992), to analysis of the construction of medical responsibility in geriatrics (Kauffman 1995), sociology began to give accounts of how otherwise hidden values inform medical decision-making. The study of local worlds and individual decision-making processes revealed how the powers and interests at stake influenced the values of a given profession, and indeed, the values of the larger society. The work of Dresser (2001) and Halpern (2001), examining the "morality of risk" in medical experiments, reinforced these findings.

Most sociological studies of bioethics have "deconstructed" the reality of the prevailing model of autonomy offered by bioethics. Studies of informed consent emphasize the way it "manufactures assent" (Anspach 1993, see also Corrigan 2003), turns moral issues into professional and technical ones (Zussman 1997; Hauschildt and DeVries 2019), or uses uncertainty to maintain medical authority (Orfali 2004). While medical ethics, a long-time stronghold of medical authority, has supposedly been challenged, most sociological works suggest that medicine was more or less successful in turning to its own purposes the attempts of others (including medical ethicists) to regulate it.

Bioethicists' work and bioethicists' expertise

Bioethicists' work

Another venue of sociological approaches concerns the new areas directly generated by the bioethics movement; for example, the studies of bioethical work in clinical ethics and research ethics committees. An oft-made criticism of bioethicists is that they are full of good ideas and policy suggestions, but that they never stop to consider how these ideas and suggestions actually work. Do end-of-life directives actually succeed in directing end-of-life care? Do ethics consultants steer corporations toward better behavior? Do elaborate rules for controlling conflicts of interest on the part of medical researchers' work? Do Institutional Review Boards (IRBs) – the American version of research ethics committees – really protect subjects of research? This kind of work, most often conducted by social scientists, allows bioethicists to see if their contributions to the biosciences are making a difference, if bioethics – measured on its own terms – is a success. This is best thought of as the evaluation research wing of bioethics and more recently around the ethical issues related to the Covid-19 pandemic (Orfali 2020).

Clinical Ethics

The hospital context has thus been the privileged location for many studies, although work on clinical ethicists or on the inner work of ethics consultations remains still scarce (Marshall 2001; Hauschildt et al. 2019; Orfali 2018). While some in the field speak pejoratively of bioethics consults as "beeper ethics" – the image here is of a bioethicist who responds to a page and rushes into a patient's room to render an ethical judgment – the work of clinical ethicists is to help caregivers, patients, and members of patients' families make decisions in circumstances that are ethically murky.

Social scientists have taken a cynical view of the role played by clinical ethicists, describing them variously as doers of the "dirty work" of medicine (Bosk 1992) and deflectors of criticism of hospitals (Chambliss 1996). For their part, clinical ethicists do not always agree on the value of their services. Their efforts at self-assessment are hampered by the lack of a clear definition of what counts as success in bioethics consultation. Is it level of satisfaction? If so, whose satisfaction? Clients? Families? Caregivers? Judged by this criterion, clinical ethicists seem to have little effect – the 1995 SUPPORT study showed that even well-planned ethics interventions at the end of life did little to improve the satisfaction of any of the participants. Yet, more recent interdisciplinary studies by Schniederman et al. (2003) showed that ethics consultation significantly reduced the use of life-sustaining treatments *and* was regarded as helpful by a majority of nurses, patients, surrogates, and physicians.

The role of a clinical bioethicist resembles that of a public defender in the American legal system. The formal role of each is to represent the interests of a client in a large and confusing organization, but both must also maintain good relationships with other members of that organization, many of whom are working against their clients. Given this situation, both are inclined to represent the interests of professionals and institutions over those who are merely passing through – patients and families (Feeley 1979). Their work is often associated with messy emotional, relational, or spiritual/religious issues: Bosk (1992), for example, describes genetic counselors as a "mop-up service" – a way for physicians to delegate the awkward task of dealing with distraught parents. Evans (2002), in his study of the role of bioethicists in the public debate over human genetic engineering, analyzed how they claimed jurisdiction over an area once controlled by theologians.

Finally, clinical bioethicists in the US seem to be doing a form of social work or dispute resolution: listening to patients (or staff), suggesting options, finding ways to reconcile individual and institutional agendas. Picking up some of the "dirty work" (Hughes 1958) of medicine might well lead bioethicists to finally become another subordinate profession in the medically-dominated division of labor as shown by these approaches.

Research Ethics

Many studies look at Institutional Review Boards (Keith-Spiegel et al., (2005), examining both the characteristics of IRBs and their decision-making processes (Bosk and De Vries 2008; Stark 2012). After their survey of a stratified sample of IRB administrators, De Vries and Forsberg (2002: 213) concluded:

> "A close look at the composition and workload of IRBs shows that not all voices are represented in board deliberations, that the existing structure of IRBs inclines researchers and research institutions to put their interests before the interests of the subjects of research, and that there are too few staff to monitor the many protocols IRBs are required to manage."

The most popular method of examining IRB *decisions* has been to watch how several different IRBs respond to the same protocol. In the 1980s these studies were done with "mock" protocols (Goldman and Katz 1982) or with "mock IRBs." In the 1990s, with the rise of multi-center trials, there was less need to create mock protocols – researchers were gaining first-hand experience with different IRB reactions to the same protocols, and a few of these researchers began to analyze and write about the variations they saw (Silverman et al. 2001; Stair et al., 2001).

Studies of informed consent and recruitment include analysis of the readability of consent forms (Goldstein et al. 1996), in-depth studies of subjects' understanding of what their consent involved (Corrigan 2003), and surrogate consent for people with dementia to problems with broad consent for the use of blood donations to a biobank (De Vries et al. 2013; Tomlinson et al. 2015). For the most part, researchers interested in questions about conflicts of interest have studied administrative rules and procedures. In 2000, Cho and her colleagues studied policies on faculty conflicts of interest at 89 universities in the US. They discovered wide variation in the management of these conflicts and concluded that this variation "may cause unnecessary confusion among potential industrial partners or competition among universities for corporate sponsorship that could erode academic standards" (Cho et al. 2000: 2203). Ethnographic studies on scientists conducting research with human embryonic stem cells by Wainwright, Williams and their colleagues (2007) are another example of social science's growing interest in research ethics. Other lines of work include the study of therapeutic misconception (Henderson et al. 2006; Kim et al. 2009) and the experience of research subjects and the professional roles of those involved, as well as key research practices when pharmaceutical drug studies are used as an alternative to standard medical care (Fischer 2009).

The professionalization of bioethical expertise

The question of what moral expertise is and what legitimizes someone to speak as a "bioethicist" remains an ongoing issue within bioethics which has gained increased attention from a sociological perspective (De Vries et al. 2009). While bioethics has been widely institutionalized in the US, bioethicists' struggle to find a collectively acceptable way of organizing themselves has been more challenging than the creation of an intellectual framework. Despite establishing training programs, occupational associations, graduate programs, and journals all over the country, there has been an ongoing debate about what credentials should be required for those working in hospital ethics committees and institutional review boards that review and approve research involving human subjects. Hospital accreditation in the US requires institutions to have an ethics committee, normally made up of various health and social work professionals, local clergy, community members, and administrators.

What qualifies one to participate in ethical decision-making? In the late 1990s the credentials of ethics committee members were debated on the "biomed-l listserv." The discussion reflected the ambivalence about professionalization among bioethicists at that time. It began with a simple question: do any members of the hospital ethics committee need to be licensed/certified? The responses varied. At one end were those suspicious of licensing; others found licensure to be a useful tool. Still others reflected on the problem of credentialing in bioethics because, given the different backgrounds of participants, there could be no unified basis for judging the competency of any candidate. In the case of this "profession in transition," the task of separating sheep from goats was complicated by the fact that the best-known bioethicists have not had professional training in bioethics. The founders of bioethics come from a variety of backgrounds, with degrees in philosophy, medicine, theology, and law. When interviewed in 1992 (by Raymond DeVries), many of these "original bioethicists" insisted that the proper way to become a bioethicist was to first get an advanced degree in one of these fields and then to come into bioethics. They justified this position by explaining that bioethics was a rich, interdisciplinary field that drew some of its best insights from the conversation between disciplines. To narrow the focus of training to bioethics would diminish the field.

The need for certification continued to be debated by bioethicists through the first decade of the new century. In 1998, the ASBH adopted and published the report of the Task Force on Standards for Bioethics Consultation, a report that takes a strong stand *against* certification. The Task Force rejected certification for a number of reasons, including: 1) a fear that certification would increase the risk of displacing providers and patients as the primary moral decision makers, and 2) concern that certification could undermine the disciplinary diversity of bioethics (see American Society for Bioethics and Humanities 1998; Aulisio et al. 2000; Churchill 1999). Around the same time, however, the National Bioethics Advisory Council – in its report *Ethical and Policy Issues in Research Involving Human Participants* (2001) – recommended that "all investigators, IRB members, and IRB staff should be certified prior to conducting or reviewing research involving human participants."

As the field grew, and bioethics consultation became more established in medical centers, attitudes about certification began to change, in ways that sociologists of the professions would expect. With no way to separate "real" bioethicists from "pretenders" (Anspach 2010), the demand for an agreed upon professional identity became critical and led many bioethicists to rethink their stance on professional education. As a result, university-based masters and PhD programs in bioethics flourished (Lee and McCarty 2016). The ASBH continued to explore the possibility of certifying ethics consultants, and in 2018, after several task forces considered the question (Horner et al. 2020), the organization moved ahead with the creation of a certification program (https://asbh.org/certification/content-outline).

A survey of the "coming generation" in bioethics (Parnami et al. 2012) found that the bioethicists of the future are finding their way to the profession in a number of different ways and availing themselves of the many new programs created to train those seeking a career in bioethics. Among the reasons given for pursuing bioethics training are personal encounters with the health care system, having an undergraduate course in bioethics, and the desire to add knowledge of bioethics to an existing career. Would-be bioethicists expressed frustration with the plethora of possible pathways to a bioethics career, including masters' programs, certification, acquiring a PhD in a related field, or obtaining a PhD in bioethics. Members of the coming generation also expressed frustration with the job market for those with graduate level training in bioethics, pointing out the absence of a clear pipeline from educational programs to jobs in bioethics consultation or the regulation of research. The professionalization of bioethics is altering not only the nature of bioethical expertise, but also its authority in American health care, moving the field from its original critical, "prophetic" role, to a more "priestly" role that affirms medical authority (Hauschildt and DeVries 2019).

Conclusion

Medical sociology and bioethics came into being in the second half of the twentieth century and in the same place – namely the US – with a similar focus on patient rights, and neither paid attention to the other. When sociologists began to examine this new field of bioethics, they often were critical of the enterprise, pointing to the limits of "a monistic conception of ethical universalism ... coupled with a tendency to disregard context" (Fox and Swazey 2008). The recurrent social science critique of bioethics has hampered a more theoretical and richer empirical approach to the emergence and development of bioethics. At the same time, it has helped construct and identify bioethics as a new territory, a distinctive object (Callahan 1999) to study. One of the early collection of essays on the relationship between bioethics and social science (De Vries and Subedi 1998) was a strongly critical appraisal of the bioethical enterprise and a call for more convergence between the two as conceptualized by Zussman (2000). In 2001, a second anthology appeared (Hoffmaster 2001), using qualitative research methods that called attention to the multiple contexts that generated both bioethics problems and debates about those problems. Recent social scientific examinations of bioethics (De Vries et al. 2007; Evans 2014; Kingori et al. 2013) move towards a clearer identification of the ways bioethics can extend sociological knowledge by exploring the social history of ethical problem solving, the way moral boundaries (Feuillet Liger et al. 2013) are negotiated in biomedicine and issues of ethics policies in different cultural contexts (Feuillet Liger et al. 2013; Myser 2011). We are now past the point where that argument must be made: for better or for worse, the social sciences are now part of the interdisciplinary bioethical enterprise. Bosk (2008), for example, uses the ethnographic lens of sociology to look at the emergent social organization of the everyday ethical dilemmas of clinical care and research and, at the same time, looks at ethnography through the lens of ethics. Others advocate for a normative approach beyond bioethics, a so called "sociology of bio-knowledge" (Petersen 2013).

Of course (as sociologists would predict) the place of social science in bioethics varies by cultural and social context. In the Netherlands and Belgium, the creation of "empirical bioethics" has given social science an established voice in the bioethical conversation (Borry et al. 2005; Stolper et al. 2020; Van der Scheer and Widdershoven 2004). In France, bioethics is analyzed in Foucault's terms of "bio -politics"

(Fassin 2012). In North America and the UK, social science methods are widely used in bioethics, but social scientists remain, to a certain extent, strangers to the field (De Vries 2004; Hedgecoe 2004). There are advantages to both insider and outsider statuses. We North Americans who stand at a distance from bioethics can take comfort in Simmel's (Simmel [1908] 1971) observation that the stranger "is freer practically and theoretically ... he surveys conditions with less prejudice [and] is not tied down in his action by habit, piety, and precedent." Simmel pointed out that those who do not "own the soil" are in a unique position, one that combines nearness and distance, indifference and involvement, a social location that allows them to become the recipients of a "most surprising openness" from group members.

On the other hand, there are undeniable benefits that come with "owning the soil" of bioethics. The collaborative work that gets done under the rubric of empirical bioethics moves the important ideas of philosophical bioethics into the real world of medicine and medical research where human beings live and work and help and harm each other (Borry et al. 2004; De Vries 2017; Molewijk et al. 2003). This tension between the "voice in the wilderness" (that no one hears) and "going native" (thereby losing the distinctive, critical perspective offered by sociology) can be used productively: distance allows challenges to the common-sense of bioethics, and closeness allows the analyses of social scientists to be incorporated into the work of bioethicists (Zussman 2000; De Vries et al. 2007).

Finally, bioethics can be viewed as an unsettled field, a project of modernity itself, a constant and tense relationship between reason and subject. Our Western culture evolved not from irrationality to rationality but from an integrated view of the universe, considered (in the Enlightenment model) as both rational and created by God, to a growing separation between the objective and subjective universes (Touraine 1995). The bioethical enterprise can be viewed as the reformulation of modernity, no longer a quest for a unified world or principle – be it rationalization, cultural identity, or any other principle – but as an inevitable tension between rationalization and individualism or subjectivism. If one component wins over the other, rationalization becomes an instrument of power and individualism a negative cultural identity (fundamentalism, nationalism, etc.). So, in a sense, the sociological critics of bioethics are both right and wrong: bioethics, as a critique of modernity, can only retain its vitality and be renewed by remaining unsettled, evolving in an ongoing process of disagreement and temporary consensus.

Notes

1 E. Durkheim. 1920. "Introduction à la morale," Revue Philosophique, 89.

2 Michel Foucault, *La Volonté de savoir. Histoire de la sexualité*, vol. 1, Paris, Gallimard, 1976, chapitre V, "Droit de mort et pouvoir sur la vie," p. 182.

3 Glaser and Strauss 1964; Quint 1972 and others. Even in medical literature a fair number of articles around truth-telling for example in cancer wards emerge at the same time.

4 There is a need in our society for a policy of deciding care according to individual situations as *the parties most involved* feel is correct (*ibid.*).

5 *In re Quinlan* (70 N.J. 10, 355 A.2d 647 (NJ 1976).

6 The two authors participated in this two-day meeting.

7 The two authors co-organized this very first session in Durban followed by a second session, in 2010 at the ISA world congress in Goteborg, Sweden. (The ISA World Congress takes place every four years).

8 From 2000 to 2013, there were 2314 bioethics and applied ethics degrees granted. (Tia Powell & Melissa Kurtz, Graduate School Programs in Bioethics, *Hastings Center: Bioethics Wire* (Sept. 2014).

References

American Society for Bioethics and Humanities. 1998. *Core Competencies for Health Care Ethics Consultation.* Glenview, IL: American Society for Bioethics and Humanities.

Annas, Georges J. 1993. *Standard of Care: The Law of American Bioethics.* New York: Oxford University Press.

Annas, Georges J. 2004. "Culture of Life' Politics at the Bedside-The Case of Terri Schiavo." *New England Journal of Medicine* 352: 1710–1715.

Annas, Georges J and Frances H Miller. 1994. "The Empire of Death: How Culture and Economics Affect Informed Consent in the US, the UK, and in Japan." *American Journal of Law & Medicine* 20(4): 357–394.

Anspach, Renée. 1993. *Deciding Who Lives: Fateful Choices in the Intensive Care Nursery.* Chicago, IL: University of Chicago Press.

Anspach, Renée. 2010. "The Hostile Takeover of Bioethics by Religious Conservatives and the Counteroffensive." Pp. 144–169 in *Social Movements and the Transformation of American Health*, edited by C. Banaszak-Holl Jane, R. Levitsky Sandra, and N. Zald Mayer. Oxford: Oxford University Press.

Aulisio, Mark, Robert Arnold, and Stuart Youngner. 2000. "Health Care Ethics Consultation: A Position Paper from the Society for Health and Human Values–Society for Bioethics Consultation Task Force on Standards for Bioethics Consultation." *Annals of Internal Medicine* 133(1):59–69.

Beauchamp, Tom and James Childress. 1979. *Principles of Biomedical Ethics.* New York: Oxford University Press.

The Belmont Report. 1979. http://ohsr.od.nih.gov/guidelines/belmont.html

Borry, Pascal, Paul Schotsmans, and Kris Dierickx. 2004. "What Is the Role of Empirical Research in Bioethical Reflection and Decision-making? an Ethical Analysis." *Medicine, Health Care and Philosophy* 7(1):41–53.

Borry, Pascal, Paul Schotsmans, and Kris Dierickx. 2005. "The Birth of the Empirical Turn in Bioethics." *Bioethics* 19(1):49–71.

Bosk, Charles. 1979. *Forgive and Remember: Managing Medical Failure.* Chicago, IL: University of Chicago Press.

Bosk, Charles. 1992. *All God's Mistakes: Genetic Counseling in a Pediatric Hospital.* Chicago, IL: University of Chicago Press.

Bosk, Charles. 2002. "Now that We Have the Data. What Was the Question?" *American Journal of Bioethics* 2(4):21–23.

Bosk, Charles. 2007. "The Sociological Imagination." Pp. 398–410 in *The Handbook of Medical Sociology*, 5th ed., edited by E. Bird Chloe, Conrad Peter, and M. Fremont Allen. Upper Saddle River, NJ: Prentice Hall.

Bosk C. 2008. *What Would You Do?: Juggling Bioethics and Ethnography*. Chicago, IL.: University of Chicago Press.

Bosk, Charles and Raymond De Vries. 2008. "Bureaucracies of Mass Deception: Institutional Review Boards and the Ethics of Ethnographic Research." Pp 187–206 in *What Would You Do? the Collision of Ethics and Ethnography, Bosk, Charles*. Chicago, IL: University of Chicago Press.

Bosk, Charles and Joel Frader. 1998. "Institutional Ethics Committees: Sociological Oxymoron, Empirical Black Box." Pp. 94–116 in *Bioethics and Society: Constructing the Ethical Enterprise*, edited by DeVries, Raymond and Subedi Janardan. Upper Saddle River, NJ: Prentice Hall.

Botti, Simona, Kristina Orfali, and Sheena Iyengar. 2010. "Tragic Choices: Autonomy and Emotional Responses to Medical Decision Making." *Journal of Consumer Research* 36:337–352.

Bury, Michael R. 1982. "Chronic Illness as Biographical Disruption." *Sociology of Health & Illness* 4(2):167–182.

Callahan, Daniel. 1999. "The Social Sciences and the Task of Bioethics." *Daedalus* 128(4):275–294.

Capron, Alexander M. 1999. "What Contributions Have Social Science and the Law Made to the Development of Policy on Bioethics?" *Daedalus* 128(4):295–325.

Chambliss, Daniel. 1996. *Beyond Caring: Hospitals, Nurses, and the Social Organization of Ethics*. Chicago, IL: University of Chicago Press.

Charmaz, Kathy. 1991. *Good Days, Bad Days: The Self in Chronic Illness and Time*. New Brunswick, NJ: Rutgers University Press.

Charon, Rita and Martha Montello. 2002. *Stories Matter. The Role of Narrative in Medical Ethics*. New York: Routledge.

Cho, Mildred, Ryo Shohara, Anna Schissel, and Rennie Drummond. 2000. "Policies on Faculty Conflicts of Interest at US Universities." *Journal of American Medical Association* (17): 2203–2208.

Churchill, Larry R. 1999. "Are We Professionals? A Critical Look at the Social Role of Bioethicists." *Daedalus* 128(4):253–274.

Clark, Jack, Deborah A. Potter, and John B. McKinlay. 1991. "Bringing Social Structure Back into Clinical Decision Making." *Social Science & Medicine* 32:853–866.

Cobbs v. Grant, 502 P. 2d 1 (Cal 1972).

Cockerham, William (ed.) 2001. *The Blackwell Companion to Medical Sociology*. Oxford: Blackwell.

Corrigan, Oona. 2003. "Empty Ethics: The Problem with Informed Consent." *Sociology of Health & Illness* 25(7):768–792.

Cruzan v. Missouri Department of Health, 497 U.S. 261 (1990).

De Vries, Raymond. 2004. "How Can We Help? from 'Sociology In' Bioethics to 'Sociology Of' Bioethics." *Journal of Law, Medicine and Ethics* 32(2): 279–292.

De Vries, Raymond. 2017. "Regarding Bioethics: A Sociology of Morality." *Perspectives in Biology and Medicine* 60(1):74–92.

De Vries, Raymond, Robert Dingwall, and Kristina Orfali. 2009. "The Moral Organization of the Professions: Bioethics in the United States and France." *Journal of Contemporary Sociology* 57(4):555–579.

De Vries, Raymond and Carl P Forsberg. 2002. "What Do IRBs Look Like, What Kind of Support Do They Receive?" *Accountability in Research* 9:199–216.

De Vries, Raymond, Kerry A Ryan, Aimée Stancyk, Paul S Appelbaum, Laura Damschroder, David S Knopman, and Scott Y H Kim. 2013. "Public's Approach to Surrogate Consent for Dementia Research: Cautious Pragmatism." *The American Journal of Geriatric Psychiatry* 21(4):364–372.

De Vries, Raymond and Janatdan Subedi (eds.). 1998. *Bioethics and Society: Constructing the Ethical Enterprise*. Upper Saddle River, NJ: Prentice Hall.

De Vries, Raymond, Leigh Turner, Kristina Orfali, and Charles Bosk (eds.). 2007. *The View from Here, Bioethics and the Social Sciences*. Oxford: Blackwell.

Dresser, Rebecca. 2001. *When Science Offers Salvation: Patient Advocacy and Research Ethics*. New York: Oxford University Press.

Evans, John H. 2002. *Playing God? Human Genetic Engineering and the Rationalization of Public Bioethical Debate*. Chicago, IL: University of Chicago Press.

Evans, John H. 2014. *The History and Future of Bioethics: A Sociological View*. New York: Oxford.

Faden, Ruth R. 2004. "Bioethics: A Field in Transition." *Journal of Law, Medicine and Ethics* 32(2):276–278.

Fassin, Eric. 2012. "*Introduction. Sous La Bioéthique, La Bio-politique*." http://www.raison-publique.fr/article523.html

Feeley, Malcolm M. 1979. *The Process Is the Punishment: Handling Cases in a Lower Criminal Court*. New York: Russell Sage.

Feuillet-Liger, Brigitte and Kristina Orfali (eds.). 2018. *The Reality of Human Dignity in Bioethics and Law: Comparative Perspectives*. Dordrecht: Springer.

Feuillet-Liger, Brigitte, Kristina Orfali, and Thérèse Callus (eds.). 2013. *Families and End of Life Treatment. An International Perspective*. Paris: Bruylant.

Fischer, Jill A. 2009. *Medical Research for Hire: The Political Economy of Pharmaceutical Clinical Trials*. New Brunswick, NJ: Rutgers University Press.

Foucault, Michel. 1976. Volonté de savoir. Histoire de la sexualité. vol. 1, chapitre V, "*Droit De Mort Et Pouvoir Sur La Vie*." Paris: Gallimard.

Fox, Renée C. 1959. *Experiment Perilous: Physicians and Patients Facing the Unknown*. Glencoe, IL: Free Press. mm.

Fox, Renée C and Judith Swazey. 1974. *The Courage to Fail: A Social View of Organ Transplant and Dialysis*. Chicago, IL: University of Chicago Press.

Fox, Renée C and Judith Swazey. 2005. "Examining American Bioethics: Its Problems and Prospects. Quo Vadis? Mapping the Future of Bioethics." *Cambridge Quarterly of Health Care Ethics* 14:361–373.

Fox, Renée C and Judith Swazey. 2008. *Observing Bioethics*. New York: Oxford University Press.

Goldman, Jerry and Martin Katz. 1982. "Inconsistency and Institutional Review Boards." *Journal American Medical Association* 248:197–202.

Goldstein, Adam, Pamela Frasier, Peter Curtis, Alfred Reid, and Nancy E. Kreher. 1996. "Consent Form Readability in University-Sponsored Research." *Journal of Family Practice* 42:606–611.

Gray, Radford H. 1975. *Human Subjects in Medical Experimentation: A Sociological Study of the Conduct and Regulation of Research*. New York: Wiley.

Guillemin, Jeanne H and Lynda L Holmstrom. 1986. *Mixed Blessings: Intensive Care for Newborns*. New York: Oxford University Press.

Halpern, Sydney. 2001. "Constructing Moral Boundaries: Public Discourse on Human Experimentation in Twentieth-Century America." Pp. 69–89 in *Bioethics in Social Context*, edited by Barry Hoffmaster. Philadelphia, PA: Temple University Press.

Hauschildt, Katrina and Raymond DeVries. 2019. "Reinforcing Medical Authority: Clinical Ethics Consultation and the Resolution of Conflicts in Treatment Decisions." *Sociology of Health & Illness* 42(2):307–326.

Hedgecoe, Adam. 2004. "Critical Bioethics: Beyond the Social Science Critique of Applied Ethics." *Bioethics* 18(2):120–143.

Heimer, Carol A and Lisa R Staffen. 1998. *For the Sake of Children: The Social Organization of Responsibility in the Hospital and in the Home.* Chicago, IL: University of Chicago Press.

Henderson, G. Michele Easter, Catherine Zimmer, Nancy King, Arlene Davis, Barbara Rothschild et al. 2006. "Therapeutic misconception in early phase gene transfer trials." *Social Science & Medicine* 62(1):239–53.

Hoffmaster, Barry (ed.). 2001. *Bioethics in Social Context.* Philadelphia, PA: Temple University Press.

Horner, Claire, Andrew Childress, Sophia Fantus, and Janet Malek. 2020. "What the HEC-C? an Analysis of the Healthcare Ethics Consultant-Certified Program: One Year I." *The American Journal of Bioethics* 20:3, 9–18.

Hughes, Everett C. 1958. *Men and Their Work.* Glencoe, IL: Free Press.

In re Quinlan, 70 NJ 10 (1976).

Jonsen, Albert R. 1998. *The Birth of Bioethics.* New York: Oxford University Press.

Kauffman, Sharon R. 1995. "Decision Making, Responsibility and Advocacy in Geriatric Medicine." *Gerontologist* 35:481–488.

Keirns, Carla, Michael Fetters, and Raymond De Vries. 2009. "Bioethics and Medical Education." Pp. 174–190 in *Handbook of the Sociology of Medical Education*, edited by C. Brosnan and B. Turner. London: Routledge.

Keith-Spiegel, Patricia and Gerald P. Koocher. 2005. "The IRB Paradox: Could the Protectors Also Encourage Deceit?" *Ethics & Behavior* 15: 339–349.

Kim, Scott, Lauren Schrock, Renee M. Wilson, Samuel A. Frank, Robert G. Holloway, Karl Kieburtz and Raymond G. De Vries. 2009. "An approach to evaluating the therapeutic misconception." *IRB*, 31(5), 7–14.

Kingori, Patricia, Kristina Orfali, and DeVries Raymond. 2013. "Bioethics in the Field." *Social Science & Medicine* 98:260–263.

Lee, Lisa M. and Frances A. McCarty. 2016. "Emergence of a Discipline? Growth in U.S. Postsecondary Bioethics Degrees." *Hastings Center Report* 46(2):19–21.

Marshall, Patricia. 2001. "A Contextual Approach to Clinical Ethics Consultation." Pp. 137–152 in *Bioethics in Social Context*, edited by Barry Hoffmaster. Philadelphia, PA: Temple University Press.

Molewijk, Albert C., Anne Stiggelbout, Willem Otten, Helen Dupuis, and Job Kievit. 2003. "Implicit Normativity in Evidence-based Medicine: A Plea for Integrated Empirical Ethics Research." *Health Care Analysis* 11:69–92.

Morreim, E. Haavi. 2001. "From the Clinics to the Courts: The Role Evidence Should Play in Litigating Medical Care." *Journal of Health Politics, Policy and Law* 26(2):409–428.

Muller, Jessica H. 1991. "Shades of Blue: The Negotiation of Limited Codes by Medical Residents." *Social Science & Medicine* 34:885–898.

Myser, Catherine (ed.). 2011. *The Social Functions of Bioethics around the Globe.* Oxford: University of Oxford Press.

Ogien, Ruwen. 2018. "Human Dignity: A Notion that Provides More Confusion than Clarity." Pp. 283–286 in *The Reality of Human Dignity in Law and Bioethics*, edited by Feuillet-Liger Brigitte and Kristina Orfali. Berlin: Springer.

Orfali, Kristina. 2004. "Parental Role and Medical Decision Making: Fact or Fiction? A Comparative Study of French and American Practices in Neonatal Intensive Care Units." *Social Science & Medicine* 58:2009–2022.

Orfali, Kristina. 2017. "Extreme Prematurity: Creating Iatrogenic Lives." *The American Journal of Bioethics* 17(8):34–35.

Orfali, Kristina. 2018. "Getting the Story Straight: Clinical Ethics as a Distinctive Field." *The American Journal of Bioethics* 18(6):62–64.

Orfali, Kristina and Elisa J. Gordon. 2004. "Autonomy Gone Awry: A Cross-Cultural Study of Parent's Experiences in Neonatal Intensive Care Units." *Theoretical Medicine* 25:329–365.

Orfali, Kristina. 2020. "Getting to the Truth: Ethics, Trust and Triage in United States versus Europe during the Covid-19 Pandemic." *The Hastings Center Report* (forthcoming).

Parnami, Sonali, Katherine Lin, Kathryn Bondy Fessler, Erica Blom, Matthew Sullivan, and De Vries Raymond. 2012. "From Pioneers To Professionals." *Cambridge Quarterly of Healthcare Ethics* 21:104–115.

Patient Self Determination Act of 1990, *101st Congress (1989–1990)*, https://www.congress.gov/bill/101st-congress/house-bill/4449

Petersen, Alan. 2013. "From Bioethics to a Sociology of Bio-knowledge." *Social Science & Medicine* 98:264–270.

Rothman, David. 1991. *Strangers at the Bedside.* New York: Basic Books.

Schneider, Carl E. 1998. *The Practice of Autonomy, Patients, Doctors and Medical Decision.* New York: Oxford University Press.

Schneiderman, L., T. Glimer, H. D. Teetzel, D. O. Dugan, J. Blustein, R. Cranford, K. B. Briggs, G. I. Komatsu, P. Goodman-Crews, F. Cohn, and E. W. W Young. 2003. "Effects of Ethics Consultations on Non-Beneficial Life Sustaining Treatments in the Intensive Care Setting: A Randomized Controlled Trial." *Journal of American Medical Association* 290(9):1166–1172.

Sheehan, Mark and Dunn Michael. 2013. "On the Nature and Sociology of Bioethics." *Health Care Analysis* 21:54–69.

Silverman, Henry, Sara C Hull, and Jeremy Sugarman. 2001. "Variability among Institutional Review Boards' Decisions within the Context of a Multi-Center Trial." *Critical Care Medicine* 29:235–241.

Simmel, Georg. [1908] 1971. "Der Fremde" ["The Stranger"] Pp. 685–691 in *Soziologie* [Sociology]. Munich and Liepzig: Duncker and Humblot. Translated and reprinted in Georg Simmel, *On Individuality and Social Forms: Selected Writings*, pp. 143–149, Donald Levine (ed.). Chicago, IL: University of Chicago Press.

Stair, Thomas, Caitlin Reed, Michael Radeos, Greg Koski, and Carlos A. Camargo; MARC investigators. Multicenter Research Collaboration. 2001. "Variation in Institutional Review Board Responses to a Standard Protocol for a Multicenter Trial." *Academic Emergency Medicine* 8:636–641.

Stark, Laura. 2012. *Behind Closed Doors: IRBs and the Making of Ethical Research.* Chicago, IL: University of Chicago Press.

Stevens, Tina M L. 2000. *Bioethics in America: Origin and Cultural Politics.* Baltimore, MD: John Hopkins University Press.

Stolper, Margreet, Reidar Pedersen, and Bert Molewijk. 2020. "Examining the Doing of Ethics Support Staff. A Dialogical Approach toward Assessing the Quality of Facilitators of Moral Case Deliberation." *The American Journal of Bioethics* 20(3):42–44.

Strauss, Anselm, Shizuko Fagerhaugh, Barbara Suczek, and Carolyn Wiener. 1985. *The Social Organization of Medical Work.* Chicago, IL: University of Chicago Press.

Strauss, Anselm and Barney G. Glaser. 1975. *Chronic Illness and the Quality of Life.* St. Louis, MO: Mosby.

Strong Philip M. 1979. "Sociological imperialism and the profession of medicine. A critical examination of the thesis of medical imperialism." *Social Science & Medicine,* Mar; 13A (2):199–215

The SUPPORT Principal Investigators. 1995. "A Controlled Trial to Improve Care for Seriously Ill Hospitalized Patients: The Study to Understand Prognoses and Preferences for Outcomes and Risks of Treatments (SUPPORT)." *Journal of American Medical Association* 274:1591–1598.

Tomlinson, Tom, Raymond De Vries, Kerry Ryan, Myra Kim Hyungjin, Nicole Lehpamer, and Scott Y H Kim. 2015. "Moral Concerns and the Willingness to Donate to a Research Biobank." *Journal of American Medical Association* 313(4):417–419.

Touraine, Alain. 1995. *Critique of Modernity.* Oxford: Blackwell.

Turner, Leigh. 2009. "Anthropological and Sociological Critiques of Bioethics." *Journal of Bioethical Inquiry* 6(1):83–98.

Van der Scheer, Lieke and Guy Widdershoven. 2004. "Integrated Empirical Ethics: Loss of Normativity?" *Medicine, Health Care and Philosophy* 7:71–79.

Wainwright, Steven P, Clare Williams, Mike Michael, Bobbie Frasides, and Alen Cribb. 2007. "Ethical Boundary-work in the Embryonic Stem Cell Laboratory." Pp. 67–82 in *The View from Here, Bioethics and the Social Sciences*, edited by Raymond DeVries, Leigh Turner, Kristina Orfali, and Charles Bosk. Oxford: Blackwell.

Wolf, Suzan M. 2004. "Law & Bioethics: From Values to Violence." *Journal of Law, Medicine and Ethics* 32:293–306.

Wolpe, Paul R. 1998. "The Triumph of Autonomy in American Bioethics: A Sociological View." Pp. 38–59 in *Bioethics and Society: Constructing the Ethical Enterprise*, edited by Raymond DeVries and Janardan Subedi. Upper Saddle River, NJ: Prentice Hall.

Zussman, Robert. 1997. *Intensive Care.* Chicago, IL: The University of Chicago Press.

Zussman, Robert. 2000. "The Contributions of Sociology to Medical Ethics." *Hastings Center Report* 10(1):7–11.

Part II

Theoretical Approaches

6

The Sociology of the Body

Sarah Nettleton

In Tom Stoppard's (1967) play Rosencrantz and Guildenstern are Dead, the two central characters lament the precariousness of their lives. Rosencrantz seeks solace in life's only certainty when he comments that "the only beginning is birth and the only end is death – if we can't count on that what can we count on?" To this he might have added that he could reliably count on the fact that he had a body. The "fact" that we are born, have a body, and then die is of course something that does seem to be beyond question. It is something that we can hold on to, as we live in a world that appears to be ever more uncertain and ever more risky (Shilling and Mellor 2017).

But is this fact so obvious? Ironically, the more sophisticated our medical, technological, and scientific knowledge of bodies becomes, the more uncertain we are as to what the body actually is. For example, technological innovations can disrupt boundaries between the physical (or seemingly natural) and social body. With the development of assisted conception, when does birth begin? With the development of life-extending technologies, when does the life of a physical body end? With the development of prosthetic technologies, what constitutes a "pure" human? It seems the old certainties around birth, life, and death are becoming increasingly unstable. It is perhaps not surprising, therefore, that attempts to understand the social and ethical significance of the body have become central to sociological debates. Attempts to develop a sociological appreciation of the body important in the subdiscipline of the sociology of health and illness. Health, disease and illness are fundamentally embodied experiences that are embedded in social contexts (Nettleton 2020). How bodies are conceptualized, maintained, monitored and managed is therefore profoundly political and so contentious. The aim of this chapter is to delineate some of the key developments in the sociological theorizing of the body and to assess their significance for a number of substantive issues in medical sociology. To meet this aim, the chapter will first review the main perspectives on the sociology of the body and social theorists who have informed each of these approaches. Second, the

The Wiley Blackwell Companion to Medical Sociology, First Edition. Edited by William C. Cockerham.

chapter will outline the parameters of the sociology of embodiment or perhaps more appropriately an embodied sociology. Concepts which have emerged from these debates such as flexible immunity bodies, body projects, biovalue and virtual bodies will also be discussed. Finally, a number of substantive issues which are central to medical sociology will be considered to highlight the merits of incorporating the body into the analysis of matters associated with health and illness. These issues are: illness and injury, body work, and embodied health inequalities.

Sociological Perspectives on the Sociology of the Body

There is a substantial literature on the sociology of the body which spans a range of perspectives. There are, however, alternative ways in which the body is understood and analyzed, with the most obvious approaches being rooted within the physical sciences and classified as being part of a naturalistic perspective (Shilling 2012). In this chapter, however, we will focus on three main sociological approaches. First, those which draw attention to the social regulation of the body, especially the way in which social institutions regulate, control, monitor, and use bodies. Our bodies are highly politicized. Whilst we might like to think that we own and have control of our own bodies and what we do with and to them, we do not. What we can do with our bodies is constrained by legal diktats and social norms, as is evident in contemporary debates on topics such as euthanasia, organ transplantation, and abortion. Feminist scholars have illustrated ways in which medicine has for centuries controlled the bodies of women (Martin 1989; Mason 2013; Ussher 2006). Regulatory practices further constrain bodies through processes of categorization which can be difficult to resist, a readily obvious example is the imposition of static gender categories often rooted in biological essentialism (Connell 2012). A view that prompts important questions about the ontology of the body.

A second perspective within the sociology of the body focuses on the ontology of the body. A number of theorists have asked the question: What exactly is the body? Their answer is that in late modern societies we seem to have become increasingly uncertain as to what the body actually is. For most sociologists the body is to a greater or lesser extent socially constructed. However, there are a number of variants of this view, with some arguing that the body is simply a fabrication (Armstrong 1983) – an effect of its discursive context – while others maintain that bodies display certain characteristics (e.g. mannerisms, gait, shape) which are influenced by social and cultural factors. Productive conceptual frameworks however recognize the interplay between the biological body and social relations. Reflecting gender for example, and the "gender-biology nexus" Annandale and her colleagues (2018), outline a theoretical framework that takes into account the "gender-shaping of biology" and the "biologic-shaping of gender" seeing these as co-"constitutive shaping processes." This approach is helpful not least because it moves beyond an ontological impasse but also helps us appreciated how gender inequalities in health operate (Williams and Bendelow 1998).

The third approach pays more attention to the way the body is experienced or lived. Whilst this phenomenological orientation accepts that the body is to some extent socially fashioned, it argues that sociology must take account of what the body, or rather embodied actor, actually does. In this sense it is perhaps more accurately described as a sociology of embodiment or embodied sociology rather than a sociology of the body. This approach to the study of the body has gained much currency, particularly in relation to illness (Carel 2016; Leder 1990). It has to some extent emerged as a result of creative debates within this field of study which have attempted to counter the dominant structural approach that concentrates on the social regulation of bodies. This research, which has outlined the ways in which bodies are socially regulated however, remains crucial for our understanding of the body in society.

Social Regulation of Bodies

In his book *Regulating Bodies*, Turner (1992) suggests that late modern societies are moving toward what he refers to as a "somatic society;" that is, a social system in which the body constitutes the central field of political and cultural activity. The major concerns of society are becoming less to do with increasing production, as was the case in industrial capitalism, and more to do with the regulation of bodies. Turner (1992: 12–13) writes:

> our major political preoccupations are how to regulate the spaces between bodies, to monitor the interfaces between bodies, societies and cultures ... We want to close up bodies by promoting safe sex, sex education, free condoms and clean needles. We are concerned about whether the human population of the world can survive global pollution. The somatic society is thus crucially, perhaps critically structured around regulating bodies.

The concerns of the somatic society are also evidenced by the way in which contemporary political movements such as, pro- and anti-abortion campaigns, debates about fertility and infertility, and disabilities coalesce around body matters (Ettorre 2010), as do politics of environmentalism all of which highlight our embodied vulnerabilities (Bulter 2015). Bodies are regulated within society through the institutions of governance notably law, religion, and medicine. The role of religion, law, and medicine is especially evident at the birth and death of bodies. As society became more secularized it also become more medicalized, with medicine now serving a moral as well as a clinical function (Busfield 2017).

Developing an analytical framework which works at two levels – the bodies of individuals and the bodies of populations – Turner (2008) identifies four basic social tasks which are central to social order. We might refer to these as the four "r" s. First, reproduction, which refers to the creation of institutions that govern populations over time to ensure the satisfaction of physical needs, for example the control of sexuality. Second, the need for the regulation of bodies, particularly medical surveillance and the control of crime. Third, restraint, which refers to the inner self and inducements to control desire and passion in the interests of social organization. Fourth, the representation of the body, which refers to its physical presentation on the world's stage.

Turner's conceptualization of these four "r"s owes a great deal to the ideas of Foucault, especially his writings on normalization and surveillance. These draw attention to the ways in which bodies are monitored, assessed, and corrected within modern institutions. A central theme which runs through Foucault's (1976, 1979) work is that the shift from pre-modern to modern forms of society involved the displacement of what he terms sovereign power, wherein power resided in the body of the monarch, by disciplinary power, wherein power is invested in the bodies of the wider population. Disciplinary power refers to the way in which bodies are regulated, trained, maintained, and understood; it is most evident in social institutions such as schools, prisons, and hospitals. Disciplinary power works at two levels. First, individual bodies are trained and observed. Foucault refers to this as the anatomo-politics of the human body. Second, and concurrently, populations are monitored. He refers to this process as "regulatory controls: a bio-politics of the population" (Foucault 1981: 139). It is these two levels – the individual and the population – which form the basis of Turner's arguments about regulating bodies that we have discussed above. Foucault argues that it is within social institutions that knowledge of bodies is produced. For example, the observation of bodies in prisons yielded a body of knowledge we now know as criminology, the observation of bodies in hospitals contributed to biomedical science, epidemiological surveys of communities generate knowledge of health risk factors. In fact, it was the discourse of pathological medicine in the eighteenth century which formed the basis of the bodies in Western society that we have come to be familiar with today.

The surveillance and more especially self-surveillance of bodies has dispersed exponentially since Foucault was writing, but not in ways that his thesis would anticipate. Not least because technologies have become networked through a multiplicity of digital self-monitoring and self-tracking devices that generate data on individuals everyday bodily practices such as, sleeping, walking, running, eating and breathing. These data may be of value not only to individuals keen to reflect on their own bodily practices, but also to commercial enterprises who harvest vast quantities of data from populations for analysis and marketing. The digital health sector emerges as a major aspect of the contemporary political economy of health, where profits are made from tracking data such that sociologists now speak of "digital bodies," "quantified bodies" and "the quantified self" (Lupton 2016; Prainsack 2017). Bodies become entangled in digitized networks opening up the potential for generation of novel categorizations of somatic groupings around levels of fitness, weight, diets, sexual practices, alcohol use, and so on. These categorizations may in turn may be classed, racialized, and gendered. Digitized bio-political data is therefore generating somatic social categories suspectable to new modes of regulation.

Through these discussions, we can see that the regulation of bodies is crucial to the maintenance of social order. This observation forms the basis of Mary Douglas's (1966, 1970) classic scholarship on the representation of the symbolic body. The ideas of Douglas – an anthropologist – have been drawn upon extensively by medical sociologists. She argues that the perception of the physical body is mediated by the social body. The body provides a basis for classification, and in turn the organization of the social system reflects how the body is perceived.

> The social body constrains the way the physical body is perceived. The physical experience of the body, always modified by the social categories through which it is known,

> sustains a particular view of society. There is a continual exchange of meanings between the two kinds of bodily experience so that each reinforces the categories of the other. As a result of this interaction the body itself is a highly restricted medium of expression. (Douglas 1970: xiii)

Thus, according to Douglas (1966), the body forms a central component of any classificatory system. Working within a Durkheimian tradition she maintains that all societies have elements of both the sacred and the profane, and that demarcation between the two is fundamental to the functioning of social systems. Thus, societies respond to disorder by developing classificatory systems which can designate certain phenomena as matter out of place. "Where there is dirt there is system ... This idea of dirt takes us straight into the field of symbolism and promises a link-up with more obviously symbolic systems of purity" (Douglas 1966: 35). Anything which transcends social, or bodily, boundaries will be regarded as pollution. Ideas, therefore, about bodily hygiene tell us as much about our cultural assumptions as they do about the "real" body and our medical knowledge of it. Furthermore, any boundaries that are perceived to be vulnerable or permeable will need to be carefully regulated or monitored to prevent transgressions (Nettleton 1988; Longhurst 2001). Bodies that transcend boundaries can be politically vulnerable, most especially where politicians invoke symbolic and cultural representations of bodies deemed as "out of place" as we see in the politics of migration, borders and popular nationalism.

Boundaries and classificatory systems play into discrimination that is both enacted (Shields 2017) and lived. For instance, a qualitative study of Arab Canadian immigrant women found that living in a new country, experiencing isolation and alienation of the body and bodily practices such as infant feeding, eating exercising and so on became sites of frustration (Oleschuk and Vallianatos 2019). The authors found that women talked in terms of embodied boundaries in two ways. One, they framed their bodies in relation to their own bodies when living in their home country and/or in relation to Arab women still living there which portrayed ways of living or a former sense of themselves now lost. Two they also framed their bodies in relation to the dominant images of Canadian women from whom they felt alienated and wanted to resist. The authors suggest that this embodied boundary talk reveals both the structural pressures of immigration, while it also enables them "to reframe the impact of those pressures (i.e. their weight gain and poor eating and exercise habits) into a narrative of immigration based on dignity."

Social changes have bodily correlates in that what bodies are permitted to do, and how people use their bodies, is contingent upon social context. The work of Elias (1978, 1982) demonstrates this on a grand scale. Elias is concerned with the link between the state and state formations and the behaviors and manners of the sociology of the body the individual. He offers a figurational sociology; this means that he works at the level of social configurations, rather than societies. In fact, for Elias, societies are the outcome of the interactions of individuals. In his studies of "The Civilizing Process" (first published in 1939 in German), Elias (1978) examines in detail changes in manners, etiquette, codes of conduct, ways of dressing, ways of sleeping, ways of eating, and changing ideas about shame and decency associated with bodies. According to Elias, the civilizing process began in the Middle Ages within court societies where social mobility became more fluid and people's futures could be determined not only by their birthrights, as had been the case under the feudal system, but also by the extent to which they were in favor with the sovereign or their advisors. In short, people were more inclined to be on their best behavior. Medieval personalities were characteristically unpredictable and emotional, they were inclined to be indulgent, and there were virtually no codes surrounding bodily functions.

However, within court societies, codes of body management were developed and copious manuals were written on how to and where to sleep and with whom, how to behave at meals, appropriate locations for defecation, and so on. Changes in behavior impacted on social relations and, as social relations transformed, so the compulsions exerted over others became internalized. This process, according to Elias, was accelerated in the sixteenth century. His analysis reveals how greater self-control over behaviors was associated with the body and a heightened sense of shame and delicacy:

> The individual is compelled to regulate his [sic] conduct in an increasingly differentiated, more even and more stable manner ... The more complex and stable control of conduct is increasingly instilled in the individual from his earliest years as an automatism, a self-compulsion that he cannot resist. (Elias 1982: 232–233)

This civilizing process involves three key progressive processes (Shilling 2012): socialization, rationalization, and individualization. Socialization refers to the way in which people are encouraged to hide away their natural functions. Thus, the body comes to be regarded more in social rather than natural terms. In fact, we find many natural functions offensive or distasteful; for example, if someone sitting next to us on a bus vomits over our clothes or if someone willingly urinates in an "inappropriate" part of our house. Rationalization implies that we have become more rational as opposed to emotional and are able to control our feelings. Finally, individualization highlights the extent to which we have come to see our bodies as encasing ourselves as separate from others. It is important, therefore, that we maintain a socially acceptable distance between ourselves and others. Furthermore, how we "manage" and "present" our bodies (Butler 1990; Goffman 1959) has become especially salient in a late modern context. Some argue that this is because the body has become a prime site for the formation and maintenance of the modern self and identity.

Bodies in Late Modern Societies

Sociological theorists have argued that a key feature of such late modern societies is risk (Beck 1992; Douglas 1986; Giddens 1991). Doubt, Giddens argues, is a pervasive feature which permeates into everyday life. Our self and identity are a continuous embodied reflexive process (Crossley 2006) where we continually revise our biographical narratives. The reflexive self is one that relies on a vast array of advice and information provided by a myriad of sources.

What has all this got to do with the body? Well, a number of theorists have suggested that the body has come to form one of the main sites through which people develop their social identities. Whilst the environment and the social world seem to be "out of control," the body becomes something of an anchor. Giddens points out that the self is embodied and so the regularized control of the body is a fundamental means whereby a biography of self – identity is maintained. Giddens (1991: 218) states:

> The body used to be one aspect of nature, governed in a fundamental way by processes only marginally subject to human intervention. The body was a "given," the often inconvenient and inadequate seat of the self. With the increasing invasion of the body by abstract systems all this becomes altered. The body, like the self, becomes a site of interaction, appropriation and re-appropriation, linking reflexively organised processes and systematically ordered expert knowledge. [...] Once thought to be the locus of the soul ... the body has become fully available to be "worked upon by the influences of high modernity" [...]. In the conceptual space between these, we find more and more guidebooks and practical manuals to do with health, diet, appearance, exercise, love-making and many other things.

According to this thesis, therefore, we are more uncertain about our bodies; we perceive them to be more pliable and are actively seeking to alter, improve, and refine them.

Flexible Immunity Bodies

The idea that contemporary societies are characterized by change and adaptability has also been articulated by Emily Martin (1994) in her empirical study of contemporary ideas about immunity in North America. By way of data collected via interviews, analyses of documents, participant observation, and informal exchanges, she (Martin 1994: xvii) found that "flexibility is an object of desire for nearly everyone's personality, body and organization." Flexibility is associated with the notion of the immune system which now underpins our thinking about the body, organizations, machines, politics, and so on. In her interviews with ordinary men and women, the idea of developing a strong immune system appeared to be in common currency. To be effective, that is to protect the body against the threats of disease and illness, the immune system must be able to change and constantly adapt.

These notions of immunity found on the street reflect those found in laboratory science where immunological understandings of immunity transformed from understanding of an immune "self" working to defend and discriminate against the foreign "non-self" (Tauber 1995). Tauber documents the fragmentation of the self-versus-non-self (S/NS) system, as immunological understandings of, for example autoimmunity, chimerism, transplantation and parasitism come to see the immune system reconfigured as an "immune-nervous system" with the creative capacity to be "over-written."

Cohen (2009) in his book *A Body Worth Defending* finds congruence between judicial, political and biological cultures. Network conceptions of immunity displace bounded systems in all these spheres in ways that have led scholars to reflect on immune-political life (Davis et al. 2016) and the begin to forge a "biopolitics of immunity" (Brown and Nettleton 2018). Brown points to the merits of Italian philosopher

Esposito's (2008) notion of an "immunity paradigm" in which the political and biological become inextricably intertwined. While modernist notions of immunity implied enclosure, protection and defense, we now recognize that immunity also requires a degree of openness, "hospitable forms of immunity" that can "preserve life" (Esposito 2008: 53–54). Perhaps, the most readily obvious examples are organ transplantation and vaccination. The latter involving the introduction of a pathogen for individual and collective benefit, something Durkheim (1982) recognized when writing about how by inoculating ourselves with smallpox, where a vaccine increases our chances of survival through collective, herd immunity. The biopolitics of immunity are foregrounded in these and other immunological matters, for example debates on antibiotics and antimicrobial resistance are found to manifest as debates on public politics and personal responsibility (Brown and Nettleton 2017, 2018). What this scholarship offers is not only provides a valuable analysis of late modernity but also reveals how our accounts and interpretations of our bodies are historically and socially contingent, and that they are not "immune" from broader social transformations (see also the discussion about the work of Elias above). How we experience our bodies is invariably social, and one of the central thrusts of modern times is the sociology of the body that we feel compelled to work at creating a flexible and therefore adaptable and socially acceptable body.

The Body as a Project

Shilling (2012) also argues that the body might best be conceptualized as a "body project"; an unfinished biological and social phenomenon, which is transformed, within limits, as a result of its participation in society. The body is in a continual state of "unfinishedness;" the body is "seen" as an entity which is in the process of becoming; a project which should be worked at and accomplished as part of an individual "self-identity" (Shilling 2012: 4). Body projects become more sophisticated and more complex in a context where there is both the knowledge and technology to transform them in ways that in the past might have been regarded as the province of fiction. There is a vast array of medical technologies and procedures to choose from if we want to shape, alter, and recreate our bodies – from various forms of techniques to "assist" conception, to gene therapies, to forms of cosmetic surgery and so on.

These projects are also gendered as illustrated by Brumberg's (1998) feminist historical analysis of adolescent girls where she finds the contemporary imperative to perfect the appearance of the body displaces the constraints imposed by the social conventions and restrictions placed on young women in the nineteenth century. There is, of course, an irony here. As we expand our freedoms, knowledge, technologies and expertise, to alter bodies we become more uncertain and insecure we become about what the body actually is and what its boundaries are. And yet it also seems that as the opportunities to work on our bodies proliferate they coalesce around a limited range of repertoires that are rooted in ideologies of individualism. This is evidenced by Gill et al.'s (2005) study of body projects and the regulation of masculinity. Based on 140 qualitative interviews with men aged between 15 and 35 from differing regions in the UK sampled to ensure representation of class, race, and sexual orientation found the authors found "an extraordinary *homogeneity*" ran through the men's talk (p. 56). There was a shared set of discourses that were consistently embraced the merits of: individualism and being different; libertarianism and having an autonomous body, rejection of vanity and narcissism, the value of being well balanced and not obsessional and the importance of being a morally responsible body. Men's body and identity talk the authors argue is structured by a "grammar of individualism" (p. 57).

Bio-value and Virtual Bodies

Whilst the above discussion has highlighted the body as an unfinished and malleable entity which has become central to the formation of the late modern reflexive self, other postmodern analyses have suggested that the body is not so much uncertain as un/hyperreal. In other words, the body has disappeared – there is no distinction between bodies and the images of bodies. Drawing on the work of Baudrillard, Frank (1992) challenges the conventional idea that the body of the patient forms the basis of medical practice. It is the image of the body which now forms the basis of medical care.

> Real diagnostic work takes place away from the patient; bedside is secondary to screen side. For diagnostic and even treatment purposes, the image on the screen becomes the "true" patient, of which the bedridden body is an imperfect replicant, less worthy of attention. In the screens' simulations our initial certainty of the real (the body) becomes lost in hyperreal images that are better than the real body. (Frank 1992: 83)

The "Visible Human Project" (VHP), described on the US National Library of Medicine, National Institutes of Health website as:

> the creation of complete, anatomically detailed, three-dimensional representations of the normal male and female human bodies. Acquisition of transverse CT, MR and cryosection images of representative male and female cadavers has been completed. The male was sectioned at one millimeter intervals, the female at one-third of a millimeter intervals. (National Library of Medicine 2008)

Fascinated by this undertaking, Catherine Waldby (2000) subjects the VHP to sociological scrutiny and highlights some intriguing features. Not only do images of the inner reaches of the body become accessible to a wide audience, but also the transformation of bodies into a "digital substance" contributes to the blurring of boundaries between the real and the unreal, the private and the public, and the dead and the living (Waldby 2000: 6). She argues that the whole exercise represents a further extension of Foucault's notion of bio-power. The VHP is at once a means of both examining and experimenting on the body and, therefore, it is also a means by which knowledge of bodies is generated and circulated.

In addition, the establishment of knowledge contributes to the production of "surplus value" in that there are significant commercial interests that benefit through the related production of medical technologies be they equipment, drugs, and so on. This is what Waldby calls "biovalue," which refers to the yield of vitality produced by the biotechnological reformulation of living processes" (Waldby 2002: 310). Two factors precipitate the generation of biovalue. First, the hope that biotechnologies will result in a better understanding and thereby treatment of disease. Second, the pursuit of exchange value of biomedical commodities – be they patents or pills – that are the yield of the interventions. Indeed, biovalue is "increasingly assimilated into capital value, and configured according to the demands of commercial economies" (Waldby 2000: 34).

The counterpart to the VHP, observes Waldby, is the Human Genome Project (HGP) in that both projects are means by which the body comes to form a database, an archive and so a source of bioinformation. The digitization of bodies however further complicates the dualism between virtual and real bodies presumed in the work of Frank and Waldby. The infiltration of the bodies of the relatively mobile and relatively wealthy by smart, wearable biosensor technologies creates further scope for biovalue and commodification of bodies as evidenced through on-line platforms that harvest biodata, such as *23andMe* and other genetic testing organizations (Saukko 2018).

Historically, perhaps one of the most profound impacts of the production of images is in relation to pregnancy. Barbera Duden (1993) argues that the use of technologies which enable the fetus to be visually represented has contributed to the transformation of an unborn fetus into a life. The imagining of the unborn has meant that the fetus has become an emblem, a "billboard image." Her study addresses the following puzzles: How did the female peritoneum acquire transparency? What set of circumstances made the skinning of women acceptable and inspired public concern for what happens in her innards? And pertinently: how was it possible to mobilize so many women as uncomplaining agents of this skinning and as willing? (Duden 1993: 7). In an amazingly short space of time, "the scan" became a routine and ubiquitous experience for most pregnant women in many Western societies. This prompts tensions between the way the body is experienced or lived and the way the body is observed and described by "medical experts" (Dumit 2010). This tension is explored empirically by Lie and her colleagues (2019) in their study of parents' experiences of an in-utero MRI (iuMRI) device that has been developed to increase accuracy of diagnosis of foetal brain abnormalities, it is not therefore used routinely but accessed in addition to ultrasound anomaly scanning. From their analysis of the parents experiences they conclude that while, the "'medical' gaze may work to separate the foetal body from its social identity" by contrast "the 'parental' gaze often does the opposite, reconstructing or reinforcing foetal and parental identities" (p. 376). Thus the lived experiential, embodied view of the body is retained even in instances where it becomes reduced to representation in a digitized form.

Sociology of Embodiment

A sociology of embodiment has developed out of a critique that the literature on the body has failed to incorporate the voices of bodies as they are experienced or lived (James and Hockey 2007). Drawing on phenomenological analyses, this approach proposes that much of the existing literature has failed to challenge a whole series of dualisms such as: the split between mind and body; culture and nature; and reason and emotion. Such socially created dualisms are pernicious, not only because they are false, but also because they serve to reinforce ideologies and social hierarchies.

"These dualisms," Bendelow and Williams (1998: 1) argue, "have been mapped onto the gendered division of labour in which men, historically, have been allied with the mind, culture and the public realm of production, whilst women have been tied to their bodies, nature, and the private sphere of domestic reproduction." But most important, from a sociological point of view they hinder any effective theorizing which must assume the inextricable interaction and oneness of mind and body. Studies of pain and emotion have, perhaps more than any other, revealed that the body and the mind are not separate entities (Bendelow and Williams 1998).

Phenomenology: The "Lived Body"

The phenomenological perspective focuses on the "lived body" and the idea that consciousness is invariably embedded within the body. The human being is an embodied social agent. The work of Merleau-Ponty, in particular his text *The Phenomenology of Perception* has been revisited, and it is regarded by many as critical to our appreciation of embodiment (Crossley 1995, 2006; Csordas 1994). Essentially, he argued that all human perception is embodied; we cannot perceive anything, and our senses cannot function independently of our bodies. This does not imply that they are somehow glued together, as the Cartesian notion of the body might suggest, but rather there is something of an oscillation between the two. This idea forms the basis of the notion of "embodiment." As Merleau-Ponty (1962) writes:

> Men [sic] taken as a concrete being is not a psyche joined to an organism, but movement to and fro of existence which at one time allows itself to take corporeal form and at others moves toward personal acts ... It is never a question of the incomprehensive meeting of two casualties, nor of a collision between the order of causes and that of ends. But by an imperceptible twist an organic process issues into human behaviour, an instinctive act changes direction and becomes a sentiment, or conversely a human act becomes torpid and is continued absent-mindedly in the form of a reflex. (Merleau-Ponty 1962: 88, cited by Turner 1992: 56)

Thus, while the notion that embodied consciousness is central here, it is also highlighted that we are not always conscious or aware of our bodily actions. We do not routinely tell our body to put one leg in front of the other if we want to walk, or to breathe in through our nose if we want to smell a rose. The body in this sense is "taken for granted," or as Leder puts it, the body is "absent." Whilst in one sense the body is the most abiding and inescapable presence in our lives, it is also characterized by its absence. That is, one's own body is rarely the thematic object of experience ... the body, as a ground of experience ... tends to recede from direct experience (Leder 1990: 1).

Within this perspective, the lived body is presumed to both construct and be constructed by, and within, the lifeworld. The lived body is an intentional entity which gives rise to this world. As Leder (1992: 25) writes elsewhere:

> in a significant sense, the lived body helps to constitute this world as experienced. We cannot understand the meaning and form of objects without reference to bodily powers

> through which we engage them – our senses, motility, language, desires. The lived body is not just one thing in the world but a way in which the world comes to be.

We can see therefore that it is analytically possible to make a distinction between having a body, doing a body, and being a body. Turner (1992) and others have found the German distinction between Leib and *Körper* to be instructive here. The former refers to the experiential, animated, or living body (the body-for-itself), the latter refers to the objective, instrumental, exterior body (the body-in-itself).

This approach highlights that the concept of the "lived body" and the notion of "embodiment" remind us that the self and the body are not separate and that experience is invariably, whether consciously or not, embodied. As Csordas (1994: 10) has argued, the body is the "existential ground of culture and self," and therefore he prefers the notion of "embodiment" to "the body," as the former implies something more than a material entity. It is rather a "methodological field defined by perceptual experience and mode of presence and engagement in the world." This idea that the self is embodied is also taken up by Giddens (1991: 56–57), who also emphasizes the notion of day-to-day praxis. The body is not an external entity but is experienced in practical ways when coping with external events and situations.

How we handle our bodies in social situations is crucial to our self and identity and has been extensively studied by Goffman, symbolic interactionists, and ethnomethodologists (Heritage 1984). Indeed, the study of the management of bodies in everyday life and how this serves to structure the self and social relations has a long and important history within sociology. It highlights the preciousness of the body as well as the remarkable ability of humans to sustain bodily control through everyday situations.

Marrying the work of theorists such as Foucault and Giddens with the insights of the early interactionists, Nick Crossley (2006) has developed the particularly useful concept of "reflexive embodiment." Premised on Cooley's (1902) notion of the "looking glass self" and Mead's (1967) suggestion that we care about, and are influenced by, how we think other people see us, Crossley's thesis is that humans are not merely subjects of regulation but are active agents whose thoughts, actions, and intentions are embedded within social networks. Embodied agents have the capacity to reflect upon themselves and such reflection involves an assessment of what they believe other people (the "generalized other") think of them.

> "Reflexive embodiment" refers to the capacity and tendency to perceive, emote about, reflect and act upon one's own body; to practices of body modification and maintenance; and to "body image." Reflexivity entails that the object and subject of perception, thought, feeling, desire or action are the same. (Crossley 2006: 1)

This notion is central to the experience of health and illness, not least because so many bodily practices and techniques are associated with the maintenance and reproduction of bodies to ensure good health and to manage illness. Many of these themes and issues have been explored by sociologists who have studied how people experience illness to explore how bodies are "lived;" how bodies are visualized especially in virtual, digitized spaces then colonized by commercial agencies to generate value and how embodiment shaped by socio-political power relations.

The Sociology of the Body: Some Illustrative Issues

Illness and Lived Bodies

The literature on the experience of chronic illness and disability drew attention to many of the themes discussed above prior to the more recent emergence of the body and embodiment literature, most particularly the fundamental link between the self and the body. A number of researchers (Broom et al. 2015; Charmaz 2000) have documented how this occurs in the case of chronic illness. Here the relationship between the body and self can be seriously disrupted. Simon Williams (1996) has illustrated this well by drawing on the findings of research into chronic illness. He demonstrates how the experience of chronic illness involves a move from an "initial" state of embodiment (a state in which the body is taken for granted in the course of everyday life) to an oscillation between states of (dys)embodiment (embodiment in a dysfunctional state) and "re-embodiment."

Attempts to move from a dys-embodied state to a re-embodied state require a considerable amount of biographical work as a result of what Bury (1982) calls "biographical disruption" and can prompt people to engage in what Gareth Williams (1984) terms "narrative reconstruction." Disruptions and reconstructions are neither isolated nor linear, for while illness may disrupt a biographical trajectory it is more likely to be a series of "ruptures" without clear beginnings, middles or ends. As Riessman (2015: 1057) puts it: "Illness by its very nature disrupts any pretense of temporal continuity, for it lacks the coherence that permits us to identify linkages between cause and effect, before and after."

Crucially these notions of biographical disruption and narrative reconstruction should not be understood as purely cognitive or mental processes. Engman (2019) asserts that the analytic purchase of these concepts has been so enduring precisely because of their implicit embodied basis and suggests that this needs to be made more explicit. From her empirical study of 36 post-operative organ transplant recipients she finds the salience of biographical disruption as meaningful feature of the illness experience, depends on the degree to which the participants bodily changes involved a distinctive shift between the "intentions of the body and its capacity to manifest those intensions." In cases where bodily intentions could not be acted upon, in other words the bodies constrained action this was more likely to trigger the articulation of a biographical disruption, than in cases where bodily changes could be incorporated into day to day lives.

> When illness pierces a subject's embodied orientation towards the world, she loses the foundation on which day-to-day life is built. The inability to perform habitual behaviours that results is, essentially, an inability to utilize all of the accumulated embodied knowledge that previously organized daily life. It is no wonder that this prompts people to re-evaluate the ways that they project themselves into the future – stripped of one's ability to enact routine behaviours, the future is necessarily uncertain. (Engman 2019: 126)

The materiality of embodiment is therefore salient and helps to collapse dualisms between the body as object and subject both as it is experienced and as it is worked upon.

Body Work

As Twigg and her colleagues (2011) argued book on the body in health and social care, the material body is essential to any adequate analysis of health care in practice.

> Body work is work that focuses directly on the bodies of others: assessing, diagnosing, handling, treating, manipulating, and monitoring bodies, that thus become the object of the worker's labour. It is a component part of a wide range of occupations. It is a central part of healthcare, through the work of doctors, nurses, dentists, hygienists, paramedics and physiotherapists. (Twigg et al. 2011: 171)

Medicine, health, care, and the body are inextricably interlinked. Analyses of, or policies on, health and social care which overlook the messy realities of the body will invariably be wanting. The rationalistic approach which has tended to dominate policy debates, "presents a bleached out, abstract, dry account that takes little cognizance of the messy, swampy, emotional world of the body and its feelings" and Twigg suggests that a focus on the body "promises to bring the world of policy into much closer and direct engagement with its central subject" (Twigg 2006: 173).

In what ways can theorizations on the body and embodiment help us to make sense of health care in practice? There are some excellent qualitative studies of health care work within formal settings that can help us answer this question. Julia Lawton's (1998) study of care within a hospice is an excellent example. Her ethnographic study sets out to understand why it is that some patients remain within the hospice to die whilst others are more likely to be discharged and sent home to die. To address this health policy puzzle, Lawton argues we need to focus on the body of the dying person. She found that those patients cared for within the hospice were those whose bodies became unbounded. By this she means that the diseases they were suffering from involved a particular type of bodily deterioration and disintegration requiring very specific forms of symptom control, the most common examples being:

> incontinence of urine and faeces, uncontrolled vomiting (including faecal vomit), fungating tumours (the rotting away of a tumour site on the surface of the skin) and weeping limbs which resulted from the development of gross oedema in the patient's legs or arms. (Lawton 1998: 128)

It is these forms of bodily (dys)functions that people living in Western society cannot tolerate rather than the process of dying itself. Indeed, in those cases where the boundedness of their bodies could be reinstated, patients would be discharged. To address the question of why unbounded bodies are unacceptable in Western society, Lawton draws upon much of the sociological theorizing outlined above – especially the work of Douglas and Elias. The unbounded body is perceived symbolically, according to Douglas, as a source of dirt – it is matter out of place. The increasingly "civilized" body, according to Elias, has become "individualized" and private, and the "natural" functions of the body are removed from public view.

The fact that natural or intimate bodily functions are problematic for health care practitioners is also been explored by Lawler (1991), who again draws upon the ideas developed by Elias and Douglas in her study of nursing care in an Australian hospital. Quintessentially, the work of nurses is about caring for bodies. This becomes a problem when nurses have to attend to those bodily functions (defecating, grooming, etc.) which in a "civilized" society have become taboo. Consequently, nurses have to learn how to negotiate social boundaries and create new contexts so that both the patient and the nurse can avoid feelings of shame and embarrassment. There is a further fascinating finding highlighted in Lawton's study, and this relates to the link that we have discussed above between the notion of self and physical body. The two are meshed together. Lawton's work demonstrates that even where there is a "competent" mind, the lack of bodily controls (Nettleton and Watson 1998: 14–17) affects a person's capacity to continue with their life projects or their reflexive self. In fact, patients who had the least control over their bodily functions exhibited behavior which suggested a total loss of self and social identity once their bodies became severely and irreversibly unbounded. Take Lawton's account of Deborah, for example:

> When Deborah's bodily deterioration escalated, I observed that she had suddenly become a lot more withdrawn. After she had been on the ward for a couple of days she started asking for the curtains to be drawn around her bed to give her more privacy. A day or so later she stopped talking altogether, unless it was really necessary (to ask for a commode, for example), even when her family and other visitors were present. Deborah spent the remaining ten days of her life either sleeping or staring blankly into space. She refused all food and drink ... One of the hospice doctors concluded that "for all intents and purposes she [had] shut herself off in a frustrated and irreversible silence." (Lawton 1998: 129)

We see how the bounded body is foundational to the representation and reproduction of a coherent self in the context of societies that extol individualism and where the independent, autonomous body is privileged.

Embodiment Inequalities in Health

A basic tenet of medical sociology is that social circumstances – in particular material and social deprivation – become inscribed in people's bodies. In other words, it is argued that health status is socially determined. The reasons why social circumstances, and more especially social inequalities, impact upon health status have been researched and debated for over centuries. By the turn of the millennium sociologists began to theorize about the links between the sociology of embodiment and health inequalities in ways that provide us with important clues as to why health is socially patterned. Freund (1990) argued that people express "somatically" the conditions of their existence. "Emotional modes of being" he writes are very likely to be linked to structural position.

> Subjectivity, social activity and the social structural contexts interpenetrate. It is this relationship that comes to be physically embodied in many ways. Irregularity of breathing may accompany muscular tension and experiences of ontological insecurity and the anger or fear that is part of this insecurity. (Freund 1990: 461)

This link becomes evident when we mesh together the "lived body" and the structural perspectives on the body. How people experience their structural context, the meanings and interpretations, they ascribe to it, in turn impacts their physical bodies (Peacock et al. 2014).

It seems, then, that unequal societies equate to unhealthy societies (Wilkinson and Pickett 2010), or rather unequal societies, are associated with unhealthy bodies. This is not just a result of material deprivation and poverty – the harmful effects of poor housing, poor food, and living conditions per se – though these are undoubtedly important. But what is also important is one's socio-economic position. Essentially, those people who are lower down the social hierarchy and who have the least control over their circumstances are more likely to be ill. They are more likely to experience prolonged stress and negative emotions, which in turn have physiological consequences. This psychosocial perspective on health inequalities points to a growing body of research that demonstrates how certain aspects of social life, such as a sense of control, perceived social status, strength of affiliations, self-esteem, feelings of ontological insecurity, and so on, lead to variations in health outcomes (Bartley 2016; Elstad 1998).

It seems that how people reflect upon, emote about, and internalize their social position and social circumstances is critical. Drawing from work in physiological anthropology, in particular studies of non-human primates, researchers have found that primates who were lower down the social hierarchy, and most importantly had least control and power, exhibited more detrimental physiological changes in times of stress. Authors have argued this may help explain the fact that numerous studies have consistently found that people in social environments with limited autonomy and control over their circumstances suffer proportionately poor health. The key issue here is the degree of social cohesion. Greater social cohesion means people are more likely to feel secure and "supported" and are less likely to respond negatively when they have to face difficulties or uncertainties. In turn, it is social inequality that serves to undermine social cohesion and the quality of the social fabric (Wilkinson and Pickett 2010)

Through a comprehensive analysis of research that documents the various pathways by which austerity and neo-liberal policies come to be embodied into health outcomes, Sparke (2017) develops the notion "biological sub-citizenship." This extends Rose and Novas's (2005) concept of "biological citizenship" articulated to describe how novel forms of citizenship, sociality and collective activism are anchored in and coalesce around shared x (often genetic) characteristics. The prefix "sub" shifts the emphasis from shared biological characteristics and highlights instead "how ill-health embodies changing conditions of political-economic subordination" (Sparke 2017: 287). Sparke writes that,

> a concept of biological sub-citizenship is useful precisely because it provides a relational way of theorizing how such embodied outcomes of austerity actively prevent people from becoming fully enfranchised biological citizens. It thereby allows us to re-evaluate ideas about enfranchisement into biological citizenship in relation to dynamics producing differentials of disenfranchisement. (p. 288)

While shared biologies may bring citizens together (biological citizenship), the privileging of global markets combined with neo-liberal economic, health and social policies that systematically disadvantage particular groups can lead to exclusion, exploitation, extraction and so exacerbate precarious embodiment (biological sub-citizenship).

Conclusion

This chapter has reviewed some of the key theoretical perspectives within the literature on the sociology of the body and the sociology of embodiment. Drawing on these approaches, it has discussed a number of substantive issues which are of interest to those working within medical sociology. Thus, it has attempted to show that a "sociology of the body" and an "embodied sociology" have made an important contribution to matters which have traditionally been of interest to this field of study. A key theme running through this chapter is that the more knowledge and information we have about bodies, the more uncertain we become as to what bodies actually are. Certainties about seemingly immutable processes associated with birth and death, for example, become questioned. Furthermore, how we experience and live our bodies has also become central to how we think about our*selves*. Bodies are politicized both in terms of identities, and also in terms of how they are monitored and marginalized, regulated and relegated, empowered and excluded. Any comprehensive analysis of the experience of health, illness, or health care should take cognizance of the body (whatever that is!) itself.

References

Annandale, Ellen, Maria Wiklund, and Hammarström Anne. 2018. "Theorising Women's Health and Health Inequalities: Shaping Processes of the 'Gender-biology Nexus'." *Global Health Action* 11: 87–96.

Armstrong, David. 1983. *Political Anatomy of the Body: Medical Knowledge in Britain in the Twentieth Century*. Cambridge: Cambridge University Press.

Bartley, Mel. 2016. *Health Inequality: An Introduction to Concepts, Theories and Methods*. London: John Wiley & Sons.

Beck, Ulrich. 1992. *Risk Society: Towards a New Modernity*. London: Sage.

Bendelow, Gill and Simon J. Williams (eds.). 1998. *Emotions in Social Life: Critical Themes and Contemporary Issues*. London: Routledge.

Broom, A. F., E. R. Kirby, J. Adams, and K. M. Refshauge. 2015. "On Illegitimacy, Suffering and Recognition: A Diary Study of Women Living with Chronic Pain." *Sociology* 49(4): 712–731.

Brown, Nik and Sarah Nettleton. 2017. "Bugs in the Blog: Immunitary Moralism in Antimicrobial Resistance (AMR)." *Social Theory & Health* 15(3): 302–322.

Brown, Nik and Sarah Nettleton. 2018. "Economic Imaginaries of the Anti-biosis: Between 'Economies of Resistance' and the 'Resistance of Economies'." *Palgrave Communications* 4(1): 1–8.

Brumberg, Joan, Jacobs. 1998. *The Body Project: An Intimate History of American Girls*. New York: Vintage Press.

Bury, Mike. 1982. Chronic illness as biographical disruption. *Sociology of Health & Illness* 4(2): 167–182.

Busfield, Joan. 2017. "The Concept of Medicalisation Reassessed." *Sociology of Health & Illness* 39(5): 759–774.

Butler, Judith. 1990. *Gender Trouble: Feminism and the Subversion of Identity*. London: Routledge.

Butler, Judith. 2015. *Notes toward a Performative Theory of Assembly*. Boston, MA: Harvard University Press.

Carel, Havi. 2016. *Phenomenology of Illness*. Oxford: Oxford University Press.

Charmaz, Kathy. 2000. "Experiencing Chronic Illness." Pp. 277–292 in *The Handbook of Social Studies in Health and Medicine*, edited by Gary L. Albrecht, Ray Fitzpatrick, and Susan C. Scrimshaw. London: Sage.

Cohen, Ed. 2009. *A Body Worth Defending: Immunity, Biopolitics, and the Apotheosis of the Modern Body*. Durham, NC: Duke University Press.

Connell, Raewyn. 2012. "Gender, Health and Theory: Conceptualizing the Issue, in Local and World Perspective." *Social Science & Medicine* 74(11): 1675–1683.

Cooley, C. H. 1902. *Human Nature and Social Order*. New York: Charles Scribner & Sons.

Crossley, Nick. 1995. "Merleau-Ponty, the Elusive Body and Carnal Sociology." *Body & Society* 1(1): 43–64.

Crossley, Nick. 2006. *Reflexive Embodiment in Contemporary Society*. Maidenhead: Open University Press.

Csordas, Thomas J. 1994. *Embodiment and Experience: The Existential Ground of Culture and Self*. Cambridge: Cambridge University Press.

Davis, Mark, Paul. Flowers, Lohm Davina, Waller Emily, and Stephenson Niamh. 2016. "Immunity, Biopolitics and Pandemics: Public and Individual Responses to the Threat to Life." *Body & Society* 22(4): 130–154.

Douglas, Mary. 1966. *Purity and Danger: An Analysis of the Concepts of Pollution and Taboo*. London: Routledge and Kegan Paul.

Douglas, Mary. 1970. *Natural Symbols: Explorations in Cosmology*. London: Cresset Press.

Douglas, Mary. 1986. *Risk Acceptability according to the Social Sciences*. London: Routledge and Kegan Paul.

Duden, Barbera. 1993. *Disembodying Women: Perspectives on Pregnancy and the Unborn*. London: Harvard University Press.

Dumit, Josef. 2010. "A Digital Image of the Category of the Person." Pp. 367–376 in *A Reader in Medical Anthropology: Theoretical Trajectories, Emergent Realities*, edited by Byron J. Good, M.J. Michael, Sarah S. Willen Fischer, and Mary-Jo Del Vecchio Good. Oxford: Wiley-Blackwell.

Durkheim, Emile. 1982. *Rules of Sociological Method*, edited by S. Lukes, translated by W. D. Halls. New York: The Free Press.

Elias, Norbert. 1978. *The Civilizing Process. Vol. 1: The History of Manners*. Oxford: Blackwell.

Elias, Norbert. 1982. *The Civilizing Process. Vol. 2: State Formation and Civilization*. Oxford: Blackwell.

Elstad, Jon I. 1998. "The Psycho-Social Perspective on Social Inequalities in Health." *Sociology of Health & Illness* 20(5): 598–618.

Engman, Athena. 2019. "Embodiment and the Foundation of Biographical Disruption." *Social Science & Medicine* 225: 120–127.

Esposito, Roberto. 2008. *Bios: Biopolitics and Philosophy*. Minnesota, MI: University of Minnesota Press.

Ettorre, Elizabeth (eds). 2010. *Culture, Bodies and the Sociology of Health*. Farnham: Ashgate Publishing.

Foucault, Michel. 1976. *The Birth of the Clinic: An Archaeology of Medical Perception.* London: Tavistock.

Foucault, Michel. 1979. *Discipline and Punish: The Birth of the Prison.* Harmondsworth: Penguin.

Foucault, Michel. 1981. *The History of Sexuality: An Introduction.* Harmondsworth: Penguin.

Frank, Arthur W. 1992. "Twin Nightmares of the Medical Simulacrum: Jean Baudrillard and David Cronenberg." in *Jean Baudrillard: The Disappearance of Art and Politics,* edited by Willaim Stearns and William Chaloupka. London: Macmillan.

Freund, Pete E. S. 1990. "The Expressive Body: A Common Ground for the Sociology of Emotions and Health and Illness." *Sociology of Health & Illness* 12(4): 452–477.

Giddens, Anthony. 1991. *Modernity and Self-Identity: Self and Society in the Late Modern Age.* Cambridge: Polity Press.

Gill, R., Henwood, K. and McLean, C., 2005. Body Projects and the Regulation of Normative Masculinity. *Body & Society* 11(1): 37–62.

Goffman, Ervin. 1959. *The Presentation of Self in Everyday Life.* Harmondsworth: Penguin.

Heritage, John. 1984. *Garfinkel and Ethnomethodology.* Cambridge: Polity Press.

James, Alison and Jenny Hockey. 2007. *Embodying Health Identities.* Basingstoke: Palgrave Macmillan.

Lawler, Jocalyn. 1991. *Behind the Screens: Nursing Somology and the Problem of the Body.* London: Churchill Livingstone.

Lawton, Julia. 1998. "Contemporary Hospice Care: The Sequestration of the Unbounded Body and 'Dirty Dying'." *Sociology of Health & Illness* 20(2): 121–143.

Leder, Drew. 1990. *The Absent Body.* Chicago, IL: Chicago University Press.

Leder, Drew. 1992. "Introduction." Pp. 1–12 in *The Body in Medical Thought and Practice,* edited by Drew Leder. London: Kluwer Academic.

Lie, Mabel, Ruth Graham, Stephen Robson, and Paul Griffiths. 2019. "'He Looks Gorgeous'–iu MR Images and the Transforming of Foetal and Parental Identities." *Sociology of Health & Illness* 41(2): 360–377.

Longhurst, Robyn. 2001. *Bodies: Exploring Fluid Boundaries.* London: Routledge.

Lupton, Deborah. 2016. *The Quantified Self.* London: John Wiley & Sons.

Martin, Emily. 1989. *The Woman in the Body: A Cultural Analysis of Reproduction.* Milton Keynes: Open University Press.

Martin, Emily. 1994. *Flexible Bodies: The Role of Immunity in American Culture from the Days of Polio to the Age of AIDS.* Boston, MA: Beacon Press.

Mason, Katherine. 2013. "Social Stratification and the Body: Gender, Race, and Class." *Sociology Compass* 7(8): 686–698.

Mead, George Herbert. 1967. *Mind, Self and Society.* Chicago, IL: Chicago University Press.

National Library of Medicine. 2008. "The Visible Human Project." National Library of Medicine, US National Institutes of Health. Retrieved online 1/13/2008 at: www.nlmnih.gov/research/visible/visible_human.htm.

Merleau-Ponty, Maurice. 1962. *Phenomenology of Perception.* London: Routledge.

Nettleton, Sarah. 1988. "Protecting a Vulnerable Margin: Towards an Analysis of How the Mouth Came to Be Separated from the Body." *Sociology of Health & Illness* 10(2): 156–169.

Nettleton, Sarah. 2020. *The Sociology of Health and Illness,* 4th ed. Cambridge: Polity Press.

Nettleton, Sarah and Jonathon Watson (eds.). 1998. *The Body in Everyday Life.* London: Routledge.

Oleschuk, Merin and Helen Vallianatos. 2019. "Body Talk and Boundary Work among Arab Canadian Immigrant Women." *Qualitative Sociology* 42: 87–614.

Peacock, Marion, Bissell Paul, and Jenny Owen. 2014. Dependency Denied: Health Inequalities in the Neo-liberal Era. *Social Science & Medicine* 118: 173–180.

Prainsack, Barbara. 2017. *Personalised Medicine: Empowered Patients in the 21st Century?* New York: New York University Press.

Riessman, Catherine Kohler. 2015. "Ruptures and Sutures: Time, Audience and Identity in an Illness Narrative." *Sociology of Health & Illness* 37(7): 1055–1071.

Rose, Nikolas and Carlos Novas. 2005. "Biological Citizenship." Pp. 439–463 in *Global Assemblages: Technology, Politics, and Ethics as Anthropological Problems*, edited by A. Ong and S. Collier. Oxford: Blackwell.

Saukko, Paula. 2018. "Digital Health–a New Medical Cosmology? The Case of 23andMe Online Genetic Testing Platform." *Sociology of Health & Illness* 40(8): 1312–1326.

Shields, Rob. 2017. "Expanding the Borders of the Sociological Imagination: Spatial Difference and Social Inequality." *Current Sociology* 65(4): 533–552.

Shilling, Chris. 2012. *The Body and Social Theory*, 3rd ed. London: Sage.

Shilling, Chris and Philip Mellor. 2017. *Uncovering Social Life: Critical Perspectives from Sociology*. London: Routledge.

Sparke, Matthew. 2017. "Austerity and the Embodiment of Neoliberalism as Ill-health: Towards a Theory of Biological Sub-citizenship." *Social Science & Medicine* 187: 287–295.

Stoppard, Tom. 1967. *Rosencrantz and Guildenstern are Dead*. London: Faber and Faber.

Tauber, Alfred I. 1995. "Postmodernism and Immune Selfhood." *Science in Context* 8(4): 579–607.

Turner, Bryan S. 1992. *Regulating Bodies: Essays in Medical Sociology*. London: Routledge.

Turner, Bryan S. 2008. *The Body and Society*, 3rd ed. Oxford: Blackwell.

Twigg, Julia. 2006. *The Body in Health and Social Care*. Basingstoke: Palgrave Macmillan.

Twigg, Julia, Carol Wolkowitz, Rachel Cohen, and Sarah Nettleton. 2011. "Conceptualising Body Work in Health and Social Care." *Sociology of Health & Illness* 33(2): 171–188.

Ussher, Jane. 2006. *Managing the Monstrous Feminine: Regulating the Reproductive Body*. London: Routledge.

Waldby, Catherine. 2000. *The Visible Human Project: Informatic Bodies and Post – Human Medicine*. London: Routledge.

Waldby, Catherine. 2002. "Stem Cells, Tissue Cultures and the Production of Biovalue." *Health* 6(3): 305–323.

Wilkinson, Richard and Kate Pickett. 2010. *The Spirit Level: Why Inequality Is Bad from Everyone*. London: Penguin Books.

Williams, Gareth. 1984. "The Genesis of Chronic Illness: Narrative Reconstruction." *Sociology of Health & Illness* 6(2): 175–200.

Williams, Simon. 1996. "The Vicissitudes of Embodiment across the Chronic Illness Trajectory." *Body & Society* 2: 23–47.

Williams, Simon and Bendelow Gillian. 1998. *The Lived Body: Sociological Themes, Embodied Issues*. London: Routledge.

7

Biomedicalization Revisited

Adele E. Clarke, Melanie Jeske, Laura Mamo, and Janet K. Shim

In the late 1990s, five medical sociologists began meeting as a research group at the University of California, San Francisco. All our projects focused on then-emergent phenomena in late-twentieth-century biomedicine, and we were grappling, individually and collectively, with the inadequacies of medicalization theory. As a major theory in medical sociology and anthropology, medicalization posits that the jurisdiction, authority and practices of professional Western medicine have been expanding to include conditions not previously considered "medical" (Zola 1972). We agreed, but were concerned that the concept did not engage recent dramatic expansions of technoscience[1] within and beyond biomedicine, and implications of computer and information sciences for the organization of biomedicine per se. Related disconnects among medical sociology, anthropology and history as well as interdisciplinary fields such as science and technology studies, feminist theory, body studies, and cultural studies also concerned us.

Together we began analyzing shifting processes of biomedicine and key elements in the development of "the biomedicalization of life itself (human, plant, and animal)… often imaged as a juggernaut of technological imperatives" (Clarke 1998: 275). We defined *bio*medicalization as the increasing reliance of medical organization, practices and treatments on technoscientific innovations (e.g. MRIs, CAT scans, new pharmaceuticals) and the reorganization of biomedicine itself from the inside out through application of computer and information sciences (e.g. computerized patient records). We then published largely conceptual articles centered around five newly framed key processes of biomedicalization (Clarke et al. 2000, 2003) and a book of empirical studies (Clarke et al. 2010).

The concept of biomedicalization was soon widely taken up – across disciplines and transnationally. Google Scholar lists 7,140 publications under the concept since

The Wiley Blackwell Companion to Medical Sociology, First Edition. Edited by William C. Cockerham.

our earliest publication in 2000; together our 2003 and 2010 publications have been cited more than 2500 times (searched 23 May 2020).

This chapter first delineates our basic concept of biomedicalization and its five key processes. We then describe highlights in the career of the concept of biomedicalization since 2010, including brief overviews of special issues of journals in other disciplines and languages. Next we focus on three major topics examined by other scholars through biomedicalization lenses: the media; medical devices and technologies; and (often overlapping) precision medicine and precision public health. Each topic demonstrates precisely *how* the five key processes of biomedicalization specifically *and unevenly* took shape. Significantly, each topic features ever stronger patterns of what we called *stratified biomedicalization* – inequalities due to differential access to and use of high-tech biomedicine and its organization. We conclude with discussion of current issues in biomedicalization including COVID-19 and climate change, and note anticipated future directions.

The Concept of Biomedicalization

We viewed the concept of biomedicalization as the "next generation" to medicalization, noting that earlier patterns producing medicalization and its practices do not disappear but often shift, become marginalized, and/or are displaced (Clarke et al. 2000, 2003). We asserted a historiography: the rise of Western scientific medicine fully established the medical sector of the US political economy by the end of World War II, constituting the first "social transformation of American medicine" (Starr 1982). Then, in ongoing processes called *medicalization*, the jurisdiction, authority, and practices of medicine began expanding, redefining areas once deemed moral, social, or legal problems (such as alcoholism, drug addiction, and obesity) as medical problems (e.g. Conrad 1975; Zola 1972), constituting a second transformation. Demedicalization processes also occur (Fox 1977). Since around 1985, dramatic and especially technoscientific changes in the constitution, organization, and practices of contemporary biomedicine have coalesced into *biomedicalization*, the third major transformation of American medicine.[2]

Biomedicalization continues today, organized around five key interactive processes outlined in our early work. These are:

1. a new biopolitical economy of medicine, health, illness, living, and dying together forming increasingly dense and elaborate arenas in which biomedical knowledges, technologies (including pharmaceuticals), devices, services, and biocapital are ever more co-constituted;
2. a new and intensifying focus on health (in addition to illness, disease, and injury), on optimization and enhancement of bodies and health by technoscientific means, and on elaboration of risk and surveillance at individual, group,[3] and population levels;
3. technoscientization of biomedical practices where interventions for treatment and enhancement are progressively more reliant on sciences and technologies, are conceived in those very terms, and are ever more promptly applied, often displacing lower tech and less costly alternatives;

4. transformations of biomedical knowledge production, information management, distribution, and consumption especially through applications of computer and information sciences and enhanced media coverage; and
5. transformations of bodies and the production of new technoscientific identities, again at individual, group, or population levels, potentially foundational for social movement formation.

Together, these five processes both constitute and produce biomedicalization. While descriptive, these processes may also be used as a set of analytics. As heuristics to think with, researchers can *ask whether and how each of these processes pertains to their topic of inquiry*.

Further, just as medicalization practices typically emphasize exercising *control over* medical phenomena – diseases, illnesses, injuries, bodily malfunctions – in contrast, biomedicalization practices emphasize *transformations of* such medical phenomena and of bodies *per se*. Such transformations are largely accomplished through sooner-rather-than-later technoscientific interventions not only for treatment but also increasingly for prevention, enhancement, and digitized means of monitoring.

The crux of the concept of biomedicalization is that biomedicine broadly conceived is increasingly and rapidly transforming from the inside out. The life sciences and technosciences which undergird and inform biomedicine are also similarly organizationally remade. Significantly, both biomedical practices *and institutions* are being transformed through old and new social-organizational-technological (especially digital) arrangements. Together they intervene in health, illness, healing, the organization of medical care, embodiment, and how we think about and live "life itself."[4]

Our synthetic concept of *bio*medicalization asserted changes in biomedical domains, signaled by adding the *bio* to do several kinds of work. First and foremost, it signals the increasing importance of *biological sciences* (also referred to as the life sciences) to biomedicine. Second, the *bio* signals that issues of *biopower* and *biopolitics* theorized by Foucault are integral to *bio*medicalization. Foucault (1973, 1984, 2008) argued that biopower exerts diffuse and continuous surveillance and control over living bodies – individuals, groups, and populations. Extending Foucault, Rose (2007) theorized "vital politics" as the profound reframing of the life sciences based on new molecular level understandings, including new forms of production created by molecularization.

"Vital politics" then led to the third way that "bio" informs biomedicalization – our key process of a new *biopolitical economy* of medicine, health, and illness. The terms "bioeconomy" and "biocapital" (Cooper 2008; Sunder Rajan 2017) capture how segments of financial capital have been integrated with biological sciences and technologies, biomedicine, megacorporate pharmaceutical and biotechnological industries.

For Sunder Rajan (2012), this "lively capital" involves both the commercialization of the life sciences, and the lively affects – excitement and desires – generated when such commercialization makes promises about improving embodiment, health – and life itself. It is a key part of "speculative capitalism," extensions of venture capital (high risk investment) into biotech domains. Thompson's (2013) term "promissory capital" asserts that much stem cell, genetics, and regenerative research falls within this domain, offering *promises* of future products that may or may not be fulfilled. *Key here, the future-oriented hopefulness — and hype — so characteristic of "lively capital" further legitimate biomedicalization.*

Significant for biomedicalization theory, Cooper and Waldby (2014) analyze "clinical labor" done by tissue donors, research subjects and consumers in clinical trials, surrogacy, and assisted reproduction in this emerging global bioeconomy (paid, underpaid and unpaid), central to generating new products and treatments. Clinical labor is a distinctive form of labor that produces "biovalue," value generated through biotech manipulations usually at cellular or molecular levels of living processes to generate new products and treatments such as stem cell therapies (Waldby 2002: 310).

In sum, biological sciences, biopower, and bioeconomies, biocapital, and biovalue can be understood as forming emergent and already dense theoretical webs within which our concept of biomedicalization and its five key processes make even deeper sense. Thus the trends we identified in 2003 have not only been sustained but theoretically elaborated. Importantly, they have also been taken up to delineate *empirical* specificities.

Our 2010 edited book, *Biomedicalization: Technoscience, Health and Illness in the US*, brought together empirical articles on each of our and others' research projects that inspired our collective theorizing and empirically grounded our conceptual development of biomedicalization. Wide-ranging projects examined new translations of risk into diagnostic and treatment practices (Shim, Shostak, Orr); use of pharmaceuticals, devices and technologies for newly defined medical subjects (Mamo, Fishman, Fosket, Kahn); and impacts of digital imaging and visual cultures on (bio) medicine (Clarke, Joyce). Important here, the book presaged the three major topics in recent biomedicalization scholarship we review below in "Biomedicalization in Practice."

The Career of Biomedicalization

Related Concepts: The Four "Izations"

In addition to medicalization (Conrad 1975; Zola 1972) and biomedicalization (Clarke et al. 2000, 2003, 2010), two additional "izations" are significant here: geneticization (Hedgecoe 1998; Lippman 1991), and pharmaceuticalization (Williams et al. 2008).

Lippman (1991: 19) coined the concept *geneticization* to signify when differences between individuals are simplistically reduced, "with most disorders, behaviors and physiological variations defined, at least, as genetic in origin… Through this process, human *biology* is incorrectly equated with human *genetics*." Geneticization was at the heart of critiques of the U.S. Human Genome Project (Bell and Figert 2015: 31). However, Hedgecoe (1998) found Lippman's and others' essentially solely negative views of geneticization unsophisticated and unproductive, seeking instead to provide more depth as a process, and offer a multi-faceted research manifesto. A vast amount of research ensued, some discussed below.

In sociology, Williams, Martin and Gabe (2011: 710) view *pharmaceuticalization* as "heterogeneous socio-technical processes" operating at multiple macro- and micro-levels, often partial or incomplete. Key dynamics related to expansions of pharmaceutical jurisdiction include: redefinition of health "problems" as having pharmaceutical solutions, including in the media and popular culture; creation of new consumer markets; producing new techno-social identities; and mobilizations of patient/consumer groups around drugs.

Pharmaceuticalization recognizes the outsized role of the pharmaceutical industry in dissemination of information, research, and provision of biomedicine and over-the-counter (OTC) healthcare. While physicians remain gatekeepers, pharmaceutical advertising is rampant – including to physicians themselves – and OTC medications and products are increasingly available and profitable. Anthropologists' studies of pharmaceuticalization examine intersections of pharmaceutical industries, clinical medicine, NGOs, and patients that produce individual well-being as a commodity, a distinct achievement for some, while others dwell in clinical limbo or altogether outside treatment (Biehl 2006; Petryna and Kleinman 2006; Whitmarsh 2008).

The concept of biomedicalization, we believe, generically subsumes geneticization and pharmaceuticalization, especially through constitutive processes of technoscientization and transformations of biomedical knowledge production and consumption. Both are, in principal, technoscience-based forms of biomedicine, hence sub-parts of biomedicalization as a more inclusive concept. But in so claiming, we also emphasize that biomedicalization in no way automatically displaces geneticization or pharmaceuticalization (or any other technoscientific transformation) analytically. Rather, the process having primacy of *analytic* place should be an *empirical question* in any research project.

Bell and Figert's (2015) valuable co-edited book, *Reimagining (Bio)medicalization, Pharmaceuticals and Genetics: Old Critiques and New Engagements*, helps in understanding these issues. Rather than pitting these concepts against each other, Bell and Figert judiciously discuss them as "the 4 'izations.'" Each is illustrated through sections on stratified (bio)medicalization vis-à-vis gender and race, pharmaceutical technologies and regimes, genetics/omics of race, and social determinants of health. Most striking about the volume – and literatures reviewed below – is the proliferation and relentlessness of stratifying effects accomplished through "the 4 'izations.'"

Journal Special Issues on Biomedicalization Topics

Several special issues of journals have focused on biomedicalization, including multi-disciplinary and transnational uptakes of the concept. *Technogenarians: Studying Health and Illness through an Ageing, Science, and Technology Lens* (Joyce and Loe 2011) expands aging studies through biomedicalization, constructing elders not as passive consumers, but as "technogenarians" creatively adapting technologies to fit their needs.

Second, "The Biomedicalization of Brazilian Bodies: Anthropological Perspectives" (Löwy and Sanabria 2016) examines (in Portuguese) how biomedical techniques are taken up across divergent structural constraints afforded by private and public health. Analyzing specific "local biologies" (Lock 2001), articles reveal pervasive violence particularly directed at women's bodies, exceptional forms of care under extreme precarity, and the symbolic capital afforded by consumption of "things medical" as signifying modernity and citizenship. Heavily stratified, biomedicine in Brazil unevenly spans from lavish "boutique biomedicalization for optimization" to bare life and "letting die" (e.g. Scheper-Hughes 1992).

Third, in a special issue of the British journal *Medical Anthropology Theory*, Moyer and Nguyen (2016: i–ii, v) ask: "What if… 'biomedicalization' (Clarke et al. 2003) is to the twenty-first century as industrialization was to the nineteenth?" While industrialization relied on surplus labor to produce value, biomedicalization hinges on "*how harnessing vital bodily substances produces value.*" They note that "struggles over biomedicalization are not limited to white middle-class concerns… they enfold global multitudes." Contributions focus on ethnographies of clinical trials of drugs based on such "bodily substances" in the global South and research on *resistance to biomedicalization*, including challenging the term "noncompliance" as devaluing other forms of clinical assessment, and two radical disability movements.

Finally, transnational uptake of biomedicalization has also furthered analysis of biocapital as biovalue in Brazil (Iriart and Merhy 2017), the biomedicalization of trans bodies and kinship in Northeast Asia (Hsu 2013), comparison of biomedicalized treatments of Type 2 diabetes in the US and Japan (Armstrong-Hough 2018), the biomedicalization of death in Spain (Flores-Pons and Iniguez-Rueda 2012), and a set of five projects on biomedicalization in Norway.[5]

Biomedicalization in Practice

Three substantive areas where biomedicalization has recently been empirically pursued in depth analytically and likely will continue are: health media; innovative medical devices and technologies; and precision medicine and public health.

Biomedicalization and the Media

Clarke (2010) argued that past and present developments of "things medical" are not only accompanied by and reflected in popular visual cultural iconography, but also continue to be in part generated and produced by and through them. Visual iconography includes paintings, photographs, advertisements, packaging materials, books, pamphlets, comic books, magazine images, plays, movies, television shows, etc. As images and objects become constitutive of medical knowledge and practices, they become *healthscapes*: ways of grasping, through words, images, and material culture, patterned changes in sites of health and medicine.[6]

Framing their work explicitly through biomedicalization, Briggs and Hallin (2016) coined the term *biomediatization* as the core process examined in their book *Making Health Public: How News Coverage Is Remaking Media, Medicine, and Contemporary Life*. They ask (2016: 5, emphasis added): "What would happen if we imagined 'the media' as taking up residence in clinics, hospitals, pharmaceutical corporations, and public health offices, *seeing health professionals as embedded in media spheres?*" Their answer is that *biomediatization* (defined as the co-production of medical objects and subjects through complex entanglements between epistemologies, technologies, biologies, and political economies) is *relentless and pervasive.*[7]

Briggs and Hallin's innovation – years before COVID-19 – is understanding and portraying biomediatization as routinely part of our contemporary world, and that *media and health domains are transforming each other*. News coverage of health constitutes a high proportion of all news, and *even before COVID-19* about half of people studied carefully attended to that news. Implications of biomediatization for social justice are elaborated.

Italian scholars Neresini, Crabu, and Di Buccio (2019: 8–9) developed a sophisticated quantitative means of testing our biomedicalization hypothesis in the media. In reporting on health, illness and medicine in newspapers in the UK (*The Guardian)* and Italy (*la Repubblica)* from 1984 to 2017, they found an overall "trend toward the 'biomedicalization of the press,'" with heightened framing of health and medicine issues as matters for technoscientific intervention.

Theoretically the authors echo Clarke (2010) and Briggs and Hallin (2016), emphasizing that the media are a *constitutive environment shaping biomedicalization processes*. Biomedicalization grew in centrality on three dimensions: 1) health and well-being as matters of *individual commitment* to self-monitoring and surveillance (governmentality through optimization); 2) biomedicine as a large, *technoscientific enterprise*; and 3) tensions in national health systems regarding trade-offs between universal health coverage and fiscal sustainability. Individually, media provide resources for gaining "somatic expertise" (Rose 2007) important in generating "the quantified self" (Lupton 2016).

Increased medical press coverage also assures the potency of media voices in controversies. For example, Bhatia (2018) and Bhatia and Campo-Engelstein (2018) studied biomedicalization of social egg freezing (SEF) wherein women bank their oocytes for later use to avoid compromised fertility of aging, comparing ethical opinions of professional organizations in different regions. While the European Society of Human Reproduction and Embryology condoned SEF for reproductive autonomy and justice reasons, the American Society for Reproductive Medicine discouraged it based on insufficient data and concerns about raising false hopes. The British profession took a statist pronatalist perspective. In contrast, US media intervened: While the American profession did *not* endorse SEF, it effectively unleashed "*unrestrained commercialization of SEF*" (Bhatia and Campo-Engelstein 2018: 866). Despite professional opposition, SEF became socially acceptable in the US.

In addition, there is an extant literature on how pharmaceutical advertising is co-produced with public relations, social media, and other "tech" firms generating an ethos of biomedicalization as "lifestyle" engagement, often as neoliberal individualism (e.g. Sulik 2009, 2011). In sum, not only are the media of signal importance in enhancing biomedicalization, but also in demonstrating *how* they are co-constitutive.

Biomedicalization and Biomedical Technologies

The proliferation of biomedical technologies over the past half century has profoundly shaped how we understand, intervene in, and actively resist technoscientific approaches to bodies and lives. The escalating introduction of new biomedical technologies across the spectrum of biomedicine – from the lab bench to patients bedsides, homes, and bodies (e.g. via wearable devices, and home DNA testing) – continues to reshape what we call the *technoscientization of biomedicine*. Biomedical technologies include those we interact with in healthcare settings and those behind the scenes, more invisible (e.g. surveillance technologies in refugee camps).

While Clarke and colleagues (2003) discussed several areas of technoscientization, much has since changed within biomedical infrastructures and practices. Considerable scholarship empirically examines these areas. Here, we selectively consider three broad domains: data technologies (including artificial intelligence, electronic health records, and algorithms), biomedical technologies used in the clinic and at home, and technologies developed for research laboratories.

Algorithmic Care: AI, Electronic Health Records, and Predictive Technologies

Recent sociological scholarship has attended to how automated technologies, such as artificial intelligence (AI) and algorithms, are imbued with social values and power relations, contributing to and exacerbating extant social inequalities through automation of discrimination (Benjamin 2019; Eubanks 2018; Noble 2018). Increasing data-fication of society – mobilization of "data" for various social means – has led to considerable "hype" surrounding data of all kinds. This is driving their often invisible collection, analysis, and use in social institutions including education, law enforcement and criminal justice, surveillance, and healthcare.

In health and healthcare, introduction of data-fication processes and technologies raises important questions about what technologies, created by and for whom, for which purposes, where developed, anticipated and unintended consequences, as well as the values and power relations they make visible. Efforts to integrate disparate patient electronic health record systems, for example, and the mining of this data to offer new insights on the nature of patient and population health, allow for seemingly ever-expanding data sets to be collected on those in healthcare system databases. Yet, these also raise serious issues of data privacy and potential misuse.

Moreover, they enable the ostensibly "automatic" generation of risk: simply by entering data in these systems, patients are flagged as being at risk for conditions often unrelated to the purpose of their visit, thereby triggering new forms of risk assessment and resulting illness management. As genomic testing results are increasingly integrated in electronic health records, new questions emerge about the reach of these data forms and privacy. As ethics organizations, committees, and some bioethicists take up narrow questions of informed consent, doctor–patient relations, etc., others are calling for a more incisive bioethics that addresses questions of community care and social justice (e.g. Mamo and Fishman 2013; Nelson 2016; Reardon 2017; Jeske 2020).

Further, these data systems extend far beyond collecting data on patient health and outcomes; increasingly they are used to further organizational and economic ends. As healthcare costs rise, hospital systems seek data-driven methods to ensure quality care and harness cost. Cruz's (2018) research, for example, describes how anxieties over the performance, quality, and value of social institutions has resulted in quantification of performance metrics. This pattern has turned to "data-driven" accountability reform through quantification of quality in healthcare systems.

Often incentivized by federal health agencies and their regulatory powers, such efforts also discipline clinicians' work, creating new forms of governmentality affecting patients as well (Martin et al. 2013). Moreover, Winslow (2020) reveals how implementation of quality metrics in healthcare systems too often have unintended consequences, shifting attention away from the bedside. Her study of an urban hospital emergency department demonstrates how increased emphasis on measuring quality results in what she calls *protocolization*, whereby accountability tasks and metrics displace patient care. In a similar setting, Darling (2016) ironically found that clinicians often find protocol work-arounds and take on additional *eligibilitization* tasks to better care for patients.

Beyond healthcare delivery data lay an abundance of "*lifestyle* health data" collection tools. Smartphones integrate gathering health data (e.g. step counters), if not for some immediate purpose, for the promise that such data has future value (Rab Alam 2016). Health – and our ability to track, manage, and optimize it – are built into the very infrastructures of technologies used in daily life, highlighting the ever-expanding reach of biomedicine, and potential expansions of biomedicalization.

Biomedical Technologies and the Expanding Clinic

Over the past 20 years, do-it-yourself (DIY) care technologies have become prominent in how people practice health and medicine in the US (Greene 2016). Both biotech companies and healthcare systems have harnessed this "culture of health and wellness." While "lay" people have long developed their own approaches to caring for themselves, at times embracing or rejecting biomedicine (Joyce and Jeske 2019), harnessing the DIY approach has become important for those working in and capitalizing on new and vast biomedical markets. Here innovators push for expanding (and expanded insurance coverage of) at-home diagnostic technologies (e.g. doc-in-a-box, direct to laboratory testing for HPV and high risk genotypes), virtual systems for care delivery (e.g. telemedicine services), and tracking technologies that report vitals and other health measures to clinicians for remote monitoring. Even "open" production of pharmaceuticals (e.g. insulin) in home and community settings is underway (Foti in prep.).

While virtual and DIY effors may promote democratization of biomedicine and decrease utilization of certain clinical services, physical healthcare facilities are still primary sites for seeking and receiving healthcare, and clinicians continue to be gatekeepers for accessing diagnoses and care regimens (Lupton and Jutel 2015). As such, healthcare remains a key site of stratification and inequality, particularly as new technologies reshape how care is accessed and delivered.

Electronic health records and other data technologies are one facet, but so too are technologies that test, surveil, and diagnose patients (Drust 2020; Lupton and Jutel 2015; Sachnowski 2013), as well as those implanted in their bodies (Oudshoorn 2020). Patients entering the clinic are greeted by measurement technologies (electronic thermometers, blood pressure cuffs, and scales) and those making the "inside" visible (increasingly portable/hand-held x-rays, MRIs, CT scans, and digitized diagnostic cameras). This technoscientized care provides individual health data, alerting both patients and providers to new possible risk categories, as well as potential pharmaceutical and care management regimens.

Such technoscientific transformations not only shape care delivery but also patients' expectations. Mamo's (2007) work demonstrated that users can subvert technologies for their own purposes, especially when *not* imagined as intended users. The ability to perform as "expected" and maximize healthcare encounters has been described as a *regime of patienthood* (Joyce et al. 2020; Joyce and Jeske 2019) requiring what Shim (2010) calls "cultural health capital." Shim's concept highlights how the positionality and articulateness of patients impacts patient-provider interactions. Patients' abilities to signal their concerns, competencies, and compliance have implications for how providers approach and invest time with them.

Sulik (2009, 2011) describes how immersion in biomedicine generates "technoscientific illness identities," new forms rooted in biomedical knowledge, advanced technology, and risk surveillance. As clinical (and research) genomic testing have expanded, patients (and research subjects) face new choices about how much they want to know about their genomic risks — decisions often implicating others, as well as their own technoscientific identities. However, choice about permitting data collection is eroding as tissue sampling and data sharing become invisible requisites of informed consent for care.

Telemedicine is an increasingly attractive option for managing healthcare costs, both reducing "unnecessary" clinical visits (Oudshoorn 2011), as well as an alternative in times of crisis when healthcare facilities pose new risks. Writing this chapter amid the COVID-19 pandemic, we are witness to a historic moment in which demand for telehealth applications skyrocketed. In a matter of *weeks*, the rate of using various tele applications in large healthcare systems which had hovered at 2–3% of patient visits leapt to 55% (ACP Hospitalist 2020).

Prior to the pandemic, telemedicine was important in abortion care (e.g. Grindlay et al. 2013). The availability of these alternatives raises crucial questions about who has access to human care, and who is defaulted to distanced and automated services, despite evidence showing human interaction may be critical to effective care (Pugh 2018). As new technologies mediate (and may substitute for) interpersonal interaction, quality care relies heavily on patients to properly use technologies to care for themselves, creating new burdens for patients (Oudshoorn 2011).

Biomedical Technologies in the Lab

Biomedicalization also turns analytic attention to less obvious spaces where new biomedical technologies shape how and what we know about human health and disease. Since the 1980s, advances in biotechnology and genetic engineering have dramatically changed the landscapes of the biosciences (Sunder Rajan 2012, 2017; Thompson 2013). In bioscience laboratories, human cells and models take on new meanings as they stand in as proxies for the complexities of the human condition. Such advances promise to increase detection of risk factors for disease, and treat diseases faster and more effectively – creating a regime of hope and hype in which we are always already anticipating benefits of such advances (Adams et al. 2009).

Yet despite sustained investment – and hype – surrounding such work, few applications that improve health have emerged. The significant expense of these technologies and procedures, alongside uncertainties of such investments, results in deepening public-private partnerships and imperatives toward commercialization of academic biomedical research, particularly as pharmaceutical and biotechnology companies have defunded their own research and development arms (Croissant and Smith-Doerr 2008; Robinson 2019). The promotion of new partnerships and arrangements in recent translational medicine initiatives makes visible how industry interests are increasingly intertwined with state and academic agendas (Jeske in prep.), while the *absence of investment* in other areas is often invisible.

Biomedical technologies in laboratory settings include models, devices, and tests used to understand human health and disease. They are often quite separate from living human bodies, represented instead by proxy non-human model organisms or, if human materials are present, by fragmented forms of DNA, cells, or tissues. Yet the knowledge created using these tools produces the knowledge base for much of what we know about human conditions. Unpacking the construction of these models and tools, and how they do and do not capture social difference, has been a critical contribution of biomedicalization scholarship, highlighting the inherently social nature of biomedicine. Well documented decisions about inclusion in biomedical research and the structure of clinical trials shape to whom results are applicable, and who we have and do not have knowledge about (Epstein 2007; Fisher 2011, 2020).

Moreover, beliefs about difference become embedded within biomedical tools. For example, Braun's (2014) important study of the spirometer demonstrates how slavery-era racist assumptions about lung function continue to shape how lung health is understood differentially according to race today. Thus, laboratories and their technologies become key sites where inequalities are exacerbated. Moreover, such technologies become dangerously invisible, seemingly objective tools, part of the hidden infrastructures of biomedical research. Yet they have been shaped by decisions about what to model and which differences "really" matter.

Significantly, the proliferation of technologies on each of the three technological fronts discussed here (datafication, biomedical technologies and laboratory technologies) enables elaborating visions for personalized precision medicine – the new forefront of biomedicine (e.g. Prainsack 2017).

Biomedicalization, Precision Medicine and Precision Public Health

The concept of biomedicalization has been taken up to understand shifts in medicine and public health knowledge and practices, especially how biomedicalizing processes are constitutive of clinical and population health sciences. Building on existing data-driven approaches in epidemiology and population health, precision medicine (PM) and precision public health (PPH) seek to mobilize information technology and data science to assess and improve health at individual and population levels (Dowell et al. 2016; Khoury et al. 2016; Weeramanthri et al. 2018).

This *datafication* – big data approaches to medicine and public health – includes clinical and genomic information as well as social, environmental, and behavioral factors contributing to differential rates of morbidity and mortality in populations. While PM emphasizes the use of genomic data in clinical care, PPH is a biomedicalized version of public health surveillance. In recent years, these have intensified in form, reach, and scope. PPH, for example, integrates multiple data sets and uses technosciences often in real-time to prevent, track, and respond to outbreaks, addressing spatial inequities through targeted interventions, and improving overall health and disease prevention. In fact, tracing and understanding where and how biomedicalization is enacted in and through PM and PPH reveal that in the twenty-first century, the two domains of clinical medicine and medical science on the one hand, and public health research and practice on the other, are increasingly continuous and mutually constitutive.

Reflecting biomedicalization processes, PM and PPH shape what kinds of subjects and "risks" come to matter, what problems are deemed important, which solutions are framed (e.g. Marshall 2009), what technologies are built, based on which assumptions (Benjamin 2013, 2019), and ultimately what kinds of futures are deemed possible and desirable. PM and PPH are biomedical imaginaries ultimately shaping what many hope for, expect, and fear from science, technology, and medicine (McNeil et al. 2017: 457F).

Moving away from "one-size-fits-all" medicine to tailored treatments and prevention, the biomedicalization of PM and PPH drive ongoing investments in bioinformatics and data infrastructures, despite the fact that "the exuberance that characterized the emergence of venture sciences such as pharmacogenomics and personal genomics has not been fully met" (Juengst et al. 2016; Tutton 2014: 167; Meagher et al. 2017).

Reflecting biomedicalization, the imaginary of "precision" in medicine and public health and its constituent concepts – practices, and discourses as well as actors, institutions, networks, values and cultures – also shape subjectivities and identities. This precision imaginary belongs to a particular "anticipatory regime," where new technologies promise to lead to biomedical breakthroughs, always "just around the corner – coming soon" (Adams et al. 2009: 258). As Adams and colleagues (2009: 257) remind us, "such anticipations are not only diagnostic; they are productive," generating investments. Thus biomedicalization can be seen in medicine and public health approaches where pharmaceutical, biotech, healthcare and technology companies invest in each other, and sell and distribute products, commodities and information to individuals, entities, and governments that can most afford to pay.

As UCSF Professor of Medicine Kirsten Bibbins-Domingo argues, PPH will "telescope down" into the genome, microbiome, and epigenetic profiles of individuals and then "back out" to family, community, and larger social/environmental contexts (Precision Public Health Summit 2016: 6). In future, data from multiple sources may be integrated and brought to bear on pressing public health issues. For instance, epigenetic data could be brought together with environmental data on air quality, and epidemiological data to address asthma rates as well as environmental injustices that disproportionately affect low-income communities and communities of color (Aufray et al. 2016).

Epidemiological data (e.g. surveillance data, registries, infectious disease rates, surveys and other data collection tools) have long been a crucial aspect of public health research and practice. In contrast, information-driven, technologized strategies termed PPH emerged as biomedicalized approaches including "digital epidemiology" (Salathe et al. 2012), "infodemiology" (Eysenbach 2009), "digital pharmacovigilance" (Salathe 2016), and others. As Norton (2013) demonstrates, public health surveys are instruments of biomedicalization.

The COVID-19 pandemic reveals this in real-time as PM and PPH approaches immediately ramped up to surveille, contain, and prevent further spread of the pandemic. Researchers utilizing the virus's genomic signatures track their spread globally, as well as identifying potential therapeutic targets for treatments. Disparities in COVID infection and outcomes have predictably led to possibilities of genetic variations in susceptibility. Genomic databases, enabled by artificial intelligence (AI) data mining platforms, seek to identify potential genetic variants that might confer differential risk of infection or sequelae.

Public health entities also utilize unconventional data sets such as internet search trends and cell phone GPS data to track flows of people, exposures, and movements of health risks. Technology product companies fast became the new faces of public health as digital temperatures and biometric data are combined with cell phone information into an "internet-of-things" triangulated data collection to specify sites of risk and illness. The combination of data-related skills and technologies (e.g. in epidemiology, data linkage, informatics, and communications) and the ability to aggregate, analyze, visualize, and make available high quality data, larger or linked, in close to real time, are at the heart of PPH (Weeramanthri et al. 2018: 3), much like epidemiology lay at the heart of traditional public health (Shim 2014).

Stratified Biomedicalization In/of Precision Medicine and Precision Public Health

Many scholars in sociology, anthropology and science studies examine stratifications productive of medical and public health knowledge and practices. *Stratified biomedicalization* often serves as an anchoring framework for examining mutual imbrications of race, gender, class, and other social differences alongside the construction of the premises and promises of PM and PPH.

Some critically analyze empirical situations where human differences are increasingly, and more "precisely," characterized, identified, monitored, leveraged, and often monetized. In the language of Troy Duster (2006), biomedicine more generally and precision medicine specifically sort and stratify. Biomedicalization thus provides a twinning logic for cooptation and disciplining, inclusion and exclusion, which selects for and promotes different differences for scrutiny, intervention, or neglect. Others, such as Mamo and Epstein (2014, 2016), examine how sociotechnical trajectories of HPV vaccination exemplify direct-to-consumer disease awareness and advertising campaigns of biomedicalization, and how vaccination has become an unevenly distributed public health approach to cancer prevention.

The uneven distribution of biomedicalization across social groups continues as a defining feature of twenty-first-century biomedicine and public health. The stratifying dynamics of biomedicalization occur as some people and groups, mostly higher-income and residing in high-resource countries, are over-exposed to biomedical interventions. Others, mostly low income or poor, living in high-income or low resource countries, are under-exposed – unless they are subjects in clinical research trials (Fisher 2020; Whitmarsh 2008).

Many communities, especially Black, immigrant, and other communities of color in the US, have long been objects of medical neglect of various kinds, under-resourced in terms of medical and other health care services. Simultaneously, they are over-exposed to racism and racist claims about bodies (e.g. Kahn 2013), and exploitative practices in medical research (e.g. Reverby 2012).

In *Body & Soul* and *The Social Life of DNA*, sociologist Alondra Nelson (2011, 2016) engages what we refer to as stratified biomedicalization, offering an important corrective regarding those over-exposed to injustice. Black communities in particular have long engaged science and technology as activist, social movement organizers, genetic information consumers *and* as scientists, medical providers, and researchers. In *The Social Life of DNA*, Nelson (2016) documents how Black people currently use direct-to-consumer genetic tests to actively engage this knowledge. Cost/benefit analyses of the social benefits, risks and harms) are assessed not for individuals but for community justice goals. They anticipate potential harmful use by law enforcement and criminal justice, while carefully moving forward to leverage "data" for purposes that re-center justice and power, specifically for reparations or reconciliation.

The social lives of technosciences, including DNA, have profoundly shaped public health, implicating race and racism, ability and disability, and the containment and surveillance not just of risk and disease but identities, bodies, lives and communities more generally. For example, Bliss (2015: 177, 2018) shows how "classification in public health, government-sponsored industry and the public creates a system in which people are recognized by and recognize themselves in terms of new biomedical technologies of the gene." She argues that interacting processes of geneticization and racialization drive such biomedicalization. Thereby, individuals and groups simultaneously understand themselves to be in need of biomedical expertise and intervention, yet are also prevented from seeing the social and political conditions shaping their health and lives.

Similarly, Vasquez and Garcia-Deister's (2019: 107) examination of the Mexican genome reveals how genome projects globally intersect with economic goals of nation-states; however, "Mexican samples have frequently been re-branded as the source of flexible, pan-ethnic 'Latino' or 'Latin American' DNA." Stratified biomedicalization leads not only to the racialization of ancestry in current projects, but is also viewed as a strategy for states, NGOs, private-public partners, and various health care entities to address health inequities.

Leveraging the biomedicalization framework, Hatch (2016) too traces scientific racism embedded within the rise of a metabolic fetish and politics. As costs of diabetes and its "risk factors" become "a political problem for those who govern" (2016: 7), the state, researchers, and healthcare institutions seek to combine new forms of molecularization, risk assessment, surveillance, and individual- and population-level interventions. These simultaneously produce ideas about metabolic syndrome and racial difference. One example offered is the quest for diabetes prescription drugs targeted for African Americans that simultaneously reproduce African Americans as a risk category. The accompanying rhetoric centers on equitable access to pharmacologic and other treatments for a population who disproportionately suffers from a serious and often lethal chronic condition, and who are disproportionately underserved. This rhetoric promotes the notion that race is biological and genetic while eliding the unequal impacts of racialized agricultural capitalism and food politics.

Kahn (2010, 2013) examines how precision medicine *as* racialized medicine has a decidedly pharmacological bent. BiDil was the first drug approved by the US Food and Drug Administration with a race-specific indication – to treat heart failure among "black" patients. Kahn's analysis exemplifies several biomedicalization framework arguments. Conditions of possibility for making BiDil as a racially specific drug included a biopolitical economy where biomedical knowledges, biotechnologies, health services, and biocapital are increasingly co-constituted, and an intensified focus on population-level differences leading to practices of risk and surveillance. Despite its makers' failure to fully translate the promise of the drug to meet the needs of a racially defined market, BiDil opened new markets. It became a model for analyzing data by race and using categories of race and ethnicity to exploit niche markets and promote commercial interests.

Even where precision medicine explicitly seeks a more expansive and inclusionary ambit (by also including behavioral, environmental, and social determinants), research has fallen short. Shim et al. (2014a; 2014b) found that genomic research, that even includes social determinants of health use concepts of race and ancestry that potentially undermine both the validity of self-defined sociocultural affiliations and the explanatory potentials of social inequalities as *causes* of health inequalities.

In analyzing scientists' conceptions of differences and disparities in gene-environment interaction (GEI) studies, Shim and colleagues also found that scientists characterize race, ethnicity, and ancestry using combinations of self-identified measures with genetic measures of continental ancestry. However, they perceive the latter measures to be far more precise and desirable for methodological reasons. Ultimately, GEI scientists' expansive conceptualizations of the environment yielded to imperatives to molecularize. Environmental phenomena affecting disease incidence were thereby re-defined solely in terms of their molecular components (Darling et al. 2016).

Thus "precision" imperatives, combined with the paucity of methods to include social and political processes that shape health, narrowly funneled knowledge productive efforts (Ackerman et al. 2016, 2017). The technosciences of precision medicine and public health drive both a meticulously molecularized and data-fied quest for essential biological differences *simultaneously paired with* the elision of the social, here racialization and racial hierarchies as sources of health disparities. If cooptative inclusion and strategic exclusion are modes of racialized (or racist) *medicalization*, then the double-sided molecularization and elision of race in precision medicine are a preeminent mode of twenty-first-century *biomedicalization.*

The rhetorical efforts and scientific practices of researchers to study genetic ancestry as genomic variation and as disease risk seem to be race-blind on their face. Yet they encode and reinforce deeply racialized understandings of health and its production and distribution. As Hatch (2016: 113) observes, these forms of color-blindness, the making-invisible made possible through the molecularization of race, constitutes "a new racial formation." In contrast, as Nelson (2016) shows, if we shift the empirical grounding and focus on *community engagements* with technoscience, the intersections of genetics, surveillance, data and data security, liberation, justice and inclusion, and other social processes are shown to be co-productive.

Alleviating health disparities has been central to proposals for PPH. The Precision Public Health Summit (2016: 16), co-sponsored by the University of California, San Francisco, the Obama White House, and the Bill & Melinda Gates Foundation, asked: How might precision approaches be leveraged to improve health equity? Following Obama's precision medicine initiative and the All of Us initiative, Summit organizers similarly argued that public health will be able to capitalize on new precision medicine approaches by "creat[ing] new tools for capturing the data needed to measure the environmental and social aspects of health at the population level." Data collection, integration, and real-time analyses were deemed the means of achieving more equitable public health outcomes by precisely targeting "meaningful intervention and prevention" (Precision Public Health Summit 2016: 12).

Significantly, this vision for a more equitable future requires large-scale investments in data infrastructures and analytic capacities, so that "large swaths of seemingly disparate data sets" (Precision Public Health Summit 2016: 14) can be integrated and shared among diverse stakeholders. Yet again, funding is channeled into the tech sector rather than healthier housing and improved community infrastructures.

Further, in their analyses of PPH and its application to spatial dynamics of cancer prevention in San Francisco, Kenney and Mamo (2019) argue that such approaches can loop back to re-create similar forms of targeted surveillance and containment strategies to twentieth-century medicalization practices. Yet the increased investment in data collection and infrastructure for precision approaches may ultimately not be the best approach for addressing health disparities or creating health equity because it leaves the social determinants of health and root causes of unjust health disparities largely untouched. Biomedicalization, with its concomitant big data technosciences, may be able to spatially and genomically target interventions at the population level, but is also important to anticipate other harmful travels. The solutions of PPH – increased surveillance and data gathering, biomedical interventions, and targeted risk-reduction strategies – may exacerbate the very inequalities they seek to address: further stigmatizing already marginalized populations without changing their social and economic circumstances; and shifting funding and attention away from strategies for addressing health disparities that are not framed explicitly in the terms of biomedicine or bioinformatics (Kenney and Mamo 2019).

Conclusions: Current Issues in Biomedicalization

While futures of biomedicalization will likely involve issues discussed above and others, to conclude we feature two current directions we are confronting and beginning to parse.

Stratified Biomedicalization and COVID-19

"*There's no money in being prepared for a pandemic.*"[8]

As noted, *stratified biomedicalization* is essentially *differential access to and use of high-tech biomedicine and its means of organization.* The current COVID-19 pandemic all too vividly demonstrates how profoundly stratified health care is in the US, especially access to biomedicine and its technoscientific tools. The statistics are damning.

Native Americans suffer the second highest infection rate per capita in the US; even after votes and promises were made, tribes still had to sue the US over delays in COVID response funding.[9] In the largely working-class Latinx Mission District of San Francisco, 90% of those infected "could not work from home" because they were in food service or construction trades.[10] In Iowa, Latinos were 20% of cases but only 6% of the population; in Washington State they were 31% of cases and 13% of the population.[11] In San Francisco, more than half of COVID deaths were Asian-American, despite their being only one third of the population.[12]

For African-Americans, losses are profound and on-going. In Louisiana, blacks account for 70% of the deaths but 33% of the population,[13] due in part to Mardi Gras *not* being cancelled as the epidemic first hit (Villarosa 2020). Bias in virus care also haunts black families and communities: black people who visited hospitals with COVID-19 symptoms in February and March were less likely to be tested or treated than white patients.[14] More nursing home outbreaks occurred in predominantly Black facilities which had less protective gear for staff; in one, staff were given plastic raincoats![15]

Inextricably intersectional class and race divides are the underlying problems. Race and income have long been the largest factors in determining who lives and who dies.[16] For Americans living in poverty, keeping six feet apart is a luxury beyond reach – inmates, farm workers, detained immigrants, Native Americans and homeless families.[17] A newspaper headline trumpeted: "COVID-19's Race and Class Warfare," is exposing "the savagery of American democracy and the economic carnage it has always countenanced."[18]

Yet health scholars and practitioners have studied and understood these problems and inequities *for decades*. None of these practices are new. "*We are looking at societal policies, driven by institutional racism, that are producing the results that they were intended to produce*" (Villarosa 2020: 39; Bayer and Galea 2015). Biomedicalization allows us to see how bioeconomies shape where health care is located, in what forms, who does and does not have access, who benefits most and who is excluded. Further, it allows us to interrogate the technosciences of possibility, such as whether a vaccine will be available to all or will some merely continue as objects of disease surveillance. These are among the issues facing the next generation of scholars.

Biomedicalization, the Environment and Climate Change

Second, the climate crisis currently facing the world requires understanding its socio- and geopolitical roots and the potentials of technoscience and biomedicine to begin to accomplish needed changes. The biomedicalization of public health as PPH has marginalized environmental considerations, focusing instead on individual factors (Luna 2007). "The proportion of NIH-funded projects with the words 'public' or 'population' in their title... dropped by 90% over the past 10 years (Bayer and Galea 2015: 501). Environmental racism also enters here, making people living near pollution sources more vulnerable – often people of color: "[T]he risks of death from COVID-19 are also affected by long-term exposure to air pollution" (Villarosa 2020: 38).

Recent analyses that the climate crisis *is a health crisis* demand that biomedicine reckon with coming catastrophes (Manning 2020). Some medical schools are gearing up to include curricula on biomedicalized treatment of acute and chronic climate-related illnesses due to fires (respiratory), flooding (water contamination and mold) and related disorders. Pharmacists are learning that grabbing computers with listings of patients' prescriptions or saving such lists to the cloud can also save lives. But technology will not save us if we don't understand how to use it to address environmental justice concerns.

Seemingly one trade-off of such biomedicalization is that enhanced safety precautions come at the price of extended surveillance, recently named "surveillance capitalism" (Zuboff 2019). For example, percentages of residents staying home on a given day of the COVID pandemic were calculated by analysis of cellphone location data.[19] Whether enacting policies that actually limit environmental degradation and remove environmental threats from residential areas – enacting environmental justice – will occur remains a major question and quest.

In sum, we anticipate continued elaboration of biomedicalization – and research on it, "bio," "medicine," and "in between" that is increasingly transdisciplinary and transnational (Löwy 2011). The scientization of medicine has been uneven across specialties, hence we anticipate the clinic will become as rich a site as the laboratory has been (e.g. Latimer 2013). The clinic will also be the site of application of new forms of biovalue generated by emerging biomedicalized interventions based on harnessing vital bodily substances to address both disease and enhancement. We can also anticipate a flood of "outbreak science," much of it seeking biomedicalization of risks as well as treatments. But perhaps the most fundamental issues are transnational political-economic choices of intensified investments in the potentials of high-tech biomedicalized PPH compared with investments in basic public health strategies such as clean water, sanitary housing, waste management – and, radically, clean air – to avoid further stratified biomedicalization.

Notes

1 "Technoscience" indicates that science and technology are not easily distinguishable as "basic" and "applied," but should be understood as co-constitutive and hybrid (Latour 1987), intensified of late through enhanced integration of computer and information sciences.

2 Our view, then, as now, is that while biomedicalization is increasingly common, both *medicalization* (e.g., Conrad 1975, 2007; Zola 1972) and *demedicalization* (Fox 1977) also continue (Clarke et al. 2010).

3 On "niche standardization," see Epstein (2007).

4 For an overview, see Table 1: "The Shift from Medicalization to Biomedicalization" in (Clarke et al. (2003): 168–169; (2010): 53–54).

5 See https://www.med.uio.no/helsam/english/research/projects/biomedicalization-inside-out.

6 In generating this concept, she drew upon Appadurai's (Appadurai 1996: 33–35) scapes.

7 Briggs and Hallin also co-organized an international interdisciplinary conference at UC Berkeley, "Circulating Health: Mediatization and the (Im)Mobilization of Medical Subjectivity" in 2017, with a session on "Mediatization vis-à-vis Biomedicalization".

8 *The New York Times*, 8 May 2020, p. A29.
9 *The New York Times*, 2 May 2020, p. A9.
10 *The San Francisco Chronicle*, 5 May 2020, pp. A6–A7.
11 *The New York Times*, 8 May 2020, p. A12.
12 *The San Francisco Chronicle*, 20 May 2020, pp. A1, A8.
13 *The New York Times*, 19 April 2020, pp. SR14–15.
14 *The New York Times*, 11 May 2020, pp. A1, A9.
15 *The New York Times*, 22 May 2020, pp. A1, A8.
16 *The New York Times*, 5 May 2020, p. A13.
17 *The New York Times*, 13 April 2020, p. A1, A15.
18 *The New York Times*, 4 May 2020, p. A 23.
19 *The New York Times*, 14 May 2020, p. A10.

References

Ackerman, Sara L., Katherine Weatherford Darling, Sandra Soo-Jin Lee, Robert A. Hiatt, and Janet K. Shim. 2016. "Accounting for Complexity: Gene-Environment Interactions and the Moral Economy of Quantification." *Science, Technology & Human Values* 41(2): 194–218.

Ackerman, Sara L., Katherine Weatherford Darling, Sandra Soo-Jin Lee, Robert A. Hiatt, and Janet K. Shim. 2017. "The Ethics of Translational Science: Imagining Public Benefit in Gene-Environment Interaction Research." *Engaging Science, Technology, and Society* 3: 351–374.

ACP Hospitalist. 2020, 1 April. "Talking about COVID-19 with Bob Wachter." ACP Hospitalist Weekly. Retrieved from http://www.acphospitalist.org/weekly/archives/2020/04/01/4.htm

Adams, Vincanne, Michelle Murphy, and Adele Clarke. 2009. "Anticipation: Technoscience, Life, Affect, Temporality." *Subjectivity* 28(1): 246–265.

Appadurai, Arjun. 1996. *Modernity at Large: Cultural Dimensions of Globalization.* Minneapolis, MN: University of Minnesota Press.

Armstrong-Hough, Mari. 2018. *Biomedicalization and the Practice of Culture: Globalization and Type 2 Diabetes in the United States and Japan.* Durham, NC: University of North Carolina Press.

Auffray, Charles, Timothy Caulfield, Julian L. Griffin, Muin J. Khoury, James R. Lupski, and Matthias Schwab. 2016. "From Genomic Medicine to Precision Medicine: Highlights of 2015." *Genome Medicine* 8(12): 1–3.

Bayer, Ronald, and Sandro Galea. 2015. "Public Health in the Precision-Medicine Era." *New England Journal of Medicine* 373: 499–501.

Bell, Susan E., and Anne E. Figert (Eds.). 2015. *Reimagining (Bio)Medicalization, Pharmaceuticals and Genetics: Old Critiques and New Engagements.* New York: Routledge.

Benjamin, Ruha. 2013. *People's Science: Bodies and Rights on the Stem Cell Frontier.* Palo Alto, CA: Stanford University Press.

Benjamin, Ruja. 2019. *Race After Technology: Abolitionist Tools for the New Jim Code.* New York: John Wiley & Sons.

Bhatia, Rajani. 2018. *Gender before Birth: Sex Selection in a Transnational Context.* Seattle: University of Washington Press.

Bhatia, Rajani, and Lisa Campo-Engelstein. 2018. "The Biomedicalization of Social Egg Freezing: A Comparative Analysis of European and American Professional Ethics Opinions and U.S. News and Popular Media." *Science, Technology, & Human Values* 43(5): 864–887.

Biehl, João. 2006. "Pharmaceutical Governance." Pp. 206–239 In *Global Pharmaceuticals: Ethics, Markets, Practices*, edited by Adriana Petryna, Andrew Lakoff and Arthur Kleinman. Durham, NC: Duke University Press.

Bliss, Catherine. 2015. Biomedicalization and the new science of race. In *(Bio) Medicalization, Pharmaceuticals and Genetics: Old Critiques and new Engagements*, edited by Susan E. Bell and Anne E. Figert, pp. 175–196. New York: Routledge.

Bliss, Catherine. 2018. "Biomedicalization in the Postgenomic Age." In *Routledge Handbook of Genomics, Health and Society*, edited by Sahra Gibbon, Barbara Prainsack, Stephen Hilgartner, Janelle Lamoreaux, Pp. 15-23 New York: Taylor and Francis.

Braun, Lindsay. 2014. *Breathing Race into the Machine: The Surprising Career of the Spirometer from Plantation to Genetics.* Minneapolis, MI: University of Minnesota Press.

Briggs, Charles, and Daniel Hallin. 2016. *Making Health Public: How News Coverage Is Remaking Media, Medicine, and Contemporary Life.* London: Routledge.

Clarke, Adele E. 1998. *Disciplining Reproduction: Modernity, American Life Sciences and the "Problems of Sex"*. Berkeley, CA: University of California Press.

Clarke, Adele E. 2010. "From the Rise of Medicine to Biomedicalization: U.S. Healthscapes and Iconography c1890-Present." In *Biomedicalization: Technoscience and Transformations of Health and Illness in the U.S.*, edited by Adele E. Clarke, Jennifer Fosket, Laura Mamo, Janet K. Shim and Jennifer Fishman, pp. 104–146. Durham, NC: Duke University Press.

Clarke, Adele E., Jennifer Fosket, Laura Mamo, Janet K. Shim, and Jennifer Fishman (Eds.). 2010. *Biomedicalization: Technoscience and Transformations of Health and Illness in the U.S.* Durham, NC: Duke University Press.

Clarke, Adele E., Janet Shim, Jennifer Fosket, Jennifer Fishman, and Laura Mamo. 2000. "Technoscience and the New Biomedicalization: Western Roots, Global Rhizomes." *Sciences Sociales et Sante* 18(2): 11–42.

Clarke, Adele E., Janet K. Shim, Laura Mamo, Jennifer Ruth Fosket, and Jennifer R. Fishman. 2003. "Biomedicalization: Technoscientific Transformations of Health, Illness, and US Biomedicine." *American Sociological Review* 68(April): 161–194.

Conrad, Peter. 1975. "The Discovery of Hyperkinesis: Notes on the Medicalization of Deviant Behavior." *Social Problems* 23: 12–21.

Conrad, Peter. 2007. *The Medicalization of Society: On the Transformation of Human Conditions into Treatable Disorders.* Baltimore, MD: Johns Hopkins University Press.

Cooper, Melinda. 2008. *Life as Surplus: Biotechnology and Capitalism in the Neoliberal Era.* Seattle: University of Washington Press.

Cooper, Melinda, and Catherine Waldby. 2014. *Clinical Labor: Tissue Donors and Research Subjects in the Global Bioeconomy.* Durham, NC: Duke University Press.

Croissant, Jennifer L., and Laurel Smith-Doerr. 2008. "Organizational Contexts of Science: Boundaries and Relationships between University and Industry." Pp 691–718 In *The Handbook of Science and Technology Studies*, 3rd, edited by Edward J. Hackett, Olga Amsterdamska, Michael Lynch and Judith Wajcman. Cambridge, MA: MIT Press.

Cruz, Taylor. 2018. Reform by Numbers: Accountability and the Sociotechnical Transformation of American Medicine. Doctoral dissertation in Sociology, University of California, San Francisco.

Darling, Katherine W. 2016. Ongoing Crisis: Managing HIV as a Chronic Condition in Biomedicalized Bureaucracies. Doctoral dissertation in Sociology, University of California, San Francisco.

Darling, Katherine Weatherford, Sara L. Ackerman, Robert A. Hiatt, Sandra Soo-Jin Lee, and Janet K. Shim. 2016. "Enacting the Molecular Imperative: How Gene-Environment Interaction Research Links Bodies and Environments in the Post-Genomic Age." *Social Science & Medicine* 155: 51–60.

Dowell, Scott F., David Blazes, and Susan Desmond-Hellmann. 2016. "Four Steps to Precision Public Health." *Nature* 540: 89–91.

Drust, William A. 2020. "Recapturing Control: Robotics and the Shift from Medicalized to Biomedicalized Surgery." *Sociological Focus* 53(2): 207–219.

Duster, Troy. 2006. "Comparative Perspectives and Competing Explanations: Taking on the Newly Configured Reductionist Challenge to Sociology." *American Sociological Review* 71: 1–15.

Epstein, Steven. 2007. *Inclusion: The Politics of Difference in Medical Research.* Chicago, IL: University of Chicago Press.

Eubanks, Virginia. 2018. *Automating Inequality: How High-Tech Tools Profile, Police, and Punish the Poor.* New York: St: Martin's Press.

Eysenbach, G. 2009. "Infodemiology and Infoveillance: Framework for an Emerging Set of Public Health Informatics Methods to Analyze Search, Communication and Publication Behavior on the Internet." *Journal of Medical Internet Research* 11(1): e11. 10.2196/jmir.1157.

Fisher, Jill A. 2011. *Gender and the Science of Difference: Cultural Politics of Contemporary Science and Medicine.* Chicago, IL: Rutgers University Press.

Fisher, Jill A. 2020. *Adverse Events: Race, Inequality, and the Testing of New Pharmaceuticals.* New York: New York University Press.

Flores-Pons, Gemma, and Lupicinio Iniguez-Rueda. 2012. "La Biomedicalizacion de la Muerte: Una Revision." [Biomedicalization of Death: A Review.] *Anales de Psicologia* 28(3): 929–938.

Foti, Nicole. In prep. The Struggle for Insulin: Community Science, Activism and the Enterprise to Open Source Pharmaceutical Knowledge. Dissertation in sociology, University of California, San Francisco.

Foucault, Michel. 1973. *The Birth of the Clinic: An Archaeology of Medical Perception.* New York: Pantheon.

Foucault, Michel. 1984. "Biopower." Pp. 258–289 In *The Foucault Reader*, edited by Paul Rabinow. New York: Pantheon.

Foucault, Michel. 2008. *Birth of the Biopolitical: Lectures at the College de France.* Trans. Graham Burchell. New York: Palgrave Macmillan.

Fox, Renee C. 1977. "The Medicalization and Demedicalization of American Society." *Daedalus* 106(1): 9–22.

Greene, Jeremy A. 2016. "Do-It-Yourself Medical Devices – Technology and Empowerment in American Health Care." *New England Journal of Medicine* 374(4): 305–308.

Grindlay, Kate, Kathleen Lane, and Daniel Grossman. 2013. "Women's and providers' experiences with medical abortion provided through telemedicine: A qualitative study." *Women's Health Issues* 23(2): e117-e122.

Hatch, Anthony Ryan. 2016. *Blood Sugar: Racial Pharmacology and Food Justice in Black America.* Minneapolis, MN: University of Minnesota Press.

Hedgecoe, Adam. 1998. "Geneticization, Medicalization and Polemics." *Medicine, Health Care, and Philosophy* 1(3): 235–243.

Hsu, Stephanie. 2013. "Transsexual Empire, Trans Postcoloniality: The Biomedicalization of the Trans Body and the Cultural Politics of Trans Kinship in Northeast Asia and Asian America." *Scholar and Feminist Online* Issue 11(3).

Iriart, Celia, and Emerson Merhy. 2017. "Inter-capitalistic Disputes, Biomedicalization and Hegemonic Medical Model." *Interface - Communication, Saude, Education* 21(63). https://doi.org/10.1590/1807-57622016.0808.

Jeske, Mel. In prep. Humans and Organs on Chips: Modeling the Body in the Translational Era. Doctoral Dissertation in Sociology, University of California, San Francisco, CA.

Jeske, Melanie. 2020. "Lessons from Theranos: Changing Narratives of Individual Ethics in Science and Engineering." *Engaging Science, Technology and Society* 6: 306–311.

Joyce, Kelly, Jennifer E. James, and Mel Jeske. 2020. "Regimes of Patienthood: Developing an Intersectional Concept to Theorize Illness Experiences." *Engaging Science, Technology & Society* 6: 185–192.

Joyce, Kelly, and Mel Jeske. 2019. "Revisiting the Sick Role: Performing Regimes of Patienthood in the 21st Century." *Sociological Viewpoints* 33: 70–90.

Joyce, Kelly, and Meika Loe (eds.). 2011. *Technogenarians: Studying Health and Illness Through an Ageing, Science, and Technology Lens.* New York: Wiley.

Juengst, Eric, Michelle L. McGowan, Jennifer R. Fishman, and R. A. Settersten Jr. 2016. "From 'Personalized' to 'Precision' Medicine: The Ethical and Social Implications of Rhetorical Reform in Genomic Medicine." *Hastings Center Report* 46: 21–33.

Kahn, Jonathan. 2010. "Surrogate Markers and Surrogate Marketing in Biomedicine: The Regulatory Etiology and Commercial Progression of an 'Ethnic' Drug." Pp. 263–288 in *Biomedicalization: Technoscience and Transformations of Health and Illness in the U.S.*, edited by Adele E. Clarke, Jennifer Fosket, Laura Mamo, Janet K. Shim and Jennifer Fishman. Durham, NC: Duke University Press.

Kahn, Jonathan. 2013. *Race in a Bottle: The Story of BiDil and Racialized Medicine in a Post-genomic age.* New York: Columbia University Press.

Kenney, Martha, and Laura Mamo. 2019. "The Imaginary of Precision Public Health." *Medical Humanities.* 10.1136/medhum-2018-011597.

Khoury, Muin J., Michael F. Iademarco, and William T. Riley. 2016. "Precision Public Health for the Era of Precision Medicine." *American Journal of Prevention Medicine* 50(3): 398–401.

Latimer, Joanna. 2013. *The Gene, The Clinic and the Family: Diagnosing Dysmorphology, Reviving Medical Dominance.* London: Routledge.

Latour, Bruno. 1987. *Science in Action: How to Follow Scientists and Engineers through Society.* Cambridge, MA: Harvard University Press.

Lippman, Abby. 1991. "Prenatal Genetic Testing and Screening: Constructing Needs and Reinforcing Inequities." *American Journal of Law & Medicine* 17: 15–50.

Lock, Margaret. 2001. "The Tempering of Medical Anthropology: Troubling Natural Categories." *Medical Anthropology Quarterly* 15(4): 478–492.

Löwy, Ilana. 2011. "Historiography of Biomedicine: 'Bio,' 'Medicine,' and In Between." *Isis* 102(1): 116–122.

Löwy, Ilana, and Emelia Sanabria (eds.). 2016. "The Biomedicalization of Brazilian Bodies: Anthropological Perspectives" *História, Ciências, Saúde-Manguinhos* 23(1): 14–16.

Luna, Marcos. 2007. *The Biomedicalization of Public Health and the Marginalization of the Environment: A Policy History from the Environment to the Hospital and Back Again.* Newark, DE: University of Delaware Press.

Lupton, Deborah. 2016. *The Quantified Self: A Sociology of Self-Tracking.* Cambridge: Polity Press.

Lupton, Deborah, and Annemarie Jutel. 2015. "'It's Like Having a Physician in your Pocket!' A Critical Analysis Of Self-Diagnosis Smartphone Apps." *Social Science & Medicine* 133: 128–135.

Mamo, Laura. 2007. *Queering Reproduction: Achieving Pregnancy in the Age of Technoscience.* Durham, NC: Duke University Press.

Mamo, Laura, and Steven Epstein. 2014. "The Pharmaceuticalization of Sexual Risk: Vaccine Development and the New Politics of Cancer Prevention." *Social Science & Medicine* 101: 155–165.

Mamo, Laura, and Steven Epstein. 2016. "The New Sexual Politics of Cancer: Oncoviruses, Disease Prevention, and Sexual Health Promotion." *BioSocieties* 12(3): 367–391.

Mamo, Laura, and Jennifer R. Fishman. 2013. "Why justice? Introduction to the Special Issue on Entanglements of Science, Ethics, and Justice." *Science, Technology, & Human Values* 38(2): 159–175.

Manning, Cyril. 2020. "The Climate Crisis is a Health Crisis: Medicine Must Reckon with the Coming Catastrophe." UCSF Magazine (Winter):12–13.

Marshall, Barbara L. 2009. "Sexual Medicine, Sexual Bodies and the 'Pharmaceutical Imagination'." *Science as Culture* 18(2): 133–149.

Martin, Graham P., Myles Leslie, Joel Minion, Janet Willars, and Mary Dixon-Woods. 2013. "Between Surveillance and Subjectification: Professionals and the Governance of Quality and Patient Safety in English Hospitals." *Social Science & Medicine* 99: 80–88.

McNeil, Maureen, Michael Arribas-Ayllon, Joan Haran, Adrian Mackenzie, and Richard Tutton. 2017. "Conceptualizing Imaginaries of Science, Technology, and Society." Pp. 435–464 In *The Handbook of Science and Technology Studies*, edited by Ulrika Felt, Rayvon Fouche, Clark A. Miller and Laurel Smith-Doerr. Cambridge, MA/ London: MIT Press.

Meagher, Karen M., Michelle L. McGowan, Richard A. Settersten, Jennifer R. Fishman, and Eric T. Juengst. 2017. "Precisely Where Are We Going? Charting the New Terrain of Precision Prevention." *Annual Review of Genomics and Human Genetics* 18: 369–387.

Moyer, Eileen, and Vinh-Kim Nguyen (Guest Eds.). 2016. "Is the 21st Century the Age of Biomedicalization?" *Medical Anthropology Theory* 3(1): i–vii.

Nelson, Alondra. 2011. *Body and Soul: The Black Panther Party and the Fight Against Medical Discrimination.* Minneapolis, MI: University of Minnesota Press.

Nelson, Alondra. 2016. *The Social Life of DNA: Race, Reparations, and Reconciliation after the Genome.* Boston, MA: Beacon Press.

Neresini, Frederico, Stefano Crabu, and Emanuele Di Buccio. 2019. "Tracking Biomedicalization in the Media: Public Discourses on Health and Medicine in the UK and Italy, 1984–2017." *Social Science & Medicine* 243(1–11): 112621.

Noble, Safiya U. 2018. *Algorithms of Oppression: How Search Engines Reinforce Racism.* New York: New York University Press.

Norton, Aaron T. 2013. "Surveying Risk Subjects: Public Health Surveys as Instruments of Biomedicalization." *BioSocieties* 8(3): 265–288.

Oudshoorn, Nelly. 2011. *Telecare Technologies and the Transformation of Healthcare.* London: Palgrave Macmillan/Springer.

Oudshoorn, Nelly. 2020. *Resilient Cyborgs: Living and Dying with Pacemakers and Defibrillators.* London: Palgrave Macmillan.

Petryna, Adriana, and Arthur Kleinman. 2006. "The Pharmaceutical Nexus." Pp. 1–32 In *Global Pharmaceuticals: Ethics, Markets, Practices*, edited by Adriana Petryna, Andrew Lakoff and Arthur Kleinman. Durham, NC: Duke University Press.

Prainsack, Barbara. 2017. *Personalized Medicine: Empowered Patients in the 21st Century?* New York: New York University Press.

Precision Public Health Summit. 2016. *Summit Report: June 6–7, 2016*. San Francisco, CA: University of California.

Pugh,Allison.2018.AutomatedHealthCareOffersFreedomfromShame,ButIsItWhatPatients Need?TheNewYorker,May22.https://www.newyorker.com/tech/annals-of-technology/automated-health-care-offers-freedom-from-shame-but-is-it-what-patients-need

Rab Alam, Sonia. 2016. Promissory Failures: How Consumer Health Technologies Build Value, Infrastructures, and the Future in the Present. Doctoral Dissertation in Sociology, University of California, San Francisco.

Reardon, Jenny. 2017. *The Postgenomic Condition: Ethics, Justice, and Knowledge After the Genome*. Chicago, IL: University of Chicago Press.

Reverby, Susan M. (Ed.). 2012. *Tuskegee's Truths: Rethinking the Tuskegee Syphilis Study*. Durham, NC: University of North Carolina Press.

Robinson, Mark Dennis. 2019. *The Market in Mind: How Financialization Is Shaping Neuroscience, Translational Medicine, and Innovation in Biotechnology*. Cambridge, MA: MIT Press.

Rose, Nikolas. 2007. *The Politics of Life Itself. Biomedicine, Power, and Subjectivity in the Twenty-first Century*. Princeton, NJ: Princeton University Press.

Sachnowski, Alan V. 2013. "Biomedicalization of Cardiac Risk." *Intersect: The Stanford Journal of Science, Technology, and Society* 6(1): 1–14.

Salathe, Marcel. 2016. "Digital Pharmacovigilance and Disease Surveillance: Combining Traditional and Big-Data Systems for Better Public Health." *Journal of Infectious Diseases* 214(Supp. 4): S399-S403.

Salathe, Marcel, Linus Bengtsson, Todd J. Bodnar, Devon D. Brewer, John S. Brownstein, Caroline Buckee, Ellsworth M. Campbell, Ciro Cattuto, Shashank Khandelwal, Patricia L. Mabry, and Alessandro Vespignani. 2012. "Digital Epidemiology." *PLoS Computational Biology* 8(7): e1002616.

Scheper-Hughes, Nancy. 1992. *Death without Weeping: The Violence of Everyday Life in Brazil*. Berkeley: University of California Press.

Shim, Janet K. 2010. "Cultural Health Capital: A Theoretical Approach To Understanding Health Care Interactions and The Dynamics of Unequal Treatment." *Journal of Health and Social Behavior* 51(1): 1–15.

Shim, Janet K. 2014. *Heart-Sick: The Politics of Risk, Inequality, and Heart Disease*. New York: NYU Press.

Shim, Janet K., Sara L. Ackerman, Katherine Weatherford Darling, Robert A. Hiatt, and Sandra Soo-Jin Lee. 2014b. "Race and Ancestry in the Age of Inclusion: Technique and Meaning in Post-Genomic Science." *Journal of Health and Social Behavior* 55(4): 504–518.

Shim, Janet K., Katherine Weatherford Darling, Martine D. Lappe, L. Katherine Thomson, Sandra Soo-Jin Lee, Robert A. Hiatt, and Sara L. Ackerman. 2014a. "Homogeneity and Heterogeneity as Situational Properties: Producing—and Moving Beyond?—Race in Post-Genomic Science." *Social Studies of Science* 44(4): 579–599.

Starr, Paul. 1982. *The Social Transformation of American Medicine: The Rise of a Sovereign Profession and the Making of a Vast Industry*. New York: Basic Books.

Sulik, Gail A. 2009. "Managing Biomedical Uncertainty: The Technoscientific Illness Identity." *Sociology of Health & Illness* 31(7): 1059–1076.

Sulik, Gail A. 2011. "'Our Diagnoses, Our Selves': The Rise of the Technoscientific Illness Identity." *Sociology Compass* 5(6): 463–477.

Sunder Rajan, Kaushik (ed.). 2012. *Lively Capital: Biotechnologies, Ethics, and Governance in Global Markets.* Durham, NC: Duke University Press.

Sunder Rajan, Kaushik. 2017. *Pharmocracy: Value, Politics, and Knowledge in Global Biomedicine.* Durham, N.C.: Duke University Press.

Thompson, Charis. 2013. *Good Science: The Ethical Choreography of Stem Cell Research.* Cambridge, MA: MIT Press.

Tutton, Richard. 2014. *Genomics and the Reimagining of Personalized Medicine.* Farnham, England: Ashgate Pubs.

Vasquez, Emily E., and Vivette García-Deister. 2019. "Mexican Samples, Latino DNA: The Trajectory of a National Genome in Transnational Science." *Engaging Science, Technology, and Society* 5: 107–134.

Villarosa, Linda. 2020. "Who Lives? Who Dies? How Covid-19 has Revealed the Deadly Realities of a Racially Polarized America." New York Times Magazine, 3 May, pp. 34–39, 50.

Waldby, Catherine. 2002. "Stem Cells, Tissue Cultures and the Production of Biovalue." *Health* 6(3): 305–323.

Weeramanthri, Stephen, Hugh Dawkins, Gareth Baynam, Matthew Bellgard, Ori Gudes, and James Bernard Semmens. 2018. "Editorial: Precision Public Health." *Frontiers in Public Health* 6(121). 10.3389/fpubh.2018.00121.

Whitmarsh, Ian. 2008. *Biomedical Ambiguity: Race, Asthma, and the Contested Meaning of Genetic Research in the Caribbean.* Ithaca, NY: Cornell University Press.

Williams, Simon J., Jonathan Gabe, and Peter Davis. 2008. "The Sociology of Pharmaceuticals: Progress and Prospects." *Sociology of Health & Illness* 30(6): 813–824.

Williams, Simon J., Paul Martin, and Jonathan Gabe. 2011. "The Pharmaceuticalization of Society: A Framework for Analysis." *Sociology of Health & Illness* 33(5): 710–725.

Winslow, Rosalie. 2020. "Failing the Metric but Saving Lives: The Protocolization of Sepsis Treatment Through Quality Measurement." *Social Science & Medicine* 253 (1–10): 115982.

Zola, Irving Kenneth. 1972. "Medicine as an Institution of Social Control." *Sociological Review* 20: 487–504.

Zuboff, Shoshana. 2019. *The Age of Surveillance Capitalism.* New York: Hachette.

8

Health Lifestyles
Bringing Structure Back

William C. Cockerham

In past historical periods, people more or less took their health for granted. That is, they were either healthy or unhealthy, and that simply was the way life had turned out for them. But this attitude has changed. Health today is viewed as an achievement – something that people are supposed to *work* at to enhance their quality of life or risk illness and premature death if they do not (Clarke et al. 2010). The primary mechanism by which health is manufactured or undermined in contemporary society is through health-related lifestyles. Most individuals begin life healthy, but their living conditions and lifestyle practices impact on their prospects for maintaining their health throughout their lives. Consequently, the study of health lifestyles has become an important area of research in medical sociology that will be discussed in this chapter.

Health lifestyles can be defined as collective patterns of health-related behavior based on choices from options available to people according to their life chances (Cockerham 2005, 2021a, 2021b). This definition incorporates the dialectical relationship between life choices and life chances proposed by Weber in his lifestyle concept (Weber 1978 [1922]: 926–39, [1978 [1922]: 531–39]). Health lifestyle choices, as is the case for other types of lifestyles, are voluntary, but life chances – which primarily represent class position – either empower or constrain choices as choices and chances work off each other in tandem to determine behavioral outcomes. In a Weberian context, life choices are a proxy for the exercise of agency and life chances are a form of structure.

Sociologists were slow to recognize the importance of lifestyles on behavior and, ultimately, on health. One reason may have been the influence of Thorstein Veblen's (1994 [1899]) classic, the *Theory of the Leisure Class*, which linked the term "lifestyle" to upper-class ways of living. We now know, as Giddens (1991: 6) pointed

---

The Wiley Blackwell Companion to Medical Sociology, First Edition. Edited by William C. Cockerham.

out, that it would be a major error to suppose that only those in more privileged material circumstances have a lifestyle. Everyone has a lifestyle, even the poorest of the poor. It may not be "stylish," but it nonetheless is a style of life. Moreover, as Giddens (1991), Turner (1992), and others (Clarke et al. 2010, 2003) concluded, lifestyle options have become integrated with physical regimens or routine practices that affect the body one way or another.

For example, the epidemiological transition from acute to chronic illnesses as the major cause of death throughout most of the world places greater emphasis on the relationship between lifestyles and health. This is because chronic diseases – namely, heart disease, cancer, stroke, diabetes, and the like – can not be cured by medical treatment, and health lifestyle practices, such as smoking, alcohol and drug abuse, eating high-fat foods, and lack of exercise can cause health problems and end life prematurely. Unhealthy lifestyle practices like smoking can cause lung cancer, and the afflicted person is likely to die from it regardless of what a doctor may do to forestall the eventuality. Moreover, newly emerging infectious diseases like COVID-19 show that lifestyles are also important causal factors in the transmission of viruses, as seen in "stay-at-home" and "social distancing" preventive strategies. What this means is that the responsibility for avoiding both chronic and infectious diseases ultimately falls on one's self through healthy lifestyle practices. Consequently, achieving a healthy lifestyle has become more of a life or (time of) death option at this time in history.

The Agency-structure Debate

As greater recognition of the role of lifestyles in determining health has emerged, the need for an applicable theory led to the development of health lifestyle theory by the author (Cockerham 2005, 2021b). Any theoretical conceptualization of health lifestyles, however, is affected by the agency–structure debate. The relative contributions of agency and structure in influencing social behavior have been *the* central sociological question since the beginning of the discipline. As Archer (1995: 1) explains: "the vexatious task of understanding the linkage between 'structure and agency' will always retain this centrality because it derives from what society intrinsically is." People make decisions about their behavior (agency) within the confines of a particular social structure that influences the behavior chosen. However, medical sociologists paid little attention to the agency–structure debate in the twentieth century, although it is clearly relevant to theoretical discussions of health and lifestyles. When applied to health lifestyles, the question becomes whether the decisions people make concerning food, exercise, smoking, and the like are mainly a matter of individual choice or are principally molded by structural variables such as social class position and gender.

It is crucial in analyzing any exercise of *agency* that the actor could have acted otherwise is a particular situation if he or she had chosen to do so (Bhaskar 1998). Emirbayer and Mische (1998) suggest, accordingly, that human agency consists of three different elements: (1) *iteration* (the selective reactivation of past patterns of thought and action), (2) *projectivity* (the imaginative generation of possible future trajectories of action in which structures of thought and action may be creatively reconfigured), and (3) *practical evaluation* (the capacity to make effective and normative judgments among alternative possibilities). Agency can thus be considered a process in which individuals recall their past, imagine their future actions, critically evaluate their present circumstances, and choose their behavior based upon their assessment of the situation.

William Sewell (1992: 19) provides a definition of *structures* as "sets of mutually sustaining schemas and resources that empower or constrain social action and tend to be reproduced by that social action." Schemas are transposable rules or procedures applied to the enactment of social life. Resources are of two types, either human (e.g. physical strength, dexterity, knowledge) or non-human (naturally occurring or manufactured) that can be used to enhance or maintain power. Sewell equates resources with the power to influence action consistent with Giddens' (1984) notion of the duality of structure as both constraining and enabling. This duality, while correct, nonetheless contains a contradiction. The enabling function suggests resources increase the range and style of options from which the actor can choose, but constraint means that resources invariably limit choices to what is possible.

Although agency theorists maintain that agency will never be entirely determined by structure, it is also clear that "there is no hypothetical moment in which agency actually gets 'free' of structure; it is not, in other words, some pure Kantian transcendental free will" (Emirbayer and Mische 1998: 1004). This is because, as Bauman (1999) observes, individual choices in *all* circumstances are confined by two sets of constraints: (1) choosing from among what is available and (2) social roles or codes telling the individual the rank order and appropriateness of preferences. People do have the capability to act independently of the social structures in their lives, but the occasions on which they do so appear to be rare. Moreover, in situations such as the COVID-19 pandemic, in which individual choices are constrained by "social distancing" and stay-at-home" orders or requirements to wear masks, structural influences dominate the exercise of agency in health matters. In such circumstances, there is a limited ability to choose otherwise.

Max Weber and Pierre Bourdieu: Bringing Back Structure

Weber

Much of what we know about lifestyles has its theoretical origins in the early twentieth-century work of Max Weber (1978 [1922]). Weber's conceptualization of the dialectical interplay between life choices and life chances as the two primary components of lifestyles seems to accord a dominant role to choice. People have needs, goals, identities, and desires that they match against their chances and probabilities for acquiring; they then select a lifestyle based on their assessments and the reality of their circumstances (Cockerham et al. 1997:325). Therefore, when we consider Weber's influence on conceptualizing health lifestyles, we find that conditions external to the individual like norms, life chances, and other structural dimensions are often submerged in relation to the more robust role for agency or choice (Cockerham 2021a, 2021b). As Frohlich, Corin, and Potvin (2001:782) earlier pointed out:

"When lifestyle is currently discussed within the sociomedical discourse, there is a decided tendency for it to be used in reference to individual behavioural patterns that affect disease status," thereby neglecting its collective (structural) characteristics. In this context, health lifestyles are individually constructed forms of behaviors. This type of approach is an example of Archer's (1995) notion of "upwards conflation" in which individuals are seen as exercising power in a one-way, upwards fashion in society that seems incapable of acting back to influence them.

According to Ringer (2004), Weber never abandoned his commitment to the rational individual as key to understanding social action; however, his theory of action extended well beyond this foundation. Ringer (2004:178) states:

> From 1910 on, Weber explicitly distinguished the work of the sociologist from that of the historian. He thought it possible to detect "regularities" in the realm of social action, cases in which similar "meanings" lead to similar "progressions" of behavior. Sociology, he argued, is concerned with such "types" of progressions, ... [and] develops ... typological concepts and seeks general rules about events.

The bridge from agency to structure for Weber was his construction of "ideal types" that were conceptual entities existing beyond the individual, such as his model of bureaucracy or conceptualizations of macro-level processes like the spread of formal rationality in Western society (Kalberg 1994). Ideal types represented a progression from individuals to structures that allowed him to make general statements about collective patterns of social behavior. For example, in *The Protestant Ethic and the Spirit of Capitalism* (1958), Weber emphasized macrostructure in a mostly "top-down" fashion by showing how social institutions (Calvinist religion) and widespread belief systems (the spirit of capitalism) were powerful forces in shaping the thoughts and behavior of individuals (Sibeon 2004). As Weber (1958:55) himself states: "In order that a manner of life well adapted to the peculiarities of capitalism ... could come to dominate others, it had to originate somewhere, and not in isolated individuals alone, but as a way of life common to whole groups of men."

Therefore, Weber's approach to social action does not favor the individual to the neglect of external conditions; instead, it is multidimensional, which is one of his great strengths as a theorist. Alexander (1983: 55) discusses "normative force as the other major environment of the individual act" and details Weber's multidimensional perspective in his early writings, his retreat from multidimensionality, and his return to it as a mature scholar. Mommsen (1989), like Alexander, Kalberg, and Ringer, also credits Weber with a multidimensional approach to social action. Mommsen (1989:151) finds that even though Weber emphasized the innovative deeds of individuals, he repeatedly pointed out that social processes are largely determined by rigid institutional structures and that individuals are usually helpless against them because, as a rule, their economic interests require adaptation and conformity with the social order. Mommsen (1989: 150) says this about Weber's view of social action:

> He persistently emphasized the key role played by individual action ... Yet at the same time he argued again and again that the life-conduct of individuals is largely determined by socio-economic conditions beyond their control; the average person at any rate has little choice other than to adapt his or her life-conduct to the prevailing social and

economic circumstances; conformity to given conditions and traditions is likely to be the individual's normal reaction.

Consequently, even though the lifestyle concept and others by Weber may reflect an individualist and agency-oriented outlook, major Weberian scholars recognize he did not view patterns of social action as the uncoordinated practices of disconnected individuals (Kalberg 1994; Mommsen 1989; Ringer 2004). Instead, he saw social action in terms of regularities and uniformities repeated by numerous actors over time. As Kalberg (1994: 30) explains, the manner in which the natural random flow of action is transformed into regularities constitutes one of Weber's most basic and central themes. Such regularities evolve in connection to collectivities, such as membership in a particular status group. Kalberg (1994: 30) therefore observes that: "In spite of his methodological individualism, ... Weber never viewed social life as an 'aimless drift' of solitary action-orientations." His focus was not on the way in which people act individually but on how they act in concert, which inescapably leads back to structure.

Bourdieu

In contrast to Weber, Bourdieu (1984) emphasizes the role of structure to the detriment of agency. Examples are seen in his depiction of social class and habitus. He views social class position as the most important determinant of a lifestyle in an assessment that can also be applied to health lifestyles (Cockerham 2021a, 2021b). The structural significance of class position is confirmed in the enduring outcome of better health at the top of *any* class structure and lessening health in descending order the closer toward the bottom (Clouston et al. 2015; Cockerham 2005, 2013, 2021a, 2021b; Rees Jones et al. 2011; Lee et al. 2018; McGovern and Nazroo 2015; Missinne et al. 2015). However, class is not a simple one-dimensional variable. Although some models depict class or socioeconomic status (SES) as a unitary concept or single element, others focus on the different components of SES (education, income, and occupational prestige) and treat them as having distinct or multidimensional effects (Bollen et al. 2001).

Bourdieu (1984: 106) likewise maintains that a social class is not defined by a single or base property, but rather by the structure of the relationships between all pertinent properties, which gives a specific value to each property and to the effects they exert on practices. In order to account for the diversity of lifestyle practices, Bourdieu (1984: 107) suggested that it is necessary to "break with linear thinking, which only recognizes the simple, ordinal structures of direct determination, and endeavor to construct the networks of interrelated relationships which are present in each of the factors."

Therefore, it is the relationships between the various factors or variables comprising the structural features of a particular social class and their lifestyle that is important. Bourdieu maintains that the variables that constitute the constructed class are not equal or dependent upon each other to the same extent; instead, the structure of a class is determined by those variables that have the greatest functional weight. While each component is essential and necessary in providing a representative class-based structure, some variables carry more predictive power (functional weight) as seen in the strength of education's effects on health lifestyles in the US and similarly occupation in Europe (Andrews et al. 2017; Cockerham 2021; Lawrence 2017). However, even though income, education, and occupation are distinct variables providing differing dimensions of social stratification, they are inter-related and structurally connected to each other (Adler et al. 1994; Bollen et al. 2001).

Class position enters into an individual's consideration in Bourdieu's approach to lifestyles with his concept of habitus. The notion of habitus originates with Aristotle, who used the term to describe a profoundly entrenched character attribute (Cockerham 2018; Hinote 2014; Wacquant 2016). Husserl (1989 [1952]: 266–93) centuries later used "habitus" to refer to habitual action that is intuitively followed and anticipated. The concept has since been expanded by Bourdieu (1977: 72–95) to serve as his core explanation for the agency–structure relationship in lifestyle dispositions (Bourdieu 1984: 169–225). Bourdieu (1990: 53) defines habitus as "systems of durable, transposable dispositions, structured structures predisposed to operate as structuring structures, that is, as principles which generate and organize practices and representations that can be objectively adapted to their outcomes without presupposing a conscious aiming at ends or an express mastery of the operations necessary in order to attain them." Stated more simply, the habitus is a cognitive map or set of perceptions in the mind that routinely guides and evaluates a person's choices and options. It is imparted to the individual through socialization that brings the individual an awareness of the social reality of external social structures, such as class position and its accompanying lifestyle. As a class-based view of reality, the habitus provides enduring dispositions toward acting in particular ways deemed appropriate by society at large and/or some class or group therein. Included are dispositions that can be carried out even without giving them a great deal of thought in advance. They are simply habitual ways of acting when performing routine tasks.

Any theory of health lifestyles needs to account for the operations of structure and not just agency. The remainder of this chapter will consider the author's (Cockerham 2005, 2013, 2021a, 2021b) health lifestyle paradigm. While agency is important, it will be argued that structural conditions can act back on individuals and configure their lifestyle patterns in particular ways. Agency allows them to reject or modify these patterns, but structure limits the options that are available and shapes the decisions that are made. It therefore appears that health lifestyles are not the uncoordinated behaviors of disconnected individuals, but are personal routines that merge into an aggregate form representative of specific groups and classes.

A Health Lifestyles Model

Weber associated lifestyles not with individuals but with status groups, thereby treating them as a collective social phenomenon. Weber maintained that status groups are aggregates of people with similar status and class backgrounds, and they originate through a sharing of similar lifestyles. People who wish to be part of a particular status group are required to adopt the appropriate lifestyle if they want to be accepted by those in that group. Status groups are stratified according to their patterns of consumption. These patterns not only establish differences between groups, but they also *express* differences that are already in place (Bourdieu 1984). Health lifestyles are a form of consumption in that the health that is produced is used for something, such as a longer life, work, or enhanced enjoyment of one's physical being (Cockerham 2005). Moreover, health lifestyles are supported by an extensive health products industry of goods and services (e.g. running shoes, sports clothing, diet plans and vitamin supplements, health foods, health club and spa memberships) promoting consumption as an inherent component of participation.

However, while the term health lifestyle is meant to encompass a general way of healthy living, there has been discussion over whether or not there is an overall "health lifestyle." The best evidence suggests that for many people their health lifestyle can be characterized as either generally positive or negative, but for others – perhaps most individuals – both good and bad practices occur in the same lifestyle (Burdette et al. 2017; Cockerham 2021; Cockerham et al. 2017; Maller 2015; Mollborn and Lawrence 2018; Mollborn et al. 2014; Saint Onge and Krueger 2017). As Maller (2015: 61) points out: "In essence, most practices could be said to have both good and bad health outcomes and it is the sum total of participation in a particular set of practices that will result in the observed health outcomes of individual people or groups."

Given the need for a theoretical model of health lifestyles to explain the various facets of its operation, the author developed a paradigm that is presented in Figure 8.1. The arrows between boxes indicate hypothesized causal relationships.

Beginning with box 1, in the top right-hand corner of Figure 8.1, four categories of structural variables are listed that have the capacity to shape health lifestyles: (1) class circumstances, (2) age, gender, and race/ethnicity, (3) collectivities, and (4) living conditions. Each of these categories is suggested by a review of the research literature.

Class Circumstances

The first category of structural variables is class circumstances, which is presented as the most important influence on lifestyle forms. The close connection between class and lifestyles has been observed since the nineteenth century (Veblen 1994 [1899]). However, it remained for Weber (1978 [1922]) to produce the most insightful account of the link between lifestyles and socioeconomic status. Weber (1946) not only found that lifestyles expressed distinct differences between status groups and their adoption was a necessary feature of upward social mobility, but he also observed that influential social strata were "social carriers" of particular ways of living. These carrier strata were important causal forces in their own right as they transmitted class-specific norms, values, religious ethics, and ways of life across generations (Kalberg 1994).

The seminal study detailing class as the most decisive variable in the determination of health lifestyles is Bourdieu's (1984) *Distinction*, which included a survey of differences in sports preferences and eating habits between French professionals (upper-middle class) and the working class. Bourdieu found the working class to be more attentive to maintaining the strength of the male body than its shape, and to favor food that is both cheap and nutritious; in contrast, the professional class prefers food that is tasty, healthy, light, and low in calories. As for leisure sports

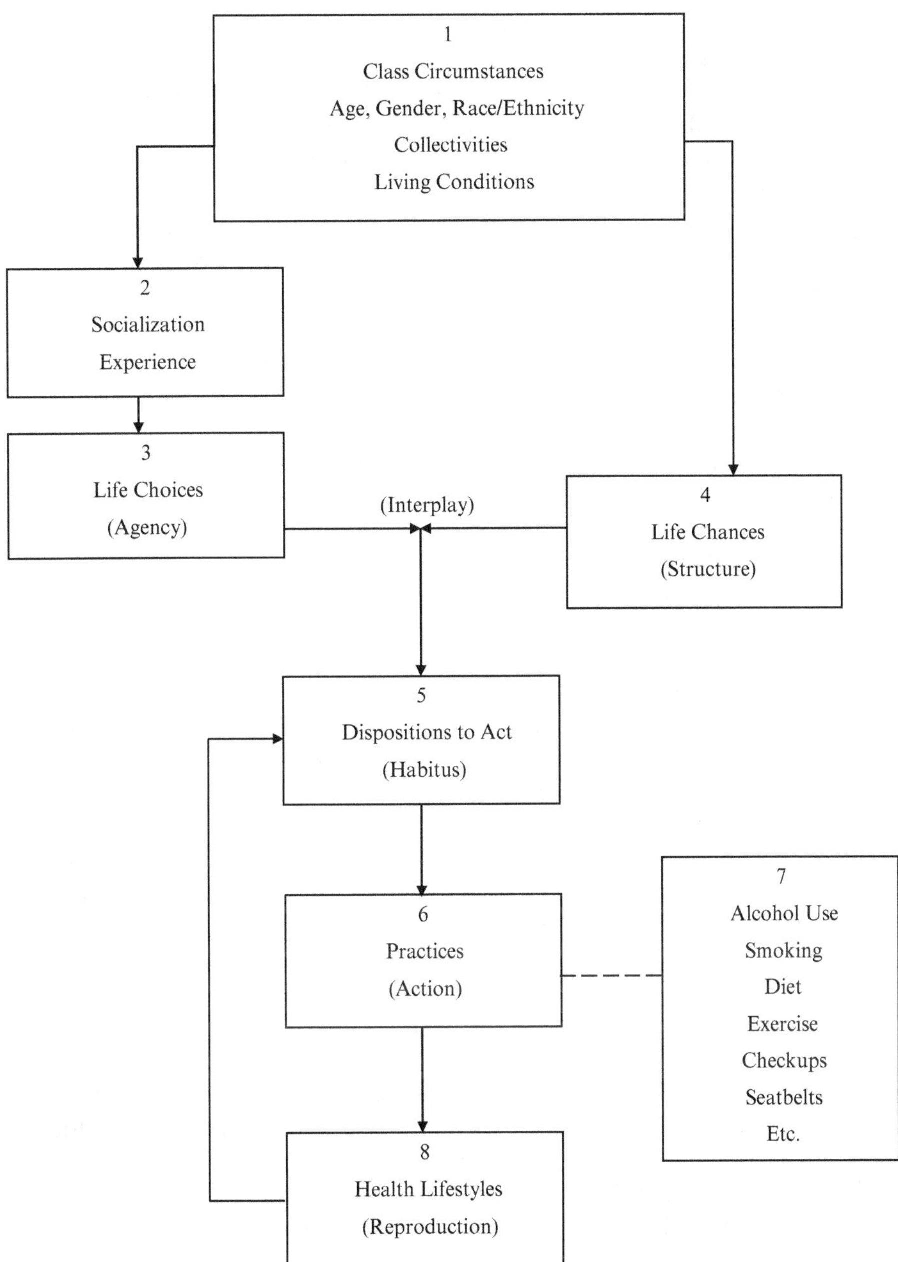

Figure 8.1 Health lifestyles paradigm.

such as sailing, skiing, golf, tennis, and horseback riding, Bourdieu noted that the working class faces not only economic barriers, but also social barriers in the form of hidden entry requirements of family tradition, obligatory dress and behavior, and early socialization. Moreover, these sports are usually practiced in exclusive locations with chosen partners and require investments of money, time, and training that the working class lacks. The working class, in contrast, opts for sports that are popular with the general public and equally accessible to all classes. These are sports like football (soccer), wrestling, and boxing that feature strength, endurance, and violence.

Thus, Bourdieu formulated the notion of "distance from necessity" that emerges as a key explanation of class differences in lifestyles. He points out that the more distant a person is from having to forage for economic necessity, the greater the resources, freedom, and time that person has to develop and refine personal tastes in line with a more privileged class status. Lower social strata, in turn, tend to adopt the tastes consistent with their class position, in which acquiring items of necessity is paramount. For example, Bourdieu (1984: 177) notes that as one rises in the social hierarchy, the proportion of income spent on food diminishes and that within the food budget, the percentage spent on heavy, fattening foods, which are also cheap – pasta, potatoes, beans, bacon, and pork – also declines, as does that spent on wine. But an increasing proportion is spent on leaner, lighter, non-fattening foods and especially fresh fruits and vegetables.

Bourdieu finds that social classes not dominated by the common interests and urgencies of making a daily living claim superiority in social and cultural tastes over those who have only fundamental levels of material well-being. "As the objective distance from necessity grows," states Bourdieu (1984: 55), "life-style increasingly becomes the product of what Weber calls a 'stylization of life,' a systematic commitment which orients and organizes the most diverse practices–the choice of a vintage or a cheese or the decoration of a holiday home in the country." The greater the social distance, the greater the refinement of practices. The relevance of the distance from necessity concept is seen in health lifestyles where classes higher on the social scale have the time and resources to analyze and adopt the healthiest practices.

Similarly, research in France by d'Houtaud and Field (1984) at the same time as Bourdieu, found that different classes also value health in different ways. Health was conceptualized as something to be cultivated for increased vitality and the enjoyment of life among the upper and middle classes, and for the capability to continue to work for the classes below them. For those closest to necessity, being unhealthy meant being unable to work and secure those necessities; however, for those whose resources placed them beyond the range of basic necessity, being unhealthy meant less enjoyment out of life. In sum, lower socioeconomic status (SES) persons viewed health mainly as a means to an end (to be able to work), while higher SES persons regarded health as an end in itself (vitality).

Furthermore, even though health lifestyle practices have a general binary character (positive or negative), such practices may not be exclusively one way or the other in differentiating between lifestyles. They may be a mixture or combination of both good and bad (Burdette et al. 2017; Cockerham et al. 2017; Maller 2015; Mollborn and Lawrence 2018; Mollborn et al. 2014; Saint Onge and Krueger 2017).

For example, even though an upper-class person may engage in health-promoting leisure-time exercise, he or she may also routinely consume rich foods or smoke (Christensen and Carpiano 2014). As Maller (2015: 61) points out: "In essence, most practices could be said to have both good and bad health outcomes and it is the sum total of participation in a particular set of practices that will result in the observed health outcomes of individual people or groups."

Overall, the lifestyles of the upper and upper-middle classes are the healthiest. Virtually every study confirms this. These classes have the highest participation in leisure-time sports and exercise, healthier diets, moderate drinking, little or no smoking, more physical checkups by physicians, and greater opportunities for rest, relaxation, and coping successfully with stress (Andersson 2015; Burdette et al. 2017; Christensen and Carpiano 2014; Cockerham 2021a, 2021b; Lee et al. 2018). The upper and upper-middle classes are also the first to have knowledge of new health risks and, because of greater resources, are most able to adopt new health strategies and practices (Phelan and Link 2013). The advantaged classes are able to move more fluidly to embrace new health behaviors, such as adopting low-cholesterol and low-carbohydrate diets. Advantaged classes were able to reduce their risk of heart disease in the US (which at one time was high relative to the lower class) so that lower-class individuals are now at greater risk. While education is a critical factor, it is, as noted, only one feature of the broader dimension of class membership that enables members of higher social strata to be healthier over the life course. The other factors are income that provides them with the financial resources to live a healthy life and occupational status that provides them with high self-esteem and a sense of responsibility.

Although capitalism is inherently a system of inequality, the paradox is that it has clearly been compatible with significant improvements in overall standards of living and health. Today in most advanced countries, traditional health indicators such as life expectancy and infant mortality have never been better. Infectious diseases that used to take the lives of young and middle-aged people have been severely diminished or curtailed, as in the case of smallpox and polio. COVID-19, however, emerged as a major pandemic in 2019 that was particularly deadly for those with heart and breathing problems and the elderly. Nevertheless, advances in medical care like organ transplants have saved lives, progress in reproductive health has improved fertility, and other measures like hip replacements and surgery for cataracts have enhanced the quality of some people's lives. In the process, the health and longevity of all socioeconomic groups have improved, even though the gap between the top and bottom of society not only persists but in some cases – like in Britain and the U.S. – has even increased. "General health improvement," states Michael Bury (2005: 24), "can therefore occur alongside persisting and even widening inequalities." When it comes to health lifestyles, the advantage likewise accrues to higher social strata.

Age, Gender, and Race/ethnicity

Weber did not consider other stratification variables such as age, gender, and race/ethnicity, yet contemporary empirical studies show that these variables also influence health lifestyles. Health lifestyles go through age-based transitions over the life course

(Burdette et al. 2017; Cockerham et al. 2020; Lawrence et al. 2017; Mize 2017; Mollborn et al. 2014; Mollborn and Lawrence 2018) and tend to be "locked-in" along class lines by old age (Rees Jones et al. 2011). Exercise, however, is one major health lifestyle activity that declines and is generally lost with advancing old age (Grzywacz and Marks 2001; Saint Onge and Krueger 2011). We likewise know that health lifestyles can be affected by marital status (Ross et al. 2016), diverge by gender (Cockerham 2005, 2013, 2018; Flood and Moen 2015; Lee et al. 2018), differ between racial groups (Cockerham et al. 2017), and be adversely affected by racial discrimination (Hill 2016; Sims et al. 2016; Williams and Sternthal 2010). So, while SES collectively has the most functional weight in shaping health lifestyles, such lifestyles can nevertheless be affected to varying degrees by other variables.

Collectivities

Collectivities are collections of actors linked together through particular social relationships, such as kinship, work, religion, and politics. Their shared norms, values, ideals, and social perspectives constitute intersubjective "thought communities" beyond individual subjectivity that reflect a particular collective world view (Zerubavel 1997). The notion of thought communities is akin to Mead's (1934) concept of the generalized other in that both are abstractions of the perspectives of social collectivities or groups that enter into the thinking of the individual. While people may accept, reject, or ignore the normative guidance rendered, collective views are nevertheless likely to be taken into account when choosing a course of action (Berger and Luckmann 1967). Weber (1978 [1922]) notes that concepts of collective entities have meaning in the minds of individuals, partly as something actually existing and partly as something with normative authority. "Actors," states Weber (1978 [1922]: 14), "thus in part orient their action to them, and in this role such ideas have a powerful, often a decisive, causal influence on the course of action of real individuals."

Religion is an example of a collectivity with a strong influence on the health lifestyles of its members. This is seen in the usual preference of highly religious persons and groups for positive health lifestyles since their beliefs invariably promote healthy living in the form of good nutrition, exercise, and personal hygiene, while discouraging alcohol use and smoking cigarettes (Hill et al. 2007; Idler 2014). Several studies have associated religious attendance with positive self-rankings of health in Europe (Huijts and Kraaykamp 2011 and the U.S. (Stroope and Baker 2018). However, the full extent of the relationship between religiosity and health lifestyles has yet to be fully researched.

The influence of collectivities on health lifestyles is also obvious in studies of the families, peer groups, and religion. The family typically influences how a particular person perceives his or her health situation (Cockerham 2021a). Most individuals are born into a family of significant others – significant because they provide the child with a specific social identity. This identity includes not only an appraisal of physical and intellectual characteristics but also knowledge about the family's social and medical history. In addition to learning the family's social status, perspective, and cultural orientation, the child learns about the health threats most common for the family and the measures needed to cope with them, as well as being familiarized with and observing the enactment of family health lifestyles by adult relatives.

Although the initial social world presented to children by their significant others may be weakened by later social relationships and experiences, it can nonetheless be a long-lasting influence. Parental guidance, for example, has been found to be the most important and persistent influence on the health beliefs of children and significant in shaping their health lifestyles (Mollborn et al. 2014; Mollborn and Lawrence 2018). Such influences (good or bad) seem to underlie the transition of health lifestyles as they evolve out of childhood and adolescence into adulthood (Burdette et al. 2017; Lawrence et al. 2017; Lee et al. 2018; Mize 2017; Mollborn and Lawrence 2018). Other studies find that adolescent health lifestyles not only reflect family influence but those of schools and peers, which, in the case of peers, is not necessarily positive with respect to diet, drinking, and smoking. Social status (being seen as "cool") in peer groups can offset healthy lifestyle practices learned in the home (Mollborn and Lawrence 2018; Stead et al. 2011).

Living Conditions

Living conditions are a category of structural variables pertaining to differences in the quality of housing and access to basic utilities (e.g. electricity, gas, heating, sewers, indoor plumbing, safe piped water, hot water), neighborhood facilities (e.g. grocery stores, parks, recreation), and personal safety. In the US, living in disadvantaged neighborhoods has been associated with a less positive health status (Browning and Cagney 2002, 2003), heavy drinking (Chuang et al. 2005; Hill and Angel 2005), less outdoor exercise (Grzywacz and Marks 2001), and greater obesity (Lippert 2016). For example, adolescents from poor neighborhoods are more likely to become obese during the transition to adulthood and remain obese than those who have not lived in poor neighborhoods (Lippert 2016). Consequently, living conditions can constrain or enhance health lifestyles.

Socialization and Experience

Class circumstances and the other variables shown in box 1 of Figure 8.1 provide the social context for socialization and experience as depicted by the arrow leading to box 2. This is consistent with Bourdieu's (1977) view that dispositions to act in particular ways are constructed through socialization and experience, with class position providing the social context for this process. The present model, however, adds the additional structural categories – age, gender, race/ethnicity, collectivities, and living conditions – depicted in box 1, since they may also influence the social environment within which socialization and experience occur.

Whereas primary socialization represents the imposition of society's norms and values on the individual by significant others and secondary socialization results from later training, experience is the learned outcome of day-to-day activities that comes about through social interaction and the practical exercise of agency. It is through both socialization and experience that the person acquires reflexive awareness and the capacity to perform agency, but experience – with respect to life choices – provides the essential basis for agency's practical and evaluative dimensions to evolve over time. This is especially the case as people confront new social situations and conditions.

Life Choices (Agency)

Figure 8.1 shows that socialization and experience (box 2) provides the capacity for life choices (agency) depicted in box 3. As previously noted, the term "life choices" was introduced by Weber as one of the two major components of lifestyles (the other is life chances) and refers to the self-direction of one's behavior. It is an English-language translation of *Lebensführung*, which in German literally means conducting or managing one's life. Life choices are a process of agency by which individuals critically evaluate and choose their course of action. Weber's notion of life choices differs from rational choice theory in that it accounts for both means-ends rationality and the interpretive process whereby the potential outcomes of choices are imagined, evaluated, and reconstructed in the mind (Emirbayer and Mische 1998). Weber (1946) maintained that individuals have the capacity to interpret their situation, make deliberate choices, and attach subjective meaning to their actions. All social action in his view takes place in contexts that imply both constraints and opportunities, with the actor's interpretive understanding (*Verstehen*) of the situation guiding behavioral choices (Kalberg 1994).

Life Chances (Structure)

Class circumstances and, to a lesser degree, the other variables in box 1 constitute life chances (structure) shown in box 4. Life chances are the other major component of lifestyles in Weber's model. Weber was ambiguous about what he meant by life chances, but the term is usually associated with the advantages and disadvantages of relative class situations. Dahrendorf (1979: 73) finds that the best meaning of life chances in Weber's work is the "crystallized probability of finding satisfaction for interests, wants and needs, thus the probability of the occurrence of events which bring about such satisfaction." Consequently, the higher a person's position in a class hierarchy, the better the person's life chances or probabilities for finding satisfaction and vice versa. Dahrendorf (1979: 65) adds the following clarification: "for Weber, the probability of sequences of action postulated in the concept of chance is not merely an observed and thus calculable probability, but is a probability which is invariably anchored in structural conditions." Thus a person's probabilities for satisfaction that constitute his or her life chances are based on the structural conditions in their life, especially their class position. Weber's thesis is that chance is socially determined and social structure is an arrangement of chances. Therefore, life chances represent the influence of structure in Weber's *œuvre* and this paradigm.

Choice and Chance Interplay

The arrows in Figure 8.1 indicate the dialectical interplay between life choices (box 3) and life chances (box 4). This interaction is Weber's most important contribution to conceptualizing lifestyle construction (Cockerham, Abel, and Lüschen 1993;

Cockerham et al. 1997). Choices and chances operate in tandem to determine a distinction lifestyle for individuals, groups, and classes. Life chances (structure) either constrain or enable choices (agency); agency is not passive in this process, however. As Archer (2003) explains, whether or not constraints and enablements are exercised as causal powers is based on agency choosing the practices to be activated. "Constraints," says Archer (2003: 4), "require something to constrain, and enablements something to enable." Consequently, people have to consider a course of action if their actions are to be either constrained or enabled. People therefore align their goals, needs, and desires with their probabilities for realizing them and choose a lifestyle according to their assessments of the reality of their resources and class circumstances. Unrealistic choices are not likely to succeed or be selected, while realistic choices are based upon what is structurally possible.

In this context, choices and chances are not only connected dialectically, they are also analytically distinct. As Archer (1998: 369) points out: "Because the emergent properties of structures and the actual experiences of agents are not synchronized (due to the very nature of society as an open system), then there will always be the inescapable need for a two-part account." Weber provides such a framework. He conceptualizes choice and chance as separate components in the activation and conduct of a lifestyle and merges the different functions of agency and structure without either losing their distinctiveness.

Dispositions to Act (Habitus)

Figure 8.1 shows that the interaction of life choices and life chances produces individual dispositions toward action (box 5). These dispositions constitute a habitus. The influence of exterior social structures and conditions are incorporated into the habitus, as well as the individual's own inclinations, preferences, and interpretations. The dispositions that result not only reflect established normative patterns of social behavior, but they also encompass action that is habitual and even intuitive. Through selective perception, the habitus molds aspirations and expectations into "categories of the probable" that impose perceptual boundaries on dispositions and the potential for action. "As an acquired system of generative schemes," observes Bourdieu (1990: 55), "the *habitus* makes possible the free production of all the thoughts, perceptions, actions, inherent in the particular conditions of its production – and only those."

When Bourdieu speaks of the internalization of class conditions and their transformation into personal dispositions toward action, he is describing conditions similar to Weber's concept of life chances that determine materially, socially, and culturally what is probable, possible, or impossible for a member of a particular social class or group (Swartz 1997: 104). Individuals who internalize similar life chances share the same habitus because, as Bourdieu (1977: 85) explains, they are more likely to have similar shared experiences: "Though it is impossible for *all* members of the same class (or even two of them) to have the same experiences, in the same order, it is certain that each member of the same class is more likely than any member of another class to have been confronted with the situations most frequent for members of that class." As a result, there is a high degree of affinity in health lifestyle choices among members of the same class. Bourdieu maintains that while they may depart from class standards, personal styles are never more than a deviation from a style of a class that relates back to the common style by its difference.

Even though Bourdieu allows agency some autonomy (e.g. agents are determined only to the extent they determine themselves), his emphasis on structure with respect to routine operations of the habitus clearly delineates a lesser role for agency than the individualist approach to health lifestyles. Some have argued that Bourdieu strips agency of much of its critical reflexive character (Bohman 1999). Bryan Turner and Stephen Wainwright (2003:273), however, disagree and find that Bourdieu gives "full recognition" to "agency through his notions of strategy and practices," while illustrating the influential role of institutions and resources "in shaping, constraining, and producing human agency." Simon Williams (1995) also defends Bourdieu by pointing out that the habitus does not preclude choice, and he is able to account for the relative durability of different forms of lifestyles among the social classes. As the concept of the habitus is not original to Bourdieu, even though he revitalized it, his lasting contribution may in fact be his analysis of the importance of differential and durable tastes and lifestyles that distinguish the social classes from one another.

It can also be argued that the *process* of experience rescues Bourdieu's concept of habitus from the charge of downward conflation. Through experience, agency acquires new information and rationales for prompting creativity and change by way of the habitus. As Bourdieu (Bourdieu and Wacquant 1992: 133) explains, even though experiences confirm habitus, since there is a high probability that most people encounter circumstances that are consistent with those that originally fashioned it, the habitus nevertheless "is an *open system of dispositions* that is constantly subjected to experiences, and therefore constantly affected by them in a way that reinforces or modifies its structures." Thus the habitus can be creative and initiate changes in dispositions, although this potential is not stressed in Bourdieu's work.

Bourdieu calls for the abandonment of theories that explicitly or implicitly treat people as mere bearers (*Trägers*) of structure. Yet he also maintains that the rejection of mechanistic theories of behavior does not imply that we should bestow on some creative free will the exclusive power to generally constitute the meanings of situations and determine the intentions of others. The dispositions generated by the habitus tend to be compatible with the behavioral parameters set by the wider society; therefore, usual and practical modes of behaving – not unpredictable novelty – typically prevail. Consequently, Bourdieu emphasizes structure more than agency even though he accords agency the capacity to direct behavior when motivated; otherwise, his perspective largely accounts for routine behaviors that people enact without having to analyze or even think much about unless more in-depth attention is required.

Completing the Model

Figure 8.1 shows that dispositions (box 5) produce practices (action) that are represented in box 6. The practices that result from the habitus can be based on deliberate calculations, habits, or intuition. Bourdieu (1984) helps us to realize that practices linked to health lifestyles can be so integrated into routine behavioral repertoires that they can be acted out more or less unthinkingly once established in the habitus. Bourdieu observes that people tend to adopt generalized strategies (a sense of the game) oriented toward practical ends in routine situations that they can habitually follow without stopping to analyze them. As a routinized feature of everyday life, it is therefore appropriate to view health lifestyles as guided more by a practical than an abstract logic (Williams 1995).

The four most common practices measured in studies of health lifestyles are alcohol use, smoking, diet, and exercise. These are shown in box 7 along with other practices such as physical checkups by physicians and automobile seatbelt use that comprise other typical forms of action or not taken. The practices themselves may be positive or negative, but they nonetheless comprise a person's overall pattern of health lifestyles as represented in box 8. It is important to note that these practices sometimes have a complexity of their own. Smoking tobacco in any form is harmful. Eating fresh fruits and vegetables is positive, but consuming meat can be either positive or negative depending on how it is cooked and its fat content. Relatively vigorous leisure-time exercise has more health benefits than physical activity at work because the latter is subject to stress from job demands and time schedules. In contrast, walking and other everyday forms of exercise have some value. However, measures of leisure-time exercise may not fully represent the physical activities of women who take care of children and do housework. It is therefore necessary that researchers consider the multifaceted features of health lifestyle practices into account when analyzing them.

Action (or inaction) concerning a particular health practice leads to its reproduction, modification, or nullification by the habitus through a feedback process. This is seen in Figure 8.1 by the arrow showing movement from box 8 back to box 5 and is consistent with Bourdieu's (1977, 1984) assertion that when dispositions are acted upon they tend to produce or modify the habitus from which they are derived. As conceptualized by Bourdieu, habitus is the centerpiece of the health lifestyle model.

Conclusion

A central theme of this chapter is that the individualistic paradigm of health lifestyles is too narrow and unrealistic because it fails to consider structural influences on health lifestyle choices. In order to correct this course and formulate a theory where none previously existed, a health lifestyle model is presented here that accords structure a role that is consistent with its influence in the empirical world. There are times when structure outweighs but does not negate agency and other times when structure overwhelms agency, and these situations need to be included in concepts explaining health lifestyle practices. A macrosocial orientation does not mean that action is structurally predetermined; instead, it recognizes that social structures influence the thoughts, decisions, and actions of individuals (Sibeon 2004).

The theoretical model presented here is strongly influenced by Weber and Bourdieu. Although Bourdieu, in particular, has his critics, his notion of habitus nevertheless represents a novel and logical conceptualization of the internalization of external structures in the mind and perceptual processes of the individual. The result is a registry of dispositions to act in ways that are practical and usually consistent with the socially approved behavioral pathways of the larger social order or some class or group therein. Deviant behavior, of course, is an exception.

This model of health lifestyles states that four categories of (1) structural variables, namely (a) class circumstances, (b) age, gender, and race/ethnicity, (c) collectivities, and (d) living conditions, provide the social context for (2) socialization and experience that influence (3) life choices (agency). These structural variables also collectively constitute (4) life chances (structure). Choices and chances interact and commission the formation of (5) dispositions to act (habitus), leading to (6) practices (action), involving (7) alcohol use, smoking, diets, and other health-related actions. Health practices constitute patterns of (8) health lifestyles whose reenactment results in their reproduction (or modification) through feedback to the habitus. This theory is an initial representation of the health lifestyle phenomenon and is subject to verification, change, or rejection through future empirical future. However, it has stood the test of time thus far in the research that has utilized it (see, for example, Burdette et al. 2017; Christensen and Carpiano 2014; Cockerham et al. 2020; Lawrence 2017; Lawrence et al. 2017; Maller 2015; Mize 2017; Mollborn et al. 2014; Mollborn and Lawrence 2018; Rees Jones et al. 2011; Saint Onge and Krueger 2017). It is a beginning for theoretical formulations concerning a significant aspect of day-to-day social behavior for which no other theory now exists. Moreover, it moves beyond current theoretical trends reflecting methodological individualism to bring considerations of structure consistent with the reality of everyday life back into the conceptual focus of theory in medical sociology. Finally, it shows that structure has a direct causal effect on health through lifestyle practices.

References

Adler, Nancy E., Thomas Boyce, Margaret A. Chesney, Sheldon Cohen, Susan Folkman, Robert L. Kahn, and S. Leonard Syme. 1994. "Socioeconomic Status and Health: The Challenge of the Gradient." *American Psychologist* 10: 15–24.

Alexander, Jeffrey C. 1983. *Theoretical Logic in Sociology. Vol. 3: The Classical Attempt at Theoretical Synthesis: Max Weber.* Berkeley, CA: University of California Press.

Andersson, Matthew A. 2015. "Chronic Disease at Midlife: Do Parent-Child Bonds Modify the Effect of Childhood SES?" *Journal of Health and Social Behavior* 57(3): 373–89.

Andrews, Hannah, Terrence Hill, and William C. Cockerham. 2017. "Educational Attainment and Dietary Lifestyles." *Advances in Medical Sociology* 18: 101–20.

Archer, Margaret S. 1995. *Realist Social Theory: The Morphogenetic Approach.* Cambridge: Cambridge University Press.

Archer, Margaret S. 1998. "Realism and Morphogenesis." Pp. 356–81 in *Critical Realism*, edited by M. Archer, R. Bhaskar, A. Collier, T. Lawson, and A. Norrie. London: Routledge.

Archer, Margaret S. 2003. *Structure, Agency, and the Internal Conversation.* Cambridge: Cambridge University Press.

Bauman, Zygmunt. 1999. *In Search of Politics.* Stanford, CA: Stanford University Press.

Berger, Peter L. and Thomas Luckmann. 1967. *The Social Construction of Reality*. New York: Anchor.

Bhaskar, Roy. 1998. *The Possibility of Naturalism: A Philosophical Critique of the Contemporary Human Sciences*. London: Routledge.

Bohman, James. 1999. "Practical Reason and Cultural Constraint: Agency in Bourdieu's Theory of Practice." Pp. 129–52 in *Bourdieu: A Critical Reader*, edited by R. Schusterman. Oxford: Blackwell.

Bollen, Kenneth A., Jennifer L. Glanville, and Guy Stecklov. 2001. "Socioeconomic Status and Class in Studies of Fertility and Health in Developing Countries." *Annual Review of Sociology* 27(1): 153–85.

Bourdieu, Pierre. 1977. *Outline of a Theory of Practice*, translated by R. Nice. Cambridge: Polity.

Bourdieu, Pierre. 1984. *Distinction*, translated by R. Nice. Cambridge, MA: Harvard University Press.

Bourdieu, Pierre. 1990. *The Logic of Practice*, translated by R. Nice. Stanford, CA: Stanford University Press.

Bourdieu, Pierre and Loïc Wacquant. 1992. *An Invitation to Reflexive Sociology*. Cambridge: Polity.

Browning, Christopher R. and Kathleen A. Cagney. 2002. "Neighborhood Structural Disadvantage: Collective Efficacy and Self-Rated Health in a Physical Setting." *Journal of Health and Social Behavior* 43(3): 383–99.

Browning, Christopher R. and Kathleen A. Cagney. 2003. "Moving Beyond Poverty: Neighborhood Structure, Social Processes, and Health." *Journal of Health and Social Behavior* 44(4): 552–71.

Burdette, Amy M., Belinda L. Needham, Miles G. Taylor, and Terrence D. Hill. 2017. "Health Lifestyles in Adolescence and Self-rated Health in Adulthood." *Journal of Health and Social Behavior* 58(4): 520–36.

Bury, Michael. 2005. *Health and Illness*. Cambridge: Polity.

Christensen, Vibeke T. and Richard M. Carpiano. 2014. "Social Class Differences in BMI among Danish Women: Applying Cockerham's Health Lifestyles Approach and Bourdieu's Theory of Lifestyle." *Social Science & Medicine* 112: 12–21.

Chuang, Ying-Chih, Susan T. Enett, Karl E. Bauman, and Vangie A. Foshee. 2005. "Neighborhood Influences on Adolescent Cigarette and Alcohol Use: Mediating Effects Through Parent and Peer Behaviors." *Journal of Health and Social Behavior* 46(2): 187–204.

Clarke, Adele, Laura Mamo, Jennifer Ruth Fosket, Jennifer R. Fishman, and Janet K. Shim (eds.). 2010. *Biomedicalization: Technoscience, Health and Illness in the U.S.* Durham, NC: Duke University Press.

Clarke, Adele E., Janet K. Shim, Laura Mamo, Jennifer Ruth Fosket, and Jennifer R. Fishman. 2003. "Biomedicalization: Technoscientific Transformations of Health, Illness, and U.S. Biomedicine." *American Sociological Review* 68(2): 161–94.

Clouston, Sean A. P., Marcus Richards, Dorina Caadar, and Scott M. Hofer. 2015. "Educational Inequalities in Health Behaviors at Midlife: Is There a Role for Early-Life Cognition?" *Journal of Health and Social Behavior* 56(3): 323–40.

Cockerham, William C. 2005. "Health Lifestyle Theory and the Convergence of Agency and Structure." *Journal of Health and Social Behavior* 46(1): 51–67.

Cockerham, William C. 2013. "Bourdieu and an Update of Health Lifestyle Theory." pp. 127–54 in *Medical Sociology on the Move: New Directions in Theory*, edited by William Cockerham. Dordrecht: Springer.

Cockerham, William C. 2018. "Health Lifestyles and the Search for a Gender-Specific Habitus." *Social Theory and Health* 16: 142–55.

Cockerham, William C. 2021a. *Social Causes of Health and Disease*, 3rd edition. Cambridge: Polity.

Cockerham, William C. 2021b. *Sociological Theories of Health and Illness*. New York: Routledge.

Cockerham, William C., Thomas Abel, and Günther Lüschen. 1993. "Max Weber, Formal Rationality, and Health Lifestyles." *Sociological Quarterly* 34(3): 413–25.

Cockerham, William C., Shawn Bauldry, Bryant W. Hamby, James M. Shikany, and Sejong Bae. 2017. "A Comparison of Black and White Racial Differences in Health Lifestyles and Cardiovascular Disease." *American Journal of Preventive Medicine* 52: S56–S62.

Cockerham, William C., Alfred Rütten, and Thomas Abel. 1997. "Conceptualizing Health Lifestyles: Moving Beyond Weber." *Sociological Quarterly* 38(2): 321–42.

Cockerham, William C., Joseph D. Wolfe, and Shawn Bauldry. 2020. "Health Lifestyles in Late Middle Age." *Research on Aging* 42: 34–46.

d'Houtaud, A. and Mark G. Field. 1984. "The Image of Health: Variations in Perception by Social Class in a French Population." *Sociology of Health & Illness* 6(1): 30–59.

Dahrendorf, Ralf. 1979. *Life Chances*. Chicago, IL: University of Chicago Press.

Emirbayer, Mustafa and Ann Mische. 1998. "What is Agency?" *American Journal of Sociology* 103(4): 962–1023.

Flood, Sarah M. and Phyllis Moen. 2015. "Healthy Time Use in the Encore Years: Do Work, Resources, Relations, and Gender Matter?" *Journal of Health and Social Behavior* 56(1): 74–91.

Frohlich, Katherine L., Ellen Corin, and Louise Potvin. 2001. "A Theoretical Proposal for the Relationship Between Context and Disease." *Sociology of Health & Illness* 23(6): 776–97.

Giddens, Anthony. 1984. *The Constitution of Society: Outline of the Theory of Structuration*. Cambridge: Polity.

Giddens, Anthony. 1991. *Modernity and Self-Identity*. Stanford, CA: Stanford University Press.

Grzywacz, Joseph G. and Nadine F. Marks. 2001. "Social Inequalities and Exercise During Adulthood: Toward an Ecological Perspective." *Journal of Health and Social Behavior* 42(2): 202–20.

Hill, Shirley A. 2016. *Inequality and African-American Health*. Bristol: Policy Press.

Hill, Terrence D. and Ronald J. Angel. 2005. "Neighborhood Disorder, Psychological Distress, and Heavy Drinking." *Social Science & Medicine* 61: 965–73.

Hill, Terrence D., Christopher G. Ellison, Amy M. Burdette, and Marc A. Musick. 2007. "Religious Involvement and Healthy Lifestyles: Evidence from a Survey of Texas Adults." *Annals of Behavioral Medicine* 34: 217–22.

Hinote, Brian. 2014. "Habitus, Class, and Health." Pp. 741–47 in *Wiley Blackwell Encyclopedia of Health, Illness, Behavior, and Society*, edited by William Cockerham, Robert Dingwall, and Stella Quah. Oxford: Wiley Blackwell.

Huijts, Tim and Gerbert Kraaykamp. 2011. "Religious Involvement, Religious Context, and Self-Assessed Health in Europe." *Journal of Health and Social Behavior* 52(1): 91–106.

Husserl, Edmund. 1989 [1952]. *Ideas Pertaining to a Pure Phenomenology and to a Phenomenological Philosophy*, translated by R. Rojecwicz and A. Schuwer. London: Kluwer Academic.

Idler, Ellen (ed.). 2014. *Religion as a Social Determinant of Public Health*. New York: Oxford University Press.

Kalberg, Stephen. 1994. *Max Weber's Comparative Historical Sociology*. Chicago, IL: University of Chicago Press.

Lawrence, Elizabeth M. 2017. "Why Do College Graduates Behave More Healthfully Than Those Who Are Less Educated?" *Journal of Health and Social Behavior* 58(3): 291–06.

Lawrence, Elizabeth M., Stefanie Mollborn, and Robert A. Hummer. 2017. "Health Lifestyles across the Transition to Adulthood: Implications for Health." *Social Science & Medicine* 193: 23–32.

Lee, Chioun, Vera K. Tsenkova, Jennifer M. Boylan, and Carol D. Ryff. 2018. "Gender Differences in the Pathways from Childhood Disadvantage to Metabolic Syndrome in Adulthood: An Examination of Health Lifestyles." *SSM – Population Health* 4: 216–24.

Lippert, Adam M. 2016. "Stuck in Unhealthy Places: How Entering, Exiting, and Remaining in Poor and Nonpoor Neighborhoods Is Associated with Obesity during the Transition to Adulthood." *Journal of Health and Social Behavior* 57(1): 1–21.

Maller, Cecily Jane. 2015. "Understanding Health Through Social Practices: Performance and Materiality in Everyday Life." *Sociology of Health & Illness* 37(1): 52–66.

McGovern, Pauline and James Y. Nazroo. 2015. "Patterns and Causes of Health Inequalities in Later Life: A Bourdieusian Approach." *Sociology of Health & Illness* 37(1): 143–60.

Mead, George H. 1934. *Mind, Self, and Society*. Chicago, IL: University of Chicago Press.

Missinne, Sarah, Stijn Daenekindt, and Pers Bracke. 2015. "The Social Gradient in Preventive Healthcare Use: What Can We Learn from Socially Mobile Individuals?" *Sociology of Heath & Illness* 37(6): 823–38.

Mize, Trenton D. 2017. "Profiles in Health: Multiple Roles and Health Lifestyles in Early Childhood." *Social Science & Medicine* 178: 196–205.

Mollborn, Stefanie, Laurie James-Hawkins, Elizabeth Lawrence, and Paula Fomby. 2014. "Health Lifestyles in Early Childhood." *Journal of Health and Social Behavior* 55(4): 386–402.

Mollborn, Stefanie and Elizabeth Lawrence. 2018. "Family, Peer, and School Influences in Children's Developing Health Lifestyles." *Journal of Health and Social Behavior* 59(1): 133–50.

Mommsen, Wolfgang J. 1989. *The Political and Social Theory of Max Weber*. Cambridge: Polity.

Phelan, Jo C. and Bruce G. Link. 2013. "Fundamental Cause Theory." Pp. 105–126 in *Medical Sociology on the Move: New Directions in Theory*, edited by William Cockerham. Dordrecht: Springer.

Rees Jones, Ian, Olia Papocosta, Peter H. Whincup, S. Goya Wannamethee, and Richard W. Morris. 2011. "Class and Lifestyle 'Lock-in' among Middle-Aged and Older Men: A Multiple Correspondence Analysis of the British Regional Heart Study." *Sociology of Health & Illness* 33(3): 399–419.

Ringer, Fritz. 2004. *Max Weber: An Intellectual Biography*. Chicago, IL: University of Chicago Press.

Ross, Catherine E., Terrence D. Hill, and John Mirowsky. 2016. "Reconceptualizing Health Lifestyles: The Case of Marriage." *Sociology of Health Care* 34: 243–60.

Saint Onge, Jarron M. and Patrick M. Krueger. 2011. "Education and Racial-Ethnic Differences in Types of Exercise in the United States." *Journal of Health and Social Behavior* 52(2): 197–211.

Saint Onge, Jarron M. and Patrick M. Krueger. 2017. "Health Lifestyle Behaviors among US Adults." *SSM – Population Health* 3: 89–98.

Sewell, William H. 1992. "A Theory of Structure: Duality, Agency, and Transformation." *American Journal of Sociology* 98(1): 1–29.

Sibeon, Roger. 2004. *Rethinking Social Theory.* London: Sage.

Sims, Mario, Ana V. Diez-Roux, Samson Y. Gebreab, Allison Brenner, Patricia Dubbert, Sharon Wyatt, Marino Bruce, DeMarc Hickson, Tom Payne, and Herman Taylor. 2016. "Perceived Discrimination is Associated with Health Behaviours among African-Americans in the Jackson Heart Study." *Journal of Epidemiology and Community Health* 70(2): 187–94.

Stead, Martine, Laura McDermott, Anne Marie MacKintosh, and Ashley Adamson. 2011. "Why Healthy Eating is Bad for Young People's Health: Identity, Belonging and Food." *Social Science & Medicine* 72: 1121–39.

Stroope, Samuel and Joseph O. Baker. 2018. "Whose Moral Community? Religiosity, Secularity, and Self-rated Health across Communal Religious Contexts." *Journal of Health and Social Behavior* 59(2): 185–99.

Swartz, David. 1997. *Culture and Power: The Sociology of Pierre Bourdieu.* Chicago, IL: University of Chicago Press.

Turner, Bryan S. 1992. *Regulating Bodies: Essays in Medical Sociology.* London: Routledge.

Turner, Bryan S. and Steven P. Wainwright. 2003. "Corps de Ballet: The Case of the Injured Dancer." *Sociology of Health & Illness* 25(2): 269–88.

Veblen, Thorstein. 1994 [1899]. *Theory of the Leisure Class.* New York: Dover.

Wacquant, Loïc. 2016. "A Concise Genealogy and Anatomy of Habitus." *Sociological Review* 64(1): 64–72.

Weber, Max. 1946. *From Max Weber Essays in Sociology*, translated and edited by Hans H. Gerth and C. Wright Mills. New York: Oxford University Press.

Weber, Max. 1958. *The Protestant Ethic and the Spirit of Capitalism*, translated by T. Parsons. New York: Free Press.

Weber, Max. 1978 [1922]. *Economy and Society*, Vol. 2, translated and edited by G. Roth and C. Wittich. Berkeley, CA: University of California Press.

Williams, David R. and Michelle Sternthal. 2010. "Understanding Racial- Ethnic Disparities in Health: Sociological Contributions." *Journal of Health and Social Behavior* 51(extra issue): S15–S27.

Williams, Simon J. 1995. "Theorising Class, Health and Lifestyles: Can Bourdieu Help Us?" *Sociology of Health & Illness* 17(5): 577–604.

Zerubavel, Eviatar. 1997. *Social Mindscapes.* Cambridge, MA: Harvard University Press.

9

The Life Course Perspective

Kim M. Shuey and Andrea E. Willson

Over the past few decades, *life course* has become a well-known and often used term, not only in academic research but also among members of the general public. Life course is an intuitive phrase that brings to mind, very simply, the course of an individual's life, from birth to death. Going well beyond this lay understanding, however, the Life Course Perspective provides a conceptual framework for both descriptive and explanatory research, tools for the identification and formulation of research problems, and strategies for research design and analysis (Elder et al. 2003). Whether referred to as a theoretical framework, a perspective, or a framework of inquiry, life course principles and concepts provide a lens with which to view the social world that, once discovered, makes it difficult to see things otherwise. Aspects of the Life Course Perspective, as originally formulated in Sociology, can be found in various disciplines, with similar and sometimes overlapping concepts the result of the over-time cross fertilization of ideas. This includes life course epidemiology, which notably has elaborated and tested life course socioeconomic models of health (e.g. Ben-Shlomo and Kuh 2002), and research in human development and psychology. Key life course concepts that have been utilized by various disciplines, such as trajectories and transitions, are rarely situated within or connected to a broader, overarching life course framework. This framework provides a myriad of tools and insights that help us identify questions aimed at more holistically investigating the nuances and complexities of aspects of the social world, including health.

The aim of this chapter is therefore to delineate key aspects of the Life Course Perspective and to assess their significance and contribution to the field of medical sociology. We are not the first to write about the contribution of life course research more generally and there are certainly more thorough and detailed accounts (see, for example Mayer 2009). Our aim here is to provide both a resource that is accessible to those who are unfamiliar with a life course approach, as well as to provide a summation of the utility of the framework for health research and help

The Wiley Blackwell Companion to Medical Sociology, First Edition. Edited by William C. Cockerham.

spark some new ideas for those who are. The chapter provides an overview of the field, discussing the emergence of the Life Course Perspective and its key principles, some salient issues in life course research, and some of the unique contributions of this approach to examining the social world. Throughout the chapter we provide empirical examples of its application and contribution (or potential contribution) to medical sociology.

The Life Course Perspective

The theoretical foundations of the Life Course Perspective in sociology go back a long way to the work of C. Wright Mills, who wrote the influential *Sociological Imagination* in 1959. Mills urged the study of the intersection of history, social change, and the individual biography in order for us to understand how the personal predicaments we face as individuals primarily have social causes. In the two decades to follow, theorists such as Cain introduced the term life course to refer to the successive stages and statuses that individuals occupy as they age (Cain 1964). Other aging scholars, such as Riley (1979) and Neugarten (1970), contributed to the development of a life course perspective through their discussion of the social and historical influences on the individual life course and the guidance that age norms and expectations provided for individuals to map out the course of their lives (for discussion see Elder 1994; Marshall and Mueller 2003). In addition to these theoretical roots, broader societal developments, such as greater longevity and changing age structures, as well as pragmatic changes such as the availability of longitudinal data that followed samples of children as they aged, provided greater opportunity to examine changes across the span of an individual's life and raised previously unanswerable questions about how lives are influenced by social change and historical circumstances (for discussion see Elder et al. 2003). From these roots came Glen Elder's (1974, 1994, 1998)) penultimate assembly and theorizing of a systematic life course paradigm that outlines a number of guiding principles and concepts which ground life course sociology. This includes the foundational five life course principles clearly outlined by Elder and colleagues (Elder et al. 2003) that will be incorporated into the discussion that follows.

Although often referred to as the Life Course Perspective, there is no consensus on whether the set of principles and approaches that it provides represents a perspective, a theoretical orientation, a paradigm, or a framework. For many life course scholars, it represents a flexible, orienting framework that provides theoretical and conceptual tools that are applicable across a variety of domains, rather than a rigid explanatory theory (Shanahan and Macmillan 2008). Regardless of its name, life course today has established a firm footing within sociology, and coupled with diverse theories and approaches, has been utilized to investigate a myriad of research topics and domains of study. From its origins in the 1960s and 1970s, its influence as a guiding framework has grown, with the annual number of publications incorporating life course increasing over time. For example, key word searches of the interdisciplinary database Scopus show a 30-fold increase over the past 20 years from less than 50 publications in 1990 to approximately 400 in 2009 (Billari 2009), and, based on the authors' review, over 1,500 in 2019. In addition to the growth of life course research both within sociology and across disciplines, since the 2000s we have seen the establishment of numerous edited volumes and research outlets targeted specifically at life course researchers, including two volumes of the *Handbook of the Life Course* (2003, 2016), at least two journals specifically dedicated to life course research (*Advances in Life Course Research* and *Longitudinal and Life Course Studies*), the establishment of longitudinal data sources facilitating life course research (for example, *The National Longitudinal Study of Adolescent to Adult Health*), as well as numerous professional associations such as the *Society for Longitudinal and Life Course Studies* and association sections supporting life course scholarship (see Bynner 2016 for discussion of the growth of longitudinal research and life course study). As the principles and dimensions of a life course framework encourage a holistic approach to understanding the social world, life course research is inherently an interdisciplinary undertaking that incorporates the expertise of scholars in other areas of study. Thus, its long reaching influence has cut across disciplines and facilitated the growth of interdisciplinary research across fields such as anthropology, criminology, epidemiology, history, health sciences, and psychology.

One main contribution of the life course perspective is its emphasis on *temporality* in sociological investigation (Elder et al. 2003; Heinz and Kruger 2001). Most familiar and prolific is research that focuses on the micro level, examining temporality in the form of individual biography and life history within intra-individual pathways across time. As the lives of individuals are situated within a broader historical and social context, the life course principle of *time and place* highlights the essential link between individual biography, history, and the broader social and political context that both constrains individual action and provides opportunities (Elder et al. 2003; Giele and Elder 1998; Settersten 2003b). A unique objective of life course research is its commitment to a multi-level approach that draws connections across analytic levels, linking micro, meso, and macro-level social phenomena rather than privileging one approach at the exclusion of the other (Elder et al. 2003; Hagestad and Dannefer 2001; Heinz 2009; Mayer 2009). We next turn to a more detailed discussion of key tenants and contributions of the Life Course Perspective and their relevance and importance for advancing the field of medical sociology.

Life Course Principles and Their Application

If we think about society as an onion we can visualize peeling back the multiple layers of influence that the social world has on its individual members. Sometimes referred to as macro-level or distal factors, the outer skin represents broader societal-level forces of influence such as historical events, policy, culture, systems of inequality, and demographic change. The next layer of the onion, the more proximal meso-level sphere of influence, includes more immediate social contexts such as family, workplace, community, or school. At the core is the micro or individual level, comprised of both individual development and change across the course of one's life, as well as the individual perceptions, behaviors, and meanings that are uniquely attached to these experiences (for a review see Shanahan and Macmillan 2008). Each interconnected layer represents a unique "point of entry" for studying a particular social phenomenon (Elder et al. 2003). From a researcher's chosen starting point, the life course perspective encourages the acknowledgment and conceptualization of "linking" mechanisms that reveal interdependencies and cross-level interactions (see Bernardi, Huinink, and Settersten, Jr. 2019; Hagestad 2003). Regardless of point of entry, researchers must appreciate and acknowledge the multilevel complexities of the problem at hand and solutions that go beyond the individual biography. Ignoring these linkages by considering one level in isolation can result in inaccurate, inconsistent, and overly simplistic understandings of the lived experiences of individuals (Connidis 2014; Shanahan and Macmillan 2008). Because of the proliferation and familiarity of research focused on individual experiences at the micro-level, we shall begin our discussion of life course principles and contributions here as well.

Dynamics of the Individual Life Course

The conceptualization of the individual life course and its various dimensions, such as health, as a *dynamic process* that unfolds over time is a key contribution of life course studies. Use of the term "dynamic" has gained popularity in recent decades, partly as a response to the challenges faced by early research attempts to understand phenomena such as health inequality using static point-in-time estimates or short-term longitudinal data capturing only a small portion of the life course. Life course research acknowledges the complex, changing nature of individual biography over time associated with the changing influence of the social world (Dannefer et al. 2016; Willson and Shuey 2016).

One important conceptual and empirical direction of life course research involves taking a long-term view of human lives to understand the sources of stability or change in experiences occurring over time as we age. Conceptually rooted in the field of human development, Elder's (Elder 1985, 1994; Elder et al. 2003) life course principle of *life span development* recognizes that aging is a process that occurs from birth to death, and as a result, an emphasis is placed on the importance of considering intra-individual development across the life course by observing individuals across all its stages, from early life into adolescence, adulthood, and later life. Long term longitudinal panel data or life history data allow researchers to study lives over time in order to understand the linkages between earlier and later life experiences. Importantly, this approach calls for a shift away from more static "age-specific" studies of particular life stages, such as old age, in favor of research that takes a longer view and incorporates the processes through which earlier experiences shape individual biography (Marshall and Mueller 2003).

A number of principles and organizing concepts have developed within life course scholarship which facilitate this long term, dynamic view of individual lives. Over the course of one's life, individuals experience a multitude of *transitions*, which involve a change in a particular status or role that occurs over a bounded period of time, often with long-term consequences (George 1993). Transitions, such as becoming a parent or entering the labor force, becoming an adult or a cancer patient, can be crisp or blurred, smooth or rough. Smooth transitions can create stability across other aspects of the life course, such as health, while others, including those that occur in the absence of support from social institutions and social networks, can create a sudden change in the future course of one's life. Transitions that create a substantial change in life direction can be conceptualized as *turning points* (see Elder et al. 2003), and they are sometimes studied in order to better understand why an individual's life might end up quite differently than it began. Transitions provide a window through which we are able to observe lives both temporally prior and subsequent and studying them allows us to identify qualitative variations in experience across individuals and groups along dimensions of social inequality.

To this end, Elder's principle of *timing* emphasizes that the timing of transitions and life events can have important, lifelong implications by shaping subsequent experiences and future transitions (Elder et al. 2003). For example, Elder's (1974) classic study on entry into the service during World War II shows that variations in the timing of entry had a significant impact on whether the experience was perceived negatively as a life disruption or created opportunities for overcoming earlier disadvantages. Structured variations in the timing of transitions, as well as the order (or sequence) in which they occur, helps explain why the same social phenomena can have varying effects across groups of individuals, perpetuating social inequalities. Examining the timing or sequence of transitions within a population at the aggregate level gives us a sense of the average time or age at which a particular transition occurs. When combined with individual data, this can help reveal the extent to which experiencing transitions either "on" or "off" time can lead to unequal outcomes and maintain broader systems of inequality (e.g. O'Rand and Elman 2004).

Life course scholars conceptualize the individual life course as consisting of a series of interconnected transitions that form a social pathway of experiences across multiple life domains such as work, health, education, and family over time, with the duration of time in between transitions lending shape and order to the pathway (Elder 1985; Hagestad 1990). The individual life course is often viewed as a *trajectory* within which individual transitions, such as experiencing a health event or work disability, are embedded. Thinking about transitions linked together across time as people age helps us identify patterns of experience that are unique in form and meaning and allows us to contextualize a current state or status within a longer history. This holistic view allows us to better understand the processes whereby individuals and groups maintain advantages in health or financial resources, for example, or experience growing disadvantage over time as they age.

To that end, within sociology theories such as Cumulative Advantage, Cumulative Dis/Advantage, and Cumulative Inequality have been under development in various forms since the 1990s (Crystal and Shea 1990; Dannefer 1987, 2003, 2020; Ferraro and Shippee 2009; O'Rand 1996). Generally speaking, these theories of accumulation outline a process whereby early-life advantages provide greater opportunities to access additional resources and to avoid sources of adversity. In contrast, the experience of early-life disadvantage generates exposure to a chain of risks resulting in further losses over time (O'Rand 2006). Aimed at a better understanding of the connections in experiences and resources across the individual life course leading to the reproduction of social inequality at the societal level, these theoretical concepts emphasize the dynamics of change over the life course whereby initial relative advantage generates further advantage and greater divergence in resources across individuals over time. Smaller initial differences in resources in early life grow larger over time, magnifying differences and making it increasingly difficult for the individuals and groups starting out disadvantaged to catch up. Thus, with age, the process of the accumulation of advantages and disadvantages at the individual level (see Dannefer 2008, 2020) generates greater within-cohort inequality at the population level (Crystal and Shea 1990; Diprete and Eirich 2006).

Theories of accumulation have sometimes been critiqued as being overly deterministic, suggesting a path dependent process that begins early in life and is unamenable to change (for discussion of the various forms of accumulation see Diprete and Eirich 2006). Recent elaborations such as Ferraro and Shippee's (2009) theory of Cumulative Inequality more explicitly examines the potential for change across the life course as a result of the dynamic interaction between early life status and social institutions across the life course, which creates the potential for acquisition or loss of resources. They emphasize that both the timing and duration of exposure to risk are important to the accumulation of disadvantage and highlight the importance of *human agency*, one of Elder's key life course principles. Building on existing conceptualizations of human agency (see for example Clausen 1991; Giddens 1984; Sewel 1992), Elder emphasizes that "individuals construct their own life course through the choices and actions they take within the opportunities and constraints of history and social circumstance" (Elder et al. 2003: 11). These include the advantages and disadvantages associated with race, class, gender, and age, with a more privileged social location providing greater opportunities to make choices that determine future pathways (Hitlin and Elder 2007a, 2007b). Others have argued that it is more accurate to understand agency as constituted by social structure rather than constrained by it, as social institutions and culture form the parameters around the ways in which individuals understand the world and forms goals and aspirations (Dannefer 2008, 2020). Regardless, across the life course individuals are not passively acted upon by social structures, but engage in willful action or choices in order to shape their lives based on the alternatives they perceive, the resources at their disposal, and institutional structures that provide the opportunity to do so (Heinz 2009; Marshall 2005).

Medical Sociology and the Individual Life Course

The necessarily brief discussion above outlines some of the conceptual tools that the life course perspective provides to help us understand the dynamic nature of the individual life course, calling our attention to life course research's unique focus on intra-individual stability and change across the life span, as opposed to a more narrow, static focus on single events or states (Mayer 2009). We next provide some examples of the contribution of micro-level life course concepts to medical sociology before turning to a discussion of the connection between the individual life course and broader social conditions in the following sections.

Within medical sociology, the principle of *agency within constraints* is evident in health research based on Health Lifestyle Theory, which emphasizes that health-related behaviors may be enabled or constrained by individual life chances (Cockerham 2005). Several recent empirical studies have suggested the importance of both social influences and human agency in the clustering of health behaviors and their "embeddedness within social structures, groups, and identities" (e.g. Mollborn and Lawrence 2018: 133; Burdette et al. 2017). In a similar vein, Thoits (2006) urges researchers to focus more attention on the ways individuals use personal agency in coping efforts and problem-solving and emphasizes that the unequal distribution of coping resources by social status helps to explain how inequalities in mental health are maintained and amplified over the life course. In part inspired by Thoits to "bring the person back into the study of social life and cumulative inequality", Schafer and colleagues' research reveals that personal agency leads to different interpretations of early adversity and hope that the future will improve, but nonetheless these experiences of early adversity dampen agency in the long run (Schafer et al. 2011: 1079).

Transitions are one of the most analyzed life course concepts, and research demonstrates the importance of the timing, sequencing, and density of key transitions for health and well-being (see George 1993). Research often focuses on the consequences of transitions, and non-normative or "off-time" transitions are of particular interest because of their potentially negative health implications. For example, stress research finds that the effect of transitions that occur early in the life course may have lasting impacts, such as the effects of parental divorce on children's mental health trajectories (Strohschein 2005), and that unexpected premarital first births are negative for mothers' mental health (Carlson and Williams 2011). The period of the life course that has come to be known as emerging adulthood has received much attention because of the density of major transitions occurring within a relatively short period. Research has examined the potential health effects of both the order in which individuals complete key transitions and the timing and delay of these transitions in relation to societal expectations (George 2003. Other research has examined continuity in health and health behaviors over the course of the transition to adulthood (e.g. Becnel and Williams 2019).

Investigating how life events and experiences such as the transition to adulthood unfold over time, creating differences across individuals in long term trajectories, is the emphasis of a large and rapidly growing body of research. Trajectory research is generally interested in how past experiences affect one's future, as well as how change in one circumstance may lead to change in another. A dynamic account of health across the life course, for example, can be achieved by focusing on individual patterns of health stability and change, characterized by dimensions including timing, sequence, and for some measures of health, reversibility. Cumulative Inequality and Cumulative Dis/Advantage theories have been influential in framing research on the long-term effects of the accumulation of various forms of advantage and disadvantage on health and the resulting amplification of health inequalities within cohorts. Early research emerged 30 years ago following Crystal and Shea's (1990) study documenting cumulative economic inequality over the life course. The framework was subsequently applied to health outcomes and remains influential today, evidenced by the 2020 *Journals of Gerontology: Social Sciences* Special Issue: Cumulative Dis/Advantage: Innovations in Research and Theory (Vol. 75, 6). A large literature on the health returns to socioeconomic resources and childhood experiences suggests an accumulative process that widens health disparities between advantaged and disadvantaged groups with age (e.g. Brown et al. 2012; Ferraro, Schafer, and Wilkinson, 2016; Willson et al. 2007).

Empirically investigating trajectories has been accomplished in a number of ways, including examinations of individual-level data from panel studies, aggregate trajectories at the population level, or by coding life history data or archival data organized to reveal temporal patterns (Clipp et al. 1992; Lynch and Taylor 2016). Trajectories of data operating across biographical and historical time may examine repeated measures of the same phenomenon, such as self-rated health or body mass index, or sequences of different types of life events, such as transitions between school completion and employment. Growth-curve models and latent class analysis are two commonly used statistical techniques allowing researchers to examine how factors such as early origins, the experience of economic disadvantage, levels of education, as well as characteristics such as gender and race/ethnicity, affect health and well-being over time (see Lynch and Taylor 2016 for a methodological review). Although much trajectory research is quantitative, that is not exclusively the case. For example, a path-breaking study by Clipp and colleagues (1992) used inductive logic to construct typologies of unique patterns of health that differed in the timing, sequence, and direction of change. More recently, intensive biographical interview data has enabled investigation of how structure and agency interact to shape the pathways of a person's life course, an approach that could be extended to include experiences of health (see Hollstein 2019).

Research on health trajectories has moved our knowledge of the social determinants of health from static snapshots of health at one point in time to a better understanding of the complex factors shaping health over the long-term. For example, research suggests that the health effects of negative experiences, such as divorce, may change over the life course, with initial short-term negative effects on mental health dissipating over time as adults adapt to change (e.g. Leopold 2018). Importantly, the resources that affect health also change over time. For example, we know that there is a strong association between high, stable socioeconomic status and men's physical health in middle age, but recent research has demonstrated upward mobility to the middle class is similarly beneficial to men's health in middle age (Frech and Damaske 2019). In addition, individual trajectories are not set in stone, and pathways may be altered, positively or negatively (George 2003; Shuey and Willson 2014). For example, Watkins-Hayes' (2019) decade-long research on women living with HIV/AIDS reveals the transformative process that may occur following a diagnosis with HIV/AIDS. For some disadvantaged women, an HIV diagnosis is a *turning point*, providing access to help and resources they otherwise would not have and, ironically, allows them to improve their overall health and safety. Finally, trajectory research also demonstrates that not everyone benefits equally from socioeconomic resources as they age. Racial disparities in wealth play a major role in inequality across several measures of health, and there are also diminishing returns to wealth for the health of black Americans (Boen et al. 2020).

Meso-level Context and Medical Sociology

As the individual life course does not occur in isolation from the social structures within which individual pathways are embedded, investigating the dynamics of individual lives represents only one part of the contribution of the life course perspective to understanding the social world. Elder's life course principle of *time and place* focuses attention on the broader social context within which individual biographies are embedded (Elder et al. 2003). Situated between the individual and broader societal forces are the more proximal, central settings of our everyday lives which connect individuals to larger systems of stratification and inequality (Settersten 2003b; Shanahan and Macmillan 2008). These meso-level contexts are comprised of social institutions such as work organizations, communities, and schools, as well as interpersonal settings such as families and peer groups. They shape key transitions and longer-term trajectories, defining the normative pathway of various social roles. Situating individual outcomes within meso-level contexts are important for understanding their contribution to stratification and the mechanisms through which this occurs.

For example, schools are embedded within a broader educational system that contains variations in funding and governance, ranging from tax-funded public systems to private institutions governed by independent organizations. Mechanisms for distributing resources affect funding levels and resource adequacy within schools, such as student-teacher ratios, which set the context for student success, aspirations, and future educational and work trajectories of individual students (Crosnoe and Benner 2016). More directly, characteristics of schools, such as average level of parent education, have effects on indicators of the health of adolescents, such as body mass index (Niu, Hoyt, and Pachucki 2019). In adulthood, the social organization of work is a context that strongly shapes life chances and quality of life, and its effect on well-being extends well beyond individual experiences in particular jobs to the ways the structure and institutionalization of work intersect with other aspects of workers' lives (Tausig 2013). For example, so profound is the effect of this context that the changes to the structure of work time among employees has been found to predict changes in health-related behavior, such as sleep, and subsequent measures of well-being (Moen et al. 2011).

Families and peer groups, arguably even more proximate in their influence, are embedded in broader systems of stratification such as race, class, and gender that shape their influence on the individual life course. Perhaps the most studied contexts, and the subject of Elder's life course principle of *linked lives*, are the family relationships within which individuals are embedded, often for long periods of time. The connections to others with whom we are closely linked in turn affects our own actions, transitions, and pathways across the life course. A classic example of the effects that the transition of one family member has on other members can be seen in the transition to parenthood, which creates a *counter-transition* (Burton and Bengtson 1985) to grandparenthood for the older generation and changing relations between partners. The timing and quality of shared transitions and experiences have *ripple effects* (Hagestad 1981) on the lives of other members of the family unit beyond just the individual at its epicenter, similar to a pebble (or conversely a large rock!) dropped into a pond. Lives lived interdependently are often the medium through which larger socio-historical changes are expressed and addressed (Elder et al. 2003). This interdependence means that families are impacted both by macro-level forces and by the individual experiences of its members. Families are a primary source of both opportunities and constraints on our abilities to make choices and take action. Because our lives are tied to family members and significant others at all times, individual agency primarily exists within these relationships, which may limit or enable agentic behavior that affects health (Landes and Settersten 2019).

For example, events that produce strain for one family member may in turn change the roles and situations of others in the family, such as when the unemployment of one family member leads other family members to enter the labor force, introducing new strains to that family member and perhaps, depending on the timing in the life course, interrupting that family member's educational pathway (Milkie 2010). Similarly, when a family member's poor health requires caregiving, the balance of roles and resources within the family is affected. Research suggests that poor parental health may create important role changes for children that affect their success in school and subsequently has long-term implications for health (Boardman et al. 2012).

A multitude of studies provide evidence of the role of family environment in the health (both physical and emotional/mental) and longevity of its members. A central question addressed by much of this research is just how influential the family is in defining the life course of children (Uhlenberg and Mueller 2003). However, "family context" is complex and may include family structure, the quality of relationships between family members, and family resources, including economic capital, social capital, and cultural capital (Uhlenberg and Mueller 2003). To add even further complexity, all of these aspects of context may be fluid and dynamic during childhood. For example, increasing economic hardship during childhood has been found to increase children's internalizing and externalizing problems, and this may be at least partially explained by parents' stress (Yuan and Vogt 2008). In the longer term, the experience of persistent economic hardship during childhood has enduring negative effects on health into midlife, but when families move out of this hardship the risk of poor health in adulthood may be reduced (Shuey and Willson 2014).

An emerging area developing out of this interest in the long-term influence of families on health over the life course focuses on the intergenerational transmission of health inequality. Long-term panel surveys, such as the Panel Study of Income Dynamics (PSID) and the National Longitudinal Study of Adolescent to Adult Health (Add Health), have made possible the observation of prospective measures of early life environment as well as indicators of health in parent and adult child generations at roughly the same stage of the life course. Work in this area continues to develop as research demonstrates continuity in parental and child health (Bauldry et al. 2016; Garbarski 2014; Hardie and Turney 2017; Mollborn and Lawrence 2018; Shuey et al. 2020; Willson and Shuey 2018). A large proportion of the association between the health of multiple generations is not due to genetic factors, but reflects shared familial and environmental factors, the accumulation of early exposures, and the transmission of status, resources, and health practices across generations within one's family of origin (Ferraro 2016; Madsen et al. 2014; Piraino et al. 2014; Thompson 2014). The intergenerational transmission of health is relevant for understanding the cumulative relationship between various resources and health, as this process begins with the passing of social, economic and biological resources from parent to child and points to the importance of incorporating family context into health studies, as well as health into the study of family processes (Willson and Shuey 2018).

At the Macro Level

Elder's life course principle of *time and place* also points to the importance of considering the influence of *macro-level* social forces on the course of individual lives. These include significant historical events, policies and actions of social institutions such as states and governments, and aggregate trends such as population aging and changing normative life course patterns (see Heinz and Kruger 2001; Shanahan and Macmillan 2008). Although it is more commonly used in reference to individual lives, at the macro-level the term *life course* can be understood as a social institution that consists of a sequence of transitions influenced the social policies of governments and nation states across life periods such as education, work, childrearing, and retirement (Mayer 2009; Mayer and Schoepflin 1989). The broader macro context guiding the timing and sequence of entry and exit from social roles across life domains such as work and family consists of formal age-based policies that define transitions such as adulthood and retirement, structured sets of inequalities that are reinforced by social institutions such as labor markets, combined with informal social norms that set the cultural context of peoples' lives (for discussion see Settersten 2003b; Shanahan and Macmillan 2008). In addition, the generosity of a country's transfers and services designed to ensure a basic level of social well-being for its citizens, as famously classified within the welfare state typology of Esping-Andersen (1990, 1999), gives us a broad sense of the degree to which states build social safety nets that smooth out the risks encountered across the life course at key transition points, such as unemployment or disability (Diewald 2016; O'Rand 2006). The patterning of life course transitions, such as those into and out of education and work, is stratified not only across state and country context, but also along lines of race, class, gender, sexuality and disability status as a result of social policy configurations of welfare states and government institutions, policies and discriminatory practices of labor markets and organizations, as well as interpersonal dynamics of social exclusion. All of these macro-level forces form the unique historical context within which people lives, and health, are embedded and unfold over time.

In practice, if considered at all, macro social contexts are often conceptualized as static instead of dynamic processes. Changing cultural norms, policies, stratification systems, as well as broader social change and new technological developments impact individuals' lives over time (Hagestad and Dannefer 2001). To start, life course scholars have noted a number of potential changes in the over-time patterning of the life course associated with other macro level changes such as globalization and the changing economy that have the potential to significantly influence the shape of individual pathways. The over-time reduction in formal age-based structuring via the policies of social organization and institutions (de-institutionalization) has resulted in greater variation in the timing and sequencing of life transitions (de-standardization) and an increase in the synchronous number of states or forms of life activity (de-chronologization) (see Bruckner and Mayer 2005; Settersten 2003b). Rather than experiencing separate life segments (such as education and work) independently and sequentially, contemporaneous trends suggest a larger number of transitions within work and family trajectories, occurring at more dispersed ages.

Here, cohort studies are an important tool to help us identify the effects of broader context on individual lives and to disentangle macro and micro level determinants. Age-period-cohort (APC) models are a classic longitudinal design aimed at separating cohort differences from the confounding influences of age-related and period (time of measurement) effects (see Bynner 2016). They have the potential to address theoretically motivated life course questions about mechanisms of social change created by forces such as *cohort succession*, for example, whereby the degree to which successive cohorts follow different life course patterns influences the degree of social change (Alwin and Ryan 2003; Elder and George 2016). Combined with other life course principles such as *timing*, comparing cohorts can help us to understand how exposure to macro level forces and changing social conditions affects cohort members differently depending on the age at which they experienced the change. Studying cohorts also can help us to understand historical changes in life course transitions, including their timing and sequencing, as well as how changing economic, policy, and institutional contexts differently affect particular populations and their exposure to risks or opportunities (Dannefer 2020). Cohort analysis, both in medical sociology and sociology more generally, typically falls short, focusing on descriptive differences across cohorts rather than theorizing social change and its impact on individual lives (Elder and George 2016)

Medical Sociology and the Macro-level Context

Macro-level contexts have received less attention in health research than micro-level characteristics and individual experiences. Research that does examine the implications of macro forces such as welfare state characteristics for health inequalities, or studies of cohort differences in health, are often not explicitly guided by a life course perspective. However, research on welfare state characteristics and health inequality, for example, clearly demonstrates the importance of the life course principle of time and place for health. These studies reveal the importance of considering social policies more broadly, such as economic assistance, pensions, and parental leave, as health policy, and most studies find that more generous social policies are associated with more positive health outcomes for the population as a whole, not only those who receive the benefits (see Bergqvist et al. 2013 for review). The policy context within which individuals live their lives plays an important role in smoothing out the life course risks individuals face – a risk may not lead to an adversity based on intervening macro level forces, such as welfare state policies (see Diewald 2016 for a review). For example, risks in the labor market, such as job insecurity and unemployment, may be buffered by social assistance and social services that prevent poverty and in the longer term, are protective of health. The cultural foundations of welfare states shape which life course risks are given priority as well as whether it is the prevention of risk or the buffering of adversity that is prioritized (Diewald 2016). In addition, as evidenced in research on post-Soviet Russia, macro-level ideologies influencing social policies and culture also play a role in supporting or undermining positive health lifestyles, which influence chronic disease and life expectancy (Cockerham et al. 2002).

A comparative framework is often critical to address questions about the effects of macro context on individual outcomes and for understanding the ways in which social policy exacerbates or mitigates health inequalities (see Corna 2013 for a more complete discussion). Research framed by theories of Cumulative Dis/advantage or Cumulative Inequality usually does not explicitly acknowledge, or model, the changing risks and opportunities individuals experience as they age due to age-based public policy such as social security systems. However, access to age-based welfare state entitlements and universal healthcare plays a critical role in the well-being of older people, in particular those who lacked resources earlier in the life course (Quesnel-Vallée et al. 2016), and it is sometimes proposed as an explanation for reduced health inequality with age (House et al. 2005). Recently, cross-national research has demonstrated that the increasing intra-cohort health inequality with age found in the US may not occur in countries with more generous welfare regimes where health disparities narrow rather than widen from middle to late life (van der Linden et al. 2020).

Leveraging data on change over time at both the macro and micro levels can aid in the observation of the interplay of social policy and other macro-contexts, such as the economy, and individual health. For example, in their examination of the potential effect of China's One Child Policy on children's overweight and underweight status, He and Zheng (2017) found that over the period of 1991 to 2006, having younger siblings generally did not affect children's weight, regardless of gender. However, during a period of lower economic development, when the proportion of family income spent on food was higher, evidence emerged of an increase in first-born girls' underweight status that was mitigated by later growth in the economy.

Social context, social change, and the passage of time clearly do not affect all groups in the same way, and often overlooked is the potential for the effect of these contexts to differ by birth cohort, which reflects the timing in the life course in which social change occurs. A consideration of societal changes in culture helps to situate and understand what may seem on the surface to be individual responses to an adversity but in fact may actually reflect cohort differences in the effect of macro-level processes. For example, Pudrovska (2010) used the changing macro-level context surrounding cancer, including changing cultural conceptions of cancer, to understand why the effect of cancer on personal growth strongly depends on birth cohort. Similarly, Pavalko and colleagues (2007) find that although women's health as a whole has not changed across cohorts, societal changes that have led to an increased ability for women with physical limitations to become and remain employed explain the increase in health problems across successive cohorts of employed women.

A Life Course Lens

The goal of this chapter was to provide an outline of the Life Course Perspective as a lens through which to investigate *process*, important for advancing the field of medical sociology. Although many are familiar with various life course concepts, the tools and complexities of the framework are rarely utilized to their full potential. Through our discussion of life course sociology at the micro, meso, and macro-levels, we have highlighted ways to approach social phenomena and the study of health in a more holistic manner aimed at capturing changing and interrelated processes. Below are a few final thoughts and future directions.

A recent discussion by life course scholar Dale Dannefer (2020) provides one clear illustration of the relevance of a life course approach. Dannefer references research on *exposure*, a central concept from epidemiology that focuses on risk factors and their association with various outcomes. While this body of research often incorporates some of the life course principles outlined above, particularly duration and accumulation, it does not adequately contextualize exposure within larger social systems. To do so requires investigating the ways in which the meso-level contexts within which individuals live their lives generate exposure to risks, as well as the ways macro systems of stratification both create and reinforce inequalities in exposure. As we discussed earlier, one such context is our connections with the other people to whom we are linked, such as family members. An understanding of exposure requires attention to linked lives and the ways that these connections increase exposure to risk, or mitigate its harmful effects. Without information on these contexts and connections, research is often unable to speak to the causal mechanisms that generate exposure to risk factors and are missing an important part of the larger story.

As a second example, research on cumulative processes points to the role of agency, operating for some through resilient responses to adverse conditions that are learned within our proximal relationships and social contexts (Schafer et al. 2009). Dannefer (2020: 1257), as well, argues that investigations on exposure largely model individuals as passive "sitting-duck targets that simply absorb the repeated assaults of exposure" without taking into account human agency. For example, although we may be able to determine that on average, exposure to a particular risk is associated with a negative outcome either at present or in the future, this does not allow us to understand heterogeneity in experiences and why not everyone has the expected outcome. Individuals often diverge from the health trajectories that we expect based on their social location, and both social institutions and human agency are key for understanding well-being over the life course (Schafer et al. 2009).

Third, the importance of *timing and changing context* is clear from existing research. Because historical events and social change occurs at different points in the life course for different birth cohorts, the potential for cohort research in helping to understand how social contexts shape health is extensive (Pavalko and Caputo 2013). The importance of the intersection between individual experience and larger social institutions at a particular life stage is apparent in both the economic and health outcomes of Millennials. Millennials, the cohorts born between 1981 and 1996, have experienced delayed milestones such as marriage, children, and homeownership, in large part because they were entering the labor force during the Great Recession, which led to high rates of unemployment among these cohorts (Bialik and Fry 2019). This experience has lasting impacts on Millennials' future earnings and wealth and emerging evidence suggests these cohorts are experiencing chronic health problems earlier in the life course than their parents (Harris 2019).

Fourth, greater recognition that the relationship between social conditions and health is not unidirectional is important (Dannefer 2020; Pavalko and Caputo 2013). This includes the need for greater attention to reciprocal relationships between social contexts, such as socioeconomic conditions and health (Pavalko and Caputo 2013). Here, advancing methodologies will be important, as most current quantitative approaches assume effects flow unidirectionally from an independent variable to a dependent variable. Current statistical models typically allow for snapshots of resources from discrete periods of the life course as covariates in multivariate models to determine which period (e.g. childhood vs. adulthood) has the largest effect on later health (for discussion see Willson and Shuey 2016). Most of our conceptual frameworks do so, as well. As a result, an analysis may find support for one process over another depending on the point in the life course we observe, giving us an incomplete understanding of the outcome of interest (McLeod and Pavalko 2008; Pavalko and Caputo 2013). As George (1999: 566) encouraged over 20 years ago, we must continue to take a "long view of individual biography" to fully conceptualize the dynamic relationship between social conditions and health.

Commitment to a multi-level approach that draws connections across analytic levels, linking micro, meso, and macro-level social phenomena to understand how contexts and institutions shape the pathways of individual lives, is a unique objective of life course research. In addition, *comparisons* are a crucial tool for understanding process. Life course scholars recognize the role of systematic comparisons across historical and social contexts, across cohorts, and across groups to understand social phenomena (Settersten 2003b). Comparisons allow us to identify both normative patterns, as well as heterogeneous experiences, with intra-cohort studies allowing us to compare across individuals and groups from the same birth cohort in order to investigate the mechanisms leading to differing outcomes over time. No one study can accomplish all of the tasks outlined by a life course framework, and life course researchers are often forced to choose a starting point from which to piece together their understanding. Regardless, a life course lens offers an awareness of the ever changing interrelationships and processes that create social inequality in health and helps bring to light issues that warrant policy attention and social change.

References

Alwin, Duane F. and McCammon Ryan. 2003. "Generations, Cohorts, and Social Change." Pp. 23–50 in *Handbook of the Life Course*, edited by Jeylan T. Mortimer and Michael J. Shanahan. New York: Kluwer Academic Publishers.

Bauldry, Shawn, Michael J. Shanahan, Ross Macmillan, Richard A. Miech, Jason D. Boardman, Danielle O. Dean, and Veronica Cole. 2016. "Parental and Adolescent Health Behaviors and Pathways to Adulthood." *Social Science Research* 58: 227–42.

Becnel, Jennifer N. and Amanda L. Williams. 2019. "Using Latent Class Growth Modeling to Examine Longitudinal Patterns of Body Mass Index Change from Adolescence to Adulthood." *Journal of the Academy of Nutrition and Dietetics* 119: P1875-1881.

Ben-Shlomo, Yoav and Diana Kuh. 2002. "A Life Course Approach to Chronic Disease Epidemiology: Conceptual Models, Empirical Challenges and Interdisciplinary Perspectives." *International Journal of Epidemiology* 31(2): 285–93.

Bergqvist, Kersti, Monica Åberg Yngwe, and Olle Lundberg. 2013. "Understanding the Role of Welfare State Characteristics for Health and Inequalities – An Analytical Review." *BMC Public Health* 13: 1234–54.

Bernardi, Laura, Johannes Huinink, and Richard A. Settersten, Jr.2019. "The Life Course Cube: A Tool for Studying Lives." Advances in Life Course Research, 41: 1–3.

Bialik, Kristen and Richard Fry. 2019. "Millennial Life: How Young Adulthood Today Compares with Prior Generations." Pew Research Center: Social & Demographic Trends. https://www.pewsocialtrends.org/essay/millennial-life-how-young-adulthood-today-compares-with-prior-generations. Downloaded June 30, 2020.

Billari, Francesco. 2009. "The Life Course is Coming of Age." *Advances in Life Course Research* 14: 83–86.

Boardman, Jason D., Kari B. Alexander, Richard A. Miech, Ross MacMillan, and Michael J. Shanahan. 2012. "The Association between Parent's Health and the Educational Attainment of Their Children." *Social Science & Medicine* 75: 932–39.

Boen, Courtney, Lisa Keister, and Brian Aronson. 2020. "Beyond Net Worth: Racial Differences in Wealth Portfolios and Black-White Health Inequality across the Life Course." *Journal of Health and Social Behavior* 61(2): 153–69.

Brown, Tyson H., Angela M. O'Rand, and Daniel E. Adkins. 2012. "Race-ethnicity and Health Trajectories: Tests of Three Hypotheses across Multiple Groups and Health Outcomes." *Journal of Health and Social Behavior* 53(3): 359–77.

Bruckner, Hannah and Karl Ulrich Mayer. 2005. "De-standardization of the Life Course: What it Might Mean? And if it Means Anything, Whether it Actually Took Place?" *Advances in Life Course Research* 9: 27–53.

Burdette, Amy M., Belinda L. Needham, Miles G. Taylor, and Terrence D. Hill. 2017. "Health Lifestyles in Adolescence and Self-rated Health into Adulthood." *Journal of Health and Social Behavior* 58(4): 520–36.

Burton, Linda M. and Vern L. Bengtson. 1985. "Black Grandmothers: Issues of Timing and Continuity of Roles." Pp. 61–77 in *Sage focus editions, Vol. 74. Grandparenthood*, edited by Vern L. Bengtson and J. F. Robertson. Beverley Hills, CA: Sage Publications, Inc.

Bynner, John. 2016. "Institutionalization of Life Course Studies." Pp. 27–58 in *Handbook of the Life course, Volume II*, edited by Michael J. Shanahan, Jeylan T. Mortimer, and Monica K. Johnson. New York: Springer.

Cain, Leonard D. Jr. 1964. "Life Course and Social Structure." Pp. 272–309 in *Handbook of Modern Sociology*, edited by R.E.L. Faris. Chicago, IL: Rand McNally.

Carlson, Daniel L. and Kristi Williams. 2011. "Parenthood, Life Course Expectations, and Mental Health." *Society and Mental Health* 1(1): 20–40.

Clausen, John A. 1991. "Adolescent Competence and the Shaping of the Life Course." *American Journal of Sociology* 96(4): 805–42.

Clipp, Elizabeth Colerick, Eliza K. Pavalko, and Glen H. Elder Jr. 1992. "Trajectories of Health: In Concept and Empirical Pattern." *Behavior, Health and Aging* 2(3): 159–79.

Cockerham, William C. 2005. "Health Lifestyle Theory and the Convergence of Agency and Structure." *Journal of Health and Social Behavior* 46: 51–67.

Cockerham, William C., M. Christine Snead, and Derek F. DeWaal. 2002. "Health Lifestyles in Russia and the Socialist Heritage." *Journal of Health and Social Behavior* 43: 42–55.

Connidis, Ingrid A. 2014. "Age Relations and Family Ties over the Life Course: Spanning the Macro-Micro Divide." *Research in Human Development* 11(4): 291–308.

Corna, Laurie M. 2013. "A Life Course Perspective on Socioeconomic Inequalities in Health: A Critical Review of Conceptual Frameworks." *Advances in Life Course Research* 18: 150–59.

Crosnoe, Robert and April D. Benner. 2016. "Educational Pathways." Pp. 179–200 in *Handbook of the Life course, Volume II*, edited by Michael J. Shanahan, Jeylan Mortimer, and Monica K. Johnson. New York: Springer.

Crystal, Stephen and Dennis Shea. 1990. "Cumulative Advantage, Cumulative Disadvantage, and Inequality among Elderly People." *The Gerontologist* 30: 437–43.

Dannefer, Dale. 1987. "Aging as Intercohort Differentiation: Accentuation, the Matthew Effect, and the Life Course." *Sociological Forum* 2: 211–36.

Dannefer, Dale. 2003. "Cumulative Advantage/disadvantage and the Life Course: Cross-fertilizing Age and Social Science Theory." *The Journals of Gerontology, Series B: Psychological Sciences and Social Sciences* 58: S327–S337.

Dannefer, Dale. 2008. "The Waters We Swim: Everyday Social Processes, Macro-structural Realities, and Human Aging." Pp. 3–22 in *Social Structure and Aging: Continuing Challenges*, edited by K. Warner Schaie and Ronald P. Abeles. New York: Springer.

Dannefer, Dale. 2020. "Systemic and Reflexive: Foundations of Cumulative Dis/Advantage and Life-Course Processes." *The Journals of Gerontology, Series B: Psychological Sciences and Social Sciences* 75(6): 1249–63.

Dannefer, Dale, Jessica Kelley-Moore, and Wenxuan Huang. 2016. "Opening the Social: Sociological Imagination in Life Course Studies." Pp. 91–96 in *Handbook of the Life course, Volume II*, edited by Michael J. Shanahan, Jeylan T. Mortimer, and Monica K. Johnson. New York: Springer.

der Linden, Van, Bernadette Wilhelmina Antonia, Boris Cheval, Stefan Sieber, Dan Orsholits, Idris Guessous, Silvia Stringhini, Rainer Gabriel, Marja Aartsen, David Blane, Delphine Courvoisier, Claudine Burton-Jeangros, Matthias Kliegel, and Stephane Cullati. 2020. "Life Course Socioeconomic Conditions and Frailty at Older Ages." *The Journals of Gerontology: Series B* 75(6): 1348–57.

Diewald, Martin. 2016. "Life Course Risks and Welfare States` Risk Management." Pp. 677–88 in *Handbook of the Life course, Volume II*, edited by Michael J. Shanahan, Jeylan T. Mortimer, and Monica K. Johnson. New York: Springer.

Diprete, Thomas A. and Gregory M. Eirich. 2006. "Cumulative Advantage as a Mechanism for Inequality: A Review of Theoretical and Empirical Developments." *Annual Review of Sociology* 32: 271–97.

Elder, Glen H. Jr. 1974. *Children of the Great Depression: Social Change in Life Experiences*. Chicago, IL: University of Chicago Press.

Elder, Glen H. Jr. 1985. "Perspectives on the Life Course." Pp. 23–49 in *Life Course Dynamics*, edited by Glen. H. Elder Jr. Ithaca, NY: Cornell University Press.

Elder, Glen H. Jr. 1994. "Time, Human Agency, and Social Change: Perspectives on the Life Course." *Social Psychology Quarterly* 57: 4–15.

Elder, Glen H. Jr. 1998. "Life Course and Human Development." Pp. 939–91 in *Handbook of Child Psychology*, edited by W. Damon. New York: Wiley.

Elder, Glen H. Jr. and Linda George. 2016. "Age, Cohorts, and the Life Course." Pp. 59–86 in *Handbook of the Life course*, Vol. II, edited by Michael J. Shanahan, Jeylan T. Mortimer, and Monica K. Johnson. New York: Springer.

Elder, Glen H., Monica Kirkpatrick Johnson, and Robert Crosnoe. 2003. "The Emergence and Development of Life Course Theory." Pp. 3–19 in *Handbook of the Life Course*, edited by Jeylan T. Mortimer and Michael J. Shanahan. New York: Kluwer Academic Publishers.

Esping-Andersen, Gosta. 1990. *The Three Worlds of Welfare Capitalism*. Princeton, NJ: Princeton University Press.

Esping-Andersen, Gosta. 1999. *Social Foundations of Postindustrial Economies*. New York: Oxford University Press.

Ferraro, Kenneth F. 2016. "Life Course Lens on Aging and Health." Pp. 389–406 in *Handbook of the Life course, Volume II*, edited by Michael J. Shanahan, Jeylan T. Mortimer, and Monica K. Johnson. New York: Springer.

Ferraro, Kenneth F., Markus H. Schafer, and Lindsay R. Wilkinson. 2016. "Childhood Disadvantage and Health Problems in Middle and Later Life: Early Imprints on Physical Health?" *American Sociological Review* 81: 107–33.

Ferraro, Kenneth F. and Tetyana P. Shippee. 2009. "Aging and Cumulative Inequality: How Does Inequality Get Under the Skin?" *The Gerontologist* 49: 333–43.

Frech, Adrianne and Sarah Damaske. 2019. "Men's Income Trajectories and Physical and Mental Health at Midlife." *American Journal of Sociology* 124: 1372–412.

Garbarski, Dana. 2014. "The Interplay between Child and Maternal Health: Reciprocal Relationships and Cumulative Disadvantage During Childhood and Adolescence." *Journal of Health and Social Behavior* 55(1): 91–106. 10.1177/0022146513513225.

George, Linda. 1993. "Sociological Perspectives on Life Transitions." *Annual Review of Sociology* 19: 353–73.

George, Linda K. 1999. "Life-Course Perspectives on Mental Health." Pp. 565–83 in *Handbook of the Sociology of Mental Health*, edited by Carol S. Aneshensel, and Jo C. Phelan. New York: Kluwer/Plenum.

George, Linda K. 2003. "What Life-Course Perspectives Offer the Study of Aging and Health." Pp. 161–88 in *Invitation to the the Life Course: Toward New Understandings of Later Life*, edited by Richard A. Settersten, Jr. Amityville, NY: Baywood Publishing Company.

Giddens, Anthony. 1984. *The Constitution of Society: Outline of the Theory of Structuration*. Los Angeles, CA: University of California Press.

Giele, Janet and Glen H. Elder Jr. 1998. "Life Course Research: Development of a Field." Pp. 5–27 in *Methods of Life Course Research: Qualitative and Quantitative Approaches*, edited by Janet Giele and Glen H. Elder. Thousand Oaks, CA: Sage.

Hagestad, Gunhild. 1981. "Problems and Promises in the Social Psychology of Intergenerational Relations." Pp. 11–46 in *Aging – Stability and Change in the Family*, edited by Robert W. Fogel and James G. March. New York: Academic Press.

Hagestad, Gunhild O. 1990. "Social Perspectives on the Life Course." Pp. 151–68 in *Handbook of Aging and the Social Sciences*, Vol. III, edited by Robert H. Binstock and Linda K. George. San Diego, CA: Academic Press.

Hagestad, Gunhild O. 2003. "Interdependent Lives and Relationships in Changing Times: A Life-Course View of Families and Aging." Pp. 135–59 in *Invitation to the Life Course: Toward New Understandings of Later Life*, edited by Richard Settersten. Farmingdale, NY: Baywood.

Hagestad, Gunhild O. and Dale Dannefer. 2001. "Concepts and Theories of Aging: Beyond Microfication in Social Science Approaches." Pp. 3–21 in *Handbook of Aging and the Social Sciences*, 5th edited by Robert H. Binstock and Linda K. George. San Diego, CA: Academic Press.

Hardie, Jessica Halliday and Kristin Turney. 2017. "The Intergenerational Consequences of Parental Health Limitations." *Journal of Marriage and Family* 79: 801–15.

Harris, Kathleen Mullan. 2019. "Intergenerational Transmission of Health: New Data from the Add Health Parent Study." Presented at the Conference on Caregiving and

Family Well-being in Later Life, Bowling Green State University, Bowling Green, OH, April 25, 2019.

He, Wei and Hui Zheng. 2017. "Under the One Child Policy Regime in China: Did Having Younger Sibling(s) Increase the Risk of Overweight and Underweight?" *Asian Population Studies* 13: 267–91.

Heinz, Walter. 2009. "Status Passages as Micro-macro Linkages in Life course Research." Pp. 473–86 in *The Life Course Reader: Individuals and Societies across Time*, edited by Walter R. Heinz, Johannes Huinink, and Ansgar Weymann. New York: Campus Verlag.

Heinz, Walter R. and Helga Kruger. 2001. "Life Course: Innovations and Challenges for Social Research." *Current Sociology* 49(2): 29–45.

Hitlin, Steven and Glen H. Elder Jr. 2007a. "Agency: An Empirical Model of an Abstract Concept." *Advances in Life Course Research* 11: 33–67.

Hitlin, Steven and Glen H. Elder Jr. 2007b. "Time, Self, and the Curiously Abstract Concept of Agency." *Sociological Theory* 25(2): 170–91.

Hollstein, Betina. 2019. "What Autobiographical Narratives Tell Us About the Life Course. Contributions of Qualitative Sequential Analytical Methods." *Advances in Life Course Research* 41.

House, James S., Paula M. Lantz, and Pamela Herd. 2005. "Continuity and Change in the Social Stratification in Aging and Health over the Life Course: Evidence from a Nationally Representative Longitudinal Study from 1986-2001/2002." *The Journals of Gerontology, Series B: Psychological Sciences and Social Sciences* 60: S15-S26.

Landes, Scott D. and Richard A. Settersten Jr. 2019. "The Inseparability of Human Agency and Linked Lives." *Advances in Life Course Research* 42.

Leopold, Thomas. 2018. "Gender Differences in the Consequences of Divorce: A Study of Multiple Outcomes." *Demography* 55: 769–97.

Lynch, Scott M. and Miles G. Taylor. 2016. "Trajectory Models in Aging Research." Pp. 23–51 in *Handbook of Aging and the Social Sciences*, 8th edition edited by Linda K. George and Kenneth F. Ferraro. San Diego, CA: Academic Press.

Madsen, Mia, Per K. Andersen, Mette Gerster, Anne-Marie N. Andersen, Kaare Christensen, and Merete Osler. 2014. "Are the Educational Differences in Incidence of Cardiovascular Disease Explained by Underlying Familial Factors? A Twin Study." *Social Science & Medicine* 118: 182–90.

Marshall, Victor W. 2005. "Agency, Events, and Structure at the End of the Life Course." Pp. 57–91 in *Advances in Life Course Research, Vol. 10*, edited by René Levy, Paolo Ghisletta, Jeane-Marie Le Goff, Dario Spini, and Eric Widmer

Marshall, Victor W. and Margaret M. Mueller. 2003. "Theoretical Roots of the Life Course Perspective." Pp. 3–32 in *Social Dynamics of the Life Course*, edited by Walter R. Heinz and Victor W. Marshall. New York: Aldine De Gruyter.

Mayer, Karl Ulrich. 2009. "New Directions in Life Course Research." *Annual Review of Sociology* 35: 413–33.

Mayer, Karl Ulrich and Urs Schoepflin. 1989. "The State and the Life Course." *Annual Review of Sociology* 15: 187–209.

McLeod, Jane D. and Eliza K. Pavalko. 2008. "From Selection Effects to Reciprocal Processes: What Does Attention to the Life Course Offer?" *Advances in Life Course Research* 13: 75–104.

Milkie, Melissa. 2010. "The Stress Process Model: Some Family-Level Considerations." Pp. 93–108 in *Advances in the Conceptualization of the Stress Process: Essays in*

Honor of Leonard I. Pearlin, edited by William R. Avison, Carol S. Aneshensel, Scott Schieman, and Blair Wheaton. New York: Springer.

Pudrovska, Tetyanna. 2010. "Why is Cancer More Depressing for Men than Women among Older White Adults?" *Social Forces* 89: 535–58.

Moen, Phyllis, Erin L. Kelly, Eric Tranby, and Quinlei Huang. 2011. "Changing Work, Changing Health: Can Real Work-Time Flexibility Promote Health Behaviors and Well-Being?" *Journal of Health and Social Behavior* 52(4): 404–29.

Mollborn, Stefanie and Elizabeth Lawrence. 2018. "Family, Peer, and School Influences on Children's Developing Health Lifestyles." *Journal of Health and Social Behavior* 59(1): 133–50.

Handbook of the Life Course. 2003. Edited by Jeylan T. Mortimer and Michael J. Shanahan. New York: Kluwer Academic Publishers.

Neugarten, Bernice L. 1970. "Dynamics of the Transition of Middle Age to Old Age." *Journal of Geriatric Psychiatry* 4(1): 71–87.

Niu, Li, Lindsay T. Hoyt, and Mark C. Pachucki. 2019. "Context Matters: Adolescent Neighborhood and School Influences on Young Adult Body Mass Index." *Journal of Adolescent Health* 64(3): 405–10.

O'Rand, Angela M. 1996. "The Precious and the Precocious: Understanding Cumulative Disadvantage and Cumulative Advantage over the Life Course." *The Gerontologist* 36(2): 230–38.

O'Rand, Angela M. 2006. "Stratification and the Life Course: Life Course Capital, Life Course Risks, and Social Inequality." Pp. 145–62 in *Handbook of Aging and the Social Sciences*, 6th edition edited by Robert H. Binstock and Linda K. George. Burlington, MA: Academic Press.

O'Rand, Angela M. and Cheryl Elman. 2004. "The Race is to the Swift: Socioeconomic Origins, Adult Education, and Wage Attainment." *American Journal of Sociology* 110(1): 123–60.

Pavalko, Eliza K. and Jennifer Caputo. 2013. "Social Inequality and Health across the Life Course." *American Behavioral Scientist* 57(8): 1040–56.

Pavalko, Eliza K., Fang Gong, and J. Scott Long. 2007. "Women's Work, Cohort Change, and Health." *Journal of Health and Social Behavior* 48: 352–68.

Piraino, Patrizio, Sean Muller, Jeanne Cilliers, and Johan Fourie. 2014. "The Transmission of Longevity across Generations: The Case of the Settler Cape Colony." *Research in Social Stratification and Mobility* 35: 105–19.

Quesnel-Vallée, Amélie, Andrea Willson, and Sandra Reiter-Campeau. 2016. "Health Inequalities among Older Adults in Developed Countries: Reconciling Theories and Policy Approaches." Pp. 483–502 in *Handbook of Aging and the Social Sciences*, 8th edited by Linda George and Kenneth Ferraro. New York: Academic Press.

Riley, Matilda White. 1979. "Introduction: Life-Course Perspectives." Pp. 3–13 in *Aging from Birth to Death*, edited by Matilda White Riley. Boulder, CO: Westview.

Schafer, Marcus H., Kenneth F. Ferraro, and Sarah A. Mustillo. 2011. "Children of Misfortune: Early Adversity and Cumulative Inequality in Perceived Life Trajectories." *American Journal of Sociology* 116: 1053–91.

Schafer, Marcus H., Tetyana Pylypiv Shippee, and Kenneth F. Ferraro. 2009. "When Does Disadvantage Not Accumulate? Toward a Sociological Conceptualization of Resilience." *Swiss Journal of Sociology* 35(2): 231–51.

Settersten, Richard A. Jr. 2003b. "Age Structuring and the Rhythm of the Life Course." Pp. 81–98 in *Handbook of the Life Course*, edited by Jeylan T. Mortimer and Michael J. Shanahan. New York: Kluwer Academic Publishers.

Sewel, William H. Jr. 1992. "A Theory of Structure: Duality, Agency, and Transformation." *American Journal of Sociology* 9: 1–29.

Shanahan, Michael and Ross Macmillan. 2008. *Biography and the Sociological Imagination: Contexts and Contingencies.* New York: Norton.

Handbook of the Life Course, Volume II. 2016. Edited by Michael J. Shanahan, Jeylan T. Mortimer, and Monica Kirkpatrick Johnson. New York: Springer.

Shuey, Kim and Andrea Willson. 2014. "Economic Hardship in Childhood and Adult Health Trajectories: An Alternative Approach to Investigating Life-course Processes." *Advances in Life Course Research* 22: 49–61.

Shuey, Kim M., Andrea E. Willson, and Travis Hackshaw. 2020. "Family Structure and Parents' Health: Implications for the Reproduction of Health Inequality across Generations." *Journal of Family Issues, Forthcoming.* Online release August 17, 2020. https://doi.org/10.1177/0192513X20946350

Strohschein, Lisa. 2005. "Parental Divorce and Child Mental Health Trajectories." *Journal of Marriage and Family* 67(5): 1286–1300.

Tausig, Mark. 2013. "The Sociology of Work and Well-being." Pp. 433–56 in *Handbook of the Sociology of Mental Health*, 2nd edition edited by Carol S. Aneshensel, Jo C. Phelan, and Alex Bierman. New York: Springer.

Thoits, Peggy A. 2006. "Personal Agency in the Stress Process." *Journal of Health and Social Behavior* 47(4): 309–23.

Thompson, Owen. 2014. "Genetic Mechanisms in the Intergenerational Transmission of Health." *Journal of Health Economics* 35: 132–46.

Uhlenberg, Peter and Margaret Mueller. 2003. "Family Context and Individual Well-Being: Patterns and Mechanisms in Life Course Perspective." Pp. 123–48 in *Handbook of the Life Course*, edited by Jeylan T. Mortimer and Michael J. Shanahan. New York: Kluwer Academic Publishers.

Watkins-Hayes, Celeste. 2019. *Remaking a Life: How Women Living with HIV/AIDS Confront Inequality.* Oakland, CA: University of California Press.

Willson, Andrea E. and Kim M. Shuey. 2016. "Life Course Pathways of Economic Hardship and Mobility and Midlife Trajectories of Health." *Journal of Health and Social Behavior* 57: 407–22.

Willson, Andrea E. and Kim M. Shuey. 2018. "A Longitudinal Analysis of the Intergenerational Transmission of Health Inequality." *The Journals of Gerontology Series B: Psychological Sciences and Social Sciences* 74(1): 181–91.

Willson, Andrea E., Kim M. Shuey, and Glen H. Elder Jr. 2007. "Cumulative Advantage Processes as Mechanisms of Inequality in Life Course Health." *American Journal of Sociology* 112(6): 1886–1924.

Yuan, Anastasia and S. Vogt. 2008. "Exploring the Changes in Economic Hardship and Children's Well-being over Time: The "Linked Lives" of Parents and Children." *Advances in Life Course Research* 13: 321–41.

10

Social Capital and Health

Lijun Song and Yvonne Chen

The idea of social capital has a long history in the social sciences. Its intellectual origin is under debate. Some quote sociological predecessors, including Emile Durkheim, Talcott Parsons, Karl Marx, Frederick Engels, Max Weber, and Georg Simmel (Portes and Sensenbrenner 1993). Some cite economists, such as David Hume, Edmund Burke, and Adam Smith (Woolcock 1998). Others name philosophers such as John Dewey (Farr 2004). According to Putnam (2000), the term social capital first appeared in a 1916 article by Lyda Judson Hanifan, an education reformer.

Despite competing claims to its nativity, social capital has grown into a popular paradigm during the last three decades. As is the case with new concepts, it has triggered extensive debates due to its diverse definitions, which inevitably result in controversial operationalization, divergent measurement, disparate mechanisms, mixed evidence, various implications, and arduous challenges. A general consensus does exist on the four key figures who popularized this concept and stimulated its theoretical development during the 1980s and the early 1990s, including three sociologists, Pierre Bourdieu (1986 [1983]), Nan Lin (1982, 2001), and James S. Coleman (1988, 1990), and one political scientist, Robert D. Putnam (1993, 2000).

Social capital as a theoretical tool has gained burgeoning acceptance in the health sciences. A search of the Web of Science for articles with "social capital" and "health" in their topics showed an accelerating popularity from the middle 1990s (see Figure 10.1). There was only one such article in 1994. But the number rose to 25 in 1999, jumped to 224 in 2009, and remained above 540 in 2018 and 2019. Despite its substantial development, this literature is dominated by Putnam's notion partly because of its political implications and quick measurements in secondary data (Foley and Edwards 1999). The original contributions of sociological theories have been relatively understated but increasingly appreciated and extended (Moore et al. 2005; Pevalin 2003; Song 2013a; Song et al. 2010; Webber and Huxley 2004).

The Wiley Blackwell Companion to Medical Sociology, First Edition. Edited by William C. Cockerham.

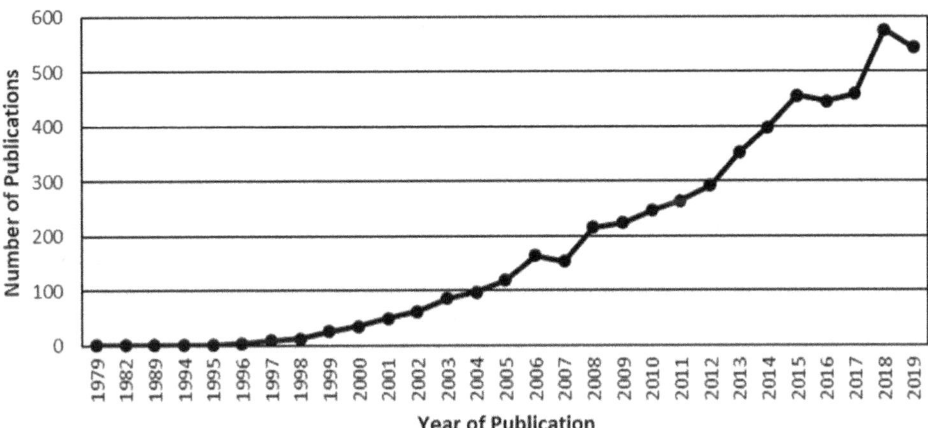

Figure 10.1 Articles with "social capital" and "health" in their topics: Web of Science (1979–2019).

In this chapter, our goal is to provide a selective review and highlight social capital as a significant social antecedent of health from a sociological perspective. We first introduce social capital concepts advanced by Bourdieu, Lin, Coleman, and Putnam. We then turn to the theoretical extension and empirical application of these four approaches to health. We conclude with challenges and future research directions. Social capital is one of the most acknowledged contributions from sociology to social science and public discourse during the last three decades (Portes 1998). Considering its intrinsic sociological nature, sociologists should play a crucial role in further refining social capital and its relationship with health.

Social Capital: Four Theoretical Approaches

Bourdieu: Exclusive Resources from Durable Networks

Bourdieu pioneered in theorizing social capital. He introduced it in his French version of *Distinction* in 1979 (Adam and Rončević 2003; Bourdieu 1984), and published his theory in a chapter in French in 1983 and later in English in 1986. He defines and distinguishes social capital from its sources and returns in the forms of other types of capital at the individual level, and emphasizes its cross-space network embeddedness and exclusive nature. However, he lacks attention to its operationalization and measurement.

Contending that the unequal distribution of capital determines the production and reproduction of social structure, Bourdieu identifies three essential forms of capital: economic, cultural, and social. Economic and cultural capital are personally owned. Social capital is embedded in social networks. It is "the aggregate of the actual or potential resources which are linked to possession of a durable network of more or less institutionalized relationships of mutual acquaintance and recognition – or in other words, to membership in a group – which provides each of its members with the backing of the collectivity-owned capital, a 'credential' which entitles them to credit, in the various senses of the word" (Bourdieu 1986 [1983]: 248–249). Its volume depends on two elements: network size and network members' (alters') capital.

Sources and returns of social capital are the other two forms of capital. Stratification is reproduced through the conversion between the three forms of capital. Despite such convertibility, social capital exerts its independent effects. "These effects, in which spontaneous sociology readily perceives the work of 'connections,' are particularly visible in all cases in which different individuals obtain very unequal profits from virtually equivalent (economic or cultural) capital, depending on the extent to which they can mobilize by proxy the capital of a group (a family, the alumni of an elite school, a select club, the aristocracy, etc.) that is more or less constituted as such and more or less rich in capital" (1986 [1983]: 256).

Networks of relationships are based on "material and symbolic exchanges" and spread across diverse contexts including physical, economic, and social space. Their establishment and maintenance requires "investment strategies, individual or collective," one of which is social exclusion. Social institutions legitimate within-group exchanges and exclude members whose mistakes threaten group interests.

Lin: Resources Embedded in Social Networks

Lin provides his fully developed theoretical scheme on social capital in a book (2001), which builds upon social resources theory he developed in the late 1970s and early 1980s (1982). He grounds his definition in the tradition of personal capital theories (e.g. Marx's capital, human and cultural capital). He typologizes social capital, offers falsifiable operationalization and measurement, and theorizes its structural and networking sources, mechanisms, and instrumental and expressive returns at the individual level.

Lin defines social capital as "resources embedded in a social structure that are accessed and/or mobilized in purposive actions" and operationally as "resources embedded in social networks accessed and used by actors for actions" (2001: 25, 29). In contrast with personal capital as resources individuals (egos) control, social capital is resources (e.g. wealth, power, reputation, and social networks) that alters (including alters in cyberspace) possess and ego can gain access to through direct or indirect ties. It has two types: accessed (resources available from alters) and mobilized (resources from alters ego uses). Assuming that alters' resources hinge upon their positions in the hierarchical social structure, Lin and colleagues developed a position generator to map alters' or accessed status (Lin and Dumin 1986; Lin et al. 2001). This instrument asks ego to identify alters associated with a sample of occupations salient in a society. Lin stresses three dimensions of accessed status: extensity (the size of different positions alters occupy), upper reachability (alters' highest position), and heterogeneity (the status range between alters' highest and lowest positions). Accessed social capital can also be measured as status of alters ego discusses important matter with using the name generator and as the total kinds of concrete resources available from alters using the resource generator (Burt 1984; Song and Chang 2012; Van der Gaag and Snijders 2005). Mobilized social capital is indicated by status of alters ego uses.

Lin proposes two sources of social capital: structural and networking (2001). Structural sources include ego's prior hierarchical roles or positions, both ascribed (e.g. gender, race/ethnicity, family origins) and achieved (e.g. socioeconomic status or SES). Networking sources refer to network locations (weak ties and closeness to social bridges). Ego's positions and network locations positively affect social capital. Their positive effects are moderated by three macro-level structural factors (the number of hierarchical levels and the equal distribution of occupants and resources across levels) respectively in negative and positive directions. Besides, collective assets such as trust and norms can either foster or restrict social capital.

Lin lists four mechanisms (information, influence, social credentials, and group identity) for instrumental (e.g. wealth, power, and reputation) and expressive (e.g. health and life satisfaction) returns to social capital. He recognizes that the two forms of returns fortify each other but his theory focuses on instrumental returns. The two forms of returns depend on tie strength. As Lin argues, social capital derived from weak ties creates more instrumental returns, while that embedded in strong ties produces more expressive returns. He criticizes Bourdieu and Coleman for their emphasis on exclusive or closed networks.

Social capital and macro-level "institutional fields" influences each other (Lin 2001). On the one hand, an institutional field regulates and constrains its members' access to and use of social capital by legitimating certain norms of social interaction. On the other hand, members can establish alternative norms and transform the existing institutional field through activating and mobilizing social capital.

Lin's initial efforts were geared toward an individual-level analysis. He later extends his theory to the macro level (2008). He distinguishes two forms of social capital for a collectivity (e.g. associations, organizations, communities, regions, or nation-states): internal (resources provided by its members), and external (resources from other collectivities).

Coleman: Functional Social-structural Resources

Coleman's article on the role of social capital in the creation of human capital called multidisciplinary attention to this term (1988). Then, he devoted one chapter to analyzing social capital, including a functionalist definition, diverse operationalization, and structural and networking sources (1990). He emphasizes its positive function as a public good at the collective level.

Coleman defines social capital by its function. "It is not a single entity, but a variety of different entities having two characteristics in common: They all consist of some aspect of a social structure, and they facilitate certain actions of individuals who are within that structure. Like other forms of capital, social capital is productive, making possible the achievement of certain ends that would not be attainable in its absence" (1990: 302). He justified his broad functionalist definition by its utility in explaining multiple outcomes and bridging the micro- and macro-levels.

A catch-all definition leads to diverse operationalization. Coleman lists six forms of social capital: (1) obligations, expectations of reciprocity, and trustworthiness, (2) information potential, (3) norms and effective sanctions, (4) authority relations, (5) appropriable social organizations, and (6) intentional organizations (1990). He hesitates about the value of social capital as a quantifiable concept. In his work on dropout rates (1988), he measures family social capital as the presence of parents, the number of siblings, and mother's expectation for child's education and community social capital as the presence of religiously based high schools and students' religious attendance.

Coleman discusses five structural and networking sources of social capital: network closure, stability of social structure, altruistic and collectivistic ideology, affluence, and government support (1990). The first three factors increase social capital but the other two factors do the opposite. He maintains that social capital has positive functions at both individual (as a private good) and collective levels (as a public good). But he emphasizes its public good aspect. He briefly mentions the importance of social capital as patient-doctor trust for access to medical care. He also recognizes that social capital can have negative functions (e.g. effective sanctions may constrain certain actions).

Putnam: Facilitating Features of Social Organization

Putnam's work on social capital and democracy appeared in 1993. His 1995 article, "Bowling Alone," and its expansion into a book of the same main title in 2000 popularized the term social capital beyond the academic community. Drawing upon Coleman's work, he proposes a functionalist definition and diverse operationalization. He constructs a state-level index and discusses structural sources. He typologizes social capital and underlines its public good aspect.

Putnam defines social capital initially as "features of social organization, such as trust, norms and networks that can improve the efficiency of society by facilitating coordinated actions" (1993: 167) and later as "connections among individuals – social networks and the norms of reciprocity and trustworthiness that arise from them" (2000: 19). Social connections can be formal (e.g. memberships and participation in formal organizations and activities) and informal (e.g. participation with family, friends, and neighbors in social and leisure activities). The norms of reciprocity and trust can be specific and generalized, and the generalized aspect is Putnam's focus. He develops a state-level social capital index, containing 14 items covering areas such as community organizational life, engagement in public affairs, community volunteerism, informal sociability, and social trust. He observes an overall decline of social capital in American society and attributes that decline to multiple factors, such as time and financial pressure, suburbanization, electronic entertainment, and generational change. He doubts the potential of small groups, social movements, and telecommunications including the Internet to offset that decline.

Putnam distinguishes two types of social capital: bonding (exclusive) and bridging (inclusive) (2000). The former exists in relationships connecting homogeneous individuals and the latter relationships linking heterogeneous persons. The former enhances within-group reciprocity and solidarity, and the latter helps obtain external goods from outside groups. He warns that the former can create between-group enmity. Lin criticizes Putnam's typology from a strict social network perspective, arguing that bonding and bridging are properties of social networks instead of social capital (2008).

Similar to Coleman, Putnam thinks of social capital as both a private and a public good but emphasizes the latter (2000). He discusses its positive functions in various areas including education and children's welfare, neighborhood safety and productivity, economic development, health and happiness, democracy, and tolerance and equality. He also mentions its negative functions in terms of its use for corruption, sectarianism, ethnocentrism, and antisocial behaviors.

Summary: A Tale of Two Schools

All the four scholars agree that social capital is resources derived from social relationships and operates net of other forms of capital. However, their definitions and operationalization diverge from one another. Their work exemplifies two schools of theoretical perspectives: the network-based conflict perspective of Bourdieu and Lin, and the normative (or communal) functionalist perspective of Coleman and Putnam.

Bourdieu's and Lin's network-based conflict approaches are more refined and precise, distinguishing social capital from its antecedents and yields for individuals (Adam and Rončević 2003; Cook 2005; Portes 1998). They treat social capital as a scarce asset with social networks across multiple spaces as its preconditions. They stress its role in the production and reproduction of social stratification, and theorize inequalities in its access and returns. They highlight the conversion between personal advantages, in particular personal capital, and social capital. Their work differs in three ways. First, Lin applies a stronger network perspective and develops a network instrument to measure social capital, while Bourdieu lacks attention to operationalization and measurement. Second, in the creation of social capital, Bourdieu underlies durable ties, network closure, and social exclusion, while Lin weak ties and network bridging. Third, Lin analyzes the links between micro-, meso-, and macrostructures of society.

In contrast, Coleman and Putnam apply a normative functionalist perspective. They provide broad definitions and diverse operationalization. Putnam's three forms of social capital overlap with the six forms Coleman identifies. Their proposed measurement captures social integration or social cohesion but not social networks. They emphasize social capital more as a public good. They mention its negative functions in terms of its misuse and unintended consequences. Their work receives more critiques. Their tautological arguments of social capital as both a cause and an effect mingles social capital with its sources and outcomes (Lin 2001; Portes 1998). Their diverse forms of social capital operate through different mechanisms and influence each other in unclear causal orders. Such "everything but the kitchen sink" conceptualization creates difficulties for theoretical development and empirical research (Cook 2005). In addition, some critics argue against specifying trust and norms of reciprocity as subjective components of social capital (Cook 2005; Foley and Edwards 1999; Lin 2001; Portes 1998). They maintain that social capital is neutral, objective, and rooted in social relationships, which contributes to its unique heuristic values. Next, we review the applications of each approach in the health literature.

Social Capital and Health: Theoretical Development and Empirical Evidence

Bourdieu: Inconsistent Applications

The theoretical utility of Bourdieu's work for health has been increasingly recognized. Applications of his work, however, are controversial. Scholars adopt different parts of his theory and operationalize and measure social capital in inconsistent ways, many of which reflect Coleman's and Putnam's approaches.

Ziersch underlines Bourdieu's notion of social capital as individual resources and decomposes it into sources (informal and formal networks, and values such as trust, reciprocity, and safety) and outcomes (help, acceptance, civic actions, and control) (2005). Her community study in Australia shows inconsistent associations between neighborhood-based social capital indicators and physical and mental health.

In contrast, Carpiano treats Bourdieu's notion as neighborhood resources with Putnam's idea as a precondition (2006). His model lists four forms of social capital (neighborhood organization participation, informal social control, social support, and social leverage) and neighborhood attachment as a moderator. His community study in Los Angeles finds inconsistent associations between social capital indicators and health behaviors and general health and inconsistent moderating effects of neighborhood attachment (2007).

Stephens credits Ziersch and Carpiano for disentangling sources and outcomes of social capital (2008). However, she criticizes them for departing from Bourdieu by constraining attention to geographical locations, omitting broader social issues on social inequalities and social exclusion, and measuring social capital as existing concepts using secondary quantitative data. Her qualitative interviews in New Zealand show social connections beyond neighborhoods, unequal access to social connections between the deprived and non-deprived, and people's competition for valuable connections and other resources including health services.

Some scholars apply Bourdieu's typology of capital. A community study in England examines economic and social capital (low sense of loneliness, desire to move, meeting with neighbors, and sense of community), and finds that economic capital and one social capital indicator (low sense of loneliness) have independent negative associations with psychological morbidity (Gatrell et al. 2004). A community study in Canada captures social classes based on economic, cultural, and social capital (trust in community members, trust in politicians, sense of community, low sense of loneliness, networking with neighbors, volunteerism, voting, and voluntary membership) and reports a positive association between social classes and health conditions (Veenstra 2007). A community study in Belgium demonstrates the positive associations of the three forms of capital with general physical and mental health but results vary by the two indicators of social capital (neighborhood social cohesion and social support) (Pinxten and Lievens

2014). A study of 15 European countries shows the positive association of social capital (number of social activities) with health care utilization net of economic and cultural capital (Paccoud et al. 2020).

Some scholars propose capital interplay theory based on Bourdieu's capital conversion argument (Veenstra and Abel 2015, 2019). They identify three types of capital interplay: acquisition (one form of capital generates another), transmission (one person's capital contributes to another person's), and multiplier (one form of capital multiplies the effect of another). Their study of young men in Switzerland supports only the capital acquisition argument. Parents' objectified cultural capital and economic and social capital (ties to influential people) mediate the association between their institutionalized cultural capital and young men's general health (Veenstra and Abel 2015). Opposite to the capital multiplier argument, the positive association between institutionalized cultural capital of young men and their health is stronger when parents have lower institutionalized cultural capital and social capital. Compensatory capital interplay is proposed as the explanation.

Lin: Rigorous Applications and Extension

Lin's approach is stricter and more fully developed, which facilitates its methodological and theoretical growth and empirical applications in the health literature. The methodological growth is the refined measurement of social capital. The theoretical growth includes coherently articulated mechanisms, the integration of his theory with other theories, challenges to its assumptions, and the emergence of its competing theory, social cost theory.

Lin operationalizes accessed social capital as accessed status. The concept of accessed status and its measurement has been expanded. Song provides a binary typology: absolute (alters' status) and relative (alters' status relative to ego's) (2015a). Lin's work examines the former. Song uses diversity and extensity respectively to refer to Lin's idea of extensity and heterogeneity (2012). Apart from diversity, extensity, and upper reachability, two more attributes of absolute accessed status are examined in the health literature: average and lower reachability (alters' average and lowest status) (Song 2011, 2015a; Song and Chang 2012). In contrast, relative higher or lower accessed status is objectively calculated as the size and proportion of alters' positions ranked higher or lower than ego's and subjectively measured as ego's perceived lower or higher status relative to alters (Song 2015a, forthcoming; Song and Pettis 2018). Diverse mechanisms are proposed for the protective health effect of alters' resources, including 1) influencing macro-level health policy decision-making, 2) advancing objective or SES attainment, 3) promoting subjective status attainment, 4) providing social support, 5) facilitating help seeking, 6) encouraging healthy norms and lifestyles, 7) improving access to health care and insurance, 8) acting as social credentials, 9) decreasing stress exposure, 10) reinforcing psychological resources, and 11) boosting the immune system (Song et al. 2018; Song and Pettis 2018).

Most existing empirical studies measure absolute accessed status through the position or name generator and demonstrate its positive role for health across societies:

mental health and health information search in the US; general health and healthy body weight in Montreal, Canada; general health, mental health, and health literacy in Taiwan; and general health in Belgium (e.g., Lee et al. 2017; Moore et al. 2011, 2009b; Song 2011; Song and Chang 2012; Song and Lin 2009; Verhaeghe et al. 2012; Yang et al. 2013). Three community studies respectively in the UK, Japan, and rural China measure accessed social capital through the resource generator and report its positive associations respectively with mental health, general health and health-related quality of life (Kobayashi et al. 2013; Sun et al. 2017; Webber and Huxley 2007). A two-wave longitudinal clinical study in the UK shows no evidence for the role of accessed resources in the course of depression (Webber et al. 2011).

Some studies investigate the indirect, mediating, and interaction effects of accessed status. A couple of US studies report that absolute accessed status is indirectly associated with mental health and body weight through subjective status and health lifestyle (Song 2011; Song et al. 2017). A few studies in the US and Montreal of Canada find that absolute accessed status mediates the associations between more upstream factors (age, gender, race/ethnicity, SES, neighborhood advantage, social integration, social cohesion, psychological resources) and health outcomes (Haines et al. 2011; Moore et al. 2014a; Song 2011; Song et al. 2017).

The analysis of the interaction effect of accessed status requires the combination of Lin's theory with other theories or perspectives. Song and Lin (2009) propose a pair of competing explanations on the interaction between personal and social capital. The compensation effect proposition expects people with lower status to need, mobilize, and benefits more from alters' resources, while the cumulative advantage proposition anticipates those with higher status to invest, mobilize, and benefit from alters' resources more successfully. Supporting the former proposition, the positive association between accessed occupations and mental health is stronger for those with lower education in Taiwan (Song and Lin 2009). Also, accessed status interacts with gender. Accessed education is associated with body weight ratings negatively for women but positively for men in the US (Song et al. 2017). Arguably alters' resources help produce and reproduce the gendered body weight norm at the network level. Accessed resources is positively associated with health (health-related quality of life in rural China and general health in urban Japan) more strongly for women (Kobayashi et al. 2013; Sun et al. 2017). Arguably women seek and mobilize resources from social contacts more actively than men. A community study in Canada documents accessed status as a stress buffer (Mandelbaum et al. 2018). The diversity of accessed occupations negatively moderates the positive association between maternal stress and children's emotional overeating.

Social cost theory recently emerges in competition with Lin's social capital theory (Song, Forthcoming; Song et al. 2018; Song and Pettis 2018). Lin's theory emphasizes the bright side of accessed status as a resource source and builds on the social resources assumption that alters' resources are valuable and protective. Social cost theory highlights the dark side of accessed status as a source of detrimental social expenses and rests on the social expenses assumption. Three mechanisms are possible for the harmful role of absolute accessed status and relative higher accessed status and the protective role of relative lower accessed status: upward or negative social comparison, receipt of harmful resources, and burdensome networking investment and expenses. Song argues that the social resources assumption can apply more to instrumental and objective outcomes but the social expenses assumption expressive, subjective, and evaluative outcomes. Three single-society studies examine the double-edged role of accessed status. Findings on mental health in urban China and South Korea support social cost theory (Lee and Kawachi 2017; Song 2015b). Findings from South Korea and Montreal show that the double-edged role varies by gender and education in the prediction of mental health and psychological resources (Lee and Kawachi 2017; Moore et al. 2009a).

Song further proposes three institutional explanations to predict the varying explanatory power of the two competing theories: collectivistic advantage, collectivistic disadvantage, and inequality structure (Song 2014a, 2015a; Song, Forthcoming; Song et al. 2018; Song and Pettis 2018). The collectivistic advantage explanation anticipates that social capital theory applies more to collectivistic societies but social cost theory individualistic societies, while the collectivistic disadvantage explanation predicts the opposite. The inequality structure explanation expects that social capital theory applies to more egalitarian societies and social cost theory more unequal societies. Song and colleagues use data simultaneously collected from three societies (the US, urban China, and Taiwan) and examine the associations of accessed status with depression, life satisfaction, and self-reported health limitation (Song 2014a, 2015a; Song, Forthcoming; Song and Pettis 2018). The collectivistic disadvantage explanation and the inequality structure explanation receives tentatively more evidence respectively in the analysis of mental and physical health. Methodologically, some indicators of accessed status (average and lower reachability) fit more to social capital theory but some (higher reachability and relative higher accessed status) social cost theory.

In addition, social capital exists in electronic networks. Social capital in online mothers' networks influence mothers' and their children's health through the provision of social support (Drentea and Moren-Cross 2005). Social capital among vaccine-refusing mothers provides social support and validation during online discussion (Reich 2018).

Coleman: Neighborhood, Family, and Workplace

Many scholars fail to recognize that Putnam's work draws upon Coleman's. They cite only Putnam's work when analyzing his three forms of social capital that overlap with the six forms Coleman distinguishes. We review studies here that cite and extend Coleman's idea to health in three life domains: neighborhood, family, and workplace.

Sampson and colleagues develop a neighborhood-level collective efficacy theory (Sampson et al. 1999, 1997). It redefines social capital as shared expectations for action among neighbors. Collective efficacy has three elements: informal social control (neighbors are counted on to intervene), social cohesion (neighborhood is close-knit; neighbors help each other, get along, and share values), and trust (neighbors can be trusted). It is measured as the aggregation of individual responses. It is spatially dynamic in that it spills over between surrounding neighborhoods.

Collective efficacy is expected to protect health by depressing health risks in neighborhoods, creating stress buffers such as social support and safety nets, and maintaining and achieving health-relevant resources (Drukker et al. 2005). Results are mixed. Drukker and colleagues (2003) analyze mental and general health of one grade of primary school students in Maastricht, the Netherlands, and find a positive association only between informal social control and mental health. Drukker and colleagues (2005) further compare these students with children aged 12 in Chicago. The three elements of collective efficacy are positively associated with perceived health for the Dutch sample but only for the Hispanic subsample in Chicago. Another study from Chicago measures the combination of reciprocal exchange and local voluntary participation at the neighborhood level (Morenoff 2003). Neighborhood internal social capital protects birth weight and mediates the effect of neighborhood poverty and residential mobility. Also, social capital from surrounding neighborhoods predicts birth weight more strongly for focal neighborhoods with more internal social capital. A US study reports the positive association between a latent collective efficacy factor and children's general health with family functioning as a mediator (Fan and Chen 2012). A longitudinal study in Los Angeles documents the negative effect of a collective efficacy scale on body weight increase only among women (Ullmann et al. 2013). A study in Pennsylvania finds the positive association between collective efficacy (neighbors' collective neighborhood improvement efforts) and African-American women's use of mammography (Dean et al. 2014). A Dutch study documents the positive association between neighborhood social cohesion and health with physical activity as a mediator (Mohnen et al. 2012).

Some scholars investigate both family and community social capital. A longitudinal study of young people in England finds that mental health is positively associated with family social capital (parental relationships, evening meal with family, and parental surveillance) but not with community social capital (parental involvement at school, sociability, and involvement in activities outside home) (Rothon et al. 2012). A community study in China reports that family (parent-child interaction and parental monitoring) and community (social cohesion, trust, sense of belonging, neighbors' care about and attention to children) social capital negatively mediate the positive association between parental migration and depression (Wu et al. 2015).

Some scholars examine workplace social capital (Suzuki et al. 2010). Using data of workers in Okayama, Japan, they measure trust and reciprocity at the individual and company levels. With the exception of company reciprocity, all the other three indicators are positively associated with workers' health.

Putnam: Expansive Applications and Mixed Evidence

Kawachi and colleagues first applied Putnam's idea of social capital and reported its mediating effect on the income inequality-mortality relationship in 1997. A huge body of empirical applications have emerged since then. Results are mixed, varying with forms, indicators and levels of social capital, outcomes, units of analysis, data sources, populations, and societies. There is stronger evidence for the salubrious effects of trust and individual social capital.

Putnam's three forms of social capital are divided into the structural (social connections) and cognitive (trust and norms of reciprocity) dimensions (Bain and Hicks 1998). His bonding and bridging social capital is grouped into horizontal (between people of equals) and vertical or linking dimensions (between people interacting across institutionalized power gradients) (Islam et al. 2006; Szreter and Woolcock 2004). Going beyond his focus on the state level, scholars measure both individual social capital, which exerts a compositional effect, and ecological social capital (usually as the aggregation of individual responses at the community, state, and country level) which has a contextual impact (Poortinga 2006).

Different possible mechanisms link different levels of social capital to health (Kawachi 1999; Kawachi et al. 1999a, 1999b). Pathways for individual and neighborhood social capital overlap, including social support, healthy norms and behaviors, social engagement, psychological resources, and physiological and biological mechanisms. Pathways for neighborhood social capital further include informal social control, local services and facilities, and collective socialization. State social capital operates through egalitarianism-oriented political participation and policymaking.

At the individual level, a US longitudinal study reports that only one out of five social capital indicators, neighbor trust, decreases major depression (Fujiwara and Kawachi 2008a). In a US adult twins study, only one out of four social capital indicators, neighbor trust, is consistently positively related to one out of four health outcomes among both monozygotic and dizygotic twins (Fujiwara and Kawachi 2008b). In two British longitudinal studies, only one out of three social capital indicators, generalized trust, is positively associated with psychological and general health (Giordano et al. 2012; Giordano and Lindström 2011). A longitudinal study in rural Malawi measures four indicators of social participation (Myroniuk and Anglewicz 2015). Varying by gender, age, health outcome, and indicator of social participation, its results show that social participation predicts better physical health but worse mental health. A study of 78 countries measures three forms of social capital: particularized and generalized trust, and social participation (Glanville and Story 2018). All three forms are positively associated with general health. One specific indicator of each trust factor also positively interacts with social participation.

At the neighborhood level, the association between death rates and social capital varies by cause of death, race/ethnicity, gender, and social capital indicator in Chicago (Lochner et al. 2003). At the US state level, all three social capital indicators – civic engagement, generalized trust, and reciprocity – are positively associated with general health, and the first two indicators are negatively related to total mortality rates (Kawachi et al. 1999a, 1997). One US study measures two county social capital scales using five indicators and two state social capital scales using ten indicators (Kim et al. 2006a). State social capital predicts negatively obesity and physical inactivity, while county social capital physical inactivity. American Indians/Alaska Natives (versus whites) benefit less from both levels of social capital in the prediction of obesity. Another US study captures county social capital using three indices and six indicators and state social capital using five indices and twenty-seven indicators (Lee and Kim 2013). It demonstrates the acceptable validity of most indices but reports their varying associations with population health outcomes.

Many studies analyze multilevel social capital. In a US study, three out of six individual social capital indicators and community bonding (instead of bridging) social capital are positively associated with general health (Kim et al. 2006). In a community study in Japan, elderly people's dental status is positively associated with individual and community horizontal (instead of vertical) social capital (Aida et al. 2009). In a study of China, individual bonding trust is positively associated with general health in both rural and urban China, individual and county bridging trust do so only in urban China, but social participation has no effect (Meng and Chen 2014). In a study of 45 countries, individual and national voluntary participation and individual trust are positively associated with general health (Mansyur et al. 2008). In a study of 22 European countries, individual (instead of national) civic participation and generalized trust predict better general health (Poortinga 2006). In a study of 35 European countries, individual (instead of national) trust is positively associated with general health (Campos-Matos et al. 2016). In a study of 69 countries, individual and national trust positively predict general health and interact with each other (Jen et al. 2010).

In addition, social capital can be detrimental directly or indirectly through across-level interaction (for a review see Villalonga-Olives and Kawachi 2017). In a community study on individual social capital in Sweden, high social participation combined with low trust is positively associated high alcohol consumption among men (Lindström 2005). In a study of 40 US communities, community trust protects health for high-trust individuals but damages health for low-trust individuals (Subramanian et al. 2002). In a study of India, community intragroup bonding (instead of intergroup binding) ties are negatively associated with women's antenatal care use and children's complete immunization, and they benefit individuals with lower intragroup bonding ties but hurt those with higher such ties (Story 2014). In two studies of respectively 22 and 35 European countries, higher national social capital protects health for individuals with high social capital but hurt those with lower social capital (Campos-Matos et al. 2016; Poortinga 2006). In a study of 45 countries, the protective effects of individual and national voluntary participation decrease respectively with the increase of national and individual voluntary participation (Mansyur et al. 2008). Such interaction effects also vary by country subgroup.

Simultaneous Applications of Diverse Approaches

Some scholars, explicitly or implicitly, apply diverse approaches to social capital simultaneously to health. In a US study, social participation is associated with mental health only indirectly through average reachability of accessed status (Song 2011). In a British study, all three forms of social capital (trust, social activities with friends and relatives, and absolute accessed classes) are positively associated with general health and mediate the effect of neighborhood deprivation (Verhaeghe and Tampubolon 2012). A Canadian study compares two trust factors with five forms of social capital (diversity of accessed status, group membership, geographic-based close family and friend ties, and neighborhood social capital) (Carpiano and Fitterer 2014). Only the two trust factors are consistently positively associated with general and mental health. They are also positively associated with all forms of social capital with the exception of geographic-based close family ties. In a study in Belgium, regular smoking is negatively associated with structural (instead of cognitive) family social capital and cognitive school (instead of community) social capital (De Clercq et al. 2014). A study from India analyzes six forms of social capital at both the individual and community levels: intergroup bridging ties, intragroup bonding ties, political participation, accessed status, neighborhood cohesion, and collective efficacy (Story 2014). Only individual accessed status and community intergroup bridging ties are consistently positively associated with all three types of health care utilization. A study of 17 European countries measures four forms of social capital: frequency and size of informal social connections, participation in social groups, trust in institutions, and sense of belonging (Pinillos-Franco and Kawachi 2018). Varying by gender, results show that the last three forms (with the exception of religious participation) are positively associated with general health.

Three studies draw data from the same longitudinal three-wave community survey in Montreal but measure social capital differently. One study uses the first wave of data and captures six forms of social capital: core ties and core tie diversity (measured through the name generator), general and neighborhood network capital (measured through the position generator), generalized trust, neighbor trust, neighborhood cohesion, and neighborhood and general social participation (Bassett and Moore 2013). Four forms of social capital (core tie diversity, generalized trust, neighbor trust, and neighborhood cohesion) are negatively associated with depressive symptoms. The other two studies employ all the three waves of data. One of them measures four forms of social capital (accessed status, accessed kin ties, generalized trust, and social participation) and controls for social isolation (Wu et al. 2018). The risk of obesity is negatively associated with the diversity of accessed status and generalized trust but positively associated with accessed kin ties. The other study includes social isolation into the measurement of social capital (diversity of accessed status, generalized trust, neighbor trust, and social participation) (Moore and Carpiano 2019). Varying by the form of social capital, gender, and health outcome, results show stable relationships of the same social capital measures over time, weak relationships between different social capital measures, lack of upstream social capital measures, and a more salient social capital-health relationship among women than among men.

Challenges and Future Directions

Social capital has opened up a burgeoning multidisciplinary health research literature during the last three decades. Four scholars – Bourdieu, Lin, Coleman, and Putnam – have contributed to the theoretical construction of social capital from different perspectives. Among them, Putnam's notion has captured more attention. Sociological theories are relatively understudied but have increasingly enjoyed fruitful applications and extensions. Despite its enormous progress, this literature now faces challenges in its future theoretical and methodological growth.

Four theoretical challenges require future efforts: the relationship with other network-based concepts, rival theories competing with social capital theories, theories on the non-direct roles of social capital, and the convergence of different social capital theories. First, social capital is a relatively new network-based concept and its relationship with longer-established network-based concepts (e.g. social networks, social cohesion, social integration, and social support) remains a challenge

(Berkman et al. 2000; Pescosolido 2007). Lin's stricter conceptualization allows us to distinguish his idea of social capital from these longer-established concepts and theorize their causal relationships with each other (Song 2013a, 2019; Song et al. 2011). The normative functionalist perspective as well as some scholars' extension of Bourdieu's approach, however, subsume these longer-established concepts under the umbrella of social capital, which spotlights these concepts but blurs their distinction from and relationships with social capital. Such equalization pours old wine into new bottles, endangers the added theoretical value of social capital, and mixes social capital with its sources and outcomes (Kawachi et al. 2004; Lin 2001; Portes 1998). Since each of these longer-established concepts already has a complex relationship with health (Moen et al. 1989; Song 2013b, 2014b; Song and Chen 2014), results on the social capital-heath relationship are unsurprisingly very complicated, which hinders theoretical synthesis and development. Scholars should draw upon the research traditions on these longer-established concepts. Theories and evidence in these traditions can inform and facilitate social capital research. For example, the three perspectives respectively on the positive, negative, and varying health effect of social integration (role enhancement, role strain, and role context) can help explain some mixed results on social capital conceived as social participation (Moen et al. 1989).

Second, facing the growing evidence on the detrimental effects of empirical indicators of social capital, we demand rival theories that compete with social capital theories. The social capital theories are based on the assumption that empirical indicators of social capital should be beneficial and protective. They are inadequate to explain the unexpected detrimental effects. Social capital is a concept at the theoretical level. It is not social capital but its empirical indicators that play puzzling double-edged roles for health. Competing theories in combination with social capital theories will help address such double-edged roles. Song recently attempts to propose social cost theory in contrast with Lin's social capital theory to theorize the harmful impact of accessed status (Song, Forthcoming; Song and Pettis 2018), which needs further empirical testing. Scholars applying the normative functionalist perspective speculate arguments for the adverse findings but have not formulated a systematic competing theory (Villalonga-Olives and Kawachi 2017). This perspective's broad definitions add difficulties for the formulation of competing theories.

Third, we require more theories on the non-direct effects of social capital: interacting, mediating, and indirect effects. We need to build institutional theories to explain the varying results between societies. Song develops three institutional explanations for the varying explanatory power of social capital and social cost theories across society (Song, Forthcoming; Song and Pettis 2018). Her efforts, however, are limited to only two institutional factors (relational culture and inequality structure) and her secondary data only three societies. Scholars extending Putnam's approach to the country level employ data from a large size of societies, ranging from 22 to 78. Some of them mention possible institutional moderators (e.g. culture, democracy, welfare policies, and economic development) (Jen et al. 2010; Mansyur et al. 2008). But they neither provide theoretical elaboration nor conduct any direct examination. The above review suggests other moderators. Scholars taking the network-based conflict perspective theorize the interaction of social capital with personal capital and gender (e.g. Song and Lin 2009; Song et al. 2017; Veenstra and Abel 2015). Naturally flow-ing from this perspective, future research should explore how other network-based factors and other stratifiers interplay with social capital. Scholars applying the normative functionalist perspective find rich results on diverse sociodemographic moderators (e.g. age, gender, and race/ethnicity) but explanations are not clear enough. Relevant sociological theories can help organize such results into a theoretical guiding framework (Song 2013a; Song et al. 2010). The extension of Putnam's approach to cross-level social capital interaction also generates mixed results, which need more theoretical elaboration. In addition, to fully understand disease-specific results and embed social capital into the health production process, more theoretical efforts are desired to jointly map the mediating and indirect effects of social capital on various health outcomes (Moore and Carpiano 2019; Moore et al. 2014a; Song 2011; Song et al. 2017). The normative functionalist perspective's broad definitions create more challenges in the theorization of these non-direct effects.

Furthermore, leaving behind all the debates on the nature and definitions of social capital, some scholars have put different approaches to social capital into simultaneous examination (Carpiano and Fitterer 2014; Moore and Carpiano 2019; Verhaeghe and Tampubolon 2012). Their attempts reconcile diverse approaches into an inclusive investigation and create social integration and social cohesion to some degree between previously exclusive social capital research communities. Their findings clarify that social capital constructs conceived by different perspectives are conceptually distinct. The publication of their work seems to signal that we are now gradually leaving the age of social capital opposition and entering the harmonious age of social capital pluralism. Their integration efforts, however, also illustrate the obstacles on the way to social capital pluralism. It is arduous to combine different approaches. Each approach, in particular the normative functionalist approaches that offer broad definitions, is already complicated enough in terms of measures and mechanisms. The social capital research paradigm may become ever expanding and then too gigantic to be clearly comprehended and productively moved forward. An appropriate combination of different approaches also requires measures consistent with these approaches. Due to data limitations, however, scholars use some proxy indicators of network-based social capital (e.g. tie strength and social isolation) or use only a limited number of measures (Moore and Carpiano 2019; Wu et al. 2018). Ideally, future theory-driven first-hand data collection will facilitate the simultaneous investigation of diverse approaches.

Finally, apart from theoretical challenges, we also face methodological ones. Bourdieu's theory lacks explicit operationalization and measurement of social capital, which restricts its extension to health and produces controversial theoretical and empirical applications. Instead of measuring social capital as in the normative functionalist approaches or other established network-based factors (Carpiano 2006; Pinxten and Lievens 2014; Veenstra 2007; Ziersch 2005), Bourdieu's two elements of social capital (network size and alters' capital) are more consistent with Lin's notion and measurement. Bourdieu's and Lin's approaches have converged in recent work on the interplay between social and personal capital on health (Song and Lin 2009; Song et al. 2017; Veenstra and Abel 2015). In the examination of Lin's theory (as well as social cost theory), for the purpose of generalizability and stronger causal inferences, we need longitudinal research designs that contain diverse network instruments, multiple indicators of absolute and relative accessed status, dynamics of disease and illness, and potential antecedents and mechanisms (Song et al. 2010; Webber et al. 2011). We also need to go beyond the qualitative applications of Lin's theory in the cyberspace and quantitatively capture online social capital (Drentea and Moren-Cross 2005; Reich 2018). In addition, we need to analyze Lin's idea of mobilized and macro-level social capital. The normative functionalist perspective receives much more attention but also generate much more mixed results partly due to the use of diverse measures of social capital at multiple levels, some of which go beyond Coleman's or Putnam's original interests. Future research needs to conduct theory-driven longitudinal data collection, derive more consistent measures from secondary data, and make more efforts to validate these multilevel measures (Lee and Kim 2013).

References

Adam, Frane and Borut Rončević. 2003. "Social Capital: Recent Debates and Research Trends." *Social Science Information* 42: 155–83.

Aida, Jun, Tomoya Hanibuchi, Miyo Nakade, Hiroshi Hirai, Ken Osaka, and Katsunori Kondo. 2009. "The Different Effects of Vertical Social Capital and Horizontal Social Capital on Dental Status: A Multilevel Analysis." *Social Science & Medicine* 69(4): 512–18.

Bain, K. and N. Hicks. 1998. "Building Social Capital and Reaching Out to Excluded Groups: The Challenge of Partnerships." Paper presented at CELAM meeting on the Struggle against Poverty towards the Turn of the Millennium, Washington DC.

Bassett, Emma and Spencer Moore. 2013. "Social Capital and Depressive Symptoms: The Association of Psychosocial and Network Dimensions of Social Capital with Depressive Symptoms in Montreal, Canada." *Social Science & Medicine* 86: 96–102.

Berkman, Lisa F., Thomas Glass, Ian Brissette, and Teresa E. Seeman. 2000. "From Social Integration to Health: Durkheim in the New Millennium." *Social Science and Medicine* 51: 843–57.

Bourdieu, Pierre. 1984. *Distinction: A Social Critique of the Judgment of Taste.* London and New York: Routledge and Kegan Paul.

Bourdieu, Pierre. 1986 [1983]. "The Forms of Capital." Pp. 241–58 in *Handbook of Theory and Research for the Sociology of Education*, edited by J. G. Richardson. Westport, CT: Greenwood Press.

Burt, Ronald S. 1984. "Network Items and the General Social Survey." *Social Networks* 6: 293–339.

Campos-Matos, Inês, SV Subramanian, and Ichiro Kawachi. 2016. "The 'Dark Side' of Social Capital: Trust and Self-Rated Health in European Countries." *The European Journal of Public Health* 26(1): 90–5.

Carpiano, Richard M. 2006. "Toward a Neighborhood Resource-Based Theory of Social Capital for Health: Can Bourdieu and Sociology Help?" *Social Science & Medicine* 62: 165–75.

Carpiano, Richard M. 2007. "Neighborhood Social Capital and Adult Health: An Empirical Test of a Bourdieu-Based Model." *Health and Place* 13(3): 639–55.

Carpiano, Richard M and Lisa M Fitterer. 2014. "Questions of Trust in Health Research on Social Capital: What Aspects of Personal Network Social Capital Do They Measure?" *Social Science & Medicine* 116: 225–34.

Coleman, James S. 1988. "Social Capital in the Creation of Human Capital." *American Journal of Sociology* 94: 95–121.

Coleman, James S. 1990. *Foundations of Social Theory.* Cambridge: Belknap Press of Harvard University Press.

Cook, Karen Schweers. 2005. "Networks, Norms, and Trust: The Social Psychology of Social Capital." *Social Psychology Quarterly* 68: 4–14.

De Clercq, Bart, Timo-Kolja Pfoertner, Frank J Elgar, Anne Hublet, and Lea Maes. 2014. "Social Capital and Adolescent Smoking in Schools and Communities: A Cross-Classified Multilevel Analysis." *Social Science & Medicine* 119: 81–7.

Dean, Lorraine, S. V. Subramanian, David R. Williams, Katrina Armstrong, Camille Zubrinsky Charles, and Ichiro Kawachi. 2014. "The Role of Social Capital in African-American Women's Use of Mammography." *Social Science & Medicine* 104: 148–56.

Drentea, Patricia and Jennifer L. Moren-Cross. 2005. "Social Capital and Social Support on the Web: The Case of an Internet Mother Site." *Sociology of Health and Illness* 27: 920–43.

Drukker, Marjan, Stephen L. Buka, Charles Kaplan, Kwame McKenzie, and Van Os. Jim. 2005. "Social Capital and Young Adolescents' Perceived Health in Different Sociocultural Settings." *Social Science & Medicine* 61: 185–98.

Drukker, Marjan, Charles Kaplan, Frans Feron, and Van Os. Jim. 2003. "Children's Health-Related Quality of Life, Neighborhood Socio-Economic Deprivation and Social Capital: A Contextual Analysis." *Social Science & Medicine* 57: 825–41.

Fan, Yingling and Qian Chen. 2012. "Family Functioning as a Mediator between Neighborhood Conditions and Children's Health: Evidence from a National Survey in the United States." *Social Science & Medicine* 74(12): 1939–47.

Farr, James. 2004. "Social Capital: A Conceptual History." *Political Theory* 32: 6–33.

Foley, Michael W. and Bob Edwards. 1999. "Is It Time to Disinvest in Social Capital?" *Journal of Public Policy* 19: 141–73.

Fujiwara, Takeo and Ichiro Kawachi. 2008a. "A Prospective Study of Individual-Level Social Capital and Major Depression in the United States." *Journal of Epidemiology and Community Health* 62: 627–33.

Gatrell, Anthony C., Jennie Popay, and Carol Thomas. 2004. "Mapping the Determinants of Health Inequalities in Social Space: Can Bourdieu Help Us?" *Health & Place* 10(3): 245–57.

Giordano, Giuseppe Nicola, Jonas Björk, and Martin Lindström. 2012. "Social Capital and Self-Rated Health – A Study of Temporal (Causal) Relationships." *Social Science & Medicine* 75(2): 340–8.

Giordano, Giuseppe Nicola and Martin Lindström. 2011. "Social Capital and Change in Psychological Health Over Time." *Social Science & Medicine* 72(8): 1219–27.

Glanville, Jennifer L. and William T. Story. 2018. "Social Capital and Self-Rated Health: Clarifying the Role of Trust." *Social Science Research* 71: 98–108.

Haines, Valerie A., John J. Beggs, and Jeanne S. Hurlbert. 2011. "Neighborhood Disadvantage, Network Social Capital, and Depressive Symptoms." *Journal of Health and Social Behavior* 52(1): 58–73.

Islam, M. Kamrul, Juan Merlo, Ichiro Kawachi, Martin Lindstrom, and Ulf-G. Gerdtham. 2006. "Social Capital and Health: Does Egalitarianism Matter? A Literature Review." *International Journal for Equity in Health* 5: 3. https://doi.org/10.1186/1475-9276-5-3

Jen, Min Hua, Erik R. Sund, Ron Johnston, and Kelvyn Jones. 2010. "Trustful Societies, Trustful Individuals, and Health: An Analysis of Self-Rated Health and Social Trust Using the World Value Survey." *Health and Place* 16(5): 1022–29.

Kawachi, Ichiro. 1999. "Social Capital and Community Effects on Population and Individual Health." *Annals of the New York Academy of Sciences* 896: 120–30.

Kawachi, Ichiro, B. P. Kennedy, and R. Glass. 1999a. "Social Capital and Self-Rated Health: A Contextual Analysis." *American Journal of Public Health* 89: 1187–93.

Kawachi, Ichiro, B. P. Kennedy, K. Lochner, and D. Prothrow-Stith. 1997. "Social Capital, Income Inequality, and Mortality." *American Journal of Public Health* 87: 1491–8.

Kawachi, Ichiro, B. P. Kennedy, and Richard Wilkinson (eds.). 1999b. *Income Inequality and Health: A Reader.* New York: New Press.

Kawachi, Ichiro, Daniel Kim, Adam Coutts, and S. V. Subramanian. 2004. "Commentary: Reconciling the Three Accounts of Social Capital." *International Journal of Epidemiology* 33: 682–90.

Kim, Daniel, S. V. Subramanian, Steven L. Gortmaker, and Ichiro Kawachi. 2006a. "US State- and County-Level Social Capital in Relation to Obesity and Physical Inactivity: A Multilevel, Multivariable Analysis." *Social Science & Medicine* 63: 1045–59.

Kim, Daniel, S.V. Subramanian, and Ichiro Kawachi. 2006b. "Bonding versus0 Bridging Social Capital and Their Associations with Self-Rated Health: A Multilevel Analysis of 40 US Communities." *Journal of Epidemiology and Community Health* 60: 116–22.

Kobayashi, Tomoko, Ichiro Kawachi, Toshihide Iwase, Etsuji Suzuki, and Soshi Takao. 2013. "Individual-level Social Capital and Self-rated Health in Japan: An Application of the Resource Generator." *Social Science & Medicine* 85: 32–7.

Lee, Chioun, Dana A. Glei, Noreen Goldman, and Maxine Weinstein. 2017. "Children's Education and Parents' Trajectories of Depressive Symptoms." *Journal of Health and Social Behavior* 58(1): 86–101.

Lee, Chul-Joo and Daniel Kim. 2013. "A Comparative Analysis of the Validity of Us State-and County-Level Social Capital Measures and Their Associations with Population Health." *Social Indicators Research* 111(1): 307–26.

Lee, Min-Ah and Ichiro Kawachi. 2017. "The Company You Keep: Is Socialising with Higher-Status People Bad for Mental Health?" *Sociology of Health & Illness* 39(7): 1206–26.

Lin, Nan. 1982. "Social Resources and Instrumental Action." Pp. 131–45 in *Social Structure and Network Analysis*, edited by P. V. Marsden and N. Lin. Beverly Hills, CA: Sage.

Lin, Nan. 2001. *Social Capital: A Theory of Social Structure and Action.* Cambridge: Cambridge University Press.

Lin, Nan. 2008. "A Network Theory of Social Capital." Pp. 50–69 in *Handbook on Social Capital*, edited by D. Castiglione, J. van Deth, and G. Wolleb. Oxford: Oxford University Press.

Lin, Nan and Mary Dumin. 1986. "Access to Occupations through Social Ties." *Social Networks* 8: 365–85.

Lin, Nan, Yang-Chih Fu, and Ray-May Hsung. 2001. "The Position Generator: A Measurement Technique for Investigations of Social Capital." Pp. 57–81 in *Social Capital: Theory and Research*, edited by Nan Lin, Karen Cook, and Ronald S. Burt. New York: Aldine de Gruyter.

Lindström, Martin. 2005. "Social Capital, the Miniaturization of Community and High Alcohol Consumption: A Population-Based Study." *Alcohol & Alcoholism* 40(6): 556–62.

Lochner, Kimberly A., Ichiro Kawachi, Robert T. Brennan, and Stephen L. Buka. 2003. "Social Capital and Neighborhood Mortality Rates in Chicago." *Social Science & Medicine* 56: 1797–805.

Mandelbaum, Jennifer, Spencer Moore, Patricia P Silveira, Michael J Meaney, Robert D Levitan, and Laurette Dubé. 2018. "Does Social Capital Moderate the Association between Children's Emotional Overeating and Parental Stress? A Cross-Sectional Study of the Stress-Buffering Hypothesis in A Sample of Mother-Child Dyads." *Social Science & Medicine*. https://doi.org/10.1016/j.socscimed.2018.12.023

Mansyur, Carol, Benjamin C. Amick, Ronald B. Harrist, and Luisa Franzini. 2008. "Social Capital, Income Inequality, and Self-Rated Health in 45 Countries." *Social Science & Medicine* 66: 43–56.

Meng, Tianguang and He Chen. 2014. "A Multilevel Analysis of Social Capital and Self-Rated Health: Evidence from China." *Health & Place* 27: 38–44.

Moen, Phyllis, Donna Dempster-McClain, and Robin M. Williams Jr. 1989. "Social Integration and Longevity: An Event History Analysis of Women's Roles and Resilience." *American Sociological Review* 54(4): 635–47.

Mohnen, Sigrid M., Beate Völker, Henk Flap, and Peter P. Groenewegen. 2012. "Health-Related Behavior as a Mechanism behind the Relationship between Neighborhood Social Capital and Individual Health - a Multilevel Analysis." *BMC Public Health* 12(1): 116.

Moore, Spencer, Ulf Bockenholt, Mark Daniel, Katherine Frohlich, Yan Kestens, and Lucie Richard. 2011. "Social Capital and Core Network Ties: A Validation Study of Individual-Level Social Capital Measures and Their Association with Extra- and Intra-Neighborhood Ties, and Self-Rated Health." *Health and Place* 17(2): 536–44.

Moore, Spencer and Richard M. Carpiano. 2019. "Measures of Personal Social Capital over Time: A Path Analysis Assessing Longitudinal Associations among Cognitive, Structural, and Network Elements of Social Capital in Women and Men Separately." *Social Science & Medicine*. https://doi.org/10.1016/j.socscimed.2019.02.023

Moore, Spencer, Mark Daniel, Lise Gauvin, and Laurette Dubé. 2009a. "Not All Social Capital Is Good Capital." *Health and Place* 15(4): 1071–77.

Moore, Spencer, Mark Daniel, Catherine Paquet, Laurette Dubé, and Lise Gauvin. 2009b. "Association of Individual Network Social Capital with Abdominal Adiposity, Overweight and Obesity." *Journal of Public Health* 31(1): 175–83.

Moore, Spencer, Alan Shiell, Penelope Hawe, and Valerie A Haines. 2005. "The Privileging of Communitarian Ideas: Citation Practices and the Translation of Social Capital into Public Health Research." *American Journal of Public Health* 95(8): 1330–7.

Moore, Spencer, Steven Stewart, and Ana Teixeira. 2014a. "Decomposing Social Capital Inequalities in Health." *Journal of Epidemiology and Community Health* 68(3): 233–38.

Morenoff, Jeffrey. 2003. "Neighborhood Mechanisms and the Spatial Dynamics of Birth Weight." *American Journal of Sociology* 108(5): 976–1017.

Myroniuk, Tyler W and Philip Anglewicz. 2015. "Does Social Participation Predict Better Health? A Longitudinal Study in Rural Malawi." *Journal of Health and Social Behavior* 56(4): 552–73.

Paccoud, Ivana, James Nazroo, and Anja Leist. 2020. "A Bourdieusian Approach to Class-Related Inequalities: The Role of Capitals and Capital Structure in the Utilisation of Healthcare Services in Later Life." *Sociology of Health & Illness* 42(3): 510–25.

Pescosolido, Bernice A. 2007. "Sociology of Social Networks." Pp. 208–17 in *21st Century Sociology: A Reference Book*, edited by Clifton D. Bryant and Dennis L. Peck. Thousand Oaks, CA: Sage.

Pevalin, David. 2003. "More to Social Capital than Putnam." *British Journal of Psychiatry* 182: 172–73.

Pinillos-Franco, Sara and Ichiro Kawachi. 2018. "The Relationship between Social Capital and Self-Rated Health: A Gendered Analysis of 17 European Countries." *Social Science & Medicine* 219: 30–5.

Pinxten, Wouter and John Lievens. 2014. "The Importance of Economic, Social and Cultural Capital in Understanding Health Inequalities: Using a Bourdieu-Based Approach in Research on Physical and Mental Health Perceptions." *Sociology of Health & Illness* 36(7): 1095–110.

Poortinga, Wouter. 2006. "Social Capital: An Individual or Collective Resource for Health?" *Social Science & Medicine* 62: 292–302.

Portes, Alejandro. 1998. "Social Capital: Its Origins and Applications in Modern Sociology." *Annual Review of Sociology* 24: 1–24.

Portes, Alejandro and Julia Sensenbrenner. 1993. "Embeddedness and Immigration: Notes on the Social Determinants of Economic Action." *American Journal of Sociology* 98: 1320–50.

Putnam, Robert D. 1993. *Making Democracy Work: Civic Traditions in Modern Italy.* Princeton, NJ: Princeton University Press.

Putnam, Robert D. 1995. "Bowling Alone: America's Declining Social Capital." *Journal of Democracy* 6: 65–78.

Putnam, Robert D. 2000. *Bowling Alone: The Collapse and Revival of American Community.* New York: Simon and Schuster.

Reich, Jennifer A. 2018. "'We are Fierce, Independent Thinkers and Intelligent': Social Capital and Stigma Management among Mothers Who Refuse Vaccines." *Social Science & Medicine:112015.* https://doi.org/10.1016/j.socscimed.2018.10.027

Rothon, Catherine, Laura Goodwin, and Stephen Stansfeld. 2012. "Family Social Support, Community 'Social Capital' and Adolescents' Mental Health and Educational Outcomes: A Longitudinal Study in England." *Social Psychiatry and Psychiatric Epidemiology* 47(5): 697–709.

Sampson, Robert J., Jeffrey D. Morenoff, and Felton Earls. 1999. "Beyond Social Capital: Spatial Dynamics of Collective Efficacy for Children." *American Sociological Review* 64: 633–60.

Sampson, Robert J., Stephen W. Raudenbush, and Felton Earls. 1997. "Neighborhoods and Violent Crime: A Multilevel Study of Collective Efficacy." *Science* 277: 918–24.

Song, Lijun. 2011. "Social Capital and Psychological Distress." *Journal of Health and Social Behavior* 52(4): 478–92.

Song, Lijun. 2012. "Raising Network Resources while Raising Children? Access to Social Capital by Parenthood Status, Gender, and Marital Status." *Social Networks* 34(2): 241–52.

Song, Lijun. 2013a. "Social Capital and Health." Pp. 223–57 in *Medical Sociology on the Move: New Directions in Theory*, edited by William C. Cockerham. Dordrecht, the Netherlands: Springer.

Song, Lijun. 2013b. "Institutional Embeddedness of Network Embeddedness in the Workplace: Social Integration at Work and Employee's Health across Three Societies." *Research in the Sociology of Work* 24: 323–56.

Song, Lijun. 2014a. "Bright and Dark Sides of Who You Know in the Evaluation of Well-Being: Social Capital and Life Satisfaction across Three Societies." Pp. 259–78 in *Social Capital and Its Institutional Contingency: A Study of the United States, Taiwan and China*, edited by Nan Lin, Yang-Chih Fu, and Chih-Jou Chen. London: Routledge.

Song, Lijun. 2014b. "Is Unsolicited Support Protective or Destructive in Collectivistic Culture? Receipt of Unsolicited Job Leads in Urban China." *Society and Mental Health* 4(3): 235–54.

Song, Lijun. 2015a. "Does Knowing People in the Positional Hierarchy Protect or Hurt? Social Capital, Comparative Reference Group, and Depression in Two Societies." *Social Science and Medicine* 136–137(9): 117–27.

Song, Lijun. 2015b. "Does Knowing People in Authority Protect or Hurt? Authoritative Contacts and Depression in Urban China." *American Behavioral Scientist* 59(9): 1173–88.

Song, Lijun. 2019. "Nan Lin and Social Support." in Pp. 78–106 in *Social Capital, Social Support and Stratification: An Analysis of the Sociology of Nan Lin*, edited by R.S. Burt, Y. Bian, L. Song, and N. Lin. London: Edward Elgar Publishing.

Song, Lijun Forthcoming. "Social Capital, Social Cost, and Relational Culture in Three Societies." *Social Psychology Quarterly.*

Song, Lijun and Tian-Yun Chang. 2012. "Do Resources of Network Members Help in Help Seeking? Social Capital and Health Information Search." *Social Networks* 34(4): 658–69.

Song, Lijun and Wenhong Chen. 2014. "Does Receiving Unsolicited Support Help or Hurt? Receipt of Unsolicited Job Leads and Depression." *Journal of Health and Social Behavior* 55(2): 144–60.

Song, Lijun, Cleothia G. Frazier, and Philip J. Pettis. 2018. "Do Network Members' Resources Generate Health Inequality? Social Capital Theory and Beyond." Pp. 233–53 in *Handbook of Social Capital and Health*, edited by S. Folland and E. Nauenberg. London: Edward Elgar Ltd.

Song, Lijun and Nan Lin. 2009. "Social Capital and Health Inequality: Evidence from Taiwan." *Journal of Health and Social Behavior* 50(2): 149–63.

Song, Lijun and Philip J. Pettis. 2018. "Does Whom You Know in the Status Hierarchy Prevent or Trigger Health Limitation? Institutional Embeddedness of Social Capital and Social Cost Theories in Three Societies." *Social Science & Medicine.* https://doi.org/10.1016/j.socscimed.2018.09.035

Song, Lijun, Philip J. Pettis, and Bhumika Piya. 2017. "Does Your Body Know Who You Know? Multiple Roles of Network Members' Socioeconomic Status for Body Weight Ratings." *Sociological Perspectives* 60(6): 997–1018.

Song, Lijun, Joonmo Son, and Nan Lin. 2010. "Social Capital and Health." Pp. 184–210 in *The New Companion to Medical Sociology*, edited by William C. Cockerham. Oxford: Wiley-Blackwell.

Song, Lijun, Joonmo Son, and Nan Lin. 2011. "Social Support." Pp. 116–28 in *The Sage Handbook of Social Network Analysis*, edited by J. Scott and P. J. Carrington. London: SAGE.

Stephens, Christine. 2008. "Social Capital in Its Place: Using Social Theory to Understand Social Capital and Inequalities in Health." *Social Science & Medicine* 66: 1174–84.

Story, William T. 2014. "Social Capital and the Utilization of Maternal and Child Health Services in India: A Multilevel Analysis." *Health & Place* 28: 73–84.

Subramanian, Subu V, Daniel J Kim, and Ichiro Kawachi. 2002. "Social Trust and Self-Rated Health in U.S. Communities: A Multilevel Analysis." *Journal of Urban Health* 79(1): S21-S34.

Sun, Xiaojie, Kun Liu, and Martin Webber. 2017. "Individual Social Capital and Health-related Quality of Life among Older Rural Chinese." *Aging and Society* 37(2): 221–42.

Suzuki, Etsuji, Soshi Takao, S. V. Subramanian, Hirokazu Komatsu, Hiroyuki Doi, and Ichiro Kawachi. 2010. "Does Low Workplace Social Capital Have Detrimental Effect on Workers' Health?" *Social Science & Medicine* 70(9): 1367–72.

Szreter, Simon and Michael Woolcock. 2004. "Health by Association? Social Capital, Social Theory, and the Political Economy of Public Health." *International Journal of Epidemiology* 33: 650–67.

Takeo, Fujiwara and Ichiro Kawachi. 2008b. "Social Capital and Health: A Study of Adult Twins in the US." *American Journal of Preventive Medicine* 35: 139–44.

Ullmann, S. Heidi, Noreen Goldman, and Anne R. Pebley. 2013. "Contextual Factors and Weight Change over Time: A Comparison between U.S. Hispanics and Other Population Sub-Groups." *Social Science & Medicine* 90: 40–8.

Van der Gaag, Martin P. J. and Tom A. B. Snijders. 2005. "The Resource Generator: Social Capital Quantification with Concrete Items." *Social Networks* 27: 1–27.

Veenstra, Gerry. 2007. "Social Space, Social Class and Bourdieu: Health Inequalities in British Columbia, Canada." *Health & Place* 13(1): 14–31.

Veenstra, Gerry and Thomas Abel. 2015. "Capital Interplays and the Self-Rated Health of Young Men: Results from a Cross-Sectional Study in Switzerland." *International Journal for Equity in Health* 14(1): 38.

Veenstra, Gerry and Thomas Abel. 2019. "Capital Interplays and Social Inequalities in Health." *Scandinavian Journal of Public Health* 47(6): 631–4.

Verhaeghe, Pieter-Paul, Elise Pattyn, Piet Bracke, Mieke Verhaeghe, and Van De Putte Bart. 2012. "The Association between Network Social Capital and Self-rated Health: Pouring Old Wine in New Bottles?" *Health and Place* 18(2): 358–65.

Verhaeghe, Pieter-Paul and Gindo Tampubolon. 2012. "Individual Social Capital, Neighbourhood Deprivation, and Self-Rated Health in England." *Social Science & Medicine* 75(2): 349–57.

Villalonga-Olives, E and Ichiro Kawachi. 2017. "The Dark Side of Social Capital: A Systematic Review of the Negative Health Effects of Social Capital." *Social Science & Medicine* 194: 105–27.

Webber, Martin, Peter Huxley, and Tirril Harris. 2011. "Social Capital and the Course of Depression: Six-Month Prospective Cohort Study." *Journal of Affective Disorders* 129(1): 149–57.

Webber, Martin P. and Peter Huxley. 2004. "Mental Health and Social Capitals (Letter)." *British Journal of Psychiatry* 184: 185–86.

Webber, Martin P. and Peter Huxley. 2007. "Measuring Access to Social Capital: The Validity and Reliability of the Resource Generator-UK and Its Association with Common Mental Disorder." *Social Science & Medicine* 65: 481–92.

Woolcock, Michael. 1998. "Social Capital and Economic Development: Toward a Theoretical Synthesis and Policy Framework." *Theory and Science* 27: 151–208.

Wu, Qiaobing, Deping Lu, and Mi Kang. 2015. "Social Capital and the Mental Health of Children in Rural China with Different Experiences of Parental Migration." *Social Science & Medicine* 132: 270–77.

Wu, Yun-Hsuan, Spencer Moore, and Laurette Dube. 2018. "Social Capital and Obesity among Adults: Longitudinal Findings from the Montreal Neighborhood Networks and Healthy Aging Panel." *Preventive Medicine* 111: 366–70.

Yang, Hsieh-Hua, Shu-Chen Kuo, and Hung-Jen Yang Jui-Chen. 2013. "Social Capital and Health Literacy in Taiwan." *Health* 5(5): 898–902.

Ziersch, Anna M. 2005. "Health Implications of Access to Social Capital: Findings from an Australian Study." *Social Science & Medicine* 61: 2119–31.

Part III

Health and Social Inequality

11

Health and Social Class

Jarron M. Saint Onge and Patrick M. Krueger

Introduction

Social class, or socioeconomic status (SES), has major implications for health and survival. Higher SES is consistently linked with better health. For example, those with a baccalaureate degree live about six years longer than those with secondary school degrees (Krueger et al. 2015). Social class disparities in health are substantial and persist across time, place, and generations. Low wages or poor standards of living are distressing in their own right but are especially invidious because they also diminish opportunities for long, healthy lives.

This chapter focuses on the diverse mechanisms that link social class to health. Social class works through the physical environment, social context, socialization experiences, and health behaviors to shape health and mortality outcomes (Adler et al. 1994). An understanding of the links between social class and health requires an examination of the theoretical and practical research that defines social class, its measurement, and the mechanisms linking them. Drawing on literature primarily focused on high-income countries, we take two primary approaches to understanding the relationship between health and social class. We consider the theoretical links between social standing and health that maintain ongoing health disparities. Second, we draw on the policy implications of social class as a lever for increasing health equity.

Conceptualizing Health and Class

Social Class/Socioeconomic Status

Social class is a multi-faceted concept, which presents challenges in conceptualization and measurement (Hummer and Lariscy 2011; Krueger and Burgard 2011). Diverse intellectual traditions invoke the terms *class* or *socioeconomic status* – we

The Wiley Blackwell Companion to Medical Sociology, First Edition. Edited by William C. Cockerham.

will use the two terms interchangeably. Historical definitions have transitioned from two-class frameworks (e.g. Marx [1867] 2007) into multi-dimensional frameworks that reflect the complexity of the stratification of modern societies (DiPrete and Grusky 1990; Wright 1998). Indeed, SES includes pecuniary resources like earnings and wealth, occupational status, the cognitive skills and knowledge that increase with education, and even the embodiment of tastes, manners, or accents (Bourdieu 1984). Moreover, these dimensions of SES often – but not always – bundle together. Individuals with higher status may have multiple privileges including access to higher status goods, respect and accolades, preferential treatment, and advantaged relationships with those in positions of authority (e.g. police officers, judges, and employers) (Magee and Galinsky 2008). This section provides an overview of some of the broad ways the literature conceptualizes social class/SES.

Education is the most commonly used indicator of human capital – formal schooling supports the acquisition of skills and cognitive abilities that can support efforts to achieve better health (Mirowsky and Ross 2003). Among measures of SES, education has a distinctive advantage – education is often fixed relatively early in adulthood, does not decline during bouts of poor health as might wealth or income, and can still be measured even for those individuals who are out of the labor force. As such, it can be somewhat more straightforward to compare education across demographic groups including age, birth cohorts, race, or gender. Further, higher levels of education can expand opportunities to other dimensions of SES, including jobs that pay higher wages or come with higher status. Despite those strengths, the measurement of education is complicated by limited information on the quality of education attained, whether the prestige of the educational institution matters for health, and by a lack of understanding of the value of years of schooling relative to specific credentials (e.g. a college degree) (Ross and Mirowsky 1999; Zajacova and Montez 2017).

Occupational status reflects the social positions of individuals based on where they work – a central activity for many adults in high-income countries. The esteem or resources that drive the status associated with an occupation are measured in diverse ways. Some measures focus on the average earnings and education that travel with an education (Nam and Boyd 2004), while others focus on the degree to which some occupations are esteemed by the general public (Nakao and Treas 1994). Some measures have multiple dimensions that attempt to account for income, education, along with other characteristics such as the sex and marital status of typical employees (Hollingshead 2011), and other scales combine the income and education of an occupation along with the prestige, and social and cultural capital associated with a given occupation (Duncan 1961; Hauser and Warren 1997; Oakes and Rossi 2003).

Across Europe and the UK, there have been recent, systematic efforts to create harmonized measures of occupational status (Erikson and Goldthorpe 1992; Wright 2005). For example, the European Socio-Economic Classification (ESeC) is an innovative categorical measure of schema based on employment relations. The ESeC overcomes several previous limitations by providing validated, cross-national comparisons that distinguishes between frequently omitted employment categories (e.g. self-employed, involuntarily excluded from the labor force) to link social patterns across life chances (Rose and Harrison 2014).

Pecuniary resources – including income, wealth, and assets like housing, automobiles, or property – are also linked to health and mortality. Simply, income and financial resources increase opportunities and abilities to purchase health promoting goods and services (e.g. health care, gym memberships). Additional income matters for health and survival outcomes even among those who are not in poverty. Successive increases in income are associated with lower mortality, even among those who are well above the poverty threshold (Chetty et al. 2016). Oakes and Rossi (2003) encourage researchers to recognize the breadth of material assets that are associated with health. Individuals can have multiple sources of income or wealth, and the amount they receive from those sources can fluctuate over the life course, making cross-sectional links with health misleading (Krueger et al. 2003).

Household dynamics also matter. For example, indicators that include a husband's resources show stronger SES-mortality relationships for women (Beebe-Dimmer et al. 2004). Measures such as wealth or material goods may capture the accumulation of assets over the life course, and ignoring wealth may result in underestimating the true differences in economic resources across subpopulations (Bond Huie et al. 2003; Conley 2009; Kahn and Fazio 2005). Further, debt is also associated with poor physical and mental health – especially if that debt comes with high interest rates (Drentea and Lavrakas 2000; Sun and Houle 2020; Walsemann et al. 2019)

Conceptualizing Health

There are diverse ways to conceptualize and measure health – each of which imply specific social or biomedical etiologies and present both benefits and challenges to measurement. Researchers often consider mortality the gold standard measure of poor health, because it is both irreversible and objective. Indeed, it is typically straightforward to ascertain whether a person is dead, and high-income countries have relatively accurate and complete vital statistics systems that capture mortality statistics. However, even all-cause mortality remains subject to errors in linkage studies (e.g. studies that link survey data to prospective mortality) and those errors may depend on respondent characteristics (Brown et al. 2019, Lariscy 2011, Rostron et al. 2010). Although shorter lives suggest that individuals have been deprived of the value of those years, the clinical or biomedical etiology associated with all-cause mortality – say where deaths from automobile accidents and breast cancers are lumped together – may be unclear. Sociologists sometimes focus on cause-specific mortality, but there may be errors in the ascertainment of the underlying cause of death and those errors may vary across groups or geographic areas (Anderson 2011).

Sociologists routinely use self-rated health – a Likert scale item that typically includes the categories: "poor," "fair," "good," "very good," and "excellent." Self-rated health is correlated with prospective mortality, even after adjusting for physicians' diagnoses and health behaviors (Benyamini et al. 1999; Idler and Kasl 1991). Self-rated health is useful as a global measure of health because it predicts survival and is easy to collect in surveys, but it offers minimal insight into the biomedical etiology of health or disease and is plagued by differing subjective interpretations across ethnic groups (Viruell-Fuentes et al. 2011).

Health behaviors provide insight into how individuals employ some agency in the translation of social statuses into health (Cockerham 2005; Pampel et al. 2010). Health behaviors, such as cigarette smoking, substance use, exercise, diets, and preventive health measures are major drivers of health and survival (Mokdad et al. 2004), but are often undertaken for reasons beyond health including pleasure, maintenance of subgroup identities, or class distinction (Bourdieu 1984; Brandt 2007). Accordingly, research has begun to consider how health behaviors group together into broader health lifestyles across the life course with implications beyond individual behaviors (Cockerham et al. 2020; Mollborn and Lawrence 2018; Saint Onge and Krueger 2017). While health behaviors are frequently self-reported, ongoing efforts to include objective data will likely present opportunities to more accurately measure the association between SES and health behaviors.

Specific medical conditions (e.g. asthma, diabetes, depression, fractures) are routinely considered in sociological research. Physician decision making and diagnosis often varies by the class, race, and gender of the patient (Lutfey and Freese 2005; Lutfey et al. 2013). Indeed, the influence of social factors on diagnosis is an important insight from sociology, which begs for a deeper understanding of the social factors that shape the apparent association between SES and health outcomes.

Social research increasingly incorporates biological markers of metabolic, cardiovascular, or immune functioning to understand how class "gets under the skin" (Harris and Schorpp 2018). New techniques of collecting (e.g. saliva samples, dried blood spots) and analyzing those measures facilitate their inclusion in large population samples (McDade, Williams and Snodgrass 2007). An advantage of these measures is that they may capture pathology before it manifests in specific medical conditions or mortality, and they may clarify the mechanisms that link social and biological processes. Social research also considers how genetic markers for unhealthy behaviors (e.g. smoking) or disease risk (e.g. Alzheimer's disease) may shape outcomes differently depending on social contexts (Boardman et al. 2008; Liu et al. 2019; Wedow et al. 2018). Yet, the collection of complex biological data such as genetic sequencing, telomere lengths or CT scans, especially over time, is often limited to small samples due to expense.

Concerns with Causality

A persistent concern in research on the association between social class and health is ascertaining causality. There are both theoretical perspectives and empirical evidence to suggest that both health and SES affect each other over the life course. For example, some individuals may move to lower status and less physically demanding occupations after becoming disabled (Moore and Hayward 1990). And poor health in early life is associated with lower socioeconomic attainment in later life (Currie and Goodman 2020; Haas 2006). Most vexingly in the US, where health insurance is neither universal nor of consistently high quality, poor health is an important driver of bankruptcies and lost income (Himmelstein et al. 2009).

That said, there is some evidence that suggests that the association between SES and health may be causal. For example, one natural experiment finds that mandatory schooling laws have been associated with lower mortality rates for the exposed cohorts, while a randomized experiment has found that housing vouchers that require that individuals move to middle class neighborhoods are associated with reduced obesity (Lleras-Muney 2005; Ludwig et al. 2011). Other studies have found that the association between education and mortality remains after adjusting for a broad set of observable confounders (Cutler and Lleras-Muney 2008; Kawachi et al. 2010). In sum, researchers should attend to complex measurements and dynamics whereby poor health and low SES may cause each other in complicated ways.

Theoretical Frameworks

This section reviews some of the most prominent theoretical frameworks that describe the association between social class/SES and health.

Material Resources and Material Deprivation

Poverty has direct links to poor health and shorter lives (Miech et al. 2006; Oh 2001). Particularly in less developed countries, large portions of the populations lack access to basic health needs, shortening lives. Individuals who live in poverty are least able to access clean water, adequate nutrition, or sanitation. Material deprivation increases poor health conditions and complications due to increased exposures to communicable diseases and heightened risk of compromised immune systems. This association is further exacerbated by a lack of adequate health care access. Moreover, the poverty and health relationship is cyclical – poverty is associated with heath compromising behaviors and poor health, which contributes to poverty and the transmission of poverty across generations. As an example, those individuals with the lowest incomes and least access to health insurance in the US are also most likely to go bankrupt after major health shocks – reinforcing a cycle between poverty and poor health (Himmelstein et al. 2009). Thus, some scholars highlight the importance of understanding the "causes of the causes" of poor health, to disrupt the patterns of disadvantage (Rose 1992).

Inequality and Relative Deprivation

Relative deprivation also matters for health, especially in wealthy countries where a majority of individuals have adequate incomes that meet basic health and nutrition needs (Eibner and Evans 2005; Wilkinson 2005). Indeed, the graded association between SES and health persists even among those with adequate material resources (Adler et al. 1994). The links between SES and health may be less about the absolute measure of SES and more about the ability of higher status individuals to mobilize resources to more efficiently pursue health (Sen 1992).

At the contextual (e.g. county, state, or local-level), income inequality is associated with lower levels of social cohesion, cooperation, social investment, and public resources for those who are relatively disadvantaged (Franzini et al. 2005; Kawachi and Kennedy 2006). Greater income inequality may also lead to political polarization that reduces support for redistributive policies, resulting in a weaker social safety net and less spending on the poor (Piketty 2015). Some, however, have questioned the impacts of social inequality on health (Lynch et al. 2004). Deaton and Lubotsky (2003) suggest that the association between income inequality and health may be confounded by the racial composition of areas, which is a unique form of inequality separate from income inequality. Others have shown that relative inequality fails to explain SES- smoking disparities across the European Union (Pampel 2002) or individual risks of obesity (Chang and Christakis 2005).

At the individual level, relatively lower position may result in lower perceived status. Lower relative standing may lead to frustration, stress, and adverse health (Festinger 1954; Wilkinson 2001). Analogous work on non-human primates has demonstrated the physiological and psychological advantages of higher status and status stability (Marmot and Sapolsky 2014). Exposure to chronic stress through economic strain, insecure employment, or low social control have direct links to negative physiological responses (Adler and Ostrove 1999; Matthews and Gallo 2011). The Whitehall studies have documented how lower prestige jobs have higher rates of mortality, even after accounting for income and education (Marmot 1994; Marmot et al. 1991). Higher social standing and occupational prestige are associated with psychosocial well-being, through sense of control, job satisfaction, job security, and favorable work environments. Even among those with relatively high incomes, debt and low levels of wealth may cause anxiety, psychological distress, and reduced investments in one's health (Krueger and Chang 2008).

A limitation to this approach is that few studies include measures of relative standing, and instead focus on objective indicators of income or education. Perceptions of relative deprivation and inequality also require that individuals assume a reference group – but studies seldom have respondents state explicitly which reference group they are using. It is not clear how individuals consider geographic region, peer groups, or race/ethnic status when determining their social positioning.

Neighborhood SES

Residential neighborhoods shape access to health-related resources within a specific geographic area (Bernard et al. 2007). Indeed, lower SES neighborhoods have fewer physical, institutional, and social resources to support health. Higher SES individuals tend to live in areas marked by less crowding, higher levels of safety, infrastructures that promote exercise (e.g. sidewalks, parks, adequate lighting), clean drinking water, and less exposure to toxic or noxious environments. Higher status neighborhoods also have better access to institutions that promote health, like grocery stories, exercise facilities, parks, and well-funded local schools that dedicate resources to support the health promotion of children.

Neighborhoods can also provide social resources. Higher SES neighborhoods may also support health promoting norms, social capital, social networks that encourage healthy behaviors and accurate health knowledge, and collective efficacy that can support health (Rios et al. 2012). Independent of individual level characteristics, exposure to negative neighborhood conditions can be a source of chronic stress, resulting in unhealthy behaviors or adverse physiological responses that increase the risk of poor health (Steptoe and Feldman 2001). Yet, additional work needs to consider that neighborhood SES may have varying effects on health across different sociodemographic groups (Denney et al. 2018; Eschbach et al. 2004).

Human Capital

Human capital includes both innate factors such as cognitive functions and motivation, but also investments in the education or skills that one can gain through time and labor (Becker 2009). Human capital suggests that more educated individuals have greater access to knowledge and the ability to seek out knowledge about healthy behaviors (e.g. diets or physical activity), current medical knowledge, or medication adherence (Mirowsky and Ross 2003). Human capital also provides a sense of personal control and self-efficacy that individuals can use to solve problems such as navigating complex behavioral landscapes or health care systems or quitting unhealthy behaviors (Mirowsky and Ross 2003). Higher levels of education are also associated with trust in scientific discoveries that may benefit health.

Human capital may impact incentives to invest in health due to expectations of an improved future health and life opportunities (Cutler and Lleras-Muney 2010). More educated individuals may be willing to delay gratification (i.e. assume a lower discount rate), allowing them to take steps in the present that, while difficult, may yield health benefits well into the future (e.g. exercise and preventive health care). Conversely, lower SES individuals may have less faith that they have control over their health or that unhealthy behaviors are important in the face of adverse conditions that increase their early risk of death (Blaxter 2003)

Social Capital and Social Relationships

Individuals with higher SES – but especially those with higher levels of education or higher status occupations – typically also have better access to social capital and advantageous social networks. Social capital, or the non-material resources that allows individuals to secure benefits through social membership in existing social structures, can function at individual or community levels (Coleman 1994; Portes 1998). Higher social capital includes mutual trust, reciprocity, and social norms that encourage healthy behavior, access to health services, and psychological support (Kawachi et al. 2008). Social capital also presents opportunities for constructive coping alternatives to unhealthy behaviors (Ross and Wu 1995). More affluent neighborhoods, with higher levels of social capital, are associated with lower rates of homicide and all-cause mortality (Sampson et al. 1997).

Social networks influence health primarily through direct support, behavioral influence, access to resources, social involvement, and person-to-person contagion pathways (Smith and Christakis 2008). Peer behaviors are important drivers of the initiation, usage, and cessation of health behaviors such as smoking, substance use, preventive health care, or unhealthy diets. For example, Christakis and Fowler (2007) demonstrate the socially contagious spread of obesity through social networks. Further, social networks have the potential to provide financial, physical and emotional support that can reduce stress or mitigate some of the complications associated with health conditions (Berkman 1995). On-going research is needed to further understand the unique contributions of multiple definitions of social capital and social networks, as well as distinguishing whether social capital is independent of SES (e.g. Carpiano 2006).

Cultural Capital

Cultural capital are the resources that classes use to signal membership, set boundaries around their values or preferences, and distinguish themselves from others (Bourdieu and Wacquant 2013). Cultural capital theories emphasizes the tastes and values that are cultivated in elite settings, such as affluent families, high status schools, or through participation in the fine arts (DiMaggio 1982). Education is often central to theories about cultural capital. While education teaches skills as noted by human capital perspectives, cultural capital theories note that higher levels of education also favor and validate the skills and values learned within higher status families (Lareau 2011). The tastes and preferences learned through education are reflections of class differences and may help to legitimate class stratification. A critique of cultural capital perspectives is that non-high status groups also have sets of tastes and values that they enact to distinguish themselves from other groups, and may not necessarily interpret higher status practices as superior or desirable, in part due to lower returns to accepting those practices (Roscigno and Ainsworth-Darnell 1999)

Cultural capital perspectives often focus on health behaviors as outcomes. Individuals use health behaviors to enact their tastes and values, depending on the resources available to them (Cockerham 2005). For example, education is positively associated with participation in fitness sports (e.g. running, weight lifting) and facilities based sports (e.g. golf, tennis), but inversely associated with participation in team sports (e.g. football, basketball) (Saint Onge and Krueger 2011). Further, there is some evidence that status groups use smoking, like tastes in music, to distinguish themselves from others. Cigarette smoking is lower among those who listen to classical music, a genre preferred by higher SES adults, whereas smoking is higher among those who listen to music genres that are preferred by lower SES adults (Pampel 2006).

SES is also linked to cultural health capital, a distinct form of cultural capital that refers to a repertoire of skills and attributes that patients deploy in disease management and health care settings (Shim 2010). Patients use cultural health capital to mobilize resources such as medical vocabulary and communication skills to collaborate with health care professionals about diagnosis and treatment plans. Lower SES individuals may experience a mismatch between provider expectations and the more limited cultural and social resources available to those patients. While some have demonstrated that lower SES groups also use cultural health capital (e.g. international prescription drug purchases) in limited access situations (e.g. lack of insurance; government assistance programs), these forms of cultural health capital have perceived limitations in achieving health equity (Madden 2015).

Diffusion of Innovation

Innovation and diffusion describe how health-related ideas and behaviors move through the population along class lines (Rogers 2010). Sociological research has long demonstrated how lower status groups update the knowledge and behaviors of higher status groups, even as they fall from fashion in higher status groups (Simmel 1971; Veblen [1899] 2005). Higher SES individuals tend to be early adopters of new medical technologies, treatments, and health behaviors, and are often the first to cease using risky technologies or treatments, and to quit unhealthy behaviors (Glied and Lleras-Muney 2008; Link 2008).

For example, high SES individuals were early adopters of cigarette smoking, in part due to advertising campaigns that extolled the health benefits and fashionableness of smoking (Brandt 2007). The SES gradient in smoking reversed, however, when high SES groups became aware of the risks of smoking and began to quit, even as lower status individuals continued the uptake of smoking (Brandt 2007; Pampel 2002). A similar pattern emerged with obesity around the globe. Initially, obesity was most common among higher status groups as jobs became more sedentary and fast food and prepared meals became more widely available (Cutler et al. 2003). However, the gradient reversed as the global obesity pandemic continued – higher status groups found ways to control their weight, whereas higher body mass became seen as a form of status among lower SES groups (Pampel et al. 2012).

Fundamental Causes

Fundamental cause theories suggest that social conditions, including SES, are determinants of health outcomes (Link and Phelan 1995). This perspective makes three primary claims: First, higher levels of SES confer power, knowledge, and resources that individuals can use flexibly to pursue better health. Second, SES works through multiple pathways to affect health, and those pathways change over time. For example, access to adequate sanitation may have accounted for SES disparities before modern sewage systems made those available to everyone. But in more recent times, higher status individuals may sustain their advantages by more quickly adopting new medical interventions like statins or vaccinations for human papilloma virus (Chang and Lauderdale 2009; Polonijo and Carpiano 2013). Third, because power, knowledge, and resources are flexible resources, higher SES individuals can use them to reduce mortality from diverse causes (Masters et al. 2015; Phelan et al. 2004).

Lutfey and Freese (2005) have important refinements to fundamental cause theory. For example, even though most mechanisms may link high SES individuals to better health in a given context, some "countervailing mechanisms" may work in the opposite direction. For example, some high-status women may manipulate their insulin intake to achieve weight loss – thinness may be especially valued in higher status groups, but manipulating their insulin to do so may incur health risks. In other cases, higher status individuals may be most likely to receive new medical technologies, even if they would provide greater benefits to lower status individuals. For example, lower status individuals may benefit most from automated insulin pumps that ensure adequate management of diabetes, even with minimal knowledge or resources. But higher status individuals – who have the income and medical knowledge to manage their diabetes – may be more likely to receive automated insulin pumps.

Life Course

The timing and succession of social conditions throughout the life course can have broad impacts on health (Ben-Shlomo and Kuh 2002, Elder et al. 2003). Numerous studies have linked exposure to social disadvantage – including low

SES and poverty – in utero, at birth, and throughout childhood to poor health in adulthood (Elo and Preston 1992; Finch and Crimmins 2004; Gluckman et al. 2008). Life course perspectives illuminate how lower SES can both leave enduring biological imprints that affect health far into the future and increase exposure to accumulated disadvantages over the life course. For example, repeated exposures to poor conditions through lower SES are associated with future adverse health through reduced immunity, poorer access to adequate nutrition, increased stress responses, and a limited ability to maintain physiological stability (Dowd et al. 2009; McEwen and Seeman 1999).

The life course perspective emphasizes varying impacts of SES over one's life by addressing sensitive periods of social and biological exposures; the accumulation of social disadvantages; early life SES influences on later life; and how adult SES may moderate the impacts of earlier life course exposures. Yet, challenges remain in matching the critical periods in the life course with the relevant SES indicators and subsequent health conditions – this is especially difficult given that childhood SES has varying impacts on health across demographic groups (Montez and Hayward 2011).

Discussion

We have described the major theoretical frameworks that social research uses to explore the association between SES and health in high-income countries. Beyond theory, the impact of SES on population health is substantial. We could save hundreds of thousands of lives each year by eliminating poverty, reducing income inequality, and increasing educational attainment (Galea et al. 2011; Krueger et al. 2015). We conclude our paper with a discussion of policy approaches to mitigating the association between SES and health.

Policies that target those with the lowest incomes may result in improved health. Transfers to young children (e.g. investments in health care, economic resources, and early education) are associated with substantial improvements in later life health and earnings. Improving neighborhoods for younger children also has the potential for long term gains in both SES and subsequent health (Campbell et al. 2014; Chetty and Hendren 2018). In the US, the Earned Income Tax Credit, a refundable tax credit for the working poor, has been linked to better education and future earnings for children (Bastian and Michelmore 2018), as well as improved birth and health outcomes (Evans and Garthwaite 2014; Markowitz et al. 2017). Among adults in the US, a 10% increase in the minimum wage is associated with a 4% reduction in non-drug suicide mortality for adults with high school or less education (Dow et al. 2019). Ongoing systematic studies are required to understand how various tax credit programs (e.g. WTC in the UK or the CWB in Canada) and minimum wage legislations matter across geographic locations and economies.

Education policy remains promising, given evidence that those with the lowest education would receive the greatest benefits from improved education (Cutler and Lleras-Muney 2010). Moreover, the economic value of the longer, healthier lives associated with high school and college degrees may be greater than the economic benefits of those degrees (Krueger et al. 2019). Distressingly, educational disparities have widened over time (Marmot 2015; Masters et al. 2012; Miech et al. 2011), and gains in life expectancy in the US have largely accrued to the most educated in recent decades (Sasson and Hayward 2019).

Unfortunately, access to and benefits of education are not equal across all groups. Each additional year of education provides smaller mortality reductions for African Americans than for whites, potentially indicating how broader structural conditions and perceptions of employers influence the SES-health relationship (Montez et al. 2012). However, policies that support the health of the least educated (e.g. stronger safety nets, anti-tobacco legislation) have narrowed educational gradients in mortality, suggesting the importance of state and federal policies in reducing educational gradients in survival (Montez et al. 2019).

Occupations can impact health through increased access to income, material resources (e.g. health insurance), social standing, and psychosocial pathways (Marmot et al. 1997). Unemployment or precarious employment is linked to negative health behaviors, often described as "deaths of despair" in the US (Case and Deaton 2020). State and national policies use training programs and skills building to urge individuals to seek employment. Policies also shape job safety in both high status and low status jobs, and psychosocial factors linked to jobs are increasingly a priority (Siegrist et al. 2010). In high-income countries, employers, unions, and governments may work to reduce stress, ensure living wages, support efforts for workplace balance, and increase job control with the potentials to reduce absenteeism and health care costs, while improving productivity.

Policies can also target health outcomes more directly. Although health care access may not necessarily reduce SES inequalities (Smith et al. 1990), better access to insurance may lead to earlier preventive care, while increased education coupled with access may lead to more effective care (Dunlop, Coyte and McIsaac 2000). Insights into the SES-health relationship are more commonly becoming integrated into the formal medical establishment and practice of medicine. An emphasis on social determinants of health and cross-sector collaboration are increasingly moving beyond clinical health solutions to increase access to major SES-health related resources such as housing, transportation, and food (Marmot and Allen 2014; Tait et al. 2018). Addressing the factors that both bring people into the health care system and that compromise interventions have the potential to lead to better health care outcomes.

Other policies target health behaviors directly, although health promotion efforts that are not aimed specifically at low SES individuals have the potential to increase SES disparities. Nonetheless, restrictions on indoor smoking and increases in cigarette taxes lead to lower initiation and reduced smoking, especially among the least educated (Brandt 2007; Martire et al. 2011). Physical activity promotion has focused on increasing incentives or opportunities for exercise in schools, workplaces, and communities. School design, supervision, and curricula can increase children's physical activity (Sallis et al. 2001). Workplace promotion programs also improve health behaviors, albeit with more mixed results (Baicker et al. 2010).

While we have focused on the role of SES on mortality, health behaviors, or chronic conditions, additional policies should further contextualize the association between SES and health. For example, addressing potential SES disparities is important in rapidly evolving social situations (Norris et al. 2008). Individuals with fewer socioeconomic resources may be less able to get through challenges associated with climate change, terrorist attacks, natural disasters, or pandemics with their health intact. Lower SES individuals are at higher risk because they lack the resources to "buy out" of high-risk situations. Ongoing efforts need to recognize the potential damages of limited job flexibility, few savings, unstable incomes, precariously sited neighborhoods, inabilities to relocate, reduced effective coping strategies, and greater social isolation.

Overall, SES disparities in health are a vibrant topic of study in sociology with significant impacts for the health of our population. Efforts to reduce disparities will require the attention of multiple disciplines to identify the diverse pathways that link SES to health behaviors, health, and mortality. Ongoing efforts to narrow SES disparities in health via public investments or social policies will require innovative approaches to ensure that the benefits do not simply go to the most advantaged. Understanding and publicizing ongoing SES disparities in health is a key part of the process to reduce health inequities.

References

Adler, Nancy E., Thomas Boyce, Margaret A. Chesney, Sheldon Cohen, Susan Folkman, Robert L. Kahn, and S. Leonard Syme. 1994. "Socioeconomic Status and Health: The Challenge of the Gradient." *American Psychologist* 49(1): 15.

Adler, Nancy E and Joan M Ostrove. 1999. "Socioeconomic Status and Health: What We Know and What We Don't." *Annals of the New York Academy of Sciences* 896(1): 3–15.

Anderson, Robert N. 2011. "Coding and Classifying Causes of Death: Trends and International Differences." Pp. 467–89. in *International Handbook of Adult Mortality*, edited by R. G. Rogers and E. M. Crimmins. New York: Springer.

Baicker, Katherine, David Cutler, and Zirui Song. 2010. "Workplace Wellness Programs Can Generate Savings." *Health Affairs* 29(2): 304–11.

Bastian, Jacob and Katherine Michelmore. 2018. "The Long-Term Impact of the Earned Income Tax Credit on Children's Education and Employment Outcomes." *Journal of Labor Economics* 36(4): 1127–63.

Becker, Gary S. 2009. *Human Capital: A Theoretical and Empirical Analysis, with Special Reference to Education.* Chicago, IL: University of Chicago Press.

Beebe-Dimmer, Jennifer, John W. Lynch, Gavin Turrell, Stephanie Lustgarten, Trivellore Raghunathan, and George A. Kaplan. 2004. "Childhood and Adult Socioeconomic Conditions and 31-Year Mortality Risk in Women." *American Journal of Epidemiology* 159(5): 481–90.

Ben-Shlomo, Yoav and Diana Kuh. 2002. "A Life Course Approach to Chronic Disease Epidemiology: Conceptual Models, Empirical Challenges and Interdisciplinary Perspectives." *International Journal of Epidemiology* 31(2): 285–93.

Benyamini, Yael, Elaine A. Leventhal, and Howard Leventhal. 1999. "Self-Assessments of Health: What Do People Know That Predicts Their Mortality?" *Research on Aging* 21: 477–500.

Berkman, Lisa F. 1995. "The Role of Social Relations in Health Promotion." *Psychosomatic Medicine* 57(3): 245–54.

Bernard, Paul, Rana Charafeddine, Katherine L. Frohlich, Mark Daniel, Yan Kestens, and Louise Potvin. 2007. "Health Inequalities and Place: A Theoretical Conception of Neighbourhood." *Social Science & Medicine* 65(9): 1839–52.

Blaxter, Mildred. 2003. *Health and Lifestyles*. London: Routledge.

Boardman, Jason D., Jarron M. Saint Onge, Brett C. Haberstick, David S. Timberlake, and John K. Hewitt. 2008. "Do Schools Moderate the Genetic Determinants of Smoking?" *Behavior Genetics* 38(3): 234–46.

Bond Huie, Stephanie A., Patrick M. Krueger, Richard G. Rogers, and Robert A. Hummer. 2003. "Wealth, Race, and Mortality." *Social Science Quarterly* 84: 667–84.

Bourdieu, Pierre. 1984. *Distinction: A Social Critique of the Judgment of Taste*. Translated by R. Nice. Cambridge, MA: Harvard University Press.

Bourdieu, Pierre and Loïc Wacquant. 2013. "Symbolic Capital and Social Classses." Journal of Classical Sociology 13(2): 292–302.

Brandt, Allan M. 2007. *The Cigarette Century: The Rise, Fall, and Deadly Persistence of the Product That Defined America*. New York: Basic Books (AZ).

Brown, Dustin C., Joseph T. Lariscy, and Lucie Kalousová. 2019. "Comparability of Mortality Estimates from Social Surveys and Vital Statistics Data in the United States." *Population Research and Policy Review* 38(3): 371–401.

Campbell, Frances, Gabriella Conti, James J. Heckman, Seong Hyeok Moon, Rodrigo Pinto, Elizabeth Pungello, and Yi Pan. 2014. "Early Childhood Investments Substantially Boost Adult Health." *Science* 343(6178): 1478–85.

Carpiano, Richard M. 2006. "Toward a Neighborhood Resource-Based Theory of Social Capital for Health: Can Bourdieu and Sociology Help?" *Social Science & Medicine* 62(1): 165–75.

Case, Anne and Angus Deaton. 2020. *Deaths of Despair and the Future of Capitalism*. Princeton, NJ: Princeton University Press.

Chang, Virginia W. and Nicholas A. Christakis. 2005. "Income Inequality and Weight Status in US Metropolitan Areas." *Social Science & Medicine* 61(1): 83–96.

Chang, Virginia W. and Diane S. Lauderdale. 2009. "Fundamental Cause Theory, Technological Innovation, and Health Disparities: The Case of Cholesterol in the Era of Statins." *Journal of Health and Social Behavior* 50: 245–60.

Chetty, Raj and Nathaniel Hendren. 2018. "The Impacts of Neighborhoods on Intergenerational Mobility I: Childhood Exposure Effects*." *The Quarterly Journal of Economics* 133(3): 1107–62.

Chetty, Raj, Michael Stepner, Sarah Abraham, Shelby Lin, Benjamin Scuderi, Nicholas Turner, Augustin Bergeron, and David Cutler. 2016. "The Association between Income and Life Expectancy in the United States, 2001-2014." *JAMA* 315(16): 1750–66.

Christakis, Nicholas A. and James H. Fowler. 2007. "The Spread of Obesity in a Large Social Network over 32 Years." *New England Journal of Medicine* 357(4): 370–79.

Cockerham, William C. 2005. "Health Lifestyle Theory and the Convergence of Agency and Structure." *Journal of Health and Social Behavior* 46(1): 51–67.

Cockerham, William C, Joseph D. Wolfe, and Shawn Bauldry. 2020. "Health Lifestyles in Late Middle Age." *Research on Aging* 42(1): 34–46.

Coleman, James S. 1994. *Foundations of Social Theory*. Cambridge, MA: Harvard University Press.

Conley, Dalton. 2009. *Being Black, Living in the Red: Race, Wealth and Social Policy in America, 2nd Ed*. Berkeley, CA: University of California Press.

Currie, Janet and Joshua Goodman. 2020. "Parental Socioeconomic Status, Child Health, and Human Capital." Pp. 239–48 in *The Economics of Education*, edited by S. Bradley and C. Green. Academic Press.

Cutler, David M., Edward L. Glaeser, and Jesse M. Shapiro. 2003. "Why Have Americans Become More Obese?" *The Journal of Economic Perspectives* 17(3): 93–118.

Cutler, David M. and Adriana Lleras-Muney. 2008. "Education and Health: Evaluating Theories and Evidence." in *Making Americans Healthier: Social and Economic Policy as Health Policy*, edited by R. F. Schoeni, J. S. House, G. A. Kaplan, and H. Pollack. New York: Russell Sage Foundation.

Cutler, David M. and Adriana Lleras-Muney. 2010. "Understanding Differences in Health Behaviors by Education." *Journal of Health Economics* 29(1): 1–28.

Deaton, Angus and Darren Lubotsky. 2003. "Mortality, Inequality and Race in American Cities and States." *Social Science & Medicine* 56(6): 1139–53.

Denney, Justin T, Jarron M. Saint Onge, and Jeff A. Dennis. 2018. "Neighborhood Concentrated Disadvantage and Adult Mortality: Insights for Racial and Ethnic Differences." *Population Research and Policy Review* 37(2): 301–21.

DiMaggio, Paul. 1982. "Cultural Capital and School Success: The Impact of Status Culture Participation on the Grades of U.S. High School Students." *American Sociological Review* 47: 189–201.

DiPrete, Thomas A. and David B. Grusky. 1990. "Structure and Trend in the Process of Stratification for American Men and Women." *American Journal of Sociology* 96(1): 107–43.

Dow, William H., Anna Godøy, Christopher A. Lowenstein, and Michael Reich. 2019. "Can Economic Policies Reduce Deaths of Despair?" Vol. 0898-2937. National Bureau of Economic Research.

Dowd, Jennifer Beam, Anna Zajacova, and Allison Aiello. 2009. "Early Origins of Health Disparities: Burden of Infection, Health, and Socioeconomic Status in U.S. Children." *Social Science & Medicine* 68(4): 699–707.

Drentea, Patricia and Paul J. Lavrakas. 2000. "Over the Limit: The Association among Health, Race and Debt." *Social Science & Medicine* 50(4): 517–29.

Duncan, Otis Dudley. 1961. "A Socioeconomic Index for All Occupations." Pp. 109–61. in *Occupations and Social Status*, edited by A. J. Reiss Jr. New York: Free Press.

Dunlop, Sheryl, Peter C. Coyte, and McIsaac Warren. 2000. "Socio-Economic Status and the Utilisation of Physicians' Services: Results from the Canadian National Population Health Survey." *Social Science & Medicine* 51(1): 123–33.

Eibner, Christine and William N. Evans. 2005. "Relative Deprivation, Poor Health Habits, and Mortality." *Journal of Human Resources* 40(3): 591–620.

Elder, Glen H, Monica Kirkpatrick Johnson, and Robert Crosnoe. 2003. "The Emergence and Development of Life Course Theory." Pp. 3–19. In: Mortimer Jeylan T., Shanahan Michael J. (eds) *Handbook of the Life Course. Handbooks of Sociology and Social Research.* Boston, MA: Springer,

Elo, Irma T and Samuel H Preston. 1992. "Effects of Early-Life Conditions on Adult Mortality: A Review." *Population Index*. 58(2): 186–212.

Erikson, Robert and John H. Goldthorpe. 1992. *The Constant Flux: A Study of Class Mobility in Industrial Societies*. Oxford: Clarendon Press.

Eschbach, Karl, Glenn V. Ostir, Kushang V. Patel, Kyriakos S. Markides, and James S. Goodwin. 2004. "Neighborhood Context and Mortality among Older Mexican Americans: Is There a Barrio Advantage?" *American Journal of Public Health* 94(10): 1807–12.

Evans, William N. and Craig L. Garthwaite. 2014. "Giving Mom a Break: The Impact of Higher Eitc Payments on Maternal Health." *American Economic Journal: Economic Policy* 6(2): 258–90.

Festinger, Leon. 1954. "A Theory of Social Comparison Processes." *Human Relations* 7(2): 117–40.

Finch, Caleb E. and Eileen M. Crimmins. 2004. "Inflammatory Exposure and Historical Changes in Human Life-Spans." *Science* 305(5691): 1736–39.

Franzini, Luisa, Margaret Caughy, William Spears, and Maria Eugenia Fernandez Esquer. 2005. "Neighborhood Economic Conditions, Social Processes, and Self-Rated Health: A Multilevel Latent Variables Model." *Social Science & Medicine* 61: 1135–50.

Galea, Sandro, Melissa Tracy, Katherine J. Hoggatt, Charles DiMaggio, and Adam Karpati. 2011. "Estimated Deaths Attributable to Social Factors in the United States." *American Journal of Public Health* 101(8): 1456–65.

Glied, Sherry and Adriana Lleras-Muney. 2008. "Technological Innovation and Inequality in Health." *Demography* 45(3): 741–61.

Gluckman, Peter D., Mark A. Hanson, Cyrus Cooper, and Kent L. Thornburg. 2008. "Effect of in Utero and Early-Life Conditions on Adult Health and Disease." *New England Journal of Medicine* 359(1): 61–73.

Haas, Steven A. 2006. "Health Selection and the Process of Social Stratification: The Effect of Childhood Health on Socioeconomic Attainment." *Journal of Health and Social Behavior* 47: 339–54.

Harris, Kathleen Mullan and Kristen M. Schorpp. 2018. "Integrating Biomarkers in Social Stratification and Health Research." *Annual Review of Sociology* 44(1): 361–86.

Hauser, Robert M and John Robert Warren. 1997. "Socioeconomic Indexes for Occupations: A Review, Update, and Critique." *Sociological Methodology* 27(1): 177–298.

Himmelstein, David U., Deborah Thorne, Elizabeth Warren, and Steffie Woolhandler. 2009. "Medical Bankruptcy in the United States, 2007: Results of a National Study." *The American Journal of Medicine* 122(8): 741–46.

Hollingshead, August B. 2011. "Four Factor Index of Social Status." *Yale Journal of Sociology* 8: 21–51.

Hummer, Robert A and Joseph T. Lariscy. 2011. "Educational Attainment and Adult Mortality." Pp. 241–61. in *International Handbood of Adult Mortality*, edited by R. G. Rogers and E. M. Crimmins. New York: Springer.

Idler, Ellen L. and Stanislav Kasl. 1991. "Health Perceptions and Survival: Do Global Evaluations of Health Status Really Predict Mortality?" *Journals of Gerontology: Social Sciences* 46: S55-S65.

Kahn, Joan R. and Elena M. Fazio. 2005. "Economic Status over the Life Course and Racial Disparities in Health." *Journal of Gerontology: Social Sciences* 60B: 76–84.

Kawachi, Ichiro, Nancy E. Adler, and William H. Dow. 2010. "Money, Schooling, and Health: Mechanisms and Causal Evidence." *Annals of the New York Academy of Sciences* 1186(1): 56–68.

Kawachi, Ichiro and Bruce P. Kennedy. 2006. *The Health of Nations:. Why Inequality Is Harmful to Your Health.* New York: New Press.

Kawachi, Ichiro, S. V. Subramanian, and Daniel Kim. 2008. "Social Capital and Health A Decade of Progress and Beyond." Pp. 1–26 in *Social Capital and Health.* Edited by Ichiro Kawachi, S. V. Subramanian, and Daniel Kim. New York: Springer.

Krueger, Patrick M. and Sarah A. Burgard. 2011. "Work, Occupation, Income, and Mortality." Pp. 263–88 in *International Handbood of Adult Mortality*, edited by R. G. Rogers and E. M. Crimmins. New York: Springer.

Krueger, Patrick M. and Virginia W. Chang. 2008. "Being Poor and Coping with Stress: Health Behaviors and the Risk of Death." *American Journal of Public Health* 98: 889–96.

Krueger, Patrick M., Ilham A. Dehry, and Virginia W. Chang. 2019. "The Economic Value of Education for Longer Lives and Reduced Disability." *The Milbank Quarterly* 97(1): 48–73.

Krueger, Patrick M., Richard G. Rogers, Robert A. Hummer, Felicia B. LeClere, and Stephanie A. Bond-Huie. 2003. "Socioeconomic Status and Age: The Effect of Income Sources and Portfolios on Adult Mortality in the United States." *Sociological Forum* 18(3): 465–82.

Krueger, Patrick M., Melanie K. Tran, Robert A. Hummer, and Virginia W. Chang. 2015. "Mortality Attributable to Low Levels of Education in the United States." *PloS One* 10(7): e0131809.

Lareau, Annette. 2011. *Unequal Childhoods: Class, Race, and Family Life*. Berkeley, CA: University of California Press.

Lariscy, Joseph T. 2011. "Differential Record Linkage by Hispanic Ethnicity and Age in Linked Mortality Studies: Implications for the Epidemiologic Paradox." *Journal of Aging and Health* 23(8): 1263–84.

Link, Bruce G. 2008. "Epidemiological Sociology and the Social Shaping of Population Health." *Journal of Health and Social Behavior* 49(4): 367–84.

Link, Bruce G. and Jo Phelan. 1995. "Social Conditions as Fundamental Causes of Disease." *Journal of Health and Social Behavior* 35: 80–94.

Liu, Mengzhen, Yu Jiang, Robbee Wedow, Yue Li, et al. 2019. "Association Studies of up to 1.2 Million Individuals Yield New Insights into the Genetic Etiology of Tobacco and Alcohol Use." *Nature Genetics* 51(2): 237–44. 10.1038/s41588-018-0307-5.

Lleras-Muney, Adriana. 2005. "The Relationship between Education and Adult Mortality in the United States." *Review of Economic Studies* 72: 189–221.

Ludwig, Jens, Lisa Sanbonmatsu, Lisa Gennetian, Emma Adam, Greg J. Duncan, Lawrence F. Katz, Ronald C. Kessler, Jeffrey R. Kling, Stacy Tessler Lindau, Robert C. Whitaker, and Thomas W. McDade. 2011. "Neighborhoods, Obesity, and Diabetes — A Randomized Social Experiment." *New England Journal of Medicine* 365(16): 1509–19.

Lutfey, Karen and Jeremy Freese. 2005. "Toward Some Fundamentals of Fundamental Causality: Socioeconomic Status and Health in the Routine Clinic Visit for Diabetes." *American Journal of Sociology* 110(5): 1326–72.

Lutfey, Karen E., Eric Gerstenberger, and John B. McKinlay. 2013. "Physician Styles of Patient Management as a Potential Source of Disparities: Cluster Analysis from a Factorial Experiment." *Health Services Research* 48(3): 1116–34.

Lynch, John, George Davey Smith, Sam A.M. Harper, Marianne Hillemeier, Nancy Ross, George A. Kaplan, and Michael Wolfson. 2004. "Is Income Inequality a Determinant of Population Health? Part 1. A Systematic Review." *The Milbank Quarterly* 82(1): 5–99.

Madden, Erin Fanning. 2015. "Cultural Health Capital on the Margins: Cultural Resources for Navigating Healthcare in Communities with Limited Access." *Social Science & Medicine* 133: 145–52.

Magee, Joe C. and Adam D. Galinsky. 2008. "Social Hierarcy: The Self-Reinforcing Nature of Power and Status." *The Academy of Management Annals* 2(1): 351–98.

Markowitz, Sara, Kelli A. Komro, Melvin D. Livingston, Otto Lenhart, and Alexander C. Wagenaar. 2017. "Effects of State-Level Earned Income Tax Credit Laws in the US. On Maternal Health Behaviors and Infant Health Outcomes." *Social Science & Medicine* 194: 67–75.

Marmot, Michael. 2015. "The Health Gap: The Challenge of an Unequal World." *The Lancet* 386(10011): 2442–44.

Marmot, Michael and Jessica J. Allen. 2014. "Social Determinants of Health Equity." *American Journal of Public Health* 104(S4): S517-S19.

Marmot, Michael G. 1994. "Social Differentials in Health within and between Populations." *Daedalus* 123(4): 197–216.

Marmot, Michael G, Hans Bosma, Harry Hemingway, Eric Brunner, and Stephen Stansfeld. 1997. "Contribution of Job Control and Other Risk Factors to Social Variations in Coronary Heart Disease Incidence." *The Lancet* 350(9073): 235–39.

Marmot, Michael G and Robert Sapolsky. 2014. "Of Baboons and Men: Social Circumstances, Biology, and the Social Gradient in Health." In Sociality, hierarchy, health: Comparative biodemography: Papers from a workshop.

Marmot, Michael G, Stephen Stansfeld, Chandra Patel, Fiona North, Jenny Head, Ian White, Eric Brunner, Amanda Feeney, and G Davey Smith. 1991. "Health Inequalities among British Civil Servants: The Whitehall Ii Study." *The Lancet* 337(8754): 1387–93.

Martire, Kristy A, Richard P. Mattick, Christopher M. Doran, and D. Hall Wayne. 2011. "Cigarette Tax and Public Health: What Are the Implications of Financially Stressed Smokers for the Effects of Price Increases on Smoking Prevalence?" *Addiction* 106(3): 622–30.

Marx, Karl. [1867] 2007. *Capital: A Critique of Political Economy*, Vol. 1. New York: Cosimo, Inc.

Masters, Ryan K., Robert A. Hummer, and Daniel A. Powers. 2012. "Educational Differences in U.S. Adult Mortality: A Cohort Perspective." *American Sociological Review* 77: 548–72.

Masters, Ryan K., Bruce G. Link, and Jo Phelan. 2015. "Temporal Changes in Educaion Gradients of 'Preventable' Mortality: A Test of Fundamental Cause Theory." *Social Science & Medicine* 127: 19–28.

Matthews, Karen A. and Linda C. Gallo. 2011. "Psychological Perspectives on Pathways Linking Socioeconomic Status and Physical Health." *Annual Review of Psychology* 62: 501–30.

McDade, Thomas W., Sharon Williams, and J. Josh Snodgrass. 2007. "What a Drop Can Do: Dried Blood Spots as a Minimally Invasive Method for Integrating Biomarkers into Population-Based Research." *Demography* 44(4): 899–925.

McEwen, Bruce S. and Teresa Seeman. 1999. "Protective and Damaging Effects of Mediators of Stress: Elaborating and Testing the Concepts of Allostasis and Allostatic Load." *Annals of the New York Academy of Sciences* 896(1): 30–47.

Miech, Richard, Fred Pampel, Jinyoung Kim, and Richard G. Rogers. 2011. "The Enduring Association between Education and Mortality: TheRole of Widening and Narrowing Disparities." *American Sociological Review* 76(6): 913–34.

Miech, Richard A., Shiriki K. Kumanyika, Nicolas Stettler, Bruce G. Link, Jo C. Phelan, and Virginia W. Chang. 2006. "Trends in the Association of Poverty with Overweight among U.S. Adolescents, 1971-2004." *Journal of the American Medical Association* 295(20): 2385–93.

Mirowsky, John and Catherine E. Ross. 2003. *Education, Social Status, and Health*. New York: Aldine de Gruyter.

Mokdad, Ali H., James S. Marks, Donna F. Stroup, and Julie L. Gerberding. 2004. "Actual Causes of Death in the United States, 2000." *Journal of the American Medical Association* 291(10): 1238–45.

Mollborn, Stefanie and Elizabeth Lawrence. 2018. "Family, Peer, and School Influences on Children's Developing Health Lifestyles." *Journal of Health and Social Behavior* 59(1): 133–50.

Montez, Jennifer Karas and Mark D. Hayward. 2011. "Early Life Conditions and Later Life Mortality." Pp. 187–206. in *International Handbood of Adult Mortality*, edited by R. G. Rogers and E. M. Crimmins. New York: Springer.

Montez, Jennifer Karas, Robert A. Hummer, and Mark D. Hayward. 2012. "Educational Attainment and Adult Mortality in the United States: A Systematic Analysis of Functional Form." *Demography* 49(1): 315–36.

Montez, Jennifer Karas, Anna Zajacova, Mark D. Hayward, Steven H. Woolf, Derek Chapman, and Jason Beckfield. 2019. "Educational Disparities in Adult Mortality across US States: How Do They Differ, and Have They Changed since the Mid-1980s?" *Demography* 56(2): 621–44.

Moore, David E. and Mark D. Hayward. 1990. "Occupational Careers and Mortality of Elderly Men." *Demography* 27(1): 31–53.

Nakao, Keiko and Judith Treas. 1994. "Updating Occupational Prestige and Socioeconomic Scores: How the New Measures Measure Up." *Sociological Methodology* 24: 1–72.

Nam, Charles B. and Monica Boyd. 2004. "Occupational Status in 2000: Over a Century of Census-Based Measurement." *Population Research and Policy Review* 23: 327–58.

Norris, Fran H., Susan P. Stevens, Betty Pfefferbaum, Karen F. Wyche, and Rose L. Pfefferbaum. 2008. "Community Resilience as a Metaphor, Theory, Set of Capacities, and Strategy for Disaster Readiness." *American Journal of Community Psychology* 41(1-2): 127–50.

Oakes, J. Michael and Peter H. Rossi. 2003. "The Measurement of Ses in Health Research: Current Practice and Steps toward a New Approach." *Social Science & Medicine* 56(4): 769–84.

Oh, Hyun Joo. 2001. "An Exploration of the Influence of Householf Poverty Spells on Mortality Risk." *Journal of Marriage and Family* 63(1): 224–34.

Pampel, Fred C. 2002. "Inequality, Diffusion, and the Status Gradient in Smoking." *Social Problems* 49(1): 35–57.

Pampel, Fred C. 2006. "Socioeconomic Distinction, Cultural Tastes, and Cigarette Smoking." *Social Science Quarterly* 87(1): 19–35.

Pampel, Fred C., Justin T. Denney, and Patrick M. Krueger. 2012. "Obesity, Ses, and Economic Development: A Test of the Reversal Hypothesis." *Social Science & Medicine* 74(7): 1073–81.

Pampel, Fred C., Patrick M. Krueger, and Justin T. Denney. 2010. "Socioeconomic Disparities in Health Behaviors." *Annual Review of Sociology* 36: 349–70.

Phelan, Jo, Bruce G. Link, Ana V. Diez-Rouz, Ichiro Kawachi, and Bruce Levin. 2004. "'Fundamental Causes' of Social Inequalities in Mortality: A Test of the Theory." *Journal of Health and Social Behavior* 45: 265–85.

Piketty, Thomas. 2015. *The Economics of Inequality*. Cambridge, MA: Harvard University Press.

Polonijo, Andrea N. and Richard M. Carpiano. 2013. "Social Inequalities in Adolescent Human Papillomavirus (Hpv) Vaccination: A Test of Fundamental Cause Theory." *Social Science & Medicine* 82: 115–25.

Portes, Alejandro. 1998. "Social Capital: Its Origins and Applications in Modern Sociology." *Annual Review of Sociology* 24(1): 1–24.

Rios, Rebeca, Leona S. Aiken, and Alex Zautra. 2012. "Neighborhood Contexts and the Mediating Role of Neighborhood Social Cohesion on Health and Psychological Distress among Hispanic and Non-Hispanic Residents." *Annals of Behavioral Medicine* 43(1): 50–61.

Rogers, Everett M. 2010. *Diffusion of Innovations*. New York: Simon and Schuster.

Roscigno, Vincent J. and James W. Ainsworth-Darnell. 1999. "Race, Cultural Capital, and Educational Resources: Persistent Inequalities and Achievement Returns." *Sociology of Education* 72(3): 158–78.

Rose, David and Eric Harrison. 2014. *Social Class in Europe: An Introduction to the European Socio-Economic Classification*, Vol. 10. New York: Routledge.

Rose, Geoffrey. 1992. *Individuals and Populations. The Strategy of Preventive Medicine*. Oxford: Oxford University Press.

Ross, Catherine E. and John Mirowsky. 1999. "Refining the Association between Education and Health: The Effects of Quantity, Credential, and Selectivity." *Demography* 36: 445–60.

Ross, Catherine E and Chia-ling Wu. 1995. "The Links between Education and Health." *American Sociological Review*. 60(5): 719–45.

Rostron, Brian L, Elizabeth Arias, and John L Boies. 2010. "Education Reporting and Classification on Death Certificates in the United States."

Saint Onge, Jarron M. and Patrick M. Krueger. 2011. "Education and Racial-Ethnic Differences in Types of Exercise in the United States." *Journal of Health and Social Behavior* 52(2): 197–211.

Saint Onge, Jarron M. and Patrick M. Krueger. 2017. "Health Lifestyle Behaviors among U.S. Adults." *SSM - Population Health* 3: 89–98.

Sallis, James F., Terry L. Conway, Judith J. Prochaska, Thomas L. McKenzie, Simon J. Marshall, and Marianne Brown. 2001. "The Association of School Environments with Youth Physical Activity." *American Journal of Public Health* 91(4): 618.

Sampson, Robert J., Stephen W. Raudenbush, and Felton Earls. 1997. "Neighborhoods and Violent Crime: A Multilevel Study of Collective Efficacy." *Science* 277(5328): 918–24.

Sasson, Isaac and Mark D. Hayward. 2019. "Association between Educational Attainment and Causes of Death among White and Black Us Adults, 2010-2017." *Jama* 322(8): 756–63.

Sen, Amartya Kumar. 1992. *Inequality Reexamined*. New York: Oxford University Press.

Shim, Janet K. 2010. "Cultural Health Capital: A Theoretical Approach to Understanding Health Care Interactions and the Dynamics of Unequal Treatment." *Journal of Health and Social Behavior* 51(1): 1–15.

Siegrist, Johannes, Joan Benach, Abigail McKnight, Peter Goldblatt, and Carles Muntaner. 2010. *Employment Arrangements, Work Conditions and Health Inequalities: Report on New Evidence on Health Inequality Reduction, Produced by Task Group 2 for the Strategic Review of Health Inequalities Post 2010*. London: Marmot Review.

Simmel, Georg. 1971. *On Individuality and Social Forms: Selected Writings*. Chicago, IL: University of Chicago Press.

Smith, G Davey, Mel Bartley, and David Blane. 1990. "The Black Report on Socioeconomic Inequalities in Health 10 Years On." *BMJ: British Medical Journal* 301(6748): 373.

Smith, Kirsten P. and Nicholas A. Christakis. 2008. "Social Networks and Health." *Annual Review of Sociology* 34(1): 405–29.

Steptoe, A. and P. J. Feldman. 2001. "Neighborhood Problems as Sources of Chronic Stress: Development of a Measure of Neighborhood Problems, and Associations with Socioeconomic Status and Health." *Annals of Behavioral Medicince* 23(3): 177–85.

Sun, Amy Ruining and Jason N. Houle. 2020. "Trajectories of Unsecured Debt across the Life Course and Mental Health at Midlife." *Society and Mental Health* 10(1): 61–79.

Tait, Margaret E., Oktawia P. Wójcik, Alonzo L. Plough, and John R. Lumpkin. 2018. "Building a Culture of Health in Our Changing Climate." *American Journal of Public Health* 108(S2): S64-S65.

Veblen, Thorstein. [1899] 2005. *The Theory of the Leisure Class: An Economic Study of Institutions*. Delhi: Aakar Books.

Viruell-Fuentes, Edna A., Jeffrey D. Morenoff, David R. Williams, and James S. House. 2011. "Language of Interview, Self-Rated Health, and the Other Latino Health Puzzle." *American Journal of Public Health* 101(7): 1306–13.

Walsemann, Katrina M, Jennifer A. Ailshire, and Caroline Sten Hartnett. 2019. "The Other Student Debt Crisis: How Borrowing to Pay for a Child's College Education Relates to Parents' Mental Health at Midlife." *The Journals of Gerontology: Series B*. 75(7): 1494–1503.

Wedow, Robbee, Meghan Zacher, Brooke M. Huibregtse, Kathleen Mullan Harris, Benjamin W Domingue, and Jason D. Boardman. 2018. "Education, Smoking, and Cohort Change: Forwarding a Multidimensional Theory of the Environmental Moderation of Genetic Effects." *American Sociological Review* 83(4): 802–32.

Wilkinson, Richard G. 2001. *Mind the Gap: Hierarchies, Health and Human Evolution*. New Haven, CT: Yale University Press.

Wilkinson, Richard G. 2005. *The Impact of Inequality: How to Make Sick Societies Healthier*. New York: The New Press.

Wright, Erik Olin. 1998. *The Debate on Classes*, Vol. 20. New York: Verso.

Wright, Erik Olin. 2005. *Approaches to Class Analysis*. New York: Cambridge University Press.

Zajacova, Anna and Jennifer Karas Montez. 2017. "The Health Penalty of the Ged: Testing the Role of Noncognitive Skills, Health Behaviors, and Economic Factors." *Social Science Quarterly* 98(1): 1–15.

12

Health and Gender

Ellen Annandale

Social relations of gender interact with the biological body to shape patterns of morbidity and mortality and the experience of health and illness of men and women, boys and girls around the world. This interplay is complex, multifaceted, constantly changing and often belies simplistic notions of binary differences between males and females as determinants of health status. The highly political nature of "gender and health" within academia and in the wider public sphere means that research is deeply infolded within real world politics and this has a significant influence on how problems are conceptualized and studied. As Schofield (2002: 29) recounts, the "different meanings associated with 'gender and health' reflect the ways in which various interests brought their claims forward." How gender is theorized and the concepts that researchers deploy are therefore not mere technical issues; they matter because they reflect the interests of different communities which bring particular collectives of "gender" into being.

The chapter begins by outlining the origins and development of research on gender and health status, from its roots in feminism and the concern with women's health through to a more gender inclusive focus which includes men and, to a lesser degree to date, other gender identities. Threaded through this condensed history we find highly charged debates about how we should comprehend gender itself. Erstwhile conceptions of gender as a social factor, distinct from, but ultimately predicated on, binary biological difference between two distinct groups of males and females have begun to give way as activists and gender theorists alike forefront gender fluidity, challenge cisgender partiality in research, seek to make gender non-binary identities transparent, and highlight the complex intersection of the biological and the social in the production of health and illness. Following this discussion, the chapter charts international variations in differences in life expectancy and explores some of the explanations for them. This is done through by an analysis of changing patterns of health status in selected regional and national contexts. In this discussion,

The Wiley Blackwell Companion to Medical Sociology, First Edition. Edited by William C. Cockerham.

some aspects of the changing social relations of gender and the lives of men and women are considered, particularly as they relate to longevity. Taking the HIV/AIDS and COVID-19 (SARS-CoV-2) pandemics as brief illustrations, the final part of the chapter explores the interplay of biological and the social factors in the production of health.

From "Women's Health" to "Gender and Health"

In its origins, the study of gender and health was synonymous with women's health. Sociological research on this theme stems back at least to the nineteenth-century, when Harriet Martineau (1861) depicted in detail the associations between women's maladies and their station in life and Charlotte Perkins Gilman (1973[1892]) pronounced to women that they had "so far lived and suffered in a man-made world." But it took the radical politics of the 1960s and 1970s, of which the women's movement was a vital part, to establish health on the political and academic agenda as feminists sought to demonstrate that illness among women is socially constructed rather than, as conventionally believed, biologically given (Annandale 2009; Ruzek 1979). This included contesting the treatment of women in health systems dominated by men, especially where reproductive health was concerned (Dreifus 1978). In the mid-1980s, Clarke 1983: 65) depicted the conflation of sex/gender in biomedically authorized practices as a form of sexism which produces "harrowing complications" when dealing with health and illness.

The sex/gender distinction introduced into feminism in the 1970s (Oakley 1972; Rubin 1975) was a major stimulus to research because it afforded analysts the capacity to challenge the pejoration of the binary script which, past and present alike, has fashioned woman's being as analogous to the biological body, itself conceived as inferior to that of man. Given that women's experience of oppression has turned historically on denigration of the biological body, the theoretical appetite was justifiably to place social (gender), rather than biological (sex), analytic center-stage. This galvanized the argument that causes of health/ill-health are predominantly social and the effect of women's disadvantage within the dominion of men, initially with reference to the global north (see, for example, Gove and Hughes 1979; Nathanson 1975; Verbrugge 1985) and subsequently the global south (e.g. Okojie 1994; Vlassoff 1994). Auspicious though the sex/gender distinction was, and arguably, in many ways still is, the social and the biological became unduly separated as attention turned towards social and biological difference between men and women, boys and girls (Annandale 2009; Schofield 2004).

Given the associations drawn between women's physical and mental health problems and stresses and burdens, in the domestic realm and the workplace, and patriarchy in all its forms (Doyal 1995; Rowbotham 1973), male power and control over women's lives was brought to the heart of the research agenda. The limitation was that although a great deal had been written about men and masculinity, this was only from the vantage of its impact on women and girls. Men's experience *qua* men was over-looked. For instance, Susan Faludi (2000: 14) wrote that since women only "see men guarding the fort, they don't see how the culture of the fort shapes men." Male privilege (especially when accompanied by privileges of class and majority ethnic status) is unmarked and hence invisible to scrutiny. As was increasingly pointed out from around the mid-1990s, many men may then fail to recognize their lives in gendered terms because their experience is represented as the norm (Kimmel 1990; Robinson 2000).

These observations reworked the research agenda as many social scientists began to explore patriarchy (and patriarchies) and associated norms of masculinity as problematic not only for women's health, but also for men's (see, e.g. Courtenay 2011). By proposing that masculinity takes multiple forms and bringing the concepts of hegemonic and subordinated masculinities to the fore, Connell's (1995) agenda-setting book, *Masculinities* inspired a swathe of new research. It was argued that the hegemonic form of masculinity is problematic because it comprises a dual system of power: by legitimating sub-ordination and super-ordination, it not only subordinates most women, but also many men (Kimmel and Wade 2018; Messerschmidt 2018, 2019).

Research was advanced that living up to culturally exalted ideals of stoicism, strength and the avoidance of weakness is injurious *both* men's *and* women's health across the world (Courtenay 2011). Since illness can be experienced as a form of weakness by men it has been associated with the failure to admit to symptoms and to seek help when needed (Höhn et al. 2020; Wadham 2002), as well as with suicide when ideals cannot be lived up to (Adinkrah 2012; Cleary 2012). Research in resource poor settings, such as the Philippines and Pakistan, points to extremes such as men selling a kidney on illegal markets in order to re-establish their position as family breadwinner when exploitative labor conditions provide no alternative. Health can be severely compromised post-surgery under such circumstances, due, for example, to lack of adequate healthcare follow-up, and accompanied by stigma and ridicule, and a weakened body desired by neither employers, nor by future wives (Yea 2011; Yousaf and Purkayastha 2015). (Of course, women may also come to see a kidney as their only productive asset, as Boyce 2006 finds in South Africa).

The economic downturn and associated rise in under- and un-employment amongst working class and otherwise disenfranchised men associated with neoliberal economic policies (Walker and Roberts 2018) is considered by some to have prompted a "crisis of masculinity" and the formation of "compensatory hypermasculinities" in reaction to "social positions lacking economic power" (Messerschmidt 2019: 87; see also, Kimmel 2017). As Gourarier (2019) writes, alongside this, advances made by women in the spheres of education and employment in many countries of the global north has nurtured the feeling amongst some men that masculinity has been sacrificed on the altar of gender equality.

When men's self-identification as the newly the disadvantaged group is accompanied by an aggrieved sense of entitlement, the potential for the rise of antifeminist politics is ripe (Connell 2005). There can be serious consequences for women's mental and physical health if men seek to shore up and restore their power through gender-based violence (GBV) against people who identify as women (Burns 2017), as witnessed through the international *#metoo* movement which, as Corbin (2018) relates, has not only increased men's accountability for sexual harassment and assault, but also inspired a backlash. "Toxic assemblages" comprising a complex blend of "orthodox alignments of power and dominance" with tropes of victimhood and "beta masculinity" have arisen (Ging 2017: 638). These assemblages operate in the public sphere and, importantly, not only in person but also through online social media in misogynistic personal attacks against individual women (Ging 2017). Underscoring the scale of GBV as a public health problem, the WHO (2019) reports (based on 2013 data) that 35% of women worldwide experience physical and/or sexual violence in their lifetime, with many serious, long-term negative mental and physical health sequelae.

The foregoing discussion indicates that the branching out of the roots of gender and health to include men's health is not without tensions. If our concern becomes appreciating men's problems, then this can neglect men as part of the problem in relation to women's health, something which is especially important in parts of the world where marked inequalities in access to power and resources render women vulnerable to conditions such as HIV and the mental and physical health consequences of interpersonal violence (Sprague 2018; UNAIDS 2019), as discussed. However, there are also positives: a more inclusive approach to gender and health encourages us to question assumptions that particular health problems *belong* to either men (e.g. heart disease, workplace stress) or to women (e.g. mental ill-health, anorexia, and other weight problems) (Annandale et al. 2007). It also prompts us to think about the experience of health, illness, and health care as at least potentially cross-cutting what are still commonly constructed as given divides of biological sex and social gender in complex and often contested ways.

Despite the opening up of gender and health research to include men, until very recently it has focused almost exclusively on normatively sexed and gendered bodies, in the process constructing a "hyper-gendered world" of males and females (Westbrook and Saperstein 2015: 534). Survey research in particular has been heavily cisgendered and concerned with those people whose gender identity matches the biological sex they were assigned at birth and those who have a gender identity or perform a gender role considered appropriately for this "sex." But, with reference to the introductory remarks of the chapter, as societal conceptions of gender have changed so too have research approaches. The gradual recognition, if not yet acceptance, of transgender and transgender rights across a number of countries (Michelson and Harrison 2020) has led to a slow awareness of the association between trans identities and health status.

A great deal of this research has quite rightly been concerned with access to and discrimination in healthcare (e.g. Institute of Medicine 2011; Vincent 2018), though there is a slowly growing body of studies on health status (to date focused mostly on populations within countries of the global north). For example, based on data from the US *National Transgender Discrimination Survey* (NTDS), Miller and Grollman (2015) report significant associations between self-reported "gender-conformity"/"gender nonconformity," transphobic discrimination and health self-harming behaviours amongst American adults. Over two-thirds (71%) of their sample of just over 4,000 transgender adults reported exposure to "everyday" discrimination. Health-harming was substantial: 44% had attempted suicide and 27% reported abuse of drugs/alcohol. Moreover, the more transgender persons felt that others read them as trans/gender-nonconforming, the greater was the likelihood of self/health-harming behaviors.

This leads Miller and Grollman (2015) to conclude that the social and health costs of gender nonconformity within the US are high and the consequences far reaching. Also for the USA, but using CDC Behavioral Risk Factor Surveillance System data, Lagos (2018) found that, compared to cisgender men (the reference group for the analysis), gender-nonconforming trans respondents showed significantly higher odds of reporting poor self-rated health than any other gender identity group (this remained almost twice as high after demographic, socio-economic and behavioral factors were adjusted for in analysis). Once again, this underscores that gender is a power relation which is at once definitional in the sense of who is allowed membership to gender categories in everyday life, and social structural with real life health consequences for individuals subject to gender-based discrimination. Taking us back to the point made earlier, about the infolding of gender research with politics within the academic and wider public sphere, transgender identity has also been the subject of quite vociferous debate within feminism for some time. On the one hand, a wide body of feminist writing, originating in queer activism of the 1990s, endorses gender plurality and accords respect to transgender women (Connell 2002). On the other hand, radical feminists, and especially radical lesbian feminists (notably, Jeffreys 2014; Raymond 1994 [1979]); have argued that transgender not only relies on but also reinforces an inappropriate biological essentialism which overlooks that gender is not biological but a political system of male domination. Thus, protagonist Sheila Jeffreys (2014: 7) depicts "transgenderism" as "a ruthless appropriation of women's experience and existence."

This debate speaks once again to the highly political nature of gender identities and gender categories used in research instruments. As Singer (2015) argues, new ways of enumerating gender enables persons who identify as transgender or as gender non-binary to both numerically and politically "count" in health status research. But, as he also points out, "transgender" has the tendency to become a catch-all category. This is exemplified in the popular notion of the "trans umbrella" under which a proliferative collective of "non-conforming" trans-binary (transmen, transwomen) and trans non-binary (e.g. gender queer, gender fluid) identities shelter, eliding significant ways of being that tend to be compared in analysis to the heteronormative binary of male/female. To an extent this echoes the dilemma of quantitative research generally of how to operationalize identity categories so that they accurately reflect the complexity of experience, but the stakes are especially high in the politically charged arena of gender and health (the same may be said of ethnicity and health). The time when researchers in the field of gender and health status are willing and able to fully address LGBTQAI + identities still seems a way off. Yet, ultimately, as Singer (2015: 58) relates for sex and gender, however formed, "demographic categories are double-edged swords in that they are necessary for the redirection of resources toward socially marginalized people," but, at the same time, "they often constitute the conditions of containment of these same people." This observation is fitting as we turn now to look at international variations in differences in life expectancy where we overwhelmingly rely upon data which treats gender as a male/female binary.

International Variations in Longevity

Women's longer average life expectancy compared to men has become an accepted fact of across the world. This is borne out for average life expectancy in 2016 (WHO 2020a) for all World Health Organization (WHO) member states. However, as the figures in Table 12.1 illustrate, the extent of women's greater longevity varies considerably, from just under two years in Zimbabwe and Pakistan, to almost 11 years in the Russian Federation and 9.5 years in the war-torn Syrian Arab Republic, where many men have been engaged in deadly armed conflict in the civil war since 2011 (the probability of dying between ages 15 and 60 for males is over three times that of females in Syria). There are also marked differences in life expectancy between men and between women across nations. For instance, in Zimbabwe, men and women die on average before reaching their late 50s and early 60s respectively, while in Australia, France, Japan and Sweden they can anticipate living into their early to mid-80s. Healthy life expectancies also present a stark picture: while Australian men and women can expect to live relatively healthy lives into their early to mid-70s, the equivalent decade for Zimbabwean men and women is the early to mid-50s (WHO 2020a).

Since the data in Table 12.1 concern 2016, they are a snapshot in recent time. Significant gender-related changes have been taking place globally since the last quarter of the twentieth-century. In different parts of the world and in different ways, new social relations of gender, gender expectations and patterns of equality and inequality between men and woman and boys and girls are emerging from gender-related change, which are reflected in new configurations of mortality and

Table 12.1 Life expectancy at Birth for Males and Females (Years), 2016.

Country	Males	Females	Difference(F-M)
Australia	81.0	84.8	+3.8
Democratic Republic Congo	58.9	62.0	+3.1
France	80.1	85.7	+5.6
Japan	81.1	87.1	+6.0
Latvia	70.6	79.6	+9.0
Liberia	62.0	63.9	+1.9
Pakistan	65.7	67.4	+1.7
Russian Federation	66.4	77.2	+10.8
Sierra Leone	52.5	53.8	+1.3
Sweden	80.6	84.1	+3.5
Syrian Arab Republic	59.4	68.9	+9.5
Ukraine	67.6	77.1	+9.5
UK	79.7	83.2	+3.5
USA	76.1	81.1	+5.0
Zimbabwe	59.6	63.1	+3.5

Source: WHO. 2020. *World Health Statistics 2020. Monitoring health for the SDGs, sustainable development goals*. Geneva: World Health Organization. Annex 2. Part 1.

morbidity. While these are not easily summarized, several broad regional trends can be highlighted. For limitations of space, in what follows, the focus is on two illustrations of change, the reducing gap in the affluent west and the large gap in some countries of Eastern Europe.

Changes in Life Expectancy in the Affluent West: A Reducing Gap

The hundred or so years from roughly the 1880s to around the 1970s were a period of gradually increasing female longevity advantage in much of the affluent West. In England and Wales, for example, the number of extra years, on average, that a female might expect to live at birth compared to a male rose from around 2.0 years for those born in 1841, to 3.6 years for those born in 1910, to 4.4 years for those born in 1950, and to a peak of 6.9 years for those born in 1969 (Office for National Statistics 2007; Yuen 2005). In the USA, females born in 1900 could expect to live, on average, 2.0 years longer than their male counterparts. This rose to 5.5 years for those born in 1950, to reach a sizable over 7 years for those born in 1970 (NCHS 2007). The female longevity advantage grew from 3.6 years for Australian females, and from about 3 years for Canadian females, born at the start of the twentieth-century, to a projected 7.0 and 7.1 years respectively for those born in the early 1980s (AIHW 2006; Statistics Canada 2001).

However, the late 1960s and early 1970s marked an historical peak as this female longevity advantage began to be chipped away during the last quarter of the twentieth- and into the twenty-first century. Life expectancy at birth continued to grow for both males and females over the period (though as discussed below, there was stagnation after 2011). But, as we can see for the UK and USA in Table 12.2, the gap between them has been reducing. Principally, this has been due to swifter increases for males than for females (Raleigh 2019). (Similar patterns can be observed for other countries, see e.g., Dinges and Weigl 2016). Table 12.3 shows more detailed data for average "years gained" by men and women across the different regions of Europe between 1980 and 2008. The first thing to note is that, with very few exceptions, male gains were larger than those of females. Second,

Table 12.2 The life expectancy gap (Years) 1969–2016.

UK		1971	1981	1991	2001	2016
	Men	69.1	70.8	73.2	75.7	79.7
	Women	75.3	76.8	78.7	80.4	83.2
	Gap	6.2	6.0	5.5	4.7	3.5
USA		**1970**	**1980**	**1990**	**2000**	**2016**
	Men	67.1	70.0	71.8	74.1	76.2
	Women	74.1	77.4	78.8	79.3	81.1
	Gap	7.0	7.4	7.0	5.2	4.9

Sources: Health United States, 2018 (National Center for Health Statistics, 2019) https://www.ons.gov.uk/peoplepopulationandcommunity/birthsdeathsandmarriages/lifeexpectancies/datasets/nationallifetablesunitedkingdomreferencetables

Table 12.3 Number of years (at birth) gained 1980, 1990 and 2000, by sex and region of Europe.

		1980–1900	1990–2000	2000–2008
North	Men	1.5	2.7	2.0
	Women	0.9	1.5	1.6
West	Men	2.2	2.4	2.7
	Women	2.2	1.8	1.9
South	Men	2.2	1.9	1.8
	Women	2.6	1.6	1.7

Source: Andeev et al. (2011), Figure 22.

somewhat different patterns are observable by region. In the North (e.g. Iceland, Sweden, Denmark) and the West (e.g. France, Germany, the UK), men consistently gained more years over the period. But in the South (e.g. Greece, Italy, Croatia), women gained slightly more years between 1980 and 1990 and men slightly more years thereafter.

This still leaves the question of what we might attribute the reducing life expectancy gap to. And, in particular, it raises the issue of whether gender-related social change in societies over the period may provide at least part of the explanation. Very generally put, if, as previously discussed, conventional masculinity is associated with health-damaging behaviours and femininity with health-enhancing behaviors, we might expect that "if men quit conventional masculinity and, or if women adopt it" (Månsdotter et al. 2006: 616), and insofar as these behaviours are associated with mortality, we might expect this to account at least in part for the reducing life expectancy gap. From a detailed analysis of national data on 24 causes of death for Sweden, Sundberg and colleagues (2018) identified three patterns of change in related to the reducing gender gap: where male mortality declines more swiftly than female; where male mortality for some diseases declines, while female mortality for some diseases increases; and where there are increases in some causes of death for both men and women, but the increase disproportionately affects women. They find the first pattern to be crucial, with reductions in deaths from circulatory diseases (especially ischaemic heart disease) and smoking-related deaths the most important factor. Cigarette smoking appears to have been a key factor. Social mores against women's smoking began to loosen in the West in the late 1920s and into 1930s (Waldron 1991) as cigarettes were marketed to, and taken up by, women as "torches of freedom" (Amos and Haglund 2000). As already observed, the narrowing gap in life expectancy generally began in the 1970s, by which time, women who were to become regular smokers coming of age during these earlier decades would be in their 60s and 70s (depending on when they started to smoke) and already potentially subject to tobacco's negative effects (Annandale 2014). Conversely, by the 1970s, male smoking rates were already declining in many countries.

As we have seen, even though the gender gap has narrowed, the life expectancy of women and men at birth in high-income countries has grown from the early nineteenth-century. For example, it almost doubled in the UK between 1841 and 2011 (ONS 2015). However, in a quite remarkable turnaround, some high income countries have experienced slowing or stalling improvements in life expectancy recently, and even downturns for some sub-groups. As Hiam and colleagues (2018: 406) express, "life expectancy is the most important social statistic that any country produces about itself and it is often an early sign of wider societal problems," which undoubtedly explains why the slowdown is the focus of a lot of attention at the present time. But it is particularly of interest for the discussion in this chapter because, in some of countries, the decelerations, and especially declines, have been of a greater magnitude for women than for men (Raleigh 2019).

In an analysis of 28 high-income OECD (Organization for Economic Co-operation and Development) countries, Raleigh (2019) shows that the slowdown in life improvement has been especially marked in the USA (see also, Marmot et al. 2020; Woolf and Schoomaker 2019), though it is also noteworthy in the UK, France, Sweden and the Netherlands. For most European countries, life expectancy at birth increased more slowly over 2011–2016 than it did over 2006–2011, though the magnitude of the slowdown has generally been greater for women than for men (Raleigh 2019). Correspondingly, Ho and Hendi (2018) chronicle an average decline of 0.21 years for women, compared to 0.18 years for men, based on their analysis of 18 OECD member countries between 2014 and 2015.

Since the UK particularly stands out for this pattern of gender difference, it makes a useful case study of what might – only time will tell – turn out to be a significant trend. It is particularly important to appreciate that the slowing of life expectancy across and within the constituent counties of the UK has occurred in the context of a major increase in socio-economic inequalities in morbidity and mortality (see, e.g. Joyce and Xu. 2019). For example, life expectancy differences between the least and most deprived deciles (geographic areas) of England grew from 9.1% to 9.5% for men and from 6.8% to 7.7% for women, between 2010–2012 and 2018–2018 (Marmot et al. 2020). But most significantly for our interest, although improvement has slowed for people in the most affluent areas of the UK, in the most deprived areas, life expectancy has stalled for men, and actually declined for women since 2011 (Marshall et al. 2019). Over this same time period, women in the most deprived areas of England saw a decrease of 0.3 years in life expectancy, while those in the top decile saw an increase of 0.5 years. For men, life expectancy increased in all deciles, but the magnitude varied from 0.2 years in the most deprived area to between 0.5–0.7 years in the six least deprived areas (Marmot et al. 2020). Older women have shouldered most of the deceleration. Older women seem to be especially impacted. Between the periods 2012–2014 and 2013–2015, life expectancy fell from 6.88 to 6.80 years for women over age 85 in England and Wales (the equivalent figures for men were 5.85 and 5.84 years) (Hiam et al. 2018).

As already noted, UK women stand out as doing particularly poorly both in terms of absolute life expectancy and in their zero improvement over the time period 2000 to 2017. In an analysis of 22 selected comparator countries by Marshall and colleagues (2019), they rank 19th above only Denmark and the USA. Indeed, the life expectancy of women in England and Wales has not progressed as well as it has for women in other high-income countries since the 1970s (Leon et al. 2019). From findings such as these Hiam et al. (2018: 406) conclude that, "the fact that the changes have systematically harmed women more than men, and the very elderly more than the younger elderly, suggests that it is those who have less access to resources of all kinds that have been hardest hit." They explain that far from being a "temporary aberration," these changes point to the negative impact of government austerity policies on the health of the most vulnerable (Hiam et al. 2018: 404). Although it is not possible to go into detail here, this discussion of the slowdown in life expectancy denotes that, for a complete understanding, we need to take account of the intersection of gender (in this instance, expressed as males and females) with age and socio-economic status (Choo and Ferree 2010).

This section has briefly explored the chipping away of the female longevity advantage since the 1970s in the affluent West, alongside, in very recent years, the stagnation of the long historical trend of rising life-expectancy. While, in this situation, women are disproportionately impacted, in what follows we observe the obverse: a mortality crisis that has excessively affected men.

Changes in Life Expectancy in Eastern Europe

As shown above in Table 12.1, with a gap favoring women of at least 8 years, the Russian Federation and some other post-Soviet states have experienced the largest male/female gender gap in life-expectancy in world. As is now well documented, the "Russian mortality crisis" began in the mid-1960s and continued throughout most of the twentieth-century. Between 1965 and 1984, male life expectancy decreased from 64.4 to 61.7 years while women's stagnated, merely rising from 73.0 to 73.8 years. Gorbachev's mid- to late-1980s anti-alcohol campaign had the direct effect of reducing the gap and returning male life expectancy to mid-1960s levels. But the most remarkable change was the sharp decline in life expectancy, especially for men, in the aftermath of the collapse of communism over in the early 1990s; by 1994 life expectancy had dropped to 71.7 years for women and to a remarkable 57.4 years for men (Timonin et al. 2017).

Although less dramatic, these changes were reflected in other post-Soviet states (Gerry et al. 2018; Parsons 2014). Conspicuously, mortality rates were, and continue to be, especially high for cardiovascular disease (CVD) and injuries and concentrated in middle-aged adults, especially men (Shkolnikov et al. 2001). The winter of 1993–1994 saw the most extreme spike in mortality in modern times (Parsons 2014). Underscoring the magnitude of this, Stuckler and Basu (2013: 21,39) observe that "ten million men disappeared in the early 1990s" in deaths that continue to "haunt the nation."

The pertinent question, of course, is *why* did men disproportionately suffer during this time? The answer is found in their dislocation in the transition from the former state-managed economy to a market economy. Arguably the driver was less the transition itself – for then we would not expect the deaths to have been concentrated in men – than the policy choices that were made in managing it (Stuckler and Basu 2013). Stuckler and Basu (2013) point specifically to the collapse of employment in the Soviet non-industrial settlements (*mono-gorod*); that is, towns with only one industry dominated by male employment, such as the lumber mills in Pitkyaranta and nickel factories in Norlisk. Towns were bankrupted and people stranded with no hope for the future. Relatively young, working age, working class men began to die at alarming rates from heart disease, alcohol poisoning, and suicide. From interviews with women and men aged 55–70 (those most at risk of dying) undertaken between 2006 and 2007, Parsons (2014) explores Muscovites' experiences and accounts of life in the early 1990s. The crux of her argument is that feeling "unneeded" (*ne nuzhny*) was a distal driver of the mortality crisis. "Being unneeded," she argues, "translates social collapse into bodily death from cardiovascular disease and alcohol-related causes" (Parsons 2014: 11). As she continues, when the state fell so did the social connections people had worked within in the social system, leaving chaos and disorder, social isolation and powerlessness. Although women were seen by Parsons' respondents to have borne the brunt of the transition due to loss of work and childcare, they were nonetheless clear that men become more "unneeded" than women did, leading her to argue, as widely supported by others (e.g. Kossova et al. 2020; Razvodovsky 2018), that men turned to alcohol as they "tried to repair a sense of neededness by drinking." But they died "unconnected, unbound, unmoored" (Parsons 2014: 24). Although women were not unaffected by the same experiences, they were protected by being "needed" in the family.

Although the gender gap in life expectancy in Russia and other East European countries continued after the immediate transition period of the early 1990s and remains large, it began to decline over the subsequent period along with rising life expectancy from around 2003. In all instances, for the selected countries shown in Table 12.4, men have gained more years than women over the period 2000–2016. Thus, although it is to a different degree, and male life expectancy in particular is much lower, as in the countries of the West considered earlier, it is mostly improvements for men that explain the reduced gap in recent years. The recovery in life expectancy has been most marked for those of working age and associated with a decline in mortality from cardiovascular disease, especially for women (Timonin et al. 2017). But these overall improvements do not completely take away from the large existing gender gaps. As Razvodovsky (2018) analyses for Russia, although there have been fluctuations in both alcohol-consumption (in this instance, binge-drinking), they have mirrored the gender gap in all-cause mortality throughout 1959–2015, clearly indicating that changes in drinking underlie

Table 12.4 Life expectancy at birth (years) for males and female, selected Eastern Europe countries, 2000–2016.

	2000			2010			2016			Yrs gained	
	M	F	F-M	M	F	F-M	M	F	F-M	M	F
Estonia	65.5	76.2	10.7	70.9	80.5	9.6	73.0	82.1	9.1	7.5	5.9
Kazakhstan	58.4	69.7	11.3	62.6	72.4	9.8	66.8	75.3	8.5	8.4	5.6
Latvia	64.8	75.9	11.1	67.8	77.9	10.1	70.6	79.6	9.0	5.8	3.7
Russian Fed.	58.7	72.0	13.3	63.0	74.8	11.8	66.4	77.2	10.8	7.7	5.2
Ukraine	62.0	73.1	11.1	64.9	74.8	9.9	67.6	77.1	9.5	5.6	4.0
Hungary	67.6	76.2	8.6	70.5	78.2	7.7	72.3	79.4	7.1	4.7	3.2
Poland	69.5	77.9	8.4	72.1	80.4	8.3	73.8	81.6	7.8	4.3	3.7

Source: WHO Global Health Observatory. *Life Expectancy at Birth (years).* https://www.who.int/data/gho/data/indicators/indicator-details/GHO/life-expectancy-at-birth-(years)

the gender gap in mortality. This is further supported by Kossova and colleagues (2020) who established that, although reductions in the gender gap were associated with increases in per capita income across 77 regions of Russia over 1998–2015, the volume of alcohol consumed is the largest predictor of the extent of the gap at different points in time.

The foregoing analysis of the relatively small and reducing gender gap in life expectancy in the affluent West and the large and persisting, but declining gap in some countries of Eastern Europe has pointed to two things. First, that longevity is not only highly sensitive to social change in general but to its gender dimensions in particular. Second, although women, on average, still live longer than men (though with considerable international variation in extent), in regard to these parts of the world, the decreasing gap in recent years is explicable by gradual improvements in men's longevity. It indicates that the lives and health of women and men, boys and girls are highly sensitive to macro level socio-economic and cultural changes within societies. Political and social factors are undoubtedly key drivers of the associations between gender and health status. But this does not mean that biological factors are not also important, we will now be addressed.

The Interaction of Social and Biological Factors

Research on gender and health status has tended to take the social as its focus to the relative neglect of biological factors. However, in recent years, social scientists, and also some biologists, have begun to explore interaction of the social and the biological, or what some have conceptualised as the "biosocial" (see, e.g. Fausto-Sterling 2012; Meloni et al. 2018). Frost (2016), for example, has sought to demonstrate that humans are "biosocial creatures," emphasising the body's becoming as it actively engages with its physical and social environment. Although the natural and the social are inextricably intertwined, within the field of gender and health status, the characteristic approach to research has been to decompose or separate out their relative influence on women's and men's health (Krieger 2003).

As Payne (2006: 22) explains, "there are relatively few conditions which affect the health of men and women which are not influenced by biology in some way, even if this influence is minor." Biological sex differences render males and females differentially vulnerable to some causes of death, such as prostate disease in men and cancer of the cervix and the womb in women. But, significantly, biology seems also appears to play a role in conditions which both males and females experience alike. For instance, lung function matures more slowly in the male foetus which gives rise to more respiratory distress syndromes and lung-related injuries in newborns. Gene expression appears to make women more vulnerable to lung cancer, since they have higher rates of this condition at the same levels of smoking (Payne and Doyal 2015; Snow 2010). The female sex hormone oestrogen protects against the risk of cardiovascular disease amongst women in the reproductive years (Bird and Rieker 2008; Payne 2006), and the male hormone testosterone can be associated with weakened immunity and elevated risk of virus effects on the bodies of men. Yet, as we will see through the illustrations which follow, it is important to appreciate these factors do not crudely determine health and longevity. Rather, biologically shaped advantages or disadvantages are mediated by the gender dynamics which influence health behaviours and access to economic and cultural resources, as already been pointed to in the chapter. This is explored in what follows through the two brief illustrations of HIV/AIDS and COVID-19 (SARS-CoV-2).

In 2018, 37.9 people worldwide were living with HIV (WHO 2020b). Most of those affected live in low-to-middle income countries, with the majority concentrated in sub-Saharan Africa where there is a female/male ratio of 1.7. Adolescent girls and young women (aged 15 to 24) are especially vulnerable being 2.4 more likely to acquire HIV than their male peers (UNAIDS 2020). There is a combination of reasons for the gender difference in infection and mortality from HIV/AIDS internationally. First, biology is important. HIV is transmitted by contact with blood, semen, vaginal fluid, rectal fluid and breast milk entering a person's blood stream by crossing a mucus membrane (e.g. of the vagina, tip of the penis, rectum, or open sores/cuts) or by direct injection. Vitally, biology exposes females to higher risk of heterosexual transmission of HIV during intercourse. Viral load is higher in sperm than in vaginal secretions and the surface area of the mucus membranes exposed to the virus is higher in females (Masquelier and Reniers 2018). Second, and crucially, unequal power relations expose girls and women to infection through domestic and sexual abuse by male partners and their lack of ability to make free decisions about their sexual and reproductive health. For example, from their interviews with young women (aged 18–24) in Johannesburg, South Africa, Pettifor and colleagues (Pettifor et al. 2012) found a disconnect between expectations and actual experiences. Although they expected their intimate relationships to encompass women's financial independence, freedom, and the power to make their own decisions, most respondents were in relationships characterised by intimate partner violence, infidelity and lack of condom use. Outside of sub-Saharan Africa, many of the people with HIV/AIDS are part of "marginalized communities," for example, sex workers and transwomen. The risk of living with HIV for the latter group is around 19 times higher compared to other women and they are at particular risk of GBV, including rape which risks virus transmission (UNAIDS 2020).

But, notably, in Africa, the higher incidence of HIV amongst women and girls co-exists with a reduction in AIDS deaths as they have gained more years of life with the disease. The roll out of ART (antiretroviral therapy), consisting of a combination antiretroviral drugs to suppress the HIV virus and stop the progression of HIV disease (especially in its early stages) has been important here. ART prevents virus replication, improves survival, and reduces the risk of onward infection and is therefore effective in reducing death and improving survival. The greater decline in mortality amongst women than men in Africa has been attributed to HIV higher testing, take-up of ART and engagement with health care. For example, in Zimbabwe, 80% of women, compared to 62% of men reported having been tested in 2015 (Masquelier and Reniers 2018) and research points consistently to a relationship between normative expectations of masculinity men's reluctance to use heath care services and access ART (see, e.g. Sileo et al. 2018; Skovdal et al. 2011).

This short consideration of HIV/AIDS points quite clearly to the interaction of social and biological factors in the production of morbidity and mortality for men and women, boys and girls: women are biologically more susceptible (in heterosexual transmission which predominates in Africa where global incidence is the highest), but social, gender-related factors are also critical. Gender power relations and expectations make women and girls vulnerable to infection, but expectations of masculinity can deter men in seeking treatment and prolonging their lives.

At the time of writing (in Spring 2020), the world is in the midst of the COVID-19 pandemic which began in Wuhan, China in December 2019 and then spread to other parts of the world in early 2020. While it is too early to be conclusive on many aspects of the pandemic, it has been clear almost from the start that although men (and boys) and women (and girls) seem equally likely to be infected in the majority of countries, men are more likely to die from the disease than women. Thus, Table 12.5 shows that as of June 2020, men represented the majority of deaths, in some cases by a large margin, in almost all countries with the exception of the seeming anomaly of Canada. Sex differences in biology are being forwarded as a critical part of the explanation. Specifically, the angiotensin converting enzyme 2 receptor (ACE2), which has higher levels in men, seems an important risk for severe COVID-19 (Gagliardi et al. 2020; Gebhard et al. 2020; *Global 50/50 Initiative* 2020; Wenham et al. 2020). Since SARS-Cov-2 binds to ACE2, a membrane-bound protein expressed in several bodily tissues, such as vital organs (e.g. heart, lungs, gut and kidneys), it is a possible explanation for higher deaths amongst men (Gebhard et al. 2020). Women, by comparision, have a more robust immune response. But, although this seems to be important, it is not likely to provide the complete explanation for higher male mortality after infection. Comorbidities (underlying conditions) seem to be important to the body's response to the COVID-19, particularly high blood pressure, CVD and some lung diseases (such as COPD, chronic obstructive pulmonary disease) which tend to have higher age-specific incidence men than in women (Gebhard et al. 2020).

As with the wider discussion of gender differences in mortality in the chapter, cigarette smoking, which is higher in men; acting on symptoms, which men may possibility delay acting on more than women, given what we know about gender and help-seeking generally (discussed earlier); and exposure to unhealthy polluted

Table 12.5 Proportion of deaths from COVID-19 by sex (selected countries) as of 11 June 2020.

	Men	Women
Albania	65	35
Bangladesh	77	23
Canada	46	54
China	64	36
England	57	42
Germany	55	45
Italy	59	41
Philippines	63	37
Pakistan	74	26
Ukraine	55	45

Source: The Global 50/50 Initiative https://globalhealth5050.org/covid19/sex-disaggregated-data-tracker

environments, which in some parts of the world may impact men more than women, may play a role here (*Global 50/50 Initiative* 2020; Wenham et al. 2020).

It also needs to be appreciated that COVID-10 deaths have been deeply patterned by socio-economic status and ethnicity. To take the UK as an example, the most deprived areas of the UK have experienced age-standardized death rates of 128.3 per 100,000 population, compared to 58.8 in more affluent areas (ONS 2020). From Table 12.6 we see that, within England and Wales, Black men have been almost three time more likely to die than White men, and Black women over twice more likely to die than White women during the January–March 2020 timeframe. All other minority ethnic groups are also experiencing higher death rates than Whites. COVID-19 is therefore exacerbating existing health inequalities. How gender (male/female), ethnicity and socio-economic status might interact with each other is, however, not fully clear at the present time, though research by *Public Health England* (2020) reports that in terms of gender disparity, working age men diagnosed with the virus are twice as likely to die than women after taking ethnicity and deprivation level into account (though occupation and comorbidities explain some of the difference).

But it is also important to look beyond mortality when considering COVID-19 and gender and health status. There has, for example, been worldwide concern that GBV has increased exponentially during the crisis as women worldwide have been forced into "lockdown" in domestic environments with their abusers, so much so that the WHO has referred to a "shadow pandemic" of abuse against women (UN Women 2020a, 2020b). In France, reports of domestic violence have increased by 30%, in Argentina emergency calls have increased by 24%, and in Singapore helpline calls are 33% higher than before the pandemic (UN Women 2020b). In conclusion, we can return to the discussion of HIV/AIDS, since, as Small and colleagues (2020) advise, there are lessons to be learned for COVID-19, especially for women's experience in low-and-middle-income countries. Small et al. (2020) presage an unprecedented threat to women's health. Pandemics make it difficult for women to access sexual and reproductive health services, including modern contraceptives and are also likely to compromise HIV positive women's capacity

Table 12.6 Age-standardized rates for deaths involving COVID-19 by sex and ethnic group, per 100,000 people in England and Wales occurring between January 3–March 5 2020.

	Male	Female
White	87.0	52.0
Mixed	144.4	75.9
Indian	157.5	86.8
Bangladeshi/Pakistani	191.0	100.8
Chinese	119.4	65.4
Black	255.7	119.4
Other	167.7	83.4

Source: ONS *Coronavirus (COVID-19) roundup*.

https://www.ons.gov.uk/peoplepopulationandcommunity/healthandsocialcare/conditionsanddiseases/articles/coronaviruscovid19roundup/2020-03-26#ethnicgroup access ART. Deaths from COVID-19 have (to date) occurred disproportionately in high income and upper middle income countries, but food insecurity is likely to precipitate a crisis of food security, hunger and malnutrition within populations least affected so far by the disease itself, with women and children bearing the brunt (Lancet Global Health 2020).

Conclusion

This chapter has explored the variety of ways in which gender is associated with health status. Tracing how research approaches have changed over time has highlighted the complex intersections between real world gender politics and academic approaches, as exemplified by debates around how gender itself should be understood and conceptualized by researchers. We have also observed how the changing dynamics of gender relations through time and in different parts of the world impact the health status of women and men, girls internationally. Specifically, even though women still on average tend to live longer than men, the life expectancy gap shows marked global variations and different gender trajectories which are intimately connected with the socio-economic conditions of a society. Finally, we have explored the ways in which social gender-related and biological sex-related factors interact in the production of health.

References

Adinkrah, Mensah. 2012. "Better Dead than Dishonored: Masculinity and Male Suicidal Behavior in Contemporary Ghana." *Social Science & Medicine* 74(4): 474–81.

AIHW. 2006. *Australia's Health 2006*. Canberra: AIHW.

Amos, Amanda and Margarethe Haglund. 2000. "From Social Taboo to "Torch of Freedom": The Marketing of Cigarettes to Women." *Tobacco Control* 9: 3–8.

Annandale, Ellen. 2009. *Women's Health and Social Change*. London: Routledge.

Annandale, Ellen. 2014. *The Sociology of Health and Medicine*, 2nd. Cambridge: Polity.

Annandale, Ellen, Janet Harvey, Debbie Cavers, and Mary Dixon-Woods. 2007. "Gender and Access to Healthcare in the UK: A Critical Interpretive Synthesis of the Literature." *Evidence and Policy* 3(4): 463–86.

Avdeev, Alexandre, Tatiana Eremenko, Patrick Festy, Joelle Gaymu, Nathalie Le Bouteilec and Sabine Springer. 2011. ""Populations and Demographic Trends of European Countries, 1980–2010." *Population-E* 66(1): 9–130.

Bird, Chloe and Patricia Rieker. 2008. *Gender and Health. The Effects of Constrained Choices and Social Policies*. Cambridge: Cambridge University Press.

Boyce, Gerard. 2006. "Potential Gender Dimensions of a Kidney Trafficking Market in South Africa." *Agenda. Empowering Women for Gender Equality* 70: 58–66.

Burns, Jim. 2017. "Biopolitics, Toxic Masculinities, Disavowed Histories, and Youth Radicalization." *Peace Review* 29(2): 176–83.

Choo, Hae Yoen and Myra Marx Ferree. 2010. "Practising Intersectionality in Sociological Research: A Critical Analysis of Inclusions, Interactions, and Institutions in the Study of Inequalities." *Sociological Theory* 28(2): 129–49.

Clarke, Juanne. 1983. "Sexism, Feminism and Medicalism." *Sociology of Health & Illness* 5(1): 62–83.
Cleary, Anne. 2012. "Suicidal Action, Emotional Expression, and the Performance of Masculinities." *Social Science & Medicine* 74(4): 498–505.
Connell, Raewyn. 2002. "Transsexual Women and Feminist Thought: Toward New Understanding and New Politics." *Signs* 37(4): 857–81.
Connell, R. W. 1995. *Masculinities.* Cambridge: Polity Press.
Connell, R. W. 2005. "Change among the Gatekeepers: Men, Masculinities, and Gender Equality in the Global Arena." *Signs* 30(3): 1801–25.
Corbin, Hope J. 2018. "Health Promotion and #metoo: Meeting Men Where They Are." *Health Promotion International* 33: 921–4.
Courtenay, Will. 2011. *Dying to Be Men.* London: Routledge.
Dinges, Martin and Andreas Weigl (eds.). 2016. *Gender-specific Life Expectancy in Europe 1850–2010.* Stuttgart: Franz Steiner Verlag.
Doyal, Lesley. 1995. *What Makes Women Sick.* London: Macmillan.
Dreifus, Claudia (ed.). 1978. *Seizing Our Bodies. The Politics of Women's Health.* New York: Vintage Books.
Faludi, S. 2000. *Stiffed. The Betrayal of American Men.* New York: Vintage.
Fausto-Sterling, Anne. 2012. *Sex/Gender. Biology in a Social World.* London: Routledge.
Frost, Samantha. 2016. *Biocultural Creatures.* Durham, NC: Duke University Press.
Gagliardi, Maria Cristina, Paolo Tieri, Ortona Elena, and Anna Ruggieri. 2020. "ACE2 Expression and Sex Disparity in COVID-19." *Cell Death Discovery* 6: 37. https://doi.org/10.1038/s41420-020-0276-1
Gebhard, Catherine, Vera Regitz-Zagrosek, Hannelore K. Neuhauser, Rosemary Morgan, and Sabra L. Klein. 2020. "Impact of Sex and Gender on COVID-19 Outcomes in Europe." *Biology of Sex Differences* 11(29). https://doi.org/10.1186/s13293-020-00304-9
Gerry, Christopher, Yulia Raskina, and Daria Tsyplakova. 2018. "Convergence or Divergence? Life Expectancy Patterns in Post-communist Countries, 1959–2010." *Social Indicators Research* 140: 309–32.
Gilman, Charlotte Perkins. 1973[1892]. *The Yellow Wallpaper.* New York: The Feminist Press.
Ging, Debbie. 2017. "Alphas, Betas, and Incels: Theorizing the Masculinities of the Manosphere." *Men and Masculinities* 22(4): 638–57.
Gourarier, Mélanie. 2019. "Undoing the Crisis of Masculinity." in Pp. 186–9 *Feminist Perspectives on Teaching Masculinities*, edited by S. Magaraggia, G. Maurerer, and M. Schmidbaur. London: Routledge.
Gove, Walter and Michael Hughes. 1979. "Possible Causes of the Apparent Sex Differences in Physical Health: An Empirical Investigation." *American Sociological Review* 44(1): 126–46.
Hiam, Lucinda, Dominic Harrison, Martin McKee, and Danny Dorling. 2018. "Why Is Life Expectancy in England and Wales Stalling?" *Journal of Epidemiology and Community Health* 72: 404–08.
Ho, Jessica and Arun Hendi. 2018. "Recent Trends in Life Expectancy across High Income Countries: Retrospective Observational Study." *British Medical Journal* 362: k2562. http://dx.doi.org/10.1136/bmj.k2562
Höhn, Andreas, Jutta Gampe, Rune Lindahl-Jacobsen, Kaare Christensen and Anna Oksuyzan. 2020. "Do Men Avoid Seeking Medical Advice? A Register-based Analysis of Gender-specific Changes in Primary Healthcare Use after First Hospitalisation at Ages 60+ in Denmark." *Journal of Epidemiology and Community Health.* 10.1136/jech-2019-213435 1

Institute of Medicine. 2011. *The Health of Lesbian, Gay, Bisexual, and Transgender People: Building a Foundation for Better Understanding.* Washington DC: National Academies Press. Original research.

Jeffreys, Sheila. 2014. *Gender Hurts. A Feminist Analysis of the Politics of Transgenderism.* London: Routledge.

Joyce, Robert and Xiaowei Xu. 2019. *Inequalities in the Twenty-first Century: Introducing the IFS Deaton Review.* London: Institute of Fiscal Studies.

Kimmel, Michael. 1990. "After Fifteen Years: The Impact of the Sociology of Masculinity on the Masculinity of Sociology." in Pp. 93–109 *Men, Masculinities and Social Theory,* edited by J. Hearn and D. Morgan. London: Unwin Hyman.

Kimmel, Michael. 2017. *Angry White Men,* 2nd edn. New York: Bold Type Books.

Kimmel, Michael and Lisa Wade. 2018. "Ask a Feminist: Michael Kimmel and Lisa Wade Discuss Toxic Masculinity." *Signs* 44(1): 233–54.

Kossova, Tatiana, Elena Kossova, and Maria Sheluntcova. 2020. "Gender Gap in Life Expectancy in Russia: The Role of Alcohol Consumption." *Social Policy and Society* 19(1): 37–53.

Krieger, Nancy. 2003. "Gender, Sexes, and Health: What are the Connections – And Why Does It Matter?" *International Journal of Epidemiology* 32: 652–57.

Lagos, Danya. 2018. "Looking at Population Health beyond 'Male' and 'Female': Implications of Transgender Identity and Gender Nonconformity for Population Health." *Demography* 55: 2097–117.

Lancet Global Health. Editorial. 2020. "Food Insecurity Will Be the Sting in the Tail of COVID-19." Vol 8 e737 https://www.thelancet.com/journals/langlo/article/PIIS2214-109X(20)30228-X/fulltext

Leon, David A., Dmitry A. Jdanov, and Vladimir M Shkolnikov. 2019. "Trends in Life Expectancy and Age-specific Mortality in England and Wales, 1970–2016, in Comparison with a Set of 22 High-income Countries: An Analysis of Vital Statistics Data." *Lancet Public Health* 4: e575–82.

Månsdotter, Anna, Lars Lindholm, Michael Lundberg, Anna Winkvist and Ann Ohman. 2006. "Parental Share in Public and Domestic Spheres: A Population Study on Gender Equality, Death, and Sickness." *Journal of Epidemiology and Community Health* 60: 616–20.

Marmot, Michael, Jessica Allen, Tammy Boyce, Peter Goldblatt and Joana Morrison. 2020. *Health Equity in England: The Marmot Review 10 Years On.* London: Institute for Health Equity.

Marshall, Louise, David Finch, Liz Cairncross, and Jo Bibby. 2019. *Mortality and Life Expectancy Trends in the UK: Stalling Progress.* London: The Health Foundation.

Martineau, Harriet. 1861. *Health, Husbandry, and Handicraft.* London: Bradbury and Evans.

Masquelier, Bruno and Georges Reniers. 2018. "AIDS and the Gender Gap in Life Expectancy in Africa." *Population and Societies* 554(4). https://www.ined.fr/en/publications/editions/population-and-societies/aids-and-the-gender-gap-in-life-expectancy-in-africa

Meloni, Maurizio, John Cromby, Des Fitzgerald, and Stephanie Lloyd (eds.). 2018. *The Palgrave Handbook of Biology and Society.* London: Palgrave.

Messerschmidt, James W. 2018. *Hegemonic Masculinity: Formulation, Reformulation, and Amplification.* Lanham: Rowman and Littlefield.

Messerschmidt, James W. 2019. "The Salience of 'Hegemonic Masculinity'." *Men and Masculinities* 22(1): 85–91.

Michelson, Melissa and Brian Harrison. 2020. *Transforming Prejudice. Identity, Fear and Transgender Rights.* Oxford: Oxford University Press.

Miller, Lisa and Eric Anthony Grollman. 2015. "The Social Costs of Gender Nonconformity for Transgender Adults: Implications for Discrimination and Health." *Sociological Forum* 30(3): 809–31.

Nathanson, Constance. 1975. "Illness and the Feminine Role: A Theoretical Review." *Social Science & Medicine* 9(2): 57–62.

NCHS. 2007. *Health, United States, 2007.* Hyattsville, MD: National Center for Health Statistics.

Oakley, Ann. 1972. *Sex, Gender and Society.* London: Temple Smith.

Office for National Statistics (ONS). 2007. *Social Trends 37.* London: The Stationery Office.

Okojie, Christiana E. E. 1994. "Gender Inequalities in Health in the Third World." *Social Science & Medicine* 39(9): 1237–47.

ONS. 2015. "How Has Life Expectancy Changed over Time?" https://www.ons.gov.uk/peoplepopulationandcommunity/birthsdeathsandmarriages/lifeexpectancies/articles/howhaslifeexpectancychangedovertime/2015-09-09. Accessed 1 June 2020.

ONS. 2020. Statistical Bulletin. Deaths involving COVID-19 by local area and socioeconomic deprivation: deaths occurring between 1 March and 31 May 2020. https://www.ons.gov.uk/peoplepopulationandcommunity/birthsdeathsandmarriages/deaths/bulletins/deathsinvolvingcovid19bylocalareasanddeprivation/deathsoccurringbetween1marchand31may2020 Accessed 12 June 2020.

Parsons, Michelle A. 2014. *Dying Unneeded: The Cultural Context of the Russian Mortality Crisis.* Nashville, TN: Vanderbilt University Press.

Payne, Sarah. 2006. *The Health of Men and Women.* Cambridge: Polity Press.

Payne, Sarah and Lesley Doyal. 2015. "Women, Men and Health." in Pp. 1328–42 *The Oxford Textbook of Global Public Health*, 6th edn. edited by R. Detels, M. Gulliford, Q. A. Karim, and C. Chuan. Oxford: Oxford University Press.

Pettifor, Audrey, Catherine MacPhail, Althea D Anderson, and Suzanne Maman. 2012. "If I Buy the Kellogg's Then He Should [Buy] the Milk': Young Women's Perspectives on Relationship Dynamics, Gender Power and HIV Risk in Johannesburg, South Africa." *Culture, Health & Sexuality* 14(5/6): 477–90.

Raleigh, Venna S. 2019. Trends in Life Expectancy in EU and Other OECD Countries: Why are Improvements Slowing? OECD Health Working Paper No. 108. https://www.oecd-ilibrary.org/social-issues-migration-health/trends-in-life-expectancy-in-eu-and-other-oecd-countries_223159ab-en. Accessed 1 June 2020.

Raymond, Janice. 1994 [1979]. *The Transsexual Empire: The Making of the She-Male.* New York: Teachers' College Press.

Razvodovsky, Yury Evgeny. 2018. "Binge Drinking and Gender Gap in all-Cause Mortality in Russia." *Acta Scientific Medical Sciences* 2(3): 18–19.

Robinson, Sally. 2000. *Marked Men: White Men in Crisis.* New York: Columbia University Press.

Rowbotham, Sheila. 1973. *Woman's Consciousness in a Man's World.* London: Pelican.

Rubin, Gayle. 1975. "The Traffic in Women: Notes on the 'Political Economy' of Sex." in Pp. 157–201 *Toward an Anthropology of Women*, edited by Rayna R. Reiter. London: Monthly Review Press.

Ruzek, Sheryl Burt. 1979. *The Women's Health Movement.* New York: Praeger.

Schofield, T. 2004. *Boutique Health? Gender and Equity in Health Policy.* Australian Policy Institute Commissioned Paper Series 2004/08. University of Sydney.

Schofield, Toni. 2002. "What Does 'Gender and Health' Mean?" *Health Sociology Review* 11(1–2): 29–38.

Shkolnikov, Vladimir, Martin McKee, and David Leon. 2001. "Changes in Life Expectancy in Russia in the Mid-1990s." *Lancet* 357: 917–21.

Sileo, Katelyn, Rebecca Fielding-Miller, Shari Dworkin, and Paul Fleming 2018. "What Role Do Masculine Norms Play in Men's HIV Testing in Sub-Saharan Africa?: A Scoping Review." *AIDS and Behavior* 22: 2468–79.

Singer, T. Benjamin. 2015. "The Profusion of Things. The 'Transgender' Matrix and Demographic Imaginaries in US Public Health." *Transgender Studies Quarterly* 2(1): 58–76.

Skovdal, Morten, Catherine Campbell, Claudius Madanhire, Zivai Mupambireyi, Constance Nyamukapa, and Simon Gregson. 2011."Masculinity as a Barrier to Men's Use of HIV Services in Zimbabwe." Globalization and Health 7: 13 http://www.globalizationandhealth.com/content/7/1/13

Small, Eusebius, Bonita B. Sharma, and Silviya Pavlova Nikolova. 2020. "Covid-19 and Gender and LMICs: Potential Lessons from HIV Pandemic." *AIDS and Behavior.* https:doi.org10 https:doi.org10 https:doi.org10

Snow, Rachel. 2010. "The Social Body: Gender and the Burden of Disease." in Pp. 47–69 *Gender Equity in Health*, edited by G. Sen and P. Östlin. London: Routledge.

Sprague, Courtenay. 2018. *Gender and HIV in South Africa.* London: Palgrave Macmillan.

Statistics Canada. 2001. "Death – Shifting Tends." *Health Reports* 12(3): 41–6.

Stuckler, David and Sanjay Basu 2013. *The Body Economic.* London: Penguin.

Sundberg, Louise, Neda Agahi, Johan Fritzell, and Stefan Fors. 2018. "Why Is the Gender Gap in Life Expectancy Decreasing? the Impact of Age- and Cause-specific Mortality in Sweden 1997–2014." *International Journal of Public Health* 63: 673–81.

Timonin, Sergy, Inna Danilova, Andreev Evgeny, and Vladimir Shkolnikov. 2017. "Recent Mortality Trend Reversal in Russia: Are Regions following the Same Tempo?" *European Journal of Population* 33: 733–63.

UN Women. 2020a. *Policy Brief. The Impact of COVID-19 on Women.* New York: United Nations.

UN Women. 2020b. *COVID-19 and Ending Violence against Women and Girls.* https://www.unwomen.org/-media/headquarters/attachments/sections/library/publications/2020/issue-brief-covid-19-and-ending-violence-against-women-and-girls-en.pdf?la=en&vs=5006. Accessed 12 June 2020.

UNAIDS. 2020. We've Got the Power. Women, Adolescent Girls and the HIV Response. Accessed 12 June 2020.

UNAIDS (Joint United Nations Programme on HIV and AIDS). 2019. Women and HIV. A spotlight on adolescent girls and young women. Acessed 12 June 2020.

Verbrugge, Lois. 1985. "Gender and Health: An Update on Hyptheses and Evidence." *Journal of Health and Social Behavior* 26(Sept): 156–82.

Vincent, Ben. 2018. *Transgender Health: A Practitioner's Guide to Binary and Non-Binary Trans Patient Care.* London: Jessica Kingsley Publishers.

Vlassoff, Carol. 1994. "Gender Inequalities in Health in the Third World: Uncharted Ground." *Social Science & Medicine* 39(9): 1249–59.

Wadham, Ben. 2002. "Global Men's Health and the Crisis of Western Masculinity." in Pp. 69–82 *Changing Men's Practices in a Globalized World*, edited by P. Pease and K. Pringle. London: Zed Books.

Waldron, Ingrid. 1991. "Patterns and Causes of Gender Differences in Smoking." *Social Science & Medicine* 32(9): 989–1005.

Walker, Charlie and Steven Roberts (eds.). 2018. *Masculinity, Labour, and Neoliberalism.* London: Palgrave.

Wenham, Clare, Julia Smith, and Rosemary Morgan, on behalf of the Gender and COVID-19 Working Group. 2020. "COVID-19: The Gendered Impacts of the Outbreak". The Lancet https://doi.org/10.1016/S0140-6736(20)30526-2

Westbrook, Laurel and Aliya Saperstein. 2015. "New Categories are Not Enough: Rethinking the Measurement of Sex and Gender in Social Surveys." *Gender and Society* 29(4): 534–60.

WHO. 2020a. *World Health Statistics 2020. Monitoring Health for the SDGs, Sustainable Development Goals.* Geneva: WHO.

WHO. 2020b. Number of people (all ages) living with HIV. https://www.who.int/gho/hiv/epidemic_status/cases_all/en. Accessed 18 June 2020.

Woolf, Steven H. and Heidi Schoomaker. 2019. "Life Expectancy and Mortality Rates in the United States, 1959-2017." *Journal of American Medical Association* 332(20): 1996–2016.

World Health Organisation (WHO). 2019. Intimate Partner and Sexual Violence against Women. Evidence Brief. https://apps.who.int/iris/bitstream/handle/10665/329889/WHO-RHR-19.16-eng.pdf?ua=1 Accessed 12 June 2020.

Yea, Sallie. 2011. "Masculinity under the Knife: Filipino Men, Trafficking and the Black Organ Market in Manila, the Philippines." *Gender, Place and Culture* 22(1): 123–42.

Yousaf, Farhan Navid and Bandana Purkayastha. 2015. "I Am Only Half Alive': Organ-trafficking in Pakistan amid Interlocking Oppressions." *International Sociology* 30(6): 637–53.

Yuen, Peter. 2005. *Compendium of Health Statistics 2005–2006*. London: Office of Health Economics.

13

Health, Ethnicity, and Race

Hannah Bradby and James Y. Nazroo

Medical sociology, as a sub-field of sociology, can trace its genesis from the founding fathers – Weber, Durkheim, Bourdieu, Goffman – who deployed theoretical insights to demonstrate the sociological character of society's approach to health, illness and medicine (see Chapter 2). While various theoretical concepts have subsequently been applied to issues of ethnicity and race, they were not identified as foundational at the inception of sociological theory. In addition to its roots in sociological theory, medical sociology can trace its development to epidemiology and social medicine, where the social stratification of health outcomes in terms of class and gender has been measured and modelled to inform clinical and public health policy and practice. As in mainstream sociology, epidemiological approaches to health and illness have lacked analytic development around ethnic and racial categories, with social class, area of residence, employment status, and gender having dominated the approach. Neither sociological theory nor epidemiological models have offered a means of capturing the complexity of ethnicity and race as culture, structure, identity and process, all of which are relevant for understanding health and illness. While sociological theorization of race and ethnicity has tended to be subordinate to consideration of class and gender, Critical Race Theory has offered intersectionality as a metaphor for how multiple identities and structures interact.

Sociological disinterest in race and ethnicity is due both to the theoretical primacy of occupational and class structures and because of the highly contested nature of race as both a popular and a scientific concept. Despite widespread rejection of race as a scientific concept, it persists in both scientific and popular discourse, referring to ideas that cannot be entirely encompassed by alternatives such as ethnicity or diversity (Bradby 2012). This chapter does not seek to fix definitions of race and ethnicity as sociological concepts, but rather to show their historical and cultural specificities by discussing research on the relationship between ethnicity, race, health and illness, illustrated with evidence from the US and the UK to consider how understandings have developed over the past two decades.

The Wiley Blackwell Companion to Medical Sociology, First Edition. Edited by William C. Cockerham.

The chapter falls into seven sections. First we interrogate the role of *slavery* and *empire* in *migration* as critical context for what *race* and *ethnicity* mean in US and UK contexts respectively, before noting how *culture* became a key issue in debates on the ways in which ethnicity and race relate to health and health experiences. Second, we consider the ways in which ethnic and racial categories are used in official data in the US and UK, which leads into the third section summarizing the patterns of stratification of health outcomes from UK and US published sources. Fourth, we assess what these data tell us about inequalities in health and critique the development of crude explanatory models. Fifth, we evaluate the evidence on how ethnicity influences the use and experience of health services, including the role that culture plays. Sixth, we touch on the relationship between migration, ethnicity, and health work, considering how the trans-global processes that brought about the creation of ethnic minority groups in Anglophone countries have also staffed the health care industry. Finally, we return to the theoretical treatment of this topic to consider whether, given our critique of existing data, the sociological problematic has been adequately described.

Slavery and Migration

Although slavery has been illegal in the US since the second half of the nineteenth century, its influence persists in terms of the current meaning of race and it has played an important role in determining current lines of social stratification. The system of indentured and slave labor was responsible for the transport of large numbers of people from West Africa to the US as slaves – estimates vary from 9 to 20 million – as well as smaller numbers of indentured servants from Scotland, Ireland, England, and Germany. The majority of Black slaves were used in agricultural work in the Southern States, a fact that is reflected in the greater proportion of African Americans in the South compared with the North that persists today. Migration over the past four centuries accounts for the presence of almost all of the US population, with the exception of about 2% who are descendants of indigent populations. The US is a land of migrants where old historical allegiances were abandoned in the construction and celebration of the "new world," yet "melting pot" multiculturalism has tended to include European, and especially Protestant, immigrants and exclude Africans and Native Americans. While the American dream depends on the ideal that anyone can succeed in the US, policy introduced from 2019 ensures that refugees seeking asylum from Latin America are forced to await court hearings in Mexico. After extended waiting times in often violent Mexican border towns, the vast majority of applications for asylum from Honduras, Cuba, Guatemala and Venezuela are refused, in what is seen as a deliberately hostile anti-immigrant policy.

Empire and Migration

Britain was involved in the Atlantic slave trade, and substantially benefited from it. While some migration from overseas colonies occurred as a result, the UK was not a major destination for slave labor and slavery was not institutionalized in the UK. While the British Isles have long received immigrants, particularly in urban, maritime centers, mass migration of non-White groups to the UK only occurred after World War II (1939–1945) when British colonials were invited to make good the labor shortage in the "mother country". The character of migration to the UK has been shaped by the legacy of its empire, a massive global power in the nineteenth century, which transmitted cultural and linguistic influence overseas so that labor migrants were familiar with the English language and aspects of British culture. While racist attitudes and practices shaped the experience of many immigrants to the UK, there was no formal outlawing of racial discrimination enacted until 1965. The White British ethnic majority sees itself as non-immigrant, or assumes origins traceable to Norman immigration ten centuries ago. The attitude to immigrants, particularly in the 1950s and 1960s, was "assimilationist;" where immigrants were welcomed or tolerated, there was an assumption that they would wish to become "British" and integrate into the ethnic majority population. Imperial British history has contributed to an assumption that "Britishness," with its particular blend of individualism, establishment Christianity, and phlegmatism, would be embraced as a superior way of life by immigrants and their descendants. The rejection of, or exclusion from, aspects of British life by immigrants was interpreted as the failure of minorities to assimilate. Multicultural social and educational policies that acknowledged, celebrated, and maintained features of a range of different ethnic and religious identities were introduced in the 1990s to promote integration, if not assimilation. Multi-cultural educational initiatives have been criticized as promoting separatism and failing to acknowledge the role of racism in marginalizing and stigmatizing and racializing ethnic minority groups. In this chapter we refer to ethnic minority groups which are socially constructed classifications, that may be adopted by administrative systems and that are also claimed for self-identification. Ethnic groups are subject to processes of racialization which suggests that shared cultural and linguistic traits arise from a biological basis that is genetically heritable (Bradby 1995, 2003).

Twenty-first-century European politics has seen the rise of anti-migrant populism, whereby immigrants are held accountable for the effects of austerity and welfare retractions. Xenophobic policies have been enacted by mainstream political parties, for instance the UK coalition government of 2012 enacted "hostile environment" policies, aimed at impeding daily life for immigrants who had not been granted residency, in the expectation that they would leave the UK voluntarily. These policies have had the intended negative effects and not only on forced migrants whose asylum applications have been refused, but also for commonwealth citizens who arrived in the twentieth century from the Caribbean – the so-called Windrush generation. Anti-migrant politics played a key role in the Brexit referendum of 2016 and the subsequent years of divisive debate about how to achieve the UK's exit from the European Union. Minority culture has been pathologized as problematic in preventing assimilation, and immigrants have been held responsible for scarcity in UK welfare and healthcare provision with culture (like ethnicity) regularly identified as something that minorities have, but the mainstream (White) majority does not.

Culture

The role allocated to culture as both marker and cause of ethnic or racial difference can be contrasted between the US and UK. In the US, residential segregation underpins many other aspects of racialized inequality (Massey and Denton 1993), whereas in the UK, the extent to which inequality can be characterized as segregation continues to be debated (McCulloch 2007) and cultural difference carries more weight as both explanation and cause.

The plurality of a melting pot of culture as a rhetorical ideal (if not a lived norm) in the US, the Atlantic slave trade, and the internal movement of slaves west during the "second passage" effectively destroyed the cultural patterns of the enslaved. Discrimination against people of African origin in the US has not focused on the content of minority culture, but rather has relied on biologically justified racism. This discrimination resembles divisions of class in the British context, where an assumption about the inherent nature of difference between groups is deep-seated and difficult to shift. The UK pattern of cultural difference justifying discrimination assumes that minorities could and should change their culture in favor of the majority, ignoring the important role that culture may play in people's identity and in constituting supportive networks.

To avoid deterministic thinking, culture needs to be thought of as potentially but not necessarily both positive *and* negative: some aspects of culture such as religion, dress, diet, marriage practices and family formation, are significant for people's sense of themselves in a way that is often (but not always) positive and supportive in material and symbolic terms. That is to say culture is important for a sense of identity and belonging and may also have some protective effects in the face of poverty and marginalization. The negative experience of an aspect of culture cannot be directly linked to a negative health outcome, but rather must be considered in socioeconomic context. For instance, multi-generational living that is, sharing a house with one's own or one's spouse's relatives, that is characteristic of some South Asian cultures, may or may not be experienced as supportive. The positive or negative health effects of that cultural practice are shaped by the socioeconomic context in which they are lived out. In the example of shared housing the material and economic circumstances of the accommodation in terms of overcrowding, access to safe outdoor space etc. are crucial: the cultural practice itself does not determine the health effect.

In the analysis of inequality, the view of cultural identity has tended to be overly and inappropriately simplified, serving to divert attention away from structural inequalities. When culture is discussed as if it features only for minorities (and never the majority), it can be used as a euphemism for referring to a problematic deviation from the majority – culture becomes no more than "a tool for blaming black people within popular ideology and in research" (Donovan 1986: 45). As a result, minorities are seen as the authors of their own disadvantage and culture comes to be identified as a, or even the, cause of that disadvantage.

In the US and the UK much of the evidence for inequalities in health within and between ethnic groups comes from official data sets and large-scale surveys. Using a "complicated view of culture" as part of a definition of ethnicity in social surveys presents both conceptual and technical challenges (Bradby 2003), which means that simplified proxies are inevitably employed. We discuss these proxies and the data that they have generated next.

Defining the Terms of the Discussion: What Do "Ethnicity" and "Race" Mean?

Ethnicity and race are difficult concepts to discuss with precision, since their meanings are highly charged politically, have been subject to change over recent history, and, like many sociological concepts, have scientific as well as popular usage, and the two do not always coincide. Furthermore, there are differences in the uses of these terms in different social settings; thus, discussing ethnicity or race in the US can have different implications compared with their discussion in the UK. Some of the contrasts between the UK and the US can be understood in terms of the history of empire and colonization, the role of institutionalized slavery, migration, and their implications for the construction of the social problem of ethnic and racial difference in contemporary society, as described above. While we have offered various definitions of race (Bradby 2012) and ethnicity (Bradby 1995, 2003), published research tends to rely on administrative definitions that underpin routine data. These administrative definitions consist of compromised classifications born of pragmatic responses to political and policy priorities, some of which we describe below.

Official Data on Ethnic and Racial Categories

The use of ethnic and racial categories in official data in the US and the UK and the changes in usage over time have been described elsewhere (Nazroo and Williams 2005). Racialized categories have been deployed in the US since the first census in 1790, whereas ethnic categories have been used in the last three UK censuses – 1991, 2001 and 2011. In both the US and the UK, the classification system has changed from census to census to reflect both changing patterns of migration and the development of ideas about racialized differences. In the US, alterations to the legal status of racialized groups have been key, as for instance with the disappearance of slave as a category of enumeration between the censuses of 1860 and 1870, following the abolition of slavery in the intervening years.

The terms *ethnic* and *racial* are sometimes used as synonyms, but they are used in distinct ways in official data. UK data only report on ethnicity and there are no racial classifications, whereas US data use both racial and ethnic classifications. The distinction between race and ethnicity is based on convention rather than theoretical or empirical data and cannot be justified except through the historical development of categories.

Official Data

In the US official data includes racial and ethnic categories, while in the UK official ethnic categories have been used since the 1990s but no racial categories exist. In both settings the categorizations have been debated and have been subject to change over time. Current categorizations have political and epistemological implications for what ethnic and racial groupings mean for health and healthcare; the adoption of particular categories means that they become normalized, with a concomitant shift in our understanding. While a critical epistemological approach to racialized and ethnic categories is an important aspect of medical sociology, the categories used for routine and register data are also discussed as administrative terms, as part of the landscape in which medical sociology research is undertaken.

US Official Data

Racial classifications were crucial for administering the system of slavery and, subsequently, racial segregation, including the prohibition on interracial marriage. Historically, the legal distinction between the free and the slave, and then between subjugated Black and subordinating White, distinguished unambiguously between Black and White, preserving privileged White access to property, education, employment, housing, and other resources. The illegality of intermarriage coexisted with sexual unions (often exploitative of the enslaved) producing a substantial mixed population, while White privilege created a strong incentive for light-skinned people of mixed origins to pass as White. First documented in the 1850 Census, people with Black and White parents were formally treated as Black according to the "one drop rule," whereby membership of the White race was limited to those without any Black ancestors. The Black–White line was thus preserved in law, in race theory, and in popular culture, but not in the genealogical legacies of the population (Perlmann and Waters 2002: 5).

The system of racial classification operating for Native Americans and Hispanic Americans relies on another logic, since this group was not subject to institutionalized slavery. Tribal membership was defined for official purposes by the proportion of an individual's ancestors who were tribal members (with the proportion required for membership differing between tribes), plus recognition of that individual as a member of the tribe by other tribe members. The rules for Hispanic Americans, descended from mixed populations in Latin America, differed again and have been constituted as a separate category through the use of a Spanish language question in the US census (Perlmann and Waters 2002: 6).

Racial classification of Black, White, Native, and Hispanic Americans has played a key role in defining the structural and symbolic aspects of the American population and ethnicity has tended to reinforce White advantage. Ethnicity is similar to race in that it is often assigned involuntarily through heredity, although for White minorities its expression is voluntaristic. The consumption of special foods and the celebration of particular holidays offer White Americans an ethnic identity and mark belonging to a community, but a highly unconstrained personal choice over the adoption of these practices is retained (Waters 1990: 151). Ethnicity generally operates as both a resource and a liability (Jenkins 1995), yet for White minorities little effort is put into sustaining group cohesion and if sexist, racist, constraining aspects of an ethnicity are encountered, the voluntary nature of participation means that the liability can be abandoned relatively easily. This is the crucial difference between race and ethnicity: for suburban Whites, ethnicity lacks social costs, provides enjoyment, and is chosen voluntarily, none of which is true for non-White Americans (Waters 1990).

Racial minorities cannot exercise choice in the same way as "ethnics," particularly White ethnics. If one's ethnicity is a voluntaristic, personal matter it can be difficult to see that other groups are subject to political, societal forces that are not a matter of individual choice. White European immigrants (certain exclusions for Italians and Irish notwithstanding) have never faced the systematic legal and official discrimination experienced by Blacks, Hispanics, and Asians in America. Ethnic identification for White Americans is voluntaristic and unaccompanied by discrimination or prejudice yet those who emphasize, for instance, an Italian or Irish ethnicity often presume equivalence with a racial identity, conceiving of both ethnicity and race as biologically rooted, ascribing identities to others, especially based on skin color. White minorities can enjoy the voluntary aspects of ethnic traditions, but because ethnic and racialized divisions are presumed to be equivalent, the rise of White suburban ethnic identification can exacerbate racial tensions (Waters 1990: 167).

UK Official Data

Until the 1991 Census, country of birth was typically used in UK official statistics as a proxy for ethnicity or race, with the clear implication that racial and ethnic minorities were "foreign," despite the majority also being British citizens. As post-World War II migration became more distant, the inadequacies of this approach for identifying growing numbers of UK-born minorities became increasingly obvious, and a question about ethnic identity was introduced in the 1991 Census. The question was updated for the 2001 and 2011 Censuses with respondents asked to select a category to describe their ethnic identity from a list. The question varied slightly across the countries of the UK, with the following categories used in England and Wales:

- **White** – English/Welsh/Scottish/Northern Irish/British, Irish, Gypsy or Irish Traveller, Any other White (write in)
- **Mixed** or **Multiple ethnic groups** – White and Black Caribbean or White and Black African or White and Asian or Any Other Mixed background (write in)
- **Asian** or **Asian British** – Indian or Pakistani or Bangladeshi or Chinese or Any Other Asian background (write in)
- **Black** or **Black British** – Caribbean or African or Any Other Black background (write in)
- **Other ethnic group** – Arab or Any Other (write in)

Compared with the 2001 categories, the 2011 list had the addition of "Gypsy or Irish Traveller" under the "White" category, and "Arab" under the "Other ethnic group" category. In 2001 the "Chinese" category was moved from "Chinese or other ethnic group" to a separate category under "Asian/Asian British" with the consequence that figures for "Asian other" and broad Asian ethnic groups are not directly comparable between 2001 and 2011.

Respondents were expected to select a single main category that applied to them (the first descriptor for each bullet point, shown in bold above), and then to choose a subcategory from the options that follow. This official categorization of a diverse population has no historical legal definition on which to draw and compounds a number of aspects of ethnicity pertinent to UK race relations, including nationality, country of birth, geographical origin, and skin color. Notable here is the emergence of the "Mixed" and "White Irish" categories between the 1991 and 2001 Censuses, and of the "Gypsy" and "Arab" categories between the 2001 and 2011 Censuses in response to popular and policy concerns. Inevitably, this form of classification contains compromises, for example all individuals from sub-Saharan Africa are covered by a single category, as are all those claiming an Indian identity. Such compromises reflect the ways in which ethnicity is conceptualized and the dimensions of an ethnic identity that are currently perceived to be of policy importance. For example, a question on religious identity was included in the 2001 England and Wales census for the first time, as religion became increasingly significant on the public policy agenda.

The lack of institutionalized racial categories in the UK means that classifications inevitably reflect powerfully felt racialized folk typologies that both constrain and inform people's identities. Conceiving a classification that usefully captures the experience of identity without promoting the essentializing of difference has proved difficult. Critiques of the homogenizing assumptions of pan-ethnic classifications (for example, Zsembik and Fennel 2005) suggest that lessons from previous work have not been learned.

In the next section we describe, in general terms, the patterning of ethnic/racial disparities in health and point to the implications of crude quantitative classificatory schemes for explanatory models. Arguably, the use of broad classifications as proxies for ethnic or cultural group has hindered the development of sophisticated explanatory models for inequalities in health and allowed the persistence of crude stereotyped explanations (Nazroo and Williams 2005: 239).

Inequalities in Health in the US and UK

Differences in health across ethnic groups, in terms of both morbidity (the presence of illness and disease) and mortality, have been repeatedly documented in the UK (Erens et al. 2001; Harding and Maxwell 1997; Marmot et al. 1984; Wild et al. 2007) and the US (Davey Smith et al. 1998; Sorlie et al. 1995, 1992; Williams 2001). Health is, of course, a multidimensional and complex concept (Blaxter 1990), yet in statistics it is often reduced to death and/or specific disease categories (such as coronary heart disease, hypertension, or diabetes). In the UK, mortality data are not available by ethnic group, but country of birth is recorded on death certificates and mortality rates have been published by country of birth using data around the 1971, 1981, and 1991 Censuses and, to a more limited extent, the 2001 and 2011 Censuses (Wallace and Kulu 2015). Given the relatively recent mass migration to the UK, analyses of mortality by country of birth have typically been taken to indicate *ethnic* inequalities in health. However, despite being statistically robust, these findings cannot be extrapolated unproblematically to ethnic categories, not least because the experiences of UK-born ethnic minority people are likely to differ from those of migrants.

Although the UK does not record mortality data by ethnicity, there has been a growth in data on ethnic differences in morbidity over the last three decades. A broad measure of self-reported general health has repeatedly shown ethnic minority people to have an increased risk of poor health compared with White people, but with considerable variation across specific groups. For example, compared with the White English group, Bangladeshi people have a more than three times higher risk of saying that their health is fair or bad rather than good, with a figure of more than two times higher for Pakistani people and almost two times higher for Indian and Black Caribbean people (Nazroo 2004). These ethnic differences in health emerge from early adulthood and increase dramatically with increasing age, with the result that the level of reporting fair or bad health, rather than good health, for White English people aged 61–70 is equivalent to that of Caribbean and Indian people aged 46–50, Pakistani people aged 36–40 and Bangladeshi people aged 26–30 (Nazroo 2004).

The extent of the difference in health varies across health conditions as well as across ethnic groups. In more detail, morbidity and mortality data have identified the following kinds of differences in health across ethnic groups (in comparison to White British groups):

- Higher, but variable, rates of diabetes across all non-White groups.
- Higher rates of heart disease among "South Asian" people, but particularly among Bangladeshi and Pakistani people.
- Higher rates of hypertension and stroke among Caribbean and African people.
- Higher rates of admission to psychiatric hospitals with a diagnosis of psychotic illness for Black Caribbean and Black African people.
- Higher rates of suicide among young women born in South Asia, or, more particularly, born in India.
- Higher rates of sexually transmitted illnesses among Black Caribbean people.
- Higher rates of congenital abnormality and childhood disability among Muslim children.

In the US, there is a similar heterogeneity of outcomes across racial and ethnic groups (Nazroo and Williams 2005; Sorlie et al. 1995). Mortality rates for non-Hispanic Black people are more than twice as high as those for non-Hispanic White people until early old age, when the gap begins to narrow. A similar pattern is found for Native Americans, though differences are smaller at younger ages, and the improvement relative to non-Hispanic White people at older ages is clearer. Mortality rates for Hispanic people are generally lower than those of non-Hispanic Whites, though the differences are small at younger ages. Rates for Asian/Pacific Islanders are uniformly lower than those for non-Hispanic Whites.

The favorable position of Hispanic people, given their relatively poor socioeconomic position, has generated considerable research interest. It has been suggested that these findings reflect: a "protective" Hispanic culture; health selection, whereby only the healthiest migrate to the US; and/or poor data quality, with under-coverage of denominators and inaccuracies in the reporting of numerators (see Nazroo and

Williams 2005 for a review). Indeed, there are important limitations linked to the quality of these mortality data for all groups. The numerator for the officially reported death rates in the US comes from death certificates, and it is estimated that officials who record racial and ethnic status on the death certificate misclassify as many as 26% of self-identified American Indians, 18% of Asians and Pacific Islanders, and 10% of Hispanics, with misclassifications largely allocated to White/non-Hispanic categories (Sorlie et al. 1992). This undercount in the numerator suppresses the death rates for the minority groups and slightly inflates the death rates for non-Hispanic Whites.

In both the US and the UK, problems with the denominator can also affect the quality of mortality statistics. Census data are used to calculate the denominators for mortality rates and a denominator that has an undercount inflates the obtained rate in exact proportion to the undercount. Although the overall undercount for the US and UK populations is relatively small, it is much higher for non-Whites. For example, in the US, an examination of the 2010 Census data suggests that for all minority groups the rate of omission from the count was higher than for Non-Hispanic White people, with a rate of 9.3% of those in any Black category, compared with 3.8% of Non-Hispanic White people, and the rates of omission from the Census count were particularly high for Black men aged 18–29 (15.6%) and Black men aged 30–49 (16.7%) (O'Hare 2019). Thus, all of the officially reported morbidity and mortality rates for minority groups are likely to be too high.

The heterogeneity found in mortality and morbidity rates parallels the heterogeneity in migration, settlement, and socioeconomic experiences. There is a need to reflect the diversity of experience in data collection, making efforts to contact an appropriate range of people, while remaining aware of, and sensitive to, potential ethnic differences within groups since we cannot assume that all Pacific Islanders, or all Hispanics, or all South Asians are equivalent.

Explaining Ethnic/Racial Inequalities in Health

How can we make sense of the data showing differences in health across these broad race/ethnic groups? There is a strong temptation to read meaning directly into the categories the statistical data provide. Just as we might say that Pakistani men have high rates of unemployment, or Black American families are more likely to be headed by a single parent, so we might say that Bangladeshi people have poor health. It is then straightforward to go from this simple description to seeking an explanation for poor health in the nature of what it is to be (in this example) Bangladeshi. The impulse to resort to explanation based on an understanding of a reified category, stripped of contextual meaning and stereotyped, is strong. Just as we might seek explanations for higher rates of single parenthood in Black cultures, we can seek explanations for high rates of a specific illness or disease in the culture or genetic profile of the race/ethnic category associated with the higher rate. As illness and disease are commonly understood to result from biological processes and health behaviors, culture and genetics are favored as the explanatory variable for minority group difference when we see a diversity of outcomes across ethnic groups or across disease categories. So, if Pakistani people have high rates of heart disease, but Caribbean people do not, how can this be explained on the basis of an ethnic disadvantage? And if the low rates of respiratory illness and lung cancer among Pakistani people can be explained as a consequence of low rates of smoking, cannot "their" high rates of cardiovascular disease be similarly explained as a consequence of cultural traits? In such a context, it is unsurprising that research on the relationship between ethnicity/race and health often focuses on the "exotic" in terms of both outcomes and the search for explanation.

Rather, if we are to develop adequate explanatory models for ethnic differences in health, we have to consider how the categories we use reflect heterogeneous social identities and how they relate to wider social and economic inequalities. In the UK, there has been a long tradition of investigating inequalities in health associated with factors such as class, residential area (for example, see the collection in Gordon et al. 1999), and gender (Annandale and Hunt 1999), producing strong evidence that these health disparities are a consequence of socioeconomic inequalities (Marmot and Wilkinson 2005). Historically, this work did not inform investigations of ethnic inequalities in health, perhaps due to the impact of Marmot and colleagues' (1984) study of immigrant mortality rates. Published shortly after the Black Report (Townsend and Davidson 1982) had put socioeconomic inequalities in health on the research agenda, this study used the combination of British census and death certificate data to explore the relationship between country of birth and mortality rates (Marmot et al. 1984). A central finding was that there was no relationship between occupational class and mortality for immigrant groups, even though there was a clear relationship for those born in the UK. It was concluded that differences in socioeconomic position could not explain the higher mortality rates found in some migrant groups in the UK (Marmot et al. 1984).

From 1984, it took more than a decade for socioeconomic position to reappear in published UK data exploring the relationship between ethnicity and health. Conclusions drawn from analysis of immigrant mortality data did not appear to support a socioeconomic explanation for the different rates of mortality across immigrant and non-immigrant groups (Harding and Maxwell 1997). Therefore many continued to claim that socioeconomic inequalities make a minimal, or non-existent, contribution to ethnic inequalities in health (Wild and McKeigue 1997). Such denials of the relevance of socioeconomic inequalities to ethnic inequalities in health can be interrogated first by considering the limitations of quantitative empirical models. The sociological significance of ethnicity and race cannot be straightforwardly captured in ethnic classifications. The role played by history, contemporary political and social situations, local context, generation and period since migration, and so forth, is difficult to encapsulate in the proxies used, and is easily ignored when using crudely quantified categories that result in ethnicity being operationalized in fixed and reified terms. Furthermore, there is a lamentable lack of good, or often any, data on economic position in health studies, let alone data that can deal with other elements of social disadvantage faced by ethnic minority groups, such as inequalities related to geography and experiences of racial discrimination and harassment.

Despite the limitations of the data, there is now a consensus that a socioeconomic patterning of health is present within ethnic groups in developed countries. Analysis of the US Multiple Risk Factor Intervention Trial (MRFIT) data showed that all causes of mortality rates over its 16-year follow-up period had a very clear relationship to median income in the area of residence of respondents for both Black and White men. Mortality rates increased with decreasing income, resulting in a twofold difference in mortality rates between those in the top ($27,500 or higher) and those in the bottom (less than $10,000) annual income bands for both Black and White men (Davey Smith et al. 1998). Similarly, in data from England, rates of reporting fair or bad general health by household income show a clear relationship between reported general health and income for each of several ethnic groups included (Nazroo 2003). These analyses point to heterogeneity within broad ethnic groupings in health: for example, Black Americans in better socioeconomic positions have better health. There is nothing inevitable, or inherent, in the link between being Black American or being British Bangladeshi and a greater risk of mortality and morbidity. There is an urgent need to move beyond explanations that appeal to, and further cement, assumptions of essentialized and fixed ethnic or race effects.

If socioeconomic position is related to health within groups, it seems probable that inequalities in socioeconomic position across ethnic groups might be related to ethnic inequalities in health. Here the interpretation of data becomes more contentious. In most analyses, once adjustments for socioeconomic position have been made, there is a clear and often large reduction in risk for ethnic/racial minority groups. For example, analysis of the US MRFIT data showed that standardizing for mean household income in area of residence greatly reduced the relative risk for all causes of mortality of Black compared with White men – it dropped from 1.47 to 1.19, thereby statistically explaining about two thirds of the elevated mortality risk among Black men with this income measure (Davey Smith et al. 1998). Nevertheless, in such analyses, for most groups and for most health outcomes, differences remain once the adjustment for the socioeconomic indicator has been made. Here again, it is important to recognize the limitations of such quantitative models. The process of standardizing for socioeconomic position when making comparisons across groups assumes that all necessary factors are accounted for by the measures available (Kaufman et al. 1997, 1998). Evidence from both the US and the UK indicates this assumption may be fallacious. An analysis of ethnic differences in income within class groups showed that, within each class group, ethnic minority people had a smaller income than White people (Nazroo 2001). Indeed, for the poorest group – Pakistani and Bangladeshi people – differences were twofold and equivalent in size to the difference between the richest and poorest class groups in the White population. Similar findings have been reported in the US. For example, within occupational groups, White people have higher incomes than Black people; once below the poverty line, Black people are more likely to remain in this situation than White people, and, within income strata, Black people have considerably lower wealth levels than White people and are less likely to be home owners (Oliver and Shapiro 1995). The implication of this is clear: Using either single or crude indicators of socioeconomic position does not "control out" the impact of socioeconomic position. Within any given level of a particular socioeconomic measure, the circumstances of minority people are less favorable than those of White people. Nevertheless, research typically presents data that are "standardized" for socioeconomic position, allowing both the author and reader to mistakenly assume that all that is left is an ethnic/race effect, often attributed to "cultural" or "genetic" difference.

In addition, these kinds of analyses reflect current socioeconomic position only, since data assessing the effect of accumulation of disadvantage across life domains and across the life course are rarely or not available. Importantly, data on other forms of social disadvantage are also not included. In fact, in the US, UK and elsewhere, research has demonstrated the links between health and experiences of racism and discrimination. US research has shown a relationship between self-reported experiences of racial harassment and a greater likelihood of reporting various measures of ill health, including hypertension, psychological distress, poorer self-rated health, and days spent unwell in bed (Krieger 2000; Krieger and Sidney 1996; Williams et al. 2003). In the UK, there is a growing body of evidence that both physical and mental health are adversely affected by: experiences of racial harassment; fear of experiencing racial harassment; experiences of discrimination; and the belief that there is general prejudice and discrimination against ethnic minority people (Karlsen and Nazroo 2002a, 2002b, 2004; Karlsen et al. 2005). These "indicators" of racism and discrimination reflect general perceptions of society as racist (belief that minority groups are discriminated against, fear of racism), personal threat (fear of racism and experiences of harassment), and experiences of events that undermine status and identity (experiences of harassment and experiences of discrimination). And these effects have been found to accumulate across domains of exposure to racism and discrimination, and over time (Wallace et al. 2016).

Related to this, there is also evidence that the aggregation of ethnic minority people in areas with those of similar ethnicity is beneficial, particularly for mental health, once the effects of area deprivation are controlled for (Bécares et al. 2009). This is likely to operate through a combination of feelings of increased security (lower exposure to racial harassment and discrimination) and increased social support. Indeed, there is some evidence demonstrating that ethnic minority people rate the areas where they live much more highly than would be implied by official indices of deprivation precisely because these are locations where a sense of inclusive community for people like them has developed (Bajekal et al. 2004).

In summary, although a concern with the detailed etiology of specific conditions occurring at higher rates for particular ethnic groups might lead to a focus on the putative proximal causes of biological change (genetic and behavioral differences), research on distal social and economic causes shows clearly that these are key drivers of ethnic differences in health. But this is not just a simple reflection of class disadvantage, as the complex and multidimensional nature of the economic and social inequalities faced by ethnic minority people are refracted through processes of racialization. If such inequalities are to be effectively addressed, specific policy responses are required, implying a fundamental rethink of approaches to race, ethnicity and migration.

Experience and Use of Health Services

When inequalities by ethnic or racialized group are found in health outcomes, the presumption that minority groups are accessing services incorrectly has been made. For instance in both the US (Almeida et al. 2018) and the UK (Kelly et al. 2009) – minority ethnic women have low birth weight babies compared to the general population – a trend that has not shifted over time. When low birth weights were becoming apparent in the 1980s, there was a tendency to assume that ethnic minority pregnant women's late presentation for ante-natal care was responsible; a line of reasoning that absolved the healthcare providers of responsibility for poor birth outcomes of ethnic/racial minorities. However the investigation of usage of healthcare services by ethic/racial minorities has also opened up a field of research. The quality of experience when using health services is a matter of social justice, regardless of resultant health outcomes. In addition to offering an equitable service, health professionals should play a role in ameliorating existing inequalities, whereas in practice, existing ethnic/racial inequalities in health may be aggravated by inequity in access to good quality services. In the US, ethnic/racial inequalities in access to and quality of health care have been repeatedly documented, with inequalities that are consistent across a range of outcomes and types of providers. An Institute of Medicine (IOM) study, requested by Congress, identified ethnic/racial differences in health care insurance status as a key determinant of these inequalities (Smedley et al. 2003). However, the primary focus of the IOM study was on non-access-related factors and the authors noted that while inequalities diminish significantly when insurance status and socioeconomic factors are controlled, some typically remain. Suggested explanations for the remaining inequalities included: characteristics of institutions (such as language barriers and time pressures on physicians); behaviors of practitioners (such as prejudice against or uncertainty with ethnic/racial minorities); and behaviors of patients (such as non-compliance and delay in seeking care) (Smedley et al. 2003).

The IOM report also noted that the studies of ethnic/racial inequalities in health care that controlled for insurance status had only done so at a crude level, without accounting for the ethnic/racial differences in the extent of coverage provided (Smedley et al. 2003). Thus, ethnic minorities are likely to have less comprehensive coverage than White Americans and, consequently, to have a more limited choice of providers, health care settings, and types of services. This confirms the point that ethnic inequalities in health are driven by socioeconomic inequalities. One way of testing whether differences in health care insurance coverage explain inequalities in health care is to examine the extent of ethnic/racial inequalities in health care systems with more comprehensive access. Studies of health care provided by the US military do support the possibility that universal access to health care eliminates the inequalities found in other systems (Smedley et al. 2003).

The publicly funded British National Health Service (NHS) provides (almost) free and universal access to health care, so one might expect ethnic inequalities in access to quality health care to be minimal, or at least smaller than those in the US. However, the benefits of universal access may be offset by the existence of widespread institutional racism in UK public services. Insofar as there is evidence from the UK, it supports the possibility that inequalities in access to health care are not present, but there are inequalities in the quality of care received, supportive of an institutional racism hypothesis. So, UK studies show an equal or greater use across ethnic minority groups of primary care health services (except possibly in the case of Chinese people), although some inequalities exist for use of hospital services and marked inequalities exist for dental services (Nazroo et al. 2009). Similarly, for conditions managed in primary care it seems that the outcomes of care (levels of undiagnosed or poorly managed illness) are as good for ethnic minority people as they are for White English people (Nazroo et al. 2009). This may result from the provision, through the NHS, of publicly funded primary care with universal access and standardized treatment protocols that results in greater equality of access and outcomes across ethnic groups. Nevertheless, the experience of care seems poorer for ethnic minority people. In primary care, ethnic minority people are more likely to be dissatisfied with various aspects of the care received (Airey et al. 1999; Rudat 1994), to wait longer for an appointment (Airey et al. 1999), and to face language barriers during the consultation (Rudat 1994). And there is a convincing body of evidence suggesting that the higher admission rate of Black people for severe mental illness is disproportionate and reflects the ways in which they are racialized (Nazroo et al. 2020).

The evidence from the UK does, then, support the possibility of institutional racism, indicating that regardless of individual professionals' intentions, health services have discriminatory effects. The concept of institutional racism remains contested, not least by medical professionals, and the mechanisms through which organizational processes discriminate are difficult to describe and therefore to reform. Health services operate in the context of broader social and economic processes and understanding persistent institutional racism is a crucial element of tackling intractable inequalities at a time when overt racism in public services is proscribed and relatively rare. The role of racism in producing these consistent findings is highly contested and, even where its role is accepted, the conceptual challenges of understanding its operation as a structural, institutional and interpersonal process are significant (Bradby 2010; Nazroo et al. 2020).

While the role of racism in healthcare is difficult to research for various reasons (Bradby et al 2019), significant work has been done under the heading of "culture," particularly in the field of mental health there is a large literature querying the cross-cultural validity of psychiatric diagnostic practices. The concern is that members of different ethnic groups will have different symptomatic experiences when mentally ill, because of cultural differences in the idioms used to express mental distress. For example, it has been suggested that South Asian people in the UK may experience particular "culture-bound" syndromes: that is, a cluster of symptoms that is restricted to a particular culture, such as *sinking heart* (Krause 1989), which consequently may not be identified as mentally ill by standard diagnostic practices and research instruments. Kleinman (1987) argues that the different idioms for expressing mental distress in different cultures allows for a "category fallacy," where the use of a category of illness that was developed in one cultural group fails to identify ill people in another cultural group, because it lacks coherence in that culture. While the Western category of depression is treated as if it were universal, the idioms of mental distress in a non-Western group may be sufficiently different for Western diagnostic practices to fail. Indeed, it has been argued that Western depression amounts to a culturally specific diagnosis (Jadhav 1996).

Small-scale empirical work with British Pakistanis has identified an expression of mental distress described as "thinking too much in my heart" (Fenton and Sadiq-Sangster 1996). While this was found to correlate strongly with the expression of most of the standard Western symptoms of depression, some of these standard symptoms were not present (those relating to a loss of meaning in life and self-worth), suggesting that the form that the disease took was different. Fenton and Sadiq-Sangster point out that "thinking too much in my heart" was not only a symptom but the core experience of the illness, raising the possibility that there were more fundamental differences between this illness and depression. Nazroo and O'Connor (2002) found similar differences, but also important commonalities, indicating that cultural differences may not lie in broader constructs of mental illness but in the detail of the idioms used to express distress. Qualitative analysis of accounts of mental distress demonstrates that people of Pakistani origin living in the UK show considerable fluency across different symbolic domains and refutes the suggestion that culture-bound metaphors or similes might determine patterns of help-seeking and health care use (Mallinson and Popay 2007).

Ethnic minority cultural practices and religious beliefs can prompt particular health behaviors but, as with the ethnic majority, minorities' non-medical practices tend to be used alongside medical advice which is attributed considerable respect (Bradby 1997). In considering the effect of culture on health service use by ethnic minorities, the culture of the health service providers and the organizational culture should be considered. A major barrier to getting access to good quality health care is the lack of common language between patient and staff. Greenhalgh et al. (2007) show how organizational features of a sample of general practices in London influenced whether interpretation services were available.

Migrant and Minority Staff in the Health Services

In both the US and the UK, migrants have filled crucial labor shortages, thereby maintaining health services. For those migrants who also are a member of a racialized minority, the experience of discrimination is routine and this is true of low-paid staff doing cleaning or catering work as well as skilled medical migrants. From the US, there is evidence that White patients treated by White doctors are less likely to report medical errors than White patients treated by non-White doctors. In a nationally representative data set, the likelihood of reporting medical error does not vary among non-White patients according to their ethnic or racial concordance with the physician (Stepanikova 2006: 3065). The systematically lower status of non-White doctors compared with White doctors is the explanation offered for White patients' greater preparedness to report medical error. This echoes the suggestion that the class position of the skilled migrant doctors who have maintained the NHS in the UK has been mediated by discrimination, leaving them in a "pariah" position compared with other doctors (Kyriakides and Virdee 2003: 296). Indeed, while the proportion of NHS staff who have an ethnic minority background was 22% in 2016, only 6.7% of senior managers were from an ethnic minority background (NHS 2016). Ethnic minority staff in the NHS were significantly more likely to be disciplined than white staff members and were significantly more likely to experience discrimination, harassment, bullying or abuse from other staff at work. from colleagues, and from their managers (NHS 2016).

Wealthy nations continue to attract qualified, skilled medical practitioners from poorer countries, who can ill afford to lose them (Bradby 2014). The ethics of global medical migration are fraught, involving as they do issues around the freedom of movement, equal opportunities to employment, and the regulation of health care markets, but the injustice of wealthy populations profiting from the education provided by poor populations is inescapable (Bradby 2016).

Conclusion

The conditions leading to health and to illness, the experience of illness, and the seeking of health care are all, in a sociological analysis, best understood as a dimension and a product of social relations. The ways in which ethnicity and racism play out in the social relations of health, illness, and health care are both complex and, at times, subtle. As an identity which is both self-ascribed and imposed by others, ethnicity or race comes into play differentially according to actors' own choices, and is dependent on the context in which those choices are exercised. Individual identities reflect structural dimensions of society, with individuals' range of choices being differentially constrained. Both structural and identity aspects of ethnicity and race develop over time, so being Muslim, Irish or Polish carry different meanings now compared with 50 years ago, in the US as well as the UK. Slavery is identified as being an important context for understanding racial categories in the US and the resonance of empire is highly relevant to ethnicity in the UK.

The terminology of quantitative analysis can give the misleading impression that the causal effects of an essentialized notion of ethnicity can be identified by using statistical controls for so-called confounders. Appreciating the racialized nature of social relations implies that structure and identity are inflected by race and there is no means of stepping outside or beyond this process: There is no "un-raced" body, just as there is no body free of gender. The misinterpretation of the implications of "controlling for" socioeconomic status in statistical models has led to the attribution of health disparities to the racial or ethnic character of the minority population. The concept of intersectionality underlines that race is irreducible to class or gender, and, having gained widespread traction in terms of rhetoric, is beginning to be applied to the empirical study of sociological processes around health and illness (Hankivsky 2012). Culture, particularly in the UK context, has become a euphemism for "problematic difference," which in its usage is difficult to distinguish from biologically determined race talk. Thus, the health deficits of minority ethnic or racial groups have all too frequently been understood as the direct effect of the content of the minority culture, and the effects of racism, poverty, and other exclusions are lost from view.

Despite its abuse, culture needs to be retained as an analytic term, given its immense importance for identity, but, as has been noted, it needs to be adequately complicated (Bradby 2003; Hillier and Kelleher 1996). Culture should be understood as a property of organizations, as well as of individuals, if the effects of institutional racism are to be mapped, and the interactions of minority and majority practices must be given equal consideration in an effort to understand culture through the life course.

References

Airey, C., S. Bruster, B. Erens, S. Lilley, K. Pickering, and L. Pitson. 1999. *National Surveys of NHS Patients: General Practice 1998*. London: NHS Executive.

Almeida, J., L. Bécares, K. Erbetta, V. R. Bettegowda, and I. B. Ahluwalia. 2018. "Racial Ethnic Inequities in Low Birth Weight and Preterm Birth: The Role of Multiple Forms of Stress." *Maternal and Child Health Journal* 22: 1154–63.

Annandale, Ellen and Kate Hunt (eds.). 1999. *Gender Inequalities in Health*. Buckingham: Open University Press.

Bajekal, Madhavi, David Blane, Ini Grewal, Saffron Karlsen, and James Nazroo. 2004. "Ethnic Differences in Influences on Quality of Life at Older Ages: A Quantitative Analysis." *Ageing and Society* 24(5): 709–28.

Bécares, Laia, James Nazroo, and Mai Stafford. 2009. "The Buffering Effects of Ethnic Density on Experienced Racism and Health." *Health & Place* 15(3): 700–08.

Blaxter, Mildred. 1990. *Health and Lifestyles*. London: Tavistock/Routledge.

Bradby, Hannah. 1995. "Ethnicity: Not A Black and White Issue. A Research Note." *Sociology of Health & Illness* 17: 405–17.

Bradby, Hannah. 1997. "Health, Heating and Heart Attacks: Glaswegian Punjabi Women's Thinking about Everyday Food." Pp. 211–33 in *Food Health and Identity* edited by P. Caplan. London: Routledge.

Bradby, Hannah. 2003. "Describing Ethnicity in Health Research." *Ethnicity and Health* 8(1): 5–13.

Bradby, Hannah. 2010. "Institutional Racism in Mental Health Services: The Consequences of Compromised Conceptualization." *Sociological Research Online*, 15, 8.

Bradby, Hannah. 2012. Racism, Ethnicity, Health and Society. in *eLS*. John Wiley & Sons, Ltd: Chichester. DOI: 10.1002/9780470015902.a0005660.pub2

Bradby, Hannah. 2014. "International Medical Migration: A Critical Conceptual Review of the Global Movements of Doctors and Nurses." *Health* 18(6): 580–96.

Bradby, Hannah. 2016. "Medical Migration and the Global Politics of Equality." Pp. 491–507 in *The Edinburgh Companion to the Critical Medical Humanities*, edited by Anne Whitehead, Angela Woods, Sarah Atkinson, Jane Macnaughton, and Jennifer Richards. Edinburgh: Edinburgh University Press.

BradbyHannah, Suruchi Thapar-Björkert, Sarah Hamed, and Beth Maina Ahlberg. 2019. "Undoing the Unspeakable: Researching Racism in Swedish Healthcare Using a Participatory Process to Build Dialogue." *Health Research Policy and Systems* 17, 43. Doi: 10.1186/s12961-019-0443-0

Davey Smith, George, James D. Neaton, Deborah Wentworth, Rose Stamler, and Jeremiah Stamler. 1998. "Mortality Differences between Black and White Men in the USA: Contribution of Income and Other Risk Factors among Men Screened for the MRFIT." *Lancet* 351: 934–39.

Donovan, Jenny. 1986. *We Don't Buy Sickness, It Just Comes: Health, Illness and Health Care in the Lives of Black People in England*. Aldershot: Gower.

Erens, Bob, Paola Primatesta, and Gillian Prior. 2001. *Health Survey for England 1999: The Health of Minority Ethnic Groups*. London: The Stationery Office.

Fenton, Steve and Azra Sadiq-Sangster. 1996. "Culture, Relativism and the Expression of Mental Distress: South Asian Women in Britain." *Sociology of Health & Illness* 2: 66–85.

Gordon, David, Mary Shaw, Danny Dorling, and George Davey Smith (eds.). 1999. *Inequalities in Health: The Evidence Presented to the Independent Inquiry into Inequalities in Health, Chaired by Sir Donald Acheson*. Bristol: Policy Press.

Greenhalgh, Trisha, Christopher Voisey, and Nadia Robb. 2007. "Interpreted Consultations as 'Business as Usual'? an Analysis of Organisational Routines in General Practices." *Sociology of Health & Illness* 29(6): 931–54.

Hankivsky, Olena. 2012. "Women's Health, Men's Health, and Gender and Health: Implications of Intersectionality." *Social Science & Medicine* 74(11): 1712–20.

Harding, Seeromanie and Rory Maxwell. 1997. "Differences in the Mortality of Migrants." Pp. in F. Drever and M. Whitehead (eds.), *Health Inequalities: Decennial Supplement Series DS No. 15*. London: The Stationery Office.

Hillier, Sheila and David Kelleher. 1996. "Culture, Ethnicity and the Politics of Health." Pp. 1–10 in David Kelleher and Sheila Hillier (eds.), *Researching Cultural Differences in Health*. London: Routledge.

Jadhav, Shushrut. 1996. "The Cultural Origins of Western Depression." *International Journal of Social Psychiatry* 42(4): 269–86.

Jenkins, Richard. 1995. "Rethinking Ethnicity." *Ethnic and Racial Studies* 17(2): 197–224.

Karlsen, Saffron and James Y. Nazroo. 2002a. "Agency and Structure: The Impact of Ethnic Identity and Racism on the Health of Ethnic Minority People." *Sociology of Health & Illness* 24: 1–20.

Karlsen, Saffron and James Y. Nazroo. 2002b. "The Relationship between Racial Discrimination, Social Class and Health among Ethnic Minority Groups." *American Journal of Public Health* 92: 624–31.

Karlsen, Saffron and James Y. Nazroo. 2004. "Fear of Racism and Health." *Journal of Epidemiology and Community Health* 58: 1017–18.

Karlsen, Saffron, James Y. Nazroo, Kwame McKenzie, Kam Bhui, and Scott Weich. 2005. "Racism, Psychosis and Common Mental Disorder among Ethnic Minority Groups in England." *Psychological Medicine* 35(12): 1795–803.

Kaufman, Joy S., R. S. Cooper, and D. L. McGee. 1997. "Socioeconomic Status and Health in Blacks and Whites: The Problem of Residual Confounding and the Resiliency of Race." *Epidemiology* 8(6): 621–28.

Kaufman, Joy S., A. E. Long, Y. Liao, R. S. Cooper, and D. L. McGee. 1998. "The Relation between Income and Mortality in US Blacks and Whites." *Epidemiology* 9(2): 147–55.

Kelly, Y., L. Panico, M. Bartley, M. Marmot, J. Nazroo, and A. Sacker. 2009. "Why Does Birthweight Vary among Ethnic Groups in the UK? Findings from the Millennium Cohort Study." *Journal of Public Health*, 31(1), 131–37.

Kleinman, Arthur. 1987. "Anthropology and Psychiatry: The Role of Culture in Cross-Cultural Research on Illness." *British Journal of Psychiatry* 151: 447–54.

Krause, Inga-Britt. 1989. "Sinking Heart: A Punjabi Communication of Distress." *Social Science & Medicine* 29(4): 563–75.

Krieger, Nancy. 2000. "Discrimination and Health." Pp. 36–75 in *Social Epidemiology*, edited by Lisa F. Berkman and Kawachi Ichiro. Oxford: Oxford University Press.

Krieger, Nancy and Stephen Sidney. 1996. "Racial Discrimination and Blood Pressure: The CARDIA Study of Young Black and White Adults." *American Journal of Public Health* 86(10): 1370–78.

Kyriakides, Christopher and Satnam Virdee. 2003. "Migrant Labour, Racism and the British National Health Service." *Ethnicity and Health* 8(4): 283–305.

Mallinson, Sara and Jennie Popay. 2007. "Describing Depression: Ethnicity and the Use of Somatic Imagery in Accounts of Mental Distress." *Sociology of Health & Illness* 29(6): 857–71.

Marmot, Michael and Richard G. Wilkinson (eds.). 2005. *Social Determinants of Health*, 2nd edition. Oxford: Oxford University Press.

Marmot, Michael G., Abraham M. Adelstein, and L. Bulusu, and OPCS. 1984. *Immigrant Mortality in England and Wales 1970–78: Causes of Death by Country of Birth*. London: HMSO.

Massey, Douglas S. and Nancy A. Denton. 1993. *American Apartheid: Segregation and the Making of the Underclass*. Cambridge, MA: Harvard University Press.

McCulloch, Andrew. 2007. "The Changing Structure of Ethnic Diversity and Segregation in England, 1991–2001." *Environment and Planning* 39(4): 909–27.

National Center for Health Statistics (NCHS). 1994. *Vital Statistics of the United States, 1990. Vol. 2: Mortality, Part A*. Washington, DC: Public Health Service.

Nazroo, James. 2004. "Ethnic Disparities in Aging Health: What Can We Learn from the United Kingdom?" Pp. 677–702 in *Critical Perspectives on Racial and Ethnic Differentials in Health in Late Life*, edited by N. Anderson, R. Bulatao, and B. Cohen. Washington, DC: National Academies Press.

Nazroo, James Y. 1997. *The Health of Britain's Ethnic Minorities: Findings from a National Survey*. London: Policy Studies Institute.

Nazroo, James Y. 2001. *Ethnicity, Class and Health*. London: Policy Studies Institute.

Nazroo, James Y. 2003. "The Structuring of Ethnic Inequalities in Health: Economic Position, Racial Discrimination and Racism." *American Journal of Public Health* 93(2): 277–84.

Nazroo, James Y. and William O'Connor. 2002. "Idioms of Mental Distress." Pp. 29–39 in *Ethnic Differences in the Context and Experience of Psychiatric Illness: A Qualitative Study*, edited by W. O. Connor and J. Nazroo. London: The Stationery Office.

Nazroo, James Y. and David R. Williams. 2005. "The Social Determination of Ethnic/Racial Inequalities in Health." Pp. 238–66 in *Social Determinants of Health*, 2nd edition, edited by M. Marmot and R. G. Wilkinson. Oxford: Oxford University Press.

Nazroo, J.Y., K.S. Bhui, and J. Rhodes. 2020. "Where Next for Understanding Race/ethnic Inequalities in Severe Mental Illness? Structural, Interpersonal and Institutional Racism." *Sociology of Health & Illness*. 42(2): 262–76.

Nazroo, J.Y., E. Falaschetti, M. Pierce, and P. Primatesta. 2009. "Ethnic Inequalities in Access to and Outcomes of Healthcare: Analysis of the Health Survey for England." *Journal of Epidemiology and Community Health* 63(12): 1022–27.

NHS 2016. "*The Workforce Race Equality Standard*." UK: National Health Service England.

O'Hare, William P. 2019. "Understanding Who Was Missed in the 2010 Census." Data and Demographic Services, LLC. https://www.prb.org/understanding-who-was-missed-in-the-2010-census

Oliver, Melvin L. and Thomas M. Shapiro. 1995. *Black Wealth/White Wealth: A New Perspective on Racial Inequality*. New York: Routledge.

Perlmann, Joel and Mary C. Waters. 2002. "Introduction." Pp. 1–30 in, *The New Race Question: How the Census Counts Multiracial Individuals*, edited by J. Perlmann and M. C. Waters. New York: Russell Sage Foundation.

Rudat, K. 1994. *Black and Minority Ethnic Groups in England: Health and Lifestyles*. London: Health Education Authority.

Smedley, Brian D., Adrienne Y. Stith, and Alan R. Nelson (eds.). 2003. *Unequal Treatment: Confronting Racial and Ethnic Disparities in Health Care*. Washington: Institute of Medicine of the National Academies.

Sorlie, Paul, Eugene Rogot, Roger Anderson, Norman J. Johnson, and Eric Backlund. 1992. "Black–White Mortality Differences by Family Income." *Lancet* 340: 346–50.

Sorlie, Paul D., Eric Backlund, and J. Keller. 1995. "US Mortality by Economic, Demographic and Social Characteristics: The National Longitudinal Mortality Study." *American Journal of Public Health* 85: 949–56.

Stepanikova, Irena. 2006. "Patient–Physician Racial and Ethnic Concordance and Perceived Medical Errors." *Social Science & Medicine* 63: 3060–66.

Townsend, Peter and Nick Davidson. 1982. *Inequalities in Health: The Black Report*. London: Penguin.

Wallace, Matthew and Hill Kulu. 2015. "Mortality among Immigrants in England and Wales by Major Causes of Death, 1971-2012: A LongitudinalAnalysis of Register-based Data." *Social Science & Medicine* 47: 209–21.

Wallace, Stephanie, James Nazroo, and Bécares Laia. 2016. "Cumulative Effect of Racial Discrimination on the Mental Health of Ethnic Minorities in the United Kingdom." *American Journal of Public Health* 106(7): 1294–300

Waters, Mary C. 1990. *Ethnic Options: Choosing Identities in America.* Berkeley, CA: University of California Press.

Wild, Sarah and McKeigue Paul. 1997. "Cross-Sectional Analysis of Mortality by Country of Birth in England and Wales." *British Medical Journal* 314: 705–10.

Wild, S.H., C. Fischbacher, A. Brock, C. Griffiths, and R. Bhopal. 2007. "Mortality from All Causes and Circulatory Disease by Country of Birth in England and Wales 2001–2003." *Journal of Public Health* 29(2):191–98.

Williams, David R. 2001. "Racial Variations in Adult Health Status: Patterns, Paradoxes and Prospects." Pp. 371–410 in *America Becoming: Racial Trends and Their Consequences*, edited by N. J. Smelser, W. J. Wilson, and F. Mitchell. Washington, DC: National Academy Press.

Williams, David R., Harold W. Neighbors, and James S. Jackson. 2003. "Racial/Ethnic Discrimination and Health: Findings from Community Studies." *American Journal of Public Health* 93(2): 200–08.

Zsembik, Barbara A. and Dana Fennel. 2005. "Ethnic Variation in Health and the Determinants of Health among Latinos." *Social Science & Medicine* 61: 53–63.

14

African American Health

Christy L. Erving and Lacee A. Satcher

This chapter explores the health of individuals of African descent living in the U.S. Historically, African Americans were the largest racial minority in the U.S., having been surpassed by individuals of Hispanic descent in 2003 (U.S. Census Bureau 2003). The most recent estimates indicate that African Americans represent 13.4% of the U.S. population (U.S. Census Bureau 2020). The unique sociohistorical context of African Americans' arrival on U.S. soil differs from all other racial minorities and still contributes to this demographic group's contemporary health patterns. The majority of African Americans currently residing in the U.S. are descendants of West Africans who were introduced to the U.S. via the transatlantic slave trade. This circumstance is crucial for providing an in-depth sociological understanding of the health of African Americans, as this group remains at the bottom of the racial social hierarchy to this day.

One of the first comprehensive sociological studies of African American health was conducted by W.E.B. DuBois, an American sociologist, historian, and civil rights activist. Dubois recognized over a century ago that Black-White differences in health were due in large part to the disparate environments these racial groups inhabit. Using national mortality data, in the 11th Annual Conference for the "Study of the Negro Problem" at Atlanta University, DuBois lamented the following regarding the causes of Blacks' relatively higher mortality rates vis-à-vis Whites:

> The Conference does not find any adequate scientific warrant for the assumption that the Negro race is inferior to other races in physical build or vitality. The present differences in mortality seem to be sufficiently explained by conditions of life; and physical measurements prove the Negro a normal human being capable of average human accomplishments. [Excerpt from *The Health and Physique of the Negro American* (1906)]

The Wiley Blackwell Companion to Medical Sociology, First Edition. Edited by William C. Cockerham.

Over one hundred years later, we arrive at a similar conclusion. Despite advancements in healthcare quality and access, medical technology, education, business, and the labor market, Blacks still die younger and experience disproportionately higher rates of most physical health problems. In this chapter, we provide an overview of the "conditions of life" that prevent millions of Black Americans from reaching their "human accomplishments." First, we begin by providing conceptual clarification for the specific population of focus in this chapter.

Who are African Americans?

Throughout the text, we use various terms to make reference to individuals of African descent. We use the term "Black American" to refer to all individuals of African descent living in the U.S. The term "African American" refers to a subset of Blacks who were born in the U.S., and whose ancestors were introduced to the American context via the transatlantic slave trade. We use the term "Caribbean Black" to refer to individuals of African descent living in the U.S. with immediate Caribbean ancestry. Individuals of African descent who migrated from countries in the Caribbean are distinct ethnic groups subsumed under this broader umbrella term. Accordingly, we view Caribbean Blacks as a pan-ethnic group comprised of individuals from various Caribbean nations (e.g. Haiti, Jamaica, Barbados). We use the term "African immigrants" to refer to individuals who were born in sub-Saharan African nations (e.g. Nigeria, Cameroon, Ethiopia) and voluntarily migrated to the U.S. Though most sociological literature focuses on African Americans, we discuss the growing ethnic diversity of the Black population and implications for how we understand race and health later in the chapter.

A Sociology of African American Health?

To assess the "prevalence" of sociological empirical research on African American health, we conducted a search of articles published since the year 2000 in the major U.S. medical sociology research outlet: *Journal of Health and Social Behavior*. As shown in Figure 14.1, between 2000 and 2019, 15 articles were published focusing exclusively on Black Americans. Another 54 articles were published comparing Black Americans to other racial groups. These articles are inclusive of various health topics including physical health, psychological health, healthcare utilization, and perceptions of as well as interactions within the health care system.

To broaden our search to generalist journals, we conducted the same search in arguably the top four U.S. generalist sociology journals: *American Sociological Review, American Journal of Sociology, Social Forces*, and *Social Problems*. We recognize that excellent research is being published in other outlets, but we conducted this search for illustrative purposes as it reflects what sociology deems "premier" research. The results of our search are presented in Table 14.1. Collectively, this search produced a yield of eighteen studies over a nineteen-year period published *across all four top sociology publications*. This paucity of literature published in

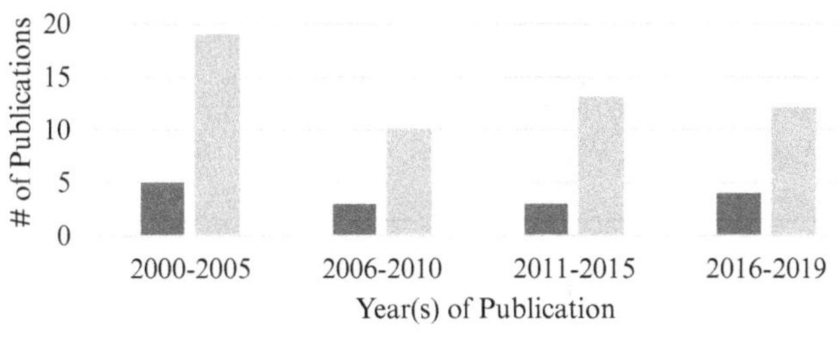

Figure 14.1 Journal of Health and Social Behavior (2000–2019) Articles Focused on Black Americans.

Table 14.1 Articles focused on Black American Health Issues in the Top Four Sociology Generalist Journals in the U.S. 2000–2019.

Journal	Number of Articles focused on Black American Health	Author Last Names (Year of Publication)	Article Title
American Sociological Review	5	Hayward, Miles, Crimmins, and Yang (2000)	The Significance of Socioeconomic Status in Explaining the Racial Gap in Chronic Health Conditions
		Elwert and Christakis (2006)	Widowhood and Race
		Williams, Sassler, Frech, Addo, and Cooksey (2011)	Nonmarital Childbearing, Union History, and Women's Health at Midlife
		Barr, Gordon Simons, and Beach (2018)	Sharing the Burden of the Transition to Adulthood: African American Young Adults' Transition Challenges and Their Mother's Health Risk
		Danya (2019)	Hearing Gender: Voice-Based Gender Classification Processes and Transgender Health Inequality
American Journal of Sociology	2	Monk (2015)	The Cost of Color: Skin Color, Discrimination, and Health among African-Americans
		Elman, McGuire, and London (2019)	Disease, Plantation Development, and Race-Related Differences in Fertility in the Early Twentieth-Century American South

(*Continued*)

Table 14.1 *Con.*

Journal	Number of Articles focused on Black American Health	Author Last Names (Year of Publication)	Article Title
Social Forces	6	Read and Emerson (2005)	Racial Context, Black Immigration and the U.S. Black/White Health Disparity
		Chang et al. (2009)	Neighborhood Racial Isolation, Disorder, and Obesity
		Coverdill, Lopez, and Petrie (2011)	Race, Ethnicity, and the Quality of Life in America, 1972-2008
		Cheng, Hamilton, Missari, and Ma (2014)	Sexual Subjectivity among Adolescent Girls: Social Disadvantage and Young Adult Outcomes
		Dupre (2016)	Race, Marital History, and Risks for Stroke in U.S. Older Adults
		Brown (2018)	Racial Stratification, Immigration, and Health Inequality: A Life Course-Intersectional Approach
Social Problems	5	Schnittker et al. (2005)	Are African Americans Really Less Willing to Use Health Care?
		Pampel (2009)	The Persistence of Educational Disparities in Smoking
		Wildeman (2012)	Imprisonment and Infant Mortality
		Roth and Henley (2012)	Unequal Motherhood: Racial-Ethnic and Socioeconomic Disparities in Cesarean Sections in the United States
		Anderson (2017)	Racial Residential Segregation and the Distribution of Health-Related Organizations in Urban Neighborhoods

high impact sociology journals suggests that U.S. sociological research does not consider African American Health a mainstream topic of investigation, despite persistent racial disparities in health.

Given the dearth of sociological research on African Americans' health, this review is necessarily interdisciplinary, incorporating insights from sociology as well as social work, epidemiology, public health, and psychology. We consider this interdisciplinary work to have sociological relevance; thus, we hope these other perspectives will spur future research that engages theories, concepts, and findings within *and* beyond sociology. We organize the remainder of the chapter into three sections: In the first section, we describe health patterns between Black Americans and other racial groups in the U.S., with a primary focus on Black-White differences in health, as reflected in the broader sociological literature. We then describe the causal factors underlying these disparities. The second section explores variation in the health profiles of Black Americans by other sociodemographic factors (e.g. gender, ethnicity, sexual orientation). The last section addresses counterintuitive findings with regards to psychological health among African Americans.

The Health of Black Americans within a Comparative Framework

For virtually every dimension of physical health, Black Americans fare worse than Whites and other racial minorities (the exception is Native Americans, who experience poor health at similar rates as Blacks). In 2017, African Americans had a life expectancy of 75.3 years compared to 76.9 years for Native Americans, 78.8 years for Whites, 81.8 for Hispanic Americans, and 87.1 for Asian Americans (Arias and Xu 2019). Therefore, Blacks not only lag behind Whites by 3.5 years, but Black-Hispanic and Black-Asian disparities are even larger at 6.5 years and 11.8 years, respectively.[1] These disparities in life chances begin from birth: African American babies are 2.23 times more likely to die before their first birthday than their White counterparts (Arias and Jiaquan 2019). Dispelling the myth that these early-life deaths are attributable to socioeconomic disadvantage, recent data reveals that Black babies born to college-educated mothers have a higher risk of dying before one year of age than White babies born to mothers with a high school education (Singh and Yu 2019).

In addition to shorter life spans, Blacks spend more years living with disabilities that limit their mobility in mid-to-late life (Brown et al. 2012). Using longitudinal data from the Health and Retirement Study (1992–2004), Brown and colleagues (2012) report that Black Americans between 53 to 73 years of age experience significantly greater functional limitations relative to their similarly aged White counterparts. Functional limitations ranged from difficulty with walking one block to raising arms above one's shoulders. Similar trends emerge for other health outcomes. For example, Blacks have overall higher rates of obesity (Boardman et al. 2005), stroke (Dupre 2016), and report lower self-rated health relative to their White counterparts (Cunningham et al. 2017).

Black Americans also experience disparities in access to healthcare, quality of care received, and interactions with medical professionals.[2] For example, 94.6% of Whites have health insurance while 90.3% of Blacks are insured (U.S. Census Bureau 2019). In terms of hospitalization, Blacks have a longer length of stay and are more likely to die post-hospitalization (Ferraro and Shippee 2008). Nevertheless, compared to Whites, African Americans report greater willingness to seek treatment, higher levels of optimism regarding treatment expectations (Schnittker et al. 2005), and more prosocial attitudes regarding vaccinations (Polonijo et al. 2016).

Despite positive expectations regarding the utility of the health care system, the reality of the care Blacks receive often falls short. Older adults living in majority Black nursing homes are less likely to receive influenza vaccination than majority White ones; hence, Blacks residing in nursing homes are more susceptible to influenza, an illness than can be fatal at older ages (Strully 2011). In terms of perceptions of interactions within the health care system, race concordance in the doctor-patient relationship increases patient satisfaction with the care received (LaVeist and Nuru-Jeter 2002; Malat 2001). One study showed that approximately 67% of Blacks perceive "somewhat often" or "very often" occurrence of racism in clinical encounters with non-Black medical doctors (Malat and Hamilton 2006). Perhaps not surprisingly, Black respondents' belief in frequent racism from non-Black medical doctors was associated with the desire to have a Black doctor. The implication is that further investment in the training of Black physicians might increase the (perceived) quality of care for Black Americans. In addition, non-Black physicians should receive professional training that would enable them to establish rapport with their Black patients to ensure a positive experience in race discordant doctor-patient relationships. This is especially critical, as White clinicians tend to hold negative implicit biases towards Black patients which, in turn, leads to lower quality care (Stepanikova 2012; van Ryn 2016).

Why do we observe savage inequalities in health and health care between Blacks and Whites? We submit that these racial differences are entrenched in structural arrangements that disadvantage Blacks while advantaging Whites. In addition, social psychological factors interact with structural factors to impinge upon perceptions, beliefs, motivations, and expectations with regards to one's own health. Accordingly, we organize our discussion around these two interrelated causal forces underlying Black-White health disparities.

Structural Explanations

Macro-level structures and social institutions can ameliorate or perpetuate disparities in health. Though the health care system as a social institution is a most obvious culprit, other systems of inequality also merit scrutiny. Here, we direct our attention to racial residential segregation and the criminal justice system, as these two institutions are powerful drivers of health and contribute to Black-White health disparities in insidious ways. Drawing from life course theory, we also describe how structural advantages and disadvantages accumulate over the life course to produce health differentials between Blacks and Whites.

Racial residential segregation. Despite the passing of The Civil Rights Act of 1964 prohibiting segregation, most major U.S. cities remain racially residentially segregated. As of 2010, Black Americans are residentially hyper-segregated from their White peers in 52 metropolitan areas (Massey and Tannen 2015). Referred to as both the structural linchpin of racial stratification (Massey and Tannen 2016) and a fundamental cause of health disparities (Williams and Collins 2001), racial residential segregation is problematic because it diminishes access to health-related resources in majority Black neighborhoods, including food resources, physical fitness facilities, health care facilities, and social services (Anderson 2017).

Disparities related to racial residential segregation highlight how the neighborhood context influences health. The racial composition and poverty rate of a neighborhood has been linked to a variety of health outcomes. Walton (2009) found that racial residential segregation in combination with concentrated poverty was associated with low birth weight for children born to Black mothers. Interestingly, the same study reported that living in high density Asian residential areas was health-protective, and highly segregated Hispanic neighborhoods had a null effect on low birth weight for Hispanic children. This suggests that the hyper-segregation of Black Americans in the U.S. is uniquely disadvantageous in ways that other racialized segregation patterns are not. In a seven-year study, Fauth and colleagues (2008) examined how movement from a high to low poverty neighborhood affected the physical health of Blacks and Latinos in Yonkers, New York. After a court-ordered neighborhood mobility program was implemented, a group of Black and Latino households transitioned from high poverty neighborhoods to townhouses in low poverty areas. The study found that at seven-year follow up, residents of the low poverty neighborhood reported significantly better health than the "stayers" who remained in low income housing in poverty-stricken neighborhoods.

Beyond considering the racial composition and socioeconomic features of the neighborhood, mechanisms through which neighborhoods affect individual health include social cohesion, social networks, social control, collective efficacy, institutional resources, and the physical environment (Arcaya et al. 2016; Chang et al. 2009; Kravitz-Wirtz 2016; Sampson et al. 2002). The collective characteristics of neighborhoods have the capacity to affect individual health and health-risk behaviors. For example, deteriorated housing conditions (e.g., maintenance deficiencies and crowding) *and* low levels of perceived social cohesion partially explained higher prevalence of asthma in Black and Puerto Rican households compared to White households in New York City (Rosenbaum 2008).

Research in environmental justice has interrogated how neighborhoods shape health via the disproportionate burden of environmentally hazardous industry siting and pollution. This injustice occurs most commonly in low-income communities of color (McKane et al. 2018; Woo et al. 2019) and increases asthma, cancer, and birth defect rates (Ghosh-Dastidar et al. 2014; Ringquist 2005). Further, recent research on food justice has shown that African American neighborhoods, in addition to being food deserts, are food swamps (i.e. neighborhoods with a high density of high-calorie fast food and junk food retailers relative to healthy food retailers) that positively predict obesity and hospitalization rates among diabetic adults (Cooksey, Schwartz, and Brownell 2017; Phillips and Rodriguez 2019). Additionally, Black urban neighborhoods are disproportionately exposed to large-scale tobacco (i.e. menthol cigarettes) and alcohol marketing and advertisement relative to more rural, White neighborhoods (Lee et al. 2015; McKee et al. 2011). This is especially impactful as targeted alcohol advertisement in Black neighborhoods is positively associated with problem drinking among Black women (Kwate and Meyer 2009). In sum, the residential areas occupied by Blacks and Whites are fundamentally unequal, which leads to a host of health problems disproportionately endured by Black Americans.

Criminal Justice System. Due, in part, to racially biased policies (e.g. "Stop and Frisk" in New York) and over-policing in Black urban areas, Black Americans are dramatically overrepresented in America's jails, prisons, and probation systems. The rate of imprisonment for Black women is nearly twice as high as White women, and Black men are nearly six times more likely to be imprisoned than White men (Bronson and Carson 2019). In fact, lifetime incarceration rates projections for men born in 2003 forecast that nearly one-third of Black men will experience incarceration in their lifetime, compared to 6% of White men (Bonczar 2003).

Given disproportionately higher rates of incarceration for Blacks, the criminal justice system contributes profoundly to health disparities. Contact with the criminal justice system is consequential not only for the health of "offenders," but also the health of those with familial or romantic ties to offenders. Direct or indirect contact with the criminal justice system has negative effects on life expectancy, mortality, morbidity (e.g. diabetes, high blood pressure, and asthma), and psychological distress (Lee and Wildeman 2013; Patterson 2013; Sewell and Jefferson 2016; Turney 2014). Moreover, incarcerated individuals and their families are likely to have poor health before contact with the criminal justice system (due to poverty and racial marginalization), and the considerable unmet needs in physical and mental health services in prisons exacerbate health concerns while creating new health problems (Wildeman and Muller 2012). Additionally, after incarceration, individuals tend to experience a spike in mortality and morbidity due to stigma and stress-related diseases (Wildeman and Muller 2012).

Parental incarceration is detrimental to child and maternal health. With Black men experiencing the highest incarceration rates of all race-gender groups in the U.S., their Black children are disproportionately affected by imprisonment. For example, Wildeman (2012) showed a direct association between parental (primarily paternal) incarceration and early infant mortality risk. The underlying mechanisms linking these two phenomena are diminished paternal financial contribution to family life which may induce financial strain and other related stressors for an expectant mother. This work also demonstrates the importance of the in utero environment and its implications for the health of the most vulnerable population: children.

Life Course Cumulative Disadvantage. Advantages and disadvantages accrue over the life course that disadvantage most Blacks while advantaging even the poorest Whites. According to cumulative disadvantage theory, early life experiences are influential factors in how cohorts become differentiated over time, especially across race and social class (see Chapter 9 for an in-depth discussion of The Life Course Perspective). This differentiation impacts life outcomes and contributes to current racial health disparities (Brown et al. 2012, 2016; Warner and Hayward 2006). Much of these early life disadvantages are manifestations of structural racism, including household poverty, low parental education attainment, and lack of wealth. Cumulative exposure to economic conditions that increase stress over the life course have damaging health effects, especially coupled with racial differences in the health returns of certain health-promoting resources such as education, income, and wealth (Boen 2016). Early life may be an especially critical period in which disparities emerge because of the sensitivity of organ and regulatory system development. Moreover, lack of access to healthcare and health education in early life as a result of racial inequality compounds the health complications that may emerge due to early life disadvantages.

Early life social adversity is consequential to the health of Black Americans at relatively early ages (Hayward and Gorman 2004; Simons et al. 2019). For example, Hargrove (2018) showed that Black adolescent girls tend to have higher body mass index (BMI) than their White female counterparts, and this disparity increases as they transition into early adulthood. In mid-to-late life, Umberson and colleagues (2014) found that childhood adversity is especially salient for Black men which, in turns, negatively impacts their health and partly explains their relatively poor health compared to White men. These childhood adversities include family economic hardship, not knowing one's father, parental death, as well as living in a household with someone with a mental health problem, a drinking problem, or exhibiting violent behavior. As a result of childhood adversity, Black men were more likely to experience relational strains in adulthood that, in turn, negatively influenced their health (Umberson et al. 2014).

Social Psychological Explanations

Social psychological explanations of health disparities explore how perception, meaning, and interpretation of illness differ across racial groups. Furthermore, a *sociological* social psychological perspective draws attention to how these processes link macro dimensions of inequality to physiological responses and physical disease (McLeod et al. 2014). Here, we describe specific psychological processes most relevant for understanding the physical health of African Americans: health behaviors, stress exposure, and psychosocial resources.

Health Behaviors. Epidemiological perspectives emphasize individual health behaviors for explaining population differences in health. Relative to their White counterparts, Blacks have higher rates of sedentary lifestyle, lower rates of recommended fruit and vegetable intake, are more likely to eat a high-fat carbohydrate-rich diet, and report similar smoking rates in adulthood (Pampel 2008; Rehm et al. 2016; Seixas et al. 2017); in quantitative studies, these differences in health behavior occasionally "explain" Black-White health disparities. Though participation in health behaviors are often described as agentic acts rooted in personal motivation and prioritization, a health lifestyles perspective argues that health-related behaviors are constrained by social structures. In other words, such behaviors are based on options available in accordance with one's life chances which are largely determined by social status. Such statuses (e.g. economic, racial) have the ability to constrain or facilitate lifestyle "choices" (Cockerham et al. 2017; see Chapter 8 for an in-depth discussion).

For example, Ray's (2017) study of Black and White middle class respondents showed that perceptions of the racial composition of the neighborhood was associated with physical activity; more specifically, Black women were less likely to engage in leisure-time physical activity if they perceived their neighborhood as predominantly Black. As such, it appears that middle class Black women were less likely to participate in physical activity because of concerns regarding safety. This finding speaks to how both the structural reality of lower levels of safety and the perception of danger both impact the decision-making process of exercising among Black women. On the other hand, the same study found that Black men were *less* likely to be physically active in neighborhoods they perceived as predominantly White, which is likely linked to the hyper-surveillance of Black men in these spaces and potential for harassment by law enforcement.

Stress Exposure. Stress refers to "socio-environmental demands that tax or exceed individual's ordinary capacity to adapt" or "the absence of the means to attain sought-after ends" (Pearlin and Bierman 2013: 326). Consistent with stress theory's prediction that individuals of lower status will experience greater stress exposure (Pearlin and Bierman 2013), Black Americans report higher levels of generalized stress than their White counterparts, and in turn, stress contributes to explaining Black-White health differentials (Sternthal et al. 2011). The most commonly studied stressor as it pertains to African American health is racial discrimination. We view racial discrimination as a structural reality sourced in racism and enacted within and across social institutions (e.g. K-12 education, in the workplace), reinforced by social policies that disproportionately target racial and ethnic minorities (e.g. the "War on Drugs"), and sedimented as a normative, but often invisible, feature of contemporary U.S. society (Jones 2000). Nevertheless, the extant literature centers on the perceptual and interpersonal dimensions of racial discrimination. The everyday and major discrimination scales are the most widely used in the sociological literature (Williams et al. 1997).[3] These scales include several items to ascertain perceptions of unfair treatment across various social contexts such as being followed in stores, not receiving a promotion at work, and being unfairly denied a loan (Williams et al. 1997).

Perceived discrimination is associated with an array of physical health outcomes including self-rated health, all-cause mortality, hypertension, asthma, breast cancer, and inflammation (Christie-Mizell, Leslie, and Hearne 2017; Bratter and Gorman 2011; Cobb et al. 2020; Lewis et al. 2015). A recent review of the literature on stress-related biosocial mechanisms of discrimination and African American health by Goosby et al. (2018) suggests that interpersonal racism experienced regularly by African Americans often become embodied and increase cardiovascular "wear and tear" over the life course. Not only is experiencing racial discrimination associated with poor health for African Americans (Monk 2015), but reporting multiple forms of discrimination (e.g. on the basis of race, gender, and sexuality) is more harmful to health than experiencing one discrimination form (Grollman 2012).

Relatedly, some recent work has shown that police contact can be a source of stress for Black Americans. Perception of unfairness in interactions with police serves as an exemplar of a perceptual measure that is rooted in a broader structural reality of racial bias (i.e. anti-blackness) among police officers. This source of stress may be especially heightened in the context of increased media attention on the deaths of unarmed Black Americans at the hands of law enforcement officers tasked with the responsibility of protecting (not killing) the citizenry. In a Nashville-based study, McFarland and colleagues (2018) found that Black men were three times more likely to report both personal and vicarious unfair treatment by police than their White male counterparts. The study also identified a positive association between perceived unfair treatment by police and shortened telomere length, a stress-related indicator of biological aging, among Black men but not White men. That exposure to problematic interactions with police can affect Blacks on a physiological level is tragic.

While Black men appear particularly vulnerable to negative interactions with law enforcement, Black women with children disproportionately experience parental stress (compared to White mothers) (Nomaguchi and House 2013). These stressors include giving up more of life than expected to care for the child, behavioral problems in the child, and anger with the child. The parental stress

Black mothers feel increases in the years between the child being enrolled in kindergarten through third grade (Nomaguchi and House 2013). More work is needed to assess whether this source of parental role strain is linked to the physical health profiles of Black women.

While discrimination is the most widely studied stressor among African Americans, other stressors have gained traction in the literature. For example, goal-striving stress refers to "the discrepancy between aspirations and achievement, weighted by the subjective probability of success and the level of disappointment experienced if goals are not reached" (Sellers and Neighbors 2008; Sellers et al. 2012). Sellers and colleagues (2012) found that goal striving success was associated with hypertension, higher BMI, physical conditions, and diminished self-rated health among Blacks and Whites. A more recent study established a positive association between high levels of goal-striving stress and chronic kidney disease among Blacks residing in Jackson, Mississippi (Cain et al. 2019). This stress exposure attempts to capture the near universal desire to obtain the American ideals of success and achievement; thus, goal-striving may make Black Americans particularly vulnerable, as they face a variety of structural barriers and constraints that often prohibit them from fully realizing the coveted American dream. Relatedly, as Black Americans attempt to identify approaches to coping with stress exposures, their health may be further compromised. For example, Black American men of lower socioeconomic position who engage in high effort coping characterized by determination, persistence, and hard work (i.e., John Henryism) experience higher rates of hypertension (Subramanyan et al. 2013).

The weathering hypothesis suggests that continuous exposure to stress (and having to cope with stress) from birth through mid-life creates a health vulnerability for Black women that increases their chances of their children experiencing low birth weight and early life mortality; this health vulnerability is especially salient in the 20s through early 30s, an age-at-birth that is considered most socially normative (Geronimus 1992). Though originally applied to birth outcomes among Black women, the weathering hypothesis has more recently been applied to understanding physical health disparities across the life course for women and men of different racial groups. The biological impact of chronic stress exposure can, in fact, accelerate aging among Black and other minority populations (Geronimus et al. 2006). Even in childhood (between ages 2 and 10), Blacks experience biological manifestations of stress (e.g. low grade inflammation) at a greater rate relative to Whites (Schmeer and Jacob 2018).

Given higher mortality rates of Black Americans, recent work has also called attention to how familial loss may also indicate stress exposure due to the loss of social support and, potentially, financial support. The loss of a relative or child disproportionately befalls Black Americans; in addition, these experiences of death tend to occur much earlier in the life course (e.g. prior to the age of 30) for Blacks than Whites (Umberson 2017). That this unique source of social disadvantage is more likely to occur among Black Americans suggests that it could instigate racial health disparities.

Psychosocial Resources. Despite disproportionately higher levels of stress exposure, Black Americans also possess psychosocial resources that are, under some circumstances, health-protective. Though psychosocial resources do not tend to explain health differences *between* Blacks and Whites, they can be salubrious for Blacks and may thus provide insight for prevention and intervention programs. Widely studied resources in sociological research include self-concept (e.g. self-esteem, mastery), coping, and social support (Pearlin and Bierman 2013). Other relevant psychosocial resources for Black Americans include religiosity (Taylor et al. 2012) and racial identity (Christie-Mizell et al. 2017). Due to space constraints, we focus our comments on social support. Social support from family members is especially critical for African Americans, as it is associated with lower arterial blood pressure (Dressler and Bindon 2000), higher self-rated health (Erving 2018), as well as fewer chronic and acute health conditions (Erving 2018). Kin support is also positively associated with mammography screening (Kang and Bloom 1993), occult blood stool examination (Kang and Bloom 1993), and smoking cessation (Lacey et al. 1993). As such, it appears that social support from relatives profoundly influences health as well as encourages health care utilization for Black Americans. Nevertheless, the "dark side" of social relationships can be detrimental to physical health, particularly negative interactions with family members (Erving 2018) and low romantic relationship quality (Barr et al. 2013). The depletion of social support via the death of a spouse also adversely affects health, though the health effect of widowhood tends to be more pronounced among Whites (Dupre 2016; Elwert and Christakis 2006). Overall, more research is necessary to ascertain the extent to which psychosocial resources can mitigate the negative impact of stress exposure on the physical health of African Americans.

Health Patterns within the Black American Population

Over the past twenty years, our knowledge of the underlying explanations for Blacks' poor health has increased. More research, however, is needed, as some explanations are found wanting. As opposed to a racial group comparison approach (e.g. Black-White differences), more intra-racial research is needed to examine the unique determinants of Blacks' health. In fact, an intersectional perspective argues that we cannot adequately understand the health of Black Americans without examining how racialized oppression intersects with other stratification systems including, but not limited to, socioeconomic status (SES), gender, nativity, ethnicity, and sexual orientation (Brown et al. 2016; Collins 2019; Gómez and López 2013). Below, we provide a brief overview of these status variations in Blacks' health in hopes of infusing additional nuance into the discussion surrounding African American health.

Socioeconomic Status

Consistent with a social stratification perspective, higher SES individuals (e.g., college educated, higher income, and occupational prestige) are in better health than their lower SES counterparts. This association is more equivocal among African Americans. Turner, Hale, and Brown (2017) showed, on one hand, that income was inversely associated with chronic conditions for Blacks. On the other hand, there was no significant association between several SES indicators (e.g. education, occupational prestige, wealth, childhood SES) and health (i.e. chronic conditions, allostatic load).

Consistent with the broader literature, higher SES was consistently associated with improved health among White Americans. These results lend empirical support to the notion that the health returns to higher socioeconomic achievement is a given for Whites and negligible for African Americans. Furthermore, unique stressors associated with middle class status for Black Americans prevent them from fully enjoying the benefits of economic privilege (Jackson and Stewart 2003; Thomas 2015).

Gender

Black women tend to be in poorer health than their male counterparts (Erving 2011; Read and Gorman 2006). For example, Read and Gorman (2006) showed that Black women experienced more functional limitations and were more likely to report their health as fair or poor relative to Black men, even after adjustments for SES, health behaviors, and health care access. A major limitation of survey data, however, is the use of community samples which yields an undercount of the Black male population due to their relatively high institutionalization rates in the racially biased U.S. carceral system (Patterson and Wildeman 2015). There are also unique sources of disadvantage relevant to Black women. For example, they have the highest maternal mortality rates of any racial group in the U.S.; in fact, the rate at which Black women die during childbirth is closer to the maternal mortality rates of upper-middle income countries such as Brazil, Botswana, South Africa, Venezuela, and Turkey (Novoa and Taylor 2018). Also, Black women are more likely to have cesarean births which are associated with negative outcomes for both the mother and the child (Roth and Henley 2012). Compared to their White female counterparts, Black women are also less likely to receive medical services when experiencing infertility, even after adjusting for income, education, and private insurance status (Greil et al. 2011).

Nativity and Ethnicity

The increasing U.S. Black immigrant population has changed what it means to be Black in the U.S. (Anderson and López 2018; Hamilton 2019). The growth of the Black immigrant population has precipitated more ethnic diversity among Black Americans, with half of Black immigrants hailing from Caribbean area countries and 39% having origins in sub-Saharan African nations (Anderson and López 2018). Due to concerted data collection efforts capturing ethnic diversity within the Black American population, we know much more about the health and social experiences of Blacks of Caribbean descent compared to African immigrants. The advent of the National Survey of American Life (NSAL) in particular provided sufficient sample size for meaningful analyses of Blacks of Caribbean descent. We recognize significant ethnic diversity among "Caribbean Blacks" and "Africans" as these pan-ethnic categories represent over 26 countries in the Caribbean region and 46 countries in the sub-Saharan African region, respectively.

On average, Black immigrants have better physical health and lower mortality relative to U.S.-born African Americans (Hamilton 2014; Read and Emerson 2005). Furthermore, African immigrants are in relatively better health than Caribbean-born Black immigrants (Hamilton and Hummer 2011; Read and Emerson 2005). In addition, increased length of time in the U.S. is associated with a decline in self-rated health for Caribbean-born immigrants but an *increase* in self-rated health among African-born immigrants (Hamilton 2019). Consistent with the broader immigrant health literature, second-generation Caribbean Blacks experienced relatively higher rates of cardiovascular, respiratory, and pain-related conditions relative to their first-generation co-ethnic counterparts (Carlisle 2012). A jarring transition occurs among the children of Black immigrants: by the second generation, the health of Black "ethnics" mirrors those of African Americans (Erving 2011). This transition to poor health is, at least in part, attributable to negative acculturation (e.g. the adoption of negative health behaviors such as smoking) as well as anti-Blackness and racial inequality in the American milieu.

Sexual Minority Status

Examinations of the intersections of race, gender identity, and sexuality among Black Americans and how their unique social location shapes health is a small but growing research area. Much of the work on sexual minority health does not take into account how the experience of LGBTQIA + status (i.e. lesbian, gay, bisexual, transgender/trans, queer or questioning, intersex, asexual, and agender)[4] is also complicated by other social statuses, particularly race. Among sexual minorities, Black and Latinx queer or gender non-conforming individuals report the highest prevalence of lifetime suicide attempts (Meyer et al. 2008; O'Donnell, Meyer, and Schwartz 2011) and Black nongender conforming individuals, particularly Black transwomen, are increasingly subject to interpersonal violence and subsequent institutional and state devaluation of their lives (Dinno 2017; Teal 2015). In fact, the average life expectancy for a Black transwoman is 35 years (Vincent 2017).

Recent research exploring Black LGBT health has shown the divergence of health outcomes and barriers to health care access for Black members of the LGBT community. Black gay and bisexual men report feeling marginalized and blamed for these health disparities by U.S. medical practitioners (Bryant 2016). Battle and colleagues (2013) show that having a regular physician is important for older Black gay men in maintaining their overall mental health. Relatedly, Ortiz et al. (2016) find that Black lesbian and bisexual women have lower prevalence of "excellent" self-rated physical health compared to Black gay men, and not having a medical healthcare provider was a factor that negatively impacted their self-rated health. Additionally, being single was positively related to self-rated health for Black LGBT women, while Black LGBT men's self-rated health benefitted from at least some college education (Ortiz et al. 2016). Black trans men experience chronic illnesses such as recurrent tendonitis, migraine headaches, diabetes, and depression at disproportionately high rates (Poteat and Follins 2016), and many trans men also report structural barriers such as lack of health insurance and economic difficulties that keep them from receiving treatment for chronic conditions. Lassiter's (2016) systematic literature review on Black bisexual health revealed that Black bisexual women experienced a range of physical and mental health conditions (e.g. STIs, reproductive coercion, depression, posttraumatic stress disorder) more than their heterosexual counterparts. Unfortunately, much of the sociological research examining the health of Black LGBTQIA + individuals is published in journals outside of the discipline, and most commonly in public health and social work. While it is encouraging that research on the health of Black sexual minorities is being conducted, this revelation suggests that mainstream medical sociology should include Black LGBTQIA + populations in explorations of Black Americans' health.

Is Mental Health an Exception to the Rule?

Despite historic and contemporary discrimination as well as disproportionate exposure to stress and economic disadvantage, African Americans experience similar or lower rates of mental disorder vis-à-vis White Americans. Often referred to as the Black-White Mental Health Paradox, sociological research in this area has sought to identifying explanatory mechanisms underlying this paradox including social support (Kiecolt, Hughes, and Keith 2008; Mouzon 2013, 2014), emotional reliance (Erving and Thomas 2018), resilience (Keyes 2009), and self-esteem (Louie and Wheaton 2019). These explanations have fallen short, with some scholars critiquing the Eurocentric measures of mental health in the Diagnostic and Statistical Manual of Mental Disorders (DSM) (Brown 2003) and developing race-specific mental health problems that fall outside of traditional psychiatric disorders (e.g. suppressed anger exppression or extreme racial paranoia; see Brown 2003). Thus, measurement bias may undercount mental health prevalence among Black Americans. Alternatively, perhaps it is problematic to assume poor mental health among Black Americans, as this group has made strides in various social domains *in spite of* institutional and interpersonal racism.

Despite overall lower rates of mental disorder among Blacks, relative to Whites, they are also more likely to be misdiagnosed with serious mental health problems like schizophrenia (Neighbors et al. 2003). This reflects a racial bias in clinician assessments whereby patients exhibiting similar symptomatology receive differential diagnosis by race. Given the standardization of diagnostic criteria for mental disorders as outlined in the DSM, this racial bias is particularly problematic and somewhat surprising. Access to quality mental health care is also an issue facing even the most high status Black Americans. For example, an audit study assessing potential race, class, and gender distinctions in access to mental health care (operationalized as being offered an appointment with a psychotherapist) found that White middle class help seekers (28%) were more likely to be offered an appointment with a psychotherapist than Black middle class help seekers (17%) (Kugelmass 2016). Overall, the literature lends empirical support for a mental health advantage in an epidemiological sense, but a mental health care access and utilization disadvantage among Blacks relative to Whites.

Conclusion

As we enter the third decade of the twenty-first century, Blacks and Whites in the U.S. still experience unequal social worlds that, in turn, sustain health disparities. As this chapter suggests, sociology and other related disciplines are amassing an impressive knowledge base regarding the social and environmental factors contributing to African American health. Nevertheless, thoughtful integration of sociological theories and perspectives from multiple research areas will provide a more robust understanding of health disparities. For example, stress theory in combination with health lifestyles and the cumulative disadvantage perspective may illuminate the interrelationships among stress exposure, health behaviors, and social disadvantage over the life course and how they collectively impinge on the health of Black Americans.

Despite the focus on African Americans in this chapter, the lives of Blacks and Whites are inextricably linked by their coexistence and interdependence in the U.S. As Dubois (1906) eloquently stated, "The health of the whole country depends in no little degree upon the health of Negroes." As such, the health of African Americans is a *national* public health issue. To improve the health of African Americans, the health care system remains a key institution in which to address health care disparities. Perhaps more critically, social policies are needed to dismantle inequality in America's social institutions such as the criminal justice system and de facto segregation in residential areas and public schools.

Notes

1 There is cause for some optimism. The Black-White gap in all-cause mortality narrowed considerably between 1999 (33%) and 2015 (16%) (Cunningham et al. 2017).

2 For a comprehensive discussion of racial disparities in healthcare, see the Institute of Medicine's 2002 report *Unequal Treatment: Confronting Racial and Ethnic Disparities in Health Care.*

3 There is, however, some gender bias in this measure, which underestimates discrimination for Black women (Harnois and Ifatunji 2011).

4 The LGBTQIA + acronym is ever-changing, as well as what sexual identity each letter represents. For more insights on LGBTQIA + sexual identities, see Human Rights Campaign (2020).

References

Anderson, Kathryn Freeman. 2017. "Racial Residential Segregation and the Distribution of Health-related Organizations in Urban Neighborhoods." *Social Problems* 64(2): 256–76.

Anderson, M. and G. López. 2018. "Key Facts about Black Immigrants in the U.S." Pew Research Center. Retrieved from http://www.pewresearch.org/fact-tank/2018/01/24/key-facts-about-black-immigrants-in-the-u-s.

Arcaya, Mariana C., Reginald D. Tucker-Seeley, Rockli Kim, Alina Schnake-Mahl, So Marvin, and S. V. Subramanian. 2016. "Research on Neighborhood Effects on Health in the United States: A Systematic Review of Study Characteristics." *Social Science & Medicine* 168: 16–29.

Arias, Elizabeth and Xu Jiaquan. 2019. "United States Life Tables, 2017." *National Vital Statistics Reports* 68(7).

Barr, Ashley B., Leslie Gordon Simons, Ronald L. Simons, and Steven R. H. Beach. 2018. "Sharing the Burden of the Transition to Adulthood: African American Young Ad ults' Transition Challenges and Their Mothers' Health Risk." *American Sociological Review* 83(1): 143–72.

Barr, Ashley B., Elizabeth Culatta, and Ronald L. Simons. 2013."Romantic Relationships and Health among African American Young Adults: Linking Patterns of Relationship Quality over Time to Changes in Physical and Mental Health." *Journal of Health and Social Behavior* 54(3): 369–85.

Battle, Juan, Jessie Daniels, Antonio Pastrana Jr, Carlene Buchanan Turner, and Alexis Espinoza. 2013. "Never Too Old to Feel Good: Happiness and Health among a National Sample of Older Black Gay Men." *Spectrum: A Journal on Black Men* 2(1): 1–18.

Boardman, Jason D., Jarron M. Saint Onge, Richard G. Rogers, and Justin T. Denney. 2005. "Race Differentials in Obesity: The Impact of Place." *Journal of Health and Social Behavior* 46(3): 229–43.

Boen, Courtney. 2016. "The Role of Socioeconomic Factors in Black-White Health Inequities across the Life Course: Point-In-Time Measures, Long-Term Exposures, and Differential Health Returns." *Social Science & Medicine* 170: 63–76.

Bonczar, Thomas P. 2003. *Prevalence of Imprisonment in the U.S. Population, 1974–2001* Washington, DC: U.S. Department of Justice. Bureau of Justice Statistics Special Report.

Bratter, Jenifer L. and Bridget K. Gorman. 2011. "Is Discrimination an Equal Opportunity Risk? Racial Experiences, Socioeconomic Status, and Health Status among Black and White Adults." *Journal of Health and Social Behavior* 52(3): 365–82.

Brown, Tony N. 2003. "Critical Race Theory Speaks to the Sociology of Mental Health: Mental Health Problems Produced by Racial Stratification." *Journal of Health and Social Behavior* 44(3): 292–301.

Brown, Tyson H. 2018. "Racial Stratification, Immigration, and Health Inequality: A Life Course-Intersectional Approach." Social Forces 96(4): 1507–1539.

Brown, Tyson H., Angela M. O'Rand, and Daniel E. Adkins. 2012. "Race-ethnicity and Health Trajectories: Tests of Three Hypotheses across Multiple Groups and Health Outcomes." *Journal of Health and Social Behavior* 53(3): 359–77.

Brown, Tyson H., Liana J. Richardson, Taylor W. Hargrove, and Courtney S. Thomas. 2016. "Using Multiple-hierarchy Stratification to Understand Health Inequalities: The Intersecting Consequences of Race, Gender, SES, and Age." *Journal of Health and Social Behavior* 57(2): 200–22.

Bryant, Dante' D. 2016. "Status Quo: Intersectionality Theory, Afrocentric Paradigms, and Meeting the Healthcare Needs of Gay and Bisexual African American Men." Pp. 121–36 in *Black LGBT Health in the United States: The Intersection of Race, Gender, and Sexual Orientation* edited by L.D. Follins and J. M. Lassiter. Lanham, MD: Lexington Books.

Cain, Loretta R., LáShauntá Glover, Bessie Young, and Mario Sims. 2019. "Goal-striving Stress Is Associated with Chronic Kidney Disease among Participants in the Jackson Heart Study." *Journal of Racial and Ethnic Health Disparities* 6(1): 64–69.

Campaign Human Rights. 2020. Glossary of Terms. Retrieved 4/14/20 at https://www.hrc.org/resources/glossary-of-terms

Carlisle, Shauna K. 2012. "Nativity Differences in Chronic Health Conditions Etween Nationally Representative Samples of Asian American, Latino American, and Afro-Caribbean American Respondents." *Journal of Immigrant and Minority Health* 14(6): 903–11.

Chang, Virginia W., Amy E. Hillier, and Neil K. Mehta. 2009. "Neighborhood Racial Isolation, Disorder and Obesity." *Social Forces* 87(4): 2063–92.

Cheng, Simon, Laura Hamilton, Stacy Missari, and Josef (Kuo-Hsun) Ma. 2014. "Sexual Subjectivity among Adolescent Girls: Social Disadvantage and Young Adult Outcomes." *Social Forces* 93(2): 515–44.

Christie-Mizell, André, Erika T. A. Leslie, and Brittany N. Hearne. 2017. "Self-rated Health, Discrimination, and Racial Group Identity: The Consequences of Ethnicity and Nativity among Black Americans." *Journal of African American Studies* 21: 643–64.

Cobb, Ryon J., Lauren J. Parker, and Roland J. Thorpe. 2020. "Self-reported Instances of Major Discrimination, Race/Ethnicity, and Inflammation among Older Adults: Evidence from the Health and Retirement Study." *The Journals of Gerontology, Series A* 75(2): 291–96.

Cockerham, William C., Bryant W. Shawn Bauldry, James M. Shikany Hamby, and Sejong Bae. 2017. "A Comparison of Black and White Racial Differences in Health Lifestyles and Cardiovascular Disease." *American Journal of Preventive Medicine* 52(S1): S56–S62.

Collins, Patricia Hill. 2019. *Intersectionality as Critical Social Theory*. Durham, NC: Duke University Press.

Cooksey-Stowers, Kristen, Marlene B. Schwartz, and Kelly D. Brownell. 2017. "Food Swamps Predict Obesity Rates Better than Food Deserts in the United States." *International Journal of Environmental Research and Public Health* 14(11): 1366–86.

Coverdill, James E., Carlos A. Lopez, and Michelle A. Petrie. 2011. "Race, Ethnicity and the Quality of Life in America, 1972–2008." *Social Forces* 89(3): 783–806.

Cunningham, Timothy J., Janet B. Croft, Yong Liu, Lu Hua, Paul I. Eke, and Wayne H. Giles. 2017. "Vital Signs: Racial Disparities in Age-specific Mortality among Blacks or African Americans–United States, 1999-2015." *MMWR* 66 (17): 444–56.

Danya, Lagos. 2019. "Hearing Gender: Voice-Based Gender Classification Processes and Transgender Health Inequality." *American Sociological Review* 84(5): 801–27.

Dinno, Alexis. 2017. "Homicide Rates of Transgender Individuals in the United States: 2010–2014." *American Journal of Public Health* 107(9): 1441–47.

Dressler, William W. and James R. Bindon. 2000. "The Health Consequences of Cultural Consonance: Cultural Dimensions of Lifestyle, Social Support, and Arterial Blood Pressure in an African American Community." *American Anthropologist* 102(2): 244–60.

DuBois, William and Edward Burghardt. 1906. *The Health and Physique of the Negro American*. Atlanta, GA: Atlanta University Press.

Dupre, Matthew E. 2016. "Race, Marital History, and Risks for Stroke in U.S. Older Adults." *Social Forces* 95(1): 439–68.

Elman, Cheryl, Robert A. McGuire, and Andrew S. London. 2019. "Disease, Plantation Development, and Race-Related Differences in Fertility in the Early Twentieth-Century American South." *American Journal of Sociology* 124(5): 1327–71.

Elwert, Felix and Nicholas A. Christakis. 2006. "Widowhood and Race." *American Sociological Review* 71(1): 16–41.

Erving, Christy L. 2011. "Gender and Physical Health: A Study of African American and Caribbean Black Adults." *Journal of Health and Social Behavior* 52(3): 383–99.

Erving, Christy L. 2018. "Ethnic and Nativity Differences in the Social Support-Physical Health Association among Black Americans." *Journal of Immigrant and Minority Health* 20(1): 124–39.

Erving, Christy L. and Courtney S. Thomas. 2018. "Race, Emotional Reliance, and Mental Health." *Society and Mental Health* 8(1): 69–83.

Fauth, Rebecca C., Tama Leventhal, and Jeanne Brooks-Gunn. 2008. "Seven Years Later: Effects of a Neighborhood Mobility Program on Poor Black and Latino Adults' Well-being." *Journal of Health and Social Behavior* 49(2): 119–30.

Ferraro, Kenneth F. and Tetyana Pylypiv Shippee. 2008. "Black and White Chains of Risk for Hospitalization over 20 Years." *Journal of Health and Social Behavior* 49(2): 193–207.

Geronimus, Arline T. 1992. "The Weathering Hypothesis and the Health of African-American Women and Infants: Evidence and Speculations." *Ethnicity & Disease* 2(3): 207–21.

Geronimus, Arline T., Margaret Hicken, Danya Keene, and John Bound. 2006. ""Weathering" and Age Patterns of Allostatic Load Scores among Blacks and Whites in the United States." *American Journal of Public Health* 96(5): 826–33.

Ghosh-Dastidar, Bonnie, Deborah Cohen, Shannon N. Gerald Hunter, Christina Huang Zenk, Robin Beckman, and Tamara Dubowitz. 2014. "Distance to Store, Food Prices, and Obesity in Urban Food Deserts." *American Journal of Preventive Medicine* 47(5): 587–95.

Gómez, Laura E. and Nancy López. 2013. *Mapping "Race": Critical Approaches to Health Disparities Research.* New Brunswick, NJ: Rutgers University Press.

Goosby, Bridget J., Jacob E. Cheadle, and Colter Mitchell. 2018. "Stress-related Biosocial Mechanisms of Discrimination and African American Health Inequities." *Annual Review of Sociology* 44: 319–40.

Greil, Arthur L., Julia McQuillan, Karina M. Shreffler, Katherine M. Johnson, and Kathleen S. Slauson-Blevins. 2011. "Race-Ethnicity and Medical Services for Infertility: Stratified Reproduction in a Population-based Sample of U.S. Women." *Journal of Health and Social Behavior* 52(4): 493–509.

Grollman, Eric Anthony. 2012. "Multiple Forms of Perceived Discrimination and Health among Adolescents and Young Adults." *Journal of Health and Social Behavior* 53(2): 199–214.

Hamilton, Tod G. 2014. "Do Country-of-Origin Characteristics Help Explain Variation in Health among Black Immigrants in the United States?" *Social Science Quarterly* 95(3): 817–34.

Hamilton, Tod G. 2019. *Immigration and the Remaking of Black America.* New York: Russell Sage Foundation.

Hamilton, Tod G. and Robert A. Hummer. 2011. "Immigration and the Health of US Black Adults: Does Country of Origin Matter?" *Social Science & Medicine* 73(10): 1551–60.

Hargrove, Taylor W. 2018. "Intersecting Social Inequalities and Body Mass Index Trajectories from Adolescence to Early Adulthood." *Journal of Health and Social Behavior* 59(1): 56–73.

Harnois, Catherine E. and Mosi Ifatunji. 2011. "Gendered Measures, Gendered Models: Toward an Intersectional Analysis of Interpersonal Racial Discrimination." *Ethnic and Racial Studies* 34(6): 1006–28.

Hayward, Mark D. and Bridget K. Gorman. 2004. "The Long Armof Childhood: The Influence of Early-Life Social Conditions on Men's Mortality." *Demography* 41: 87–107.

Hayward, Mark D., Toni P. Miles, Eileen M. Crimmins, and Yu Yang. 2000. "The Significance of Socioeconomic Status in Explaining The Racial Gap in Chronic Health Conditions." *American Sociological Review* 65(6): 910–30.

Jackson, Pamela Braboy and Quincy Thomas Stewart. 2003. "A Research Agenda for the Black Middle Class: Work Stress, Survival Strategies, and Mental Health." *Journal of Health and Social Behavior* 44: 442–55.

Jay, Turner, R., Tony N. Brown, and William Beardall Hale. 2017. "Race, Socioeconomic Position, and Physical Health: A Descriptive Analysis." *Journal of Health and Social Behavior* 58(1): 23–36.

Jennifer, Bronson and E. Ann. Carson. 2019. *"Prisoners in 2017."* Washington, DC: Bureau of Justice Statistics.

Jones, Camara Phyllis. 2000. "Levels of Racism: A Theoretic Framework and A Gardner's Tale." *American Journal of Public Health* 90(8): 1212–15.

Kang, Soo Hyang and Joan R. Bloom. 1993. "Social Support and Cancer Screening among Older Black Americans." *JNCI: Journal of the National Cancer Institute* 85(9): 737–42.

Keyes, Corey L. M. 2009. "The Black–White Paradox in Health: Flourishing in the Face of Social Inequality and Discrimination." *Journal of Personality* 77(6): 1677–706.

Kiecolt, Jill, K., Michael Hughes, and Verna M. Keith. 2008. "Race, Social Relationships, and Mental Health." *Personal Relationships* 15(2): 229–45.

Kravitz-Wirtz, Nicole. 2016. "Cumulative Effects of Growing up in Separate and Unequal Neighborhoods on Racial Disparities in Self-Rated Health in Early Adulthood." *Journal of Health and Social Behavior* 57(4): 453–70.

Kugelmass, Heather. 2016. "'Sorry, I'm Not Accepting New Patients': An Audit Study of Access to Mental Health Care." *Journal of Health and Social Behavior* 57(2): 168–83.

Kwate, Naa, A. Oyo, and Ilan H. Meyer. 2009. "Association between Residential Exposure to Outdoor Alcohol Advertising and Problem Drinking among African American Women in New York City." *American Journal of Public Health* 99(2): 228–30.

Lacey, Loretta P., Clara Manfredi, Richard B. George Balch, Karen Allen Warnecke, and Constance Edwards. 1993."Social Support in Smoking Cessation among Black Women in Chicago Public Housing." *Public Health Reports* 108(3): 387–94

Lassiter, Jonathan Mathias. 2016. "Black Bisexual Women's Health in the United States: A Systematic Literature Review." Pp. 25–38 in *Black LGBT Health in the United States: The Intersection of Race, Gender, and Sexual Orientation*, edited by L. D. Follins and J. M. Lassiter. Lanham, MD: Lexington Books.

LaVeist, Thomas A. and Amani Nuru-Jeter. 2002. "Is Doctor-Patient Race Concordance Associated with Greater Satisfaction with Care?" *Journal of Health and Social Behavior* 43(3): 296–306.

Lee, Hedwig and Christopher Wildeman. 2013. "Things Fall Apart: Health Consequences of Mass Imprisonment for African American Women." *The Review of Black Political Economy* 40(1): 39–52.

Lee, Joseph G. L., Shyanika W. Rose Lisa Henriksen, Sarah Moreland-Russell, and Kurt M. Ribisl. 2015. "A Systematic Review of Neighborhood Disparities in Point-Of-Sale Tobacco Marketing." *American Journal of Public Health* 105(9): e8–e18.

Lewis, Tené T., Courtney D. Cogburn, and David R. Williams. 2015. "Self-reported Experiences of Discrimination and Health: Scientific Advances, Ongoing Controversies, and Emerging Issues." *Annual Review of Clinical Psychology* 11: 407–40.

Louie, Patricia and Blair Wheaton. 2019. "The Black-White Paradox Revisited: Understanding the Role of Counterbalancing Mechanisms during Adolescence." *Journal of Health and Social Behavior* 60(2): 169–87.

Malat, Jennifer. 2001. "Social Distance and Patients' Rating of Healthcare Providers." *Journal of Health and Social Behavior* 42(4): 360–72.

Malat, Jennifer and Mary Ann Hamilton. 2006. "Preference for Same-Race Health Care Providers and Perceptions of Interpersonal Discrimination in Health Care." *Journal of Health and Social Behavior* 47(2): 173–87.

Massey, Douglas S. and Jonathan Tannen. 2015. "A Research Note on Trends in Black Hypersegregation." *Social Forces* 52: 1025–34.

Massey, Douglas S. and Jonathan Tannen. 2016. "Segregation, Race, and the Social Worlds of Rich and Poor." Pp. 13–33 in *The Dynamics of Opportunity in America: Evidence and Perspectives*, edited by I. Kirsch and H. Braun. New York: Educational Testing Service.

McFarland, Michael J., John Taylor, Cheryl AS McFarland, and Katherine L. Friedman. 2018. "Perceived Unfair Treatment by Police, Race, and Telomere Length: A Nashville Community-Based Sample of Black and White Men." *Journal of Health and Social Behavior* 59(4): 585–600.

McKane, Rachel G., Lacee A. Satcher, Stacey L. Houston, and David J. Hess. 2018. "Race, Class, and Space: An Intersectional Approach to Environmental Justice in New York City." *Environmental Sociology* 4(1): 79–92.

McKee, Pat, Rhonda Jones-Webb, Peter Hannan, and Lan Pham. 2011. "Malt Liquor Marketing in Inner Cities: The Role of Neighborhood Racial Composition." *Journal of Ethnicity in Substance Abuse* 10(1): 24–38.

McLeod, Jane D., Christy Erving, and Jennifer Caputo. 2014. "Health Inequalities." Pp. 715–42 in *Handbook of the Social Psychology of Inequality*, edited by J. D. McLeod, E. J. Lawler, and M. Schwalbe. New York: Springer.

Meyer, Ilan H., Jessica Dietrich, and Sharon Schwartz. 2008. "Lifetime Prevalence of Mental Disorders and Suicide Attempts in Diverse Lesbian, Gay, and Bisexual Populations." *American Journal of Public Health* 98(6): 1004–06.

Monk, Ellis P. 2015. "The Cost of Color: Skin Color, Discrimination, and Health among African-Americans." *American Journal of Sociology* 121(2): 396–444.

Mouzon, Dawne M. 2013. "Can Family Relationships Explain the Race Paradox in Mental Health?" *Journal of Marriage and Family* 75(2): 470–85.

Mouzon, Dawne M. 2014. "Relationships of Choice: Can Friendships or Fictive Kinships Explain the Race Paradox in Mental Health?" *Social Science Research* 44: 32–43.

Neighbors, Harold W., Steven J. Trierweiler, Briggett C. Ford, and Jordana R. Muroff. 2003. "Racial Differences in DSM Diagnosis Using A Semi-Structured Instrument: The Importance of Clinical Judgment in the Diagnosis of African Americans." *Journal of Health and Social Behavior* 44(3): 237–56.

Nomaguchi, Kei and Amanda N. House. 2013. "Racial-ethnic Disparities in Maternal Parenting Stress: The Role of Structural Disadvantages and Parenting Values." *Journal of Health and Social Behavior* 54(3): 386–404.

Novoa, Cristina and Jamila Taylor. 2018. "Exploring African Americans' High Maternal and Infant Death Rates." *Center for American Progress*. Retrieved online 3/15/20 at: https://www.americanprogress.org/issues/early-childhood/reports/2018/02/01/445576/exploring-african-americans-high-maternal-infant-death-rates

O'Donnell, Shannon, Ilan H. Meyer, and Sharon Schwartz. 2011. "Increased Risk of Suicide Attempts among Black and Latino Lesbians, Gay Men, and Bisexuals." *American Journal of Public Health* 101(6): 1055–59.

Ortiz, Kasim, Angelique Harris, Kenneth Maurice Pass, and Devon Tyrone Wade. 2016. "Perceptions of Health: Self-Rated Health among Black LGB People." Pp. 185–202 in *Black LGBT Health in the United States: The Intersection of Race, Gender, and Sexual Orientation*, edited by L. D. Follins and J. M. Lassiter. Lanham, MD: Lexington Books.

Pampel, Fred C. 2009. "The Persistence of Educational Disparities in Smoking." *Social Problems* 56(3): 526–542.

Pampel, Fred C. 2008. "Racial Convergence in Cigarette Use from Adolescence to the Mid-Thirties." *Journal of Health and Social Behavior* 49(4): 484–98.

Patterson, Evelyn J. 2013. "Life on the inside and Death on the Outside: Complexities in Health Disparities inside and outside U.S. Prisons." *Prison Legal News* 24(4): 24–25.

Patterson, Evelyn J. and Christopher Wildeman. 2015. "Mass Imprisonment and the Life Course Revisited: Cumulative Years Spent Imprisoned and Marked for Working-Age Black and White Men." *Social Science Research* 53: 325–37.

Pearlin, Leonard I. and Alex Bierman. 2013. "Current Issues and Future Directions in Research into the Stress Process." Pp. 325–40 in *Handbook of the Sociology of Mental Health, Second Edition*, edited by C. S. Aneshensel, J. C. Phelan, and A. Bierman. Dordrecht: Springer.

Phillips, Aryn Z. and Hector P. Rodriguez. 2019. "Adults with Diabetes Residing in 'Food Swamps' Have Higher Hospitalization Rates." *Health Services Research* 54: 217–25.

Polonijo, Andrea N., Richard M. Carpiano, Paul L. Reiter, and Noel T. Brewer. 2016. "Socioeconomic and Racial-Ethnic Disparities in Prosocial Health Attitudes: The Case of Human Papillomavirus (HPV) Vaccination for Adolescent Males." *Journal of Health and Social Behavior* 57(3): 390–406.

Poteat, Tonia C. and Lourdes Dolores Follins. 2016. "Narratives of Health among Black Trans Men: An Exploratory Intersectional Analysis." Pp. 73–85 in *Black LGBT Health in the United States: The Intersection of Race, Gender, and Sexual Orientation*, edited by L.D. Follins and J. M. Lassiter. Lanham, MD: Lexington Books.

Ray, Rashawn. 2017. "Black People Don't Exercise in My Neighborhood: Perceived Racial Composition and Leisure-Time Physical Activity among Middle Class Blacks and Whites." *Social Science Research* 66:42–57.

Read, Jen'nan Ghazal, and Bridget K. Gorman. 2006. "Gender Inequalities in US Adult Health: The Interplay of Race and Ethnicity." *Social Science & Medicine* 62(5): 1045–65.

Read, Jen'nan Ghazal, and Michael O. Emerson. 2005. "Racial Context, Black Immigration and the US Black/White Health Disparity." *Social Forces* 84(1): 181–99.

Rehm, Colin D., José Peñalvo, Ashkan Afshin, and Dariush Mozaffarian. 2016. "Dietary Intake Among US Adults, 1999-2012." *JAMA* 315(23): 2542–53.

Ringquist, Evan J. 2005. "Assessing Evidence of Environmental Inequities: A Meta-Analysis." *Journal of Policy Analysis and Management: The Journal of the Association for Public Policy Analysis and Management* 24(2): 223–47.

Rosenbaum, Emily. 2008. "Racial/ethnic Differences in Asthma Prevalence: The Role of Housing and Neighborhood Environments." *Journal of Health and Social Behavior* 49(2): 131–45.

Roth, Louise Marie and Megan M. Henley. 2012. "Unequal Motherhood: Racial-Ethnic and Socioeconomic Disparities in Cesarean Sections in the United States." *Social Problems* 59(2): 207–27.

Sampson, Robert J., Jeffrey D. Morenoff, and Thomas Gannon-Rowley. 2002. "Assessing "Neighborhood Effects": Social Processes and New Directions in Research." *Annual Review of Sociology* 28(1): 443–78.

Schmeer, Kammi K. and Jacob Tarrence. 2018. "Racial-ethnic Disparities in Inflammation: Evidence of Weathering in Childhood?" *Journal of Health and Social Behavior* 59(3): 411–28.

Schnittker, Jason, Bernice A. Pescosolido, and Thomas W. Croghan. 2005. "Are African Americans Really Less Willing to Use Health Care?" *Social Problems* 52(2): 255–71.

Seixas, Azizi, Dwayne A. Henclewood, Aisha T. Langford, Samy I. McFarlane, Ferdinand Zizi, and Girardin Jean-Louis. 2017. "Differentials and Combined Effects of Physical Activity Profiles and Prohealth Behaviors on Diabetes Prevalence among Blacks and Whites in the US Population: A Novel Bayesian Belief Network Machine Learning Analysis." *Journal of Diabetes Research* Vol. 2017: 10.

Sellers, Sherrill L. and Harold W. Neighbors. 2008. "Effects of Goal-Striving Stress on the Mental Health of Black Americans." *Journal of Health and Social Behavior* 49(1): 92–103.

Sellers, Sherrill L., Harold W. Neighbors, Rong Zhang, and James S. Jackson. 2012. "The Impact of Goal-Striving Stress on Physical Health of White Americans, African Americans, and Caribbean Blacks." *Ethnicity & Disease* 22(1): 21–8.

Sewell, Abigail A. and Kevin Jefferson. 2016. "Collateral Damage: The Health Effects of Invasive Police Encounters in New York City." *Journal of Urban Health* 93(1): 42–67.

Simons, Ronald L., Steven R. Lei Man-Kit, Ashley B. Beach, Frederick X. Gibbons Barr, and Robert A. Philibert. 2019. "Testing Life Course Models Whereby Juvenile and Adult Adversity Combine to Influence Speed of Biological Aging." *Journal of Health and Social Behavior* 60(3): 291–308.

Singh, Gopal K. and Stella M. Yu. 2019. "Infant Mortality in the United States, 1915-2017: Large Social Inequalities Persisted for over a Century." *International Journal of Maternal and Child Health and AIDS* 8(1): 19–31.

Stepanikova, Irena. 2012. "Racial-ethnic Biases, Time Pressure, and Medical Decisions." *Journal of Health and Social Behavior* 53(3): 329–43.

Sternthal, Michelle J., Natalie Slopen, and David R. Williams. 2011. "Racial Disparities in Health: How Much Does Stress Really Matter?" *Du Bois Review: Social Science Research on Race* 8(1): 95–113.

Strully, Kate W. 2011. "Health Care Segregation and Race Disparities in Infectious Disease: The Case of Nursing Homes and Seasonal Influenza Vaccinations." *Journal of Health and Social Behavior* 52(4): 510–26.

Subramanyam, Malavika A., Sherman A. James, Ana V. Diez-Roux, DeMarc A. Hickson, et al. 2013. "Socioeconomic Status, John Henryism and Blood Pressure among African-Americans in the Jackson Heart Study." *Social Science & Medicine* 93: 139–46.

Taylor, Robert Joseph, Linda M. Chatters, and Jamie M. Abelson. 2012. "Religious Involvement and DSM IV 12-month and Lifetime Major Depressive Disorder among African Americans." *The Journal of Nervous and Mental Disease* 200(10): 856–62.

Teal, Janae L. 2015. "'Black Trans Bodies are Under Attack': Gender Non-Conforming Homicide Victims in the US 1995–2014." PhD dissertation, Humboldt State University.

Thomas, Courtney S. 2015. "A New Look at the Black Middle Class: Research Trends and Challenges." *Sociological Focus* 48(3): 191–207.

Turney, Kristin. 2014. "Stress Proliferation across Generations? Examining the Relationship between Parental Incarceration and Childhood Health." *Journal of Health and Social Behavior* 55: 302–19.

Umberson, Debra. 2017. "Black Deaths Matter: Race, Relationship Loss, and Effects on Survivors." *Journal of Health and Social Behavior* 58(4): 405–20.

Umberson, Debra, Patricia A. Kristi Williams, Hui Liu Thomas, and Mieke Beth Thomeer. 2014. "Race, Gender, and Chains of Disadvantage: Childhood Adversity, Social Relationships, and Health." *Journal of Health and Social Behavior* 55(1): 20–38.

United States Census Bureau. 2003. Population Profile of the United States: Dynamic Version – Living, Working, and Growing in the USA Retrieved online 3/8/2020 at https://www.census.gov/population/pop-profile/dynamic/profiledynamic.pdf.

United States Census Bureau. 2019. Health Insurance Coverage in the United States:2018. Retrieved online 3/9/2020 at https://www.census.gov/content/dam/Census/library/publications/2019/demo/p60-267.pdf

United States Census Bureau. 2020. Quick Facts: Table. Retrieved online 3/8/2020 at https://www.census.gov/quickfacts/fact/table/US/PST045218.

van Ryn, Michelle. 2016. "Unintended Bias in Health Care: Strategies for Providing More Equitable Care." Minnesota Medicine: Clinical and Health Affairs. March/April 2016. 40–46.

Vincent, Addison Rose. 2017. "State of Emergency Continues for Trans Women of Color." *Huffpost*. Retrieved online 3/14/20 at: https://www.huffpost.com/entry/the-state-of-emergency-co_b_7981580.

Walton, Emily. 2009. "Residential Segregation and Birth Weight among Racial and Ethnic Minorities in the United States." *Journal of Health and Social Behavior* 50(4): 427–42

Warner, David F. and Mark D. Hayward. 2006. "Early-life Origins of the Race Gap in Men's Mortality." *Journal of Health and Social Behavior* 47(3): 209–26.

Wildeman, Christopher. 2012. "Imprisonment and Infant Mortality." *Social Problems* 59(2): 228–57.

Wildeman, Christopher and Christopher Muller. 2012. "Mass Imprisonment and Inequality in Health and Family Life." *Annual Review of Law and Social Science* 8: 11–30.

Williams, Kristi, Sharon Sassler, Adrianne Frech, Fenaba Addo, and Elizabeth Cooksey. 2011. "Nonmarital Childbearing, Union History, and Women's Health at Midlife." *American Sociological Review* 76(3): 465–86.

Williams, David R. and Chiquita Collins. 2001. "Racial Residential Segregation: A Fundamental Cause of Racial Disparities in Health." *Public Health Reports* 116(5): 404–16.

Williams, David R., Yu Yan, James S. Jackson, and Norman B. Anderson. 1997. "Racial Differences in Physical and Mental Health: Socio-economic Status, Stress and Discrimination." *Journal of Health Psychology* 2(3): 335–51.

Woo, Bongki, Nicole Kravitz-Wirtz, Victoria Sass, Kyle Crowder, Samantha Teixeira, and David T. Takeuchi. 2019. "Residential Segregation and Racial/ethnic Disparities in Ambient Air Pollution." *Race and Social Problems* 11(1): 60–67.

15

Latinos and Equity in Health Care Access in the US

Ronald J. Angel and Jacqueline L. Angel

The Affordable Care Act (ACA) that was passed on March 23, 2010 during the Obama Administration was the latest of a few noble attempts that have been made in US history to extend health care coverage to the large number of Americans who are underinsured. Prior attempts did not come close to passage, and universal coverage has remained an elusive holy grail. The ACA legislation, which faced universal Republican opposition, represented a compromise that acknowledged the reality of the health insurance industry's central role in the economy. Proposals for single-payer or government funded options have never gained traction in the US. Even ten years after its passage the compromised version of expanded health care introduced by the ACA continues to be the target of vehement opposition. In 2016 Donald Trump campaigned on the promise to immediately repeal Obamacare and replace it with something better, the specifics or even the generalities of which were never revealed. The intent appears really to have been to return to the traditional employment-based private health insurance system that inevitably left many individuals without adequate or continuous coverage (Jacobs and Skocpol 2016).

Despite the 5th Federal Circuit Court's rejection of the individual mandate and Congress' failure to enforce the penalty for not having coverage, as well as ongoing court challenges to other aspects of the law, the Affordable Care Act remains the law of the land, and although many individuals have lost the coverage they originally gained under the law, many more have at least minimal coverage. Insurers cannot deny coverage on the basis of pre-existing conditions and the children of parents with coverage can remain on their parent's policy until age 26. The health care exchanges continue to operate, and low-income individuals continue

The Wiley Blackwell Companion to Medical Sociology, First Edition. Edited by William C. Cockerham.

to receive subsidies to purchase coverage. All but 14 states have expanded their Medicaid programs to cover adults under age 65 with incomes below 133% of poverty.

The ACA, then, has clearly been a success in extending coverage to a large number of vulnerable individuals whose health and even whose lives would otherwise be at risk. The number of minority Americans, including Latinos, who were uninsured dropped between 2013 when the ACA began offering coverage and 2017, although the proportion of Latinos without coverage remains far above that of other groups (Berchick et al. 2019). Despite improvements, the ACA has not succeeded in guaranteeing universal coverage. Approximately 27.5 million Americans continued to lack adequate coverage in 2018. Latinos remain at particularly elevated risk of lacking coverage. In 2018 approximately one in five (21.7%) were uninsured for the entire year compared to 8.5% of the total population (Berchick et al. 2019).

In the face of continuing hostility to the ACA and attempts to extend coverage to those who are most vulnerable generally, it is possible that progress toward greater coverage may be stalled for many more decades as it was after President Truman's original proposals for reform. If the history of health care reform reflects something basic about our political culture and the strength of the opposition, any possibility of a public option or the expansion of Medicare to the entire population seems remote. Which suggests that at least for the foreseeable future the situation will remain largely as it is and the vulnerabilities that certain individuals and groups face in gaining coverage must be addressed in a more piecemeal fashion. That means dealing with a health insurance regime that is based on private, employment-based health care coverage, and a publicly funded safety net. Such a system works well for those who are employed in a job that offers a high-quality family health plan, while it places serious obstacles to even basic coverage in the way of those without work or those in jobs that do not offer coverage or only do so at a prohibitive cost.

The problem with such an employment-based system is not inherent in the system itself. Germany's health insurance system is based on employment and privately purchased insurance, but it is universal nonetheless (Busse et al. 2017). Universal coverage is not solely a reflection of a nation's wealth, but a reflection of its political culture and moral stance toward the welfare of its citizens. In Germany one is required to have insurance, a requirement that the ACA introduced, but that remains in legal limbo. As a consequence, many Americans of all ages remain uninsured, a situation that is to a large degree alleviated when one turns 65 and qualifies for Medicare. Even then, though, as we discuss further, lacking access to Medicaid supplemental insurance leaves many older Americans, and especially older Latinos, inadequately covered. Low-income pregnant and lactating women and their young children have access to Medicaid and State Children's Health Insurance Programs (SCHIP) and other public and voluntary local options, but in those states that have not expanded Medicaid, low-income childless adults have no options other than charity or care in emergency rooms, or doing without the care they need.

The reality of the situation in the US, then, is that access to high-quality health care means having a good job that provides not only a high salary, but also retirement and family health plans. Unfortunately, access to such jobs is not equally distributed in the population. Certain individuals and groups defined by the intersection of various identities are disproportionately excluded from access to the necessities of a healthy and fulfilling life (Estes 2001). As we discuss further below, individuals and groups with impaired educational opportunities or relevant social capital are excluded from high-paying and prestigious positions, which means that they are denied access to the sort of high-quality and continuous health care that optimizes health. In what follows we focus specifically on Latinos, primarily those of Mexican origin, a group which makes up over 60% of the total Latino population and one that is at seriously elevated risk of lacking health insurance.

By now, several years of research have begun to identify those structural and individual factors that place certain Latinos at particularly elevated risk of no or inadequate health care coverage. The objective of that research is to develop a sophisticated understanding of how gender, marital status, living arrangements, immigration status, the age at which one arrived in the US, and more influence health insurance coverage and access to health care. One major theme that we develop relates to the consequences of Latinos' long life expectancy combined with impaired medical care access for Latino families and for health care policy generally. Latinos, again primarily those of Mexican origin, have life expectancies that are greater at birth and at age 65 than those of non-Latino whites. Yet many of the years that they live past 65 are characterized by ill health and functional impairments, placing them at serious need of health care but also placing them at serious risk of not receiving the care they need (Angel et al. 2015).

Health Care Coverage across the Life Course

Let us begin by reviewing life-course patterns of public and private health care coverage for Latinos in the US and compare the correlates of different levels of coverage among Latinos, blacks and non-Latino whites. One of the major problems that our employment-based insurance system presents relates not only to the fact that many jobs do not include affordable family coverage, but the fact that in recent years even if they offer coverage employers are shifting a larger fraction of the cost to their employees (Collins, Radley, and Baumgartner 2019). As a consequence, it is not uncommon that some members of a family are covered while others are not. Publicly-funded programs are part of the problem. While Medicaid and the State Children's Health Insurance Program (SCHIP) provide coverage for pregnant women, infants, and children in families with incomes even somewhat above the federal poverty line, no similar programs exist for non-disabled adults in states that have not expanded Medicaid. In the absence of coverage purchased on the exchanges many low-income adults go without care or incur crushing medical debt. Even middle-class families are at risk of financial ruin in the case of serious illness if they do not have adequate coverage. In the U.S. today medical debt is a leading cause of bankruptcy (Himmelstein et al. 2019).

Children under 18

The health care financing system of the US is stratified by age in ways that have important implications for Latinos and other low-income groups. One serious implication of the age stratification of health care financing is that given a finite economic pie and inevitable fiscal limitations, different age groups necessarily compete for limited resources (Torres-Gil and Angel 2019). For individuals under 18, and especially for very young children, Medicaid, SCHIP, and other programs pay for preventive and acute care. Yet, although 43% of Medicaid participants are children in poor families, over two-thirds of Medicaid revenues go to pay for the long-term care of elderly and disabled individuals (Rudowitz et al. 2019). As the population ages the competition for Medicaid funding can only increase.

Latino, as well as black children, are heavily dependent on Medicaid. Table 15.1 presents data on various sources of health insurance coverage for Latino and black children. The analyses are based on 2017 data from the Census Bureau's Current Population Survey. The table shows that in that year 52% of black, 57% of Mexican-origin, 46% of Cuban American, and 56% of Puerto Rican children under 18 were covered by Medicaid. Unfortunately, Medicaid does not guarantee coverage to all children. The table shows that 5% of black, 8% of Mexican-origin, 5% of Cuban American, and 3% of Puerto Rican children had no coverage of any sort. In Texas, approximately 13% of children under 18 lacked insurance coverage in 2016, a rate more than twice as high as non-Latino white and black children (Every Texan 2020). In Texas, teenagers are far less likely to be receiving Medicaid than in Illinois or Massachusetts (Angel et al. 2006), Employer-based coverage is particularly low among Mexican-origin children. While 67% of non-Latino white children are covered by a parent's policy, only 33% of Mexican-origin children are on a parent's plan.

Adulthood: High Vulnerability

Adulthood presents serious health care coverage risks for able-bodied adults of all races and ethnicities, but that risk is highest for blacks and Latinos, and again especially for Mexican-origin adults. In the US, unlike Germany, employment does not

Table 15.1 Selected Type of Health Insurance Coverage By Race and Latino Ethnicity Under 18 year, 2016[1].

Type of Coverage	Non-Latino White	Non-Latino Black	Mexican American	Puerto Rican	Cuban American
Employer	64.1%	36.1%	33.7%	40.6%	43.0%
Medicaid	26.8%	58.3%	56.2%	52.6%	45.5%
None	3.8%	4.3%	8.0%	3.6%	4.2%

[1]Respondents were asked to indicate all forms of coverage they had. Categories may overlap.
Note: Weighted percentages
Source: US Census Bureau, Current Population Survey, 2017.

Table 15.2 Selected Type of Health Insurance Coverage By Race and Latino Ethnicity Aged 18–64 years, 2016[1].

Type of Coverage	Non-Latino White	Non-Latino Black	Mexican American	Puerto Rican	Cuban American
Employer	67.4%	52.2%	47.0%	52.9%	48.8%
Medicare	4.1%	5.6%	2.4%	4.7%	2.9%
Medicaid	12.1%	24.3%	18.4%	26.4%	14.4%
None	8.7%	15.2%	27.7%	11.6%	19.7%

[1]Respondents were asked to indicate all forms of coverage they had. Categories may overlap.
Note: Weighted percentages
Source: US Census Bureau, Current Population Survey, 2017.

guarantee coverage. A combination of unemployment, part-time employment, and employment in jobs that do not provide affordable coverage means that large fractions of minority adults have no coverage of any sort. Table 15.2 presents data on sources of coverage for adults 18 to 64 in 2017. It reveals that while 69% of non-Latino white adults (18–64 year) had employer-sponsored health care coverage, only 55% of black, 50% of Cuban-origin, 52% of Puerto Rican, and 46% of Mexican-origin adults had such coverage. Public programs, including Medicaid in states that have expanded the program, do not cover large fractions of the adult population. Although a substantial fraction of minority adults receive care through Medicaid, among all groups rather large percentages report no coverage, a situation which is particularly serious for blacks and Latinos. The lack of any form of coverage is particularly serious among Mexican-origin adults, 28% of whom report that they have no health insurance of any sort.

These patterns of health care coverage clearly underscore the complexity of the health care coverage system in the US and the serious vulnerability in creates for minority group members in general, and for Mexican-origin Latinos in particular. These vulnerabilities are exacerbated by labor market disadvantages, immigration status, language difficulties, and other barriers that increase the risk of inadequate coverage. Individual risk factors such as low educational levels and consequent low-income jobs interact with other structural factors related to the labor force to increase Latino's risk of lacking health care coverage. Mexican-origin adults are far less likely than any other group to be employed in managerial or professional occupations (Angel et al. 2009). On the other hand, they are over-represented in the service sector in which they are usually not offered employer-sponsored health insurance, or in which the premiums required for individual or family coverage place such coverage out of reach (Angel et al. 2009).

Maturity: Incomplete Universal Coverage

In our age stratified health care coverage regime, reaching 65 means that one arrives at the realm of universal coverage, but once again the data reveal significant group differences in the extent of that universal coverage. The third row in Table 15.3,

Table 15.3 Selected Type of Health Insurance Coverage By Race and Latino Ethnicity for 65 years and Over, 2016.

Type of Coverage	Non-Latino White	Non-Latino Black	Mexican American	Puerto Rican	Cuban American
Employer	33.0%	30.9%	21.5%	23.9%	11.8%
Medicare	96.8%	94.6%	91.6%	96.6%	95.7%
Medicaid	11.0%	25.9%	28.2%	30.0%	42.0%
None	0.3%	1.2%	3.8%	0.5%	1.5%
Total (in thousands)	197,297	40,128	24,786	3,848	2,085

[1]Respondents were asked to indicate all forms of coverage they had. Categories may overlap.
Note: Weighted percentages.
Source: US Census Bureau, Current Population Survey, 2017.

which is similar to Tables 15.1 and 15.2, clearly shows the equalizing effects of Medicare which covers over 90% of all racial and ethnic groups. Although high levels of coverage reflect the success of Medicare in addressing the needs of older Latinos, the numbers do not reveal the full reality of the situation. Latinos higher life expectancy than non-Latinos, their greater risk of chronic disease and functional limitations, and their more limited assets and income places them at elevated risk of needing medical care and other support for long periods (Angel, Angel, and Hill 2015)

Either because they cannot afford to retire, or because they are in jobs such as the professoriate in which there are few incentives to retire, a growing number of older individuals continue to work well past 65 and many continue to have access to their employer's health plan. The ability to continue working depends though on the demands of the job and one's ability to meet those demands. A professor can continue his or her research and teaching even with fairly serious chronic conditions, whereas a manual laborer cannot. While approximately 27% of non-Latino white and 24% of black older adults' report employer-based insurance, far smaller fractions of any of the three Latino groups report employer-based coverage.

Since it was enacted in 1965, Medicare has greatly increased access to vital health care for all Americans. Yet basic Medicare does not cover all of the medical expenses an individual incurs. Medicare Part A includes a sizeable deductible, and Part B includes a premium, and pays only 80% of medical services received. Other expenses, such as long-term care, eye exams, most dental care and dentures, prescription drugs, and medical devices are not covered by traditional Medicare (Centers for Medicare and Medicaid Services 2019). The introduction of Medicare Part D in 2006 created universal access to prescription drug coverage for Medicare beneficiaries. Although the program increased the number of Medicare participants with coverage for prescription drugs, Latinos are 35% less likely than non-Latino whites to have such coverage (McGarry et al. 2014a, 2014b). Recipients without supplemental private coverage, referred to as Medigap, can face the risk of bankruptcy or having to do without needed care (Narang and Nicholas 2017). In 2013, Latinos were three times less likely than non-Latino whites to have supplemental coverage (Kaiser Family Foundation 2016).

For older individuals with extremely low income and few assets, Medicaid serves as their Medigap plan. Individuals over 65 who receive Medicaid are referred to as "dual-eligibles" since they receive both Medicare and Medicaid. Depending on one's income and assets, Medicaid can pay some combination of Part B premiums, Part A and B copayments, prescription drugs, and other services not covered by Medicare (Henry J. Kaiser Family Foundation 2017). Elderly individuals with no income or assets qualify for all of these benefits.

Medicare Part C, referred to as Medicare Advantage, allows private insurers to offer consumers bundled coverage that combines Medicare Parts A and B and in many cases, prescription drug coverage (McGuire et al. 2011). Premiums differ depending on the location and type of plan and are paid by insured individuals, except in the case of Medicaid recipients (Kaiser Family Foundation 2020; Medicare.gov 2019). All states offer Medicare Advantage plans to dual-eligible Medicaid recipients, and a large fraction of Medicaid eligible older Latinos are enrolled in these plans. The reasons for this high Latino participation in Medicare Advantage is not entirely clear but may have to do with how states classify their dual-eligible Medicaid recipients. States have the option of classifying dual-eligible recipients as either partially or fully dual-eligible, based on income thresholds the state sets. The distinction has important implications for state Medicaid expenditures since states do not have to pay the full amount of acute or long-term care for partially dual-eligible recipients, expenses which they incur for fully dual-eligible beneficiaries (Atherly and Dowd 2005). Texas classifies a far larger proportion of its dual-eligible beneficiaries as partially dual-eligible than California (Angel et al. 2019). This fact may explain the relatively high enrollment in Medicare Advantage in Texas, which might increase enrollment rates for Latinos in general given the state's large Latino population (Association for Health Insurance Plans 2016; Atherly and Thorpe 2005).

Additional Structural and Individual Risk Factors

Latinos confront non-financial as well as financial obstacles to obtaining health insurance (Angel and Angel 2009a). Language difficulties represent a major barrier (Jacobs et al. 2006; Stuber and Bradley 2005). Another major barrier for Latinos, as well as for others is low health insurance literacy, which refers to a lack of understanding of the risks involved in not having adequate coverage, and a lack of understanding of how to obtain it (Velasco-Mondragon et al. 2016). Factors such as short residency in the U.S. (Vargas Bustamante et al. 2014), lacking citizenship, (Ortega, Rodriguez, and Vargas Bustamante 2015), and deportation fears (Luque et al. 2018; Paz and Massey 2016) further limit opportunities for adequate health care coverage (Angel and Angel 2006). Bureaucratic barriers are also a major obstacle to public coverage for Latinos of all ages (Stuber and Bradley 2005). These system-level factors include complicated application and renewal procedures, asset tests, and inadequate outreach efforts by agencies charged with administering health-related programs (Moreno and Mullins 2017). Let us review some of the major individual factors that increase the risk of lacking health insurance coverage among Latinos.

Education

Education is a major determinant of both health care coverage and health outcomes (Angel and Angel 2009a). Higher levels of education give one access to professional positions and high-paying jobs with benefits, including health insurance. An adequate income and health insurance means that a family receives the preventive and acute care it needs. Latinos' educational levels are on average lower than those of any other group (Angel and Angel 2009a; Torres-Gil and Angel 2019). Among Latinos gender interacts with immigration status to reduce coverage through lower levels of education. Foreign-born Mexican-origin women average 8.2 years of education compared to 11.3 years among native-born Mexican-origin women (Everett et al. 2011). Mexican-origin male immigrants average similar levels of education: (8.3%) versus 13.3% for blacks, and 13.9% for non-Latino whites. In addition to low levels of education, foreign-born Mexican-origin women face additional barriers to high-paying employment since US employers place less value on education obtained in Mexico than education received in the US (Duncan et al. 2006). The intersection of multiple barriers, then, including low levels of education, minimal English proficiency, and a lack of legal status severely constrain the employment opportunities of foreign-born Latinos over the life course (Telles and Ortiz 2008). The cumulative effect of such disadvantages results in lower retirement incomes, and consequently impaired access to adequate health insurance and medical care, among Mexican Americans in later life (Angel et al. 2014a).

Employment

Low levels of education translate directly into low status jobs. Latinos' overrepresentation in low-wage and service sector jobs means that they are less likely than those in higher-paying jobs to be offered affordable insurance options (Angel and Angel 2009a; Paz and Massey 2016; U.S. Bureau of Labor Statistics 2019a). As we mentioned before, Latinos are less likely than non-Latinos to hold professional positions. In 2018, while 40.8% of employed non-Latino whites, 31.3% of Blacks, and 53.7% of Asian workers were employed in management, professional, and related occupations, only 22.4% of employed Latinos held such positions (U.S. Bureau of Labor Statistics 2019a). Employed Latinos work as painters, construction and maintenance workers, agricultural workers, and in low-wage service occupations, including maid services and housekeeping (U.S. Bureau of Labor Statistics 2019b). Among Mexican-origin Latinos, male immigrants are heavily concentrated in agriculture (Angel et al. 2009). Latinas are more likely to work in service occupations (31.4%) than non-Latino whites (19.6%); blacks (28%) and Asians (20.8%) (U.S. Bureau of Labor Statistics 2019a).

A major determinant of access to employer-sponsored health coverage is the size of the enterprise in which one works. In general, smaller firms are less likely to offer coverage than are larger firms. In 2010 only 40.5% of firms with 3 to 9 employees offered coverage, whereas 64.7% of firms with 10 to 24 employees, and 97.4% of firms with 50 or more workers offered coverage (Agency for Healthcare Research and Quality 2010). Latinos are more likely than non-Latino whites to be employed in small firms in which they are less likely than other groups to be covered (Angel and Angel 2009a; Santos and Seitz 2000).

Data from the 2006 Employer Health Benefits Annual Survey show that health care coverage is also affected by other firm and worker characteristics. Non-unionized firms are less likely to offer coverage than are unionized firms, and low-wage and part-time workers are less likely to be offered coverage than are salaried or full-time workers (Kaiser Family Foundation 2018). In 2014 native-born Latinos were more likely than non-Latino whites to be working part-time work involuntarily. Part time employment is part of a package that includes low union membership. Latino union membership has historically been low and has been dropping (Young and Mattingly 2016). Between 1987 and 1996 union membership among employed Latinos dropped from 24.1% to 12.8% (Monheit and Vistnes 2008). By 2018 less than 10% of Latino workers were members of unions (U.S. Bureau of Labor Statistics 2019c).

Income and Wealth

Low levels of education and consequent low-wage employment results in low levels of income and assets among Latinos (Angel 2015). In 2018, the median weekly earnings of fulltime Latino male and female workers was lower than that of non-Latino white men and women. The median weekly wage for Latino women was $617 and $817 for non-Latino white women. The median for men was $720 for Latinos and $1002 for non-Latino white males (Hegewisch and Hartman 2018).

Lower lifetime earnings result in a decreased capacity to save and invest which results in truly massive ethnic disparities in accumulated wealth which persist into later life. Non-Latino white households have on average six times the wealth of Latino households, $612,000 versus $110,000 (McKernan et al. 2013). Among Latino households a far larger fraction of total wealth consists of home equity than is the case for non-Latino households for whom a larger fraction of wealth consists of stocks, bonds, and other non-housing assets (Angel and Mudrazija 2015; Angel and Mudrazijia 2011). Inadequate assets and low income are particularly serious problems among female-headed households, and they are particularly serious for minority female-headed households (Ozawa and Lee 2006).

Low lifetime earnings and impaired asset accumulation means that by the time they reach retirement age Latinos have far less in total wealth than non-Hispanic whites (Angel and Angel 2009a). Even with Medicare, low levels of disposable income can result in inadequate medical care if one cannot afford Medicare Advantage or a Medigap plan. The situation is again exacerbated by immigration status and gender. Mexican-origin immigrants are far less likely than other groups to have access to pensions or other retirement plans, which increases their risk of inadequate health care access. Unmarried Mexican American women are at particularly high risk of seriously limited financial resources in later life (Angel et al. 2014a).

But marriage is no guarantee of adequate coverage for many older Latino women. A husband who cannot afford Medigap coverage for the couple does not have the resources to pay for what Medicare does not cover out-of-pocket. Prior to retirement age, married women are at greater risk of losing coverage if their husbands lose their job or his employer drops family coverage or increases premium and out-of-pocket costs to unaffordable levels. Given their occupational vulnerabilities, Latino heads of household are at elevated risk.

One major vulnerability that many women of all races and ethnicities face results from the fact that women traditionally have married men who are older than themselves. A woman with a husband who is older than she faces a coverage of vulnerability when he retires that results from the fact that she cannot be covered by his Medicare (Angel et al. 2011). Until she reaches 65 and qualifies for her own Medicare, she finds herself in a potentially precarious situation in which coverage may be hard to find or afford. Although the ACA has provided greater possibilities for purchasing coverage on the exchanges, if the couple's resources are limited, they may not qualify for a subsidy and the wife may be left without adequate coverage.

Although the number of women who marry older men is decreasing, many women still face this health care window of vulnerability. Because women, and especially Latino women, have longer life expectancies than men they are at high risk of widowhood. Again, this is especially true for women married to older men (Angel et al. 2007). One-quarter of non-Hispanic white and African American women are covered on their husband's plans, while only 11% of Mexican-origin women are covered on their husband's plan, a situation that reflects a marginalized employment situation of many Mexican-origin husbands (Montez et al. 2009). Once again, then, multiple factors interact to place Latinas at great risk of lacking coverage at a time in life when serious health conditions become more prevalent.

Immigration Status

Latino immigrants are twice more likely to be uninsured than US born Latinos (39 vs. 17%) and non-Latinos (14%) (Krogstad and Lopez 2014). In addition to their families' of lack coverage, many immigrant children suffer additional disadvantages that increase their risk of poor health, including high poverty rates, food insecurity, and poor housing (Hamilton et al. 2011). A lack of health insurance means that Latino immigrants pay a greater share out-of-pocket for health services since they do not qualify for public assistance (Flavin et al. 2018). While Latino immigrants are generally healthier than the average citizen upon arrival in the US, their health tends to deteriorate the longer they remain in the country (Berk et al. 2000).

System-level Barriers

Individual factors interact with system-level factors to influence the likelihood that different groups will be insured privately or will receive public coverage, including Medicaid and SCHIP. An investigation of Medicaid coverage among children in Boston, Chicago, and San Antonio in 1999 revealed large differences in coverage among children of different ages, demonstrating the impact of specific state Medicaid policies (Angel et al. 2006, p. 93). In Boston, 82% of children in families with incomes below 100% of poverty received Medicaid, a figure similar to that for Chicago. In San Antonio, on the other hand, only 64% of children in families with household incomes below 100% of poverty received Medicaid. As family income increased, Medicaid participation decreased, although it remained much higher in Boston than in Chicago or San Antonio. In San Antonio, only 5% of children in families with incomes between 150% and 200% of poverty received Medicaid, compared to 35% in Chicago and 65% in Boston.

The lower rates of coverage in San Antonio at all income levels, but especially for those families with incomes between 150% and 200% of poverty, reflect more restrictive Medicare eligibility criteria in Texas compared to Illinois, and certainly to Massachusetts. Since Latinos in San Antonio are primarily of Mexican origin, one might ask if the lower rates of coverage among Mexican-origin children generally reflect the fact that this group is heavily concentrated in Texas. Data from this same study revealed that Mexican-origin children in San Antonio were less likely to be covered by any form of health insurance and far less likely to be covered by Medicaid compared to children in Chicago and Boston (Angel et al. 2006).

The consequences of lacking coverage are significant. Children in Latino families that do not have employer-sponsored health insurance or Medicaid are less likely to have a usual source of care than children in families with such coverage (Winston et al. 1999). In general, uninsured children, especially Latino, black and non-citizens are also more likely than those with health coverage to be hospitalized for preventable illnesses and their consequences (Institute of Medicine 2002). On average, uninsured children see the doctor less often for acute illnesses, and they are less likely to use prescription drugs than are children with coverage. Although inequities in access to medical care between the rich and poor have been decreased by Medicaid, poor children are still far less likely to receive dental care than children in more affluent families. Uninsured children are also less likely than insured children to be treated for conditions such as asthma and ear infections that can lead to more serious health problems (Institute of Medicine 2004).

Given their low average socioeconomic profile, Latino children are clearly at elevated risk of inadequate coverage and impaired preventive and acute care access. Because they are less likely to have a regular source of care, uninsured children are more likely than insured children to receive care in emergency rooms, community and migrant health centers, and other publicly funded health facilities. The lack of a usual source of care places these children at a high risk of undetected symptoms. Routine care received in emergency rooms is excessively expensive and may be of lower quality than that received from a physician familiar with a child's overall health (Perez et al. 2009).

Longer Lives but Sicker Lives

Given the barriers to adequate health care coverage, and consequently to adequate health care that Latinos face over the life course one would expect that they would suffer from higher levels of mortality than other more affluent groups, but this is not the case. As we have mentioned, Mexican-origin Latinos have life expectancies at birth and at older ages that are longer than those of non-Latino whites (Angel et al. 2014b). This phenomenon of low educational levels and comparatively low socioeconomic profile and a favorable mortality profile has been referred to as the "Hispanic Paradox." There has been much speculation as to the source of the paradox, including lower rates of smoking and the better general health of immigrants, but what is most puzzling, though, is that the Mexican-origin population suffers from substantial rates of obesity, hypertension, and diabetes, conditions which should increase mortality rates overall (Crimmins et al. 2007; Franzini et al. 2001; Markides and Eschbach 2005; Palloni 2007).

This paradox remains a clear mystery, but the fact of significant levels of illness and functional incapacity among older Mexican-origin individuals has been well documented (Velasco-Mondragon et al. 2016). While increased life spans have been a clear benefit of improved standards of living in most nations, long life accompanied by poor health is in many ways a mixed blessing. Longer life brings with it the possibility of longer periods of illness. The basic objective of medicine and public health is to compress morbidity into a short period just before death. Ideally one should spend most of the years she or he lives productive and in good health. Evidence for substantial compression of morbidity is contradictory, suggesting some compression with some measures and less compression with others (Cutler et al. 2013). Among Mexican-origin Latinos that ideal state of affairs appears not to hold. For this group nearly half of the years they live past 65 are plagued by ill health and functional impairments (Angel et al. 2014b). Protracted periods of illness and incapacity place serious burdens on families and society at large. The financial support of individuals with few resources who will be dependent for twenty or thirty years or even longer, in combination with the expensive medical care they require, represents a new reality that will force a reassessment of our current health care financing system, as well as the rest of our old-age welfare state programs.

Longer life spans have other important social policy implications that relate to the consequences of inequitable health care coverage. The US, like all other developed and even developing countries, is aging at an astonishing pace (Beard et al. 2016; National Center for Health Statistics 2011). Given their relatively low fertility rate non-Latino whites are aging at a faster pace than Latinos (Angel 2018). Given their younger average age, Latinos will make up a growing fraction of the labor force in the years to come (Saenz 2015). Although minority group workers will make up a growing fraction of the older population, the retired population will remain predominantly non-Latino and white. Their support, as well as the support of the rest of the population, will depend heavily on the productivity of these minority workers, a large fraction of whom will be Latinos and immigrants. If these workers are confined to low-wage occupations because of low educational levels, compounded by poor health and other disadvantages, not only will their own lives be compromised, but their potential contribution to the economy and the general welfare will be impaired (Torres-Gil and Angel 2019). This possibility introduces an ethnic dimension to our age stratified system of opportunities and health care. In the end, everyone's welfare depends on the health and education of all groups.

Conclusion

In the not too distant past health care was relatively inexpensive but medicine was limited in its effectiveness. Today medicine is highly effective at preventing and treating disease, but it has become extremely expensive. Very few individuals or families can afford to cover the costs of a serious illness out of pocket, and many would be strained to cover routine preventive services. There is ample evidence that access to regular health care is vital to the maintenance of good health and we have ample evidence that health insurance increases a family's access to that care (Institute of Medicine 2004). Most developed nations of the world guarantee access to at least basic health care to all citizens. Universal coverage can be achieved in many ways, either through direct state subsidization or through some combination of employment-based and governmental coverage. The US has developed a mixed system of employment-based coverage for the majority of citizens and their families, and a state-sponsored safety net for children and older adults with low incomes. The introduction of Medicaid and Medicare addressed two of the glaring shortcomings of the previous system by providing coverage to two highly vulnerable groups, poor children and the elderly. These programs addressed a clearly politically sensitive problem. In the world's richest nation, children and old people without access to the care they need would constitute a major embarrassment.

A major problem that has not been adequately addressed, however, is the lack of adequate access to health care among childless adults with low incomes and no access to affordable employer-based health insurance. As we and many others have documented, these individuals are disproportionately minority group members and single women. Latinos are at higher risk of lacking health care coverage than any other group. Minority children, and particularly Latino children, are consequently particularly dependent on Medicaid. Even though it is available, though, a significant fraction of Latino children who qualify on the basis of family income are not enrolled in the program (Angel and Angel 2009b). The obstacles we have mentioned, including complicated enrollment procedures, language barriers, and more contribute to this lower enrollment. The short and long-term consequences of such underutilization are serious.

President Truman's proposal in 1947 to introduce universal health insurance paid for by payroll taxes was the first of various attempts to introduce universal coverage. The bill, which became the Wagner-Murray-Dingell Bill, never made it to a vote, and later attempts, such as that by President Bill Clinton in 1993, came to naught. Prior to the ACA, Medicare and Medicaid were the only notable successes in extending coverage to large groups of people, and although the ACA was a clear step forward, it ran headlong into the same sources of opposition that were the undoing of previous attempts at universal coverage. Again, minority Americans, and especially Latinos, have been among the major losers. We must remember, though, that large numbers of non-Latino black and white families with low incomes also suffer. More equitable and broader coverage would clearly benefit Latinos, but it would also benefit other groups.

There can be little doubt that along with other low-income groups, Latinos have benefitted from the provisions of the ACA that extend care to those who would otherwise not have access. Although the ACA did not offer a public option, the exchanges allow many individuals who would have no access to coverage at a reasonable cost to purchase insurance, often with substantial subsidies. The ACA was never designed to provide universal coverage. Rather, the intent was to greatly reduce the number of uninsured. A basic requirement for universal coverage is that everyone become part of the pool of insured individuals. Young and healthy people must contribute if the system is to remain viable and provide coverage for those who are older or in worse health. Court rulings that nullified the universal mandate and that allowed states to opt out of Medicaid expansion clearly weakened the ACA's ability to extend coverage. Yet, many more individuals, including Latinos, have coverage today than they did before the bill's passage. If those groups who are opposed to the ACA in all of its aspects succeed in undermining more of its provisions, much of the progress the act made possible will be undone.

Universal health care coverage has both moral and economic justifications. The fact that large numbers of individuals in the most affluent nation in the world do not receive the basic health care they need is unacceptable in and of itself. But the practical consequences are even more serious. Given their higher fertility and immigration from Latin America, Latinos are becoming a larger fraction of the labor force. Their productivity, which depends at its foundation on education and good health, will greatly affect the productivity of the labor force of the future. Given that reality, investments in health, are necessary to insure our collective economic welfare in a nation that is becoming ever more globalized and competitive. If the moment for universal health care has not yet arrived, the reality of the need for universal care to insure our collective future will ensure that the debate will not end.

References

Agency for Healthcare Research and Quality, Center for Financing, Access and Cost Trends. 2010. Table I.B.2. 2010. "Percent of Private-sector Employees in Establishments that Offer Health Insurance by Firm Size and Selectedcharacteristics: United States, 2010." Retrieved 1/7/2020 from https://meps.ahrq.gov/data_stats/summ_tables/insr/national/series_1/2010/tib2.pdf.

Angel, Jacqueline L. 2018. "Aging Policy in a Majority-Minority Nation." *Public Policy & Aging Report* 28(1):19–23. doi: 10.1093/ppar/pry005.

Angel, Jacqueline L. and Ronald J. Angel. 2006. "Minority Group Status and Healthful Aging: Social Structure Still Matters." *American Journal of Public Health* 96: 1152–59.

Angel, Jacqueline L., Ronald J. Angel, and Philip Cantu. 2019. "Medicaid Use among Older Low-income Medicare Enrollees in California and Texas: A Tale of Two States." *Journal Health Politics, Policy and the Law* 44(6): 885–910.

Angel, Jacqueline L., Maren Jiménez, and Ronald J. Angel. 2007. "The Economic Consequences of Widowhood for Older Minority Women." *The Gerontologist* 47 (3): 222–34.

Angel, Jacqueline L, Jennifer Karas Montez, and Ronald J Angel. 2011. "A Window of Vulnerability: Health Hnsurance Coverage among Women 55 to 64 Years of Age." *Womens Health Issues* 21(1): 6–11. doi: 10.1016/j.whi.2010.07.011.

Angel, Jacqueline L. and Stipica Mudrazija. 2015. "Economic Security of Older Hispanics: The Role of Social Security and Employer-Sponsored Plans." Pp. 69–86 in Nancy

Morrow-Howell and Margaret Sherraden (eds.), *Financial Capability and Asset Holding in Later Life: A Life Course Perspective*. New York: Oxford University Press.

Angel, Jacqueline L. and Stipica Mudrazijia. 2011. *Raising the Retirement Age: Is It Fair for Low-Income Workers and Minorities? in Public Policy and Aging Report*. Washington, DC.

Angel, Jacqueline L., Kate Prickett, and Ronald J. Angel. 2014. "Sources of Retirement Security for Black, Non-Hispanic White, and Mexican-Origin Women: The Changing Roles of Marriage and Work." *Journal of Women, Politics and Policy* 35(3): 222–41.

Angel, Ronald J. 2015. "The Consequences of Social Welfare Policy for Older Hispanic Families." *Public Policy & Aging Report* 25(3): 113–16. doi: 10.1093/ppar/prv009.

Angel, Ronald J. and Jacqueline L. Angel. 2009a. *Hispanic Families at Risk: The New Economy, Work, and the Welfare State*. New York: Springer Sciences.

Angel, Ronald J., Jacqueline L. Angel, and Terrence D. Hill. 2015. "Longer Lives, Sicker Lives? Increased Longevity and Extended Disability among Mexican-Origin Elders." *The Journals of Gerontology Series B: Psychological Sciences and Social Sciences*. Doi: 10.1093/geronb/gbu158.

Angel, Ronald J., Jacqueline L. Angel, and Terrence D. Hill. 2015. "Longer Lives, Sicker Lives? Increased Longevity and Extended Disability Among Mexican-Origin Elders." *The Journals of Gerontology Series B: Psychological Sciences and Social Sciences* 70(4): 639–49.

Angel, Ronald J., Jacqueline L. Angel, and Jennifer Karas Montez. 2009. "The Work/Health Insurance Nexus: A Weak Link for Mexican-origin Men." *Social Science Quarterly* 90(5): 1112–33. doi: 10.1111/j.1540-6237.2009.00649.x.

Angel, Ronald J., Laura Lein, and Jane Henrici. 2006. *Poor Families in America's Health Care Crisis*. New York: Cambridge University Press.

Association for Health Insurance Plans. 2016. "Medicare Advantage Demographics Report, 2016." Retrieve 1/4/2020 from https://www.ahip.org/wp-content/uploads/MA_Demographics_Report_2019.pdf.

Atherly, Adam and Bryan E. Dowd. 2005. "Effect of Medicare Advantage Payments on Dually Eligible Medicare Beneficiaries." *Health Care Financing Review* 26(3): 93–104.

Atherly, Adam and Kenneth E. Thorpe. 2005. *Value of Medicare Advantage to Low-Income and Minority Medicare Beneficiaries*. Atlanta, GA: Rollins School of Public Health, Emory University.

Beard, J. R., A. Officer, I. A. de Carvalho, R. Sadana, A. M. Pot, J. P. Michel, P. Lloyd-Sherlock, J. E. Epping-Jordan, W. R. Gmeeg Peeters, J. A. Thiyagarajan Mahanani, and S. Chatterji. 2016. "The World Report on Ageing and Health: A Policy Framework for Healthy Ageing." *Lancet* 387 (10033):2145–54. doi: 10.1016/s0140-6736(15)00516-4.

Berchick, Edward R., Jessica C. Barnett, and Rachel D. Upton. 2019. *Health Insurance Coverage in the United States: 2018*. Washington, DC: U.S. Census Bureau.

Berk, Marc L., Claudia L. Schur, Leo R. Chavez, and Martin Frankel. 2000. "Health Care Use Among Undocumented Latino Immigrants." *Health Affairs* 19(4): 51–64. doi: 10.1377/hlthaff.19.4.51.

Busse, Reinhard, Miriam Blümel, Franz Knieps, and Bärnighausen. Till 2017. "Statutory Health Insurance in Germany: A Health System Shaped by 135 Years of Solidarity, Self-governance, and Competition." *The Lancet* 390 (10097): 882–97. doi: https://doi.org/10.1016/S0140-6736(17)31280-1.

Bustamante, Vargas, Jie Chen Arturo, John A. Rizzo Hai Fang, and Alexander N. Ortega. 2014. "Identifying Health Insurance Predictors and the Main Reported Reasons for Being Uninsured among US Immigrants by Legal Authorization Status." *The International Journal of Health Planning and Management* 29(1): e83–e96. doi: 10.1002/hpm.2214.

Centers for Medicare and Medicaid Services. 2019. "What's Not Covered by Part A & Part B? Retrieved 1/4/2020 from https://www.medicare.gov/what-medicare-covers/whats-not-covered-by-part-a-part-b.

Collins, Radley, and Baumgartner. 2019. "Employers Shift Higher Health-Care Costs to Workers Retrieved 1/4/2019 from https://www.wsj.com/articles/employers-shift-higher-health-care-costs-to-workers-1476194147.

Collins, Sara R. David C. Radley, and Jesse C. Baumgartner. 2019. "Trends in Employer Health Care Coverage, 2008–2018: Higher Costs for Workers and Their Families." The Commonwealth Fund. Retrieved 9/25/2020 from https://www.commonwealthfund.org/publications/2019/nov/trends-employer-health-care-coverage–2008–2018

Crimmins, Eileen M, Jung Ki Kim, Dawn E Alley, Arun Karlamangla, and Teresa Seeman. 2007. "Hispanic Paradox in Biological Risk Profiles." *American Journal of Public Health* 97(7): 1305–10.

Cutler, David M., Kaushik Ghosh, and Mary Beth Landrum. 2013. "Evidence for Significant Compression of Morbidity in the Elderly U.S. Population." NBER Working Paper No. 19268. Retrieved 1/9/2020 from https://www.nber.org/papers/w19268.pdf.

Duncan, Brian, Joseph V. Hotz, and Stephen J. Trejo. 2006. "Hispanics in the U.S. Labor Market." In *Hispanics and the Future of America*, edited by Marta Tienda and Faith Mitchell, 228–90 Washington, DC: The National Academies Press.

Estes, Carroll. 2001. *Social Policy and Aging: A Critical Perspective.* Thousand Oaks, CA: Sage.

Everett, B. G., R. G. Rogers, R. A. Hummer, and P. M. Krueger. 2011. "Trends in Educational Attainment by Race/Ethnicity, Nativity, and Sex in the United States, 1989–2005." *Ethn Racial Stud* 34(9): 1543–66. doi: 10.1080/01419870.2010.543139.

Every Texan. 2020. "Health Care: Children's Medicaid & CHIP." Retrieved 9/27/2020 from https://everytexan.org/our-work/policy-areas/health-care/health-insurance-coverage/childrens-medicaid-chip

Flavin, L., L. Zallman, D. McCormick, and J. Wesley Boyd. 2018. "Medical Expenditures on and by Immigrant Populations in the United States: A Systematic Review." *Int J Health Serv* 48(4): 601–21. doi: 10.1177/0020731418791963.

Franzini, L., J. C. Ribble, and A. M. Keddie. 2001. "Understanding the Hispanic Paradox." *Ethnicity and Disease* 11(3): 496–518.

Hamilton, Erin R., Jodi Berger Cardoso, Robert A. Hummer, and Yolanda C. Padilla. 2011. "Assimilation and Emerging Health Disparities among New Generations of U.S. Children." *Demographic Research* 25: 783–818.

Hegewisch, Ariane and Heidi Hartman. 2018. "The Gender Wage Gap: 2018 Earnings Differences by Race and Ethnicity." Retrieved 1/6/2020 from https://iwpr.org/publications/gender-wage-gap–2018

Henry J. Kaiser Family Foundation. 2017. "Dual Eligibles' Share of Medicaid Spending Retrieved 5/7/2017 from http://kff.org/medicaid/state-indicator/duals-share-of-medicaid-spending/?currentTimeframe=0&sortModel=%7B%22colId%22:%22Location%22,%22sort%22:%22asc%22%7D.

Himmelstein, D. U., R. M. Lawless, D. Thorne, P. Foohey, and S. Woolhandler. 2019. "Medical Bankruptcy: Still Common despite the Affordable Care Act." *American Journal of Public Health* 109(3): 431–33. doi: 10.2105/ajph.2018.304901.

Institute of Medicine. 2004. *Insuring America's Health: Principles and Recommendations, Insuring Health.* Washnington, DC: The National Academies Press.

Institute of Medicine, Committee on the Consequences of Uninsurance. 2002. *Health Insurance is a Family Matter.* Washington, DC: National Academies Press.

Jacobs, Elizabeth, H. M. Chen Alice, Leah S. Karliner, Niels Agger-Gupta, and Sunita Mutha. 2006. "The Need for More Research on Language Barriers in Health Care: A Proposed Research Agenda." *The Milbank Quarterly* 84(1): 111–33. doi: 10.1111/j.1468-0009.2006.00440.x.

Jacobs, Lawrence R. and Theda Skocpol. 2016. *Health Care Reform and American Politics: What Everyone Needs to Know.* Fourth ed. New York: Oxford University Press.

Kaiser Family Foundation. 2016. "Profile of Medicare Beneficiaries by Race and Ethnicity: A Chartpack Retrieved 1/4/2020 from https://www.kff.org/report-section/profile-of-medicare-beneficiaries-by-race-and-ethnicity-chartpack

Kaiser Family Foundation. 2018. "2018 Annual Survey Employer Health Benefits." Retrieved 1/6/2020 from http://files.kff.org/attachment/Report-Employer-Health-Benefits-Annual-Survey–2018.

Kaiser Family Foundation. 2020. "Figure 2: Medicare Advantage Penetration, by State, 2019." Retrieved 1/29/2020 from https://www.kff.org/medicare/issue-brief/a-dozen-facts-about-medicare-advantage-in–2019.

Krogstad, Jens Manuel and Mark Hugo Lopez. 2014. "Hispanic Immigrants More Likely to Lack Health Insurance than U.S.-born. Retrieved 1/7/2020 from https://www.pewresearch.org/fact-tank/2014/09/26/higher-share-of-hispanic-immigrants-than-u-s-born-lack-health-insurance.

Luque, John S., Caroline B. Davila Grace Soulen, and Kathleen Cartmell. 2018. "Access to Health Care for Uninsured Latina Immigrants in South Carolina." *BMC Health Services Research* 18(1): 310. doi: 10.1186/s12913-018-3138-2.

Markides, Kyriakos S. and Karl Eschbach. 2005. "Aging, Migration, and Mortality: Current Status of Research on the Hispanic Paradox." *Journal of Gerontology: Social Sciences* 60(October): S68–S75.

McGarry, Brian E., Robert L. Strawderman, and Li Yue. 2014a. "The Care Span: Lower Hispanic Participation in Medicare Part D May Reflect Program Barriers." *Health Affairs (Project Hope)* 33(5): 856–62. doi: 10.1377/hlthaff.2013.0671.

McGarry, Brian E., Robert L. Strawderman, and Li Yue. 2014b. "Lower Hispanic Participation In Medicare Part D May Reflect Program Barriers." *Health Affairs* 33(5): 856–62. doi: 10.1377/hlthaff.2013.0671.

McGuire, Thomas G., Joseph P. Newhouse, and Anna D. Sinaiko. 2011. "An Economic History of Medicare Part C." *The Milbank Quarterly* 89(2): 289–332. doi: 10.1111/j.1468-0009.2011.00629.x.

McKernan, Signe-Mary, Caroline Ratcliffe, C. Eugene Steuerle, and Sisi Zhang. 2013. "Less than Equal: Racial Disparities in Wealth." Retrieved 1/9/2020 from https://www.urban.org/sites/default/files/publication/23536/412802-less-than-equal-racial-disparities-in-wealth-accumulation.pdf

Medicare.gov. 2019. "Costs for Medicare Advantage Plans: What You Pay in a Medicare Advantage Plan." Retrieved 1/5/2020 from https://www.medicare.gov/your-medicare-costs/costs-for-medicare-advantage-plans.

Monheit, A. C. and J. P. Vistnes. 2008. "Health Insurance Enrollment Decisions: Preferences for Coverage, Worker Sorting, and Insurance Take-up." *Inquiry* 45(2): 153–67. doi: 10.5034/inquiryjrnl_45.02.153.

Montez, Jennifer Karas, Jacqueline L. Angel, and Ronald J. Angel. 2009. "Employment, Marriage, and Inequality in Health Insurance for Mexican-Origin Women." *Journal of Health and Social Behavior* 50(2): 132–48. doi: 10.1177/002214650905000202.

Moreno, Karina and Lauren Bock Mullins. 2017. "Structural Exclusion and Administrative Burden within the Affordable Care Act: An Exploratory Study of Latinos in Arizona." *Journal of Health and Human Services Administration* 40(3): 262–89.

Narang, Amol K. and Lauren Hersch Nicholas. 2017. "Out-of-pocket Spending and Financial Burden among Medicare Beneficiaries with Cancer." *JAMA Oncology* 3(6): 757–65. doi: 10.1001/jamaoncol.2016.4865.

National Center for Health Statistics. 2011. *Life Expectancy at Birth, at 65 Years of Age, and at 75 Years of Age, by Sex, Race, and Hispanic Origin: United States, Selected Years 1900–2009.* Atlanta, GA: Centers for Disease Control

Ortega, Alexander N., Hector P. Rodriguez, and Arturo Vargas Bustamante. 2015. "Policy Dilemmas in Latino Health Care and Implementation of the Affordable Care Act." *Annual Review of Public Health* 36: 525–44. doi: 10.1146/annurev-publhealth-031914-122421.

Ozawa, Martha N. and Yongwoo Lee. 2006. "The Net Worth of Female-Headed Households: A Comparison to Other Types of Households." *Family Relations* 55(1): 132–45.

Palloni, Alberto. 2007. "Health Status of Elderly Hispanics in the United States." Pp. 1–14 in Jacqueline L. Angel and Keith E. Whitfield (eds.), *The Health of Aging Hispanics: The Mexican-origin Population.* New York: Springer.

Paz, Karen and Kelly P. Massey. 2016. "Health Disparity among Latina Women: Comparison with Non-Latina Women." *Clinical Medicine Insights. Women's Health* 9 (Suppl 1):71–74. doi: 10.4137/CMWH.S38488.

Perez, Debra, Alfonso Ang, and William A. Vega. 2009. doi: "Effects of Health Insurance on Perceived Quality of Care among Latinos in the United States." *Journal of General Internal Medicine* 24(3): 555. doi: 10.1007/s11606-009-1080-z.

Rudowitz, Robin, Rachel Garfield, and Elizabeth Hinton. 2019. "10 Things to Know about Medicaid: Setting the Facts Straight." Retrieved 1/8/2020 from https://www.kff.org/medicaid/issue-brief/10-things-to-know-about-medicaid-setting-the-facts-straight.

Saenz, Rogelio. 2015. "The Demography of the Elderly in the Americas: The Case of the United States and Mexico." In *Challenges of Latino Aging in the Americas*, edited by William A. Vega, Kyriakos S. Markides, Jacqueline L. Angel, and Fernando M. Torres-Gil, 197–223. Basel: Springer International Publishing

Santos, Roberto and Patricia Seitz. 2000. "Benefit Coverage for Latino and Latina Workers." in *Moving up the Economic Ladder: Latino Workers and the Nation's Future Prosperity*, edited by Sonia M. Perez, 162–85 Washington DC: National Council of La Raza.

Stuber, Jennifer and Elizabeth Bradley. 2005. "Barriers to Medicaid Enrollment: Who Is at Risk?" *American Journal of Public Health* 95(2): 292–98. doi: 10.2105/AJPH.2002.006254.

Telles, Edward E. and Vilma Ortiz. 2008. *Generations of Exclusion: Mexican Americans, Assimilation, and Race.* New York: Russell Sage Foundation.

Torres-Gil, Juan Fernando and Jacqueline L. Angel. 2019. "The Politics of a Majority-Minority Nation: Aging, Diversity and Immigration." Edited by Toni Antonucci, *Critical Topics in an Aging Society.* New York: Sage Publishing.

U.S. Bureau of Labor Statistics. 2019a. "Household Data Annual Averages: Table 10 Employed Persons by Occupation, Race, Hispanic or Latino Ethnicity, and Sex." Retrieved 1/7/2020 from https://www.bls.gov/cps/cpsaat10.htm."

U.S. Bureau of Labor Statistics. 2019b. "Household Data Annual Averages: Table 11. Employed Persons by Detailed Occupation, Sex, Race, and Hispanic or Latino Ethnicity." Retrieved 1/7/2020 from https://www.bls.gov/cps/cpsaat11.htm.

U.S. Bureau of Labor Statistics. 2019c. "Union Membership Rate 10.5 Percent in 2018, down from 20.1 Percent in 1983." Retrieved 1/7/2020 from https://www.bls.gov/opub/

ted/2019/union-membership-rate-10-point-5-percent-in-2018-down-from-20-point-1-percent-in-1983.htm.

Velasco-Mondragon, Eduardo, Anna G. Palladino-Davis Angela Jimenez, Dawn Davis, and Jose A. Escamilla-Cejudo. 2016. "Hispanic Health in the USA: A Scoping Review of the Literature *Public Health Reviews* 37: 31-31. Doi: 10.1186/s40985-016-0043-2.

Winston, Pamela, Ronald J. Angel, Linda M. Burton, Andrew J. Lindsay Chase-Lansdale, Robert A. Moffitt Cherlin, and William Julius Wilson. 1999. *Welfare, Children, and Families: A Three-City Study, Overview and Design*. Baltimore, MD: Johns Hopkins University.

Young, Justin R. and Marybeth J. Mattingly. 2016. Underemployment among Hispanics: The Case of Involuntary Part-time Work. Monthly Labor Review, US Bureau of Labor Statistics. Retrieved 1/7/2020 from https://www.bls.gov/opub/mlr/2016/article/underemployment-among-hispanics.htm.

16

Social Policies and Health Inequalities

Amélie Quesnel-Vallée, Jaunathan Bilodeau, and Kaitlin Conway

The relationship between low social status and poor health and mortality is undoubtedly one of the most persistent empirical findings of contemporary research on population health. Across developed countries, individuals with higher socioeconomic status enjoy better health and lower mortality than individuals below them in the social structure (Antonovsky 1967; WHO 2008; Williams 1990). Moreover, this holds true whether socioeconomic status is measured as education, income or occupation, for different populations and through varied time periods, and using diverse analytic methods (Robert and House 2000).

In contrast with inequalities in health that stem from biological differences brought about by age or genetics, *social* inequalities in health are mutable and avoidable, as they are affected by public policies. In addition, they are also inherently unfair, as the preamble of the constitution of the World Health Organization states that "The enjoyment of the highest attainable standard of health is one of the fundamental rights of every human being without distinction of race, religion, political belief, economic or social condition" (World Health Organization 1948: 1).

In this chapter we focus on the last two sources of health inequalities. We will begin with a high-level overview of the field of social inequalities in health. Next, we will turn to a discussion of some of the most significant macro determinants of health (early life, housing, education, employment, and income), and draw out promising policy implications for each. Given the high volume of research produced on this topic, we have focused our review on studies offering the highest level of evidence, namely systematic reviews and meta-analyses (preferably of causal designs) (Murad et al. 2016). Finally, we end the chapter with a discussion of the rich future research opportunities offered by a focus on structural factors shaping health inequalities.

The Wiley Blackwell Companion to Medical Sociology, First Edition. Edited by William C. Cockerham.

Social Inequalities in Health

Whereas the notion of social inequalities in health has all but become common sense nowadays (Popay et al. 2003), this was not always so. In fact, increases in standards of living, medical advances and the deployment of systems of universal health insurance coverage led many in the 1960s and 1970s to expect that these inequalities in health would fade away. Yet, in the early 1980s, two seminal pieces of evidence, namely the Black Report (Townsend et al. 1982) and the Whitehall studies (Marmot et al. 1984), shattered these assumptions and heralded the onset of this prolific research enterprise. Many terms have been used to describe these associations, such as health disparities (mainly in the US), health inequities (to denote a value judgment on the unfairness of those inequalities), and social inequalities in health (a descriptive statement useful to distinguish inequalities stemming from social and other factors). For parsimony, we will refer to these inequalities in the remainder of the text as simply "health inequalities."

The Black Report (Townsend et al. 1982) was the end result of a British government-mandated Research Working Group on Inequalities in Health. Indeed, despite 30 years of strong welfare state policies, and especially the implementation of the National Health Service (NHS), Great Britain was lagging behind other comparable nations in terms of life expectancy, and the government sought to investigate on the causes of this poor performance. Mortality rates by social class over the previous century and in different countries were examined in what was arguably the first government-initiated attempt to explain trends in socioeconomic inequities in life expectancy and to relate them to policy interventions. Briefly put, this report showed that a socioeconomic gradient in life expectancy existed in the early 1900s and had persisted ever since in Great Britain. Moreover, while the diseases associated with these inequities evolved over time, the gradient itself remained mainly impervious to change and was observed in several other developed nations. In addition, the development of a universal health care (or at least coverage) system in many countries did little to lessen this gradient. Finally, individuals' lifestyles (e.g. smoking, drinking, exercising) could only explain part of the effects of socioeconomic status on mortality.

This report generated substantial political controversy in Great Britain as it challenged several assumptions that had guided policy interventions up until then (Macintyre 1997; Townsend et al. 1982). Notably, these findings dealt a strong blow to the premise that a universal health care system was a sufficient condition for the eradication of social inequities in life expectancy.[1] In addition, the report also showed a social gradient in mortality, whereby life expectancy increases linearly with each additional step in occupational class structure. Finally, these findings disputed the notion that inequalities in health concerned only the most deprived segments of society, and that interventions directed solely at these populations could successfully limit health inequalities.

But it is perhaps following the Whitehall studies that the gradient in health really struck researchers' and decision-makers' imagination the most. In these studies, Sir Marmot and his colleagues followed for close to two decades more than ten thousand British civil servants. Harnessing the fact that this population's professional status was unambiguously hierarchically ordered, Marmot found that, among males aged 40 to 64, age-standardized mortality in the lowest grades (clerical and manual) was three times as high as in the highest grade (administrative). Moreover, these findings also uncovered a gradient in mortality from the top to the bottom of this social hierarchy. Indeed, the less "fortunate" were characterized by poorer health, and this, even in the presence of the universal access to the British medical system.

Furthermore, none of the respondents could be considered materially deprived in terms of absolute poverty. Thus, these findings went beyond the Black Report in contradicting the common view that surmised that health inequalities arose because the poor suffered from the deprivation associated with their material circumstances, showing instead that they ostensibly operated across society, at all levels of the social ladder. Finally, this gradient was apparent for several illnesses, suggesting that it was caused by a prior common factor, anterior to the illnesses themselves.

These studies' main findings were replicated in the US (Pappas et al. 1993), Canada (Evans et al. 1994) and in other countries as well (Marmot et al. 1987). Furthermore, the accumulation of these results have led governments in most developed countries to designate the reduction of socioeconomic inequities in health as a primary population health goal, as stated in the World Health Organization (WHO) Rio Political Declaration on Social Determinants of Health (World Health Organization 2011).

According to the authoritative eponymous book edited by Marmot and Wilkinson (1999), the social determinants of health encompass individuals' material and psychosocial circumstances, and range from the more micro-level of health behaviors and social support to the more macro-level of unemployment rates and policies regarding food and transportation. These determinants are graphically represented in Figure 16.1 (Acheson 1998). In this figure, human populations appear at the center, and are conceptualized as being endowed with age, sex, biological and genetic characteristics. These biological factors are considered fixed and not amenable to intervention from public health policies. In contrast, the layers surrounding individuals are alterable by policy interventions. The recognition of the importance of these determinants for health cannot be understated: there has been a call from primary care practice to incorporate social determinants of health such as income in health history and risk factor assessments in addition to the more standard biological factors (Andermann 2016).

We have limited the scope of this chapter to the third and fourth layers, as they are the ones that are most pertinent to the study of social policies, which we define as "State and government interventions that contribute to the well-being of individuals and communities and foster full citizenship" (Vaillancourt et al. 2004: 313).[2] Within the realm of determinants that constitute the third layer, we restricted our analysis further to those that have received the most attention in the field, namely early life, housing, education, employment (encompassing the work environment and unemployment), and income.[3]

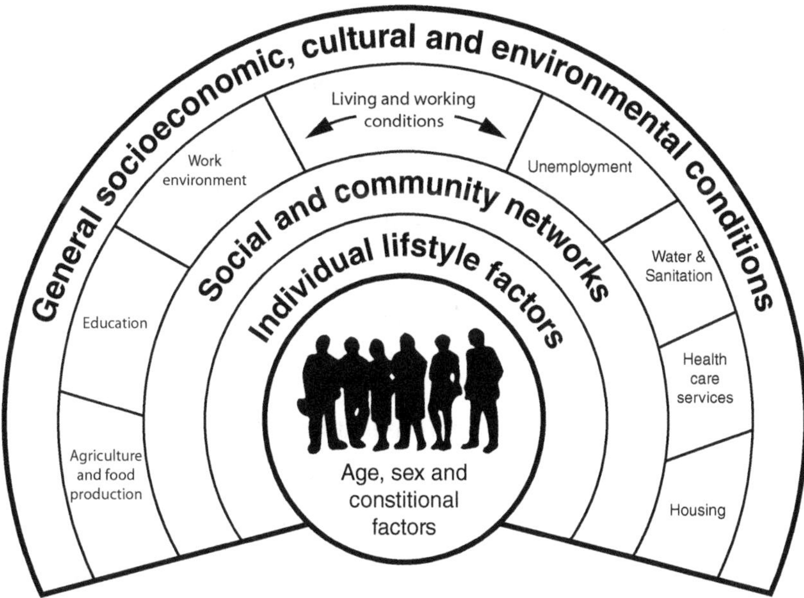

Figure 16.1 The main determinants of health.
Source: (Acheson 1998; Dahlgren and Whitehead 1991).

Social Policies and Health Inequalities

Early Life

Early childhood development which occurs in the first eight years of life (including physical, social, emotional and cognitive development) is crucial for health outcomes later in life, since it sets the stage for future health, employment potential and social relationships (WHO Commission on Social Determinants of Health 2008). Social inequalities can emerge as early as from deleterious exposures *in utero* (Wadsworth 1999). Support for this hypothesis has come notably from cohort studies of individuals having suffered through "natural experiments" of starvation, such as studies of the Dutch Famine Birth (Panel on Dietary Reference Intakes for Macronutrients, National Academy of Sciences 2002). These studies found individuals who were severely undernourished in early gestation to be at higher risk of obesity, coronary heart disease, and lower self-reported health, which suggests that they would also exhibit higher mortality in the future (Roseboom et al. 2011, 2001).

Following birth, social variations in breastfeeding can also have long-lasting effects throughout the life course. Exclusive breastfeeding is recommended for the first six months of an infant's life, as it has been linked with decreased risk of gastrointestinal tract infection and atopic eczema in the first year of life, and improved cognitive development at age 6, among other benefits (Horta et al. 2007; Horta and Victora 2013). Yet, breastfeeding rates are notoriously lower amongst socioeconomically deprived groups in developed countries, which puts additional pressure on already strained finances from the need to purchase formula, and can increase the risk of a number of nutritional and developmental deficiencies for their children (Amir and Donath 2008; Heck et al. 2006).

Finally, studies have found that adverse socioeconomic conditions during childhood were associated with greater risk of health outcomes such as poor self-reported health, cardiovascular disease and higher mortality independently of adult social circumstances (Cohen et al. 2010; Pillas et al. 2014). These findings also highlight the impact of intergenerational processes of deprivation and the fact that interventions that target parents' social inclusion, health and wellbeing will have knock-on effects on their children's health, and well into the future (Case et al. 2005).

Policy Implications

This research highlights the importance of investing now to create healthy social circumstances for children, as this can be used as "money in the bank" for future generations and to prevent the onset of processes of cumulative disadvantage (O'Rand 1996). While most women in developed countries receive adequate prenatal care, socioeconomic differences in perinatal outcomes (premature births and small-for-gestational-age babies) are still evident (Joseph et al. 2007). Nutritional differences may be at play here, and programs such as Quebec's OLO (*oeuf, lait, orange*), which provides one egg, one pint of milk and one orange a day to pregnant women in need have been found to be relatively inexpensive ways to improve perinatal outcomes among those populations (Fondation OLO. 2020). Breastfeeding can also be promoted by ensuring optimal conditions for mother-newborn bonding, and the WHO developed a certification process to recognize birthing units that follow those policy recommendations and are therefore deemed "baby-friendly" (World Health Organization 2020).

Policies aimed at stopping the circle of intergenerational disadvantage involve strengthening and improving early childhood development programs and making them universally accessible so that all children would begin school on equal footing, regardless of their social background. Other initiatives have revolved around providing adequate childcare options to parents and improved diet and nutrition for children (Black et al. 2017). Examples include the educare system in Sweden and the provision of subsidized childcare in Quebec.

Ultimately, the most efficient policies will ensure coherence across different departments such that a comprehensive approach to child health may be implemented (WHO Commission on Social Determinants of Health 2008). An example of such a concerted effort was the "Every Child Matters" agenda in Britain, which aimed at promoting children's health, safety, academic achievement, civic involvement and responsibility, and economic well-being (Government of the United Kingdom 2003).

Housing

Increasing levels of urbanization bring about new health risks such as increased air pollution as well as violence and accidents, while overcrowding facilitates the spread of infectious diseases (WHO Commission on Social Determinants of Health 2008).

In addition, studies show that the most common occupants of poor quality housing include families with children (and particularly lone-parent households), the elderly, the sick and the disabled (Murie 2008). This situation was aggravated over the past three decades by diminishing governmental funding for affordable and subsidized housing in many developed countries, including Canada, the US and the UK (Goering and Whitehead 2017; Shapcott 2008).

Inadequate housing has been associated with a number of negative health outcomes, including asthma, poisoning and injuries (Bonnefoy 2007; Lo and O'Connell 2005). Overcrowding is also harmful, as it can lead to the proliferation of infectious diseases such as tuberculosis and increased stress levels. Low-income individuals are more likely to live in these types of conditions given the limited housing options available to them (Bonnefoy 2007).

Another consequence of the welfare state retrenchment in affordable and subsidized housing (often coupled with health care reforms centered around deinstitutionalisation of mentally ill individuals) has been a secular rise in homelessness in many countries (Levinson 2004). A meta-analysis of the relationship between homelessness and health found that homeless individuals have higher mortality rates than the general population (though this is less true in Canada than in the US, due in part to universal healthcare) (Hwang 2001). The homeless are also prone to more severe diseases due to delays in seeking treatment, extreme poverty, challenges in complying with medical care, and cognitive or mental impairment. Particularly prevalent are poorly controlled chronic diseases, infectious diseases, and injuries and accidents (Schanzer et al. 2007). Finally, mental illness and substance abuse are rampant, as schizophrenia and alcoholism are disproportionately represented in the homeless male population (Ayano et al. 2019). Conversely, housing trials have demonstrated positive effects for several social and health outcomes, demonstrating that the lack of housing itself was exacerbating the consequences of many of these root causes (Baxter et al. 2019).

Policy Implications

It is therefore evident that in order to reduce social inequalities in health, affordably-priced, healthy living spaces are essential (WHO Commission on Social Determinants of Health 2008). This may include government-subsidized residential projects or programs to encourage home ownership. A recently successful example of this type of project is Housing First, which has been implemented in different cities across the US and Canada, among other countries. Results from the At Home/Chez Soi randomized control trial in Canada show the Housing First approach to be beneficial in moving homeless individuals with severe mental illness into stable housing (Aubry et al. 2015).

In addition, improved urban planning must include adequate public transport services and regulated retail planning to improve the availability and affordability of healthy foods (and limit the availability of less healthy options, like fast foods and alcohol). This is supported by evidence from a randomized control trial of participants of the US Department of Housing and Urban Development's "Moving to Opportunity," an intervention which enabled low-income families to move from areas of high-poverty to areas of low-poverty. Jackson et al. (2009) found that without harm reduction measures in place, moving to a new area still had the potential for negative mental health outcomes among participants and instead suggested investments to improve high-poverty neighbourhoods may be more beneficial to overall health outcomes (Jackson et al. 2009). Finally, these initiatives should also consider the fact that homelessness, landlessness, poverty and displaced individuals also exist in rural areas, and thus that these problems are not just the purview of urban areas.

Education

The relationship between education and health has long been documented (Cutler and Lleras-Muney. 2012; Furnee et al. 2008). The strength and persistence of this association may be due to the fact that education impacts health indirectly, through several pathways. More educated individuals are more likely to be employed full time and occupy a safer, more autonomous and more fulfilling position than their less educated counterparts (Mirowsky and Ross 2003). In contrast, the less educated are often faced with repetitive, routine, non-stimulating, and even plainly physically dangerous jobs, which increase their likelihood of poor physical and mental health (Karmakar and Breslin 2008; Vosko 2006). Individuals with poor education often occupy jobs of lower quality, which often offer lower benefits, and do not pay well (Kalleberg 2011). The better educated tend to adopt healthier lifestyle habits, including being less likely to smoke, drink or eat excessively (Cutler and Lleras-Muney. 2010; Mirowsky and Ross 2003). They are also more likely to seek routine medical care not only because of their knowledge of the importance of those behaviors, but also because they have the financial resources or insurance and social networks required to do so (Link and Phelan 1995).

Policy Implications

Given the evidence outlined above, it seems hardly surprising that one of the most effective ways to reduce health inequalities could be to invest in universal education for all (Campbell et al. 2014; Hahn and Truman 2015). In Canada, research shows that such social investments in education have indeed succeeded in improving socioeconomic position for most Canadians who underwent compulsory education (Oreopoulos 2005).

In addition, as highlighted in the early childhood section, education initiatives should begin as early as possible to foster cognitive and social development at an early age, thus improving chances of succeeding at K-12 schooling (Low et al. 2005). Low and colleagues (2005) have proposed an "Education Starts at Birth" policy scheme, which would involve combining comprehensive childcare, parental education and childhood education initiatives into a single policy goal in order to improve educational outcomes and ultimately, reduce health disparities. Similarly, the World Health Organization's Commission on the Social Determinants of Health (2008) recommended "equity from the start" integrated policies, which includes universal childcare, education and early childhood programmes for all, regardless of ability to pay.

Employment

Gainful employment is one of the most significant social activities in advanced societies both in terms of the time we devote to it over the life course, and because of its importance in providing social standing and facilitating social participation. Its impact on health is thus commensurate.

Unemployment

There is a strong and statistically robust association between unemployment and higher morbidity and mortality, especially with regards to cardiovascular disease and suicide (Roelfs et al. 2011). Poor mental health is also dynamically associated with unemployment (independent of previous mental health), as it can improve once employment is regained (Murphy and Athanasou 1999; Strandh et al. 2014). In addition, most studies show that the unemployed are also more likely to use medical services, such as visit physicians, go to hospitals or take prescription medication, which adds to the social costs related to unemployment beyond the underutilisation of human resources (Jin et al. 1997).

Despite these associations, the pathways whereby unemployment affects health remain unclear. Some have posited that the relationship between employment and health may be due to a selection effect, whereby poor health leads to higher risk of unemployment. Overall, however, the main explanatory mechanisms are thought to run causally from employment to health (Schmitz 2011; Sermet and Khlat 2004). Unemployment jeopardizes income stability, which can lead to lower standards of living and the need to borrow money and/or sell property, all of which has been associated with higher rates of depression, stress, and poor health (Bartley et al. 1999).

Another pathway could involve the psychosocial stressors inherent to unemployment. In addition to earnings, a secure job provides a daily routine, a valued status and identity, and socialization opportunities, all of which are lost during unemployment. Accordingly, decreased self-esteem, alienation and isolation are associated with unemployment (Salsali and Silverstone 2003). The impact of these stressors could also manifest itself through poor health behaviors (smoking, drinking, drug use and over-eating), which have been found to occur more frequently among the unemployed (Arcaya et al. 2014).

Work Conditions

The effects of employment on health are not limited to those who are out of work, however. Insecure, precarious or unsafe employment can also have just as negative effects on one's health as unemployment (Benach et al. 2007, 2014). In particular, precarious or contingent employment which involves "a cumulative combination of atypical employment contracts, limited social benefits, poor statutory entitlements, job insecurity, short tenure and low wages" (Lewchuk et al. 2003: 23) has indeed been associated with poorer health outcomes. Precarious jobs thus feature a combination of decreased job security, fewer benefits, lower wages and increased likelihood of hazardous work conditions, all of which can have negative effects on health (Benach et al. 2014; Joyce et al. 2010; Quesnel-Vallée et al. 2010).

Policy Implications

High rates of employment are beneficial for any government, since the population tends to be happier (and healthier), and there is more tax revenue and fewer expenditures on social benefits such as health care and unemployment insurance (Deacon 2000). Yet when unemployment does occur, the negative health effects of income loss can be mitigated by social policies through unemployment benefits, as was demonstrated in the US by Cylus and Avendano (2017), using methods allowing for causal inference.

However, policies need to go beyond approaches to reduce unemployment or simply the mitigation of income loss and consider the complex needs of unemployed individuals (who may in fact be experiencing other social problems concurrently). According to Bartley et al. (1999), governments should provide "spring boards," not simply safety nets for the unemployed, particularly in contexts with structurally high unemployment.

For example, Britain's "Welfare-to-Work" policy implemented in 1998 aimed at increasing the number of jobs available to welfare recipients, while also improving their eligibility for such positions by encouraging motivation and skill-development through training programs with generous participation incentives. Results from systematic reviews of this type of program in North America have not been positive, however. According to Gibson et al. (2017), health benefits among single parents participating in a welfare-to-work program were marginal, with ongoing poverty among participants thought to be a mediating factor.

Income

Individuals with lower income tend to experience higher morbidity and mortality (Kawachi et al. 2010). Many have found that this relationship follows a linear income gradient, whereby each additional dollar of income brings health benefits (Case et al. 2002; Currie and Stabile 2002). However, yet others have found that income has a non-linear (logarithmic) relationship with morbidity and mortality such that the positive effects of income on health mainly or only occur at lower income levels (Dowd et al. 2011), and still others have found that the effects of income on health among children in particular is largely mediated by maternal health status (Khanam et al. 2009; Propper et al. 2007).

Poverty, and the associated material deprivation, has also long been recognized as a strong determinant of poor health (Conroy et al. 2010). Those in poverty have been found to be more likely to experience higher accident mortality rates, higher degrees of activity restriction and poorer self-rated health (Direction de la santé publique 2002). They are also more likely to engage in unhealthy behaviours, such as smoking or drinking (Peretti-Watel et al. 2009). Furthermore, a systematic review of 17 studies concluded that social assistance is generally insufficient to maintain the health of socioeconomically disadvantaged populations (Shahidi et al. 2019), suggesting that these policies are not mitigating the negative effects of poverty on health inequalities.

Low income can also have significant effects on self-esteem (Salsali and Silverstone 2003) and is thus sometimes associated with high rates of suicide and depression (Patel 2001; Sher 2005). In addition, women and children tend to be disproportionately affected by low income. For instance, low income has been associated with higher infant mortality rates, higher hospital admission rates, and increased risk of injuries, illness and developmental problems among children (Kim and Saada 2013). Despite this, people with lower income have been found to have poorer access to physicians than their richer counterparts, sometimes even in countries with universal health care like Canada (Dunlop, Coyte, and McIsaac 2000).

Policy Implications

With poverty rates and inequality on the rise across developed countries, redistributive income policies should be a priority for policymakers (Pickett and Wilkinson 2015; Shaw et al. 1999). In light of the findings of the 2008 Commission on the Social Determinants of Health, there has been also been an increased push for greater equality in access to other health-improving resources. According to Michael Marmot, "relative disadvantage with respect to income translates into absolute disadvantage in empowerment and control over one's life [...] It is not what you have that is important for health, but what you can do with what you have" (Marmot 2015: 2444). As such, there is also a need for providing adequate employment, education, training, housing and childcare opportunities for low-income families in order to mitigate the effects of their social circumstances on their health (Marmot and Bell 2012; Stephen et al. 2008).

Following the 2008 Great Recession, with the rising awareness of growing income inequalities (e.g. the "Occupy" movement), and given growing concerns that technological advances could lead to a new world of work rendering many human workers obsolete, many jurisdictions have begun considering a "radical" policy shift with regards to state income support, namely the provision of basic income/guaranteed minimum income support to all. This policy has been or is being rolled out in trials in many jurisdictions, with promising effects on health inequalities (Beck, Pulkki-Brännström, and San Sebastián 2015; Forget 2011; Gibson et al. 2020)

Opportunities for the Study of Social Policy and Health Inequalities

Structural Determinants of Health Inequalities

One of the primary explanations for the persistence of health inequalities is that government policies have left most of the fundamental causes of health inequality largely unaltered (Braveman and Gottlieb 2014; Link and Phelan 1995; Mackenbach 2012). These fundamental causes share the following four characteristics (Link and Phelan 1995). First, they contribute to the apparition of several diseases. Second, they affect diseases through multiple risk factors. Third, they include access to resources that can help to prevent health risks or minimize the aftereffects of a disease once it occurs. Fourth, the association between a fundamental cause and different health outcomes persist over time through the substitution of the mechanisms involved. Because of the conflation of the social determinants of health with the causes of the unequal distribution of health, governments can miss their targets if they do not also consider the determinants of health inequalities (Graham 2004). Thus, the structuring impacts of important axes of inequalities such as gender, racism/ethnicity and social class remain significantly less integrated in health inequalities research (Gkiouleka et al. 2018).

As illustrated in Figure 16.2, the fundamental causes of health are conceptualized as part of the determinants of health inequalities. They influence the distribution of health among a population via multiple mechanisms such as exposure, vulnerability and the response to the social determinant of health (Solar and Irwin 2010). This model also highlights the role of the socioeconomic and sociopolitical context in the distribution of health among the population. This recognition has prompted calls for complementing social epidemiology with political sociology or political epidemiology (Beckfield and Krieger 2009; Krieger 2011). In this section, we will discuss some of these determinants of health inequalities. After addressing the empirical literature on the relationship between social policies and health inequalities, we will focus on gender, racism/ethnicity and social class from a social policy perspective.

The upstream causes of health inequalities have remained largely outside the research agenda until quite recently (Beckfield and Krieger 2009; Pega et al. 2013). To fill this gap, a growing number of studies have looked at the relationship between the welfare state and health inequalities, based on the assumption that countries

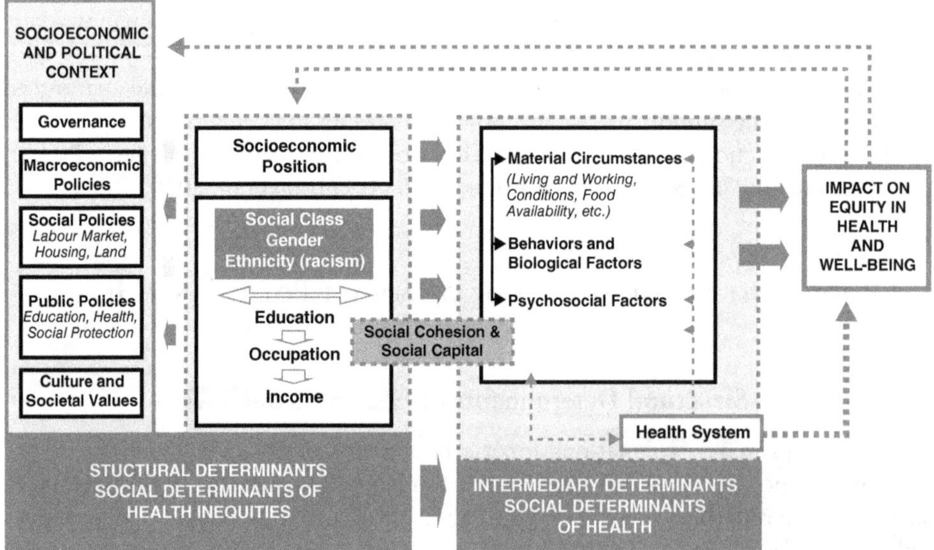

Figure 16.2 The Commission on the Social Determinants of Health conceptual framework.
Source: (Solar and Irwin 2010).

with universal and generous social policies would be the most successful in reducing socioeconomic inequalities in health. This approach is largely grounded in the typology proposed by Esping-Andersen (1990), which groups countries according to the extent to which their policies reduce the level of dependence of individuals on the labor market (i.e. decommodification) to maintain a decent standard of living, the type of social stratification and the relation between the state, the market and the family. According to Esping-Anderson, liberal countries such as the UK and the USA offer the lowest levels of decommodification, while decommodification is highest in social-democratic regimes such as Denmark and Norway. However, this typology does not lead to unambiguous support for the performance of social democratic countries in reducing health inequalities, which has been attributed to the fact that a heterogenous classification of the countries and concepts that were not developed with health as an outcome fail to explain the significant variations that may exist within the country groupings (Bergqvist et al. 2013; Brennenstuhl, Quesnel-Vallée, and McDonough 2012)

Research has also focused on the effect of public investments in health and health inequalities (Bergqvist et al. 2013). Some of these findings indicate that health inequalities are lower among countries with higher public spending and that social spending works to moderate the relationship between socioeconomic status and health (Álvarez-Gálvez and Jaime-Castillo 2018; McAllister et al. 2018; McCartney et al. 2019b). However, this research has been questioned due to its high risk of path-dependency and endogeneity.

Finally, the institutional approach focuses on how welfare institutions and specific social policies and programs affect population health and its distribution (Bergqvist et al. 2013). In an umbrella review, Pega et al. (2013) distinguishes the political approach from the individual policy approach. The political approach refers to research that link tradition and political ideology, processes, systems or institutions to population health. As an example, a 2019 umbrella review found that neoliberal restructuring increases health inequality (McCartney et al. 2019b). In turn, the individual policy approach involves studies evaluating the effect of clearly defined, specific policies on population health and health equality. According to Pega et al. (2013), the individual policy approach, which emerged in the context of evidence-based policy, would offer the most promising avenue for research on the relation between social policies and health inequality.

Indeed, the individual policy approach provides some compelling and actionable empirical evidence regarding the reduction of health inequalities. The aforementioned review from Bergqvist et al. (2013) showed that family benefits, pension benefits, economic and unemployment benefits and access to health care are beneficial for the health of the overall population and not just the most vulnerable segments or targeted population. Social policies targeting tobacco, alcohol, food and nutrition, reproductive health services, infectious disease control, the environment and work regulation also show significant effects according to a recent umbrella review (Thomson et al. 2018). The authors conclude that taxes on unhealthy food and drinks, food subsidy programs addressed to women of low socioeconomic status, and fiscal incentive schemes for childhood vaccinations are effective in reducing health inequalities. However, fiscal interventions such as taxes on tobacco and free fruit provision in schools have no overall effect on health inequalities. In turn, a 2019 umbrella review of 62 systematic reviews provides evidence that regulating tobacco, alcohol and food markets would be beneficial for population health and for reducing health inequalities when the interventions result in access restrictions, notably via taxation (Naik et al. 2019). However, regarding the field at large, an umbrella review conducted in 2019 revealed that evidence on the effect of social protection policies on health inequalities remains sparse, of low quality and of limited generality due to an emphasis on the Anglo-Saxon welfare type (Hillier-Brown et al. 2019). This suggests that much remains to be done on this front and points to a promising avenue for future research.

Throughout the next sections, we will briefly discuss the roles of gender, racism and social class in structuring health inequalities. Since the relationship between social class, gender, racism and ethnicity are already discussed in depth in Chapters 11, 12, 13, 14, and 15, we will only briefly address the relationships between these structural factors and health inequalities with a social policies lens.

Gender

The differences in mortality and morbidity between men and women are among the most consistent and well documented in medical sociology and social epidemiology literature. Although differences have begun to narrow over the years, life expectancy continues to be higher among women and they generally experience longer periods of poor health compared to men (Rieker and Read 2017).

Gender is a multidimensional and multilevel process. It subsumes a confluence of economic relations, power relations and emotional relations. It operates simultaneously at the intrapersonal, interpersonal and institutional levels (Springer et al. 2012). As shown in Figure 16.2, gender fundamentally structures socioeconomic differences between men and women. Consequently, women remain underrepresented in many of the most prestigious and influential occupations, and income inequality between men and women continues to be pervasive in many countries (Gkiouleka et al. 2018; Read and Gorman 2010). As an illustration, studies show that male-to-female transition among transgender people is associated with a decrease in salary while female-to-male transition is associated with an increase in salary (Lorber 1994; Schilt and Wiswall 2008).

Far from being a binary variable, it has been established that gender can intervene via multiple mechanisms and at different levels of analysis of the health inequalities between men and women. For example, results from a 2019 study by Homan demonstrate deleterious effects for women and men at the macro level as structural sexism increases (Homan 2019). At the mesosocial level, the effects of structural sexism would increase for women but decrease for men while no significant effect was found at the microsocial level.

More recently, studies have attempted to document how gendered welfare regimes and social policies can contribute to health inequalities. A systematic review showed that policies supporting women's participation in the labor force and decreasing their burden of care, including the provision of public services, support for families and entitlements for fathers, are all negatively related to health inequality between men and women (Palència et al. 2017). This finding is consistent with the review of McAllister et al. (2018) showing that dual-earner welfare (typically Nordic countries) are associated with less mental health inequality between women and men. Another study supports that employment incentives and private market subsidies, government spending on rehabilitation, residential and home-help services, and old-age residual and home-care services are more advantageous for men compared to women in terms of mortality reduction (Beckfield et al. 2018). However, women tend to benefit more than men in terms of all-cause mortality when it comes to social investments that stimulate job creation through public employment.

Racism

Substantial research suggests that even after adjusting for age, sex, education, income, severity of illness and other variables, health disparities based on immigrant status, race categories and ethnicity persist (Hyman 2009; Phelan and Link 2015; Williams et al. 2019). For example, black Americans have been found to have shorter life expectancies and worse health outcomes than white Americans (Phelan and Link 2015).

Like gender, racism is seen as a structural process with manifestations visible across several levels of society (Williams et al. 2019). According to Williams, racism is a "organized social system in which the dominant racial group, based on an ideology of inferiority, categorize and rank people into social groups called 'race' and uses its power to devaluate, disempower and differentially allocate valued resources and opportunities to group defined as inferior" (Williams et al. 2019: 2). This has concrete implications for health. As an illustration, a recent study showed that across all states, increasing racial inequity in unemployment was associated with a 5% increase in black infant mortality (Wallace et al. 2017).

The specific history of the USA contributed to an early research focus on the link between racism and the welfare state (Bailey et al. 2017). This connection is in line with the concept of structural racism which refers to the processes of racism rooted in the laws (local, state and federal), policies and practices of society and its institutions (Williams et al. 2019). This structural racism has knock-on effects for discrimination through mutually reinforcing systems of housing, education, employment, income, benefits, credit, media, health care, and criminal justice (Bailey et al. 2017). Thus, behind the appearance of racial neutrality, several authors have illustrated how social policies and laws can participate in structural racism via their indirect effects (Bailey et al. 2017; Hicken et al. 2018; Williams et al. 2019).

Despite rich literature related to structural racism, the specific relation between racialized public policies and health inequalities remains in the early stages. Research on structural racism has not been adequately integrated into medical and scientific literature intended to clinicians and other health professionals (Bailey et al. 2017). Recently, studies have documented the relation between racialized legal status and the role of residential segregation on health inequalities, however again the empirical support remains sparse (Asad and Clair 2018; Bailey et al. 2017). Finally, while many countries debate the use of the concept of race in their vital and national statistics, mounting evidence suggests that similar processes may be at play in their jurisdictions, requiring the consideration of these "master statuses" in their analyses (Veenstra 2019).

Social Class

There is a strong indication that social class contributes to health inequalities (Muntaner et al. 2017; Solar and Irwin 2010). Although that social class has sometimes been used interchangeably with socioeconomic status, these concepts nevertheless have different implications, as social class arises from a social status process while socioeconomic status is more anchored in the stratification perspective (McCartney et al. 2019a; Muntaner et al. 2017; Solar and Irwin 2010).

Unlike socioeconomic status, for which indicators such as education, income and occupation are easier to obtain, the relationship between social class and health inequalities is rarely explored, notably due to a lack of measures permitting to fully capture the processes relating to social class (McCartney et al. 2019a).

Little research has documented the relationship between state regimes and social class inequalities in health. Based on Wright's (1997) conceptual framework combining stratification concepts with Marxist and Weberian traditions of social class, Espelt et al. (2008) use ownership, credentials and management position as indicators of social class, and examine their relation to self-reported health and long-term illness in the various welfare regime developed by Huber et al. (1997). The results show that the least educated people had poorer perceived health and more long-term illness than the most educated people and this relationship was higher in late democracy countries. Similarly drawing on Wright's conceptual model of social class, another recent longitudinal study analyzed whether the relationship between social class and self-reported health and chronic conditions vary significantly depending on five welfare regimes (Nordic, Anglo-Saxon, Eastern, Southern, and Continental) (Muntaner et al. 2017). They divided social class into three categories: business owners with employees, self-employed or employees with high education, or self-employed or employees with low education. They found that the social class gradient in health was significantly wider in the Anglo-Saxon and Southern regimes.

Intersectionality

While we are mindful that the integration of each axis (of gender, racism/ethnicity and social class) in the study of the relationship between social policies and social inequalities has barely begun to emerge, we cannot end without mentioning the intersectional approach, which invites us to subsume this compartmentalized vision of power relation (Gkiouleka et al. 2018; Lapalme et al. 2019). The intersectional approach opts instead for an understanding of power through the intersection of different structural power systems (Lapalme et al. 2019). According to this perspective, the combination of several statuses can give rise to health inequalities that go far beyond their individual additive effect.

Despite an increased consideration of intersectionality in empirical studies on health, few studies had adopted an intersectional lens to document health inequalities and its integration in the field remains essentially theoretical (Gkiouleka et al. 2018; Lapalme et al. 2019). However, there is some evidence of the relevance of this approach among the studies presented in this chapter. For instance, Brennenstuhl et al. (2012) show that many studies found that the effect of the welfare regime on socioeconomic inequality in health differs by sex categories. Similarly, the wider social class inequality in health among late democracy observed by Espelt et al. (2008) is significantly more pronounced among women. Similar effects might be expected for combinations of statuses that tend to weaken ties to the labor market, such as non-white migrant women from countries with lower gender equity ratios (Setia et al. 2011).

Challenges of Enacting Healthy Public Policy

While this area of research has seen a massive expansion since the 1990s, it is only in the past two decades that governments have begun enacting policies that explicitly tackle health inequalities and the unequal distribution of their social determinants (Graham and Power 2004). Thus, public health policy in many countries now has broadened its mandate from a concern with population health to the protection of health equity and the promotion of health in all policies (World Health Organization 2014).

Yet, as we have discussed above, these initiatives can conflate the social determinants of health and the social processes that create an unequal distribution of those determinants in society. This confusion has led to policy perspectives that wrongly assume that addressing health determinants will also de facto reduce inequalities. Thus, while recent decades have seen population improvements in the social determinants of health (e.g. rising living standards, higher average education, lower smoking rates), with concomitant benefits in average population health, health inequalities have persisted or even increased. Many have therefore come to recommend that, to truly address health inequalities, policy agendas will have to tackle not only the social determinants of health, but also the determinants of social inequality that shape the myriad ways in which social advantage cumulates over the life course and across generations. As the last section of our chapter demonstrates, this is where future research efforts are needed, in order to support evidence-informed policies in this area.

Notes

1 Which is not to say that health systems do not contribute to health inequalities: as the weight of evidence coming from the US shows, unequal health systems can further exacerbate health inequalities. [see chapter 26].
2 See Chapter 8 for discussions of the individual lifestyle factors.
3 Given that four chapters are devoted to health systems in this book, we point the reader to Chapters 15, 26, 27, 28 for a discussion of this area of policy intervention.

References

Acheson, Donald, (ed). 1998. *Independent Inquiry into Inequalities in Health: Report.* London: The Stationery Office.

Álvarez-Gálvez, Javier and Antonio M. Jaime-Castillo. 2018. "The Impact of Social Expenditure on Health Inequalities in Europe." *Social Science & Medicine* 200: 9–18.

Amir, Lisa H. and Susan M. Donath. 2008. "Socioeconomic Status and Rates of Breastfeeding in Australia: Evidence from Three Recent National Health Surveys." *Medical Journal of Australia* 189(5): 254–56.

Andermann, Anne. 2016. "Taking Action on the Social Determinants of Health in Clinical Practice: A Framework for Health Professionals." *CMAJ : Canadian Medical Association Journal* 188(17–18): E474–83.

Antonovsky, Aaron. 1967. "Social Class, Life Expectancy and Overall Mortality." *The Milbank Memorial Fund Quarterly* 45(2): 31.

Arcaya, Mariana, M., Nicholas A. Maria Glymour, Ichiro Kawachi Christakis, and S. V. Subramanian. 2014. "Individual and Spousal Unemployment as Predictors of Smoking and Drinking Behavior." *Social Science & Medicine (1982)* 110: 89–95.

Asad, Asad L. and Matthew Clair. 2018. "Racialized Legal Status as a Social Determinant of Health." *Social Science & Medicine* 199: 19–28.

Aubry, Tim, Geoffrey Nelson, and Sam Tsemberis. 2015. "Housing First for People with Severe Mental Illness Who are Homeless: A Review of the Research and Findings from the at Home – Chez Soi Demonstration Project." *The Canadian Journal of Psychiatry* 60(11): 467–74.

Ayano, Getinet, Getachew Tesfaw, and Shegaye Shumet. 2019. The Prevalence of Schizophrenia and Other Psychotic Disorders Among Homeless People: A Systematic Review and Meta-Analysis. *BMC Psychiatry*, 19(1): 370.

Bailey, Zinzi D., Nancy Krieger, Madina Agénor, Jasmine Graves, Natalia Linos, and Mary T. Bassett. 2017. "Structural Racism and Health Inequities in the USA: Evidence and Interventions." *The Lancet* 389(10077): 1453–63.

Bartley, Mel, Jane Ferrie, and Scott M. Montgomery. 1999. "Living in a High-Unemployment Economy: Understanding the Health Consequences." Pp. 81–104 in *Social Determinants of Health*, edited by M. Marmot and R. G. Wilkinson. Oxford: Oxford University Press.

Baxter, Andrew J., Emily J. Tweed, Srinivasa Vittal Katikireddi, and Hilary Thomson. 2019. Effects of Housing First approaches on health and well-being of adults who are homeless or at risk of homelessness: systematic review and meta-analysis of randomised controlled trials. *Journal of Epidemiology and Community Health*, 73(5) : 379–387.

Beck, Simon, Anni-Maria Pulkki-Brännström, and Miguel San Sebastián. 2015. "Basic Income – Healthy Outcome? Effects on Health of an Indian Basic Income Pilot Project: A Cluster Randomised Trial:" *Journal of Development Effectiveness* 7(1).

Beckfield, Jason and Nancy Krieger. 2009. "Epi+ Demos+ Cracy: Linking Political Systems and Priorities to the Magnitude of Health Inequities – Evidence, Gaps, and a Research Agenda." *Epidemiologic Reviews* 31(1): 152–77.

Beckfield, Jason, Katherine Ann Morris, and Clare Bambra. 2018. "How Social Policy Contributes to the Distribution of Population Health: The Case of Gender Health Equity." *Scandinavian Journal of Public Health* 46(1): 6–17.

Benach, Joan, Carles Muntaner, and Vilma Santana, and Employment Conditions Knowledge Network (EMCONET). 2007. *Employment Conditions and Health Inequalities: Final Report to the WHO Commission on the Social Determinants of Health (CSDH).* Geneva: World Health Organization.

Benach, Joan, Alejandra Vives, Marcelo Amable, Christophe Vanroelen, Gemma Tarafa, and Carles Muntaner. 2014. "Precarious Employment: Understanding an Emerging Social Determinant of Health." *Annual Review of Public Health* 35: 229–53.

Bergqvist, Kersti, Monica Åberg Yngwe, and Olle Lundberg. 2013. "Understanding the Role of Welfare State Characteristics for Health and Inequalities–an Analytical Review." *BMC Public Health* 13(1): 1234.

Black, Maureen M., Susan P. Walker, C. H. Lia, Christopher T. Andersen Fernald, Ann M. DiGirolamo, Chunling Lu, Dana C. McCoy, Günther Fink, Yusra R. Shawar, Jeremy Shiffman, Amanda E. Devercelli, Quentin T. Wodon, Emily Vargas-Barón, and Sally Grantham-McGregor. 2017. "Early Childhood Development Coming of Age: Science through the Life Course." *The Lancet* 389(10064): 77–90.

Bonnefoy, Xavier. 2007. "Inadequate Housing and Health: An Overview." *International Journal of Environment and Pollution* 30(3/4): 411–29.

Braveman, Paula and Laura Gottlieb. 2014. "The Social Determinants of Health: It's Time to Consider the Causes of the Causes." *Public Health Reports* 129(Supplement 2): 19–31.

Brennenstuhl, Sarah, Amélie Quesnel-Vallée, and McDonough, Peggy. 2012. "Welfare Regimes, Population Health and Health Inequalities: A Research Synthesis." *Journal of Epidemiology and Community Health* 66(5): 397–409.

Campbell, Frances, James J. Heckman Gabriella Conti, Seong Hyeok Moon, Rodrigo Pinto, Elizabeth Pungello, and Yi Pan. 2014. "Early Childhood Investments Substantially Boost Adult Health." *Science* 343(6178): 1478–85.

Case, Anne, Angela Fertig, and Christina Paxson. 2005. "The Lasting Impact of Childhood Health and Circumstance." *Journal of Health Economics* 24(2): 365–89.

Case, Anne, Darren Lubotsky, and Christina Paxson. 2002. "Economic Status and Health in Childhood: The Origins of the Gradient." *American Economic Review* 92(5): 1308–34.

Cohen, Sheldon, Denise Janicki-Deverts, Edith Chen, and Karen A. Matthews. 2010. "Childhood Socioeconomic Status and Adult Health." *Annals of the New York Academy of Sciences* 1186(1): 37–55.

Conroy, Kathleen, Megan Sandel, and Barry Zuckerman. 2010. "Poverty Grown Up: How Childhood Socioeconomic Status Impacts Adult Health:" *Journal of Developmental & Behavioral Pediatrics* 31(2): 154–60.

Currie, Janet and Mark Stabile. 2002. *Socioeconomic Status and Health: Why Is the Relationship Stronger for Older Children? NBER-WP-9098*. Cambridge, MA: National Bureau of Economic Research.

Cutler, David and Adriana Lleras-Muney. 2012. *Education and Health: Insights from International Comparisons.* Working Paper 17738. Cambridge, MA: National Bureau of Economic Research.

Cutler, David M. and Adriana Lleras-Muney. 2010. "Understanding Differences in Health Behaviors by Education." *Journal of Health Economics* 29(1): 1–28.

Cylus, Jonathan and Mauricio Avendano. 2017. "Receiving Unemployment Benefits May Have Positive Effects On The Health Of The Unemployed." *Health Affairs* 36(2): 289–96.

Dahlgren, Goran and Margaret Whitehead. 1991. *Policies and Strategies to Promote Social Equity in Health: Background Document to WHO-Strategy Paper for Europe.* Stockholm: Institute for Futures Studies.

David, Low, M., Barbara J. Low, Elizabeth R. Baumler, and Phuong T. Huynh. 2005. "Can Education Policy Be Health Policy? Implications of Research on the Social Determinants of Health." *Journal of Health Politics, Policy and Law* 30(6): 1131–62.

Deacon, Alan. 2000. "Employment." in *The Student's Companion to Social Policy*, edited by P. Alcock, M. May, and K. Rowlingson. Oxford: Blackwell Publishing.

Direction de la santé publique. 2002. *Urban Health: A Vital Factor in Montreal's Development.* Montreal, QC: Régie régionale de la santé et des services sociaux de Montréal-Centre.

Dowd, Jennifer B., Trivellore E. Jeremy Albright, Robert F. Schoeni Raghunathan, Felicia LeClere, and George A. Kaplan. 2011. "Deeper and Wider: Income and Mortality in the USA over Three Decades." *International Journal of Epidemiology* 40(1): 183–88.

Dunlop, Sheryl, Peter C. Coyte, and McIsaac, Warren. 2000. "Socio-economic Status and the Utilisation of Physicians' Services: Results from the Canadian National Population Health Survey." *Social Science & Medicine* 51(1): 123–33.

Espelt, Albert, Carme Borrell, Maica Rodriguez-Sanz, M. Carles Muntaner, Isabel Pasarín, Joan Benach, Maartje Schaap, Anton E. Kunst, and Vicente Navarro. 2008. "Inequalities in Health by Social Class Dimensions in European Countries of Different Political Traditions." *International Journal of Epidemiology* 37(5): 1095–105.

Esping-Andersen, Gosta. 1990. *The Three Worlds of Welfare Capitalism.* Princeton, NJ: Princeton University Press.

Evans, Robert G., Morris L. Barer, and Theodore R. Marmor, (eds). 1994. *Why are Some People Healthy and Others Not? the Determinants of Health Populations.* 1st Edition. New York: Routledge.

Fondation OLO. 2020. "Notre Action." Fondation OLO. Retrieved February 21, 2020 (https://fondationolo.ca/en).

Forget, Evelyn L. 2011. "The Town with No Poverty: The Health Effects of a Canadian Guaranteed Annual Income Field Experiment." *Canadian Public Policy* 37(3): 283–305.

Furnee, Carina A., Wim Groot, and Henriëtte Maassen van den Brink. 2008. "The Health Effects of Education: A Meta-Analysis." *The European Journal of Public Health* 18(4): 417–21.

Gibson, Marcia, Wendy Hearty, and Peter Craig. 2020. "The Public Health Effects of Interventions Similar to Basic Income: A Scoping Review." *The Lancet Public Health* 5(3): e165–76.

Gibson, Marcia, Hilary Thomson, Kasia Banas, Martin J. Vittoria Lutje, Susan P. McKee, Candida Fenton Martin, Clare Bambra, and Lyndal Bond. 2017. "Welfare-to-work Interventions and Their Effects on the Mental and Physical Health of Lone Parents and Their Children." *Cochrane Database of Systematic Reviews* (8), CD009820.

Gkiouleka, Anna, Tim Huijts, Jason Beckfield, and Clare Bambra. 2018. "Understanding the Micro and Macro Politics of Health: Inequalities, Intersectionality & Institutions-A Research Agenda." *Social Science & Medicine* 200: 92–98.

Goering, John and M. E. Whitehead Christine. 2017. "Fiscal Austerity and Rental Housing Policy in the United States and United Kingdom, 2010–2016." *Housing Policy Debate* 27(6): 875–96.

Government of the United Kingdom. 2003. *Every Child Matters.* London: HM Treasury.

Graham, Hilary. 2004. "Social Determinants and Their Unequal Distribution: Clarifying Policy Understandings." *The Milbank Quarterly* 82(1): 101–24.

Graham, Hilary and Christine Power. 2004. "Childhood Disadvantage and Health Inequalities: A Framework for Policy Based on Lifecourse Research." *Child: Care, Health & Development* 30(6): 671–78.

Hahn, Robert A. and Benedict I. Truman. 2015. "Education Improves Public Health and Promotes Health Equity." *International Journal of Health Services* 45(4): 657–78.

Hassan, Murad, M., Noor Asi, Mouaz Alsawas, and Fares Alahdab. 2016. "New Evidence Pyramid." *Evidence Based Medicine* 21(4): 125–27.

Heck, Katherine E., Paula Braveman, Gilberto F. Chávez Catherine Cubbin, and John L. Kiely. 2006. "Socioeconomic Status and Breastfeeding Initiation among California Mothers." *Public Health Reports* 121(1): 51–59.

Hicken, Margaret T., Nicole Kravitz-Wirtz, Myles Durkee, and James S. Jackson. 2018. "Racial Inequalities in Health: Framing Future Research." *Social Science & Medicine* 199: 11.

Hillier-Brown, Frances, Katie Thomson, Victoria Mcgowan, Terje A. Eikemo Joanne Cairns, Diana Gil-Gonzále, and Clare Bambra. 2019. "The Effects of Social Protection Policies on Health Inequalities: Evidence from Systematic Reviews." *Scandinavian Journal of Public Health* 47(6): 655–65.

Homan, Patricia. 2019. "Structural Sexism and Health in the United States: A New Perspective on Health Inequality and the Gender System." *American Sociological Review* 84(3): 486–516.

Horta, Bernardo L., José C. Martines Rajiv Bahl, and Cesar G. Victora. 2007. *Evidence on the Long-Term Effects of Breastfeeding.* Geneva: World Health Organization.

Horta, Bernardo L. and Cesar G. Victora. 2013. *Short-Term Effects of Breastfeeding: A Systematic Review on the Benefits of Breastfeeding on Diarrhoea and Pneumonia Mortality.* Geneva: World Health Organization.

Huber, Evelyne, Charles Ragin, and John D. Stephens. 1997. "Comparative Welfare States Dataset." *Chapel Hill: NC: Northwestern University, University of North Carolina.*

Hwang, Stephen W. 2001. "Homelessness and Health." *CMAJ: Canadian Medical Association Journal* 164(2): 229–33.

Hyman, Ilene. 2009. *Racism as a Determinant of Immigrant Health.* Ottawa, ON: Strategic Initiatives and Innovations Directorate of the Public Health Agency of Canada.

Jackson, Lois, Lynn Langille, Renee Lyons, Jean Hughes, Debbie Martin, and Viola Winstanley. 2009. "Does Moving from A High-Poverty to Lower-Poverty Neighborhood Improve Mental Health? A Realist Review of 'Moving to Opportunity." *Health & Place* 15(4): 961–70.

Jin, Robert L., Chandrakant P. Shah, and Tomislav J. Svoboda. 1997. "The Impact of Unemployment on Health: A Review of the Evidence." *Journal of Public Health Policy* 18(3): 275–301.

Joseph, K. S., Robert M. Liston, Linda Dodds, Leanne Dahlgren, and Alexander C. Allen. 2007. "Socioeconomic Status and Perinatal Outcomes in a Setting with Universal Access to Essential Health Care Services." *CMAJ : Canadian Medical Association Journal* 177(6): 583–90.

Joyce, Kerry, Julia A. Critchley Roman Pabayo, and Clare Bambra. 2010. "Flexible Working Conditions and Their Effects on Employee Health and Wellbeing." *Cochrane Database of Systematic Reviews* (2), CD008009.

Kalleberg, Arne L. 2011. *Good Jobs, Bad Jobs: The Rise of Polarized and Precarious Employment Systems in the United States, 1970s to 2000s.* New York: Russell Sage Foundation.

Karmakar, Sunita D. and F. Curtis Breslin. 2008. "The Role of Educational Level and Job Characteristics on the Health of Young Adults." *Social Science & Medicine* 66(9): 2011–22.

Kawachi, Ichiro, Nancy E. Adler, and William H. Dow. 2010. "Money, Schooling, and Health: Mechanisms and Causal Evidence: Money, Schooling, and Health." *Annals of the New York Academy of Sciences* 1186(1): 56–68.

Khanam, Rasheda, Hong Son Nghiem, and Luke B. Connelly. 2009. "Child Health and the Income Gradient: Evidence from Australia." *Journal of Health Economics* 28(4): 805–17.

Kim, Daniel and Adrianna Saada. 2013. "The Social Determinants of Infant Mortality and Birth Outcomes in Western Developed Nations: A Cross-Country Systematic Review." *International Journal of Environmental Research and Public Health* 10(6): 2296–335.

Krieger, Nancy. 2011. *Epidemiology and the People's Health: Theory and Context.* Oxford: Oxford University Press.

Lapalme, Josée, Rebecca Haines-Saah, and Katherine L. Frohlich. 2019. "More than a Buzzword: How Intersectionality Can Advance Social Inequalities in Health Research." *Critical Public Health* 30(4): 1–7.

Levinson, David. 2004. "Deinstitutionalization." Pp. 110–15 in *Encyclopedia of Homelessness.* Thousand Oaks, CA: Sage Publications.

Lewchuk, Wayne, Alice de Wolff, Andy King, and Michael Polanyi. 2003. "From Job Strain to Employment Strain: Health Effects of Precarious Employment." *Just Labour* 3: 23–35.

Link, Bruce George and Jo Carol Phelan. 1995. "Social Conditions as Fundamental Causes of Disease." *Journal of Health and Social Behavior* 35: 80–94.

Lo, Bernard and Mary Ellen O'Connell, (eds). 2005. "Housing and Health." in *Ethical Considerations for Research on Housing-Related Health Hazards Involving Children.* Washington D.C.: The National Academies Press.

Lorber, Judith. 1994. *Paradoxes of Gender.* New Haven, CT: Yale University Press.

Macintyre, Sally. 1997. "The Black Report and Beyond: What are the Issues?" *Social Science & Medicine* 44(6): 723–45.

Mackenbach, Johan P. 2012. "The Persistence of Health Inequalities in Modern Welfare States: The Explanation of a Paradox." *Social Science & Medicine* 75(4): 761–69.

Marmot, Michael. 2015. "The Health Gap: The Challenge of an Unequal World." *The Lancet* 386(10011): 2442–44.

Marmot, Michael and Ruth Bell. 2012. "Fair Society, Healthy Lives." *Public Health* 126: S4–10.

Marmot, Michael and Richard G. Wilkinson, (eds). 1999. *The Social Determinants of Health.* Oxford: Oxford University Press.

Marmot, Michael Gideon, Manolis Kogevinas, and Mary Ann Elston. 1987. "Social/economic Status and Disease." *Annual Review of Public Health* 8(1): 111–35.

Marmot, Michael Gideon, Martin J. Shipley, and Geoffrey Rose. 1984. "Inequalities in Death—Specific Explanations of a General Pattern." *The Lancet* 323(8384): 1003–06.

McAllister, A., S. Fritzell, M. Almroth, L. Harber-Aschan, S. Larsson, and B. Burström. 2018. "How Do Macro-Level Structural Determinants Affect Inequalities in Mental Health? – A Systematic Review of the Literature." *International Journal for Equity in Health* 17(1): 180.

McCartney, Gerry, Mel Bartley, Ruth Dundas, Srinivasa Vittal Katikireddi, Rich Mitchell, Frank Popham, David Walsh, and Welcome Wami. 2019a. "Theorising Social Class and Its Application to the Study of Health Inequalities." *SSM-Population Health* 7, 100315.

McCartney, Gerry, Wendy Hearty, Julie Arnot, Frank Popham, Andrew Cumbers, and McMaster, Robert. 2019b. "Impact of Political Economy on Population Health: A Systematic Review of Reviews." *American Journal of Public Health* 109(6): e1–12.

Mirowsky, John and Catherine E. Ross. 2003. *Education, Social Status, and Health. Hawthorne*, New York: Aldine de Gruyter.

Muntaner, Carles, Owen Davis, Kathryn McIsaack, Lauri Kokkinen, Ketan Shankardass, and Patricia O'Campo. 2017. "Retrenched Welfare Regimes Still Lessen Social Class Inequalities in Health: A Longitudinal Analysis of the 2003–2010 EU-SILC in 23 European Countries." *International Journal of Health Services* 47(3): 410–31.

Murie, Alan. 2008. "Housing." Pp. 343–50 in *The Student's Companion to Social Policy*, edited by P. Alcock, M. May, and K. Rowlingson. Oxford: Blackwell.

Murphy, Gregory C. and James A. Athanasou. 1999. "The Effect of Unemployment on Mental Health." *Journal of Occupational and Organizational Psychology* 72(1): 83–99.

Naik, Yannish, Sharif A. Peter Baker, Taavi Tillmann Ismail, Kristin Bash, Darryl Quantz, Frances Hillier-Brown, Wikum Jayatunga, Gill Kelly, and Michelle Black. 2019. "Going Upstream–an Umbrella Review of the Macroeconomic Determinants of Health and Health Inequalities." *BMC Public Health* 19(1): 1678.

O'Rand, Angela M. 1996. "The Precious and the Precocious: Understanding Cumulative Disadvantage and Cumulative Advantage over the Life Course." *The Gerontologist* 36(2): 230–38.

Oreopoulos, Philip. 2005. *Canadian Compulsory School Laws and Their Impact on Educational Attainment and Future Earnings.* Ottawa, ON: Statistics Canada.

Palència, Laia, Deborah De Moortel, Lucía Artazcoz, María Salvador-Piedrafita, Vanessa Puig-Barrachina, Emma Hagqvist, Marisol E. Ruiz Glòria Pérez, Sara Trujillo-Alemán, and Christophe Vanroelen. 2017. "Gender Policies and Gender Inequalities in Health in Europe: Results of the SOPHIE Project." *International Journal of Health Services* 47(1): 61–82.

Panel on Dietary Reference Intakes for Macronutrients, National Academy of Sciences. 2002. *Dietary Reference Intakes for Energy, Carbohydrate, Fiber, Fat, Fatty Acids, Cholesterol, Protein, and Amino Acids (Macronutrients).* Washington D.C.: National Academies Press.

Pappas, Gregory, Susan Queen, Wilbur Hadden, and Gail Fisher. 1993. "The Increasing Disparity in Mortality between Socioeconomic Groups in the United States, 1960 and 1986." *New England Journal of Medicine* 329(2): 103–09.

Patel, Vikram. 2001. "Is Depression a Disease of Poverty? [Editorial]." *Regional Health Forum* (5): 14–23.

Pega, Frank, Ichiro Kawachi, Kumanan Rasanathan, and Olle Lundberg. 2013. "Politics, Policies and Population Health: A Commentary on Mackenbach, Hu and Looman (2013)." *Social Science & Medicine* 93: 176–79.

Peretti-Watel, Patrick, Valérie Seror, Jean Constance, and François Beck. 2009. "Poverty as a Smoking Trap." *International Journal of Drug Policy* 20(3): 230–36.

Phelan, Jo C. and Bruce G. Link. 2015. "Is Racism a Fundamental Cause of Inequalities in Health?" *Annual Review of Sociology* 41(1): 311–30.

Pickett, Kate E. and Richard G. Wilkinson. 2015. "Income Inequality and Health: A Causal Review." *Social Science & Medicine* 128: 316–26.

Pillas, Demetris, Michael Marmot, Kiyuri Naicker, Peter Goldblatt, Joana Morrison, and Hynek Pikhart. 2014. "Social Inequalities in Early Childhood Health and Development: A European-Wide Systematic Review." *Pediatric Research* 76(5): 418–24.

Popay, Jennie, Sharon Bennett, Carol Thomas, Gareth Williams, Anthony Gatrell, and Lisa Bostock. 2003. "Beyond 'Beer, Fags, Egg and Chips'? Exploring Lay Understandings of Social Inequalities in Health." *Sociology of Health & Illness* 25(1): 1–23.

Propper, Carol, John Rigg, and Simon Burgess. 2007. "Child Health: Evidence on the Roles of Family Income and Maternal Mental Health from a UK Birth Cohort." *Health Economics* 16(11): 1245–69.

Quesnel-Vallée, Amélie, Suzanne DeHaney, and Antonio Ciampi. 2010. "Temporary Work and Depressive Symptoms: A Propensity Score Analysis." *Social Science & Medicine* 70(12): 1982–87.

Read, Jen'nan Ghazal and Bridget K Gorman. 2010. "Gender and Health Inequality." *Annual Review of Sociology* 36: 371–86.

Rieker, Patricia P. and Jennan G. Read. 2017. "The Health Gender Gap: A Constrained Choice Explanation." Pp. 85–118 in *The Psychology of Gender and Health*, edited by M. Pilar Sánchez-López and R. M. Limiñana-Gras. London: Academic Press.

Robert, Stephanie A. and James S. House. 2000. "Socioeconomic Inequalities in Health: An Enduring Sociological Problem." Pp. 79–97 in *Handbook of Medical Sociology*. Vol. 5, edited by C. E. Bird, P. Conrad, and A. M. Fremont., NJ: Prentice Hall.

Roelfs, David J., Karina W. Davidson Eran Shor, and Joseph E. Schwartz. 2011. "Losing Life and Livelihood: A Systematic Review and Meta-Analysis of Unemployment and All-Cause Mortality." *Social Science & Medicine* 72(6): 840–54.

Roseboom, Tessa J., Rebecca C. Painter, F. M. Annet, Marjolein V. van Abeelen, E. Veenendaal, and Susanne R. de Rooij. 2011. "Hungry in the Womb: What are the Consequences? Lessons from the Dutch Famine." *Maturitas* 70(2): 141–45.

Roseboom, Tessa J., Jan H. P. van der Meulen, Clive Osmond, David J. P. Barker, Anita C. J. Ravelli, and Otto P. Bleker. 2001. "Adult Survival after Prenatal Exposure to the Dutch Famine 1944–45." *Paediatric and Perinatal Epidemiology* 15(3): 220–25.

Salsali, Mahnaz and Peter H. Silverstone. 2003. "Low Self-Esteem and Psychiatric Patients: Part II – The Relationship between Self-Esteem and Demographic Factors and Psychosocial Stressors in Psychiatric Patients." *Annals of General Hospital Psychiatry* 2(1): 8.

Schanzer, Bella, Patrick E. Shrout Boanerges Dominguez, and L. M. Caton Carol. 2007. "Homelessness, Health Status, and Health Care Use." *American Journal of Public Health* 97(3): 464–69.

Schilt, Kristen and Matthew Wiswall. 2008. "Before and After: Gender Transitions, Human Capital, and Workplace Experiences." *The BE Journal of Economic Analysis & Policy* 8(1).

Schmitz, Hendrik. 2011. "Why are the Unemployed in Worse Health? the Causal Effect of Unemployment on Health." *Labour Economics* 18(1): 71–78.

Sermet, Catherine and Myriam Khlat. 2004. "Health of the Unemployed in France: Literature Review." *Revue D'epidemiologie Et De Sante Publique* 52(5): 465–74.

Setia, Maninder Singh, Amélie Quesnel-Vallée, Michal Abrahamowicz, Pierre Tousignant, and John Lynch. 2011. "Access to Health-Care in Canadian Immigrants: A Longitudinal Study of the National Population Health Survey." *Health & Social Care in the Community* 19(1): 70–79.

Shahidi, Faraz V., Chantel Ramraj, Odmaa Sod-Erdene, Vincent Hildebrand, and Arjumand Siddiqi. 2019. "The Impact of Social Assistance Programs on Population Health: A Systematic Review of Research in High-Income Countries." *BMC Public Health* 19(2).

Shapcott, Michael. 2008. *Wellesley Institute National Housing Report Card 2008*. Toronto: Wellesley Institute.

Shaw, Mary, Danny Dorling, and George Davey Smith. 1999. "Poverty, Social Exclusion and Minorities." Pp. 211–39 in *Social Determinants of Health*, edited by M. Marmot and R. G. Wilkinson. Oxford: Oxford University Press.

Sher, Leo. 2005. "Per Capita Income Is Related to Suicide Rates in Men but Not in Women." *The Journal of Men's Health and Gender* 3(1).

Solar, Orielle and Alec Irwin. 2010. *A Conceptual Framework for Action on the Social Determinants of Health*. Geneva: World Health Organization.

Springer, Kristen W., Olena Hankivsky, and Lisa M. Bates. 2012. "Gender and Health: Relational, Intersectional, and Biosocial Approaches." *Social Science & Medicine* 74(11).

Stephen, McKay, P. Karen Rowlingson, Alcock, M. May, and K. Rowlingson. 2008. "Income Maintenance and Social Security." Pp. 303–10 in *The Student's Companion to Social Policy*, edited by P. Alcock, M. May, and K. Rowlingson. Oxford: Blackwell.

Strandh, Mattias, Anthony Winefield, Karina Nilsson, and Hammarström, Anne. 2014. "Unemployment and Mental Health Scarring during the Life Course." *European Journal of Public Health* 24(3): 440–45.

Thomson, Katie, Frances Hillier-Brown, Adam Todd, Courtney McNamara, Tim Huijts, and Clare Bambra. 2018. "The Effects of Public Health Policies on Health Inequalities in High-Income Countries: An Umbrella Review." *BMC Public Health* 18(1): 869.

Townsend, Peter, Nick Davison, and Margaret Whitehead. 1982. *Inequalities in Health: The Black Report.* London: Pelican Books.

Vaillancourt, Yves, Francois Aubry, Muriel Kearny, Luc Theriault, and Louise Tremblay. 2004. "The Contribution of the Social Economy Towards Healthy Social Policy Reforms in Canada: A Quebec Viewpoint." in *Social Determinants of Health: Canadian Perspectives*, edited by D. Raphael. Toronto, ON: Canadian Scholars' Press Inc.

Veenstra, Gerry. 2019. "Black, White, Black and White: Mixed Race and Health in Canada." *Ethnicity & Health* 24(2):113–24.

Vosko, Leah F. 2006. *Precarious Employment: Understanding Labour Market Insecurity in Canada.* Montreal, QC: McGill-Queens University Press.

Wadsworth, Michael. 1999. "Early Life." Pp. 44–63 in *Social Determinants of Health*, edited by M. Marmot and R. G. Wilkinson. Oxford: Oxford University Press.

Wallace, Maeve, Joia Crear-Perry, Lisa Richardson, Meshawn Tarver, and Katherine Theall. 2017. "Separate and Unequal: Structural Racism and Infant Mortality in the US." *Health & Place* 45:140–44.

WHO Commission on Social Determinants of Health, (ed). 2008. *Closing the Gap in a Generation: Health Equity through Action on the Social Determinants of Health: Commission on Social Determinants of Health Final Report.* Geneva, Switzerland: World Health Organization, Commission on Social Determinants of Health.

Williams, David R. 1990. "Socioeconomic Differentials in Health: A Review and Redirection." *Social Psychology Quarterly* 53(2): 81–99.

Williams, David R., Jourdyn A. Lawrence, and Brigette A. Davis. 2019. "Racism and Health: Evidence and Needed Research." *Annual Review of Public Health* 40: 105–25.

World Health Organization. 1948. *Constitution of the World Health Organization.* Geneva: World Health Organization.

World Health Organization. 2011. "Rio Political Declaration on Social Determinants of Health." Retrieved April 3, 2020 (https://www.who.int/sdhconference/declaration/en).

World Health Organization. 2014. *Health in All Policies: Helsinki Statement, Framework for Country Action.* Geneva: World Health Organization.

World Health Organization. 2020. "Breastfeeding." Retrieved March 26, 2020 (https://www.who.int/westernpacific/health-topics/breastfeeding).

Wright, Erik Olin. 1997. *Class Counts: Comparative Studies in Class Analysis.* New York: Cambridge University Press.

Part IV

Health and Social Relationships

17

Health and the Family

Mieke Beth Thomeer and Kirsten Ostergren Clark

Social relationships matter for health, and family members are often our longest-lasting and most salient social relationships (Umberson et al. 2010). The importance of family for health is seen from the very beginning of life in research identifying the unique role of parents on infant well-being (Catalano and Ehrenberg 2006). Family members continue to matter for health throughout the rest of the life course – from early childhood to adolescence to young adulthood to midlife and, finally, to the later years (Umberson and Thomeer 2020). The presence or absence of family and the quality of those family ties are key determinants of whether or not a person experiences a "good death" at the end of life (Granda-Cameron and Houldin 2012). Family relationships include a wide range of connections, including parents, siblings, spouses, children, grandparents, cousins, nieces and nephews, aunts and uncles, and other extended kin. There is also increased attention to chosen family (i.e. close friendships and intimate ties that perform similar functions as family members without legal or biological bonds; Mouzon 2014). Families are associated with many different health and well-being outcomes – including mental health, health behaviors, physical health, disabilities and functional limitations, biomarkers, cognitive health, and life expectancy – through multiple pathways (Umberson and Thomeer 2020). The importance of family members for health varies across sociodemographic categories (e.g. gender, sexual identity, immigration status, race/ethnicity, age, social class, geographic location), which is why researchers increasingly use an intersectional framework (Collins and Bilge 2016) alongside a life course perspective (Elder et al. 2003) when studying how and when families matter for health (Umberson and Thomeer 2020).

Most studies that consider family and health focus on one type of family relationship (e.g. adult children and their parents, cohabiting partners), a specific time in the life course (e.g. early childhood, midlife), and a specific health or well-being outcome (e.g. depressive symptoms, self-rated health). From these studies, we can

The Wiley Blackwell Companion to Medical Sociology, First Edition. Edited by William C. Cockerham.

draw three broad conclusions. First, how and why family members matter for health depends on whether considering the structural component of the relationship or the content of the relationship. Structural components include the presence and absence of specific family ties, the number of family ties, and the extent of contact with those ties, whereas content describes relationship quality and the health, socioeconomic status (SES), and other characteristics of the tie. Second, family relationships matter for health in both positive and negative ways, and, at times, family relationships do not matter for health at all (at least not in measurable ways) but associations between family and health are a statistical artifact driven by selection processes. Generalizations suggesting that family ties are always good for health are not supported by the current literature; rather, family ties are sometimes good for health, sometimes bad for health, and sometimes not at all important for health. Third, the importance of family members for health is moderated by race/ethnicity, gender, sexual identity, age, cohort, SES, geographic location, and other sociodemographic characteristics. Families are changing rapidly and unevenly, and so it should not be surprising that there is no universal story of when, why, and how families matter for health. Rather, understanding how families shape health in different ways across different social locations requires careful theoretical and empirical consideration of the specific contexts in which families are embedded. This work can then provide needed insight into the role families play in reducing or exacerbating health disparities across groups.

In this chapter, we provide an overview of this research, indicating how recent studies provide empirical support for these three takeaways. We spend most of the chapter on the first point regarding structure and content, with the other points providing further contextualization. We conclude by discussing the role of policy in the link between families and health. Although most of the research discussed focuses on the US, there is much research on the associations between health and family in many other national and cultural contexts (see Berkman et al. 2015; Jadhav and Weir 2018 for examples) and more cross-national comparisons are needed (see Glass et al. 2016 for example). Family and health research is a broad area of study with contributions from multiple disciplines and fields. Expanding our understanding of how, when, and why families matter for health has importance not only for research but also for clinical practice, community advocacy, policymaking, and family life.

How Family Structure Matters for Health

Researchers investigating the associations between family relationships and health distinguish between the structure and the content of family. Many early studies of how family members – and other social ties – matter for health focused on the presence or absence of specific family relationships and the extent to which a person has contact with those family members. Famously, Émile Durkheim (1951 [1897]), the first sociologist to theorize about the importance of family members for health, posited that family serves as protection against suicide, such that the larger the family, the lower the suicide risk. Durkheim theorized that family provides integration and regulation which buffer against suicidal thoughts or inclinations. More recent studies similarly find that suicide risk is lowest for those with family ties (e.g. people with larger families, married people; Denney et al. 2009), and that mortality risk more generally is lower for those with family–although many of these studies look only at marital status (Kang et al. 2016).

These conclusions are based on research and theories focusing on the structure of families. Structure includes the presence and absence of specific family ties, the number of family ties, and the extent of contact with those ties, with most studies looking at the presence or absence of specific ties and often conceptualizing this as family status (e.g. marital status; parental status). These family status studies conclude that married people (i.e. people with a spouse) are healthier than non-married people, but only if the spouse is actually present in the household (Fuller 2010). In contrast, by some measures, parents are less healthy than people without children, but this difference is reduced when children leave the household and parents become "empty nesters" (Grundy and Read 2015). But studies of structure involve more than just specific family statuses. They also involve the entire family network (i.e. web of family relationships surrounding an individual) and social integration with family members (i.e. overall level of involvement with family relationships). People without any family ties – defined as "kinless" – are at risk of social isolation, meaning they have sparse social networks and little to no social integration or meaningful contact with others (Margolis and Verdery 2017). Social isolation is, in turn, associated with a wide range of negative health outcomes, including greater risk of cardiovascular disease, hypertension, cancer, and depression; slower wound healing and weaker immune systems; more pain; worse cognitive health; and higher risk of premature mortality (Courtin and Knapp 2017).

Most research on family structure and health has focused on specific categories of family relationships, as discussed above with family status research. In Figure 17.1, we illustrate how the types of family ties a person has – and the salience of those ties for health – shifts throughout the life course in ways that likely matter for health. Figure 17.1 draws attention to the fact that the structure of family ties matters at every point in the life course, and that this influence is often additive and interactive such that family relationships early in life – even if no longer present in later life – leave a mark on later life health through cumulative (dis)advantage processes (Umberson et al. 2014). We divide these family ties into five main categories: families of origin (i.e. parents, siblings), extended kin (i.e. grandparents, aunts, uncles, cousins, nieces, nephews, in-laws), families of choice, intimate/sexual/romantic partners, and offspring (i.e. children, grandchildren).

Much of the research around families and health focuses on intimate or romantic partners. These studies generally suggest that the married and cohabiting are in better health than the unmarried, and those cohabiting are in worse health than the married (Rendall et al. 2011). We know much less about the health impacts of dating or "living apart together" relationships (Strohm et al. 2009). The presence or absence of intimate partners matters for more than just the intimate partners themselves; research also demonstrates that this aspect of family structure is important for children's health and well-being. Studies indicate that children living with married parents have better mental and physical health – and lower mortality – than children living with cohabiting or single parents or even grandparents (Cavanagh and Fomby 2019; Rogers et al. 2020). The instability hypothesis states that this is

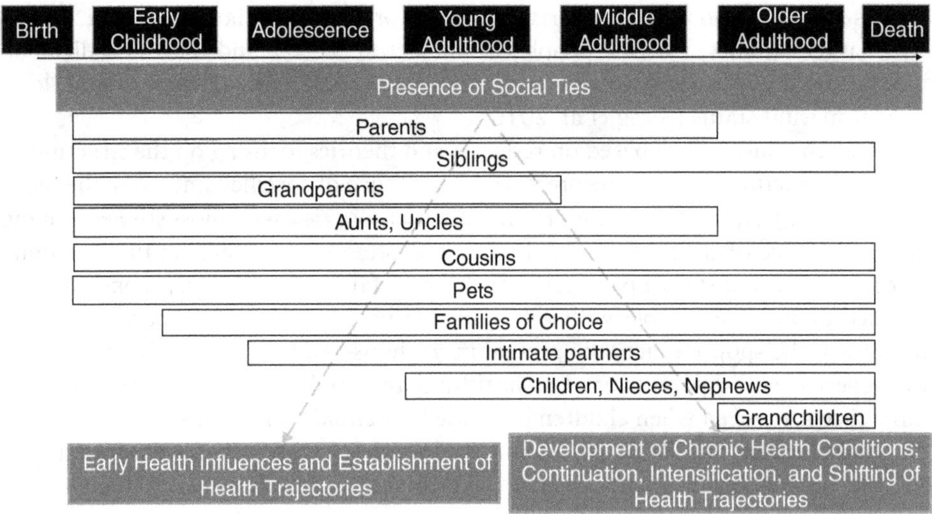

Figure 17.1 Sample Conceptual Model for How the Structure of Social Ties Influences Health Throughout the Life Course.

largely due to the greater stability associated with marriage, meaning children in married homes move less often, have more stable social network and schooling experiences, and have more certainty and less stress (Hadfield et al. 2018). Married parents also tend to have more resources, including financial resources, thus improving children's health and health care access (Sierminska 2018). Controlling for stability and resources, studies find little difference in health between children of married, cohabiting, or single parents (Cavanagh and Fomby 2019).

The attention to family stability and instability within family and health research demonstrates the negative health consequences that often – but not always – accompany the loss of a family member, such as through death, divorce, or other mechanisms. Studies have found that the death of a spouse is associated with decreased immunocompetence, worse cognitive health, higher rates of psychiatric disorders, and even increased risk of mortality especially within the first year of being widowed (see Thomeer and Umberson 2014 for overview). Deaths of other family members – including children, siblings, and parents – also take a health toll (Umberson et al. 2017). For example, one study found that experiencing the death of a sibling in childhood increased the risk of all-cause mortality over the next four decades by 71% (Bolton et al. 2017). The health impacts of these deaths are attributed to the accompanying loss of resources (e.g. social, emotional, financial) and the grief, stress, and trauma related to the death.

Loss of family members can occur through mechanisms other than death. For example, families can be separated through incarceration, military deployment, or deportation. The removal of a family member through these processes harms the well-being of the remaining family members, especially children (Turney 2014). As theorized in a life course perspective (Elder et al. 2003), the effects of family separation can have long-term ripples, even if the family is later reunited (Turney 2014).

As a notable exception, research on parental incarceration finds that the removal of abusive parents from the household is beneficial to children's health and well-being (Arditti 2012).

Looking beyond intimate partners and children, the presence, absence, or loss of other family members also has implications for health. Extended kin include grandparents, grandchildren, aunts, uncles, cousins, nieces, and nephews, and people have varying levels of contact with each of these family members. Despite the fact that each of these ties – through direct or indirect pathways – can matter for health and well-being, extended families are generally understudied (Fingerman et al. 2020). Recent demographic trends point to an urgent need to both study and contextualize the ways in which structures of extended family relationships shape health. These trends include a rise in multigenerational households (at least compared to the low levels characteristic of the 1960s forward), fewer extended kin ties due to people having less or even no children, and more blended or disrupted extended family relationships (e.g. step-grandparents, cousin's ex-spouse) (Fingerman et al. 2020).

As an example, because of increased life expectancy, grandparents and grandchildren have longer overlapping lifespans, and there is now even more overlapping years between great-grandchildren and great-grandparents (Margolis 2016). There is more frequent contact within these greater number of years, not only due to the overlapping lifespans but also because grandparents have fewer grandchildren (and more time to invest in each) and greater technological access (e.g. video calls, social media; Fingerman et al. 2020). Recent decades have seen a rise in grandchildren living with grandparents – including more grandparents with custody of their grandchildren (Margolis 2016). In fact, recent data indicate that almost 30% of all children in the US have at one time coresided with a grandparent (Amorim, Dunifon, and Pilkauskas 2017). Thus, we might expect these trends would mean grandparents and grandchildren matter more for each other's health than in the past, but research is needed to fully disentangle the health impacts of these trends.

In addition to more research on extended kin, families of choice are also worth special consideration, given their general absence in most traditional family and health research but their likely central importance to the health and well-being of marginalized groups. Families of choice, also called fictive kin or intentional families, are voluntary social relationships without biological or legal ties that serve the same function and purpose of "traditional families," including providing support, identity, socialization, and caregiving (Mouzon 2014). Studies of these families have been focused on blended families, Black families, and queer constructions of families (Nelson 2013), with this third line of research building on Weston's classic ethnography, *Families We Choose* (1997). These families of choice members may take on increased salience in a person's life, and thus increased health impact, when facing rejection by families of origin, encountering structural barriers that limit the formation of more traditionally and legally recognized family ties, or actively rejecting traditional family models for a range of political, cultural, and personal reasons.

We note a sixth developing category that could arguably be included within the families of choice category: pets. There has been increasing attention to the role of pets within families, given that about three-fifths of households own pets and – according to one survey – 80% of these households view their pets as family members (Chan 2020). Pets can be a key source of social support, a loneliness deterrent, and a motivator for spending time outside of the house and practicing self-care, as found especially in studies of older adults – including nursing home residents, older people with chronic conditions, and lesbian, gay, bisexual, and transgender older adult samples (Muraco et al. 2018; Ryan and Ziebland 2015). Evidence of health benefits of pet ownership in the general population is more limited, however, with some arguing that these weak findings cast doubt on assertions that pets should be included alongside parents, children, and extended kin as family members (Ryan and Ziebland 2015).

These diverse strands of research demonstrate the importance of looking beyond the presence or absence of specific traditionally studied family members to consider a range of family relationships including the loss and instability of those relationships. Research on family structures and health is based in demographic and social network understandings of the family, and considering how different distributions of family members matter for health should continue to be a key focus within medical sociology.

How the Content of Family Ties Matters for Health

The extent to which family structure is associated with health depends in large part on the content of the family ties. Content refers both to the dynamics occurring within the family tie and the characteristics of the tie; this includes the relationship quality of the tie as well as the health and other characteristics of the tie (e.g. having a mother who has clinical depression or a spouse who is unemployed). The structure of family ties is associated with health, as discussed in the previous section, but the reason why having family ties is generally associated with healthier outcomes than not having family ties is because most family relationships come with resources. In other words, the impact of family structure depends in large part on the content of those family ties, and certain types of content (e.g. conflict, family members with health issues) are associated with negative health outcomes and other types of content (e.g. support, family members with high educational attainment) are associated with positive health outcomes. Thus, content can provide insight into the mechanisms through which family structures matter for health, as well as the conditions under which family structures are associated with health.

In Figure 17.2, we provide a hypothetical illustration of how the content of various types of family ties a person has over their life course might be linked to their health. We focus here on two key elements of content – relationship quality and characteristics of the family member. Each of these are important characteristics of any given family member relationship, and serve both as mechanisms connecting families to health as well as moderating factors that drive heterogeneous associations between families and health.

Relationship Quality. Relationship quality is typically measured by assessing the degree of support and conflict or strain within a relationship. Social support is defined as the perception and actuality that one is cared for and has assistance available from other people, whereas social strain is the stress derived from being in

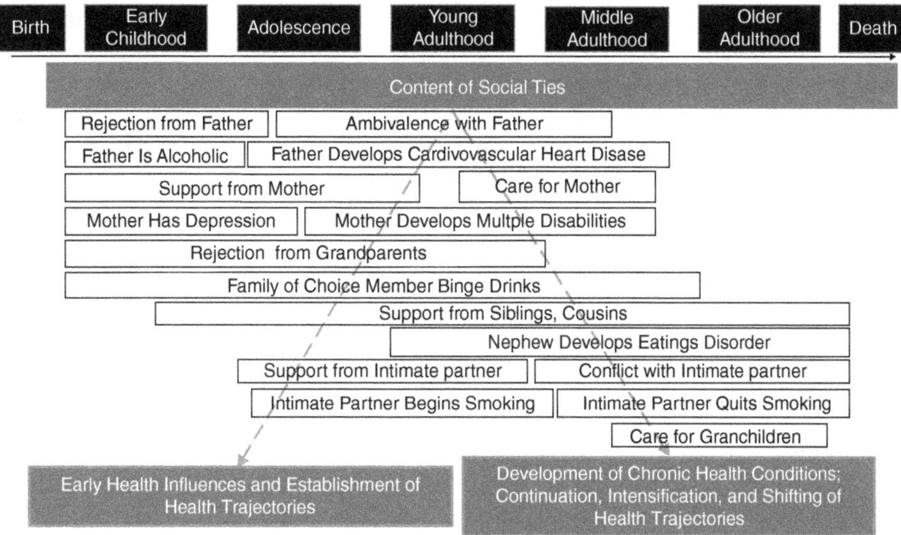

Figure 17.2 Sample Conceptual Model for How the Content of Family Ties Influences Health Throughout the Life Course.

a relationship (Umberson and Karas Montez 2010). Both social support and strain can be broadly interpreted and include a range of supportive and straining dynamics. For example, a strained relationship may include feeling irritated and frustrated with the other person or it may involve being in frequent verbal and physical altercations with them. Relationship quality is also sometimes assessed by asking the degree to which a person is satisfied with their relationship with the family member. A family relationship that is supportive and satisfying protects a person against health problems, but a relationship that involves tension, strain, and conflict is a significant source of stress and makes a person susceptible to health issues (Umberson and Montez 2010).

This general pattern of supportive family ties promoting health and conflicted family ties harming health is observed across a wide range of family member categories, including marriage, parent-child ties, and sibling relationships. For example, a meta-analysis of 126 studies found that better marital quality was related to better health across multiple outcomes, including lower risk of mortality and lower cardiovascular reactivity (Robles et al. 2014). This has led some researchers to conclude that we should not say that marriage improves health but rather specify that this generally only applies to supportive and satisfying marriages (Umberson et al. 2005; Williams 2003). Those in strained and conflicted marriages have worse health than the unmarried, including the divorced (Williams 2003). Similarly, within parenthood, satisfaction with the parent-child relationship is a key moderator in the association between parenthood and psychological well-being (Nomaguchi 2012). And for children, better relationship quality with parents is linked to better health in adolescence and adulthood (Branje et al. 2010). Sibling relationships are some of the longest lasting relationships, and people who have close and positive relationships with siblings also have higher well-being than those with strained sibling relationships (Vogt Yuan 2009). The impact of this relationship quality may be tied to relationships with other family members; for example, relationships with parents may promote or undermine relationships among siblings (Ruff et al. 2018). Thus, we need to look beyond relationship quality in any given family dyad to the entire constellation of family ties, as promoted by a family systems approach (Cox and Paley 2003).

Physiological and behavioral mechanisms together partially explain the link between relationship quality and health. Early work on the physiological link between relationship quality and health was largely based on laboratory studies, testing observations based on animal studies on humans. These studies found that supportive interactions with other family members, especially spouses, facilitated better immune functioning, wound healing, and other beneficial physiological processes, whereas stressful interactions, such as arguments, were detrimental to physiological functioning (Wilson et al. 2020). More recently, longitudinal datasets have begun including biomarkers on surveys, allowing researchers to consider how relationship quality is associated with multiple physiological processes in large nationally representative samples over time. For example, one study using the Health and Retirement Study found that the frequency of positive and negative interactions with a spouse is associated with diabetes-related biomarkers (e.g., glycosylated hemoglobin) in married men (Whisman et al. 2014).

Daily diary studies paired with biomarker collection are also a fast developing research area, equipping researchers to study respondents in their typical social environment (rather than the laboratory) and to collect more frequent and detailed data than often possible in largescale surveys. One study of 132 adolescents collected salivary cortisol, a stress hormone, throughout the day and information regarding interactions between the adolescents and their parents (Lippold et al. 2016). The researchers found that negative daily experiences with mothers were associated with higher dinner and bedtime cortisol levels, whereas positive daily experiences with fathers were linked to lower dinner cortisol levels. As predicted by an allostatic load perspective which notes that physiological systems can be worn down due to constant strain and activation of the stress system (McEwen 1998), these studies together suggest that the more chronic the family stress, the more detrimental the health outcomes. Thus, a life course perspective together with the physiological evidence indicates that constant stress from family relationships throughout the life course coupled with an absence of social support from relationships will likely have negative impacts on a person's health.

Health behaviors also serve as a mechanism linking family relationship quality and health. Health behaviors include multiple types of activities which influence health, disability, and mortality, encompassing both "risky" behaviors such as smoking and "health-benefitting" behaviors such as exercise. One behavioral pathway through which social ties influence health is social control. Social control is the direct and indirect ways in which individuals seek to influence the health of the people they know (Reczek et al. 2014). Social control occurs to a varying degree throughout the life course, although the main family source of social control depends strongly on an individual's life stage. For example, in childhood, the key sources of social control are parents and peers (Umberson et al. 2010). Parents tell their children when to go to bed and they dictate what food their children eat, in this way directly controlling their health behaviors and likely influencing their health. After childhood, parents and peers are largely replaced by spouses, intimate partners, and – eventually – adult children (Reczek et al. 2014). This is particularly the case for men, whose wives are often their main source of social control. In late adulthood, some men lose this social control when their wife dies, which can contribute to the greater negative health impact of widowhood for men compared to women (Williams 2004).

A behavioral pathway linking families and health with generally an opposite health impact involves using risky healthy behaviors as a way to cope with family-related stress. Families can be both a source of stress and a buffer against stress (Thoits 2011). People often cope with stress through health behaviors, typically unhealthy behaviors such as smoking, drinking excess alcohol, and overeating (Krueger and Chang 2008). Umberson et al. (2008) found that stress, including relationship stress from family members in childhood and adulthood, contributes to worse health behaviors in adulthood. They also found that the specific health behaviors impacted vary over the life course, such that those with relationship stress in middle adulthood are more likely to drink excessively and gain weight, whereas in late adulthood this stress contributes to more unhealthy weight loss.

Few relationships can be characterized as wholly supportive or wholly strained. Many family relationships are ambivalent – meaning the content of the relationship has conflicting elements, either being simultaneously supportive and strained or having unclear and ambiguous understandings about the nature of the relationship (Birditt et al. 2009). One study found that ambivalence was especially prevalent among relationships with in-laws, when family members have poor health, between mothers and daughters, and for adult children with poor parental relations in early life (Willson et al. 2003). Another study concluded that sibling relationships are more often marked by ambivalence than friendships, indicating that ambivalence may just be a hallmark of compulsory family ties and less common within family of choice relationships (Voorpostel and Van Der Lippe 2007). Ambivalence in the parent-child tie is related to worse health for both generations when compared to more straightforward assessments of the relationship as either supportive or strained (Fingerman et al. 2008). These studies point to the importance of examining ambivalence alongside other components of relationship quality, as well as recognizing that relationship quality can change over time and should be conceptualized as dynamic rather than static.

Characteristics of the Family Member. Another element of relationship content involves the characteristics of the family members involved in the tie. Most research within this area focuses on two key characteristics: health status and SES (e.g. employment status, educational attainment). This research demonstrates that who the family member is and what they experience has implications for the health of those within their family, as also hypothesized by the linked lives concept from the life course perspective (Carr 2018; Thomeer 2016). Health can "spread" across family relationships or "spill over" from one family member to another, as shown in social contagion studies (Christakis and Fowler 2009).

Family members often have similar health and health behavior for a number of reasons. First, family members sometimes reside (or have resided) in the same household, and this increases the likelihood that they will practice similar health behaviors and have similar health outcomes. For example, siblings and parents may be exposed to the same environmental hazards, leading to similar risks of certain health conditions as they age. This can be extended from environmental contaimments to include exposures to psychosocial risk factors, such as discrimination (Colen et al. 2019). Second, and generally specific to intimate partners and families of choice relationships, assortative mating (or friendship) practices contribute to people with similar health and health behaviors forming relationships. For example, non-drinkers often date and marry non-drinkers, and spouses with highly divergent drinking practices have an increased risk of divorce (Reczek et al. 2016). Assortative mating practices, together with genetic processes, also contribute to similarities in health between biological relatives (Clarke et al. 2019). Third, as implied by the use of the word contagion, health and health behaviors might spread among family relationships through the sharing and transference of norms, beliefs, values, and even moods. Seeing an adult child regularly go to the gym might encourage a parent to purchase their own membership, and being married to someone who quits smoking might also contribute to quitting smoking for one's self (Margolis and Wright 2016). Due to these different processes, studies find similarities in health and health behavior across family members in multiple outcomes, including obesity, alcohol use, smoking behavior, and mental health (Christakis and Fowler 2008).

As a fourth mechanism, health also matters because family members' health status can either prompt the need for caregiving or other forms of support or can limit the availability of support – and increase the stress – from that family tie (Thomeer 2016). Although caregiving has been shown to have some positive impacts on health and well-being (Freedman et al. 2014), much more research attention has been paid to the negative health impacts of caregiving (Vitaliano, Zhang and Scanlan 2003). The health costs of caregiving are often attributed to the fact that caregiving is a chronic and unpredictable stressor, and caregivers often note that they are exhausted, have too much to do, and too little time for themselves (Pinquart and Sörensen 2003). Caregiving for family members can lead to problems balancing work and other responsibilities, described as role engulfment – meaning all other roles a person has (e.g. employee, student, parent) becomes subsumed by the caregiving role (Skaff and Pearlin 1992). Living longer means an increase in the possibility of having multiple complex family relationships with people who require caregiving. A life course perspective notes that parenting, and specifically parenting a child with an intellectual or developmental disability (IDD), means there may not be an end to their role as caregiver (Lunsky et al. 2017). These linked lives result in parents negotiating a balance of caring for a child who may never be fully independent as an adult, maintaining relationships with – and sometimes caring for – other family members, and navigating their own health concerns as they themselves age (Marsack and Perry 2018).

Research has also identified the importance of SES of family members in shaping other family member's health and well-being. This research extends studies that show that one's own SES matters for health (Zajacova and Lawrence 2018). Most of this research considers how the financial well-being and educational attainments of parents benefits their children's health (Mossakowski 2015). But more recent studies identify that children's educational attainment also benefits the health of their later-life parents (Wolfe 2019). For example, parents with children who completed college have significantly lower levels of depressive symptoms than parents without college-educated children (Yahirun et al. 2020). Spousal education, combined with one's own education, is associated with married adults' self-rated health (Brown et al. 2014). Other elements of SES also matter for family member's health, including income, wealth, debt, educational attainment, employment status, and occupation, and these can each be an important resource or a source of stress. There is evidence that unemployment decreases the mental health of spouses almost as much as it does for the unemployed person (Marcus 2013). Researchers should continue to investigate how various components of SES and other characteristics of the family member shape the health of others within the family.

The Good, the Bad, and the Non-existent Ways Families Matter for Health

Whether considering structure or content of families – and regardless of the specific components of family considered – it is clear that the impact of families on health is far from simple to summarize. There just is not broad empirical support for claims such as "Marriage benefits health" or "Parenting young children damages well-being." As already discussed above, sometimes family members benefit health. The presence of family members who are able to provide support, care, and other resources (e.g. money, housing, knowledge) is beneficial, and the absence of those family members can be harmful. "Kinless" people may find close ties with friends who can offer and provide assistance and support. Even when an adult with health needs has children or a spouse, if the state of that relationship is rocky or the child or spouse is unable to provide care, families of choice members or extended family can be a needed source of care. The type of family tie is likely not important, as long as that family member is supportive, present, committed, and able and willing to provide those resources. This is why studies often find that the benefit of family members on health is conditioned on whether or not that family member provides support and on the level of commitment people have to a particular family relationship (Perelli-Harris et al. 2018).

But not all family members provide resources, and in fact – as discussed above when mentioning strain and social contagion – there are many ways that families harm health. At the most extreme are abusive or negligent family members whose negative impacts on health are experienced throughout the life course, but perhaps most consequentially in childhood and in later life. Childhood experiences with abusive family members are linked to poor health both during the experience of abuse and cumulatively as the person ages (Lünnemann et al. 2019). And older people who may be more dependent on only a few family members are especially vulnerable to the negative health impacts of abuse and neglect (Orfila et al. 2018). But even ambivalent relationships with family members, which are a mix of support and strain, can have negative health consequences, perhaps especially if these are family members who are traditionally expected to be supportive (e.g. mother, spouse).

At the same time, sometimes observed associations between family and health are actually a result of third-variable explanations. Statements such as "Parental divorce hurts the health of children" assume a causal association between divorce and children's health. Yet social scientists who have carefully investigated this assumption find evidence that this association could be non-causal. One issue is that many of the same factors that predispose people to divorce (e.g. poverty, mental disorders) also negatively impact children's health; therefore, researchers interested in the impact of divorce on children's health need to rule out the possibility that these confounders drive the association (Amato and Anthony 2014). One way social scientists have addressed this issue is through matching techniques which reduce imbalance, model dependence, and the influence of confounding variables, providing insight into long-assumed causal family-health linkages. For example, in one study, researchers matched families based on several factors known to be associated with risk of divorce (e.g. couple's socioeconomic status, couple's marital conflict, mother's depression). After comparing divorced parents and married parents with similar divorce risk factors, they found that parents who were divorced had children with more health issues, suggesting that the link between divorce and children's health might be causal (Weaver and Schofield 2015). These matching techniques have also been used in studies considering whether or not marriage actually improves health. For example, one study found that once propensities for marriage were taken into account, married adults were only modestly healthier than unmarried adults both physically and mentally – casting doubt on claims that marriage and health are causally related (Tumin and Zheng 2018).

Matching techniques are just one way to address issues of selection and confounding. Matching methods come with limitations, including only being able to match based on observable characteristics and difficulty satisfying model assumptions (Sekhon 2009). But because family and health researchers are increasingly concerned with causal inference techniques, multiple types of strategies are gaining popularity, including fixed effect models, placebo regressions, and inverse-probability-weighted estimation of marginal structural models (Gangl 2010). Some researchers make use of natural experiments, searching for events or conditions (e.g. natural disasters, public policies) that allow the population to – somewhat randomly – be divided into treatment and control groups. For example, prior to 2015, same-sex marriage laws in the US were highly variable across states, and comparing the health and experiences of same-sex married and unmarried couples in states that allowed same-sex marriage to unmarried same-sex couples in states that did not provides insight into the health benefits of marriage (Everett et al. 2016). Similar studies have found that health benefits of same-sex marriage laws actually extend beyond the same-sex couples themselves to unpartnered sexual minority people—including one study that found lower rates of suicide attempts among sexual minority adolescents in states with legally-recognized same-sex marriage (Raifman et al. 2017).

Families and their meaning for health are complex, and research investigating this should be theoretically driven and methodologically appropriate. Conclusions about the impact of families on health should be based on careful consideration of multiple studies conducted using a wide array of methods and data sources. This nuanced approach to studying the family should not be read as a privileging of any one approach, but rather a call to consider multiple types of studies (e.g. ethnography, longitudinal survey analysis) as in conversation with each other.

Social Locations of Families Shape How, When, and Why They Matter for Health

Families and health research is also difficult to summarize because these relationships need to be contextualized within their social location. Family relationships have heterogeneous effects on health, with this association conditioned on several sociodemographic factors – including age, cohort, race/ethnicity, gender, sexual identity, and social class, just to name a few. As discussed in a family diversity perspective (Collins 1998; Stacey 2012), there are multiple family structures and lived experiences of family, and these different structures and experiences are strongly shaped by social position which in turn structure the impact of family relationships on health. For example, Black adults are less likely to be married than White adults, but are more likely to have beneficial extended kin and family of choice networks (Waite and Das 2010). Women are less likely to be married at every age compared to men, with this especially pronounced at older ages with more women widows than men, and report more strain within their marriages (Liu and Umberson 2008). Those with low educational attainment have smaller family networks on average and are less likely to be married and more likely to be divorced than those with high education (Waite and Das 2010). Until 2015, sexual minority adults were legally banned from marriage in many states, and they continue to be less likely to have children than heterosexual men and women (Reczek 2020). Older adults have smaller networks than younger adults and are more likely to be socially isolated (Waite and Das 2010).

Families are a social determinant of health (Russell, Coleman, and Ganong 2018). As such, different distributions of various family ties – both in terms of structure and content – within a population can play a role in understanding health disparities. Heterogeneous effects of families on health across groups may also play a role in explaining health disparities. Gender scholars have long argued that women receive more health costs and fewer health benefits from marriage than men – as well as more health costs from parenthood–and that this underlies gender disparities in health seen at the population level (Gove 1972; Williams 2003). Additionally, due to systemic racism, Black people experience higher rates of family stress in childhood, and this helps explain racial disparities in health and mortality and throughout the life course (Umberson et al. 2014). Sexual minority adults seem to receive fewer benefits from marriage than heterosexual people, which could partially explain sexual minority-based health disparities (Solazzo, Gorman. and Denney 2020).

But we should not revert to a family deficit model, viewing some groups as having "deficient" families which necessarily drive health disparities. A family diversity model notes that – for some groups – family structures and their content are adaptive to the specific needs and environments of those groups and thus may provide a buffer against stressors and structural disadvantages. Lower rates of marriage within a community may signify a rejection of the gender inequality that often accompanies heterosexual marriages and an embrace of non-traditional and more egalitarian relationships. It may also indicate supportive environments for single adults. Scholars have suggested that marriage is "greedy," such that married people invest within their immediate family but overlook extended kin and community members (Gerstel and Sarkisian 2006). A low prevalence of marriage may mean flourishing of non-marital supports – with positive benefits for the health of all in a society – and thus research fixated on only one type of family structure as important for health and well-being may miss the benefits of other models. Instead, family and health researchers should carefully contextualize families within their specific social location and also their historical period.

Implications for Policy and Practice

Public policy is a key driver of the persistent association between family relationships and health. For example, spousal access to employer-sponsored health insurance and tax benefits for married couples facilitates the positive association between marriage and well-being. This can become self-fulfilling, for even while governments enact policies that strengthen the association between marriage and health, they also base policies, programs, and legal decisions on the known fact that marriage benefits health. Indeed, this was a key argument in legal discussions of whether the US should federally recognize same-sex marriage, citing studies showing that marriage improves health (Perone 2015). Similarly, cities and states fund marriage promotion programs for single parents, often with the stated goal of improving the health of children (Lichter, Batson, and Brown 2004). Our health care system relies on the work of family members to provide caregiving for older adults (Feinberg et al. 2011), making the absence of family at later life— an increasingly common state (Margolis and Verdery 2017)— an incredible health risk (Shankar et al. 2011). More public supports for older adults would make family less impactful for health at these older ages (although still important for emotional well-being and support). Yet we also have policies that weaken the association between families and health – or even contribute to families having negative impacts on health. Parenthood, especially single motherhood, is associated with worse well-being in the US, but this is not the case in countries with more comprehensive safety nets (e.g. paid parental leave, subsidized childcare) (Glass et al. 2016). Thus, associations between parenthood and poor health in the US are artifacts of the specific US context and policies. Changing these policies would likely alter the association between parenthood and health.

Public policy is thus a key lever through which to influence the associations between family and health, and public policy (and social structures more broadly) have incredible power within this area, even when policies and structures do not have obvious implications for families or health. Changes to health care, education, immigration, and criminal justice, to name a few, can shift what families look like and how, when, and why they matter for health. Even beyond public policies, changes in corporate policies, religious institutions, and nonprofit services can shape the associations between families and health. For example, many churches have loosened policies around divorce and remarriage, providing more welcoming environments for single parents and blended families. Yet traditional church teachings around gender and sexuality provide a key backdrop through which same-sex couples and other sexual and gender minority-member families face stigma, leading to possible negative outcomes for themselves and their family members (Boppana and Gross 2019). Researchers interested in family and health should not confine their analysis to households, but consider the roles of workplaces, schools, neighborhoods, hospitals, places of worship, and the many other organizations and institutions that shape health and family life.

Conclusion

Studying families and health has been a central focus of medical sociologists, with this work providing support for the claim that families are a social determinant of health. Future work on how the family matters for health should continue to emphasize the contextual factors that shape this influence – including possibilities that selection factors rather than causal factors drive some of these relationships. Although there is no universal story of when, why, and how families matter for health, continuing to interrogate the myriad ways that families are important can provide insight into health patterns within the population. We specifically issue a call for more research placing family ties in context with one another and in context of the overall life course. Family relationships do not occur in isolation but different family relationships likely interact with each other in ways that matter for health. For example, a supportive aunt might buffer the negative impact of a stressful father, or a mother may be providing care for a young child while also providing care for an aging parent. These interacting and compounding social ties need to be studied together in order to best make sense of these relationships. Similarly, family relationships need to be studied from a life course perspective, examining how family relationships might have particular salience at specific life course stages (e.g. critical periods) and how the impacts of family ties shift and accumulate as people age. There is a particular research need to explore more about how relationships early in life "spill over" to impact health and relationships later in life. Studying family relationships in this way requires using methods and theories from multiple different perspectives, including social network analysis and life course approaches (Perry et al. 2018; Shanahan et al. 2016). It also requires identifying and adapting to demographic changes in the family, rather than assuming the current trajectory of family life will continue. Research on family and health is a rich and growing area, with a strong legacy of past and current research and much room for innovation and insights to come.

References

Amato, Paul R. and Christopher J. Anthony. 2014. "Estimating the Effects of Parental Divorce and Death with Fixed Effects Models." *Journal of Marriage and Family* 76(2): 370–86.

Amorim, Mariana, Rachel Dunifon, and Natasha Pilkauskas. 2017. "The Magnitude and Timing of Grandparental Coresidence during Childhood in the United States." *Demographic Research* 37: 1695–706.

Arditti, Joyce A. 2012. "Child Trauma within the Context of Parental Incarceration: A Family Process Perspective." *Journal of Family Theory & Review* 4(3): 181–219.

Berkman, Lisa F., M. Yuhui Zheng, Maria Glymour, Mauricio Avendano, Axel Börsch-Supan, and Erika L Sabbath. 2015. "Mothering Alone: Cross-National Comparisons of Later-Life Disability and Health among Women Who Were Single Mothers." *Journal of Epidemiology and Community Health* 69(9): 865–72.

Birditt, Kira S., Laura M. Miller, Karen L. Fingerman, and Eva S. Lefkowitz. 2009. "Tensions in the Parent and Adult Child Relationship: Links to Solidarity and Ambivalence." *Psychology and Aging* 24(2): 287–95.

Bolton, James M., Rae Spiwak, and Jitender Sareen. 2017. "Consequences of Sibling Death: Problematic, Potentially Predictable, and Poorly Managed." *JAMA Pediatrics* 171(6): 519–20.

Boppana, Shilpa and Alan M. Gross. 2019. "The Impact of Religiosity on the Psychological Well-Being of LGBT Christians." *Journal of Gay & Lesbian Mental Health* 23(4): 412–26.

Branje, Susan J.T., William W. Hale, Tom Frijns, and H.J. Meeus Wim. 2010. "Longitudinal Associations between Perceived Parent-Child Relationship Quality and Depressive Symptoms in Adolescence." *Journal of Abnormal Child Psychology* 38(6): 751–63.

Brown, Dustin C., Robert A. Hummer, and Mark D. Hayward. 2014. "The Importance of Spousal Education for the Self-Rated Health of Married Adults in the United States." *Population Research and Policy Review* 33(1): 127–51.

Carr, Deborah. 2018. "The Linked Lives Principle in Life Course Studies: Classic Approaches and Contemporary Advances." Pp. 41–63 in *Social Networks and the Life Course*, Alwin, Duane F., Felmlee, Diane Helen, Kreager, Derek A. (Eds.). New York: Springer.

Catalano, P.M. and H.M. Ehrenberg. 2006. "The Short-and Long-Term Implications of Maternal Obesity on the Mother and Her Offspring." *BJOG: An International Journal of Obstetrics & Gynaecology* 113(10): 1126–33.

Cavanagh, Shannon E. and Paula Fomby. 2019. "Family Instability in the Lives of American Children." *Annual Review of Sociology* 45: 493–513.

Chan, Melissa. 2020. "Pets are Part of Our Families. Now They're Part of Our Divorces, Too," in *Time Magazine*. New York: TIME USA LLC.

Christakis, Nicholas A. and James H. Fowler. 2008. "The Collective Dynamics of Smoking in a Large Social Network." *New England Journal of Medicine* 358(21): 2249–58.

Christakis, Nicholas A. and James H. Fowler. 2009. *Connected: The Surprising Power of Our Social Networks and How They Shape Our Lives*. New York: Little, Brown Spark.

Clarke, Toni-Kim, Mark J. Adams, David M. Howard, Charley Xia, Gail Davies, Caroline Hayward, Archie Campbell, Sandosh Padmanabhan, Blair H. Smith, and Alison Murray. 2019. "Genetic and Shared Couple Environmental Contributions to Smoking and Alcohol Use in the UK Population." *Molecular Psychiatry* 1–11.

Colen, Cynthia G., Qi Li, Corinne Reczek, and David R. Williams. 2019. "The Intergenerational Transmission of Discrimination: Children's Experiences of Unfair Treatment and Their Mothers' Health at Midlife." *Journal of Health and Social Behavior* 60(4): 474–92.

Collins, Patricia Hill. 1998. "It's All in the Family: Intersections of Gender, Race, and Nation." *Hypatia* 13(3): 62–82.

Collins, Patricia Hill and Sirma Bilge. 2016. *Intersectionality*. Cambridge: John Wiley & Sons.

Courtin, Emilie and Martin Knapp. 2017. "Social Isolation, Loneliness and Health in Old Age: A Scoping Review." *Health & Social Care in the Community* 25(3): 799–812.

Cox, Martha J. and Blair Paley. 2003. "Understanding Families as Systems." *Current Directions in Psychological Science* 12(5): 193–96.

Denney, Justin T., Richard G. Rogers, Patrick M. Krueger, and Tim Wadsworth. 2009. "Adult Suicide Mortality in the United States: Marital Status, Family Size, Socioeconomic Status, and Differences by Sex." *Social Science Quarterly* 90(5): 1167–85.

Durkheim, E. 1951 [1897]. *Suicide*. New York: Free Press.

Elder, Glen H., Monica Kirkpatrick Johnson, and Robert Crosnoe. 2003. "The Emergence and Development of Life Course Theory." Pp. 3–19 in *Handbook of the Life Course*, Jeylan T. Mortimer; Michael J. Shanahan (eds.). New York: Springer.

Everett, Bethany G., Mark L. Hatzenbuehler, and Tonda L. Hughes. 2016. "The Impact of Civil Union Legislation on Minority Stress, Depression, and Hazardous Drinking in A Diverse Sample of Sexual-Minority Women: A Quasi-Natural Experiment." *Social Science & Medicine* 169: 180–90.

Feinberg, Lynn, Susan C. Reinhard, Ari Houser, and Rita Choula. 2011. "Valuing the Invaluable: 2011 Update, the Growing Contributions and Costs of Family Caregiving." *Washington, DC: AARP Public Policy Institute* 32: 1–28.

Fingerman, Karen L., Meng Huo, and Kira S. Birditt. 2020. "A Decade of Research on Intergenerational Ties: Technological, Economic, Political, and Demographic Changes." *Journal of Marriage and Family* 82(1): 383–403.

Fingerman, Karen L., Eva S. Lefkowitz Lindsay Pitzer, Kira S. Birditt, and Daniel Mroczek. 2008. "Ambivalent Relationship Qualities between Adults and Their Parents: Implications for the Well-Being of Both Parties." *The Journals of Gerontology Series B* 63(6): P362–P371.

Freedman, Vicki A., Jennifer C. Cornman, and Deborah Carr. 2014. "Is Spousal Caregiving Associated with Enhanced Well-Being? New Evidence from the Panel Study of Income Dynamics." *Journals of Gerontology Series B* 69(6): 861–69.

Fuller, Theodore D. 2010. "Relationship Status, Health, and Health Behavior: An Examination of Cohabiters and Commuters." *Sociological Perspectives* 53(2): 221–45.

Gangl, Markus. 2010. "Causal Inference in Sociological Research." *Annual Review of Sociology* 36, 21–47.

Gerstel, Naomi and Natalia Sarkisian. 2006. "Marriage: The Good, the Bad, and the Greedy." *Contexts* 5(4): 16–21.

Glass, Jennifer, Robin W. Simon, and Matthew A. Andersson. 2016. "Parenthood and Happiness: Effects of Work-Family Reconciliation Policies in 22 OECD Countries." *American Journal of Sociology* 122(3): 886–929.

Gove, Walter R. 1972. "The Relationship between Sex Roles, Marital Status, and Mental Illness." *Social Forces* 51(1): 34–44.

Granda-Cameron, Clara and Arlene Houldin. 2012. "Concept Analysis of Good Death in Terminally Ill Patients." *American Journal of Hospice and Palliative Medicine* 29(8): 632–39.

Grundy, Emily and Sanna Read. 2015. "Pathways from Fertility History to Later Life Health: Results from Analyses of the English Longitudinal Study of Ageing." *Demographic Research* 32: 107–46.

Hadfield, Kristin, Margaret Amos, Michael Ungar, Julie Gosselin, and Lawrence Ganong. 2018. "Do Changes to Family Structure Affect Child and Family Outcomes? A Systematic Review of the Instability Hypothesis." *Journal of Family Theory & Review* 10(1): 87–110.

Jadhav, Apoorva and David Weir. 2018. "Widowhood and Depression in a Cross-National Perspective: Evidence from the United States, Europe, Korea, and China." *The Journals of Gerontology: Series B* 73(8): e143–e153.

Kang, Jeong-han, Jibum Kim, and Min-Ah Lee. 2016. "Marital Status and Mortality: Does Family Structure in Childhood Matter?" *Social Science & Medicine* 159: 152–60.

Krueger, Patrick M. and Virginia W. Chang. 2008. "Being Poor and Coping with Stress: Health Behaviors and the Risk of Death." *American Journal of Public Health* 98(5): 889–96.

Lichter, Daniel T., Christie D. Batson, and J. Brian Brown. 2004. "Welfare Reform and Marriage Promotion: The Marital Expectations and Desires of Single and Cohabiting Mothers." *Social Service Review* 78(1): 2–25.

Lippold, Melissa A., Susan M. McHale, Kelly D. Davis, David M. Almeida, and Rosalind B. King. 2016. "Experiences with Parents and Youth Physical Health Symptoms and Cortisol: A Daily Diary Investigation." *Journal of Research on Adolescence* 26(2): 226–40.

Liu, Hui and Debra J. Umberson. 2008. "The Times They are a Changin': Marital Status and Health Differentials from 1972 to 2003." *Journal of Health and Social Behavior* 49(3): 239–53.

Lünnemann, M.K.M., F.C.P. Van der Horst, M.P.C.M. Luijk Peter Prinzie, and M. Steketee. 2019. "The Intergenerational Impact of Trauma and Family Violence on Parents and Their Children." *Child Abuse & Neglect* 96: 1–12.

Lunsky, Yona, Suzanne Robinson, Ashleigh Blinkhorn, and Ouellette-Kuntz, Hélène. 2017. "Parents of Adults with Intellectual and Developmental Disabilities (IDD) and Compound Caregiving Responsibilities." *Journal of Child and Family Studies* 26(5): 1374–79.

Marcus, Jan. 2013. "The Effect of Unemployment on the Mental Health of Spouses–Evidence from Plant Closures in Germany." *Journal of Health Economics* 32(3): 546–58.

Margolis, Rachel. 2016. "The Changing Demography of Grandparenthood." *Journal of Marriage and Family* 78(3): 610–22.

Margolis, Rachel and Ashton M. Verdery. 2017. "Older Adults without Close Kin in the United States." *The Journals of Gerontology: Series B* 72(4): 688–93.

Margolis, Rachel and Laura Wright. 2016. "Better off Alone than with a Smoker: The Influence of Partner's Smoking Behavior in Later Life." *Journals of Gerontology Series B* 71(4): 687–97.

Marsack, Christina N. and Tam E. Perry. 2018. "Aging in Place in Every Community: Social Exclusion Experiences of Parents of Adult Children with Autism Spectrum Disorder." *Research on Aging* 40(6): 535–57.

McEwen, Bruce S. 1998. "Stress, Adaptation, and Disease: Allostasis and Allostatic Load." *Annals of the New York Academy of Sciences* 840(1): 33–44.

Mossakowski, Krysia N. 2015. "Disadvantaged Family Background and Depression among Young Adults in the United States: The Roles of Chronic Stress and Self-Esteem." *Stress and Health* 31(1): 52–62.

Mouzon, Dawne M. 2014. "Relationships of Choice: Can Friendships or Fictive Kinships Explain the Race Paradox in Mental Health?" *Social Science Research* 44: 32–43.

Muraco, Anna, Jennifer Putney, Chengshi Shiu, and Karen I. Fredriksen-Goldsen. 2018. "Lifesaving in Every Way: The Role of Companion Animals in the Lives of Older Lesbian, Gay, Bisexual, and Transgender Adults Age 50 and Over." *Research on Aging* 40(9): 859–82.

Nelson, Margaret K. 2013. "Fictive Kin, Families We Choose, and Voluntary Kin: What Does the Discourse Tell Us?" *Journal of Family Theory & Review* 5(4): 259–81.

Nomaguchi, Kei M. 2012. "Parenthood and Psychological Well-Being: Clarifying the Role of Child Age and Parent–Child Relationship Quality." *Social Science Research* 41(2): 489–98.

Orfila, Francesc, Montserrat Coma-Solé, Marta Cabanas, Francisco Cegri-Lombardo, Anna Moleras-Serra, and Enriqueta Pujol-Ribera. 2018. "Family Caregiver Mistreatment of the Elderly: Prevalence of Risk and Associated Factors." *BMC Public Health* 18(1): 167.

Perelli-Harris, Brienna, Stefanie Hoherz, Fenaba Addo, Trude Lappegård, Ann Evans, Sharon Sassler, and Marta Styrc. 2018. "Do Marriage and Cohabitation Provide Benefits to Health in Mid-Life? the Role of Childhood Selection Mechanisms and Partnership Characteristics across Countries." *Population Research and Policy Review* 37(5): 703–28.

Perone, Angela K. 2015. "Health Implications of the Supreme Court's Obergefell Vs. Hodges Marriage Equality Decision." *LGBT Health* 2(3): 196–99.

Perry, Brea L., Bernice A. Pescosolido, and Stephen P. Borgatti. 2018. *Egocentric Network Analysis: Foundations, Methods, and Models*, Vol. 44. Cambridge: Cambridge University Press.

Pinquart, Martin and Sörensen, Silvia. 2003. "Associations of Stressors and Uplifts of Caregiving with Caregiver Burden and Depressive Mood: A Meta-Analysis." *The Journals of Gerontology Series B* 58(2): P112–P128.

Raifman, Julia, S. Ellen Moscoe, Bryn Austin, and McConnell, Margaret. 2017. "Difference-in-differences Analysis of the Association between State Same-Sex Marriage Policies and Adolescent Suicide Attempts." *JAMA Pediatrics* 171(4): 350–56.

Reczek, Corinne. 2020. "Sexual-and Gender-Minority Families: A 2010 to 2020 Decade in Review." *Journal of Marriage and Family* 82(1): 300–25.

Reczek, Corinne, Tetyana Pudrovska, Deborah Carr, Mieke Beth Thomeer, and Debra Umberson. 2016. "Marital Histories and Heavy Alcohol Use among Older Adults." *Journal of Health and Social Behavior* 57(1): 77–96.

Reczek, Corinne, Mieke Beth Thomeer, Amy C. Lodge, Debra Umberson, and Megan Underhill. 2014. "Diet and Exercise in Parenthood: A Social Control Perspective." *Journal of Marriage and Family* 76(5): 1047–62.

Rendall, Michael S., Margaret M. Weden, Melissa M. Favreault, and Hilary Waldron. 2011. "The Protective Effect of Marriage for Survival: A Review and Update." *Demography* 48(2): 481–506.

Robles, Theodore F., Richard B. Slatcher, Joseph M. Trombello, and Meghan M. McGinn. 2014. "Marital Quality and Health: A Meta-Analytic Review." *Psychological Bulletin* 140(1): 140.

Rogers, Richard G., Robert A. Hummer, Andrea M. Tilstra, Elizabeth M. Lawrence, and Stefanie Mollborn. 2020. "Family Structure and Early Life Mortality in the United States." Journal of Marriage and Family OnlineFirst 82: 1159–77.

Ruff, Saralyn C., Jared A. Durtschi, and Randal D. Day. 2018. "Family Subsystems Predicting Adolescents' Perceptions of Sibling Relationship Quality over Time." *Journal of Marital and Family Therapy* 44(3): 527–42.

Russell, Luke T., Marilyn Coleman, and Lawrence Ganong. 2018. "Conceptualizing Family Structure in a Social Determinants of Health Framework." *Journal of Family Theory & Review* 10(4): 735–48.

Ryan, Sara and Sue Ziebland. 2015. "On Interviewing People with Pets: Reflections from Qualitative Research on People with Long-Term Conditions." *Sociology of Health & Illness* 37(1): 67–80.

Sekhon, Jasjeet S. 2009. "Opiates for the Matches: Matching Methods for Causal Inference." *Annual Review of Political Science* 12: 487–508.

Shanahan, Michael J., Jeylan T. Mortimer, and Monica Kirkpatrick Johnson. 2016. *Handbook of the Life Course*. New York: Springer.

Shankar, Aparna, Anne McMunn, James Banks, and Andrew Steptoe. 2011. "Loneliness, Social Isolation, and Behavioral and Biological Health Indicators in Older Adults." *Health Psychology* 30(4): 377–85.

Sierminska, Eva. 2018. "The 'Wealth-Being' of Single Parents." Pp. 51–80 in *The Triple Bind of Single-Parent Families*, edited by Rense Nieuwenhuis Laurie C. Maldonado. Chicago, IL: Bristol University Press,

Skaff, Marilyn M. and Leonard I. Pearlin. 1992. "Caregiving: Role Engulfment and the Loss of Self." *The Gerontologist* 32(5): 656–64.

Solazzo, Alexa, Bridget Gorman, and Justin Denney. 2020. "Does Sexual Orientation Complicate the Relationship between Marital Status and Gender with Self-Rated Health and Cardiovascular Disease?" *Demography*, 57: 599–626.

Stacey, Judith. 2012. *Unhitched: Love, Marriage, and Family Values from West Hollywood to Western China*. New York: NYU Press.

Strohm, Charles Q., Judith A. Seltzer, Susan D. Cochran, and Vickie M. Mays. 2009. "'Living Apart Together' Relationships in the United States." *Demographic Research* 21: 177–214.

Thoits, Peggy A. 2011. "Mechanisms Linking Social Ties and Support to Physical and Mental Health." *Journal of Health and Social Behavior* 52(2): 145–61.

Thomeer, Mieke Beth. 2016. "Multiple Chronic Conditions, Spouse's Depressive Symptoms, and Gender within Marriage." *Journal of Health and Social Behavior* 57(1): 59–76.

Thomeer, Mieke Beth and Debra Umberson. 2014. "Widowhood." Pp. 7126–30 in *Encyclopedia of Quality of Life and Well-Being Research*, edited by A. C. Michalos. New York: Springer.

Tumin, Dmitry and Hui Zheng. 2018. "Do the Health Benefits of Marriage Depend on the Likelihood of Marriage?" *Journal of Marriage and Family* 80(3): 622–36.

Turney, Kristin. 2014. "Stress Proliferation across Generations? Examining the Relationship between Parental Incarceration and Childhood Health." *Journal of Health and Social Behavior* 55(3): 302–19.

Umberson, Debra, Robert Crosnoe, and Corinne Reczek. 2010. "Social Relationships and Health Behavior across the Life Course." *Annual Review of Sociology* 36: 139–57.

Umberson, Debra, Patricia A. Kristi Williams, Hui Liu Thomas, and Mieke Beth Thomeer. 2014. "Race, Gender, and Chains of Disadvantage: Childhood Adversity, Social Relationships, and Health." *Journal of Health and Social Behavior* 55(1): 20–38.

Umberson, Debra, Hui Liu, and Corinne Reczek. 2008. "Stress and Health Behaviour over the Life Course." *Advances in Life Course Research* 13: 19–44.

Umberson, Debra and Jennifer Karas Montez. 2010. "Social Relationships and Health: A Flashpoint for Health Policy." *Journal of Health and Social Behavior* 51(1_suppl): S54–S66.

Umberson, Debra, Julie Skalamera Olson, Robert Crosnoe, Hui Liu, Tetyana Pudrovska, and Rachel Donnelly. 2017. "Death of Family Members as an Overlooked Source of Racial Disadvantage in the United States." *Proceedings of the National Academy of Sciences* 114(5): 915–20.

Umberson, Debra and Mieke Beth Thomeer. 2020. "Family Matters: Research on Family Ties and Health, 2010 to 2020." *Journal of Marriage and Family* 82(1): 404–19.

Umberson, Debra, Kristi Williams, Daniel A Powers, Meichu D Chen, and Anna M Campbell. 2005. "As Good as It Gets? A Life Course Perspective on Marital Quality." *Social Forces* 84(1): 493–511.

Vitaliano, Peter P., Jianping Zhang, and James M. Scanlan. 2003. "Is Caregiving Hazardous to One's Physical Health? A Meta-Analysis." *Psychological Bulletin* 129(6): 946–72.

Vogt Yuan, Anastasia S. 2009. "Sibling Relationships and Adolescents' Mental Health: The Interrelationship of Structure and Quality." *Journal of Family Issues* 30(9): 1221–44.

Voorpostel, Marieke and Van Der Lippe, Tanja. 2007. "Support between Siblings and between Friends: Two Worlds Apart?" *Journal of Marriage and Family* 69(5): 1271–82.

Waite, Linda and Aniruddha Das. 2010. "Families, Social Life, and Well-Being at Older Ages." *Demography* 47(1): S87–S109.

Weaver, Jennifer M. and Thomas J Schofield. 2015. "Mediation and Moderation of Divorce Effects on Children's Behavior Problems." *Journal of Family Psychology* 29(1): 39–48.

Weston, Kath. 1997. *Families We Choose: Lesbians, Gays, Kinship*. New York: Columbia University Press.

Whisman, Mark A, Li Angela, David A Sbarra, and Charles L Raison. 2014. "Marital Quality and Diabetes: Results from the Health and Retirement Study." *Health Psychology* 33(8): 832–40.

Williams, Kristi. 2003. "Has the Future of Marriage Arrived? A Contemporary Examination of Gender, Marriage, and Psychological Well-Being." *Journal of Health and Social Behavior* 44(4): 470–87.

Williams, Kristi. 2004. "The Transition to Widowhood and the Social Regulation of Health: Consequences for Health and Health Risk Behavior." *The Journals of Gerontology Series B* 59(6): S343–S49.

Willson, Andrea E., Kim M. Shuey, and Glen H. Elder Jr. 2003. "Ambivalence in the Relationship of Adult Children to Aging Parents and in-Laws." *Journal of Marriage and Family* 65(4): 1055–72.

Wilson, Stephanie J., Brittney E. Bailey, Williams B. Malarkey, and Janice K. Kiecolt-Glaser. 2020. "Linking Marital Support to Aging-Related Biomarkers: Both Age and Marital Quality Matter." Journals of Gerontology Series B OnlineFirst.

Wolfe, Joseph D. 2019. "Age, Cohort, and Social Change: Parental and Spousal Education and White Women's Health Limitations from 1967 to 2012." *Research on Aging* 41(2): 186–210.

Yahirun, Jenjira J., Connor M. Sheehan, and Krysia N. Mossakowski. 2020. "Depression in Later Life: The Role of Adult Children's College Education for Older Parents' Mental Health in the United States." *The Journals of Gerontology: Series B* 75(2): 389–402.

Zajacova, Anna and Elizabeth M. Lawrence. 2018. "The Relationship between Education and Health: Reducing Disparities through a Contextual Approach." *Annual Review of Public Health* 39: 273–89.

18

Health and Religion

Ellen Idler

The social scientific study of health's association with religion remains as lively as ever, since the first chapter on the topic in this series was published in 2010. That chapter (Idler 2010) attempted to review the important sociological research on religion and health, going back necessarily to Durkheim's *Suicide* (Durkheim (1897) 1979). Topics in that earlier chapter included theories, methods, study design, and the results of studies and descriptions of explanatory mechanisms: social support, social control, and selection. There were also sections on health-related harms caused by religion, controversies that have arisen among researchers, and religion's role in generating new approaches to social and health care. The chapter's overall framework was that religion serves as a predictor of health status, and also has a role in the organization and practice of medicine and public health. There are developments in both of these research areas.

The present chapter will act as an update to this background, and is limited to research published in the last decade. It has in fact been a period of flourishing for the research, with new developments in theory and methods, and a deeper development of the research of the prior decades. There has by no means been a lessening of interest in the topic, certainly not in the era of the COVID-19 pandemic.

The chapter will be organized into four parts. *Populations* will review the new research from population-based studies on health outcomes, with the emphasis on representative studies. *Practices* will discuss the new emphasis on material practice and "lived religion" as factors in health. *Politics* will raise issues of controversy in health and religion, which are often related to harms to health caused by religion. Finally, work on *Partnerships* between organizations in religion and in public health is attracting new interest.

Two important frameworks underlie or form a backdrop for the last decade of research, giving a new set of assumptions or context to the work that has emerged during the decade. The first backdrop is the increasing secularization of Western

The Wiley Blackwell Companion to Medical Sociology, First Edition. Edited by William C. Cockerham.

societies. Growing interest and expertise in the demography of religion has demonstrated ever more clearly that religious affiliation and religious practice have been declining from one generation to the next in the US. This pattern of lower attendance at religious services for each younger cohort has long been recognized in Western Europe, but until recently was still debated in the US (Berger et al. 2008; Torpey 2010). New research shows that there is no longer any question that the US population is becoming more secular as well (Pew Research Center, June 13, 2018; Voas and Chaves 2016). One implication of secularizing societies is that the proportion of respondents who are influenced by religious participation is shrinking, and therefore the number of individuals subject to any health-related effects of religion, be they positive (protective) or negative (harms), is also shrinking. This backdrop of secularization contrasts the review of recent research with that of an earlier, perhaps more naïve period.

The second backdrop is the theoretical shift in conceptualizing the relationship between religion and health. As research in public health and social epidemiology is increasingly organized around the social determinants of health perspective (Marmot 2005), inequalities or disparities in income, education, and wealth within a population are now seen as the most powerful forces in shaping population health, more important even than the availability or quality of health care. The World Health Organization's Commission on the Social Determinants of Health (2008) defined them as: "… the circumstances in which people are born, grow up, live, work and age, and the systems put in place to deal with illness. These circumstances are in turn shaped by a wider set of forces: economics, social policies, and politics." This is now the paradigm for public health research and practice: that the most powerful determinants of population health are income and wealth inequality, status and power differences, and race and racism. The WHO Report does not mention religion as one of the social determinants of health, despite its role as a "… circumstance in which people are born …". Especially given the WHO focus on health in the global South, the omission of the presence and influence of religion – in the part of the world where religious observance remains very high, or even near-universal in some societies – ignores a fundamental aspect of social life. The argument for including religion among the social determinants of public health draws on life course epidemiology, and forms a second backdrop for conceptualizing religion as one among the many social forces in health (Idler 2014).

This chapter is being written in the midst of the COVID-19 pandemic, in a US state with the second-highest number of deaths in the country, and which is still in lockdown. Religion has been a real flashpoint in the societal response to COVID-19. The dominant narrative in the mainstream press has been one in which religion has been a risk-increasing force, often through defiance of state-imposed prohibitions on gathering for religious services. There is also an important counter-narrative of religion's role in protecting public health and caring for those who are the most vulnerable. The presence of chaplains in intensive care units caring for those dying alone, and the actions of faith-based organizations in setting up field hospitals, are two examples of this counter-narrative. The following four sections – Populations, Practices, Politics, and Partnerships – will each include what is known about that aspect of religion's response to COVID-19.

Populations

In this section we will review significant studies from the past ten years that have added to our knowledge of religion as a population health determinant. The emphasis will be on research with population-based (not patient or non-random) samples. To jump quickly to the conclusion, while both the theoretical frameworks and the methods for longitudinal analysis have become more sophisticated in the past decade, the results of the research have remained largely the same: attendance at religious services, regardless of faith tradition, has a significant protective effect against all-cause mortality. This effect is partially mediated by better health behaviors and greater social ties but it remains significantly protective in fully adjusted models.

The adoption of a social determinants perspective that includes religion brings a life course perspective to the fore in three ways: first, it directs our attention to the "circumstances in which people are born;" second, it mandates the use of longitudinal methods; and third, it forces us to consider the ways in which religion may be connected to the other social determinants of health, in complex ways.

The religious observance level of parents is a feature of early life (along with the income and education of the parents) that children are subject to. Besides the social connection to a religious congregation, observant families may have distinct dietary practices, or norms regarding smoking, alcohol use, or sexual activity that set them apart from secular families, in ways that may be relevant to health. This is an early life-course exposure on which there has been only a small amount of research to date (Burdette et al. 2012; Burdette and Pilhauskas 2012), making it a promising area of future investigation (Iles-Caven et al. 2019).

As noted above, both older and more recent studies of representative population-based samples have found adult respondents with more frequent religious attendance to have a consistently lower hazard of all-cause mortality. Examples include analyses of the Third National Health and Nutrition Examination Survey (NHANES) (Pantell et al. 2013), the Health and Retirement Study (HRS) (Idler et al. 2017), the Nurses' Health Study (NHS) (Li et al. 2016a), the Black Women's Health Study (BWHS) (VanderWeele et al. 2017), and the Mexican Health and Aging Study (MHAS) (Hill et al. 2020). Protective effects of frequent religious attendance in these studies, after adjustment for confounders and mediators, ranged from 20% to 40% lower hazards for all-cause mortality.

Since the original linkage of religion and mortality, in Durkheim's *Suicide* (Durkheim (1897) 1979), there has been a long tradition, continuing to the present, of research on suicide, a specific cause of death inherently linked to social factors. A meta-analysis of nine studies conducted in 2015 found a 62% reduced risk of completed suicide among the more religious in several cultures around the world (Wu et al. 2015). Linking the World Health Organization mortality data with the World Values Survey (WVS) across 42 countries, Hsieh (2017) found that religion had protective effects against suicide in countries in Latin America, English-speaking countries, and parts of Europe, but aggravating effects in the more secular regions of East Asia and western and southern Europe. In the US, where religiosity remains relatively high and the association is protective, the opioid crisis (Case and Deaton 2015) has provoked consideration of the role of religion in this other, still-ongoing, public health crisis (Case and Deaton 2020). Chen and colleagues (2020) analyzed data from the Health Professionals Follow-Up Study (HPFS) and the Nurses' Health Study II (NHSII); they found a 68% lower hazard of "deaths of despair" – suicide or death from substance abuse – in those participants reporting higher religious service attendance at baseline (Chen et al. 2020). In this specific cause of death, as with all-cause mortality, results from studies done in the past decade do not differ much from the findings of previous studies, although they are arguably much stronger in terms of analytic methods such as marginal structural modeling and time-varying covariates (e.g. Li et al. 2016b) or the geographic scope of data collection (e.g. Hsieh 2017).

With respect to outcomes other than mortality, there has also been continued research on a range of physical and mental health measures. Das and Nairn (2016) analyzed biodemographic data from the National Social Life, Health, and Aging Project (NSHAP) to test if religious attendance was related to stress and biological "weathering" in this older sample; results showed that frequent religious attendance was significantly associated with more favorable inflammatory and cardiovascular, but not metabolic measures, for both men and women. An analysis of disability data from the HRS found that weekly or more frequent attendance at religious services was associated with up to 5.1 years of additional life expectancy, and up to 4.3 additional years of disability-free life expectancy (Ofstedahl et al. 2019). The HRS-related SHARE study (Survey of Health, Ageing and Retirement in Europe) similarly found protective effects of "taking part in a religious organization" for both activity limitation and also current symptoms of depression (Ahrenfelt et al. 2017). Two recent studies of the incidence of depression, one using data from the HRS and one using the Nurses' Health Study, found a 29% reduced risk (Li et al. 2016a) and a 35% reduced risk (Ronneberg et al. 2016), respectively, of non-depressed frequent attenders developing depression compared with non-depressed but less frequent attenders. With these morbidity outcomes, as with the mortality outcomes, the new research has findings that do not differ much from earlier research, but the availability of biomarker data, and the development of more sophisticated methods for modelling repeated measures data has increased the rigor of the work.

There is also new and more global research on measures of general health and well-being. A large study by the Pew Research Center (January 2019) used data from the World Values Survey, the International Social Survey Programme (ISSP) and their own data from the US to analyze the cross-sectional association of individual religiousness (which they categorized as "actively affiliated," "inactive," and "unaffiliated") and multiple measures of self-reported health and well-being in 35 countries around the world. While there were substantial between-country differences, overall the actively religiously affiliated were more likely to say they were "very happy", were in "good health," did not smoke, avoided frequent drinking, exercised several times per week, belonged to at least one other nonreligious organization, and always voted in national elections; they were not less likely to be obese. In all of these studies of both mortality and morbidity, a point that has been left implicit until now is that the operative aspect of religiousness that is shown repeatedly to have protective effects on health is religious attendance or affiliation, or in other words, the active engagement with a religious community, rather than more private, less social aspects of religiousness like spirituality, private prayer, or feeling that religion is important. This is a consistent finding in decades of research; it strengthens the need to consider religion a *social* determinant of health.

Research has also continued on the question of the causal mechanisms, or mediators, of the association. Particular areas of concern, especially given the ongoing public health crises of the opioid epidemic and the COVID pandemic, are the connections of religion to substance abuse and social isolation. One analysis of the National Comorbidity Study Replication showed that, compared with stable religiosity from childhood to adulthood, either a significant increase or a significant decrease in religiosity was associated with greater substance use and misuse (of alcohol, tobacco, and illicit drugs) (Moscati and Mezuk 2014). A recent review of research in this area notes that the large majority of addiction treatment programs in the US contain a component of spirituality, and that 84% of scientific studies show that faith is positively associated with both prevention and recovery from substance use (Grim and Grim 2019).

Similarly, religious participation has been linked to the protective factor of quantitatively and qualitatively greater social ties. An NSHAP analysis showed that older couples with homogeneous patterns of religious attendance had higher-quality marriages on several dimensions (Schafer and Kwon 2017); analysis of the Nurses' Health Study showed a 47% lower risk of divorce or separation for frequent attenders compared with never attenders (Li et al. 2018); and a study of the National Survey of Families and Households showed that adult children who attended services more frequently were significantly more likely to be providing care to their elderly parents (King et al. 2013). Thus, recent evidence continues to support the link of religious participation with the two primary mechanisms most often tested in mortality studies: better health practices and more robust social network ties.

Does the theoretical backdrop of including religion as a social determinant of health advance the impact of these studies? The answer is both yes, and not yet. Yes – in that some measures of religion are increasingly included in data collection for large population-based surveys, and that the study designs, methods of analysis, and quality of journal placement have been strengthened. It seems today to be a more mainstream, less marginal area of research. But this is only a first step in exploiting the utility of theory. For a social determinants of health approach to have a real impact on the study of religion's effect on health, we must undertake a consideration of the relationship between religion and the other social determinants whose health effects are well known: income, education, race/ethnicity, and gender. Sociologists refer to the study of the interacting effects of race, class, and gender as intersectionality (McCall 2005). What is needed is to ask questions such as: is religion's effect on health independent of those of education, income, race, and gender, or is it in some way dependent or contingent on them? Does it exacerbate their effects? Mitigate them? Is it a causal, mediating, pathway for other social determinants? Or the reverse? Research on religious discrimination (Samari 2016; Alang 2016; Vang et al. 2019), religion and economic attitudes and wealth (de Pablo 2019; Giuso et al. 2003), and religion and marital status (Das and Nairn 2016) shows how complex these associations are. Religion is profoundly connected with life chances in the US and other countries, advantaging some religions and disadvantaging others. Until these associations are fully investigated in the context of health outcomes we will have neither a complete picture of any of the traditional social determinants of population health, nor of religion.

The second backdrop to this research is the increasing rate of secularization, especially in Western European countries, some of which are reaching extremely low levels of religious observance (Idler 2020). Scholars have tied the decline of the importance of religion to other broad social changes, including the decline in fertility and the changing social role of women (Lesthaeghe 2014), and rising income, education, health care, and social security in developed countries (Paldam and Gundlach 2013). Regardless of the causes of secularization, however, the process appears to be immutable, proceeding from one generation's lower levels of religiosity to the next generation's even lower levels (Twenge et al. 2015) resulting in pronounced age differences in religiosity in most countries around the world (Pew Research Pew Research Center 2018a). Thus, while the significant positive effect of religious observance on health in the research we have reviewed for the past decade has not changed much from earlier studies, the proportion of the population to which it applies is aging and also growing continually smaller. There is some suggestive evidence of this with intra-individual change: analysis of General Social Survey (GSS) data from 1973 to 2012 shows that individuals who report disaffiliating from the religious tradition of their childhood report poorer self-rated health and general well-being compared with both those who were continuously affiliated and continuously nonaffiliated (Fenelon and Danielsen 2017). In another analysis of GSS data over the same period, other authors find that the overall positive association of religious attendance with self-rated health remains strong for men but declines in strength for women, and this is mostly explained by women's increases in education (Mukerjee and Venugopal 2018).

A third suggestive study showing the erosion of the association explores the associations between religion and self-rated health and mortality and shows that they are dependent on the overall religiosity of the society. Stavrova (2015) finds, in a study of 59 countries, that religion is positively associated with better self-rated health and decreased mortality, but only in countries where religious participation is the norm. As a group these studies point to the importance of considering a future context of declining individual and societal religious observance. Another implication is that as the numbers of religiously observant individuals in a population declines, the remaining religiously observant are stratified by age and gender especially, but also by race and immigration status. As a minority, the religiously observant may become increasingly stigmatized as old, female, nonwhite, immigrant, and less educated, or some combination of these (Bruce 2016).

The role of religion in the response to COVID-19 has been multi-faceted and high-profile. Any measurable religious differentials in COVID-19-related mortality or morbidity outcomes at the population level must await future research. But certainly the spread of the virus in religious settings has been much in the news. This underscores the importance of considering religion as a social determinant of health, but it is ironic that the aspect of religion that has made it a protective factor in research to date – the social dimension – is precisely the reason that it constitutes a risk in an infectious disease pandemic. Religious communities congregate in large groups and participate in practices that, in the current conditions, promote not the supportive social solidarity that is the basis of the protective association, but the transmission of a highly contagious virus that is a still-increasing cause of serious illness and death.

To sum up then, research on religion in the past decade has advanced in several ways, although the general picture of religious participation as a protective factor in population health has not changed much from earlier research. There have been important advances in methodology for longitudinal research, and increased availability of at least a small amount of data on religion in large population-based surveys, giving an increasing confidence in the size and consistency of the effect. Considering religion as a social determinant of health, in concert with other population health determinants, will be a necessary next step for future research, but that research will take place under conditions of lower levels of exposure to religion, as the secularization of many societies around the world proceeds.

Practices

Religious practices are an important, but under-studied way to understand the health effects of religious participation. This section will make an argument for the importance of considering practices and rituals as key to understanding the impact of religion on health by giving examples of existing research on their health effects, which are generally positive. But religious practices have been at the center of the transmission of epidemics in the past, notably during the Ebola outbreak, as they are again today during the COVID-19 pandemic.

Religious practices accompany both birth and death in most, if not all religious traditions, and other religious practices or rituals may be performed as frequently several times per day by religious adherents. Rituals have a cyclical character. There are daily, weekly, annual, and life course cycles, which could be thought of as regular exposures to a particular experience (Idler 2013). Moreover, the experience of participating in a religious ritual or practice has a physical dimension; the body is involved in an experience that unites the physical, spiritual, emotional, and cognitive. In some ways that is the purpose of rituals, to create the time and place for those wholistic, unifying, integrative experiences (Rappaport 1999).

For a ritual or practice to have a demonstrable effect on population health, it must be widely practiced by ordinary members of a faith tradition, not just the priests, religious leaders, or members of orders. Any single religious tradition will have multiple religious practices, and any single ritual can be practiced by many different religious traditions, albeit in different ways. Some widely-practiced rituals in many faith traditions include pilgrimages, fasting, or prayer. Some religious practices have been studied for their health effects (Idler 2014). Circumcision in infancy or childhood is a foundational ritual for both Judaism and Islam (Seeman 2014); population studies show that higher rates of circumcision are associated with lower rates of HIV/AIDS infection, and also with lower cervical cancer rates for the female partners of circumcised males (Drain et al. 2006). Vegetarianism is a daily religious practice for many faith traditions including Hinduism, Buddhism, and Seventh Day Adventism (Grant and Montenegro 2014); the health benefits of a vegetarian diet are well-known (Willett 2003). Attendance at weekly religious services, a feature of the monotheistic religious traditions of Judaism, Christianity, and Islam, has been most-studied aspect of a religious practice as a factor in health; its protective effects on health are often attributed to the social interaction and support of the religious group but it is itself the site for the performance of rituals such as baptism, communion, prayer, or chanting (Idler 2011). Rituals that revolve on an annual cycle, such as Christmas or Ramadan, have also been studied for their health effects (Idler and Kasl 1992; An-Na'im 2014). Most, although not all, of the studies of rituals and practices find protective effects on health, as might be expected by their close connection to attendance at religious services (Idler 2011). The practice of religious rituals can embed an individual in expectable cycles of performance, and provide a continuous sense of identity throughout the life course. This may be especially beneficial in old age, when memory and cognition may decline, while deeply rooted memories remain strong.

A notable example of the negative role of religious ritual in health was the 2014 West African Ebola crisis, where religion was right at the heart of the epidemic, initially as a cause of the spread of the disease, and eventually as a key solution. In the beginning, traditional religious burial practices that involved intimate contact of grieving relatives with the deceased were quickly spreading the disease (Brainard et al. 2016). One notable case was that of a well-known pharmacist who died of Ebola and was buried by his family. Following the funeral, 28 persons contracted the virus themselves, most of them also members of his family who had carried and or touched his body during the funeral (Curran et al. 2016). The World Health Organization's protocol for the "safe" burial of Ebola victims was not being practiced; even families of the deceased who were aware of the risk of traditional practices disregarded the guidelines because they were thought to be disrespectful to their loved ones.

The current COVID-19 pandemic has upended many aspects of religious practice. At this writing in early summer 2020, churches, temples, and mosques have begun to reopen in just a few states in the US, after nearly universally moving to online services. Religious gatherings are an example of the type of mass gatherings that have been associated with rapid spreading of the virus (Quadri 2020). One well-documented spreading event occurred early in the pandemic in South Korea, where members of the Shincheonji Church of Jesus sought to avoid testing because of their religious beliefs, but where 5200 were eventually found to test positive (Statista 2020). Another occurred at a church in Arkansas in March 2020; the pastor and spouse both became infected, and transmitted the infection to 35 persons before they became symptomatic; three of their parishioners died (James et al. 2020).

An important feature of religious gatherings in many faith traditions is vocal music, performed by the entire congregation, or by choirs or chanters. One of the earliest spreading events in the US was at a church in Washington State; the 60-member Skagit Valley Chorale, none of whom were showing symptoms, held a rehearsal March 10, following which 28 members tested positive and 2 died (CNN April 1, 2020). Singing (or yelling) projects aerosolized droplets from deep in the lungs, and thus is far more likely to spread more virus particles, and to spread them further, than simple speaking. Moreover, singing synchronizes breathing, such that all singers are breathing out, and then breathing in each other's exhalations simultaneously – clearly a deeply risky practice. There are few worship services in the US that do not include choral music and/or congregational singing (Chaves 2004). In the absence of public health guidance on singing in religious services, a number of professional choir organizations (sacred and secular) have been providing webinars and documents, but it is not yet known how well that guidance will be followed.

The COVID-19 pandemic has called forth responses from every sector of our society and affected every aspect of life, including, quite profoundly, religious practices and rituals, particularly those performed in mass gatherings. Religious practices have played a role during plagues throughout history, as a normal response to human suffering. But only recently have scientific medicine and epidemiology allowed us to specify the role religion has played in increasing and/or decreasing risk of transmission of the virus. Thus religious practices take on a heightened meaning in infectious disease outbreaks, but they have a role to play in health in other times as well.

Politics

The political dimensions of the religion – health relationship have not received much attention in previous research, but the current climate of political polarization in the US has fault lines that run parallel to religious divides, and it seems essential to bring the issues forward in any contemporary discussion of religion and health. The COVID-19 pandemic, especially, is bringing these tensions to the fore, although they have been there in the background all along.

One way these issues line up coincides with the backdrop of secularization. The generational pattern of secularization, with each successive cohort reporting less religious affiliation, effectively stratifies religiosity by age (Pew Research Center, June 13, 2018). In both the US and Western Europe, religious people are older, and also more politically and socially conservative than younger and more secular generations (Phalet et al. 2018). Western European young adults, who are very secular, are more liberal about social issues such as same-sex marriage and legal abortion, and are more accepting of Muslims and Jews compared with Eastern Europeans, who are more religious (Pew Research Center, October 29, 2018). An analysis of the US General Social Survey from 1972 to 2012 shows a strong trend, beginning in the late 1980s, of the growth of the non-religiously-affiliated from 7% in 1987 to 20% in 2012. When the trend is stratified by political views, there is very little increase in the "no religious affiliation" group among political conservatives from the baseline in 1987 to 2012, but an increase from less than 20% to more than 30% among political liberals during the same time period, with moderates in between (Hout and Fischer 2014). Thus the religiously unaffiliated in the US and Europe are younger, more educated, more politically liberal, more racially diverse, and also more religiously diverse, in that there are larger proportions of Muslims and Hindus, and fewer Christians among the young (Pew Research Center, June 13, 2018).

Prior to the COVID-19 pandemic, there were many health and sexuality-related issues on which religious conservatives differed from mainline Protestants and the increasingly secular population. Faith-linked controversies have surrounded family planning, abortion, reproductive technology, immunization, stigmatized sexuality and gender identity, violence against women, and end of life issues (Doebler 2015; Tomkins et al. 2015). Some of these controversies have been exploited as wedge issues for advantage in national politics. Many, if not all of these health policy differences have put religious conservatives at odds with public health policies and recommendations, leading to an often contentious, mistrusting relationship between public health officials and parts of the faith community.

The COVID-19 pandemic has surfaced these tensions dramatically. Religion's role in the response to the pandemic in the US and around the world has been much in the news. Throughout history, minority religious groups have been blamed for outbreaks of disease, as Jews were in the Middle Ages in Europe (Pamuk 2020) and Muslims are today in India (Berkley Center, June 3, 2020). This tendency to blame religious persons and/or persons from foreign countries as "the other" portrays these groups as dangerous transmitters of contagion. Observers are seeing the rise of conspiracy theories from extremist groups, many of which involve elements of religion (Berkley Center for Religion, Peace, and World Affairs2020a). Thus while on the one hand, religious minorities may be victimized as carriers of contagion, there are other instances where religious groups have ignored public health recommendations, resulting in actions that put religious group members – and other members of the public – at risk for transmission of the virus. Funerals and large public worship services, for example, have been held despite local and state public health directives on mass gatherings, social distancing, and masks, with considerable media coverage (Stack, April 29, 2020; James et al. 2020).

Conservative religious voices in the US and elsewhere have made an argument against public health authorities' directives during the pandemic on the grounds of constitutional protections of religious freedom (Berkley Center, May 7, 2020), further politicizing the issue. On May 20, 2020, after significant delays, the US Centers for Disease Control and Prevention (CDC) issued guidance for the reopening of numerous institutions, including schools, child-care facilities, restaurants, and mass transit, but did not provide guidance for religious institutions. According to the *Washington Post*, guidance for religious institutions was held back at the direction of the White House (Sun, Dawsey and Boorstein, May 20, 2020). Two days later, CDC's "Interim Guidance for Communities of Faith" was released (CDC 2020), although it oddly says nothing about the nearly universal practice of singing, arguably the riskiest aspect of a worship service. On June 1, the Supreme Court decided 5-4 to deny an application by a California church challenging Governor Gavin Newsom's Stay-at-Home order and phased reopening plan for religious worship gatherings (Seeman 2020). Writing for the majority, Chief Justice John Roberts argued that religious institutions were not being discriminated against in having more restrictive guidelines than the reopening for banks, laundromats, or stores, because such institutions (unlike religious gatherings) do not have large numbers of people congregating for sustained periods of time; rather, religious services more closely resemble the mass gatherings of lectures, concerts, or sporting events, which have similar restrictions. It is notable that it was a close decision, with four justices dissenting.

It should be said that these high-profile political events are somewhat at odds with US nationally representative survey data showing that fewer than 10% of Americans think that in-person religious services should be permitted without restrictions on size or social distancing during the pandemic, including a majority of Evangelical Christians and Republicans (Beyerlein and Nirenberg 2020). As we will see in the next part of the paper, religious groups are also playing a very constructive role in combatting the pandemic in the US, but the politicization of religion in this period by leaders of government is both aggressive and unfortunate.

Looking ahead, it is foreseeable that some religious groups will mobilize against the vaccine for COVID-19 when it becomes available (Berkley Center May 31, 2020). A 20-year-long anti-vaccination movement in the US has often taken advantage of religious exemption clauses in state laws (McDuffie 2020) and the number of unvaccinated children enrolled in kindergarten, particularly for the very contagious disease of measles, is growing, albeit still a small percentage (Mellerson et al. 2018). Most states offer a religious exemption in addition to a medical exemption to enroll children in kindergarten without one or more vaccinations; the number claiming religious exemptions is far greater than the number claiming medical exemptions (Mellerson et al. 2018). This troubling trend is growing, despite the complete absence of doctrine in any of the world's religious traditions prohibiting vaccination (Grabenstein 2013). The World Health Organization listed "vaccine hesitancy" as one of the top ten threats to global health in 2019 (WHO 2019), well before the onset of Covid-19 and the attendant, on-going search for a vaccine.

These events could lead the secular public to form impressions of religious people in general as anti-scientific, and/or politically focused on individual rights and freedoms rather than having concern for the safety of the collective and the protection of others. This message of conflict between religion and public health (science) has unfortunately been a dominant narrative in the media during the COVID-19 pandemic to date.

Partnerships

The subject of this chapter, the relationship between religion and health, has a social reality on both the individual and the institutional level. The intersection of these social spheres at the individual level can be studied in the form of individual health outcomes, as reviewed in the first two sections of the chapter, on "Populations" and "Practices." Religious participation appears from the extant research to offer individuals the health benefits of supportive social ties and the regulation of health lifestyles that result in measurable health advantages compared with those who do not participate. The latter two parts of this chapter focus on "Politics" and "Partnerships," and they shift our gaze from the individual to the way that health care and public health institutions interface and interact with religious institutions. In the previous section on "Politics" we saw the conflict and contention that has to a certain extent existed between these two sectors, and which has been recently exacerbated by the COVID-19 pandemic. In this final section we focus on more constructive associations and partnerships where mutual interests are recognized and acted upon.

A prominent example of the intersection of religion and health care is the role of the hospital chaplain. Chaplains are clergy with special training who work in health care settings, often with the most seriously ill patients in hospitals. They are credentialed by their respective religious organizations, but their workplace and colleagues are in an entirely different institution, with a mission quite different from their own. In her history of the institution of chaplaincy, Cadge notes that this is a "profession in process" (2012), in that chaplains working in increasingly secular but simultaneously religiously diversifying health care settings, have been actively adapting their role. In a diary study of palliative care chaplains, we found that encounters and conversations with patients and their families covered a wide range of topics ranging from practical matters to ultimate concerns, and that – perhaps surprisingly – prayer, religious sacraments, and discussion of explicitly religious/spiritual issues were found in only a small minority of encounters (Idler et al. 2015).

With the advent of COVID-19 and the resulting strict isolation of victims in hospital intensive care units where many have died, chaplains have come to the fore in media accounts. Major stories in the news have featured their work, most poignantly as the only person present when a patient dies (Dias 2020); these stories have recounted the creative use of technology to allow family members to say goodbye to their loved one that they cannot be with. A report by the London School of Economics defines a large role for religious practice in assuring "a good death" from COVID-19 in UK National Health Service hospitals (Bear et al. 2020). Cadge notes that, while the number of people who are members of religious congregations is on the decline, the role of chaplains is growing, as evidenced by the growth of training programs in theological schools, and the number of people reporting contact with a chaplain (Cadge 2020).

There are partnerships of religion with public health, as well as with medicine. A special section of the *American Journal of Public Health* in March 2019 featured examples of such partnerships at the state level (the Faithful Families nutrition project in North Carolina), national level (an H1N1 flu vaccination program), and global level (faith community response to the Ebola and HIV crises) (Blevins et al. 2019; Hardison-Moody and Yao 2019; Idler et al. 2019; Kiser and Lovelace 2019).

The story of the Ebola outbreak in West Africa was raised earlier in this chapter as an example of the harm brought to the population by unsafe religious burial practices that spread the virus. But that was not the end of the story – what happened next was a dramatic reversal that was the result of a partnership between faith-based organizations and public health authorities. Representatives of Islamic and Christian groups responded to burial contagiousness by playing an important role in revising the World Health Organization's guidelines for not just "safe", but "safe and dignified" burials that would be acceptable to bereaved families who needed to honor their dead, and at the same time maintain a safe physical distance.

Revising the WHO guidelines was a first step, but getting the message to individual imams and pastors throughout the affected countries was an additional challenge. In Sierra Leone, a national faith-based organization called Focus 1000 met this challenge. Founded by Dr. Mohammad Jalloh, a pediatrician who had worked for a number of years with the World Health Organization, Focus 1000 had already established local groups of Christian and Muslim faithful in every district in Sierra Leone before the outbreak. In a two-day meeting, leaders from this Inter-religious Council searched the Quran and the Bible for teachings that would be relevant to a time of epidemic. These groups – the Islamic Action Group (ISLAG) and the Christian Action Group (CHRISTAG) – disseminated the guidance developed by the Inter-religious Council of Sierra Leone to local communities (Blevins et al. 2019). An exhibit at the CDC's David Sencer Museum displayed one of the Qurans and one of the Bibles that had been used by the religious leaders at the meeting, complete with post-it notes and handwriting in the margins. (One is able to see, for instance, the word "quarantine" written beside an underlined text in the book of Leviticus in the Bible). Those passages became the basis for sermons, khutbahs, and lessons that could be distributed to all faith communities, from national to regional to local mosques or churches. This interfaith meeting took place in late 2014, at the very peak of the epidemic, concurrent with the release of the revised guidelines for safe and dignified burials. Three weeks after these events began the rapid decline in cases. The faith community's actions, which in the early stages had been an accelerant for the epidemic, then became an important braking mechanism.

The faith community's response to the COVID-19 pandemic in the US and abroad has been swift and multifaceted. In New York City, for example, the Hasidic Jewish Orthodox community has been a leader in plasma donations, accounting for half of all donations (Berkley Center, June 6, 2020). The Sikh community made and delivered more than 145,000 (vegetarian) meals in 10 weeks to New York City hospital workers (Krishna 2020). Twenty-four Christian churches, mostly in Black and Hispanic neighborhoods in Brooklyn and the Bronx, opened COVID-19 testing sites in partnership with the State Department of Health (Kuruvilla 2020). There are many other examples of the direct provision of health and social services by faith communities during this pandemic.

Another important role has been advisory, in working with the CDC and other public health authorities to provide resources for faith communities. For example, the Joint Statement from the National Muslim Task Force on COVID-19 "... strongly recommends that Muslims in North America make every effort to support self-quarantine and social distancing as advised by your local, regional, state, and national public health or government authorities" (National Muslim Task Force 2020). Early in the pandemic much of the focus was on helping local congregations to live-stream their services so that members could participate safely from home. Significant repositories of resources for faith communities based on CDC and WHO guidelines were established at several sites, including the Emory University Interfaith Health Program, the Georgetown University Berkley Center for Religion, Peace, and World Affairs, Practical Resources for Churches, Imana, the Islamic Medical Association of North America, and the Union for Reformed Judaism.

There are also significant international partnerships between public health authorities and faith-based organizations in low resource countries. The WHO has an Information Network for Epidemics and Faith-Based Communities that has been providing guidance through documents and webinars, focused especially on supporting health care workers, many of them employees of faith-based health services, and supporting their mission to care for vulnerable populations Both in the US and in global contexts, religious institutions have taken an official stance in partnership and cooperation with national and international public health organizations. By contrast, the cases of conflict and even defiance discussed earlier appear localized and isolated. In a webinar organized by the Berkley Center, several faith-based health workers in Africa, reflecting on lessons they had learned from the Ebola crisis and were now applying in the COVID-19 epidemic were asked, how did they see their relationship with the World Health Organization? Sister Barbara, head of a hospital in Liberia, said simply, "We are blessed [to work with them]."

In webinars and Zoom calls with faith leaders confronting the COVID-19 pandemic, one recurrent theme in their remarks is the value of past experience in partnerships with public health organizations. In Sierra Leone, it was the pre-existence of the ISLAG and CHRISTAG networks that allowed them to be brought together rapidly and to work together successfully during the Ebola crisis; these faith leaders from very different religious traditions already knew and trusted one another and the faith-based organizations that brought them together. The basis of trust that exists between faith communities and the health sector has been essential to the provision of care for people living with HIV/AIDS, as well as the initial response to Ebola (Blevins, Jalloh, Robinson 2019). Trust requires interaction over a long period, to see the outcomes of cooperation, making it difficult to create trusted organizational partnerships from nothing at the moment of a crisis. In the JLI/CCIH survey mentioned above, 63% of the participants (leaders of faith-based organizations) mentioned the need for preventing stigma and fear (maintaining trust) almost as often as the need for protective gear and preparedness for outbreaks and surge demand. Combining existing social networks with trusted relationships is a uniquely valuable asset of faith-based organizations in a crisis such as the current one where events are happening quickly and the needs are urgent. Organizations that are long time members of their communities are likely to have the largest amount of these assets.

The partnership of public health and religion is a sociological example of two social institutions with very different structures, functions, roles, support, histories, and missions, that have nevertheless found alignments of at least some of their interests and have been able to work together at that intersection. One way to increase the likelihood of finding those mutual interests could be through interdisciplinary professional education for leaders in both groups, so that identifying shared perspectives becomes easier. These partnerships will likely be increasingly called on as the COVID-19 pandemic and those that follow it spread, particularly in low resource countries.

Conclusion

The study of religion as a social determinant of health is both individual and institutional. At the individual level, several decades of research and many recent studies show a positive association, in that higher levels of religious participation are associated with better health outcomes, particularly lower mortality from all causes, and that religious practices generally benefit health. At the institutional level the association is both politically contentious at times and cooperatively partnering at others. These associations are set against a backdrop of secularization and declining religious participation in many countries around the world, suggesting fewer of both the assets and the liabilities from this source in the future. Despite this decline, the area of research on religion and health has remained of interest to serious researchers and of ever-better quality of data and methods. The current pandemic of COVID-19 has been quite revealing of the multifarious response of religious organizations to the crisis, most of which has been well-aligned and not at odds with the guidance of the public health community.

References

Ahrenfeldt, Linda Juel, Sören Möller, Karen Andersen-Ranberg, Astrid Roll Vitved, Rune Lindahl-Jacobsen, and Niels Christian Hvidt. 2017. "Religiousness and Health in Europe." *European Journal of Epidemiology* 32: 921–9.

Alang, Sirry. 2016. "Islamophobia and Public Health in the United States." *American Journal of Public Health* 106(11): 1920–5.

An-Na'im, Abdullahi. 2014. "Fasting in Islam." Pp. 77–81 in *Religion as a Social Determinant of Public Health*, edited by Ellen Idler. New York: Oxford University Press.

Bear, Laura. et al. 2020. *"A Good Death" during the Covid-19 Pandemic in the UK: A Report on Key Findings and Recommendations.* London: London School of Economics and Political Science.

Berger, Peter, Grace Davie, and Edie Fokas. 2008. *Religious America, Secular Europe? A Theme and Variations.* Burlington, VT: Ashgate.

Berkley Center for Religion, Peace, and World Affairs. April 6, 2020a. "Covid-19: Impact on Extremism?" Washington, DC: Georgetown University.

Berkley Center for Religion, Peace, and World Affairs. May 7, 2020b. "Tensions Between Understanding of Religious Freedom and Public Health Directives and Authority." Washington, DC: Georgetown University.

Berkley Center for Religion, Peace, and World Affairs. May 31, 2020c. "The COVID-19 Vaccine Challenge: Faith Fears?" Washington, DC: Georgetown University.

Berkley Center for Religion, Peace, and World Affairs. June 3, 2020d. "Rising Stigma Amid the Pandemic: India's Muslim Community." Washington, DC: Georgetown University.

Berkley Center for Religion, Peace, and World Affairs. June 6, 2020e. "Turning Tragedy into Hope: Hasidic Jews Donate Lifesaving Plasma." Washington, DC: Georgetown University.

Beyerlein, Kraig and David Nirenberg. 2020. "For Most Churchgoers, Controversy between Religious Freedom and Public Health is not Real." *USA Today*, June 2, 2020.

Blevins, John, Mohamed Jalloh, and David Robinson. 2019. "Faith and Global Health Practice in Ebola and HIV Emergencies." *American Journal of Public Health* 109(3): 379–84.

Brainard, Julii, Lee Hooper, Katherine Pond, Kelly Edmunds, and Paul Hunter. 2016. "Risk Factors for Transmission of Ebola or Marburg Virus Disease: A Systematic Review and Meta-analysis." *International Journal of Epidemiology* 46(1): 102–16.

Bruce, S. 2016. "The Sociology of Late Secularization: Social Divisions and Religiosity." *The British Journal of Sociology* 67(4): 613–31.

Burdette, Amy and Natasha Pilhauskas. 2012. "Maternal Religious Involvement and Breastfeeding Initiation and Duration." *American Journal of Public Health* 102(10): 1865–8.

Burdette, Amy, Janet Weeks, Terrence Hill, and Isaac Eberstein. 2012. "Maternal Religions Attendance and Low Birth Weight." *Social Science & Medicine* 74: 1961–7.

Cadge, Wendy. 2012. *Paging God: Religion in the Halls of Medicine.* Chicago, IL: University of Chicago Press.

Cadge, Wendy. 2020. "The Rise of the Chaplains." The Atlantic. May 17, 2020. https://www.theatlantic.com/ideas/archive/2020/05/why-americans-are-turning-chaplains-during-pandemic/611767

Case, Anne and Angus Deaton. 2015. "Rising Morbidity and Mortality in Midlife among White Non-Hispanic Americans in the 21st Century." *Proceedings of the National Academy of Sciences* 112(49): 15078–83.

Case, Anne and Angus Deaton. 2020. *Deaths of Despair: And the Future of Capitalism.* Princeton, NJ: Princeton University Press.

Centers for Disease Control and Prevention. May 23, 2020. "Coronavirus Disease 2019 (COVID-19) Interim Guidance for Communities of Faith". https://www.cdc.gov/coronavirus/2019-ncov/community/faith-based.html

Chaves, Mark. 2004. *Congregations in America*. Cambridge, MA: Harvard University Press.

Chen, Ying, Howard Koh, Ichiro Kawachi, Michael Botticelli, and VanderWeele. Tyler. 2020. "Religious Service Attendance and Deaths Related to Drugs, Alcohol, and Suicide among US Health Care Professionals." *JAMA Psychiatry Published online May* 6: 2020. 10.1001/jamapsychiatry.2020.0175.

CNN. 2020. https://www.cnn.com/2020/04/01/us/washington-choir-practice-coronavirus-deaths/index.html

Curran, Kathryn. et al. 2016. "Cluster of Ebola Virus Disease Linked to a Single Funeral – Moyamba District, Sierra Leone, 2014." *Morbidity and Mortality Weekly Report* 65(8): 202–5.

Das, Aniruddha and Stephanie Nairn. 2016. "Religious Attendance and Physiological Problems in Late Life." *Journals of Gerontology: Social Sciences* 71(2): 291–308.

de Pablo, José Navarro. 2019. "The Religious Composition of Top Income and Wealth Groups, A Global Overview." *Journal of Religion and Demography* 6: 282–98.

Dias, Elizabeth. 2020. "In the Pandemic, as Ever, 'I Will Give You Rest'". *New York Times* June 7, 2020.

Doebler, Stefanie. 2015. "Relationships between Religion and Two Forms of Homonegativity in Europe – A Multilevel Analysis of Effects of Believing, Belonging and Religious Practice." *PLoS One* 10(8): e133538. 10.1371/journal.pone.0133538.

Drain, Paul, Daniel Halperin, James Hughes, Jeffrey Klausner, and Robert Bailey. 2006. "Male Circumcision, Religion, and Infectious Diseases: An Ecologic Analysis of 118 Developing Countries." *BMC Infectious Diseases* 6(1). 10.1186/1471–2334–6–172.

Durkheim, Emile. (1897) 1979. *Suicide*. Glencoe, IL: Free Press.

Fenelon, Andrew and Sabrina Danielsen. 2017. "Leaving My Religion: Understanding the Relationship Between Religious Disaffiliation, Health and Well-Being." *Social Science Research* 57: 49–62.

Giuso, Luigi, Paola Sapienza, and Luigi Zingales. 2003. "People's Opium? Religion and Economic Attitudes." *Journal of Monetary Economics* 50: 225–82.

Grabenstein, John D. 2013. "What the World's Religions Teach, Applied to Vaccines and Immune Globulins." *Vaccine* 31: 2011–23.

Grant, George and Jose Montenegro. 2014. "Vegetarianism in Seventh-Day Adventism." Pp. 49–54 in *Religion as a Social Determinant of Public Health*, edited by Ellen Idler. New York: Oxford University Press.

Grim, Brian and Melissa Grim. 2019. "Belief, Behavior, and Belonging: How Faith is Indispensable in Preventing and Recovering from Substance Abuse." *Journal of Religion and Health* 58(5): 1713–50.

Hardison-Moody, Annie and Julia Yao. 2019. "Faithful Families, Thriving Communities: Bridging Faith and Health through a State-Level Partnership." *American Journal of Public Health* 109(3): 363–8.

Hill, Terrence, J. Saenz, and S. Rote. 2020. "Religious Participation and Mortality Risk in Mexico." *Journals of Gerontology: Social Sciences* 75(5): 1053–61.

Hout, Michael and Claude Fischer. 2014. "Explaining Why More Americans have No Religious Preference: Political Backlash and Generational Succession." 1978–2012. *Sociological Science* 1: 423–47.

Hsieh, Ning. 2017. "A Global Perspective on Religious Participation and Suicide." *Journal of Health and Social Behavior* 58(3): 322–39.

Idler, Ellen. 2020. "Religion and aging in the global context of secularization: patterns, processes, consequences." Pp. 255–68 in *Handbook of Aging and the Social Sciences*, 9th Edition, edited by Kenneth F. Ferraro and Deborah Carr. London: Elsevier.

Idler, Ellen. 2010. "Health and Religion." Pp. 133–58 in *The New Blackwell Companion to Medical Sociology*, edited by William Cockerham. Oxford: Wiley-Blackwell.

Idler, Ellen. 2011. "Religion and Adult Mortality." Pp. 345–77 in *International Handbook of Adult Mortality*, edited by Richard Rogers and Eileen Crimmins. Dordrecht: Springer.

Idler, Ellen. 2013. "Ritual and Practice." Pp. 329–48 in *APA Handbooks in Psychology: APA Handbook of Psychology, Religion, and Spirituality: Vol 1. Context, Theory, and Research*, Assoc. edited by Kenneth Pargament, Julie Exline, and James W. Jones. Washington, DC: American Psychological Association.

Idler, Ellen (ed.). 2014. *Religion as a Social Determinant of Public Health*. New York: Oxford University Press.

Idler, Ellen, Zachary Binney, George Grant, Molly Perkins, and Tammie Quest. 2015. "Practical Matters and Ultimate Concerns, 'Doing' and 'Being': A Diary Study of the Chaplain's Role in the Care of the Seriously Ill in an Urban Acute Care Hospital." *Journal for the Scientific Study of Religion* 54(4): 722–38.

Idler, Ellen, John Blevins, Mimi Kiser, and Carol Hogue. 2017. "Religion, a Social Determinant of Mortality? A 10-Year Follow-Up of the Health and Retirement Study." *PLoS One* 12(12): e0189134. (https://doi.org/10.1371/journal.pone.0189134).

Idler, Ellen, Jeff Levin, Tyler VanderWeele, and Anwar Khan. 2019. "Partnerships Between Public Health Agencies and Faith Communities." *American Journal of Public Health* 109(3): 346–7.

Idler, Ellen L. and Stanislav Kasl. 1992. "Religion, Disability, Depression and the Timing of Death." *American Journal of Sociology* 97: 1052–79.

Iles-Caven, Yasmin, Steven Gregory, Kate Northstone, and Jean Golding. 2019. "Longitudinal Data on Parental Religious Behaviour and Beliefs from the Avon Longitudinal Study of Parents and Children (ALSPAC)." *Wellcome Open Research* 4, 38. (https://doi.org/10.12688/wellcomeopenres.15127.1).

James, Allison, Lesli Eagle, Cassandra Phillips, D. Stephen Hedges, Cathie Bodenhamer, Robin Brown, J. Gary Wheeler, and Hannah Kirking. 2020. "High COVID-19 Attack Rate among Attendees at Events at a Church – Arkansas, March 2020." *Morbidity and Mortality Weekly Report* 69(May): 19, 2020.

King, Valerie, Maggie Ledwell, and Jennifer Pearce-Morris. 2013. "Religion and Ties between Adult Children and their Parents." *Journals of Gerontology: Social Sciences* 68(5): 825–36.

Kiser, Mimi and Kay Lovelace. 2019. "A National Network of Public Health and Faith-Based Organizations to Increase Influenza Prevention among Hard-to-Reach Populations." *American Journal of Public Health* 109(3): 371–7.

Krishna, Priya. 2020. "How to Feed Crowds in a Protest or Pandemic? The Sikhs Know." New York Times June 8, 2020.

Kuruvilla, Carol. 2020. "New York Churches Open COVID-19 Testing Sites in Push to Reach Minority Communities." *Huffington Post* May 15, 2020.

Lesthaeghe, Ron. 2014. "The Second Demographic Transition: A Concise Overview of its Development." *PNAS* 111(51): 18112–15.

Li, Shanshan, L. D. Kubzansky, and Tyler VanderWeele. 2018. "Religious Service Attendance, Divorce, and Remarriage among US Nurses in Mid and Late Life." *PLoS One* 13(12): e0207778.

Li, Shanshan, Olivia Okereke, Shun-Chiao Chang, Ichiro Kawachi, and VanderWeele. Tyler. 2016a. "Religious Service Attendance and Lower Depression among Women – A Prospective Cohort Study." *Annals of Behavioral Medicine* 50: 876–84.

Li, Shanshan, Meir Stampfer, David Williams, and Tyler VanderWeele. 2016b. "Association of Religious Service Attendance with Mortality among Women." *JAMA Internal Medicine* 176(6): 777–85.

McCall, Leslie. 2005. "The Complexity of Intersectionality." *Signs: Journal of Women in Culture and Society* 30(3): 1771–800.

McDuffie, David. 2020. "Sacred Immunity: Religion, Vaccines, and the Protection of Public Health in America." *Journal of Public Health: From Theory to Practice.* https://doi.org/10.1007/s10389-020-01254-7.

Marmot, Michael and Richard Wilkinson. 2005. *Social Determinants of Health*, 2nd Edition. London: Oxford University Press.

Mellerson, Jenelle, Choppell Maxwell, Cynthia Knighton, Jennifer Kriss, Ranee Seither, and Carla Black. October 12, 2018. "Vaccination Coverage for Selected Vaccines and Exemption Rates among Children in Kindergarten – United States, 2017–18 School Year." *Morbidity and Mortality Weekly Report* 67(40): 1115–22.

Moscati, Arden and Briana Mezuk. 2014. "Losing Faith and Finding Religion: Religiosity over the Life Course and Substance Use and Abuse." *Drug and Alcohol Dependence* 136(Mar): 127–34.

Mukerjee, Swati and Arun Venugopal. 2018. "Religiosity and Health through the Decades: Is There a Gender Difference?" *American Journal of Health Promotion* 32(4): 1028–41.

National Muslim Task Force. 2020. "Joint Statement from the National Muslim Task Force on COVID-19 Regarding the Global Coronavirus Pandemic." https://www.cair.com/wp-content/uploads/2020/03/National-Muslim-Task-Force-Statement-on-COVID19.pdf

Ofstedahl, Mary Beth, Chi-Tsun Chiu, Carol Jagger, Yasuhiko Saito, and Zachary Zimmer. 2019. "Religion, Life Expectancy, and Disability-Free Life Expectancy among Older Women and Men in the United States." *Journals of Gerontology: Social Sciences* 74(8): 3107–e118.

Paldam, Martin and Erich Gundlach. 2013. "The Religious Transition. A Long-Run Perspective." *Public Choice* 156: 105–23.

Pamuk, Orhan. 2020. "What Plague Novels Tell Us". *New York Times Sunday Review*, April 26, 2020: 6.

Pantell, Matthew, David Rehkopf, Douglas Jutte, S. Leonard Syme, John Balmes, and Nancy Adler. 2013. "Social Isolation: A Predictor of Mortality Comparable to Traditional Clinical Risk Factors." *American Journal of Public Health* 103(11): 2056–62.

Pew Research Center, June 13, 2018a. *The Age Gap in Religion around the World.*

Pew Research Center, October 29, 2018b. *Eastern and Western Europeans differ on importance of religion, views of minorities, and key social issues.*

Pew Research Center, January 31, 2019. *Religion's Relationship to Happiness, Civic Engagement and Health around the World.*

Phalet, K., F. Fleischmann, and J. Hillekens. 2018. "Religious Identity and Acculturation of Immigrant Minority Youth." *European Psychologist* 23(1): 32–43.

Quadri, Sayed. 2020. "COVID-19 and Religious Congregations: Implications for Spread of Novel Pathogens." *International Journal of Infectious Diseases* 96: 219–21.

Rappaport, Roy. 1999. *Ritual and Religion in the Making of Humanity.* New York: Cambridge University Press.

Ronneberg, Corina, Edward Alan Miller, Elizabeth Dugan, and Frank Porell. 2016. "The Protective Effects of Religiosity on Depression: A 2-Year Prospective Study." *The Gerontologist* 56(3): 421–31.

Samari, Goleen. 2016. "Islamophobia and Public Health in the United States." *American Journal of Public Health* 106(11): 1920–25.

Schafer, Markus and Soyoung Kwon. 2017. "Religious Heterogamy and Partnership Quality in Later Life." *Journals of Gerontology: Social Sciences* 74(7): 1266–77.

Seeman, Don. 2014. "Circumcision in Judaism: The Sign of the Covenant." Pp. 85–90 in *Religion as a Social Determinant of Public Health*, edited by Ellen Idler. New York: Oxford University Press.

Seeman, Evan. 2020. "U.S. Supreme Court Upholds California's COVID-19 Restrictions on Religious Worship." The National Law Review. http://www.natlawreview.com

Stack, Liam. April 29, 2020. "2,500 Mourners Jam a Hasidic Funeral, Creating a Flash Point for de Blasio." New York Times https://nyti.ms/3aOp05N

Statista. 2020. https://www.statista.com/statistics/1103080/south-korea-covid-19-cases-related-to-shincheonji-church

Stavrova, Olga. 2015. "Religion, Self-Rated Health, and Mortality: Whether Religiosity Delays Death Depends on the Cultural Context." *Social Psychological and Personality Science* 6(8): 911–22.

Sun, Lena, Josh Dawsey, and Michelle Boorstein. May 20, 2020. "Reopening Guidance for Churches Delayed after White House and CDC Disagree." *Washington Post*.

Tomkins, Jean Duff, Atallah Fitzgibbon, Azza Karam, Edward Mills, Keith Munnings, Sally Smith, Shreelata Rao Seshadri, Avraham Steinberg, Robert Vitillo, and Philemon Yugi. 2015. "Controversies in Faith and Health Care." *The Lancet* 386: 1776–85.

Torpey, J. 2010. "American Exceptionalism?" Pp. 141–59 in *The New Blackwell Companion to the Sociology of Religion*, edited by Bryan S. Turner. Chichester: Blackwell.

Twenge, Jean, Julie Exline, Joshua Grubbs, Ramya Sastry, and W. Keith Campbell. 2015. "Generational and Time Period Differences in American Adolescents' Religions Orientation, 1966-2014." *PLoS One* 10(5): e0121454. 10.1371/journal.pone.0121454.

VanderWeele, Tyler, Jeffrey Yu, Yvette Cozier, Lauren Wise, M. Austin Argentieri, Lynn Rosenberg, Julie Palmer, and Alexandra Shields. 2017. "Attendance at Religious Services, Prayer, Religious Coping, and Religious/Spiritual Identity as Predictors of All-Cause Mortality in the Black Women's Health Study." *American Journal of Epidemiology* 185(7): 515–22.

Vang, Zoua, Feng Hou, and Katharine Elder. 2019. ""Perceived Religious Discrimination, Religiosity, and Life Satisfaction." *Journal of Happiness Studies* 20(6): 1913–32.

Voas, David and Mark Chaves. 2016. "Is the United States a Counterexample to the Secularization Thesis?." *American Journal of Sociology* 121(5): 1517–56.

Willett, Walter. 2003. "Lessons from Dietary Studies in Adventists and Questions for the Future." *American Journal of Clinical Nutrition* 78(3 Suppl): 539S–543S.

World Health Organization. 2019. "Ten Threats to Global Health in 2019." https://www.who.int/news-room/feature-stories/ten-threats-to-global-health-in–2019

World Health Organization Commission on the Social Determinants of Health. 2008. *Closing the gap in a generation: Health equity through action on the social determinants of health.* Geneva: WHO.

Wu, Andrew, Jing-Yu Wang, and Cun-Xian Jia. 2015. "Religion and Completed Suicide: A Meta-Analysis." *PLoS One* 10(6): e0131715. 10.1371/journal.pone.0131715.

19

Migration and Health

Elyas Bakhtiari

Our health is shaped by the social contexts in which we live. This is one of the core findings from decades of medical sociology and population health research, and it raises a range of questions about how housing, job opportunities, environmental exposures, food access, social relationships, cultural norms, and other aspects of our local environments influence our health and well-being. But what happens when people leave one social context for another? The phenomenon of migration has proven both promising and perplexing to researchers interested in understanding the social causes of health and illness.

In the abstract, migration provides a unique quasi-experimental opportunity for empirically linking social conditions and health, as individuals move from one set of social exposures to another. But the reality of migration is complicated. Who migrates, and how they migrate, is shaped by a variety of factors that can select migrants to have very different characteristics than their non-migrant counterparts, making population health analyses complex. Where migrants end up, and how they fare once they arrive, is also tied to a myriad of factors, including national-level immigration policies and other determinants in the context of reception. In a field of research accustomed to comparing outcomes across definable groups or populations, understanding migrant health requires analyzing a unique and dynamic process. The determinants of migrant health vary before, during, and after migration, and are shaped by a wide variety of social factors in both the contexts in which migrants are leaving and arriving.

Disentangling the web of causal pathways linking migration and health outcomes is becoming more important to medicine and public health as movement across borders becomes more common. The number of international migrants has increased in recent decades, and the relative size of the migrant populations in many destination countries of Europe and North America is as high as at any point in history (United Nations 2020). This is not only of concern to researchers and practitioners

The Wiley Blackwell Companion to Medical Sociology, First Edition. Edited by William C. Cockerham.

tasked with understanding and treating the health of immigrant populations, but the dynamics of migrant health are increasingly relevant to researchers focused on other dimensions of population health inequality, particularly racial and ethnic disparities in outcomes. As an influx of migrants changes the demographics of longstanding groups, comparisons become less straightforward and must account for the intersecting influences of migration status, race, ethnicity, socioeconomic position, and gender. Consider, for example, the effect of migration on racial disparities in the US context, which is increasingly shaped by the influx of African and Caribbean black immigrants, whose high levels of education and good overall health can change the health profile of the black population.

As migration has increased, it has also become more central to political and social dynamics in both sending and receiving countries. The rise of right-wing populism in many migrant destination countries in Europe and the US has been tied to discourse about immigration, and in some cases it has been followed by policies aimed at restricting migration or controlling immigrants (Yılmaz 2012). This has created a growing set of risk factors that can affect the social ties, stress experiences, care utilization, and broader social determinants of existing migrant populations, and it is reconfiguring societies in ways that affects the medical care and health risks of non-migrant populations as well. The determinants of population health for both migrants and their descendants extend beyond health policy to the various immigration policies and political institutions that shape their entry, exit, and experiences in the destination context.

In this shifting social environment, the focus of immigrant health research is also changing. This chapter begins with an overview of the subfield's initial quest to explain the selection of healthy migrants and the post-migration deterioration in health status often seen with greater duration of residence. It then turns to recent research that has documented the heterogeneity in migrant health patterns, moving from questions solely about proximate risk factors–such as health behaviors and individualistic selection processes–toward more upstream determinants of migrant health trajectories. As the field moves further upstream, sociologists are particularly well-suited to address such questions about the political and social structures that shape migrant health throughout the migration and integration process.

Selection and Duration Effects

Early research on migration and health was dominated by efforts to explain what is often referred to as the "immigrant health paradox" or the "healthy immigrant effect." The apparent paradox consists of two relatively persistent empirical findings. First, new immigrant populations tend to be healthier than their non-migrant counterparts, and often relatively healthy compared to the native-born population in the destination context. This is considered paradoxical in part because immigrant populations, particularly in the US, tend to have characteristics that typically are associated with poor health and early mortality, such as lower socioeconomic status and experiences of discrimination and marginalization (Dubowitz et al. 2010; Ruiz et al. 2013). Researchers have replicated this finding using a range of health measures, including self-reported health, adult and infant mortality, birth weight, and specific disease categories (Jasso et al. 2004; Landale et al. 2000; Palloni and Arias 2004; Singh and Miller 2004; Teitler, Martinson, and Reichman 2017).

The second empirical finding in the immigrant health paradox literature is a tendency for health outcomes to become worse with duration of residence (Cho et al. 2004; Hamilton and Hummer 2011; Rumbaut 1997). Numerous studies have found that the children of immigrants have worse health and mortality outcomes than their parents, and even among the first-generation of immigrants, indicators of health often become worse with greater duration of residence in the destination context, sometimes within as few as ten years. Research on this phenomenon has origins in studies of Latin American immigration to the US, but the general pattern of healthy new immigrants and changes in health status post-migration has been found across multiple immigrant groups and a variety of destination countries (Huijts and Kraaykamp 2012; Li and Hummer 2014; Urquia et al. 2010).

Selection of Healthy Migrants

Research on the "immigrant health paradox" has been primarily motivated by two questions. Why are new immigrants so healthy? And what happens after migration that can change the health profiles of immigrant populations with duration of residence in a new context? Researchers have often answered the first question by attributing initial migrant health patterns to a combination of selection processes that shape the health and demographic profiles of migrant populations. This can occur before and during the migration process via the selection of migrants who are already healthy or whose demographic and social characteristics are associated with better health. Because movement across long distances can be taxing and challenging, individuals who are disabled, dealing with chronic health problems, or critically ill are less able to migrate (Jasso et al. 2004; Kennedy et al. 2006). The resulting demographic distribution of the migrant population therefore omits the less healthy tail of the origin country population. Similarly, migration can be financially demanding or driven by employment opportunities, and migrants in some cases may be disproportionately younger or of a higher socioeconomic status than non-migrants, which is also conducive to better health profiles (Riosmena et al. 2017). For a variety of reasons, the population distribution of migrants tends to look very different from the population distributions of their home country as well as their destination country.

Evidence for health selection occurring before migration is widespread. At the national level, the general pattern of better health for new immigrants has been found across major destination countries other than the US, including the UK, Canada, Australia, and Europe (Boulogne et al. 2012; Guendelman et al. 1999; Kennedy et al. 2006; Malmusi et al. 2010). There is also evidence of health selection among internal migrants (i.e. migrants who move within a country rather than between countries) in a variety of contexts (Chen 2011; Lu 2008; León-Pérez 2019). The selection of healthy internal migrants suggests at least a portion of the healthy immigrant effect is related to demographic selection tied to the barriers and burdens of movement, rather than social or cultural differences that may confound comparisons of international migrants.

Selection processes may continue after the initial migration. Researchers in the US have found evidence of the self-selection of return migrants. Migration is not always a one-way journey, and in some cases migrants return to their origin countries later in life, particularly if their initial motivation for migrating was employment. This can create another selection point in which individuals who are older and at greater risk for poor health are more likely to migrate home, possibly skewing mortality statistics because their eventual deaths are recorded in their origin context (Abraído-Lanza et al. 1999; Palloni and Arias 2004). This is sometimes referred to as the "salmon" bias (Bostean 2012; Turra and Elo 2008), alluding to the desire many migrants have to return to their origin countries late in life, much like salmon return to the rivers in which they were born to spawn at the end of their lifecycle. Because this leads to an "undercount" of migrant population mortality in the destination country, some researchers have argued the healthy immigrant effect in mortality statistics may be a data artifact.

These selection processes may coincide with selection on behavioral or cultural traits, sometimes referred to as "protective cultural buffering," that may be conducive to healthier behaviors (Dubowitz et al. 2010; Palloni and Arias 2004; Riosmena et al. 2017). There is evidence that migrants to the US, particular Hispanic migrants, are less likely to smoke and drink than their native-born counterparts, have healthier diets, and exhibit other behaviors that may explain a portion of the healthy immigrant effect (Blue and Fenelon 2011; Fenelon 2013; Lariscy et al. 2015). This is sometimes interpreted as tied to cultural differences between countries, but it might also be driven by selection in which migrants' health behaviors differ from non-migrants in their origin contexts.

Health Deterioration with Duration

The second question, about why migrant health often declines with post-migration duration of residence, has proven more complicated to answer. One of the most popular theoretical explanations has focused on behavioral changes that increase rates of smoking, drinking, poor dietary habits, and other risk factors (Abraído-Lanza et al. 2005). Often referred to as the "acculturation hypothesis," this line of research argues that acculturation into US society erodes a "cultural buffer" and leads to unhealthy behaviors that resemble the health behavior patterns of the native-born population. Despite some evidence for all types of selection discussed above, differential patterns of health behaviors were arguably a central focus in early research focused on the post-migration health declines, particularly for Latino immigrants to the US.

There is evidence that changes in health behaviors play a role in post-migration duration effects. Increased rates of tobacco use in particular may explain a substantial portion of health and mortality differences across generations among Mexican and other Hispanic populations (Blue and Fenelon 2011; Fenelon 2013; Lariscy et al. 2015). Although this was developed in the context of Hispanic migration to the US, the acculturation explanation has been used for a variety of immigrant groups and in other destination contexts, often as a stand in for general changes in health outcomes associated with duration of residence (Huijts and Kraaykamp 2012).

Although there is evidence for changes in culturally-influenced health behaviors, this particular theoretical explanation has faced growing scrutiny and critique. Cultural change is endogenous to a broader social context in which migrants experience new social status, resource access, legal standing, and other social conditions. Research that relies on duration of residence as a proxy for acculturation may overlook a range of confounding changes that occur after migration. Acculturation itself is often heavily influenced by a range of social and demographic factors, such as socioeconomic status, network ties, and other social experiences. To revisit changes in smoking behavior as an explanation for duration effects, there is variation in smoking patterns within migrant populations that suggest multiple moderators between acculturation and smoking outcomes. Social support from friends, for instance, is associated with lower rates of smoking among Latino immigrant men, but not Latina immigrant women (Alcántara et al. 2015).

Another issue in acculturation models is the linear assumption built into the modeling. A large body of sociological work on immigrant integration argues that contemporary migrants take divergent or "segmented" paths of assimilation and acculturation (Rumbaut 1994; Portes and Rumbaut 2006). Although the linear model of increasing social and cultural integration may fit for some migrants, others experience either "downward assimilation" into a permanent urban underclass or pursue economic mobility while maintaining national and ethnic community ties (Portes et al. 2005; Stepick and Stepick 2010). The pathways depend in part on social context, experiences of racism, and other structural constraints. Health trajectories also appear to be segmented. For instance, Latino immigrants who perceive themselves as experiencing downward social mobility after migration are more likely to exhibit poor health outcomes (Alcántara, Chen, and Alegría 2014). Growing evidence suggests acculturation often affects health in conjunction with material hardship and processes of cumulative disadvantage, pointing toward either segmented trajectories or multicausal mechanisms that extend beyond cultural change (Allen et al. 2014; Riosmena et al. 2015).

Increasingly, scholars have argued that research on migrant health over-relies on acculturation – and by implication, cultural explanations – and have called for shifting focus toward factors tied to stuctural conditions to understand post-migration health trajectories (Abraído-Lanza et al. 2006; Acevedo-Garcia et al. 2012; Finch et al. 2004; Holmes 2006). This has directed explanations toward other exposures and changes also associated with duration of residence, such as stress associated with discrimination and integration (Finch et al. 2001), increased knowledge about health problems and access to medical care (Gorman et al. 2010), and other social determinants that align with general research on the social causes of health and health inequalities.

Heterogeneity in Migrant Health Research

Although evidence for health selection and duration effects among migrants is widespread, particularly in the US context, it is not entirely consistent or generalizable. Recent research questions have shifted from understanding general selection and duration processes to analyzing variation in patterns of migrant population health.

Variation Across Migrant Populations

One of the most significant sources of variation in patterns of migrant health is origin country context. It is true that the healthy immigrant effect has been documented among a variety of immigrant populations, but the degree of health selection is not always the same, and for some populations there is little or no evidence of health selection at all. For instance, studies suggest that the healthy immigrant effect may not be present for Arab immigrants to the US, and in some cases Arab immigrants report poorer self-rated health than their US-born counterparts (Abdulrahim and Baker 2009; Read et al. 2005).

Even within immigrant pan-ethnic populations for which the healthy immigrant effect is found, there is considerable within-category heterogeneity and sensitivity to group definitions. Although the general population of Asian and Pacific Islander immigrants are more likely to report good health than US-born Asian and Pacific Islander adults, analyses of subpopulations reveal variation between Japanese, Chinese, Filipino, Korean, Asian Indian, Pacific Islander, and Vietnamese migrants (Frisbie et al. 2001). Similarly, despite widespread evidence of the healthy immigrant effect among Hispanic immigrants, there is no evidence of health selection for Puerto Ricans and Cubans, and the effect size differs between sending country subpopulations (Cho et al. 2004).

While aspects of the selection process are sometimes treated as generalizable – for instance, Jasso et al. (2004) attempt to incorporate health into a cost-benefit equation predicting migration likelihood – there is increasing evidence of heterogeneity in selection processes based in part on characteristics of the immigrant populations and their origin countries. An analysis of the New Immigrant Survey 2003 cohort found significant variation in likelihood of selection by region of origin, related in part to the socioeconomic profiles of immigrant streams (Akresh and Frank 2008). Health selection rates may also vary by gender (Singh Setia et al. 2011). An examination of Mexican immigrants found women were less likely to experience positive health selection but also had smaller health declines over time than men (Gorman et al. 2010). The role of health selection in the migration process also can depend on the reasons for migration, age at the time of migration, and dimensions of health (Lu 2008). Macro-social characteristics of the origin countries also matter. The degree of economic development and the level of economic inequality in the origin country is not only associated with initial health selection, but also with post-migration trajectories (Hamilton and Kawachi 2013; Van Hook and Stamper Balistreri 2007).

Variation Across and Within Cohorts

Variation among migrant populations is not only shaped by where they are coming from, but also by the migration processes that drive their movement across borders. Scholars of immigration often distinguish between types of migration based on the push and pull forces that initiate movement. Many of the assumptions about health selection derive from research about voluntary labor migration, in which individual decisions about employment opportunities play a role in the selection of migrants. The experiences of involuntary migrants and refugees, who are often driven from their homes by conflict or disaster, are very different. Selection processes work differently when entire families have little choice but to undertake arduous and sometimes dangerous journeys. Involuntary migrants typically have worse health than economic migrants (DesMeules et al. 2005). Refugees arrive in destination contexts with serious mental and physical health problems shaped by both the conditions of their home country and risks embedded in their migration trajectories (Stathopoulou et al. 2019). This transition sometimes involves periods in refugee camps, where the spread of infectious disease and the lack of traditional medical care can create unique health risks (Eiset and Wejse 2017).

Even within broad categories of migrant types, health selection can be shaped by visa requirements, transnational social networks, and other factors that may influence who migrates and who stays behind. In the US, health selection tends to be less evident among family-based visa entrants but more evident among employment-based visa entrants, likely because family reunification programs expand the demographic diversity of migrants to include older or less-healthy family members (Akresh and Frank 2008; Ro et al. 2016). Similarly, a study in the UK found that immigrants who migrated for employment, family, and study reasons had better health outcomes than the native-born population, but people who migrated to seek asylum had worse health outcomes (Giuntella et al. 2018).

Migration flows between countries change over time, leading to differences in the characteristics of various arrival cohorts that shape their health profiles. A portion of the apparent downward trend in health status associated with duration of residence among Hispanic migrants may actually be related to differences among arrival cohorts, as the most recent cohorts from Latin America report better health than previous cohorts (Hamilton et al. 2015). Relative health and mortality advantages also differ across the life course. Although foreign-born Mexicans over 65 have a mortality advantage relative to US-born whites, the same is not true for younger Mexican migrants (Fenelon et al. 2017). Disentangling age, period, and cohort effects makes it challenging to pinpoint the unique health consequences associated with duration of residence.

Within a cohort, the age of migration can play a big role in post-migration trajectories. Immigration scholars often distinguish migrants who arrive to a country at a relatively young age as the 1.5 generation–indicating that their social experiences fit in between the first-generation of foreign born immigrants and their second-generation descendants. Immigrants who arrive at a young age are often oriented more toward the destination context than older arrivals and quicker to "assimilate" in terms of language acquisition, identity formation, and other indicators (Rumbaut 2004). This appears to apply to the deleterious effects of duration of residence, as well.Post-migration declines in health are more evident for migrants who arrived at an early age when measured by birth outcomes (Teitler, Martinson, and Reichman 2015), obesity (Roshania et al. 2008), and health behaviors such as smoking (Wilkinson et al. 2005).

Variation Across Destination Contexts

There also appears to be a great deal of variation in migrant health patterns across destination contexts. Attempts to compare migrant health patterns across destination contexts in Europe have found mixed results, with older migrants in France, Germany, the Netherlands, Sweden, and Switzerland actually reporting worse self-perceived health (Solé-Auró and Crimmins 2008). A review of international literature found a general tendency for migrants to exhibit disadvantaged risk profiles (making them prone to hypertension, chronic conditions, and obesity), however, overall migrant disease patterns vary widely based on country of origin, country of destination, characteristics of the migrant, and the health outcome being measured (McKay et al. 2003).

The conclusions of cross-national comparison can vary depending on whether duration of residence is accounted for or not, as well as the health indicator being studied. Although migrants often fare better on measures of physical health, first-generation migrants may have worse mental health than the second generation and the native-born population across contexts (Levecque and Rossem 2015). In Europe, between-group comparisons of immigrants and non-immigrants on self-rated health shows wide variation in patterns, including worse immigrant health in some contexts. However, isolating the comparison to new immigrants shows patterns of relatively good health after controlling for age and socioeconomic indicators.

Patterns of migrant health also vary across local destination contexts within a country. As Hispanic migrants have shifted from settling primarily in "traditional gateway" cities to new destinations throughout the US, researchers have found variation in the Hispanic mortality advantage across contexts, with evidence of a larger health advantage in new destination contexts (Fenelon 2017; Brazil 2017). Structural and social characteristics of the destination context may manifest in health outcome patterns. Migrants living in ethnic enclaves have better health outcomes than their counterparts living in neighborhoods with few migrants or high levels of ethnic/racial segregation (Cagney et al. 2007; Eschbach et al. 2004; Osypuk et al. 2010). Living in a neighborhood with a higher proportion of immigrants is also associated with better diets for Hispanic and Chinese migrants, although it is unclear whether this extends to other health behaviors or is consistent across immigrant groups (Osypuk et al. 2009).

Historical context also matters. Although most migration and health research is based on studies in the US after a shift in migration policy in 1965, migration was equally relevant to social life in the early twenieth century. Studying historical patterns is challenging due to limited data sources, yet there is some evidence that migrant health trajectories were very different for arrivals to the US from Europe in the early 1900s. Contrary to today's trends, new migrants in this era tended to have worse rates of childhood mortality than the US-born white population, but rates improved with duration of residence (Bakhtiari 2018). Differences in disease profiles may play a role, with infectious disease representing a more immediate risk in the context of reception in the early 1900s. But it also highlights potential differences in integration opportunities and relative racial status of European immigrants in the early 20th century versus migrants from Asia, Africa, and Central/South America today.

Moving Migrant Health Research Upstream

As researchers have uncovered heterogeneity in patterns of migrant health–in both selection and duration effects–questions have shifted from attempting to understand a single epidemiological paradox to instead explaining the variation among migrant health trajectories. This represents a much-needed movement "upstream" in the migrant health literature, which has arguably been disproportionately focused on proximate risk factors, health behaviors in particular. As Link and Phelan (1995; 1996) argue, certain social conditions can act as a "fundamental" cause of health and health inequalities, in part because they persist even as more proximate "downstream" risk factors, linking mechanisms, and even diseases change across time and place. Immigrant health research has been remarkably disconnected from this influential theory – a "Web of Science" search of the term "immigrant health" returns 11,186 articles published between 1989 and 2017, only three of which directly reference "fundamental cause" theory – yet scholars are increasingly asking similar questions about the "risk of risks" or "causes of causes" that shape health for migrant populations.

This has involved greater attention to the structural factors that shape post-migration life, such as intersectional inequality, institutionalized racism, and experiences of discrimination (Acevedo-Garcia et al. 2012; Finch et al. 2004; Holmes 2006; Yoo et al. 2009). Moreover, sociological research on immigration and race have long focused on aspects of the context of reception – the social, political, and economic environment into which individuals and groups migrate – that play a major role in organizing the life chances of new arrivals (Portes and Böröcz 1989). As outlined below, researchers have begun to pinpoint characteristics of the destination context that shape immigrant health trajectories, and one of the remaining challenges is integrating this research with broader sociological insights about the social lives of immigrant populations.

Immigration Policy

It is impossible to fully understand the selection of migrants without considering the immigration policies that create barriers or pathways to movement between various contexts. Many countries have historically built health selection directly into their immigration policies via health screenings designed to deny entry to migrants with disability or disease (Chiswick et al. 2008). One of the first steps in the transition from ship at the iconic Ellis Island port of entry to the US in the early twentieth century was a medical examination. Although health screening policies are often framed in the interest of public health and preventing the spread of disease, they have at times been deployed in ways to stigmatize and exclude undesired groups of immigrants. For instance, medical inspections of immigrants and medicalized labeling of immigrant groups varied across ports of entry to the US in the early 1900s, often in conjunction with nativist sentiment and racialized depictions of various immigrant populations, particularly Central and Eastern European Jewish immigrants (Markel and Stern 1999). Similarly, health inspections, quarantines, and forced treatment played a significant role in shaping early policy and social exclusion at the US-Mexico border (Mckiernan-Gonzalez 2012).

Medical screenings are still present in immigration policy today. The Centers for Disease Control mandates medical examinations for all refugees entering the US, and migrants applying for temporary entry may be required to undergo medical examination at the discretion of immigration officials. However, direct medical screening plays only a small part in the structural selection of migrants. Any policies that alter the possibility of movement across borders have the potential to shape the demographic selection of resultant immigrant populations. Evidence of this is seen in variation across immigrant visa types, which suggests lower barriers to entry can reduce health selection effects. Similarly, broader attempts at restricting immigration can increase health selection, as policy barriers create another filter that favors younger, higher-SES, and healthier migrants.

However, restrictive immigration policies can theoretically drive paradoxical effects. While restrictive immigration policies may select healthier initial populations, they can exacerbate risk factors that can lead to more significant post-migration declines and worse overall immigrant population health. Cross-national comparison of different national approaches to immigration provide some evidence of the negative health effects associated with restrictive immigration policy. Immigrants in European countries classified as "exclusionist" have worse self-rated health than immigrants in countries with "assimilationist" or "multi-cultural" approaches (Malmusi 2015). Similar associations between restrictive or exclusionary immigration policy and poor health have been found in research on mortality differences (Ikram et al. 2015) and birth outcomes, such as low birth weight and preterm birth (Villalonga-Olives, Kawachi, and von Steinbüchel 2016).

In the US, a militarized immigration policy and state-level variation in documentation requirements have created unique natural experiments for measuring the mechanisms through which immigration policy, particularly enforcement and deportation, affect health. Detention and deportation efforts have increased substantially, creating a climate of fear and stress for many immigrant populations, both documented and undocumented (Hacker et al. 2011). Individual immigration workplace raids are often militarized events that create high levels of stress for social networks that extend beyond targeted undocumented immigrants. For instance, in the months after one of the largest federal raids on undocumented migrants in Postville, Iowa, increased rates of low birth weight births were observed not just for foreign-born Latina migrants who were among the primary targets of the raid, but also for US-born Latina mothers who were part of the broader community in the area (Novak et al. 2017). Beyond individual raids, state-level variation in restrictive immigration laws can also result in stress-related increases in adverse birth outcomes (Torche and Sirois 2019) and other health outcomes sensitive to the stress response. Fear of deportation has been associated with worse self-rated health, cardiovascular health, mental health outcomes, and other measures of health and well-being among undocumented migrants and their children (Perreira and Pedroza 2019; Torres et al. 2018; Venkataramani et al. 2017). Effects are particularly pronounced among children who were left behind after the deportation of a parent (Allen et al. 2015).

Another pathway through which immigration policy, particularly enforcement and restriction, can affect post-migration health is via changes in health and illness behaviors. The passage of restrictive local policies can increase distrust of health services, resulting in delayed and worse care for immigrants (Hacker et al. 2011; Pedraza et al. 2017; Rhodes et al. 2015). Mistrust often extends beyond direct interactions with providers to broader institutions in which they are embedded. When the state is enacting targeted restrictions against immigrant populations, they may become wary of other sources of state support, such as health and social benefits. For instances, increases in deportation rates have reduced immigrant enrollment in Medicaid and Special Supplemental Nutrition Program for Women, Infants, and Children (Vargas 2015; Vargas and Pirog 2016). Again, effects often extend beyond undocumented immigrants to their broader foreign-born and US-born coethnic communities. Much of the research on the health consequences of deportation and restrictive immigrant policy has focused on Latino immigrants, and effects may differ for Asian and other immigrant populations (Young et al. 2019).

Immigrant Integration Policy

It is important to distinguish between immigration policy, which is concerned with controlling the flows of movement into a country, and other policies and programs that focus on the incorporation of immigrants once they arrive. Institutionalized efforts to facilitate the incorporation of immigrant groups can be beneficial to the health of immigrants, as well as their descendants. For instance, European countries that adopt policies to protect immigrant groups from discrimination – measured using the Migrant Integration Policy Index (MIPEX) assessment of immigration policy components – tend to have lower relative health inequalities than countries with fewer protections (Bakhtiari et al. 2018). This pattern extends across both self-rated health and activity limitations, and it includes both first-generation and second-generation immigrant populations. As seen in scholarship on restrictive immigration policy, the effects of incorporation approaches are often not just seen in immigrant population health, but also in the health of the co-ethnic descendants of immigrants. Similar health benefits tied to integration policy can be seen with birth outcomes, with higher naturalization rates thought to reduce risk associated with stress, discrimination, and lack of social capital (Bollini et al. 2009).

In the US, the battle over the Deferred Action for Childhood Arrivals (DACA) has provided a natural experiment for measuring the health consequences of various approaches to integration across generations. The DACA program provided temporary work permits and deportation amnesty for undocumented migrants who met certain conditions, and evidence from the post-implementation period suggests this executive action improved the mental health of DACA-eligible immigrants as well as the children of DACA-eligible mothers (Hainmueller et al. 2017; Venkataramani et al. 2017).

Access to the welfare state–both health care services and other forms of public support–is another area of integration policy that varies across countries. Ability to access medical care is a major determinant of migrant health trajectories, and there is substantial variation across countries in the degree of access granted to migrant populations (Olafsdottir and Bakhtiari 2015). Undocumented migrants, in particular, are frequently constructed as undeserving of inclusion in the political and moral community that has access to healthcare and other social services (Willen

2012b). Across the European Union, the majority of countries with universal health care for citizens either deny care to undocumented migrants altogether or provide access only to emergency care, with only a handful offering access to care beyond emergency treatment (Cuadra 2012)

Exclusionary discourse often extends beyond distinctions based on legal citizenship to framings of "public charge" or "moral hazard" concerns that portray migrants as potential freeloaders of health services and burdens on the state and society (Park 2011). The US has a long history of political discourse about immigrants as burdens on the state, which has not only led to the exclusion of undocumented migrants from some public programs but also manifested in strict bureaucratic barriers and fraud detection programs for publicly funded medical services. Even in countries with universal healthcare policies, undocumented migrants are often portrayed as public burdens in ways that can influence bureaucratic obstacles, provider discrimination, and other intangible barriers to healthcare access for documented and undocumented migrants (Larchanché 2012; Willen 2012a).

Racialized Discrimination

Although policy is an important upstream determinant of migrant health trajectories, other social conditions in the destination context also shape downstream health risks for migrants. Population health research has identified discrimination as a major source of stress for ethnic and racial minority populations, and it has become a significant mechanism for explaining disparities in outcomes (Krieger 2014). Many migrant populations deal with intersecting forms of discrimination. Anti-immigrant discrimination or stigma can be a major source of stress for migrant groups. In fact, dealing with anti-immigrant discrimination or "othering" may offer an alternative to the acculturation framework for understanding inter-generational health changes (Morey 2018; Viruell-Fuentes 2007).

Many immigrant groups also encounter racialized discrimination as they navigate the ethno-racial hierarchy of their new countries. Ostensible anti-immigrant sentiment may actually be a cover for broader racialized discrimination that targets and affects US-born members of the same ethnic or racial groups. Black immigrants to the US from Africa and the Caribbean encounter an environment of systemic anti-black racism that shapes dramatic post-migration declines in health for some groups, despite relatively high levels of health selection (Hamilton and Hummer 2011; Read and Emerson 2005). Variation across sending countries suggests the dynamic of health selection and post-migration decline is larger among black migrants who have not previously lived as a minority in a racial hierarchy (Read and Emerson 2005). Black immigrants from European countries already exhibit poor health profiles, perhaps reflecting existing effects of living as a racial minority (Read, Emerson, and Tarlov 2005).

These intersecting forms of discrimination are important as migrant populations are incorporated into broader research on population health disparities. Some migrant populations to the US, such as Hispanic and Arab migrants, are formally classified as white, yet their experiences of racialized discrimination expose them to similar risk factors that are of concern when studying racial disparities in health. For instance, in the period immediately after the attacks of September 11, 2001, there was a dramatic increase in racialized discrimination and violence against Arab populations, and the resulting experiences of stress were likely responsible for an increase in low birth weight births (Lauderdale 2006). There is in fact considerable heterogeneity in health outcomes within the official white category, driven in part by racialized status and associated health risks faced by Hispanic and Middle Eastern immigrant populations (Asad and Clair 2018; Read et al. 2020).

Transnational Social Ties

Migrant health research is understandably focused on upstream risk factors, but a unique set of resources may also play a role in shaping migrant health trajectories. Most notably, transnational social ties may act as a resource for helping migrants cope with stress, access health information, and prevent or respond to disease in other ways. Transnational ties can influence health behaviors, care utilization, and may play a role in physical health outcomes (Villa-Torres et al. 2017). Migrants may be particularly reliant on social ties, both transnational and local, to access both informal and formal sources of health care from their origin countries when faced with barriers to access in the destination context (Menjívar 2002; Wang and Kwak 2015). In fact, the health effects of transnational social ties may be a relatively understudied driver of the "healthy immigrant effect," in that it can provide a source of medical information and treatment and social support not measured in conventional surveys or health records.

Future Directions

This chapter began with a review of research on the longstanding epidemiological puzzle regarding why migrants tend to be healthier than expected and why health may deteriorate with duration of residence. Recent research demonstrating heterogeneity in migrant health patterns has provided more complex answers about selection and duration phenomena and has raised new questions about the determinants of migrant health outcomes before, during, and after migration. As scholars look for future directions in the field, sociologists are uniquely qualified to answer questions that hinge on complex understandings of the process of migration and the broader social and political contexts in which migration occurs.

For instance, there is already a shift underway to move beyond the linear acculturation model to explain changes to migrant health associated with duration of residence. There are many mechanisms involved other than cultural behaviors – including stress responses, social support, resource access, care access, etc. – and even when health and illness behaviors change, the structural context of reception plays a role in shaping patterns of behaviors. Drawing on a rich literature on the sociology of immigration and race/ethnicity can provide alternative frameworks for understanding how life changes for migrants after migration.

There are also gaps within the medical sociology literature that have implications for our understanding of migrant health. Because so much early scholarship revolved around explaining the paradox of healthy migrants, research has focused disproportionately on proximate risk factors and selection mechanisms, while other population health research has continued to move upstream to address questions of causality. Migrant health research has been disconnected from influential theoretical perspectives like fundamental cause theory and similar frameworks for explaining disparities in outcomes, yet questions about the "cause of causes" are increasingly relevant. A burgeoning subfield focused on the political economy of health also offers new empirical directions for migration and health research. This directs theoretical attention even further upstream to the national and global institutions that shape health, including immigration policy regimes, the welfare state, and consequences of globalized capitalism (Bakhtiari et al. 2018; Beckfield et al. 2015). The growing availability of historical and cross-national datasets opens new avenues for addressing these questions through a comparative empirical framework.

Robust data is limited, however, and moving in new directions is hampered in part by remaining methodological challenges. By now it is clear that standard between-group comparisons involving migrants insufficiently capture the dynamics of selection and duration effects that shape health trajectories. Yet many data sources, including health records, often lack data on duration of residence and other migration characteristics. This not only limits our ability to assess migrant health, but it matters for all research on health inequalities in contexts where migrants make up a growing share of the population.

Current trends suggest addressing such theoretical and methodological issues will become more important in coming decades. Rates of global migration are projected to increase due to climate change and accompanying social unrest. At the same time, migration has become a prominent driver of national politics in many destination countries, as far-right groups have gained influence and put migrants in their crosshairs. As these two trends continue to intersect, understanding the political and social determinants of migrant health will be crucial to medicine, public health, and sociology.

References

Abdulrahim, Sawsan and Wayne Baker. 2009. "Differences in Self-Rated Health by Immigrant Status and Language Preference among Arab Americans in the Detroit Metropolitan Area." *Social Science & Medicine* 68: 2097–103.

Abraído-Lanza, Ana F., Adria N. Armbrister, Karen R. Flórez, and Alejandra N. Aguirre. 2006. "Toward a Theory-Driven Model of Acculturation in Public Health Research." *American Journal of Public Health* 96(8): 1342–6.

Abraído-Lanza, Ana F., Maria T. Chao, and Karen R. Flórez. 2005. "Do Healthy Behaviors Decline with Greater Acculturation?: Implications for the Latino Mortality Paradox." *Social Science & Medicine* 61: 1243–55.

Abraído-Lanza, Ana F., B. P. Dohrenwend, D. S. Ng-Mak, and J. B. Turner. 1999. "The Latino Mortality Paradox: A Test of The" Salmon Bias" and Healthy Migrant Hypotheses." *American Journal of Public Health* 89(10): 1543–8.

Acevedo-Garcia, Dolores, Emma V. Sanchez-Vaznaugh, Edna A. Viruell-Fuentes, and Joanna Almeida. 2012. "Integrating Social Epidemiology into Immigrant Health Research: A Cross-National Framework." *Social Science & Medicine* 75: 2060–8.

Akresh, Ilana Redstone and Reanne Frank. 2008. "Health Selection Among New Immigrants." *American Journal of Public Health* 98(11): 2058–64.

Alcántara, Carmela, Chih-Nan Chen, and MargaritaAlegría. 2014. "Do Post-Migration Perceptions of Social Mobility Matter for Latino Immigrant Health?" *Social Science & Medicine* 101: 94–106.

Alcántara, Carmela, Kristine M. Molina, and Ichiro Kawachi. 2015. "Transnational, Social, and Neighborhood Ties and Smoking among Latino Immigrants: Does Gender Matter?" *American Journal of Public Health* 105(4): 741–9.

Allen, Brian, Erica M. Cisneros, and Alexandra Tellez. 2015. "The Children Left Behind: The Impact of Parental Deportation on Mental Health." *Journal of Child and Family Studies* 24(2): 386–92.

Allen, Jennifer Dacey, Caitlin Caspi, May Yang, Bryan Leyva, Anne M. Stoddard, Sara Tamers, Reginald D. Tucker-Seeley, and Glorian C. Sorensen. 2014. "Pathways between Acculturation and Health Behaviors among Residents of Low-Income Housing: The Mediating Role of Social and Contextual Factors." *Social Science & Medicine* 123: 26–36.

Asad, Asad L. and Matthew Clair. 2018. "Racialized Legal Status as a Social Determinant of Health." *Social Science & Medicine* 199: 19–28.

Bakhtiari, Elyas. 2018. "Immigrant Health Trajectories in Historical Context: Insights from European Immigrant Childhood Mortality in 1910." *SSM – Population Health* 5(August): 138–46.

Bakhtiari, Elyas, Sigrun Olafsdottir, and Jason Beckfield. 2018. "Institutions, Incorporation, and Inequality: The Case of Minority Health Inequalities in Europe." *Journal of Health and Social Behavior* 59(2): 248–67.

Beckfield, Jason, Clare Bambra, Terje A. Eikemo, Tim Huijts, Courtney McNamara, and Claus Wendt. 2015. "An Institutional Theory of Welfare State Effects on the Distribution of Population Health." *Social Theory & Health* 13(3): 227–44.

Blue, Laura and Andrew Fenelon. 2011. "Explaining Low Mortality among Us Immigrants Relative to Native-Born Americans: The Role of Smoking." *International Journal of Epidemiology* 40(3): 786–93.

Bollini, Paola, Sandro Pampallona, Philippe Wanner, and Bruce Kupelnick. 2009. "Pregnancy Outcome of Migrant Women and Integration Policy: A Systematic Review of the International Literature." *Social Science & Medicine* 68: 452–61.

Bostean, Georgiana. 2012. "Does Selective Migration Explain the Hispanic Paradox? A Comparative Analysis of Mexicans in the US And Mexico." *Journal of Immigrant and Minority Health* 15(3): 624–35.

Boulogne, Roxane, Eric Jougla, Yves Breem, Anton E. Kunst, and Grégoire Rey. 2012. "Mortality Differences between the Foreign-Born and Locally-Born Population in France (2004–2007)." *Social Science & Medicine* 74: 1213–23.

Brazil, Noli. 2017. "Spatial Variation in the Hispanic Paradox: Mortality Rates in New and Established Hispanic US Destinations." *Population, Space and Place* 23: e1968.

Cagney, Kathleen A., Christopher R. Browning, and Danielle M. Wallace. 2007. "The Latino Paradox in Neighborhood Context: The Case of Asthma and Other Respiratory Conditions." *American Journal of Public Health* 97(5): 919–25.

Chen, Juan. 2011. "Internal Migration and Health: Re-Examining the Healthy Migrant Phenomenon in China." *Social Science & Medicine* 72: 1294–301.

Chiswick, Barry R, Yew Liang Lee, and Paul W Miller. 2008. "Immigrant Selection Systems and Immigrant Health." *Contemporary Economic Policy* 26(4): 555–78.

Cho, Youngtae, W., Parker Frisbie, Robert A Hummer, and Richard G Rogers. 2004. "Nativity, Duration of Residence, and the Health of Hispanic Adults in the United States." *International Migration Review* 38(1): 184–211.

Cuadra, Carin Björngren. 2012. "Right of Access to Health Care for Undocumented Migrants in EU: A Comparative Study of National Policies." *The European Journal of Public Health* 22(2): 267–71.

DesMeules, Marie, Jenny Gold, Sarah McDermott, Zhenyuan Cao, Jennifer Payne, Bryan Lafrance, Bilkis Vissandjée, Erich Kliewer, and Yang Mao. 2005. "Disparities in Mortality Patterns among Canadian Immigrants and Refugees, 1980–1998: Results of a National Cohort Study." *Journal of Immigrant and Minority Health* 7(4): 221–32.

Dubowitz, Tamara, L., M Bates, and D. Acevedo-Garcia. 2010. ""The Latino Health Paradox: Looking at the Intersection of Sociology and Health." Pp. 106–23." in *Handbook of Medical Sociology*, 6th edition, edited by Chloe Bird, Peter Conrad, Allen Fremont, and Stefan Timmermans. Nashville, TN: Vanderbilt University Press.

Eiset, Andreas Halgreen and Christian Wejse. 2017. "Review of Infectious Diseases in Refugees and Asylum Seekers Current Status and Going Forward." *Public Health Reviews* 38: 221–32.

Eschbach, Karl, Glenn V. Ostir, Kushang V. Patel, Kyriakos S. Markides, and James S. Goodwin. 2004. "Neighborhood Context and Mortality among Older Mexican Americans: Is There a Barrio Advantage?" *American Journal of Public Health* 94(10): 1807–12.

Fenelon, Andrew. 2013. "Revisiting the Hispanic Paradox in the United States: The Role of Smoking." *Social Science & Medicine* 82: 1–9.

Fenelon, Andrew. 2017. "Rethinking the Hispanic Paradox: The Mortality Experience of Mexican Immigrants in Traditional Gateways and New Destinations." *International Migration Review* 51(3): 567–99.

Fenelon, Andrew, Juanita J. Chinn, and Robert N. Anderson. 2017. "A Comprehensive Analysis of the Mortality Experience of Hispanic Subgroups in the United States: Variation by Age, Country of Origin, and Nativity." *SSM – Population Health* 3(December): 245–54.

Finch, Brian Karl, Reanne Frank, and William A Vega. 2004. "Acculturation and Acculturation Stress: A Social-Epidemiological Approach to Mexican Migrant Farmworkers' Health." *International Migration Review* 38(1): 236–62.

Finch, Brian Karl, Robert A. Hummer, Bohdan Kol, and William A. Vega. 2001. "The Role of Discrimination and Acculturative Stress in the Physical Health of Mexican-Origin Adults." *Hispanic Journal of Behavioral Sciences* 23(4): 399–429.

Frisbie, W. Parker, Youngtae Cho, and Robert A. Hummer. 2001. "Immigration and the Health of Asian and Pacific Islander Adults in the United States." *American Journal of Epidemiology* 153(4): 372–80.

Giuntella, O., Z. L. Kone, I. Ruiz, and C. Vargas-Silva. 2018. "Reason for Immigration and Immigrants' Health." *Public Health* 158(May): 102–9.

Gorman, Bridget K., Jen'nan Ghazal Read, and Patrick M. Krueger. 2010. "Gender, Acculturation, and Health among Mexican Americans." *Journal of Health and Social Behavior* 51(4): 440–57.

Guendelman, Sylvia, Pierre Buekens, Beatrice Blondel, Monique Kaminski, Francis C. Notzon, and Godelieve Masuy-Stroobant. 1999. "Birth Outcomes of Immigrant Women in the United States, France, and Belgium." *Maternal and Child Health Journal* 3(4): 177–87.

Hacker, Karen, Jocelyn Chu, Carolyn Leung, Robert Marra, Alex Pirie, Mohamed Brahimi, Margaret English, Joshua Beckmann, Dolores Acevedo-Garcia, and Robert P. Marlin. 2011. "The Impact of Immigration and Customs Enforcement on Immigrant Health:

Perceptions of Immigrants in Everett, Massachusetts, USA." *Social Science & Medicine* 73: 586–94.

Hainmueller, Jens, Duncan Lawrence, Linna Martén, Bernard Black, Lucila Figueroa, Michael Hotard, Tomás R. Jiménez, et al. 2017. "Protecting Unauthorized Immigrant Mothers Improves Their Children's Mental Health." *Science* 357(6355): 1041–4.

Hamilton, Tod G. and Robert A. Hummer. 2011. "Immigration and the Health of U.S. Black Adults: Does Country of Origin Matter?" *Social Science & Medicine* 73: 1551–60.

Hamilton, Tod G. and Ichiro Kawachi. 2013. "Changes in Income Inequality and the Health of Immigrants." *Social Science & Medicine* 80: 57–66.

Hamilton, Tod G., Tia Palermo, and Tiffany L. Green. 2015. "Health Assimilation among Hispanic Immigrants in the United States: The Impact of Ignoring Arrival-Cohort Effects." *Journal of Health and Social Behavior* 56(4): 460–77.

Holmes, Seth M. 2006. "An Ethnographic Study of the Social Context of Migrant Health in the United States." *PLoS Med* 3(10): e448.

Huijts, Tim and Gerbert Kraaykamp. 2012. "Immigrants' Health in Europe: A Cross-Classified Multilevel Approach to Examine Origin Country, Destination Country, and Community Effects." *International Migration Review* 46(1): 101–37.

Ikram, Umar Z., Davide Malmusi, Knud Juel, Grégoire Rey, and Anton E. Kunst. 2015. "Association between Integration Policies and Immigrants' Mortality: An Explorative Study across Three European Countries." *PLoS ONE* 10(6): e0129916.

Jasso, Guillermina, Douglas S. Massey, Mark Rosenzweig, and James P. Smith. 2004. "Immigrant Health: Selectivity and Acculturation." Pp. 227–66 in *Critical Perspectives on Racial and Ethnic Differences in Health in Late Life*, edited by N. B. Anderson, R. B. Bulato, and B. Cohen. Washington D.C.: National Academy Press.

Kennedy, Steven, James Ted McDonald, and Nicholas Biddle. 2006. "*The Healthy Immigrant Effect and Immigrant Selection: Evidence from Four Countries.*" *Social and Economic Dimensions of an Aging Population Research Papers*, Vol. 164. Ontario, Canada: McMaster University.

Krieger, Nancy. 2014. "Discrimination and Health Inequities." *International Journal of Health Services* 44(4): 643–710.

Landale, Nancy S., R. S. Oropesa, and Bridget K. Gorman. 2000. "Migration and Infant Death: Assimilation or Selective Migration among Puerto Ricans?" *American Sociological Review* 65(6): 888–909.

Larchanché, Stéphanie. 2012. "Intangible Obstacles: Health Implications of Stigmatization, Structural Violence, and Fear among Undocumented Immigrants in France." *Social Science & Medicine* 74: 858–63.

Lariscy, Joseph T., Robert A. Hummer, and Mark D. Hayward. 2015. "Hispanic Older Adult Mortality in the United States: New Estimates and an Assessment of Factors Shaping the Hispanic Paradox." *Demography* 52: 1–14.

Lauderdale, Diane S. 2006. "Birth Outcomes for Arabic-Named Women in California before and after September 11." *Demography* 43: 185–201.

León-Pérez, Gabriela. 2019. "Internal Migration and the Health of Indigenous Mexicans: A Longitudinal Study." *SSM - Population Health* 8(August): 100407.

Levecque, Katia and RonanVan Rossem. 2015. "Depression in Europe: Does Migrant Integration Have Mental Health Payoffs? A Cross-National Comparison of 20 European Countries." *Ethnicity & Health* 20(1): 49–65.

Li, Jing and Robert A. Hummer. 2014. "The Relationship between Duration of U.S. Residence, Educational Attainment, and Adult Health among Asian Immigrants." *Population Research and Policy Review* 34(1): 49–76.

Link, Bruce G. and Jo C. Phelan. 1995. "Social Conditions as Fundamental Causes of Disease." *Journal of Health and Social Behavior* 1: 80–94.

Link, Bruce G. and Jo C. Phelan. 1996. "Understanding Sociodemographic Differences in Health–The Role of Fundamental Social Causes." *American Journal of Public Health* 86(4): 471–3.

Lu, Yao. 2008. "Test of the 'Healthy Migrant Hypothesis': A Longitudinal Analysis of Health Selectivity of Internal Migration in Indonesia." *Social Science & Medicine* 67: 1331–9.

Malmusi, Davide. 2015. "Immigrants' Health and Health Inequality by Type of Integration Policies in European Countries." *The European Journal of Public Health* 25(2): 293–9.

Malmusi, Davide, Carme Borrell, and Joan Benach. 2010. "Migration-Related Health Inequalities: Showing the Complex Interactions between Gender, Social Class and Place of Origin." *Social Science & Medicine* 71: 1610–19.

Markel, Howard and Alexandra Minna Stern. 1999. "Which Face? Whose Nation? Immigration, Public Health, and the Construction of Disease at America's Ports and Borders, 1891-1928." *American Behavioral Scientist* 42(9): 1314–31.

McKay, Laura, Sally Macintyre, and Anne Ellaway. 2003. *Migration and Health: A Review of the International Literature*. Glasgow: Medical Research Council Social & Public Health Sciences Unit.

Mckiernan-Gonzalez, John. 2012. *Fevered Measures: Public Health and Race at the Texas-Mexico Border, 1848–1942*. Durham, NC: Duke University Press.

Menjívar, Cecilia. 2002. "The Ties that Heal: Guatemalan Immigrant Women's Networks and Medical Treatment." *International Migration Review* 36(2): 437–66.

Morey, Brittany N. 2018. "Mechanisms by Which Anti-Immigrant Stigma Exacerbates Racial/Ethnic Health Disparities." *American Journal of Public Health* 108(4): 460–3.

Novak, Nicole L., Arline T. Geronimus, and Aresha M. Martinez-Cardoso. 2017. "Change in Birth Outcomes among Infants Born to Latina Mothers after a Major Immigration Raid." *International Journal of Epidemiology* 46(3): 839–49.

Olafsdottir, Sigrun and Elyas Bakhtiari. 2015. ""Citizenship and Healthcare Policy." Pp. 561-77." in *The Palgrave International Handbook of Healthcare Policy and Governance*, edited by Robert H. Ellen Kuhlmann, Ivy Blank, Lynn Bourgeault, and Claus Wendt. London: Palgrave.

Osypuk, Theresa L., Lisa M. Bates, and Dolores Acevedo-Garcia. 2010. "Another Mexican Birthweight Paradox? the Role of Residential Enclaves and Neighborhood Poverty in the Birthweight of Mexican-Origin Infants." *Social Science & Medicine* 70: 550–60.

Osypuk, Theresa L., Ana V. Diez Roux, Craig Hadley, and Namratha R. Kandula. 2009. "Are Immigrant Enclaves Healthy Places to Live? the Multi-Ethnic Study of Atherosclerosis." *Social Science & Medicine* 69: 110–20.

Palloni, Alberto and Elizabeth Arias. 2004. "Paradox Lost: Explaining the Hispanic Adult Mortality Advantage." *Demography* 41: 385–415.

Park, Lisa S. H. 2011. *Entitled to Nothing: The Struggle for Immigrant Health Care in the Age of Welfare Reform*. New York: NYU Press.

Pedraza, Franciso I., Vanessa Cruz Nichols, and Alana M. W. LeBrón. 2017. "Cautious Citizenship: The Deterring Effect of Immigration Issue Salience on Health Care Use and Bureaucratic Interactions among Latino US Citizens." *Journal of Health Politics, Policy and Law* 42(5): 925–60.

Perreira, Krista M. and Juan M. Pedroza. 2019. "Policies of Exclusion: Implications for the Health of Immigrants and Their Children." *Annual Review of Public Health* 40(1): 147–66.

Portes, Alejandro, P. Fernandez-Kelly, and W. Haller. 2005. "Segmented Assimilation on the Ground: The New Second Generation in Early Adulthood." *Ethnic and Racial Studies* 28(6): 1000–40.

Portes, Alejandro and JózsefBöröcz. 1989. "Contemporary Immigration: Theoretical Perspectives on Its Determinants and Modes of Incorporation." *International Migration Review* 23(3): 606–30.

Portes, Alejandro and Ruben G. Rumbaut. 2006. *Immigrant America: A Portrait*. Oakland, CA: University of California Press.

Read, Jen'nan Ghazal, Benjamin Amick, and Katharine M. Donato. 2005. "Arab Immigrants: A New Case for Ethnicity and Health?" *Social Science & Medicine* 61: 77–82.

Read, Jen'nan Ghazal and Michael O. Emerson. 2005. "Racial Context, Black Immigration and the U.S. Black/White Health Disparity." *Social Forces* 84(1): 181–99.

Read, Jen'nan Ghazal, Michael O. Emerson, and Alvin Tarlov. 2005. "Implications of Black Immigrant Health for US Racial Disparities in Health." *Journal of Immigrant Health* 7(3): 205–12.

Read, Jen'nan Ghazal, Jessica S. West, and Christina Kamis. 2020. "Immigration and Health among Non-Hispanic Whites: The Impact of Arrival Cohort and Region of Birth." *Social Science & Medicine* 246: 112754.

Rhodes, Scott D., Florence M. Lilli Mann, Eunyoung Song Simán, Jorge Alonzo, Mario Downs, Emma Lawlor, et al. 2015. "The Impact of Local Immigration Enforcement Policies on the Health of Immigrant Hispanics/Latinos in the United States." *American Journal of Public Health* 105(2): 329–37.

Riosmena, Fernando, Bethany G. Everett, Richard G. Rogers, and Jeff A. Dennis. 2015. "Negative Acculturation and Nothing More? Cumulative Disadvantage and Mortality during the Immigrant Adaptation Process among Latinos in the United States." *International Migration Review* 49(2): 443–78.

Riosmena, Fernando, Randall Kuhn, and Warren C. Jochem. 2017. "Explaining the Immigrant Health Advantage: Self-Selection and Protection in Health-Related Factors among Five Major National-Origin Immigrant Groups in the United States." *Demography* 54: 175–200.

Ro, Annie, Nancy L. Fleischer, and Bridgette Blebu. 2016. "An Examination of Health Selection among US Immigrants Using Multi-National Data." *Social Science & Medicine* 158: 114–21.

Roshania, Reshma, KM Venkat Narayan, and Reena Oza-Frank. 2008. "Age at Arrival and Risk of Obesity among US Immigrants." *Obesity* 16(12): 2669–75.

Ruiz, John M., Patrick Steffen, and Timothy B. Smith. 2013. "Hispanic Mortality Paradox: A Systematic Review and Meta-Analysis of the Longitudinal Literature." *American Journal of Public Health* 103(3): e52–e60.

Rumbaut, Rubén G. 1994. "The Crucible Within: Ethnic Identity, Self-Esteem, and Segmented Assimilation among Children of Immigrants." *International Migration Review* 28(4): 748–94.

Rumbaut, Rubén G. 1997. "Assimilation and Its Discontents: Between Rhetoric and Reality." *International Migration Review* 31(4): 923–60.

Rumbaut, Rubén G. 2004. "Ages, Life Stages, and Generational Cohorts: Decomposing the Immigrant First and Second Generations in the United States." *International Migration Review* 38(3): 1160–205.

Setia, Singh, John Lynch Maninder, Michal Abrahamowicz, Pierre Tousignant, and Amelie Quesnel-Vallee. 2011. "Self-Rated Health in Canadian Immigrants: Analysis of the Longitudinal Survey of Immigrants to Canada." *Health & Place, Geographies of Care* 17(2): 658–70.

Singh, Gopal K and Barry A Miller. 2004. "Health, Life Expectancy, and Mortality Patterns among Immigrant Populations in the United States." *Canadian Journal of Public Health* 95(3): I14–21.

Solé-Auró, Aïda and Eileen M Crimmins. 2008. "Health of Immigrants in European Countries." *International Migration Review* 42(4): 861–76.

Stathopoulou, Theoni, Lydia Avrami, Anastasia Kostaki, Jennifer Cavounidis, and Terje Andreas Eikemo. 2019. "Safety, Health and Trauma among Newly Arrived Refugees in Greece." *Journal of Refugee Studies* 32(Special_Issue_1): i22–i35.

Stepick, Alex and Carol Dutton Stepick. 2010. "The Complexities and Confusions of Segmented Assimilation." *Ethnic and Racial Studies* 33(7): 1149–67.

Teitler, Julien, Melissa Martinson, and Nancy E. Reichman. 2017. "Does Life in the United States Take a Toll on Health? Duration of Residence and Birthweight among Six Decades of Immigrants." *International Migration Review* 51(1): 37–66.

Torche, Florencia and Catherine Sirois. 2019. "Restrictive Immigration Law and Birth Outcomes of Immigrant Women." *American Journal of Epidemiology* 188(1): 24–33.

Torres, Jacqueline M., Robert B. Julianna Deardorff, Kim G. Gunier, Abbey Alkon Harley, Katherine Kogut, and Brenda Eskenazi. 2018. "Worry about Deportation and Cardiovascular Disease Risk Factors among Adult Women: The Center for the Health Assessment of Mothers and Children of Salinas Study." *Annals of Behavioral Medicine* 52(2): 186–93.

Turra, Cassio M and Irma T Elo. 2008. "The Impact of Salmon Bias on the Hispanic Mortality Advantage: New Evidence from Social Security Data." *Population Research and Policy Review* 27(5): 515–30.

United Nations. 2020. "International Migrant Stock 2019." United Nations Population Division. Retrieved February 28, 2020. https://www.un.org/en/development/desa/population/migration/data/estimates2/estimates19.asp

Urquia, M., J. Frank, R. Moineddin, and R. Glazier. 2010. "Immigrants' Duration of Residence and Adverse Birth Outcomes: A Population-Based Study." *BJOG: An International Journal of Obstetrics & Gynaecology* 117(5): 591–601.

Van Hook, Jennifer and Kelly Stamper Balistreri. 2007. "Immigrant Generation, Socioeconomic Status, and Economic Development of Countries of Origin: A Longitudinal Study of Body Mass Index among Children." *Social Science & Medicine* 65: 976–89.

Vargas, Edward D. 2015. "Immigration Enforcement and Mixed-Status Families: The Effects of Risk of Deportation on Medicaid Use." *Children and Youth Services Review* 57(October): 83–9.

Vargas, Edward D. and Maureen A. Pirog. 2016. "Mixed-Status Families and WIC Uptake: The Effects of Risk of Deportation on Program Use." *Social Science Quarterly* 97(3): 555–72.

Venkataramani, Atheendar S., Sachin J. Shah, Rourke O'Brien, Ichiro Kawachi, and Alexander C. Tsai. 2017. "Health Consequences of the US Deferred Action for Childhood Arrivals (DACA) Immigration Programme: A Quasi-Experimental Study." *The Lancet Public Health* 2(4) April. https://doi.org/10.1016/S2468-2667(17)30047-6.

Villalonga-Olives, E., I. Kawachi, and N. von Steinbüchel. 2017. "Pregnancy and Birth Outcomes among Immigrant Women in the US and Europe: A Systematic Review." *Journal of Immigrant and Minority Health* 19(6): 1467–87.

Villa-Torres, Laura, Tonatiuh González-Vázquez, Paul J. Fleming, Edgar Leonel González-González, César Infante-Xibille, Rebecca Chavez, and Clare Barrington. 2017. "Transnationalism and Health: A Systematic Literature Review on the Use of Transnationalism in the Study of the Health Practices and Behaviors of Migrants." *Social Science & Medicine* 183: 70–9.

Viruell-Fuentes, Edna A. 2007. "Beyond Acculturation: Immigration, Discrimination, and Health Research among Mexicans in the United States." *Social Science & Medicine* 65: 1524–35.

Wang, Lu and Min-Jung Kwak. 2015. "Immigration, Barriers to Healthcare and Transnational Ties: A Case Study of South Korean Immigrants in Toronto, Canada." *Social Science & Medicine* 133: 340–8.

Wilkinson, Anna V., Margaret R. Spitz, Sara S. Strom, Alexander V. Prokhorov, Carlos H. Barcenas, Yumei Cao, Katherine C. Saunders, and Melissa L. Bondy. 2005. "Effects of Nativity, Age at Migration, and Acculturation on Smoking among Adult Houston Residents of Mexican Descent." *American Journal of Public Health* 95(6): 1043–9.

Willen, Sarah S. 2012a. "How Is Health-Related 'Deservingness' Reckoned? Perspectives from Unauthorized Im/Migrants in Tel Aviv." *Social Science & Medicine* 74: 812–21.

Willen, Sarah S. 2012b. "Migration, 'Illegality,' and Health: Mapping Embodied Vulnerability and Debating Health-Related Deservingness." *Social Science & Medicine* 74: 805–11.

Yılmaz, Ferruh. 2012. "Right-Wing Hegemony and Immigration: How the Populist Far-Right Achieved Hegemony through the Immigration Debate in Europe." *Current Sociology* 60(3): 368–81.

Yoo, Hyung Chol, Gilbert C. Gee, and David Takeuchi. 2009. "Discrimination and Health among Asian American Immigrants: Disentangling Racial from Language Discrimination." *Social Science & Medicine* 68: 726–32.

Young, Maria-Elena De Trinidad, Gabriela Leon-Perez, Christine R. Wells, and Steven P. Wallace. 2019. "Inclusive State Immigrant Policies and Health Insurance among Latino, Asian/Pacific Islander, Black, and White Noncitizens in the United States." *Ethnicity & Health* 24(8): 960–72.

20

Mental Health

Teresa L. Scheid

Sociological scholarship on mental health and illness links micro-level individual experiences to macro-level structures. The exemplar is Emile Durkheim in his classic study *Suicide* where he provided empirical evidence that the most private of acts, suicide, is influenced by the level of group cohesion. Group cohesion remains a central framework for understanding mental health and illness. Sociologists continue to focus on mental health and illness in its social context, with an emphasis on the relationship between social structure and mental health. There has been continued debate over both the definition and how we can assess or measure mental health or illness. In general sociologists share a critique of biological reductionism and medicalized approaches to treatment, and agree that the meaning and experience of mental health and illness is shaped by social context. This insight leads to the sociological research which provides evidence for the ways that social statuses (social class, gender, and race) shape mental health outcomes. The stress process model posits that social context and status inequalities produce stress, which place individuals at greater risk for mental health problems. The stress process model also points to ways that social contexts and relationships can provide needed social supports. Finally, sociologists focus attention on the organization and delivery of mental health care which includes treatment, service systems, mental health law, and policy – all of which are shaped by diverse cultural contexts. These three general areas of scholarship provide the framework for my review of mental health.

Conceptualizing and Operationalizing Mental Health and Illness

Mental health and mental disorder represent two different areas of theory, research and policy implications, reflecting our common tendency to dichotomize healthy and sick, normal and abnormal, sane and insane. The World Health Organization

The Wiley Blackwell Companion to Medical Sociology, First Edition. Edited by William C. Cockerham.

defines mental health as a general state of well-being (WHO 2004). Mental health is not merely the absence of disease; it involves mastery and fulfilling social relationships. While most of us fall short of optimal well-being, those who experience mental health problems or psychological distress have been the focus of most sociological research.

In the US a medical model of mental illness or disorder is dominant, while in the UK and much of Europe a social model of disability is prevalent (I will return to the disability model at the conclusion to this section). The medical model of mental disorder views mental illness as a disease or a biological abnormality which can be diagnosed and treated. Biochemical pathways, neuropathology, genetics, and brain abnormalities are viewed as the primary sources of mental illness, and can be diagnosed with advanced brain imaging technologies. The American Psychiatric Association developed the Diagnostic and Statistical Manual (DSM). Currently in version 5, the DSM provides the classification system by which clinicians and researchers can identify (i.e. diagnose) distinct mental disorders. These disorders are assumed to be discrete (i.e. they do not overlap with one another). The classification of mental disorders is referred to as psychiatric nosology, and has always been controversial.

The DSM is used worldwide by researchers in order to provide estimates of the prevalence of mental disorder in a population. However, many sociologists have challenged the dominance of biological models of mental illness which reduce mental health problems to discrete diagnoses and minimize the role of social context. Sociologists have demonstrated that the DSM overstates the amount of mental disorder, viewing all evidence of psychiatric symptoms, regardless of their cause, as evidence of pathology. Horwitz (2002) has argued that the view that mental illnesses or disorders are brain diseases is a cultural belief and that social changes hold far more promise than biological changes for improving mental health. Rather than biology, researchers need to focus on the social causes of distress and mental disorder, i.e. those life events that are negative and uncontrollable including poverty, instability, unemployment, and neighborhood disorganization. In a series of books Horwitz and Wakefield (2007; 2012) argue that the DSM overstates the amount of mental disorder by not distinguishing normal reactions to social stressors from pathological behaviors. Of interest is that the DSM-5 eliminated a category of what had been referred to in previous iterations of the DSM as "culture-bound syndromes" which were clearly related to social context (Lefley 2017).

Revisions to the version 5 of the DSM were especially contentious, and the roots of this controversy and the ensuing political battles over DSM-5 are described by Allan Frances (2013), who led the workforce which revised version IV of the DSM. A key critique has been that with each revision of the DSM, more and more conditions are defined as "abnormal," a process Frances (2013) describes as diagnostic inflation. Diagnostic inflation is driven in part by medicalization and in part by the pharmaceutical industry, which profits from the medicalization of ordinary, or normal, conditions such as sadness or anxiety. Medicalization occurs when nonmedical problems (such as sadness) come to be defined in medical terms (such as major depressive disorder), and there is increased reliance on medical interventions for treatment. In response to various criticisms of DSM-5, the National Institute of Mental Health proposed a new classification system to be used by researchers (as opposed to clinicians, who will continue to use DSM-5 in their diagnosis of patients). The Research Domain Criteria (RDoC) is based upon the assumption that mental distress is primarily a problem residing in the brain, and research should focus on brain-imaging and neuroscience. Consequently, the RDoC represents an increased medicalization as well as further decontextualization of mental disorder and distress (Whooley 2014).

In a recent book on the DSM, Schnittker (2017: 4) argues that the disagreement over psychiatric classification is rooted in "deep ambiguity" over mental illness. This is the issue of validity; we all experience sadness (and anxiety); but is it a mental illness? The issue of reliability has to do with measurement; DSM measures of disorders demonstrate consistency on most indicators of reliability. Schnittker (2017) makes that fundamental point that categorical approaches to diagnosis assume mental illnesses have some kind of "essence" - they exist in nature, we just have to "find" them. The problem is that there is no biological marker or "psychophysical identity" for mental illness or disorder (Schnittker 2017: 218). The psychological (or psychosocial) is the Mind which includes ideas, feelings, and emotions which are all shaped by our perceptions and experiences of the world and can change over time. The Mind is qualitatively different that the Brain, and has no physical essence. We do know they interact, for example stress can produce the same effects as aging in the hippocampus portion of the brain, and over time cortisol levels change in response to a number of social factors related to stress. However, we have yet to find a clear physical or biological marker for mental illness, and "in the absence of a gold standard validity is contentious" (Schnittker 2017: 237).

Rather than a psychiatric diagnosis or psychiatric nosology, the other way to assess mental health or illness is to use a continuum, such as commonly utilized scales for psychological well-being or distress. With a continuum one is assessing levels, or degrees, of mental health or distress. The idea is that over time all of us will move back and forth between relative mental health to some degree of mental distress, generally tied to the social context which influences our levels of stress. Indices assess not only the problem, but the severity and frequency along a continuum (Mirowsky and Ross 2002). The psycho-social model of mental illness (dominant until the 1970s) was based upon a continuum definition of mental health and illness where the boundary between health and illness was fluid and subject to social and environmental influences. That is, it was widely accepted that anyone could become "sick" if subject to the right conditions, or environmental stressors. The diathesis-stress hypothesis asserts that stressful environments can trigger biological vulnerabilities. Keyes (2017) offers a sociological continuum which conceptualizes mental health as "flourishing;" in contrast poor mental health which is described as "languishing." The "Complete State Paradigm" (as Keyes refers to it) includes continuum measures of both mental health and mental disorder. This is a model which moves to a more useful approach to understanding the mental health profile of a given community or population.

Rather than discrete diseases, mental health disorders may be better understood as syndromes characterized by a diverse array of symptoms. The types of symptoms vary by social context and cultural background. Schnittker (2017) describes recent research in bootstrap taxometrics, which assess dimensionality by the observation of symptoms. The difference between major or minor depression is quantitative, not qualitative. Various types of depression are not caused by different things, and clinical judgement is critical to determining if medical intervention is necessary to alleviate the symptoms of depression and to reduce the risk of suicide. Even schizophrenia is dimensional given the wide number of symptoms and different biological markers observed world-wide. However, a key issue has to do with the relationship between symptoms and diagnosis, which is critical to both research and clinical practice and points to a growing area of research – the Sociology of Diagnosis.

Diagnosis is critical as it affects access to care. A recent study in the US found that consistent with previous research, women have higher rates of symptoms of anxiety, and also have higher rates of a clinical diagnosis of anxiety. However, Blacks have higher rates of anxiety symptoms compared to whites and Native Americans or Hispanics, but the lowest rates of an anxiety diagnosis (Vandermiden and Esala 2019). This finding is in accord with previous research that with the same symptoms, Black men are more likely to be diagnosed with schizophrenia while white men more likely to be diagnosed as bi-polar (Neighbors et al. 2003). In support of sociological arguments about the importance of social context, Vandermiden and Esala (2019) found that individuals who experience violence, unsafe neighborhoods, poverty, and unstable housing are more likely to experience anxiety – but less likely to receive a diagnosis of anxiety, even controlling for access to care.

Rather than individual pathology, sociologists focus on the social context of illness and treatment. In examining the role of social structure and culture on social distress, sociologists have empathized the importance of social reactions to behavior. Traditionally, sociologists have viewed mental disorder as deviance from institutional expectations – often referred to as social reaction theory. Social reaction, or labelling theory, asks two fundamental questions: who is labeled mentally ill, and what are the consequences of these labels (Link and Phelan 2017)? Labeling theory has been described as "radically sociological" because it views mental illness as "created and sustained by society itself" (Thoits 2010: 121). The label of "mentally ill" involves negative stereotypes and is highly stigmatized, often resulting in outright discrimination.

The question of the universality or culturally specific nature of mental illness presents a test of medical etiology which asserts that the source of mental illness is biological, neurological, biochemical or genetic. If the cause of mental illness is organic (i.e. biological) in nature, then such behaviors will be invariant across different cultures. While all cultures characterize some forms of behavior as mental illness or disorder, there is disagreement over whether specific categories of mental illness are indeed universal. Kleinman and Goode's now classic (1985) cross cultural study of depression found that symptoms of depression vary, as does the experience of sadness, failure, and loss. Cross cultural research also challenges the widely held belief that rates of schizophrenia are culturally invariant (Morgan, McKenzie and Fearon 2008). At the same time, globalization is reducing cultural variability; Waters (2010) provides a number of examples of the ways in which conceptions of mental health and illness have been "westernized."

We do know that social conditions and environments are critical in not only understanding what constitutes a mental health problem, but in the course and outcome of mental health problems. For example, The World Health Organization

(2004) has documented that individuals with a diagnosis of schizophrenia do better in less developed (not more developed) countries. While the mechanisms by which the social environment influences mental health has not been thoroughly studied (Morgan, McKenzie and Fearon 2008), the World Health Organization posits the higher levels of stress and lower social supports in industrialized societies are critical (Lefley 2017). An important distinction in understanding cross-cultural differences in mental health is the degree of social cohesiveness (Horwitz 1982). Individualist societies value autonomy and individual rights, but generate higher levels of isolation and loneliness, and individuals with mental health problems experience more symptom severity and poorer rates of relapse and recovery. Communal societies provide greater group cohesion and social supports; consequently, individuals with even severe mental disorders such as schizophrenia do better over time (Lefley 2017).

The disability model of mental health links disability to relationships and structures in society, rather than in the individual (Keith and Keith 2013; Spandler et al. 2015). Disability is not just a matter of individual health (or psychiatric symptoms), rather the roots of disability lie in society. Disabilities are made worse by society's inability to either provide or create supportive environments (Keith and Keith 2013). Under a medical model, emphasis is placed on diagnosis, treatment, and cure. Under a disability model, there is recognition that mental health problems often involve long term impairment and loss of functioning... no matter what the "cause" of the disability. A view of mental health problems as disabilities is firmly grounded in a social model of health and points to the importance of modifying social structures so as to promote the capacities and strengths of individuals, ideals that have been emphasized by the movement to recovery (which I will address more fully later). Viewing mental illness as a disability expands the focus for "treatment" to the wider society, and the social sources of disability, which can also potentially mitigate the stigma of being labelled as "mentally ill" and hence biologically "different."

In conclusion, whether mental health problems are understood as illnesses, psychiatric disorders, psychological distress, disability, or the result of processes of social reaction and labeling, social context plays a vital role in how these problems are defined, experienced, and treated. Having valuable social roles is clearly critical to both recovery and improved quality of life. I turn to a summary of the extensive sociological research on the role of social context in understanding the development and experience of mental health problems.

Social Context, Status, and Stress[1]

One of the most consistent research findings has been the inverse relationship between social class and various types of mental disorder (Eaton and Muntaner 2017). There are three major explanations for finding that those in the lower social classes have higher rates of mental distress: social causation, social selection, and social reaction. Social causation refers to the reality that those in the lower classes are subject to higher levels of stress as a consequence of poverty and economic instability. This stress or instability results in higher levels of mental distress. Social selection (or drift) occurs when individuals with mental health problems are less able to  complete education or sustain employment and consequently fall (or drift down) to a lower social class position. Social reaction explanations argue that the restricted opportunities available to those in the lower classes lead to less mastery or a sense of personal efficacy and higher levels of fatalism, resulting in higher levels of depression  (for women), psychological distress (for racial and ethnic minorities), or substance abuse (for men). While there is some evidence for social selection in that certainly some individuals with mental health problems do indeed "drift" down the socio-economic ladder, the prevailing evidence has been for social causation and social reaction. It is one's social class position that provides access to resources which then influence one's risk for mental health problems rather than the fact that mental health problems determine socio-economic status or class position.

Sociologists have contributed a great deal to our understanding of how diverse socio-cultural and demographic groups experience and respond to mental health problems. There is extensive research on the role played by social status categories including gender, race, ethnicity, and age. Marriage, divorce, work, unemployment, and neighborhood are also important factors which influence mental health. What unites much of this research is a focus on the role played by social stress and social support, which is increasingly referred to as the stress process model. The stress process model has been developed and elaborated by leading sociologists since the 1970s and a concise description is provided by Turner (2013). The model posits that social characteristics (gender, race/ethnicity, socioeconomic position, neighborhood disadvantage, and segregation/integration) directly influence exposures to stress, the social resources to deal with stress, and the personal resources to cope with stress. The social resources include social supports and network ties while the personal resources include mastery, self esteem, resilience, and mattering to others. Obviously, one's personal resources for coping are influenced by social supports and network ties as well as one's social status. Exposure to stress in turn triggers social resources and personal resources for coping with stress. Exposure to stress, coping mechanisms, and social supports then all have direct effects on mental health. What we have learned in the past 40 years of research on the stress process is that it is vital to include multiple measures of stress. In the 1970s life event scales were primarily used; researchers now include recent eventful stressors, daily hassles, chronic stress, lifetime trauma, and discrimination (Turner 2013). It is also important to include multiple outcomes, including mental health disorder, psychological distress, and substance abuse problems.

Stress is an important source of mental health distress and it is "generated and conditioned by social factors" (Turner 2013: 182). Consequently, the treatment of mental health problems cannot be directed solely at the individual; interventions must be aimed at reducing the health disparities which result in increased exposure to stress, less mastery and resiliency for disadvantaged and minority groups, or those with less power relative to the majority. Social position and relative power play important roles in access to those social resources which can both decrease vulnerability to stress as well as help anyone to cope with stress.

Social context defines not only the sources of stress, but also the social relationships within which stress is developed and mitigated. Sociologists have contributed a great deal to our understanding of social support, which we know can buffer the effects of stress and also improve mental health. Social ties and supports provide a sense of belonging as well as concrete resources (i.e. emotional and tangible supports). While addressing the structural sources of stress is clearly necessary, improving access to social resources and social supports can improve mental health outcomes. In addition to describing sources of stress and social support, considerations of social context situate stress that accompanies social status (i.e. social class, gender, race, age, sexual orientation) as well as role occupancy (i.e. spouse, worker).

Researchers are also concerned with the measurability of stress and major life events; there is recognition that the meaning of an event exhibits great social variability (Aneshensel 1992). Simple life event scales that add up the number of stressful life events one experiences fail to capture how the same event is experienced in different ways by different individuals and groups. The social environment prior to such common life transitions as job loss and divorce is far more consequential than either the transition itself or the coping strategies utilized by an individual (Wheaton and Montazer 2017). For example, a divorce may be experienced by one person as devastating, resulting in the loss of a significant other, social position, family and friends. Severe depression may thus be a likely outcome as that individual may feel grief and guilt, as well as the painful necessity of reconstructing their lives. However, if the marriage was especially stressful, or involved emotional and/or physical abuse, divorce may be a welcome release and may produce a sense of freedom, autonomy and mastery. Research on the effects of divorce examines whether the divorce was a temporary crisis, or a chronic strain due to the loss of financial and/or emotional stability. Chronic stress arises from continuous and persistent social environmental conditions and is more important in understanding mental health than acute stressors (Wheaton and Montazer 2017).

In addition to stress, sociologists have focused a great deal of attention on social support networks, that is, the role played by family and friends in helping an individual cope with stress – or in exposing an individual to additional stressors. We may receive primarily emotional support (love, empathy, understanding); structural forms of support such as money, or a place to live; or a combination. Structural forms of support are also referred to as tangible and/or instrumental support. While there is much theoretical attention given to how social support can reduce mental disturbance, Thoits (1995) has argued that researchers have not examined the intervening mechanisms by which social support influences one's ability to cope, or the selection of coping mechanisms, or how social support affects feelings of self-esteem and mastery (which are so crucial to mental health). Furthermore, Thoits (1995) notes that we do not understand how one's existing social network and perceived social support influences help seeking behaviors. Often a families' shame, or ignorance of the reality of mental illness can prohibit them from seeking out professional help. Alternatively, a family with a good bit of positive experience with professional care-providers may routinely access mental health services, hence forestalling future problems due to stressful events.

A final issue needing further research is how stress affects social support. Many events that are considered stressful (i.e. divorce or unemployment) can also have negative impacts on social support by altering the social networks that individuals are embedded in. Thoits (2011) addresses the various ways in which social support can mediate stress life events. First, she notes that we need to distinguish between everyday social supports from stress related social supports. Everyday supports are cumulative, and can help reduce the occurrence of stress events and also contribute to a sense of perceived supports, positive well-being, and self-esteem which can all help alleviate the negative effects of stress. In contrast, stress related social support is more focused and consists of problem related social supports which do help with the effects of a stressful situation. Second, Thoits (2011) argues we also need to distinguish between two groups of supporters: significant others and similar others. Significant others may not be familiar with the source of the stress or stressor, and while they can offer various forms of social supports, their role in reducing the effects of the stressor may be limited. In contrast similar others are those who have familiarity with the source of the stressor and can provide empathy, information, and advice. For example, during a divorce one's significant others (family members) may not be empathic or understanding, though they can help with the financial impact of a divorce. Fellow divorcees or co-workers may have more insight and empathy, and will constitute a more concrete social support network.

A major source of stress is unemployment; there is strong aggregate support for the positive relationship between unemployment and lower mental health. Warner (1985) has argued that the effects of extended unemployment – isolation, withdrawal, anxiety, and depression – are similar to the symptoms commonly associated with schizophrenia. At the same time, work can also be a major source of stress, especially when work decreases individual opportunities for autonomy and self control or when work is a source of anxiety. Workers in jobs with little discretion over their work (low in autonomy and control) experience higher rates of depression, as well as a loss of self-esteem. These types of job experiences are more common among the lower and working classes. Furthermore, job control and decision latitude are also important to a sense of mastery – which we have seen is important to one's mental health. In a recent article, Schneider and Harknett (2019) examine the mental health consequences of unstable work schedules among service workers. Precarious work creates work-life conflicts with negative effects on psychological distress, sleep, and happiness. With COVID-19 we have all experienced heightened work instability as well as greater work-life conflicts. However, opportunities to work at home may also reduce job related stress by giving workers greater autonomy and control over their work.

Levels of control and mastery are also important to understanding gender differences in mental illness and disorder. Women have higher levels of mood disorder, anxiety, and depression while men exhibit higher rates of personality disorder and substance abuse. Drawing on the theories of Emile Durkheim, Schwartz (1991) focuses on the social context of depression and differentiates between levels of integration and regulation. Altruism, or other oriented valuative preferences, is associated with high levels of group integration while fatalism, a belief that one has little control, is associated with high degrees of regulation whereby others in fact do control an individual's choices and actions. Girls are socialized to be both other oriented and to accept strong normative controls over their behavior (the most obvious example is rules governing sexual behavior). These dual conditions of high integration and high regulation produce both altruism and fatalism, which results in lowered self-esteem in response to stress. Girls are more dependent on others for self-worth and valuation, and thus more likely to feel helpless and powerless and to have lower self-esteem. Anger may also be turned inward, and all of these conditions are consistent with the etiology of depression (Schwartz 1991).

Boys, on the other hand, are socialized in a context with less emphasis on group membership (low integration or egoism in Durkheim's terminology) as well as lower levels of normative regulation on behavior (or anomie). Consequently, males are more likely to display anti-social behaviors in response to stress. That is, they are more likely to act out, to display aggressive or hostile behavior, or to resist normative authority and seek to actively break rules systems. Schwartz (1991) refers to her theory as the norm hypothesis, and contrasts it with the more traditional role stress hypothesis. The role stress argument is that women experience higher levels of mental distress because their traditional roles, their changing roles, and conflict between the two types of roles produce higher levels of stress for which women were inadequately prepared.

An individual's social involvement and investment in meaningful role relationships clearly plays an important role in mental health. The key to the positive role played by multiple role identities is that we have different sources of satisfaction and opportunities to develop a sense of efficacy and mastery. Likewise, multiple roles provide additional opportunities for social support. For example, married people report consistently better mental health outcomes, due primarily to their higher levels of social and emotional support. Yet the quality of the relationship as well as the division of labor (both housework and paid work) are important conditions that cannot be ignored. Chronic stressors (poverty, unemployment, marital and family disruption, discrimination and poor physical health) fall disproportionately on minority groups. In addition to the stress of racism, Blacks are also disproportionately concentrated in the lower social classes, making it difficult to untangle the separate effects of class and race on mental health. Members of minority groups face higher levels of stigma, as well as conflicting cultural messages as they are expected to conform to the values and standards of the dominant "white" culture. Racism and discrimination are significant sources of stress. However, the effects of racism are also moderated by identity, with individuals for whom race (or ethnicity) is a central identity experiencing lower levels of distress due to discrimination (Mossakowski 2003; Sellers et al. 2003). There is a need for more research on the mental health experiences of minority youth because they are vulnerable to stress and mental disorder. The reality that approximately three of five Black children grows up in poverty, and in neighborhoods considered less than desirable, obviously has serious mental health implications. At the same time, recent movements for racial justice may have created an important "buffer" in that youth in general are less likely to hold racist views and minority youth have a stronger sense of racial identity, leading to higher levels of self-esteem and lower levels of psychological distress.

Social class, gender, race and ethnicity are interrelated in a complex manner with multiple feedback loops, and the effects of multiple minority statuses (social class, gender, race, sexuality) is referred to as intersectionality. Intersectionality begins with the idea that social identities are multiple and interlocking and provides a "framework for understanding how multiple social identities intersect at the micro level of experience to reflect interlocking systems of power and privilege" (Bowleg

2012, 1267). Female and Black are two social statuses that are socially devalued, and African American women are more likely to live in poverty than white women. African American women also face demanding social networks, which may be a unique source of stress, rather than a coping resource. Keith and Brown (2017) provide a theoretical model for understanding how these intersecting social statuses affect the mental health of African American women which emphases the complex inter-relationship between race, gender, and SES. Mental well-being is influenced by not only the primary social statues of race, gender, and SES but other social statuses including age, marriage, mothering, and employment. This comprehensive model could also be used in comparative research on the mental health of women world-wide.

There is a growing literature on the mental health of immigrants (Takeuchi 2016). While migration and immigrant status clearly constitute a chronic strain, foreign-born Hispanics have been found to have better mental health than native born Hispanics, despite their lower SES and educational attainment. In a recent study, Diaz and Nino (2019) examine whether family ties help explain this paradox and find that feeling close to one's family reduced the risk of depression and anxiety, but that having higher levels of family responsibility increased mental distress. We again see evidence for the important interaction between social roles, identity, and mental health outcomes. Immigration is a global issue, as is racial inequality, and there is clearly a need for more comparative research.

In addition to social class, gender, race and ethnicity, social position is also structured by age and changing social roles. In addition to the persistent finding that mental health is linked to social class, researchers have also found that mental health and distress vary across the life course with younger and older individuals experiencing higher levels of mental distress and those in their middle years have the highest levels of mental well-being (Mirowsky and Ross 2017). Levels of control or mastery provide an answer: younger people face a great deal of uncertainty as they navigate education, jobs, and relationships. Older adults face the loss of social status due to retirement, poorer physical health, and loss of social relationships. Adults in their middle years are at their "peak" in terms of career, income, and family stability. Lin et al., (2019) found that for older adults, divorce was neither a temporary crisis or a chronic strain, instead older divorcees (and those widowed) gradually adjusted to their new life conditions.

In summary, exposure to stress in not randomly distributed (Carr 2014); stress reflects social patterns of inequality. Social class is the most important determinant of both exposure to, and responses to stress. Those in lower SES groups are subject to higher levels of chronic stress, that is, their social environments subject them to more stressful conditions and also limit the coping resources available to deal with chronic strains (such as poverty). Social class can also affect one's sense of control over the conditions in life, and therefore self-esteem and mastery. Lifelong exposure to stress (including poverty, sexism, and racism) can erode self-efficacy; furthermore, if stressors cannot be controlled than a belief in personal control (self-efficacy) may even be detrimental and may negatively impact mental health (Aneshensel 1992). Chronic strains can also lead to stress proliferation, where those facing adversity are a greater risk for facing additional adversity (Carr 2014). Covid-19 is clearly a chronic stressor, with devastating effects on health, well-being, and employment. With Covid-19, we have seen that those workers who are deemed

"essential" are both higher status (physicians) but also lower status (nursing home aides) and they all face not only greater risks of contracting the virus, but also job related stress. At the same time, many sectors of the economy have been closed with workers being furloughed and/or laid off. The uncertain prospects for the future (as of this writing in the summer of 2019) is a major stressor for all of us, and has already had a marked impact on mental health with rising rates of depression, anxiety, and suicide. In response, we look to the mental health care delivery system for assistance.

Mental Health Care and Treatment

Mental health care must be understood in terms of its wider social context: the care and treatment provided to individuals with mental health problems reflects wider social values and priorities. Specifically, widely held values and beliefs about mental health and attitudes toward the mentally ill as well as professional treatment preferences will shape the political climate, economic priorities, and the type of services available. The mental health system, i.e. the network of organizations, services, and health care professionals, will change as these normative preferences change. It is for this reason that it is so difficult to achieve consensus on what type of system of care will work, and why it is so difficult to implement change (Mechanic 2006). Currently we are experiencing three normative frameworks (or institutional demands) for treatment: medicalization, recovery, and increased institutionalized care. In addition, people with mental health problems fall into three groups (Mechanic 2006). First are those with acute mental health problems such as normal depression following a loss or some other stressful event. Second are those with acute mental health problems that are more severe, or those with chronic conditions but who can maintain normal role functions. The third group are those with serious, chronic mental diseases which involve significant functional disability. Treatment for the first and second groups consists primarily of medication and some therapy, with the second group seeking recovery. It is the third group of individuals, those with severe and persistent or severe mental health problems, who pose the major problem for mental health delivery systems as they face significant functional limitations and need a broad array of services. In the current post-deinstitutionalization era most care for those with serious mental health problems is provided in the community, rather than the hospital (Scheid 2016). However, we are witnessing competing normative demands for recovery and community integration as well as increased social controls (or restrictions) over those with severe mental disorders.

Medicalization of "Normal" Mental Health Problems

The majority of us will suffer from some form of acute mental health problem as well as psychological distress. The dominant form of medical treatment for mental distress involves medications, and this treatment is reinforced by managed care and its reliance on cost effective, clinically efficacious treatment. The growing reliance on the use of primary care physicians to diagnosis and treat mental health problems also reinforces the use of medications, as opposed to therapy with a specialty mental health provider. A major finding of the National Comorbidity Survey Replication is that while more people are being treated for mental health problems by general medical providers, the adequacy of this treatment has declined (Kessler 2010). In keeping with the medicalization of mental health care most people with mental health problems receive medication, which is the primary expenditure for mental health care in Medicaid. The "worried well" and are also likely to be *overtreated* with psychiatric medications, while those with more severe mental health problems are less likely to receive adequate treatment (Frances 2013).

Peter Conrad (2007) originated research on the medicalization of mental health problems and provides an analysis of the social forces propelling medicalization. The reliance on a medical model of mental distress, where behavior is defined as a medical problem or illness and treatment is delegated to medical professionals, is one force propelling medicalization. Recent decades have seen tremendous expansion in the use of psychiatric medications for both adults and children, with a great deal of critical analysis aimed at the pharmaceutical industry and the role it has played in marketing drugs for mental health problems to the public. Pharmaceuticals not only market drugs, they market diseases (referred as disease branding) such as anxiety disorder and use public media to encourage individuals to seek treatment for what are fairly normal responses to life stressors.

Another force promoting medicalization is "the way in which we finance human services" (Conrad 2007: 160). Reimbursement for treatment is tied to a clinical diagnosis, reinforcing the biomedical model and reliance upon DSM categories to differentiate those who require treatment and those who do not. Furthermore, treatments must be found to be clinically efficacious, a standard which can be easily met with clinical drug trails and not so easily met with therapy or counseling. The essential criticism of medicalization is that treatment is always focused on the individual, and not on the social context in which mental health problems develop and are treated. There is a rich tradition in the Sociology of Mental Health which examines the ways in which various mental health problems have been and are medicalized, as well as on the dominance of the medical model in mental health treatment. For example, Smith (2014) interviewed 20 psychiatrists and found that despite intensive training in psychoanalysis, the majority adhered to a medical model of treatment and relied upon medications.

Trends propelling medicalization exist globally; Waters (2010) describes how the Japanese had a culture of sadness, but the ability to bear melancholy (sadness) was seen as a source of strength. However, in the 1990s given an economic downturn, economic insecurity, and overwork, rates of suicide increased. Pharmaceutical companies capitalized on this and marketed depression as the "cold of the soul" which could be easily treated with anti-depressants, a clear example of disease branding and pharmaceutically driven medicalization.

Recovery and Empowerment

Recovery builds on the ideals of consumer empowerment, and is based on an advocacy model first introduced by Rose and Black (1985). While a focus on patient rights was certainly important to the original community care movement, empowerment pushed the idea of client autonomy to emphasize the individual's right to advocate for their own care and assume control over the direction of their own treatment. Some advocates of empowerment even rejected professional intervention, building upon critiques of both biomedical and psychosocial rehabilitation models which ultimately wanted clients to conform to professional definitions of mental health (Paulson 1992). The concept of empowerment has evolved from independence from the system to choice within the system (McLean 2000: 837). While recovery is certainly not essential for empowerment (one can advocate for one's services and not seek recovery), recovery has become the dominant normative demand – used by stakeholders, advocates, and consumers world-wide.

Recovery involves both a reduction in psychiatric symptoms (recovery from illness) as well as recovery within illness with client level determined quality of life (Dobransky 2014). The development of psychosocial conditions for leading a fulfilling life (hope, connection, empowerment) as well as the external conditions which allow individuals to lead a productive life are necessary for recovery (Jacobson and Greenley 2001; Jacobson 2004). As such recovery is a fairly broad and ambiguous term that can serve as an umbrella for many different kinds of services. Recovery can mean an expanded service model as once an individual's symptoms are stabilized they will have an increased need for social supports and skills building programs. However, recovery can also mean reduced reliance (and cost savings) on service systems when defined as meeting certain limited functional goals. Recovery can be used as a yardstick for improved client outcomes, with little commitment to creating the kind of therapeutic environments where recovery can be fostered (Spandler and Stickley 2011). As described more fully by Jacobson (2004) there have been a number of efforts to develop recovery based "best practices" and standards for care and these standards are often tied to funding for service provision

Recovery is fundamentally a social process, not a clinical outcome and involves improved quality of life (Keith and Keith 2013). Yanos et al. (2007) provide a nice theoretical framework for understanding recovery – emphasizing the role of social structure and individual agency rather than biological explanations. They argue that the personal agency of those with severe mental health problems, such as coping mechanisms and the ability to set and strive for goals, is constrained by current social structures, including poverty, legal restrictions, a lack of affordable housing, distressed neighborhoods, and the routinized practices of stigma and discrimination which in turn create further stress, hopelessness and anomie. Whether mental health systems can truly promote recovery depends on whether resources are invested into the kinds of supportive services so necessary to community stability. Community care in most localities is marginal at best, and many individuals with severe mental health problems are isolated with few friends or social supports (Keith and Keith 2013). The stigma of mental illness also plays an important role in contributed to the exclusion and control of those with more serious mental illnesses. An important idea developed by sociologists is that mental health treatment often involves social control rather than therapeutic care. The current "criminalization" of those with mental health problems is an obvious indication of a generalized societal preference for social control.

Social Control Imperatives

The issue of social control is important to understanding the treatment of those with more severe mental health problems. The power asymmetry between patient and provider is heightened by the association of mental illness with incomprehensibility, unintelligibility, irrationality or incompetence (Horwitz 1982). "Treatment" has been viewed as little more than a medical justification for confinement (Foucault 1988 (1965)), and medication has also been used as a form of social control in that it controls behavior deemed undesirable. Central is continued debate over the social control of those with alleged mental illnesses is the role of mandated community treatment (Bonnie and Monahan 2005; Testa and West 2010). Also referred to as outpatient commitment, or assisted outpatient treatment, mandated community treatment involves the use of leverage (or benign coercion) to elicit compliance with treatment from those with serious mental illness. In exchange for compliance with treatment demands in the community, various forms of leverage are used to avoid negative events such as hospitalization or incarceration, or to gain access to positive events such as the provision of housing or transportation. Both negative and positive forms of leverage are fairly common (Bonnie and Monahan 2005), and some coercion can be beneficial. However, leverage should be rare (Swanson et al. 2006) and used to expand, rather than constrict patient choice (Bonnie and Monahan 2005). Adherents of recovery models are also critical of involuntary commitment given their emphasis on self-directed treatment and choice (Henwood 2008). Wales and Hiday (2006) argue that we need to replace PLC (persuasion, leverage, or coercion) with tender loving care (TLC) – or improved patient centered treatment and assertive outreach.

The dearth of community supports remains a central issue in renewed calls for expanded civil commitment criteria. Sederer and Sharfstein (2014) provide a very concise summary of exactly what kinds of community based services individuals with serious mental health problems need – the issue is how to provide the diverse array of needed services and supports in an era of cost-containment and restricted funding. In the wake of even more recent violent events, calls for greater recovery efforts as well as stronger controls over those with mental health disabilities in the community poses a central policy dilemma (Miller and Hanson 2016). The belief that individuals with mental illnesses are dangerous is a prevailing stereo-type, and leads to public support for more coercive forms of treatment as well as a disinclination to fund the kinds of social supports needed for community integration and recovery.

Mental Health Policy and Stigma

The stigma attached to mental illness is a major source of inertia in policy making (Mechanic et al. 2014; McSween 2002), and is a barrier to treatment and social supports. A stigma is an attribute that is discrediting and involves stereo-types which can result in active discrimination. Countless surveys have demonstrated that many people believe those with mental illnesses are dangerous, unpredictable, can never be normal, cannot be talked with, and do not make good employees. Not only does the stigma of mental illness carry negative moral connotations, it can result in social isolation and withdrawal of the stigmatized individual and ultimately outright discrimination (Link and Phelan 2001).

Sociologists make an important distinction between public stigma and private and self stigma. Public stigma involves stereotyping, prejudice, and discrimination – self stigma is the internalization of public stigma and results in a devalued sense of self. Link (1987) has demonstrated how individuals who are labelled "mentally ill" internalize the negative attributes associated with the label and expect to be rejected, resulting in demoralization and unemployment. A potentially positive effect of the label of mentally ill is the receipt of treatment or services. Rosenfield (1997) found that treatment benefits eroded over time while the stigma of being a mental health recipient led to a lower quality of life. More recent research points to the same problems (Dobransky 2014; Marcussen and Ritter 2016), with self-stigma leading to increased social marginalization (Harkness et al. 2016). Sociologists have turned their attention to stigma resistance in order to combat the negative consequences of public stigma. Thoits (2011) identifies two resistance strategies: challenging and deflecting. Challenging involves attempts to change the views of others while deflecting involves efforts to distance oneself from the negative label (i.e. I'm not like that). Challenging strategies can be used by advocates and consumers groups and can ultimately overcome public stigma, while deflecting strategies can be used to reduce self-stigma.

Pescosolido (2013) provides a concise summary of the empirical research on how people view mental illness and the stigma of mental illness. The first basic finding is that in general the public is more open to the recognition and treatment of mental health problems. The second basic finding is that the stigma of mental illness has not changed much over time, and that the association of mental illness with dangerousness and violence has actually increased. Third, whether the focus is on the "label" of mentally ill or the behavior, social reactions involve stigma. Finally, while viewing mental illnesses as having a genetic basis has led to increased public support for treatment (especially medications), those who believe mental health problems have a biological basis report higher levels of stigma. The most recent research on stigma involves cross-national research and preliminary findings show an important link between cultural levels of stigma and individual stigma. Pescosolido (2013: 15) concludes that "stigma is fundamentally a social phenomenon rooted in social relationships and shaped by the culture and structure of society."

Concluding Thoughts

Public policy is driven in part by the identification of problems that need to be solved and part of the reason for the dearth of a coherent mental health policy is disagreement over the nature of the problem (Mechanic et al. 2014). As we saw in Part I of this essay, there is no consensus on what mental illness is, or how to measure it. This leads to problems when we try to assess the sources of mental health problems in different groups and populations (Part II). Despite decades of research we still lack a clear understanding of the mental health status of major minority groups, in part due to differing methodologies and operationalization of mental health outcomes (Williams et al. 2017). In the absence of a common understanding of mental illness, stigmatized conceptions prevail. While there is wide recognition of the negative mental health consequences of social dislocation and trauma, there is little political will to deal with the needs of the most marginalized groups in all societies – those who are disabled by their mental health problems, as we saw in Part III.

Funding for mental health care is not market driven but results from governmental policies which impact not only health, but the provision of necessary social supports including income maintenance, housing, transportation, and employment policy. Mental health and primary health care systems are also poorly integrated, with primary care providers increasingly providing mental health treatment in the form of medications but with little training in mental health therapy. For those with disabling mental health problems, issues of system fragmentation occur not only within the mental health system and in the interface between mental and physical health systems, but in the integration of the mental health system with other service systems including social support or welfare systems, education, and the criminal justice system. The need for coordinated mental health as well as medical services will continue to put pressures on health care service systems, which will increase with the growing proportion of the population that is elderly, and minority. Globally few resources are provided to mental health, with much of that money being directed toward more acute mental health problems, especially in developed countries. In poorer countries there is more emphasis on those individuals with the greatest mental health needs, and often more creative solutions (Lefley 2017).

The mental health of minority groups and the reality of mental health disparities also necessitates treatment systems that are culturally competent. Culturally competent providers are able to provide for patient centered care and understand the impact of an individual's culture on both the diagnoses and experience of mental health problems. Mental health treatment seeks not only to reduce psychiatric symptoms, but also to improve social functioning. As such, treatment often emphasizes "normalization," whereby the client is able to live a normal life in the community. While what is defined as "normal" is culturally specific and valued, "almost all cultures recognize an official sanctioned Western medical and mental health system" (Lefley 2017: 146). The focus on biologically oriented explanations and reliance on psychiatric medications is a major obstacle to culturally appropriate, integrated mental health support systems. Instead, an understanding of mental health problems as a type of disability can lead to treatment options which improve personal agency as well as addressing needed structural changes to allow for meaningful recovery and improved quality of life. Rather than illness, the focus needs to be on mental health. Meaningful social relationships are an indication of well-being (World Health Organization 2004) and far too many individuals with mental health problems are isolated due to the stigma of mental illness. Reducing stigma, increasing social supports, and community integration all require that we focus on social structures as the source of mental health problems, and not solely on the individual.

Increasing attention is being paid to the combined as well as the cumulative effects of stress over the life course, as well as recent work on macro level contextual sources of stress, including economic recession, terrorism, and disasters. There are also important cohort effects, with social context shaping the experiences of each generation. Recent cohorts have grown up in a society dominated by fears over terrorism and mass shootings, and political debates over gun control and violence. Baby Boomers (now entering retirement) have faced different kinds of stressors than

Millennials, who are entering a very uncertain future with COVID-19 and a world wide depression. If nothing else, COVID-19 has awakened us to the reality that sources of illness, disability, and stress lie outside of our control.

Note

1 The processes by which social context and status influence mental health are similar to those which affect physical health and readers are directed to chapters in Part II of this volume for more detailed discussions of social class, gender, race and ethnicity.

References

Aneshensel, Carol S. 1992. "Social Stress: Theory and Research." *Annual Review of Sociology* 18: 15–38.

Bonnie, Richard. J. and John Monahan. 2005. "From Coercion to Contract: Reframing the Debate on Mandated Community Treatment for People with Mental Disorders." *Law and Human Behavior* 29: 485–503.

Bowleg, Lisa. 2012. "The Problem with the Phrase: Women and Minorities: Intersectionalilty – An Important Theoretical framework for Public Health." *American Journal of Public Health* 112(7): 1267–73.

Carr, Deborah. 2014. *Worried Sick: How Stress Hurts Us and How to Bounce Back*. New Brunswick, NJ: Rutgers University Press.

Conrad, Peter. 2007. *The Medicalization of Society: On the Transformation of Human Conditions into Treatable Disorders*. Baltimore, MD: John Hopkins University Press.

Diaz, Christina J. and Michael Nino. 2019. "Familism and the Hispanic Health Advantage: The Role of Immigrant Status." *Journal of Health and Social Behavior* 60(3): 273–89.

Dobransky, Kerry M. 2014. *Managing Madness in the Community: The Challenge of Contemporary Mental Health Care*. New Brunswick, NJ: Rutgers University Press.

Eaton, William W. and Carles Muntaner. 2017. "Socioeconomic Stratification and Mental Disorder." Pp. 239–65 in *A Handbook for the Study of Mental Health*, 3rd Edition, edited by T. L. Scheid and E. R. Wright. Cambridge: Cambridge University Press.

Foucault, Michel. 1988 (1965). *Madness and Civilization: A History of Insanity in the Age of Reason*. New York: Vintage Books.

Frances, Allan. 2013. *Saving Normal: An Insider's Revolt Against Out-of-Control Psychiatric Diagnosis, DSM-5, big Pharma, and the Medicalization of Ordinary Life*. New York: Harper Collins.

Harkness, Sarah K., Amy Krosta, and Bernice Pescosolido. 2016. "The Self-Stigma of Psychiatric Patients: Implications for Identities, Emotions, and the Life Course." Pp. 207–334 in *50 Years After Deinstitutionalization: Mental Illness in Contemporary Communities. Advances in Medical Sociology*, Vol. 17, edited by B. L. Perry. Bingley: Emerald.

Henwood, B. 2008. "Involuntary Inpatient Commitment in the Context of Mental Health Recovery." *American Journal of Psychiatric Rehabilitation* 11(3): 253–66.

Horwitz, Allan. 1982. *The Social Control of Mental Illness*. New York: Academic Press.

Horwitz, Allan V. 2002. *Creating Mental Illness*. Chicago, IL: University of Chicago Press.

Horwitz, Allan V. and Jerome C. Wakefield. 2007. *The Loss of Sadness: How Psychiatry Transformed Normal Sorrow into Depressive Disorder*. New York: Oxford University Press.

Horwitz, Allan V. and Jerome C. Wakefield. 2012. *All We Have to Fear is Fear Itself: Psychiatry's Transformations of Natural Anxieties into Mental Disorders.* New York: Oxford University Press.

Keith, Heather E. and Kenneth D. Keith. 2013. *Intellectual Disability: Ethics, Dehumanization, and a New Moral Community.* Malden, MA: Whiley-Blackwell.

Keith, Verna and Diane Brown. 2017. "African American Women and Well-Being: The Intersection of Race, Gender, and Socioeconomic Status." Pp. 304–21 in *A Handbook for the Sociology of Mental Health*, 3rd Edition, edited by T. L. Scheid and E. R. Wright. Cambridge: Cambridge University Press.

Kessler, Ronald C. 2010. "The Prevalence of Mental Illness." Pp. 46–63 in *A Handbook for the Sociology of Mental Health*, edited by T. L. Scheid and T. N. Brown. New York: Cambridge University Press.

Keyes, Corey L. M. 2017. "The Dual Continuum Model: The Foundation of the Sociology of Mental Health and Mental Illness." Pp. 66–81 in *A Handbook for the Sociology of Mental Health*, 3rd Edition, edited by T. L. Scheid and E. R. Wright. Cambridge: Cambridge University Press.

Kleinman, Arthur and Barbara Good (eds.). 1985. *Cultural and Depression.* Berkeley, CA: University of California Press.

Lefley, Harriet P. 2017. "Mental Health in Cross-Cultural Context." Pp. 145–72 in *A Handbook for the Sociology of Mental Health*, 3rd Edition, edited by T. L. Scheid and E. R. Wright. Cambridge: Cambridge University Press.

Lin, I. Fen, Susan L. Brown, Matthew R. Wright, and Anna M. Hammersmith. 2019. "Depressive Symptoms Following Later Life Marital Dissolution and Subsequent Reparenting." *Journal of Health and Social Behavior* 60(2): 153–68.

Link, Bruce G. 1987. "Understanding Labeling Effects in the Area of Mental Disorder: An Assessment of the Effects of Expectations of Rejection." *American Sociological Review* 52(1): 96–112.

Link, Bruce G. and Jo C. Phelan. 2001. "Conceptualizing Stigma." *Annual Review of Sociology* 27: 363–85.

Link, Bruce G. and Jo C. Phelan. 2017. "Labeling and Stigma." Pp. 393–408 in *A Handbook for the Sociology of Mental Health*, edited by T. L. Scheid and E. R. Wright. Cambridge: Cambridge University Press.

Marcussen, Kristen and Christian Ritter. 2016. "Revisiting the Relationships Among Community Mental Health Services, Stigma, and Well-Being." Pp. 177–206 in *50 Years After Deinstitutionalization: Mental Illness in Contemporary Communities. Advances in Medical Sociology*, Vol. 17, edited by B. L. Perry. Bingley: Emerald.

McLean, Athena H. 2000. "From Ex-Patient Alternatives to Consumer Options: Consequences of Consumerism for Psychiatric Consumers and the Ex-Patient Movement." *International Journal of Health Services* 30: 821–47.

McSween, Jean L. 2002. "The Role of Group Interest, Identity, and Stigma in Determining Mental Health Policy Preferences." *Journal of Health Politics, Policy, and Law* 27: 773–800.

Mechanic, David. 2006. *The Truth About Health Care: Why Reform is Not Working in the U.S.* New Brunswich, NJ: Rutgers University Press.

Mechanic, David, Donna D. McAlpine, and David A. Rochefort. 2014. *Mental Health and Social Policy: Beyond Managed Care.* 6th Edition. Boston, MA: Pearson Publishing.

Miller, Dinah and Annette Hanson. 2016. *Committed: The Battle over Involuntary Psychiatric Care.* Baltimore, MD: Johns Hopkins University Press.

Mirowsky, J. and Catherine E. Ross. 2017. "Well-Being Across the Life Course." Pp. 338–57 in *A Handbook for the Sociology of Mental Health*, edited by T. L. Scheid and E. R. Wright. Cambridge: Cambridge University Press.

Mirowsky, John and Catherine E. Ross. 2002. "Measurement for a Human Science." *Journal of Health and Social Behavior* 43(2): 152–70.

Morgan, Craig, Kwame McKenzie, and Paul Fearon. 2008. *Society and Psychosis*. Cambridge: Cambridge University Press.

Mossakowski, Krysia N. 2003. "Coping with Perceived Discrimination: Does Ethnic Identitiy Protect Mental Health?" *Journal of Health and Social Behavior* 44(3): 318–31.

Neighbors, Harold W., Steven J. Trierweiler, Brigget Ford, and Jordan Muroff. 2003. "Racial Differences in the Diagnostic Statistical Manual Diagnosis in Using a Semi-Structured Instrument: The Importance of Clinical Judgement in the Diagnosis of African Americans." *Journal of Health and Social Behavior* 44(Special Issue): 237–55.

Nora, Jacobson. 2004. *In Recovery: The Making of Mental Health Policy*. Nashville, TN: Vanderbilt University Press.

Nora, Jacobson and Diane Greenley. 2001. "What is recovery? A Conceptual Model and Explication." *Psychiatric Services* 52(4): 482–5.

Paulson, R. 1992. "Advocacy and Empowerment: Mental Health Care in the Community." *Community Mental Health Journal* 28: 70–1.

Pescosolido, Bernice A. 2013. "The Public Stigma of Mental Illness: What Do We Think; What Do We Know; What Can We Prove?" *Journal of Health and Social Behavior* 54(1): 1–21.

Rose, S. P. and B. L. Black. 1985. *Advocacy and Empowerment: Mental Health Care in the Community*. Boston: Routledge and Kegan Paul.

Rosenfield, Sarah. 1997. "Labeling Mental Illness: The Effects of Received Services and Perceived Stigma on Life Satisfaction." *American Sociological Review* 62(4): 660–72.

Scheid, Teresa L. 2016. "An Institutional Analysis of Public Sector Mental Health in the Post-Deinstitutionalization Era." Pp. 63–90 in *50 Years After Deinstitutionalization: Mental Illness in Contemporary Communities. Advances in Medical Sociology*, Vol. 17, edited by B. L. Perry. Bingley: Emerald.

Schneider, Daniel and Kristen Harknett. 2019. "Consequences of Routine Work-Schedule Instability for Worker Health and Well Being." *American Sociological Review* 84(1): 82–114.

Schnittker, Jason. 2017. *The Diagnostic System: Why the Classification of Psychiatric Disorders is Necessary, Difficult, and Never Settled*. New York: Columbia University Press.

Schwartz, Sharon. 1991. "Women and Depression: A Durkheimian Perspective." *Social Science and Medicine* 32: 127–40.

Sederer, L. I. and S. S. Sharfstein. 2014. "Fixing the Troubled Mental Health System." *JAMA* 10:1001/jama.2014.10369.

Sellers, Robert M., Cleopatra H. Caldwell, K. H. Schmeel-Cone, and Marc A. Zimmerman. 2003. "Racial Identity, Racial Discrimination, Perceived Stress, and Psychological Distress Among African American Youth." *Journal of Health and Social Behavior* 43: 302–17.

Smith, Dena T. 2014. "The Diminished Resistance to Medicalization in Psychiatry: Psychoanalysis Meets the Medical Model of Mental Illness." *Society and Mental Health* 4(2): 75–91.

Spandler, Helen, Jill Anderson, and Bob Sapey. 2015. *Distress and Disability: Madness and the Politics of Disablement*. Bristol: Policy Press.

Spandler, Helen. and Theo Stickley. 2011. "No Hope Without Compassion: The Importance of Compassion in Recovery-Focused Mental Health Services." *Journal of Mental Health* 20: 555–66.

Swanson, Jeffrey W., Robert A. Van Dorn, John Monahan, and Marvin Swartz. 2006. "Violence and Leveraged Community Treatment for Persons with Mental Disorders." *American Journal of Psychiatry* 163: 1404–11.

Takeuchi, David T. 2016. "Vintage Wine in New Bottles: Infusing Select Ideas in the Study of Immigration, Immigrants, and Mental Health." *Journal of Health and Social Behavior* 57(4): 423–35.

Testa, Megan and Sara G. West. 2010. "Civil Commitment in the United States." *Psychiatry* 7(10): 30–40.

Thoits, Peggy A. 1995. "Stress, Coping, and Social Support Processes: Where are We? What Next?" *Journal of Health and Social Behavior* (Extra Issue): 53–79.

Thoits, Peggy A. 2010. "Sociological Approaches to Mental Illness." Pp. 106–124 in *A Handbook for the Study of Mental Health: Social Contexts, Theories, and Systems*, 2nd edition, edited by T.L. Scheid and T.N. Brown. New York: Cambridge University Press.

Thoits, Peggy A. 2011. "Mechanisms Linking Social Ties and Support to Physical and Mental Health." *Journal of Health and Social Behavior* 52(2): 145–61.

Turner, R. Jay. 2013. "Understanding Health Disparities: The Relevance of the Stress Process Model." *Society and Mental Health* 3(4): 170–86.

Vandermiden, Jennifer and Jennifer J. Esala. 2019. "Beyond Symptoms: Race and Gender Predict Anxiety Disorder Diagnosis." *Society and Mental Health* 9(2): 111–25.

Wales Heathcote and Virginia A. Hiday. 2006. "PLC or TLC: Is Outpatient Commitment the/an Answer?" *International Journal of Law and Psychiatry* 29(6): 451–68.

Warner, Richard. 1985. *Recovery from Schizophrenia: Psychiatry and Political Economy.* London: Routledge and Kegan Paul.

Waters, Ethan. 2010. *Crazy Like Us: The Globalization of the American Psyche.* New York: Free Press.

Wheaton, Blair and Shirin Montazer. 2017. "Studying Stress sin the Twenty-First Century: An Update of Stress Concepts and Research." Pp. 180–206 in *A Handbook for the Sociology of Mental Health*, edited by T. L. Scheid and E. R. Wright. Cambridge: Cambridge University Press.

Whooley, Owen. 2014. "Nosological Reflections: The Failure of DSM-5, the Emergence of RDoc, and the Decontextualization of Mental Distress." *Society and Mental Health* 4(2): 92–110.

Williams, David R., Manuela Costa, and Jacinata P Leavell. 2017. "Race and Mental Health." Pp. 281–303 in *A Handbook for the Sociology of Mental Health*, edited by T. L. Scheid and E. R. Wright. Cambridge: Cambridge University Press.

World Health Organization. 2004. *Promoting Mental Health: Concepts, Emerging Evidence, Practice.* Geneva: World Health Organization.

Yanos, Phillip T., Edward L. Knight, and David Roe. 2007. "Recognizing a Role for Structure and Agency: Integrating Sociological Perspectives into the Study of Recovery From Severe Mental Illness." Pp. 407–33 in *Mental Health, Social Mirror*, edited by W. R. Avison, J. D. McLeod, and B. A. Pescosolido. New York: Springer.

Part V

Health and Disease

21

Emerging Infectious Diseases

Ron Barrett

From December 31, 2019 to January 2, 2020 Chinese authorities first reported a cluster of 44 patients diagnosed with a pneumonia of unknown etiology in Wuhan, a city of more than 11 million people, capital of the Hubei province, and major economic hub of central China (WHO 2020). By January 7, a novel coronavirus had been identified, which would eventually be named SARS-CoV-2, and COVID-19 for the associated disease. By January 20, 282 cases had been detected in China, Thailand, Japan, and Republic of Korea. From these four countries, the disease quickly spread throughout the world.

At the time of this publication, more than 86 million cases of COVID-19 have been reported in 218 countries, resulting in more than 1.9 million deaths (Johns Hopkins 2020). Although China initially bore the brunt of this disease, the Spring months of 2020 saw the numbers shift to the US, which currently has the highest number of cases and deaths at 21.6 million and 360 thousand, respectively. In addition, national and regional responses to the disease, in the form of various quarantine, isolation, and shutdown measures, have resulted in major economic recessions, massive unemployment, and forecasts of 42–66 million children falling into extreme poverty within the first year of the pandemic (United Nations 2020).

Although the COVID-19 pandemic is far from over at the time of this book's publication, the virus presents key lessons for the medical social sciences that will remain relevant and timely long after it recedes, as it will for future pandemics. Chief among them are the social determinants of infectious diseases. While it is certainly useful to study the molecular and genetic properties of pathogens, human practices, and human environments, are primary drivers in the emergence, evolution, and spread of all our infectious diseases.

With human determinants in mind, this chapter presents a social history and prehistory of infectious disease pandemics. Beginning with a critical analysis of the so-called "emerging" infectious diseases, it will highlight the major roles of social

The Wiley Blackwell Companion to Medical Sociology, First Edition. Edited by William C. Cockerham.

ecology and political economics in human infections from the Paleolithic to the present day. All of this will be framed within three epidemiological transitions occurring during the Neolithic, the Industrial Revolution, and the accelerated globalization we see today. Throughout these three transitions, we will see how human modes of subsistence, settlement, and social organization determined the major increases and declines rises of infectious pandemics over the last 10 thousand years. We will also see how the recent biosocial concept of syndemics is the *sine qua non* of the Third Epidemiological Transition, of which COVID-19 is but one of many pandemics to come.

Forgotten Precedents and Emergence of Emerging Infections

When teaching about infectious diseases, I often begin discussion with this question: What makes an infectious disease an *emerging* infectious disease? In addition to descriptions of danger and rapid transmission, the most common responses are that emerging infections are new and unprecedented. I then unpack these latter descriptors, explaining that many newly identified diseases have been around a while, most often in non-human animal hosts, but sometimes in human populations as well. When there is a significant lag time between initial human infections and scientific attention, it is usually because the disease had been present in a poor and socially marginalized population. It is for this reason that some global health researchers cynically joke that an infectious disease becomes an *emerging* infectious disease when the first white guy gets it (Barrett and Armelagos 2013).

The joke, of course, is not funny. But unfortunately, it is often quite true. Wealthy societies, and the scientific institutions within them, often ignore diseases of poverty, labeling them as rare, exotic, or "tropical," if they are even aware of them at all. This was the case for HIV/AIDS, which had been infecting people in central and western Africa for decades before it was finally discovered in small group of hospitalized patients in New York City and California (CDC 1981; Zhu et al. 1998). The bacterium responsible for Legionnaire's disease was first identified at a Pennsylvania convention in 1976 (Meyer 1983). Only then, did researchers discover that the Legionella bacterium had been infecting people with unspecified pneumonias for many years. 1976 was also the year of the first Ebola epidemic in Zaire, now the Central African Republic (Garrett 1994). But even this deadly disease escaped the public attention of wealthy societies for two decades, including eight additional outbreaks, until related viruses were found in US and European primate research facilities (Barrett 2015). I also explain to my students that, when the pathogens (the viruses, bacteria, and parasites that cause disease) are indeed newcomers to the human population, the conditions of their arrival and spread are not unprecedented. History is full of precedents for even the newest of human infections, and this year, I countered the claims of politicians and journalists that COVID-19 is unprecedented. The recent history of the twenty-first century provides clear precedents involving closely related coronaviruses: the SARS pandemic of 2003 and the more virulent MERS pandemic of 2015 (Cui et al. 2019; Song et al. 2019). Both of these diseases entered the human population through the same kinds of human subsistence and economic activities. Both were spread via the same human behaviors in the same human environments. And both generated the same varieties of individual and social responses, for better and worse.

Given these histories, why do so many people and politicians believe that the COVID-19 pandemic is unprecedented? Or perhaps the better question is: Why have the precedents been forgotten? To better answer these questions, we must turn to the events that led to the phrase, emerging infectious diseases. Here, we will find three closely connected social trends: modernism, recentism, and isolationism.

The twentieth century saw an incredible surge of technological developments, including medical technologies such as antibiotics and vaccinations. It also saw a major decline in infectious disease mortality, so much that most societies saw major population increases despite major declines in fertility (Omran 1971). However, along with these developments came the modernist belief that new and improved technologies, linked with industrial development, were the first and final cures for major human problems. This was the especially the case for how industrialized societies viewed infectious diseases in the four decades after World War II. Sir Macfarlane Burnet, the pioneering Australian virologist and Nobel laureate, famously described the middle of the twentieth century as "... the end of one of the most important social revolutions in history, the virtual elimination of the infectious diseases as a significant factor in social life" (Burnet 1962: iii). As president of the American Association of Medical Colleges, Robert Petersdorf predicted that there would be little role for infectious disease specialists in the next century, unless, as he put it, they would "spend their time culturing one another" (Petersdorf 1986: 478). Statements like these echoed a common consensus among western scientists that infectious diseases would soon become a problem of the past in the developed (read, industrialized) world and this would also be the case for the underdeveloped once it became sufficiently industrialized. Governments shared this modernist view, shifting research and resources from the control of infectious to noninfectious diseases.

Microbes are the ultimate critics of modernity, and by the 1990's, three microbial trends occurred to shatter this view. Dozens of newly discovered pathogens appeared in human populations (Amyes 2001). In wealthy societies, there was a resurgence of diseases, such as tuberculosis, that had previously been in decline (Farmer 1997). And pathogenic bacteria were evolving antibiotic resistance faster than new drugs were being discovered, prompting one researcher to suggest that the world was entering a post-antibiotic era (Garrett 1994).

In response to these trends, the US Institute of Medicine (IOM) published a major report entitled, *Emerging Infections* (Lederburg et al. 1992). In addition, the US Centers for Disease Control and Prevention (CDC) sponsored a new peer-reviewed journal, Emerging *Infectious Diseases*. As with the efforts themselves, the intended purpose of these titles was to refocus attention and resources to the prevention and control of infectious diseases and bring public attention to a neglected area of global health. Their goals were also less modernist:

> It is unrealistic to expect that humankind will win a complete victory over the multitude of existing microbial diseases, or over those that will emerge in the future. ... Still, there are many steps that scientists, educators, public health officials, policymakers, and others can and should be taking to improve our odds in this ongoing struggle. With diligence and concerted action at many levels, the threats posed by infectious diseases can be, if not eliminated, at least significantly moderated (Lederburg et al. 1992: 32).

This was also around the time that the European and North American public first became aware of the Ebola virus with blockbuster movies like Outbreak and bestselling books like *The Hot Zone* (Preston 1994). These and other popular media presented gruesome, zombie-like depictions of this disease, emphasizing exotic origins in the Dark Continent, and suggesting that the virus could easily spread to a backyard near you. For many consumers of this media message, emerging infectious evoked an image of monsters on the doorstep of the developed world.

This oscillation of risk perceptions, between disregard and dread of infectious diseases, was not simply due to the rise and fall of modernist assumptions. Linked to these assumptions was a strong current of recentism, a tendency to focus on recent histories at the expense of understanding earlier histories. If more people had been aware of the earlier history of declining infections in nineteenth and early twentieth centuries, they would have known that the largest portion of these declines occurred before the advent of antibiotics and most vaccinations; that improved nutrition, sanitation, and improved living conditions – rather than new medical technologies – were the greatest contributors to these declines (McKeown 1988).

There was also a strong current of isolationist thinking that obscured awareness of how interconnected the world had become. With the accelerated globalization that has been occurring during that time and today, there are no truly isolated societies. Thus, any epidemic is a potential pandemic because a pathogen can spread from a poor person to a wealthy person, anywhere around the world, in less than a day. Consequently, all infectious diseases are problems for the wealthy as well as the poor. When they become problems for the wealthy, the "emerging infection" is often an emerging awareness of a long-standing threat within a single, global disease ecology.

The oscillations have continued since the 1990's, moving between disregard to dread and back to disregard through the emergence of Zika and West Nile viruses, the evolution of drug resistant tuberculosis (MDRTB and XDRTB) bacteria, the dodged bullets of highly pathogenic influenzas, eleven additional Ebola epidemics, and two notable coronavirus outbreaks. At the moment of this book's publication, the world is facing a major pandemic with the opportunity to learn many important lessons. To learn these lessons, we must cast aside some previous assumptions and view the social dynamics as well as the biological dynamics of the situation from a global, deep-time perspective.

From Emerging to Converging Infections in Three Epidemiological Transitions

The Classic Model of epidemiological transitions was first proposed to explain a major demographic shift associated with industrial economic development in affluent societies of the late nineteenth and early twentieth centuries: an exponential increase in total population despite declining fertility rates (Omran 1971). The obvious remaining explanation was that these same societies had undergone significant mortality declines. But Omran pushed the model beyond demography alone to examine "the complex change in patterns of health and disease and on the interactions between these patterns and the demographic, economic, and sociological determinants and consequences" (1971: 510). Omran then gathered historical data to demonstrate that these mortality declines were primarily due to declining infectious diseases, particularly in childhood, despite lesser increases in noninfectious diseases. Taken on the whole, these populations increased because more children had survived to adulthood.

This Classic Model was a significant contribution to the interdisciplinary study of health determinants across recent historical periods. Most notably, it paved the way for the studies of McKeown and others regarding the role of changing living patterns on human disease susceptibility (McKeown 1988). However, the model has at least two significant shortcomings when applied to a broader set of health transitions. Its first shortcoming is historical: the presentation of a single transition gives a false impression that that pre-industrial societies had always suffered from high rates of infectious diseases. Its second shortcoming is economic: although Omran presents a delayed transition model for developing nations, the classic transition suggests that poorer nations will achieve the same mortality gains once they become sufficiently industrialized.

To address these shortcomings, my colleagues and I expanded the epidemiological transition framework (Barrett and Armelagos 2013; Barrett et al. 1998). Based on studies of contemporary hunting gathering populations, and paleopathological evidence from ancient societies undergoing the transition from nomadic foraging to sedentary agriculture, we demonstrate that acute infections did not have a major health impact during our first one hundred millennia as biological modern humans. Moreover, the first truly emerging infections – i.e. acute infections as a major cause of human mortality – began in the Neolithic rather than the 1990's, with first instances of agricultural intensification and their concomitant changes in settlement and social organization. This was the First Epidemiological Transition. Omran's later, classic model, was the Second Epidemiological Transition. A major implication of these two transitions was that, prior to the trappings of our so-called "modern civilizations," human lives had not always been nasty, brutish, and short.

The Third Epidemiological Transition addresses the second, economic shortcoming of Omran's classic model. Contrary to the optimistic predictions for developing nations, those that underwent a Second Transition after World War II never caught up with their more affluent counterparts (Riley 2005). Despite initial gains, by the turn of the twenty-first century, most of the developing world had converged into a "high mortality club" with life expectancies between 50 and 60 years of age, while the developed world converged into "low mortality club" with life expectancies around 75 years of age (Bloom and Canning 2007). For most poor societies, the health benefits Second Transition had come too little and too late. Meanwhile, these same societies had experienced the increased problems associated with this transition: rising chronic degenerative diseases, and aging populations due to rapid urbanization.

Consequently, much of the world is in a crossover between post-First and post-Second Transition disease patterns, a situation that has been characterized as "the worst of all worlds" (Bradley 1993). Furthermore, with the globalization of human disease ecologies, the worst and best of worlds are converging into a single world, thus setting the stage for the Third Epidemiological Transition.

As a consequence of this globalization, syndemics are most distinctive feature of the Third Transitions. A syndemic occurs when people have two or more diseases, and the interactions between them increase morbidity and mortality to a greater degree than the sum of their separate effects (Singer and Clair 2003; Weaver et al. 2016). We see syndemics at both individual and population levels: (1) in examples of co-occurring noninfectious diseases such as diabetes, heart disease, and renal failure, and, (2) in examples of co-occurring infectious diseases, such as HIV with TB, hepatitis B with hepatitis D, and many of the influenzas with many of the bacterial pneumonias (Singer 2010). And most significantly, we see syndemics in the emerging infectious diseases as they have been formally defined: new infections, resurging infections, and drug resistant infections.

New Infections: Coronaviruses and Chronic Degenerative Diseases

Between 1940 and 2004, over 330 novel human pathogens were discovered (Jones et al. 2008). Detection bias accounts for some of these discoveries, but phylogenetic analyses confirm that most of these pathogens are indeed new to our species, and most of these having recently made the jump from non-human animal populations. Based on these data, much attention has been focused on transmission via human subsistence practices, ranging from the more "exotic" examples of bushmeat hunting and wet markets, to the more mainstream (and far more prevalent) risks associated with industrial food production (Loyd-Smith 2009; Wolfe et al. 2005). These practices are major contributors to the invasion of new pathogens, but they are only part of the equation. Host conditions also play a major role.

Epidemics involving the highly pathogenic coronaviruses, Severe Acute Respiratory Syndrome (SARS) and Middle East Respiratory Syndrome (MERS), provide important lessons about the role of host conditions at the earliest stages of pathogen invasion. Among SARS cases In Hong Kong, Taiwan, and Toronto, comorbidity with chronic diseases such as chronic obstructive pulmonary disease (COPD), cardiac disease, diabetes, and chronic renal failure was associated with significantly higher rates of infection among nonmedical workers and much higher case fatality rates, especially among people over 60 years of age (Booth et al. 2003; Chen et al. 2005; Leung et al. 2004).

These comorbid associations were even stronger during the MERS pandemic. Among the first 47 detected cases of Middle East respiratory syndrome (MERS), 45 were comorbid with at least one major chronic noninfectious medical condition, the most prevalent of which were diabetes, hypertension, and chronic heart and renal diseases (Assiri et al. 2013). It should be noted that case fatality rates increased with age and were highest among people over 60 years.

While the first SARS epidemic lasted only seven months, the MERS epidemic continued for several years, providing additional time for the virus to adapt to human host populations. With this in mind, it is important to note changes in patient demography following the early stages of the epidemic. From the ninth to the thirteenth months, the percentage of elderly among the cumulative total of MERS cases declined from 81% to 67% and comorbidity declined from 97% to 76% (WHO MERS-CoV Research Group 2013). In addition, while the sex ratio remained skewed toward males, it shifted significantly from > 9 : 1 to 6.5 : 1 with a substantial rise in the number of female cases. Following this shift, the demographic characteristics of human hosts have changed little up through the end of 2015 (Zumla et al. 2015). Human to human transmission has been largely restricted to hospital settings. Most community transmission has occurred between animals and humans.

These host demographic patterns make sense, given the role of susceptible populations as likely pathways for the initial entry of zoonotic pathogens into human populations. This "invasion" process does not typically happen all at once, but rather in a stepwise fashion. Anderson and MAY (1986) describe these steps as: (1) initial establishment, involving animal-human transmission; (2) persistence, involving human-human transmission; and, (3) spread, involving sustained transmission within and between human populations. The first two steps best describe the early months of the SARS and MERS epidemics, with animal-human, and limited human-human transmissibility, but no sustained human-human transmission. That the epidemiology of MERS had shifted from higher risk to broader groups suggests that the virus is becoming better adapted to human populations – a troubling possibility.

It is at these earlier stages of pathogen invasion that susceptible populations create evolutionary opportunities for pathogens that are not yet fully adapted for transmission to and from human tissues. Chronic diseases often compromise immunity thereby lowering the threshold for the establishment and transmission of pathogens. These conditions are also associated with diminished physical activity and lung excursion, two major risk factors for respiratory infection (Hespanhol and Barbara 2020). And insofar as some chronic conditions are associated with increased respiratory secretions and cough, they can create what is sometimes known as the "cloud effect" which enhances the airborne dissemination of microorganisms into local environments (Sherertz et al. 1996; Stein 2011).

All of these factors underscore the syndemic potential of chronic diseases to facilitate the emergence of novel infections in human populations. And not surprisingly, all of these factors are highly relevant to the COVID-19 pandemic, which is essentially a worldwide syndemic between an acute, novel infection and a growing list of chronic, noninfectious diseases.

Resurging Infections: Tuberculosis and Diabetes

The aforementioned links between novel coronaviruses and diabetes mellitus (DM) are preceded by a broader set of long-standing associations between respiratory infections and metabolic disease. This can be traced back to the early decades of the Second Epidemiological Transition, when TB presented the greatest infectious disease threat. Here, autopsies revealed lung tubercles in 40–50% of DM patients in three 19th century European populations (Root 1934). In the 1920's, a sample of 750 US adolescents with juvenile diabetes in the 1920's were between 13 and 16 times more likely to develop primary tuberculosis in comparison to control groups (Root 1934).[1] The same study reports increasing rates of TB mortality among adult DM patients, despite significant declines in overall TB mortality within the same population.

While not as dramatic as the nineteenth and early twentieth century observations, more recent studies still reveal significant associations between DM and TB diseases (Baker et al. 2011). A meta-analysis of 13 observational studies between 1974 and 2007 found that diabetes was associated with a relative risk of 3.11 for TB infection (95% CI, 2.27–4.46), and that the relative risk increased to 4.4 when adjusted for smoking (Jeon and Murray 2008). Most of these studies did not distinguish between Type I and Type II diabetes, though with random sampling, it is reasonable to infer a higher percentage of adult onset cases, drawing from higher overall rates of Type II DM than from those of earlier studies.

Considering the common pathologies of all diabetic diseases, it is well known that hyperglycemia can lead to pathologies associated with lower resistance to infection (Jafar et al. 2016; Casqueiro et al. 2016). These include impaired production of cytokines and lowered macrophage activity associated with the depletion of vitamin co-factors required for effective immune responses. At the same time, hyperglycemia can exacerbate bacterial colonization and growth in host tissues. There are clear physiological links from diabetes to tuberculosis, just as there are with diabetes and other respiratory, skin, and soft tissue infections.

Socioeconomic status is a strong mediating factor for tuberculosis and diabetes, and there is strong evidence that this is also the case for the interaction between these two diseases. In the aforementioned Jeon and Murray (2008) meta-analysis, three studies that accounted for socioeconomic variables confirmed the well-known associations between TB and poverty in their respective study populations, variously considering the effects of income, education, veteran status, and health insurance coverage (Coker 2006; Pablos-Mendez 1997; Perez et al. 2006). Two of these studies treated these social variables as confounders to understanding the associations between TB and diabetes alone, but Perez and others took additional steps toward analyzing the effects of social variables on the strength of the disease interactions (2006). The study compared different populations living in US-Mexico border regions with those living in non-border regions. Interestingly, people of all races with diabetes were more likely to have TB in border than non-border regions, but the association was reversed for Hispanic people with diabetes. Moreover, living in the border region was not a risk factor for TB when adjusting for all other social factors. These findings strongly suggest that the links between TB and diabetes are social as well as physiological.

In many ways, tuberculosis is an exemplar for the syndemic nature of today's re-emerging infections. The TB pathogen, *Mycobacterium. tuberculosis*, has long been associated with the highest rates of infectious disease mortality, and it is estimated that 24% of the world's population has been exposed to it in some way (Rein, Houben and Dodd 2016). Yet 30% of the world does not have tuberculosis, a testament to the proposition that the TB disease is not caused by the mycobacterium alone, but rather in combination with the right host and the right environmental conditions. Tuberculosis is an obligate syndemic disease.

Even before the bacterium was discovered, medical researchers were recognizing the syndemic nature of tuberculosis in relation to a chronic noninfectious disease (Root 1934). But with the decline of TB in the Second Epidemiological Transition, these lessons were largely forgotten or ignored. This awareness is remerging with the return of TB and other long-standing infections as significant threats to affluent populations in the Third Epidemiological Transition.

Drug Resistant Infections: MRSA, Long Term Care, and The

The history of antibiotic resistance is as long (or rather, as short) as the use of the drugs themselves. Many of these resistance mechanisms have been around since bacteria first began excreting compounds to compete with one another. But the human production of these compounds and their derivatives have greatly increased directional selection toward further resistance. From penicillin in the early 1940's to daptomycin in the early 2000's, most antibiotics have faced drug resistance within a decade of their widespread deployment (Brown and Wright 2016; Davies and Davies 2011). Today, the human population consumes more than 100 thousand tons of antibiotics annually, but as with many of our other drug habits, we consume these substances with ever diminishing returns as the rates of bacterial evolution have outpaced those of human discovery and invention.

Among the more prevalent of bacterial pathogens, *Staphylococcus aureus* has been notably quick to acquire drug resistance. In the early 1940's, it was the first pathogen discovered to have acquired penicillin resistance in clinical and community settings (Amyes 2001). Methicillin resistant *Staph. aureus* (MRSA) followed in 1961, only two years after the deployment of this second line antibiotic. Still, MRSA remained a relatively rare infection for more than two decades, appearing mainly among cancer patients undergoing chemotherapy. Then, in the 1980's, MRSA rates increased appeared among the first generation of AIDS patients and elderly residents of nursing homes in affluent nations such as the US (Barrett et al. 1998).

From the early 1990s to the early 2000s, MRSA increased from 20–25% to more than 70% of all *Staph. aureus* isolates discovered in US hospitals, and the infection became endemic to nursing homes and long-term care facilities (Marshall and Levy 2011). During the same period, the definition of MRSA has been expanded to include *Staph.* resistance to all beta-lactam antibiotics, inclusive of all penicillin-like drugs, including commonly prescribed cephalosporins, and carbapenems. Today, MRSA strains are among the most commonly identified multidrug resistant pathogens in four continents, including North America.

Given the rapid adaptability and global prevalence of these strains, MRSA could be considered the proverbial "canary in the coal mine" for future forms of antibiotic resistance. Thinking of the future, while recalling the past lessons of tuberculosis, we should not be surprised to find that multi-drug resistant TB (MDRTB) is significantly associated with Type II diabetes in certain US populations (Fisher-Hoch et al. 2008). Building on the lessons of the Second Transition, we know that proper nutrition has always been among the best preventatives for both TB and diabetes. And faced with the emergence of MDR and XDRTB in the Third Transition, there may be few other treatments available.

Aging Societies, Urbanization, and Poverty

It is very important to examine how aging plays a major role in all major disease trends of the Third Epidemiological Transition. Recall that the framework of epidemiological transitions is based on major demographic transitions. The major demographics of the Third Epidemiological Transition is a rapid increase in the percentage of elderly people. This increase is certainly occurring in well-developed (read, wealthy) societies. The most recent impact of this can be seen in the COVID mortality for the US and the European Union, where the vast majority of deaths have occurred among the elderly (Rothan and Byrareddy 2020).

Yet we should also note that the demographic trend toward aging societies, with its higher mortality for COVID and other infections, is also occurring in the up and coming, and so-called "second world" nations of China, India, and Brazil (Johns Hopkins 2020). Furthermore, in terms of absolute numbers, this aging trend is most prevalent in most underdeveloped (read, poor) societies (Kinsella and Velkoff 2001). Here, the reason for the aging trend is not that people are living longer because they are healthier. It is because fertility declines have shifted the ratios of younger to older people – a decreasing percentage of younger people entails an increasing percentage older people over time. It also entails an increasing percentage of older people with a much greater risk of contracting infectious diseases.

Why the fertility decline? The primary driver is urbanization, for which the geometry of space and the economy of subsistence requires fewer children. By the standards of human geographers, most of the world's population live in urban environments (Dye 2008). This urbanization, however, does not entail better living for the world's poorer societies. Urban slums have concentrated human populations to a much greater degree than occurred during the First Epidemiological Transition, with environments bereft of clean water and sanitation, and stressors, both physical and psychological, that decrease immunity and increase vulnerability to disease.

Add to this, the importance of mobility for urban survival, and traditional three-generation, extended families shrink to "modern" three-generation, nuclearized families. This may work in wealthier urban societies that have the finances to support professional caregiving and other supports. But poorer urban societies are faced with the double dilemma of diminished financial resources as well as diminishing social resources. With this, they must face an increasing percentage of vulnerable older people within their families. Multiply these challenges by the majority of the world's population, and we have the demographic and economic conditions for most "emerging infections" of the Third Epidemiological Transition.

Conclusion

Emerging infectious diseases was a well-intended phrase to bring attention and resources to a major global health problem. But this attention tended to focus on the characteristics of pathogens over those of people and their environments. Additionally, it rarely accounted for the deeper social histories leading up to these events. This chapter addresses these issues with an expanded framework of epidemiological transitions, demonstrating that many new diseases, like COVID-19, are fundamentally social. Their determinants are mainly human, persisting for many centuries to the present day.

The more complex version of this story involves multiple, nonlinear trajectories and the different ways that rich and poor societies have experienced these transitions. For some societies, health conditions have changed very little since the First Transition. Many others experienced later and more attenuated Second Transitions. At a worldwide level, the First and Second Transitions have never been complete. Now, with the globalization of human disease ecologies, these incomplete trends have converged, bringing together infectious and chronic disease patterns, each having a synergistic effect on the other. As such, the current challenge of emerging infections might be better described as *converging* infections, syndemics within a global disease ecology.

Note

1 The higher rates were among adolescents older than 15 years of age, suggesting that the duration of diabetes may be an independent variable in the risk of TB infection and or manifestation of secondary pneumonia.

References

Amyes, Sebastian. 2001. *Magic Bullets, Lost Horizons: The Rise and Fall of Antibiotics.* New York: Taylor & Francis.

Anderson, Roy M. and Robert M. MAY. 1986. “The Invasion, Persistence and Spread of Infectious Diseases within Animal and Plant Communities.” *Philosophical Transactions of the Royal Society of London Series B-Biological Sciences* 314(1167): 533–70.

Assiri, Abdullah, Jaffar A. Al-Tawfiq, Abdullah A. Al-Rabeeah, Fahad A. Al-Rabiah, Sami Al-Hajjar, Ali Al-Barrak, Hesham Flemban, Wafa N. Al-Nassir, Hanan H. Balkhy, Rafat F. Al-Hakeem, Hatem Q. Makhdoom, Alimuddin I. Zumla, and Ziad A. Memish. 2013. “Epidemiological, Demographic, and Clinical Characteristics of 47 Cases of Middle East Respiratory Syndrome Coronavirus Disease from Saudi Arabia: A Descriptive Study.” *Lancet Infectious Diseases* 13(9): 752–61.

Baker, Meghan A., Anthony D. Harries, Christie Y. Jeon, Jessica E. Hart, Anil Kapur, Knut Loennroth, Salah-Eddine Ottmani, Sunali D. Goonesekera, and Megan B. Murray. 2011. “The Impact of Diabetes on Tuberculosis Treatment Outcomes: A Systematic Review.” *BMC Medicine* 9: 81.

Barrett, Ron. 2015. "The Specter of Ebola: Epidemiological Transitions and the Zombie Apocalypse." Pp. 279–94 in *New Directions in Biocultural Anthropology*, edited by M. Zuckerman and D. Martin. New York: Wiley-Blackwell.

Barrett, Ron and George Armelagos. 2013. *An Unnatural History of Emerging Infections*. Oxford: Oxford University Press.

Barrett, Ronald, Christopher W. Kuzawa, Thomas. McDade, and George J. Armelagos. 1998. "Emerging Infectious Disease and the Third Epidemiological Transition." Pp. 247–71 in *Annual Review of Anthropology*. Vol. 27, ed. W. Durham. Palo Alto, CA: Annual Reviews Inc.

Bloom, David E. and David Canning. 2007. "Mortality Traps and the Dynamics of Health Transitions." *Proceedings of the National Academy of Sciences* 104(41):16044–9.

Booth, C. M., L. M. Matukas, G. A. Tomlinson, A. R. Rachlis, D. B. Rose, H. A. Dwosh, S. L. Walmsley, T. Mazzulli, M. Avendano, P. Derkach, I. E. Ephtimios, I. Kitai, B. D. Mederski, S. B. Shadowitz, W. L. Gold, L. A. Hawryluck, E. Rea, J. S. Chenkin, D. W. Cescon, S. M. Poutanen, and A. S. Detsky. 2003. "Clinical Features and Short-Term Outcomes of 144 Patients with SARS in the Greater Toronto Area." *Jama-Journal of the American Medical Association* 289(21): 2801–9.

Bradley, DJ. 1993. "Environmental and Health Problems of Developing Countries." in *1993* Environmental Change and Human Health, *Ciba Foundation Symposium 175*. Ciba Foundation.

Brown, Eric D. and Gerard D. Wright. 2016. "Antibacterial Drug Discovery in the Resistance Era." *Nature* 529(7586): 336–43.

Burnet, Mcfarlane. 1962. *Natural History of Infectious Disease*. Cambridge: Cambridge University Press.

Casqueiro, Juliana, Janine Casqueiro, and Cresio Alves. 2016. "Infections in Patients with Diabetes Mellitus: A Review of Pathogenesis." *Indian Journal of Endocrinology and Metabolism* 16(Suppl. 1): S27–36.

CDC (Centers for Disease Control and Prevention). 1981. "Kaposi's Sarcoma and Pneumocystis Pneumonia among Homosexual Men - New York City and California." *Morbidity and Mortality Weekly Report* 30: 305–8.

Chen, K. T., S. J. Twu, H. L. Chang, Y. C. Wu, C. T. Chen, T. H. Lin, S. J. Olsen, S. F. Dowell, and I. J. Su. 2005. "SARS in Taiwan: An Overview and Lessons Learned." *International Journal of Infectious Diseases* 9(2): 77–85.

Coker, R., M. McKee, R. Atun, B. Dimitrova, E. Dodonova, S. Kuznetsov, and F. Drobniewski. 2006. "Risk Factors for Pulmonary Tuberculosis in Russia: Case-Control Study." *British Medical Journal* 332(7533): 85–7.

Cui, Jie, Fang Li, and Zheng-Li Shi. 2019. "Origin and Evolution of Pathogenic Coronaviruses." *Nature Reviews Microbiology* 17(3): 181–92.

Davies, Julian and Dorothy Davies. 2010. "Origins and Evolution of Antibiotic Resistance." *Microbiology and Molecular Biology Reviews* 74(3): 417–33.

Dye, Christopher. 2008. "Health and Urban Living." *Science* 319: 766–9.

Farmer, P. 1997. "Social Scientists and the New Tuberculosis." *Social Science & Medicine* 44(3): 347–58.

Fisher-Hoch, Susan P., Erin Whitney, Joseph B. Mccormick, Gonzalo Crespo, Brian Smith, Mohammad H. Rahbar, and Blanca I. Restrepo. 2008. "Type 2 Diabetes and Multidrug-Resistant Tuberculosis." *Scandinavian Journal of Infectious Diseases* 40(11–12): 888–93.

Garrett, Laurie. 1994. *The Coming Plague: Newly Emerging Diseases in a World Out of Balance*. New York: Farrar Straus and Giroux.

Hespanhol, Venceslau and Cristina Barbara. 2020. "Pneumonia Mortality, Comorbidities Matter?" *Pulmonology* 26(3): 123–9.

Hopkins, Johns. 2020. "COVID-19 Dashboard by the Center for Systems Science and Engineering (CSSE) and Johns Hopkins University (JHU)." https://coronavirus.jhu.edu/map.html.

Jafar, N., H. Edriss, and K. Nugent. 2016. "The Effect of Short-Term Hyperglycemia on the Innate Immune System." *American Journal of Medical Sciences* 351(2): 201–11.

Jeon, Christie Y. and Megan B. Murray. 2008. "Diabetes Mellitus Increases the Risk of Active Tuberculosis: A Systematic Review of 13 Observational Studies." *Plos Medicine* 5(7): 1091–101.

Jones, K. E., N. G. Patel, M. A. Levy, A. Storeygard, D. Balk, J. L. Gittleman, and P. Daszak. 2008. "Global Trends in Emerging Infectious Diseases." *Nature* 451(7181): 990–3.

Kinsella, Kevin and Victoria A. Velkoff. 2001. *An Aging World: 2001.* 95/01-1. Washington D.C.: U.S. Census Bureau.

Lederburg, J., R. E. Shope, and S. C. Oaks. 1992. *Emerging Infections: Microbial Threats to Health in the United States.* Washington, D.C.: Institute of Medicine, National Academy Press.

Leung, G. M., P. H. Chung, T. Tsang, W. Lim, S. K. K. Chan, P. Chau, C. A. Donnelly, A. C. Ghani, C. Fraser, S. Riley, N. M. Ferguson, R. M. Anderson, Y. I. Law, T. Mok, T. Ng, A. Fu, P. Y. Leung, J. S. M. Peiris, T. H. Lam, and A. J. Hedley. 2004. "SARS-CoV Antibody Prevalence in All Hong Kong Patient Contacts." *Emerging Infectious Diseases* 10(9): 1653–6.

Lloyd-Smith, James O., Dylan George, Kim M. Pepin, Virginia E. Pitzer, Juliet R. C. Pulliam, Andrew P. Dobson, Peter J. Hudson, and Bryan T. Grenfell. 2009. "Epidemic Dynamics at the Human-Animal Interface." *Science* 326(5958): 1362–7.

Marshall, Bonnie M. and Stuart B. Levy. 2011. "Food Animals and Antimicrobials: Impacts on Human Health." *Clinical Microbiology Reviews* 24(4): 718–33.

McKeown, T. 1988. *The Origins of Human Disease.* Oxford: Basil Blackwell.

Meyer, R. D. 1983. "Legionella Infections – A Review of 5 Years of Research." *Reviews of Infectious Diseases* 5(2): 258–78.

Omran, A. R. 1971. "The Epidemiologic Transition: A Theory of the Epidemiology of Population Change." *Millbank Memorial Fund Quarterly* 49(4): 509–38.

PablosMendez, A., J. Blustein, and C. A. Knirsch. 1997. "The Role of Diabetes Mellitus in the Higher Prevalence of Tuberculosis among Hispanics." *American Journal of Public Health* 87(4): 574–9.

Perez, A., H. S. Brown, and B. I. Restrepo. 2006. "Association between Tuberculosis and Diabetes in the Mexican Border and Non-Border Regions of Texas." *American Journal of Tropical Medicine and Hygiene* 74(4): 604–11.

Preston, Richard. 1994. *The Hot Zone.* New York: Random House.

Riley, J. C. 2005. "The Timing and Pace of Health Transitions around the World." *Population and Development Review* 31(4): 741–64.

Root, H. F. 1934. "The Association of Diabetes and Tuberculosis." *New England Journal of Medicine* 210: 1–13.

Rothan, Hussin A. and Siddappa N. Byrareddy. 2020. "The Epidemiology and Pathogenesis of Coronavirus Disease (COVID-19) Outbreak." *Journal of Autoimmunity* 109: 102433.

Sherertz, R. J., D. R. Reagan, K. D. Hampton, K. L. Robertson, S. A. Streed, H. M. Hoen, R. Thomas, and J. M. Gwaltney. 1996. "A Cloud Adult: The Staphylococcus Aureus – Virus Interaction Revisited." *Annals of Internal Medicine* 124(6): 539–47.

Singer, Merrill. 2010. "Pathogen-Pathogen Interaction: A Syndemic Model of Complex Biosocial Processes in Disease." *Virulence* 1(1): 10–18.

Singer, Merrill and Scott Clair. 2003. "Syndemics and Public Health: Reconceptualizing Disease in Bio-Social Context." *Medical Anthropology Quarterly* 17(4): 423–41.

Song, Zhiqi, Yanfeng Xu, Linlin Bao, Ling Zhang, Yu Pin, Qu Yajin, Hua Zhu, Wenjie Zhao, Yunlin Han, and Chuan Qin. 2019. "From SARS to MERS, Thrusting Coronaviruses into the Spotlight." *Viruses-Basel* 11(1): 59.

Stein, Richard A. 2011. "Super-Spreaders in Infectious Diseases." *International Journal of Infectious Diseases* 15(8): E510–13.

United Nations. 2020. *Policy Brief: The Impact of COVID-19 on Children.*

Weaver, Lesley Jo, Ron Barrett, and Mark Nichter. 2016. "Introduction to Syndemics and Comorbidity." *Medical Anthropology Quarterly* 30(4): 435–41.

WHO (World Health Organization). 2020. Novel Coronavirus (2019-NCoV) Situation Report-1 21 January 2020. Retrieved July 11, 2020. (https://www.who.int/docs/default-source/coronaviruse/situation-reports/20200121-sitrep-1-2019-ncov.pdf?sfvrsn=20a99c10_4).

WHO MERS-CoV Research Group. 2013. "State of Knowledge and Data Gaps of Middle East Respiratory Syndrone Coronavirus." *PLOS Current Outbreaks* 1: 1–36.

Wolfe, N. D., P. Daszak, A. M. Kilpatrick, and D. S. Burke. 2005. "Bushmeat Hunting Deforestation, and Prediction of Zoonoses Emergence." *Emerging Infectious Diseases* 11(12): 1822–7.

Zhu, T., B. T. Korber, A. J. Nahmias, E. Hooper, P. M. Sharp, and D. D. Ho. 1998. "An African HIV-1 Sequence from 1959 and Implications for the Origin of the Epidemic." *Nature* 391(6667): 594–7.

Zumla, Alimuddin, David S. Hui, and Stanley Perlman. 2015. "Middle East Respiratory Syndrome." *Lancet* 386(9997): 995–1007.

22

Beyond the Lost Self

Old Insights and New Horizons in the Sociology of Chronic Illness

Alexandra C. H. Nowakowski

The sociology of chronic illness includes many theories and studies of how persistent health challenges intersect with social life. This subfield has expanded in recent decades. Multiple factors have spurred interest in exploring causes and consequences of chronicity using the sociological imagination. These include the increasing prevalence of common conditions like Type II diabetes and Alzheimer's disease, deepening awareness of the challenges people with chronicity face, expanding innovations in disease management across clinical and community settings, and evolving policy on the public and private insurance coverage of disease management services. Across these diverse areas, an enduring sociological theme persists: chronic illness as constant negotiation of loss of self.

This attention to how the self and the surrounding world interact first drew me to sociological inquiry on chronicity. Having lived my whole life in the spaces between being defined entirely by chronic disease and wanting to define myself beyond my illness, I found both intellectual and emotional resonance with the idea that I could mourn things my disease stole while finding new opportunities in what remained. As I read more sociological literature on chronic illness, I quickly found the framework that would define most of my scholarship: the notion of losing oneself to the ravages of illness, and finding oneself anew in the resulting journey. "Loss of Self: A Fundamental Form of Suffering in the Chronically Ill" (Charmaz 1983) still guides my explorations of both my own and others' data.

Moreover, the evolution of this classic work into nuanced reflections on "Experiencing Chronic Illness" (Charmaz 2000) represents broader shifts in sociology exploring how much illness can evolve across the life course. So it seems fitting that

The Wiley Blackwell Companion to Medical Sociology, First Edition. Edited by William C. Cockerham.

I am taking over for Dr. Kathy Charmaz – whose work inspired my own – in offering an overview of scholarship on chronic illness. My own life illustrates many of the principles Charmaz's work represents. It thus affords me a unique perspective on the history and evolution of chronic illness inquiry. Here I offer a critical review that celebrates past achievements, challenges present beliefs, captures emerging directions, and considers future opportunities.

Evolution of the Field

Discourse on the loss of self inspired broader inquiry about illness and identity in early literature about persistent disease. Foundational scholarship in this area described biographical disruptions (Bury 1982), in which sickness produces feelings of derailment in achieving life goals. This concept translated the classic "sick role" construct, which explored expectations for extrinsic behavior during illness, into reflections on intrinsic biography (Lubkin, Morof, and Larsen 2006). As the sick role model has evolved, so too has inquiry on the social meanings of illness (Cockerham 2014).

Further work on illness and identity explored how a disrupted biography results in perceptions of nothing being normal, and thus adjustment to new concepts of normalcy. This process of illness management became a key model for how people newer to chronicity negotiate transitions in their identities and biographies alike (Charmaz 2000). This work began to intersect with scholarship on adaptive techniques (Cahill and Eggleston 1994) in which people with disabling conditions use strategies to facilitate daily activities. Notions of illness management as conscious work both within and beyond clinical settings appeared across these areas (Corbin and Strauss 1985). These writings offered portraits of adjustment to new illness experiences, and changes that occur in the process.

Understanding how chronicity may produce a loss of self also requires understanding how identities form. Consequently, early advancements in the field involved attention to chronic stress and how its impact on health builds with time. The stress process model (Pearlin 1981) illuminates how challenges in negotiating social expectations can both come from and result in chronic illness. Specific threads in this research included theoretical and mechanical explanations of allostatic load (McEwen and Seeman 1999) and the physical and chemical burden of accumulated stress and weathering (Geronimus 1992) resulting in the gradual erosion of health from allostasis. From these early models, interest grew in the social origins of stressors that can harm health (Turner 2009).

Scholarship on the fundamental social causes of health began to include exploration of illness experiences (Link and Phelan 1995). It gradually shifted away from individual and small group explanations toward structural insights into this variability. Attention to how structural disadvantage and resulting from stress focused increasingly on lifelong processes. Initial scholarship on cumulative advantage and disadvantage (Dannefer 2003) shifted into thinking about cumulative inequality as a whole (Ferraro and Shippee 2009). Research moved away from simpler models into more complex approaches to understanding the development and progression of persistent illness (Freese 2008). Attention increased to genetic origins of chronicity (Clarke et al. 2003) and to the potential social consequences of genetic factors (Davison et al. 1994). Scholarship on chronic illness also began assessing relationships between social, mental, and physical health experiences more creatively. As more social scientists used theory on cumulative inequality, they also developed innovative ways of modeling it.

These innovations included quantitative modeling frameworks like hierarchical linear modeling (Taylor 2008) and structural equation modeling (Taylor and Lynch 2004) demonstrating how different levels of influence can shape trajectories of chronic illness. Likewise, quantitative modeling techniques expanded to address reciprocity between health states and other sociological constructs, and the evolution in these relationships (Dush et al. 2013). Markov or Monte Carlo simulation models (Pudrovska and Anishkin 2015) began to appear in quantitative studies on chronic illness to capture these complexities.

Richer qualitative inquiry on chronicity complemented these quantitative advancements. Patient narratives presented opportunities for analyzing things like critical illness, in which health reaches crisis from unmanaged disease (Rier 2000); and inchoate feelings, in which people sense impending crisis and feel dissonant (Karp 2017). Accounts by scholars who occupied patient roles themselves also outlined the process and challenges of illness management (Bury 2001). These narratives affirmed the value of patient perspectives for health care providers (Littlewood 2003).

Partly because of this emphasis on storytelling, both qualitative and quantitative inquiry on chronicity evolved to include creative data visualizations. Sometimes these were contributed by patients themselves—for example, by drawing feelings about particular events (Cook and Wright 1995). Others were generated by computer modeling programs using parameter estimate data (Hahn et al. 2010). Still others were generated by geospatial analysis programs, resulting in outputs like zip code maps of disease risk (Ory et al. 2013). Additional works bridged geographic coordinates with perceptions of community boundaries to explore chronicity in neighborhood context (Basta et al. 2010). These techniques also stimulated interest in visualizations themselves as sources for data on chronicity. PhotoVoice projects in which patients photographed community health indicators were an early example (Wang and Hannes 2009).

Early efforts to visualize chronic illness and its social contexts made space for previously marginalized voices in scholarship. These usually focused on lower income populations experiencing intersecting structural disadvantages in addition to widespread disease. This work helped sociology shift away from privileged perspectives on chronicity in both academic literature and clinical care. Sociological critiques of public health models like successful aging (Holstein and Minkler 2003) emerged in response to limited understanding of structural inequality in life course scholarship. Progressive illness had rarely appeared in early medical sociology literature, despite offering an ideal way to study changes in health over time. Scholarship by researchers familiar with lifelong disease and its cumulative consequences began to emerge (Nowakowski 2019). These works were increasingly based on the experiences of researchers who were themselves patients (Rier 2010).

Current Landscape

Sociology is presently moving beyond these early accounts from marginalized people. Researchers have long called attention to ageism as both a fundamental cause and social consequence of chronicity (Phelan and Link 2005). Presently the field includes diverse work on getting older with chronic disease. However, many conditions perceived as childhood diseases remain excluded from the literature on aging (Schwaiger 2009). This also illustrates growing sociological understanding that what constitutes successful disease and illness management may differ between people over time (Taylor and Bury 2007).

Sociologists have consequently begun incorporating concepts of person-centered medicine – the idea popularized in the mid-1990s that individuals may have unique care needs (May 2011). Literature on chronic illness management has begun to emphasize goal setting as a specific element of person-centeredness in health care, both generally and specifically for people with persistent conditions (Alexander et al. 2012). Emphasizing patient agency in setting goals and making decisions has brought sociological research opportunities and challenges (Bury 2010).

This increased attention to continuous processes also extends far beyond the specific context of person-centered medicine. Sociologists have begun to understand experiences like addiction and recovery as disease processes rather than purely behavioral matters (Wilson 2007). Literature on eating disorders has followed a similar path (D'Abundo and Chally 2004). More physiological processes have also appeared in chronic disease sociology. Research on chronic inflammation has proliferated, focusing on both origins of inflammation itself (Nowakowski and Sumerau 2015) and its consequences for health (Nowakowski et al. 2016). Likewise, research exploring how genetics predict and shape health over time in response to complex circumstances has expanded. Biopsychosocial data collection and analysis on chronicity has become more common. Panel datasets like the National Social Life, Health, and Aging Project (Waite et al. 2007) and National Health and Aging Trends Survey (Kasper and Freedman 2014) have supported these efforts. These datasets help scientists understand diverse influences on chronicity, including time and place (Mayer 2009).

Concepts of community in chronic disease scholarship have continued to broaden. Research on neighborhoods and health has grown, showing how community intersects with chronicity (Duncan and Kawachi 2018). Analyses by Census tract and zip code continue to appear, as do studies requiring people to define neighborhood boundaries themselves (Diez Roux 2004). Other approaches to understanding chronicity in neighborhood context have also developed. These include attention to food service areas (Kwate 2008) and how community foodways may prevent or exacerbate disease symptoms (Burdette and Hill 2008). Research in school settings has also increased, whether for community K-12 schools or higher education institutions (Williams 2000). Across these contexts, inquiry on conditions like asthma and diabetes has called attention to rarer diseases (Browning and Cagney 2002).

Current illness literature also addresses intersections between community and family. Several studies take whole family approaches to engagement (Ross and Mirowsky 2001). This work looks at experiences and perspectives of multiple generations in understanding community patterns of chronicity (Hill et al. 2005). Family activities

– like childbearing, adopting, parenting, grandparenting, and fostering – increasingly appear in sociological studies of chronic illness (Bruhn and Rebach 2014). Caregiving and caregiver burden were early focus areas. Studies about care work inspired broad thinking about these roles – and how they can be reciprocal rather than one-way (Nowakowski and Sumerau 2017a). Sociology now includes more diverse perspectives on how people with chronicity live and behave (Pierret 2003).

Critical thinking about illness itself has also increased. Scholars now question what it means to be sick (Aujoulat et al. 2008) and think about how sickness and wellness can coexist. Some of my own work reflects on these themes (Nowakowski 2016a). I and others have used autoethnography to contribute novel insights on chronic illness. Such approaches include attention to daily ups and downs of living with chronicity (Nowakowski 2016b). This work has reframed illness management as a lifelong process rather than a brief adjustment. Invisible illness also features in autoethnography on chronicity (Thomas 2007). Populations previously treated as invisible by scholars have also become a focus (Aspinall 2001).

Recent chronicity research also pays more intersectional attention to social justice issues. Invisible illnesses with social origins have facilitated these changes. Research on Alzheimer's and other dementias – conditions often made worse by social isolation and marginalization – has become common. Broader inquiry on discrimination stress and its consequences has continued to expand. Likewise, greater attention has been paid to chronicity at the end of life. This includes death and dying as a general phenomenon (Seale 1998). It also includes specific processes by which people enter progressive decline (Hebert and Schulz 2006), the mechanisms through which they receive care (Exley and Allen 2007), and their experiences along the way (McPherson et al. 2007). Premature death and lifelong disability from chronic ailments resulting from violence have also gained attention (Williams 2004).

Sociologists have begun to explore chronicity resulting from structural and individual violence alike. Police violence, both generally and specifically in Black communities, has emerged in life course scholarship (Collins 2009). Studies address not only experiences of Black victims of police brutality, but also those of families and friends from multiple generations (Sewell 2017). Likewise, sociologists have explored chronic health challenges faced by sexual abuse survivors. These outcomes include both persistent mental health conditions like generalized anxiety and post-traumatic stress disorder (Taylor and Jason 2002) and chronic physical ones like autoimmune disease and constant pain (Radomsky 2014). Domestic violence beyond sexual abuse has also gained focus in social epidemiology of chronic illness. This literature includes emotional forms of violence as well as purely physical ones (Willis and Elmer 2007).

Sociological literature now addresses chronic health consequences from many types of violence. Social violence against fat people has been explored in detail (Lupton 2018). Yet less attention has gone to other non-physical violence that produces chronic health consequences for heavier individuals (Thille 2019). Medicalization of fatness itself now receives increased attention (Saguy and Almeling 2008). Likewise, research now includes environmental forms of violence and their lasting consequences. Fat studies literature has inspired this work by showing how environmental injustice can fundamentally cause health outcomes previously associated with fatness itself (Moffat 2010).

Scholars have also explored social origins of chronic outcomes in communities like Flint, Michigan (Miller and Wesley 2016) and the Standing Rock tribal reservation in North Dakota (Carter and Kruzic 2017). Both communities experience frequent illness from ongoing environmental abuses, including poisoned water. Like communities impacted by other forms of violence, indigenous peoples have formed social movements in response to these shared traumas (Gilio-Whitaker 2019). The #NoDAPL, #MeToo, and #BlackLivesMatter movements have all addressed chronicity stemming from constant structural and individual violence (Brown et al. 2017). These activist traditions have increasingly appeared in sociological scholarship on chronic illness.

Patient activism and advocacy have also inspired scientists to ask new questions about illness. Health social movements (Brown et al. 2010) have appeared frequently in research. These movements and the ways social scientists study them have become increasingly intersectional. Examples include increased attention to broader LGBTQIA + community experiences, and more nuanced inquiry on how lesbian/gay/bisexual and trans/nonbinary experiences may converge and diverge (Fish 2008). Research with queer and trans populations also illustrates greater attention to cultural and linguistic competency in disease management (Fredriksen-Goldsen et al. 2014). Present approaches to this topic go beyond stereotypical notions of what these terms mean (Wilkinson 2015). Yet likewise, research on chronicity in both foreign born and second language populations has expanded (Yee, Marshall, and Vo 2007). Migrant health has become a focus, as has the stressful life of undocumented residents (Kahn et al. 2017).

These topics have also fostered research on policies for accommodating people with chronic diseases (Quadagno 2010). The Affordable Care Act (ACA) of 2010 – and subsequent attempts to dismantle it – has featured prominently in sociological scholarship on policy approaches to chronic disease (Lanford and Quadagno 2016). Experiences of foreign born individuals with chronic conditions have drawn attention to injustice in health care access and outcomes (Williams and Sternthal 2010). Likewise, attention to lifelong diseases and childhood chronicity has grown in response to the preexisting conditions mandate in ACA (Carlson et al. 2014). Sociologists now explore what being left out of health policy means for everyday life with chronicity, in addition to continuing research on early mortality.

Emerging Areas

Notions of labeling also characterize several emerging areas in chronic disease sociology. Debate over coverage for preexisting conditions in ACA has stimulated interest in how people become labeled as sick (Vargas 2016). This process involves both formal and informal activities. Formally, sociology of diagnosis explores how people receive condition labels that at once establish and transform identity (Jutel 2009). Informally, patient experience literature – including a dedicated interdisciplinary journal – describes long and complex journeys to diagnosis (Nettleton 2006). Literature on contested illness has grown in both of these areas (McGann et al. 2011). Sociologists now describe how diagnosis and treatment often prove difficult for people with contested conditions (Fair 2010). This material also shows how contested conditions and patients who have them often remain marginalized even after diagnosis (Moore 2014).

Newer research includes illness experiences of populations with otherwise contested and marginalized identities (Swoboda 2006). Literature on chronic illness among queer, trans, and intersex people is now available (Witten 2004). These studies offer snapshots of community experiences, and some describe illness across the whole life course (Witten 2014). Panel studies like Aging with Pride (Fredriksen-Goldsen et al. 2015) provide rich data on chronic illness as people age. These datasets show how identity and health can influence each other (Wentling et al. 2008). Intersex and nonbinary experience are also starting to appear in research, as are bisexuality and asexuality. Panel datasets with detailed information about identity also demonstrate intersectionality in life course minority health (Richardson and Brown 2016). These data highlight queer, trans, and intersex voices along with other marginalizing experiences like disability (Warner and Brown 2011).

Research increasingly describes how disability develops and progresses in marginalized people with chronic conditions (Brown et al. 2016). Likewise, scholars continue to explore how disability is similar to and different from functional limitation (Grönvik 2009). As new approaches for managing some conditions involving physical and cognitive functioning changes become available (Putnam 2002), this literature may keep growing. Therapies like stem cell transplants, laboratory grown organs, prenatal surgeries for birth differences, and implantable mechanical organs have already begun shaping dialogue on functional limitation (Howe 2011). People with conditions like spina bifida, a birth difference in which the spinal column does not close fully during development, may experience life differently than their predecessors (Waggoner 2013). These changes may result from early clinical services, social responses to those interventions, and treatment outcomes alike (Brown et al. 2011).

Generational patterns in illness have also begun to appear in research. Recent literature addresses how different generations are living with chronicity (Warren-Findlow et al. 2010) and how socially linked conditions may be passed down from one generation to another (Wickrama, Conger, and Todd Abraham 2005). Existing generational research addresses Type 2 diabetes, tobacco associated conditions, and other health experiences that have behavioral components (Bowers and Yehuda 2016). However, sociologists have illustrated that behavioral risk factors often result from fundamental social causes (Phelan et al. 2010). This literature also describes connections between social and behavioral factors in causing and managing chronicity. Additionally, studies of generational patterns increasing describe illness management as a lifelong process that never stops evolving (Willson et al. 2007).

Newer literature on chronicity also deals with multiple generations within families and communities; other work examines relationships themselves within and across generations. Reciprocal illness management in life partnerships represents an emerging focus (Nowakowski and Sumerau 2017b). Some research looks at caregiver support and mutual caregiving. This work includes a variety of caregivers – not only partners, but also children, parents, friends, colleagues, neighbors, community members, and specialized professionals (Drentea 2007). The social and behavioral normalcy of caregiving has become a major theme.

Normalizing things previously considered deviant has become an important pattern in chronic illness sociology. The classic medicalization concept describes how health experiences are defined as medical conditions and thereby subjected to medical authority (Conrad 1992). This model has dominated over the past three decades. Demedicalization, wherein medical authority cedes control over specific health related experiences, has now begun to gain prominence (Adler and Adler 2007). Characteristics like autism, blindness, intersex physiognomy, dwarfism, fatness, and queer sexuality are increasingly contested as medical conditions. Multiple rounds of demedicalization and remedicalization can occur, framing things once again as diseases (Conrad and Angell 2004). Patient advocates have long recommended viewing such characteristics simply as life experiences that may or may not produce particular health needs.

Thinking critically about what should be considered a disease demands attention to detail in research. Although characteristics like deafness and tallness may involve no health concerns whatsoever, these experiences may also result from underlying diseases or related interventions. An intersex person may undergo hysterectomy because of chronic bleeding and pain from endometriosis, an autoimmune disease where uterine lining invades other tissues. People can develop endometriosis whether or not they are intersex (Labuski 2015). Being very tall may or may not relate to living with Marfan syndrome, a connective tissue condition often causing tall stature (Heath 2007). Newer research addresses subtleties in how health experiences can impact both appearance and identity (Jones 2020).

Studies of marginalized groups are also inspiring creativity in life course research. Newer approaches to studying chronicity include collaborative autoethnography, biomonitoring with enrichment interviews, clinical encounter observation, relationship partner surveys, and electronic medical records review (Carpiano 2009). These techniques also offer new ways to frame and organize scholarship. Options for studying persistent illness now include arts based research, community based research, and trauma informed research (Hesse-Biber and Leavy 2010).

Trauma has gained much attention in research on illness. This focus area presently includes inquiry on mass trauma, like the September 11 World Trade Center and Pentagon bombings, and its diverse health consequences over time. Early findings from these disasters include numerous conditions, from obstructive pulmonary diseases to post-traumatic stress disorder to oral cancers (Adams et al. 2006). Other research describes military and campus sexual trauma as origins of post-traumatic stress and associated conditions like autoimmunity (Chivers-Wilson 2006). Work on sexual health includes attention to abuse of people whose conditions impact genital functioning and/or arousal patterns (Lindsey 2015).

Sometimes chronic conditions themselves can also cause trauma. Diseases causing significant suffering and/or early mortality can do so even with good medical management. Yet more diseases are shifting from terminal to chronic, changing the meaning of living with lifelong illness (Sanderson et al. 2011). HIV is a good example in the US – among those with access to health insurance and advanced therapies (Baumgartner 2007). Conditions like sickle cell disease (SCD) and cystic fibrosis (CF) are also beginning to follow that path (Duggleby et al. 2010). In SCD, red blood cells form in crescent shapes and stick together. In CF, mucus becomes sticky like rubber cement and harbors infection. Writing this chapter seems fitting because I am living its content. I do not have SCD, but I do have CF.

I thus have vast experience with another research area: patient navigation for chronic care. I often help CF patients and their families find and use available resources to manage the condition. Sometimes this involves helping people identify appropriate clinicians, or discuss newer therapies. Other times it means counseling patients who feel overwhelmed and afraid, or who deal with multiple traumas like transphobia and poverty.

Patient navigation research involves a variety of identity and selfhood issues. Work on CF often addresses organ transplantation – particularly the lungs but also other affected organs including the heart, liver, and kidneys (Lowton 2003). CF patients with transplants often describe ambiguity in thinking about self and connecting with others. Recipients of double lung transplants, for example, still have CF but often experience different pulmonary issues. These changes in how people experience illness are not at all unique to CF.

Sometimes a transplant also cures an underlying condition entirely. When my father got a new liver, it cured the problem that made him sick. My father's rapid adjustment to living with idiopathic nonalcoholic cirrhosis – massive liver damage from unknown causes – ended after only six weeks on the transplant list. In the months before his transplant, my father and I had briefly crossed paths in the land of fatal progressive disease. I simultaneously treasure that kinship and feel glad it ended. Moreover, I value what my family learned about teamwork and its value for illness management.

I thus see how teamwork matters for chronic disease sociology. This includes both teamwork in health care and teamwork in research itself (Stuckler and Siegel 2011). Both health care and social research are exploring how team medicine can help people with chronic conditions achieve goals in ways that feel right for their circumstances. Work on team science also explores how collaboration can improve disease prevention and management (Kitto et al. 2011). Sociological journals are publishing interdisciplinary team science, just as interdisciplinary journals are publishing sociological work on chronicity. I and others who occupy the dual roles of patient and scientist often reflect on the value of patient science and leadership in research.

Future Directions

Team science is becoming a focus area in chronic disease sociology. It also invites rethinking teamwork itself in sociomedical research. As patient narratives appear more in academic literature, and patients find ourselves also becoming scientists, researchers can view teamwork as a way to include voices that offer different perspectives. This framing can include classic medical sociology themes: interface between illness and identity, and how these patterns shape social responses to chronic disease.

New research questions in illness and identity are also possible. Face transplants, a novel approach to managing chronic consequences from serious injuries or aggressive cancers, can show how body changes impact sense of self (Shilling 2007).

Certainly other body parts contribute to identity as well, and thus require identity work when transplanted (Nowakowski and Sumerau 2018). Yet face transplants introduce some unique cognitive and social experiences. Sociology offers multiple frameworks for understanding these transitions in personal biography and social interaction.

Reproductive organ transplants can be another focus area in chronic disease research. Conditions treatable with transplants may include endometriosis, polycystic ovary syndrome, uterine fibroids, vascular dysfunction, and various types of cancers (Nettleton 2010). Transplants may also help transsex and intersex people with particular life goals like pregnancy (Ettorre 2016 and may pose persistent health implications related to organ rejection. Literature on assisted reproduction has only recently included trans and intersex people and chronic conditions that may be more common in these groups (Lampe et al. 2019). Likewise, scholars have only begun to explore organ transplants as a way for people to have children. Research can show how transplants may create more options for people with chronic diseases.

Conditions leading to transplant also need more research. Medicinal and recreational cannabis research has begun to address how people experience and treat painful chronic conditions (Weiss and Lonnquist 2017). Research on clinical and community uses of cannabis in disease management should also explore related social justice issues and their consequences (Pedersen and Sandberg 2013). Medicinal cannabis may help society move away from mass imprisonment and the mental and behavioral health problems it causes (O'Brien 2013).

Gun violence is another important area related to drugs, prisons, and chronic disease. Sociology should address topics like chronic fear and its impact on health. This includes conditions resulting from perpetual fear, both broadly and more specifically for people of color impacted by multiple injustices (Lankford 2016). School health and its long term consequences are another way to study gun violence and chronic disease (Muschert 2007). Overall, there are many opportunities to explore how social justice issues and chronic health conditions influence one another over time (Turner 2005).

Social justice movements themselves have also created new options for research on chronic disease. Health care choices for sex and gender minority patients have diversified as community visibility has increased (Johnson 2015). People of all ages can access sophisticated hormonal regimens and surgical techniques more easily (Mayer et al. 2014). Such access requires financial resources, and is therefore a social justice issue (Geist et al. 2017). And even with access to quality care, people may experience unexpected health impacts from taking hormones or having surgery. Likewise, barriers to gender affirming care may have harmful consequences (Johnson 2019).

Puberty blockers, an increasingly common approach to helping trans and nonbinary youth be well during adulthood, offer an exciting chance to study life course health. Sociologists should study direct health consequences of puberty suppression treatment, including both harmful and helpful impacts (Roberts and Cronshaw 2017). Researchers should also investigate how these therapies may prevent problems that trans and nonbinary people might otherwise develop (Wolfe 2018). These may include conditions related to chronic social and cognitive stress, like metabolic syndrome and various dementias.

Likewise, as nonconsensual surgeries performed on intersex youth become less common thanks to advocacy efforts and policy changes (Davis 2015), sociologists should explore how simply letting bodies be can prevent harm. The experiences of both intersex and endosex individuals who embrace their birth anatomy and those who choose to alter it later should be compared (Davis and Evans 2018). The lives of intersex people with various health conditions and experiences of marginalization should be thoroughly described (Lucal 2008). Sociologists should likewise continue investigating how genetics impact the origins and outcomes of different physical and chemical characteristics leading people to identify as intersex (Monro 2010), and how these shape health over time.

Social researchers should also explore new genetic approaches to preventing and managing disease. Gene editing technologies like CRISPR pose questions about the nature of disease and what actually makes us who we are (Wainwright et al. 2009). Illness and identity literature should expand to cover scenarios like being conceived with the genetics for a particular condition (Petersen 2006), but avoiding the disease because of gene editing. Life course health outcomes from gene editing may shape the social meaning of living with chronic disease.

Therapies targeting products rather than encoding of genes should also be studied. Current genetic therapies address the more distant consequences of gene encoding (Duster 2001). They usually target the composition and/or functioning of proteins coded by specific genetic material. Research on CF illustrates how gene classification and associated therapeutic approaches is shaping social understanding of specific diseases (Hedgecoe 2003). This work also shows how genetic therapies may impact social life and its perceived value – especially with questions of "whose deaths matter" (Armstrong et al. 2006).

While I was drafting this chapter, the triple combination CF protein modulator therapy Trikafta got regulatory approval. Indeed, modulators for proteins and genes that control their production are becoming available. As new therapies for chronic conditions are developed, the social meanings of progressive diseases may shift. Researchers interested in geneticization and its relationship to disease outcomes should study these changes. There will also be opportunities to study patients who get left behind. Trikafta may help some 90% of CF patients worldwide. My specific genetic mutations place me in other 10%.

Whether this "leaves me out" is a fascinating sociological question. Currently I cannot access modulator therapies. However, because of how my disease progressed before these drugs were available, I might find more harm than benefit in taking modulators anyway. The available modulator that might work for me (Kalydeco) is already known to stress the kidneys. Because I have chronic CF kidney disease, my providers and I doubt Kalydeco would do more harm than good unless my lungs got much worse. So although I cannot take modulators, I cherish the benefits I derive from my current care. I would rather keep my original kidneys and deal with more challenges in lung health as I age.

That said, I can make these choices because of several types of privilege. Having options to voice treatment preferences, see providers honor those preferences, and pay for the care I get are privileges few chronic disease patients have in the US (Prior 2003). Sociologists should gather data from people with chronic diseases who remain excluded from health care in various ways (Reid 2017). Likewise, the experiences of people previously not represented in research on lifelong disease should be explored (Thomas 2010). A variety of communities need more attention in future research.

Immigrant and foreign born populations with chronic conditions should be a focus. The unmet medical needs of people born outside the US have recently gotten media exposure. People are being deported because of reversals in health care exceptions to immigration law for migrants with complex diseases (Hacker et al. 2011). This has introduced new hardships for deeply marginalized families (Portes et al. 2012). Research on how immigration policy and outcomes shape families' ability to cope with chronic illness is much needed.

Family dynamics beyond immigration also invite novel inquiry on chronicity trajectories. Polyamorous families represent one possible thread. Historically, literature on chronic disease management within intimate relationships has focused on relationship partners who only have romantic and sexual intimacy with one another. Yet current data suggest that polyamory appears at least as commonly among people living with chronic conditions as it does in the general US population (Iantaffi 2010). Poly dynamics also intersect with other nuances in family composition like the phenomenon of "chosen family" in queer and trans community (Bigner 2013). These intersections of social location related to sexualities and congruent identities inspire innovation in chronic disease inquiry.

Likewise, stories are emerging in popular media about how sex and gender identity can evolve over time and impact chronic care needs. Examples include how using hormone replacement therapy may interact with medication regimens for certain chronic conditions (Braun et al. 2017). People receiving organ transplants as part of general chronic disease care may also need to adjust their hormone therapy to avoid complications (Hoch et al. 2016). These experiences should be studied across the whole lifespan. Researchers should examine how balancing transition-related care and other health needs impacts both personal development and family relationships as people age.

The life course idea itself should also be explored more. Although human life expectancy has been fairly consistent between generations in many industrialized societies, people with progressive diseases are living longer thanks to medical advancements (Settersten and Angel 2011). Scholars now describe conditions once considered to be pediatric or otherwise terminal using different vocabulary (Thorne et al. 2002). I see this happening firsthand within the CF community, and observe it secondhand for other conditions. So I see how concepts of inclusion and exclusion in aging have gained new meaning. These changes come from people with progressive diseases reaching older ages, and health care that helps them do so (Higgs et al. 2003). Clinical trials and related research thus offer unique opportunities for sociomedical research on living and aging with chronicity.

Likewise, broader health technology advancements are a good area to study. Mobile technologies are helping people with chronic conditions connect with one another (Locker 2008). This is invaluable for CF patients because cross-infection concerns limit our ability to interact directly (Lowton and Gabe 2003). Smartphone apps and advocacy websites help us access and use resources for self-care (Kanter et al. 2019). Online resources allow aging patients to get multiple kinds of support simultaneously (Porter et al. 2019). They have also increased options for working and earning money for people with functional limitations and/or frequent hospitalizations (Edwards and Boxall 2010. Yet these technologies are also changing demands on time and expectations of ability (Harries et al. 2019). Sociologists should explore how the benefits and drawbacks of mobile technologies impact people with chronic diseases.

Finally, these recommendations show how chronicity – whether progressive or not – includes diverse health experiences and care needs. Chronic conditions evolve over time just as people do, which can bring unexpected challenges along with surprising opportunities (Bury 2013). This adjustment process often involves renegotiating our very sense of self (Charmaz 2019). We may do this in different ways, like getting tattoos (Koller and Bullo 2019) or playing sports (Atkinson 2019). But the changing and often unpredictable experience of aging with chronic illness generally causes feelings of losing old selves and gaining new ones (Franklin et al. 2019).

As a child being tested for CF, I would never have predicted that the disease my family so feared would one day inspire my most important social connections and impacts. In losing myself as healthy in the eyes of others (Kirk and Hinton 2019), I have found the most important aspects of who I am and what I contribute. I have also come to understand what being healthy means contextually as someone aging with a progressive condition. So the "illness transformations" concept I and colleagues have described should remain a focus in chronic disease sociology (Nowakowski and Sumerau 2019).

References

Adams, Richard E., Joseph A. Boscarino, and Sandro Galea. 2006. "Social and Psychological Resources and Health Outcomes after the World Trade Center Disaster." *Social Science & Medicine* 62(1): 176–188.

Adler, Patricia A. and Peter Adler. 2007. "The Demedicalization of Self-Injury: From Psychopathology to Sociological Deviance." *Journal of Contemporary Ethnography* 36(5): 537–570.

Alexander, Jeffrey A., Larry R. Hearld, Jessica N. Mittler, and Jillian Harvey. 2012. "Patient–Physician Role Relationships and Patient Activation among Individuals with Chronic Illness." *Health Services Research* 47(3pt1): 1201–1223.

Armstrong, Elizabeth M., Daniel P. Carpenter, and Marie Hojnacki. 2006. "Whose Deaths Matter? Mortality, Advocacy, and Attention to Disease in the Mass Media." *Journal of Health Politics, Policy and Law* 31(4): 729–772.

Aspinall, Peter J. 2001. "Operationalising the Collection of Ethnicity Data in Studies of the Sociology of Health and Illness." *Sociology of Health & Illness* 23(6): 829–862.

Atkinson, Michael (ed.). 2019. *Sport, Mental Illness and Sociology*, Vol. 11. Bingley: Emerald Publishing.

Aujoulat, Isabelle, Renzo Marcolongo, Leopoldo Bonadiman, and Alain Deccache. 2008. "Reconsidering Patient Empowerment in Cronic Illness: A Critique of Models of Self-Efficacy and Bodily Control." *Social Science & Medicine* 66(5): 1228–1239.

Basta, Luke A., Therese S. Richmond, and Douglas J. Wiebe. 2010. "Neighborhoods, Daily Activities, and Measuring Health Risks Experienced in Urban Environments." *Social Science & Medicine* 71(11): 1943–1950.

Baumgartner, Lisa M. 2007. "The Incorporation of the HIV/AIDS Identity into the Self over Time." *Qualitative Health Research* 17(7): 919–931.

Bigner, Jerry J. 2013. *An Introduction to GLBT Family Studies*. New York: Routledge.

Bowers, Mallory E. and Rachel Yehuda. 2016. "Intergenerational Transmission of Stress in Humans." *Neuropsychopharmacology* 41(1): 232.

Braun, Hannan M., Jury Candelario, Courtney L. Hanlon, Eddy R. Segura, Jesse L. Clark, Judith S. Currier, and Jordan E. Lake. 2017. "Transgender Women Living with HIV Frequently Take Antiretroviral Therapy and/or Feminizing Hormone Therapy Differently than Prescribed Due to Drug–Drug Interaction Concerns." *LGBT Health* 4(5): 371–375.

Brown, Melissa, Rashawn Ray, Ed Summers, and Neil Fraistat. 2017. "#sayhername: A Case Study of Intersectional Social Media Activism." *Ethnic and Racial Studies* 40(11): 1831–1846.

Brown, Phil, Crystal Adams, Rachel Morello-Frosch, Laura Senier, and Ruth Simpson. 2010. "Health Social Movements." Pp. 380–394 in *Handbook of Medical Sociology*, edited by Chole Bird, Peter Conrad, Alan Fremont, and Stefan Timmermans, 6th ed. Nashville, TN: Vanderbilt University Press.

Brown, Phil, Rachel Morello-Frosch, Stephen Zavestoski, Laura Senier, Rebecca Gasior Altman, Elizabeth Hoover, Sabrina McCormick, Brian Mayer, and Crystal Adams. 2011. "Health Social Movements: Advancing Traditional Medical Sociology Concepts." Pp. 117–137 in *Handbook of the Sociology of Health, Illness, and Healing*, edited by Bernice Pescosolido, Jack Martin, Jane McLeod, and Anne Rogers. New York: Springer.

Brown, Tyson H., Liana J. Richardson, Taylor W. Hargrove, and Courtney S. Thomas. 2016. "Using Multiple-Hierarchy Stratification and Life Course Approaches to Understand Health Inequalities: The Intersecting Consequences of Race, Gender, SES, and Age." *Journal of Health and Social Behavior* 57(2): 200–222.

Browning, Christopher R. and Kathleen A. Cagney. 2002. "Neighborhood Structural Disadvantage, Collective Efficacy, and Self-Rated Physical Health in an Urban Setting." *Journal of Health and Social Behavior* 43(4): 383–399.

Bruhn, John G. and Howard M. Rebach. 2014. *The Sociology of Caregiving*. New York: Springer.

Burdette, Amy M. and Terrence D. Hill. 2008. "An Examination of Processes Linking Perceived Neighborhood Disorder and Obesity." *Social Science & Medicine* 67(1): 38–46.

Bury, Michael. 1982. "Chronic Illness as Biographical Disruption." *Sociology of Health & Illness* 4(2): 167–182.

Bury, Michael. 2001. "Illness Narratives: Fact or Fiction?" *Sociology of Health & Illness* 23(3): 263–285.

Bury, Michael. 2010. "Chronic Illness, Self-Management and the Rhetoric of Empowerment." Pp. 161–179 in *New Directions in the Sociology of Chronic and Disabling Conditions*, edited by G. Scambler. London: Palgrave Macmillan.

Bury, Michael. 2013. *Health and Illness in a Changing Society*, Vol. 2. London: Routledge.

Cahill, Spencer E. and Robin Eggleston. 1994. "Managing Emotions in Public: The Case of Wheelchair Users." *Social Psychology Quarterly* 300–312.

Carlson, Daniel L., Ben Lennox Kail, Jamie L. Lynch, and Marlaina Dreher. 2014. "The Affordable Care Act, Dependent Health Insurance Coverage, and Young Adults' Health." *Sociological Inquiry* 84(2): 191–209.

Carpiano, Richard M. 2009. "Come Take a Walk with Me: The "Go-along" Interview as a Novel Method for Studying the Implications of Place for Health and Well-Being." *Health & Place* 15(1): 263–272.

Carter, Angie and Ahna Kruzic. 2017. "Centering the Commons, Creating Space for the Collective: Ecofeminist# NoDAPL Praxis in Iowa." *Journal of Social Justice* 7: 1–22.

Charmaz, Kathy. 1983. "Loss of Self: A Fundamental Form of Suffering in the Chronically Ill." *Sociology of Health & Illness* 5(2): 68–195.

Charmaz, Kathy. 2000. "Experiencing Chronic Illness." Pp. 277–292 in *Handbook of Social Studies in Health and Medicine*, edited by Gary L. Albrecht, Ray Fitzpatrick, and Susan C Scrimshaw. Thousand Oaks, CA: Sage.

Charmaz, Kathy. 2019. "Experiencing Stigma and Exclusion: The Influence of Neoliberal Perspectives, Practices, and Policies on Living with Chronic Illness and Disability." *Symbolic Interaction* 43(1): 20–45.

Chivers-Wilson, Kaitlin A. 2006. "Sexual Assault and Posttraumatic Stress Disorder: A Review of the Biological, Psychological and Sociological Factors and Treatments." *McGill Journal of Medicine* 9(2): 111–118.

Clarke, Adele E., Janet K. Shim, Laura Mamo, Jennifer Ruth Fosket, and Jennifer R. Fishman. 2003. "Biomedicalization: Technoscientific Transformations of Health, Illness, and US Biomedicine." *American Sociological Review* 68(2): 161–194.

Cockerham, William C. 2014. "Sick Role." Pp. 2118–2124 in *The Wiley Blackwell Encyclopedia of Health, Illness, Behavior, and Society*, edited by William C. Cockerham, Robert Dingwall, and Stella R. Quah. Hoboken, NJ: Wiley.

Collins, Randall. 2009. *Violence: A Micro-Sociological Theory*. Princeton, NJ: Princeton University Press.

Conrad, Peter. 1992. "Medicalization and Social Control." *Annual Review of Sociology* 18(1): 209–232.

Conrad, Peter and Alison Angell. 2004. "Homosexuality and Remedicalization." *Society* 41(5): 32–39.

Cook, Judith A. and Eric R. Wright. 1995. "Medical Sociology and the Study of Severe Mental Illness: Reflections on past Accomplishments and Directions for Future Research." *Journal of Health and Social Behavior* 35(extra issue): 95–114.

Corbin, Juliet and Anselm Strauss. 1985. "Managing Chronic Illness at Home: Three Lines of Work." *Qualitative Sociology* 8(3): 224–247.

D'Abundo, Michelle and Pamela Chally. 2004. "Struggling with Recovery: Participant Perspectives on Battling an Eating Disorder." *Qualitative Health Research* 14(8): 1094–1106.

Dannefer, Dale. 2003. "Cumulative Advantage/Disadvantage and the Life Course: Cross-Fertilizing Age and Social Science Theory." *The Journals of Gerontology Series B: Psychological Sciences and Social Sciences* 58(6): S327–S337.

Davis, Georgiann. 2015. *Contesting Intersex: The Dubious Diagnosis*. New York: New York University Press.

Davis, Georgiann and Maddie Jo Evans. 2018. "Surgically Shaping Sex: A Gender Structure Analysis of the Violation of Intersex People's Human Rights." Pp. 273–284. in *Handbook of the Sociology of Gender*, edited by Barbara Risman, Carissa Froyum, and William J. Scarborough. New York: Springer.

Davison, Charlie, Sally Macintyre, and George Davey Smith. 1994. "The Potential Social Impact of Predictive Genetic Testing for Susceptibility to Cmmon Chronic Diseases: A Review and Proposed Research Agenda." *Sociology of Health & Illness* 16(3): 340–371.

Diez Roux, Ana V. 2004. "Estimating the Neighborhood Health Effects: The Challenges of Casual Inference in a Complex World." *Social Science & Medicine* 58(10): 1953–1960.

Drentea, Patricia. 2007. "Caregiving." Pp. 401–402 in *The Blackwell Encyclopedia of Sociology*, edited by J. George Ritzer, Michael Ryan, and Betsy Thorn. Malden, MA: Blackwell.

Duggleby, Wendy, Lorraine Holtslander, Jari Kylma, Vicky Duncan, Chad Hammond, and Allison Williams. 2010. "Metasynthesis of the Hope Experience of Family Caregivers of Persons with Chronic Illness." *Qualitative Health Research* 20(2): 148–158.

Duncan, Dustin T. and Ichiro Kawachi (eds.). 2018. *Neighborhoods and Health.* New York: Oxford University Press.

Dush, Claire M. Kamp, Kammi K. Schmeer, and Miles Taylor. 2013. "Chaos as a Social Determinant of Child Health: Reciprocal Associations?" *Social Science & Medicine* 95: 69–76.

Duster, Troy. 2001. "The Sociology of Science and the Revolution in Molecular Biology." Pp. 213–226 in *The Blackwell Companion to Sociology*, edited by Judith R. Blau. Oxford: Blackwell Publishing.

Edwards, Jill and Kathy Boxall. 2010. "Adults with Cystic Fibrosis and Barriers to Employment." *Disability & Society* 25(4): 441–453.

Ettorre, Elizabeth (ed.). 2016. *Culture, Bodies and the Sociology of Health.* New York: Routledge.

Exley, Catherine and Davina Allen. 2007. "A Critical Examination of Home Care: End of Life Care as an Illustrative Case." *Social Science & Medicine* 65(11): 2317–2327.

Fair, Brian. 2010. "Morgellons: Contested Illness, Diagnostic Compromise and Medicalisation." *Sociology of Health & Illness* 32(4): 597–612.

Ferraro, Kenneth F. and Tetyana Pylypiv Shippee. 2009. "Aging and Cumulative Inequality: How Does Inequality Get under the Skin?" *The Gerontologist* 49(3): 333–343.

Fish, Julie. 2008. "Navigating Queer Street: Researching the Intersections of Lesbian, Gay, Bisexual and Trans (LGBT) Identities in Health Research." *Sociological Research Online* 13(1): 1–12.

Franklin, Marika, Sophie Lewis, Karen Willis, Anne Rogers, Annie Venville, and Lorraine Smith. 2019. "Goals for Living with a Chronic Condition: The Relevance of Temporalities, Dispositions, and Resources." *Social Science & Medicine* 233: 13–20.

Fredriksen-Goldsen, Karen I., Charles P. Hoy-Ellis, Charles A. Emlet Jayn Goldsen, and Nancy R. Hooyman. 2014. "Creating a Vision for the Future: Key Competencies and Strategies for Culturally Competent Practice with Lesbian, Gay, Bisexual, and Transgender (LGBT) Older Adults in the Health and Human Services." *Journal of Gerontological Social Work* 57(2-4): 80–107.

Fredriksen-Goldsen, Karen I., Charles P. Hoy-Ellis, Anna Muraco, Jayn Goldsen, and Hyun-Jun Kim. 2015. "The Health and Well-Being of LGBT Older Adults: Disparities, Risks, and Resilience across the Life Course." Pp. 25–53 in *The Lives of LGBT Older Adults: Understanding Challenges and Resilience*, edited by Nancy A. Orel and Christine A. Fruhauf. Washington, DC: American Psychological Association.

Freese, Jeremy. 2008. "Genetics and the Social Science Explanation of Individual Outcomes." *American Journal of Sociology* 114(S1): S1–S35.

Geist, Claudia, Megan M. Reynolds, and Marie S. Gaytán. 2017. "Unfinished Business: Disentangling Sex, Gender, and Sexuality in Sociological Research on Gender Stratification." *Sociology Compass* 11(4): e12470.

Geronimus, Arline T. 1992. "The Weathering Hypothesis and the Health of African-American Women and Infants: Evidence and Speculations." *Ethnicity & Disease* 2(3): 207–221.

Gilio-Whitaker, Dina. 2019. *As Long as Grass Grows: The Indigenous Fight for Environmental Justice, from Colonization to Standing Rock*. Boston, MA: Beacon Press.

Grönvik, Lars. 2009. "Defining Disability: Effects of Disability Concepts on Research Outcomes." *International Journal of Social Research Methodology* 12(1): 1–18.

Hacker, Karen, Jocelyn Chu, Carolyn Leung, Robert Marra, Alex Pirie, Mohamed Brahimi, Margaret English, Joshua Beckmann, Dolores Acevedo-Garcia, and Robert P. Marlin. 2011. "The Impact of Immigration and Customs Enforcement on Immigrant Health: Perceptions of Immigrants in Everett, Massachusetts, USA." *Social Science & Medicine* 73(4): 586–594.

Hahn, Elizabeth A., David Cella, Rita K. Bode, and Rachel T. Hanrahan. 2010. "Measuring Social Well-Being in People with Chronic Illness." *Social Indicators Research* 96(3): 381–401.

Harries, Tim, Ruth Rettie, and Jonathan Gabe. 2019. "Shedding New Light on the (In)compatibility of Chronic Disease Management with Everyday Life - Social Practice Theory, Mobile Technologies and the Interwoven Time-Spaces of Teenage Life." *Sociology of Health & Illness* 41(7): 1396–1409.

Heath, Deborah. 2007. "Bodies, Antibodies and Modest Interventions." Pp. 135–156 in *Technoscience: The Politics of Interventions*, edited by Kristin Asdal, Brita Brenna, and Ingunn Moser. Unipub, AS: Oslo Academic Press.

Hebert, Randy S. and Richard Schulz. 2006. "Caregiving at the End of Life." *Journal of Palliative Medicine* 9(5): 1174–1187.

Hedgecoe, Adam M. 2003. "Expansion and Uncertainty: Cystic Fibrosis, Classification and Genetics." *Sociology of Health & Illness* 25(1): 50–70.

Hesse-Biber, Sharlene N. and Patricia Leavy (eds.). 2010. *Handbook of Emergent Methods*. New York: Guilford Press.

Higgs, Paul, Martin Hyde, Richard Wiggins, and David Blane. 2003. "Researching Quality of Life in Early Old Age: The Importance of the Sociological Dimension." *Social Policy & Administration* 37(3): 239–252.

Hill, Terrence D., Catherine E. Ross, and Ronald J. Angel. 2005. "Neighborhood Disorder, Psychophysiological Distress, and Health." *Journal of Health and Social Behavior* 46(2): 170–186.

Hoch, Deborah Ann, Maya Bulman, and Dorn W. McMahon. 2016. "Cultural Sensitivity and Challenges in Management of the Transgender Patient with ESRD in Transplantation." *Progress in Transplantation* 26(1): 13–20.

Holstein, Martha B. and Meredith Minkler. 2003. "Self, Society, and the 'New Gerontology'." *The Gerontologist* 43(6): 787–796.

Howe, P. David. 2011. "Cyborg and Supercrip: The Paralympics Technology and the (Dis) empowerment of Disabled Athletes." *Sociology* 45(5): 868–882.

Iantaffi, Alessandra Alex. 2010. "Disability and Polyamory: Exploring the Edges of Inter-Dependence, Gender and Queer Issues in Non-Monogamous Relationships." Pp. 172–178 in *Understanding Non-Monogamies, Meg Barker & Darren Langdridge, eds.* New York: Routledge.

Johnson, Austin H. 2015. "Normative Accountability: How the Medical Model Influences Transgender Identities and Experiences." *Sociology Compass* 9(9): 803–813.

Johnson, Austin H. 2019. "Rejecting, Reframing, and Reintroducing: Trans People's Strategic Engagement with the Medicalisation of Gender Dysphoria." *Sociology of Health & Illness* 41(3): 517–532.

Jones, Charlotte. 2020. "Intersex, Infertility and the Future: Early Diagnoses and the Imagined Life Course." *Sociology of Health & Illness* 42(1): 143–156.

Jutel, Annemarie. 2009. "Sociology of Diagnosis: A Preliminary Review." *Sociology of Health & Illness* 31(2): 278–299.

Kahn, Sarilee, Edward Alessi, Leah Woolner, Hanna Kim, and Christina Olivieri. 2017. "Promoting the Wellbeing of Lesbian, Gay, Bisexual and Transgender Forced Migrants in Canada: Providers' Perspectives." *Culture, Health & Sexuality* 19(10): 1165–1179.

Kanter, Elisa, Jennifer L. Bevan, and Sam M. Dorros. 2019. "The Use of Online Support Groups to Seek Information about Chronic Illness: Applying the Theory of Motivated Information Management." *Communication Quarterly* 67(1): 100–121.

Karp, David A. 2017. *Speaking of Sadness: Depression, Disconnection, and the Meanings of Illness*. Oxford: Oxford University Press.

Kasper, Judith D. and Vicki A. Freedman. 2014. "Findings from the 1st Round of the National Health and Aging Trends Study (NHATS): Introduction to a Special Issue." *The Journals of Gerontology* 69B(S1): S1–S7.

Kirk, Susan and Denise Hinton. 2019. ""I'm Not What I Used to Be": A Qualitative Study Exploring How Young People Experience Being Diagnosed with A Chronic Illness." *Child: Care, Health and Development* 45(2): 216–226.

Kitto, Simon, Janice Chesters, Jill Thistlethwaite, and Scott Reeves. 2011. Sociology of Interprofessional Health Care Practice: Critical Reflections and Concrete Solutions (Health Care Issues, Costs and Access). Hauppauge, NY: Nova Science Publishers

Koller, Veronika and Stella Bullo. 2019. "'Fight like a Girl': Tattoos as Identity Constructions for Women Living with Illness." *Multimodal Communication* 8: 1. 10.1515/mc-2018-0006.

Kwate, Naa and A. Oyo. 2008. "Fried Chicken and Fresh Apples: Racial Segregation as a Fundamental Cause of Fast Food Density in Black Neighborhoods." *Health & Place* 14(1): 32–44.

Labuski, Christine. 2015. *It Hurts down There: The Bodily Imaginaries of Female Genital Pain*. New York: State University of New York Press.

Lampe, Nik M., Shannon K. Carter, and J. E. Sumerau. 2019. "Continuity and Change in Gender Frames: The Case of Transgender Reproduction." *Gender & Society* 33(6): 865–887.

Lanford, Daniel and Jill Quadagno. 2016. "Implementing ObamaCare: The Politics of Medicaid Expansion under the Affordable Care Act of 2010." *Sociological Perspectives* 59(3): 619–639.

Lankford, Adam. 2016. "Race and Mass Murder in the United States: A Social and Behavioral Analysis." *Current Sociology* 64(3): 470–490.

Lindsey, Linda L. 2015. *Gender Roles: A Sociological Perspective*. New York: Routledge.

Link, Bruce G. and Jo Phelan. 1995. "Social Conditions as Fundamental Causes of Disease." *Journal of Health and Social Behavior* 35(Extra Issue): 80–94.

Littlewood, Roland. 2003. "Why Narrative? Why Now?" *Anthropology & Medicine* 10(2): 255–61.

Locker, David. 2008. "Living with Chronic Illness." Pp. 81–92 in *Sociology as Applied to Medicine*, edited by Graham Scambler, Vol. 6. New York: Saunders/Elsevier.

Lowton, Karen. 2003. "'Double or Quits': Perceptions and Management of Organ Transplantation by Adults with Cystic Fibrosis." *Social Science & Medicine* 56(6): 1355–1367.

Lowton, Karen and Jonathan Gabe. 2003. "Life on a Slippery Slope: Perceptions of Health in Adults with Cystic Fibrosis." *Sociology of Health & Illness* 25(4): 289–319.

Lubkin, Ilene Morof and Pamala D. Larsen. 2006. *Chronic Illness: Impact and Interventions*. Sudbury, MA: Jones & Bartlett Learning.

Lucal, Betsy. 2008. "Building Boxes and Policing Boundaries: (De)constructing Intersexuality, Transgender and Bisexuality." *Sociology Compass* 2(2): 519–536.

Lupton, Deborah. 2018. *Fat.* New York: Routledge.

May, Carl. 2011. "Mundane Medicine, Therapeutic Relationships, and the Clinical Encounter: Current and Future Agendas for Sociology." Pp. 309–322 in *Handbook of the Sociology of Health, Illness, and Healing*, edited by Bernice Pescosolido, Jack Martin, Jane McLeod, and Anne Rogers. New York: Springer.

Mayer, Karl Ulrich. 2009. "New Directions in Life Course Research." *Annual Review of Sociology* 35: 413–433.

Mayer, Kenneth H., Robert Garofalo, and Harvey J. Makadon. 2014. "Promoting the Successful Development of Sexual and Gender Minority Youths." *American Journal of Public Health* 104(6): 976–981.

McEwen, Bruce S. and Teresa Seeman. 1999. "Protective and Damaging Effects of Mediators of Stress: Elaborating and Testing the Concepts of Allostasis and Allostatic Load." *Annuals of the New York Academy of Sciences* 896(1): 30–47.

McGann, P. J., David Hutson, and Barbara Katz Rothman (eds.). 2011. *Sociology of Diagnosis.* Bingley: Emerald Group Publishing.

McPherson, Christine J., Keith G. Wilson, and Mary Ann Murray. 2007. "Feeling Like a Burden: Exploring the Perspectives of Patients at the End of Life." *Social Science & Medicine* 64(2): 417–427.

Miller, DeMond Shondell and Nyjeer Wesley. 2016. "Toxic Disasters, Biopolitics, and Corrosive Communities: Guiding Principles in the Quest for Healing in Flint, Michigan." *Environmental Justice* 9(3): 69–75.

Moffat, Tina. 2010. "The 'Childhood Obesity Epidemic': Health Crisis or Social Construction?" *Medical Anthropology Quarterly* 24(1): 1–21.

Monro, Surya. 2010. "Towards a Sociology of Gender Diversity: The Indian and UK Cases." Pp. 242–259 in *Transgender Identities: Towards a Social Analysis of Gender Diversity*, edited by Sally Hines and Tam Sanger. Milton Park: Taylor & Francis Group.

Moore, Lauren Renée. 2014. "'But We're Not Hypochondriacs': The Changing Shape of Gluten-Free Dieting and the Contested Illness Experience." *Social Science & Medicine* 105: 76–83.

Muschert, Glenn W. 2007. "Research in School Shootings." *Sociology Compass* 1(1): 60–80.

Nettleton, Sarah. 2006. "'I Just Want Permission to Be Ill': Towards a Sociology of Medically Unexplained Symptoms." *Social Science & Medicine* 62(5): 1167–1178.

Nettleton, Sarah. 2010. "The Sociology of the Body." Pp. 47–68 in *The New Blackwell Companion to Medical Sociology*, edited by William C. Cockerham. Chichester: Blackwell Wiley.

Nowakowski, Alexandra CH. 2016a. "You Poor Thing: A Retrospective Autoethnography of Visible Chronic Illness as A Symbolic Vanishing Act." *Qualitative Report* 21(9): 1615–1635.

Nowakowski, Alexandra C.H. 2016b. "Hope Is a Four-Letter Word: Riding the Emotional Rollercoaster of Illness Management." *Sociology of Health & Illness* 38(6): 899–915.

Nowakowski, Alexandra C.H. 2019. "Neverland: A Critical Autoethnography of Aging with Cystic Fibrosis." *The Qualitative Report* 24(6): 1338–1360.

Nowakowski, Alexandra C.H., Katelyn Y. Graves, and J.E. Sumerau. 2016. "Mediation Analysis of Relationships between Chronic Inflammation and Quality of Life in Older Adults." *Health and Quality of Life Outcomes* 14: 46. 10.1186/s12955-016-0452-4.

Nowakowski, Alexandra C.H. and J.E. Sumerau. 2015. "Swell Foundations: Fundamental Social Causes and Chronic Inflammation." *Sociological Spectrum* 35(2): 161–178.

Nowakowski, Alexandra C.H. and J.E. Sumerau. 2017a. "Managing Chronic Illness Together." *Sociology Compass* 11(5): e12466.

Nowakowski, Alexandra C.H. and J.E. Sumerau. 2017b. "Aging Partners Managing Chronic Illness Together: Introducing the Content Collection." *Gerontology and Geriatric Medicine* 3: 1–3.

Nowakowski, Alexandra C.H. and J.E. Sumerau. 2018. "It's All Done with Mirrors: Neurological and Sociological Integration in the Case of Limb Transplants." *Clinical and Translational Neuroscience* 1–5.

Nowakowski, Alexandra C.H. and J.E. Sumerau. 2019. "Reframing Health and Illness: A Collaborative Autoethnography on the Experience of Health and Illness Transformations in the Life Course." *Sociology of Health & Illness* 41(4): 723–739.

O'Brien, Patrick K. 2013. "Medical Marijuana and Social Control: Escaping Criminalization and Embracing Medicalization." *Deviant Behavior* 34(6): 423–443.

Ory, Marcia G., SangNam Ahn, Luohua Jiang, Kate Lorig, Phillip Ritter, Diana D. Laurent, Nancy Whitelaw, and Matthew Lee Smith. 2013. "National Study of Chronic Disease Self-Management: Six-Month Outcome Findings." *Journal of Aging and Health* 25(7): 1258–1274.

Pearlin, Leonard I., Elizabeth G. Menaghan, Morton A. Lieberman, and Joseph T. Mullan. 1981. "The Stress Process." *Journal of Health and Social Behavior* 22(4): 337–356.

Pedersen, Willy and Sveinung Sandberg. 2013. "The Medicalisation of Revolt: A Sociological Analysis of Medical Cannabis Users." *Sociology of Health & Illness* 35(1): 17–32.

Petersen, Alan. 2006. "The Best Experts: The Narratives of Those Who Have a Genetic Condition." *Social Science & Medicine* 63(1): 32–42.

Phelan, Jo C. and Bruce G. Link. 2005. "Controlling Disease and Creating Disparities: A Fundamental Cause Perspective." *The Journals of Gerontology* 60B(S2): S27–S33.

Phelan, Jo C., Bruce G. Link, and Parisa Tehranifar. 2010. "Social Conditions as Fundamental Causes of Health Inequalities: Theory, Evidence, and Policy Implications." *Journal of Health and Social Behavior* 51(S1): S28–S40.

Pierret, Janine. 2003. "The Illness Experience: State of Knowledge and Perspectives for Research." *Sociology of Health & Illness* 25(3): 4–22.

Porter, Tom, Bie Nio Ong, and Tom Sanders. 2019. "Living with Multimorbidity? the Lived Experience of Multiple Chronic Conditions in Later Life." *Health* 10.1177/1363459319834997.

Portes, Alejandro, Patricia Fernández-Kelly, and Donald Light. 2012. "Life on the Edge: Immigrants Confront the American Health System." *Ethnic and Racial Studies* 35(1): 3–22.

Prior, Lindsay. 2003. "Belief, Knowledge and Expertise: The Emergence of the Lay Expert in Medical Sociology." *Sociology of Health & Illness* 25(3): 41–57.

Pudrovska, Tetyana and Andriy Anishkin. 2015. "Clarifying the Positive Association between Education and Prostate Cancer: A Monte Carlo Simulation Approach." *Journal of Applied Gerontology* 34(3): 293–316.

Putnam, Michelle. 2002. "Linking Aging Theory and Disability Models: Increasing the Potential to Explore Aging with Physical Impairment." *The Gerontologist* 42(6): 799–806.

Quadagno, Jill. 2010. "Institutions, Interest Groups, and Ideology: An Agenda for the Sociology of Health Care Reform." *Journal of Health and Social Behavior* 51(2): 125–136.

Radomsky, Nellie A. 2014. *Lost Voices: Women, Chronic Pain, and Abuse.* New York: Routledge.

Reid, Colleen. 2017. *The Wounds of Exclusion: Poverty, Women's Health, and Social Justice.* New York: Routledge.

Richardson, Liana J. and Tyson H. Brown. 2016. "(En)gendering Racial Disparities in Health Trajectories: A Life Course and Intersectional Analysis." *SSM-Population Health* 2: 425–435.

Rier, David. 2000. "The Missing Voice of the Critically Ill: A Medical Sociologist's First-Person Account." *Sociology of Health & Illness* 22(1): 68–93.

Rier, David A. 2010. "The Patient's Experience of Illness." Pp. 163–178 in *Handbook of Medical Sociology*, edited by Chloe E. Bird, Peter Conrad, Allen M. Fremont, and Stefan Timmermans. Nashville, TN: Vanderbilt University Press.

Roberts, Celia and Cron Cronshaw. 2017. "New Puberty; New Trans: Children, Pharmaceuticals and Politics." Pp. 59–84 in *Gendering Drugs*, edited by Ericka Johnson. London, UK: Palgrave Macmillan.

Ross, Catherine E. and John Mirowsky. 2001. "Neighborhood Disadvantage, Disorder, and Health." *Journal of Health and Social Behavior* 42(3): 258–276.

Saguy, Abigail C. and Rene Almeling. 2008. "Fat in the Fire? Science, the News Media, and the 'Obesity Epidemic'." *Sociological Forum* 23(1): 76–96.

Sanderson, Tessa, Michael Calnan, Marianne Morris, Pam Richards, and Sarah Hewlett. 2011. "Shifting Normalities: Interactions of Changing Conceptions of a Normal Life and the Normalisation of Symptoms in Rheumatoid Arthritis." *Sociology of Health & Illness* 33(4): 618–633.

Schwaiger, Elisabeth. 2009. "Performing Youth: Ageing, Ambiguity and Bodily Integrity." *Social Identities* 15(2): 273–284.

Seale, Clive. 1998. *Constructing Death: The Sociology of Dying and Bereavement.* Cambridge: Cambridge University Press.

Settersten, Richard A. and Jacqueline L. Angel (eds.). 2011. *Handbook of Sociology of Aging.* New York: Springer.

Sewell, Abigail A. 2017. "The Illness Associations of Police Violence: Differential Relationships by Ethnoracial Composition." *Sociological Forum* 32(S1): 975–997.

Shilling, Chris. 2007. "Sociology and the Body: Classical Traditions and New Agendas." *The Sociological Review* 55(1_suppl): 1–18.

Stuckler, David and Karen Siegel (eds.). 2011. *Sick Societies: Responding to the Global Challenge of Chronic Disease.* Oxford: Oxford University Press.

Swoboda, Debra A. 2006. "The Social Construction of Contested Illness Legitimacy: A Grounded Theory Analysis." *Qualitative Research in Psychology* 3(3): 233–51.

Taylor, David and Michael Bury. 2007. "Chronic Illness, Expert Patients and Care Transition." *Sociology of Health & Illness* 29(1): 27–45.

Taylor, Miles G. 2008. "Timing, Accumulation, and the Black/White Disability Gap in Later Life: A Test of Weathering." *Research on Aging* 30(2): 226–250.

Taylor, Miles G. and Scott M. Lynch. 2004. "Trajectories of Impairment, Social Support, and Depressive Symptoms in Later Life." *The Journals of Gerontology Series B: Psychological Sciences and Social Sciences* 59(4): S238–S246.

Taylor, Renée R. and Leonard A. Jason. 2002. "Chronic Fatigue, Abuse-Related Traumatization, and Psychiatric Disorders in a Community-Based Sample." *Social Science & Medicine* 55(2): 247–256.

Thille, Patricia. 2019. "Managing Anti-Fat Stigma in Primary Care: An Observational Study." *Health Communication* 34(8): 892–903.

Thomas, Carol. 2007. *Sociologies of Disability and Illness: Contested Ideas in Disability Studies and Medical Sociology.* London: Macmillan.

Thomas, Carol. 2010. "Medical Sociology and Disability Theory." Pp. 37–56 in *New Directions in the Sociology of Chronic and Disabling Conditions*, edited by Graham Scambler and Sasha Scambler. London: Palgrave Macmillan.

Thorne, Sally, Barbara Paterson, Sonia Acorn, Connie Canam, Gloria Joachim, and Carol Jillings. 2002. "Chronic Illness Experience: Insights from a Metastudy." *Qualitative Health Research* 12(4): 437–452.

Turner, Leigh. 2005. "Bioethics, Social Class, and the Sociological Imagination." *Cambridge Quarterly of Healthcare Ethics* 14(4): 374–378.

Turner, R. Jay. 2009. "Understanding Health Disparities: The Promise of the Stress Process Model." Pp. 3–21 in *Advances in the Conceptualization of the Stress Process: Essays in Honor of Leonard I. Pearlin*, edited by William R. Avison, Carol S. Aneshensel, Scott Schieman, and Blair Wheaton. New York: Springer.

Vargas, Robert. 2016. "How Health Navigators Legitimize the Affordable Care Act to the Uninsured Poor." *Social Science & Medicine* 165: 263–270.

Waggoner, Miranda R. 2013. "Motherhood Preconceived: The Emergence of the Preconception Health and Health Care Initiative." *Journal of Health Politics, Policy and Law* 38(2): 345–371.

Wainwright, Steven P., Clare Williams, Mike Michael, and Alan Cribb. 2009. "Stem Cells, Translational Research and the Sociology of Science." Pp. 67–84 in *The Handbook of Genetics & Society: Mapping the New Genomic Era*, edited by Paul Atkinson, Peter Glasner, and Margaret Lock. New York: Routledge.

Waite, Linda J., Edward O. Laumann, Wendy Levinson, Stacy Tessler Lindau, Martha K. McClintock, Colm A. O'Muircheartaigh, and L. Philip Schumm. 2007. "National Social Life, Health, and Aging Project (NSHAP)." *National Archive of Computerized Data on Aging*. Ann Arbor, MI.

Wang, Qingchun and Karin Hannes. 2019. "Towards a more comprehensive approach of conducting and analyzing photovoice research: An overview of sites and modalities to consider in future photovoice research." In 3rd European Congress of Qualitative Inquiry, Date: 2019/02/13-2019/02/15, Edinburgh.

Warner, David F. and Tyson H. Brown. 2011. "Understanding How Race/Ethnicity and Gender Define Age-Trajectories of Disability: An Intersectionality Approach." *Social Science & Medicine* 72(8): 1236–1248.

Warren-Findlow, Jan, Rachel B. Seymour, and Dena Shenk. 2010. "Intergenerational Transmission of Chronic Illness Self-Care: Results from the Caring for Hypertension in African American Families Study." *The Gerontologist* 51(1): 64–75.

Weiss, Gregory L. and Lynne E. Lonnquist (eds.). 2017. *The Sociology of Health, Healing, and Illness*, Vol. 9. New York: Routledge.

Wentling, Tre, Elroi Windsor, Kristen Schilt, and Betsy Lucal. 2008. "Teaching Transgender." *Teaching Sociology* 36(1): 49–57.

Wickrama, K. A. S., Rand D. Conger, and W. Todd Abraham. 2005. "Early Adversity and Later Health: The Intergenerational Transmission of Adversity through Mental Disorder and Physical Illness." *The Journals of Gerontology* 60B(S2): S125–S129.

Williams, Beverly Rosa. 2004. "Dying Young, Dying Poor: A Sociological Examination of Existential Suffering among Low-Socioeconomic Status Patients." *Journal of Palliative Medicine* 7(1): 27–37.

Williams, Clare. 2000. "Alert Assistants in Managing Chronic Illness: The Case of Mothers and Teenage Sons." *Sociology of Health & Illness* 22(2): 254–272.

Williams, David R. and Michelle Sternthal. 2010. "Understanding Racial-Ethnic Disparities in Health: Sociological Contributions." *Journal of Health and Social Behavior* 51(S1): S15–S27.

Willis, Karen F. and Shandell L. Elmer (eds.). 2007. *Society, Culture and Health – an Introduction to Sociology for Nurses*. Oxford: Oxford University Press.

Willson, Andrea E., Kim M. Shuey, and Glen H. Elder Jr. 2007. "Cumulative Advantage Processes as Mechanisms of Inequality in Life Course Health." *American Journal of Sociology* 112(6): 1886–1924.

Wilkinson, Willy. 2014. "Cultural Competency." *Transgender Studies Quarterly* 1(1-2): 68–73.

Wilson, Sarah. 2007. "'When You Have Children, You're Obliged to Live': Motherhood, Chronic Illness and Biographical Disruption." *Sociology of Health & Illness* 29(4): 610–626.

Witten, Tarynn M. 2004. "Life Course Analysis – the Courage to Search for Something More: Middle Adulthood Issues in the Transgender and Intersex Community." *Journal of Human Behavior in the Social Environment* 8(2–3): 189–224.

Witten, Tarynn M. 2014. "It's Not All Darkness: Robustness, Resilience, and Successful Transgender Aging." *LGBT Health* 1(1): 24–33.

Wolfe, Atticus. 2018. "Transgender Inclusive and Specific Health Care." *Public Health Review* 1(1): 1–8.

Yee, June Ying, Zack Marshall, and Vo. Tess. 2014. "Challenging Neo-Colonialism and Essentialism: Incorporating Hybridity into New Conceptualizations of Settlement Service Delivery with Lesbian, Gay, Bisexual, Trans, and Queer Immigrant Young People." *Critical Social Work* 15(1): 88–103.

Part VI

Health Care Delivery

23

Health Professions and Occupations

Jason Adam Wasserman and Brian Philip Hinote

The word "profession" is used very loosely in common parlance, often referring to whatever sort of work someone does to earn a living. However, the ordinary use of this term belies a more complex and nuanced picture. In sociological terms, professions represent a specific form of work characterized by expertise, altruism, self-regulation, and community. Yet even these parameters are highly contested. Some even charge that distinguishing professions from other forms of work is elitist (Monteiro 2015). Some assert that the altruism of professions is under assault from the forces of commercialization (Pellegrino 1989), while others suggest that the image of altruism has always been something of a commodity (Cruess 2006). And while expert knowledge has always distinguished professional work, the democratization of knowledge, deskilling of professionals, and growing skepticism of expertise itself all accompany recent post-industrial shifts in health professions and occupations.

Sociological insights are especially important for understanding contemporary health professions, which stand at a critical historical juncture. The discovery of the germ enabled medical interventions that that could be commodified at unprecedented levels of scale (Hinote and Wasserman 2012; Starr 1982; Wasserman and Hinote 2011). The power and prestige accompanying this success redefined professional medicine and its auxiliary occupations throughout the twentieth century. More recently, however, the epidemiological transition has disrupted health care and its various professional groups. Chronic diseases today fail to conform to the prerequisites of modernity, since they exhibit complex causal profiles and diffuse, unpredictable outcomes (Beck 1992, 1994; Hinote and Wasserman 2013; Wasserman and Hinote 2010). What it means to practice medicine today is therefore radically different than even 50 years ago, not only (and not even primarily) in terms of technological complexity, but because the ambiguities introduced by chronic disease have punctured medicine's professional terrain in ways that reshape its relationship with patients, with nursing and other health professions, and even with its own expertise.

The Wiley Blackwell Companion to Medical Sociology, First Edition. Edited by William C. Cockerham.

In this complex social landscape, where the definitions and parameters of professions have become even more ambiguous and contested, sociological analysis of health professions is more important than ever. The incalculable nature of health risks and complex disease outcomes require greater interprofessional collaboration as ailments traverse organ systems and professional specialties, as disease trajectories span greater periods of the life course; and as physiological, psychosocial, and existential concerns increasingly converge in our understanding of health and illness. Not only is the work of patient care shifting; so too are professional communities themselves. As different professions and occupations jostle for position, thereby intersecting and interfering with each other, sociological analysis must illuminate various manifestations of power that shape the interwoven processes of professionalization and deprofessionalization over time.

In this chapter, we first review classic and contemporary sociological analyses of health professions, highlighting how different theoretical frameworks help identify various important features of these phenomena. These include functionalist accounts of professions as value-based communities, as well as more critical accounts that frame professions in terms of power. We then turn to two areas where such accounts are useful for understanding contemporary health care professions. The first involves comparatively macro-level discussion of the evolution of medicine, nursing, and physician assistants, each on a distinct professionalization trajectory. Here, we examine social and historical factors that constrained or enabled professionalization in different ways, at different paces, and within different socio-historical moments. Second, we examine interprofessional teamwork as an interactional space in which these broad structural conditions play out in the social interactions of physicians, nurses, and other allied health professionals themselves. We conclude with reflections on what a sociological perspective suggests about the future.

Sociological Theories of Professions in Health and Healthcare

Traditionally, the sociological study of professions coalesced around at least three axes: structure, process, and power. While different theoretical traditions obviously lean more heavily on one or more of these, they are often difficult to separate. Structural functionalist accounts tend to focus primarily on the distinctive characteristics of professions as social phenomena, but it is impossible to ignore the processual *qua* evolutionary features that are explicit or implicit in many of these accounts. Similarly, few socio-historical accounts that focus on the developmental processes of health professions can ignore how forces of power shaped the evolution of medicine and nursing, or their relationships with each other.

Professions and Professionalization

Of course, in a broad sense, we can describe professions (and even contemporary conflicts between professions) as fundamentally rooted in processes of specialization and the division of labor (see Durkheim 1933 [1997]). That is, as functions of labor continue to subdivide, gaining efficiency and success, at least some portions of that work become more technically sophisticated. Professions take up this end of the labor spectrum as work becomes increasingly cognitive and rooted in knowledge systems, and increasingly separated from the physical work that may be paired with their expert judgments. Judges draw, for example, on legal theory and precedent to hand down sentences to the convicted, while others in this system handcuff and jail those defendants. Similarly, physicians assess symptoms and order tests, medications, and common procedures that today are nearly always performed by nurses, physician assistants, respiratory or physical therapists, social workers, and so on.

Other classic sociological accounts emphasize professions as rooted in some combination of shared altruism and expertise. Parsons (1939), for example, argued that professions offer a functional counterbalance to capitalism where they rise above self-interested motivations (though he takes care not to romanticize professionals as selfless per se, suggesting rather that altruism is an implicit prerequisite of professional work itself). He thus characterizes professions as the products of various social forces:

> The professional type is the institutional framework in which many of our most important social functions are carried on, notably the pursuit of science and liberal learning and its practical application in medicine, technology, law and teaching... Certain features of our received traditions of thought, notably concentration of attention on the problem of self-interest with its related false dichotomy of concrete egoistic and altruistic motives, has served seriously to obscure the importance of these other elements, notably rationality, specificity of function and universalism. (Parsons 1939: 467)

For Parsons, the kind of altruism that characterized professions such as medicine was not an internal personal quality of a doctor, but a rational functionalist mandate of the larger society in which medicine needs to operate with at least some relative degree of independence from commercial interests.

Without ignoring underlying forces of power and prestige, Weber ([1922] 1978) too offers a quasi-functionalist account, particularly with respect to the important question of professional values. Though he wrote less explicitly about them, Weber clearly analyzed professions as a product of Western rationalization. In contrast to current discussions of deprofessionalization, which tend to lay blame on increasingly bureaucratic and management-heavy health systems, he suggested that "professionalization and bureaucratization are *not* antithetical" (Ritzer 1975: 627, italics original). As the examples above suggest, a profession *qua* expertise can fit well within a bureaucratic system, where the task of work is stratified into cognitive and physical divisions of labor. Weber also suggested that an ethic of responsibility served as a sufficient substitution for earlier social forms organized around religious cosmologies within labor sectors of secular modern societies (see Turner 1995).

Early functionalist accounts also generated a list of characteristics for professions that, with some variation, have become widely accepted (see for example, Goode 1957; Reed and Evans 1987). These include:

- Shared identity
- Shared values and norms

- Specialized body of knowledge
- Collective autonomy
- Practice autonomy for its members
- Clear boundaries for membership
- Control of access to the profession
- An obligation of service

In these, we can see the characteristics of many health professions coming into focus. Medicine itself embodies all of these and is widely considered the most professional form of health care work.[1] For example, physicians share a sense of identity captured in various symbols and clothing; talk in jargon that few outsiders can understand; collectively attest to shared values, including swearing an oath at their graduations; and govern the standards of medical school curricula and practice licensure.

Although they follow different historical trajectories, other health professional groups exhibit trends consistent with professionalization as a sociohistorical process. For example, nursing has increasingly professionalized, but is still moving incrementally toward the professional ideal type. Today, the profession largely controls nursing education and licensure, and its members have a shared sense of identity. It has also articulated specialized knowledge around the cognitive and theoretical features of patient care in contradistinction to the curative functions of medicine (though some argue that nursing is less developed than medicine on this account, pointing toward ongoing processes of professionalization). Nurses also enjoy relatively limited practice autonomy, though this too has been growing, particularly for those who become nurse practitioners, the first program for which was established in 1965 (www.aanp.org).

The notion that professions have a "service orientation that supersedes proprietary interest" (Reed and Evans 1987: 3279) is potentially controversial, particularly where expected altruism collides with economic realities. Conceptualizing this as a collective obligation of the profession as a whole, however, shapes it less as a form altruism per se, and more as a *quid pro quo* social arrangement that is ultimately economically beneficial. This kind of "social contract" perspective focuses on the explicit and implicit agreements that a profession enters into with society at large. Cruess (2006), for example, suggests that commitment to professional values like altruism are exchanged for, among other things, explicit legal protections and implicit forms of public trust that are essential to the profession's viability. The social contract view sits at an interesting juncture in sociological theory. The exchanges supposed by such a contractual model certainly hint of functionalism, where professions harmonize their needs with those of the broader society. But the metaphor of a contract also suggests that opposing sides are in a negotiation for their own interests, something which directs us also to examine forces of social conflict in the formation of professions.

Surely, the economic advantages leveraged by professionalization are impossible to overlook. This naturally suggests a more critical account of what they are, how they are shaped, and why they look and behave as they do. Indeed, the history of the medical profession entreats such an analysis. As far back as the 1600s, when Nicolas Culpepper translated the London College of Physicians' *London Pharmacopaeia* from Latin to English, he was reviled and ostracized by his fellow practitioners.[2] Culpepper's was an explicitly political act, a direct and conscious assault on the hoarding of expert knowledge by physicians and the resulting public dependence on the medical profession. However, as medicine gained increasing interventional efficacy, those sorts of professional assertions of power only escalated, thereby deepening the boundaries between physicians and lay people.

Prior to the discovery of the germ, allopathic medicine still dominated the landscape of health and healing, but it existed amidst a far more pluralistic set of other medical professions. Their limited ability to actually cure disease left allopathic physicians in a state of relative equality with homeopaths, botanicals, and hydropaths, particularly with respect to the construction of expertise (Flannery 2002; Kaptchuk and Eisenberg 2001). But as the commodities of medical intervention became more successful, those interventions also became more valuable. In response, allopathic medicine established clearer norms and professional strictures that they leveraged in advocating for legislative action protecting these commodities. The first AMA code of medical ethics in 1847, for example, articulates medicine as a fundamentally moral enterprise, but the majority of the document is conspicuously focused on the professional community and the relationships of physicians to each other. It notably states that,

> ... no one can be considered as a regular practitioner or a fit associate in consultation, whose practice is based on an exclusive dogma, to the rejection of the accumulated experience of the profession, and of the aids actually furnished by anatomy, physiology, pathology, and organic chemistry (American Medical Association 1848: 19).

As professionalization unfolded, the generally positive relationships between "regular" and "irregular" practitioners (where allopaths and homeopaths routinely consulted with one another) began to decay. Uproar and fiery debate around the non-consultation clause in the AMA Code of Ethics erupted throughout the 1880s and 1890s, but opponents of the 1847 code offered little defense of "irregulars" per se. Rather they argued that scientific evidence in place of orthodoxy should define practice standards, often scoffing at the idea of consulting with homeopaths in the process (Warner 1999). Eventually sectarian practitioners could no longer qualify for medical licensure at all, in no small part due to the closure of most homeopathic medical schools following the 1910 Flexner report, which assessed the academic standards of US Medical Schools. In this story, we can clearly see various ways in which the profession as a form of social power was leveraged to protect its economic interests.

Sociological frameworks that focus on power add much to understanding professionalization in medicine and other health professions (as others discuss below). A broadly Marxist framework would characterize not only the obvious attempts to circumscribe the commercial terrain of the profession as driven by economic interest, but suggest similar motivations behind the core values around which it professes to be organized, including altruism itself. Such a frame has intuitive appeal, particularly where public trust in physicians represents a valuable commodity and inspires a belief that physicians act out of altruistic concern for patients (Hughes 1958). These perceptions are undeniably profitable. On this account, Bryan Turner (1995: 137) notes that "a satisfactory explanation of professionalization as an occupational strategy will come eventually to depend upon both Weberian and Marxist perspectives." While the various historical exercises of material and ideological power extinguished some forms of medical practice, or nearly so, as we discuss below, they also allowed other occupations to emerge and supplement medicine, provided their positions of subservience remained clear.

Friedson (1970) offers the most popular classic account of professions as systems of social closure (i.e. exclusion). He focuses heavily on medicine's legal and political moves as it professionalized throughout the late nineteenth and early twentieth centuries, noting that "The foundation of medicine's control over its work is... clearly political in character, involving the aid of the state in establishing and maintaining the profession's preeminence" (Friedson 1970: 23). While state authority to grant protections to a professional body implies its ultimate authority to retract those privileges, Friedson's analysis underscores how the medical profession has navigated, if not infiltrated, state functions. In the US, for example, he writes, "While obviously... the state has ultimate authority in matters of licensing and prosecution of practitioners, much of its authority has either been given to the AMA or has been based on the advice of the AMA" (Friedson 1970 : 29). Indeed, even with managed health care, the US is still predominantly characterized by the "professional model," which offers a great deal of latitude to physicians to collectively define practice terrain and to individually exercise clinical judgment within it (Light 2013). Moreover, even in state-managed health care systems, Friedson notes that the inaccessibility of physicians' expert knowledge among state administrators renders a comparatively high degree of professional autonomy to physicians.

Additionally, medicalization, or the process by which phenomenon not previously understood through the lens of illness come to be seen that way, has profoundly transformed medicine's professional terrain (Conrad 1992). Childbirth, for example, transitioned from a home-based experience under the purview of lay midwives from one's own community, to a highly technocratic experience largely occurring within a hospital system under the direction of a physician (Drife 2002). Moreover, increasing technological capacities for intervention drove physicians to seek new markets for intervention. Wertz and Wertz (2009: 208) note that even the naming of the new specialty of "obstetrics" represented an assertion of professional power: "The renaming of the practice of midwifery symbolized doctors' new sense of themselves as professional actors." As a result of the combination of their authoritative claim over knowledge regarding disease and a legal monopoly on treatment practices, professional power represents a key influence (though not the only one) in the process of medicalization.

Of course, the claims inherent in the classic accounts of professions above face numerous counter-examples in health and medicine today. Individuals outside of medicine seem to increasingly define the terms of disease and illness experience, and navigate ways to confront them, often without reference to professional medicine at all. One need only to look at the variety of lifestyle enclaves purporting one theory or another about how to be healthy. Nor does the profession of medicine today reflect the above characterizations of monolithic power. Indeed, Friedson penned his classic work at the tail end of an historical period sometimes referred to as the "golden era of medicine," a moment where both professional prestige and professional autonomy were at a crescendo. We have arguably since witnessed a deprofessionalization of medicine, where its power, autonomy, and prestige have all contracted in observable ways. We will explore these further below.

Professions and Identity

While the focus of the sociology of professions has centered on its structures, functions, power, and conflict, sociological inquiry at the intersections of professions and self are also important. For instance, we can understand work as a set of different kinds of activities. Bellah et al. (1996) famously distinguish a taxonomy of work consisting of job, career, and calling. The higher order forms of work contain the lower order ones (i.e. callings are usually also careers and jobs), but not the other way around (i.e. a job is not necessarily a career or calling). The notion of calling intersects with that of profession in that a calling inherently involves work with a sense of moral meaning. And in this way, a profession involves something more deeply personal than other forms of work, something that is connected to one's sense of a moral life. Indeed, when prospective students apply to medical school, they are asked to articulate, in various ways, why medicine is their calling, or how it is intimately connected to who they are as a person.

Robert Merton (1957) examines these notions, particularly in analyzing the processes by which medical students take up new ideas about who they are in the course of their training. He notes that the acquisition of professional norms and values is a functional imperative of the work of doctoring. However, because professional ideals may be permanently out of reach with respect to the realities of practice, Merton (1957: 72) writes, "Medical education can be conceived as facing the task of enabling students to learn *how to blend* incompatible or potentially incompatible norms into a functionally consistent whole."

Today, those in academic medicine focus heavily on the notion of "professional identity formation," and often draw on frameworks of socialization and other interactional theories. Cruess et al. (2015), for example, characterize professional identity formation in medicine beginning with trainees' engagement of the profession through "legitimate peripheral participation," to which they bring their existing personal identities. That is, trainees are at first welcomed as observers or minor assistants, and still largely stand as outsiders to professional practice. As interactions proceed, however, they begin to be negotiated, a stage where implicit and explicit propositions are accepted, compromised, or rejected altogether. Over time, and with the repetition of practice, full participation is achieved and professional identities crystallize (though never fully stop evolving).

Notions of cognitive apprenticeship and the hidden curriculum feature strongly in these sorts of socialization models (Hafferty and Franks 1994). That is, becoming a physician is not merely a matter of mastering a specialized knowledge about disease and the body, but also a process by which the ethos of medicine is inculcated into the individual professional. Over time, trainees not only learn the knowledge necessary to diagnose and treat illness, but their own "way of being" a professional, a construct that inherently involves negotiation of one's personal identity and the norms of the wider professional community. Later, we will return to these concepts to examine how identity constructs amidst shifting professional roles and expectations complicate interprofessional teamwork at a time in the history of disease when it is most needed.

Deprofessionalization and Countervailing Power

The privileges enjoyed by physicians in the golden era of medicine arguably began to recede in the 1970s. While some contend that professional medicine's continued hegemonic control of medical knowledge diminishes claims of deprofessionalization (Friedson 1989), Light (1991: 500) notes that "rank-and-file physicians no longer have the control over their work that they did in the late 1960s." Numerous different social forces mobilized to constrain physicians' professional autonomy throughout the 1970s and 1980s, including the rise of managed care systems aiming (though ostensibly failing) to control skyrocketing health care costs (Reed and Evans 1987). Increasing technological capacity and the epidemiological ascendancy of chronic illness amplified the costs of health care, though arguably without proportionally good outcomes. Much of medical science's advance during this period appeared to extend illness and dying trajectories, but with cures for fewer and fewer diseases. Not only have institutions and insurers managed medical care, but physicians are now typically employees of practices rather than owners of them. Costs and bureaucratic complexity have promoted marked decreases in practice ownership by physicians. As a result, we see more clinicians in large practices, or their wholesale employment by large health systems (Kane 2015). Meanwhile, within those employment models, physicians' work is often measured by metrics that assess efficiency and volume, like Relative Value Unit (RVU) schemas (Midkiff and Cordaro 2012).

It is tempting to interpret deprofessionalization, particularly in light of the power exercised by professional medicine in the late nineteenth and early twentieth centuries, as a victory for rebalancing power in health care divisions of labor. After all, these trends ostensibly correspond with the rise of patient-centered care and deference to patient autonomy in medical decision-making. But closer analysis calls this into question. Reed and Evans (1987), for example, worry that diminished autonomy for physicians will atrophy skills of clinical judgement within the profession itself. Moreover, recall the structural functionalist account where the distancing of medicine from commercial interests is critical for public trust, but also requires high degrees of professional autonomy, or at least freedom from oversight by institutional systems with primarily financial concerns. It is impossible to ignore the irony of the push by large health systems to promote "patient-centered care," while at the same time enforcing patient quotas and incentivizing interventional volume. At best, the deprofessionalization of medicine appears to be displacing the power of the profession with that of corporations.

In the last decade or more, perhaps the most significant countervailing power attenuating the professional dominance of physicians has come from the decentering of expertise and movements of patient empowerment (Vinson 2016). This is also closely connected to the epidemiological transition, which has rendered questions about how to be healthy increasingly complex and unverifiable. The clearly beneficial interventions of infectious disease gave way to various contested theories of diet and exercise that *may* prevent or delay chronic disease, or to long-term management of chronic disease symptoms with no prospect of cure (Wasserman and Hinote 2011). The expert authority of medicine in this context is decidedly less impressive, while the public appears decidedly more ambivalent about expert advice. The anti-vaccine movement, for example, involves the exercise of power as collective populism in the context of decentralizing health knowledge (Hinote and Wasserman 2020). Other health social movements manifest in similar fashion, made possible by the uncertainty of risk and knowledge in the contemporary health landscape.

Yet amidst the many social forces diminishing its professional dominance over the last fifty years, medicine deployed countervailing powers of its own, particularly in the form of hegemonic control of the clinical moment. Vinson (2016) highlights how the uptake of patient-centered care among professional medicine itself also can represent a reassertion of medical authority in the clinical encounter. In particular, discourses of patient empowerment can be redefined as a practitioner strategy for patient rapport and compliance, as well as promoting the efficiency of encounters to achieve the bureaucratic and commercial expectations of the institution. Ultimately, Vinson (2016: 1375) concludes "the use of patient empowerment discourse to shape patient participation is an exercise of physician authority, and represents a mechanism by which the medical profession resists the countervailing power of patient consumerism."

Perhaps an even more starkly ironic example of the appropriation of patient empowerment comes in the area of bioethics. The discipline of bioethics ostensibly emerged from the momentum of the Civil Rights Movement and countercultural revolutions of the 1960s, and in response to cases of medical paternalism that shocked the increasingly individualist sensibilities of the public by the 1970s (e.g. Karen Ann Quinlan and Dax Cowart). The overriding concern with patient autonomy eventually culminated in the Patient Self Determination Act of 1990, presumably marking a turn away from the beneficent paternalism at the center of medical ethics through the 1960s.

Professional medicine responded to these efforts with countervailing forces in at least two ways. The first concerned how broader bioethical mandates toward "respect for persons" and "dignity" were whittled into the construct of autonomy, and then further how this was clinically operationalized as decision-making capacity (Wasserman and Navin 2018). The result was that "who" counted in clinical bioethics became a narrower set of persons. To qualify as a person, one had, not coincidentally, to sufficiently demonstrate the kind of means-ends way of thinking that is characteristic of science and medicine in the first place. The second concerned how clinical bioethics became institutionalized as a consultation service operating within the health care system. A study of clinical ethics consultation by Hauschildt and De Vries (2020: 320) notes that the institutionalization of bioethics in the clinical setting, where it is often performed by clinicians themselves, has promoted a reframing of many ethical questions in terms of "technical judgements that rely on the technical expertise of clinicians." Further, even where clinical ethicists operate with an ostensible degree of independence, "they do not often pose significant challenges to physician authority" (Hauschildt and De Vries 2020: 320). In the end, it appears as though the gains made by the patients' rights movement have been at least significantly offset by countervailing powers aimed at retaining professional dominance.

An Analysis of Health Professions at Two Levels of Scale

As described above, various theoretical frameworks are useful for illuminating the social character of health professions, ranging from structures and functions; to their dynamic interplay with social contexts over time; to their inherent conflicts; and to the ways in which they intersect their members' identities. In this section we explore health professions at two distinct levels of scale by drawing from some of these frameworks. The first involves the intersections of medicine, nursing, and physician assistants as professions that both complement and compete with each other. The second involves interprofessional teamwork as an embodied, interpersonal space in which professions (in the form of professional identities) are involved in dynamic, often symbolic, exchanges.

Professions in Contest: Physicians, Nurses, and Physician Assistants

We have briefly mentioned the history of medicine and nursing in our account of significant sociological paradigms above. Here, we will focus more intently on nurses and physician assistants (PAs), as well as their interactions with professional medicine. The developmental arcs of each show how professionalization responds to social conditions of particular historical moments, but also how the contours of professions are negotiated among members and between professional groups, a process rife with power dynamics and inequality. We have seen, for example, how increasing technological sophistication promoted increasing specialization and greater interventional capacity in medicine. Combined with the various assertions of power leveraged against midwives, for example, this fostered the emergence of obstetrics as a specialty. But a sociological lens can illuminate any number of intersections between various health care professions – intersections that both inform those professions in practical ways and contribute to the development of social theory.

Medicine's matriculation to a full-fledged profession was aided significantly by the ability to commodify its services around curing disease after the discovery of the germ. Leveraging different social conditions, nurses and physician assistants exhibit different trajectories of professionalization, while professional medicine has actively opposed these trends (particularly in areas of practice autonomy). To understand these processes, we first must understand the distinct histories of nursing and PA. Nursing underwent marked shifts in professionalization in the late 1800s, around the time that professional medicine was crystallizing as a more clearly bounded, exclusive community. This was made possible, of course, by increasing specialization in medicine that pulled physicians further away from the delivery of day-to-day tasks of bedside care. Nursing professionalization in this period also drew on many of the same strategies, including the codification of its knowledge base, most notably in the form of new academic programs with elevated rigor. As in medicine, nurses appeared to be quite conscious of the prospects of professionalization. At the inauguration of Johns Hopkins nursing school in 1889, for example, the hospital superintendent Henry M. Hurd remarked, "In the eyes of the Trustees, nursing the sick is not to be considered a trade but a learned profession" (quoted in James [1979] 2001: 44). However, nursing's arc of professionalization took a different path, failing over the next century or so to emerge as a full profession (on the criteria described above) alongside medicine. In particular, while nursing increasingly defined its scope of practice, centered on a notion of caring in contradistinction to the curative work of medicine, it failed to achieve a corresponding level of practice autonomy (Tosh 2007).

Since the 1970s, nursing has witnessed more rapid change, particularly with the development of advanced nursing practice degrees. In fact, as of 2018, 23 states allowed nurse practitioners (NPs) full practice autonomy, including the authority to "evaluate patients; order and interpret diagnostic tests; and initiate and manage treatments, including prescribing medications and controlled substances" (American Association of Nurse Practitioners 2018). Despite shifts in legal statutes to facilitate practice independence, some have suggested that in the normative culture of health care institutions, the legal aspects of practice autonomy are not matched with the reality of actual independence in the clinical setting. While initially established to expand primary care, particularly for underserved populations, casting the role of nurse practitioners as "physician extenders" undersold the distinct approach of nursing toward patient care. As a result, Weiland (2008: 350) writes:

> ... each incremental expansion of NP practice has been amid a crisis whose driving force was economics. If we consider access to care as a financial concept, and if we consider NPs as a financial concept, an instrument, or object that is both cost effective and productive, then using such an available resource makes good business sense. Those external forces such as professional competition, healthcare policy, reimbursement, and state rules and regulations determine where we work, the type of patients we see, and where our practice of care extends. Practice independence in this overall environment is next to impossible.

Indeed, the AMA has openly, and with some success, opposed the expansion of nurse practitioners' and other non-physician providers' scopes of practice. In fact, a 2020 AMA article celebrated more than "50 scope of practice victories in 2019," along with the creation of, "more than 100s of advocacy tools for medicine to utilize when fighting scope expansion legislation and regulation including model bills, legislative templates, state laws analyses, issue briefs and more" (American Medical Association 2020). There were also internal conflicts within nursing related to issues of professionalization. In particular, efforts to professionalize have been criticized as not only assuming a modernist scientific paradigm that undermines the humanist underpinnings of nursing, but as also creating hierarchies within nursing that implicitly denigrate those without advanced degrees (Herdman 2001). Herdman (2001: 6) notes, "Just as the first phase of nursing professionalization in the nineteenth century was followed by proletarianization during the early twentieth century, the contemporary phase of professionalization is associated with the deskilling of some nurses."

The professionalization trajectory of PAs has both similarities and differences. Nursing has historical roots dating back nearly two centuries, and a correspondingly long discourse about its philosophies, practices, and role in health care. The first PA program was not established until 1965 to leverage the sizable number of medic-trained Vietnam veterans against the emerging shortage in primary care. Like NPs, PA programs were first established (and at about the same time) to amplify primary care, and PAs were envisioned as "physician extenders," not as independent practitioners. Unlike nursing, however, it was physicians themselves who largely fostered this new occupation. As a result, PA training hones in on a similar medical model of disease, often closely resembling medical education itself, whereas nurses have historically maintained theoretical distance from medicine (Cockerham and Hinote 2015).

In short, the PA profession was developed by physicians for physicians. This is perhaps why in 1993, Osterweis and Garfinkel (1993: 2) noted:

> the most significant difference between PAs and NPs is not the skills they learn but the general orientation or socialization toward health care and the intensity of the desire for independent practice. Apparently, PAs are comfortable in a dependent role that requires physician supervision while nurses are striving to establish independent practice.

But more recently PAs, like NPs have pushed for greater practice independence, particularly in primary care settings (Cockerham and Hinote 2015). Laws in some states have accommodated this push, giving greater independence to PAs. For example, in 2016, the State of Michigan passed House Bill 5533, which loosened the supervision requirements permitting "a PA to practice without delegation and supervision from a physician or podiatrist, provided there is a signed, compliant practice agreement between the PA and a participating physician or podiatrist" (Bosler and Reed 2018).

It is worth bearing in mind Weiland's critique above: The new latitude conferred to PAs may owe more to economic conditions in health care than a deference to their professional expertise. The professional status of PAs and NPs alike remains precarious in this way. Moreover, the AMA has specifically opposed practice autonomy for all non-physicians, but noted specifically of PAs:

> With regard to physician assistants specifically, AMA policy states that physician assistants should be authorized to provide patient care services only so long as the physician assistant is functioning under the direction and supervision of a physician or group of physicians (AMA 2018).

NPs and PAs will certainly continue to push for expansion of practice autonomy, and may indeed be aided by conditions within a health care system that continues to struggle to provide primary care access amidst growing physician shortages.

The cases of nursing and physician assistants underscore the utility of sociological frameworks, which can shed light on the status and direction of these fields. For instance, functionalist accounts underscore how these professions have been shaped by conditions of health and illness in society more generally. Such accounts highlight how the emergence of both professional groups maps to social evolutionary processes. For nursing, this begins with health science advances that multiply the functions of patient care in ways that foster increasing technical involvement from nurses, who then require more specialized training. For both NPs and PAs, shifts in physician specialization and consequent primary care shortages opened this space further in the 1960s and 1970s. But the definitive sociological characteristics of professions also illustrate that professionalization in these fields is incomplete. Other sociological accounts draw on constructs of power and conflict to show us why.

In contrast to PAs, the professionalization of nursing has also been comparatively slow. This is particularly surprising insofar as nursing has long understood itself as fundamentally distinct from medicine, while physician assistants see themselves as fully aligned with (and in many ways comparable to) physicians. Perhaps nursing's distinctive theoretical orientation, along with its more clearly delineated practice terrain, made it sufficiently targetable as something from which physicians could resist encroachment. Yet it is also difficult to ignore the gender dynamics likely at play. Nursing was founded largely by and for women and remains today dominated by women. Yet men in nursing experience gendered advantages nonetheless, including higher pay, greater prevalence in higher paying nursing specialties, and greater rates of promotion to leadership positions (Alexander 2016; Brown 2009; Cleary et al. 2019; Greene et al. 2017; Muench et al. 2015). Conversely, we are currently witnessing the feminization of physician assistants (Hooker et al. 2013), which may have implications for both internal professional dynamics, as well as exercises power and social inequality in the interprofessional landscape.

Finally, insofar as professions reflect and act as forms of power often focused on protecting and promoting economic advantage, we can understand the professionalization processes of NPs and PAs, as well as physicians' opposition, as fundamentally about class struggle. Practice autonomy for NPs and PAs would invite direct economic competition from health professionals that are currently either legally or effectively subsidiaries of the medical enterprise. Sady (2015: 6) explicates this economic contest, "experienced PAs and NPs are held hostage and unable to practice without collaborative agreements. Often, physicians demand monthly stipends (sometimes thousands of dollars) to act as a collaborator under such an agreement."

Sociology's structural-level considerations focus on professions in aggregate, and how they develop, change, and compete. Yet implied throughout is the notion that professions have a collective identity, especially where professions conceive of their community vis-à-vis distinct values, norms, and practices. This naturally entreats exploration of how individual professionals – having been socialized within the ethos, logos, and pathos of their profession – come to understand themselves as professionals, as well as how they interact with others inside and outside of their own professional group(s). Sociological analysis at the interactional level of scale can add much to the important area of interprofessional collaboration.

Sociological Perspectives on Interprofessional Collaboration

The working relationships between different health care professions is not an entirely new area of observation and analysis. The emergence of professional nursing at the end of the 1800s brought with it the need to negotiate patient care roles and the responsibilities of physicians and nurses. The notion of health care as a function of interdisciplinary teams dates at least back to the 1940s, "after effectiveness of multidisciplinary medical and surgical care teams was clearly demonstrated in World War II" (Baldwin 1996: 174). However, when professional and institutional structures were more stringently hierarchical, appeals to authority rendered questions about role boundaries less complex and more easily navigated. Health care today remains hierarchical in many ways, including authority for treatment decisions in patient care. Yet the expansion and codification of professional terrain, particularly within nursing, but also in any number of other health professions with specialized foci (e.g. physical and respiratory therapy, nutrition, etc.), have yielded a system of health care professions today that is more horizontally organized than ever before.

Since the early 1970s, both academics and various professional societies have made a more concerted effort to explicate and coordinate the structures and functions of interprofessional teams. This is not coincidental. As noted previously, the disruptions of the epidemiological transition reshaped the landscape of illness and professional roles and expectations within it. The sheer complexity and multivocality of chronic disease (which typically compels a focus on long-term management), and its more robust intersections with the personal and social life of a patient, simply require an interdisciplinary approach. As Atul Gawande (2011) summarized, "Making systems work in health care – shifting from corralling cowboys to producing pit crews – is the great task of your and my generation of clinicians and scientists."

Yet amplifying interdisciplinarity in health care has proven challenging, largely due to various aspects of professionalization. Recall that professions are existentially dependent on a specialized body of knowledge protected by disciplinary processes, including education.

> Often, neither students nor teachers from the different professions interact, rendering opportunities to learn with, from, and about each other well nigh impossible. Small wonder that students identify with their intended profession to the exclusion of others if reciprocal perceptions are, at best, ill-informed and at worst, stereotypical.
>
> (Barr and Coyle 2013: 185)

The paradox expressed here is sociologically significant: Professions depend to at least some extent on a kind of parochialism that impedes the types of collaboration necessary to promote their success in the chronic illness era. Wackerhausen (2009: 461) writes that at the micro-level:

> being an accepted member of a profession implies attuning oneself to, and consequently embodying a whole group of rules, beliefs, and habits: *a way of speaking, a way of questioning, a way of understanding and explaining, a way of seeing and valuing, a way of telling narratives*, etc. (italics are original).

Interprofessional teamwork schemas have emerged largely from within health professions, with comparatively little contribution from sociology proper. Practical models (e.g. TeamSTEPPS, AHRQ 2019) have been widely adopted. However, underneath these practical roadmaps for improving teamwork and communication are complex social and psychological dynamics, many of which intersect with or derive from the interplay of professional identities and role expectations.

Sociology therefore has much to offer in terms of a more robust analysis and understanding of the interactional space involved with interprofessional teamwork in health care. In particular, it is important to understand how the socio-historical processes of professionalization are woven into countless interactional moments in health care practice. That is, an interactional analysis can illustrate how interprofessional interactions are shaped by one's understanding of self as a nurse, a physician, or a PA, along with one's evaluations of those other professions, as well as one's perceptions of how other professions define, frame, or interpret their own profession. These interactional frames speak broadly to the ways that teams function, as well as critical issues about how they leverage diversity within interactional space.

The sociological imagination is defined, in part, by the ability to see how the broadest sociohistorical processes are manifest in the most intimate moments of our private lives (Mills 1959). In the case of professions, while sociology offers a long history and examination of those macro social and historical processes, studying how professions and professional identities feature in the day-to-day interactions of health care workers has received comparatively less attention. The prevailing approach focuses on teaching interprofessional teamwork to medical, nursing, and allied health students, or implementing frameworks like TeamSTEPPS in health care settings (AHRQ, 2019; Fox et al. 2018). Indeed, there is strong evidence that such approaches improve efficiency within health care systems and even result in better patient care. Moreover, there is substantial evidence that interprofessional teams perform better with respect to problem-solving because they can leverage their diverse experiences and skillsets (Paige 2007). This is especially true with complex problems, something which is particularly important in the era of chronic illness (Hinote and Wasserman 2020; Wasserman and Hinote 2010).

It is not enough, however, for teams simply to be experientially diverse. That diversity must be well-coordinated or it will not only be unhelpful, it can actually create problems where social and professional boundaries are reinforced rather than mitigated and traversed. Stavert and Lott (2013: 8) offer one example of how diverse specialists involved in a complex patient case resulted in worse care for the patient:

> Our team was one of nine specialty services tending to this patient in the intensive care unit (ICU), in addition to his primary providers. Physician-to-physician handoffs were frequent, with more than 40 doctors participating in the patient's care during his 11-day stay in the ICU. Our inability to easily name his disease process quickly created ambiguity about "ownership" of the patient. Well-intended multidisciplinary discussions regarding his diagnosis and potential plan of care soon devolved into fragmented, narrow, and internal deliberations within each specialty.

They conclude that something resembling the bystander effect rendered the wealth of expertise among a diverse set of practitioners ineffective or even harmful (see Latané and Darley 1968, 1970).

Even if teams are well-coordinated, research on interprofessional practice suggests only that measurable outcomes of team performance on tasks will improve. That is, well-coordinated, diverse teams will solve problems better, provide more efficient patient care, etc. But there are deeper confounding issues in the area of interprofessional interactions, where conflicts may become amplified as care becomes more complex and different professions push for greater ownership of contested occupational terrains. Writing about scientists, Gieryn (1983) noted that boundary-work also served any number of professions as a strategic resource for expansion, monopolization, and protection of autonomy. In health care, similar dynamics play out in conflicts between team members, which serve to reinforce disciplinary boundaries. These dynamics are triggered, according to McNeil et al. (2013), by many factors that frequently accompany interprofessional interaction in health care, including differential treatment; differing values; expectations of assimilation; acts of insult or humiliation; or even "simple contact," particularly in contexts where interprofessional anxiety is high. Of course, all of these are evident in health care, particularly in the escalating clashes between physicians and other health professions about scopes of practice; patient care decision-making and expertise; and the clear status differences between them.

There are numerous examples of interprofessional conflict that can emerge in the interactional moment. The continuation of the long history of devaluation of nursing work, is evidenced, for example, in the "show me your stethoscope" movement (Robbins 2015). This formed in backlash to TV host Joy Behar mocking a nurse competing in the Miss America Pageant who delivered a monologue about caring for a patient while wearing scrubs and a stethoscope, which Behar referred to as a "doctor's stethoscope." The social media storm that followed saw nurses posing with their stethoscopes and was the impetus for the formation of a new nursing advocacy organization called "Show Me Your Stethoscope" which now boasts more than 650,000 members (www.smysofficial.com).

The above discussion suggests that the development of unique practice terrain and knowledge sets complicates interprofessional expectations of assimilation, where the dependence of emerging professions on unique expertise can confound the function of a team. After all, the essence of expertise is that it is not shared by others. A professional knowledge base then inherently resists the expectations of assimilation. Yet paradoxically, where apparent similarities between professions exist, such as in the ability to provide basic primary care, there are efforts to mandate exclusion. All of these contribute to interprofessional tensions that play out within professional interactions, which are likely to escalate as health and illness become only more complex.

Conclusion

The sociology of health professions is a rich field of inquiry, ranging from the most macro-level sociohistorical considerations to the most intimate notions of identity. Classic sociological work on health professions tended to focus on their structures and functions, as well as reading professions as systems of exclusion and status protection. But increasing disease complexity following the epidemiological transition has focused a more practical lens on schemas of interaction between professionals. Certainly, the multifactorial diseases of the contemporary health landscape naturally invite health care pluralism. Amidst these shifts we have witnessed the deprofessionalization of medicine over the last 40 years. These factors have set the stage for new health professions, as well as old ones increasingly able to amplify their professional stature. In turn, we now observe examples of countervailing power as both overt policy and the hegemonies of practice. Into the future, the health professions will continue to represent novel and socially complex systems that require incisive sociological analysis across multiple analytic scales. In particular, classic models of professionalization should be revisited and reconsidered amidst new forms of pluralism and complexity in the landscape of health and health care. The classically theorized dynamics of professionalization or deprofessionalization will continue to characterize shifts in health care work, but we will also witness instances of these phenomena that defy classic models.

Clinical bioethics represents one potentially complex, emerging profession. Over the past several decades, clinical bioethics work has shifted from a pastime of professional philosophers or clinicians with side-interests in the ethics of medicine, to an increasingly codified set of practices circumscribed by a defined knowledge base. In particular, the last three decades have witnessed the following:

- The quasi-legal protection of clinical ethics terrain in the Joint Commission's requirement that every hospital have a mechanism for resolving ethics conflicts (though it stops short of specifying the architecture of that mechanism);
- The formation of a professional society for bioethics and medical humanities (the ASBH), which has elaborated core competencies for health care ethics consultation (ASBH 2011);
- The explosion of graduate degree programs specifically focused on health care ethics (Lee and McCarty 2016);
- And most recently, an official health care ethics consultant certification (HEC-C), which requires a standardized examination (Bruce et al. 2019; Horner et al. 2020).

Yet many of these efforts to solidify the boundaries of clinical ethics consultation have involved a kind of "de-skilling" in the form of the codification (and therefore potential commodification) of complex and contested epistemic and moral systems into a standardized set of technical skills. Hynds and Raho (2020: 45) note this irony:

> Arguably, the knowledge competency required by the HEC-C process, if judged from the Core References,[3] barely meets the standard for a minor in an undergraduate degree. We know of no profession that exists or could reasonably claim to exist as a profession on such a minimalist basis, least of all one whose practitioners contribute substantially and often dispositively *ex professo* to decisions about whether other individuals will live or die.

These sorts of paradoxes and complexities within professionalization characterize any number of other emerging occupations with professional potential. New sociological insights will be important for understanding how these trends evolve amidst the complexities of the post-industrial health care landscape.

Notes

1 This is despite forces of deprofessionalization over the last several decades, as we discuss later.
2 This echoes, in a less gruesome way, the anger of the clergy toward John Wycliffe, who similarly translated the Bible from Latin to English, was declared a heretic, and subsequently had both his works and his exhumed body burned (Flannery 2007).
3 I.e., the study guides for the certification exam.

References

Agency for Healthcare Research and Quality. 2019. "Guidelines for Using TeamSTEPPS Materials." Agency for Healthcare Research and Quality, Rockville, MD. https://www.ahrq.gov/teamstepps/master-trainer-registration.html

Alexander, Nanette. 2016. "Are Female Nurses Treated Differently? Yes." *The Journal of Nurse Practitioners* 12(6): 372.

American Association of Nurse Practitioners. 2018. "State Practice Environment." www.aanp.org. Accessed May 13, 2019.

American Medical Association. 1848. *Code of Medical Ethics*. Philadelphia: T. K. and P. G. Collins Printers.

American Medical Association. 2018. "Physician Assistant Scope of Practice." www.ama-assn.org. Accessed May 13, 2019.

American Medical Association. 2020. "AMA successfully fights scope of practice expansions that threaten patient safety." https://www.ama-assn.org/practice-management/payment-delivery-models/ama-successfully-fights-scope-practice-expansions, Accessed February 25, 2020.

Baldwin, DeWitt C. 1996. "Some Historical Notes on Interdisciplinary and Interprofessional Education and Practice in Healthcare in the U.S.A." *Journal of Interprofessional Care* 10: 173–187.

Barr, Hugh, and Julia Coyle. 2013. "Introducing Interprofessional Education." Pp. 185–196 in *Educating Health Professionals: Becoming a University Teacher*, edited by Stephen Loftus, Tania Gerzina, Joy Higgs, Megan Smith, and Elaine Duffy. Rotterdam: Sense Publishers.

Beck, Ulrich. 1992. *Risk Society*. London: Sage.

Beck, Ulrich. 1994. "The Reinvention of Politics: Towards a Theory of Reflexive Modernization." Pp. 1–55 in *Reflexive Modernization: Politics, Tradition, and Aesthetics in the Modern Social Order*, edited by U. Beck, A. Giddens, and S. Lash. Palo Alto, CA: Stanford University Press.

Bellah, Robert, Richard Madsen, William Sullivan, Ann Swidler, and Steven M. Tipton. 1996. *Habits of the Heart: Individualism and Commitment in American Life*. Berkeley, CA: University of California Press.

Bosler, Barbara, and Kathleen A. Reed. 2018. "New Roles for the Physician's Assistant and Advanced Practice Registered Nurse in Michigan." State Bar of Michigan Health Care Law Section. www.dykema.com. Accessed March 16, 2020.

Brown, Brian. 2009. "Men in Nursing: Re-Evaluating Masculinities, Re-Evaluating Gender." *Contemporary Nurse* 33: 120–129.

Bruce, Courtenay R., Chris Feudtner, Daniel Davis, and Mary Beth Benner. Felicia Cohn for the Healthcare Ethics Consultant Certification Commission. 2019. "Developing, Administering, and Scoring the Healthcare Ethics Consultant Certification Examination." *Hastings Center Report* 49: 15–22.

Cleary, Michelle, Sacia West, David Arthur, Rachel Kornhaber, and Catherine Hungerford. 2019. "Women in Health Academia: Power Dynamics in Nursing, Higher Education and Research." *Journal of Advanced Nursing* 75(7): 1371–1373.

Cockerham, William C., and Brian P. Hinote. 2015. "PAs in a Changing Society: A Sociologic Perspective." *Journal of the American Academy of Physician Assistants* 28: 18–20.

Conrad, Peter. 1992. "Medicalization as Social Control." *Annual Review of Sociology* 18: 209–232.

Core Competencies Task Force. 2011. *Core Competencies for Healthcare Ethics Consultation.* (2nd ed.). Chicago, IL: American Society of Bioethics and Humanities.

Cruess, Richard L., Sylvia R. Cruess, Boudreau, J. Donald, Linda Snell, and Yvonne Steinert. 2015. "A Schematic Representation of the Professional Identity Formation and Socialization of Medical Students and Residents: A Guide for Medical Educators." *Academic Medicine* 90: 718–725.

Cruess, Sylvia R. 2006. "Professionalism and Medicine's Social Contract with Society." *Clinical Orthopaedics and Related Research* 449: 170–176.

Drife, James. 2002. "The Start of Life: A History of Obstetrics." *Postgraduate Medical Journal* 78: 311–315.

Durkheim, Emile. 1933 [1997]. *The Division of Labor in Society.* New York: The Free Press.

Flannery, Michael A. 2002. "The Early Botanical Medical Movement as a Reflection of Life, Liberty, and Literacy in Jacksonian America." *Journal of the Medical Library Association* 90: 442–454.

Flannery, Michael A. 2007. "Introduction." in *The English Physician by Nicholas Culpeper,* edited by Michael A. Flannery. Tuscaloosa, AL: University of Alabama Press.

Fox, Lanae, Robert Onders, Carol J Hermansen-Kobulnicky, Thanh-Nga Nguyen, Leena Myran, Becky Linn, and Jaime Hornecker. 2018. "Teaching interprofessional teamwork skills to health professional students: A scoping review." *Journal of Interprofessional Care* 32: 127–135.

Friedson, Eliot. 1970. *The Profession of Medicine: A Study of the Sociology of Applied Knowledge.* Chicago, IL: University of Chicago Press.

Friedson, Eliot. 1989. *Medical Work in America: Essays on Health Care.* New Haven and London: Yale University Press.

Gawande, Atul. 2011. "Cowboys and Pit Crews." New Yorker, May 26. www.newyorker.com/news/news-desk/cowboys-and-pit-crews.

Gieryn, Thomas F. 1983. "Boundary-Work and the Demarcation of Science from Non-science: Strains and Interests in Professional Ideologies of Scientists." *American Sociological Review* 48: 781–795.

Goode, William J. 1957. "Community within a Community." *American Sociological Review* 22: 194–200.

Greene, Jessica, Majeda M. El-Banna, Linda A. Briggs, and Jeongyoung Park. 2017. "Gender Differences in Nurse Practitioner Salaries." *Journal of the American Association of Nurse Practitioners* 29: 667–672.

Hafferty, Frederick W., and Ronald Franks. 1994. "The Hidden Curriculum, Ethics Teaching, and the Structure of Medical Education." *Academic Medicine* 69: 861–871.

Hauschildt, Katrina, and Raymond De Vries. 2020. "Reinforcing Medical Authority: Clinical Ethics Consultation and the Resolution of Conflicts in Treatment Decisions." *Sociology of Health & Illness* 42: 307–326.

Herdman, Elizabeth A. 2001. "The Illusion of Progress in Nursing." *Nursing Philosophy* 2: 4–13.

Hinote, Brian P., and Jason Adam Wasserman. 2013. "Reflexive Modernity and the Sociology of Health." Pp. 215–232 in *Medical Sociology on the Move: New Directions in Theory*, edited by William C. Cockerham. New York: Springer Publishers.

Hinote, Brian P., and Jason Adam Wasserman. 2020. *Social and Behavioral Science for Health Professionals*. Lanham, MD: Rowman and Littlefield.

Hooker, Roderick S., Stephen P. Robie, Jennifer M. Coombs, and James F. Cawley. 2013. "The Changing Physician Assistant Profession: A Gender Shift." *Journal of the American Association of Physician Assistants* 26: 36–44.

Horner, Claire, Andrew Childress, Sophia Fantus, and Janet Malek. 2020. "What the HEC-C? An Analysis of the Healthcare Ethics Consultant-Certified Program: One Year in." *The American Journal of Bioethics* 20: 9–18.

Hughes, Everett C. 1958 [2015]. *Men and their Work*. New Orleans: Quid Pro Quo Books.

Hynds, James A., and Joseph A. Raho. 2020. "A Profession without Expertise? Professionalization in Reverse." *American Journal of Bioethics* 20: 44–46.

James, Janet Wilson. [1979] 2001. "Isabel Hampton and the Professionalization of Nursing in the 1890s." Pp. 42–84 in *Enduring Issues in American Nursing*, edited by Ellen D. Baer, Sylvia Riker Patricia D'Antonio and Joan E. Lynaugh. New York: Springer Publishing Company.

Ritzer, George. 1975. "Professionalization, Bureaucratization and Rationalization: The Views of Max Weber." *Social Forces* 53(4): 627–634.

Kane, Carol K. 2015. "Updated Data on Physician Practice Arrangements: Inching Toward Hospital Ownership." In *Policy Research Perspectives*, American Medical Association.

Kaptchuk, Ted J., and David M. Eisenberg. 2001. "Varieties of Healing. 1. Medical Pluralism in the United States." *Annals of Internal Medicine* 135: 189–195.

Latané, Bibb, and John M. Darley. 1968. "Group Inhibition of Bystander Intervention in Emergencies." *Journal of Personality and Social Psychology* 10: 215–221.

Latané, Bibb, and John M Darley. 1970. *The Unresponsive Bystander: Why Doesn't He Help?* New York: Appelton-Century Crofts.

Lee, L. M., and F. A. McCarty. 2016. "Emergence of a discipline? Growth in US Postsecondary Bioethics Degrees." *Hastings Center Report* 46: 19–21.

Light, Donald W. 1991. "Professionalism as a Countervailing Power." *Journal of Health Politics, Policy and Law* 16(3): 499–506.

Light, Donald W. 2013. "Comparative Models of 'Health Care' Systems." Pp. 543–57 in *The Sociology of Health and Illness: Critical Perspectives*, 9th edition. edited by Peter Conrad and Valerie Leiter. New York: Worth.

McNeil, Karen Anne, Rebecca J. Mitchell, and Vicki Parker. 2013. "Interprofessional Practice and Professional Identity Threat." *Health Sociology Review* 22: 291–307.

Merton, Robert K. 1957. "Some Preliminaries to a Sociology of Medical Education." Pp. 3–79 in *The Student Physician: Introductory Studies in the Sociology of Medical Education*, edited by Robert K. Merton, George G. Reader and Patricia L. Kendall. Cambridge, MA: Harvard University Press.

Midkiff, Hurd, and Elizabeth Cordaro. 2012. "Developing Work RVUs for Production-based Physician Compensation Programs." *Healthcare Financial Management* 66: 140–145.

Mills, C. Wright. 1959. *The Sociological Imagination*. London: Oxford University Press.

Monteiro, A. Reis. 2015. "Sociology of the Professions." Pp. 47–60 in *The Teaching Profession: Present and Future*, edited by A. Reis Monteiro. Cham, Switzerland: Springer Nature.

Muench, Ulrike, Jody Sindelar, Susan H. Busch, and Peter I. Buerhaus. 2015. "Salary Differences Between Male and Female Registered Nurses in the United States." *Journal of the American Medical Association* 313: 1265–1267.

Osterweis, Marian, and Stephen Garfinkel. 1993. "The Roles of Physician Assistants and Nurse Practitioners in Primary Care: An Overview of the Issues." Pp. 1–11 in *The Roles of Physician Assistants and Nurse Practitioners in Primary Care*, edited by D. Kay Clawson and Marian Osterweis. Washington DC: Association of Academic Health Centers.

Paige, Scott E. 2007. *The Difference: How the Power of Diversity Creates Better Groups, Firms, Schools, and Societies*. Princeton, NJ: Princeton University Press.

Parsons, T. 1939. "The Professions and Social Structure." *Social Forces* 17: 457–467.

Pellegrino, Edmund D. 1989. "Character, Virtue and Self-Interest in the Ethics of the Professions." *Journal of Contemporary Health Law and Policy* 5: 53–73.

Reed, Ralph R., and Daryl Evans. 1987. "The Deprofessionalization of Medicine: Causes, Effects, Responses." *Journal of the American Medical Association* 258: 3279–3282.

Robbins, Alexandra. 2015. "Is Nursing a Talent?: You Can Bet Your Life on It." The Washington Post, September 17.

Sady, Brian. 2015. "Autonomy Now!: Why PAs, Like NPs, Need Full Practice Autonomy." *Clinician Reviews* 25(10): 6–8.

Starr, Paul. 1982. *The Social Transformation of American Medicine: The Rise of a Sovereign Profession and the Making of a Vast Industry*. New York: Basic Books.

Stavert, Robert R., and Jason P. Lott. 2013. "The Bystander Effect in Medical Care." *New England Journal of Medicine* 368: 8–9.

Tosh, Karen. 2007. "Nineteenth Century Handmaids or Twenty-First Century Partners?" *Journal of Health Organization and Management* 21: 68–78.

Turner, Bryan. 1995. *Medical Power and Social Knowledge*. London: Sage.

Vinson, Alexandra H. 2016. "'Constrained Collaboration': Patient Empowerment Discourse as Resource for Countervailing Power." *Sociology of Health & Illness* 38: 1364–1378.

Wackerhausen, Steen. 2009. "Collaboration, Professional Identity, and Reflection Across Boundaries." *Journal of Interprofessional Care* 23(5): 455–473

Warner, John Harley. 1999. "The 1880s Rebellion against the AMA Code of Ethics: Scientific Democracy and the Dissolution of Orthodoxy." in *The American Medical Ethics Revolution: How the AMA's Code of Ethics Has Transformed Physicians' Relationships to Patients, Professionals, and Society*, edited by Robert B. Baker, Arthur L. Caplan, Linda L. Emanuel and Stephen R. Latham. Baltimore, MA: Johns Hopkins University Press.

Wasserman, Jason Adam, and Brian P. Hinote. 2011. "Chronic Illness as Incalculable Risk: Scientific Uncertainty and Social Transformations in Medicine." *Social Theory and Health* 9: 41–58.

Wasserman, Jason Adam, and Mark Christopher Navin. 2018. "Capacity for Preferences: Respecting Patients with Compromised Decision Making." Hastings Center Report (May/June): 31–39.

Weber, Max. [1922] 1978. *Economy and Society*. Vol. 2. Berkeley, CA: University of California Press.

Weiland, Sandra A. 2008. "Reflections on independence in nurse practitioner practice." *Journal of the American Academy of Nurse Practitioners* 20: 345–352.

Wertz, Richard W., and Dorothy C. Wertz. 2009. "Notes on the Decline of Midwives and the Rise of Medical Obstetricians." Pp. 200–212 in *The Sociology of Health and Illness: Critical Perspectives*, 9th edition. edited by Peter Conrad and Valerie Leiter. New York: Worth.

24

Doctor–Patient Relationship

HYEYOUNG OH NELSON

The doctor-patient relationship is one of the most fundamental components of health care delivery. The interactions that take place between patients and doctors directly impact crucial aspects of health care, including patients' health care experiences, their health outcomes, and health care costs. Since the early twentieth century, social scientists have extensively explored the patient–doctor relationship, defining the nature and dynamics of the relationship, identifying the roles and responsibilities of patients and doctors, and analyzing how this relationship has transformed over time due to various micro- and macro-level changes within broader society (Boyer and Lutfey 2010; Lupton 1997; Lupton et al. 1991; Lutfey Spencer 2018; Parsons 1951; Timmermans and Oh 2010; Williams 2005). In this chapter, I explore this scholarship, providing a broad overview of the key theoretical approaches applied to the patient–doctor relationship. I review the literature on the patient–doctor relationship within medical sociology chronologically, with emphasis placed on key conceptualizations of patients' and doctors' roles as well as on how broader societal changes influenced, and accelerated, new identities and dynamics in the doctor-patient relationship over the course of the twentieth and twenty-first centuries in the United States. I then offer an empirical analysis of the pivotal role technology has played in shaping the patient–doctor relationship. Finally, I conclude with a discussion on how the patient–doctor relationship is a dynamic – and in many ways, privileged – process that is not uniformly experienced by the larger patient population.

MEDICAL PATERNALISM IN THE EARLY TWENTIETH CENTURY

In the early twentieth century, the doctor-patient relationship was one characterized by medical paternalism. Medical paternalism refers to a relationship where the "general practitioner genuinely wants the best for the patient, but believes that 

The Wiley Blackwell Companion to Medical Sociology, First Edition. Edited by William C. Cockerham.

patients often need to be guided firmly through the decision making process as they do not always know what is best for them" (McKinstry 1992: 340). Paternalism was prominent during this time period because of the identities accepted by patients and doctors. According to Talcott Parsons (1951), patients assumed the "sick role." The sick role refers to an individual who is "in a state where he is suffering or disabled or both, and possibly facing risks of worsening, which is socially defined as either 'not his fault' or something from which he cannot be expected to extricate himself by his own effort, or generally both" (Parsons 1951: 440–441).

Furthermore, he "is not, of course competent to help himself" and instead must seek "professional, technically competent help" (Parsons 1951: 441). In this context, patients were not held responsible for becoming ill, but they were responsible for seeking out medical professionals in order to recover. They were not able to make any determinations regarding their health and well-being, and instead had to place their full trust in the medical authority of physicians, granting them complete autonomy and control over all health care decisions (Reeder 1972). Even in instances where patients may question their physician or wish to seek another opinion, Parsons (1951: 438–439) stated that:

> if the patient is not satisfied with the advice his physician gives him he may properly do one of two things, first he may request a consultation, even naming the physician he wishes called in, but in that case it is physician A not the patient who must call B in, the patient may not see B independently. And above all not without A's knowledge. The other proper recourse is to terminate the relation with A and become "B's patient."

Subsequently, the patient–physician relationship was one centered on trust and full authority granted to the physician, otherwise the relationship should not persist.

The physician, therefore, was a "technical expert who by special training and experience, and by an institutionally validated status, is qualified to 'help' the patient in a situation institutionally defined as legitimate in a relative sense but as needing help" (Parsons 1951: 439). Furthermore, the physician was held responsible "for the welfare of the patient in the sense of facilitating his recovery from illness to the best of the physician's ability. In meeting this responsibility, he is expected to acquire and use high technical competence in 'medical science' and the techniques based upon it" (Parsons 1951: 447).

Their technical training, combined with the profession's institutional orientation to functional specificity, affective neutrality, and universalism, ensured their ability to properly and effectively care for the ill. As such, concerns of profit motives and physician greed could be set aside because physicians were unlike businessmen due to an institutionalized collectivity orientation that focused on the welfare of patients (Parsons 1951). This orientation guaranteed that physicians would not place financial gains above patient needs by enforcing specific behaviors, including prohibiting physicians from advertising to patients or refusing to provide care to individuals who could not afford it.

Thus, though patients were vulnerable due to an asymmetry of knowledge and power between themselves and doctors, the structuring of the medical system established numerous institutional safeguards to prevent physicians from exploiting patients (Parsons 1951). These safeguards ensured that the physician, who was given intimate access to patients' bodies and lives, would maintain a professional relationship with patients in health care delivery (Parsons 1951). The resulting patient–doctor relationship was one driven by paternalism (Beisecker and Beisecker 1993; Coulter 1997; Emanuel and Emanuel 1992), where physicians were granted full authority in care decision making with the expectation that they always acted in the best interests of patients.

Such medical paternalism remained prominent following the Second World War through the mid-1960s, which has commonly been referred to as the Golden Age of Medicine in the United States. During this period, physicians had achieved what Eliot Freidson (1970) has referred to as professional dominance, the distinguishing trait of all professions. According to Freidson (1970: XV), a profession is:

> an occupation which has assumed a dominant position in a division of labor, so that it gains control over the determination of the substance of its own work. Unlike most occupations, it is autonomous or self-directing. The occupation sustains this special status by its persuasive profession of the extraordinary trustworthiness of its members. The trustworthiness it professes naturally includes ethicality and also knowledgeable skill. In fact, the profession claims to be the most reliable authority on the nature of the reality it deals with. When its characteristic work lies in the attempt to deal with the problems people bring to it, the profession develops its own independent conception of those problems and tries to manage both client and problems in its own way.

Subsequently, professional dominance refers to a profession's ability to have full  authority and autonomy over their work. Accordingly, physicians held private, fee-for-service practices, set the qualifications of health professionals, determined interactions with patients, and controlled the relations they held with third parties, such as pharmaceutical and medical technology companies, without any external interference (Starr 1982). Physicians also held a great deal of cultural authority: they were deeply respected and experienced high levels of trust amongst the general public. The late-20th century, however, would see a widespread transformation within the provision of health care and a corresponding shift in the doctor-patient relationship, transforming the identities, responsibilities, and experiences of both patients and practitioners (Boyer and Lutfey 2010; Lupton 1997; Timmermans and Oh 2010; Williams 2005).

A Transforming Health Care Landscape: New Identities for Patients and Providers

Medical paternalism became an inaccurate characterization of the doctor-patient relationship by the latter half of the twentieth century, as the health care landscape underwent a complete transformation. Health care delivery, and the doctor-patient relationship, took on new dimensions as various parties become integral to the exchange of health care. Patients and doctors assumed different identities, ones that largely offset the asymmetry of knowledge and power associated with medical paternalism. However, before delving into the details of this new doctor-patient relationship, the following section explores changes to the broader health care system that facilitated the emergence of these new patient and provider roles.

It was during the Golden Age of Medicine when the foundations were established for a complete transformation in the distribution of health care within the United States. One major driving force was the growing commodification of medical care, which resulted in the emergence of a new medical landscape. This landscape became associated with numerous external parties (e.g. insurance companies, the pharmaceutical industry, the federal government) and with the infusion of money into the medical transaction (e.g. financial incentives, profit motives, etc.) (Light and Levine 1988). The rise of these external parties, with distinct objectives and incentives, established a new division of labor within health care provision. No longer a direct fee-for-service transaction between patient and physician, the exchange of medical care transformed into a complex marketplace encounter involving many parties (Conrad and Leiter 2004; Fennell and Alexander 1993; Light 2000).

These external parties took on tasks that were once solely performed by the physician (Casalino 2004), or new tasks that had become necessary within this unfamiliar health care landscape. The majority of these tasks were redistributed to external parties, primarily insurance companies, or to medical personnel and administrative staff within the clinical setting (Charles-Jones et al. 2003; Fennell and Alexander 1993). For instance, managers became integral to meet the new goals of cost-effectiveness and efficiency in clinics and hospitals. Managers were involved in care provision decisions, delegating duties and responsibilities of physicians, nurses, and other medical personnel in the clinical setting. These decisions were driven by goals of cost-saving and efficiency, but also resulted in new divisions of labor as the professional identities and responsibilities of health professionals were reconfigured (Charles-Jones et al. 2003).

This complex division of labor reflected the newfound requirement to be able to manage the conflicting needs of individuals inside and outside the organization (Kahn, Wolfe, Quinn, Snoek, and Rosenthal 1964). Consequently, the patient–physician relationship evolved from one dealing with patients and physicians, to one that had to account for numerous third parties. These third parties, also referred to as countervailing powers, were able to impose regulations and restrictions on physicians, threatening the professional dominance they had acquired over the first half of the 20th century (Haug 1988; Light 2000; Waitzkin 2000);[1] these groups offset the power and control physicians had amassed economically, politically and culturally (Light 2000; Light and Levine 1988) complicating the relationship between patient and doctor (Conrad and Leiter 2004; Light 2000; Waitzkin 2000).[2]

In particular, one of the most significant threats to physicians' professional dominance was the emergence of managed care companies. In the 1970s, health maintenance organizations were created to produce "efficient and fair health care" (Wallack 1992: 27) and have remained the hallmark of managed care. Managed care became a solution to the exponentially growing health care expenditure in the United States. The primary objectives of managed care were to "reduce excessive and unnecessary service utilization" to ensure efficiency (Wallack 1992: 28). Therefore, in order to meet these goals, managed care companies not only controlled costs, but also determined how physicians could practice medicine. To the dismay of both patients and physicians alike, bureaucratic rules and practices quickly became deeply entrenched in health care transactions (Hafferty and Light 1995). Patients encountered a limited choice of medical practitioners and therapies while physicians' experienced restrictions on the patients they could see and the types of treatments they could provide (Mechanic 1996). Furthermore, physicians experienced constraints to their time: limits were placed on how much time physicians could spend with patients (Mechanic 1996), resulting in increasingly shorter, impersonal clinical encounters (Mechanic 2008). Consequently, patients became increasingly disenchanted with their doctors and clinical encounters, and physicians, whom had become financially reliant on these external parties, experienced diminished professional autonomy and cultural authority.

The Rise of Patient Consumerism

This complete transformation in health care delivery gave rise to patient consumerism and a vastly different doctor-patient relationship than the one found in the early 20th century. As financial considerations became an increasingly salient issue in the exchange of medical care, physicians were now placed in an institutional position that required they balance financial considerations with the health and welfare of their patients (Rodwin 1993). This shift initiated a consumer driven model of health care (Conrad and Leiter 2004; Haug and Lavin 1983), where medical care was increasingly understood as a service that could be bought and sold, and the asymmetry of knowledge and power characteristic of patient–doctor relationships was reduced (Conrad and Leiter 2004; Haug and Lavin 1983). In this model of care provision, patients became regarded as *consumers* (Bashshur et al. 1967; Lupton 1997; Reeder 1972) and physicians as *providers* (Logan et al. 1989; Reeder 1972). Gone was the paternalistic patient–doctor relationship, and instead both parties brought "different resources to the encounter...prepared to negotiate an acceptable set of terms for the relationship," which included "agreements on both diagnosis and treatment" and resulted in "neither participant... automatically in charge" (Haug and Lavin 1981: 213).

As consumers, patients were comfortable challenging the authority of physicians, taking a proactive role in the medical decision making process at all stages of the clinical encounter—from diagnosis to payment (Charles et al. 1999; Haug and Lavin 1983; Oh 2012, 2017). Patients grew comfortable engaging in a variety of consumerist practices, which included making informed autonomous decisions, weighing financial costs when selecting both health care providers and making health care decisions, and exercising the freedom to shop, compare, purchase, and refuse providers and services (Heger Boyle and Lawler 1991; Hibbard and Weeks 1987; Lupton et al. 1991; Oh 2012, 2017). Individuals were equipped with greater bargaining and negotiation power when interacting with physicians as they were acknowledged as paying customers (Freidson 1970; Reeder 1972). While the shift towards consumerism was widespread, it is also important to note that generally individuals who tended to adopt such consumerist practices were often times "younger, more knowledgeable, more rejecting of authority in general, skeptical of physicians' service orientation, and convinced of their right to make health care decisions – who at least believe that physicians should not always be in charge" (Haug and Lavin 1981: 222).

As physicians took on the role of *providers*, and were forced to balance patient welfare with personal financial gain (Rodwin 1993), they saw the distribution of medical care as a service to be sold, in which they were in competition with other practitioners for patients (Reeder 1972). Accordingly, there was a growing fear of losing patients to competitors, which resulted in many physicians' newfound focus on patient satisfaction and patient needs (Reeder 1972). Consequently, this transformation of health care delivery resulted in a patient–doctor relationship driven much more by consumerism rather than paternalism. However, similar to the differences found across the patient populations, providers also embraced patient consumerism to varying degrees.[3] Some physicians refused patient demands, often times citing patients' inevitable lack of competency, or they tried to persuade patients, usually successfully, to adhere to their recommendations (Haug and Lavin 1981; Timmermans et al. 2018).

This emergence of greater patient consumerism (Figert 2011) was coupled with, and accelerated by, a decline in trust of physicians over the late-twentieth century. With the increased bureaucratization of medical care, the thalidomide scandal and reports of medical experimentation, and the implementation of informed consent laws (Haug and Lavin 1983; Taylor and Merrijoy 1987), doubts were cast as to whether physicians acted in patients' best interests (Reeder 1972). This erosion of trust equipped patients with even greater agency to engage in consumer practices (Campbell 1971); patients no longer hesitated to shop for a second opinion and to switch medical practitioners (Olsen et al. 1976). Consumerism was further exacerbated due to the unabated growth of health care costs, publicized malpractice lawsuits, and reports of excessive treatments and tests performed by physicians for financial gains (Gray 1997; Reeder 1972).

In this new health care landscape, patients actively sought out resources to offset the asymmetry of knowledge and power characteristic of the patient–physician relationship. Drawing from various resources, patients increasingly practiced self-diagnosis and demanded specific types of care from physicians rather than seeking out their opinions. Furthermore, with this increased erosion of trust in physicians and medicine, patients were comfortable questioning medical expertise, seeking complementary and alternative approaches to care (Winnick 2006, 2005),[4] and engaging in health social movements to elicit changes in health care provision, research and patients' rights (Brown et al. 2004; Epstein 1995). Such forms of patient engagement and autonomy, while salient, however were not uniform across the patient population. Instead, deep inequities could be found: for instance, typical users of complementary and alternative medicine and individuals at the frontlines of patient health movements – in turn largely shaping the movements' initiatives – have been predominantly white, highly educated, and of high socioeconomic status (Epstein 1995; Klawiter 1999).[5] Such inequities stemming from socio-demographic characteristics systematically render specific patient groups less able to make independent health care choices and less able to find alternative options in regards to their health and well-being. Consequently, more vulnerable patient populations are unable to gain power in clinical encounters and instead have little choice in deferring to medical practitioners for diagnosis and treatment options.

Nonetheless, with these shifts in care delivery towards a consumerist model, combined with the growing discontent among patients, physicians demonstrated a renewed commitment to regaining patient trust (Mechanic 2008) by making patients' needs central to care provision (Emanuel and Pearson 2012). For instance, providers developed ways to give patients the benefits associated with longer office visits and more personal care – ensuring physicians familiarized themselves with particular patients' needs (Mechanic 2008). Other initiatives included avoiding conflicts of interest (e.g. pharmaceutical companies offering physicians incentives to promote specific therapeutic options) and addressing recurrent problems of patient safety and medical error. In addition, pay-for-performance (P4P) initiatives, which define important objectives of care and provide financial incentives for physicians to meet these objectives, were developed and adopted in numerous clinical settings (Mechanic 2008). These initiatives were implemented to help improve the quality of health care received by patients, and to renew the trust of patients in both physicians and the health care system (Mechanic 2008).

The Shift to Patient-Centered Care

The strategies adopted by clinicians reflected another progressive shift in health care delivery: one towards patient-centered care. Patient-centered care refers to care provision that is "respectful of and representative to individual patient preferences, needs, and values and ensuring that patient values guide all clinical decisions" (Committee on Quality of Health Care in America 2001: 40). This model of care encourages patient agency, empowerment, and inclusion in medical decision making with providers. Subsequently, patient-centered care "fosters interactions in which clinicians and patients engage in two-way sharing of information; explore patients' values and preferences; help patients and their families make clinical decisions; facilitate access to appropriate care; and enable patients to follow through with often difficult behavioral changes needed to maintain or improve health" (Epstein et al. 2010: 1490).

Patient satisfaction is a central, and critical feature, to this mode of care delivery, often utilized as a metric to assess physician and care quality. Patient satisfaction measures ensure that the "physician has provided comfort, emotional support, education, and considered the patient's perspective in the synthesis of the clinical decision making process" (Kupfer and Bond 2012: 139). Studies have revealed that patient satisfaction is positively correlated with physicians foregoing medical paternalism, promoting effective communication with patients and families, and including them in the decision making process (Bernabeo and Holmboe 2013; Mast, Hall, and Roter 2008; Street Jr. et al. 2009). In recent years, financial incentives, such as reimbursement policies and determinations of physician compensation based on patient satisfaction metrics, have been established to further solidify the emphasis of care delivery on patient satisfaction and patients' experiences (Lyu et al. 2013; Manary et al. 2013).

Technology and the Doctor-Patient Relationship

Many scholars have extensively studied the driving forces that have defined and redefined the doctor-patient relationship over the course of the twentieth and twenty-first centuries. While numerous factors have played an integral role in the changing identities of doctors and patients, advancements in technology, have arguably, been the most significant. In this section, I examine how technology has directly shaped the doctor-patient relationship, starting with the internet. The internet has facilitated patients' abilities to obtain knowledge in regards to their own health and health care options (Haug 1988), vastly transforming the patient–physician relationship. The internet has given patients access to electronic health books, health forums, and other online sources that provide a wealth of information that enables patients to self-diagnose, to learn about treatment options, and to even evaluate the financial costs associated with different treatment plans (McKinlay and Marceau 2008). Studies have revealed how patients have used the internet to compare medical facilities and to learn about physicians' histories, increasing their abilities to shop around and find the best care at the cheapest price (Hibbard and Weeks 1987; Lupton et al. 1991; McKinlay and Marceau 2008). Consequently, patients were increasingly comfortable making autonomous decisions when selecting physicians, making health care choices, and selecting health insurance policies (Hibbard and Weeks 1987; Lupton et al. 1991).

Patients were now equipped with the ability to engage in self-care (Swan 2012), diagnosing themselves and actively searching for information about illnesses and treatment options prior to stepping into a physician's office (Burrows et al. 2000; Davison et al. 2000; Greene and Hibbard 2012). Patients found resources and comfort in online self-help communities (Barker 2008; Davison et al. 2000; Eng 2001; Oravec 2001), giving them a space to commiserate over shared conditions, define symptoms, discuss treatment options, evaluate experiences, provide support, and empower patients in interactions with their doctors (Barker 2008; Davison et al. 2000; Halpern 2004). Consequently, these "well-informed" and "knowledge empowered" patients began to skip the diagnostic process and instead were scheduling visits to request specific forms of treatment or medications (McKinlay and Marceau 2008).

Patients' Internet-Use: The Implications of Too Much Information

In response to these shifts in the patient–physician relationship, scholars have extensively examined this transformation in patients' approaches to care, with many bemoaning the clinical consequences of such "empowered" patients, such as the over-medicalization of conditions and the growing reports of unnecessary pharmaceutical use (Bergen et al. 2017; Butler et al. 1998; Kravitz et al. 2005; Rathert et al. 2013; Stivers 2002; Weissman et al. 2004). The literature has pointed to "well-informed" patients frequently pressuring physicians for specific medications that are not always clinically indicated (Bergen et al. 2017; Butler et al. 1998; Kravitz et al. 2005; Mangione-Smith et al. 1999; Moloney 2017; Stivers 2002). Of particular concern is the overprescribing of unnecessary antibiotics (Butler et al. 1998; Mangione-Smith et al. 1999; Nyquist et al. 1998) due to the public health implications of the misuse of antibiotics and the growing emergence of drug resistant illnesses (Mehta et al. 2014).

Much of the onus of responsibility to curb such overprescribing has been placed on physicians' shoulders, with less attention placed on the role of "informed" patients' expectations in shaping the likelihood of prescription (Heritage and Stivers 1999; Mangione-Smith et al. 2003). One approach has been the utilization of "online commentary," which refers to the process of physicians' clearly communicating to patients what they are finding during the examination (Heritage et al. 2010; Mangione-Smith et al. 2003). When practicing online commentary, physicians use specific communication techniques to show the patient "no problem" or "problem" commentary; this strategy informs patients during the clinical encounter itself as to when physicians are finding concerns that require drug intervention and when they are not (Heritage et al. 2010; Mangione-Smith et al. 2003).

It is important to note that patients' internet behaviors are not solely to be blamed for the growing concerns of unnecessary prescriptions. The pharmaceutical industry, specifically its use of direct-to-consumer advertising for marketing rather than solely advertising to providers, is a major contributing factor behind these trends (Kessler and Pines 1990). Direct-to-consumer advertising increases patients' awareness of pharmaceutical therapies, and subsequently the likelihood that they will make requests to their physicians to receive these therapies (Kravitz et al. 2005). Proponents of direct to consumer advertising highlight that these advertisements produce well-informed, proactive patients because they provide not only information on various pharmaceutical options, but also educate individuals on a variety of health conditions that they were unaware of (Holmer 1999; Weissman et al. 2004). This translates to patients becoming cognizant of, and accessing, new therapeutic options, resulting in better management of symptoms and conditions and in turn, improved health outcomes (Batchlor and Laoui 2003; Kravitz et al. 2005; Weissman et al. 2004). For instance, in the case of major depression, patients who referred to specific pharmaceutical advertisements were more likely to receive prescriptions for much needed antidepressants. This prevented initial undertreatment of the condition, which unfortunately was common among patients who did not mention an advertisement to their providers (Kravitz et al. 2005).[6]

Nevertheless, improper prescribing of pharmaceuticals is one commonly documented consequence of increased patient consumerism and agency in health care delivery. Many have argued that while technologies like the internet have helped to create more knowledgeable patients, there remains an information deficit between patients and physicians, as evidenced by these reports of patients' pressuring providers for unnecessary prescriptions. Patients often times lack proficiency in distinguishing reliable information, consequently they remain misinformed or uninformed (Henwood et al. 2003). While this may be true, it is crucial to state that patients' consumerist practices are not solely responsible for such trends, but rather numerous factors, including pharmaceutical companies, time constraints in clinical encounters, and the realities of managed care, collectively incentivize providers to repeatedly turn to pharmaceutical therapies for patient care (Moloney 2017). In Moloney's (2017) study of pharmaceutical interventions for insomnia, physicians reluctantly provided prescriptions for patients complaining of sleeplessness and insomnia. Although these clinicians would have preferred to not medicalize insomnia and to avoid prescribing drug interventions for some of their patients, patients' requests and preferences combined with insurance considerations and time limitations placed on office visits, all factored into physicians' decisions to recommend a pharmaceutical intervention.

Furthermore, while this patient-centered model of care has led to increased patient autonomy and empowerment, an asymmetry of power persists between patients and providers. Although some physicians feel compelled to provide patients with the care they desire, many physicians reject patients' findings, refuse to negotiate with them, or cultivate strategies that convince patients to accept medical expertise and adhere to provider recommended diagnosis and treatment options (Haug and Lavin 1981; Henwood et al. 2003; Timmermans et al. 2018). Accordingly, even as patients become equipped with greater knowledge, patients still commonly face an uphill battle to gain an equal voice in care provision. In addition, even with the general availability of resources such as the internet, many patients still opt to maintain a paternalistic approach to medicine and primarily seek the advice of the physician (Henwood et al. 2003; Lupton et al. 1991).

Digitized Patients: An Expectation in the 21st Century

Internet and other information technologies have taken on new meaning in the 21st century. Rather than simply being characterized as a tool for patients to engage in consumerism or to become empowered—which have previously been attributed to negatively impacting the patient–physician relationship—use of the internet and other health technologies are now expected of patients if they wish to be deemed serious about their health and well-being. Providers often anticipate that patients will welcome serving as managers of their own health and health care by seeking out the internet (Stevenson et al. 2018), sharing information and data, and using web-based personal health repositories (Lupton 2013a). With the near universal access to the internet, along with the widespread use of mobile digital devices and other digital health technologies, patients have unprecedented opportunities to engage in self-surveillance of their health by collecting and analyzing personal biometric data (e.g. heart rate, steps, glucose, sleep, etc.), as well as being able to access health information anywhere and at any time (Goggin 2011; Swan 2012).[7]

Providers have also embraced these same technologies, further reshaping health care provision (Mort et al. 2009; Oudshoorn 2011, 2012; Stevenson et al. 2018). For instance, telemedicine has emerged as a vital component of the medical system – one that fulfills the triple aim in health care (Berwick et al. 2008)[8] by positively impacting patients' health care experiences and improving patients' health outcomes at low financial costs (Perzynski et al. 2017). Telemedicine "involves using digital and other technologies to encourage patients to self-monitor their medical conditions at home, thus reducing visits to or from health care providers, and to communicate with health care providers via these technologies rather than face to face" (Lupton 2013a: 259). The end result is that patients are required to engage in regular self-monitoring and self care; such "digitizing" of bodies has become the norm and patients "become 'engaged' and 'activated,' to 'take control' of their health and to produce their own data on themselves and share these data with others as well as access the data produced by medical testing and medical records" (Lupton 2013a: 260).

Unequal Access to New Patient Identities

Discussions of greater patient consumerism, agency, and empowerment routinely tend to disregard the privileged nature of these statuses. Scholars have extensively examined how assumptions of patient-centered care and increased patient consumerism are inaccurate characterizations of many patient populations (Andreassen and Trondsen 2010; Hibbard and Cunningham 2008; Salander and Moynihan 2010; Shim 2010). The ability to adopt consumerist or digitized practices in health care delivery relies greatly on the resources available to patients (Gage-Bouchard 2017; Hibbard and Cunningham 2008). Younger, more educated, and higher income patient groups tend to favor consumerist approaches when seeking out care (Hibbard and Cunningham 2008). These findings resonate with the patient dynamics that have emerged from the widespread acceptance of information and communication technologies in health care by both patients and providers; such heavy reliance on different modes of technology have alienated individuals and exacerbated inequities among certain patient groups. For instance, self-surveillance and regular monitoring can be deeply overwhelming for patients (Lupton 2013a; Veitch 2010), resulting in resistance to, or complete abandonment of, such practices (Lupton 2013a). Women in particular have been found to experience increased anxiety and greater likelihood of adverse health outcomes due to such increased self-surveillance (Seçkin 2020).

Furthermore, studies have revealed how the elderly, underinsured, and minority patients – especially individuals who identify as African American and Latinx – are disproportionately negatively impacted by the heavy reliance on information technologies. For instance, these populations are "less likely to live in areas with a preponderance of home broadband internet or to access the patient portal" (Perzynski et al. 2017: 929). Subsequently, individuals from these groups have limited opportunities to engage in the digital practices that have increasingly been associated with "good" or "dedicated" patients. While smartphones may alleviate some of these challenges, racial and ethnic minorities and individuals with lower socioeconomic status are once again found to be at a disadvantage: these individuals are much more likely to "reach their plan's data cap" (Perzynski et al. 2017: 931) and therefore unable to utilize technologies like patient portals and data repositories when managing their own care. Such actions, or lack thereof, can result in the mislabeling of patients as "non-compliant" or "non-adherent" as providers perceive these patients as resisting or neglecting providers' recommendations and guidelines.

These inequities are unsurprising when considering Janet Shim's (2010) research, which has focused on how broader social inequalities are re-created in patient–doctor interactions through cultural health capital. Cultural health capital refers to:

> "a specialized form of cultural capital that can be leveraged in health care contexts to effectively engage with medical providers… CHC develops in and through the repeated enactment of health-related practices, such as consuming biomedical knowledge, exercising calculative and future-oriented approaches to decision-making and engaging in self-surveillance and risk-reduction practices".
>
> (Shim 2010: 3)

Patients' abilities to cultivate cultural health capital are fundamentally tied to factors including race and ethnicity, socioeconomic status, gender, and educational attainment. The ability to acquire and expand one's cultural health capital is acutely important because such capital can lead to micro-advantages that grow over time, resulting in starkly different health care experiences and outcomes (Gengler 2014; Rubin et al. 2018).

For instance, Gengler (2014) explored how parents navigated care for their children, who were diagnosed with life-threatening conditions, at an elite medical institution. Drawing on the concept of cultural health capital, Gengler (2014) found that parents tended to enter into two distinct trajectories of care engagement: care-captaining and care-entrusting. Care captaining included "negotiating with health care providers, conducting sophisticated research on available doctors, hospitals, and treatments, and successfully intervening to influence the care their children received" (Gengler 2014: 346). The end result was that parents exhibited high degrees of cultural health capital as they mobilized resources, were deeply engaged in their children's care, and they were unafraid "to hold key actors accountable, and held those actors accountable when they deemed necessary" (Gengler 2014: 346). In contrast, care-entrusting individuals left the medical decision making to the physicians, resulting in immensely different care and illness experiences within the same medical institution: care-captaining parents tended to acquire advantages throughout various stages of illness management.

This is particularly concerning because patients who cultivate more cultural health capital are able to gain more respect from providers and subsequently, are given more time and resources in clinical encounters (Fenton 2019; Shim 2010), resulting in different health care trajectories (Gage-Bouchard 2017). Patients' medical knowledge and demeanor with providers dictate the likelihood that patients will be included in the medical decision making process, whether they will be offered additional resources and information (Shim 2010), and whether clinicians will defer to patients' preferences when determining treatment protocols (Fenton 2019). In contrast, patients with less cultural health capital are often labeled as passive or negligent of their care, resulting in providers failing to "supplement the toolkit they have to optimize their own care and relationships with health professionals" (Shim 2010: 8). These interactions stymie patients' abilities to generate cultural health capital and without an ability to mobilize and cultivate such capital, inequities increase.

Similar to how the advantages of cultural health capital can accrue over time, the disadvantages associated with a lack of cultural health capital can also accumulate leading to widening gaps in health. There are critical consequences for patients who routinely experience less favorable clinical encounters and fail to receive adequate treatments (Rubin et al. 2018; Sleath and Shih 2003). Rubin and colleagues (2018) found that when dealing with chronic pain management, patients with less cultural health capital had much poorer pain management compared to their more advantaged counterparts. African American women living in poverty were especially at a disadvantage in clinical encounters; they were less likely to be asked about treatment preferences or to be included in medical decisions, and were much more likely to be written off as difficult and unable to effectively manage their own pain (Rubin et al. 2018).

Similarly, Hausmann et al. (2013) found that among patients being monitored for prescribed opioid use, African American patients had an increased likelihood for being singled out for drug testing or recommended to see a substance abuse specialist, compared to White patients. Such interactions left African American patients feeling defensive and dissatisfied with care, which had implications for their health: many of these patients reported inadequate pain management. Unsurprisingly, these negative health care experiences compounded over time can foster growing distrust, apathy, and antagonism towards health care providers and the broader health care system. What are the implications of this? The critical consequence is that patients either fail to receive the care that they need or they abandon future attempts to seek out care.

Cultural health capital, and other advantages that patients possess in clinical encounters, are typically cultivated through effective interpersonal interactions and communication skills. Studies have found that racial and ethnic minorities are more likely to be misunderstood and dismissed by providers during clinical conversations (Balsa and McGuire 2001, 2003; Balsa et al. 2005; Cooper et al. 2006; McGuire et al. 2008; Rubin et al. 2018). Subsequently, as patients face an uphill battle to be sufficiently heard and understood by clinicians, they may start to forego care, especially when treatment protocols fail to effectively manage the patient's primary concerns. However, it is also important to note that cultural health capital, patient agency and empowerment, and inclusion in decision making may not always translate to better care, as providers may inappropriately defer to patients, resulting in treatment protocols that contradict standards of care (Fenton 2019; Gengler 2014; Rand et al. 2007). For instance, in clinical encounters with parents regarding HPV vaccinations for their children, providers were more likely to defer to parents' requests to delay vaccination, especially to those utilizing greater cultural health capital. Unfortunately, this decision to delay the HPV vaccine was at odds with the Advisory Committee on Immunizations Practices' recommendation to provide the HPV vaccination to children when they turn 11 or 12 years of age (Fenton 2019). Nonetheless, generally, inclusion of patients in medical care decision making and acknowledgement of patients' agency and empowerment, result in improved health care experiences and greater patient satisfaction (Yeh, Wu, and Tung 2018).

Subsequently, it is deeply problematic that the widespread transformations in the patient–physician relationship and new patient identities that have emerged over the course of the twentieth and twenty-first centuries are unevenly distributed across the population. Many groups remain marginalized and are unable, or simply do not wish, to challenge medical authority and take on more responsibilities in care provision (Andreassen and Trondsen 2010; Salander and Moynihan 2010). Yet as the current health care landscape continues to embrace patient-centered care and has come to expect savvy, engaged, digitized, and proactive patients, many health inequities will continue to persist, if not, widen. The patient–doctor relationship has deep implications for patients' health care experiences and outcomes. Providers' perceptions of patients are crucial in shaping patients' trajectories. Consequently, when patients are perceived as disengaged, negligent, and lazy due to their lack of medical knowledge, inadequate self-monitoring, and ineffective use of technologies like the internet, with little consideration of the structural factors that shape these actions and interactions between patients and providers, there are consequences for patients' health outcomes. Therefore, it is critical for scholars to continue to examine and re-examine the patient–doctor relationship, as it is one that is not uniform but rather, a dynamic process deeply influenced by a wide array of individual and structural factors.

Notes

1 The increased role of external parties in the medical exchange could partly be attributed to changes in the actual medical field: there was a shift towards increased specialization (Light 2000; Starr 1982). The division of labor that ensued from the emergence of various subspecialties ironically made health professionals more vulnerable to external control, diminishing the dominance they had achieved during the Golden Age of Medicine (Light 2010).

2 Some examples of these countervailing powers include managed care companies, medical supply companies, medical personnel and administrative staff, pharmaceutical companies, and the federal government.

3 It is important to note that the patient–physician relationship however could never mimic a true market transaction. Donald Light (2010) discusses this distinction stating that in markets consumers should have "complete and free information" rather than "asymmetrical" information, which is common within the exchange of health care; there will always be an inherent asymmetry of knowledge between patients and physicians. This asymmetry of knowledge manifests itself regardless of patients' abilities to gain greater agency and knowledge from various sources, ranging from the internet to direct-to-consumer advertising.

4 Complementary and alternative medicines are defined as the "diagnosis, treatment and/or prevention which complements mainstream medicine by contributing to a common whole, by satisfying a demand not met by orthodoxy or by diversifying the conceptual frameworks of medicine" (Ernst et al. 1995: 506). Some of the most popular alternative treatments have been varieties of Chinese medicine (typically acupuncture), chiropractic and folk healing, and homeopathic remedies (Hartley 2002). The rise in CAM can in part be attributed to achievements of biomedicine: people live longer, however in turn they also develop difficult to treat chronic conditions (Lee-Treweek 2001). The uncertainty of biomedical knowledge is another factor, as limits in biomedical treatment options leave patients looking for alternative, less orthodox therapies (Epstein 1995). A third contributing factor has been the cost-effectiveness of such services; insurance companies have capitalized on the financial benefits of complementary and alternative medicine and have even extended some of their policies to cover particular complementary and alternative treatments for patients (Winnick Terri 2005). In response to the growing popularity of CAM, physicians supported patients' preferences for alternative therapies. Many physicians began accepting and recommending complementary and alternative medicines as a treatment course for some patients, even incorporating CAM into their own practice (Winnick 2006).

5 The difference in CAM use may be a reflection not only of a lack of resources or information that facilitates use of complementary and alternative therapies, but also that CAM services may not be physically available in particular neighborhoods (e.g. low income areas).

6 There exist critical inequities in access to prescriptions, particularly in the arena of mental health; age, insurance coverage, and patient–physician relationships all shape the likelihood of an individual receiving a prescription, resulting in some patients being undertreated and unable to access the therapies that they need (Sleath and Shih 2003).

7 Even workplaces have taken advantage of the availability of these various health technologies, encouraging workers to track various health metrics (e.g. sleep, diet, and exercise) and rewarding them (usually financially) for good health behaviors (Lupton 2013b).

8 The triple aim in health care refers to the commitment to improve patients' health care experiences, to improve the health of populations, and to reduce health care costs (health care per capita spending) (Berwick et al. 2008).

References

Andreassen, Hege and Marianne Trondsen. 2010. "The Empowered Patient and the Sociologist." *Social Theory & Health* 8(3): 280–287.

Balsa, Ana I. and Thomas G. McGuire. 2001. "Statistical Discrimination in Health Care." *Journal of Health Economics* 20: 881–907.

Balsa, Ana I. and Thomas G. McGuire. 2003. "Prejudice, Clinical Uncertainty and Stereotyping as Sources of Health Disparities." *Journal of Health Economics* 22: 89–116.

Balsa, Ana I., Thomas G. McGuire, and Lisa S. Meredith. 2005. "Testing for Statistical Discrimination in Health Care." *Health Services Research* 40: 227–252.

Barker, Kristin. 2002. "Self-Help Literature and the Making of an Illness Identity: The Case of Fibromyalgia Syndrome (FMS)." *Social Problems* 49: 279–300.

Barker, Kristin. 2008. "Electronic Support Groups, Patient-Consumers, and Medicalization: The Case of Contested Illness." *Journal of Health and Social Behavior* 49: 20–36.

Bashshur, Rashid L., Charles A. Metzner, and Carla Worden. 1967. "Consumer Satisfaction with Group Practice, the CHA Case." *American Journal of Public Health* 57: 1991–1999.

Batchlor, Elaine and Marlanne Laoui. 2003. "Pharmaceutical Promotion, Advertising, and Consumers." *Health Affairs 22 (NO. SUPPL1: Web Exclusives)*: 109–111.

Beisecker, Analee E. and Thomas D. Beisecker. 1993. "Using Metaphors to Characterize Doctor-patient Relationships: Paternalism versus Consumerism." *Health Communication* 5: 41–58.

Bergen, Clara, Rebecca K. Tanya Stivers, John Heritage Barnes, Rose McCabe, Laura Thompson, and Merran Toerrien. 2017. "Closing the Deal: A Cross-cultural Comparison of Treatment Resistance." *Health Communication* 33(11): 1–12.

Bernabeo, Elizabeth and Eric S. Holmboe. 2013. "Patients, Providers, and Systems Need to Acquire a Specific Set of Competencies to Achieve Truly Patient-Centered Care." *Health Affairs* 32(2): 250–58.

Berwick, Donald M., Thomas W. Nolan, and John Whittington. 2008. "The Triple Aim: Care, Health, and Cost." *Health Affairs* 27(3): 759–769.

Boyer, Carol A. and Karen Lutfey. 2010. "Examining Critical Health Policy Issues within and beyond the Clinical Encounter: Patient-Provider Relationships and Help-seeking Behaviors." *Journal of Health and Social Behavior* 51(S): S80-93.

Brown, Phil, Stephen Zavestoski, Sabrina McCormick, Brian Mayer, Rachel Morello-Frosch, and Rebeca Gasior Altman. 2004. "Embodied Health Movements: New Approaches to Social Movements in Health." *Sociology of Health & Illness* 26(1): 50–80.

Burrows, Roger, Sarah Nettleton, Nicholas Pleace, and Steven Muncer. 2000. "Virtual Community Care? Social Policy and the Emergence of Computer Mediated Social Support." *Information, Communication and Society* 3: 95–121.

Butler, Christopher C., Stephen Rollnick, Roisin Pill, Frances Maggs-Rapport, and Nigel Stott. 1998. "Understanding the Culture of Prescribing: Qualitative Study of General Practitioners' and Patients' Perceptions of Antibiotics for Sore Throats." *British Medical Journal* 317: 637–642.

Campbell, John L. 1971. "Working Relationships between Providers and Consumers in a Neighborhood Health Center." *American Journal of Public Health* 61: 97–103.

Casalino, Lawrence P. 2004. "Unfamiliar Tasks, Contested Jurisdictions: The Changing Organization Field of Medical Practice in the United States." *Journal of Health and Social Behavior* 45: 59–75.

Charles, Cathy, Amiram Gafni, and Tim Whelan. 1999. "Decision Making in the Physician-patient Encounter: Revisiting the Shared Treatment Decision Making Model." *Social Science & Medicine* 49: 651–661.

Charles-Jones, Huw, Joanna Latimer, and Carl May. 2003. "Transforming General Practice: The Redistribution of Medical Work in Primary Care." *Sociology of Health & Illness* 25: 71–92.

Committee on Quality of Health Care in America (Institute of Medicine). 2001. *Crossing the Quality Chasm: A New Health System for the 21st Century.* Washington, DC: National Academy Press.

Conrad, Peter and Valerie Leiter. 2004. "Medicalization, Markets and Consumers." *Journal of Health and Social Behavior* 45: 158–176.

Cooper, Lisa A., Mary Catherine Beach, Rachel L. Johnson, and Thomas S. Inui. 2006. "Delving below the Surface: Understanding How Race and Ethnicity Influence Relationships in Health Care." *Journal of General Internal Medicine* 21: S21-27.

Coulter, Angela. 1997. "Partnerships with Patients: The Pros and Cons of Shared Clinical Decision Making." *Journal of Health Services Research and Policy* 2: 112–121.

Davison, Kathryn, James Pennebaker, and Sally Dickerson. 2000. "Who Talks: The Social Psychology of Illness Support Groups." *American Psychologist* 55: 205–217.

Emanuel, Ezekiel J. and L.L. Emanuel. 1992. "Four Models of the Physician-patient Relationship." *Journal of the American Medical Association* 267: 2221–2226.

Emanuel, Ezekiel J. and Steven D. Pearson. 2012. "Physician Autonomuy and Health Care Reform." *JAMA* 307(4): 367–368.

Eng, Thomas. 2001. *The Ehealth Landscape: A Terrain Map of Emerging Information and Communication Technologies in Health and Health Care.* Princeton, NJ: Robert Wood Johnson Foundation.

Epstein, Ronald M., Kevin Fiscella, Cara S. Lesser, and Kurt C. Stange. 2010. "Why the Nation Needs a Policy Push on Patient-Centered Health Care." *Health Affairs* 29(8): 1489–1495.

Epstein, Steven. 1995. "The Construction of Lay Expertise: AIDS Activism and the Forging of Credibility in the Reform of Clinical Trials." *Science Technology Human Values* 20(4): 408–437.

Ernst, Edzard, K., L. Resch, R. Hill, A. Mitchell, M. Willoughby, and A. White. 1995. "Complementary Medicine – a Definition." *British Journal of General Practice* 45(398): 506.

Fennell, Mary L. and Jeffrey A. Alexander. 1993. "Perspectives on Organizational Change in the US Medical Care Sector." *Annual Review of Sociology* 19: 89–112.

Fenton, Anny T. 2019. "Abandoning Medical Authority: When Medical Professionals Confront Stigmatized Adolescent Sex and the Human Papillomavirus (HPV) Vaccine." *Journal of Health and Social Behavior* 60(2): 240–256.

Figert, Anne E. 2011. "The Consumer Turn in Medicalization: Future Directions with Historical Foundations." Pp. 291–307 in *Handbook of the Sociology of Health, Illness, and Healing*, edited by B. A. Pescosolido, J. K. Martin, J. D. McLeod, and A. Rogers. New York: Springer.

Freidson, E. 1970. *Profession of Medicine: A Study of the Sociology of Applied Knowledge.* New York: Harper and Row Publishers.

Gage-Bouchard, Elizabeth A. 2017. "Culture, Styles of Institutional Interactions, and Inequalities in Healthcare Experiences." *Journal of Health and Social Behavior* 58(2): 147–165.

Gengler, Amanda N. 2014. "'I Want You to Save My Kid!': Illness Management Strategies, Access, and Inequality at an Elite University Research Hospital." *Journal of Health and Social Behavior* 55(3): 342–359.

Goggin, Gerard. 2011. "Ubiquitous Apps: Politics of Openness in Global Mobile Communities." *Digital Creativity* 22(3): 148–159.

Gray, Bradford H. 1997. "Trust and Trustworthy Care in the Managed Care Era." *Health Affairs* 16: 34–49.

Greene, Jessica and Judith H. Hibbard. 2012. "Why Does Patient Activation Matter? an Examination of the Relationships between Patient Activation and Health-related Outcomes." *Journal of General Internal Medicine* 27(5): 520–526.

Hafferty, Frederic W. and Donald W. Light. 1995. "Professional Dominance and the Changing Nature of Medical Work." *Journal of Health and Social Behavior* 35: 132–153.

Halpern, Sydney A. 2004. "Medical Authority and the Culture of Rights." *Journal of Health Politics, Policy and Law* 29(4-5): 835–852.

Hartley, Heather. 2002. "The System of Alignments Challenging Physician Professional Dominance: An Elaborated Theory of Countervailing Powers." *Sociology of Health and Illness* 24: 178–207.

Haug, Marie R. 1988. "A Re-Examination of the Hypothesis of Physician Deprofessionalization." *The Milbank Quarterly* 66(Supplement 2): 48–56.

Haug, Marie R. and Bebe Lavin. 1981. "Practitioner or Patient – Who's in Charge?" *Journal of Health and Social Behavior* 22(3): 212–229.

Haug, Marie R. and Bebe Lavin. 1983. *Consumerism in Medicine.* Beverly Hills, CA: Sage Publications.

Hausmann, Leslie R. M., Shasha Gao, Edward S. Lee, and C. Kent Kwoh. 2013. "Racial Disparities in the Monitoring of Patients on Chronic Opioid Therapy." *Pain®* 154: 46–52.

Heger Boyle, Elizabeth and Edward J. Lawler. 1991. "Resolving Conflict Through Explicit Bargaining." *Social Forces* 69: 1183–1204.

Henwood, Flis, Sally Wyatt, Angie Hart, and Julie Smith. 2003. "Ignorance Is Bliss Sometimes': Constraints on the Emergence of the 'Informed Patient' in the Changing Landscapes of Health Information." *Sociology of Health & Illness* 25: 589–607.

Heritage, John, Marc N. Elliott, Tanya Stivers, Andrea Richardson, and Rita Mangione-Smith. 2010. "Reducing Inappropriate Antibiotics Prescribing: The Role of Online Commentary on Physical Examination Findings." *Patient Education and Counseling* 81(1): 119–125.

Heritage, John and Tanya Stivers. 1999. "Online Commentary in Acute Medical Visits: A Method of Shaping Patient Expectations." *Social Science and Medicine* 49: 1501–1517.

Hibbard, Judith H. and Peter J. Cunningham. 2008. "How Engaged are Consumers in Their Health and Health Care, and Why Does It Matter." *Research Brief* 8: 1–9.

Hibbard, Judith H. and Edward C. Weeks. 1987. "Consumerism in Health Care: Prevalence and Predictors." *Medical Care* 25: 1019–1032.

Holmer, Alan F. 1999. "Direct-to-Consumer Prescription Drug Advertising Builds Bridges between Patients and Physicians." *JAMA* 281: 380–382.

Kahn, Robert, Donald M. Wolfe, Robert P. Quinn, J. Diedrick Snoek, and Robert A. Rosenthal. 1964. *Organizational Stress: Studies in Role Conflict and Ambiguity.* New York: Wiley.

Kessler, David A. and Wayne L. Pines. 1990. "The Federal Regulation of Prescription Drug Advertising and Promotion." *JAMA* 264: 2409–2415.

Klawiter, Maren. 1999. "Racing for the Cure, Walking Women, and Toxic Touring: Mapping Cultures of Action within the Bay Area Terrain of Breast Cancer." *Social Problems* 46(1): 104–126.

Kravitz, Richard L., Ronald M. Epstein, Mitchell D. Feldman, Carol E. Franz, Michael S. Azari Rahman, Ladson Hinton Wilkes, and Peter Franks. 2005. "Influence of Patients' Requests for Direct-to-Consumer Advertised Antidepressants: A Randomized Controlled Trial." *JAMA* 293: 1995–2002.

Kupfer, Joel M. and Edward U. Bond. 2012. "Patient Satisfaction and Patient-Centered Care: Necessary but Not Equal." *JAMA* 308(2): 139–140.

Lee-Treweek, Geraldine. 2001. "I'm Not Ill, It's Just This Back: Osteopathic Treatment, Responsibility and Back Problems." *Health* 5: 31–49.

Light, Donald W. 2000. "The Medical Profession and Organizational Change: From Professional Dominance to Countervailing Power." Pp. 201–216 in *Handbook of Medical Sociology*, vol. 5th, edited by C. E. Bird, P. Conrad, and A. M. Fremont. Upper Saddle River, NJ: Prentice Hall.

Light, Donald W. 2010. "Health Care Professions, Markets, and Countervailing Powers." Pp. 270–289 in *Handbook of Medical Sociology*, 6th, edited by C. E. Bird, P. Conrad, A. M. Fremont, and S. Timmermans. Nashille, TN: Vanderbilt University Press.

Light, Donald W. and Sol Levine. 1988. "The Changing Character of the Medical Profession: A Theoretical Overview." *The Milbank Quarterly* 66(Supplement 2): 10–32.

Logan, John, David Green, and Alan Woodfield. 1989. *Healthy Competition*. Sydney: Centre for Independent Studies.

Lupton, Deborah. 1997. "Consumerism, Reflexivity and the Medical Encounter." *Social Science and Medicine* 45: 373–381.

Lupton, Deborah. 2013a. *Digitized Health Promotion: Personal Responsibility for Health in the Web 2.0 Era. Sydney Health & Society Group Working Paper No.5*. Sydney: Sydney Health & Society Group.

Lupton, Deborah. 2013b. "The Digitally Engaged Patient: Self-monitoring and Self-care in the Digital Health Era." *Social Theory & Health* 11(3): 256–270.

Lupton, Deborah, Cam Donaldson, and Peter Lloyd. 1991. "Caveat Emptor or Blissful Ignorance? Patients and the Consumerist Ethos." *Social Science & Medicine* 33: 559–568.

Lutfey Spencer, Karen. 2018. "Transforming Patient Compliance Research in an Era of Biomedicalization." *Journal of Health and Social Behavior* 59(2): 170–184.

Lyu, Heather, Elizabeth C. Wick, Michael Housman, Julie Ann Freischlag, and Martin A. Makary. 2013. "Patient Satisfaction as a Possible Indicator of Quality Surgical Care." *JAMA Surgery* 148(4): 362–37.

Manary, Matthew P., William Boulding, Richard Staelin, and Seth W. Glickman. 2013. "The Patient Experience and Health Outcomes." *The New England Journal of Medicine* 368: 201–203.

Mangione-Smith, Rita, Elizabeth A. McGlynn, Marc N. Elliott, Paul Krogstad, and Robert H. Brook. 1999. "The Relationship between Perceived Parental Expectations and Pediatrician Antimicrobial Prescribing Behavior." *Pediatrics* 103: 711–718.

Mangione-Smith, Rita, Tanya Stivers, Marc N. Elliott, Laurie McDonald, and John Heritage. 2003. "Online Commentary during the Physical Examination: A Communication Tool for Avoiding Inappropriate Antibiotic Prescribing?" *Social Science & Medicine* 56: 313–320.

McGuire, Thomas G., John Z. Ayanian, Daniel E. Ford, Rachel E. M. Henke, Kathryn M. Rost, and Ala M. Zaslevsky. 2008. "Testing for Statistical Discrimination by Race/

Ethnicity in Panel Data for Depression Treatment in Primary Care." *Health Services Research* 43: 531–551.

McKinlay, John and Lisa Marceau. 2008. "When There Is No Doctor: Reasons for the Disappearance of Primary Care Physicians in the US during the Early 21st Century." *Social Science & Medicine* 67: 1481–1491.

McKinstry, Brian. 1992. "Paternalism and the Doctor-patient Relationship in General Practice." *British Journal of General Practice* 42: 340–342.

Mast, Marianne Schmid, Judith A. Hall, and Debra L. Roter. 2008. "Caring and Dominance Affect Participants' Perceptions and Behaviors During a Virtual Medical Visit." *Journal of General Internal Medicine* 23(5): 523–27.

Mechanic, David. 1996. "Changing Medical Organization and the Erosion of Trust." *The Milbank Quarterly* 74: 171–189.

Mechanic, David. 2008. "Rethinking Medical Professionalism: The Role of Information Technology and Practice Innovations." *The Milbank Quarterly* 86: 327–358.

Mehta, Kishor C., Ramesh R. Dargad, Dhammraj M. Borade, and Onkar C. Swami. 2014. "Burden of Antibiotic Resistance in Common Infectious Diseases: Role of Antibiotic Combination Therapy." *Journal of Clinical and Diagnostic Research* 8(6): ME05-08.

Moloney, Mairead Eastin. 2017. "'Sometimes, It's Easier to Write the Prescription': Physician and Patient Accounts of the Reluctant Medicalization of Sleeplessness." *Sociology of Health & Illness* 39(3): 333–348.

Mort, Maggie, Tracy. Finch, and Carl May. 2009. "Making and Unmaking Telepatients: Identity and Governance in New Health Technologies." *Science, Technology & Human Values* 34(1): 9–33.

Nyquist, Ann-Christine, Ralph Gonzales, John F. Steiner, and Merle A. Sande. 1998. "Antibiotics for Children with Upper Respiratory Infections." *Journal of the American Medical Association* 280: 1401-1401.

Oh, Hyeyoung. 2012. "Consumerism in Action: How Patients and Physicians Negotiate Payment in Health Care." *Qualitative Health Research* 23(3): 385–395.

Oh, Hyeyoung. 2017. "Resisting Throughput Pressures: Physicians' and Patients' Strategies to Manage Hospital Discharge." *Journal of Health and Social Behavior* 58(1): 116–30.

Olsen, Donna M., Robert L. Kane, and Josephine Kasteler. 1976. "Medical Care as a Commodity: An Exploration of the Shopping Behaviors of Patients." *Journal of Community Health* 2(2): 85–91.

Oravec, Jo and A. Ann. 2001. "On the 'Proper Use' of the Internet: Self-help Medical Information and On-line Health Care." *Journal of Health and Social Policy* 14: 37–60.

Oudshoorn, Nelly. 2011. *Telecare Technologies and the Transformation of Healthcare.* Houdmills: Palgrave Macmillan.

Oudshoorn, Nelly. 2012. "How Places Matter: Telecare Technologies and the Changing Spatial Dimensions of Healthcare." *Social Studies of Science* 42(1): 121–142.

Parsons, Talcott. 1951. *The Social System.* New York: Routledge.

Perzynski, Adam T., Mary Joan Roach, Sarah Shick, Bill Callahan, Douglas Gunzler, David C. Randall Cebul, Anne Huml Kaelber, John Daryl Thornton, and Douglas Einstadter. 2017. "Patient Portals and Broadband Internet Inequality." *Journal of the American Medical Informatics Association* 24(5): 927–932.

Rand, Cynthia M., Laura P. Shone, Christina Albertin, Peggy Auinger, Jonathan D. Klein, and Peter G. Szilagyi. 2007. "National Health Care Visit Patterns of Adolescents: Implications for Delivery of New Adolescent Vaccines." *Archives of Pediatrics & Adolescent Medicine* 161(3): 252–259.

Rathert, Cheryl, Mary D. Wyrwich, and Suzanne A. Boren. 2013. "Patient-centered Care and Outcomes: A Systematic Review of the Literature." *Medical Care Research and Review* 70(4): 351–379.

Reeder, Leo G. 1972. "The Patient-Client as a Consumer: Some Observations on the Changing Professional-Client Relationship." *Journal of Health and Social Behavior* 13: 406–412.

Rodwin, Marc A. 1993. *Medicine Money & Morals: Physicians' Conflicts of Interest*. New York: Oxford University Press.

Rubin, Sara, Nancy Burke, Meredith Van Natta, Irene Yen, and Janet K. Shim. 2018. "Like a Fish Out of Water: Managing Chronic Pain in the Urban Safety Net." *Journal of Health and Social Behavior* 59(4): 487–500.

Salander, Pär and Clare Moynihan. 2010. ""Facilitating Patients' Hope Work through Relationship: A Critique of the Discourse of Autonomy." Pp. 113–125 in *Configuring Health Consumers: Health Work and the Imperative of Personal Responsibility*, edited by R. Harris, N. Wathen, and S. Wyatt. Houndmills: Palgrave Macmillan.

Seçkin, Gül. 2020. "Expansion of Parson's Sick Role into Cyberspace: Patient Information Consumerism and Subjective Health in a Representative Sample of U.S. Internet Users." *Social Science & Medicine* 247: 1–10.

Shim, Janet K. 2010. "Cultural Health Capital: A Theoretical Approach to Understanding Health Care Interactions and the Dynamics of Unequal Treatment." *Journal of Health and Social Behavior* 51(1): 1–15.

Sleath, Betsy and Ya-Chen Tina Shih. 2003. "Sociological Influences on Antidepressant Prescribing." *Social Science & Medicine* 56: 1335–1344.

Starr, Paul. 1982. *The Social Transformation of American Medicine*. New York: Basic Books.

Stevenson, Fiona, Laura Hall, Maureen Seguin, Helen Atherton, Rebecca Barnes, Geraldine Leydon, Catherine Pope, Elizabeth Murray, and Sue Ziebland. 2018. "General Practitioner's Use of Online Resources during Medical Visits: Managing the Boundary between inside and outside the Clinic." *Sociology of Health and Illness* 41(S1): 65–81.

Stivers, Tanya. 2002. "Participating in Decisions about Treatment: Overt Parent Pressure for Antibiotic Medication in Pediatric Encounters." *Social Science & Medicine* 54(7): 1111–1130.

Street Jr., Richard L., Gregory Makoul, Neeraj K. Arora, and Ronald M. Epstein. 2009. "How Does Communication Heal? Pathways Linking Clinician-Patient Communication to Health Outcomes." *Patient Education and Counseling* 74(3): 295–301.

Swan, Melanie. 2012. "Health 2050: The Realization of Personalized Medicine through Crowdsourcing, the Quantified Self, and the Participatory Biocitizen." *Journal of Personalized Medicine* 2(3): 93–118.

Taylor, Lathryn M. and Kelnor Merrijoy. 1987. "Informed Consent: The Physicians' Perspective." *Social Science and Medicine* 24: 135–143.

Timmermans, Stefan and Hyeyoung Oh. 2010. "The Continued Social Transformation of the Medical Profession." *Journal of Health and Social Behavior* 51(S): S94-106.

Timmermans, Stefan, Ashelee Yang, Melissa Gardner, Catherine E. Keegan, Beverly M. Yashar, Patricia Y. Fechner, Margarett Shnorhavorian, Eric Vilain, Laura A. Siminoff, and David E. Sandberg. 2018. "Does Patient-centered Care Change Genital Surgery Decisions? The Strategic Use of Clinical Uncertainty in Disorders of Sex Development Clinics." *Journal of Health and Social Behavior* 59(4): 520–535.

Veitch, Kenneth. 2010. "The Government of Healthcare and the Politics of Patient Empowerment: New Labour and the NHS Reform Agenda in England." *Law & Policy* 32(3): 313–331.

Waitzkin, Howard. 2000. ""Changing Patient-Physician Relationships in the Changing Health-Policy Environment." Pp. 271–283 in *Handbook of Medical Sociology*, vol. 5th, edited by C. E. Bird, P. Conrad, and A. M. Fremont. Upper Saddle River, NJ: Prentice Hall.

Wallack, Stanley S. 1992. "Managed Care: Practice, Pitfalls, and Potential." *Health Care Financing Review* 1991(Annual Supplement): 27–34.

Weissman, Joel S., Alvin J. David Blumenthal, Michael Newman Silk, Kinga Zapert, Robert Leitman, and Sandra Feibelmann. 2004. "Physicians Report on Patient Encounters Involving Direct-to-Consumer Advertising." *Health Affairs 23 (NO. SUPPL1: Web Exclusives)*: 219–233.

Williams, Simon J. 2005. "Parsons Revisited: From the Sick Role to ...?" *Health: An Interdisciplinary Journal for the Social Study of Health, Illness and Medicine* 9(2): 123–144.

Winnick Terri, A. 2005. "From Quackery to "Complementary" Medicine: The American Medical Profession Confronts Alternative Therapies." *Social Problems* 52(1): 38–61.

Winnick, Terri A. 2006. "Medical Doctors and Complementary and Alternative Medicine: The Context of Holistic Practice." *Health* 10: 149–173.

Yeh, Mei-Yu, Shu-ChenWu, and Tao-Hsin Tung. 2018. "The Relation between Patient Education, Patient Empowerment and Patient Satisfaction: A Cross-Sectional-Comparison Study." *Applied Nursing Research* 39: 11–17.

25

Complementary and Alternative Medicine

Eeva Sointu

Defining CAM

The term complementary and alternative medicine (CAM) encompasses a diverse array of healing practices with differing diagnostic approaches and understandings of illness. Complementary and alternative medicine is not a coherent or unified whole; forms of CAM can differ from one another in relation to their histories and geographical origins, their methods of diagnosis and treatment, but also their cultural appeal and acceptability. Furthermore, practices that may be considered complementary and alternative medicine in the West – such as Traditional Chinese Medicine, Tibetan Medicine or Ayurveda – possess long histories outside the West and can be central to systems of caring for health within the cultures from which they originate. What is often thought to unify the diverse range of CAM practices is a lack of state supported legitimacy (Cant and Sharma 1999; Saks 2003). There are, however, differences between CAM practices in terms of their relationship with, and standing within, biomedical institutions. While forms of CAM are increasingly accepted and integrated into some biomedical settings (Alameida and Gabe 2016; Fitzsimmons et al. 2019), other CAM practices exist primarily outside the biomedical mainstream.

The process of integration, and search for scientific legitimacy, is also shaping how complementary and alternative medicines are practiced (Doel and Sergott 2003; Givati 2015). There are differences between forms of CAM also in terms of professional organization. Some practices, such as acupuncture, homeopathy and herbal medicine, tend to have organized professional bodies. Others, however, lack a central professional body or are organized in a manner that is more diffuse and fragmented (Baer 2010; Givati 2015). CAM practices also vary in their

The Wiley Blackwell Companion to Medical Sociology, First Edition. Edited by William C. Cockerham.

diagnostic and therapeutic approaches. While some focus on the manipulation of the body, others revolve around meditation and breathing, and yet others contain more spiritual components, or entail the prescription of different kinds of non-biomedical remedies.

In this chapter I posit that defining the diverse complementary and alternative medicines primarily through their exclusion from the dominant, state-supported, systems of healthcare (Cant and Sharma 1999; Saks 2003) risks sidestepping the manner in which many complementary and alternative medicines capture broad cultural values around health and illness, and the self and the body. Even when institutionally marginal, CAM practices and philosophies can be culturally resonant (Sointu 2012). Many complementary and alternative medicines embrace a holistic conceptualization of health and illness that underscores the interconnectedness of the mind, the body and, at times, the spirit.

An active role allocated to the client also characterizes many CAM practices; the capacity for healing is often considered innate and available for a person in search of wellbeing. Many CAM approaches also stress self-responsibility as well as consider self-exploration and self-awareness as a means of attaining fuller well-being. Rather than physiological health only, the kind of well-being emphasized in the complementary and alternative health arena frequently encompasses feelings of personal fulfilment and happiness (Sointu 2006a, 2012). The cultural resonance of forms of CAM, and of philosophies associated with CAM, is visible today not only in the continuing popularity of different CAM practices, but also in the rise of diverse products and practices aiming at *well-being* and *wellness*. Beliefs, products and practices located with the broad category of CAM – such as mindfulness, meditation, and natural remedies – entwine with diffuse practices seeking to enhance wellness, often through the consumption of varied wellness products.

Situating CAM Historically

To understand the idea of CAM it is important to look to the past. I will start from considering the significance of the separation of health from the domain of the sacred. Health and healing were central concerns in, for example, Medieval Christianity and in popular religious movements throughout modernity. In this context, lay people were seen as capable of directly drawing on sacred power through rituals aimed at safeguarding people's material needs, including their health (McGuire 2008: 32). Throughout early modernity, the reformation movements delineated the sacred as a sphere distinct from the profane, including the body.

Locating sacred power in the hands of churches entailed efforts to discourage folk religion and ritual. Furthermore, "[c]hurch leaders' efforts to disabuse church members of their trust in the powers of religious and folk healers preceded, by several centuries, the development of modern, rational biomedicine" (McGuire 2008: 132).

What might today constitute forms of CAM – folk remedies or even the idea of lay people having access to healing power – is shaped by historical developments relating to the separation of religion and medicine into two institutionally distinct spheres. The moving of the body from the domain of the sacred to the domain of the profane also played a role in opening the body to the emerging scientific biomedical gaze (McGuire 2008).

The idea of complementary and alternative medicine is also connected with the rise of what is considered "orthodox" or conventional biomedicine. The consolidation of regular medicine – and later biomedicine – is interwoven with institutional, scientific, and legal shifts that took place throughout the nineteenth and early twentieth centuries (Baer 2001; Dew 2004). In Britain, licensing laws such as the Apothecaries Act of 1815 and the Medical Act of 1858, distinguished regular medicine from irregular healing practices. In the US, most states had enacted licensure laws favoring regular medicine by the 1890s (Baer 2001). State supported licensing laws allocated regular medicine, and medical education acquired through regular medical schools, with a degree of legitimacy unavailable to unlicensed practices.

The founding of regular medical societies – such as the American Medical Association in 1847, the Association Générale des Médicines de France in 1858, and the Canadian Medical Association in 1867 – was also integral to the development of what today is considered complementary and alternative medicine. Regular medical societies were central in the unseating of irregular practitioners from licensing boards and, consequently, from the ranks of licensed medical practitioners (Baer 2001; Porter 1999). Regular medicine gaining the upper hand in questions of licensing, gradually throughout the nineteenth century, gave rise to a state-supported system of distinguishing what was alternative and what was not. Licensing laws underscored the legitimacy of regular medicine and, simultaneously, relegated practices and practitioners not adhering to the regular medical principles to the margins (Baer 2001; Porter 1999; Saks 2003).

The shifts in licensing laws were, at least in part, driven by a desire to eradicate medical competition. After all, the nineteenth century landscapes of health and healing were characterized by medical plurality (Baer 2001). This medical plurality was partially grounded on the methods used by regular medical practitioners. The "heroic medicine" practiced by many regular doctors entailed procedures such as bleeding, cupping, leeching and blistering, or the prescription of poisons to induce vomiting. Many of the irregular healing practices – that are today considered CAM – were popular during the nineteenth century because the methods utilized by licensed medics were harmful as well as expensive (Baer 2001; Porter 1999).

The efforts of regular medical societies to eclipse irregular practice and to acquire control of the medical marketplace were, however, also supported by scientific development. Germ theory and improvements in fields such as surgery contributed to the rising success and standing of regular medicine, particularly from the latter half of the nineteenth century onwards (Porter 1999). The ascent of what would later be termed biomedicine was also entwined with economic interests. The focus on individual pathology improved the health of the workforce while, simultaneously, facilitating the ignoring of social and environmental causes, such as pollution or poverty, that also underlie ill health.

By the 1930s, medical systems across the West that had been characterized by plurality had become dominated by biomedicine (Baer 2001). State and corporate support, and the growing importance of scientific thinking, enabled regular medicine to gain the upper hand in defining medical knowledge. In contrast with the abundance of practitioners addressing ill health historically, ours is a world marked by biomedical dominance. The power of biomedicine is central to the manner in which complementary and alternative medicines are defined, perceived, and practiced. The consolidation of institutionalized biomedicine was accompanied by the exclusion of practitioners and practices that either competed with regular medicine or did not adhere to scientific ideas of pathology. Complementary and alternative medicines were, as such, created through processes of exclusion (Baer 2001; Cant and Sharma 1999; Porter 1999; Saks 2003).

CAM Today

The position of biomedicine as the primary provider of health care has, however, been eroded over the past decades. Particularly since the late 1960s, non-biomedical practices have become increasingly popular. Although usage figures vary depending on whether CAM use refers to consulting a CAM practitioner, or making use of over-the counter remedies, special diets, forms of exercise or prayer (Kristoffersen et al. 2018: 2), the complementary and alternative health field has grown considerably. The use of complementary and alternative medicines in the US has been placed at 38.3% of the population (Barnes et al. 2008: 14; Nahin et al. 2016). The most popular forms of CAM are thought to be used by as many as 68.9% of Australians (Xue et al. 2007: 644), while in Britain, 44% of the population is estimated to utilize a form of CAM at least once in their lifetime (Hunt et al. 2010: 1498).

Increasing popularity has also fostered growing professionalization, the establishment of professional bodies, as well as the entry of forms of CAM into biomedical institutions (Givati 2015; Saks 2003). Despite some forms of CAM being available through biomedical care settings, consultations with CAM practitioners are frequently paid for privately. Considerable amounts of money are spent on complementary and alternative medicines. For example, in the US in 2012, the out-of-pocket spending on complementary health approaches was estimated at $30.2 billion (Nahin et al. 2016). The growing utilization of complementary and alternative medicines has also made questions of efficacy and safety important. Many biomedical practitioners, as well as policy makers, are calling for the further study of CAM, especially through randomized controlled trials (RCT). Government initiatives around complementary and alternative medicines, such as the House of Lords 6th Select Committee Report on Complementary and Alternative Medicine in the UK in 2000, and the White House Commission on Complementary and Alternative Medicine Policy in the US in 2002, also underscored questions of efficacy, regulation and safety.

Entry into Mainstream Medicine

While biomedicine has been and continues to be a broad and diverse institution (Berg and Mol 1998; Lawrence and Weisz 1998), biomedical institutions and societies have, historically, held a negative view of complementary and alternative medicines. Up until the 1990s, medical associations actively sought to prevent doctors from working with complementary and alternative health practitioners or utilizing non-biomedical techniques (Porter 1999; Ruggie 2004; Winnick 2005). Some CAM practices have, nevertheless, gradually entered biomedical settings (Wiese et al. 2010). By 2001, nearly half of general practitioners in England provided some access to complementary and alternative medicine, with 27% making referrals to CAM practitioners (Thomas et al. 2003: 575; Thomas et al. 2001b). More than half of office-based physicians in the US recommended complementary health approaches (CHAs) to their patients in 2012 (Stussman et al. 2020).

Biomedical institutions and practitioners are not, however, unified in their views towards complementary and alternative medicines (Wardle et al. 2018). For example, general practitioners, internists, and psychiatrists have been found to recommend complementary health approaches and mind-body therapies more than other specialists (Stussman et al. 2020). Further, forms of CAM such as Tai Chi, Yoga, Healing Touch, or Reiki are often partially integrated into biomedical cancer care settings (Fitzsimmons et al. 2019), while close to half of nurses in Australia utilise CAM techniques or draw on CAM philosophies in their clinical practice (Shorofi and Arbon 2010: 232). The continuing marginality of CAM practices within integrated settings is embodied in the division of therapeutic labour and authority. Whereas areas such as diagnosis and referrals belong under the purview of biomedicine, CAM practitioners tend to work on combatting chronic complains and pain (Hollenberg 2006: 738; Mizrachi et al. 2005: 32), or focus on alleviating the side effects of biomedical treatments and on improving wellbeing (Fitzsimmons et al. 2020).

Aspects of CAM are, simultaneously, being drawn on and appropriated by biomedical practitioners (Hollenberg 2006; Hollenberg and Muzzin 2010; Sharp et al. 2018). Many biomedical practitioners favour "the selective incorporation of CM [complementary medicine] and co-optation of CM practices rather than an integrative CM and biomedical practice" (Wiese et al. 2010: 339; Wiese and Oster 2010). CAM practitioners who enter biomedical settings often need to navigate a terrain that remains critical of non-biomedical ways of understanding health (Hollenberg and Muzzin 2010; Shuval et al. 2012). The drive towards the integration of CAM treatments within biomedical settings has often been met with criticism on the part of CAM providers. This criticism underscores not only the appropriation of CAM treatments but also the loss of self-determination on the part of CAM practitioners wishing to enter the biomedical mainstream (Parusnikova 2002; Sharp et al. 2018; Wiese and Oster 2010; Wiese et al. 2010).

Who Uses CAM?

The use of complementary and alternative health practices appears to follow certain demographic trends. Chronic ill health has been found to characterize many users (Hunt et al. 2010; Ruggie 2004). Women are also more likely to turn to CAM than men (Clarke et al. 2018; Hunt et al. 2010; Keshet and Simchai 2014; Ong et al. 2002; Ruggie 2004; Thomas et al. 2001a; Xue et al. 2007). CAM use is, furthermore, thought to be more common among people with higher than average income and levels of education (Conboy et al. 2005; Hunt et al. 2010; Nahin et al. 2016; Ong et al. 2002; Ruggie 2004; Thomas and Coleman 2004; Xue et al. 2007). While in the past practices that might today be considered CAM offered the poor and the disenfranchised access to medical care, today those with lesser economic means may be "priced out of certain CAM options" (Wasserman 2014: 3).

Despite there being connections between CAM use and at least some affluence, CAM techniques are utilized across social classes. Studies indicate that CAM use is higher among white people than other racial groups (Conboy et al. 2005: 980; Hunt et al. 2010) and that there are racial differences in the type of CAM used (Johnson et al. 2018). The use of certain complementary and alternative medicines, such as traditional Chinese Medicine, Ayurveda or Tibetan medicine, can also entwine with the ethnic and cultural roots and traditions of particular communities.

Why Do People Turn to CAM?

Dissatisfaction with Conventional Medicine

The rise of complementary and alternative medicines is often seen to relate to a sense of dissatisfaction with conventional medicine (Astin 1998; Kelner 2003; Ruggie 2004; Salamonsen and Ahlzén 2018; Sharma 1992; Siahpush 1999). A focus on managing chronic ill health that biomedicine has failed to alleviate constitutes an important factor pulling people to CAM (O'Connor 2003; Ruggie 2004; Thomas et al. 2001b). Complementary and alternative medicine use has also been considered as a critique of the Parsonian "sick role;" rather than passive recipients of doctors' expertise, CAM clients are thought to desire agency in their health care and to claim a more proactive and responsible role in the treatment and prevention of ill health (Cartwright and Torr 2005; Gale 2011; Hughes 2004; Kelner 2003; Ruggie 2004; Stacey 1997; Wiles and Rosenberg 2001).

A critique of conventional medicine among CAM users may encompass additional meaning among non-white CAM users. Continuing racial discrimination within health care settings (Feagin and Bennefield 2014; Phelan and Link 2015; Shippee et al. 2012), may constitute a factor in Black Americans turning to practices outside conventional medicine, including forms of CAM. As Shippee et al. (2012: 1161) argue, "seeking CAM represents agentic action – an effort to reassert control over health care choices for Black persons who feel marginalized by discrimination in various settings."

The Appeal of Holism

Holism – treating the mind, the body and, at times, the spirit – appeals to many CAM users. In part, through connecting the mind with the body, CAM practices offer "deeper-level explanations of health and illness, linking psychological and physical dimensions of health" (Cartwright and Torr 2005: 564). The holism of complementary and alternative medicines also sets CAM apart from biomedicine. While what Anne Harrington (2008) refers to as the "physicalist" approach in biomedicine "denies the relevance of the kinds of questions people so often ask when they become ill: Why me? Why now? What next?" (Harrington 2008: 17), CAM practices tend to ascribe illness meaning. Forms of CAM allow for, and even encourage, personal interpretation of ill health and resonate with the lived experience of illness (Cartwright and Torr 2005; Harrington 2008; Sointu 2012). Complementary and alternative medicines also often stress the uniqueness of each client. Tailoring treatments to the needs and individual characteristics of clients is, furthermore, often seen to underlie the therapeutic efficacy of CAM practices. As a CAM practitioner explains, "[y]ou've got to know what you are to be able to treat it" (Sylvia – a practitioner, cited in Sointu 2012: 48–9).Through their emphasis on individual experiences and characteristics of clients, CAM practices can provide a counterpoint to standardization underlying biomedical knowledge. CAM can challenge "the extreme depersonalization and bureaucratization of regular medicine" (Porter 1999: 689). As such, the rise of CAM practices captures the growing significance of patients' own experiences, perceptions and self-assessed health needs, as well as a desire for making sense of illness beyond biomedical frameworks.

Pragmatic Mixing and Matching

Clients consult CAM practices for physical unease ranging from common colds to musculoskeletal problems, and from chronic pain to medically unexplained symptoms. However, people also turn to CAM for help in dealing with non-medical challenges and losses in life. Differing motivations of CAM use can, furthermore, exist simultaneously (Baarts and Pedersen 2009; Sointu 2006a, 2012). Importantly, complementary and alternative medicines are rarely used as substitutes for conventional care. Rather than rejecting biomedical care, many CAM users are "purposeful and pragmatic" in choosing non-biomedical practices (Connor 2004: 1703). CAM users are involved in eclectic mixing and matching of health care options (Cartwright and Torr 2005; Grace et al. 2018; Mcgregor and Peay 1996; Sirois and Gick 2002). Importantly, much CAM use is directed at health maintenance and more general *well-being* (Sointu 2006a, 2012; Stussman et al. 2015; Thomas and Coleman 2004; Wiles and Rosenberg 2001).

Well-being

While CAM practices can provide solutions to chronic medical problems, constitute forms of health maintenance, as well as offer "treats" for the mind and the body (Bishop et al. 2008; Thomas et al. 2001a), understanding CAM as primarily focused on the production of biomedical health ignores the complex cultural factors underlying the rise of the complementary health arena. The stories of clients and practitioners reveal a complex story about CAM use often aiming at a broad sense of *well-being* (Johnson et al. 2018; Sointu 2006a, 2006b, 2006c, 2012, 2013; Sointu and Woodhead 2008). Many CAM clients and practitioners are involved in searching for and providing well-being, not merely biomedical health. Understanding how clients and practitioners define well-being provides a means of accessing and analysing the social and cultural values that underlie the popularity and meaningfulness of diverse CAM practices.

The well-being offered through CAM practices is defined in different ways (Sointu 2006a, 2012). Rather than physiological health only, well-being denotes feelings of fulfilment and happiness, as well as a capacity of responding to and navigating challenges in life. Well-being entwines with feelings like optimism, and a sense of control over one's life. Well-being is also understood as harmony and balance that saturate lives marked by well-being. This kind of well-being transcends biomedical understandings of health and is, as such, difficult to measure scientifically. The notion of well-being also reconfigures medical authority and locates defining ill health more firmly in the hands of non-biomedical experts and lay people (Sointu 2012).

The well-being that many users and practitioners aspire to is frequently thought to rest on self-awareness. Being true to oneself is also often understood as the key to well-being. As a CAM client explains, well-being emerges from "being true to yourself rather than truer to the pack" (Helen – a client, cited in Sointu 2012: 49). Well-being is, furthermore, available through "reconnecting where I've been disconnected" (Ivy – a client, cited in Sointu 2012: 48). As such, listening to "wisdom within" is often seen as what facilitates access to person-specific well-being (Sointu 2006a, 2012; Sointu and Woodhead 2008). Many CAM practices emphasize and encourage clients to develop deeper *awareness* of their experiences and feelings. As a practitioner explains, "self-knowledge, self-awareness is crucial" (Sylvia – a practitioner, cited in Sointu 2012: 58). Conceptualizing well-being as connected with self-awareness normalizes, and encourages, self-exploration and reflexivity.

The valuing of self-exploration that is captured in ideas of well-being is not new. Listening to wisdom seen to lie within has, rather, been important throughout history (Taylor 1989, 1991, 1994). Today, being true to one's unique self is readily seen as "something we have to attain if we are to be true and full human beings" (Taylor 1994: 28). The ideal of inner depth resonates through everyday language; expressions like "be true to yourself," "listen to your heart," "do what is right for you" capture the normalization of inner depth and the valuing of individual authenticity. Considering the appeal and popularity of CAM as connected not with biomedical health but, rather, with values such as inner depth and self-exploration, it is possible to start to see further commonalities uniting the diverse array of CAM practices. The importance of self-reflection in many CAM practices captures the hold of the ideal of inner depth over selfhood today.

The Neoliberal Ethos and CAM

Defining well-being as not only happiness but also agency and control embodies and reproduces important social values including individual uniqueness, self-fulfilment and self-responsibility. Through the focus on self-awareness, CAM practices also readily capture reflexivity characterizing selfhood in late modernity (Giddens 1991). The ideal of wellbeing also entwines with values such as self-responsibility and agency that are increasingly important in the context of "neoliberal reason" today (Brown 2015). The valuing of "the self-regulating, self-surveillant and autonomous self" (Peacock et al. 2014: 175) that characterizes neoliberal thinking saturates also the CAM domain and, more specifically, the manner in which well-being is tied with self-responsibility and self-exploration. Simultaneously, the "narrative of responsibility" individualizes ill health and hides the social and economic causes underlying illness (Horrocks and Johnson 2014: 178; Peacock et al. 2014).

The rise of complementary and alternative medicines also echoes the importance of consumer choice imbuing social and economic landscapes today. CAM practices allow, even invite, the shopping around for suitable treatments. As such, they fit neatly into the broader consumerist frame of Western modernity (Cartwright and Torr 2005). At the same time, CAM practices are often seen as less commercial than biomedicine and even understood as free from the profit motive driving "Big Pharma" (Attwell et al. 2018). Simultaneously, a sense of self-responsibility in the management of disease and in health behavior more generally, characterizes many users (Baarts and Pedersen 2009). Being self-directed and knowledgeable about treatments and the workings of medical bureaucracies now define the manner in which many patients engage with medical settings, including complementary and alternative medicines (Shim 2010).

The empowered client who chooses to turn to CAM rather than to adhere to a more traditional biomedical patient role emerges in relation to broader neoliberal trends emphasizing self-responsibility and individual fulfillment. In a consumer society, a perpetual search for well-being is normalized and this further encourages the turn to practices like complementary and alternative medicines. The emphasis on consumer choice and personal responsibility, the availability of medical information, and the general medicalization of life (Conrad 2005) all contribute to the conditions that enable complementary and alternative medicines to flourish. Ideas of personal responsibility that resonate through the complementary and alternative health arena are also congruent with health policy developments that underscore individual responsibility for health and illness.

CAM and Class

At the same time as the notion of well-being captures and reproduces broad social values, the ideal of wellbeing also embodies possibilities and dispositions that are classed. Research shows that CAM use is more common among the more educated and affluent (Conboy et al. 2005; Hunt et al. 2010; Nahin et al. 2016; Ong et al. 2002; Ruggie 2004; Thomas and Coleman 2004; Xue et al. 2007). The dominance of the middle classes within the CAM arena connects with the cost associated with CAM treatments. Actively managing ill health through CAM can also be considered a form of "cultural health capital" (Shim 2010) that is more readily available to the more privileged. There is also an alignment between values, such as reflexivity and self-exploration, emphasised in many CAM practices and more middle class dispositions. As Illouz (2008: 150) argues, "middle-class emotional culture... has been characterized by an intense introspectiveness and reflexivity." Introspection and reflexivity are central also to the kind of wellbeing that many clients seek and that many practitioners offer (Sointu 2006a, 2012; Sointu and Woodhead 2008). Working on the self, however, requires resources, including time and money, that are more available to the more affluent (Skeggs 2004; Skeggs and Loveday 2012).

Gender and CAM

While men and women both use and practice forms of CAM, the field is dominated by women (Clarke et al. 2018; Hunt et al. 2010; Keshet and Simchai 2014; Kristoffersen et al. 2014; Ong et al. 2002; Ruggie 2004; Taylor 2010; Thomas et al. 2001a; Xue et al. 2007). The prevalence of women users and practitioners can be seen to capture gendered patterns in health care utilization more generally. Women are, for example, thought to visit conventional doctors more and to engage in healthier behaviours (Cockerham 2005; Courtenay 2000). Many complementary and alternative health practices also offer and emphasize values such as care, acceptance and empathy that have, traditionally in the West, been associated with femininity (Hochschild 2003; Keshet and Simchai 2014; Lupton 2012; Sointu 2012; Widding Isaksen 2002). As Stacey explains: "the cultures of alternative health are based upon philosophies more traditionally associated with the cultural competences of femininity: communication, caring, gentleness and natural remedies" (Stacey 1997: 216). Femininity has, in the West, also long been associated with informal, familial care (Courtenay 2000; O'Grady 2005; Young 1990).

The feminization of the CAM arena also pertains to historical developments around access to medical training and practice, and rests on the manner in which practices that are now considered CAM offered a route to medical practice to female medical practitioners. While women were generally excluded from regular medicine and medical education through the nineteenth century, irregular practices were more open to female practitioners (Baer 2001; Heggie 2015). For example, throughout the nineteenth century in the US, New York's homeopathic Women's Medical College, the American Hydropathic Institute, and Woman's Medical College in Philadelphia offered hundreds of women training in irregular healing practices (Baer 2001; Bix 2004).

Women, as well as the feminine qualities of intuition and empathy, were valued in many of the healing movements, such as the mind-cure movement, Spiritualism, and Christian Science that emerged in the late nineenth and early twentieth centuries (Baer 2001; Harrington 2008; McGuire 2008). This openness to female practitioners, and the valuing of qualities associated with femininity, contribute to the feminization of the CAM arena that continues today. However, cultural associations between CAM practices and femininity extend also to the ways in which CAM is understood as not only "irrational" but also as a form of "pampering;" qualities and behaviors that remain more readily connected with femininity. The feminization of the CAM field is important for understanding the experiences of people navigating this diverse field.

Good Practitioner

The entwining of CAM with traditional ideas of femininity can be detected also in the manner in which CAM practitioners and users conceptualize a good practitioner. For example, a client describes a good practitioner as someone who "is genuinely and utterly there, giving you complete and utter undivided attention" (Ivy – a client, cited in Sointu 2012: 74). A good practitioner "genuinely gives me the impression that she cares" (Dave – a client cited in Sointu 2012: 74). According to another client, a good practitioner is "non-judgmental and I think with non-judgmental, accepting" (Angela – a client, cited in Sointu 2012: 74). The gentleness and care of good

CAM practitioners affirm the experiences of clients and can, furthermore, remedy the silencing and powerlessness experienced especially by female clients in encounters with conventional medicine but also in patriarchal societies more broadly.

Care and acceptance feature in the manner in which many CAM practitioners also understand their work. A practitioner, for example, aims to create "a holding environment" which enables "people to find themselves, and to, you know, gain insight and awareness" (Frances – a practitioner, cited in Sointu 2012: 76) as an important part of their work. Another practitioner describes her role also in terms of facilitating awareness and empowerment: "I like to encourage people to, I suppose, find their own life and their own power, really" (June – a practitioner). The therapeutic work in many CAM practices centers on reflection and meaning-making, with good practitioners supporting clients uncovering, expressing and analyzing their experiences. The kind of care offered by good practitioners is accepting and compassionate. At the same time, a good practitioner must remain "*very* grounded themselves" and even "emotionally removed from it, from the operation" (Jan, a practitioner, cited in Sointu 2012: 74). The authenticity and empowerment that characterize the wellbeing that many clients seek shapes also how good practitioners are conceptualized. While a good practitioner "has a sort of, caring, loving approach" this care "isn't overwhelming or threatening in any way" (Bella – a client, cited in Sointu 2012: 75). Good practitioners often offer guidance rather than definitive answers. In the CAM sphere, the ultimate authority to decide on treatments and explanations is more firmly located in the hands of the client. Accordingly, good CAM practitioners are valued for utilizing "affiliative speech" that involves "showing support, expressing agreement, and acknowledging the other's contributions" (Leaper and Ayres 2007: 329). At the same time, many CAM practitioners and clients avoid "assertive speech" that entails disagreement and "directive statements" (Leaper and Ayres 2007: 329) that are more readily associated with biomedical expertise and a more traditional patient role (Sointu 2012).

Even while ideas of the good CAM practitioner connect with more traditional ideas of caring femininity, CAM practices encompass potential for challenging traditional ascriptions of femininity, especially on the part of clients (Stacey 1997; Sointu 2011, 2012; Sointu and Woodhead 2008). This is because many CAM practices encourage focusing on one's own wellbeing, rather than the wellbeing of others. While traditional ideas of femininity connect femininity with care for others (O'Grady 2005; Young 1990, many CAM practices emphasise care for the self (Sointu 2011, 2012; Sointu and Woodhead 2008). It is, as such, possible to see the CAM domain as a setting for women navigating "increasingly conflictual female roles" (McNay 1999: 110–1). The importance placed on the self, and on individual lives, contrasts 'the conventional expectation of "being there for others" that is associated with femininity' (Adkins 2002: 45).

Sociological Reflections on the Healing Produced through CAM

Despite ongoing work to establish an evidence base for forms of complementary and alternative medicine, CAM practices rarely enjoy scientific legitimacy and the standing accorded to biomedical practices (Baarts and Pedersen 2010; Barry 2006; Paterson et al. 2009). Notwithstanding the lack of scientific legitimacy, people continue turning to CAM and, what is more, find help for their concerns. As such, even without being scientifically efficacious, CAM treatments can make people feel better. Some of the therapeutic effect of CAM may relate to physiological efficacy that is yet be scientifically established. Experiences of healing may also emerge through the placebo response that can underlie the therapeutic effect of CAM practices and biomedicine alike. While often understood in negative terms – as a sham or a sugar pill influencing susceptible patients, or as the inert control against which real pharmacological compounds are measured in clinical research (Bishop et al. 2012) – it is becoming evident that placebos can play a potent, albeit poorly understood, role in all experiences of healing (Harrington 2008; Kaptchuck 2002; Thompson et al. 2009).

Improvement experienced through CAM use can include enhanced mobility, feelings of optimism and coping, and a lowered sense of anxiety (Cartwright 2007; Kelner and Wellman 1997; Sointu 2006a, 2006b, 2012; Wiles and Rosenberg 2001). CAM is thought to afford those utilizing these practices a stronger sense of control over health and health care than what may be available via conventional medicine alone (Baarts and Pedersen 2009; Cartwright and Torr 2005; Fitzsimmons et al. 2019; Johnson et al. 2019; Mcgregor and Peay 1996; Wiles and Rosenberg 2001). At the same time, CAM practitioners provide personalized services that are aligned with the individual needs of clients, and facilitate the development of personal illness narratives that transcend the "physicalist" orientation of biomedicine (Harrington 2008) and that accommodate the emotional aspects of illness experience (Cartwright and Torr 2005; Sointu 2006a, 2006b, 2012).

Healing Bodies, Feeing Bodies

While the body has, historically in the West, been understood as not only a hindrance to the operation of the mind, but also as something sinful (Grosz 1994), the body is important and positively regarded in many CAM practices (Baarts and Pedersen 2009; Gale 2011; O'Connor 2003; Sointu 2006c, 2012, 2013). The focus on the body in CAM is important for a number of reasons. First, while "our relationship to our bodies, in the normal course of events, remains largely unproblematic and taken-for-granted" (Williams and Bendelow 1998: 159), CAM can give rise to "bodily awareness" that is valued by clients (Baarts and Pedersen 2009). The awareness of the body that CAM can generate is poised to disrupt the ordinary invisibility of the body (Baarts and Pedersen 2009). Through CAM practices that focus on the body, tacit embodied experience can become a more explicit, and enduring, part of life (Baarts and Pedersen 2009: 274).

The body that CAM practitioners work on is often seen as holistically connected with the mind and, at times, the spirit. As a CAM client explains, "my body, I see it very much as reflection, or intertwined with my attitudes – they're not separate" (Kate – a client, cited in Sointu 2012: 154–4). The idea of holistic connectedness facilitates working on emotions through the body. As a practitioner puts it, "the body is a very powerful medium to reach a person, or to promote healing" (Beth – a practitioner, cited in Sointu 2012: 155). CAM practices often call on clients to recognize and attend to their bodies. As such, the holistic body tends to be conceptualized as possessing a voice as well as feelings.

At the same time, the care involved in forms of bodywork tends to be trivialized (Gimlin 2007; Twigg 2000; Twigg et al. 2011). What is more, "bodywork also borders on the more ambivalent territory of sexuality" (Twigg 2000: 390). Practitioners and clients need to navigate meaning ascribed to bodies and touch within cultural contexts where "sex is symbolically fused with the body" (Oerton 2004; Oerton and Phoenix 2001: 406). As such, tacit maintenance of bodily boundaries is important in many forms of CAM that focus on the body. The blending of bodies and touch with sex (Oerton and Phoenix 2001) accentuates the importance of trust in CAM practitioners (Twigg 2000). Furthermore, according to Oerton and Phoenix (2001), the idea of holism itself offers a means of navigating complex associations between bodies and sexuality. Understanding the body as holistically connected with the mind and the spirit, locates the body treated in CAM practices outside sexual intimacy (Oerton and Phoenix 2001: 401).

The holism of CAM practices, often considers bodies as "containers" for feeling. As a practitioner explains, "when you have unresolved emotional issues, which you don't deal with, you know, you suppress, they become – they don't disappear. They are in your body" (Anne – a practitioner, cited in Sointu 2010: 160). Bodywork makes it possible to "release some of the trauma" (Kim – a client) captured in the body. The idea of the body as a container for feeling is not new. The "body that speaks" constitutes a cultural motif rooted in Christian ideas of the healing potential of the confession (Harrington 2008: 68–9). The "body that speaks" is embodied also in Freudian psychoanalysis and the idea of the unconscious making past trauma present through physical ailments (Harrington 2008: 93–4). Today, "the body that speaks" is especially visible in the CAM domain where healing is often seen to entail bringing the trauma contained in the body to the surface (Harrington 2008). The holism of many CAM practices, thus, implicitly ties healing with the willingness and the capacity to express and analyze feelings captured in the body. As such, the holism of CAM practices entwines with ideals of reflexivity and self-responsibility. Despite the positive emphasis on the body, this holism often subtly reproduces the primacy of the self-reflexive mind over the body (Sointu 2012). The idea of the holistic body can, however, also generate experiences of authorship. Holism that links the mind with the body can ascribe ailment meaning outside biomedical interpretations as well as biomedical expertise. The holism of CAM practices can, as such, facilitate experiences of both ownership and control. The holistic body in the CAM field is, simultaneously, deeply individualistic.

CAM and Recognition

Focusing on the relational dynamics within therapeutic encounters offers another means of making sense of some of the positive experiences of CAM users. As social beings whose lives are made meaningful through responses from others (Benjamin 1988, 1990; Sayer 2011), how others relate to us, and to our concerns and ailments, matters. Affirmation given by CAM practitioners can enable self-expression which, in turn, can grant a client a voice as well as authority in defining illness.

Within the biomedical context, illness tends to be understood as "an intra-corporal lesion or abnormality" (Armstrong 2011: 802) that is "located within the anatomical frame" (Nettleton 2006: 1168). Further, it is primarily the biomedical expert, rather than a patient, who possesses the specialist knowledge to define and treat illness. CAM practices, however, allow for and even call for reflexively making sense of one's experiences and ailments. CAM can, as such, be experienced very differently compared with conventional medicine. As a client explains: "I'd been to the doctor. I didn't feel I was getting anywhere... it felt um, that like somehow you had to prove something more for doctor whereas the homeopath was more likely to take what you were saying seriously" (Sue – a client, cited in Sointu 2012: 107). The "physicalist" way of conceptualizing disease tends not to allow for the personal meaning-making that can be important to the ill (Harrington 2008).

A lack of alignment between biomedical diagnosis and the illness experience can, furthermore, challenge patients over "the validity of their own experiences" (McGuire 1996: 108). As another CAM client explains: "I used to come away questioning my own mental health if ever I went to see a doctor because of the way they received me" (Ivy – a client, cited in Sointu 2012: 109). CAM practitioners and consultations can be experienced differently to biomedicine. According to a CAM client, "when I'm with [the practitioner]... something inside me feels touched by that warmth, love, care. And it makes me feel valued in a way, somehow kind of affirms me as a person" (Kim – a client, cited in Sointu 2012: 100). Clients see good CAM practitioners as not only non-judgmental, but also skilled in hearing and addressing the individual concerns that clients bring to them (Sointu 2006a, 2012). As such, in addition to, for example, musculoskeletal manipulation or non-biomedical remedies, good CAM practitioners offer *recognition*.

Theories of recognition posit that "the establishment of one's self-understanding (one's idea of 'self' or 'subjective self-certainty') is inextricably dependent on recognition or affirmation on the part of the others" (Yar 2001: 59). Recognition, as Jessica Benjamin (1988: 12) explains, constitutes "that response from the other which makes meaningful the feelings, intensions, and actions of the self." Not only do experiences of recognition underlie the development of subjectivity and agency, experiences of recognition connect with feelings of esteem and worth (Honneth 2001; McQueen 2015). CAM practitioners who listen to and affirm their clients can – beyond any positive physiological effect that a practice may generate – give their clients experiences of recognition that, in turn validate what the client is experiencing. The recognition that CAM practitioners give clients rests on the importance that the CAM arena ascribes to self-awareness and self-expression. Experiences of recognition, and the positive effect of being recognized, are made possible through the emphasis placed on the views and the voice of the client. The social values around selfhood – the emphasis on the experiences and interpretations of the client – that saturate the CAM domain can thus also be seen as meaningful in the production of experiences of healing.

Concluding Thoughts: CAM as Culturally Resonant, Even while Institutionally Marginal

In order to understand the popularity and even the effect of forms of CAM, it is necessary to look beyond biomedical health. Cultural rather than solely medical factors underlie the rise, but also the appeal of many CAM practices. Social and cultural ideals pertaining to normal and desirable selfhood – ideals such as individualism, self-responsibility and self-fulfillment – echo through much of the complementary and alternative health sphere making CAM practices acceptable and appealing to today's health consumers.

The idea of improving health through self-management and self-responsibility (Horrocks and Johnson 2014), aligns many CAM practices also with neoliberal values. Values such as self-responsibility and reflexivity, however, also connect with cultural and economic capital that enable and encourage the utilization of complementary and alternative medicines. Values emphasized in the CAM arena – such as personal fulfillment and self-awareness – may also throw light on the appeal of CAM practices to women; the focus on personal fulfillment challenges some of the other-directedness traditionally associated with femininity. Rather than a simple sense of dissatisfaction with biomedicine or people growing increasingly narcissistic and prone to turn to therapeutic practices, the proliferation of alternative and complementary medicines is intimately entwined with configurations of gender and class (Sointu 2012).

References

Adkins, Lisa. 2002. *Revisions: Gender and Sexuality in Late Modernity.* Buckingham: Open University Press.

Almeida, Joana and Jonathan Gabe. 2016. "CAM within a Field Force of Countervailing Powers: The Case of Portugal." *Social Science & Medicine* 155: 73–81.

Armstrong, David. 2011. "Diagnosis and Nosology in Primary Care." *Social Science & Medicine* 73: 801–7.

Astin, J. A. 1998. "Why Patients Use Alternative Medicine: Results of National Study." *Journal of the American Medical Association* 279(19): 1548–53.

Attwell, Katie, Paul R. Ward, Samantha B. Meyer, Philippa J. Rokkas, and Julie Leask. 2018. ""Do-It-Yourself": Vaccine Rejection and Complementary and Alternative Medicine (CAM)." *Social Science & Medicine* 196: 106–224.

Baarts, Charlotte and Inge Kryger Pedersen. 2009. "Derivative Benefits: Exploring the Body Through Complementary and Alternative Medicine." *Sociology of Health & Illness* 31(5): 719–33.

Baarts, Charlotte and Inge Kryger Pedersen. 2010. "Fantastic Hands but No Evidence: The Construction of Expertise by Users of CAM." *Social Science & Medicine* 71: 1068–75.

Baer, Hans A.. 2001. *Biomedicine and Alternative Healing Systems in America.* Madison, WI: University of Wisconsin Press.

Baer, Hans A.. 2010. "Complementary and Alternative Medicine. Processes of Legimation, Professionalization, and Cooption." Pp. 373–90 in *New Blackwell Companion to Medical Sociology*, edited by William C. Cockerham. Oxford: Wiley-Blackwell.

Barnes, Patricia M., Barbara Bloom, and Richard L. Nahin. 2008. "Complementary and Alternative Medicine Use among Adults and Children: United States, 2007." National Health Statistics Reports, 12. U.S. Department of Health and Human Services. Hyattsville, MD: National Center for Health Statistics.

Barry, Christine. 2006. "The Role of Evidence in Alternative Medicine: Contrasting Biomedical and Anthropological Approaches." *Social Science & Medicine* 62: 2646–57.

Benjamin, Jessica. 1988. *Bonds of Love: Psychoanalysis, Feminism, and the Problem of Domination.* London and New York: Pantheon Books.

Benjamin, Jessica. 1990. "An Outline of Intersubjectivity: The Development of Recognition." *Psychoanalytic Psychology* 7: 33–46.

Berg, Marc, and Annemarie Mol. 1998. *Differences in Medicine: Unravelling Practices, Techniques, and Bodies.* Durham and London: Duke University Press.

Bishop, Felicity L., Eric E. Jacobson, Jessica R. Shaw, and J. Ted Kaptchuk. 2012. "Scientific Tools, Fake Treatments, or Triggers for Psychological Healing: How Clinical Trial Participants Conceptualise Placebos." *Social Science & Medicine* 74: 767–74.

Bishop, Felicity L., Lucy Yardley, and George T. Lewith. 2008. "Treat or Treatment: A Qualitative Study Analyzing Patients' Use of Complementary and Alternative Medicine." *American Journal of Public Heath* 98(9): 1700–05.

Brown, Wendy. 2015. *Undoing the Demos, Neoliberalism's Stealth Revolution.* New York: Zone Books.

Cant, Sarah and Ursula Sharma. 1999. *A New Medical Pluralism? Alternative Medicine, Doctors, Patients and the State.* London: UCL Press.

Cartwright, Tina. 2007. "'Getting on With Life': The Experiences of Older People Using Complementary Health Care." *Social Science & Medicine* 64: 1692–703.

Cartwright, Tina and Rebecca Torr. 2005. "Making Sense of Illness: The Experiences of Users of Complementary Medicine." *Journal of Health Psychology* 10: 559–72.

Clarke, Tainya C., Patricia M. Barnes, Lindsey I. Black, Barbara J Stussman, and Richard L. Nahin. 2018. "Use of Yoga, Meditation, and Chiropractors Among U.S. Adults Aged 18 and Over." NCHS Data Brief 325. Hyattsville, MD: National Center for Health Statistics.

Cockerham, William C. 2005. "Health Lifestyle Theory and the Convergence of Agency and Structure." *Journal of Health and Social Behavior* 46: 51–67.

Conboy, Lisa, Sonal Patel, Ted J. Kaptchuk, Bobbie Gottlieb, David Eisenberg, and Delores Acevedo-Garcia. 2005. "Sociodemographic Determinants of the Utilization of Specific Types of Complementary and Alternative Medicine: An Analysis Based on a Nationally Representative Survey Sample." *The Journal of Alternative and Complementary Medicine* 11(6): 977–94.

Connor, Linda H. 2004. "Relief, Risk and Renewal: Mixed Therapy Regimens in an Australian Suburb." *Social Science & Medicine* 59: 1695–705.

Conrad, Peter. 2005. "The Shifting Engines of Medicalization." *Journal of Health and Social Behavior* 46: 3–14.

Courtenay, Will H. 2000. "Constructions of Masculinity and Their Influence on Well-being: A Theory of Gender and Health." *Social Science and Medicine* 50: 1385–401.

Dew, Kevin. 2004. "The Regulation of Practice. Practitioners and Their Interactions with Organisations." Pp. 64–80 in *The Mainstreaming of Complementary and Alternative Medicine: Studies in Social Context*, edited by Philip Tovey, Gary Easthope and Jon Adams. London: Routledge.

Doel, Marcus A. and Jeremy Sergott. 2003. "Beyond Belief? Consumer Culture, Complementary Medicine, and the Dis-ease of Everyday Life." *Environment and Planning D: Society and Space* 21: 739–59.

Feagin, Joe, and Zinobia Bennefield. 2014. "Systemic Racism and U.S. Health Care." *Social Science & Medicine* 103: 7–14.

Fitzsimmons, Alexandra G., Deborah V. Dahlke, Caroline D. Bergeron, Kasey N. Smith, Aakash Patel, Marcia G. Ory, and Matthew L. Smith. 2019. "Impact of Complementary and Alternative Medicine Offerings on Cancer Patients' Emotional Health and Ability to Self-manage Health Conditions." *Complementary Therapies in Medicine* 43: 102–8.

Gale, Nicola Kay. 2011. "From Body-talk to Body-stories: Body Work in Complementary and Alternative Medicine." *Sociology of Health & Illness* 33(2): 237–51.

Giddens, Anthony. 1991. *Modernity and Self-Identity*. Cambridge: Polity Press.

Gimlin, Debra. 2007. "What is 'Body Work'? A Review of the Literature." *Sociology Compass* 1(1): 353–70.

Givati, Assaf. 2015. "Performing 'Pragmatic Holism': Professionalisation and the Holistic Discourse of Non-medically Qualified Acupuncturists and Homeopaths in the United Kingdom." *Health* 19(1): 34–50.

Grace, S., J. Bradbury, C. Avila, and A. Du Chesne. 2018. "'The Healthcare System is not Designed Around My Needs': How Healthcare Consumers Self-integrate Conventional and Complementary Healthcare Services." *Complementary Therapies in Clinical Practice* 32: 151–6.

Grosz, Elizabeth. 1994. *Volatile Bodies: Towards a Corporeal Feminism*. Bloomington and Indianapolis, IN: Indiana University Press.

Harrington, Anne. 2008. *The Cure Within: A History of Mind-body Medicine*. London and New York: W. W. Norton & Company.

Heggie, Vanessa. 2015. "Women Doctors and Lady Nurses: Class, Education, and the Professional Victorian Woman." *Bulletin of the History of Medicine* 89(2): 267–92.

Hochschild, Arlie R. 2003. *The Commercialization of Intimate Life: Notes from Home and Work*. Berkeley and Los Angeles, CA: University of California Press.

Hollenberg, Daniel. 2006. "Uncharted Ground: Patterns of Professional Interaction among Complementary/alternative and Biomedical Practitioners in Integrative Health Care Settings." *Social Science & Medicine* 62: 731–44.

Hollenberg, Daniel, and Linda Muzzin. 2010. "Epistemological Challenges to Integrative Medicine – An Anti-Colonial Perspective on the Combination of Complementary/alternative Medicine with Biomedicine." *Health Sociology Review* 19(1): 34–56.

Honneth, Axel. 2001. Recognition or Redistribution? Changing Perspectives on the Moral Order of Society. *Theory, Culture and Society* 18 (2–3): 43-55.

Horrocks, Christine and Sally Johnson. 2014. "A Socially Situated Approach to Inform Ways to Improve Health and Wellbeing." *Sociology of Health & Illness* 36(2): 175–86.

Hughes, Kahryn. 2004. "Health as Individual Responsibility. Possibilities and Personal Struggle." Pp. 25–46 in *The Mainstreaming of Complementary and Alternative Medicine: Studies in Social Context*, edited by Philip Tovey, Gary Easthope and Jon Adams. London: Routledge.

Hunt, K. J., H. F. Coelho, B. Wider, R. Perry, S. K. Hung, R. Terry, and E. Ernst. 2010. "Complementary and Alternative Medicine Use in England: Results from a National Survey." *International Journal of Clinical Practice* 64(11): 1496–502.

Illouz, Eva. 2008. *Saving the Modern Soul: Therapy, Emotions, and the Culture of Self-Help*. Berkley, Los Angeles, CA and London: University of California Press.

Johnson, Pamela Jo, Judy Jou, Todd H. Rockwood, and Dawn M. Upchurch. 2019. "Perceived Benefits of Using Complementary and Alternative Medicine by Race/Ethnicity Among Midlife and Older Adults in the United States." *Journal of Aging and Health* 31(8): 1376–97.

Kaptchuk, Ted J. 2002. "The Placebo Effect in Alternative Medicine: Can the Performance of a Healing Ritual Have Clinical Significance?" *Annals of Internal Medicine* 136(11): 817–25.

Kelner, Merrijoy. 2003. "The Therapeutic Relationship under Fire." Pp. 79–97 in *Complementary and Alternative Medicine: Challenge and Change*, edited by Merrijoy Kelner, Wellman Beverly, Bernice Pescosolido and Mike Saks. London: Routledge.

Kelner, Merrijoy and Beverly Wellman. 1997. "Health Care and Consumer Choice: Medical and Alternative Therapies." *Social Science & Medicine* 45(2): 203–12.

Keshet, Yael and Dalit Simchai. 2014. "The 'Gender Puzzle' of Alternative Medicine and Holistic Spirituality: A Literature Review." *Social Science & Medicine* 113: 77–86.

Kristoffersen, Agnete E., Trine Stub, Frauke Musial, Vinjar Fønnebø, Ola Lillenes, and Arne Johan Norheim. 2018. ""Prevalence and Reasons for Intentional Use of Complementary and Alternative Medicine as an Adjunct to Future Visits to a Medical Doctor for Chronic Disease." *BMC Complementary and Alternative Medicine* 18: 109.

Kristoffersen, Agnete E., Trine Stub, Anita Salmonsen, Frauke Musial, and Katarina Hamberg. 2014. "Gender Differences in Prevalence and Associations for Use of CAM in a Large Population Study." *BMC Complementary and Alternative Medicine* 14: 463.

Lawrence, Christopher, and George Weisz. 1998. "Medical Holism: The Context." Pp. 1–22 in *Greater Than the Parts: Holism in Biomedicine, 1920-1950*, eds Christopher Lawrence and George Weisz. New York and Oxford: Oxford University Press.

Leaper, Campbell and Melanie M. Ayres. 2007. "A Meta-Analytic Review of Gender Variations in Adults' Language Use: Talkativeness, Affiliative Speech, and Assertive Speech." *Personality & Social Psychology Review* 11(4): 328–63.

Lupton, Deborah. 2012. *Medicine as Culture: Illness, Disease and the Body in Western Societies*. 3rd ed. London, Thousand Oaks, CA: Sage.

McGregor, Katherine J. and Edmund R. Peay. 1996. "The Choice of Alternative Health Therapy for Health Care: Testing Some Propositions." *Social Science & Medicine* 43(9): 1317–27.

McGuire, Meredith B. 1996. "Religion and Healing the Mind/body/self." *Social Compass* 43(1): 101–16.

McGuire, Meredith B. 2008. *Lived Religion: Faith and Practice in Everyday Life*. Oxford: Oxford University Press.

McQueen, Patrick. 2015. *Subjectivity, Gender and the Struggle for Recognition*. Houndmills: Palgrave Macmillan.

McNay, Lois. 1999. Gender, Habitus and the Field: Pierre Bourdieu and the Limits of Reflexivity. *Theory, Culture and Society* 16: 95–117.

Mizrachi, Nissim, Judith T. Shuval, and Sky Gross. 2005. "Boundary at Work: Alternative Medicine in Biomedical Settings." *Sociology of Health & Illness* 27(1): 20–43.

Nahin, Richard L., Patricia M. Barnes, and Barbra J. Stussman. 2016. "Expenditures on Complementary Health Approaches: United States, 2012." National Health Statistics Reports 95. US Hyattsville, MD: National Center for Health Statistics.

Nettleton, Sarah. 2006. "'I Just Want Permission to Be Ill': Towards a sociology of medically unexplained symptoms." *Social Science & Medicine* 62: 1167–78.

O'Connor, Bonnie B. 2003. "Conceptions of the Body in Complementary and Alternative Medicine." Pp. 39–60 in *Complementary and Alternative Medicine: Challenge and Change*, edited by Merrijoy Kelner, Wellman Beverly, Bernice Pescosolido and Mike Saks. London: Routledge.

O'Grady, Helen. 2005. *Woman's Relationship with Herself: GENDER, Foucault and Therapy*. London and New York: Routledge.

Oerton, Sarah. 2004. "Bodywork boundaries: Power, politics and professionalism in therapeutic massage." *Gender, Work and Organization* 11(5): 544–65.

Oerton, Sarah, and Joanna Phoenix. 2001. "Sex/bodywork: Discourses and practices." *Sexualities* 4(4): 387–412.

Ong, Chi-Keong, Sophie Petersen, Gerard C. Bodeker, and Sarah Stewart-Brown. 2002. "Health Status of People Using Complementary and Alternative Medical Practitioner Services in 4 English Counties." *American Journal of Public Health* 92(10): 1653–56.

Parusnikova, Zuzana. 2002. "Integrative Medicine: Partnership or Control." *Studies in History and Philosophy of Biological and Biomedical Sciences* 33: 169–86.

Paterson, Charlotte, Charlotte Baarts, Laila Launsø, and Marja J. Verhoef. 2009. "Evaluating Complex Health Interventions: A Critical Analysis of the 'Outcomes' Concept." *BMC Complementary and Alternative Medicine* 9: 18–28.

Peacock, Marian, Paul Bissell, and Jenny Owen. 2014. "Dependency Denied: Health Inequalities in the Neo-Liberal Era." *Social Science & Medicine* 118: 173–80.

Phelan, Jo C. and Bruce G. Link. 2015. "Is Racism a Fundamental Cause of Inequalities in Health?" *Annual Review of Sociology* 41: 311–30.

Porter, Roy. 1999. *The Greatest Benefit to Mankind: A Medical History of Humanity from Antiquity to the Present.* New York and London: W. W. Norton & Company.

Ruggie, Mary. 2004. *Marginal to Mainstream: Alternative Medicine in America.* New York: Cambridge University Press.

Saks, Mike. 2003. *Orthodox and Alternative Medicine: Politics, Professionalisation and Health Care.* London and New York: Continuum.

Salamonsen, Anita and Rolf Ahlzén. 2018. "Epistemological Challenges in Contemporary Western Healthcare Systems Exemplified by People's Widespread Use of Complementary and Alternative Medicine." *Health* 22(4): 356–71.

Sayer, Andrew. 2011. *Why Things Matter to People: Social Science, Values and Ethical Life.* Cambridge: Cambridge University Press.

Sharma, Ursula. 1992. *Complementary Medicine Today: Practitioners and Patients.* London and New York: Tavistock/Routledge.

Sharp, Deborah, Ava Lorenc, Gene Feder, Paul Little, Sandra Hollinghurst, Stewart Mercer, and MacPherson Hugh. 2018. "'Trying to Put a Square Peg into a Round Hole': A Qualitative Study of Healthcare Professionals' Views of Integrating Complementary Medicine into Primary Care for Musculoskeletal and Mental Health Comorbidity." *BMC Complementary and Alternative Medicine* 18: 290.

Shim, Janet K. 2010. "Cultural Health Capital: A Theoretical Approach to Understanding Health Care Interactions and the Dynamics of Unequal Treatment." *Journal of Health and Social Behavior* 51(1): 1–15.

Shippee, Tetyana Pylypiv, Markus H. Schafer, and Kenneth F. Farraro. 2012. "Beyond the Barriers: Racial Discrimination and Use of Complementary and Alternative Medicine among Black Americans." *Social Science & Medicine* 74: 1155–62.

Shorofi, Sayed Afshin and Paul Arbon. 2010. "Nurses' Knowledge, Attitudes, and Professional Use of Complementary and Alternative Medicine (CAM): A Survey at Metropolitan Hospitals in Adelaide." *Complementary Therapies in Clinical Practice* 16: 229–34.

Shuval, Judith T., Revital Gross, Yael Ashkenazi, and Leora Schachter. 2012. "Integrating CAM and Biomedicine in Primary Care Settings: Physicians' Perspectives on Boundaries and Boundary Work." *Qualitative Health Research* 22: 1317–29.

Siahpush, Mohammad. 1999. "A Critical Review of the Sociology of Alternative Medicine: Research on Users, Practitioners and the Orthodoxy." *Health* 4(2): 159–78.

Sirois, Fuschia M. and Mary L. Gick. 2002. "An Investigation of the Health Beliefs and Motivations of Complementary Medicine Clients." *Social Science & Medicine* 55: 1025–37.

Skeggs, Beverley and Vik Loveday. 2014. "Struggles for Value: Value Practices, Injustice, Judgment, Affect and the Idea of Class." *British Journal of Sociology* 63(3): 472–90.

Skeggs, Beverley. 2004. *Class, Self, Culture.* London: Routledge.

Sointu, Eeva. 2006a. "The Search for Wellbeing in Alternative and Complementary Health Practices." *Sociology of Health & Illness* 28(3): 330–49.

Sointu, Eeva. 2006b. "Recognition and the Creation of Wellbeing." *Sociology* 40(3): 493–510.

Sointu, Eeva. 2006c. “Healing Bodies, Feeling Bodies: Embodiment and Alternative and Complementary Health Practices.” *Social Theory and Health* 4(3): 203–20.

Sointu, Eeva. 2010. “The Rise of an Ideal: Tracing Changing Discourses of Wellbeing.” *The Sociological Review* 53(2): 255–74.

Sointu, Eeva. 2011. “Detraditionalization, Gender, and Alternative and Complementary Medicines.” *Sociology of Health and Illness* 33(3): 356–71.

Sointu, Eeva. 2012. *Theorizing Complementary and Alternative Medicines: Wellbeing, Self, Class, Gender.* Basingstoke; New York: Palgrave Macmillan.

Sointu, Eeva. 2013. “Complementary and Alternative Medicines, Embodied Subjectivity and Experiences of Healing.” *Health* 17(5): 439–54.

Sointu, Eeva, and Linda Woodhead. 2008. “Spirituality, Gender, and Expressive Selfhood.” *Journal for the Scientific Study of Religion* 47(2): 259–76.

Stacey, Jackie. 1997. *Teratologies: A Cultural Study of Cancer.* London: Routledge.

Stussman, Barbara J., Lindsey I. Black, Patricia M. Barnes, Richard L. Nahin, and Tainya C. Clarke. 2015. “Wellness-Related Use of Common Complementary Health Approaches Among Adults: United States, 2012.” National Health Statistics Reports 85. Hyattsville, MD: National Center for Health Statistics.

Stussman, Barbara J., Richard L. Nahin, Patricia M. Barnes, and Brian W. Ward. 2020. “US Physician Recommendations to Their Patients About the Use of Complementary Health Approaches.” *The Journal of Alternative and Complementary Medicine* 26(1): 25–33. Published online Jan 2020, https://doi.org/10.1089/acm.2019.0303.

Taylor, Charles. 1989. *Sources of the Self.* Cambridge, MA: Harvard University Press.

Taylor, Charles. 1991. *The Ethics of Authenticity.* Cambridge, MA: Harvard University Press.

Taylor, Charles. 1994. “The Politics of Recognition.” Pp. 25–73 in *Multiculturalism, Examining the Politics of Recognition*, edited by Amy Gutman. Princeton, NJ: Princeton University Press.

Taylor, Scott. 2010. “Gendering in the Holistic Milieu: A Critical Realist Analysis of Homeopathic Work.” *Gender, Work & Organization* 17(4): 454–74.

Thomas, Kate and Pat Coleman. 2004. “Use of Complementary or Alternative Medicine in a General Population in Great Britain. Results from the National Omnibus Survey.” *Journal of Public Health* 26(2): 152–7.

Thomas, Kate J., Pat Coleman, and J. P. Nicholl. 2003. “Trends in Access to Complementary or Alternative Medicines via Primary Care in England:1995–2001. Results From a Follow-Up National Survey.” *Family Practice* 20: 575–7.

Thomas, Kate J., J. P. Nicholl, and Piers Coleman. 2001a. “Use and Expenditure on Complementary Medicine in England: A Population Based Survey.” *Complementary Therapies in Medicine* 9: 2–11.

Thomas, Kate J., J. P. Nicholl, and Margaret Fall. 2001b. “Access to Complementary Medicine via General Practice.” *British Journal of General Practice* 51(462): 25–30.

Thompson, Jennifer Jo, Cheryl Ritenbaugh, and Mark Nichter. 2009. “Reconsidering the Placebo Response from a Broad Anthropological Perspective.” *Culture, Medicine and Psychiatry* 33: 112–52.

Twigg, Julia. 2000. “Carework as a Form of Bodywork.” *Ageing and Society* 20: 389–411.

Twigg, Julia, Carol Wolkowitz, Rachel Lara Cohen, and Sarah Nettleton. 2011. “Conceptualising Body Work in Health and Social Care.” *Sociology of Health & Illness* 33(2): 171–88.

Wardle, Jon L., David W. Sibbritt, and Jon Adams. 2018. "Primary Care Practitioner Perceptions and Attitudes of Complementary Medicine: A Content Analysis of Free-Text Responses from a Survey of Non-Metropolitan Australian General Practitioners." *Primary Health Care Research & Development* 19: 246–55.

Wasserman, Jason Adam. 2014. "Complementary and Alternative Medicine Usage and Race." Pp. 293–6 in *The Wiley Blackwell Encyclopedia of Health, Illness, Behavior, and Society*, edited by William C. Cockerham, Robert Dingwall and Stella R. Quah. Oxford: Wiley Blackwell.

Widding Isaksen, Lise. 2002. "Toward a Sociology of (Gendered) Disgust: Images of Bodily Decay and the Social Organization of Care Work." *Journal of Family Issues* 23: 791–811.

Wiese, Marlene and Candice Oster. 2010. "Becoming Accepted: The Complementary and Alternative Practitioners' Response to the Uptake and Practice of Traditional Medicine Therapies by the Mainstream Health Sector." *Health* 14(4): 415–33.

Wiese, Marlene, Candice Oster, and Jan Pincombe. 2010. "Understanding the Emerging Relationship Between Complementary Medicine and Mainstream Health Care: A Review of the Literature." *Health* 14(3): 326–42.

Wiles, Janine and Mark W. Rosenberg. 2001. "'Gentle Caring Experience:' Seeking Alternative Health Care in Canada." *Health and Place* 7: 209–24.

Williams, Simon J. and Gillian Bendelow. 1998. *The Lived Body: Sociological Themes, Embodied Issues*. London: Routledge.

Winnick, Terri A. 2005. "From Quackery to "Complementary" Medicine: The American Medical Profession Confronts Alternative Therapies." *Social Problems* 52(1): 38–61.

Xue, Charlie C. L., Anthony L. Zhang, Vivian Lin, Cliff Da Costa, and David F. Story. 2007. "Complementary and Alternative Medicine Use in Australia: A National Population-Based Survey." *The Journal of Alternative and Complementary Medicine* 13(6): 643–50.

Yar, Majid. 2001. Recognition and the Politics of Human(e) Desire. *Theory, Culture & Society* 18 (2–3): 57–76.

Young, Iris Marion. 1990. *Throwing Like a Girl and Other Essays in Feminist Philosophy and Social Theory*. Bloomington and Indianapolis, IN: Indiana University Press.

26

American Health Care System

Reforms for Access, Outcomes and Cost Amid Legal, Legislative and Political Disputes

BERNICE A. PESCOSOLIDO AND CAROL A. BOYER

At the end of the nineteenth century the medical profession stood amid great change in America. The coming of the industrial revolution coupled with new scientific theories of medicine, the rise of the middle class professional, and the infusion of philanthropic capital created the modern profession of medicine (Pescosolido and Martin 2004). With that social transformation of American medicine (Starr 1982), the new health care system would be substantially different from the one at the beginning of the nineteenth century or even at mid-century. Further, as it continued to evolve throughout the twentieth century, the modern medical system in the US took a very different path from its European counterparts, building a mixed private and public system of care with powerful physician direction (Brown 1979; Freidson 1970; Hollingsworth 1986; Rosen 1983).

What was less anticipated but equally remarkable was the contrast between the current system and that early one. Escalating costs without equivalent medical markers of success (e.g. the relatively high infant mortality rate), increasing burden of chronic and degenerative diseases, expanding uninsured population, the unexpected challenges of the opioid epidemic and the COVID-19 pandemic, strained the system and led to major efforts to restructure the American health care system. In the early 1990s, a failed Clinton health care plan led employers and state governments to launch managed care strategies to transform the structure and financing of health services. But a public backlash against managed care by mid-decade weakened many of its objectionable utilization management practices including limiting physician choice, access to specialists, and rationing of health care services, producing what Mechanic (2004) described as "managed care lite."

The Wiley Blackwell Companion to Medical Sociology, First Edition. Edited by William C. Cockerham.

By the turn of the twenty-first century, health care costs continued to escalate, the number of uninsured increased, and health care services remained fragmented and uncoordinated. Despite public resistance, a variety of cost control strategies were implemented including "medical necessity" reviews for services, cost-sharing, limits on inpatient admissions and lengths of stay, and selective contracting with health insurers. Managed care, even if watered down, dominated national policy, covering almost two-thirds of all Medicaid beneficiaries (Medicaid and CHIP Payment and Access Commission 2017). In response, public outcry, investors' and executives' concerns, class action filings, and malpractice or employee-benefit lawsuits against managed care practices again were successful in eliminating several of the most stringent cost controlling practices (Bloche and Studdert 2004). In 2010, the Patient Protection and Affordable Care Act (ACA; Obamacare) offered systematic and comprehensive health reforms to reduce the number of uninsured. With initial successes in increasing population coverage, especially using Medicaid waivers in key states (e.g. Kentucky), this effort faced and continues to face opposition, the elimination of its critical fiscal support pillar, and threat of roll back. While efforts to overturn the ACA have failed, the impending presidential and congressional elections in 2020 and the impending appointment of a conservative Supreme Court justice hold the potential to make fundamental changes to the ACA in opposite policy directions.

This chapter provides an overview of different eras in providing health care in the US. We concentrate on current challenges and opportunities surrounding ongoing strategies to either implement or strike down all or parts of the ACA. Beginning with a review of the evolution of the American health care system focusing on physician authority in the provision of heath care, we target efforts to assure access and improve quality of care in a cost-effective manner.

The Rise of a Health Care System in the US

Historians and sociologists alike have argued that the discovery of a bacillus that caused anthrax, the routine use of antiseptics, and the introduction of anesthesia combined to produce the great break between medicine of the past and the modern form of science-based practice. While different societies embraced the new science in different ways in shaping their health care systems, industrializing countries of the US and Europe used political, social and economic mechanisms to place science-based physicians at the center of modern health care. Figure 26.1 provides a simple heuristic device charting the relative authority of physicians in the American health care system over time. As Figure 26.1 indicates, the authority and reach of modern physicians grew dramatically from the mid-1800s to 1910 and beyond. The Flexner Report, from the Carnegie Foundation, was instrumental in establishing physician authority, and gave rise to the scientific model of medical education in the US. It recommended that only medical schools following the German model of biomedical training and stronger clinical practice receive financial assistance and public support. The Rockefeller Foundation provided the infusion of capital (Brown 1979). Itinerant medicine practitioners delivering elixirs laced with opium or alcohol and other practices purging disease by cleansing the body through vomiting or elimination were outlawed. Gone also was the standard practice of "regular" physicians (i.e. the precursors of the scientific physician such as Benjamin Rush) who bled the ill person to remove tainted blood. Other alternative providers such as Granny midwives who delivered babies at home and female or minority physicians who learned medicine through apprenticeships were also eliminated through the establishment of state-based licensing laws.

Formed in 1847, the American Medical Association lobbied to direct the use of resources generated by wealthy industrialists to scientific medicine and away from well-established chiropractors and homeopaths, who were preferred providers of the Midwest farmers and the upper classes, respectively (Quadagno 2006). While backing large infusions of wealth into the emerging system of modern medicine, the industrialists did so through their newly established philanthropic foundations. Licensing laws represented the critical but minimal role of government in the US, requiring all those wanting to practice medicine to take state examinations written by the rising middle-class physicians at the newly established, scientific-based medical schools, such as Johns Hopkins University. Both aspiring and practicing medical providers not trained at modern medical schools failed the examinations and were prohibited from practicing medicine in the US (Brown 1979). Aside from passing licensing laws, governments, whether federal or state, played a minimal role, differing substantially from the European experience (Berlant 1975). With this complex of efforts, the scientific medical profession became a successful, if not total, monopoly (Berlant 1975; Collins 1979; Starr 1982).

Historically the US depended on a mix of public and private sources to provide health insurance, never establishing universal health insurance. As a result, the health care system is a patchwork of providers practicing in nonprofit, private and public sectors including solo-practitioners, incorporated groups of physicians and other clinicians, voluntary community hospitals, private and public hospitals. Major pre-paid group practice plans, initially started between 1930 and 1960, were later referred to as health maintenance organizations (HMOs, e.g. Kaiser-Permanente Medical Program), and provided an alternative structure along with wider networks of providers in managed care plans known as preferred provider organizations (PPOs). Earlier health cooperatives were established in rural areas and small communities without medical specialists or a nearby hospital to serve farming communities and workers in railroad and mining industries that developed beyond urban centers. The nonprofit sector was supplemented by a public sector that included city and county hospitals, long-term care facilities (e.g. mental hospitals, TB sanitariums), Veterans Administration System established at the end of the Civil War in the 1860s, public health nursing and specialized community clinics (e.g. the Community Mental Health Centers or CMHCs) that were established with the deinstitutionalization of patients in state mental hospitals.

Thus, the period from 1910 through 1970 represented an era of significant growth, success, and authority of the medical profession. After World War II, with the large infusion of support by the federal government for research and development and hospital construction, American physicians became the most

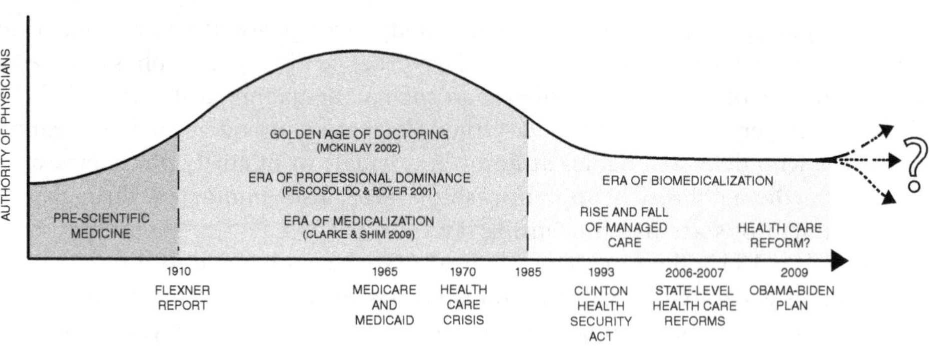

Figure 26.1 Eras in the American health care system

prominent and powerful medical professional group in the world. This era has been described by McKinlay and Marceau 2002) as the "Golden Age of Doctoring," by Clarke and her colleagues as the "Medicalization Era" (Clarke and Shim 2009), and by us, using Eliot Freidson's (1970) term, as "The Era of Professional Dominance" (see Figure 26.1). Working in a primarily private health care system, physicians determined both the nature of medical care and the arrangements under which it was provided (Freidson 1970). Physicians set their fees, worked in predominantly solo-practices, and joined the American Medical Association. The New Deal, which introduced several major economic and social programs including Social Security in response to the Great Depression of the 1930s, was not extended to the public provision of health care characteristic of health insurance systems of Europe. Beginning in the 1940s, for the most part, patients could choose the physician of their choice for treatment and purchase private health insurance or be treated in the public sector.

Adopted together in 1965, Medicare and Medicaid represented the first major governmental change in the American system. These programs, targeting different population groups, had contrasting policies and regulations, social impact and funding mechanisms. Medicare provides hospital insurance, skilled nursing home and home health care and hospice under Social Security for *all* older individuals regardless of need as well as those with disabilities or end-stage renal disease (Part A), and government-subsidized voluntary insurance for outpatient care and services (Part B). Part C offers Medicare Advantage Plans with a private insurer that incorporates Parts A, B and frequently prescription drug coverage into one comprehensive plan typically within health maintenance organizations (HMOs) or preferred provider organizations (PPOs). Part D includes partial coverage for prescription drugs. Unlike the entitlement aspect of Medicare, Medicaid is a means-tested public assistance program for low income citizens and the medically needy. Uniform federal standards for eligibility and benefits exist for Medicare, but under President Reagan's New Federalism policies, the authority about program eligibility and coverage for Medicaid beneficiaries moved from the federal to state governments (Starr 1982; Thompson 2012).

END OF UNQUESTIONED MEDICAL PROFESSION DOMINANCE

In 1970 President Richard Nixon announced the existence of a health care crisis in the US (see Figure 26.1). Although Medicare and Medicaid provided insurance coverage to several groups, these programs still left millions without health care insurance and the uninsured population was increasing. At the same time, these programs, notably Medicare, resulted in escalating costs and profit-taking at a time of rapid inflation in the economy. The two-tiered or two-class system of US health care became more prominent and rose to the forefront of policy debates. Especially evident in treating chronic illnesses such as cancer, heart disease, and degenerative illnesses that are not well addressed by the germ theory or acute care models, Americans who were better educated, had more resources and higher expectations received more sophisticated technological options denied to those without them. Yet, the middle classes increasingly questioned established practices, demanding more input. Even as the "Biomedicalization Era," (Clarke and Shim 2009, Figure 26.1) in 1985 brought dramatic and largely technoscientific changes to the practice and organization of American medicine, the public demonstrated a growing interest in both older and newer forms of complementary and integrative medicine, including midwifery, immunotherapy, acupuncture, chiropractic and homeopathy. The potential for a "second social contract" between modern medicine and society was suggested by these developments and scientific medicine's deprofessionalization; patients' rights advocacy and a growing consumer movement; anti-trust regulation for professions; and the use of integrative and holistic approaches to health care (Pescosolido and Kronenfeld 1995; Pescosolido et al. 2000). Further, health care insurance began to cover more integrative medicines, even if limited (e.g., chiropractic), and the membership of the American Medical Association plummeted in favor of specialty groups. Professional dominance was unraveling. Sociologists shifted their discussion from issues of professional dominance to corporatization, proletarianization and countervailing powers; anthropologists discussed alternative medical systems being complementary rather than competing, discussing the potential for integration; and American medical schools were being described as "vassals of the marketplace" that had retreated from their public mission (Light 1995; Light and Levine 1988; Ludmerer 1999; Unschuld 1976).

This disillusionment was not exclusive to modern medicine and, perhaps, reflected larger changes in modern society (Pescosolido and Rubin 2000). Rubin (1996) argued that the social and economic bases of modern society tarnished in the early 1970s and marked a turning point. The postwar growth that had fueled prosperity in all sectors, including medicine, diminished. A long decline in expansion resulted in the downsizing of corporations and displacement of large numbers of workers. While new jobs continued to be created, some were also increasingly part-time, temporary, low wage, and without important benefits including health insurance (Kronick and Gilmer 1999). US health care costs continued to rise at rates higher than inflation and individuals experienced greater barriers to access. Diseases, thought to have been solved, returned (e.g. tuberculosis), new ones that perplexed medical researchers and strained the limits of scientific medicine arose (e.g. HIV/AIDS, antibiotic-resistant bacterial infection) and persistent social problems plagued the country that spent the most on health care globally, but without consistently good outcomes (e.g. higher US infant mortality rate than Japan, Germany, Italy, or Singapore).

Health Care Reform of the 1990s: Managed Care, Its Backlash and Transformation

Health care became a central political issue in national electoral debates in the 1990s (see Figure 26.1). In the 1990 presidential election, Democratic candidates Bob Kerry and later Bill Clinton focused on the health care crisis which became a lightning rod among the American public. After his election, President Clinton sought major health care system reform, appointing his wife, Hillary Clinton, to chair a Task Force (1992–1994) that crafted the Clinton Health Security Act. Based on the triad of managed competition, global budget, and universal coverage, the plan sought to achieve improved access through privately provided health insurance and cost controls (Zelman 1996). The Clinton Plan proposed, for the first time, that health care in America was a right, not a privilege based on ability to pay. The Clinton Plan preserved the private nature of health care in the US while ensuring it as a public good.

While scholars, politicians and policy makers debated its merits (e.g., Relman 1993), the Clinton Health Reform Act was eventually abandoned in 1994 after lengthy and complicated recommendations in reports were issued amid strong public opposition (see Domhoff 1996; Quadagno 2006; Skocpol 1997). In its demise, the private health insurance market was transformed, nonetheless, as the private sector introduced managed care and the centralization of large health plans. Facing total health benefit costs increasing more than 20% each year (Higgins 1991), fiscal constraints from a mounting federal budget deficit and rising skepticism about the value of health care given its costs, eventually state governments also moved to a managed care approach. Different models of managed care including health management organizations (HMOs) and preferred provider organizations (PPOs) expanded over the years (National Council on Disability 2013).

By the mid- to late 1990s, the public's negative response to managed care stemmed from denials for medical services as well as court decisions, legislation, and health plan policies that challenged managed care efforts to zealously reduce costs. Many of these tightly managed cost-conscious practices with stringent utilization management, restrictive provider networks, and broad preauthorization reviews were eventually eliminated (Bloche and Studdert 2004). Beginning in 2000, preferred provider organizations (PPOs) grew, offering greater choice of providers, more flexibility in treatments for consumers and providers, and lower administrative costs for purchasers (Hurley et al. 2004). These continue to be pervasive (enrolling 44% of covered workers) and virtually eliminating HMOs and conventional or indemnity plans (Kaiser Family Foundation 2019).

The focus on cost eclipsed other problems. Managed care placed greater responsibility for providing care after a hospital discharge on individuals and families (Pescosolido and Kronenfeld 1995). It challenged the autonomy and clinical decision-making authority of physicians as services were subject to utilization management, profiling, capitated payments and financial incentives which fit uneasily with medical professional ethics (Mechanic 2004). While some discretion has been returned to physicians (Freudenheim 1999), these challenges prompted a professionalism movement that reasserted the primacy of physicians' altruistic and community-oriented duties (e.g. Hafferty and Castellani 2009).

The last two decades of the twentieth century represented an historic turn in the American health care system with the expansion of managed care that did not reduce costs but slowed the escalating growth of health care costs. The exponential growth of Medicaid managed care has been characterized as the "mass migration of Medicaid enrollees to managed care in the 1990s" (Thompson 2012). States began pursuing managed care through Medicaid channels under the Balanced Budget Act of 1997. Although managed care demonstrations did not substantiate the efficacy of managed care, Medicaid managed care grew as a policy solution from the political momentum that it could be implemented without the failures and scandals of the past (Gifford et al. 2019; Oliver 2001; Thompson 1981). This was accomplished through diverse insurance options and organizations including (Gold 1998): (1) use of a fixed prepayment, capitated or negotiated fee for a defined set of services for a specified population of enrollees; (2) insurance risk shared by a managed care organization (MCO) and/or providers to provide necessary services; (3) selective contracting with enrollees limited to a panel of providers; (4) use of primary care gatekeepers to coordinate care and control use of services; (5) utilization review to assess the appropriateness of care and provider decisions before services were provided including pre-certification, concurrent review and high-cost case management; (6) managing quality of care with clinical practice guidelines; and (7) tracking patient and organizational outcomes referred to as performance monitoring to identify poor-quality plans, care and providers.

However, along with these changes, deductibles or out-of-pocket payments in individual market plans and some employer plans made health care unaffordable for lower and moderate-income individuals and families resulting in their delaying care and creating a growing "underinsured" population (Collins et al. 2017). In the end, while managed care constrained health care cost increases under its most stringent practices, both costs and premiums rose substantially with the withdrawal of these strategies (Center for Studying Health System Change 2002; Draper et al. 2002; Strunk et al. 2001).

The Affordable Care Act: Implementation, Ongoing Reforms and Appeals

The Patient Protection and Affordable Care Act (ACA; Obamacare) in 2010 represented the most significant and complex advance in American health care policy since Medicaid and Medicare. Its policy reforms touched Medicare and Medicaid, the private health insurance industry and the health care delivery system, standing as the largest health care reform in the nation's history (Burwell 2020). Not surprisingly, it has also been the most controversial, with reforms and repeals ongoing since the day it was signed by President Barack Obama.

The ACA changed insurance eligibility, provided subsidies and offered technical assistance to individuals. The ACA's provisions for insurance expansion included reforms in the private insurance market and in Medicaid and Medicare programs. Parents could keep children on their insurance until age 26. Insurers were prohibited from imposing annual and lifetime limits on coverage and from denying insurance based on preexisting conditions. The ACA addressed parity concerns by including mental health and substance abuse treatments as essential health benefits required in insurance coverage, barred insurers from denying coverage or raising premiums for persons with pre-existing illnesses and disabilities, and provided Medicare coverage of preventive services. Medicaid coverage widened to include all lower income (138% of the federal poverty level) documented residents (Emanuel and Gluck 2020) from original categories of beneficiaries (e.g. children, the disabled, pregnant women). As incentives to the States, Medicaid coverage statewide that met essential health benefits was provided at 100% federal funding from 2014 through 2016, tapering to 90% in 2020 and subsequent years. Subsidies for private insurance premiums were provided to low income individuals and families (at or below 400% of the federal poverty level) and consumer insurance costs were limited (from 2.06% for the poorest to 9.78% for the highest income). Subsidies for deductibles were provided to those with incomes at or below 250% of the poverty line (Blumenthal et al. 2020). Government subsidies for cost-sharing to private insurers were provided, subsequently overruled by a federal judge, and accommodated by states on an individual basis (Blumenthal et al. 2020). The expansion of Medicaid with its comprehensive delivery and payment reforms has been seen to hold the potential for a "transformation from a welfare program into a pillar of national health reform and a major player in the health plan market" (Rosenbaum 2015: 1).

Structural reforms in the delivery system included ACA marketplaces (i.e. exchanges beginning with the 2014 first open enrollment period), easier access to plan comparisons, and enrollment in health insurance plans using web-based tools with the added benefit of promoting competition among insurance companies. Delivery system reforms included investments in accountable care organizations (ACOs), patient-centered medical homes (PCMHs), and health homes (HHs), which were designed to reduce fragmentation and inefficiency while improving quality of care including integrating primary care and behavioral health services. Organizations were established including the non-profit Patient-Centered Outcomes Research Institute (PCORI) to support comparative effectiveness research and monitor and improve quality of care and health system performance, while the Center for Medicare and Medicaid Innovation (CMMI) was a new agency within the Centers for Medicare and Medicaid (CMS) to conduct experiments in cost and quality reforms.

As a risk-sharing, fiscal base, the ACA included both an individual mandate requiring all Americans to have health insurance or pay a tax penalty, and, an employer mandate requiring firms with 50 or more full-time employees to provide a minimum level of health insurance coverage for their employees or pay a fine. In a 2012 Supreme Court decision on the constitutionality of the ACA and the mandate to have health insurance (*NFIB et al v. Sebelius*), the Medicaid expansion was also upheld but rendered optional for states. By January, 2020, 37 states including the District of Columbia had adopted the expansion while 14 states with Republican leadership opted not to do so. Several potential changes revolved around Medicaid waivers for substance use disorders and mental illness and work requirements for Medicaid recipients (Rudowitz et al. 2020).

Beyond the administrative, legislative and political disputes across the federal government and the states, the constitutional challenges to the ACA have been ongoing since its enactment. In one of the most critical lawsuits, *Texas v. United States*, again challenged the individual mandate. In December 2019, the Fifth Circuit Court of Appeals agreed with a lower district court ruling that the individual penalty-less mandate was not enforceable as a tax. While the 2012 Supreme Court ruling upheld the mandate as only a tax, a 2017 tax reform law zeroed out the tax, threatening the fiscal basis of the ACA. Ultimately the case will now be decided by the US Supreme Court which will hear an appeal with a decision likely in 2021 to uphold or strike down the ACA in its entirety (Blumenthal and Seervai 2019; Collins 2020). In response to the mandate challenge, six states have introduced their own mandates to create balanced and stable risk pools (Blumenthal et al. 2020).

At the ten-year anniversary in 2020, the ACA had expanded comprehensive health insurance to millions of previously uninsured Americans. By reducing the numbers of uninsured persons to historically low levels, the ACA considerably improved access to health care services (Blumenthal et al. 2020). Yet, as described above, opponents of the ACA continue to work for repeal even as three Republican-sponsored bills to repeal and replace the ACA have failed (American Health Care Act, the Better Care Reconciliation Act, Health Care Freedom Act) (Nadash et al. 2018). Further, advancing quality of care and constraining costs will continue to be challenging initiatives in MCOs. Medicaid managed care plans still face considerable uncertainty in maintaining their enrollment continuity and promoting coordinated and integrative care with potential federal and state budget cuts, waivers and changing federal regulations in Medicaid programs (Garfield et al. 2018).

A repeal of the ACA would "trigger massive disruptions throughout the US health care system" and the health care industry that is nearly 20% of the nation's economy (Collins 2020). Repealing the ACA would leave young adults uninsured through parents' health insurance plans, reduce improved health care benefits for seniors, eliminate reformed and expanded payments to doctors, hospitals and other providers, end experiments in enhanced value-based care, eliminate pre-existing health condition protections in insurance, potentially reverse the reduced racial and income inequities in health insurance coverage along with prohibited discriminatory insurance pricing, and halt the unprecedented trend in substantially reducing the nation's uninsured population (Rosenbaum 2020).

While the ACA achieved substantial reductions in the uninsured population, recent increases in the uninsured population and in insurance costs remind us of the continuing multiple social forces and policy changes at play. Ongoing electoral politics echo recurring debates and resistance among parties, the public, and the courts regarding expanded rights and legal protections in access (Oberlander 2008). Major providers in the health care system, physicians, advanced practice nurses and physician assistants, have significant responsibilities not only in improving quality of care through evidence-based practices, but also serving the public in their relationships with patients and more broadly in enhancing population health (Benatar

2001; Mechanic 2000; Mechanic and Reinhard 2002; Stevens 2001). The economic and social interdependence among the world's populations increases the likelihood of pandemics like the COVID-19 virus, and the return of old infectious diseases. Coupled with rising rates of chronic illnesses, the global burden of illness may rise.

Remaining Challenges in the American Health Care System

Although frequently characterized as one of the best in the world, the American health care system requires continuing reform to match spending with outcomes. Five issues are critical – continuing to reduce the number of uninsured, improving population health status, cost control, reinforcing the "new professional ethic" among health care clinicians, and facing threats to global health.

Challenge 1: Covering the Uninsured Population

At the time the ACA was passed in 2010 a total of 48.6 million (16%) persons of all ages lacked health insurance (DeNavas-Walt et al. 2013), the highest percentage among high income nations (Baicker and Sommers 2020). By 2016 the uninsured population had decreased to 27.3 million (8.6%), the lowest recorded US level (Cohen et al. 2019). Coverage gains were attributed to Medicaid expansion (60%) and to subsidized private insurance through the exchanges (40%) (Frean et al. 2017). More specifically, Black, Hispanic, and White adults aged 19 to 64 years old, among the highest uninsured populations, made the largest gains since the ACA's main provisions for access went into effect in 2014. Uninsured Black adults went from 24.4% in 2013 to 14.4% in 2018. Uninsured Hispanic adults declined in the same period from 40.2% to 24.9%. According to the US Census Bureau's American Community Survey, the working age adult uninsured rate fell from 20.4% in 2013 to 12.4% in 2018. Uninsured White adults declined from 14.5% in 2013 to 8.6% in 2018 (Baumgartner et al. 2020). The highest uninsured among all age groups, those aged 19 to 34 years old, declined from 46% in 2010 to 17% in 2018. Both states that expanded their Medicaid programs, as well as those that did not, reported greater insurance coverage for Black, Hispanic and White populations with coverage gains greater in expansion states (Baumgartner et al. 2020; Gunja and Collins 2019). Most importantly, insurance coverage gains translated into reduced racial and ethnic disparities in access to health care.

However, recent estimates showed an increase in the uninsured to 30.4 million (9.4%) in 2018 (Cohen et al. 2019) and insurance loss affected all three major population groups (13.7% in 2016 to 14.4% in 2018 for Blacks; 8.2% in 2016 to 8.6% in 2018 for Whites; 25.5% to 24.9% for Hispanics). That is, gains in coverage for the uninsured population under the ACA are stalling at a time when eligibility exists in statewide expanded Medicaid programs and through subsidized health insurance in the ACA exchanges. Affordability, work requirements for Medicaid coverage, and reduced funding for outreach and navigator funding to assist individual access to insurance during open enrollment periods are cited as key reasons for the recent reversals. Further, legal immigrants may choose not to enroll, especially for their children, given fears of changes in national immigration policies including the "public charge" rule (an 1882 concept determining the likelihood that an applicant for immigration may be or become dependent on government benefits being leveraged by the Trump administration to reduce immigration (Gunja and Collins 2019; Rudowitz et al. 2020).

Challenge 2: Improving Health Outcomes

Among the key provisions of the ACA to improve health outcomes were increasing access to care of greater quality in both Medicaid and private health insurance coverage, eliminating low value treatments, integrating physical and behavioral health, and advancing prevention strategies. Comprehensive reviews of health outcomes that have been conducted especially for non-elderly populations in states with Medicaid expansion have shown improved self-reported health, increased rates of diagnosing and treating chronic illnesses including diabetes, improved depression outcomes, mixed evidence on cancer stage at diagnosis, and reduced mortality among middle-aged adults (Goldin et al. 2019; Sommers et al. 2017; Soni et al. 2020). As Mechanic and Olfson (2016) highlighted the "unprecedented opportunities" for reforming the behavioral health sector, the expansion of Medicaid coverage, indeed, has led to an increased likelihood of persons with a mental health condition being insured (Thomas et al. 2018) and better access to health care services for individuals with depression including reductions in time to care and medication adherence (Fry and Sommers 2018).

In addition, ACA expansion of dependent coverage for young adults with psychosis has increased private insurance coverage, along with a reduction in public insurance for hospitalizations with uncertain coverage for rehabilitation services (Busch et al. 2019). Medicaid expansion was associated with reduction in care barriers for persons with substance use disorders as well, particularly in admissions for opioid use disorder compared to alcohol, cocaine and other substances (Maclean and Saloner 2019; Olfson et al. 2018; Saloner and Maclean 2020). Rochefort (2018) credits the ACA with these coverage expansions and service innovations.

However, these gains coincide with the lack of achieving parity in insurance coverage for behavioral health care, severe shortages of mental health professionals, rigid treatment restrictions, and worsening inequalities in the financing and organization of care for those most in need. Finally, the major question remains unanswered: How much did Medicaid expansion and reforms in private insurance or other factors contribute to improved health outcomes (Allen and Sommers 2019)?

Challenge 3: Controlling Costs: Health Care Spending in Comparative Perspective

The US has the most expensive health care system in the world, spending 17.7% of gross domestic product (GDP) on health care in 2018, nearly twice as much as the average among OECD countries. While the most recent years show a plateauing in overall health care spending, 2018 also records the largest expenditures in Medicaid in US history (Emanuel and Navathe 2020). As noted above, the critical problem is not in the highest spending levels alone, but in the several notable health outcomes that are worse in the US. Compared to many OECD countries, these poorer outcomes include lowest life expectancy, highest suicide rate, and highest rates of avoidable mortality (Emanuel and Navathe 2020; Ginsburg 2008; Tikkanen and Abrams 2020). In the US, the high costs of health care are attributed to the widespread use of new medical technologies, high chronic disease burden, high obesity rates, comparatively higher numbers of hospitalizations due to preventable causes, high rates of elective surgery, high prices of prescription drugs and treatments, and higher public expectations about treatment and services. Despite widespread beliefs, population aging plays only a minor role in the high US costs, as all advanced countries confront this demographic trend.

Efforts to control costs are disappointing. Although the US House of Representatives comprehensive drug cost control legislation passed in 2019 to counter one of these problems, it is unlikely to pass in the US Senate (Blumenthal and Seervai 2019). Accountable care organizations (ACOs) were funded under the ACA as a major voluntary initiative. They were charged to promote evidence-based medicine, coordinate delivery of inpatient and outpatient care, reduce hospitalizations, improve preventive care, and eliminate low value practices. The mechanism involved physician-led organizations partnering with other physician groups, hospitals and other providers in assuming responsibility for the total costs and quality of care for at least 5,000 Medicare beneficiaries. ACOs have achieved modest savings while maintaining or improving quality; yet it is unclear whether this results, in part, from selecting healthier populations (Blumenthal and Abrams 2020).

The modest and controversial results of delivery system reforms elicit middling support at best, with conclusions that the ACA, at least, has not made things worse. At worst, the ACA reforms have not identified critical pathways to lower costs and better outcomes (Blumenthal and Abrams 2020; Emanuel and Navathe 2020).

Challenge 4: Reinforcing the "New Professional Ethic" for Health Care Clinicians

As the organization and financing of health care changed in the US, so was the practice of medicine by physicians and other clinicians transformed in significant ways. Focusing on the profession of medicine, Starr (1982) predicted that the coming of corporate medicine and the financial behavior of large corporations in the 1980s would threaten the autonomy and power of the practicing physicians. As Figure 26.1 shows, the relative authority of physicians declined in the era of managed care (see dotted lines). But while the most stringent strategies of managed care no longer exist, physicians and other clinicians still encounter many of its controls in their practice. Treatment guidelines standardize care and reduce variations in practice that constrain independent decision-making. At the same time, an international study of the coordination of patient care for medical and health-related social needs by primary care physicians in eleven high income countries showed the US ranking only in the middle range of performance (Doty et al. 2020). Compared to physicians in other countries only 32% to 36% of US physicians had timely communication with specialists, after-hours care centers and home-based nursing care providers for managing and coordinating ongoing care. Innovative care models and a commitment by clinicians, payers and the government for improved communication and collaboration across settings are necessary solutions to address these challenges.

With the erosion of autonomy in clinical decision-making and heightened concerns about patient care, ethical dilemmas translate into balancing financial incentives with the best interests of patients amid disparities within the health care system (Grumbach et al. 1998; Hadley et al. 1999). In response, physicians reasserted their obligations. "Responsive medical professionalism" brought attention to the potential of physicians, especially given the loyalty of their patients, to recapture levels of leadership, albeit in different ways than under the era of professional dominance (Frankford and Konrad 1998). In fact, Mechanic (2000) called for a "new professional ethic" for physicians, but clearly applicable to all clinicians. This ethic focused on responsible and just patient advocacy, included enhanced collaboration with public health practitioners in assuming more responsibility for population health, required forging new partnerships and collaborations with more engaged patients, and paying greater attention to evidence-based approaches.

Challenge 5: Facing Threats to Global Health

In an increasingly interdependent world, the transmission of both infectious and chronic illnesses threatens the population health of all countries. With the growth of foreign travel and markets for international food and other products and services, diseases can spread rapidly throughout the world, resulting in high morbidity and mortality rates. With the 2019-2020 COVID-19 pandemic, the predictions of global influenza pandemics are now more than a grave and inevitable infectious disease threat; it is a reality (Osterholm 2005). In the recent past, significant threats included the "swine flu" strain (H1N1), severe acute respiratory syndrome (SARS), the avian influenza virus strain (H5N1), HIV/AIDS, tuberculosis, and the Marburg virus that did not reach pandemic proportions in the US The rapid geographic spread of COVID-19 and the sharp escalation of cases globally calls for mobilizing cross-national cooperation focusing on strengthening health system resources and public health interventions, as well as preparedness and prevention for future outbreaks.

There is substantial evidence, through the COVID-19 experience, that the research and technology for preparing for a pandemic (e.g. limited production capacity for vaccines and equipment) as well as the multinational commitment and planning to addressing the global health challenge fall far short of what is required (Osterholm 2005; Sandman and Lanard 2005). Beyond these severe limitations in production and management are three relevant social issues. First, while the growing economies of the world have generated considerable wealth enhancing the lives of many people, the income gap between the rich and poor has widened throughout the world and within the US poverty and malnutrition are associated with many of the old as well as new diseases that disproportionately affect the poor. The relationship between socioeconomic status and health and mortality is well established (Benatar 2001; Mechanic 2002; Wilkinson 1996). Even the early data on the COVID-19 pandemic reveal that Blacks in the US experienced a greater burden of disease and higher mortality rates than other groups (Dyer 2020; Yancy 2020). Second, the social values and distribution of wealth and power that have shaped health care systems throughout the world and the profession of medicine have not been mobilized to respond effectively to the growing global burden of disease. The gravity of these global problems has been documented for several years, but the priorities in health care spending, research, and treatment and services have not matched the threats (Benatar 2001). Third and finally, the relationship of politics to health has come into clear relief during the COVID-19 pandemic. From the resistance of China to allow WHO teams early access in Wuhan, the center point of the pandemic, to the US reluctance to accept international testing kits, to threatening support for the WHO, and to sidelining the CDC in favor of political actors, all raise concerns about the non-scientific forces that can shape the course of health problems and solutions.

Conclusion

Health care reform remains at the top of the political agenda in the US. However, the fundamental question is not how to improve efforts that the ACA began but whether there will be continued rollback and a complete return to pre-2010 conditions. Although the ACA has faced major constitutional challenges, legislative policy changes and continuing opposition from the federal government administration and other political opponents, the law has shown remarkable resilience (Levitt 2020). Studies of the ACA's impact on cost control, expansion of health insurance coverage and improvement in health outcomes provide important data in recognizing its success and failures, but also direction for future changes to the law. For example, when the IRS sent letters to taxpayers who had paid the tax penalty for lacking health insurance under the initial ACA requirements, not only were coverage gains in evidence but, more importantly, reductions in middle age mortality were reported (Goldin et al. 2019). While the individual mandate (and tax penalty) has been repealed at the federal level, serious questions remain about the fiscal stability of the ACA and its potential to improve population health unless it is restored at the state or federal level (Levitis 2018).

The US continues to search for strategies to contain costs, provide access to high-quality and effective care, manage care for chronic illnesses and disabilities, treat old and new infectious and viral diseases, and reconfigure professional roles and responsibilities. Although the various health care systems of the world operate under different organizing principles and evolve from unique political and social cultures, economic climates, and the roles of professional groups, many fundamental problems and challenges exist cross-nationally, similar pressures exist for health care systems arising from escalating costs, aging populations and the increased burden of diseases. As Ruggie (2009) points out, the US has much to learn from the experiences of other countries. But, wisely, she points to the limits of a naïve view that extols the virtues of other systems and advocates for wholesale adoption of their programs, policies and reforms. Countries confront different local pressures. The implicit social contract between the state, physicians, other clinicians, employers, insurers and consumers places critical limits on practice and policy decisions. Cross-nationally, public support for health care system change reflects current economic and demographic challenges. However, their support for solutions tend to cluster more directly around the history and tradition of the countries' health care arrangements (Kikuzawa et al. 2008).

References

Allen, Heidi and Benjamin D. Sommers. 2019. "Medicaid Expansion and Health: Assessing the Evidence after 5 Years." *Journal of the American Medical Association* 322: 1253–4.

Baicker, Katherine and Benjamin D. Sommers. 2020. "Insurance Access and Health Care Outcomes." In *The Trillion Dollar Revolution: How the Affordable Care Act Transformed Politics, Law, and Health Care in America*, edited by Ezekiel J. Emanuel and Abbe R. Gluck, Pp. 209–224. New York: Public Affairs.

Baumgartner, Jesse C., Sara R. Collins, David C. Radley, and Susan L. Hayes. 2020. *How the Affordable Care Act Has Narrowed Race and Ethnic Disparities in Access to Health Care.* New York: The Commonwealth Fund.

Benatar, Solomon R. 2001. "The Coming Catastrophe in International Health." *International Journal* 61: 611–31.

Berlant, Jeffrey. 1975. *Profession and Monopoly: A Study of Medicine in the United States and Great Britain.* Berkeley, CA: University of California Press.

Bloche, M. Gregg and David M. Studdert. 2004. "A Quiet Revolution: Law As Agent of Health System Change." *Health Affairs* 23: 29–42.

Blumenthal, David and Melinda Abrams. 2020. "The Affordable Care Act at 10 Years- Payment and Delivery System Reforms." *New England Journal of Medicine.* Published online, February 26. https://doi.org/10.26099/0y4q-km81.

Blumenthal, David, Melinda K. Abrams, Corinne Lewis, and Shanoor Seervai. 2020. "The ACA's Effect on Medical Practice." In *The Trillion Dollar Revolution: How the Affordable Care Act Transformed Politics, Law, and Health Care in America*, edited by Ezekiel J. Emanuel and Abbe R. Gluck, Pp. 280–293. New York: Public Affairs.

Blumenthal, David, Sara R. Collins, and Elizabeth J. Fowler. 2020. "The Affordable are Act at 10 Years- Its Coverage and Access Provisions." *New England Journal of Medicine* 382: 963–9.

Blumenthal, David and Shanoor Seervai. 2019. "Health Care in 2019: Year in Review." *To the Point* (blog). NY: Commonwealth Fund. https://doi.org/10.26099/vxpe-n134.

Brown, E. Richard. 1979. *Rockefeller Medicine Men: Medicine and Capitalism in America.* Berkeley, CA: University of California Press.

Burwell, Sylvia Mathews. 2020. "Preface." In *The Trillion Dollar Revolution: How the Affordable Care Act Transformed Politics, Law, and Health Care in America*, edited by Ezekiel J. Emanuel and Abbe R. Gluck, Pp. 1–5. New York: Public Affairs.

Busch, Susan H., Ezra Golberstein, Howard H. Goldman, Christine Loveridge, Robert E. Drake, and Ellen Meara. 2019. "Effects of ACA Expansion of Dependent Coverage on Hospital-Based Care of Young Adults with Early Psychosis." *Psychiatric Services* 70: 1027–33.

Center for Studying Health System Change. 2002. *Navigating a Changing Health System, 2001 Annual Report.* Washington, DC: Health System Change. Retrieved December 8, 2004 www.hschange.com/CONTENT/452.

Clarke, Adele and Janet Shim. 2009. "Medicalization and Biomedicalization Revisited: Technoscience and Transformations of Health and Illness." In *The Handbook of the Sociology of Health, Illness, and Healing*, edited by Bernice A. Pescosolido, Jack K. Martin, Jane McLeod and Anne Rogers, Pp. 173–200. New York: Springer.

Cohen, Robin A., Emily P. Terlizzi, and Michael E. Martinez. 2019. *Health Insurance Coverage: Early Release of Estimates from the National Health Interview Survey, 2018.* Hyattsville, MD: National Center for Health Statistics.

Collins, Randall. 1979. *The Credential Society*. New York: Academic Press.

Collins, Sara R. 2020. "The Supreme Court Denies Request for Expedited ACA Review." In *To the Point Blog, January 22: 1–5*. New York: Commonwealth Fund.

Collins, Sara R., Munira Z. Gunja, and Michelle M. Doty. 2017. *How Well Does Insurance Coverage Protect Consumers from Health Care Costs?* New York: Commonwealth Fund.

DeNavas-Walt, Caren, Bernadette D. Proctor, and Jessica C. Smith. 2013. *Income, Poverty, and Health Insurance Coverage in the United States: 2010*. Washington, DC: U.S. Census Bureau.

Domhoff, G. William. 1996. *State Autonomy or Class Dominance? Case Studies on Policy Making in America*. New York: Aldine.

Doty, Michelle M., Roosa Tikkanen, Arnav Shah, and Eric C. Schneider. 2020. "Primary Care Physicians' Role in Coordinating Medical and Health-Related Social Needs in Eleven Countries." *Health Affairs* 39: 115–23.

Draper, Debra A., Robert E. Hurley, Cara S. Lesser, and Bradley C. Strunk. 2002. "The Changing Face of Managed Care." *Health Affairs* 21: 11–23.

Dyer, Owen. 2020. "Covid-19: Black people and other minorities are hardest hit in US." *BMJ* 369: m1483.

Emanuel, Ezekiel J. and Abbe R. Gluck (eds.). 2020. *The Trillion Dollar Revolution: How the Affordable Care Act Transformed Politics, Law, and Health Care in America*. New York: Public Affairs.

Emanuel, Ezekiel J. and Amol S. Navathe. 2020. "Delivery-System Reforms: Evaluating the Effectiveness of the ACA's Delivery-System Reforms at Slowing Cost Growth and Improving Quality and Patient Experience." In *The Trillion Dollar Revolution: How the Affordable Care Act Transformed Politics, Law, and Health Care in America*, edited by Ezekiel J. Emanuel and Abbe R. Gluck, Pp. 225–249. New York: Public Affairs.

Frankford, David M. and Thomas R. Konrad. 1998. "Responsive Medical Professionalism: Integrating Education, Practice and Community in a Market-Driven Era." *Academic Medicine* 73: 138–45.

Frean, Molly, Jonathan Gruber, and Benjamin Sommers. 2017. "Premium Subsidies, the Mandate, and Medicaid Expansion: Coverage Effects of the Affordable Care Act." *Journal of Health Economics* 53: 72–86.

Freidson, Eliot. 1970. *Professional Dominance*. New York: Atherton Press.

Freudenheim, Milt. 1999. "Big HMO to Give Decisions on Care Back to Doctors." *New York Times*, November 9, pp. A1, C8.

Fry, Carrie E. and Benjamin D. Sommers. 2018. "Effect of Medicaid Expansion on Health Insurance Coverage and Access to Care Among Adults with Depression." *Psychiatric Services* 69: 1146–52.

Garfield, Rachel, Elizabeth Hinton, Elizabeth Cornachione, and Cornelia Hall. 2018. *Medicaid Managed Care Plans and Access to Care: Results from the Kaiser Family Foundation 2017 Survey of Medicaid Managed Care Plans*. San Francisco, CA: Henry J. Kaiser Family Foundation.

Gifford, Kathleen, Eileen Ellis, Aimee Lashbrook, Mike Nardone, Elizabeth Hinton, Robin Rudowitz, Maria Diaz, and Marina Tian. 2019. *A View from the States: Key Medicaid Policy Changes: Results from a 50-State Medicaid Budget Survey for State Fiscal Years 2019 and 2020*. San Francisco, CA: Henry J. Kaiser Family Foundation.

Ginsburg, Paul B. 2008. *High and Rising Health Care Costs: Demystifying U.S. Health Care Spending*. Princeton, NJ: Robert Wood Johnson Foundation.

Gold, Marsha R. 1998. "Understanding the Roots: Health Maintenance Organizations in Historical Context." Pp. 7–16 in *Contemporary Managed Care: Readings in Structure, Operations, and Public Policy*, edited by Marsha R. Gold. Chicago, IL: Health Administration Press.

Goldin, Jacob, Ithai Z. Lurie, and Janet McCubbin 2019. "*Health Insurance and Mortality: Experimental Evidence from Taxpayer Outreach.*" NBER Working Paper Series. Cambridge, MA: National Bureau of Economic Research.

Grumbach, Kevin, Dennis Osmond, Karen Vranizan, Deborah Jaffe, and Andrew B. Bindman. 1998. "Primary Care Physicians' Experience of Financial Incentives in Managed-Care Systems." *New England Journal of Medicine* 339: 1516–21.

Gunja, Munira Z. and Sara R. Collins. 2019. *Who Are the Remaining Uninsured and Why Do They Lack Coverage?* New York: Commonwealth Fund.

Hadley, Jack, Jean M. Mitchell, Daniel P. Sulmasy, and M. Gregg Bloche. 1999. "Perceived Financial Incentives, HMO Market Penetration, and Physicians' Practice Styles and Satisfaction." *Health Services Research* 34: 307–19.

Hafferty, Frederick W. and Brian Castellani. 2009. "Two Cultures – Two Ships: The Rise of a Professionalism Movement within Modern Medicine and Medical Sociology's Disappearance from the Professionalism Debate." In *The Handbook of the Sociology of Health, Illness, and Healing*, edited by Bernice A. Pescosolido, Jack K. Martin, Jane D. McLeod and Anne Rogers. New York: Springer.

Higgins, A. Foster. 1991. *Health Care Benefits Survey.* Vol. 1. New Jersey: Health Care Benefits Survey. *Journal of Health Politics, Policy and Law.* 1999. Special Issue. "The Managed Care Backlash." 24: 873–1218.

Hollingsworth, J. Rogers. 1986. *A Political Economy of Medicine: Great Britain and the United States.* Baltimore, MD: Johns Hopkins University Press.

Hurley, Robert E., Bradley C. Strunk, and Justin S. White. 2004. "The Puzzling Popularity of the PPO." *Health Affairs* 23: 56–68.

Kaiser Family Foundation. 2019. *Employer Health Benefits Survey.* San Francisco, CA: Henry J. Kaiser Family Foundation.

Kikuzawa, Saeko, Sigrun Olafsdottir, and Bernice A. Pescosolido. 2008. "Similar Pressures, Different Contexts: Public Attitudes toward Government Intervention for Health Care in 21 Nations." *Journal of Health and Social Behavior* 49: 385–99.

Kronick, Richard and Todd Gilmer. 1999. "Explaining the Decline in Health Insurance Coverage, 1979–1995." *Health Affairs* 18: 30–47.

Levitis, Jason A. 2018. "State Individual Mandates." *Center for Health Policy.* Washington, DC: Brookings Institution.

Levitt, Larry. 2020. "The Affordable Care Act's Enduring Resilience." *Journal of Health Politics, Policy and Law* 45: 609–16.

Light, Donald. 1995. "Countervailing Powers: A Framework for Professions in Transition." Pp. 25–41 in *Health Professions and the State in Europe*, edited by Terry Johnson, Gerald Larking and Mike Saks. London: Routledge.

Light, Donald and Sol Levine. 1988. "The Changing Character of the Medical Profession: A Theoretical Overview." *Milbank Quarterly* 66(Supplement): 10–32.

Ludmerer, Kenneth M. 1999. *Time to Heal: American Medical Education from the Turn of the Century to the Era of Managed Care.* New York: Oxford University Press.

Maclean, Johanna C. and Brendan Saloner. 2019. "The Effect of Public Insurance Expansions on Substance Use Disorder Treatment: Evidence from the Affordable Care Act." *Journal of Policy Analysis and Management* 38: 366–93.

McKinlay, John B. and Lisa D. Marceau. 2002. "The End of the Golden Age of Doctoring." *International Journal of Health Services* 32(2): 379–417.

Mechanic, David. 2000. "Managed Care and the Imperative for A New Professional Ethic." *Health Affairs* 19: 100–11.

Mechanic, David. 2002. "Disadvantage, Inequality, and Social Policy." *Health Affairs* 21: 48–59.

Mechanic, David. 2004. "The Rise and Fall of Managed Care." *Journal of Health and Social Behavior* 45: 76–86.

Mechanic, David and Mark Olfson. 2016. "The Relevance of the Affordable Care Act for Improving Mental Health Care." *Annual Review of Clinical Psychology* 12: 515–42.

Mechanic, David and Susan C. Reinhard. 2002. "Contributions of Nurses to Health Policy: Challenges and Opportunities." *Nursing and Health Policy Review* 1: 7–15.

Medicaid and CHIP Payment and Access Commission. 2017. *MACStats: Medicaid and CHIP Data Book*. Washington, DC: Medicaid and CHIP Payment and Access Commission.

Nadash, Pamela, Edward Alan Miller, David K. Jones, Michael K. Gusmano, and Sara Rosenbaum. 2018. "A Series of Unfortunate Events: Implications of Republican Efforts to Repeal and Replace the Affordable Care Act for Older Adults." *Journal of Aging and Social Policy* 30: 259–81.

National Council on Disability. 2013. *Medicaid Managed Care for People with Disabilities: Policy and Implementation Consideration for State and Federal Policymakers*. Washington, DC: National Council on Disability.

Oberlander, Jonathan. 2008. "The Politics of Paying for Health Reform: Zombies, Payroll Taxes, and the Holy Grail." *Health Affairs* 27(6): w544–w555.

Olfson, Mark, Melanie Wall, Colleen L. Barry, Christine Mauro, and Ramin Mojtabai. 2018. "Impact of Medicaid Expansion on Coverage and Treatment of Low-Income Adults with Substance Use Disorders." *Health Affairs* 37: 1208–15.

Oliver, Thomas R. 2001. "State Health Politics and Policy: Rhetoric, Reality, and the Challenges Ahead." In *The New Politics of State Health Policy*, edited by Robert B. Hackey and David A. Rochefort, Pp. 273–291. Lawrence, KA: University of Kansas Press.

Osterholm, Michael T. 2005. "Preparing for the Next Pandemic." *New England Journal of Medicine* 352: 1839–42.

Pescosolido, Bernice A. and Jennie J. Kronenfeld. 1995. "Sociological Understandings of Health, Illness, and Healing: The Challenge from and for Medical Sociology." *Journal of Health and Social Behavior (Extra Issue)* 35: 5–33.

Pescosolido, Bernice A. and Jack K. Martin. 2004. "Cultural Authority and the Sovereignty of American Medicine: The Role of Networks, Class and Community." *Journal of Health Politics* 29: 735–56.

Pescosolido, Bernice A., Jane D. McLeod, and Margarita Alegría. 2000. "Confronting the Second Social Contract: The Place of Medical Sociology in Research and Policy for the 21st Century." Pp. 411–26 in *The Handbook of Medical Sociology*, edited by Chloe Bird, Peter Conrad and Allen Fremont. 5th edition. Upper Saddle River, NJ: Prentice-Hall.

Pescosolido, Bernice A. and Beth A. Rubin. 2000. "The Web of Group Affiliations Revisited: Social Life, Postmodernism and Sociology." *American Sociological Review* 65: 52–76.

Quadagno, Jill. 2006. *One Nation, Uninsured: Why the U.S. Has No National Health Insurance*. New York: Oxford University Press.

Relman, Arnold S. 1993. "Controlling Costs by 'Managed Competition' – Would It Work?" *New England Journal of Medicine* 328: 133–5.

Rochefort, David A. 2018. "The Affordable Care Act and the Faltering Revolution in Behavioral Health Care." *International Journal of Health Services* 48: 223–46.

Rosen, George. 1983. *The Structure of American Medical Practice 1825–1944*. Philadelphia, PA: University of Pennsylvania Press.

Rosenbaum, Sara. 2015. "Ushering in a New Era in Medicaid Managed Care." In *To the Point Blog, July 1: 1–5*. New York: Commonwealth Fund.

Rosenbaum, Sara. 2020. "Toward Equality and the Right to Health Care." in *The Trillion Dollar Revolution: How the Affordable Care Act Transformed Politics, Law, and Health Care in America*, edited by Ezekiel J. Emanuel and Abbe R. Gluck, Pp. 311–324. New York: Public Affairs.

Rubin, Beth A. 1996. *Shifts in the Social Contract*. Thousand Oaks, CA: Pine Forge Press.

Rudowitz, Robin, Elizabeth Hinton, MaryBeth Musumeci, Samantha Artiga, and Rachel Garfield. 2020. *Medicaid: What to Watch in 2020*. San Francisco, CA: Henry J. Kaiser Family Foundation.

Ruggie, Mary. 2009. "Learning from Other Countries: Comparing Experiences and Drawing Lessons for the United States." In *The Handbook of the Sociology of Health, Illness, and Healing*, edited by Bernice A. Pescosolido, Jack K. Martin, Jane D. McLeod and Anne Rogers, Pp. 85–100. New York: Springer.

Saloner, Brendan and Johanna Maclean. 2020. "Specialty Substance Use Disorder Treatment Admissions Steadily Increased in the Four Years After Medicaid Expansion." *Health Affairs* 39: 453–61.

Sandman Peter, M. and Jody Lanard. 2005. "*Pandemic Influenza Risk Communication: The Teachable Moment*." Retrieved from www.psandman.com/col/pandemic.htm.

Skocpol, Theda. 1997. *Boomerang: Health Care Reform and the Turn Against Government*. New York: W.W. Norton and Company.

Sommers, Benjamin D., Atul A. Gawande, and Katherine Baicker. 2017. "Health Insurance Coverage and Health: What the Recent Evidence Tells Us." *New England Journal of Medicine* 377: 586–93.

Soni, Aparna, Laura R. Wherry, and Kosali I. Simon. 2020. "How Have ACA Insurance Expansions Affected Health Outcomes? Findings from the Literature." *Health Affairs* 39: 371–7.

Starr, Paul. 1982. *The Social Transformation of American Medicine*. New York: Basic Books.

Stevens, Rosemary A. 2001. "Public Roles for the Medical Profession in the United States: Beyond Theories of Decline and Fall." *Milbank Quarterly* 79: 327–53.

Strunk, Bradley C., Paul B. Ginsburg, and Jon Gabel. 2001. "Tracking Health Care Costs." *Health Affairs*, Web Exclusive. Retrieved September 26, 2001 (content.healthaffairs.org).

Thomas, Kathleen C., Adele Shartzer, Noelle K. Kurth, and Jean P. Hall. 2018. "Impact of ACA Health Reforms for People with Mental Health Conditions." *Psychiatric Services* 69: 231–4.

Thompson, Frank J. 1981. *Health Policy and the Bureaucracy*. Cambridge, MA: MIT Press.

Thompson, Frank J. 2012. *Medicaid Politics: Federalism, Policy Durability and Health Reform*. Washington, DC: Georgetown University Press.

Tikkanen, Roosa and Melinda K. Abrams. 2020. *U.S. Health Care from a Global Perspective, 2019. Higher Spending, Worse Outcomes?* New York: Commonwealth Fund.

Unschuld, Paul. 1976. "Western Medicine and Traditional Healing Systems: Competition, Cooperation, or Integration?" *Ethics in Science and Medicine* 3: 1–20.

Wilkinson Richard, G. 1996. *Unhealthy Societies: The Afflictions of Inequality*. London: Routledge.

Yancy, Clyde W. 2020. "COVID-19 and African Americans." *JAMA* 323(19): 1891–92.

Zelman, Walter A. 1996. *The Changing Health Care Marketplace*. San Francisco, CA: Jossey-Bass.

27

The British Healthcare System

Jonathan Gabe

The British National Health Service (NHS) was founded in 1948 and continues to this day to be funded primarily by direct taxation, with limited finance from social insurance contributions.[1] Health care is therefore free at the point of use. It is the largest employer in the UK, with 1.2 million people working for the NHS in England in 2017. Of these one in eight come from overseas, including a quarter of all doctors (Fitzgerald et al 2020). It is also one of the most popular institutions in the UK and there continues to be strong public support for it (Calovski and Calnan 2020). While initially established as a unified service across England, Wales, Scotland and Northern Ireland, the NHS's constituent parts have started to diverge since administrative devolution in 1999. In this chapter the focus will be on the NHS in England, which represents the largest part of the old NHS.

Like other health care systems, the NHS has evolved over time, especially under the influence of neoliberal policies. These policies were first introduced by the Conservatives under Prime Minister Margaret Thatcher in the 1980s and developed further by New Labour under Prime Ministers Tony Blair and Gordon Brown from 1997 to 2010, and more recently by Conservative administrations (from 2010–2016 in coalition with the Liberal Democrats) under David Cameron, Teresa May and Boris Johnson. This chapter will examine how the NHS has changed, partly in light of these neoliberal policies, and consider its consequences for patients and the health care professions. First, however, we need to clarify the meaning of neoliberalism.

Neoliberalism

Neoliberalism is a contested term and has been defined in a variety of ways. It has been viewed as a political economic philosophy (Schmidt 2018), an ideology (Harvey 2007), and a transnational process (neoliberalization) (Springer et al.

The Wiley Blackwell Companion to Medical Sociology, First Edition. Edited by William C. Cockerham.

2016) in a class-divided society (Harvey 2007). Neoliberalism in England, as in other Anglophone countries, has been shaped by economists like Friedrich von Hayek and Milton Friedman. In the 1980s Margaret Thatcher endorsed neoliberalism as the only solution to the economic crises and stagflation of the 1970s and it has since become so embedded that it has been accepted as "common sense" (Monaghan et al. 2018). For the sake of simplicity we can identify two overarching tenets of neoliberalism, free markets and individualism. The first of these, the free market, emphasises the primacy of the market as the most efficient form of economic and political organization. The role of the state is to set the conditions for the market to function efficiently while limiting interference in the market as much as possible and alongside this reducing government bureaucracy. This emphasis on the market, together with the goal of controlling inflation whatever the social costs and balancing the budget, shaped the government's approach to health care in England, introducing a health care market of purchasers and providers and encouraging a mixed economy of health care. It also informed the response to the global financial crisis in 2008, leading to austerity policies to reduce government debt which resulted in severe cuts to the health care budget (Monaghan et al. 2018).

The second tenet of neoliberalism is that of individualism. It is assumed that people act independently of each other and rationally pursue narrow self-interest over any mutual interest (Schmidt 2018). Self-interest is in turn linked to the idea of individuals rationally choosing between options on the basis of informed knowledge to maximise their self-interest and minimise loss (Gabe et al. 2015). When applied to health care the ideal patient is seen as responsible and informed and wanting to choose; failure to act responsibly becomes the patient's responsibility alone (Newman and Clarke 2009; Smart 2010). Choice is also linked to the policy of creating a market in health care. Choice is believed to fuel competition between health care providers, thereby enhancing quality and maximising efficiency, even in healthcare systems which are predominantly publically funded such as England (Fotaki 2007; Peckham and Sanderson 2012). As Gabe et al. state (2015: 625), "From this standpoint health and health services are viewed as commodities to be purchased by consumers in the market like any other good."

The neoliberal emphasis on individual responsibility also chimes with Foucault's notion of governmentality. Bell and Green (2016: 240) refer to this as governing at a distance; the emphasis being on "calculability; and the promotion of self-activating, disciplined, individuated subjects." Here the focus is on specific forms of government where people wilfully regulate themselves, for example by taking responsibility for their own health and well-being, rather than being overtly coerced into doing so. It has been described as a kind of "engineering of souls" which involves individuals being governed indirectly through the creation of structures of incentives rather than directly through state intervention (Schmidt 2018). Below we consider how neoliberalism has shaped three policies in the NHS in England: (1) New Managerialism, (2) Consumerism and (3) a Mixed Economy of Health Care. The consequences for health care professionals and patients will also be considered.

New Managerialism

Until relatively recently, poor NHS management, in one form or another, has regularly been blamed by governments of all political persuasions for shortcomings in the service. The Conservative administrations of the 1980s, however, attached particular weight to this assessment as it coincided with their ideological attachment to neoliberalism, with its emphasis on monetarism, professional deregulation, and the application of private-sector business principles to the public sector as a way to control expenditure. Moreover, it served the political function of distancing the Conservatives from the impact that the application of monetarist principles to public spending would have on the level of service.

In 1983 the Conservatives introduced general managers into the NHS in line with the recommendations in the Griffiths Report. The aim was to alter the organizational culture of the service by introducing features of business management, subsequently described as New Public Management, to make more efficient use of resources (Dopson 2009). Previously NHS managers, then called administrators, acted as diplomats, helping to organize the facilities and resources for professionals to get on with their work and reacting to problems as they arose. Decisions were made consensually by multi-disciplinary teams that included doctors and nurses as well as administrators. The new general managers were expected to proactively develop management plans, ensure quality of care and cost improvements, and monitor and reward staff. The policy was designed to alter the balance of power in favor of managers, at the expense of other professionals, especially doctors, whose clinical freedom to make decisions about individual patients regardless of cost had previously been a major determinant of the level of expenditure. In the new system doctors were to be more accountable to managers, who had stricter control over professional and labor costs through a system of management budgets that related workload objectives to the resources available (Hunter 1991).

Doctors were encouraged to participate in this micromanagement system and help secure and oversee the most effective use of resources. While some doctors were appointed as general managers, many were reluctant to give their unequivocal support to these developments (Cox 1991). As a result, doctors continued to exercise considerable autonomy and managers continued to lack real control over medical work (Hunter 2006).

Subsequently, in a further attempt by the Conservatives to shift the balance of power in the direction of managers, a variety of new techniques of managerial evaluation were developed. Quality assurance and performance indicators, made possible by advances in information technology, increased opportunities for the managerial determination of work content, productivity, resource use, and quality standards (Flynn 1992). Managers were also required to participate in the specification and policing of consultants (specialists) contracts (Hunter 2006). They were seen as "change agents" required to achieve demanding performance targets and were financially rewarded for doing so. They were expected to be more visible and to demonstrate more individualistic forms of leadership. In primary care, managers also came into their own, being employed to assist GPs in a variety of tasks, including commissioning services.

Under the New Labour government from 1997, managers were given further powers to challenge medicine's autonomy. The introduction of "clinical governance" as a mechanism to control doctors resulted in hospital Chief Executives becoming responsible for clinical as well as financial performance. From 1999, these Chief Executives were expected to make sure that their clinicians restricted themselves to treatments recommended on grounds of clinical and cost effectiveness by the National Institute for Clinical Excellence (NICE) (now the National Institute for Health and Care Excellence). They were also expected to comply with service guidelines for specified conditions under the National Service Frameworks (NSF). Furthermore, managers were required to provide evidence to demonstrate that doctors in their Trusts[2] were complying with these guidelines for the rolling programme of inspections being conducted by Commission for Health Improvement (Harrison and Ahmad 2000) and its successor (the Care Quality Commission). This focus on measuring service quality via metrics has been described as a shift from government to governance, because of the wider range of agencies and stakeholders involved in health service delivery (Dopson 2009).

One such metric is that of surgical performance, where surgeons in England are required to report their post-operative mortality rates on line to maximize transparency. This practice has been labelled "soft surveillance" where the logic of management discourse is internalized and doctors become involved in auditing their own practice through public reporting (Exworthy et al. 2019), demonstrating a new mentality of self-monitoring "at a distance" (Numerato et al. 2012).

It might be argued that these developments have given managers the opportunity to constrain NHS doctors as never before, along the lines identified in the proletarianization/corporatization thesis. Advocates of this position argue that doctors are being deskilled, are losing their economic independence, and are being required to work in bureaucratically organized institutions under the instruction of managers, in accordance with the requirements of advanced capitalism (McKinlay and Marceau 2002). However, as Freidson (1989) indicated, the widespread adoption of new techniques for monitoring the efficiency of performance and resource allocation does not on its own illustrate reduced professional autonomy. What really matters is whose criteria for evaluation and appraisal are adopted and who controls any actions that are taken (Elston 1991). Moreover, doctors are perfectly capable of transforming themselves into managers/clinical directors and have come to see this as a way of retaining control of the service. Having learned the language and values of management, or what has been called managerial logic (Martin et al. 2015), alongside their professional logic, doctors have been able to interpret and reframe problems, to adopt a clinical perspective on managerial issues and a managerial perspective on clinical matters (Thorne 2002). Adopting what amounts to a hybrid logic (Exworthy et al. 2019), they may be able to deflect or neutralize changes being required under the government's reform agenda or may even attempt to reshape them (Hunter 2006).

In contrast to arguments about proletarianization/corporatization, attempts to incorporate the medical profession by turning them into managers have arguably been used by doctors to enable them to re-professionalize. Creating new forms of expertise by assimilating management skills has enabled clinical directors to extend their jurisdiction and domain. The resulting differentiation between these clinical directors and other doctors may, however, lead to greater internal stratification and fragmentation of the medical profession (Thorne 2002), with a concomitant loss of power. Others have pointed out that such internal stratification does not exclusively result in growing inequalities within the medical profession. It can also provide new opportunities for lower segments of the profession such as GPs, facilitating re-positioning for some of them (Calnan and Gabe 2009; Numerato et al. 2012).

In sum, while doctors in the NHS now have to account for their actions in ways that were unthinkable four decades ago, it is far from certain that the introduction of New Public Management in the NHS has resulted in a victory for the "corporate rationalizers"(i.e. managers) over the "professional monopolists" (doctors) (Alford 1975). What is certain, however, is that the policy changes outlined above were good for the managers themselves, at least until the Coalition government under David Cameron proclaimed that it was going to "liberate" the NHS by delayering its bureaucracy, reducing management costs and empowering clinicians (Department of Health 2010). While the number of managers increased by 53% between 1975 and 1991, and doubled again between 1992 and 2002, since 2010 they have fallen back by 18% (Kings Fund 2019a). Thus numbers increased substantially for over thirty years, inspired initially by a Conservative government, only for recent Conservative (led) administrations to bare down on these numbers, allegedly in order to give more power (back) to "front line" clinicians.

Consumerism

In common with other many Western countries (Harris et al. 2010), patients in England have been encouraged by the state to become "consumers" of health care, making choices about who to consult for a health condition, which medication to accept from a GP and which surgeon to choose if they need a surgical procedure. Entwined within the rhetoric about choice are ideas about information on which choices are based. The neo-liberal discourse of choice equates the "informing process" with patient empowerment and the emergence of the "informed patient" who has a responsibility to care for him/herself (Henwood et al. 2011). It is also assumed that there is now more information available, although patients generally have less information than providers, reflecting the asymmetry of medical knowledge between doctors and their patients (Greener 2003). Furthermore, the sheer amount of information may reduce the ability to assimilate and comprehend it (Tsoukas 1997).

Arguments about "choice" also contain assumptions about the quality of evidence that is available, although such evidence is increasingly contested. For example, in 2012 there was a discussion in the UK media about the risks of taking sleeping tablets, whether some were safer than others and whether they not only led to dependence but shortened a patient's life, stemming from a paper published in a medical journal (Kripke et al. 2012). How readers responded to such coverage reportedly varied, depending on their experiential knowledge and/or appreciation of the quality of the data (Gabe et al. 2017).

Then there is the belief that doctors can still be trusted, although there is evidence to suggest that trust in medicine, as in any occupation, is increasingly conditional and has to be earned again in each health care encounter (Gabe et al. 2012), in the face of growing doubt and uncertainty in late modernity (Giddens 1994). And there are assumptions about *responsibility* and about who should be making these choices. Should patients cease to rely on the advice of a doctor, even when they are feeling extremely ill, and take responsibility for their own decisions? Indeed some have argued that that "freedom to choose" has come to be construed as an "obligation to choose" (Rose 1999). And others have pointed to the "tyranny of choice" which damages individual well-being and social relations (Baumann 2011).

The need for choice can certainly be seen as the message in a whole variety of policy initiatives introduced by governments of different political persuasions in England in recent years. It reflects the dominance of a neo-liberal consensus between the political parties in favor of self-reliance, individual responsibility, and the rule of the market.

Three policy initiatives reflecting this neo-liberal approach will be considered in turn:

(1) The Patient's Charter
(2) Choose and Book
(3) NHS Choices

The Patient's Charter was introduced in 1992 by the Conservative Government. It was one of a number of charters proposed which it was believed would transform the running of public services like the NHS and put patients in the driving seat. The Patient's Charter was designed to make the health service more responsive to patients as consumers and raise quality overall at nil cost. This was to be achieved by setting and publishing the rights and services patients could expect. New rights were established such as for the length of time one should expect to wait in an Emergency Department before being seen; the right to detailed information about quality standards; and having a complaint investigated and dealt with promptly. Critics of the Patient's Charter argued that while it might have increased patients right to information, this was not legally binding. It was also premised on the dubious assumption that making information available to patients would in and of itself change the practice of clinicians and managers (Crinson 1998). The problem with this, however, was that the medical profession and management have a vested interest in maintaining the status quo and the Patient's Charter did nothing to challenge such interests.

Choose and Book was introduced by the Labour Government for patients in England, as part of its emphasis on individual choice. Labour stressed this approach increasingly the longer they were in power, in place of policies to increase collective involvement in health care decision making (Forster and Gabe 2008). Choose and Book was a computer system which gave patients a choice about who, when and where they received care for elective surgery. Usually GPs made this decision on behalf of patients. However, after 2006, patients were offered a choice of 4–5 local providers for their hospital treatment. Initial uptake was slow, suggesting a lack of enthusiasm on the part of patients (Calnan and Gabe 2009). Subsequently it was recognised that patients' awareness of the right to choose and GPs' willingness to offer choice were slow to grow (Coulter 2010). However, where choice was offered patients responded positively, even though most chose to remain at their local hospital (Dixon et al. 2010). More recently it has been shown that poor and minority group patients were much less likely to choose private hospitals and that choice was also affected by the geographical distribution of hospitals (Beckert and Kelly 2017). In 2015 Choose and Book was replaced by the NHS e-Referral service which continues to allow patients to choose appointments with NHS hospitals in England, and also private hospitals, as long as they provide NHS services.

In addition, since 2008, English patients have been able to choose from an extended network of hospitals. These include newly established privately run *Independent Sector Treatment Centres* and other private hospitals from an approved list that provide care at the national price. Independent Sector Treatment Centres were set up with government encouragement to undertake a high volume of a limited number of operations like cataracts and hip replacements, normally undertaken by the NHS, in order to reduce waiting times for patients and increase patient choice at no financial cost to such patients. It was also expected that these centres would benefit from private sector expertise in order to introduce innovative customer focused services (Waring and Bishop 2013). Evidence from one study which interviewed clinicians working in ISTCs, however, reported some criticisms of managers for being more concerned with maximising a financial return than working in the best interests of patients. At the same time these clinicians felt that patients attending ISTCs benefited from an improved "aesthetic experience" (for example, a cleaner and more orderly reception area, private bays and high quality refreshments) and a more reliable service with fewer delays or cancellations, in line with a customer focussed ethos (Waring and Bishop 2012).

The third case is *NHS Choices* – a website set up by the Labour government following a review in 2008. It has been designed to provide comparative information for patients on a range of services provided by the NHS in England, including performance against quality indicators. As with the other policies that have been mentioned, the assumption is that patients want to exercise choice about where they are treated and even which surgeon in a particular hospital operates on them.

How might patients respond to such data? The first point is that patients vary in their "information literacy;" the skills and competence to understand the context of the information provided and its interpretation (Henwood et al. 2003). Of course, some patients with long term conditions have become "expert patients" or "experts by experience" (Jones and Pietila 2020), with regard to their condition and so may well be able to understand and find such data helpful. Others may however feel too ill to want to explore such information and thus ignore the sense of obligation to take responsibility for health care decisions that governments in England now apparently wish them to assume. And the age of the patient may also be significant. Older patients may be less used to the Internet and hence might not feel confident to use sites like NHS Choices (Exworthy et al. 2010). Overall it seems that the publication of data on clinical performance has not led the majority of patients to shop around (Coulter 2010).

Alongside these policy initiatives there is some evidence that patients wish to participate in decision making in the consultation (Elwyn et al. 2010). And this consumerism has been further encouraged by the growth of the Internet. As illustrated by the website NHS choices, the Internet is now a major resource for those seeking health information, especially women and young people (Conrad and Stults 2010), alongside patient support platforms and social media (Lupton 2018). It provides an easy source of information about medical services and general medical knowledge which helps patients to engage in consumerist behavior. Patients are now more likely to search for information about illnesses and treatment options, enabling them to *self-diagnose* before they even book an appointment to see their doctor.

Yet use of the internet has not resulted in people turning away from medical care. Instead it just signifies a need for up to date information. This in turn suggests that patients have not necessarily *lost trust* in the medical profession, as some have suggested (Elston 2009). Rather it seems that trust is no longer blind or unconditionally given to doctors, but has to be earned by them (Calnan and Rowe 2008). And it is quite possible for patients to continue to trust their doctor on this basis, while being distrusting of the local hospital or the health care system (Calnan and Rowe 2008). Furthermore, it seems that evidence of hospital performance does not increase trust. Rather it is patients' experience of whether medical staff are competent which influences trust relations in secondary care (Gabe et al. 2012). Overall it seems that patients are starting to challenge the power of medicine but the situation is complicated. While the days of unquestioning deference are over, doctors are still able to earn patients' trust.

Given the above, how is the popularity of consumerism in policy circles to be explained? One explanation is that the different government initiatives have been driven by ideology. Certainly the policies of the Conservatives seem to have been heavily influenced by a neoliberal ideology based on a belief in the value of self-reliance, individual responsibility, and the rule of the market, with sovereign consumers expressing demand on the basis of knowledge about the choices available. Yet the Conservatives did not follow this ideology to the letter, as the market they created was internal to the NHS and the service remained free at the point of use. The Labour government up to 2010 seemed to accept elements of neoliberalism (increasing individual and maximizing personal responsibility for health care), combined with a more collective approach, thus reflecting a preference for pragmatism.

An alternative approach is that the emphasis on consumerism reflects more general socioeconomic changes, encapsulated in the phrase "postFordism." From this standpoint the health service reforms described above parallel a shift from Fordist principles (mass production, universalization of welfare, mass consumption) to those of post-Fordism (flexible production techniques designed to take account of rapid changes in consumer demand and fragmented market tastes). In a post-Fordist society it is the consumers rather than the producers who call the tune. From this standpoint health care is a commodity to be purchased by consumers in the market like other goods (Gabe et al. 2015). While this approach has some value in placing the health policy changes under consideration in a broader context, it fails to distinguish between surface changes in appearance and underlying social relations.

Also there is the question of whether health care can be commodified given the uncertainties and unpredictabilities associated with it. While the rhetoric has been about enhanced consumer power, producers in the form of the medical profession and health service managers arguably continue to hold the upper hand over the users of the service.

Mixed Economy of Health Care

A further policy shaping NHS reforms is a preference for a mixed economy of health care, involving both the public and private sectors. While the health services in England, like all others in the developed world, have long had both public and private funding, planning and provision, reforms since the 1980s have attempted to shift the balance profoundly in favor of greater private-sector involvement (Mohan 2009).

One strategy for shifting the balance between the public and private sector has involved the development of policies to encourage the growth of private medicine. In the 1980s, planning controls were relaxed on the development of private hospitals and the power of local authorities to object to such developments was curtailed (Mohan and Woods 1985). Furthermore, NHS consultants' contracts were revised to enable them to undertake more private work in addition to their NHS commitments (Rayner 1987) and tax changes were introduced to encourage higher levels of private health cover (Calnan et al. 1993). Together these changes created the climate for private hospital development with the number of private hospitals increasing by 35% and the number of private beds by 40% between 1980 and 2001 (Royce 2010). Many of these hospitals were located in the prosperous South East of England, compounding rather than eliminating the geographical inequalities in the distribution of resources.

At the same time, the level of private health insurance increased from 5% of the population to a peak of 13% in 1989, with company-purchased schemes being particularly popular (Calnan et al. 1993). The popularity of private health insurance subsequently declined, only for it to recover to close to the 1989 figure in 2008 (12.4%). Thereafter numbers covered fell again, in part due to the subsequent financial crisis, until 2015 when they increased sharply by just over 2% to 10.6%. This rise has been attributed to fears about waiting times for operations, which have lengthened as a result of the funding crisis facing the NHS under the Conservative-led administration's austerity policies (Collinson 2017). Coverage has been concentrated in London and the southeast of England, with those with policies generally having professional and managerial jobs and being male, though roughly equal numbers of both sexes are actually covered (Foubister et al. 2006).

A further strategy to shift the balance between the public and private sector has involved the introduction of reforms that have facilitated greater collaboration between the two sectors. An early attempt was the Conservative government's policy of requiring NHS District Health Authorities to introduce competitive tendering for domestic, catering and laundry services in the 1980s. The intention was to challenge the monopoly of the in-house providers of services in the expectation that costs would be reduced and greater "value for money" would be achieved. In practice the financial benefits proved relatively modest, at least to start with, and the savings achieved were said to have been at the expense of quality of service (Mohan 1995).

More recently, the NHS has been encouraged to contract out patient care to the private sector. These cooperative arrangements were initially undertaken on a voluntary basis by individual Health Authorities (HAs) that did not have in-house alternatives, for example, as a result of capacity constraints. Subsequently, Conservative and Labour governments have used private hospitals as a way of reducing NHS waiting lists for non-urgent cases and those waiting more than one year. For example, the New Labour government of Tony Blair instituted a "concordat" between the NHS and the private sector in 2000 to allow patients to be treated at NHS expense in the private sector when there is no spare room in NHS hospitals. Labour also introduced Independent Treatment Centers, as noted earlier, as a way to expand private sector involvement in routine NHS work and allowed Primary Care Trusts to award contracts to private companies in addition to GPs. The subsequent Conservative-led government built on this policy in the 2012 Health and Social Care Act by allowing Clinical Commissioning Groups (which replaced Primary Care Trusts) to contract with any qualified provider (AQP), including private and third sector organizations as well as public sector bodies. The decision to introduce contracts to alternative providers was based on the assumption that the diversification of providers would result in improved efficiency through market competition (Pollock and Price 2011).

The ability of private hospitals to compete with NHS hospitals for NHS patients has resulted in a considerable increase in spending on private facilities by NHS Commissioners (PCTs and subsequently Clinical Commissioning Groups). By 2012 this amounted to 28% of inpatient income for private hospitals (Biro and Hellowell 2016) and this spending has increased subsequently. In 2018–2019 NHS Commissioners spent £9.2 billion on services delivered by the private sector (King's Fund 2019b). Moreover, during the COVID-19 pandemic, NHS England block booked 8000 private beds because of insufficient predicated capacity in the NHS. This collaboration gave the NHS access to much needed beds but it is also said to have provided financial relief to the private sector at a time of considerable uncertainty as a result of non-urgent operations being cancelled (The Lowdown 2020).

Another example of collaboration has been the development of the Private Funding Initiative (PFI). Launched by the Conservatives in early 1990s and subsequently continued by Labour and the Conservative–led administration, the aim was to encourage private capital investment in the NHS, thus increasing overall resources in the service while avoiding raising taxes or increasing public borrowing. Much of the investment was used to build new acute hospitals with 101 of the 135 built in England between 1997 and 2009 being financed under this scheme (Pollock and Price 2011). Under PFI, private companies designed, constructed, owned and operated services for a 25–30-year period, in return for an annual fee. While clinical services remained the responsibility of government, PFI was seen as permitting an element of risk to be transferred to the private sector, as building cost overruns were picked up by the private sector. Critics argued, however, that there were serious disadvantages associated with PFI-funded projects, including reduced bed numbers (substantially in excess of what would be expected from long term demand trends) – a problem which resurfaced during the 2020 COVID-19 pandemic; the need for a quicker throughput of patients; a significant reduction in spending on clinical staff, especially nurses; higher interest-rate charges compared to the cost of government borrowing, thereby putting a severe strain on hospital Trust budgets; and the creation of substantial debt over time (Mohan 2009). The Conservative government announced in 2018 that they had ended PFI, although there had been no new schemes since 2014, due to a squeeze on budgets which made it difficult for hospital Trusts to make repayments for existing PFI schemes (King's Fund 2018).

The third strategy has been to encourage competition between the NHS and the private sector. This is best illustrated by the Conservative government's willingness to encourage the NHS to expand its pay-bed provision, thereby sharpening competition for private patients and threatening the private providers' profit margins. Originally introduced in 1948 as a concession to hospital consultants, pay-beds were in decline when the Conservatives came to power in 1979, and their number continued to fall subsequently. In the late 1980s, however, the Conservatives decided to revitalize this provision in the face of increasingly severe financial constraints. The policy was also in line with their belief in generating competition between providers in order to enhance consumer choice and maximize efficiency. In 1988 it therefore used the Health and Medicines Act to relax the rules governing pay-bed charges so that hospitals could make a profit rather than simply cover costs. This propelled hospitals to upgrade their private wings or develop dedicated pay beds on NHS wards. Under Labour there was a strict cap on the number of private patients the NHS could treat. However, under recent Conservative (led) administrations this has been relaxed allowing the NHS in England to be a major provider of private health care. In 2016 it was estimated that there were 1140 pay beds in the NHS. This compares with 8,900 beds in the private sector at that time (King's Fund 2020).

These three strategies illustrate the shift to a new public/private mix of services and growing privatization – that is, the transfer of assets from the public to the private sector (Saltman 2003). The policy has been driven in part by ideological considerations, especially a reliance on neoliberalism with its emphasis on individuals exercising choice in the market. Economic and political calculations have also been important, especially the need to maximize efficiency and get value for money from existing tax revenues and in the case of New Labour, the importance of being seen to act to reduce waiting lists.

It has also been suggested that these policies illustrate a shift toward post-Fordism in the sense that Health Authorities have become "flexible firms," concentrating on core functions and buying in peripheral services from outside. While this argument is superficially attractive, it ignores the extent to which the reforms have been the result of deliberate political decisions in the face of external economic considerations and ideological preferences (Kelly 1991). Rather than simply mirroring structural developments in the economy, the shift in the balance between public and private health care provision is best seen as an attempt to erode services that people experience collectively and persuade them to act instead in terms of their own immediate self-interest.

Conclusion

This chapter has shown that while access to health care in the English NHS is still free at the point of use this health care system has changed considerably in recent times. Policies encouraging new managerialism, consumerism and a mixed economy of health care have radically reconfigured the health service. Driven by an ideological commitment to neoliberalism and faced with a financial crisis and public disquiet the Conservatives under Margaret Thatcher introduced managerialism, a Patient's Charter and policies to encourage a more pluralist economy of health care. Labour modified some of these reforms, often on pragmatic grounds, but did not try to halt the shift to greater welfare pluralism. More recent Conservative (led) administrations have taken marketization of the health service to a new level.

While some of these recent policy changes have brought certain benefits such as increasing the accountability of the medical profession, making rationing decisions explicit and creating a more responsive service, there have also been major disadvantages. Of these perhaps the most significant has been that by opening up the NHS in England to corporate interests and relying on the market and consumer choice there is a considerable risk that service will in due course be privatized at the cost of providing care at the point of need. Indeed the direction of travel seems to be towards the Americanization of the service. Whether this happens will in part depend on whether the government negotiates a trade deal with the US in the future which allows American corporations access to the English health care system, and whether the electorate's attachment to the NHS forces the government to take such a deal off the table.

In the meantime, the NHS has had to treat a considerable number of patients with COVID-19. As of mid-June 2020, the UK overall has the third highest number of recorded COVID-19 deaths in the world. Only the US and Brazil have had more and both have significantly larger populations. It is also clear that the poorest have been most affected. People living in the poorest parts of England and Wales have been dying at twice the rate of those in richer areas. When England went into lockdown in late March 65,000 retired doctors and nurses were asked to return to help the NHS cope with the health care crisis. Six so-called "nightingale hospitals" were created at speed in England, often in unused conference centres, to provide more critical care beds for around 11,000 patients to "save the NHS" from being overwhelmed. While far from fully used they have been seen as an important additional resource. More troubling has been the number of NHS staff who have died of Covid-19, especially from black and minority ethnic groups. Over 180 NHS staff have died as of early June 2020, of whom over 60% are from black and minority group backgrounds (although making up around 20% of the workforce) (Cook et al. 2020). Critics have blamed these deaths in part at least on the failure of the Conservative government to lock down sooner and for not having adequate supplies of personal protective equipment. Throughout the crisis the government has publicly expressed gratitude for the care provided by the National Health Service. This includes from the Prime Minister who was himself treated for the disease in an NHS hospital. In these circumstances further privatization is perhaps less likely, at least in the short term.

Notes

1 Parts of this chapter are based on and extend the argument in Gabe (2012).
2 Large hospitals are now self-governing Trusts with significant financial freedoms and greater autonomy than used to be the case.

References

Alford, Richard. 1975. *Health Care Politics*. Chicago, IL: University of Chicago Press.

Baumann, Zygmunt. 2011. *Collateral Damage: Social Inequalities in a Global Age*. Cambridge: Polity Press.

Beckert, Walter and E. Kelly. 2017. *Divided by Choice? Private Providers, Patient Choice and Hospital Sorting in the English National Health Service*. IFS Working Paper. School of Business, Economics and Informatics, Birkbeck College, University of London.

Bell, Kirsten and Judith Green. 2016. "On the Perils of Invoking Neoliberalism in Public Health Critique." *Critical Public Health* 26: 239–43.

Biro, Aniko and Mark Hellowell. 2016. "Public-private Sector Interactions and the Demand for Supplementary Health Insurance in the United Kingdom." *Health Policy* 120: 840–7.

Calnan, Michael, Sarah Cant, and Jonathan Gabe. 1993. *Going Private: Why People Pay for Their Health Care*. Buckingham: Open University Press.

Calnan, Michael and Jonathan Gabe. 2009. "The Restratification of Primary Care in England? A Sociological Analysis." Pp. 56–78 in *The New Sociology of the Health Service*, edited by Jonathan Gabe and Michael Calnan. London: Routledge.

Calnan, Michael and Rosemary Rowe. 2008. *Trust Matters in Health Care*. Maidenhead: Open University Press.

Calovski, Vid and Michael Calnan. 2020. "Creeping Privatisation? Examining Procurement Choices in the 'New' NHS in England." Pp. 131–54 in *Navigating Private and Public Healthcare: Experiences of Patients, Doctors and Policymakers*, edited by Fran Collyer and Karen Willis. Basingstoke: Palgrave Macmillan.

Collinson, Patrick. 2017. "Private Health Insurance Sales Surge amid NHS Crisis." *The Guardian* https://www.theguardian.com/business/2017/jan/16/private-medical-insurance-sales-surge-health-nhs

Conrad, Peter and Cheryl Stults. 2010. "The Internet and the Experience of Illness." Pp. 179–191 in *Handbook of Medical Sociology*, edited by Chloe E. Bird, Peter Conrad, Allen M. Fremont, and Stefan Timmermans. Sixth ed. Nashville, TN: Vanderbilt University Press.

Cook, Tim, Emira Kursumovic, and Simon Lennane. 2020. "Exclusive: Deaths of NHS Staff from Covid-19 Analysed." *Heath Service Journal*. https://www.hsj.co.uk/exclusive-deaths-of-nhs-staff-from-covid-19-analysed/7027471.

Coulter, Angela. 2010. "Do Patients Want to Choose and Does It Work?" *British Medical Journal* 341: 972–5.

Cox, David. 1991. "Health Service Management – A Sociological View." Pp. 89–114 in *The Sociology of the Health Service*, edited by Jonathan Gabe, Michael Calnan, and Michael Bury. London: Routledge.

Crinson, Ian. 1998. "Putting Patients First: The Continuity of the Consumerist Discourse in Health Policy: From the Radical Right to New Labour." *Critical Social Policy* 18: 227–39.

Department of Health. 2010. *Equity and Excellence. Liberating the NHS*. London: Department of Health.

Dixon, Anna, Ruth Robertson, John Appleby, Peter Burge, and Nancy Devlin. 2010. *Patient Choice: How Patients Choose and Providers Respond*. London: King's Fund.

Dopson, Susan. 2009. "Changing Forms of Managerialism in the NHS: Hierarchies, Markets and Networks." Pp. 37–55 in *The New Sociology of the Health Service*, edited by Jonathan Gabe and Michael Calnan. London: Routledge.

Elston, Mary Ann. 1991. "The Politics of Professional Power: Medicine in a Changing Health Service." Pp. 58–88 in *The Sociology of the Health Service*, edited by Jonathan Gabe, Michael Calnan, and Michael Bury. London: Routledge.

Elston, Mary Ann. 2009. "Remaking a Trustworthy Medical Profession in Twenty-first Century Britain?" Pp. 17–36 in *The New Sociology of the Health Service*, edited by Jonathan Gabe and Michael Calnan. London: Routledge.

Elwyn, Glyn, Steve Laitner, Angela Coulter, Emma Walker, Paul Watson, and Richard Thomson. 2010. "Implementing Shared Decision Making in the NHS." *British Medical Journal* 341: c5146.

Exworthy, Mark, Smith, Glenn, Gabe, Jonathan, and Jones, Ian Rees. 2010. Disclosing Clinical Performance: the Case of Cardiac Surgery. *Journal of Health, Organization and Management* 24: 571–83.

Exworthy, Mark, Jonathan Gabe, Ian Rees Jones, and Glenn Smith. 2019. "Professional Autonomy and Surveillance: The Case of Public Reporting in Cardiac Surgery." *Sociology of Health & Illness* 41(6): 1040–55.

Fitzgerald, Des., Amy Hinterberger, John Naryan, and Ros Williams. 2020. "Brexit as Heredity Redux: Imperialism, Biomedicine and the NHS in Britain." *Sociological Review* https://doi-org.ezproxy01.rhul.ac.uk/10.1177/0038026120914177.

Flynn, Robert. 1992. *Structures of Control in Health Management*. London: Routledge.

Forster, Rudolf and Jonathan Gabe. 2008. "Voice or Choice? Patient and Public Involvement in the National Health Service in England under New Labour." *International Journal of Health Services* 38: 333–56.

Fotaki, Marianna. 2007. "Patient Choice in Healthcare in the UK and Sweden: From Quasi-market and Back to Market? A Comparative Analysis of Failure in Unlearning." *Public Administration* 85: 1059–75.

Foubister, Thomas, Sarah Thompson, Elias Mossialos, and McGuire Alistair. 2006. *Private Medical Insurance in the United Kingdom*. Brussels: European Observatory on Health Systems and Policies.

Freidson, Eliot. 1989. *Medical Work in America: Essays on Health Care*. New Haven, CT: Yale University Press.

Gabe, Jonathan. 2012. "Continuity and Change in the British National Health Service." Pp 565–79 in *The Sociology of Health and Illness: Critical Perspectives*, edited by Peter Conrad and Valerie Leiter. 9th ed. New York: Worth.

Gabe, Jonathan, Mark Exworthy, Ian Rees Jones, and Glenn Smith. 2012. "Towards a Sociology of Disclosure: The Case of Surgical Performance." *Sociology Compass* 6: 908–22.

Gabe, Jonathan, Kirsten Harley, and Michael Calnan. 2015. "Healthcare Choice: Discourses, Perceptions, Experiences and Practices." *Current Sociology* 63: 623–35.

Gabe, Jonathan., Williams, Simon and Coveney, Catherine. 2017. Prescription Hypnotics in the News: a Study of UK Readers. *Social Science and Medicine* 174: 43–52.

Giddens, Anthony. 1994. "Living in a Post Traditional World." Pp. 56–109 in *Reflexive Modernization, Politics, Tradition and Aestheticism in the Modern Social Order*, edited by Ulrich Beck, Anthony Giddens, and Lash Scott. Cambridge: Polity Press.

Greener, Iain. 2003. "Patient Choice in the NHS. The View from Economic Sociology." *Social Theory and Health* 1(1): 72–89.

Harris, Roma, Nadine Wathen, and Wyatt Sally. (eds.). 2010. *Configuring Health Consumers. Health Work and the Imperative of Personal Responsibility.* Basingstoke: Palgrave Macmillan.

Harrison, Steve and Waqar Ahmad. 2000. "Medical Autonomy and the UK State." *Sociology* 34: 129–46.

Harvey, David. 2007. *A Brief History of Neoliberalism.* Oxford: Oxford University Press.

Henwood, Flis, Roma Harris, and Philippa Spoel. 2011. "Informing Health? Negotiating Logics of Choice and Care in Everyday Practices of Healthy Living." *Social Science and Medicine* 72: 2026–32.

Henwood, Flis, Sally Wyatt, Angie Hart, and Julie Smith. 2003. "'ignorance Is Bliss Sometimes': Constraints on the Emergence of the 'Informed Patient' in the Changing Landscapes of Health Information." *Sociology of Health & Illness* 25(5): 589–607.

Hunter, David. 1991. "Managing Medicine: A Response to the Crisis." *Social Science and Medicine* 32: 441–9.

Hunter, David. 2006. "From Tribalism to Corporatism." Pp. 1–23 in *Challenging Medicine*, edited by David Kelleher, Jonathan Gabe, and Gareth Williams. 2nd ed. London: Routledge.

Jones, Marjaana and Ilkka Pietila. 2020. "Personal Perspectives on Patient and Public Involvement – Stories about Becoming and Being an Expert by Experience." *Sociology of Health & Illness* 42(5): 809–24.

Kelly, Aidan. 1991. The Enterprise Culture and the Welfare State: Restructuring the Management of Health and Personal Social Services. Pp. 126–51, in Roger Burrows (ed.) *Deciphering the Enterprise Culture.* London: Routledge.

King's Fund. 2019a. *NHS Staffing Numbers.* London: Kings Fund.

King's Fund. 2018. *Budget 2018: What It Means for Health and Social Care.* London: Kings Fund.

King's Fund. 2019b. *Is the NHS Being Privatised?* London: Kings Fund.

King's Fund. 2020. *NHS Hospital Bed Numbers: Past, Present and Future.* London: Kings Fund.

Kripke, Daniel., Langer, Robert and Kine, Lawrence. 2012. Hypnotics' Association with Mortality or Cancer: a Matched Cohort Study. *British Medical Journal Open* 358: e000850

The Lowdown. 2020. *NHS England's Deal a Life-saver – Even for Private Hospitals* https://lowdownnhs.info/private-providers/nhs-englands-deal-a-life-saver-even-for-private-hospitals

Lupton, Deborah. 2018. *Digital Health: Critical and Cross-disciplinary Perspectives.* London: Routledge.

Martin, Graham P, Natalie Armstrong, Emma-Louise Aveling, Georgia Herbert, and Mary Dixon-Woods. 2015. "Professionalisation Redundant, Reshaped or Reinvigorated? Realizing the 'Third Logic' in Contemporary Health Care." *Journal of Health and Social Behavior* 56(3): 378–97.

McKinlay, John and Lisa Marceau. 2002. "The End of the Golden Age of Doctoring." *International Journal of Health Services* 32: 379–416.

Mohan, John. 1995. *A National Health Service? The Restructuring of Health Care in Britain since 1979.* Basingstoke: Macmillan.

Mohan, John. 2009. "Visions of Privatisation. New Labour and the Reconstruction of the NHS." Pp. 79–98 in *The New Sociology of the Health Service*, Jonathan Gabe and Michael Calnan. London: Routledge.

Mohan, John and Kevin Woods. 1985. "Restructuring Health Care: The Social Geography of Public and Private Health Care under the British Government." *International Journal of Health Services* 15: 197–215.

Monaghan, Lee, Andrea Bombak, and Emma Rich. 2018. "Obesity, Neoliberalism and Epidemic Psychology: Critical Commentary and Alternative Approaches to Public Health." *Critical Public Health* 28: 498–508.

Newman, Janet and John Clarke. 2009. *Public, Politics and Power.* London: Sage.

Numerato, Dino, Domenico Salvatore, and Giovanni Fattore. 2012. "The Impact of Management on Medical Professionalism: A Review." *Sociology of Health & Illness* 34: 626–44.

Peckham, Stephen and Marie Sanderson. 2012. "Patient Choice: A Contemporary Policy Story." Pp. 219–32 in *Shaping Health Policy*, edited by Mark Exworthy, Stephen Peckham, Martin Powell, and Alson Hann. Bristol: Policy Press.

Pollock, Allyson and David Price. 2011. "The Final Frontier: The UK's New Coalition Government Turns the English National Health Service over to the Global Health Care Market." *Health Sociology Review* 20: 294–305.

Rayner, Geoff. 1987. "Lessons from America? Commercialization and Growth of Private Medicine in Britain." *International Journal of Health Services* 17: 197–216.

Rose, Nicholas. 1999. *Powers of Freedom: Reframing Political Thought.* Cambridge: Cambridge University Press.

Royce, Robert. 2010. *A Study of the Dynamics of the Private Health Care Market in the United Kingdom with Particular Reference to the Impact of the British United Provident Association (BUPA) Provider and Benefit Initiatives. Unpublished Doctoral Thesis.* Swansea: Swansea University.

Saltman, Richard. 2003. "Melting Public-private Boundaries in European Health Systems." *European Journal of Public Health* 13: 24–9.

Schmidt, Vivien. A. 2018. "Ideas and the Rise of Neoliberalism in Europe." Pp 69–92 in *The Sage Handbook of Neoliberalism*, edited by Damien Cahill, Melinda Cooper, Martin Konings, and David Primrose. London: Sage.

Smart, Barry. 2010. *Consumer Society: Critcal Issues, Environmental Consequences.* London: Sage.

Springer, Simon, Kean Birch, and MacLeavy Julia. (eds.). 2016. *The Routledge Handbook of Neoliberalism.* New York: Routledge.

Thorne, Marie. 2002. "Colonizing the New World of NHS Management: The Shifting Power of Professionals." *Health Service Management Research* 15: 14–26.

Tsoukas, Haridimos. 1997. "The Tyranny of Light." *Futures* 29: 827–43.

Waring, Justin and Simon Bishop. 2012. "Going Private: Clinicians' Experiences of Working in UK Independent Sector Centres." *Health Policy* 104: 172–8.

Waring, Justin and Simon Bishop. 2013. "McDonaldization or Commercial Re-stratification: Corporatization and the Multimodal Organisation of English Doctors." *Social Science and Medicine* 82: 147–55.

28

The Chinese Health Care System

Lei Jin and Chenyu Ye

China has been grappling with the challenge of providing its vast population with quality healthcare at acceptable costs. Like many countries all over the world, the central issue lies in the role of the state versus the market in the financing and provision of healthcare. As China experienced large-scale social and political changes in the past decades, the emphasis has oscillated between the state and the market, with important implications for both the provision of health care and the health of the Chinese population (Yip and Hsiao 2020). In this chapter, we first provide an overview of the current configuration of China's health care system. We then trace the development of the health care system since the establishment of the People's Republic of China 70 years ago, focusing on the role of the state and market. Finally, we discuss the existing challenges in China's health care system, with an emphasis on how medical sociology may contribute to understanding these issues.

The Current Configuration of China's Health Care System

Health Care Providers

In China, rural and urban residents seek health care in different types of organizations. Township health centers, village health stations, and county hospitals serve the rural population. In urban areas, secondary and tertiary hospitals provide most of the outpatient and inpatient care (Yip et al. 2010). Chinese hospitals are classified into three grades and within each grade they are further divided into levels A, B, and C, according to their performance, technological sophistication, and quality of personnel. The A-level tertiary hospitals are considered the best in the country; inpatient beds and consultation with doctors in these hospitals are highly sought after. In addition to hospitals, community health centers and stations provide routine

The Wiley Blackwell Companion to Medical Sociology, First Edition. Edited by William C. Cockerham.

outpatient care to the urban population (Bhattacharyya et al. 2011). Independent outpatient clinics, which are a relatively new organizational form, may be located in either urban or rural areas and provided roughly 8.5% of all outpatient care in 2018 (National Commission of Health 2019).

In 2018, the Chinese health care system employed 3.6 million doctors and 4.1 million licensed nurses. Around 45% of Chinese doctors do not have a bachelor's degree (high school or lower, 1.4%; vocational training school, 15%; junior college, 28%); 42% of doctors had a bachelor's degree and another 13% had a postgraduate degree. The diversity in Chinese doctors' educational background largely resulted from a number of innovative programs of medical education introduced in the 1960s and 1970s, which aimed to train health care personnel quickly so as to expand basic medical services. For example, a large number of rural residents, typically with only a few years of education, were given very basic medical training so that they could serve the rural communities in which they lived. Vocational medical schools were also established to provide two to three years of medical training to individuals with a junior high school education. In the 1980s, China started to shift the focus of medical education to the tertiary level. At the time of writing, individuals can go through two to three years of medical training after high school and become a licensed assistant doctor, or go through five to eight years of training after high school and become a licensed doctor. Around 80% of nurses received their training in junior colleges (49%) or vocational nursing schools (30%) (National Commission of Health 2019). The distribution of health care resources between urban and rural populations is highly unequal. In 2018, the average number of inpatient beds per 1,000 people was 8.7 in cities and 4.56 in rural areas; the average number of doctors per 1,000 people was 4.01 in cities and 1.82 in rural areas. The distribution of more highly educated medical personnel is also very unequal. About 76% of doctors working in hospitals had a bachelor's or postgraduate degree, but only 29% of those working in township health centers were educated at the tertiary level (National Commission of Health 2019).

Most of the health care in China is provided by public not-for-profit organizations. Although 28% of all hospitals were private-for-profit, they tended to be small and specialty-based, and in 2018 accounted for only 7.5% of outpatient and 9.4% of inpatient care provided in hospitals. Almost all township health centers and over 75% of community health centers are not-for-profit. The for-profit sector plays a more important role in delivering outpatient care. About a quarter of village health stations and more than 90% of outpatient clinics are private-for-profit.

In 2017, the for-profit sector accounted for about 14% of outpatient and 18% of inpatient care; about 17% of doctors and 14% of nurses worked in privately run health care organizations (National Commission of Health 2018). Table 28.1 shows the five major types of health care organizations mentioned above, the shares of inpatient and outpatient care they provided, and the percentage of for-profit organizations in each type in 2018.

The Financing of Health Care

Prior to 2016, rural and urban residents were covered by different types of public health care insurance programs. As of 2015, 95% of the rural population was covered by the new cooperative medical scheme (NCMS), which was jointly funded

Table 28.1 Five major types of healthcare organizations in China; their numbers, the shares of outpatient and inpatient care they provided, and the percentage of for-profit organizations in each type in 2018.

	Number	% Outpatient care	% Inpatient care	% For profit
Hospitals	33,009	43	79	38
Village health stations	622,001	20	—	23
Township health centers	36,461	13	16	—
Outpatient clinics	215,018	9.7	—	90
Community health centers (stations)	34,997	9.6	1.4	22

Source: National Commission of Health (2019).

by the central and local government (80%) and rural residents (20%) (National Commission of Health and Family Planning 2016). NCMS is managed by county governments and the risk pooling takes place at county level. Regional variations exist in the contributions to and benefits of the NCMS programs, but most of the programs emphasize relief for catastrophic health care spending rather than providing a comprehensive benefits package (Wagstaff et al. 2009; Yip and Hsiao 2009). In cities, most urban residents were covered by the urban basic medical insurance programs or urban employees' basic medical insurance scheme (National Commission of Health and Family Planning 2016). For the employed, the employers contribute 6% and the employees contribute 2% of the salary as the insurance premium. The premium for those who do not have a job is subsidized by the local government (Lin et al. 2009). Again, contributions to and benefits of the urban insurance programs vary from one locale to the other. Typically, compared with rural schemes, urban schemes offered higher reimbursement rates and better access to health care facilities and enjoyed larger risk pools.

In 2016, in order to reduce urban/rural inequality, the Chinese government started the initiative to integrate the schemes for rural and urban residents, i.e. the new cooperative medical scheme and urban basic medical insurance, into the urban and rural residents' basic medical insurance system (URRBMI) and as of 2018, the integration has been completed in all but seven provinces in China (National Healthcare Security Administration 2019). The new scheme typically offers several levels of premiums with corresponding levels of benefits and pools risk at higher levels than previous schemes, often at the prefecture level. On average, in 2018, the reimbursement rates for inpatient expenditure were 72% for employed and 56% for non-employed urban and rural residents (National Healthcare Security Administration 2019). In 2018, total health care spending was about 6.57% of China's GDP, 28% of which came from government spending, 44% from social risk pooling, and the out-of-pocket spending of individual citizens made up the remaining 28% (National Commission of Health 2019). Despite the integration of urban and rural insurance schemes, large gaps still exist between urban and rural residents in terms of their utilization of health care resources. For example, in

2018, the per capita health care spending of urban residents was ¥2046 (US$295), approximately twice as much as that of rural residents (¥1240 (US$179)) (National Commission of Health 2019).

Traditional Chinese Medicine

Traditional Chinese medicine (TCM) is an established component in China's health care system. In early 1950s, just a few years after the establishment of the communist regime, the Chinese government started to emphasize TCM as a counterbalance to Western medicine. TCM was seen as a valuable component of a national cultural heritage and was invoked to balance the influence of the imperial West and the professional elites who aligned themselves with Western influences. At the same time, China suffered from a severe shortage of medical expertise and had to mobilize all types of medical personnel, including those who practiced Chinese medicine. With the support of the Chinese state, TCM grew tremendously and became deeply embedded in China's health care system. Currently the practice of TCM is supervised by its own administrative infrastructure in the Ministry of Health, and Chinese medicine practitioners have their own professional associations and journals. Independent Chinese medicine colleges and vocational schools train future practitioners (Scheid 2002). As of 2018, there were 4939 hospitals specializing in TCM and around 700,000 Chinese medicine doctors provided about 13% of health care (National Commission of Health 2019). During the current COVID-19 epidemic, Chinese medicine featured prominently in the officially recommended treatment regimen (National Administration of Traditional Chinese Medicine 2020).

Despite the importance of TCM in China's health care system, its legitimacy and relevance as an effective healing system have been constantly challenged in a modernizing society. In the first half of the twentieth century, as China gradually came into contact with modern science and medical technology, skepticism over the effectiveness of TCM grew. Intellectual elites who advocated the modernization of China rejected TCM as unscientific and outdated (Scheid 2002; Tang, Liu, and Ma 2008). In the latter half of the twentieth century, despite the commitment of the Chinese state to the development of TCM, the skepticism remained. On the one hand, TCM was emphasized as a cherished cultural tradition. On the other, the state has always advocated reforming TCM according to modern scientific principles (Scheid 2002). However, decades of research and efforts at integrating TCM into the framework of modern science have largely failed; its theories "remained inexplicable to science" (Tang et al. 2008: 1939). At the same time, both supporters and detractors of TCM have questioned whether TCM can and should be made scientific, how it can be made more scientific, and whether it would lose its essence if reformed according to scientific principles (Farquhar 1987; Quah 2003; Scheid 2002). Some of these debates were no longer limited to the academic arena and became highly visible in the public media. During recent decades, as China increasingly opened up to the rest of the world, TCM has been facing more competition from biomedicine, and its jurisdiction has become more circumscribed (Scheid 2002). As a result, the utilization of TCM has declined in recent decades, especially in urban areas (Jin 2010).

THE EVOLUTION OF CHINA'S HEALTH CARE SYSTEM: 1949–NOW

To understand the current configuration of the health care system in China, and, in particular, the system's major challenges, it is necessary to examine its evolution since 1949, when the People's Republic of China was established. In the past seven decades, China has experienced large-scale political and social changes, which led to dramatic changes of the institutional basis of China's health care system and consequently the system itself. From 1949 to 1978, a centralized health care system was established, with its institutional basis in the centralized economic and social organizations of the communist state. Starting from 1978, as the unfolding of marketization reforms eroded its institutional basis, important components of the centralized systems disintegrated. In the early 2000s, the Chinese government renewed its efforts to improve China's health care system and largely succeeded in building publicly administered and subsidized health care insurance programs with almost universal coverage. But the development in other segments of China's health care system was uneven. In the following sections, we briefly review the three phases of evolution of China's health care system.

The Establishment of a Centralized Health Care System: 1949–1978

In 1949, after the Japanese invasion and years of civil war, modern medicine was virtually non-existent in China except in a few large cities. The health conditions of the Chinese people were among the worst in the world. The estimated life expectancy was around 35, and 20% of infants died during the first year of their lives (Banister 1991; Blumenthal and Hsiao 2005). During the 1950s and 1960s, separate health care systems were developed for rural and urban residents.

During the 1950s, with the consolidation of the rule of the Chinese Communist Party, Chinese society was reorganized; the new institutions in rural and urban areas became the basis for the new health care system. In rural areas, people's communes were established so that farm land was collectively owned. The communes organized agricultural production such that peasants were assigned tasks by the commune and the output of their labor was also distributed by the commune. In cities, most working age adults belonged to publicly owned work units. Street-level committees monitored the life of those who were not employed by work units (Banister 1991; Walder 1986).

The main components of the rural system were barefoot doctors, the cooperative medical scheme, and the three-tier referral system (Banister 1991). To compensate for the severe shortage of health care personnel in rural China, a large number of farmers went through three to six months of basic medical training and became community health care workers, providing preventive care such as immunization and treating common illnesses. They were called "barefoot doctors" because many of them worked as farmers when they were not practicing medicine. By 1978, there were 1.6 million barefoot doctors staffing village health stations (Zhang and Unschuld 2008). The second component of the rural health care system was the cooperative medical scheme, which was a basic health insurance system for farmers. Agricultural communes, which organized collective farming, also operated the cooperative medical scheme, in which a portion of the communes' output was set aside to partially compensate barefoot doctors and reimburse farmers' health care costs. Finally, the three-tier referral system consisted of village health stations, township health centers, and county hospitals (Banister 1991; Blumenthal and Hsiao 2005).

Empirical studies have shown that the training and quality of barefoot doctors, and the abilities of communes to support medical personnel and cover health care costs significantly correlated with the level of economic development and proximity to urban centers of a commune. The rural health care system by no means met all the health care needs of rural residents, but it provided basic health care and a safety net to a vast rural population that previously had virtually no access to modern medicine (Banister 1991). As such, in the 1970s, the Chinese system was held up by the WHO and the UN as a model for the provision of basic health care in developing countries (Blumenthal and Hsiao 2005).

In cities, public hospitals provided both inpatient and outpatient services. The health care costs of urban residents and their families were covered on a fee-for-service basis by their workplaces under the government insurance scheme and labor insurance scheme. The two schemes combined to cover around 70% of urban residents (Liu 2002). For both schemes, the health care costs of urban workers and their families were covered by their employers, who were typically state-owned or collectively owned enterprises.

The Chinese health care system developed during the first three decades of the People's Republic of China was credited to have contributed to tremendous achievement in population health. By the end of the 1970s, average life expectancy reached 68 years and infant mortality rate dropped to 64 per 1,000 live births (Blumenthal and Hsiao 2005). During this period of time, however, the improvement of population health and the development of the health care system had also suffered setbacks. In particular, the massive famines of 1958–1960, mostly caused by political and economic turmoil, claimed an estimated 20–30 million lives. In addition, during the Cultural Revolution, when political factions struggled for dominance, universities and medical schools were closed for five years and faculty and students were sent to the countryside. As a result, the training of elite medical personnel and medical research was stopped (Banister 1991).

Moreover, toward the end of the 1970s, the centralized health care system was faced with several problems. In particular, in cities, because participants were reimbursed on a fee-for-service basis, the cost of running the two insurance schemes for urban workers increased rapidly, at an annual rate of 18% from 1979–1985 (Liu 2002). In rural areas, the cooperative medical schemes suffered from poor management, inefficiency and corruption in many instances. In addition, since doctors in all levels of public hospitals were paid a fixed salary, they had little incentive to serve their patients well, which strained the patient-doctor relationship (Banister 1991). These problems were part of the impetus for efforts to reform the health care system in the 1980s.

The Disintegration and Transformation of the Centralized Health Care System: 1978–2003

In 1978, market reforms were initiated to revitalize China's stagnant state-controlled economy; the state retreated from the operation of all sectors of the economy, including health care. The pre-reform health care system became greatly weakened, which exacerbated existing problems and created new challenges. In rural areas, by the end of 1983, the collective system of people's communes and the production teams largely disappeared, replaced by each household farming its own leased land and retaining all the earnings. The reform was very successful in improving agricultural output and efficiency, and in raising the living standard of the rural population. But it also dismantled the institutional basis of the rural health care system. As collective farming disappeared, the cooperative medical scheme (CMS) collapsed. The 1990s witnessed several attempts to resurrect the CMS scheme, but these efforts failed to achieve widespread coverage. The coverage rate of CMS went down from over 90% in 1978 to around 5% in 1984 and stayed at a low level throughout the 1990s. Most rural residents were left without access to any forms of health care insurance (Blumenthal and Hsiao 2005).

In cities, as a large number of unprofitable state-owned enterprises lost the financial backing of the government, they could no longer cover the health care costs of their workers. At the same time, the rapidly growing private sector generally did not offer coverage of health care costs (Liu 2002). The urban health care reform, initiated in 1997, aimed to replace medical insurance organized at the level of the workplace with one organized at the level of a city, called the urban employee's basic medical insurance. It was hoped that the new scheme would cover workers in both state-owned enterprises and the private sector, thereby boosting the overall coverage rate. The reform succeeded in implementing city-wide insurance schemes, but failed to increase overall coverage. The percentage of urban residents with insurance coverage gradually declined to around 49% in late 1990s (Blumenthal and Hsiao 2005).

As the economic reforms unfolded, the Chinese government started to withdraw from financing the provision of health care in the mid-1980s. The share of total health care spending paid for by the government declined from 36% in 1980 to around 16% in 1999 (National Commission of Health 2019). In 1999, among the general hospitals run by the Ministry of Health, transfers from the government accounted for only 6% of total outlays (National Healthcare Security Administration 2019). Consequently, hospitals and other health care providers had to rely on the sales of health care services and products to cover their expenses. To assure access to basic health care services, the government continued to set the prices of routine clinical visits and standard diagnostic tests and pharmaceuticals below cost. However, profits from new drugs, tests, and technology were permitted, so that health care organizations remained financially viable. The financing and pricing policies created distorted incentives for health care providers, who favored prescribing costly new drugs and high-technological services, at the expense of providing basic health care services. Over-prescription of drugs and diagnostic tests was widespread, and hospitals competed to introduce high-technological devices. As a result, China's health care expenditure has increased at 16% per year since the 1990s, which is 7% faster than the growth of its gross domestic product (Yip et al. 2010).

In addition to over-prescription, the profit motive and lack of accountability measures led to other unethical practices, such as accepting (sometimes exhorting) briberies from patients, taking kickbacks from the makers and suppliers of drugs and medical equipment, and selling counterfeit or expired drugs (Yip et al. 2010). These unethical practices greatly compromised patients' trust, which resulted in escalating tension and conflicts, often violent, between patients and providers (Zhang and Sleeboom-Faulkner 2011). Moreover, the health care system was highly fragmented and lacked a functioning referral system, because providers had an incentive to hold on to their patients rather than referring them to other levels of health care organizations. Patients therefore preferred to seek care in top-ranking hospitals, which became overcrowded, while lower-level health care organizations did not have enough patients. The utilization of the system's available capacity was inefficient and the level of patient satisfaction was low (Bhattacharyya et al. 2011; Yip et al. 2010). In addition, the neglect of primary care and lack of a functioning referral system did not match the needs of a population with an increasing prevalence of chronic diseases (Yip et al. 2010).

As insurance coverage and governmental health care input declined, the burden of health care costs borne by individual citizens increased. Whereas out-of-pocket spending accounted for 20% of the total health care spending in 1980, the share went up to 60% in 2000 (National Commission of Health 2019). As costs rose, health care became less affordable. Moreover, the ability to obtain health care services increasingly came to depend on a person's economic resources, which exacerbated social inequality in access and utilization of health care (Blumenthal and Hsiao 2005). For example, among those who needed, but failed to get, an outpatient visit, the percentage who did not see a doctor because they could not afford it steadily increased from 5% in 1993 to 19% in 2003. In addition, the percentage of individuals who could not afford outpatient visits when needed grew at a faster rate among low-income groups (Ministry of Health 2004). It was also not unusual for catastrophic health care spending to push households into poverty. A 2006 study estimated that using US$1 as the poverty line, health expenditure increased poverty rates from 13.5% to 16.2% in China (van Doorslaer et al. 2006).

At the beginning of the twenty-first century, China's health care system was beset with such problems as lack of affordability, patient–doctor conflicts, inequality, inefficiency, and wastefulness. Critics of the health care system have argued that the improvement in population health stagnated and that gaps in health outcomes between the rich and poor widened between 1980 and 2000, and that the chaotic health care system was partially to blame (Blumenthal and Hsiao 2005).

Recent Reforms of China's Health Care System: 2003–Present

In the early 2000s, the Chinese government started to put more emphasis on developing social welfare programs, including health care financing and provision, as a response to rising public discontent. The crisis caused by severe acute respiratory syndrome (SARS) in 2003 highlighted the weaknesses of the Chinese health care system and served as a further impetus for change (Blumenthal and Hsiao 2005). Since 2003, the government has significantly increased health care spending (Bhattacharyya et al. 2011) and focused on expanding the coverage of social health care insurance programs and strengthening primary health care capacities. In 2009, the State Council of China set forth a proposal of comprehensive health care reforms, with the goal of providing safe, effective, convenient, and affordable basic care for all citizens by 2020. In the following years, public spending on health care increased rapidly; from 2008 to 2017, government health care expenditure quadrupled to 1.52 trillion Yuan (Yip et al. 2019). Other efforts were directed at reforming public hospitals, building a functioning referral system, realigning provider incentives, and improving the quality of healthcare personnel. The achievements from the large-scale campaign to address the problems in China's health care system have been uneven. With generous infusion of public funds, the expansion of SHI programs has been largely successful. On the other hand, other reform efforts, especially those highly dependent on their adaptation in the existing institutional environment, tended to unfold slowly and have generally not achieved intended results. Interestingly, during this stage of the evolution of China's health care system, the role of the state and market have both been emphasized. The expansion of the SHI programs relied on the infusion of public funds and the organizational capacities of local and central government. At the same time, policy initiatives have sought to utilize market mechanisms to improve health care. For example, to motivate public hospitals to improve care delivery, policies have been implemented to encourage the expansion of private provision of health care so as to increase the extent of market competition. In addition, measures have been taken to untie physicians from the public hospitals in which they work so that they may also choose to work in private hospitals or medical groups. Below we discuss some significant reform measures and their impacts (Yip and Hsiao 2020).

The Expansion of Social Health Care Insurance Programs

In 2003, the Chinese government started to experiment with the new cooperative medical scheme in rural areas. The scheme was heavily subsidized by the government and quickly spread (Wagstaff et al. 2009). In urban areas, in addition to workers, the basic medical insurance was expanded to cover residents who were not employed. With government subsidies for the urban indigent, the program also grew rapidly. By 2013, SHI programs in rural and urban areas covered more than 95% of rural and urban residents, and the high coverage rates have been sustained since. Early assessments showed that the expanding SHI programs increased Chinese citizens' access to medical care. The utilization of health care services increased (Ministry of Health 2009a; Wagstaff et al. 2009), and the proportion of individual who did not seek medical care when needed because they could not afford it declined (Ministry of Health 2009a). However, it was also found that the reimbursement rates were generally quite low (Ministry of Health 2009a) and the expansion of insurance coverage did not lead to a decrease in individual citizens' out-of-pocket health care spending, mostly because of inefficiencies in the health care system (Wagstaff et al. 2009). Since 2009, further infusion of large amounts of public funds in the SHI programs has led to reducing co-payment rates, increasing reimbursement rate, expanding coverage of eligible health care services and further insurance against catastrophic health care spending. A recent investigation of household health care spending from 2010 and 2016 found increasing utilization of inpatient and outpatient care, increasing reimbursement rates of hospital care and declining proportions of households with catastrophic health care spending (defined as out-of-pocket payments for health care constituting 40% or more of households' total consumption expenditure net of food). Moreover, poorer households seemed to

have benefited more than richer households. For example, from 2010 to 2016, the reimbursement rate of inpatient care increased 14.2% for the 25% of the households with the lowest household income, as compared to 10.7% for the richest 25% of households; the incidence of catastrophic health care spending decreased 6.1% for the poorest 25% of households, as compared to a reduction of 2.7% among the richest households. Glaring inequality still exists in reimbursement rate and incidence of catastrophic health care spending; for example, in 2016, the reimbursement rate of inpatient care is 50.2% for households in the top quartile of the income distribution and only 38.0% for households in the bottom quartile (mostly because richer households were enrolled in insurance programs with more favorable reimbursement policies). The incidence of catastrophic spending is 7.3% and 16.8% respectively for the top and bottom quartiles of the households. However, the gaps have become narrower during the recent years (Yip et al. 2019).

The expansion of SHI programs has had many positive impacts, but the programs still suffer from some problems. First, as of 2018, more than 280 million rural residents have migrated to cities in search of better economic opportunities. Although most of the migrants are covered by the NCMS offered in their home villages, they cannot benefit from these programs in cities. Until 2016, only about 20% of migrants to cities took part in urban employee basic medical insurance scheme (Ministry of Human Resources and Social Security 2017), leaving a large gap in the effective coverage of health care insurance in China. In 2015, the Chinese government started to seek to expand the portability of insurance benefits within and across provinces, with the explicit purposes of maintaining effective coverage of rural-to-urban migrants (Yip et al. 2019). However, the development seemed to have been quite uneven and as of now, most rural-to-urban migrant do not have access to the health insurance scheme that they registered with. Moreover, some municipalities used a variety of strategies to discourage migrants from using the public services, including health care services, that they are entitled to in cities (Chan and O'Brien 2019). Second, the SHI programs have experienced some financial problems. During the early days of the SHI programs, inefficiency in the administration of the insurance schemes led to huge surpluses in the insurance funds; for example, in 2009, the cumulative surplus of the urban basic medical insurance scheme was 1.16 times higher than its total revenues. The huge sums of unspent money prevent enrollees from benefiting from high levels of health care protection and potentially provide opportunities for fraud and abuse of the system (Gu 2010). However, since 2012, the balance of medical insurance funds has been decreasing quickly. In 2017, some local schemes suffered from deficits, while the schemes in several other areas were projected to lapse into deficits (Ministry of Human Resources and Social Security 2018). As China is ageing quickly, the financial sustainability of the SHI funds has been called into question.

Building Primary Health Care Based Referral System

As China experienced the epidemiological transition from acute to chronic diseases and as its population aged rapidly, the burden of non-communicable diseases (NCDs) has also grown quickly. Recent studies have shown that the management of NCDs has been far from optimal in China, which may be attributed to the weak primary care provision and the lack of a functioning referral system (Yip et al. 2019). Moreover, during public health emergencies such as the recent outbreak of the COVID-19 virus in Wuhan, China, people swarmed to tertiary hospitals for testing and treatment, despite the fact that uncomplicated cases can be managed in lower-level health care facilities. This gravely strained the resources at the tertiary hospitals and elevated the risks of cross infection. Strengthening the provision of primary health care and building a functioning referral system are therefore important and urgent tasks.

The Chinese government has intensified its efforts to build the primary health care capacity and a functioning referral system. Since 2003, the government has invested heavily in building the infrastructure of a nationwide network of community health centers and stations, subsidizing preventive health care provided in primary health care facilities and training health care personnel for primary care facilities. The heavy investment, however, has not achieved the intended results of building a functioning referral system centered on providers of primary health care. From 2009 to 2017, outpatient visits increased at an annual rate of 12.2% in tertiary hospitals, but only at 4.4% in primary health care facilities. As a result, the share of outpatient visits to primary health care facilities decreased relative to tertiary hospitals. Patient still overwhelmingly preferred to seek care in hospitals, especially tertiary hospitals (Yip et al. 2019). The low utilization rate of primary care facilities may mainly be attributed to patients' lack of financial incentives to seek care as well as their perception of low quality of care in these facilities, which has been substantiated in empirical studies (Bhattacharyya et al. 2011).

In 2015, the Chinese government renewed its effort to strengthen primary health care provision. Further policy guidelines were issued to encourage the development of alliances between hospitals and primary health care facilities so as to build a tiered referral system. According to the guidelines, higher-level hospitals can provide training, technical support and expedited channels of referral for lower-level facilities that in turn, serve as points of contact and sources of patients to upper-level hospitals. Members of such alliances would be bound together with shared management and economic interests. In 2016, the government started to promote the role of family doctors and encourage urban and rural residents to register with family doctors who are designated with the tasks of providing preventive and basic health care services and serving as gatekeepers. The implementation of these policy initiative, however, is still at an early stage. Evidence has shown that these initiatives have yet to be implemented as they were intended to. Although many alliances have been built, they tended to be loose networks led by hospitals, with little shared responsibilities, planning or financial interests. Moreover, although registration with family doctors has become widespread, few family doctors were qualified and motivated to take up their designated responsibilities (Yip et al. 2019). Further evaluation is needed to assess whether these policy initiatives will be refined to achieve the desired outcomes.

Public Hospital Reforms

China's public hospitals are the most important provider of health care, employing 77% of medical personnel and owning 74% of all hospital beds (National Commission of Health 2019). Public hospitals are complex organizations with deeply entrenched interests both within and outside of the organizations. Scholars have argued that the Ministry of Health, hospital managers, and doctors have formed a "medical axis-of-power" devoted to serving their own interests instead of public welfare (Hsiao 2007). Public hospitals also embody many contradictions. Financially, although they are public in name, less than 10% of the operating costs of public hospitals came from public funds, and so they are actually driven by profit motives. On the other hand, in terms of governance, they follow the bureaucratic model of state-owned organizations and enterprises and typically feature rigid and hierarchical control; moreover, they are also required to serve public welfare goals envisioned by their administrative superiors (Guan, Qi, and Liu 2016; Yip and Fu 2020). These contradictions resulted in complicated and often convoluted incentives and practice of managers and staff. The reforms of public hospitals are therefore seen as the most difficult part of the overall health care reforms. Since 2012, public hospital reforms have targeted hospital governance, personnel management and compensation structure. These reform measures ran against the entrenched interests and incentives in public hospitals and are met with many challenges. These difficulties in fact reflect more broadly the inherent contradictions in an economic system that emphasizes the primacy of centralized control but also prizes economic efficiency.

The priority of public hospital reforms lay in the restructuring the distorted financial incentives of hospitals and physicians. In 2012, the central government launched the initiative to eliminate the 15% mark-up of pharmaceuticals, first in county hospitals and then in city hospitals. As discussed above, because the government set the rate of medical services at very low levels but allowed a 15% mark-up of drugs, hospitals have to rely on the sale of drugs for financial survival, which resulted in rapidly escalating health care costs. Drug sales made up 40% of hospital revenues, as compared to an average of 16% in OECD countries. By design, the zero mark-up drug policy sought to control health care expenditure in public hospitals and the shortfall in hospital revenues after the policy would be made up by increases in fees for some medical services and procedures, local government fiscal subsidies and improvement in hospital efficiency. Initial assessment of the policy revealed that drug expenditure did decline but the growth of total hospital expenditure continued unabated. Hospitals recovered the losses in drug sales through increasing diagnostic tests and volumes of medical services, not through efficiency gains or increases in local government subsidies (Yip and Fu 2020).

In 2012, the central government also directed local governments to carry out pilot reform projects. By 2015, several models of public hospital reform emerged from local experiments and one of them, from the city of Sanming in Southeast China, was particularly promising. The Sanming model gave hospital administrators more autonomy in managing the day-to-day affairs of hospitals, revised price schedule to increase physician fees, negotiated with pharmaceutical companies to reduce drug costs, and tied the compensation of administrators and physicians to appropriate sets of performance-based measures rather than hospital profits. The Sanming experiment reduced health care expenditure without sacrificing the quality or volume of health care. Moreover, physician income more than doubled from 2011 to 2014 (Yip et al. 2019). The success of the Sanming model, combined with the mixed results from the zero mark-up drug policy, illustrated the importance of implementing comprehensive measure that target different aspects of hospital government and incentive structure, rather than just one specific incentive. The central government has since sought to replicate the Sanming model across China but the progress has so far been very slow. Scholars have argued that the Sanming success stemmed from the convergence of a number of features of local bureaucracy (He 2018); the replicability of the Sanming model in other locales in China is still uncertain.

Another aspect of public hospital reforms is to untether physicians from the hospitals in which they practice, by allowing them to practice at multiple sites, including private hospitals and clinics. Chinese physicians are much more dependent on the organizations in which they work than their Western colleagues (Jin 2017). Legally, prior to 2009, physicians were required to register with one organization and can work only in that organization. In practice, doctors in China's public hospitals are almost always employees of the hospitals; rank-and-file doctors are supervised by their department heads, who are in turn managed by higher-level officials who may or may not be medical doctors. Typically, these doctors have few external alternatives to advance their career and interests and have to rely heavily on their departments and hospitals for income and opportunities to move up the career ladder (Bloom, Han, and Li 2001). In 2009, regulations were changed such that physicians were allowed to register and practice at multiple sites (Ministry of Health 2009b), but this policy stayed largely dormant for a few years before it was further operationalized and promoted in 2017. The goals of the multi-site practice policy were to give physicians more autonomy so as to raise their morale and income, and to supply the growing private health care sector with manpower (Ministry of Health 2009b). However, public hospitals have little incentives to allow their physicians to engage in multi-site practice.

In 2018, the authors conducted a survey of around 800 physicians in 17 tertiary and secondary hospitals in three large cities, in which 84% of the physicians reported that they supported multi-site practice, whereas only 23% perceived that their hospitals would be receptive to their staff engaging in multi-site practice. Given the dependence of Chinese physicians on their hospitals, although hospitals were explicitly prohibited from preventing their doctors from taking up multi-site practice, they still have many hidden tactics to discourage their physicians from benefiting from the policy. As a result, only a small number of physicians with large bargaining power were able to entertain the idea of keeping their positions in public hospitals and practicing at private hospitals/clinics. For most other physicians, choosing multi-site practice effectively means giving up the positions in public hospitals and switching to private medical groups. Because of the dominance of public hospitals in China's health care sector, physicians are typically reluctant to formally leave public hospitals. The policy of multi-site practice, therefore, has not achieved its intended purposes of freeing physicians from hospitals.

Reforming Professional Training: Standardizing Residency Training

As discussed above, there is tremendous diversity in the training and quality of Chinese physicians. In 2013, standardized residency training programs were launched to improve the quality of medical training for physicians. Initially three years of residency training was mandated for those who finished five years of undergraduate medical training (Zhu, Li, and Chen 2016). In 2016, additional years of training for specialists were introduced. Standardized residency training programs grew rapidly. By the end of 2018, there were more than 400,000 physicians-in-training taking part in residency programs in 859 training bases (National Healthcare Security Administration 2019). Despite the rapid growth, the new training system is still faced with many gaps and challenges. Specifically, the quality of residency training is highly dependent on the local institutional configuration and organizational environment and therefore is still highly variable. Residents often complained that they were used as cheap labor dealing with high-intensity but low-skilled work and received little systematic hands-on training of medical techniques. Subsidies to residency programs are typically insufficient and as a result, residents often have to endure years of heavy workload with very low compensation. Moreover, residents may receive unequal treatment, with those who have the prospect to work in the hospitals in which they receive training being treated more favorably. As a result of these problems, recent research has shown that the morale of medical residents is generally low and their enthusiasm in pursuing a career in clinical practice has declined (Lien et al. 2016).

Discussion

Since the early 2000s, several rounds of health care reforms have targeted both the financing and delivery of health care in China, and the outcomes have been mixed. On one hand, the expansion of the social health insurance programs has been largely successful, resulting in almost universal coverage of China's vast rural and urban populations. Moreover, the further refinement of the SHI programs during the past 10 years seems to have benefited the economically disadvantaged more and contributed to diminishing the socioeconomic gaps in reimbursement rates and rates of catastrophic health care spending. Since early 2000s, population health has steadily improved; from 2000 to 2018, life expectancy has increased from 71.4 years to 76.7 years (World Bank 2019a) and the infant mortality rate declined from 28 deaths to 7.4 deaths per 1000 live births (World Bank 2019b). On the other hand, reform efforts directed at building primary care-based referral system, realigning provider incentives, and improving the quality of medical professionals have generally been progressing slowly. With the exception of some local successes, these reform efforts have not yet achieved their intended results.

The Chinese health care system is still plagued by a number of problems: lack of proper provision of primary and preventive care for population with high prevalence of chronic conditions; lack of a functioning referral system; convoluted financial incentives for hospitals and physicians; lack of functioning standardized training programs of physicians. These shortcomings resulted in rapidly increasing health care costs, suboptimal care and low patient satisfaction, and in particular, further strained the already deteriorating patient-doctor relationship. From 2000 to 2014, violence against medical professionals grew at an annual rate of 11% (Du et al. 2020); a recent study found that 56% of physicians reported experiencing workplace violence during the previous year (Tian et al. 2020). The patient-doctor relationship is the gateway through which patients come into contact with the health care system and the problems of health care system get reflected and may even be amplified in the patient-doctor relationship. The best way to improve the patient-doctor relationship and restore patients' trust in doctors is to build an efficient and credible health care system (Xu 2014).

It is worth noting that sociological perspectives have been largely absent in the study of China's health care system and health care reforms. Existing studies are mostly empirical policy analyses motivated by economic perspectives. However, as a recent review pointed out, the experience of recent health care reforms has shown that as the current reforms are increasingly tackling complex aspects of the health care system, only pouring public funds into health care provision is no longer sufficient for the success of reform efforts and may even aggravate the existing inefficiencies. Rather, it is important to consider the institutional environment in which policies are implemented. Against such a backdrop, sociological perspectives may be particularly helpful in both understanding the institutional environment and actions and reactions of stakeholders in the environment. For example, as discussed above, as a component of public hospital reforms, the policy of multi-site practice aims to untie doctors from hospitals and was based on the consideration that once doctors are allowed to practice in multiple sites, they would pursue such opportunities, motivated by economic interests.

However, to understand the actual impact of the policy, we need to recognize that although driven by profits, the organization of public hospitals are still mostly following the "*danwei*" model, prevalent during the era of centralized planning, under which hospitals retain strong control over their employees and at the same time may provide many benefits, such as housing and child care to the employees (Henderson 1984). Physicians are embedded in the social and power relations and governance structure implied in the *danwei* model and contingent on their positions, there is great variability in physicians' abilities and willingness to take advantages of the opportunities afforded by the new policy and growing private health care sector. This example illustrates that by focusing on (but not limited to) the institutional environment, sociological studies may offer in-depth and realistic understanding of the impact of policy initiatives. The current health care reforms, therefore, provide fertile ground for sociological investigation, which in turn may advance theoretical and empirical research in areas such as medical sociology, sociology of professions and organizational studies.

As we write this chapter, the COVID-19 virus is ravaging the world. The epidemic has revealed shortcomings in China's health care system, such as the lack of functioning referral system, as discussed above. It may also have significant impacts on the health care system. For example, it has been observed that most public and private hospitals, like many other business, suffered severe economic hardship during the epidemic, which may lead to the restructuring of the health care sector in years to come. More importantly, the epidemic has illustrated that the functioning of a health care system is highly dependent on the social context and political system in which it is embedded. In China's case, a fairly rigid public health alert system had been set up to report new infections since the 2003 SARS epidemic. However, although at this point, exact details of what happened is unknown, it seems that during the early days of the epidemic, the large and multi-layered bureaucracy of China's government ignored the alerts and missed the opportunity to take early action to stop the spread of infection for the political goals of maintaining social stability and protecting economic activities.

On the other hand, as the new infection started to spread and its threat became apparent, the Chinese government locked down Wuhan, a city with a population of ten million where the earliest cases emerged. In addition, the whole population of China was ordered to stay in their homes and local communities exercised close monitoring of their residents and any outsiders. Such strict measures restricting population movements, at great economic and social costs, effectively contained the infection in Wuhan and a few of its surrounding cities. So far there has been no large-scale outbreak of the virus in other parts of China. The Chinese government was able to exercise such drastic lockdown and quarantine measures because it can exercise it formidable mobilization capacities and control the society and people (He 2020).

After seventy years' evolution, the current health care system in China boasts almost universal coverage of China's vast population, but is still plagued by serious problems in both the financing and delivery of health care remain. Reforms targeting different aspects of the health care system are still unfolding and these reform efforts have been continuously adjusted according to the outcomes of previous efforts. Rigorous examination is needed to assess the processes and outcomes of the reform efforts. Sociologists can and should play a more important role in examining and evaluating these changes.

References

Banister, Judith. 1991. *China's Changing Population*. Stanford University Press.

Bhattacharyya, Onil, Yin Delu, Sabrina T. Wong, and Chen Bowen. 2011. "Evolution of Primary Care in China 1997–2009." *Health Policy* 100(2–3): 174–180.

Bloom, Gerald, Leiya Han, and Xiang Li. 2001. "How Health Workers Earn a Living in China." *Human Resources for Health Development Journal* 5(1–3): 25–38.

Blumenthal, David and William Hsiao. 2005. "Privatization and Its Discontents — The Evolving Chinese Health Care System." *New England Journal of Medicine* 353: 1165–1170.

Chan, Alexsia T. and Kevin J. O'Brien. 2019. "Phantom Services: Deflecting Migrant Workers in China." *The China Journal* 81: 103–122.

Du, Yuxian, David J. Wenxin Wang, Shinduk Lee Washburn, Samuel D. Towne, Hao Zhang, and Jay E. Maddock. 2020. "Violence against Healthcare Workers and Other Serious Responses to Medical Disputes in China: Surveys of Patients at 12 Public Hospitals." *BMC Health Services Research* 20(1): 253.

Farquhar, Judith. 1987. "Problems of Knowledge in Contemporary Chinese Medical Discourse." *Social Science & Medicine* 24(12): 1013–1021.

Gu, Xin. 2010. "On the Level of Fund Balance in China's Urban and Rural Public Healthcare Insurance." *Journal of Graduate School of Chinese Academy of Social Sciences* 5: 53–61.

Guan, Xiao, Lin Qi, and Longfei Liu. 2016. "Controversy in Public Hospital Reforms in China." *The Lancet Global Health* 4(4): e240.

He, Alex Jingwei. 2018. "Manoeuvring within a Fragmented Bureaucracy: Policy Entrepreneurship in China's Local Healthcare Reform." *The China Quarterly* 236: 1088–1110.

He, Jingwei. 2020. "China's State Machinery Will Beat Coronavirus Crisis, but at What Cost?" *South China Morning Post*, February 1.

Henderson, Gail. 1984. *The Chinese Hospital: A Socialist Work Unit*. New Haven, CT: Yale University Press.

Hsiao, William C. 2007. "The Political Economy of Chinese Health Reform." *Health Economics, Policy and Law* 2(03): 241–249.

Jin, Lei. 2010. "From Mainstream to Marginal? Trends in the Use of Chinese Medicine in China from 1991 to 2004." *Social Science & Medicine* 71(6): 1063–1067.

Jin, Lei. 2017. "Physician Autonomy and the Paradox of Rationalization: Clinical Pathways in China's Public Hospitals." *Sociology of Development* 3(3): 295–322.

Lien, Selina S., Russell O. Kosik, Angela P. Fan, Lei Huang, Xudong Zhao, Xiaojie Chang, Yuhwa Wang, and Qi Chen. 2016. "10-Year Trends in the Production and Attrition of Chinese Medical Graduates: An Analysis of Nationwide Data." *The Lancet* 388: S11.

Lin, Wanchuan, Gordon G. Liu, and Gang Chen. 2009. "The Urban Resident Basic Medical Insurance: A Landmark Reform Towards Universal Coverage in China." *Health Economics* 18(S2): S83–S96.

Liu, Yuanli. 2002. "Reforming China's Urban Health Insurance System." *Health Policy* 60(2): 133–150.

Ministry of Health. 2004. *Chinese National Health Services Survey: 2003*. Beijing: Union Medical School Press.

Ministry of Health. 2009a. *Chinese National Health Services Survey: 2008*. Beijing: Union Medical School Press.

Ministry of Health. 2009b. "Circular of the Ministry of Health on Issues Related to Doctors' Multi-Site Practice." Retrieved May 11, 2020 (http://www.gov.cn/zwgk/2009-09/16/content_1418981.htm).

Ministry of Human Resources and Social Security. 2017. *Bulletin on the Development of Human Resources and Social Security 2016*.

Ministry of Human Resources and Social Security. 2018. *Bulletin on the Development of Human Resources and Social Security 2017*.

National Administration of Traditional Chinese Medicine. 2020. "Experience of Treating Novel Coronavirus Pneumonia by TCM." Retrieved May 11, 2020 (http://www.satcm.gov.cn/xinxifabu/meitibaodao/2020-04-01/14418.html).

National Commission of Health. 2018. *Health Statistics Yearbook of China*. Beijing: Peking Union Medical University Press.

National Commission of Health. 2019. *Health Statistics Yearbook of China*. Beijing: Peking Union Medical University Press.

National Commission of Health and Family Planning. 2016. *Health Statistics Yearbook of China*. Beijing: Peking Union Medical University Press.

National Healthcare Security Administration. 2019. "Medical Insurance Statistics Bulletin 2018." Retrieved May 11, 2020 (http://www.nhsa.gov.cn/art/2019/6/30/art_7_1477.html).

Quah, Stella R. 2003. "Traditional Healing Systems and the Ethos of Science." *Social Science & Medicine* 57(10): 1997–2012.

Scheid, Volker. 2002. *Chinese Medicine in Contemporary China: Plurality and Synthesis*. Durham, NC: Duke University Press.

Tang, Jin-Ling, Bao-Yan Liu, and Kan-Wen Ma. 2008. "Traditional Chinese Medicine." *The Lancet* 372(9654): 1938–1940.

Tian, Yusheng, Yuchen Yue, Jianjian Wang, Ting Luo, Li Yamin, and Jiansong Zhou. 2020. "Workplace Violence against Hospital Healthcare Workers in China: A National WeChat-Based Survey." *BMC Public Health* 20(1): 582.

van Doorslaer, Eddy, Owen O'Donnell, Ravi P. Rannan-Eliya, Aparnaa Somanathan, Shiva Raj Adhikari, Charu C. Garg, Deni Harbianto, Alejandro N. Herrin, Mohammed Nazmul Huq, Shamsia Ibragimova, Anup Karan, Chiu Wan Ng, Badri Raj Pande, Rachel Racelis, Sihai Tao, Keith Tin, Kanjana Tisayaticom, Laksono Trisnantoro, Chitpranee Vasavid, and Yuxin Zhao. 2006. "Effect of Payments for Health Care on Poverty Estimates in 11 Countries in Asia: An Analysis of Household Survey Data." *Lancet* 368(9544): 1357–1364.

Wagstaff, Adam, Magnus Lindelow, Gao Jun, Xu Ling, and Qian Juncheng. 2009. "Extending Health Insurance to the Rural Population: An Impact Evaluation of China's New Cooperative Medical Scheme." *Journal of Health Economics* 28(1): 1–19.

Walder, Andrew G. 1986. *Communist Neo-Traditionalism: Work and Authority in Chinese Indusrty*. Berkeley, CA: University of California Press.

World Bank. 2019a. "Life Expectancy at Birth, Total (Years) - China | Data." Retrieved May 11, 2020 (https://data.worldbank.org/indicator/SP.DYN.LE00.IN?locations=CN).

World Bank. 2019b. "Mortality Rate, Infant (Per 1,000 Live Births) - China | Data." Retrieved May 11, 2020 (https://data.worldbank.org/indicator/SP.DYN.IMRT.IN?locations=CN).

Xu, Weixian. 2014. "Violence against Doctors in China." *The Lancet* 384(9945): 745.

Yip, Winnie, William Chi-Man, Qingyue Meng Hsiao, Wen Chen, and Xiaoming Sun. 2010. "Realignment of Incentives for Health-Care Providers in China." *The Lancet* 375(9720): 1120–1130.

Yip, Winnie, Fu Hongqiao, Angela T. Chen, Tiemin Zhai, Weiyan Jian, Xu Roman, Jay Pan, Hu Min, Zhongliang Zhou, Qiulin Chen, Wenhui Mao, Qiang Sun, and Wen Chen. 2019. "10 Years of Health-Care Reform in China: Progress and Gaps in Universal Health Coverage." *The Lancet* 394(10204): 1192–1204.

Yip, Winnie Chi-Man and Hongqiao Fu. 2020. "Public Hospital Reforms in China: Progress and Challenges." Pp. 261–280 in *World Scientific Series in Global Health Economics and Public Policy*. Vol. 1. WORLD SCIENTIFIC.

Yip, Winnie Chi-Man and William C. Hsiao. 2009. "Non-Evidence-Based Policy: How Effective Is China's New Cooperative Medical Scheme in Reducing Medical Impoverishment?" *Social Science & Medicine* 68(2): 201–209.

Yip, Winnie Chi-Man and William C. Hsiao. 2020. "What Drove the Cycles of Chinese Health System Reforms?" Pp. 5–23 in *World Scientific Series in Global Health Economics and Public Policy*. Vol. 1. WORLD SCIENTIFIC.

Zhang, Xinqing and Margaret Sleeboom-Faulkner. 2011. "Tensions between Medical Professionals and Patients in Mainland China." *Cambridge Quarterly of Healthcare Ethics* 20: 1–8.

Zhang, Daqing and Paul U. Unschuld. 2008. "China's Barefoot Doctor: Past, Present, and Future." *The Lancet* 372(9653): 1865–67.

Zhu, Jiming, Wenkai Li, and Lincoln Chen. 2016. "Doctors in China: Improving Quality through Modernisation of Residency Education." *The Lancet* 388(10054): 1922–1929.

Author Index

The Wiley Blackwell Companion to Medical Sociology, First Edition. Edited by William C. Cockerham.

Subject Index

The Wiley Blackwell Companion to Medical Sociology, First Edition. Edited by William C. Cockerham.

CPSIA information can be obtained
at www.ICGtesting.com
Printed in the USA
BVHW012251200822
645059BV00003B/56